HOW WAR CAME

HOW WAR CAME

THE IMMEDIATE ORIGINS OF THE SECOND WORLD WAR, 1 9 3 8 – 1 9 3 9

Donald Cameron Watt

PANTHEON BOOKS NEW YORK

All rights reserved under International and Pan-American Copyright
Conventions. Published in the United States by Pantheon Books, a
division of Random House, Inc., New York. Originally published in
hardcover in the United States by Pantheon Books, a division of
Random House, Inc., and in Great Britain by William Heinemann Ltd.,
London in 1989.

Library of Congress Cataloging-in-Publication Data

Watt, Donald Cameron.
How war came.
Bibliography. p.
Includes index.
1. World War, 1939–1945—Causes. I. Title.
D741.W36   1989   940.53'11   89-8802
ISBN 0-679-73093-1

Manufactured in the United States of America

Pantheon Paperback Edition

Credits appear on pages 710 and 711.

for Felicia

CONTENTS

PREFACE AND ACKNOWLEDGEMENTS

The drive to write this book began on September 2 and 3, 1939, when, as an eleven-year-old schoolboy, I helped my father and his colleagues fill sand-bags in one of the great sand quarries outside Rugby, the Midland marketing town. It grew enormously in strength two years later when, lazing in the summer on the banks of the school close, with the scent of new-mown grass in the air, I read for the first time an account of the British retreat to Dunkirk. How could a British army have come to find itself in so near-disastrous a position? How could things have been allowed to go so far?

My need to understand drove me to wangle, connive, volunteer and out-compete my fellow conscripts to a posting to British Troops, Austria as an acting sergeant in Field Security, concerned with the tail-end of denazification, with keeping an eye on the wilder and madder edges of the political spectrum, firstly among the inhabitants of Styria, then among the tides of refugees from south-eastern Europe that the political processes from 1943 onwards were washing westwards out of Romania, Hungary, Yugoslavia, Czechoslovakia and the Ukraine. I learnt almost immediately that the realities of Central European politics covered a very wide range of attitudes, virtuous and vicious, unimaginable to a teenage schoolboy in an isolated and blockaded island between his eleventh and seventeenth birthdays.

The Social Democratic political policeman who regarded the neo-Nazis, whose first underground stirrings became known in the winter of 1947, as the rankest of amateurs; the veteran of the Jewish brigade who, from sheer need to know, kept tabs on the revival of Catholic anti-semitism; the Hungarian Anglophile and liberal Count who first gave me a rough guide to the political differences between the refugees of 1943, 1944, 1945 and 1946 in preparation for the flood of 1947; the broken disciple of Maček, the Croat leader, who for shame at the excesses committed in Croatia's name by Anton Pavelič and his followers, only admitted to being a Croat himself in his blackest moments; the Catholic anti-Nazi lawyer; the village gendarme who regarded all politicians as equally dire acts of God; the ultra-nationalist doctor (his family came from the South Tyrol), an ex-Reichswehr surgeon, who overcame his Anglophobia to dress my poisoned toe: all of these increased my desire to understand, while at the same time increasing my awareness of the complexities to be understood. Few, if any of them, fitted the stereotypes of my imagining.

From the army, my desire to understand drove me to read Politics, Philosophy and Economics, taking the international history of the inter-war years as my special subject. (History in Oxford ended then in 1914. In the twenty-five years since my father had emerged from uniform at the end of a previous world war to read first Classics and then History, the terminal date had advanced from 1870, some thirty-four years. But, apart from a special paper on the Anglo-French Entente, there was nothing for the would-be historian of the twentieth century.) I had the good fortune to sit at the feet of a generation whose historical interests had been developed by service, often at Bletchley Park, or in SOE. Christopher Seton-Watson, my tutor, guided my reading. Finally, with the aid of John Wheeler-Bennett, I left Oxford to join the small British editorial team working alongside equally small American and French teams to screen and edit for publication the captured archives of the German Foreign Ministry.

Here I worked in parallel, the first historian to read the Foreign Ministry files for the period 1933–7 (later to be published as Series C of *Documents on German Foreign Policy*) while at the same time devilling for the editors-in-chief on volumes V–X of Series D, especially on volumes VI and VII which ran from March to September 1939. I helped collate the documents with those already published in Series III of *Documents on British Foreign Policy* and with the Italian series published by Mario Toscano, then the doyen of European historians of diplomacy. I drafted editorial notes incorporating evidence cited in the Tokyo war crimes trials.

From working alongside my French and American colleagues I discovered how grossly inadequate in technical terms was the education of which I was so proud; and all the time my understanding grew of how fragmentary in evidential terms, and how unsatisfactory in human terms was the accepted orthodoxy of the time. The son of a school-master, a great, if self-effacing teacher, I found the language employed to comment upon the motives and comprehensions underlying British policy reminiscent of an end-of-term report. When I moved to London, and a senior professor of Diplomatic History, a terrifying female (popularly supposed to breakfast off young assistant lecturers), expressed disdain and contempt for my interest in how and why the war had come, I held my peace. My own professor supported me and gave me my head, as I began to write a series of articles on individual episodes, publishing documents, re-examining relationships, rather than dashing into a new monograph that I instinctively felt to be premature (no doubt my Aberdonian heritage at work).

The steady release of material, especially after the easing of the fifty-year restrictions on access to British records, brought an increasing stream of would-be graduate students to London; all took part in our graduate seminar, as did an increasing number of visiting scholars. It was my good fortune to have a succession of first-class students, whose abilities and time gave them understanding and knowledge of the new British archives to a degree which the increasing load of teaching, supervisory and administrative/policy duties made it very difficult for me to match. Whatever they acquired from my supervision, I more than matched in learning from them.

I began the first attempt to write this book in the late 1960s. Three things made me put it aside: the absence of any serious French evidence, the difficulty of making sense of the Soviets, and my complete dissatisfaction with the received version of American policy. Since then, the work of Jean-Baptiste Duroselle and the French school of international historians gathered around the periodical *Relations Internationales*, many of whom took part in a series of Anglo-French conferences which I attended, and the publication of *Documents Diplomatiques Français* have enormously altered the position so far as the French evidence is concerned. Indeed, the French evidence has enabled a re-examination of the course of events in the Balkans in the same period.

On the American side, the work of younger British and German historians in interpreting the American and British evidence, untrammelled by the political traditions which made a re-evaluation of Roosevelt and Hull's conduct of foreign policy so difficult for their American contemporaries, has completely changed the picture.

Even the Soviet position has become clearer. And where the small powers are concerned the work of the Italian historian Alfredo Breccia on Yugoslavia, of the German historian Hoppe on Bulgaria, of the Finnish historian Seppo Myllieniemi on the Baltic states, and the Dutch historian Ger van Roon on the Oslo and Benelux states, has changed the position completely.

Much of the best work in that first draft has already been published by me, as separate articles, as contributions to various *Festschrifts*, or as conference papers. One aspect, the role of the British, French, German,

Italian and Polish staffs, I dealt with in my 1973 Lees-Knowles lectures at Cambridge, and published in 1975 as *Too Serious a Business: European Armies and the Approach of the Second World War*. This book is directed at a more general, less academic audience. I have attempted to tell the story of how the Second World War began from the direct evidence left by those whose actions (and inactions) played a part in that beginning. I have used not only the official records but, where possible, the private papers, letters, and diaries, the reminiscences, published and unpublished, of the political and professional makers of policy and their advisers in all the countries involved.

The Second World War began in Europe in the first days of September 1939 (despite the cataloguers of the Library of Congress who date its beginning to December 7, 1941). It began as the result of a breakdown of the European international system; its progress brought in the Soviet Union and the United States, and the Japanese chose, disastrously as it turned out, to take advantage of it, to advance their own, very different, claims to Asian and Pacific hegemony, against the European colonial presence, and against the trading and cultural interests of Britain and the United States. But the processes which involved them in the attempt to dominate China, although they were to converge with what was happening in Europe in 1938–41, are separate and peculiar to Asia and the Pacific.

Both the United States of America and the Soviet Union were to be drawn into the fighting. Both played their part, and chose their sides, in 1939. For very different reasons, and by very different processes, both countries decided not to commit their military forces to conflict in 1939. Their role was important, but it was a supporting role, not a starring one. They were fortunate to be able to make such a choice. The smaller powers of Europe could not. Willy-nilly they found themselves directly involved. The narrator must therefore pay attention to their actions, their dilemmas, their fits of courage and caution: the resolute Turks, the determined Greeks; the hesitant and divided Yugoslavs, the excitable Romanians, the cautious Bulgarians, the craven Hungarians, the unhappy Czechs, Slovaks and Ruthenes trying to preserve some residue of national identity in a world which had abandoned them in the autumn of 1938; the determined but deserted Finns; the Latvians, Lithuanians and Estonians, doomed to absorption by their Soviet neighbours; the Scandinavians, Dutch, Belgians and Swiss, set on preserving their neutrality. Those states, by their actions, added to the uncertainty, the confusion and the breakdown of power and resolution which opened the way for Hitler's attack on Poland. They command the narrator's attention as much as do Roosevelt and Stalin.

This is not a story of men whose actions are determined by large, impersonal forces. The forces are there, but the stuff of history is humanity. Impersonal forces only figure in this narrative in so far as they formed part of the perceptions of the individual actors. History is lived through and, for the fortunate, survived by people. Their actions, their failures to act, their hesitations, their perceptions, their judgments, their misunderstandings, misperceptions and mistakes act and interact upon each other across political, social and cultural divisions. So far as space allows, the narrative tries to record the political and cultural atmosphere of the eleven months between September 30, 1938 and September 3, 1939.

Not being a linguist of genius, nor the possessor of a bottomless purse and unlimited time, I have had to rely on other scholars for evidence in most of the languages of Eastern Europe and of Japan. But I have also benefited greatly from the work of my former students, most notably Sidney Aster, Uri Bialer, James Compton, John R. Fox, Gerry van Kessell, John Koliopoulis, the late Frank Marzari, Lawrence Pratt, John Pritchard, Elizabeth Ann Radice, Angela Raspin, Norman Rose, Donald Rotunda, Wesley Wark and Robert Young. Their number is a measure of my good fortune. Mrs Marion Yates, Anne Lane and John Hermann have helped me enormously, finding material and photographs. Other scholars to whom I owe special thanks for aid and encouragement are Anthony Adamthwaite, Martin Alexander, Corelli Barnet, Henryk Batowski, Roy Bridge, Clifton Child, Alvin Coox, David Dilks, Kenneth Duke, Margaret Gowing, Jonathan Haslam, Dov Lungu, Alastair Parker, Enrico Serra and Zara Steiner. At LSE, Ian Nish and Anthony Polonsky helped me with the Japanese and Polish sources and interpretations. Kenneth Bourne lent me encouragement, and taught me by his own example how to extract the utmost from the evidence. I must also salute the Honourable Miss Margaret Lambert under whose guidance I discovered I could read Italian, and who opened my eyes to scholarship at its most meticulous. For encouragement, assistance and advancement my debt is most strong towards the dead, Mario Toscano, Llewellyn Woodward and most of all to Norton Medlicott, who appointed me to LSE.

I have also to thank the staffs of the libraries of Aberdeen University, the British Library of Political and Economic Science, the University of Birmingham Library, Churchill College, Cambridge, Cambridge University Library, the Library of the Foreign and Commonwealth Office, and of the Ministry of Defence, the National Library of Scotland, the Bodleian Library, the Institut für Zeitgeschichte in Munich, the German Historical Institute, the Institut Français, the Institute of

Historical Research, the Library of the School of Slavonic and East European Studies, the Sikorski Institute, the Liddell Hart Military Archives Centre, King's College, London, and the National Maritime Library.

I have also benefited from consulting over the years the memories of the late Lord Strang, Lord Brimelow, Lord Gladwyn, Lord Stanfield, the late Sir Robert Craigie, Sir Frank Roberts, Sir Fitzroy Maclean, and the late Lady Loraine, widow of Sir Percy Loraine.

My thanks are also due to my editor, the tactful and meticulous Jane Carr.

HOW WAR CAME

CHAPTER 1

MAY 1945: EUROPE'S END

It was raining over the Lüneburg Heath. Winds from off the North Sea whipped drizzle across the stunted pines and fir trees. On one bare patch amidst the trees stood a small weatherbeaten tent, 10 feet by 20 in ground plan with room inside only for a wooden kitchen table covered by a blue cloth. There were two microphones on the table, and between them stood an inkstand with one ordinary steel-nibbed pen. Nearby was a caravan, the mobile home from which Monty – Field Marshal Sir Bernard Montgomery – had fought his war and commanded his armies ever since the tides of war had begun to turn against the now defeated, devastated and divided Germany.

At five o'clock of that afternoon, May 4, 1945, a small group of German officers arrived outside the caravan. At their head was the grey-faced General-Admiral von Friedeburg, a leather coat over his admiral's uniform, a battered peaked soldier's hat on his head. With him was General Kinzel, Chief of Staff to the German armed forces in northern Germany, magnificent in a green Wehrmacht greatcoat with brilliant red lapels, a monocle screwed into one eye, the epitome of the old Prussian army, dominating still the small cluster of staff officers who accompanied him, drab and huddled in German army grey. They stood disconsolate and shivering in the rain, surrounded by an excited bevy of Allied press correspondents and photographers, as the Admiral disappeared into Monty's caravan.

A few minutes later he re-emerged. Again the group waited. Finally Montgomery appeared at the door of the caravan, in immaculate British army battledress, red staff tabs on his lapels, a field marshal's baton on his shoulder straps. As always, his personality, electric, jaunty, like that of an eternal captain of games in some minor Victorian public school, carrying his bat after a winning innings at cricket, dominated and held the attention of those who waited. As he walked, with his inimitable swagger, past the waiting Allied reporters, his inability to resist playing to any audience overcame for a moment his sense of occasion. 'This is the moment,' he said out of the corner of his mouth. Then he entered the tent, sat down, with a wave of his hand invited the German officers to sit also, adjusted his horn-rimmed spectacles, opened the sheaf of papers he carried in his hand and began to read aloud: 'Instrument of Surrender of all German armed forces in Holland, in north-west Germany, including all islands, and in Denmark. 1. The German Command agrees . . .'

When the reading was over, the German officers, grey and stone of face, signed one after the other: General-Admiral von Friedeburg; General Kinzel; Rear Admiral Wagner; General Pauhle.

Finally, Montgomery took up the pen. 'And now,' he said, 'I will sign on behalf of the Supreme Allied Commander, General Eisenhower.' In his clear, round, simple hand he wrote, 'B. L. Montgomery, Field Marshal. 4 May 1945, 1830 hrs.' The fighting was over.

The scene was to be repeated: in Italy between Field Marshal Alexander and General Wolff; in southern Germany; in the east with the Russians in the ruins of Berlin; and finally in the small red schoolhouse outside Reims where General Eisenhower had his Supreme Headquarters in the west. The junketing, the mafeking, the mixture of formal ceremony and prayer and orgiastic, riotous release with which Britain and America celebrated VE night, Victory in Europe, were not to come for another four days. But for the opposed forces of the two belligerents who had made the German-Polish dispute over Danzig and the Polish Corridor a world-wide conflagration, five years and nine months before, the war was over. There remained only the ruins, the misery, the task of immediate survival, and finally the slow, immensely slow, task of economic and physical reconstruction. There remained also the unavoidable task of investigation, identification, trial, and, where appropriate, punishment.

For, contrary to what some historians are now beginning to argue, whether from an instinctive bent towards apologetics, or in an attempt at an inhuman detachment or from an exaggerated respect for the role of accident in history, the Second World War *was* willed to happen. Not perhaps in the way it did: miscalculation, misinformation and mistaken intentions all enter into the process by which it came about. But a war against Britain and France, the conquest and subjugation of Poland, and the physical elimination of its gypsy and Jewish communities, all that Hitler conceived, all that his minions and followers for their thousand and one different motives – lust for power, pride in race and name, ambition, fear, greed, that peculiar German virtue, obedience to death (*Kadavergehorsamkeit*) – did in interpretation of and obedience to his concepts, was willed, aided and abetted, and acquiesced in by a multitude of accomplices, German and non-German. Some were caught and tried. Many were not. What they did, the ruins, the hunger, the hatred, the destruction they created and which was created to defeat them, Europe could only survive and overcome as the day of Nazi defeat withdrew into time.

In May 1945, Europe was near death. Over the whole continent from the North Sea to the banks of the Volga its cities lay in ruins. Its transportation system was shattered, its rolling stock scattered the length and breadth of the continent, rusting in sidings, burnt out by the edge of the track where carriages and wagons had been tipped to clear the rails after air attack or sabotage had wrecked them. Europe's bridges were largely in ruins, its rivers bridged instead by the temporary structures of the victorious armies. Its factories lay roofless and gaping to the sky, and when the war ended the spring was almost over without the farmers having been able to plough and sow. The green fields of France and Germany were spotted with dead cows, stomachs bloated, four legs stiffly in the air, a feast for flies and a breeding ground for pestilence.

What mostly caught the eye as one travelled through Europe after the ceasefire were the bones of the cities. Germany was worst hit, its cities, from Cologne to Dresden, from Hamburg to Berlin, grey heaps of rubble in the bright sunshine which followed the bleak weather of early May. France and Belgium had come off comparatively lightly except for the battlegrounds of Normandy, the coastal towns and the areas around the big industrial complexes. Even here sudden gaps among the houses of a roadside village would show where a couple of Tiger tanks or a company of Panzergrenadiers had sought to hold up the Allied advance or where the vengeful bands of the Maquis had cornered their erstwhile persecutors.

Much of the Netherlands had been under water since the winter of 1944, and the Dutch had been reduced to eating tulip bulbs in an effort to avoid starvation. Italy and the whole of the Eastern Front were in far worse shape. A swathe of destruction marked the progress of the Allied forces in Italy from Salerno to the plains of northern Italy, while from the banks of the Volga and the gates of Moscow and Leningrad to the borders of Austria and the plains of central Germany, the advance and retreat of war had left hardly a city or town unscathed.

The ruins of Europe were matched by the wreck of European society and government as they had existed before the war. The Third Republic in France had collapsed in defeat and voted itself out of existence in the summer of 1940. Its collaborationist, authoritarian successor, the shameful descendants of the French patriots, Déroulède and Gambetta, had passed into the oblivion of treason trials and organized purges. The Belgian monarchy and its supporters lay under the suspicion of collaboration during captivity. The German state, down to its least municipal authority, had been deprived of power and disbanded by the occupying powers. The Austrian state, destroyed by Hitler in 1938 and resurrected by an Allied decision in 1943, had two governments, one in Vienna sponsored by the Russians, and one, largely self-constituted, under American protection in Salzburg.

East of Germany the Soviets had supplanted or were in the process of overthrowing entirely the pre-war governments of Eastern Europe. The Baltic states had disappeared entirely into the Union of Soviet and Socialist Republics in 1940. In Yugoslavia the victorious partisan leader, Marshal Tito, was agreeing with reluctance and reservations to accept representatives of the pre-war democratic parties into his government. The young king, Peter, remained in exile. In Greece the Communist partisans of the ELAS, having devoted most of their wartime efforts to eliminating the non-Communist armed bands, had already attempted to seize power by a coup in December 1944 only to find that they had been abandoned by Stalin to a British occupation determined to restore the legitimate monarchy and a reasonable semblance of government by voluntary rather than enforced consent.

Italy lay as in 1920, before Mussolini seized power, divided between Socialist and Communist anti-clericals and the mass strength of the Catholic Church and Italian industrial society, still monarchist and authoritarian by sympathy, but convinced by twenty years of Fascism that neither the monarchy nor corporative politics was the answer to their problems, and ready for a return to that personal factionalism which had been the bane of Italian politics since the twelfth-century renaissance.

This, however, was at the highest level of politics. The ordinary life of Europeans was governed by the fantastic upheavals of total war. It is quite impossible to obtain accurate figures of the casualties Europe suffered in the five and a half years of war. At various times upwards of forty million men served in the embattled forces of the European powers, not including twelve and a half million more from the Soviet Union. Five and a half million or more of them died in action, over and above a Soviet death toll of a further seven and a half million. Civilian casualties in Europe probably brought the figure up to ten million. The Soviet Union suffered an estimated two and a half million civilian deaths. The statistics for wounded, missing, deaths through disease and so on are unobtainable. Between four and a half and six million Jews, 70 per cent or more of Europe's pre-war Jewish population, and a rather higher percentage of European gypsies were murdered as a matter of policy. For those who survived, there could be no forgiveness for so ultimate a crime.

The war brought with it immense enforced movements of population. Nearly seven million forced labourers were imported into Germany between 1942 and 1944. The unfortunate Baltic Germans were shipped backwards and forwards across Europe with the changes and turns of German resettlement policies. Over ten million Germans were driven out of Eastern Europe in 1945–6, mainly from Poland and Czechoslovakia. As the guns ceased firing, the roads of Europe pullulated with populations on the move, walking, cycling, pushing perambulators, driving carts laden with household utensils and personal belongings, trekking less in hope than in hopelessness, searching for some point of reference where perhaps a new beginning could be made. They found little to aid them in the task. Europe's cities, the whole fabric of urban industrial life, were as much casualties of war as they were.

The worst, because the most irredeemable, losses to Europe were those suffered in the field of art and architecture. The works the Nazis plundered could be and were restored, or at least the best known and most famous. Even those that were looted or 'liberated', as the phrase went, by the individually greedy among the Allied armies, would turn up sooner or later among the art and junk shops of Europe and America. But the lost paintings, the monasteries and old cities, gutted by bomb, shell or fire, could never properly be restored; and despite the care that was taken to put some of the more mobile treasures out of harm's way before the fighting began, to store paintings in caves, statues in cellars, jewels and silver in disused railway tunnels, despite the work of the British and American Monuments, Fine Arts and Archives officers, despite the orders given personally by Roosevelt and Churchill to spare cultural treasures as much as possible and to avoid occupying listed monuments, despite the work of the German *Kunstschutz* and the Italian officials in similar organizations, a major part of Europe's treasures, the creations of more than twenty-five centuries of successive civilizations, has disappeared for ever.

In Russia the great eleventh-century monastery and cathedral at Kiev, the Elizabeth-palais and the Alexander-palais at Tsarskoe Selo; the Granavity Palace, the Church of Spas-Mereditsky, built in 1148 with the cycle of fresco paintings, the most celebrated examples of ancient Russian painting; the Cathedral of the Transfiguration at Chernigov, the best of Russia's Byzantine buildings – all completely destroyed.

In Poland, almost the whole of medieval Danzig; the medieval centre of Warsaw, the old market square, St John's Cathedral, the baroque palaces of Lazienski and Krasinski, the fifteenth-century Gothic church of the Holy Virgin; in Poznan, the beautiful cathedral; in Lwow, the seventeenth-century church of the Bernardine monks, the flower of early baroque in Poland – all were totally destroyed.

In the Netherlands, in Rotterdam, all but the tower of the Groote Kirk of St Lawrence, the beautiful medieval centre of Middelburg, and many of the best buildings of the same period in Arnhem, Nymwegen, Sluis and Venlo; in Belgium, the Church of St Catherine and the Town Hall at Hoogstraaten, the Reliquary of St Gertrude, the most remarkable example of Flemish Gothic goldsmith's work, the carved sixteenth-century reredos at Bocholt, the fourteenth-century Benedictine Church of St Gertrude at Louvain, most of the old town at Tournai – all destroyed.

In France, the town of St Malo, largely composed of seventeenth- and eighteenth-century houses, lay in ruins, as did the church and two beautiful towers of Notre Dame in St Lô. In Caen Allied shells and bombs completely destroyed the twelfth-century Church of St Gilles, the perfect spire of the Church of St Pierre, the City Hall and the castle. Large parts of the cathedral at Rouen; the medieval section of Beauvais round the old tenth-century church; the twelfth-century cathedral of St Die; the whole waterfront of the Vieux Port in Marseilles – all destroyed.

Budapest, with its loveliest of bridges and the Royal Palace, completely destroyed. In Vienna, bombs directed at that obvious military centre, Schönbrunn Palace, blew the western end of the delicate Gloriette to bits; the Belvedere, built for Marlborough's ally, Prince Eugene of Savoy, was damaged; incendiaries burnt out the roof of St Stephen's Cathedral, Vienna's beloved Alte Steffel, and the Opera; the Liechtenstein Stadtpalais and the grand baroque palace of the Schwarzenbergs were destroyed.

Britain, like Austria, came off comparatively lightly save for the cities of London, Coventry and Plymouth. Despite the deliberate attempts to destroy it by the Luftwaffe in the so-called 'Baedeker' raids of 1943–4, the beautiful eighteenth-century town of Bath only suffered minor damage. The precincts of Canterbury were hit in another Baedeker raid. Worse losses were the cathedral at Coventry, St Andrew's Church at Plymouth, the Tudor St Peter's Hospital at Bristol and the fifteenth-century church at St Mary le Port. Worst hit of all were the London churches, Chelsea Old Church, All Hallows, St Bride's, Fleet Street, St Lawrence Jewry, St Clement Danes, and many others; and the great halls of the city, the Guildhall, Merchant Taylors' and the Charterhouse.

The worst losses were in Italy and in Germany. The city of Ancona was fought over bitterly, and the Church of Santa Maria della Misericordia and much else destroyed. The ancient Cathedral of Benvento was severely damaged in the fighting following the Allied landing at Salerno. When the Germans evacuated Naples, already battered by Allied bombing, they mined the ruins as they left. The great Church of Santa Chiara was burnt out. As the 'red hot rake of the battle line' (Churchill's words) was drawn up the peninsula, the Allies destroyed the famous monastery of Monte Cassino, and the towns of Cori, Nervi, Palestrino, Frascati and Viterbo all suffered. The Germans deliberately shelled the little medieval town of San Gimignano after they had evacuated it. Forno, Pescara, Faenza were all damaged, and Rimini, with the great Church of San Francesco, Alberti's masterpiece, was damaged. Paintings, frescoes, altarpieces and painted ceilings were minor casualties. The worst damage was suffered by Florence, declared an open city by Hitler to save it from destruction. To bar Allied troops from crossing the River Arno, all Florence's bridges save the Ponte Vecchio, including the beautiful Ponte Santà Trinità, were destroyed. To bar the road to the Ponte Vecchio the Germans levelled the old medieval city where Dante lived, the Primo Cerchio of the Middle Ages, and mined the ruins. In chalk, below Dante's statue in the Colonnade of the Uffizi, an unknown hand scrawled

> *In sul passo dell'Arno*
> *I tedeschi hanno lasciato*
> *I recordi della loro civiltà.*

('In their passage of the Arno the Germans have left the record of their civilization'.)

This was the bitter comment of war. For Germany suffered as badly, if not worse than any other country save Poland.

The City Hall at Aachen; St Gereon, the beautiful Romanesque St Maria im Capitol, Gross St Martin, the City Hall and much of the Cathedral itself in Cologne; the fourteenth-century Gothic Town Hall, the City Wine House, the thirteenth-century Church of St Ludges in Münster; the old market place, and the Electoral Palace at Mainz; the town centre and the Kesselstedtpalais at Trier; the old city centre at Darmstadt; the square, and the Alte Markt, the City Hall and the Domplatz at Frankfurt; the Stiftskirche and the two palaces, one sixteenth-, one eighteenth-century, at Stuttgart; the city centre, rich in old houses, at Ulm; the Venetian and Mirror rooms in the Residenz at

Würzburg, masterpiece of the great baroque architect Balthasar Neumann; the medieval centre, the market place, the Frauenkirche and the Spital der Heiligen Geist at Nuremberg; St Anne Damen Stifts-kirche, masterpiece of the high baroque architects, the Asan brothers; the Town Hall and sixteenth-century centre at Augsburg; the Kaiser-haus and St Andrew's Church at Hildesheim; the centre of Goethe's Dresden; the old area around the Binnenhofen with the Katheriner-kirche in Hamburg; almost all the old houses in the Altstadt and the five famous churches and the main building of the Schloss Herrenhausen in Hanover; most of medieval Lübeck; the Castle of the Teutonic Knights at Königsberg; the beautiful rococo house of Mon Bijou, the Charlot-tenburg and the Hohenzollern Schloss in Berlin.

These are only a few of the buildings listed as 'destroyed', 'ruined', and 'gutted to the outer shell' in the reports of the British and American Monuments, Fine Arts and Archives officers who had the heartbreak-ing task of surveying, reporting, and where possible salvaging those parts of the heritage of Europe which the warriors had spared.

It would be easy enough to extend this catalogue, but to add names to more names is the job of an accountant rather than a historian. What Europe lost through the war was a great part of its history and an immense treasury of delight and joy for all generations to come. To destroy the relics of the past is, even in small things, a kind of amputation, a self-mutilation not so much of limbs as of the memory and the imagination. To destroy buildings, paintings and sculptures on the scale they were destroyed in the years of the Second World War – the work of craftsmen, carpenters, painters, wood-carvers, sculptors and writers of ten centuries, conceived in joy and brought forth with a delight which remained to fill all those who came to see them through the generations that followed – was an act which made those creations as though they had never been and impoverished all who were to come. To walk through the mountains of fire-blackened rubble where once the centres of medieval cities stood and to realize this was not the random outcome of ill-directed bombing, but deliberate, is to feel the presence once again of barbarism. The courage and determination of the airmen who dropped the bombs, riding high above the searchlights and anti-aircraft fire, but not always high enough to escape destruction, battling with the night fighters, are beyond question. But to what end was this courage directed by those who planned the raids? It is difficult to argue that the war was one whit the closer to being won for this destruction. But those who live in Europe are infinitely the poorer. In these years Europe not only destroyed much of her heritage; she performed what amounted to a partial prefrontal lobotomy.

In the months immediately after the war ended, however, it was the concentration camps that struck Europeans most deeply. Belsen and Buchenwald became household names. Few there were who had not seen, at least on the newsreels, the pitiful survivors of the camps, their thin, impossibly elongated legs and arms, their blank hollow eyes, and the desperate filth around them, seeming to justify almost any infamy committed against those who were responsible. As the fuller details, the sadism and the beatings, the mass sterilizations, the gas chambers, the forced labour and the medical experiments, gradually became known, Europe recoiled in horror and disgust. Worse possibly was the ghoulish utilitarianism of the concentration camp managers, displayed in the piles of baled human hair for stuffing cheap mattresses, the heaps of gold fillings which went to swell the Nazi gold reserves, the clusters of spectacles and eyeglasses that were all that remained of those whom the guards had gassed and incinerated. All over Europe the camps were found. All over Europe their guards, their commandants and super-visors, and the men who had organized and administered them were sought, too often in vain. Allied security forces in Europe kept by them a register, the size of a London telephone directory, of names of men and women wanted on war crimes charges. It had over twenty thousand entries. In many cases there were merely the names of units: the XYZ Company of an SS Grenadier Division wanted for the massacre of the inhabitants – men, women and children – of a village in Bosnia; a certain infantry regiment, D Company, wanted for the shooting of hostages in Galicia; and so on, and so on. To this day there are men in Europe, going about their business, working as doctors, dentists, garage mechanics, farm hands, who took part during these years in unspeakable cruelties and bestialities. Many are living in retirement. Only time can finally eliminate them.

These are all personal tragedies, endless in number, endlessly re-peated. Europe collectively had lost more than this. The war had begun with Europe's two strongest powers, industrial Germany and imperial Britain, at war. At its end Germany was devastated and Britain bankrupt. The armies of two non-European powers, the Russian and American superpowers, met in Europe's centre. The United States and the Soviet Union were neither of them European powers in the strictest sense. Both had emerged to enter world politics in the eighteenth century, Russia at the beginning, America at the end of the century. Both had developed internally in considerable isolation from the main currents of European social, intellectual and cultural developments. As Europe had entered its century of revolutions, America had cut herself off by presidential proclamation, Russia by police powers. Each had developed its own brand of agrarian populist radicalism, idealizing the direct political democracy of the town meeting, or the direct economic democracy of the workers' co-operative. Their dominant regimes differed very greatly, American democracy being a republican variant of eighteenth-century British limited monarchy, Russian autocracy a theocratic variant of eighteenth-century German benevolent despotism. What both had in common, by the time Soviet Communism and New Deal Federal democracy had replaced the systems of the nineteenth century, was a universalist ideology and a consequent conviction of the invariable and exclusive correctness of their own methods and approach, which was quite unlike anything which survived in Europe in 1945 where even the native brands of totalitarianism were national and particularist rather than universalist. There was no European Nazi or Fascist party. The European Socialist parties had failed manifestly to collaborate. The European Communist parties had only been kept in unity by the severest and closest of Russian control which, now that they were achieving power through much of Eastern Europe, was going to have to be even more closely exercised, rather than the reverse.

At war's end Europe lay divided between the soldiers of Soviet Russia and those of the United States. Two British armies and one French were all that remained of Europe's power, with the share in the occupation of Central Europe that their survival had won them. Inevitably the superpowers were to disagree on the maintenance of European security and the future of Europe's still immense industrial potential. Their disagreement was to harden into a new conflict and confrontation, but without fighting. Europe occupied in 1945 was to become Europe garrisoned. And the still imperial powers of the Western European coasts – Belgium, the Netherlands, France and Britain – were to lose all but the fractional residues of their empires as power finally left Europe, and the rest of the world returned gradually to the polycentrism it had enjoyed before the great European outpouring had begun.

Portugal had begun that outpouring in the fifteenth century, her painted caravels edging down the coasts of Africa to break finally into the Indian Ocean. Portugal remained neutral throughout the war, and Portugal was the last to abandon her colonial empire. The continent of Europe lay divided between the two superpowers, tied in varying degrees of tightness, politically, socially, financially, or economically, into one or other of the rival systems. Europe conquered had become Europe revived. But Europe revived was still Europe garrisoned.

CHAPTER 2

THE PRELIMINARIES TO EUROPE'S SUICIDE

The devastation of Europe in 1945 was in no way novel or unprecedented. Europe had known destruction on this scale before, in 1918. The devastation had not been so widespread; at least not in Western Europe, where it had been confined to a broad swathe running through northern France and Flanders. But where war had struck, the destruction wrought in 1914–18 had been, if anything, more intense than that of the years 1939–45, as visitors to the battlefields of the Western Front of 1914–18 and of 1940–4 in France frequently remarked. The death toll was at least as large; in fact, for France and Britain it was much larger in the hecatombs of Verdun, the Somme, and Passchendaele than it was to be in the fighting of the Second World War. The death toll in the East was larger in 1941–5, but only marginally if the casualties of the Russian Civil War are added to those of the years 1914–17.

The political upheavals of 1917–19 in Europe were, if anything, even more drastic than those which followed the Soviet victories of 1944–5. However, they were not so lasting in their effect. Empires disappeared in 1919 and new successor states were born. A *macédoine* of young and weak nations sprang up where once had lain the borderlands of the Hapsburg, Ottoman and Tsarist empires. But 1944–5 saw Soviet Russian power establish itself at the core of pre-war Europe. Who holds Bohemia holds Europe, Bismarck wrote. In 1945 the Soviet armies held Bohemia – they were to hold it for the next 45 years.

Despite all this, there is good warrant for saying that Europe in 1919 experienced much of what she was to know again in 1945. Her harvests were small, her young men killed or mutilated, her treasuries exhausted, and her power in the world had to take second place to the immense financial and industrial wealth of the United States, as it did to its huge levels of manpower. When the peace conference met at Versailles, President Wilson of the United States spoke with the authority of the only man who controlled armies of fresh untried young men in numbers hardly yet tapped by the battlefields of 1918. Tied by no secret agreements, or none that he recognized, he inspired himself and his entourage with a contempt and distaste for those who were to be his associates at the peace conference almost as severe as that which he reserved for the defeated German enemy. His were the words and ideals with which those attending the Conference of Peace were forced to concern themselves by virtue of the manner in which he had negotiated the armistice with Germany and by virtue of his belief that he spoke for the common people of Europe as well as of the United States. In 1919 as in 1945 Europe lay under the shadow of American power, but in 1919 it was to be withdrawn and Europe, then the focal point of all but two of the great powers of the world, was to have another chance.

From 1815 to 1914, the European powers had dominated the globe, financing its development, planting it with colonies, girdling it with railways, steamship lines and wireless communications, absorbing all but the Americas into their various imperial spheres. Two nations, Italy and Germany, had unified themselves without a major war, by virtue of a common system of conventions and negotiations known as the 'Concert system' or the balance of power. Conflicts there had been in plenty, but they had always been localized by the skill and limited objectives of the participants.

In 1914 the system had broken down under the strain of a new set of national leaders who understood neither its rules nor, once they had broken them, how the system could be reconstituted. What was disastrous for Europe was not so much the outbreak of the First World War, but the inability or unwillingness of anyone in the seats of power and authority to bring the war to an early end. For four and a quarter years Europe's leaders had ravaged its wealth and manhood like violent, compulsive drunks, feeding their peoples on nationalist and racialist hatred as a way of justifying the terrible casualties they suffered. The European great powers ended one Europe, dissolving, dissipating and destroying the system on which its dominant position in the world rested.

Yet, in 1919, the European system did seem to have won a second chance. President Wilson failed to carry his country into the new League of Nations, wrecking his health in the effort. Civil war ravaged the Soviet Union, leaving it weak, suspicious and isolated, behind a barrier of neutral, if not antipathetic, nations. The European powers – Britain, France, Germany and Italy – confronted one another over a prostrate but recovering Europe. They put their seal on this recovery at the Swiss lakeside city of Locarno in 1925, when Britain and Italy guaranteed the Franco-German frontier, and the French and German

Foreign Ministers, Aristide Briand and Gustav Stresemann, seemed to have celebrated the end of three hundred years of Franco-German conflict. The celebration was followed by a serious effort to tackle the question of European disarmament, and a rather less serious treaty to 'outlaw the use of war as an instrument of national policy', important because it bore the name of the American Secretary of State, Frank Kellogg, and marked the offered return of the United States to participation in international politics for a further, progressively less hopeful, five years.

Nevertheless, by 1928 Europe seemed to have recovered from its first great war. Democratic governments ruled in Germany and France. The pound was back on the gold standard, even if the penalty was a long-term deflation of Britain's economy. Her government was embarking on a substantial programme of welfare expenditure. Her investments overseas were approaching the 1914 figure, even though this was now dwarfed by America's immense investments abroad. The Dawes Plan had gone much of the way towards solving the problems of German reparations payments. Britain and France were gradually repaying their war debts to the United States. The League of Nations was functioning in Geneva, having stopped what might have been a nasty little war between Greece and Bulgaria in 1925. The preparatory commission for the World Disarmament Conference was also meeting in Geneva with American and, for the first time in 1928, Soviet participation. The worst threat to peace seemed to lie in Anglo-American naval rivalry; this too was to be settled within a year.

And yet there were portents on the horizon. Italy, the victor deprived of what her nationalists regarded as the spoils of victory, had abandoned parliamentary democracy in 1922 and was now a Fascist state under Benito Mussolini. Fascist gangsters raised their ugly heads in France. In Germany Hitler was writing his second book, his party revived and disciplined after the collapse of the 1923 putsch, much more evenly distributed nationally than before, waiting for the hour to come. Squalid terrorism disfigured the Balkans where Italians financed and trained the International Macedonian Revolutionary Organization to terrorize Bulgaria, and extremist Croats to disrupt the state of Yugoslavia. In Austria relations between the two largest parties, the Christian Social Party and the Socialists, were already on the verge of civil war. In Poland, Marshal Pilsudski had thrown out the politicians and installed a junta of radical colonels of a kind with which the world was to become only too familiar long before the end of the twentieth century. The streets of Europe were beginning to familiarize themselves with political violence, with political armies in uniform, with shouted salutes, with the gun and the rubber truncheon. Under cover of the prosperity and the noble speeches on peace and disarmament, civilization in Europe, desperately shaken by defeat and economic disaster, was tiptoeing steadily backwards towards the abyss.

Central to this was the abiding influence of the experience of war. The years 1914–18 had taken a whole generation of bourgeois sons and students and made them into officers and masters in a tradition of aristocracy heavily overladen with the brutality of the old-style professional armies. It had conferred on them high ideals, camaraderie, an inability to relate to all but small groups, platoons, companies, free corps, a taste for living dangerously, and a familiarity with violence.

For many confronted with defeat and the collapse of the home front the experience was too much, especially when their newly won status as commanders, givers of orders which had to be obeyed, was challenged by members of social classes or minority groups they regarded as below them – peasants, trades unionists, revolutionary workers, Jews, Poles, Irish. Demobilized, they turned to violence rather than to petty clerkdom or minor managerial jobs – professional posts of the kind for which, without a world war, they would have been marked. In Italy, they gravitated naturally to the *Fasci di Combattimento*; in Germany they thronged into the *Freikorps*, the *Einwohnerwehr*, the multifarious nationalist splinter parties among which the Nazis were only one of the smallest, the paramilitary organizations and the illegal armies. To those whom they regarded as traitors or as dangerous to the State they meted out violence and assassination. Inflation wiped out their capital and the savings of their parents, their chance of status and their hope of careers.

More fortunate than her European neighbours, Britain exported her hardest hit cases to Ireland, Palestine, Rhodesia and elsewhere. The guns which in Germany were turned on the left-wing Spartacists, could be used by Britain to maintain order in India in decent obscurity and without creating the scars of civil war. Outwardly, Europe presented a view of peace, tranquillity and prosperity. But behind the façade lurked the rats, ready, given half a chance, to kill and destroy, to remake the chaos and anarchy, the comradeship, dedication and adventure of war.

The collapse was not long in coming. It began early in 1929 when the flow of American investment which had kept Europe's wheels turning began to be diverted to speculation in the great Wall Street boom. Unemployment rose in Germany and the terms negotiated by the American banker Young for the further settlement of Germany's reparation obligations struck much of German banking and industry as impossibly onerous. In their imagined extremity they turned to the German parliamentary nationalists, and they in turn, struck by the growth of the Nazi party in Parliament in the elections of 1929, turned to the Nazis. The moneybags of German industry were opened to Hitler, and as unemployment climbed, so did Nazi strength.

In October 1929 the stock market in Wall Street crashed. The first days of the crash were spectacular. But they were followed by an even steadier decline which pulled the props from under every government and financial organization in Europe save only the Bank of France. Gustav Stresemann died that same month. Five months later the 'Great Coalition', which united German Social Democrats with the parliamentary right, finally disintegrated and President von Hindenburg found himself forced to nominate a minority government to govern by exercise of the emergency presidential powers. His new Chancellor, Heinrich Brüning, was still a democrat. His rivals were not. Germany lurched steadily into civil strife and towards a dictatorship exercised by a real dictator. Brüning turned rashly to seeking success in the field of foreign policy adequate to enable him to win over a majority of the German Parliament to his side again. The moment could hardly have been worse chosen.

Brüning's Foreign Minister, Julius Curtius, launched an idea which was to strike a blow for the union of Germany and Austria that the Treaty of Versailles had forbidden: to negotiate a customs union between the two countries. But when the news of his proposal leaked out, in March 1931, it provoked the French into bitter resistance. The Austrians were already negotiating for a loan in Paris; and in May the largest Austrian bank had to be supported by Austrian government action to avoid its going into bankruptcy. Germany's own financial position was none too safe, and the internal necessity of a tough new budget was balanced by the obvious need to diminish German reparations payments. Money began to leave Germany in a steadily increasing flood, and the Government's credit was rapidly exhausting itself. The Bank of England stepped into the breach to buttress both Austria and Germany, and President Hoover proposed a twelve-month moratorium on all inter-governmental payments.

The French, however, would not play. For a vital fortnight they argued and delayed. The strain on the Reichsmark regained and increased its original vigour. In July the Darmstadter and National Bank, one of the two largest banks in Germany, closed its doors. Then pressure shifted dramatically to London despite credits from America and repeated consultation with Germany, France and Italy. The Labour Government in Britain broke over the necessary measures of economy, and Ramsay MacDonald formed a new National Coalition of the Conservatives, the Labour ministers who supported him, and the

Liberals. Even this was not adequate. Six weeks afterwards Britain abandoned the gold standard and embarked on a series of cuts in government expenditure which were to leave her and her empire militarily defenceless against possible aggression and to cause mutiny in the Home Fleet, for the first time since the Spithead mutinies of 1798.

It was at this very precise moment, far away on the other side of the globe, that the first shots were fired in the preliminary skirmishes of the Second World War. Since the breakdown of the Chinese empire at the end of the nineteenth century, the Chinese nation had known weakness, civil war and revolution. Her central government had been helpless against foreign pressure, her provinces ruled by individual warlords, generals of varying faiths and degrees of civilization, maintaining power only by their possession of the *ultima ratio regum*, obedient guns. No wonder that Mao Tse-tung, leading the infant Chinese Communist Party out of the shambles of the abortive urban revolution of 1927 into the long flight which was to make of it something undreamt of by Karl Marx and unimaginable by Lenin, wrote 'All power grows from the end of a gun'. It was not his party, however, but the Chinese 'bourgeois' nationalist Kuomintang, led by the Soviet-trained soldier, Chiang Kai-shek, who knitted the Chinese provinces together again so that by 1929 his power and influence was beginning to lap over into Manchuria, northernmost province of China and virtually a Japanese economic colony, where Japanese troops had been guarding the railroads ever since Japan's defeat of Russia in 1905.

On the night of September 4, 1931 at Mukden, the capital of Southern Manchuria, a conspiratorially organized group of Japanese officers staged an 'incident', which led the Japanese forces in Manchuria to occupy the whole province and to proclaim it an independent state, Manchukuo, with the last Manchu emperor of China at its head. Unable to restrain them, the Japanese Cabinet resigned, making way for one more in tune with the sentiments of these new military nationalists. Ships of the Japanese navy answered a Chinese boycott of Japanese goods with an amphibious operation at Shanghai in January 1932. Their marines ran into determined Chinese opposition, an armistice only interposing itself when both sides had fought themselves to a standstill. Through all of this the League of Nations debated, attempted to mediate, and investigated. But even the carefully conciliatory proposals for a settlement put forward in the autumn of 1932 by Lord Lytton, the English chairman of the League's investigating commission, could not prevent the new Japanese Government, totally nationalist in its own self-righteousness, from taking Japan out of the League of Nations. British and American interests in the Far East had been served notice. For Britain at least the anxieties of her Pacific dominions and the threat to her own very considerable interests in China were to be an abiding distraction from threats closer to home, in Europe and in the Mediterranean, in the years to come.

The collapse of the Austro-German customs union project had left France temporarily the leader of Europe. Hers was, however, a leadership by default, by weakness, by negation. French power was the power to obstruct, to deny. Creative power she lacked entirely, and the strength of the franc on which this power rested was steadily eroded as the pound recovered after the abandonment of the gold standard. Attempting to force through an economic reconstruction of the Balkans with a £10 million sterling loan to back it, the French only succeeded in alienating the Italians. Mussolini sacked his pro-French Foreign Minister, Count Grandi, sending him to comparative exile in the Italian Embassy in London, and devoted his conspiratorial talents (which were as considerable as those more statesmanlike were lacking to him) to capturing control of Austria and to fomenting the hatred of Hungary against her victorious neighbours, Romania, Czechoslovakia and Yugoslavia. The Soviet Union, equally suspicious, backed away from any close association with France; and Britain, recovering rapidly from the nadir of her fortunes in 1931, found herself moving steadily into the position of arbiter between France and Germany.

This increase in British power would not have mattered had the British Government and people been able to see beyond their own immediate economic problems and the desirability of disarmament to recognize what was happening in Germany, and the crucial importance of this for the future well-being of Europe as a whole. At least the French understood the essential importance for the tranquillity of Europe of maintaining a balance of control as against the largest, most industrially powerful and most politically undeveloped nation in Europe. Their difficulty in persuading others lay partially in the extreme nationalist character of their own arguments, and partly in their inability, after Briand's death, to see beyond the problem of controlling Germany. They were thus to contribute both to British and to German unreason, distracting British opinion by the obstacles they placed in the way of a reduction in armaments by agreement, a cause to which every party in Britain had to some degree been forced to pledge support, and providing extreme German nationalists with arguments with which to attack their own governments. In fact, it would not have been true at any time to say that a majority of Germans saw the cause of their extreme economic discontent in foreign machinations. It was rather that the forces which actually exerted power in Germany during this period came in part to seek success in foreign policy as a means of providing them with new prestige to replace that which their inability to solve Germany's internal problems had lost them. The only forces directly interested in foreign policy success for its own sake were the industrialists and financiers for whom the ending of reparations was desirable, and the current army leadership, who wished to see an end to the special restrictions on Germany's armed forces incorporated in the Treaty of Versailles. By December 1932, both these aims had been achieved. Yet only two months later Hitler had been made Chancellor of Germany.

It took the President of Germany, Field Marshal von Hindenburg, and his private supporters four major steps in eight months to reach this point. The first was the dismissal of Brüning, the appointment of the right-wing cavalryman, the former Military Attaché in Washington, Franz von Papen, as Chancellor, and the lifting of the ban imposed on Hitler's storm-troopers by Brüning in April 1932. The second step was the suppression of the Government of the State of Prussia, the largest state in the nominally Federal Germany, by von Papen. The third was the replacement of von Papen by the army's leader and nominee, General Kurt von Schleicher, in December 1932. The fourth, von Papen's revenge, was the poisoning of Hindenburg's mind against von Schleicher, the bringing together of Hitler and the nationalists, and the virtual blackmailing of Hindenburg into appointing Hitler Chancellor of a coalition cabinet. During these eight months the Nazi share of electoral support in Germany rose in the Reichstag elections of July 1932 to an all-time high of 37.8 per cent of the votes cast, to fall in November to 33.1 per cent of the votes cast. Hindenburg himself was re-elected president in March 1932 with over nineteen million votes to eleven and a half million cast for Hitler. Unemployment remained steady at six million, nearly a quarter of the working population.

No single one of these four major steps was caused, or indeed prevented, by success or failure in the field of German foreign policy. Hindenburg removed Brüning from office in the hope of securing a right-wing parliamentary coalition, and as a reaction against Brüning's attempts to deal with the problem of the heavy subsidies that were being paid in the form of high grain prices to the inefficient large-scale Junker farmers of eastern Prussia. Von Papen fell because he was unable either to secure a parliamentary coalition or to govern efficiently and maintain order without one. General von Schleicher thought he saw the possibility of an effective coalition in the separation of the trades unions from the Socialist party and the capture of the dissidents in the ranks of the Nazi party itself. He fell because he failed in this, lost Hindenburg's confidence, and laid himself open to von Papen's intrigues. In spite of his expressed contempt for the 'Bohemian Corporal', as he referred to Hitler, von Papen nevertheless 'persuaded' Hindenburg to accept Hitler as Chancellor of a cabinet that only contained one other Nazi, Goering, out of twelve, with von Papen himself as Deputy Chancellor.

During these eight months the British press and governmental opinion watched events in Germany in fascinated but almost total incomprehension. Some were apprehensive of a revived German nationalism of the type they had been taught by the propaganda and experience of 1914–18 to distrust and oppose. Some could only discuss German affairs in terms of social categories which disguised the daemonic and charismatic character of Hitler himself. Others fell easy or uneasy victims to that charisma. Yet others shared von Papen's illusion that that dynamism, that charisma, would be contained by the more hierarchical elements in German political society. Few saw that this was the last moment in which to dismantle whatever controls the international system still made enforceable against Germany. An end to reparations and an advance in disarmament seemed the only desirable achievements. To achieve these required steady, persistent diplomacy – at the world disarmament conference which finally opened at Geneva in February 1932, and at Lausanne in July 1932.

By December 1932 British and American pressure had brought the French to concede an end to the Versailles restrictions on German armaments, and full equality of rights within a system of international security. It proved to be easy to concede the first, impossible to secure the second. Meanwhile the Nazi storm troops, the SA, marched, the streets of Germany's cities echoed to crossfire between the SA, Communists, *Stahlhelm* and *Reichsbanner*, paramilitary organizations attached to the major parties. The police did nothing. The guns that were used in Germany's streets were to be employed, as the price of national unity, against her neighbours in Europe. There was little a world disarmament conference, liberal aspirations notwithstanding, could do about this, though even Hitler took a little time before he realized that Europe had no policemen in its international streets either, and that the British Government's view of their role varied between that of a town planner and that of a traffic warden.

With Hitler s appointment as Chancellor, the world was six and a half years away from war, and ill-prepared for it. Of all the European great powers probably only the Soviet Union had the manpower under arms to wage a major war, and the Soviet Union was plunged deep in the fight for collectivization and the first Five Year Plan, its peasantry bitterly resisting the amalgamation of their farms and the confiscation of their livestock, preferring slaughter, death and mass deportation to obedience. France's mass armies and air force were already obsolescent, unable to live in the air with the aircraft being designed in Italy, Germany and Britain. The French High Command was sunk in the siege-warfare mentality of Verdun and the trenches, and slow-moving offensives for which the war material and ammunition were lacking. Britain was in an even worse state. During the 1920s her three services had barely existed on budgets cut to the bone. In 1931 and 1932 all kinds of normal current expenditure on her armed forces had been postponed to achieve the reduction in government expenditure necessary to persuade foreign investors to keep the pound afloat. In 1933, for the third year running, the Chiefs of Staff warned that the level of Britain's armed forces and their state of preparedness was not adequate to defend Britain or her overseas dominions and possessions against foreign attack.

It was to take Hitler four years to destroy any chance of or basis for opposition to him in Germany. In March 1933 he was to use the destruction of the Reichstag by a fire started by a single mentally unstable arsonist to obliterate the parties of the left, driving some of their leaders into exile and imprisoning others in concentration camps. By the summer of 1933 he had broken the Catholic centre party, driving its leaders into exile in Rome, and negotiating a new concordat with the Vatican. There followed the absorption (*Gleichschaltung*) into the Nazi party of the democratic and marginally democratic parties of the right and all their supporting organizations. In the summer of 1934, by a pre-emptive strike in alliance with the German army, he broke the power of the Nazi left and their hopes of a genuine revolution which would replace the German army with a people's army based on the SA. All the multifarious professional organizations, trades unions and so on which made Germany a plural society were abolished or nazified.

That same summer the aged President von Hindenburg died. By a coup of breathtaking daring, Hitler established himself as head of state, demanding and receiving the oaths of loyalty to the State from all officers and civil servants in the State's employ. In the meantime, a new Nazi organization, half thugs, half ideologues, the SS, was expanding to take over or parallel the organs of state, absorbing the police, challenging the State's intelligence services, and subverting the loyalties of the senior figures in the bureaucracy where it could. In the summer of 1936 Hitler attempted to take over control of German industry, to mobilize it for war and for the withstanding of blockade. Hjalmar Schacht, the banker and economic innovator who had remobilized German capital and repudiated Germany's external obligations, laying the basis for Hitler's political survival in 1933–5, found himself steadily challenged and driven out of power by Goering, head of the new Four Year Plan.

In 1938 Hitler took advantage of a combined intrigue between Goering and the SS against the army leadership to take over control of the German armed forces himself. At the same time he pushed his favourite, Joachim von Ribbentrop, into control of the Foreign Ministry. In the autumn of 1938, the new Army Chief of Staff, General Beck, trying in vain to rally his fellow officers against Hitler, was driven into resignation. By October 1938 Hitler had entire control over the greatest and most powerful nation in Europe. He controlled most of their sources of information. His one failure had been with the churches. In 1933 his attempt to control the Lutheran Church had caused the breakaway of a large section, which had become the Confessional Church. And his attempt to break the Catholic Church in 1937 had ended in a Mexican stand-off. Individual Catholic nuns and priests were martyred. The Church survived. Resistance to Hitler continued, but of necessity it was clandestine, ill-organized, and laboured under the stigma, in the most law-respecting nation in Europe, of treason.

One of Hitler's earliest actions was to order his military men to produce by 1938 armed forces so strong that he could use them to make German power felt in the world. In the meantime he turned to diplomacy and subversion to attain his first ends, those of freeing Germany from all the restraints imposed by Versailles. In October 1933 he took Germany out of the League of Nations and the disarmament conference. In January 1934 he secured his eastern frontier by a non-aggression agreement with Poland, the most trigger-happy of his neighbours, and began his courtship of Italy and Britain. But the summer of 1934 was a disastrous one for him. Despite his approaches to Mussolini, the coup his wild men had been preparing in Austria misfired and Mussolini moved Italian troops to the Brenner Pass as a warning. The murder of Engelbert Dollfuss, the Austrian Chancellor, during the coup revolted Europe. In France a strong Foreign Minister, Louis Barthou, turned towards Italy and the Soviet Union, to prepare a diplomatic alliance which would permanently fence Germany in against any new attempts at expansion. Croat terrorists put an end to Barthou as he greeted King Alexander of Yugoslavia in Marseilles. His successor, Pierre Laval, followed the main outline of his plans, though he gave Italy the pre-eminence Barthou had given the Soviet Union and aimed at a front which could be used to negotiate with rather than to restrain Hitler. In January 1935 he and Mussolini concerted plans for discussion if Hitler proclaimed any new act, and in February Britain produced a new scheme designed to bring Hitler back to the fold of multilateral security.

Hitler evaded their combined pressure, proclaiming German rearmament and an end to the restrictive military clauses of Versailles before French and Italian plans were co-ordinated. Two British ministers, Sir John Simon and Anthony Eden, travelled to Berlin at the end of March 1935, to be harangued for two days on Hitler's desire for peace and his conceptions of a European settlement. Exhausted and shaken, Sir John Simon still felt there was enough hope of bringing Hitler back to the fold for him to restrain France and Italy (at the conference they called at Stresa in April 1935) from discussing any more drastic measures, though military conversations between the French and Italian General Staffs were to follow in June. Laval felt obliged to conclude the pact with the Soviet Union which Barthou had projected, and the Soviets completed the ring around Hitler by a second pact with Czechoslovakia to become operative as soon as France activated her own alliance with Czechoslovakia. Once again Germany was hemmed in by the threat of a two-front war.

Only Britain would not see things in this drastic light, while Italy could not resist cashing in on her key position in France's plans. In June a German delegation came to London to discuss questions of naval disarmament, essential in Britain's eyes to the maintenance of her position in the Pacific. Their leader, Joachim von Ribbentrop, confronted the British at the opening meeting with a blunt alternative: either an agreement with Germany which fixed German naval strength at 35 per cent of that of Britain or an end to the talks. The British Cabinet accepted, not realizing or even discussing the diplomatic consequences of their action in Europe. For Hitler the subsequent Anglo-German Naval Agreement represented the concentration of German strength on dominion in Central and Eastern Europe and an act of demonstrative disassociation by Britain from any resistance to these plans. It was a voluntary sacrifice of any plans to challenge Britain on the world's oceans, plans which he believed had condemned imperial Germany to British hostility and defeat. To France the signature of the agreement on the 120th anniversary of her defeat at Waterloo at the hands of Wellington and Blücher was a deliberate insult. To Mussolini it was an act of hypocrisy which made him the more determined to snatch at empire in Abyssinia.

Contemporary writers blamed Britain for breaking the so-called Stresa front and legitimizing by a new agreement the German breach of the disarmament clauses of Versailles. But in retrospect it is clear that it was Mussolini's determination to attack Abyssinia and the decision of the British Cabinet to lead the League of Nations into resistance to this – a breach of the League Covenant – that destroyed any hopes of the Stresa front continuing. Laval did his twisty best to keep his two associate nations together. But he could resolve neither their differences nor his own difficulties. Italy had agreed to oppose a German attack on Austria by force whereas Britain adamantly refused to accept any more commitments in Europe; yet Italy was clearly in breach of the Covenant and half Laval's own country and Cabinet clamoured for France to support Britain and the League against her. Laval's efforts to produce a compromise pulled down both himself and the unfortunate Sir Samuel Hoare who had succeeded Sir John Simon as British Foreign Secretary in June 1935. But they did not prevent the British from evolving a new scheme to bring Hitler back to the fold nor Hitler from once again forestalling them by taking what they were about to offer by unilateral action.

The gage he seized was the demilitarized zone on Germany's western frontier along the Rhine, demilitarized at Versailles to ensure that a future Franco-German war would be fought on German soil, not French. There was no French military riposte to his action, none ever having been planned; and the crisis passed in a diplomatic flurry whose only consequence was the opening of Staff talks, at a very limited level, between France and Britain.

In France the June elections produced a victory for the new Popular Front of Radical Socialists, Socialists and Communists. But they were hostile to Italian Fascism rather than to Germany and more intent on domestic reforms than on international action. Their main effort was to weaken the franc still further and prevent the launch of any coherent French rearmament programme. Hitler, meanwhile, was settling back to launch a new Four Year Plan for rearmament and the development of low-grade ores or synthetic substitutes for those raw materials of modern war which could be interrupted by blockade. An autarchic Germany, free from reliance on foreign sources of oil, rubber and so on, was his aim. At the same time, work was begun on fortifications on Germany's western frontier, the West Wall or Siegfried line. In the course of this second phase, Nazi control over Germany's war economy was greatly strengthened. Otherwise Germany was to be quiescent for eighteen months.

In July 1936 civil war flared in Spain. Italy, victorious in Abyssinia in May, the League sanctions defeated and ended, answered at once the Spanish military junta's call for aid. Hitler, lured at first by the idea of taking over Spain's British-owned copper and wolfram mines, followed suit more discreetly. The Soviets, even more discreetly at first, began aid to the Republican Government. Driven by fears of a Franco-Italian clash, Britain and France proposed agreement on non-intervention and the establishment of a committee to regulate this. Within a year several divisions of Italian 'volunteers' were fighting in Spain, the German Condor Legion was trying out many of the tactics of the Blitzkrieg on a real enemy and Republican Spain was flooded with Soviet military and political 'advisers'. The Non-Intervention Committee was successful in preventing any escalation of the civil war into the major war in the Mediterranean that Hitler, and possibly Stalin, hoped to provoke. Its record in preventing intervention was less successful. Hitler used the war to grapple Mussolini to him with psychological bonds Mussolini was never able to break, and to launch an anti-Communist campaign which provided a bridge to Japan in the Far East.

Throughout 1937 Hitler brooded and waited his time. At last, in November, he took advantage of a conference called to iron out an inter-service dispute on the allocation of armour-plate to speak his mind to his generals. Germany, he said, had to solve her need for *Lebensraum*, by acquiring territory contiguous to her own within the next few years. As a first step she had to deal with Austria and Czechoslovakia. She could expect no support from Britain and France whom he described as 'hate-crazed antagonists' of Germany and all she stood for. The best year for this action he estimated would be 1942, when Germany's rearmament programme would have the maximum advantage over the rearmament of Britain and France. It might, he thought, be possible to act earlier, in one of two eventualities: either if a war should break out between France and Italy in the Mediterranean as a result of the civil war in Spain, or if a civil war should occur in France itself.

This revelation of his plans struck the professional part of his audience with dismay. War with France and the Soviet Union, and their Czechoslovak ally was something they had been preparing for (though not with any great enthusiasm) since the signature in May 1935 of the Franco-Soviet and Czechoslovak pacts. But war with Britain – it was almost axiomatic with them – meant defeat for Germany. Hitler and his entourage realized that they would have to get rid of these men of little heart. In February 1938 they struck. Field Marshal von Blomberg, the Minister for War, was shamed into resignation by the revelation that his new bride had a dubious past. General von Fritsch, the Chief of Army Staff, was framed on a homosexual charge. When the dust cleared, Hitler was found to have converted the Ministry of War into a new agency, the Supreme Command of the Armed Forces, OKW in its German initials, with himself at its head and his two creatures, Generals Keitel and Jodl, as his deputies. The purge went further, however. Baron von Neurath, the Foreign Minister, was removed to the chairmanship of a new Reichs Council, which never met. In his place Hitler promoted Joachim von Ribbentrop, his Ambassador to Great Britain, formerly a peripatetic champagne salesman, who had impressed the Nazis with his air of belonging by right to that international society they knew only from the illustrated papers and the novels of Vicki Baum and her imitators. (The aristocratic 'von' was a dubious acquisition from an aunt.) Two independent-minded ambassadors, Ulrich von Hassell in Rome and Hans Trautmann in China, were removed from office. Herbert von Dirksen in Tokyo was recalled but his stepmother, who had once tried to launch the Führer in Berlin society, secured his posting to London. Franz von Papen in Vienna was also recalled. It was his efforts to avert this end to his career which put Hitler in the way of his next great coup in foreign affairs.

Franz von Papen, Chancellor before Schleicher, Vice Chancellor to Hitler in 1933, Catholic, aristocratic, a perpetual intriguer, perpetually unsuccessful, had nearly come unstuck at the time of the 'night of the long knives' in 1934 when his secretary, Edgar Jung, was murdered by the SS. To save himself he had accepted Hitler's proposal that he should head the German Legation in Vienna to clear up the mess left after Dollfuss's murder. Once in Vienna he had devoted himself to cultivating the so-called 'respectable national opposition' to Dollfuss's successor, Kurt von Schuschnigg, and to attempting to control the Austrian Nazis who hoped for more extreme methods. An Austro-German 'Gentleman's Agreement' was signed by Schuschnigg in 1936, whereby he promised to take into his cabinet representatives of the 'national opposition'; but his pressure had been insufficient to satisfy the hotheads of the Austrian Nazi party, whose plans for a second *coup d'état* fell into the hands of the Austrian police when they raided the Austrian Nazi headquarters in Vienna in January 1938.

To put off his recall and prevent Schuschnigg from using the evidence his police had captured, von Papen hit on the masterstroke of a meeting between Schuschnigg and Hitler at Berchtesgaden. Struck by the scheme, Hitler agreed; and when the unsuspecting Austrian Chancellor arrived he was bullied unmercifully by Hitler, with much display of military plans and martial pomp, to take into his cabinet two 'respectable' Nazi fellow travellers. Alone and isolated, he agreed to do what he could. But on his return to Austria he conceived of the device of a plebiscite, organized to show to the world the degree of Austrian resistance to the idea of a union with Germany, and the degree of popular support he, Schuschnigg, enjoyed.

Inevitably, intelligence of his intentions reached Hitler's ears before he was ready to act. Threatened with a publicly humiliating defeat of his Austrian policy, Hitler ordered military preparations for the invasion of Austria, the cancellation of the plebiscite, and, a day later, Schuschnigg's resignation and his replacement by the fellow traveller, Artur Seyss-Inquart (hanged in 1946, and justifiably so, for his record as wartime Gauleiter of the Netherlands). On March 12, 1938, German troops crossed into Austria. A day later Hitler proclaimed the union of Austria and Germany.

Next on his programme of November 1937 was Czechoslovakia, its frontier defences now decisively turned by the moving of German troops on to its southern boundaries. While Hitler was still mulling over his plans for dealing with her – he began by instructing Konrad Henlein, on the German payroll since 1935, always to push his demands on the Czech Government one stage further than the Czechs could be expected to concede – an incident in the Czech frontier lands swung the Führer into a decision to take out Czechoslovakia that year. On the weekend of May 20–1, 1938, spurred by mysterious and untrue intelligence reports of major German troop moves towards their former borders with Austria, the Czech Government recalled one class of reservists to the colours. Britain made diplomatic representations in Berlin, Hitler was forced to deny that he had any intention of attacking Czechoslovakia, and the world press proclaimed his withdrawal, once his bluff had been called.

Such comments were both ill-timed and ill-conceived. The open humiliation determined Hitler to 'smash Czechoslovakia at the first available opportunity'. After two days' conference with his military chiefs, orders to this end were issued to the German armed forces on May 30. The German press launched a gradual crescendo of attack on the Czech Government designed to create an atmosphere for attack by October 1.

It was at this point that the British Government took a hand. In February 1934 a committee of senior civil servants and military advisers had pinpointed a rearming Germany as the main future threat to Britain's security. In the autumn of 1935, recommending a comprehensive scheme for British rearmament, they had named 1939 as the year of maximum danger. The rearmament programme itself had been launched in 1936, by which time it was becoming uncomfortably clear that Britain's world-wide interests were also threatened by Italy in the Mediterranean and by Japanese expansion in the Far East. By the spring of 1937 it was also becoming clear to the British Cabinet not only that the escalating costs of the rearmament programme were threatening Britain's full economic recovery from the slump of 1931 and with this her financial capacity for sustaining a long war against Germany, but also that, even when the rearmament programme was completed, the forces at Britain's disposal could never be adequate to deal with three potential enemy states as widely separated from one another's spheres of operation as were Germany, Italy and Japan. It seemed almost essential to attempt to limit the causes of conflict and to 'appease' as far as possible one or more of the potential enemies. One enemy less would be as major an accretion of strength as one resoundingly defeated, though cabinet discussions which reached this point of argument usually concluded gloomily that to diminish the number of Britain's potential enemies was a lot easier to conceive than to achieve.

The annexation of Austria sounded the tocsins of alarm in London. Little love for Czechoslovakia lodged in the hearts of the British Cabinet. The Chiefs of Staff issued a categorical warning that war in 1938 would entail the gravest risks of British defeat. The dominions were at best lukewarm, if not actively hostile to war over the Czecho-slovak issue. The Cabinet had already recognized south-eastern Europe as an area where the expansion of German influence might be restrained but could not be stopped. Lord Halifax, closest associate of the Prime Minister, Neville Chamberlain, had said as much to Hitler in Novem-ber 1937. The danger lay in the French alliance with Czechoslovakia and in the possible escalation of Czech-German conflict within Czecho-slovakia into a war with Germany; or so, at least, ran the thinking of Neville Chamberlain and his Cabinet. The French would have to be persuaded to get the Czechs to see sense. Failing that, and by mid-June it was clear that that had failed, Britain would have to do something.

That 'something' took the form of the dispatch to Czechoslovakia early in August 1938 of a British 'mediator'. As a device it was singularly ill-conceived. The mediator himself, Lord Runciman, an expert in industrial disputes in Britain and a former Cabinet Minister, had one card in his hand. He knew from clandestine contacts with Henlein that the Sudeten German leader was out of sympathy with Hitler's stated objectives, hoping to become the first German prime minister of Czechoslovakia rather than a mere Gauleiter over a Sudeten German appendix to Germany. The SS had, however, outflanked him and brought his extremists under their control. Runciman, therefore, could only make the rounds in Czechoslovakia, a faintly comic figure reminiscent, in the self-satisfied uprightness of his bearing and his vague air of puzzlement among all these bewildering Central Europeans, of the film comedian Stan Laurel. His mission served only to occupy the month of August, a month in which nothing could happen as the German military planning was not yet complete.

In British eyes the period of maximum danger was expected for the first week of September, the week of the annual Nazi party rally at Nuremberg. This was a grandiosely theatrical occasion, with its thousands of marching and wheeling formations: soldiers, the Reichs Labour Service with their uniforms and highly polished spades, German Maidens, gymnasts, all shouting slogans in massive unison under the September sun, and massing in the searchlights of the night-time displays. It seemed only too likely to drive the Führer (depicted in London as a man whom the emotion of the moment and the urgings of the extremists among his entourage might carry away) into proclaiming an open attack on Czechoslovakia. To avert that development, Neville Chamberlain, though over seventy and never having previously set foot in an aeroplane, was prepared to fly to Germany to appeal personally to Hitler.

However, Hitler's speech at Nuremberg, which coincided with the breakdown of Henlein's negotiations with the Czechs, was intended only as the first step in the final escalation into conflict. It was nevertheless alarming enough to lead Chamberlain to put his plan into operation. Three times he flew to Germany, dismounting apparently unshaken to confer with the Führer at Berchtesgaden, at Godesberg and at Munich. After Godesberg, the negotiations trembled on the verge of breakdown. The Czechs mobilized, the British fleet mobilized, gasmasks were issued and air-raid trenches dug in London's parks. But an appeal by Chamberlain to Mussolini, to persuade Hitler to meet Chamberlain once more, provided Hitler with an occasion he could only have neglected at the cost of the world's recognizing that what he wanted was not justice for the Sudeten Germans but war on the Czechs; war with France and Britain would have followed; and for this he was not yet ready. Nor, as the dismal reception given by the people of Berlin on the evening of September 27 to what was intended to be a martial parade through the city under the eyes of the Führer, made only too clear, were the German people. Hitler was forced to confer rather than fight.

The conference at Munich stripped Czechoslovakia of her fortified frontier areas and broke the Czechoslovakian state into its federal components – Czechia, Slovakia, and a minuscule appendix in the curve of the Carpathian mountains known alternatively as Ruthenia or the Carpatho-Ukraine. Czechoslovakia's other neighbours, Poland and Hungary, also pressed claims. The Czechs bowed sadly to their inevitable passage into Germany's sphere of hegemony. And on the morning of September 30, shortly before his return to a deeply divided Britain, Neville Chamberlain persuaded Hitler to sign a declaration of Anglo-German friendship. This was the famed piece of paper he waved in the air as he descended from the aeroplane which had brought him back from Germany to Hendon airport. He read it aloud to the waiting microphones and before the newsreel cameras. He read it again to a House of Commons of whom all but a handful were prepared to wallow in an ecstasy of relief at their release from the imminence of war.

This was its text: 'We, the German Führer and Chancellor, and the British Prime Minister, have had a further meeting today, and are agreed in recognizing that the question of Anglo-German relations is of the first importance for the two countries and Europe.

'We regard the agreement signed last night and the Anglo-German Naval Agreement as symbolic of the desire of our two peoples never to go to war with one another again.

'We are resolved that the method of consultation shall be the method adopted to deal with any other questions which may concern our two countries and we are determined to continue our efforts to remove possible sources of differences, and thus to contribute to ensure the peace of Europe.'

Before twelve months had passed, Germany and Britain were at war.

CHAPTER 3

HITLER PLANS A NEW WAR

The world celebrated the Munich Agreement as Hitler's greatest victory. In the British Parliament, Churchill, Anthony Eden and Duff Cooper (the First Lord of the Admiralty, who resigned his office rather than lend his agreement to so dishonourable an action) attacked it bitterly. At one stroke the French position in Central Europe had been shattered. 'Who holds Bohemia, holds Europe', it was said. Bohemia – Czechoslovakia – now lay defenceless in Hitler's grasp, stripped of her frontier fortifications, devoid of allies. In Prague, people walked the streets in shock and dismay. M. Daladier, the French Prime Minister, felt the Munich Agreement to be so great a defeat that he is said at first to have taken the crowd which welcomed him at Le Bourget airfield on his return from Munich as a vengeful mob.

Yet Hitler regarded Munich as a defeat. 'That senile old rascal', Neville Chamberlain,[1] with his governess's manner and his bourgeois indecisiveness, had defeated him. When Hitler had stood on the balcony of the Reichs Chancellery three days earlier to inspect the troops about to launch the assault on Czechoslovakia, the Berlin crowds had greeted him glumly, silently. When Chamberlain drove through the streets of Munich the crowds shouted for joy and relief, threw flowers, and even shouted '*Heil* Chamberlain'. Truly, Hitler's career as the 'supreme War Lord of all time', as the sycophants of the years to come were to call him, had begun inauspiciously. Instead of leading his victorious troops in triumphal victory into Prague, he had to content himself with following in their wake into Eger, Karlsbad, Friedland, and Krumau. It took him three days even to bring himself to do this, and his first excursion into his newly won dominions lasted all of a day, October 3.[2] He repeated the experience the following day. But his mood was grim and black, and only the tumultuous applause which greeted him could bring from him a smile of acknowledgement.

It was in this atmosphere of rage, frustration, and fury, with the thwarting of his first major move towards the realization of his aims, that Hitler now bent himself to ponder his next move. To understand this, to see how the course of events over the next twelve months was to be set, we must look a little further into the mind and character of this extraordinary man, whose visions and motivations were to involve all Europe, all the world, in so terrible and so destructive a war. The details of his birth and early career are all now sufficiently well known. Born the son of an Austrian customs officer, a 'drop out' from school at fifteen years of age, a layabout in Vienna and Munich, living off his pension as the son of a civil servant and the proceeds of sales of his dull, uninspired drawings; a war hero in a minor way, corporal in a Bavarian regiment running messages under fire between battalion headquarters and the front, wounded, gassed, decorated with the Iron Cross (first class); thereafter paid political agitator and army spy, extremist party leader and street corner speaker, unsuccessful putschist, surviving until President von Hindenburg was blackmailed into offering him the Chancellorship after Germany's economic collapse, mass unemployment and right-wing money had enabled him to create a mass party; all this is known. But behind this façade of fact observers at the time and historians thereafter have discerned so many different Hitlers as to remind one of nothing so much as Max Beerbohm's caricature of Homer, forty or more faces rising above and beside one another on the head and shoulders of a wandering Greek bard, tunic-clad, besandalled and clutching a lyre.

His appearance is still part of the universal mythology: the dark lock falling across the forehead, the ridiculous toothbrush moustache, and the square face so often pulled into a grimace of determination, are all recorded in a thousand photographs. But these are static records of the man. They do not convey how hypnotic his eyes could be, the charm which he could command on occasion, the curious quality of coarseness which the society hostesses of Berlin, especially Frau von Dirksen, stepmother of the German Ambassador to Britain in the years 1938–9, tried so hard to overlay. Nor do they convey the vulgarity of the Upper Austrian accent with which he spoke German, the note of barely controlled hysteria that crackled in his voice when he spoke in public, or the way in which his rather unattractive personality expanded and flowered when he was addressing large responsive audiences. Not that he ever looked at them and saw their members as they really were, the ordinary, common, neighbourly people of what is, in more normal times, one of the most comfortable and civilized nations in Europe. When he spoke he communed with the spirit of German history as he saw it and his audience became abstract heroic figures infused with the same daemon. Hence the sense of almost sexual frustration when they failed to respond (as on September 27, 1938) to his vision of history. Most of the time, however, cowed by the carefully stage-managed theatricality of uniforms, floodlights and burning torches, ritual chanting, war songs and brass bands, his audiences bent and swayed as he willed them to, and followed blindly behind him into a war which was to divide and destroy their country. Such was the power of his imagination, which was for him the reality within which he lived.

Apart from his imagination and his oratory, he still remains an appallingly third-rate character. Nobility of thought and expression, clarity of language, and depth of understanding and perception were qualities he lacked entirely. His private life was devoid of even the shadow of greatness. In his relations with women, apart from his unhappy attempt to play substitute father to his niece, Geli Raubal (who escaped from his incestuous attentions into suicide), he seems to have sought only the unthinking adulation that as a boy he enjoyed from his mother. He had no real friends, only allies and followers. And although he made room in his private pantheon for his Italian confrère, Benito Mussolini, he seems never to have related to him in any way. Some friends he had despite himself: Rudolf Hess, Max Amann, his publisher, and Heinrich Hoffmann, his photographer. But only one person, Eva Braun, seems to have penetrated to the heart of his essential isolation; and all she found there was self-destruction by poison and petrol.

This is the side of Hitler that it is so difficult to relate to the Hitler of so many historians, filled with a vision of German world dominance, the successive steps towards which unfolded in a long-matured programme, set in action once he had achieved power. There is nothing in Hitler's previous record to show that he was capable of so long and sustained an effort of foresight and planning. Nor, despite the popularly held beliefs to the contrary, is there anything in his one published work, *Mein Kampf*, which can be identified as an original draft of a programme to which his later actions were to conform. *Mein Kampf* is an exposé of Hitler's political ideas and methodologies, not a programme in any meaningful sense of the word, and still less a 'blueprint' for aggression. It shows the calibre of the man, his political ethic, the visions to which he wanted reality to correspond, the methods and political manœuvres he thought would, by their conformity to the innate nature of politics, be right to employ against the enemies of his vision. But for his success in achieving power in 1933, few would ever even have known of its existence, let alone have read it. Such programmatic elements as can be found in Hitler's foreign policy between 1933 and 1938 were imposed upon him by external fact, not internal vision.

Realization of this has led a smaller number of historians to identify his vision and aims with those of the German nationalists he replaced in power, and to depict him instead as the master of improvisation, the Machiavellian, the player of the game always returning and dominating the services of his opponents, short-term in all he did, reacting only to the external stimuli of the world around him and his Reich. Again, however, the picture is a little difficult to reconcile with his known sloth and lassitude, the long periods of inactivity, the waiting and probing, the lengthy exposés of his plans to his political and military deputies made, for example, on November 5, 1937[3] and on May 23, 1939[4] or with the lengthy political preambles with which he insisted that his military orders, from mid-1937 onwards, should be introduced. True, he often did not carry out the aims he announced on these occasions in the way he intended to. True, there are definite attempts in all these documents and exposés to counter the feeling he knew his audiences entertained, that he was pitting Germany against enemies which would in the long run prove too strong for her, as they had once before in 1914–18. But the speeches and the orders were clearly intended to set forth his aims and how he planned to achieve them. To that extent they represent a programme, or rather a series of directives. They are not, however, consistent enough in direction to be taken for more than this, and yet are too specific to be dismissed as less.

Adolf Hitler, it has to be remembered, approached politics as the ignorant outsider. His viewpoint was that of the pothouse politician, the café critic. What he knew of politics, both domestic and European, he took entirely from the press of pre-war Vienna and post-war Munich. To the natural crudities and over-simplicies of his sources of information, he added the resentment of the small-town bourgeois, the déclassé's belief in conspiracy and corruption as political norms, and the violence of the adolescent rebel against over-strict parental authority. Of his account of his childhood in Mein Kampf one of the few parts that rings true is that section which depicts his father, now retired, unsuccessful in his first attempt at running a homestead, turned in on his family with no outlet for his abundant energies, and violently and aggressively imposing his authority upon the young Adolf.

Then, suddenly, in Adolf's thirteenth year the parental tyrant died. Within two years Hitler had also escaped the tyranny of school and embarked on a life which was one long succession of evasions of authority and discipline. He left Vienna for Munich to escape conscription into the Hapsburg army. He always hated the Hapsburg state, possibly identifying it, subconsciously, with the unthinking authority of his father, its servant. Yet he needed a substitute authority; this he found in the orderliness of the Munich bourgeois, to whose mores he easily adapted. Not for him the flowing tie, the unkempt hair of the Munich artist or art-taster. He dressed in Munich as soberly and staidly as any bank clerk, dependent on his manager's approval for existence, let alone promotion. And when war came in August 1914 he threw himself into the camaraderie, the discipline and the purpose of a front-line infantry unit.

This cocoonlike existence, warm, dedicated, purposive, tolerant of all eccentricities, was destroyed by the defeat of Germany and the revolutionary disturbances that followed. Thenceforward Hitler lapsed into the life of a man to whom all authority and external direction was basically intolerable. He took over and dominated the infant Nazi party, riding roughshod over its original committee of self-educated artisans. He challenged the authority of the Bavarian Government and denounced far and wide that in power in Berlin. In small matters, too, in any dealings with authority, he dragged his feet. Deprived of Austrian citizenship in 1924 he did nothing to acquire German citizenship until he embarked on his brief career as an official in Braunschweig in 1932, when it became a political embarrassment. He never paid income tax. He manœuvred out of his party all who questioned or opposed his authority. Only the German President, the aged Field Marshal von Hindenburg, won his reluctant deference. And once that aged warrior died he took steps to secure that all oaths of loyalty to the German state were pledged to him in person as Führer and Reichs Chancellor.

Meanwhile he reasoned and rationalized his own methods, his combination of indolence and intuition. There are three kinds of secrecy, he once remarked, 'secrets that one communicates to one other trusted individual, *unter vier Augen* [between four eyes]; secrets that one holds in one's own breast; and ideas that one retains in the depths of one's consciousness since the time is not yet ripe thoroughly to think them through.' His programme was thus at best a sombre dream filled with half-formulated intuitions, a potter's workshop rather than an architect's filing cabinet. And his best and most successful period was that between 1934 and 1937 when, after the ignominious failure of his efforts to force the pace over Austria, he sat back and waited for events to light up in him that spark of intuition as to where and when to make his next move which made him so quickly the dominant figure in Europe. His almost instinctive sense of timing was based on the same source as that from which he originally formed his views of politics, from his reading of the press. While his Foreign Ministry laboriously concocted summaries of the foreign press of the powers, which reached him, to his contempt,[5] weeks after the event, his *Reichspresschef*, Otto Dietrich, reported daily on the tone of comment in the leading newspapers of Europe. From this he derived a shrewd idea of the limits of their tolerance and support, how they could be confused by their own double standard of morality, and beguiled into endorsing his actions if only they were accompanied by appeals to justice, peace and the reconstruction of Europe.

His successful reliance on the tone of the foreign press as a means of measuring his own freedom of action depended on three other factors: the extent to which his other sources of information agreed with or confirmed his own intuitions in this matter; the degree to which the European press accurately reflected the movements of opinion in their own countries; and the degree to which he could curb or control his own innate impatience, which had betrayed him into near-disaster both in 1923 in the Bierkeller putsch and in 1934 over Austria. None of these three factors was to remain constant in the years 1938–9. Together they were to lead him into a war whose initial victories were to make his eventual ruin inevitable.

Since 1937 his discussions of his plans were filled with an increasing sense of the urgent passage of time. In his speech of November 1937, which he said was to be regarded as his last will and testament if he died, he put the years 1943–5 as the latest date for action. If the Führer was still living, he said, it was his unalterable decision to solve Germany's problem of space (*Lebensraum*) by then. He repeated this view during the 1938 crisis and returned to it in 1939. No German statesman could solve the problem for longer than fifteen to twenty years, he said in May 1939. And in August he repeated this even more strongly.[6] 'No one will ever again have the confidence of the whole German people as I have. . . . My existence is therefore a factor of great value. I can be eliminated at any time, by a criminal or a lunatic.' And again, 'our economic situation is such that we can only hold out a few more years. . . . All these favourable circumstances will no longer prevail in two or three years' time. No one knows how much longer I shall live.' And again in November,[7] 'Time is working for our adversaries.' Fear of his own death mixed with fear of the progress of British and French rearmament and economic recovery led to the feeling that the sands were running out on him. History would not wait. None of his family lived to be very old, he told the propaganda chiefs of the Nazi party in 1937.[8] It was therefore necessary to solve the problem of living space as soon as possible, so that it could happen in his lifetime. Later generations would no longer be able to do this.

His belief that destiny waits on no man was thus profoundly to inhibit his intuition and undermine the patience with which he had watched and waited his moment in his first five years of power. But other factors were also at work. The most disastrous of these was a personal one, in the form of his Foreign Minister, Joachim von Ribbentrop. Neither his contemporaries nor historians have dealt kindly with this man. Hitler's own choice of him is an adequate commentary on the reliability of the Führer's intuition. Vain, arrogant, pompous and empty-headed are among the kinder epithets which have been showered upon him. Nazis of long standing in the party despised and condemned a man who had only joined the year before it achieved power. Diplomatists regarded him as an empty and dangerous fool who told Hitler what he wanted to hear and made him deaf to the evidence of danger. Historians have suggested that the war of 1939 should be called Ribbentrop's war because he, more than anyone else, did his best to bring it about. 'A combination of vanity, stupidity and superficiality,' wrote Sir Nevile Henderson, British Ambassador in Berlin.[9]

Yet, in relation to the Nazi leadership, Ribbentrop had an immense advantage. Goering alone excepted, they were provincial nobodies, with no experience of *le grand monde* outside Germany whatever. When Hitler came to power, his only two other acquaintances who fitted into the Europe of international café society with its curious mixture of smartness, wealth and power, that Europe which comprehended both Vicki Baum and the glossy magazines as well as that hand-book of Europe's hereditary aristocracy the *Almanach de Gotha*, were Kurt Luedecke, the *Weltbummler* (global pub-crawler) who made the mistake of earning Goering's enmity,[10] and the Harvard-educated art dealer and pianist, 'Putzi' Hanfstaengel, who had no real political ambitions.[11] To the mass of Hitler's entourage, as to the Führer himself, the world of power and the establishment was unsettlingly forbidding. Von Ribbentrop, the ex-champagne salesman, with his knowledge of English and French, his ceaseless name-dropping, his air of polished cosmopolitanism, impressed them like a confidence trickster intent on selling Brooklyn Bridge to the small-town hicks up for their first uneasy glimpse of the lights of the metropolis. Ribbentrop was to worm his way steadily into Hitler's confidence, until even Goering was embattled against him.

The irony of all this is that socially Ribbentrop was a complete fraud. The 'von' in his name was less genuine than even the most dubious of Lloyd George's knighthoods. The eternal parvenu, Sir Horace Rumbold called him 'a contemptible and disastrous cad'.[12] The London society rumour was that he had had the German Ambassador, Leopold von Hoesch, poisoned to gain the Embassy.[13] The famous occasion on which he greeted King George VI with the Nazi salute did nothing to ease his acceptance. People invited him once, or visited the massive German Embassy to see the opulent vulgarity of his new decorations – but not twice. His overbearing manner, arrogance, rudeness and spitefulness were too much for them.

Moreover, Ribbentrop seems genuinely to have believed that a secret aristocratic oligarchy ruled in Britain. He pinned his hopes on the unfortunate Edward VIII, whose ill-advised visit to Hitler shortly after his abdication and marriage to Mrs Simpson, Ribbentrop always regarded as a great personal triumph. By the beginning of 1938, however, he had come to regard his Embassy as a total failure,[14] and, spiteful and petty as ever, had turned against Britain which he now reported to Hitler to be both permanently hostile to and jealous of Germany's rise to power and senilely impotent to do anything effective to counter it. Throughout the twelve months after Munich, Ribbentrop fed Hitler's willing ears with abuse and denigration of the British Government, whose every move he interpreted as toothless bluff and empty bravado. In his speech of November 23, 1939, Hitler said he was disturbed by the 'stronger and stronger appearance of the British'. The Englishman, he said, 'is a tough opponent.' His surprise and alarm are a measure of the degree to which Ribbentrop had misled him over the previous eighteen months. If Hitler's intuition and grasp of the limits to which his potential opponents might be expected to go, skills which had stood him in such good stead over the previous four years, deserted him in 1939, Ribbentrop bears a great deal of the responsibility.

A measure of responsibility must also be ascribed to the British press. Much of the information on which Hitler fed his intuition came from his appreciation of the terms in which the European press formulated its discussion of international problems. After Munich the British press, especially *The Times* and the popular dailies, as a matter of policy did all they could to restrain the gradual movement of British opinion away from the overwhelming relief with which the avoidance of war at Munich had been greeted, towards a grimly determined acceptance of war as inevitable. By July and August 1939 the bulk of British opinion had indeed come to accept war as almost inevitable, though there was a deep distrust of Neville Chamberlain, who, it was felt, might still be prepared to purchase a further year's grace at the expense of British honour. Little or nothing of this appeared in the press, though it was to erupt violently on the second day of September 1939. Once again Hitler's intuition had plenty on which to feed, but all of it was misleading.

Hitler's anger after Munich was directed primarily against Britain and against Chamberlain. On the night of September 29–30, 1938, when he saw Mussolini off on the train back to Italy, he spoke of the inevitability of war with Britain and France.[15] During his meeting with Chamberlain on the morning of September 30, he sat looking pale and uneasy, answering the British Prime Minister's remarks with an absentminded 'Ja', and hesitated noticeably before signing his name to the declaration Chamberlain sprang upon him.[16] As the world press celebrated Munich, so his anger grew. If Chamberlain was to be fêted as the man who had saved Europe from war, who then was threatening Europe with war, but he, Adolf Hitler? If Chamberlain was the angel of peace, who but he was cast as the serpent? Day by day, his anger mounted, feeding itself on an added belief that the British were interfering in the working of the commission charged with outlining the new German-Czechoslovak frontiers.

Chamberlain's use of the radio against him no doubt increased Hitler's anger (a German translation of Chamberlain's appeal for peace had been broadcast over the increasingly powerful transmitters of Radio Luxemburg, control over whose programming had been acquired clandestinely by British intelligence interests in 1936).[17]

The debate on Munich in the British House of Commons added fuel to Hitler's ire. By October 5, no word of praise for Chamberlain had fallen from his lips, and the Premier was reduced to pleading for some word of appreciation. Hitler gave it in his speech that day at the Palace of Sport in Berlin, in the course of a thirty-minute address, in an oblique reference to the 'two other great statesmen' who, besides his 'true great friend' Mussolini, had played their part in the agreement. But he followed it with a personal attack on Eden and Duff Cooper and a grandiose claim that his programme of self-assistance was quite different from that of his predecessor continually passing the begging bowl from conference to conference.[18] And on October 9 at Saarbrücken[19] he openly attacked Britain, saying that it was time for her to put aside the seduction of the Versailles period. 'We Germans will no longer endure such governessy interference. Britain should mind her own business and worry about her own troubles,' of which she had plenty, such as the Arab revolt in Palestine.

The course of the crisis of September 1938, and the soundings made of German opinion by the organs of Goebbels' Ministry of Propaganda and by the SS and the Gestapo, had convinced Hitler of the need to change the tone of German propaganda. German crowds had fêted and cheered Chamberlain on his visits to Berchtesgaden, Godesberg and Munich: not, as journalistic opponents of appeasement had argued, because they saw in Chamberlain a tool come to give them what they wanted in Czechoslovakia; but because they believed he came to preserve peace. Goebbels' efforts to fill Germans with hatred for the Czechs had failed, as had the war march through Berlin on September 27. To bring the German people to enthusiastically and determinedly embrace war, that war which Hitler believed alone could prove them fit to dominate Europe (and 'tomorrow the world'), a campaign of psychological preparation would be necessary.

Goebbels' immediate orders to the media were to stress Hitler's role at Munich as the victor for peace. Large sections of German opinion made this the basis for their identification with him. Now they would have to be converted to the idea of war, power, and dominion. On November 10, in front of an audience of four hundred German journalists and publicists, headed by Goebbels, Rosenberg, Max Amann, his publisher and head of the Reichs Chamber for the Press, and Otto Dietrich, his Press Chief, Hitler delivered, in secret, the new message.[20] For years, he said, he had had to preach only peace; this had been the only way to nerve the German public to follow him. Now it was necessary to convince them that some things, if they could not be secured by peace, must be secured by force. The 'inner voice' of the German people had to be brought to the point where they themselves began to clamour for force. The gramophone record of peace was now played out.

'I am the greatest German that ever lived' – Hitler to Schuschnigg at Berchtesgaden, 1938.

At the same time, Goebbels' propaganda machine was switched to build up the image of the armed forces, and to popularize the idea of *Lebensraum*.[21] Germany was among the 'have-not' nations; she needed space, space to breathe, space to spread, space to colonize, space to dominate; Germany was involved in a class war between the nations; Germany's enemies, encircling her, stood in the way. While Hitler spent time talking to groups of German officers, Goebbels was working to ensure that German opinion would come to see Britain as the enemy standing in the way of German wealth, power and dominion. Hitler's anger against Britain was to become part of the inner voice of the German people.

As Hitler himself brooded over Britain's rejection of his friendship, as he saw it, his anger became infused with a contemptuous dismissal of Britain's resolution and power and Chamberlain's determination under fire. This anger came to dominate his plans for the next six months. His contempt led him to believe that Britain would back off from a future challenge.

For the next six months the world's press was to be filled with rumours and reports of the Führer's plans and intentions. Poland, Memel, the Ukraine, Romania, the Netherlands, all were to be named as his targets. In reality, however, during this entire period his thoughts were turning to war with Britain, to driving her from the Continent and ending her infernal and interminable interference in Germany's main sphere of influence. The first steps in this planning had already been taken in May 1938, under the impact of the 'weekend' crisis.

The yardstick of Hitler's intentions towards Britain was always his policy on the German navy. In his earliest years of political activity he had eagerly followed the attacks on the naval policy of the Kaiser and his Admiral, Grand Admiral von Tirpitz, launched by the disgruntled naval officer and prolific writer of polemics, Captain Persius.[22] In *Mein Kampf* Hitler had castigated the Kaiser for gratuitously adding Britain to the list of Germany's enemies by challenging her at sea, when he should have been concentrating his efforts against Germany's hereditary enemy, France, and against Tsarist Russia. Among his first actions upon coming to power was to inform Admiral Raeder, Chief of the German Naval Staff, that he intended to offer the British a deal by which the German navy was kept at a third of the strength of the Royal Navy. This offer Ribbentrop translated into the Anglo-German Naval Agreement of 1935, which Chamberlain specifically named in the draft Anglo-German agreement he produced on the morning of September 30.

It is thus of the utmost significance that it was on May 24, 1938, in the aftermath of the 'weekend' crisis, that Hitler had his naval adjutant instruct Admiral Raeder completely to revise the current shipbuilding plans for the German navy, as 'the Führer must reckon Britain permanently among his enemies.'[23] The task was undertaken with considerable reluctance by the Naval Staff, among whom it had long been doctrine that war with Britain spelt defeat for Germany. In November relations between Admiral Raeder and Hitler flared up, Hitler bitterly criticizing the navy for the weakness of the two new battleships *Bismarck* and *Tirpitz* then approaching their launch. Their guns were too small, their speed too low, they did not carry enough armour. Goaded beyond endurance, Raeder jumped to his feet, demanded that Hitler accept his resignation and stormed from the room. Hitler, however, ran after him and soothed him.[24] The navy's new construction plan was ready a month later, to be named the Z-plan, and was easily accepted by Hitler. On January 6 he ordered that it be given overall priority in the allocation of raw materials, armour-plate, and so on over the other two services.[25] German armour-plate, instead of being put into tanks to overrun the cornfields of the Ukraine and the oil of the Caucasus, was to go into battle cruisers, commerce destroyers, submarines and super-*Bismarcks* of 60,000 tons and upwards.[26] With such a navy, as Raeder wrote in despair on September 3, 1939,[27] when the outbreak of war with Britain four years too soon forced the abandonment of the Z-plan, the chances of 'solving the British problem permanently' would have been good.

It was against this background that Hitler began planning his next moves against Britain. On the diplomatic front there were to be three major enterprises, woven together to make one grand design. In the first place, the left-over remnants of Czechoslovakia must be tidied up, and Bohemia and Prague be brought under German rule. This was a mere 'mopping up' operation, which should also take in the return of Memel to Germany. Secondly, agreement must be reached with Poland over Danzig and the Corridor to tie Poland firmly to Germany as an opponent of Russia. There must be no question of a re-activation of the Franco-Polish alliance, or of the Poles waiting to see who won before they decided to join the victors. Poland must be negotiated into Germany's camp. Thirdly, Japan and Italy must be linked with Germany in a military alliance. The presence of Japanese forces in Manchuria and Mongolia was already acting as a restraining influence on the Soviet Union. A military alliance would separate and distract British power and divert American attention from Europe. The military alliance was to be supplemented by staff talks on a common war, to be fought by Italy and Germany against Britain and France, the aim of which would be the military defeat of France and the consequent expulsion of British power and influence from the Continent.

The one thing this grand design lacked, for obvious reasons, was a timetable. In the first place Hitler had still not made the mental transition from waiting for events to provide his intuition with recognizable moments for action (the attitude which had stood him in such good stead in his earlier years in power) to deliberately manipulating international politics himself so as to produce such moments. He had, in fact, passed from the one to the other during the summer months of 1938, but he had not yet made the major adjustments in his mental approach which the change in method called for. Crudely put, his success in timing had come in the past because he had only to watch and wait. His intuition could function unhampered. After the summer of 1938 his intuition was to be inhibited by his involvement in the events he was trying to manipulate. And at manipulation, especially of the many variables involved in his post-Munich designs, he was a good deal less than competent, whilst Ribbentrop was no good whatever. Multilateral manipulation, if one may call it that, of international events is a job for a professional diplomatist not a shallow, superficial, ignorant and prejudiced amateur. One cannot expect someone trained on a child's piano to give even an adequate performance on a church organ. The main diplomatic triumphs to come Hitler's way in 1939 had been prepared for him by his professional diplomatists (though Ribbentrop, as usual, took all the credit).

This lack of a timetable is the main reason why the grand design was to go so wrong. No effort was made to orchestrate or synchronize its various parts. Ribbentrop's contribution consisted of sudden and highly dramatized descents by special train, on Milan, on Vienna, on Warsaw. Indeed, historians may well remember the Hitler era as the last days of the time when the train was the instrument of state. The newsreels of the 1930s are filled with scenes of ceremonies at railway stations. The great steam engine moves majestically to a halt, past the waiting dignitaries with their frockcoats, top hats, uniforms and medals. To the orchestration of steam, hissing from the pistons, numbing the ears and obscuring the view, the red carpet is unrolled precisely, to the door of the great man's carriage. The door is flung open. The statesman emerges, pauses at the head of the carriage steps, for the cameras. Then he advances, sometimes severe, sometimes smiling, to meet his hosts. Salutes, *Heil* Hitlers, handshakes, polite chitchat. The station-master is presented. Then the party strolls to the waiting limousines and inspects a guard of honour, all flashing buttons and clashing rifle butts. Then comes the serious business of the visit.

The meeting over, there follows the retreat to the station. The dignity and pomp fold into themselves like tulips at night-fall, as the massive presence of the locomotive reasserts itself. The final camera shot shows the visitor at his carriage window, waving austerely to his hosts below him on the platform. Only the spectators hear the noise, the power, the slow explosion of departure.

Charles Chaplin was to parody such a scene in *The Great Dictator*. Small wonder its showing was banned in Hitler's Europe. No one would have been more anxious to ban it than Ribbentrop. He preferred always to arrive in uniform if protocol allowed, to sport an empty arrogant stare, his jaw set at what he fondly imagined to be a suitably determined angle, characteristic of the great defender of the Führer's noble cause he imagined himself to be. But he had a passion for trains, which he was able to indulge to the full during the war years, following Hitler in his own special train wherever the Führer went through the Europe he had conquered. But his taste for the dramatic arrival, followed by the equally dramatized signature of the treaty, was to be sadly starved until August 1939; and his carefully prepared *coup de théâtre* flopped for lack of supporting players.

The end towards which all this diplomatic activity was directed can be deduced from the military directive issued by Hitler's dogsbody in the OKW, General Keitel, on November 26, 1938,[28] when Hitler could still believe that his various diplomatic plans were going successfully. The military-political basis of this directive, which was to govern discussions between the German High Command and the Italians, was war by Germany and Italy against France and Britain with the object of knocking out France; this, wrote Keitel, according to Hitler's 'detailed instructions', would deprive Britain of her bases on the Continent and leave her to face Germany and Italy alone. Italy's task was to occupy the Balearic Islands and threaten the whole Anglo-French position in North Africa and the Middle East. French North Africa was to be attacked, Corsica captured, Gibraltar eliminated. Italy was also to guard Germany's rear by joining Hungary in sending forces against Poland if any threat to Germany came from that direction.

The German task was to attack the French frontier between the Moselle and the Rhine and break through the Maginot line. Artillery experiments against the Czech fortifications had shown that the heavy-calibre artillery employed by Germany could destroy Maginot-line-type fortifications. Training films were made of the work and regularly shown to senior German officers. Ribbentrop was so cock-a-hoop with the discovery that he boasted of the matter to the Polish Ambassador in Berlin, Józef Lipski,[29] at the end of October. Once France was knocked out, the Luftwaffe and the German navy would concentrate on block-ading Britain. What was to happen thereafter the memorandum did not say. It was presumably one of the secrets in Hitler's mind which he had not yet thought through to the end.

These military orders also lacked a timetable. Indeed, the evidence suggests that Hitler had not yet decided how the various courses he was considering, or that were being urged upon him, should be fitted together. His intuition, overwhelmed perhaps by his anger with Britain, was silent. How seriously was he considering other options? Others were being urged upon him by Ribbentrop's rivals, Goering and the SS especially, as will be seen. But lacking a genuine record of what was said, and by whom, in his endless nocturnal conferences and table talk, we shall probably never know the full extent of the rival factions. There are some small indications that the army contained a group that wished to turn against the Soviet Union.[30] Within the German Foreign Ministry there were also survivors from the days of Weimar Germany's *Ostpolitik*, the union of the two pariahs of Europe against Poland and the territorial settlement in Eastern Europe. But Hitler's planning never mentions the Soviet Union as a factor to be taken into account.

Which leaves us with a surprising question. What was the Soviet Union supposed to be doing while all this was going on? She was still nominally an ally of France, even if she had been totally neglected by the French and British before Munich and excluded from the conference itself. The exclusion of the Soviet Union as a serious military factor from Hitler's calculations was nothing new. Even as far back as the summer of 1937, the military orders he then had issued[31] gave no sign of considering the Soviet Union as a serious military factor. He made little or no reference to the Soviet Union at the Hossbach Conference in November 1937. The revised military orders of December 1937[32] made no mention of the Soviet armed forces as a major factor against which any measures needed to be taken. Even in the various military drafts from 1938 which comprise the planning for the attack on Russia's then ally, Czechoslovakia, there is little or no serious consideration given to the necessity of meeting any military threat from the Soviet Union. Unless it is assumed that Hitler had already had assurances from Stalin of his benevolent neutrality (an assumption which would have done away with the need for the tortuous and uncertain negotiations of May–August 1939 which led to Ribbentrop's last great coup, the conclusion of the Nazi-Soviet Pact), there can only be one possible explanation for this: Hitler did not take the Soviet Union seriously as a military power. He knew the Soviet navy to be greatly inferior to the

German fleet in the Baltic. The Red Air Force had no bases from which German territory could be seriously threatened. There was no common frontier across which the Red Army might attack. And he had been persuaded by the SS leader, Heydrich (moving spirit behind the creation of the SS intelligence and security service, the *Sicherheitsdienst*), that the purges of 1937, which Heydrich had fed with a dossier of forged documents passed to the Soviets via the ever-gullible Czech president, Dr Beneš,[33] had crippled the Red Army's leadership.

Poland was another matter; against her Italian and Hungarian forces could be deployed. While Hitler turned his thoughts westward, Russia, militarily, was a null. Only if he was to attack Poland and look for a common frontier with the Soviet Union would it be necessary for him to consider Soviet power. Until then the Soviet Union was simply a useful bogey with which to make other people's flesh crawl. But a serious military threat, apparently, in Hitler's eyes at least, she was not.

So the plans went forward and the Führer brooded. And Ribbentrop began to play the great Machiavelli. He did not do it very well.

CHAPTER 4

RIBBENTROP IN DIFFICULTIES

Ribbentrop's first check came at the hands of the Italians, his partners in the Axis. On October 23, in the course of a telephone conversation with Count Ciano, the Italian Foreign Minister, he suddenly announced his impending visit to Rome. The Führer, he said, had empowered him to convey a personal message to the Duce. He was planning to arrive in Rome in four days' time to deliver it.[1] The Italian reaction was cold, uneasy and suspicious. Whatever the feelings of Benito Mussolini for Hitler, he and Count Ciano, his son-in-law, despised von Ribbentrop. 'You have only to look at his head,' said Mussolini, 'to see he has a little brain.'[2] 'Vain, frivolous and loquacious' was Ciano's verdict. Both men had had more than their bellyful of him when Hitler visited Rome in May 1938. Determined to mark the beginning of his foreign ministry with a new coup, he had harried Ciano through the five-day visit with successive drafts of a military alliance, producing them from his pockets with the relentless dexterity of a third-rate conjuror at a holiday show on a seaside pier.[3] But they disliked his manners on the telephone still more. 'Sooner or later we shall have to call a halt to this tendency for a new political technique of *coups de téléphone*,' noted Ciano in his diary.[4]

Ribbentrop's sense of timing was, as usual, impeccably inaccurate. Back in April 1938, Mussolini had succeeded in extracting from the British their agreement finally to recognize the Italian conquest of Abyssinia.[5] This achievement had cost him two years of pressure, in Spain, in North Africa, and on Britain's most sensitive nerve, in the Palestine conflict between Jew and Arab which had opened with the Arab revolt of 1936. Anthony Eden had resigned rather than negotiate under such pressure, coupled as it was in his case with a campaign of personal vilification unprecedented in those days. But by a characteristic piece of ineptness – Count Ciano was, in his own way, quite as incompetent a diplomatist as Ribbentrop – it was only after the signature of the treaty that the Italians woke up to the fact that the

British had made their ratification of the treaty dependent on the prior abandonment by the Italians of all their various forms of pressure on Britain, including the withdrawal of their troops from Spain.

The British Cabinet was, however, determined to press ahead with the ratification. They believed, on Foreign Office evidence,[6] that Mussolini had in fact abandoned all intervention on behalf of the extreme Arab nationalists. Bari radio had ceased the worst of its propaganda. Mussolini was about to withdraw about half the Italian infantry forces in Spain. By the middle of October they had apparently concluded that more could not be asked for without driving Mussolini into Hitler's arms. On October 26, Lord Perth, the British Ambassador to Rome, was instructed to tell Ciano that the British Cabinet had decided to ratify the Anglo-Italian Agreement.[7] Lord Perth was able to break this happy news to the Italian Foreign Minister a few hours before Ribbentrop arrived in Rome.[8] Ciano was able to see Mussolini and tell him of this news before he met Ribbentrop.

Ribbentrop was to show himself a long way from having plumbed the minds of his hosts. Between him and Count Ciano there was little love lost. Ciano shared the instinctive dislike felt by all Italians for the Nazi aping of old-style Prussian militarism. While each had his own sense of the theatrical – Ciano enjoyed strutting in uniform and donning the grave insolent face of one who dominates the destinies of the world, as much as Ribbentrop did – Ribbentrop's continuous efforts to upstage Ciano were resented bitterly. For Ciano the language and pomp of Fascist imperialism were parts of a role to be played whenever the public demanded it. The remainder of the time his own immense vanity was tempered by the acutest of Latin cynicism and realism. Ribbentrop struck him alternatively as a hypocrite and a fanatical fool, with his perpetual talk of war, war, war.[9] Either way he was dangerous, to be avoided if possible, to be watched with great care and suspicion if encounter was inevitable.

Mussolini's attitude was altogether more complicated. For Ribbentrop he had nothing but contempt. But for Hitler, that was another story. Inside that fatuous exterior, so reminiscent of the bullfrog the caricaturists of the West so often discerned in him, there were two very different personalities at odds with one another. The one hankered after public acclaim and the power to arouse that acclaim. Trained as a journalist, Mussolini saw politics essentially in terms of newspaper headlines, and he would do almost anything to command them. Precisely what he should do to earn these headlines depended on what others were doing. If the salvation of peace and the mediation of conflict were what the public applauded then Mussolini would play the dove of peace itself, hardly able to become airborne for the weight of the olive branches in his beak. If the aggressive assertion of national interest, the voice of war, the trampling down of the proud democracies who dared to try to legislate what he, Benito Mussolini, should or should not do, looked like earning more space in the world press then, bellicose, he would play Caesar and ride roughshod over any power in his way, provided that it was small enough to warrant his anticipating an easy victory (he was not always as good a judge of this as the occasion demanded). He was also the senior dictator, the first to achieve victory for Fascism in Europe. Pride and vainglory made him instinctively seek centre-stage, whatever play happened to be occupying the other actors at the moment.

Yet, alongside this swaggering Ratapoil, this master of braggadocio of the pen, lived an insecure and frightened co-tenant. Mussolini had eagerly embraced the doctrines of Bergson, of Marinetti, of Gabriele d'Annunzio. He believed as ardently as they that violence was the rule of life, that action was itself a philosophy, that stagnation and inactivity showed their practitioners to be moving through decadence to death. Only, in his innermost soul, Mussolini, this other Mussolini, was miserably aware that he was not the man of action he desired, how desperately, to be. With his mouth, as with his pen (for he continued to write regularly for the press after his seizure of power), he could dare as desperate deeds as any man. But, in practice, that was a very different matter. Hesitant, anxious, uncertain, he vacillated from one side to the other, such native resolution as he possessed being sicklied over, less by the 'pale cast of thought' than the desperate anxiety of one who feels he has nowhere to go but down, and no resources to fall back on once his reputed strength is challenged. As so often with such men, he hid his weakness and caution behind a blustering cynicism. But he betrayed his meanness of disposition by his ready recourse to anonymous letters as a means of attacking those he disliked. He could hardly be described as lovable. But in the grubby and sordid anxieties of this, his second soul, he is far less alien, far more human than his darkly neurotic partner north of the Alps.

Where Germany was concerned, Mussolini laboured in addition under a desperate guilt complex. For Hitler he felt both dislike and admiration. He was not very much impressed by Hitler as a person. At their first meeting in Venice in June 1934, he dismissed him as a man of limited consequence. But as Hitler proceeded from gamble to gamble, from triumph to triumph, not at the expense of Greeks or Ethiopians, but at the expense of France and Britain, so Mussolini came to see in Hitler all that he wished, so desperately wished, to be himself. And since Hitler was so clearly all Mussolini's desires told him a historic personality should be, it followed that he was going to conquer. This idea came to obsess Mussolini. His visit to Berlin in September 1937 marked the point of no return in this obsession. He was even driven to exercise his execrable German on the masses of Berliners corralled by the usual Nazi methods to provide an audience for the spectacle laid on for him at the Maifeld; fortunately for his sense of dignity a heavy rainfall rendered his speech inaudible as well as unintelligible to his audience. He was to talk of the spectacle years afterwards. It left an undying impression upon him.

It also made him much more sensitive in his relations with Germany to imagined slights and rudenesses, and to threats to his own power and position. Hitler's annexation of Austria swung him back again into bitter, suspicious and grandiloquent talk of putting himself at the head of a European coalition against Germany. But only for a moment. For there was another, even stronger tug on his feelings. In 1915 Italy had abandoned her alliance with Germany and Austria-Hungary to fight, for material reward, against them. In his capacity as Socialist journalist turned chauvinist, Mussolini had played his part in this turnaround. To judge by his subsequent remarks, it had left him extremely sensitive to charges of treachery against those to whom Italy was allied. 'We must always bear ourselves so that they cannot call us *Berater*' (*Verräter*, i.e. traitors), he told Ciano. Besides, there was always the vexed question, was Hitler the man of destiny he seemed? Until 1940 Mussolini was never quite sure.

Ribbentrop's arrival in Rome found Mussolini in one of his more sensitive moods and Ciano at his most antipathetic. Ciano met him at the Grand Hotel, true Vicki Baum territory, the evening of his arrival, October 27. Ribbentrop was at his most apocalyptic, prophesying war in the course of the next few years.[10] They continued their discussion the following morning, with Ribbentrop outlining his ideas in much more detail. He had come, he said, to propose a defensive alliance of Germany, Italy and Japan. The Führer was convinced that there would be war in four to five years' time. Britain and France already had detailed military agreements (this was not true). It was time for the Axis to do likewise.[11] Ciano had heard the same arguments and had received a copy of the latest draft of the tripartite treaty from the Japanese the previous day.[12] He remained unimpressed. Leaving Ribbentrop, he went at once to the Palazzo Venezia, where Mussolini would receive Ribbentrop in the afternoon. He persuaded Mussolini that the alliance was not urgent. It would be highly unpopular with the Italian people in general, who were violently anti-German at this moment.

This argument struck Mussolini forcibly. Ribbentrop's proposal became at once unreal, an exercise in competitive bombast. That afternoon, when Ribbentrop repeated his arguments, the Duce elaborated them.[13] Of course there was going to be war with Britain and France. The trend of history pointed that way. The break between the democracies and dictatorships was irreparable. He recognized the fate of the two dictatorships was at stake. An alliance between them already existed in all but name. It was a sacred pledge between friends. And yet, he continued, switching from rhodomontade to reality, was this precisely the moment for it? The fact had to be faced that Germany was hardly popular with important sections of Italian opinion. The idea had to be allowed to mature.

Ribbentrop was visibly taken aback. Could the Italian people, he asked, not recognize the immense accession of strength an alliance would bring to them? Germany had already mobilized 400,000 men on the French frontier at the time of Munich (this was the greatest of lies). If they were combined with the arms of Italy, led by the Führer and the Duce, the alliance should be irresistible. Mussolini agreed. Yet the conditions for an alliance must mature. However, when the time was ripe, he continued, easily trumping Ribbentrop's ace, it should not be a purely defensive alliance. No one was thinking of attacking the totalitarian states. No, it must be an alliance to change the world. And the following morning Mussolini sat down to compose a reply to the formal proposal which he gave to Ribbentrop the same afternoon. Crestfallen, disappointed and unable to hide his disappointment, Ribbentrop had to take the train back to Berlin.

Ribbentrop had good reason to be disappointed. Not only were the Italian arguments palpably specious, save for the unanswerable realism with which Mussolini had punctured the sweep of his fantasy (no one today or tomorrow is in a position to attack the totalitarian states), but Ciano had rubbed the whole thing in by enquiring pointedly how his arguments could be reconciled with the proposal put to the Italians on October 11 by Reichsmarschall Goering via the Prince of Hesse for a four-power pact with Britain and France.[14] Nothing more was to be heard of this proposal, the first of Goering's attempts to conduct an alternative foreign policy to that of von Ribbentrop. But Ciano had derived malicious glee from Ribbentrop's obvious ignorance of the whole proposal; and the assurances Ciano gave him after dinner on October 28, that solidarity between the Axis powers was total without a written document, were hardly what he had come to Rome to hear. He did not even have the satisfaction of an official communiqué to deal with his meeting with Mussolini. It must have been a long and disconsolate journey back to Berlin.

Mussolini, by contrast, would seem to have enjoyed himself hugely. His ego was still buoyed up by his belief that he had played a critical role as a peacemaker at Munich. He enjoyed being courted by Germany and Britain. He enjoyed still more putting the detestable Ribbentrop in his place. The British were about to recognize his victory in Ethiopia. The French had already anticipated them in accrediting a new ambassador on October 4 to 'the King of Italy and Emperor of Abyssinia'. He was preparing his peculiarly beastly sets of measures against persons who were in no position to strike back, the Italian Jews[15] and the Albanians. 'I was born never to leave the Italians in peace,' he bragged to the applause of the Fascist Grand Council. 'First Africa, now Spain, tomorrow something else.'[16] He was in the process of at last replacing the hated Chamber of Deputies, the last relic of Italian parliamentarian-ism, by a Chamber of the Fasces and the Corporations. And he was working himself up for another attack on the 'cowardly and disgusting *bourgeois*'.[17] He foresaw, he told Ciano, a period of *détente*[18] in Europe; but not for the French. As soon as the British had finally ratified their treaty with Italy, the heat would be on the French. They had done their best to bury the hatchet, and had in fact nominated their Ambassador in Berlin, the suave André François-Poncet, as their new Ambassador in Rome, in the hope that he would prove as successful in establishing good personal relations with Mussolini as he had with the Führer; all in vain. 'I shall do everything to help him break his head. I don't like the man,' said the Duce;[19] and he went on to discuss Italian demands: neutralization and a condominium over Djibouti, capital of French Somaliland and railhead for Ethiopia's only railway to the sea; Tunisia to have a similar regime; Corsica to become Italian; likewise Nice.[20] The million Italians living in France were to be recalled.[21] François-Poncet was to be snubbed and humiliated.

Mussolini would have been the more pleased with Ribbentrop's disappointment had he realized what encouragement the Chief of the Italian Army Staff, General Pariani, had been giving the Germans, as he would have been angered by the very low opinion of the military value of an alliance with Italy entertained by the German General Staff. But Mussolini's control over the Italian armed forces was always pre-carious. During the pre-Fascist era they had owed their allegiance directly to the King. Under Fascism they remained a separate, virtually closed corporation despising the mass of Fascists as vulgar and ridicu-lous civilians of ignoble birth, whilst individually they were prepared to crawl with flattery to Mussolini in the hope of advancement. Mussolini had, if anything, made confusion worse confounded by adding in 1925 a new post of Chief of the General Staff above the Chiefs of Staff of the three services. In 1938 this was occupied, as it had been since 1925, by Marshal Badoglio, the victor of Vittorio Veneto, Italy's only military victory in the First World War. But by 1938 Mussolini had succeeded in stripping the post of all power. Badoglio consoled himself with a continuing sense of his own indispensability in war. In the meantime he lived in honorific desuetude.

But Mussolini by this very action had reduced his chances of controlling the actions of the individual services. And General Pariani was obsessed by the threat to Italy he perceived from the Western democracies. His estimates of their strength, profoundly pessimistic as they were, appalled him. Since August 1938 when he had visited Hitler,[22] he had been urging the closest of Staff contacts and co-ordination between the two Axis powers. Talks were arranged in the last days of the Munich crisis. But the summoning of the conference overtook them before they could actually be convened and in the event the only contacts that took place were between the signals staff of the two armies concerned to arrange a common cipher by which they could communicate.[23] In the following weeks Pariani became more and more importunate in his representations to the unfortunate German Military Attaché in Rome until the German army authorities told him to avoid any further contacts on this issue.[24] As the German assessment back in April 1938 had been that Italy became a liability as soon as Britain was numbered among Germany's enemies,[25] this view is understandable. It made Ribbentrop's task no easier, however, even after a formula had been evolved to keep the Italians happy.

On his return to Berlin, Ribbentrop was to be greeted with more discouragement. The draft of the alliance he had taken to Rome represented a modification of one originally produced by the Japanese army. This had come to him through a man who was for a long time his closest associate among the foreign diplomatists in Berlin: Major-General Hiroshi Oshima who, after long service as Japanese Military Attaché, had taken over as Ambassador in Berlin the day Ribbentrop left for Rome. General Oshima, a short, thick-set man, was so enthusiastically pro-German as to be a byword among his own people. His father, a former Minister of War, himself a general and an admirer of imperial Germany, was a member of the Emperor's Privy Council for much of the Second World War. But Oshima junior was not only pro-German; he was pro-Nazi, something his father disapproved of profoundly. Pronouncedly anti-Soviet as a result of service with the Japanese interventionist forces in Siberia in 1918–19, he had served as an Assistant Military Attaché in Berlin in 1921–3. He had disliked the politics and society of the Weimar Republic. On his return as Military

Attaché to Germany in 1934, he had been overwhelmed by the change in German society, and could admit no imperfections in the Nazi system. In the Gaimusho, the Japanese Foreign Office, they referred to him as the German Ambassador in Berlin. His diplomatic colleagues in Berlin found him more than a little trying in his devotion to Ribbentrop and his unswerving hostility towards the Soviet Union. He was, however, highly regarded by the Japanese army leadership for his obstinacy as a negotiator and for his devotion to the cause of Japanese expansionism. Apart from his admiration for von Ribbentrop, he struck his colleagues as intelligent and tough, and he seems to have won their reluctant admiration for his ability to 'hold his liquor'.

Oshima had been the architect of the original anti-Comintern pact signed in November 1936, which he had fought through a long year's negotiations against the resistance of both Foreign Ministry and Wehrmacht leadership on the German side and the opposition of his own Ambassador Shigenori Togo, and the Gaimusho in Japan.[26] He had twice approached the Germans in 1937 with proposals to transform this pact into a military agreement, and had tried yet again in January 1938 after consultation with Ribbentrop, only to have the proposal squashed by Togo. In June 1938, after his rebuff in Rome, Ribbentrop had approached Oshima yet again with a proposal for a military alliance. To avoid the Embassy, Oshima sent the proposal back to Tokyo with a staff officer temporarily seconded to Berlin to learn German, General Yukio Kasahara.

The Japanese army was gaining the upper hand in Tokyo politics, and after a month's deliberations the Inner Cabinet decided to go ahead. They were, however, distinctly worried by the wide scope of the pact Ribbentrop proposed. The Japanese Navy Minister had no desire to see his ageing fleet dragged into battle against Britain and America to serve some purely German design in Central Europe. They insisted, there-fore, that the scope of the pact be limited to the Soviet Union; and they asked for a considerable limitation on the obligation to go to their ally's assistance.[27] General Kasahara returned to Berlin on September 20. And Oshima gave Ribbentrop the news.

At this point the Japanese Ambassador in Berlin was informed for the first time of the negotiations. His furious expostulations were cut short and he was transferred to Moscow. General Oshima was appointed as his successor. Behind this lay a successful conspiracy between the ideologists of Japanese expansion in the Japanese army, and a younger group of some fifty members of the Japanese Foreign Ministry led by Toshio Shiratori, former Japanese Minister to Sweden. Kasahara, brother-in-law to Kazushige Ugaki, the Foreign Minister, denounced

Togo as so anti-Nazi as to be virtually *persona non grata* in Berlin. The intrigue succeeded, but the price was the limitation of any alliance with Germany to operations against the Soviet Union.

The draft treaty which Ribbentrop proposed the Italians should sign was thus in the main a Japanese draft, somewhat roughly amended. Early in November Oshima and Ribbentrop met Friedrich Gaus, head of the German Foreign Ministry's legal department, and concocted a new version which they sent off to Tokyo.[28] The Japanese Inner Cabinet were again convened to examine it. They met on November 11 in inauspicious circumstances.[29] The effort to conquer China had clearly failed and Generalissimo Chiang Kai-shek, despite numerous defeats, despite the Japanese occupation of the entire Chinese sea-coast and the provinces bordering on the sea, despite the loss of the capitals, Peking and Nanking, was still firmly in control. The principal Chinese collaborationist, Wang Chin-wei, once Chiang's principal rival for the leadership of the Chinese nationalist movement, the Kuomintang, had fled to Hong Kong, expelled from the party. Soviet and Western aid was clearly the main reason why Chiang refused to accept the various Japanese overtures for an agreement. Something would have to be done to deter this aid from reaching Chiang. Thus ran the reasoning of the Japanese Minister for War, General Itagaki, as did, in rather weaker vein, the views of the Foreign Minister and the Prime Minister, Prince Konoye. On the other hand the Navy Minister, Admiral Yonai, remained adamantly opposed to any involvement with the Axis powers. To his mind they were totally untrustworthy and were earning the mounting hostility of Britain and the United States. If Japan signed a pact with the Axis she would at the least share the odium they were attracting, and might well find herself at war through no choice of her own.[30]

Prince Konoye had in fact just received evidence of this. On November 1, Sir Robert Craigie, the astute, tough and perceptive British Ambassador in Tokyo, had warned him that any attempt to strengthen the anti-Comintern pact would be interpreted as a move against Britain, just as the conclusion of the pact itself had been.[31] Craigie was, in appearance, almost a caricature of the stuffy inhibited British diplomatist. But he was in fact extremely well informed, both from open and clandestine sources, as to what was going on in the Japanese Cabinet. He was a superb negotiator with an immense confidence in his own professional abilities. And if he ever lacked resolution it was made up for by his formidable wife, the daughter of an American diplomatist, a Virginian who terrorized her husband's staff and before whom even American admirals had been known to withdraw defeated. Sir Robert could be relied on to apply every means of pressure available to him; and his American colleague, Joseph Grew, architect of the reform and professionalization of the American diplomatic service before his transfer to Tokyo in 1931, could be relied on to support him.

It is hardly surprising, therefore, that the Japanese Cabinet (which on October 29 had replaced those who had appointed Oshima) should have begun to back-pedal. Oshima received one telegram to say that the Cabinet accepted the idea of a treaty in principle but that its scope was to be confined to the Soviet Union. Only if Britain and France joined the Soviet Union in an attack on one of the signatories, or if France went Communist, was the alliance to operate against them. Oshima protested bitterly, and the Minister of War, General Itagaki, driven by the extremists among his younger officers (as a younger officer he had played the same role in Manchuria in 1931), backed him. As Oshima had already altered the instructions given to him in September, the Cabinet was faced with an impasse. Indeed, Oshima was to go to Rome in December on his own initiative and at Ribbentrop's request to urge Mussolini to join the pact. No new instructions could be evolved in Tokyo.

Then, on January 4, the Japanese Cabinet resigned. Prince Konoye was succeeded by the taciturn Baron Kuchiro Hiranuma (so reticent even by Japanese standards as to earn the nickname of the Japanese Calvin Coolidge) and the entire problem had to be examined all over again.

Baron Hiranuma had inherited most of Prince Konoye's Cabinet, including General Itagaki, Admiral Yonai (the Navy Minister) and Foreign Minister Arita. As Prime Minister he was to chair a succession of meetings on the problem of the pact; but he had already given his pledge to Arita to resign rather than yield to army pressure to extend the anti-Comintern pact to waging war against England and France. This pledge was needed. The extreme nationalists did not hesitate to threaten him and Arita with assassination. Even Prince Chichibu, the Emperor's brother, could not convince them of the folly of allying Japan with Germany against Britain. The Emperor's own advisers, Prince Saionji and Admiral Saito, the Lord Keeper of the Privy Seal, were also threatened. In February 1939 talk spread in Tokyo of a military revolt more extensive than that of February 1936, in which attacks had been made on Admiral Suzuki (then Grand Chamberlain), Prince Saionji, the Prime Minister and Admiral Saito. Kerekiyo Takahashi, the Minister of Finance, and General Watanabe, the Inspector General of Military Training, had been killed. Admiral Yonai took this talk seriously enough to hold a large contingent of bluejackets ready to land in Tokyo to resist any army mutineers. And the talk receded for the moment.

In the meantime the endless search for a formula, so characteristic of the Japanese political system of this period, continued. Itagaki urged and pressed his colleagues. He was backed by the unexpected support of the Minister of Finance, desperate for anything that would end the drain on Japan's resources provoked by the endless war in China. The younger army officers fretted, plotted and cursed the westernized liberal advisers around the Emperor. Yonai remained obdurate, the full strength of the navy behind him. And Arita strove unavailingly to bring Oshima and his diplomatic colleague, Toshio Shiratori, the Ambassador in Rome, to present a balanced viewpoint to the governments to which they were accredited. Oshima and Shiratori were unmoved. It was difficult to know, said Arita despairingly in March, whether Oshima was a Japanese or a German diplomat. And Shiratori, on whose behalf the younger nationalists in the Foreign Ministry had petitioned Prince Konoye to make him Foreign Minister the previous September, was unwilling to give his rival any help. When Arita instructed them to make it clear that Japan was only prepared to sign the alliance if it was directed against Moscow, Shiratori advised Count Ciano to reject the proposal.

In desperation Arita put together a special three-man mission under the former Japanese Minister to Poland, Nobafumi Ito, and sent them to Rome and Berlin by sea with a new draft of the pact and detailed instructions to explain Tokyo's standpoint. Oshima responded by lobbying the other Japanese diplomatists in Europe, first on visits to the various missions in Europe and then, while the Ito commission was actually in Berlin, calling a conference of all heads of missions in Europe to meet in Berlin to confront Ito. Neither of these devices was successful. Meanwhile time was passing and Ribbentrop was no nearer his grand coup than he had been in October. Had Ribbentrop, or for that matter the Italians, realized the true state of division in Tokyo, where in March the Emperor himself was to intervene to strengthen the resolve of the Cabinet against any widening of the proposed alliance, they might have cut their losses earlier. But they believed what Oshima and Shiratori told them; the more so as the Japanese army faction took good care to provide the German Embassy in Tokyo with supporting evidence. However, it was to become gradually more and more clear that, for all his intriguing, Oshima could not deliver; he could only postpone a realization of his impotence.

The Italians, it was true, had changed their tune. Ratification of the Anglo-Italian treaty came on November 16. Two days earlier Count

Ciano wrote to the Italian Ambassador in London, Dino Grandi.[32] The Duce was determined not to rest on his laurels for a moment. Italy would demand a condominium in Tunisia and Somaliland, reversion of the Addis Ababa-Djibouti railway, and a seat on the Suez Canal Board. It was Grandi's job to prepare the British. The new French Ambassador was kept kicking his heels until November 29 and then given a display of Italian Fascist hauteur, exaggerated, according to Ciano, by the Duce's heavy cold.[33] The new Italian Ambassador in Paris was told by Rome to wait on events. They came the next day. As Count Ciano spoke in the Fascist Chamber, a speech he had been working on since November 19, 'there burst out a veritable storm of acclamations and shouts of "Tunis, Corsica, Nice, Savoy". Spontaneously, the deputies gave voice to their aspirations, which are those of the whole people.' Or so at least Ciano confided to his diary.[34]

The Duce was trying what he called 'Sudeten methods' on the French. This did his ego good at first ('a great day for the regime', he remarked to Ciano), as did the flood of letters and telegrams of congratulations which his missions organized from all over Italy. The attack on France also distracted attention from his preparations to annex Albania. But a week later he was beginning to have second thoughts. Press warfare was all very well; but there was no sign of French concessions, nor, for that matter, of British willingness to mediate. The largely defunct agreements concluded between Mussolini and Laval in January 1935 were officially denounced on December 7, 1938 to the accompaniment of new polemics. But there was still no sign of concessions from Paris or London. In London, speaking to the House of Commons on December 19, Chamberlain emphasized the cordiality of relations between Britain and France.[35] And Lord Perth, the British Ambassador, more than hinted that Chamberlain might feel himself obliged to cancel his forthcoming visit to Rome, if the anti-French demonstrations continued.[36] M. Daladier, the French Premier, made an extremely tough speech on Christmas Day. And Mussolini retired to his villa at Rocca della Caminata to consider the matter further. He told Ciano of his decision on New Year's Day. Italy would sign the tripartite alliance. The following day Ciano communicated the Italian decision to Ribbentrop.[37] The news was no doubt very welcome, but it was almost immediately vitiated by the fall of Prince Konoye's Cabinet in Tokyo. Ribbentrop's timetable in regard to the military alliance had gone very askew.

Nor were his negotiations with Poland any happier. Since the death of the Polish dictator, Marshal Pilsudski, in May 1935, with whom Hitler had concluded the non-aggression pact in January of the preceding year, power in Poland was shared between five men: President Ignacy Mościcky; the Premier, Slawoj-Skladkowski; the Vice-Premier, Eugeniusz Kwiatkowski; Marshal Edouard Smigly-Rydz, the Commander-in-Chief of the Polish army; and Colonel Józef Beck, the Foreign Minister. These men had one thing in common. They had seen Poland reborn after a century or more of partition. They had been born citizens of the three empires, Austria-Hungary, imperial Germany or Tsarist Russia. They were, moreover, like many other nationalist leaders, products of a social as well as a national revolution. They were not from the Polish aristocracy. They had fought for the independence of Poland during the First World War. Under Pilsudski they had striven for a greater Poland, with Lithuania, White Russia and the Ukraine, only to see their dream collapse before the advent of the Red Army. They had broken that same Red Army before the gates of Warsaw in 1920. They had had setbacks; but they had never known conquest. Courage, flair, heroism, devouring ambition, all these they had in abundance; realism and worst-case analysis, let alone defeatism or appeasement, were alien to them entirely. Of the junta Colonel Beck enjoyed an almost total monopoly in the conduct and formulation of Poland's foreign policy. In 1938 he was 45 years old, born in the old Hapsburg empire, the son of a provincial lawyer, of a family that had originally been Flemish. In the early years of Poland's independence he had led a curiously shadowy career in Polish espionage. His name was linked with that of Boris Savinkov, the *émigré* Russian Socialist who ran an espionage and terrorist organization inside Russia in the early 1920s. In 1923 the French expelled him from Paris where he was serving as Polish Military Attaché, under suspicion of spying for Germany. Returning to Poland, he first became Marshal Pilsudski's hatchet man and then his *Chef de Cabinet* in the Polish Ministry of War. In 1932 Pilsudski had made him Foreign Minister.

His appearance was as foxy as his character was devious and two-faced. He was devouringly ambitious and arrogantly unrealistic in his judgment of the strength of Poland's international position. Like Count Ciano, he was exceedingly well informed. The Polish intelligence services were among the best in Europe, and were outstandingly well informed about the Soviet Union, exchanging information with, among others, the Japanese, with whom they worked closely in their analysis of Soviet military dispositions. They had, in addition, cracked the German Enigma cipher machine, although it is far from clear whether this included the diplomatic codes, or what material the German armed forces, in times of peace, entrusted to radio rather than to couriers or land-lines. In any case, the Germans changed the

Enigma code in September 1938. The new system was not to be broken until 1939. More effective was the regular interception (*Operation Wozek*) of German mail as it crossed the Polish Corridor in sealed trains.[38]

Like Ciano, Beck was incompetent as Foreign Minister though, to be fair, his country laboured under much greater difficulties than did Italy. In negotiation his style varied from a legalistic stonewalling to an arrogant imposition of conditions. His conduct of Polish foreign policy during the Czech crisis left Poland without a friend in Europe. 'If Hitler was to march into Poland,' wrote Commander Stephen King-Hall (otherwise a consistent opponent of Nazi Germany) in his famous *Newsletter*, 'I would say *Sieg Heil.*' This was after the Poles had demanded the cession to them of the coalmining area of Teschen, presenting an ultimatum to the Czechs the day the Munich settlement was announced. The demand seemed so like kicking a man when he was down that Poland was to become the scapegoat for all the guilt feelings that lurked below the surface of public approval for the Munich settlement in Britain. But then Britain's behaviour in the Czech crisis had not impressed Colonel Beck. In common with most Central Europeans he saw the outcome of the Munich crisis as a mark of British withdrawal from Central Europe – even perhaps of a partial retreat from her previous domination of European politics.

British opinion would have been the more agitated if it had been able to follow Beck's next intrigue. On the acceptance of the Munich Agreement, the Czechs had also been forced to yield to pressure from the other nationalities that made up the Czechoslovak state and accept the establishment of separate governments in Slovakia and in the extreme eastern tip of Czechoslovakia in the area known as Ruthenia or the Carpatho-Ukraine. In Ruthenia the politically active were divided between a nominally pro-Russian group, of whose leaders the first Premier turned out to be in Hungarian pay, and a group dreaming of a greater Ukrainian state, to take in the three million Ukrainian minority in southern Poland, and, eventually, the Soviet Ukraine. Their leader, Vološin, turned naturally to Berlin. Polish intelligence was well aware that the stirrings of Ukrainian nationalism, which were now apparent in the Carpatho-Ukraine, were fomented from Germany. A Ukrainian legion had been organized and trained by the German military intelligence, the *Abwehr*, since May 1938. The German Consulate in Cracow was a known source of funds and instructions to Ukrainian nationalists in southern Poland, where demonstrations in support of the new autonomous Ukrainian Czech state had taken place in October in Lwow.[39]

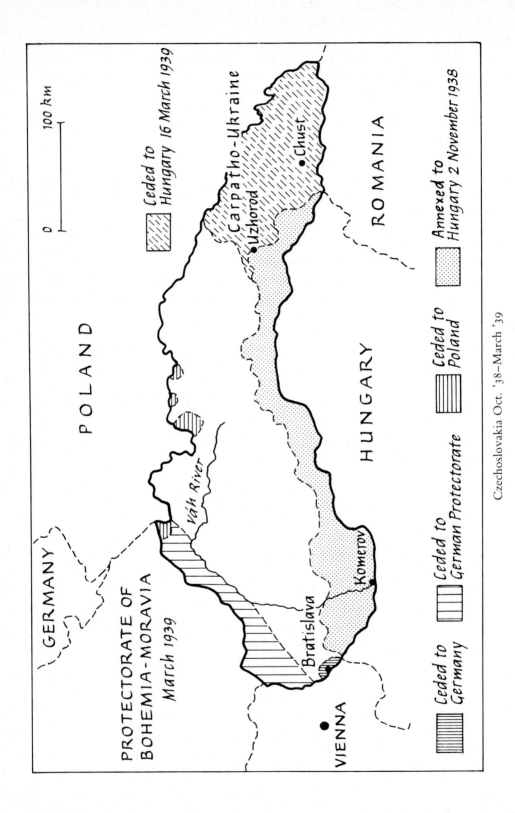

GERMANY

POLAND

PROTECTORATE OF
BOHEMIA-MORAVIA
March 1939

Váh River

Carpatho-Ukraine

Uzhorod

Chust

Bratislava

Komerov

VIENNA

HUNGARY

ROMANIA

0   100 km

Ceded to
Hungary 16 March 1939

Annexed to
Hungary 2 November 1938

Ceded to
German Protectorate

Ceded to
Poland

Ceded to
Germany

Czechoslovakia Oct. '38–March '39

The case of the Carpatho-Ukraine, in its own way, and to the misery and ruin of those who believed in it, exemplifies the problems which Ribbentrop was attempting to manipulate. In its small and embryo form it embodied the hopes, fears and dreams of an independent Ukrainian nation. The Ukrainian communities in the New World were as fired and ready to pump in money and hope as ever the Zionists in America were into Eretz Israel or the Boston, Chicago and New York Irish into the IRA.[40] The substantial Ukrainian minority in Poland, as politically disadvantaged as they were well organized, thrilled to the idea of an autonomous state, even one based on the backwoods nowhere that was Chust.[41] In addition to the German army *Abwehr*'s long-standing but quiet and minimalist subsidy to the survivors of the Cossack state of 1917–18, Heydrich and Himmler had been building up links between their own intelligence service, the SD, and both White Russians and Ukrainians. Radio Vienna was a centre of Slovak and Ukrainian broadcasts to the oppressed peoples of the old Czech state struggling to be free.[42] Seeing a means of thwarting and confusing Ribbentrop, Goering was pushing for German exploitation of its alleged resources.[43]

Inevitably all this leaked abroad. On December 13, Coulondre, the French Ambassador, provided the French with a lengthy first-hand survey of the work of the 'National Union of the Ukraine' organized from 79 Mecklenburg Street in Berlin.[44] The Ukraine was to become a German vassal state, with or without Polish acquiescence.[45] In October, before leaving for Rome, Coulondre's predecessor, François-Poncet, had reported on the White Russian branch of the SD led by a former Tsarist Guards cavalry officer, and another Tsarist officer, Tavaritzky, from a Russian regiment of less social standing, married to the sister of one of Himmler's adjutants.[46] There was talk in London and Paris of a new revolution in Russia, an internal disintegration of the Soviet machine.[47] Foreign Office and Quai d'Orsay officials remained more than sceptical. But the Soviets, picking this up and reading the constant speculation in the European press over plans for the Ukraine, can be forgiven for thinking the risk father to the thought, not realizing that the more they denied any foreign access to Russia and the Russian people, the more they fed the suspicions that they had something to hide.

In the meantime Ribbentrop only alarmed and angered the Poles. Józef Beck had always been under the sway of geopolitical writings. From his mentor, Marshal Pilsudski, he had adopted the idea that Poland could only survive if she maintained her independence between, and neutrality towards, Germany and Russia. But he needed more than this. In the aftermath of the German-Polish Non-Aggression Pact he seems to have conceived the idea of creating a great bloc of powers under Polish leadership stretching from Scandinavia to the Adriatic as a permanent entity between Germany and the Soviet Union.[48] He broached the idea of this *intermarium*, as he called it, this 'third Europe', to Count Ciano when he visited Rome in March 1938.[49] His visits to Sweden, Denmark, Norway, Latvia and Estonia in the summer of 1938 were part of the same scheme, as was the effort he put into persuading Hungary to confine her claims on Czechoslovakia to the Carpatho-Ukraine and into persuading Romania to accept this. By this means a common Hungarian-Polish frontier would be established, and a bloc of Hungary, Poland, Yugoslavia and Romania would, with Italian aid, be able to withstand most kinds of pressure in Central Europe.

The plan for a joint Polish-Hungarian action was already well under way early in October. The initiative came originally from the Hungarians. It is difficult to write about the regime in command of Hungary at this time with anything but contempt. The regime of Admiral Horthy led a nation with a long and idiosyncratic history, divided from its neighbours by a language quite unlike either the Slavonic tongues of Serbs and Croats in the south, Czechs, Slovaks, Ruthenes, Ukrainians and Poles in the north or the Latinized Slav mix of Romania. The Hungarian kingdom had borne the brunt of the long onslaught of the Ottoman on Central Europe. It had survived by assimilating to its race any and all who would adopt its language and religion, making second-class citizens of all – Jews, Germans, Romanians – who would not. With the defeat of the Central Powers in 1918, the kingdom of Hungary had been shorn of much of its historic territory, losing Transylvania to Romania. It had survived one of the most bloodthirsty of Bolshevik insurrections outside Russia, as well as the White Terror which had followed. The monarchy, symbol of national continuity, was preserved in a regency, headed by a former Admiral in the Austro-Hungarian navy, Horthy. Its foreign policy centred on the revision of the 1919 treaties, and was the cement holding together the 'Little Entente' of Czechoslovakia and Yugoslavia.

Under the timorous, arthritic regime of Admiral Horthy the Hungarians lived, as only Hungarians could, lives of passion and enjoyment tempered by continuous economic crises, largely indifferent to successive governments, divided by religion, prey to the external politics of small groups of the violent and alienated dreaming of Hungary's past. The Horthy regime preserved the authoritarianism and the secret police of Hapsburg days. It has been called Fascist, partly as an insult. Truly Fascist it was not, though its own home-grown Fascists waited around on street corners as their analogues did throughout Europe and the Levant in the inter-war years.

Throughout the summer of 1938 the Hungarian regime had been pressed by Goering, Ribbentrop and Hitler to join the coming war against Czechoslovakia. Characteristically pusillanimous, it had hesitated and dithered until suddenly Chamberlain's descent upon Munich made it too late. Lacking even the 'courage' displayed by the Poles over Teschen, they faced again the possibility that they had missed their chance. At the beginning of October Count Csáky, the Hungarian Foreign Minister, appeared in Warsaw. On October 7 he met Colonel Beck.[50] Beck, uncertain of German plans, encouraged the Hungarians to take the lead. Together they hatched a plot. Polish forces disguised as 'volunteers' or 'free corps' were to enter the Carpatho-Ukraine from the north, Hungarian 'volunteers' from the south. On October 18–20, Colonel Beck visited Romania to try to square the Romanians, but in vain.[51] Thereafter the Poles withdrew, giving the Hungarians active encouragement but reserving their own fire for a succession of bitter protests to the Germans over the activities of Polish Ukrainian refugees in Germany, the encouragement given them by various German authorities and the propaganda they were directing on Vienna radio towards both Carpatho-Ukraine and the Ukrainian minority in Poland.[52] The Hungarians went ahead with their plans, only to be frustrated by a direct warning from Germany on November 21.[53] The essence of the plot lay in the destabilization of the infant Ruthenian Government by co-ordinated subversive action. The Poles duly carried out their side of the bargain, the Polish General Staff wisely refusing any combined action.[54] The Hungarians, using the so-called Ragged Guards (*Rongyos Garda*), a ragamuffin group of extreme Fascists and unemployed men, raised in the summer of 1935 by Miklos Kozma, then Minister of the Interior, followed suit.[55] This first raid, on October 11, was a disaster. They were ambushed by Czech troops and lost half of the group, killed or captured by the Czechs, who threatened to execute their prisoners if such raids continued.[56]

On November 2, in response to the Hungarian appeal, Germany and Italy awarded Hungary most of the areas along the Slovak and Ruthenian borders with Hungary including the capital, Uzhgorod; these awards fell as far short of Hungary's demands as of Beck's expectations. Beck, despite his failure in October to persuade the Romanians to share in a partition of Ruthenia, continued his pressure on Budapest.[57] Timid as ever, the Hungarians sought diplomatic aid and aircraft from Italy[58] and four Polish army corps to take out the Czech army.[59] Beck had no desire to challenge Hitler head-on; the Polish

General Staff thought it impossible. If Hungary could engineer any kind of appeal from a Ruthenian body, then Poland would act to restrain any Romanian intervention. The action of the Polish irregulars on Ruthenia's northern boundaries continued. On November 17 the leaders of the Ragged Guards were told to start operations within twenty-four hours.[60] Incompetent as ever, the Hungarians published the news of a Ruthenian appeal for Hungarian intervention a day too soon.[61] Berlin was alerted. A furious Hitler gave Budapest an ultimatum. Any action against Ruthenia would be regarded as an unfriendly act. Two German diplomats toured the Carpatho-Ukraine, as Vološin and his supporters now insisted Ruthenia should be called.[62] Beck's dreams of a 'Third Europe' were at an end.

Ribbentrop had already made his first move towards anchoring Poland into the German sphere. He invited the Polish Ambassador to Germany, Józef Lipski, who had been trying to meet him to complain about Vienna's pro-Ukrainian propaganda, to make a special trip to Berchtesgaden (involving a long and uncomfortable train journey and disembarkation on a typical German country railway station, with no platform, a long drop off the high carriage steps and a walk across bare railway tracks to the station building). He then whisked him off to the Grand Hotel, a tourist hotel lying under the shadow of the great hill on which Hitler had built his 'eagle's nest', to overlook Austria, and plied him with lunch. His guest remained unmoved. He had long ago made himself impervious to German pressures much more subtle and sophisticated than those now employed by Ribbentrop.

Józef Lipski was, in fact, born in Germany, in Breslau, and went to school near his family's estates in German-occupied Poland. Childhood as a Pole in Germany, subject to all the pressures towards Germanization to which so many of his fellows succumbed, had made him fastidious, controlled and aloof. He was sustained by a family tradition of service to Poland going back to the sixteenth century, and was reared in this tradition by his deeply religious, cultivated, kind but demanding mother. At school Józef learned German history and German literature, and spoke German. At home his mother, with seven languages at her command, taught him French and English and, above all, the history and language of Poland. He was naturally outgoing and convivial with his friends. But he learned to hold his tongue and his counsel; and the German intelligence who watched and listened in on all foreign diplomatists in Germany rarely caught him out.

Throughout the disastrous year which followed Munich he remained unperturbed, in control, unflappable. He regarded the maintenance of good relations with Germany as of the utmost importance for his country. He had in fact played a large hand in making the German-Polish Declaration of 1934. He was prepared to use the unstable personalities that made up the Nazi leadership, to flatter their pride and show concern for their susceptibilities. He was not, however, at any time ready to compromise the sovereign rights and honour of his country. He was to need all his courage, control, urbanity and determination to give nothing away in the negotiations which were to follow.

Lunch and the subsequent conversation that day at Berchtesgaden lasted three hours.[63] It took Ribbentrop some time to get to the point, and when he did he was portentously secretive. What he had to propose was so secret that it should be kept between only Lipski, Beck and himself. (His staffer, Walter Hewel, headed his note of the conversation for those three only.) He asked Lipski to report orally to Beck because otherwise there was a great danger that the matter might leak out. He would like Beck to come to Berlin to discuss the matter with him. Indeed 'our Polish friends' had a standing invitation to visit Berlin.

What he, Ribbentrop, had to propose was nothing less than a complete settlement (*eine Gesamtlösung*) of all possible points of friction between Poland and Germany. First of all, Danzig must return to Germany. Secondly, Germany must have East Prussia linked by land with the rest of Germany by extra-territorial *Autobahn* and rail connections. Poland would join the anti-Comintern pact and receive an extra-territorial road and railway and a free port in the Danzig area. The German-Polish treaty would be extended from ten to twenty-five years and each country would guarantee the other's frontiers. Lipski listened in silence. When Ribbentrop had finished he reminded him of Hitler's pledge given him on November 5, 1937, and repeated by Hitler on January 14, 1938 to Colonel Beck, that there would be no change in the legal status of Danzig; Danzig lived from Poland, and without the Polish hinterland it would be nothing. Poland had never interfered in Danzig's affairs, however, and had always recognized its German character. He could see no possibility of an agreement involving the reunion of Danzig with Germany. The Polish people could never be prevailed on to accept it. He promised, none the less, to report on the conversation to Colonel Beck. He took the train back to Warsaw the next day.

In Warsaw Lipski spoke to Colonel Beck and to Count Szembek.[64] He was very pessimistic. He thought that the Germans were determined to annex Danzig. One could postpone discussion and avoid the evil day but sooner or later they would return to the charge. Goering understood how things were, that Danzig cut off from its hinterland would perish; but Ribbentrop showed no understanding at all. Szembek noted that the German Gauleiter of Danzig, Forster, who had just been to see Hitler and had been flown back to Danzig in the Führer's private plane, had been organizing a number of meetings since his return on the theme that things were going to get better and better.[65] It looked as if the Germans were determined to take Danzig.

Lipski was unable to see Ribbentrop again until the middle of November. He then unfolded to him the instructions he had brought back from Warsaw.[66] The conversation was friendly enough,[67] though the content of Lipski's message was inevitably disappointing. He made what Ribbentrop characterized as a 'verbose' statement about the importance of Danzig for Poland. If the Danzig question was opened, he warned, German-Polish relations would be seriously endangered. This apparently hit Ribbentrop rather hard as he in turn emphasized the difficulty for Hitler of recognizing the Polish Corridor. He was in no way trying to treat Poland as he had treated Dr Beneš and Czechoslovakia. German policy on Poland was conceived on very broad lines and his sole idea was to achieve stable relations between the two countries. Lipski proposed a new agreement replacing the League of Nations statute over Danzig by a bilateral agreement. Ribbentrop dismissed this. If Beck would reflect on his suggestions at leisure, then Ribbentrop was sure he would come to accept them. Lipski returned once more to Warsaw to report.

He came to Warsaw in a rather better mood than on his previous visit.[68] Two hints Ribbentrop had dropped, that the proposal was his own idea and not Hitler's, and that he had been trying to find a way to fulfil Hitler's conviction of the necessity of good relations between these two countries, cheered him immensely. Moreover, he felt Poland was much less isolated and Germany more so than in October. Perhaps, he suggested, Ribbentrop should be invited to Warsaw and treated to a full display of Polish military power and ceremony. Beck was even more sanguine and inclined to think that Ribbentrop was overplaying his hand. He was encouraged in this by an interview he had on November 22 with Hans Adolf von Moltke, the German Ambassador in Poland, during which von Moltke said that Ribbentrop had paid great attention to Lipski's remarks and had taken due cognizance of his declaration on Danzig.[69] He also said that he had always warned Ribbentrop how important Danzig was to the Poles. Germany, he said, had been under the influence of false information. If von Moltke did make such remarks he was far too discreet to put them into his own report of the meeting[70] which dealt with quite other matters. Beck's fatal euphoria was settling in again.

He was the more pleased in that he was just about to pull off a new coup, the signature of a joint declaration with the Soviet Union.[71] In view of Ribbentrop's invitation to Poland to join the anti-Comintern pact, this was a direct snub to Ribbentrop. At the time of its signature the Deputy Chief of the Polish General Staff, General Fabrycy, was in Germany talking to Marshal Goering, who not only got a great deal of malicious pleasure out of the snub to Ribbentrop, his enemy and rival, but also made reassuring noises about Germany's attitude to a common Polish-Hungarian frontier.[72] It was time, Beck felt, to clear away all the misunderstandings Ribbentrop's amateurish incompetence was causing. He must be invited to Warsaw. Lipski could sweeten the invitation by indicating that Poland was prepared to talk about the *Autobahn*. But on Danzig there could be no yielding.[73]

Beck was in for a rude surprise. Hitler was already beginning to lose patience with his procrastination. Nor had the Polish pact with the Soviets or the evidence of the clandestine Polish inspiration behind the Hungarian plans for a coup against the Carpatho-Ukraine inspired him with any great admiration for Colonel Beck. Worst of all in its effect on him was the increasing pressure being put on the German minority in western Poland. This pressure was being felt with increasing ferocity by the German minority in Poland proper since the Governor, the *Voivode* of Polish Silesia, Dr Grażyński, had stepped up his policy of weakening the agricultural sector of the German minority by economic means and replacing them with Polish peasants. On October 10,[74] the German press had been commanded to suppress all reports of Polish action against the German minority, but the extension of the Polish pressure to the German minority in Teschen, Poland's share of the carve-up of Czechoslovakia, enabled the anti-Polish elements in Hitler's entourage to go over to the attack. On November 12, SS Oberführer Behrends, the head of the *Volksdeutsche Mittelstelle*, the SS office charged with relations with and subversion among the German minorities of Eastern Europe, evaded Ribbentrop, and enlisted Rudolf Hess's old tutor at Munich, the geopolitician Karl Haushofer, in support. Haushofer buttonholed Hitler at the christening party for Hess's youngest child, and held forth at length on the woes of the Germans in Poland. Hitler replied that he did not intend to put up with 'the conduct of his Eastern neighbours towards his fellow Germans' for much longer.[75] Towards the end of November Hitler in fact ordered military preparations for a sudden occupation of Danzig. Early in December, German local newspapers along the German-Polish frontiers were authorized to report incidents and to comment on their possible consequences.[76]

Hitler's entourage at this time contained two schools of thought on Danzig and Poland. The one favoured what they chose to call the 'little solution', a military coup against Danzig. The most ardent supporter of this was naturally the Nazi Gauleiter of Danzig, Herr Forster. Opposed to him was the group which wanted a more far-reaching solution, a group led by Goering himself, and also containing the Gauleiter of East Prussia, Erich Koch. This latter is a shadowy figure in accounts of Nazi Germany. Once a member of the German Communist Party, he had crossed over to the Nazis in the 1920s. Violently anti-Russian, he wanted Poland to be offered compensation at the expense of the Soviet Union. At this time he was most concerned to combat those who, like Himmler, Behrends, Goebbels and Forster, were urging Hitler into war – war against Poland, war against Britain, what did it matter? 'We are trying to plead the cause of sanity, of moderation,' Koch told the League of Nations High Commissioner for Danzig, the Swiss, Carl Burckhardt, meeting him in mid-December in Ribbentrop's antechamber.[77] 'We need the Poles, they need us. Goering will support you since you have arrived to calm the lunatics . . . a European war would be the end of everything, a madness. Colonies, what nonsense. . . . You will see how difficult it is to create animosity against the British; these are criminals who influence the Führer in this direction . . . never a European war, never. It is against Asia that one must fight.'

An extraordinary outburst, but revealing in its hysteria. It was only wrong in one respect: Hitler was still really determined against Britain. Forster, Goebbels and Behrends might incense him against Poland and move him to prepare the army for a coup against Danzig and the Memel. But he was still prepared to woo the Poles, as Ribbentrop, partisan of the large solution as a pre-condition for his own pet war against Britain, urged him. Beck, however, continued to clasp his illusions. While Ribbentrop was prepared to wait until he came to Warsaw for one final appeal, Beck precipitated his own encounter with Hitler. He approached von Moltke in Warsaw to say that he would be passing through Berlin on his return from spending the Christmas holiday in Monte Carlo.[78] He would be prepared to stop over for unofficial talks with Ribbentrop to prepare the way for the latter's visit to Warsaw. Ribbentrop accepted the idea with alacrity. But instead of seeing Ribbentrop in Berlin, Beck found himself whisked off to Berchtesgaden, to see Hitler.[79] He carried the meeting off well. But he was shaken by the experience. On his return to Warsaw he found it necessary to warn the President and Marshal Smigly-Rydz that there were alarming symptoms which could 'well result in war'.[80]

The most alarming symptom, in his view, was Hitler's insistence on raising the idea of Danzig's return to Germany, 'in accordance with the will of its population'. True, Hitler promised full protection of Poland's economic interests. But for Beck, and for Polish opinion, this could only mean putting Poland's economy into Germany's hands and ceding Polish independence. He told Ribbentrop the following day[81] that he saw no possibility of an agreement along these lines and warned that the actions of the Nazi regime in Danzig could well provoke a crisis. Ribbentrop's generous offer to support Polish ambitions in the Ukraine, he passed off with a laugh. The only scrap of hope he had to cling to was Hitler's assurance that Poland would not be confronted with any more *faits accomplis*.

His experience at Berchtesgaden left Beck with two convictions. It was essential to mend his fences with the British and the French.[82] How he must have regretted the snub he had administered to an unofficial French invitation to visit Paris on his return from Monte Carlo! Secondly, he was convinced that nothing must be done to break contact with the Germans. Ribbentrop's visit must take place, despite the naïveté of his approach.

For his part Ribbentrop still seems to have nurtured the illusion that the Poles would understand the weakness of their general position, and would finally accept the role of junior partner that Hitler was offering them. On January 22, with Goering's aid, he succeeded in fending off severe pressure from OKW and military circles, who argued strongly for an abandonment of negotiations and the adoption of military measures against Poland. The occasion was apparently a major military meeting which he addressed in Goering's presence, a record of which fell into Czech hands through intelligence sources.[83] The military argued that French military weakness would be as commanding in the summer of 1939, when the Siegfried line, the German fortifications in the west, was finished, as it had been in September 1938, especially in view of France's commitment to a defensive strategy; that Britain would continue to be restrained by German superiority in the air; that Russia would be unlikely to intervene in a German-Polish conflict, as her officer corps had been decimated, her war industries were inadequate, and she was distracted in the Far East; that the Ukrainian issue could be used decisively against Poland; indeed it could be used to cause Russia great difficulties. The East could be divided, in the German interest of 'divide and rule' between a rump Poland (shorn of its German- and Ukrainian-inhabited areas), Great Ukraine and Russia. A war against Poland would be very popular among both army and people, whereas a war against the West with Italy as Germany's ally had no support whatever.

Ribbentrop's counter-arguments laid great weight on Germany acting in concert with Italy and Japan. She was not yet strong enough to act on her own. If she attacked Poland and Russia in 1939 Italy would be exposed to the combined weight of the Western democracies, and Germany would find herself isolated. Moreover, in the year or two it would take to get a decision in the East, Germany would have committed her war industry and armaments while those of the West were still developing their strength. At the end Germany could well find herself, under Western pressures, having to give up what she won in the East. Germany's superiority in armaments, especially in the air, would no longer be available as a permanent threat to back her dynamic foreign policy.

From this Ribbentrop concluded that Germany had to act in step with Italy and Japan. He expected a Mediterranean decision which would demand of Germany a readiness to stand 100 per cent on Italy's side. This would cause France to yield without conflict, at least to Italy's minimum demands. As long as France was not dealt with, the Axis must strive to keep France and Britain apart. He thought there was a 40 per cent probability of war against the West in 1939, and a 60 per cent probability Britain and France might yield. If they yielded then the Axis position in Spain, Tunisia, Corsica and Minorca would be greatly strengthened. The next stage would come in 1940, its successful outcome the acquisition of colonies. Ribbentrop laid great weight on the need for Polish neutrality to be completely guaranteed. This made it essential to put the brake on the Ukrainian affair and to moderate the tempo at which the rest of Czechoslovakia was to be absorbed into the German sphere of power.

Ribbentrop's arguments apparently carried the day, especially with General Keitel and General von Brauchitsch. It was decided that the Danzig question should not be raised during his visit to Warsaw. Forster was not present at this meeting, but it was noticed that the *Danziger Vorposten*, usually regarded as his mouthpiece, had suggested on January 21 that the Danzigers would do well to maintain their city's status as a free city.[84] He was in fact instructed to withhold any new measures until after Ribbentrop's return from Warsaw.[85]

The Poles had planned to give Ribbentrop a full dose of pomp and ceremony.[86] From the moment his train steamed into the gloom of the main railway station in Warsaw, its partially finished buildings covered with swastikas, Ribbentrop found himself caught in a programme so tightly planned as to demand the celerity of a quick-change artist. A magnificent reception at the Polish Foreign Ministry, an old palace dating from the seventeenth century, a reception by President

Mościcky, a full military display, a reception at the German Embassy, and numerous other functions ran him ragged and played upon his nerves. The sudden outburst of press reports that a German trade mission was *en route* for Moscow by rail caught him just before his visit to President Mościcky, when his nerves were at their tautest. He exploded. This was deliberate sabotage. The mission, which had just reached Warsaw, was recalled, and Ribbentrop went off to meet the Polish President who talked to him severely, ignoring the flattery Ribbentrop lavished on Marshal Smigly-Rydz.

Severest of all was Colonel Beck.[87] Poland could never consent to the reunion of Danzig with Germany. It would give Germany control over Poland's economic life and with it control over Polish national policy. An extra-territorial *Autobahn* across the Corridor was categorically rejected. One could not expect Poland to part with tangible rights in exchange for mere assurances. Hitler's remarks at Berchtesgaden had made the worst possible impression. Poland could not join the anti-Comintern pact. Beck accused Ribbentrop of reverting to the policy of Stresemann in making a distinction between Germany's western and eastern frontiers. And he warned Ribbentrop against misrepresenting his experience in Warsaw in an optimistic form to Hitler. The warning was ignored. Ribbentrop's only minute of the conversations[88] depicted a cringing Beck offering to consider the German proposals further, both on Danzig and on the Ukraine. He reported to Hitler that Poland was prepared in principle to accept a new settlement regarding Danzig and the Corridor.[89] In his speech to the Reichstag on January 30, therefore, Hitler paid tribute to German-Polish friendship as one of the reassuring factors in the political life of Europe.[90]

In reality Ribbentrop was furious.[91] Since Munich, where he had been largely a cipher, his plans had gone totally astray. The agreement with Japan and Italy was nowhere near conclusion. The settlement with the Poles was as far away as ever, and he was caught empty-handed between two groups in Hitler's entourage who hated him equally – Goering, Koch and Hans Frank on the one side, Goebbels, Himmler and Forster on the other. He cannot but have rejoiced in the scandal which broke out in the first week of February over Goebbels' involvement with the actress Lida Baarova; Himmler, Goering and Rosenberg all united to curse him. When Goebbels threatened divorce Hitler was forced to intervene personally to forbid it and to expel Baarova from Germany.

Ribbentrop's sole success in this period had been the signature of the Franco-German Declaration on December 6, 1938. Even this had turned to ashes in his mouth, as his visit to Paris had been greeted coldly by the Parisians. Nevertheless he felt that something had been achieved by it. He had not, it was true, succeeded in driving a wedge between France and Britain. The British had encouraged the whole process, and had been kept fully informed at every step. But he had, so he believed, extracted from M. Bonnet, the French Foreign Minister, a guarantee that Germany would have a free hand in the East.

Of all the diplomatic moves undertaken during the years of Hitler's power, the Franco-German Declaration must be the most hollow and futile. It was, in fact, a complete non-event, born of Ribbentrop's lust for coups and Bonnet's annoyance and pique at the conclusion of the Anglo-German Declaration of September 30. This had been concluded without any consultation with Daladier, the French Premier, or Bonnet, who had been left to learn of it from the French afternoon newspapers on their return to Paris from Munich. Daladier's under-standable chagrin had led to an exchange of correspondence with Chamberlain, in the course of which the British Prime Minister had suggested a Franco-German declaration on similar lines.[92] But for the moment Daladier had somewhat grander ideas.

Edouard Daladier was a Provençal, whose accent sang through his every word though, like his fellow Provençals, he was niggardly with them, being solid and taciturn by nature. He had the reputation of being what in the political life of the Third Republic passed for a 'strong man'. But this was a false reputation. He looked solid enough. He could give an impression of massive calm, of reliance on the great French virtues of patriotism, honour and steadfastness under fire. But when the crunch came he lost his nerve, he delayed, he hesitated, he was indecisive. Once already the crunch had come for him, in February 1934. On that terrible day when the riotous bands of the French anti-parliamentary right threatened to storm across the Seine and take the Assemblée Nationale by assault, the police had held them magnificently. M. Daladier, however, had resigned. It had taken him four long years to work his way back into power; but he had not acquired any more backbone on the way.

He was, in any case, more familiar with issues of war than foreign policy. His heart was in the right place. He detested the dictatorship while dreaming vaguely of a settlement with Hitler as between veterans of the First World War. Munich he regarded as a major defeat. To avoid it turning into a disaster there was only one course to be followed: to cleave to Britain. On this his Cabinet, though otherwise divided, were agreed.

But to which Britain should he cleave? His Foreign Minister, Georges Bonnet, had no doubt. Britain was represented in Paris by Sir

Eric Phipps, Britain's former Ambassador in Berlin. He and Sir Robert Vansittart's wives were sisters. Otherwise they had nothing in common. Phipps was set on the avoidance of war. In October 1938 he persuaded Bonnet to purge the Quai d'Orsay of its hawks. The senior professional head, the Secretary General to the Quai d'Orsay, Alexis St Léger Léger, was too deep in Daladier's confidence to be vulnerable. Bonnet pretended to Phipps that he and Léger saw eye to eye. Phipps' comment[93] was 'in that case the eyes must be astigmatic'. Other officials were less gifted. To Phipps' delight, Bonnet rid the Quai d'Orsay of its two most hawkish, if most Anglophile of officials. René Massigli was summarily packed off to represent his country in Ankara. Pierre Comert, head of the Quai d'Orsay press department, was transferred to the American department. Bonnet was less able to do anything with Charles Corbin, the French Ambassador in London, who remained a determined opponent of any weakness towards Germany on either side of the Channel.

The Munich conference had apparently revived French memories of the Four-Power Pact intended to regulate the peace of Europe, which their Government had signed in 1933. To rekindle this it would be very necessary to repair relations with Italy. On October 3, three days after Munich, it was decided to send a new ambassador to Italy. M. Robert Coulondre was to move from Moscow, where his talents were being wasted on attempting to achieve a collaboration with the Soviet Union which the French intelligence service, the Deuxième Bureau, had advised was militarily pointless, and sent to Berlin. Perhaps Ribbentrop could come to Paris. In any case, something must be done.

Thoughts of a four-power pact were also crossing German minds, but not, as we have seen, that of von Ribbentrop. The mission undertaken by Prince Philip of Hesse to Rome was apparently believed by the German Foreign Minister to be in order to square Mussolini about a visit by him, von Ribbentrop, to Paris.[94] It was in fact to advance Goering's idea of a four-power pact. However, a Franco-German declaration could well be a first stage to this; and although M. François-Poncet suggested this in a visit to the German Foreign Ministry on October 13,[95] the first real initiative was in fact taken by Hitler.

On October 19, M. François-Poncet was invited by Hitler to Berchtesgaden to make his adieux before taking up his new appointment in Rome.[96] As a special mark of favour, Hitler not only put his personal plane at the French Ambassador's disposal, but received him in his special 'eagle's nest' high in the Alps above Berchtesgaden. From below the house appeared like an observatory perched on a great pile of boulders. The approach road swung up the mountain in a series of fantastically engineered curves ending in a courtyard. Bronze gates opened into a long tunnel ending in a roomy lift lined with copper plate. The lift rose some 300 feet through the living rock to emerge suddenly in the eagle's nest itself, a vast series of rooms each with one wall of plate-glass windows looking across a sheer drop of 2,000 feet to an immense panorama of mountains, at whose base lay the castle rock and spire-filled city of Salzburg. Every point of access was guarded by machine-gunners. The effect on visitors was always overwhelming. Grandiose, savage, uncaring, the mountains stared back. Humanity was invisible at their feet. And the bourgeois comforts which Hitler chose to press on his visitors – the many armchairs, the logs burning in the immense fireplace – did little to modify this impression.

Hitler received the Frenchmen (the Ambassador was accompanied by his Air Attaché, Captain Paul Stehlin) with tea. They found Hitler pale and tired-looking and easily beguiled from his initial amiability into a tirade against the British. But he had himself well in hand for the rest of the conversation, playing the calm, moderate, conciliatory statesman to perfection. The French Ambassador proposed formally the mutual recognition of frontiers by France and Germany, a step which would bind Hitler formally to accept the verdict of Versailles on Alsace-Lorraine. This could be recognized by Italy and Britain; thus the Four-Power Pact would be revived. Hitler was pleased and instructed Ribbentrop to work out a formula. So was M. François-Poncet. With immense periphrasis, with weighty warnings as to Hitler's inconstancy of character, he recommended acceptance. And M. Bonnet accepted.[97] Indeed, he claimed later that it was his own idea.[98]

It is at this stage that fate on the one hand and the ambitions of M. Bonnet and Herr von Ribbentrop on the other intervened. Fate's role was greatly to exacerbate relations between Germany and Britain in the British reaction to the anti-Jewish pogrom carried out in Germany on the night of November 10, and by the Italian advancing of claims for Corsica, Nice and Tunisia on France. All hope of a four-power pact went by the board. Nevertheless, the two Foreign Ministers persisted with the plans for Ribbentrop to visit Paris, the German for reasons of prestige. He collected diplomatic coups like an ambitious Red Indian warrior counted scalps. But Bonnet? His motives are more obscure.

It has been M. Bonnet's fate never to be able to inspire total confidence in any audience to which he addressed himself. He has, no doubt, reinforced his fate by the manner in which in successive memoirs he has remodelled his own version of the past. Slight of build and sallow of complexion, his narrow face and habitually lugubrious expression greeted many statesmen, ambassadors and politicians. Even his eldest and closest associates seem never to have been quite sure about him. In this case, however, he seems simply to have been pursuing a short-term advantage. He was certainly put out by the delay of a month which was to ensue. For Ribbentrop did not accept an invitation to come to Paris until November 21, and the visit itself did not take place until December 6, a wave of strikes in Paris having caused a further postponement.

Ribbentrop arrived in Paris on the morning of December 6, bringing with him a large retinue of experts, none of whose services was needed except to add to the impressiveness of the occasion. The conversation followed the usual form, a long harangue from Ribbentrop modelled carefully on the style of his master, a lengthy interjection from M. Bonnet on the subject of Franco-Italian relations and an exchange of views on a series of largely unrelated questions of foreign policy. The conversation was conducted partly in French and partly in German, Ribbentrop speaking both languages, with the ubiquitous Paul-Otto Schmidt, interpreter extraordinary to the German Foreign Ministry and to Hitler, interpreting from German into French.[99] No interpretation was made from French into German.

At one point, according to the later German versions of their meetings, M. Bonnet stated to von Ribbentrop that by Munich France had declared that she was no longer interested in the fate of Eastern Europe. France would respect the German sphere of influence. Bonnet and Léger have consistently denied this. They certainly cannot have meant to imply that France was disinterested in what remained of the Little Entente. The French Cabinet, already concerned at the degree to which Germany was invading France's traditional markets in Yugoslavia and Romania, was about to launch a new effort to regain France's financial and economic influence in the Balkans. Bonnet may in fact only have been referring to the guarantee for Czechoslovakia. Ribbentrop chose to understand him as referring to Poland also. Franco-Polish relations were not at their best at that time and Bonnet's remarks in the German version are ambiguous. Whatever he said, Bonnet was soon to have to change his position, under pressure, in the French Chamber. The event passed unnoticed by von Ribbentrop. With his illusions intact he returned to Berlin. The one triumph of his year, however, was not to be of any comfort to him for long.

CHAPTER 5

REARMAMENT AND SETTLEMENT: CHAMBERLAIN AFTER MUNICH

After Hitler, Neville Chamberlain is perhaps the single most important individual in the events of 1939. Faced with the forbidding volume of literature and judgment already extant on the character and personality of the Prime Minister of Britain at this date, how can the historian's spirits (or, for that matter, those of his readers) fail to sink? Yet the necessity of coming to grips with the problem is ineluctable. Chamberlain's character and personality are central to the story of how war came to Europe in 1939. In 1939 he dominated British political life. His Cabinet respected him. His parliamentary majority, marshalled, even dragooned, by Captain Margesson, then Conservative Chief Whip, followed him unquestioningly, stirred by appeals to their loyalty as well as to their fear of political ostracism. In the country, large numbers revered him as the man who had saved the world from war, a view which the newsreels (and twenty million British citizens went to the cinema every week), with what strikes us now as their insufferably gung-ho and hurrah-patriotic commentators, assiduously encouraged. Most of the press echoed this. All hint of controversy was kept from the radio too. To attack Chamberlain was caddish, ignoble, disloyal, subversive: it smacked of warmongering; it was impossibly old-fashioned; to some it was even irreverent, if not positively satanic. After Munich the headmaster of my preparatory school addressed the school-children. People would tell us, he said, that Mr Chamberlain had done something dishonourable and wrong. We were not to believe them. He had been sent by God to preserve the peace of the world. What he had done was noble and Christian and we were never to forget that. Such was Neville Chamberlain's strength in Britain.

And yet it is extremely difficult to like Neville Chamberlain. His public personality lacked warmth, though the few friends he had were close and intimate. He remains cold and distant, and his gift for arousing hostility among those who study him has outlived his death. It is true that many of his detractors come now, as they did during his lifetime, from what (copying G. B. Shaw's Henry Higgins) could be called the 'undeserving left'. Those sheaves of anonymous pamphlets pouring hotly from the presses of Mr Victor Gollancz from 1939 onwards, their authors concealed behind noble Roman pseudonyms (Michael Foot, later leader of the Labour Party, then a Beaverbrook journalist, was one), have had a constant stream of successors from that day to this, a surprisingly large number of them recently from the United States. But their analyses lean heavily on theories of social and economic conditioning so blanket in their scope that most of Chamberlain's Conservative opponents are equally covered by them. He has accumulated more than his due share of jeers and gibes – a mediocre man with a little mind, a good Lord Mayor of Birmingham in a bad year, and so on. In very justice the historian who is attempting to achieve historical objectivity has to recall facts in his favour.

It is of course nonsense to depict him as ignorant of European politics. True, he had none of the firsthand knowledge of the intricacies of Berlin, Vienna, Prague or Budapest possessed by the largely radical-minded correspondents of the European press, or of those senior academic historians who led the offensive against him before and after his death. But then it is not usual for a British premier or foreign minister to possess such firsthand knowledge or to be recruited from such milieux. Lord Salisbury was not such a man. Nor was Lord Curzon. That is why they had expert advisers, saw Foreign Office telegrams and dispatches and so on, and were served by the clandestine sources of information provided by the Secret Intelligence Service, the radio and communications monitoring and cryptographic branches, and other such secret agencies. Mr Chamberlain and his Foreign Secretary, Lord Halifax, read such reports assiduously, as their memoirs, their papers and their biographies abundantly prove. Injudicious they may have been, ignorant never.

Nor was Neville Chamberlain in any way attracted by Nazism or beguiled by Hitler himself, though he rashly once gave reason to believe that he was when he referred publicly to Hitler having pledged his word. He had been at the centre of the British rearmament effort since its inception in 1934 and had urged and pressed it forward, expressly relating it to the threat from Germany. In 1937 he had roundly denounced Germany as the main disturber of European peace in a letter to Henry Morgenthau, the US Secretary of the Treasury.[1] His closest adviser during these years was Sir Warren Fisher, a man as virulently opposed to Nazi Germany as any in Britain.[2] There is abundant evidence to show he doubted and distrusted Hitler's sincerity at every turn.

Indeed, that was precisely the trouble. So much of Chamberlain's thinking, so much of his analysis, was conditional, tentative, contingent. He doubted; but he was never certain. He distrusted; but he did not totally disbelieve. He saw a threat; but he did not recognize a certainty. To do all this he would have had to have been a fatalist, a pre-destinarian, a pessimist. He was none of these things; his hatred of war, related in his mind to both the banker's and the butcher's bill for the First World War, made it impossible. The sense that a new war was inevitable had its hold over him, as it had over virtually everyone in Britain. But he found it abhorrent, and fought against it.

He was, too, an impatient man, impatient of men who could not see things as clearly as he believed he saw them, impatient of men who struck him as believing outmoded concepts or bureaucratic procedures to be more important than the avoidance of war, impatient of men who sought refuge from the unbearable dilemmas of decision in striking moral attitudes or pretending that the dilemmas did not exist. He had been reared in a family tradition of accepting responsibility; and he went on accepting and bearing responsibility far beyond the limits of reason. This was indeed one of the reasons for his dominance in and over his party. He was relentless, sanguine, a most efficient dispatcher of business, impelled always to act and to decide and never afraid of taking an unwelcome or unpopular decision. For those who were not as he was, who opposed him, he had little but contempt, which was fed by the reports on their contacts, their sources of finance, even their intercepted telephone conversations, with which his sources in MI5, especially the ubiquitous Sir Joseph Ball, provided him, and one of his least attractive attributes, especially in the House of Commons, was the freedom with which he showed this contempt.

Chamberlain had other equally unattractive attributes which go a long way to explain the animosities he always aroused. His demeanour was not only jaunty and self-satisfied in public; it was often intolerably smug. It was not so much that he was conceited as that, as Scottish parlance has it, he had a good conceit of himself; but the English rarely succeed in distinguishing between these two qualities. His worst attribute, that for which he has suffered most, was his distrust and dislike of public opinion. He appears to have regarded the public as too easily swayed by emotion to be trusted with the full facts, and too chauvinistic to be relied on to keep their heads in moments of crisis. So he concealed much of the truth from them, and he justified and defended his actions in absolutist terms, when in fact he was himself swayed by very different arguments. There must always be a fairly wide gap between the arguments that governments use behind closed doors and their public defence of them. Never was the gap as wide or as absolute as under Neville Chamberlain. The existence of the gap was known or sensed by many. It has much to do with the plethora of privately circulating newsletters, from the now grossly over-praised *The Week*, run by a member of the British Communist Party, Claud Cockburn,[3] and Commander Stephen King-Hall's *Newsletter*, to some extraordinary productions of the extreme right.

Chamberlain dominated his Cabinet, or all but one member of it. This was his close friend, Edward Wood, Viscount Halifax, the Foreign Secretary. Of immense height, bony, even gawky sometimes, with a long, saturnine, 'damnably Puritan face', Halifax approached politics with a sense of obligation to public service which came from his training, a sense of detachment which was the result of his intellectual powers as well as of his height, and a need to feel morally justified in what he was doing which stemmed from the Anglo-Catholic faith he practised. These three virtues, or psychological assets, might have been expected to give him a solidity, a certainty which would have been of immense advantage to the Cabinet. And indeed he slept very soundly of nights. But in fact they worked at odds with one another. His intellectual powers were great; he had a brilliant career at Oxford (to this day, his portrait stares down quizzically, sympathetically, slightly pityingly, from the wall of the Great Hall at All Souls College, Oxford, on the Fellows and the candidates for the Fellowship examinations). But his intellect only conveyed doubt and uncertainty, an ability always to see every side of a question. Indeed, an exasperated senior diplomat once said that Halifax could see at least three more facets to any diamond than the jewellers who cut it had placed there.

Nor was his religion any help. He prayed, regularly and repeatedly; his reliance on what the American Ambassador, Joseph Kennedy, once angrily called 'All that God stuff' was notorious. But he only rarely achieved certainty. Most of his tenure of the Foreign Office was filled with an endless examination and re-examination of the questions which he had to decide, until somehow, in some way, his conscience told him that a particular decision was right and morally just. Then he was unshakeable. Beneath the intellect and the judiciousness there was a streak of ruthlessness. But for much of the time he was undecided, and under continuous pressure. No other office in the British Cabinet breeds pressures on a weak and undecided tenant in quite the way the Foreign Office does. Not that Halifax yielded to pressure, though he was known to be open to it. But he could be, and was, subject to attacks of alarmism, verging on panic. Many of the most important decisions regarding British policy in the eleven months after Munich were the result of such panic.

Nevertheless, Halifax inspired regard, respect and even affection, where Chamberlain did not. In May 1940 the Labour leadership briefly would have preferred to serve under his rather than Churchill's leadership. Fortunately for the world they were not given the opportunity of choice. For Halifax could not have been the inspiration of Britain's survival: he could not inspire his way out of a paper bag. His gifts for self-projection, such as they were, were personal, reserved for meetings face-to-face.

Apart from Halifax, the only other real strength in Chamberlain's Cabinet was provided by a cluster of failed Foreign Secretaries: Sir John Simon and Sir Samuel Hoare; Sir Thomas Inskip, a lawyer who for three years had been overlord for defence matters; the go-getting Jewish businessman, Leslie Hore-Belisha, who was Minister for War; Oliver Stanley, President of the Board of Trade; and Sir Kingsley Wood, the Air Minister. Simon at this time was Chancellor of the Exchequer, still striving to keep the cost of rearmament down to a tolerable level, earning from one angry Air Marshal the comment that his main aim seemed to be to preserve enough money in Britain to pay an indemnity after Britain had been defeated. Hoare was able and shrewd but accident-prone. Inskip, a lawyer a little out of his depth, achieved unjustified immortality as 'Caligula's horse' for his unexpected appointment as Minister for the Co-ordination of Defence in 1936.

Oliver Stanley, Samuel Hoare, Leslie Hore-Belisha and Sir Kingsley Wood were to head the hawkish element in the Cabinet, at least until Halifax took the lead. Stanley had come the closest to resigning over Munich. On October 3 he had warned Chamberlain[4] that he could only regard the Munich settlement as an uneasy truce and that any attempt to lull public opinion would provoke him publicly to express his scepticism as to Nazi promises and his fears as to Nazi policy. Chamberlain found him irresolute, unstable and too prone to threaten resignation.

Hore-Belisha was doing his best to reform and make ready for war an army which had been the poor relation of the services for too long; its senior offices were stuffed with dead wood. Neither his Jewishness nor his gift for publicity in a service which regarded both with equal hostility made his job any easier, and his steady progress brought about equally steady progress towards political suicide. With Inskip, he was to be the principal target of a revolt by the Young Turks among the junior ministers in Chamberlain's Cabinet in December 1938; though, unlike Inskip, who was shifted sideways to the Ministry for Commonwealth Relations, he escaped unscathed – for the moment.

In many ways Sir Kingsley Wood was the solidest man in the Cabinet, and his words carried the most weight, in Cabinet discussions, after the Prime Minister's. In 1938 he was a dove, an appeaser. In 1939, he knew war was coming; the air force would be ready.

Behind the disagreements within the Cabinet, and much of Whitehall, there were four elements which all held in common. The first was the memory of the four ghastly years, 1914–18. These years had seen the decimation – and more – of a generation of Britons. The losses of the war were remembered every year, on November 11, at 11 a.m. when, irrespective of the day of the week or the press of business, all activity stopped for two minutes. Those losses were, in most cases, intensely personal. Sons, husbands, lovers, fathers, school friends, neighbours, work-mates, all were missed and mourned. The daily lists of dead and wounded in the newspapers, the terror aroused by the appearance of a post office delivery man with a telegram, the empty faces of those who returned, these memories were mingled with fears of a new war which would begin with death and destruction by bombs and poison gas rained from the sky. To these were added the memories and myths of the lost golden days of Edwardian greatness, vanished along with the financial supremacy that had been sold for American arms to outweigh German industrial superiority. A new war might well bring about defeat through bankruptcy.

To these worries were added those of 1931, memories of the vulnerability of sterling to short-term financial panic. In 1937 and 1938 Britain was still buying much more from abroad than she sold, even allowing for all the invisible items of trade, financial services, earnings from shipping, insurance and so on. All of these depended on a revival of world trade, as did the re-employment of those thrown out of work by the collapse of Britain's own primary industries, and the key to this was a rise in demand for the basic commodities – wheat, sugar, coal, rubber, sisal, tin and so on – upon which depended the well-being of Britain's colonial empire. An increase in world trade depended on an end to the closed economies of America and Germany, and to subsidized exports where prices were manipulated by devaluation or exchange control.

Third in the list was a common consciousness of the disparity between Britain's commitments and the resources available to defend them. Rearmament was essential in order to end the vulnerability, especially to air attack, which made British diplomatic pressure for peace, British efforts to defuse potential crises, not credible to those who had to be deterred. British power could never be adequate to face concurrent wars in Europe, the Mediterranean and the Far East. Britain needed fewer enemies; she needed, too, a measure of disarmament or arms control, especially in the air. But rearmament which weakened Britain's capacity to fight and win a long war was unwise. The dilemma lay in the need for rearmament to be visible and impressive, if it was to deter war. As war became seemingly more imminent, so the fears of bankruptcy, the gloomy prognostications of the Treasury, were progressively set aside. By December 1940, they had come true. Lend-lease provided the remedy; but in 1938 lend-lease was unimaginable.

The last, in these days of moral relativism, and in a world which, for better or worse, has ceased to uphold the moral values of nineteenth-century Europe, is the most difficult to explain. Chamberlain, the majority of British opinion with him, believed that peace was the normal state of relations between nations, and that that peace depended upon the observance by those nations of a number of rules and conventions of international behaviour, of which keeping one's word, and respect for the rights and interests of other nations were the most important. Not that these rules, like those of football, for instance, were not sometimes violated; but the adoption of a course of behaviour which ignored or flouted them could only be taken as criminal, marking the violator as one who was totally determined on war and conquest. Whatever the inner debates in Whitehall might have turned on, such violation was, after all, the reason which took Britain united into the war against Germany in 1914. It was this feeling which had so incensed, and which had been so exploited by, the Sovietophobes of the period 1917–30. Peace was a moral issue, it was true. But the defence of 'civilization', the codeword for this complex of beliefs and attitudes, could, as a matter of hard necessity, override the avoidance of war.

Neville Chamberlain had returned from Munich to the kind of triumph that even successful politicians can only dream of. It is hardly surprising, therefore, that even he was carried away by it. The Anglo-German Agreement which he had sprung on Hitler that morning of September 30 was intended as a test. 'If he signs it and sticks to it that will be fine,' he told Lord Dunglass, his private secretary. 'But if he breaks it that will convince the Americans of the kind of man he is.'[5] In the House of Commons on October 6, he asked that remarks made in the euphoria of the moment should not be taken too literally. As the euphoria ebbed away, Chamberlain was left with two convictions. First, that the utmost must be done to exploit the Anglo-German Agreement and to build towards a European settlement: Germany's economic isolation had to be broken down. Second, that the circumstances which forced Munich upon Britain must not be left unrepaired. The first of these demanded the taking up of contacts with Hitler and

Mussolini. The second demanded that everything possible be done to strengthen France and to accelerate the process of British rearmament. It also demanded, though it took Halifax a long time to convince Chamberlain of this, a mending of the fences with Soviet Russia.

Halifax's view of Munich was quite simple. It was horrid and humiliating – but yet better than a European war. He did not believe that Hitler wanted a war with Britain. Beyond this he was fascinated and repelled by him. Nazism he regarded as repellent, pagan and to be destroyed, if possible, deterred and restrained if not. The danger of a major European war had lain in the combination of French military weakness with commitments in Eastern Europe and the consequent miscalculations (and the knock-on effect, as in 1914) which might follow. This was now removed. Hitler would have plenty on his hands consolidating his position in Central Europe. As for Eastern Europe, Halifax was convinced that it should not be allowed to pass under German economic domination, if that meant its inclusion in the same totally closed economic realm which Germany itself already constituted. The economies of Eastern Europe should be strengthened against such pressure. Britain was not in the game of building up Germany's powers to make war. Austria, Hungary, Czechoslovakia and Poland might fall to German influence. Romania, Greece, Turkey and Yugoslavia were another matter.

Since the spring of 1938, the Foreign Office had been pressing for the use of British money and economic strength to buttress the economies of those countries against too great a dependence on Germany. An inter-departmental committee, headed by Sir Frederick Leith-Ross, gave Greece first priority. Romania, the barrier to German or Italian pressure on Turkey, came second. Early in September 1938, an Anglo-Romanian Payments Agreement had revitalized trade between the two countries. British trade and influence were steadily outstripping those of Germany in Bucharest.

In the meantime, another effort had to be made to defuse tension, and to recover some of the moral ground lost at Munich. Britain's task was to reach a settlement on Germany's western frontiers and acquire the strength to hold it; similar tasks awaited her in the Mediterranean where the ratification of the pact with Italy should be followed by the strengthening of British relations with Greece, Turkey, Egypt, Portugal and with Spain, where Franco's victory now seemed inevitable. Relations with the United States were of great importance. To prevent any danger of a German-Soviet *rapprochement*, good relations had to be maintained with the Soviet Union. Poland would 'fall more and more into the German orbit', as she was unable to reach agreement with the

Soviet Union. But Russia, 'for good or evil, is part of Europe and we cannot ignore her existence.'[6]

This, however, was a programme for inaction and Chamberlain was impatient. He was far from accepting the belief of his more gullible followers, whose letters of congratulation continued to descend on him and his unfortunate wife by the sackload, that he had secured 'peace in our time'. 'We have avoided the greatest catastrophe,' he wrote to his sister Hilda,[7] 'but we are very little nearer the time when we can put all thoughts of war out of our minds. . . . The conciliation part of the policy', he added, 'is as important as the rearming.' His mind running firmly on a European settlement, he was resolved to explore both possible paths, that of direct negotiations with Germany and that of an indirect approach via Italy. It was also of extreme importance to see France strengthened, since French weakness had done so much to bring about the near-disaster which Munich had averted. These three lines of approach were to be taken up simultaneously.

The Italian question was fairly easily dealt with. The only real difficulty was the acute pressure which Mussolini and Ciano put on Britain through the British Ambassador in Rome, Lord Perth (Eric Drummond). Lord Perth had once been the brightest star in the Foreign Office firmament. As Private Secretary to Lord Balfour, Lloyd George's Foreign Secretary in the last two desperate years of the First World War, the young Drummond had travelled everywhere with him, and everywhere his charm, his drive, his attention to administrative detail, and his intelligence had commended him to all who met him. Once Sir Maurice Hankey had contemptuously refused the Secretary Generalship of the new League of Nations, he had been a natural choice for the post, given that the first Secretary General was to be a British nominee. He had held the post for thirteen years, putting its administration on a sound international basis. But he had not been quite as successful at that most difficult of all tasks of which the later Lord Hankey was such a master: guiding the policy of an organization from the position of its Secretary. He had left the League of Nations with great professions of goodwill on all sides, but an equally strong conviction that he had not perhaps been the overwhelming success which was expected of him in view of his prior record. The Rome Embassy at a time when Britain and Italy were still close associates was a more than adequate reward for a man who was an ardent Italophile and a devout Catholic.

Unfortunately for the new peer (he succeeded to the title of Earl of Perth in 1935), relations between the two countries were heading for disaster. The onset of the Italo-Abyssinian crisis might have been expected to make of Lord Perth an ardent advocate of taking a strong British line with the erring dictator, at odds with the League of Nations. It did not, for two reasons. Perth had always seen the League as an association of the great powers and their European clients. The admission of what he regarded as half-civilized countries like Abyssinia, a state which attempted to seek shelter in the League against the legitimate interests of the great powers, in his view made a mockery of the League. Moreover, Perth was one of the large company of ambassadors to whom the maintenance of good relations between their own government and that to which they are accredited becomes the only command they recognize. Perth became incapable of advising his government to stand firm when that was required.

Two further complications impaired his effectiveness. The security of his Embassy was fatally breached by the Italian secret service, a fact which he totally refused to recognize, even when Lady Perth's tiara vanished from the Embassy safe. His every report, his every instruction lay on Ciano's or Mussolini's desk within days of his receiving or issuing it, often before he had acted on it. And his judgment was fatally clouded by a family tragedy in the autumn of 1935 which bore on him night and day from then on. Eric Drummond, star of the Foreign Service, became Lord Perth, suppliant, over-anxious, compliant to all the pressures the Italians would bring to bear on him.

What Count Ciano in fact presented, on October 3,[8] was a peremptory demand that Britain ratify the Anglo-Italian Agreement or agree to do so, by October 6. Otherwise the Italian Government would be forced to 'take certain actions which up to now they had definitely refused.' This, Perth explained, could well mean at least the withdrawal of the Italian Ambassador, and was likely to mean a formal alliance with Germany.[9] This was too much for Halifax. There were still large numbers of Italian 'volunteers' and aircraft in Spain, and Spanish nationalist aircraft were bombing British ships. Parliament had just adjourned and would not reassemble until the beginning of November, and ratification would have to be laid before Parliament.[10] Chamberlain too was not to be pushed. He was determined to ratify the agreement, it was true; but not at breakneck speed under duress.[11] After the trouble he had faced in his own Cabinet and in Parliament over Munich, he was not inclined to run any more risks by seeming to appease Italy. British opinion in general was never inclined to allow Mussolini the latitude it was prepared to concede to Hitler.

By the end of October, the British Cabinet had, in fact, weakened. While Ciano was still being pressed to give assurances on Italian policy in Spain, especially on the bombing of British ships, the Cabinet was no longer inclined to insist. Two factors had apparently swung the decision. The first was secret information on the progress of the German drive for a tripartite military alliance. Seen in this light, Ribbentrop's visit to Italy in October took on a most sinister appearance, though Perth dismissed the idea that an alliance had been discussed (the suggestion came from his Soviet colleague, Boris Shtein) as derived only from press comments and Soviet ingenuity.[12] The second was the failure to make any progress in the direct approach to Germany. Chamberlain now conceived the idea of a personal visit to Rome. 'Rome', he wrote to his sister Hilda,[13] 'at the moment is the end of the Axis on which it is easiest to make an impression. . . . An hour or two's *tête-à-tête* with Musso might be extraordinarily valuable in making plans for talks with Germany.' An invitation was issued to him on November 16, the day the Anglo-Italian Agreement was brought into effect.[14]

Chamberlain's hopes of building on the Anglo–German Declaration had in fact got precisely nowhere. The British negotiators on the commission charged with executing the decisions of the Munich conference on the ground soon found that they were being continually ignored and excluded by the Germans. Lord Halifax made a tentative approach to the German Ambassador on October 7.[15] But the only answer he received was the insults of Hitler's speech at Saarbrücken,[16] and a series of violent attacks in the German press on the 'Churchill–Eden–Duff Cooper clique' and on British rearmament. The British Embassy took great care to see that these attacks were fully reported.[17] The cue was set by two violent letters[18] written to Lord Halifax by Sir Nevile Henderson, the British Ambassador, before he went on leave, a leave which through illness was to extend until the middle of February 1939. If Henderson could write, 'I never want to work with Germans again . . . the monstrous incubus of Hitler, Himmler, Ribbentrop and Co.' and the 'real and very immediate peril' of the German air force which 'is immensely powerful and far superior to our own', his staff, who thought him almost wickedly and deceitfully optimistic in his normal reportage,[19] could be relied on to depict the real sense of official Nazi Germany towards Britain without flinching. The German press campaign was in fact deliberate and inspired, as the German Ambassador in London found when he protested privately.[20]

Private approaches, such as those made by George Steward, Chief Press Officer to the Prime Minister, to Dr Hesse, head of the German News Agency in London (to the fury of the Foreign Office, who heard of it from MI5), were equally unsuccessful in the face of this campaign.[21] Nor were the efforts of Sir Samuel Hoare and Leslie

Burgin, the Minister of Transport, to charm the German Ambassador during successive weekends in the country in the second half of October any more successful. Herr von Dirksen only set out the general course of the ideas expressed to him: an Anglo-German agreement including agreement on armaments and on the 'humanizing' of air warfare (no poison gas, no bombing of cities), a colonial settlement, possibly even a guarantee against attack from the Soviet Union as part of a disarmament agreement;[22] but in vain. This last is often cited by Soviet historians as proof of their thesis that the Cabinet was obsessed by the urge to provoke a German-Soviet conflict. Taken in their proper context, Hoare's ill-chosen remarks make it clear that the offer of a guarantee was intended to disarm any German arguments that Soviet strength in the air necessitated the maintenance of a large German Luftwaffe. Like the British guarantee to France in 1925 at the time of Locarno, it was intended not as a means of defeating Russia but of controlling Germany. Soviet historians, who have still not entirely abandoned the belief that Locarno was intended as a preliminary to a new Western war of intervention against the Soviet Union, would not find such an argument convincing. The valueless nature of the contemporary British guarantee for Czechoslovakia, to which they so often call attention, shows, however, that to many British negotiators such guarantees are only too often a form of diplomatic legerdemain, intended for their psychological effect only. More hope seemed to lie in the economic approach.

The Chamberlain Cabinet and the Foreign Office's economic advisers had always been prone to attribute much of Hitler's intransigence to German economic weakness, though the belief that trade excluded war was not confined to them. A German economic delegation passed through London *en route* for Dublin on October 17 and 18. Sir Frederick Leith-Ross, the economic adviser to the Cabinet, pressed the leader of the delegation, Counsellor Rüter,[23] on the prospect of four-power economic co-operation to stimulate reciprocal trade and to ease Germany's foreign-currency position so as to make three-cornered trade deals, especially between Germany, south-east Europe and British, French and Dutch colonies, possible. This was far from being the payment of Danegeld Soviet historians have seen it as. If accepted it would have destroyed German hopes of adding the Balkans to their economic empire.

But Britain's main hopes, it was to emerge, were pinned less on south-east Europe than on Anglo-German co-operation in China and the Far East. The Germans, however, were not interested in genuine co-operation, but in using bogus concessions over tariffs (bogus because not tariffs but German exchange control was the real issue) to force further entry into Britain's colonial markets, and in trying to negotiate concessions on debts, especially those which would enable them to 'adjust their economy to prepare for a war against Britain'. The talks were continued for two reasons: so long as Germany continued to trade with Britain, buying British coal and textiles, the terms of the Anglo-German financial agreements gave Britain a limited control over and insight into Germany's financial position. Moreover, Britain's rearmament effort benefited from the machine tools and machinery Britain bought in return. Britain continued to press for talks, though with increasing scepticism as to their outcome. Negotiations on a coal cartel, and contacts between the Federation of British Industry and the Reichsgruppe Industrie continued.

Any hopes that might have been still flickering were extinguished, or should have been, by the events of November 10 in Germany, the 'night of the plate-glass windows', the *Kristallnacht*, the great pogrom. On October 6, the German Government had cancelled all passports held by German Jews, in preparation for their being stamped with a red 'J', an inch and a quarter in height. This measure had been insisted on by the Swiss authorities as a means of restricting the immigration of Jews from Germany and Austria without having to impose visa requirements on all German citizens. As a result, the Polish Government insisted that all passports of Polish citizens living abroad should lose their validity unless they bore a new inspection stamp. The measure principally affected, as it is difficult to believe it was not intended to affect, the seventy thousand or more Polish Jews living in Germany. On October 20, therefore, the German Ministry of the Interior began the wholesale deportation of Polish Jews. Some fifteen thousand Polish Jews were collected in trucks, brought to the German border and pushed across the frontier. The Polish frontier-guards refused to admit them and threatened to open fire on them. Some seven thousand or more were trapped for days without food or shelter between the frontier posts. Among them were the parents of Herschel Grynzspan, a seventeen-year-old Polish Jew studying in Paris.

Maddened by the news of their sufferings, young Grynzspan bought a revolver and, on the morning of November 7, went to the German Embassy. Accosting a stranger in the Embassy courtyard, he demanded to see the Ambassador. In a hurry, the stranger, who was the Ambassador, Count von Welczeck himself, referred him to the chancellery of the Embassy. Entering the office, Grynzspan drew his revolver and fired several shots at the first Embassy official he saw, a young Third Secretary, Ernst von Rath, and then surrendered. Hitler sent his own personal doctor and a surgeon to Paris, but von Rath died from his wounds the following morning.

In the small hours of Thursday, November 10, the SA, quiescent since the violent suppression of their leadership in 1934, were given their head. All over Germany, synagogues were burnt or damaged, shops and offices looted, plate-glass windows smashed. Over all the great stores signs were plastered – 'Jewish property. Germans, do not buy from Jews', and so on. Twenty thousand Jews were arrested, to be incarcerated in Dachau, Oranienberg and Buchenwald; the community as a whole was fined 84 million pounds – one billion Reichsmarks – in punishment. From January 1, 1939, they were to be excluded from all economic activity. The attacks were organized by Reinhard Heydrich, the ex-German naval officer who had become Himmler's right hand in building up the SS. The economic exploitation was Goering's idea, conceived in high good humour on the train hurrying back to Berlin.

The British Embassy in Germany reported extensively on the Nazi atrocity.[24] It reported, in addition, on accusations in the German press linking the Conservative Opposition, including Churchill and Duff Cooper, and the Labour Party leader, Clement Attlee, with the murder of von Rath, in photographs entitled 'Jewish murderers and their instigators!' The British press and Parliament condemned the German measures in the strongest terms. Lord Halifax dispatched an indignant note which drew from Dr Goebbels the most grudging of apologies, which, though given to Reuters News Agency, was not printed by any German paper.[25] As the German Ambassador pointed out, for the time being, any possibility of Chamberlain proposing a new approach had been brought to an end.[26]

These 'barbarities', as Chamberlain termed them in a letter of November 13, again to his sister Hilda,[27] stung Halifax into a more definite opposition to Germany. On November 10, armed with a lengthy report from an inter-departmental committee,[28] he confronted his colleagues,[29] arguing that German expansion into Eastern Europe would not contribute to peace, but would simply lock the countries concerned into Germany's economic sphere. British finance should be used to decrease their dependence on Germany by regular purchases of Romanian wheat and oil, by trade credits for Greece and Yugoslavia, by helping the Balkan countries build up their armed forces, and, so he hoped, to relieve the pressure on Italy to conform to German views. His arguments won a sympathetic hearing from his colleagues. But in practice it was not so easy. British smokers, so the tobacco companies argued, in a faintly comic series of exchanges over the next few months, would not touch Balkan tobacco. Its aroma was so coarse and distinctive that blending was impossible. To import it would require the expensive construction of separate tobacco factories and warehouses to avoid Britain's favourite Virginia tobacco being contaminated. More seriously, the Anglo-American Trade Agreement, in which, to ensure American goodwill, considerable British economic interests had been compromised, was signed on November 17. Cordell Hull, the American Secretary of State, came from a tobacco-growing state, Tennessee. Mr Hull, perennially antagonistic to, and suspicious of, Britain's trading ministries, would suspect another British trick if Britain were immediately to encourage other tobacco-producing states.

The real difficulty, however, lay in the desperate needs and exaggerated expectations of the Balkan states. King Carol of Romania came to London from November 15 to 18 with a long shopping list. Despite the most forceful support from the former British High Commissioner in Egypt, Lord Lloyd, one of those uncontrollable *lusi naturae* the British political élite throws up from time to time, all Carol secured was a trade mission and a British undertaking to purchase 200,000 tons of wheat with an option on 400,000 more at prices well above world market level.[30] An Anglo-Romanian committee was to look into the prospects of joint investment projects. But his hopes of a £30-million loan were disappointed. There was a savagely anti-German debate in Parliament at the end of November.[31] Both Oliver Stanley, President of the Board of Trade, and the ambitious Robert Hudson, junior minister in charge of the Department of Overseas Trade, came out very strongly in favour of widening the Government's power to combat German economic expansion by measures designed to prop up the economies of those countries that were threatened. But the most that could be spared – and the legislation took until February to pass – was £10 million for political credits, of which £3 million was earmarked for China, another £3 million for Iraq and Afghanistan, and £1 million each for Portugal and Egypt. To buttress the Balkans against Hitler, only £3 million was made available, £2 million for Greece and £1 million for Romania. All other aid had to be found by increasing the import into Britain of Balkan produce or by finding reasonably promising opportunities for British investment. To all such proposals, the Treasury was to turn a resolutely sceptical eye.[32]

This was, however, only one part of Halifax's new determination. On November 14 he subjected the Foreign Policy Committee to a further blast:[33] no useful purpose, he said, would be served by a resumption of Anglo-German conversations. Secret information showed that Hitler regarded Munich as a disaster. German military might had not been displayed. Instead, his own popularity in Germany had waned and that of the British Prime Minister had soared. He now regarded Britain as his prime enemy, and was completely in Ribbentrop's hands. He aimed to break Britain's alliance with France by cultivating the French. He was working on Italy and Japan to sign a military alliance to dish British power in the Mediterranean and the Far East. He was doing all he could to aggravate Britain's difficulties in the Near East and over Palestine. His propaganda machine had now singled out British rearmament as the major threat to the German people.

The Foreign Office's German informants depicted the extremists as riding high in Hitler's confidence; a new German rearmament programme had so destabilized Germany's economy that financial chaos was only a few months away, a chaos which Hitler could well seek to avoid by plunging into one of the many adventures being urged on him in the Balkans, in Asia Minor, in India or elsewhere. Hitler was quoted as saying that if Britain had not introduced conscription by the spring of 1939 they could consider Europe as lost.

Chamberlain remained sceptical towards these informants. While accepting that the extremists' star was rising, he did not believe Hitler was contemplating any immediate aggressive action against Britain. He was one of those who feared that Hitler was planning to strike eastwards in conjunction with Poland against the Ukraine. But, as he wrote to his sister Hilda on November 11,[34] he was disturbed by the continued attacks upon Britain in the German press, and 'the failure of Hitler to make the slightest gesture of friendship'. Moreover, he had come to believe that Hitler's counsellors were divided between 'moderates' and 'extremists', under whose influence he was quite capable of being stampeded into an irrational and ill-calculated 'mad-dog act' of aggression from which, like Sarajevo in 1914, a general war could well ensue.

The full Cabinet, meeting on November 30, agreed that Britain should do what it could to strengthen the moderates.[35] In the meantime, the French needed reassurance. Chamberlain's mind was turning towards Mussolini. Perhaps, as in September, the Führer's friend could be persuaded to exercise a restraining influence on Hitler. Nor was Chamberlain prepared to abandon his hopes of disarmament. To its fury the Air Staff was forced to spend Christmas drawing up yet another plan for limiting British, and German, bombing strength.

Chamberlain was soon to receive further evidence of German preparations for war. When the decision to sign the Anglo-German Naval Agreement was taken in June 1935, Stanley Baldwin, the then Prime Minister, had remarked, 'This is a signpost. If Hitler breaks it or cheats, we will know that he is going to challenge us.' At the beginning of December, the German Ambassador formally announced that his Government intended to exercise the rights granted under the agreement to build their submarine strength up to equality with that of Britain.[36] At the same time, it proposed to convert two cruisers into heavy 8-inch-gun cruisers, which they had previously told the British would be 6-inch-gun cruisers. Lord Halifax insisted that this decision could not be taken without prior consultation. That consultation took place in Berlin on December 30 and can have left the British in no doubt whatever that a denunciation of the treaty was only a matter of time; the Germans showed clearly that they had no interest in a perpetuation of the relationship they had accepted in 1935.[37]

Meanwhile the press war intensified. The German press caused particular offence by its attacks on the actions of British troops in Palestine, and on British statesmen. A particularly silly though spectacular incident came on December 13 when the German Ambassador and the German press corps in London absented themselves from the dinner given by the Foreign Press Association in honour of the Prime Minister. Herr von Dirksen felt obliged to apologize;[38] but the incident did nothing to improve matters and some of the tougher-minded members of the Cabinet began to comment publicly on the impossibility of attempting to reach an agreement with a country whose only response to friendship was insult. Accusations that British troops were committing atrocities in Palestine were taken particularly ill by those who remembered the record of the German suppression of the Herero revolt in South West Africa before 1914 and the savagery of German reprisals against the civilian population in Belgium in 1914 in response to the actions of Belgian *francs-tireurs*. Formal protests were lodged but to little effect.

It was hardly surprising, therefore, that by Christmas Chamberlain was already in a state of considerable depression. Due thought had been given to the support of France, and he and Halifax had visited Daladier and Bonnet on November 24–5. The conversations they had held had done nothing to relieve their anxieties about the state of France's armaments or the realism of the French Premier.[39] M. Daladier expected French aircraft production to rise from eighty aircraft a month to four hundred a month in six months' time, an estimate which meant a five-fold expansion at a rate which it had taken the British some two years to achieve. The remainder of the discussions reassured the British as to the lack of any further French obligations in Eastern Europe; but they also showed very clearly how little military help Britain could offer France in the event of a continental war in Europe.[40] Nevertheless,

Chamberlain felt obliged to strengthen Daladier's hand by an exchange of declarations in December in which M. Bonnet re-affirmed France's intention to come to Britain's aid in the event of unprovoked aggression and Mr Chamberlain hailed these as 'more significant than an actual Treaty';[41] the more so as Britain was not, strictly speaking, obligated to support France against the new Italian propaganda offensive.

About the only consolation Chamberlain could find lay in the progress of the British rearmament effort. Shortly after his return from Munich he had wearily turned to his defence ministers to ask what measures could be taken to improve Britain's defences – wearily, as the arguments were all familiar, the demands of the three services all competitive and conflicting, the financial limitations just as urgent as ever. There was little enough the navy could do. Its programme for 1938 and 1939 had been cut early in 1938 when the Admiralty's programme for a new two-power standard was abandoned because of reasons of expense. The best the Admiralty could do was to return to its demand that the scrapping of the Royal Sovereign battleship class, over-age and largely obsolete as they were, should be postponed. The air force came up with a very much enlarged scheme for expansion of the RAF, both in fighters and the new heavy-bomber types carrying 8,000–10,000 pounds' weight of bombs as against the 1,000–3,000 pounds carried by the existing types. With these, British bombing capacity would equal that of Germany with half the number of aircraft. The air force pointed out that German air strength as projected ran at a steady three-to-one ratio with that planned for the RAF; they did not point out that German reserves were always smaller than their front-line strength, whereas Britain planned for reserves roughly twice as large as their first line, a factor which gave the RAF much more staying power through combat than the Luftwaffe, all of whose goods were, so to speak, in the shop window.

The air force claims were so expensive as to arouse once again the opposition of Sir John Simon, in fear for the financial stability of the country. The Cabinet, despite the dilemma of rising costs, decided in favour of the heavy bomber. At the same time, however, fighter production and that of anti-aircraft guns and searchlights (the best way of diminishing Britain's vulnerability from the air of which they were so aware) were accelerated. The Air Staff, still obsessed by the idea of the strategic bombing offensive, remained unhappy. It was despite them rather than with their support that the development of Fighter Command was pushed ahead and the first steps taken towards establishing the radar stations which, with the ground-to-air control system evolved by the boffins, was to make nonsense of the contempt with which the advocates of strategic bombing dismissed the strategy of defence.

Most alarming for Mr Chamberlain, however, was the steady realization that the previous policy of starving the army and confining its role to colonial intervention was no longer possible. Nothing had weakened Britain so much *vis-à-vis* France before Munich as Britain's inability to provide more than two infantry divisions and then only some six to seven months after the outbreak of hostilities. Leslie Hore-Belisha, his War Minister, was agitating steadily for an increase in the Expeditionary Force and for the full equipment of the Territorial Volunteer Army. The mobilization in September 1938 had revealed a chaos in the mobilization procedures and a lack of vital stores throughout the army so severe as gravely to weaken the army's confidence in its own abilities to cope with a continental war without a drastic re-examination of its role and purpose in modern warfare.

But the most cogent arguments were again diplomatic and sprang from the interview with the French in November 1938. Lord Halifax was convinced by that meeting that France could not be strengthened further or encouraged to rearm more unless Britain actually appeared to be ready to offer substantial military assistance. Without it in the long run there was always a chance that France would remain neutral if Germany attacked Britain directly. These views of Lord Halifax were backed by further pressure from the British Embassy in Paris,[42] all tending to wear down Chamberlain's conviction, and that of his advisers, that Britain would have been better advised in 1914 and would be better advised now not to commit large forces to a continental strategy. By the end of December 1938 Chamberlain's convictions had been badly shaken, though he had not yet been finally driven to capitulate to the pressure of Hore-Belisha and Halifax.

He still had one hope, that of Italian intervention. On January 11 he and Halifax arrived in Rome. They had had some misgivings about going in view of the violence of the Italian campaign against France unleashed so soon after the ratification of the Anglo-Italian Agreement. It reinforced all the objections that Chamberlain's opponents had raised to the agreement as such.[43] And Lord Perth was driven to the edge of misrepresentation in his efforts to persuade the Prime Minister to go ahead.[44] The lengthy assessment which he sent to Lord Halifax at the end of the year on how to deal with Mussolini provoked Sir Alexander Cadogan, the Permanent Under Secretary, to a sardonic minute: 'The moral seems to me to be that we must show Mussolini in as friendly a manner as possible that the democracies are not on the run.'[45]

Mussolini, as it happened, had other matters on his mind. Having ratified the Anglo-Italian Agreement and denounced that of 1935 with France, having deployed all his bombast and rhetoric, he was now waiting for the 'men of Munich', in whose gutlessness he had now come to believe, to offer British mediation. Shortly before Christmas he sent Chamberlain a set of proposals intended to encourage such a move, by the 'secret channel', which had been employed at the time of Eden's resignation.[46] It ran through Adrian Dingli (an Italian lawyer, legal adviser to the Italian Embassy in London, and passionately interested in Italian claims on Malta) to Sir Joseph Ball (a lawyer and former member of MI5, with a finger in very many pies, chief adviser on policy to the Cabinet, and head of the Conservative research organization). Three memoranda were transmitted late in December 1938.[47] One dealt with Italian claims on Tunisia. A second covered the alleged determination of the British Colonial Office to suppress the '*Italianità*' of the Maltese. And one proposed Anglo-Italian economic and political co-operation both in the Balkans, based on Hungary, and in the exploitation of East Africa. There was a need to revive the Anglo-Italian clearing agreement, to enable more Italian goods to be sold in Britain,

Hitler blickt misstrauisch auf die englisch-italienische Annaherung, bei der Mussolini und Chamberlain versprechen, niemals wieder gegeneinander Krieg zu führen
'Hitler looks distrustfully at the Anglo-Italian *rapprochement*, in which Mussolini and Chamberlain promise never to make war against each other'

and to increase British coal deliveries to Italy. With the exception of Tunisia, all the other Italian claims against France were negotiable.

Mussolini and Ciano were seriously worried by the rate of German trade expansion in Eastern Europe. They had pinned their hopes on the Hungarian-Polish plot in November 1938. They feared Hungary and Yugoslavia would become German economic satellites. Ciano dreamt of a Hungarian-Yugoslav-Romanian bloc backed by Britain, France and Italy. Ciano's visit to Belgrade to further this had been a failure. But with Britain behind him things could be different. These hopes were disappointed. Chamberlain was in no mood to mediate, as he made clear from the start. He had his own hopes of Mussolini, but they did not involve any concessions, least of all on Malta.

For his part, Mussolini seems to have been rather alarmed by Chamberlain's popularity with the Italian people and the demonstrations of this popularity which accompanied his every public appearance.[48] The Prime Minister was clapped, waved at, applauded and bravoed from the moment his train steamed into Rome station, despite Mussolini's deliberate refusal either to organize the crowds or to publish the route the Prime Minister was to take to his meeting with Mussolini at the Palazzo Venezia. The warmth of the Roman crowds was in fact the most favourable memory the British Premier was to take away from his meeting with Mussolini.

The conversations themselves, though cordial on the surface, took place across an abyss. 'How far away are these people. It is another world,' was Ciano's reaction.[49] 'These men are not made of the same stuff as the Francis Drakes and the other magnificent adventurers who created their empire. These after all are the tired sons of a long line of rich men and they will lose their empire,' replied Mussolini. The contrast between the young and vigorous men of action of the Fascist world and the old and tired statesmen of the decadent West was a favourite theme of Mussolini's, curiously at odds with the realities. In fact, Mussolini and Ciano (once the daring young airman) were both, by now, chubby chairbound urbanites, fit only for the sports of the boudoir (if fit for any at all), and then only in regimented moderation. Chamberlain and Halifax were both men of very considerable physical stamina. As was the custom among English politicians of that generation, they were men who took great amounts of open-air exercise, including a great deal of walking over irregular countryside. Chamberlain was a keen golfer and fisherman. Halifax relaxed by long walks through his native Yorkshire. Both men, unlike Mussolini and Ciano, could wander freely anywhere on holiday, with only the single police detective their rank made obligatory. Mussolini needed a police bodyguard the size of an infantry platoon. As so often, Mussolini was the principal victim of his own rhetoric.

Given Chamberlain's refusal to play the mediator, there was little for Mussolini to offer save pomp and rhetoric. The role he chose to affect was that of the serious statesman, the famous chin bowed now towards the floor, now pointed towards the ceiling. Count Ciano interpreted. In his statesmanlike role he was a man of peace, though not unfortunately of Chamberlain's peace. He offered no help on the Jewish question, he lied through his teeth over the recent dispatch of reinforcements for the Italian air forces in Spain, he did not give an inch on the question of Franco-Italian relations, and he refused to produce anything but anodynes to allay the anxieties Chamberlain expressed regarding the possibility of a new German offensive eastwards. This was all wrapped up in a cloud of historico-philosophical metaphysics through which Chamberlain groped his careful way, returning again and again to the points on which he sought reassurances but finding none.

Relations remained friendly. But a doorway to an Anglo-German meeting Chamberlain most emphatically did not find in Rome; not a doorway, not a key, not even the vaguest of directions.[50] Sanguine as always, he returned to his train on January 14 and steamed back through Italy and France. His immediate impressions were ecstatic. 'A very wonderful visit,' he wrote to his sister.[51] 'I have achieved all I expected to get and more. . . . I am satisfied that the journey has definitely strengthened the chances of peace.' But he had nothing to set against Lord Halifax's dawning percipience of Mussolini's essentially second-rate uselessness. Nor had he anything to set against the increasingly alarming reports coming from British and French intelligence sources as to the outlines of Hitler's next move. Within a fortnight these reports were to produce a new crisis.

Indeed, the visit seemed to have confirmed much of the British establishment in its belief that Mussolini was firmly in Germany's camp. The military planners began to discuss a pre-emptive strike against Italy in the event of war against Germany and Italy. The Maltese received a new constitutional charter which placed almost dictatorial powers in the hands of the Governor. The pro-Italian agitators who had been expelled in 1936 and 1938 were barred from re-entry to Malta and her anti-aircraft defences were reinforced. Fortifications were begun on the road from Italian-occupied Libya into Egypt at Sidi Barrani and Mersa Matrûh. Nor did Mussolini help matters. On February 4, speaking to the Fascist Grand Council, he claimed that Italy could not be truly independent as a nation until she had an opening on the Atlantic, and had broken out of the 'prison of the Mediterranean sea' by a 'march to the ocean'.[52] Britain, custodian of the gate to the Atlantic, Gibraltar, was unimpressed. Firmness, if not intransigence, was now the note of a series of speeches made by prominent Cabinet members over the period from January 27 to February 6. They represented a warning to Germany rather than Italy, and were born of the 'war scare' (which will be examined in the next chapter). But they were not lost on Mussolini.

CHAPTER 6

LORD HALIFAX IS ALARMED

As December 1938 shaded into January of the new year the conviction grew in the British Foreign Office that Hitler was up to something, that he was planning a new adventure. Since October, Sir Nevile Henderson, British Ambassador in Berlin, had been away from his post on sick leave. He had left in a state of severe gloom, for once, his usual sanguine spirits depressed and anxious, especially at the great disparity between British and German air strength, the refusal of the Air Ministry to take the problem seriously, and the prospect of the Luftwaffe being used as a

'Europe can look forward to a christmas of peace', says Hitler

big stick to enforce a 'Pax Germanica'. In his absence, the Berlin Embassy staff, who normally regarded the Ambassador as inclined deliberately to misrepresent matters in his reports to London, did their best to open Lord Halifax's eyes to the realities of Berlin. From mid-November a series of reports called attention to the depths of anti-British feeling expressed by the German press, and to the mounting evidence that Hitler was actively planning some new exploit.

The bulk of the Embassy's evidence seems to have come from the members of the growing opposition to Hitler within the German Staff and among the old Prussian aristocracy. Henderson himself was on familiar terms with the rather equivocal opposition within the Foreign Ministry, centred around Ernst von Weizsäcker. This included the brothers Kordt, Erich in Berlin and Theo in the London Embassy. Theo was in regular contact with MI5, though he did not tell them everything. Others were closer to the genuine opposition, to Ewald von Kleist-Schmenzin (who had tried desperately and at great risk to his life to warn Chamberlain in August and September 1938), to Fabrian von Schlabrendorff, of the German General Staff, and to other, more shadowy figures in the German Air Ministry and in the Army Staff. Karl Goerdeler, the former Burgomaster of Leipzig, and Reichs Commissar for Price Control in the mid-1930s, is the most frequently named. Other names are Hjalmar Schacht, the mysterious Ritter (known by a pun on his name as 'K' for 'knight', the English equivalent of *Ritter*), and General von Reichenau and General von Kluge. Hermann Rauschning, the former Nazi Gauleiter of Danzig who, having broken with Hitler, had published the sensational and now somewhat questionable accounts of his meetings with Hitler, *Hitler Speaks*, is another of those named as sources in the British records.

The Embassy staff were aided by men such as T. P. Conwell-Evans,[1] the British former professor of English at the University of Königsberg, who had interpreted for David Lloyd George on his visit to Hitler in 1936. Their reports were added to by those that reached the Foreign Office from the Secret Intelligence Service, from the monitoring of German radio communications and from the private intelligence service built up for Sir Robert Vansittart by a former Air Attaché in Berlin, Colonel Christie.

The very nature of this kind of information and activity debars the historian from any accurate knowledge of all that these clandestine sources were reporting. It is nevertheless surprising how accurate much of their information was. The Foreign Office thus knew of Hitler's secret speech to the German press in November.[2] They were informed of the plans for a *coup de main* against Danzig.[3] They had accurate and alarming information on the state of German aircraft production,[4] and the growth of the German army.[5] They had, moreover, an ever-increasing flow of reports linking together the strains to which the German economy was subject, Hitler's bitterness and hostility towards Britain and the growth in influence of the so-called extremists among his entourage; military intelligence produced a picture of a German army rapidly approaching total mobilization so that Hitler was on the verge of being able to order a major military action in any direction at very short notice. Means, motive and mentality, according to these reports, combined to depict a Hitler capable, at any moment, of a new irrational and uncalculated aggression, a 'mad dog act', as it was put in Cabinet on December 21.[6] But when and where would he strike? Eastwards, towards the Ukraine, or westwards perhaps, against the Netherlands or Britain? As the new year broke, the latter seemed, to some at least, increasingly less improbable.

The accumulation of evidence as to Hitler's hostility towards Britain had, as we here see, already provoked Halifax into an assault on his Cabinet colleagues. A new avalanche had begun with the return from his post as First Secretary to the British Embassy in Berlin of Ivone Kirkpatrick, who was to rise to be permanent Under Secretary at the time of Suez, and show himself Eden's staunchest support in that disastrous enterprise. Kirkpatrick had been warned, shortly before he left Berlin, by 'a former civil servant close to General Beck', the mysterious Ritter, in fact, that Hitler was planning a sudden air attack on London. This could occur in as little time as three weeks. Kirkpatrick's successors in the Berlin Embassy warned that Hitler, 'drunk with his resounding successes, thirsting for more political adventure and confronted with growing economic and domestic discontent', could well be provoked into another adventure. Ribbentrop was said to regard Britain as ripe for further blackmail.[7]

On January 23 Halifax suddenly convened the Foreign Policy Committee of the Cabinet.[8] They were confronted with a Foreign Office memorandum on 'Possible German intentions'.[9] Hitler, it was reported, was about to launch a pre-emptive strike against Britain in the form of an all-out air attack on London or by a prior invasion of the Netherlands to give him air bases close enough to Britain to destroy her cities by air. Preparations were said to be fixed to begin on February 21. Halifax himself was sceptical of these reports, as was Sir Alexander Cadogan; members of the Cabinet, especially Chamberlain, were equally sceptical. But the sources on which the reports were based had so far proved reliable and trustworthy. The Foreign Office Committee and the full Cabinet[10] felt they could not be ignored. War seemed imminent. Lord Halifax was therefore driven to compose a long dispatch to Washington for President Roosevelt's private information.[11] And the Cabinet began to consider what should be done in the event of a German invasion of the Netherlands. The military authorities, who had already been asked to comment on France's ability to withstand Germany,[12] should Britain, as in September 1938, only be able to send two divisions to her aid, found themselves in a cleft stick. They had already come to the belief that only a full-scale military commitment would give the French the backbone to resist Hitler.[13] But the army was still formally incapable of any but the most marginal of interventions on the Continent. War with Germany over the Netherlands would not save them from being overrun. Yet it was clearly quite impossible for them to abandon the Netherlands to their fate. If Germany invaded the Netherlands Britain would have to go to war.

A great deal followed from this. France, and Belgium, would have to be approached and asked for support. This would have to be followed by Staff talks. These would commit Britain to major military intervention on the Continent, something which had been religiously excluded up to that date. Moreover, it would be ridiculous only to envisage war with Germany. Germany and Italy would have to be treated as one, and planning would have to cover the Mediterranean and the Middle East.

Viewed from Britain, the picture of a war against Germany and Italy with only France as an ally was an extremely gloomy one. It was expected that every state which could stay neutral would do so. Soviet strength was dismissed as being in no condition to wage war effectively. To blockade Germany would be difficult, if not impossible, though Italy was obviously much more vulnerable. Except at sea, British and French forces would be considerably inferior to those of Germany, and until this balance was redressed, the war would inevitably be defensive. Britain's air defences at home were still far from adequate, especially as far as anti-aircraft guns and searchlights were concerned. Fighter Command was still very weak and the first radar screens only just in the process of construction. Nevertheless, it seemed that war was inevitable if Germany attacked. At the end of January, therefore, diplomatic approaches were made to France, the Netherlands and to Belgium.

The extent of the change this crisis brought about in British military thinking cannot be over-stressed. For years now the army had been starved of weapons and sustained only to fight a colonial war against Italian troops in Africa. At best all Britain could offer France at Munich was two divisions of infantry, a drop in the bucket against the hundred-odd divisions Germany was raising. For years the view had been expressed that Britain must never fight a major military campaign on the Continent again. Peripheral, amphibious strategy was the key to Britain's defeat of Napoleon, so it was argued, and what Britain needed therefore was a mobile, highly professional army, a 'Gold Medal' army. Give continental generals large armies and there would be more Sommes, more Passchendaeles, more massacres of infantrymen sent to attack machine guns, mines and barbed wire on foot. Yet now Britain was committing itself to a continental defence of France. The Chiefs of Staff grumbled, and Hore-Belisha, with Halifax's determined backing, prepared to strike for an enlargement of the army, even for conscription. And all for the reports which Halifax produced to a doubting Cabinet and Prime Minister.

Yet it now seems clear that these reports were untrue. The Luftwaffe may have been playing with air attacks on Britain as a planning exercise. But it had no plans for this as a substitute for an orthodox war. The idea of an attack on the Netherlands does not appear in any German Staff plan, so far located, until after the conquest of Poland. The British intelligence reports on this were quite quite wrong. The French Deuxième Bureau received similar reports.[14] The Dutch were equally worried, the more so as Kirkpatrick's report seems to have been passed on to them by the British Minister in The Hague, Sir Neville Bland.[15] Similar rumours reached the American Minister in The Hague.[16] General Gamelin, the French Chief of Army Staff, saw in these reports a way of killing two birds with one stone. Britain could be made to enter a major military commitment on the Continent. Britain could bully Belgium into ending her 'neutralist' stance and into opening military Staff talks with France. Gamelin spoke to Mr Hore-Belisha on January 1.[17] But he did not invent the rumours. These reports, and this would seem particularly true of the information relayed to Sir Robert Vansittart's 'Germanophile' informants,[18] must have been deliberately engineered from the German side to produce an effect on Britain.

Who then were the sources of these reports? Their true identity will probably never be known. But it is possible to hazard a guess as to their original begetter: Hans Oster, deputy to Admiral Canaris, head of the *Abwehr* – or someone like him, a member of the secret opposition to Hitler. This group had come together before Munich as part of the army's reaction to the charges of homosexuality trumped up by the Nazis against General von Fritsch. In the weeks before Munich they had stirred up and organized a considerable part of the army leadership into planning a coup against Hitler. Whatever chances that coup had of success were destroyed by Chamberlain's offer to come to Munich. The majority of the conspirators retired into bafflement and reluctant admiration of the Führer's judgment. This was particularly the case among the officers of the pre-Nazi regular army. A minority, among them Oster and other hardcore dissidents, plotted on. By no means all of them have as yet come forward. Histories and studies of the German opposition always leapfrog the years between Munich and the outbreak of war. This plant upon the British has all the hallmarks of Oster's other known actions. It was semi-treasonable. But so was the warning he transmitted in May 1940 to the Dutch that German invasion was imminent.[19] And it was exaggerated to strike the most sensitive nerve of those whom it was intended to stir to action.

Hans Oster was excellently placed for such activity; the more so as *Abwehr* agents under his control had thoroughly penetrated the centre of British secret intelligence operations against Germany in the Netherlands.[20] As Canaris' deputy, he could act in secret and without responsibility. Brave, sardonic, sophisticated and devious, he hid behind his slightly dandyish air a mixture of patriotism, acute distaste for the barbarism of the Nazi leaders and a strong mixture of ethics and Christianity which must have sat very uneasily with the more orthodox, if that be the word, aspects of his task. It is the nature of intelligence work to attract men of unusual strength of personal convictions, exceptionally resistant to the normal pressures of social and political conformism and governed by their own highly personal sets of hates, abhorrences and taboos. For Oster these hates, these abhorrences, concentrated on the Nazis and the SS in general and on Hitler in particular. In Hitler he saw the ultimate threat to European culture. It was typical of his trade and the highly individual patriotism which inspired him that he would shrink neither from treason nor assassination to defeat and destroy this threat. Of all the known members of the opposition to Hitler, he alone combined the position, the knowledge of Britain's particular anxieties and vulnerabilities, and the personality to set such an exercise in disinformation in train.

The opposition of this hard core (most of whom were eventually to be involved in the attempted coup which failed when Hitler survived the bomb attack on his life on July 20, 1944) to Hitler and all he stood for, and against, in German law, culture and traditions cannot be questioned. They were, however, equally in favour of a revision of the Treaty of Versailles to restore Germany to the position, in geographical as well as *Machtpolitische* terms, that she had occupied in 1914. They were profoundly conservative in their attitude to international relations, looking back to the kind of embryo international system that had been emerging in the last decades before 1914 and which, to their regret, the German governments of the day had done so much to disrupt. Symptomatic of their approach was the initiative taken by Goerdeler early in December 1938 with a message to Ashton-Gwatkin of the Foreign Office's Economic Section[21] asking for a British and French commitment to the return of Danzig and the Corridor to Germany, colonial concessions, and an interest-free loan of £500 million to support a military coup being planned against Hitler. In return the new regime would, he said, recouple the German economy with the free exchange of the world, renounce the search for German hegemony in south-east Europe, guarantee the status quo in the Mediterranean and support Britain in the Far East.

Such an offer would have gone some way to satisfy what the British Government had been attempting for some time and was no doubt put together from knowledge of their desiderata. The British reaction was profoundly sceptical. 'We are to deliver the goods and Germany gives the I.O.U.s,' Sir Alexander Cadogan minuted.[22] Chamberlain would have none of it. 'These people must do their own job,' he told Cadogan.[23] The evolution of German conservative ideas through the preservation of a 'European' conservatism (with in many cases a strongly Catholic or Lutheran element) to the European federalism of the 1950s which was to take a son of the State Secretary to be President of West Germany had only just begun.

The smallness of this group in numerical terms and their membership drawn from the ranks of the old military, bureaucratic and regional intellectual élites, should not, however, cause us to dismiss them, as was so frequently done in Britain, as an unrepresentative coterie. They were only unrepresentative in that the social cohesion of the milieux in which they moved made them impervious to the police methods of penetration which had by 1938 clubbed down four successive efforts to rebuild the German Socialist movement within Germany. From British diplomatic as well as more clandestine reporting, the British Government had derived a picture of widespread discontent in Germany and anxiety at the apparently inevitable rush forward towards war. British radio propaganda was continuing to play upon this, using the powerful and apparently neutral transmitters of Radio Luxemburg especially, as Chamberlain well knew.[24] What he felt and resented was the necessity to the German opposition of the presence and actions of Britain as the only weapon, apart from a reluctant army, to counter Hitler's stranglehold over the police and media of the German state. They needed the strongest resistance to Hitler from Britain to move the army leadership to overthrow him. That support Britain's leaders, concerned more by the threat to peace involved in Hitler's expansionism and confused by the degree to which the anti-Nazi conservatives known to them seemed to share his aims, never gave them.

Before Munich the German opposition had tried gentlemanly methods to move the British Government by accurate, if desperate, warnings. This had failed. Their warnings had been ignored. Now they were trying manufacturing evidence. Their effects succeeded – but in the end not enough. They were not content, however, with making just one move. Similar information was fed directly to Professor Conwell-Evans around January 24–5 from party sources, though this time the reports spoke of Hitler planning to turn the Maginot line by attacks not only through the Low Countries but through Switzerland as well.[25]

These reports threw the Foreign Office into what was later described by the British Ambassador in Washington, who was home on leave at the time, as an 'almost unbelievable state of excitement'.[26] Halifax's appeal to Roosevelt spoke of Hitler's insensate rage against Britain and of his megalomania. Hitler might push Italy into a war with France, and then act, ostensibly as Italy's ally. He might attack Holland, bribing Poland and Japan with promises of colonial loot. He might advance impossible colonial demands in the form of an ultimatum. He might launch a sudden air attack on Britain. The danger period would be from the end of February and was linked with what Halifax believed to be the imminent conclusion of a tripartite German-Italian-Japanese alliance. Britain was about to make warning noises in public. Could Roosevelt follow suit?

Before any American reply could be received, Sir Alexander Cadogan, the Permanent Under Secretary at the Foreign Office, himself inclined to view the reports rather sceptically, wrote to The Hague suggesting that Sir Neville Bland, the British Minister in the Netherlands, should ask M. Colijn, the Dutch Foreign Minister, what credence he attached to reports of this nature.[27] But before Bland could even decipher the telegram from Cadogan, he found himself called to Colijn, who was already in a state of great alarm and excitement. Roosevelt, without consulting his Secretary of State, had just seen the Dutch Minister in Washington personally to send the Dutch Government a warning that he had received information from three separate and reliable sources that the signature of a German-Italian-Japanese alliance was imminent and that Germany was about to move westwards, possibly by provoking an attack on the Netherlands. It would depend on Britain whether or not the Netherlands stood alone.[28] Bland further reported that Colijn was coming to England in February and would like to see Halifax privately and secretly;[29] his general reaction was still one of desperate anxiety not to believe so unpleasant a report.

The American reply arrived the next morning.[30] It was short and disappointing, the work of the Secretary of State, Cordell Hull. The

American Government had received similar information, Hull told the British Chargé in Washington, in his 'normal cryptic and circumlocutory manner'. But internal opinion in America was so isolationist that the President had to proceed with great caution. No message would be forthcoming. Roosevelt was in the middle of a bitter fight with Congress over the supplementary appropriations for relief, and defence appropriations were next to come before Congress. News of French Government purchases of American fighter aircraft under development was already causing trouble. As so often, Roosevelt preferred not to force the issue at that moment.

Failing a move from Roosevelt, Halifax now moved on to press both the Dutch and the Belgians officially,[31] and to propose Staff talks to the French.[32] Again the proposal met with all too little success. The Belgian Government was divided. King Léopold, author of the Belgian declaration of neutralism in October 1936, was determined not to be involved in any new arrangements with the West. His decision naturally was binding on his Cabinet, especially his Foreign Minister and Foreign Office. They may have found the whole idea so novel as to be suspicious. Belgium isolated between a Netherlands under German attack and a France coming to the aid of the Dutch? They simply could not believe the report. As for Staff talks with the French, that was out of the question. Such talks were bound to leak out and the whole basis of Belgian neutrality would be destroyed.[33] Sir Robert Clive's insistence on Staff talks they regarded as mere bullying, and the whole basis of the British proposal struck them as extremely suspicious.

Not so, however, the Belgian Minister of Defence, General Denis, or General van den Bergen, Chief of the Belgian Army Staff. General Denis also had heard the reports of a German attack on the Netherlands being planned. He was determined to work out plans for dealing with this and he proposed to hold confidential talks with the British and French Military Attachés.[34] These do not seem to have been followed up. On February 9 the Belgian Government resigned and a new one was not formed until February 20.

To pin the French down on Staff talks was equally difficult. The French alleged that their information also covered a possible German attack via Belgium or Switzerland and they wanted these countries included in the general guarantee which they now felt that the British were about to give them.[35] The exchange of memoranda lasted until well into March. And by the time the Staff talks actually began, on March 29 in London, their whole basis had changed. Lord Halifax had recovered his nerve, and lost it all over again. And the Germans were in Prague.

The episode is none the less instructive. It shows how little confidence anyone in British Government circles had in Hitler's good intentions. The popular myth that it took the annexation of Prague to open British eyes to Hitler's essential untrustworthiness is completely untenable in the face of this evidence. It shows too the curious mixture of alarmism and excitability in which the Foreign Office, so traditionally a model of calm, so monumentally phlegmatic, actually worked at this time. It also shows how the sceptics – Cadogan, Halifax himself, even Chamberlain – could be swept away by clandestine reports and secret information, and how this alarmism could be manipulated by interested parties to produce the results they desired. It also demonstrates the remarkable unwillingness of the Belgians and the Dutch to adopt any posture other than that of an ostrich. They were to pay very severely for this blindness in May 1940.

CHAPTER 7

STALIN MAKES A SPEECH

On March 10, 1939, Josef Stalin went before the Eighteenth Congress of the Communist Party of the Soviet Union. The party delegates must have found it a novel, and unnerving, experience. It was four years since the previous Congress, four years during which the purges and the secret police had terrorized all the Russias. In 1934 nearly two thousand delegates had listened to Stalin's views on foreign policy. The Soviet Union had only just joined the League of Nations. The policy of collaborating with all kinds of bourgeois and democratic anti-Fascist forces against Hitler, the Popular Front, was still in gestation. The Soviet Union was just emerging from the isolation of the first Five Year Plan. Of those two thousand delegates of five years ago only thirty-five attended the Congress of March 1939. Eleven hundred of the remainder had been arrested for 'counter-revolutionary crimes'. Fifty-two of the seventy-one full members of the Central Committee, sixty of the sixty-eight candidate members, no longer appeared. Ninety-eight of these had been shot in the intervening years. Five members of the Politburo were dead of natural causes, two were awaiting execution. Two of their four replacements were also about to be liquidated. Show trials had pilloried and condemned to death all of Stalin's former rivals to the party leadership. Zinoviev, Kamenev, Bukharin, Tomsky, Rykov, Pyatakov and Radek were all dead, exposed as British, German, French, American, Polish or Japanese spies, diversionists or saboteurs.

The Red Army had come off equally badly. Three out of five marshals, all eleven Deputy Commissars for Defence, seventy-five out of eighty members of the Supreme Military Council, all military district commanders, thirteen of fifteen army commanders, fifty-seven out of eighty-five corps commanders, one hundred and ten of one hundred and ninety-five divisional commanders, half the officers of brigade rank, between a quarter and a half of the total officer corps had been 'purged'. For officers above the rank of colonel, in nine out of ten cases this euphemism meant that they had been shot. The Red Air Force and the Red Fleet, the officers of the Staff academies, the heads of the political sections, naval and air force constructors and designers had suffered similar losses. Two successive heads of the secret police, the organizers and directors of this purge themselves, Genrikh Yagoda and Nikolai Yezhov, had themselves been eliminated. Only Lev Davidovich Trotsky survived, in exile in Mexico, to be murdered by an NKVD agent bearing an ice-pick, in 1940. About a million party members and up to seven million others were arrested during the purges in Russia. Of these, upwards of one million had been executed, and a very large section of the remainder had disappeared into labour camps with a death rate of rather over 10 per cent per annum.

Foreign Communists in Russia suffered equally. Six hundred Germans were to be handed over by the NKVD to the Gestapo in the winter of 1939. Béla Kun, leader of the Hungarian revolution in 1919, and twelve other People's Commissars of the 1919 Revolutionary Government were arrested and executed. Two hundred Italian Communists, more than a hundred Yugoslavs, the complete leadership of the Polish Communist Party and all but a handful of the fifty thousand or so Polish refugees in Russia were shot. The Comintern was formally dissolved in 1942. But its staff and directorate, Russian and non-Russian, had been almost totally liquidated by the summer of 1939.

The Eighteenth Congress could therefore be called the Congress of the Survivors. But it was more than that. To be present in Moscow as a fraternal delegate in March 1939 meant advancement at a time when there were only two roads to survival: impenetrable stupidity, or attachment to a more prominent survivor. Survival, promotion, for this latter group depended on guessing accurately and quickly where the lightning would strike next, who of one's superiors was himself going to be on the winning side. A Congress meeting would be for all but the most impenetrably stupid among the delegates (there were many of these) a time for the most careful of calculations, the most concentrated observation of all the hundred and one signs by which a Soviet politico could sense whom to support and whom to abandon. They could not be expected to have their minds most fully attuned to what was happening in the outside world, nor to be possessed of much of the information which the Soviet press withheld from its readership for fear of impugning the official line.

The speech the Congress heard[1] from Stalin was in fact mainly devoted to the internal affairs of the Soviet Union. But these affairs were set against a background of world affairs. 'A new imperialist war has opened,' Stalin declared. The world recession of 1937 had led to a further sharpening of the imperialist struggle. A bloc of aggressor states had been formed under the title of the anti-Comintern pact which, so Stalin declared, was directed not against the Comintern or the Soviet Union, but against the Western capitalist democracies. Yet the democracies lacked the will to resist the aggressive powers. Instead they appeared eager to embroil them with the Soviet Union so that they, the Western democracies, might gain from the resultant war. As an alleged example of this, he instanced the stories the democratic press were carrying on the effect of the purges on the morale of the Soviet armed forces and the 'hullabaloo' they were making about alleged German plans to invade or subvert the Soviet Ukraine. Such reports, he said, were intended to incense the Soviet Union against Germany, to poison the atmosphere and to provoke a conflict without visible grounds. The Soviet Union, however, would remain at peace. Its guiding principle was 'not to allow our country to be drawn into conflict by warmongers who are accustomed to have others pull their chestnuts out of the fire for them.'

The speech was later to be hailed, by Molotov,[2] Ribbentrop,[3] and others following them, as the signal for the opening of Nazi-Soviet conversations. It was nothing of the sort. It marked not the opening of a new phase of Soviet foreign policy, but the end of a period of transition. As the German Ambassador noted shrewdly,[4] there was lacking the usual obligatory denunciation of the authoritarian states. Instead, the main targets of Stalin's abuse were the democratic states – Britain, France and the United States – which had destroyed the principle of collective security and were using the Ukrainian question to incite Germany against the Soviet Union. He also commented that the speech showed no deviation from the current Soviet line. Sir William Seeds, the British Ambassador, echoed his judgment.[5] The speech contained little that was new or unexpected but seemed to confirm and consecrate the principal tendencies in Soviet foreign policy. Those in Britain who believed that Soviet Russia was only awaiting an invitation to join the Western democracies should be advised to ponder Mr Stalin's advice to his party. The only dissident note was struck by the American Chargé d'affaires in Moscow, Kirk, who reported that junior members of the German Embassy in Moscow were sure that if Stalin's remarks could be put to Hitler in the proper light then something could be done to improve German-Soviet relations.[6]

Stalin's speech and the monolithic presence of the Politburo behind him as he spoke to the expectant party members concealed a debate which had raged fiercely since September 1938, and spasmodically for two years before that. The vital question debated was how the Soviet Union should break out of the trap of the anti-Comintern pact which faced her with a hostile Japan in the East and a hostile Germany in the West, planning together and co-ordinating their actions. Since the advent of Hitler to power, the Soviet Union had joined the League of Nations and pledged its support to collective security. At the same time, the weight of the surviving European Communist parties had been thrown into supporting anti-Fascist coalitions throughout Western Europe, under the general title of the Popular Front. The outbreak of civil war in Spain, with the nationalist forces being supported by Italy and Germany first with arms and then with 'volunteers', had led the Soviet Union to follow their example, if a trifle more discreetly. Arms shipments from Odessa and elsewhere were shipped in chartered shipping sailing, much of it, under the British flag. And most of the Soviet-organized 'volunteers' were genuine volunteers, unlike their German or Italian opponents. They were not, however, Soviet citizens, being drawn from the survivors of the German, Austrian, Italian and East European Communist parties, augmented by volunteers from the left-wing youth of Britain, America and Western Europe.

The architect of this policy was Maxim Litvinov, a Russian Jew married to the daughter of the celebrated British historian, Sir Sydney Low, whom he met in London during his political exile from Tsarist Russia. Litvinov had been Commissar for Foreign Affairs since 1930. He was comparatively junior in the Soviet hierarchy, a mere candidate member of the Politburo. This was his salvation, throughout the purges, as was the fact that in Tsarist days he had not even been a member of the Bolshevik Party at all. He was in fact an old Menshevik, a member of the Russian Social Democratic Party. But throughout the years up to Munich his was the sole hand in charge of Soviet foreign policy. Stalin said and did little. Perhaps he despised the paunchy, sophisticated Jew; he was capable of the most virulently anti-semitic remarks. In any case he had little knowledge of the outside world and little experience to call on. In the paranoiac world of the purges and the show trials knowledge and experience of the non-Socialist world was an automatic reason for suspicion. Stalin's directives to his secret policemen could be paraphrased as 'action on suspicion'. But an exception was always made for Litvinov and the other Menshevik members of the Soviet diplomatic services – Jakob Suritz in Paris, Ivan Maisky in London, Boris Shtein in Rome. They were certainly watched, but where their colleagues disappeared wholesale, they survived.

Nevertheless, Litvinov's line in Soviet foreign policy was not unchallenged. The principal open critic of this collective-security, popular-front policy was Stalin's right-hand man, Vyacheslav Molotov, who was to succeed Litvinov as Soviet Foreign Minister. Molotov looked like a salesman of encyclopaedias down on his luck. His mottled complexion, ingratiating smile and straggly moustache hid one of the most inexorably stupid men to hold the foreign ministership of any major power in this century. Beside him Ciano, Beck, even Ribbentrop, seem masters of intelligence, quick-witted, well informed and of impeccable judgment. He was ignorant, stupid, greedy and grasping, incurably suspicious and immovably obstinate. Like many stupid men he was cranky, pedantic even, and a bit of a bully in a coarse, peasant way. Stalin made fun of his vegetarianism and his abhorrence of alcohol. But Molotov had one indispensable virtue in Stalin's eyes: his family was completely at Stalin's mercy. Stalin had used this threat successfully to whip Molotov into line during the height of the purges. There was even a time when Stalin appears to have seriously considered purging him. But in the end he did not. Whatever the reason, Molotov was completely, unalterably loyal to Stalin himself.

After 1936 Molotov had become an occasional advocate of improving relations with Germany, of not being drawn into the anticipated collapse of the capitalist world. His advocacy coincided with Stalin's first attempt to reach an agreement with Hitler, in the secret approaches conducted immediately after the signature of the anti-Comintern pact whose secret consultative clauses the Soviets knew in detail from their intelligence service. These approaches had come to nothing.[7] Indeed the SS had provided Stalin, through the ever-gullible Czechoslovak President, Edvard Beneš, with a dossier of forged documents which had been used to justify Stalin's purge of the Soviet military leadership.[8] Instead, the Soviet representative on the Non-Intervention Committee had done his best to promote conflict between Britain and France and the Axis members of the Committee. Other Soviet agencies had done all they could to keep the war in Spain going and to eliminate all those elements on the Spanish Republican side who might have framed a compromise peace.

The course of the Munich crisis and its conclusion, a four-power conference to which the Soviet Union was not even invited, marked a major defeat for Litvinov's policy of collective security and the system of pacts which was supposed to give it teeth. Maisky's efforts in London to urge the conclusion of an Anglo-Soviet alliance, Litvinov's own appearance at Geneva and his attempts to get the Council of the League involved in the dispute were quietly ignored. Chamberlain preferred to deal with Hitler and Mussolini directly and Daladier backed him in this.

When the agreement was concluded, the Soviet Union had lost its only friend west of its own boundaries, and had been forced to learn what had happened at second hand. The Anglo-German Declaration was even worse than the Munich Agreement. Britain seemed to be giving Hitler a free hand in Central Europe. The German-French Declaration in December was added confirmation of this.

Faced with such a threat, the Soviet leadership found itself in a very difficult position. It was all very well Stalin angrily attacking the Western powers for denigrating the Red Army. By the end of 1938 he was beginning to feel the need to rebuild a competent generalship and to restore some of the Red Army's faith in its abilities. But he knew that the Soviet rearmament programme was far from in its stride yet. The Red Air Force was technically backward. The Red Fleet was embarking on a construction programme designed to transform it from a small coastal defence navy into an ocean-going navy armed with battleships and cruisers as good as any in the world. The Red Army was still evolving its tanks; in 1938 they were light and easily vulnerable to anti-tank fire. The Soviet Union faced two powerful armies, one in Germany, the other in Manchuria and Mongolia. It was vulnerable along the whole length of its European frontiers and much of its frontiers in Asia. Caution would have to be the watchword of the Soviet leadership.

Under the circumstances it would not have been at all surprising had the exclusion of the Soviet Union from the Munich Conference been followed by a major change in the management of Soviet foreign policy, the dismissal or transfer of Litvinov, a replacement of some of his senior ambassadors, or a shake-up in the Foreign Affairs Commission established as a party watchdog in spring 1938. Foreign diplomats anticipated this, and there was a spate of rumours that Litvinov's position had been seriously shaken, which kept the notoriously rumour-ridden foreign diplomatic corps in Moscow more than usually busy.[9] This was not, however, the way the Soviet system worked. Soviet diplomatists devoted themselves to 'exposing' attempts to denounce the Soviet role in the Munich crisis.[10] Litvinov's deputy, Vladimir Potemkin, remarked to Robert Coulondre, the outgoing French Ambassador, that he saw only one denouement, a fourth partition of Poland.[11] On the surface, however, the old line was maintained. Molotov's speech at the celebrations for the twenty-first anniversary of the Bolshevik revolution, a paean of praise for the Soviet Union's readiness to resist aggression and aid all states that felt themselves the victims of aggression, coupled with denunciations of the pusillanimity of the Chamberlain and Daladier regimes for their abandonment of the principles of collective security, was a typical example of this kind of propaganda.[12]

Behind this cloud of argument, however, Litvinov was still biding his time, waiting for the inevitable next German move that would, in his view, once again confront the democracies with the need either to sacrifice a vital interest for the sake of peace (something he was certain they would do), or to accept the Soviet offer of a common military alliance to resist war. Litvinov was not in any way concerned with Italy, with whom the Soviet Union maintained reasonably friendly relations, so far as Mussolini made this possible. One very significant pointer to the degree of Soviet disinterest in Italy at this date is the Soviet decision, taken in November 1938, to pull out of Spain. The military and police advisers and the hard core of the Stalinist elements in the International Brigade were withdrawn, the arms shipments ended, and the finance cut off.[13] The remains of the brigades were abandoned to be driven across into internment in France, where many were to fall into German hands in 1940.[14]

Litvinov's position was, however, under a new threat. In the autumn of 1938 Stalin had rid himself of the instrument of his purges, the infamous Nikolai Yezhov, the head of the NKVD. In his place Stalin appointed a fellow Georgian, Laurenty Beria. Beria moved cautiously. But by February 1939 he had cleaned out most of Yezhov's henchmen and executed them on charges of espionage for Britain. In their place he installed a group of fellow Georgians: Vsevolod Merkulov became his deputy and head of internal security; Vladimir Dekanosov became head of the foreign department, that is of the NKVD's foreign intelligence system. At the same time, the military intelligence wing of the Red Army, the GRU, absorbed into the NKVD at the time of the army purges, was reorganized and put under the control of the General Staff once more. Those of its networks which had survived the purges, notably that headed by the German journalist Richard Sorge in Tokyo,[15] and a smaller set which grouped itself around Rudolf von Scheliha, a German diplomatist on the staff of the German Embassy in Warsaw, were hard at work, though, according to the editors of the Soviet diplomatic documents, von Scheliha thought he was working for 'a Western intelligence agency'.[16] But the main efforts of the revived GRU were devoted to preparing for the war in the West which they believed to be imminent, building up new centres in Belgium and Switzerland.[17]

Dekanosov had a much more difficult task. Before the years of the purges there had been two parallel Soviet networks active outside the Soviet Union's frontiers, one run by the Comintern and one by the NKVD; both had recruited their agents from much the same milieu, the European Communist revolutionaries of Germany, Poland and Central Europe who had rallied to the Russian revolution in 1917. These people had been particularly hard hit by the purges. One or two had fled from 'Soviet justice'. Most had been purged, either on recall to Moscow, or murdered by the NKVD's 'mobile groups', as was Ludwig Poretsky, alias Ignace Reiss, murdered in Switzerland in September 1937.[18] Many of their agents had been abandoned. It was Dekanosov's task to identify them and re-activate them. Perhaps the most immediately useful was John Herbert King, a member of the British Foreign Office's communications department with continuous access to the diplomatic and telegraphic correspondence between London and all British diplomatic missions. Recruited in 1935 by bribery and blackmail, he was deserted in 1937 when his case officer, Theodore Maly, was recalled to Moscow. He seems to have been re-activated some time in March–April 1939.[19]

Between them, the GRU (to whose command the Soviet Military Attaché in Berlin, General Orlov, was posted in April 1939) and the NKVD also disposed of various American sources of information, such as the diplomatist Noel Field, and a range of informants in New Deal Washington. They also had access to the main Italian source of intelligence on Britain, the Italian agent who regularly burgled the safe of the British Embassy in Rome. In addition to King, they had information from Donald Maclean, then attached to the British Embassy in Paris, and controlled a considerable network of agents and 'moles' throughout Western Europe. Political intelligence as opposed to military industrial intelligence, the exploitation of which seems to have been the main task of the GRU, was passed to the Soviet Foreign Ministry. Some reports from Sorge, Scheliha and from Rudolf Herrnstadt, the German journalist in Warsaw who recruited him, have even been printed in collections of Soviet Foreign Ministry documents. What the NKVD got it kept to itself.

The most important information these informants brought to Litvinov was a detailed knowledge of the course of the German negotiations with Japan for a military alliance. Second only to this was the knowledge of Ribbentrop's negotiations with the Poles. Sorge was himself a close friend of General Ott, the German Ambassador in Tokyo. But even more important (since Ott was not officially brought into these negotiations until April 1939), Sorge's friend, Ozaki Hozumi, was a close associate of and unofficial adviser to Prince Konoye, the Japanese Premier, and to Prince Saionji, the sole survivor of the great generation of statesmen who had modernized Japan, the *Genro*. The diary of Baron

Harada, Saionji's right-hand man, shows Saionji to have been privy to the debates which split successive Japanese cabinets so fiercely. From the information which came from these two sources to Litvinov, it was clear to him that Germany was beginning to turn westwards; else Ribbentrop would have had no difficulty in accepting the Japanese formulation of the pact. From this there came a second deduction, that whatever the German intentions in fomenting the Carpatho-Ukrainian question, they were not directed against the Soviet Union, as the Western press argued.

Where Litvinov was much less well informed and more inclined to push his hypotheses too far was in his assessment of the Western press agitation about the Ukraine in the context of the Anglo-German and Franco-German declarations. Litvinov's views on the realities behind the press agitation over the alleged German plot against the Ukraine tended to vary according to his audience. He was in possession of information suggesting that there was, at least until January 1939, a strong group of German advocates of a drive against the Ukraine.[20] But he was also convinced that the agitation was part of an Anglo-French move, either separately or in conjunction, to spur Hitler into an eastward attack.[21]

The Czechs, broken by Munich, had started these stories in the first week of October 1938.[22] To them Litvinov had added his firm conviction, which Maisky supported, that Chamberlain was determined on appeasement to the bitter end.[23] Chamberlain's rejection of Soviet approaches from April 1938 onwards had convinced Litvinov that the British Prime Minister was entirely doctrinaire in his approach. This was something Litvinov, used to the rigidities of Soviet doctrine, could understand. Chamberlain would never change. There were plenty more sacrifices he could make, at the expense of others, to avoid war. He was 'psychologically prepared for another Munich',[24] in the cause of an Anglo-German settlement; Bonnet and Daladier even more so. Every British move to avoid conflict – the ending of the Non-Intervention Committee's work in Spain, the ratification of the Anglo-Italian Agreement on the Mediterranean, the acceptance of the extension of Japanese control over the islands of the South China Sea – was grist to his argument.

Moreover, his convictions were strengthened in February 1939 when he received what seems to have been a garbled version of Chamberlain's conversation with Mussolini. Chamberlain, as we have seen, hoped to persuade Mussolini to influence Hitler to call off his supposed plans to drive into the Ukraine. The report which reached Litvinov[25] depicted Chamberlain as using Mussolini as a conduit through which Hitler would learn that Britain would not intervene if Hitler attacked the Ukraine, almost the exact reverse of what Chamberlain had actually said. The conviction that Britain's main aim was to bring about a German-Soviet conflict still dominates Soviet historical writing on this period.

This belief in a British effort to 'turn the German torrent towards the east', as Potemkin expressed it to the Italian Ambassador to Moscow, Augusto Rosso, early in April 1939,[26] meant that British efforts to mend their fences with the Soviet Union aroused only the deepest of suspicions in Litvinov's breast. This was the more understandable, though none the less unfortunate, in that it had taken Halifax until early January to convince Chamberlain of the desirability of such a move. The real opportunity came, in Halifax's view, with the dispatch of a new British Ambassador, the immensely tall Sir William Seeds, to Moscow to replace the shrewd, sardonic Viscount Chilston, who was due to retire. Sir William was an enthusiast – not for the Soviet system but for the Russian people; he was also an advocate of Anglo-Soviet agreement. His Russian was good, acquired in Tsarist days as a student in Moscow.[27]

Up to that point, Halifax had been fighting an uphill task. The British had kept the Soviet Embassy up-to-date on their information on German plans for the Ukraine.[28] But the failure of the hopes originally pinned on exploitation of the Anglo-German Declaration made a mending of fences with the Soviet Union seem an obvious and sensible re-insurance. This was made the more urgent by the apparent progress of the German-Japanese talks and by the crisis in Italian relations with France.

In January 1939 there was a fresh crop of rumours of German-Soviet political talks.[29] Opinion in the Foreign Office tended to interpret these as mistaken speculations arising out of the revival of the German-Soviet economic talks. But the Foreign Office's Moscow watchers were not entirely happy with German-Soviet contacts even on the economic level. The French, always more alarmist than the British about anything which might leave Germany free to attack westwards without any worry on their eastern frontiers, consulted Sir Alexander Cadogan early in February.[30] Cadogan did his best to soothe their fears, but his own minutes reveal a distrust of Soviet intentions which he would have done well to keep in mind in the months which followed.

Sir William Seeds went to Moscow with fresh instructions to emphasize Britain's general goodwill towards the Soviet Union. He spoke to Litvinov and to President Kalinin to this end.[31] Litvinov was suspicion itself. The Russian reaction brought Ivan Maisky, the Soviet Ambassador to Britain, round to the Foreign Office in a rush. He spoke to Rab Butler, then Parliamentary Under Secretary, with some severity about the follies of Britain's policies towards Russia before and after Munich. He warned too that the Soviet Union was retreating into an isolationist position,[32] a warning that he repeated six days later to a group of British visitors to the Soviet Embassy, and to the Anglo-Russian parliamentary group. Litvinov spoke with similar severity to Seeds a week or so later.[33]

One thing particularly worried Maisky and Litvinov: that Britain might denounce the Anglo-Soviet trade agreement. How genuine this worry was in Litvinov's case it is impossible to say. Trade was handled by Mikoyan, now rapidly rising in the Soviet hierarchy, and not by Litvinov's department at all, and it is impossible to know whether he saw in Mikoyan an ally or a rival. But Maisky's comments that denunciation would have an extremely bad effect[34] were sincerely meant. Maisky had an unfortunate effect on many who met him; he was a typical emotionally left-wing intellectual, by turns aggressively and self-consciously clever and ingratiatingly silly. He profited immensely from the atmosphere of the Popular Front. He was allowed a degree of latitude in his interventions into British internal politics which would have earned any other ambassador the immediate withdrawal of recognition. But he was dedicated to the cause of Anglo-Soviet friendship and he admired elements in the British system in a way which would have ensured his immediate execution had they come to the attention of Messrs Yagoda or Yezhov in their prime.[35]

Denunciation was far from the British mind. The Cabinet planned to send Robert Hudson, Head of the Department of Overseas Trade, to Moscow in early March. That this was to be more than a narrow exercise in trade promotion is shown by the effort that was put into cultivating Maisky socially by the British Cabinet. Halifax dined with him on February 20 at the Soviet Embassy.[36] Chamberlain visited the Soviet Embassy on March 1, for the formal celebrations of the anniversary of the March revolution of 1917, the first time any British premier had visited the Soviet Embassy since that year. Four other Cabinet Ministers accompanied him. Mr Maisky was baffled.[37]

He gave vent to his doubts and suspicions in his conversations with Rab Butler and Robert Hudson. Hudson told him Britain was determined to stand up to Hitler and was quite sure Britain would win in the long run. If Maisky's doubts were shared by his superiors in Moscow, he should take immediate steps to disabuse them.[38] Such remarks were too good to be true, Maisky told Butler. He could not believe that they formed part of Chamberlain's desire to be friends with Germany and

Italy. The only explanation that he could see was that the Cabinet had at last recognized how weak Britain was and how essential it was to be linked with the might of the Soviet Union.[39]

This Soviet suspicion is quite understandable in the light of the Soviet experience over the previous year. It was, however, unfortunate. No doubt the Soviet analysis of British motives was, in part at least, correct. There *was* an element of re-insurance in the British attempt to improve relations with the Soviet Union in this period. But that element of insurance sprang from a background of increasing confidence in British strength, probably misplaced but none the less genuine, as Maisky would have realized had he spent more time cultivating friends in the Government than among its critics. It did not spring, as the Soviet analysis argued, from a consciousness of increasing British weakness. By mid-February the panic of January was giving way to an equally surprising sense of euphoria. Moreover, there were enough signs of increasing British dissatisfaction with Germany to worry German commentators.[40] It should not have been beyond the powers of Soviet diplomatists to observe them, had they not had their eyes fixed in ideological blinkers. Maisky, however, seems to have preferred, as ambassadors of totalitarian states so often do, to emphasize his own role in his reports to Moscow rather than to provide his superiors with an objective record of what was being said on the British side.

It is the more surprising in that Litvinov's attempts to produce an initiative of his own during this period cannot be said to have been crowned with very much success. Part of his policy involved an attempt to revive the *cordon sanitaire* of border states linked with the Soviets by special agreements that Chicherin, his predecessor, had erected in the 1920s.[41] The agreement with the Polish Government in November 1938 was just such a move, as the Soviet press emphasized on its publication. Each land that wants to take care of its security must reckon with the Soviet Union and can count on its support, wrote *Izvestiya*.[42]

In February Litvinov tried to secure the Balkan part of Russia's European frontiers by means of an agreement with Turkey and Romania. Meeting the Turkish Ambassador, Haidar Aktai, at a luncheon, Litvinov broached the idea of a Black Sea security pact to comprise all the powers bordering on the Black Sea. His Romanian colleague, who was also at the luncheon, was said to have treated the idea very coolly. But the Turkish Ambassador was less certain.[43] The Turks appear to have sounded out their allies in the Balkan Entente, especially the Greeks, and the matter was discussed at the annual conference of the Balkan Entente powers at Bucharest.[44] The proposal struck all these Balkan powers as an extremely unwelcome invitation to choose sides in the war they were now all coming to accept as inevitable. It was therefore rejected. Instead, Maisky made it clear to his Romanian colleague in London, Virgil Tilea, that the Soviet Union would come to Romania's aid if Germany attacked her.[45] The news was not treated with any enthusiasm in Romania, and on March 8 the Soviet news agency Tass was forced to deny that any request for assistance, military or otherwise, had been made by the Romanians.[46] Rather similar approaches had been made to the Turks, in the belief that President Ismet Inönü, a veteran of Soviet-Turkish co-operation at the time of the Turkish war of independence in 1919–20, was definitely pro-Russian.[47]

The worst defeat that Soviet policy suffered in these months was the collapse of their trade and credit negotiations with Germany. This collapse was the more upsetting in that all the initiatives had been taken from the German side. The initial idea came from the handsome, even striking, figure of Count Friedrich von der Schulenburg, the German Ambassador to the Soviet Union, a survivor of that group within the German Foreign Ministry which in the 1920s had consistently advocated German-Soviet co-operation against the West. In October, profiting from his observations of Russian feelings of isolation, he had proposed a programme of settlement in German-Soviet relations, beginning with the negotiation of a new trade agreement and a new and larger grant of credit to the Soviet Union.[48] The idea was eagerly taken up by the Soviet authorities and a new trade agreement was signed in Berlin on December 19, 1938. The ensuing negotiations over a grant of credit to the Soviet Union were initiated by the Soviets on January 10, 1939 with the request that the place of negotiation be transferred to Moscow, a request which had various political implications.[49] This the Germans refused to concede, but they did agree to send their leading financial expert, Julius Karl Schnurre, to Moscow via Warsaw.[50]

Schnurre duly left for Warsaw where his visit coincided with the pomp and ceremony of von Ribbentrop's visit. The news of Schnurre's forthcoming visit to Moscow was leaked to the French press and made the basis of far-reaching speculation on a Nazi-Soviet get-together. Furious, Ribbentrop ordered Schnurre home to Berlin.[51] The negotiations continued in Moscow, Schulenburg seeing Mikoyan early in February.[52] But early in March the German Ministry of Economics ruled that the negotiations would have to be brought to a standstill. Germany's war rearmament left her nothing like enough surplus capacity to produce deliveries on the scale of the credit proposed.[53]

The Soviet leadership seems to have pinned some hope on a political development of these negotiations. Since October 1938 anti-German propaganda in the Soviet press had largely ceased, the main weight of Soviet propaganda being turned on the Western democracies. Later in December the Soviet foreign-language press began an outright series of attacks on the Western democratic powers for inciting Germany to attack the Soviet Union over the question of the Ukraine. The attacks continued during Chamberlain's visit to Rome, from January 11 to 14.

The Soviets were misled by a lengthy conversation Hitler held with the Soviet Ambassador in Berlin on January 12. The occasion was extremely public, the New Year's greetings ceremony, postponed until January 12 so that it could be held at the new Reichs Chancellery building on the Voss-strasse adjoining the old Chancellery on the Wilhelmsplatz.[54] Today the building lies in ruins just across the wall which divides Berlin. In 1939 it was a masterpiece of Third Reich vulgar-classic, entered through two bronze doors tacked on to the old Chancellery building, covered in marble, mosaics and bronze. Hitler's own study was 80 feet long, 45 feet wide and had a 60-foot-high ceiling, with his initials worked into the door panelling. The architect was Albert Speer. Hitler's own workdesk was marble. He was to kill himself in the air-raid shelter constructed in the building's bowels; his corpse was burnt and buried in its garden where the Soviets exhumed it.

The German diplomatists present had all been forced to wear a new uniform designed by Ribbentrop with epaulettes, silver or gold lanyards and dirks, all covered in shining pieces of metal, buttons, Nazi badges and so on. The SS officers wore their white gala uniforms with silver and white army-style belts. Hitler himself appeared wearing a belt worked with gold. The Papal Nuncio, as doyen of the foreign diplomatic corps in Berlin, speaking on behalf of his colleagues, formally wished the Führer a happy and successful New Year. Hitler replied in a suitably truculent vein and then moved among the guests. With the Soviet Ambassador he spent more than three-quarters of an hour. No German record has survived of what he said, though Soviet historians often refer to this as the first stage of the Nazi approach to the conclusion of the non-aggression pact in Europe. If this represents the hopes aroused among the Soviet leadership by the meeting, then they were to be disappointed.

That such hopes *were* aroused by this conversation is suggested by the affair of the *News Chronicle* article. On January 27, after the German agreement to send Schnurre to Warsaw, the British journalist and political commentator Vernon Bartlett, who was known to have often enjoyed the confidence of the Soviet Ambassador in London, Ivan Maisky, published a sensational article in the London *News Chronicle*, a popular newspaper supported by the Quaker interests of the Cadbury family and generally regarded as the paper of the Liberal Party opposition to Chamberlain. The article alleged that the conclusion of a pact between Nazi Germany and the Soviet Union was imminent.[55] It did a great deal to fan the agitation of the French and Polish press against Schnurre's visit to Moscow and to bring about his recall. What is most significant about this article, however, is that it was taken up by the Soviet press and reprinted without any comment.[56] It is said to have been widely discussed among the inner circles of the Communist Party of the Soviet Union and among the surviving European Communists, where it was used to prepare party opinion for the idea that a deal could be struck with the Nazis, despite their previous role in Soviet propaganda as the arch-fiends of war.

If this was the Soviet hope, the subsequent interruption of the credit negotiations with Germany must have brought disillusionment. By late February the diplomatic corps in Moscow was again buzzing with rumours that Litvinov's removal from the Commissariat for Foreign Affairs was imminent. This time it was alleged that he was to go to Washington as ambassador; much of his work, it was said, was being handled by Mikoyan; and his personality was regarded as the main obstacle to the adoption by the Soviet Union of a policy of encouraging the Nazi leadership to guarantee the Soviet frontiers, presumably as part of their preparations to attack in the West.[57] The time for Litvinov's dismissal, however, had not yet come.

By the beginning of March, therefore, the Soviets had retreated in part into a suspicious and dilatory isolationism, with strong hints that they would like to see an agreement with Germany which would divert German expansionism westwards. Behind this lay a deep and abiding distrust of Britain and France. Litvinov's moves had failed to secure any marked increase in Soviet security. Beria and Dekanosov had firm control of the NKVD foreign policy apparatus. And over all sat Josef Stalin, brooding, calculating, listening, all-powerful, and about to make an error which would cost the lives of at least ten million of his countrymen, and bring his regime within a hair's breadth of collapse two summers later.

CHAPTER 8

DIVIDED COUNSELS IN WASHINGTON: ROOSEVELT BACKS BRITAIN AND FRANCE

In October 1938, Franklin Roosevelt was fifty-six years old. He was approaching the mid-term Congressional elections of his second term as President, elections which were significantly to weaken his never very effective control of Congress. Elected to the Presidency in November 1932, he had broken twelve years of Republican control of the Presidency by putting together a precarious and contradictory coalition of Southern conservatives, Midwestern agrarian radicals and progressives, and the organized, machine-politics-led minorities of the predominantly urban states of the north-east. In 1936 he had carried every state in the Union but Maine and Vermont. The following year he had thrown much of that advantage away in an effort to 'pack' the Supreme Court in his favour. His efforts, despite the enormous fountain of patronage and electoral persuasion which the New Deal offered, had coincided with a new industrial recession. The question of who would succeed him – or if anyone should succeed him – at the end of his second term was beginning to climb to the top of the private agendas of many of his closest allies and supporters, not in itself a recipe for that selfless suppression of private ambition for public good which might have eased his task as leader.

In so far as any unity existed, Roosevelt's ability to lead America so successfully for three and a quarter terms of office stemmed from his technique of dominating those he led by a mixture of the authority which any Presidential candidate inherits at the moment of election, the strength of his own personality and the secrecy which underlay his ability to be all things to all the disparate elements which made up his coalition. His closest supporters and adherents complained that he 'deliberately concealed the processes of his mind', that he never talked 'frankly even with the people' who were loyal to him.[1] His personality was overpoweringly regal; his advisers constituted a court rather than a cabinet. He displayed to them a mass of conflicting characteristics, not so much ill balanced as constantly shifting in balance. 'Inconsistent in his consistencies, cold and distant behind the apparent warmth of personality with which he could overwhelm even the most hardened visitor, listening always to some private voice whose tones we can recognise but never overhear, and whose advice we can imagine but never verify',[2] his protean, almost chameleonlike, changes, his hesitancies, his willingness to leave initiative to others, the freedom with which he abused others for not acting with the strength he was not prepared to display himself, all this is difficult to reconcile with the reputation he has enjoyed as the 'great leader' of the democracies.

And yet a great leader he certainly was. His secretiveness was displayed only to those who tried to discover how far he could be relied upon. His public personality was not only distinguished by strength and determination in his opposition to all that Nazism stood for; its hall-mark was certainty and a deep, unshakeable confidence in the wealth, the strength and the determination of the United States. He was a great patriot, not only for himself but for the United States. He also assumed that the values for which, under his leadership, the United States stood and which he advocated were those most conducive to the advancement of peace and the general interests of humanity. Those who thought in such general terms in other countries were, from time to time, shaken by the discovery that the President's identification of such values with the interests of the United States was absolute. In others, among members of the British Cabinet, for example, such absolutism induced anger, irritation and cynicism.

What is more surprising is to discover how the President's secretiveness, his distrust of his supporters, and his total confidence in his own judgment and vision were to encourage him to entertain a series of beliefs and convictions about those with whom he was dealing that left him very nearly as ill informed and as myopic in his judgment of European, indeed of world, politics as Stalin was. Like Stalin he suspected a constant conspiracy on the part of British financial interests to accept Germany's terms for a division of Europe. Like Stalin he consistently misinterpreted Neville Chamberlain's horror and fear of European war as cloaking a psychological affinity for the totalitarian powers. Like Stalin with his fears of a Baltic invasion, Roosevelt imagined strategic threats to the United States where none existed. By contrast with Stalin, however, his intelligence sources were all second-hand and, in the main, grossly unreliable. Indeed some were certainly subject to Soviet influence.

The sources in which he put most trust were seven in number. They consisted of reports from the French Deuxième Bureau sent to him by his old friend, William Bullitt, his Ambassador in Paris;[3] reports from the Polish intelligence bureau sent to him by Anthony J. Drexel Biddle IV, his Ambassador in Warsaw;[4] some information from the German opposition to Hitler which reached him through George Messersmith, a career diplomatist in the State Department who had been Consul General in Berlin and American Minister in Vienna;[5] selected items of political intelligence passed on by the British, especially in relation to the Far East; the reportage of leading American foreign correspondents in Europe; Latin American radical and fellow-travelling journalists obsessed (as a result of the impact of the Spanish Civil War on Latin America) by fears of German 'Fifth Column' activists in Latin America; and reports in *The Week*, a privately circulated newsletter coming out of London, edited by a former *Times* correspondent in Washington and Berlin, Claud Cockburn, who, under the alias of Frank Pitcairn, also worked on the editorial staff of the British Communist Party newspaper, the *Daily Worker*.[6]

Roosevelt's court was basically divided into three factions on the issues of the approaching war. Cordell Hull, his Secretary of State, the former Senator from Tennessee, had done more than anyone else to secure Roosevelt's nomination as Democratic candidate in 1932. To many he seemed Roosevelt's natural successor in 1940. The epitome, at least in looks, of the classic American statesman, slow and gentle of speech, he brooded over slights and grievances, imagined or real, hated implacably, entertained long, cold feuds which ended only when he finally 'got his man'.[7] Roosevelt gave him his head where his obsession (that all wars stemmed from economic rivalries and could be overcome by the freeing of international trade) was concerned; but he did not confide in him.

His confidence was reserved for the man he had appointed Hull's Under Secretary of State, Sumner Welles, a Grotonian like himself, who frequently repaid his confidence by directing foreign ambassadorial enquiries away from the aspects of Roosevelt's foreign policy of which Welles disapproved, thereby feeding Roosevelt's belief in the natural gutlessness of the European opponents of Fascism. Sumner Welles shared with Hull and others in the State Department – Adolf Berle, and Jay Pierrepont Moffatt, head of the European division – the conviction that America's economic recovery from the Depression depended on the recovery of world trade, and that both Britain and Germany, who had used the 1930s to build up separate economic blocks, the German system of economic autarchy and the Ottawa system of imperial preferences, were, as a result, not only potential enemies to each other, but also inimical to the United States. Britain and

Germany shared too, or so the Americans believed, a propensity to get together to the detriment of the United States. Their Marxistic analysis of the springs of war and imperialism shared a common origin with that entertained in Moscow, in the writings of turn-of-the-century British and American radicals, such as J. A. Hobson and Charles Conant, whose theories of imperialism Lenin took over, ready-made. It led them to such gems of wisdom as Hull's statement that the Ottawa agreements constituted 'the greatest injury in a commercial way that has been inflicted on the United States since I entered public life,' and Sumner Welles's 'the whole history of British imperial preference is a history of economic aggression against America.'

These views and suspicions were shared by the two strongest members of Roosevelt's Cabinet besides Hull, Henry Morgenthau, the Secretary to the Treasury, and Harold Ickes, the Secretary of the Interior. But where Hull and Welles were prepared to press 'free trade' upon the Germans and accept the consequent losses on the German market until the German system cracked under pressure, Morgenthau and Ickes were prepared to go much further. They did not, perhaps, share the confidence in Britain which Norman Davis, the State Department's leading Anglophile, professed despite everything. But they did share the outright suspicion of, and hostility towards, Germany preached by George Messersmith. Moreover neither had any qualms about expressing himself in public. Ickes was denounced in the German press as a 'Deutschenfresser', an eater of Germans, a Teutonophage.[8] Morgenthau's religion lent substance to the anti-semitic-conspiracy theories of the Nazi press.

Behind this conflict there lay, however, both an anxiety and a psychological dilemma for Roosevelt and his advisers. Was America to play the great mediator? Or was she to play the role of champion of freedom against the totalitarian powers? Much depended on which way the British Government could be expected to jump.[9] Convinced by Claud Cockburn, who had invented it, of the existence of the 'Cliveden Set', allegedly a clique of British politicians and financiers who met at Cliveden, the country seat of Lord and Lady Astor in Buckinghamshire, a 'pro-German group with heavy backing' from the City and financial interests,[10] and an ally of those Wall Street interests with whom the New Deal ideologists from the President downwards felt themselves to be at war,[11] Roosevelt faced, or thought he faced, the possibility of an Anglo-German carve-up of markets both in Europe and Latin America, from which American interests could only suffer.

These suspicions were very largely baloney. The Anglo-German economic talks of October 1938, despite attempts on the German side to doll them up for Hitler as the kind of British concession towards German hegemony in south-eastern Europe he was known to see as a basis for Anglo-German co-operation, were not only not successful but were concerned mainly with attempts to regulate Anglo-German bilateral trade. Earlier British thoughts on economic co-operation with Germany on a global scale, which remained on the back burner until Hudson's ill-chosen resurrection of the issue in his talks with the head of the German Four Year Plan, Helmut Wohltat, in July 1939, centred on co-operation in the development of central Africa. Germany was, it was true, buying heavily of Britain's imperial raw materials, so much so that any abrupt cessation would have had the most adverse effects on Britain's balance of payments. But the Cabinet was swinging strongly towards a series of measures, to which Hull was to object very strongly as they could hardly be described as 'open trading', designed to buttress the economic independence of the Balkan countries – Greece, Turkey and Romania – against Germany, measures which, as already noted, were to induce a certain sense of desperation in German governing circles in the spring of 1939.

Indeed, the failure of the Anglo-German talks led in November 1938 to the British Cabinet's decision finally to conclude the Anglo-American Trade Agreement which Hull had been pursuing for so long. The terms of the agreement were more onerous than the economic interests in the Cabinet were happy with. Oliver Stanley, President of the Board of Trade, spoke bitterly of 'intolerable' American 'dealings and tergiversations' which had brought him to 'the state of bitterness and exasperation which usually results from dealing with the American government'; and Simon, the Chancellor of the Exchequer, spoke of there being 'a limit to the demands we must concede'. But Halifax's reply, 'I am afraid the political reasons for getting a treaty must outweigh trade and economic considerations,' overruled them and the treaty was duly signed on November 2.[12] It did little to allay American suspicions of Britain, where no real reduction in imperial preferences could be detected. Nor for that matter could London detect any changes in the American tariff wall. The drop of 20 cents in the value of sterling from $4.70 to $4.50, instead of being taken as a reflection of the constant drain on sterling which underlay so much of the Treasury's reluctance to aid Germany's potential victims in Europe, was seen as a typical City trick to undercut American goods on the world market.

Roosevelt had, however, already made his choice, though, typically, he kept it hidden from his State Department advisers. The instrument of his choice was William Bullitt, his Ambassador in Paris, a friend from the days when both had been junior members of Woodrow

Wilson's administration, Roosevelt as Assistant Secretary of the Navy, Bullitt as Wilson's intermediary in the Russian Civil War. Bullitt had been practically alone among the President's advisers in condemning the tone of moral disapprobation of British policy in the Munich crisis expressed by Hull, Sumner Welles and the State Department. 'I know of nothing more dishonourable,' he had cabled Washington on September 17, 1938, 'than to urge another nation to go to war, if one is determined not to go to war on the side of that nation.'[13]

Bullitt was convinced, on the basis of information from the Deuxième Bureau, the French intelligence service, that the preponderance of German air power over that of France and Britain made the Munich 'surrender' unavoidable.[14] Together with the French Air Minister, Guy la Chambre, he conceived a scheme for France to build aircraft in Canada, in which American labour and American mass-production measures could be employed to increase the miserable output of aircraft which, riven by strikes and cottage-industry practices, was all France could achieve in 1938. His figures of German air production were confirmed by the American air hero, Colonel Lindbergh,[15] whose one-man flight across the Atlantic (and subsequent suffering with the kidnapping and murder of his young child and harrowing by the more sensation-hungry of the US press) had both made him an oracle on the balance of world air power and driven him and his wife into more or less permanent, if peripatetic, exile in Europe. Early in October Bullitt, then, returned to Washington where he spent most of the evening of October 13 unburdening himself to the President.

On October 21, Roosevelt entertained as his guest at his home, Hyde Park, an old Scottish friend, Colonel the Honourable Sir Arthur Murray, later Lord Murray of Elibank. Murray had known Roosevelt in 1917–18, when, as Assistant Military Attaché in Washington, he had, from time to time, stood in line in the clandestine communications via Colonel House and Sir William Wiseman, the head of British intelligence in the United States, by which President Wilson had communicated with the British Cabinet behind the backs of the British Ambassador to Washington and his own Ambassador in London, both of whom he distrusted. Murray, now a railway magnate in Scotland, had re-opened the friendship in 1933, on Roosevelt's election as President. In May 1936, he had stayed as the President's guest in the White House. Throughout the electoral year of 1936 he had acted as the clandestine intermediary by which the sudden appearance of Lord Runciman, then President of the Board of Trade, in the White House as Roosevelt's guest, immediately following Roosevelt's second inauguration, had been arranged.[16]

Roosevelt now opened his mind to Murray, charging him as his secret intermediary with a message to Neville Chamberlain. 'In so far as he, the President, was able to achieve it,' he wished Chamberlain to feel that, 'in the event of war with the dictators, he had the industrial resources of the American nation behind him.'[17] In a separate message to the British Air Minister, Roosevelt offered all the parts and basic materials necessary to ensure for the democracies an overwhelming superiority in the air: plates for wings, aluminium, wood and steel castings for engines, cylinder blocks, spark plugs, magnetos.[18] He advanced Bullitt's ideas of assembly lines in Canada where the separate parts of American-designed aircraft could be assembled, and proposed to speak directly to Mackenzie King, the Canadian Premier, about it.

The offer was generous – but it still displayed Roosevelt's limited grasp of international political realities. In terms of domestic politics it entailed the most desperate secrecy, not only towards the isolationist majority in Congress, but also towards his Cabinet and his Ambassadors. Roosevelt, in fact, impressed on Murray the absolute importance of keeping his proposals secret from both the British Embassy in Washington, whose security he unjustly suspected, and the American Embassy in London. The only member of his Cabinet to be informed was the Secretary of the Army, Woodring. This was itself unfortunate as he and Woodring were barely on speaking terms. Roosevelt's military advisers were horrified at the idea of diverting American defence-production capacity, and to put their security under such a strain was in itself highly hazardous.

But it was precisely this secrecy, necessitated by domestic politics, which was so severely to limit its international effectiveness. If war was to be avoided, then Hitler had to be deterred. Deterrence and secrecy are largely incompatible notions. If Hitler was to be deterred from war by the strength of British and French air power, then the fact that American aid was giving them an edge over Germany had to be made known to him. The effectiveness of Roosevelt's offer was thus limited to its impact on British morale. Here certain limitations were imposed by the inaccuracy of Roosevelt's intelligence, and doubt as to whether he could deliver the goods. In his talks with Murray he put German aircraft production at 40,000 planes a year as against 15,000 in France and 25,000 for Britain. At that date British intelligence figures of German total production were about 7,500 aircraft of all types, an estimate which was remarkably accurate as to the total figure, but doubled German bomber strength by lumping together bombers and transport planes. The actual German figures for combat aircraft were 3,300 in 1938, 4,733 in 1939. The comparable British figures were 2,827 in 1938, a figure which was to rise in 1939 to nearly 8,000, an average production of 645 a month to Germany's 691.[19] Roosevelt's figures came from Lindbergh and the French, but their grotesquely exaggerated nature cannot have inspired much confidence in British breasts in his judgment or the quality of his intelligence sources. Roosevelt believed that he could afford to divert 20,000 planes a year, or their equivalent, from US production to Britain and France.

The main effect of Roosevelt's communiqué, in fact, appears to have been on Chamberlain's morale. When Murray finally saw Chamberlain early in December, the President's message stirred the Prime Minister into warmth. American support for Roosevelt, he told Murray, could

well have a powerful deterrent effect on Hitler's advisers.[20] The new situation was one that was to give him a great deal of encouragement and to lead him towards that euphoria from which Hitler's invasion of Bohemia on March 15, 1939 was to provide so rude an awakening.

The secretiveness with which Roosevelt briefed Murray had another side to it. Nothing, the President insisted, was to be said to the British Embassy in Washington or to the American Ambassador in London, Joseph Kennedy. An Irish Catholic, steeped in the murky dealings of Boston's Irish politics, and father of the future President, Joseph Kennedy had been sent to London both to get him out of Washington, where he was anathema to Roosevelt's closest allies, and as a practical joke on the British. Instead, Kennedy had taken to London's political society like a duck to water and the British had equally taken to him. 'I'm just like that with Chamberlain. Why, Franklin himself isn't as confidential with me,' he boasted. He was right. 'Who would have thought the English could take into camp a red-headed Irishman?' Roosevelt asked Morgenthau. But he also scented danger as Kennedy's enemies fed Roosevelt with stories of Kennedy's presidential aspirations and, still worse, of Kennedy's membership of Claud Cockburn's 'Cliveden Set'.

In the meantime, Roosevelt was following Britain's lead with the French. In 1938 the French had already contracted for the purchase of a hundred Curtis P-36 fighters.[21] In November, Jean Monnet, the future architect of both the French Fourth Republic's Commissariat du Plan and of that bureaucratic élitist conspiracy which led to the establishment, first, of the European Coal and Steel Community and then of the European Common Market, arrived in Washington at the head of a purchasing mission designed to order anything up to one thousand planes in America, provided they could be delivered quickly, as Monnet's earlier enquiries had led him to believe they could be.

Roosevelt had already announced to Morgenthau his decision to build fifteen thousand aircraft a year, and to construct eight new factories near cities with pools of unemployed men. However, the idea quickly became lost, first when Roosevelt had second thoughts as to the practicability of setting up a state-owned aircraft industry to manufacture under licence, and, second, in a bureaucratic battle between Morgenthau and the War Department. Roosevelt himself seems hardly to have noticed this, being too overcome with the apocalyptic vision of German air supremacy Bullitt and the French had inflicted upon him.

On November 14, at the White House, Roosevelt spoke his mind; once again the State Department representatives were not present. He was no longer proud, he said, of the part he had played in engineering the Munich conference. The recrudescence of German power had completely re-oriented America's international relations; for the first time since the Holy Alliance of 1818, the United States faced the possibility of attack on the Atlantic side in both the northern and the southern hemispheres. Since sending a large army overseas was 'undesirable and practically out of the question', this demanded that America immediately provide a huge air force. This had to be ready before hostilities broke out; there would be no period of grace such as America had enjoyed until 1917. If America had had five thousand planes in the summer of 1938 and the capacity immediately to produce ten thousand, 'Hitler would not have dared to take the stand he did.'[22]

Roosevelt's references to the dangers of an attack on the Atlantic shores of North and South America reflected a further lapse into Comintern-fed credulity. The realities of the German position in Latin America were such as to cause Berlin considerable alarm. An attempted coup in Brazil by the extreme right-wing Integralist Party in May 1938 had collapsed amidst widespread allegations of German involvement. The German Ambassador in Brazil, Karl Ritter, an ultra-nationalist who served Hitler to the bitter end, had been declared *persona non grata*. Extremist Nazis, of the type Hitler had purged in 1934 in Germany, had produced extravagant plans for German empires in Brazil, Chile, Peru, and around the River Plate. Comintern-spread myths of the role of the Fifth Column in Spain and of the Nazi inspiration for Franco's original rising had won wide credence in South America. The Spanish Republican Government, increasingly under Soviet influence and in its last throes, was mobilizing its American sympathizers in a last desperate effort to persuade Roosevelt to repeal the embargo on arms exports to Spain. A small-scale map seemed to suggest an invasion of northern Brazil from French West Africa. Northern Brazil in turn could act as a base for a German attack on the Panama Canal.[23] Of such geopolitical fantasies was Roosevelt's first rearmament programme born.

In launching his new programme, Roosevelt had, characteristically, managed to create yet another bureaucratic conflict. Moreover, he had rung into his foreign policy process the most isolationist elements of his administration, and that part which was least under his control, the professional military men. Already, in 1938, procurement officers in the US Navy had defeated Roosevelt's efforts to strengthen the Soviet Far Eastern fleet against Japan by having two battleships built for the Soviet Union in the United States, by threatening to blacklist any American shipyard which agreed to take the order. Now Woodring, himself an isolationist from Kansas, and the army leadership had a perfect weapon by which to block any French purchases of aircraft in

America. The existing production capacity was all required to meet the American target. No military secrets could be given to a foreign power.[24]

Incensed, Morgenthau and Roosevelt hit upon the device of offering the French facilities to inspect prototypes of the planes the army had not yet accepted and which it could not therefore claim to be secret. Among them were the Curtis P-40, the Glenn-Martin 166 and 167 and the Douglas DB-7, a twin-engined bomber. It took a direct written order from Roosevelt to overcome the army's opposition to showing any foreigner (who, in their view, was probably on an espionage mission and had no real intention of buying anything) an up-to-date American aircraft.[25] On January 28, 1939, two of Monnet's assistants, Colonel Jaquin, and a French test pilot, Colonel Paul Chemidlin, both in civilian clothes and speaking English to one another, were shown the Douglas bombers at Los Angeles. Colonel Chemidlin questioned the DB-7's flying capabilities, and the Douglas test pilot, infuriated, determined to make him 'eat his words'. He took the plane, with Chemidlin aboard, into an ill-judged series of aerobatics which spun the plane into the ground. The Frenchman escaped with a broken leg; but in the emotion of the moment his colleague broke into French. Secrecy was at an end.[26]

On January 4, Roosevelt had delivered his New Year's message to Congress. 'A war which threatened to envelop the world in flames', he said, 'has been averted. But it has become increasingly clear that peace is not assured. All about us rage undeclared wars. . . . All about us are threats of new aggression.' He spoke of the change in the nature of war. 'Weapons of attack are so swift that no nation can be safe in its will to peace. . . . Survival cannot be prevented by arming after the attack begins. . . . Long before any overt military act, aggression begins with preliminaries of propaganda, subsidized penetration, the loosening of ties of goodwill, the stirring of prejudice.' 'There are many methods short of war, but stronger and more effective than mere words, of bringing home to aggressor governments the aggregate sentiments of our people.'[27] (The applause sounds thin on the BBC recording of the speech, which was broadcast in London and Paris.) On January 12, he had called for half a billion dollars to be spent on defence, the bulk on the army air force.[28] The Senate Military Affairs Committee, which included several determined isolationists, had promptly begun hearings on the message.[29] On January 23, the news of the DB-7's crash with a military representative of a foreign power on board meant that they had something to get their teeth into.

Roosevelt acted quickly to draw these teeth. The entire Senate

Military Committee was invited to the White House.[30] He told them that in 1936 the US Government had learnt that Germany, Italy and Japan had reached agreement 'to move simultaneously or to take turns' in aggressive actions against other nations. That had been strengthened 'almost every month' until they had 'today – without any question whatever – what amounts to a defensive and offensive alliance'. One way of looking at it was 'trusting that an assassin will get them', the other was to try to prevent the domination of the world 'by peaceful means'.

The first line of America's defence in the Pacific was the American Pacific islands. On the Atlantic, 'our first line is the continued independent existence of a very large group of nations.' He listed Finland, Latvia, Estonia, Lithuania, Sweden, Norway, Denmark, Holland ('with her colonies'), Belgium, Hungary, Czechoslovakia, Poland, Romania, Bulgaria, Greece, Yugoslavia, Turkey and Russia. To these he added France and England. If they had to fight and were beaten, which, given their lack of aircraft and arms, was at best a fifty-fifty chance, Europe would be lost to America as a market. The small nations would drop into Hitler's lap, followed by Africa. They would be followed by the Argentine and South America, Brazil with its 250,000 Germans, Venezuela, and Colombia which was only fifty-eight minutes' flight from the Panama Canal. Revolution in Central America could be had for between $1 million and $4 million per country. This would bring German influence into Mexico, on the very borders of the United States.

To stop this, America needed to prevent the destruction of her first lines of defence in Europe and the Mediterranean. By buying planes in America, France and Britain were helping America's aircraft manufacturers to develop methods of mass production. Their orders now would get the wheels turning so that, when the American process of appropriating the necessary funds was completed, the aircraft factories would be ready. In the meantime French and British independence would be maintained. At this point, the President was interrupted by Senator Reynolds, a conservative Democrat from North Carolina, who wanted US pressure to be turned on Mexico, which had in 1938 nationalized all American oil holdings in the country. Roosevelt shut him up without giving him his usual show of geniality.

Reynolds, Senator Gerald P. Nye of North Dakota, a Republican progressive isolationist, and Senator Champ Clark, a Democrat from Missouri, left the White House together.[31] They saw the meeting primarily as an attempt to stop them exposing the President's secretive and unconstitutional efforts to circumvent US neutrality legislation and to sell arms to a country, France, which had still to pay off the debts it had contracted buying arms from America in 1914–18. Nye was open in his protests and publicly withdrew from all executive (i.e. secret) meetings of the Military Affairs Committee.[32] One Senator was less scrupulous. The following day, banner headlines quoted Roosevelt as saying that America's frontier was on the Rhine. At subsequent press conferences on February 15 and 17, Roosevelt did his best to quieten the uproar.[33] He did not assuage the isolationists; nor did he strengthen the impact of his words in Berlin.

The strongest signal Roosevelt and Congress could have sent to Berlin was the repeal of the 1937 US Neutrality Act; in his address of January 4 to Congress, Roosevelt had accused this legislation of operating unevenly and unfairly, of giving aid to aggressor states and denying it to the victims of aggression. His speech could well have influenced Hitler to take a more pacific note in his own New Year's address. It unleashed a flood of proposals in Congress in which both advocates of all-out American aid to 'victims of aggression' (by which many in fact meant Republican Spain) and those pacifists and isolationists who wished to strengthen America's defences against being dragged into European war were equally prominent.[34]

But Roosevelt's credit in Congress was low. He had to contend not only with isolationist Senators and Congressmen, resistant to what opinion polls showed to be an increasing wave of public opinion in favour of American opposition to 'the dictatorships'; there was also a considerable volume of opinion in both houses of Congress which resented the strengthening of Federal as against State power resulting from New Deal legislation, thought Roosevelt would not object to a healthy dose of dictatorial powers for the Presidency, resented the growth in Federal patronage as a threat to their own power, and felt Congress should demonstrate its independence.

These feelings were given voice by Senator Key Pittman of Nevada, the Chairman of the Senate Foreign Relations Committee, through which all legislation on American foreign policy had to pass. Pittman was a steady, unbalanced, congenitally indiscreet alcoholic. His office in Congress boasted a refrigerator for his drink. He always had a glass in front of him at committee meetings and hearings. Alcohol made him abrupt and rough in his outbursts against Japan and Germany.[35] It did not affect his judgment of Senate opinion, but it made him cautious and roundabout in his approach to tactics and management. Nor did it enhance his authority with his fellow Senators. In October 1938 and again on January 11, 1939, he argued, indeed insisted, that Roosevelt leave the initiative to the Senate Committee for Foreign Relations.[36] Let the Committee sort out and even exhaust the impetus behind all the proposals now clamouring for senatorial attention. If the President and State Department would only hold their peace, he would be able to evolve a compromise. However, the bitterness of the public debate over the embargo on arms to Spain scared him into suspending the hearings on January 20.[37] They were not to be revived until after Hitler's march into Prague.

The appearance of toughness, and the prospect of American hostility towards Germany bringing about a revision of America's neutrality legislation, encouraged Neville Chamberlain, as it did the French, into the toughness towards Italy and euphoria which he displayed so publicly on the eve of the German march into Prague. In reality Roosevelt was not only back-pedalling over the repeal of neutrality. He and his administration were again entertaining a whole snake's nest of suspicions towards Britain.

These began (and here there is again a parallel with Stalin) with Roosevelt's reaction to the British 'war scare' of mid-January 1939. Roosevelt had already heard of the alleged German plans to invade the Netherlands in a leak from the Foreign Office to Claude Bowers, his Ambassador to Republican Spain.[38] The US Minister in The Hague, as we have seen, was well aware of all the rumours. Roosevelt saw the Dutch Minister to the United States on January 26 to convey a warning to him.[39] The following day, he had again expressed his fears that German economic penetration of Latin America would lead to political dominance.[40] He was incensed by the British suggestion that he make some public utterance which might deter Hitler, choosing to believe that the authors of the message were proposing to say nothing. The result was, ironically, that the press version of his remarks to the Senate Military Affairs Committee on January 31 was taken in London as the positive gesture Britain had requested: whereas Roosevelt simply ignored the evidence of Chamberlain's public statement of February 6 and the detailed reports Lord Halifax sent him regarding Britain's assumption of military obligations to France, Belgium, the Netherlands and Sudetenland in the event of a German attack westwards.[41]

His views were not helped by the kind of report that was reaching him from Paris, from Bowers, presiding over the last death throes of the Spanish Republican Government at St Jean de Luz,[42] or from Biddle in Warsaw.[43] Bullitt's version of Daladier's remarks on February 6,[44] stigmatizing Britain as 'a most weak reed on which to lean', and alleging that the British reaction to the reporting of a German attack on Holland had been to propose a committee of three to arbitrate the dispute (an outright untruth), cannot have helped matters. What the President or Hull made of Daladier's reported opinions, of Chamberlain (a 'desiccated stick'), George VI (a 'moron'), his Queen ('an excessively ambitious young woman who would be ready to sacrifice every other country in the world so that she might remain queen') and Eden (a 'young idiot'), one cannot guess. Roosevelt did, however, explode to Lord Lothian on January 27, and repeat himself in mid-February, to the effect that what the British needed was 'a good stiff grog' and that 'he could do nothing while Britain cringed like a coward.'[45]

In the meantime, Chamberlain's hopes were rising. As he saw it, 'the policy of appeasement was steadily succeeding'. 'There were many passages in Hitler's speech' (of January 28), he told the Commons, 'which indicated the necessity of peace for Germany.'[46] On January 28 Britain had signed a coal agreement with Germany. The Federation of British Industry was due to have talks early in March with its opposite number, the Reichsgruppe Industrie. Speaking at Birmingham, on February 22, Chamberlain referred to economic discussions leading to arms limitations and peace.[47] He conveyed a strong sense of euphoria speaking to the American Ambassador in London, Joseph Kennedy, on February 17.[48]

The State Department, fed by alarmist reports of imminent Italian military action against France, action which they believed Hitler to be aiding and abetting, were puzzled and suspicious. Messersmith thought Neville Chamberlain stupid to the point of criminality.[49] The State Department was convinced that a tripartite German-Italian-Japanese alliance had been, or was about to be, signed, and that an Italian adventure, with or without major German support, was to be launched in Africa. A stream of reports from Bullitt in Paris fuelled these fears.[50] They were, of course, fantasies. There was no tripartite agreement, no concerted action between Berlin, Rome and Tokyo and, above all, no Italian plan to launch a war against France. As for Roosevelt, he took a report in *The Week* on German troop concentrations in Carinthia on the Yugoslav border so seriously that he returned forthwith to Washington from sailing with the US Atlantic Squadron on its spring manœuvres in the Caribbean.[51] To Baron Rothschild, whom he had met on his Caribbean trip, he remarked that either 'the British Intelligence service had gone to pieces or the Administration was wilfully blind to reality.'[52] (This was, presumably, just after he had read Kennedy's telegram reporting his talk with Chamberlain, which Hull had thoughtfully sent on to USS *Houston*, Roosevelt's flagship.) Blind to reality Chamberlain was – as has been seen; but it was the reports of Hitler's forthcoming coup against Czechoslovakia that he failed to believe, not Roosevelt's Bullitt-fed fantasies about a joint German-Italian attack on Tunisia from Libya, or Cockburn's rumours (presumably intended by his informants as a *ballon d'essai* to find out just what Hitler actually was hatching).

The State Department and Hull were equally concerned by the failure of the Anglo-American Trade Agreement to produce any of the benefits, political or economic, that Hull had anticipated. In Hull's view, which he imparted both to the President and to his juniors,[53] the British were up to their old habit of double-dealing, preaching free trade but still following their traditional trade practices. Relations, he said, would become more difficult because Britain had now divined America's intentions. The State Department was particularly worried by the progress of the Anglo-German trade contacts, about which the British were providing them with so much information.[54] They distrusted both Oliver Stanley, the President of the Board of Trade, and Robert Hudson, the head of the Department of Overseas Trade – Hudson particularly. Hudson, wrote Moffatt, was 'unfriendly to American interests or at least . . . unwilling to subordinate immediate British interests with a view to obtaining a broader agreement with us in world trade . . . he has certainly encouraged the Prime Minister to seek cartel agreements with Germany. He is ready to sacrifice people to pounds sterling.'[55]

These suspicions were to last well past the events of March 1939 and were to be fed by every Cockburnesque rumour of Anglo-German contacts, including the near-disastrous reports of the Wohltat-Hudson conversations in July. Indeed, Hull remained convinced right up to September 2 that Britain would rat on Poland. In their own way, Hull and the State Department were as much the victims of their own prejudices and of Soviet-inspired reportage as were Stalin and Molotov on the one hand and the isolationists in Congress on the other. Roosevelt and Morgenthau were less open to such accusations. The German march into Prague, and the British guarantees for Poland, Greece, Romania and Turkey, persuaded them of the near-inevitability of war, the need to strengthen Britain and France by reforming, if not repealing, the neutrality legislation and the need to develop those 'measures short of war' of which Roosevelt had spoken in January.

Fortunately for Chamberlain's peace of mind, very little of this distrust and dissension came his way. If any of it reached Joseph Kennedy in London he did not pass it on. Nor was the British Ambassador in Washington sufficiently in the confidence of any of the various factions in Roosevelt's court to be apprised of it; in so far as he was aware, so long as the negotiations in Moscow hung fire, there was little he could do about it.

CHAPTER 9

HITLER ENTERS PRAGUE

At 4.30 in the morning of Wednesday, March 13, 1939 George Kennan, then a Secretary of Legation at the American Legation in Prague, was woken from sleep and called to the phone. A terrified voice announced that German troops would invade Bohemia and Moravia, the two Czech provinces of Czechoslovakia, in an hour and a half's time.[1] In all, seven German army corps were involved. The Czechs had four hours' warning from their President in Berlin and no opposition was offered. The Czech frontier guards, meticulously dressed, surrendered their posts to the German troops, then watched glumly as column after column of motorized infantry, guns and half-tracks rumbled past them towards Prague. It was snowing heavily, and no aircraft flew that morning. The Czech air force had been forbidden to take off, anyway. Pilsen was occupied almost at once.

The leading German columns reached Prague at 9 o'clock in the morning, entering past thin crowds. They consisted mainly of motor-cycle and side-car units, a light machine gun in the side car, the riders heavily waterproofed, their collars buttoned high up to their mouths to keep out the driving blizzard which greeted them, automatic rifles slung across their backs, steel helmets on their heads. They were nervous, but correct. No shots were fired. The columns of motor cycles, staff cars, and personnel carriers poured into Prague all day, and through Prague to the Slovak border and beyond. As they moved, Hitler followed, by train from Berlin, leaving at 9 a.m. as the advance units entered Prague, reaching the Sudetenland at 3 p.m., then by car through continuing blizzards to Prague, which he reached at 7.15 in the evening. He spent the night in the Hradcany Palace, showing himself on the balcony to German demonstrators the following noon. In all he spent two days in Bohemia, returning via Vienna to Berlin which he entered in triumph, the returning conqueror, on March 19.[2]

It had been a famous, bloodless victory, the culmination of more than four years' bitter planning and hatred since Dr Beneš, the Czech President, concluded a pact with the Soviet Union and urged France against Hitler at the time he re-occupied the Rhineland. But it left him cold. He rarely spoke of it thereafter. He had no especial vengeance to wreak on the Czechs, as he was to tread down the Poles, and plan to destroy the British. Under the attentions of the *Sicherheitsdienst* and Reinhard Heydrich, the Czechs in general were to have a less easy time. Five thousand arrests were made in the first few days and the number of suicides rose steeply. But this was no more than normal under the beneficent rule of the Thousand Year Reich. Somehow Hitler's victory had gone sour at the moment of its achievement. It was to spell complete defeat for the more far-reaching plans he had been maturing through the winter.

The diplomatic and political side of the take-over of Bohemia was in fact an extremely badly botched job. For once it does not seem to have been entirely Ribbentrop's fault, though he certainly played his part. The real job of political preparation had been left to the SS, working through the *Volksdeutsche Mittelstelle* and Heydrich's *Sicherheitsdienst*. Goering had a hand in it too. The worst bungling, however, was that of the group in Vienna entrusted with fomenting the Slovak and Ruthene separatists against the Czechs. This group comprised Artur Seyss-Inquart, who had been appointed Viceroy for Austria in reward for his role in its Anschluss, and Josef Bürckel, then Gauleiter of Vienna. Hitler's former troubleshooter in matters Austrian, the engineer Wilhelm Keppler, acted with them in their ham-handed interventions in Slovak affairs.

It is far from clear that Hitler had any other motive for occupying the Czech lands and declaring a protectorate over them than sheer bloody-mindedness at not having been able to have his war at Czechoslovakia's expense in September 1938. Even then, it is not at all clear at what point he decided to finish with the Czechs. The initial military orders for action against Czechoslovakia issued in October 1938[3] were entirely conditional, a preparation for action in case rump-Czechoslovakia pursued an anti-German policy. Hitler himself inclined at this stage to the idea of maintaining Czecho-Slovakia as one state.[4] It was Goering who saw advantages in separating the Slovak from the Czech parts, linking the idea with an air base in Slovakia for operations against the East.[5] He was supported by Karl-Hermann Frank, former leader of the extremist wing of the Sudeten Germans,[6] and the whole debate can well be seen as part of Goering's pressure for a far-reaching settlement with Poland, preparatory to a general drive eastwards. Hitler's plans matured more slowly. In mid-October he choked Goering off a bit while

Ribbentrop dealt with the Czech Foreign Minister.[7] Even when the military orders against Czechoslovakia were modified in December to provide for a peaceful occupation,[8] there is still no implication that this was an imminent operation or that Hitler had hardened against the Czechs.

Hitler's mind probably changed as he became more personally involved with the negotiations with Colonel Beck over a Polish settlement. When Beck came to Berchtesgaden in early January Ribbentrop hinted very heavily to him that Polish concessions over Danzig could be compensated at Slovakia's expense.[9] At the same time German subversive activity among the Ruthenians slackened off. On January 16, 1939 Hitler spoke his mind rather more clearly to Count Csáky, the Hungarian Foreign Minister, talking of a politico-territorial solution with Polish and Hungarian participation, a precisely timed operation with Poland, Hungary and Germany working together like a football team. Nothing could be done before March, he said.[10]

The problem Hitler faced was a complex one. After Munich, the Czechoslovak state transformed itself. In 1918 it had been formed as a union of five provinces of the old Austrian empire, the crownlands of the old Czech crown, Bohemia, Moravia and Silesia, being joined by the Slovaks, who had hitherto formed part of the Kingdom of Hungary, and the Ruthenes, a mixture of Slav and Ukrainian peasants in the east of what had been the Hapsburg province of Galicia. Pre-Munich Czechoslovakia was a state dominated by the Czechs as the largest and best educated of the three groups. For twenty years Czech officials assumed extensive, almost colonial-style responsibility for affairs in the Slovak and Ruthene provinces. They achieved much but antagonized many Slovaks by their zeal, their tactless assumption of superiority and their didactic manners. A strong Slovak autonomous movement centred around certain Catholic Slovak priests; a paramilitary wing, the so-called Hlinka Guards, sprang up, held at bay only by the satisfaction of the bulk of the Slovak population with the economic benefits of Czech dominance.

After Munich the Slovak political parties came together at Zilina on October 3. They were persuaded for the moment to accept the transformation of Czechoslovakia into a federation of three states, Bohemia-Moravia, Slovakia and Ruthenia. A five-man Cabinet under Monsignor Tiso, the leader of the pre-Munich autonomous movement, was set up in Bratislava. All parties were dissolved. The Hlinka Guards with their black tunic, breeches and boots, came to dominate the streets and the German minority were given a special office for German affairs under their leader, Franz Karmasin.

Ruthenia presented an even odder picture. Its population consisted of about half a million Ruthenian peasants, about a hundred thousand or more Hungarians and about ninety thousand Jews. The Hungarians lived in the southern plains, the Ruthenes in the comparatively infertile, heavily wooded north, on the southern flanks of the great Carpathian mountains. Before Munich there had been little political activity in the region. After Munich the inhabitants divided partly along religious lines, those who followed the Orthodox faith calling themselves the 'Ruthenian National Council', those who followed the Uniate Church calling themselves the 'Ukrainian National Council'. 'Ukrainians' looked to a great Ukrainian state uniting Czech Ruthenia with the Ukrainian minority-dominated provinces of southern Poland, 'Ruthenians' to autonomy or eventual union with the Russian Ukraine. On October 9 these two groups came together in a meeting at the small town of Uzhgorod and formed a six-man Ministry with three 'Ruthenes', two 'Ukrainians', and a neutral. Within a fortnight the three 'Ruthenians' had quarrelled with their colleagues. Brody, the Premier, was arrested, allegedly for being in Hungarian pay, and his colleagues fled to Hungary. A new three-man Cabinet, all 'Ukrainians', took office with Father Vološin, a Uniate priest, as Premier, and Julius Revay, a former Social Democrat Deputy, as his Foreign Minister. Almost immediately the Germans and Italians, meeting in Vienna, awarded all of the plains, including the only two towns, to Hungary. Ruthenia was left as a series of narrow valleys running into the Carpathians with only one road. The seat of government was shifted to the large village of Chust. In mid-November, as already related, Germany had to intervene to prevent a Hungarian annexation of all that remained of Ruthenia.

In the meantime, the central Government was also re-organized. On November 30 Dr Emil Hácha, a shy and retiring old man who had been President of the Czech Supreme Court, a man of great sense of duty, a scholar, deeply religious and totally unambitious for himself, became President. He appointed a new Cabinet headed by the tough-minded Czech, Dr Rudolf Beran, former leader of the Czech Agrarians, with the former Czech Ambassador in Rome, František Chvalkovský, as Foreign Minister, the piratical General Syrovy, hero of the Czech Legion's epic march across Siberia in 1918, one eye permanently covered with a black patch, as Minister for Defence, and the Slovak, Karol Sidor, head of the Hlinka Guards, as Deputy Premier.

Before the proper formation of the new Czechoslovak state the disruptive elements of the *Volksdeutsche Mittelstelle* (*VdM*) and the *Sicherheitsdienst* (*SD*) were already at work. SS Colonel Behrends of the *VdM* won in November the right to co-ordinate and control subversion in Ruthenia, which now renamed itself the Carpatho-Ukraine.[11] He had a lot to build on. Ever since the collapse of the independent Ukraine in 1918 at the hands of the Poles and the Red Army, Ukrainian refugees had been on the payroll of one or other clandestine German agency. The main centres of Ukrainian activity in 1938 were in Berlin where the German army financed the extremist Ukrainian terrorist organization, the OUM;[12] in Poland; and in Vienna, where the radio became a centre of Ukrainian propaganda. Russian NKVD agents had caught and assassinated the Ukrainian leader, Eugene Konovalets, in Rotterdam in 1938; but his organization was still open to use for espionage and subversive purposes. Now their main attention was centred on the Carpatho-Ukraine. A Ukrainian para-military organization, the Sič, was recruited from the more adventurous and ambitious of the young peasants, clothed in sky-blue uniform and given small arms training by the reluctant Czech regular troops in Ruthenia. Wilhelm Keppler signed a treaty for the monopoly exploitation of Ruthenia's natural resources.[13] A German Consulate was opened in Chust, and a highly unpleasant German journalist, Kleiss, was sent, ostensibly as correspondent of the *Völkischer Beobachter*, actually as an *SD* representative.[14]

The *SD* also had its finger in the Slovak pie. Money was made available to finance the travels of Dr Ďurčanský and other Slovak officials who wished to visit Germany.[15] But none of them could really be called the *SD*'s man in the sense of being responsive to German initiatives. Nor was it possible to look for an alternative while Hitler remained undecided as to what to do. The turning point in his thinking seems to have come after the Beck visit, whether as a means of satisfying the Poles by allowing the absorption of Ruthenia into Hungary and the formation of the common frontier between Poland and Hungary that both sides had so often asked for, whether as a means of scaring the Poles, or whether from sheer impatience is not clear. (It is also possible that the German economy needed the infusion of Czech currency reserves, and command of Czech heavy industry to step up the rate of German rearmament. Czech-made tanks were to play their part in the campaign in France in 1940.) What does seem to be clear is that there was nothing in the behaviour of the Czech Government which lent itself to a change in Hitler's policy. Indeed he was remarkably kind (for him) to the Czech Cabinet after the march into Prague, keeping its members in office for a time and then paying their pensions, which he would hardly have done if they had offended him.

Whatever his motives, he gave the go-ahead towards the end of

January. A warning reached the French early in February that German action against Prague would come in six weeks.[16] Walter Schellenberg of the *SD* was charged to plan internal disruption;[17] and looking around for disruptive elements in Slovakia, Goering hit on the figure of Professor Dr Voitech Tuka. This worthy gentleman and extreme Slovak nationalist had been tried and sentenced by the Czechs on charges of high treason and espionage in 1929 and only released in 1938, having lost his sight in prison. On February 9, the ubiquitous Herr Karmasin brought him to Berlin to meet Goering.[18] From Goering he went on to Hitler and Ribbentrop. He was treated to the usual harangue, full of dark threats and forebodings, but in essence Hitler's message was perfectly clear. He was about to deal with the Czechs. If Slovakia chose to cleave to the Czechs then he would leave her to be shared between Poland and Hungary. If she chose to declare her independence then he would protect her.[19] Tuka retired to Slovakia. This heavily built old bore with his large aquiline nose and prissy smile was not the man the Germans wanted. He had little or no political sense and no organizing ability whatever. Moreover, he could no more keep a secret than fly. The steady flow of German visitors to his house, whom he received without any limits either of discretion or prudence, served one purpose only, to alarm the Czechs in Prague. Within a fortnight the German Consul in Bratislava was reporting that he was politically dead with very few followers. Moreover he was complacently satisfied with the current Slovak Government.[20] This was not the view of the Vienna radio agitators,[21] but it was to be proven correct.

The Germans turned to other Slovak Ministers: Truchinsky, the Minister of Trade; and Pruzinsky, the Minister of Economics, who saw Goering.[22] Their ablest contact was undoubtedly the young Slovak propaganda chief, Alexander Mach. But they were to have a very hard time getting any Slovak to act as they wanted. It was fortunate therefore that weak nerves in Prague were to do their work for them.

On January 21, 1939 the Slovak Government had presented its programme to the Slovak Assembly.[23] It said nothing of the Czechoslovak state, much of 'our state, our new state, our Slovak state'. The central Czech Government was greatly alarmed by three things: by this, by the German efforts to subvert the radical nationalist Slovaks, and by the propaganda for complete Slovak independence from Czechoslovakia put out by Mach and others.[24] On March 1 they confronted three Slovak representatives, Karol Sidor and two others, to discuss Slovak requests on the division of revenue and the introduction of more Slovak officers and soldiers into the Czechoslovak units stationed in Slovakia.[25] Premier Beran insisted on exacting from the

Slovak Cabinet a statement of loyalty to the Czechoslovak state as an essential preliminary to any discussion of details. Dr Chvalkovský, the Foreign Minister, said that the Czechs would do nothing to hinder a proclamation of independence by the Slovaks. But they could not have it both ways: either the Slovaks were part of the Czechoslovak state or they were not. Foreign diplomatists were prophesying the breakup of Czechoslovakia in a matter of weeks or, at best, months. Czechoslovakia was simply becoming an object not a subject in international politics. As Sidor refused all undertakings, saying that the Slovaks stuck fast to the constitutional grant of autonomy to them, Beran, the next day, formally demanded an official Slovak statement in favour of the Czechoslovak state, the dismissal of Mach, and an abandonment of the Slovak military requests.

On March 6 the Slovak Cabinet meeting with the President of the Slovak Assembly and the Party Chairman decided to insist on the proper application of the constitutional law granting Slovak autonomy.[26] Sidor was instructed to reject the Czech demands. This was enough. From Vienna the advocates of a disruption of Czechoslovakia scented the kill. The following day Artur Seyss-Inquart descended on Tiso and Sidor from Vienna.[27] What would the Slovaks do, he demanded, if Hitler intervened against the Czechs? Tiso replied: We are decided to move towards the independence of Slovakia at our own pace. Seyss-Inquart replied that it was often necessary to jump rather than to go at a reasoned pace. Tiso, that massive-shouldered priest, remained adamant, however.

The rumours continued to fly. The Prague Government, apparently believing that a Slovak declaration of independence was imminent, decided to act to forestall it. As over-heated Hlinka Guards demonstrated, there was a small-scale riot in Bratislava. Dr Chvalkovský had apparently formed the view, from a meeting with the German Chargé d'affaires in Prague, that the Slovaks were acting without German support. When Sidor returned to Prague to meet the Czechoslovak Cabinet, of which he was a member, the Czechs acted. Once Sidor had refused either to confirm or deny the rumours of a Slovak declaration of independence, Beran lured him outside the Cabinet room and had him arrested. At the same time the Czechoslovak police in Bratislava occupied the Slovak Government offices and arrested some two to three hundred prominent Slovak personalities, mainly from the Hlinka Guards, including Mach and Tuka, and deported them into Bohemia. At midnight President Hácha published a decree dissolving the Tiso Cabinet and appointing the moderate Jan Sivak, Minister of Education in Tiso's Cabinet, as the new Premier. Czech troops then moved into

Slovakia in more strength. Sidor protested so bitterly at his arrest that the Czechs freed him and allowed him to return to Bratislava.[28]

The next day, March 10, passed quietly, apart from a few demonstrations by small groups of Hlinka Guards whom the Czechs wisely left alone.[29] In the evening the deposed Tiso Cabinet met together with Sidor in the Jesuit presbytery in Bratislava to which Tiso was confined by the Czechs. Under Sidor's advice and in the hope of offering the Czechs a way off the hook on which they had impaled themselves, those assembled decided to offer the Czechs two alternatives, either a new Tiso cabinet or one under Sidor. The unfortunate Mr Sivak, the Czech nominee, had been caught by the crisis at Rome, attending the coronation of the new Pope, Pius XII. Early on the morning of March 11, President Hácha accepted a new Cabinet under Carol Sidor.[30]

In the meantime the Germans were busy organizing their version of events. On the evening of March 10, members of the German minority demonstrated their solidarity with the dismissed Cabinet.[31] Dr Ďurčanský, the SD-subsidized Minister, had fled to Vienna in a car provided by the German Consul in Bratislava. That night he broadcast on Vienna radio, urging the Hlinka Guards to fight the Czechs and saying that they could rely on German support.[32] In Slovakia his efforts were countered by Sidor, who stated that the crisis had been cleared up and, as Commander of the Hlinka Guards, ordered them to obey his authority.[33]

The following morning the German orchestration came out strongly in support of the downtrodden Slovaks. 'Return to the old Czech methods', 'Prague is terrorizing Slovakia' ran the headlines in the *Völkischer Beobachter*.[34] All the German press announced that Tiso had appealed to Germany for help and declared that Germany still recognized the legitimacy of his Government. Unfortunately no such appeal had as yet been issued. It was now for the SD and the Vienna cabal to organize this appeal.

This was to prove very difficult. Tiso left Bratislava for his canon's post at Banovce, remarking as he left, 'Now I can have a little peace. I do not want to be the Seyss-Inquart of my nation.'[35] He had already refused to issue an appeal to Hitler when SD emissaries pressed this on him.[36] The Germans alleged that he had authorized Ďurčanský to act for him and gave circulation to a telegram sent in his name from Vienna appealing for German intervention.[37] But their own subsequent behaviour shows this to be false. On the night of March 11/12 at 3 in the morning. Seyss-Inquart, Bürckel and Keppler, flown in from Berlin to Vienna, and then taken by car to the Slovak border to find out what was going wrong, descended on Bratislava to interview Sidor. It was a long, cold car drive they had, and they had warmed themselves liberally with schnapps on the way.[38] Monumentally calm in the face of this intrusion, Sidor explained that the Slovak National Party had decided not to proclaim independence suddenly. The drunken Bürckel demanded that Sidor immediately proclaim Slovak independence on the somewhat curious ground that Hitler had already been informed that he had made such a proclamation, and the Führer must not be embarrassed or deceived; Sidor stuck to his guns and Keppler and the others returned disconsolate to Vienna.

On March 12 nevertheless Hitler decided to go ahead.[39] The OKW (Supreme Command of the Armed Forces) drafted conditions for an ultimatum.[40] The Hungarians were informed that Germany had withdrawn her protection from Ruthenia.[41] And the astute observer of the German press could notice a marked change in German propaganda against the Czechs. No longer were the sufferings of the Slovaks alleged. Instead the theme was the 'sufferings' of the German minority at the hands of the brutal and barbaric Czechs.

That evening Keppler made one last effort. The exhausted Tiso was got out of his canonical bed at Banovce by two German officials. He was to go at once with them to Vienna, and then fly to Berlin as Hitler's guest. Tiso sent them away, protesting that he had had no sleep for three nights.[42] When the German Consul intervened to guarantee the authenticity of the invitation, Tiso decided.[43] Instead of heading for Berlin he returned to Bratislava to consult Sidor, his successor. The new Slovak Cabinet, augmented once again by the Speaker of the Slovak Assembly and the Party Chairman, decided to send Tiso to Berlin to discover what was in Hitler's mind and to report back.[44] 'Not as a fugitive imploring Hitler's help but as a legitimate envoy of a legitimate Cabinet,'[45] Tiso then left for Berlin.

It was of little avail. Hitler was at his most truculent.[46] He was going to settle with the Czechs. What would the Slovaks do? They could choose independence now and Germany would guarantee their security, or they could stay with the Czechs; in which case Hitler washed his hands of them. He would abandon them to their destiny, probably to occupation by Poland and Hungary. He wanted a decision at once – *Blitzschnell!* At the crucial moment Ribbentrop handed Hitler a 'message' to the effect that Hungarian troops were moving towards the Slovakian borders. This was certainly a lie. Tiso remained unmoved, solid, bull-like. He said very little, simply that he would have to have time to consult. He phoned Bratislava to arrange for the Slovak Assembly to meet the next day. Hitler then left him to Ribbentrop, who pressed him to broadcast a statement of Slovak independence for which

Ribbentrop had thoughtfully prepared a text. Nor was this the end of Ribbentrop's forethought. He also presented Tiso with a telegram, drafted by Keppler, which Tiso was to send to Hitler, inviting the Führer to 'protect' Slovakia's frontiers. Tiso at once smelt a rat. 'Protect' to him meant legal protection, that Slovakia would be a German protectorate. Even the *SD*-subsidized Ďurčanský backed him in resisting this demand. They argued with Ribbentrop until past 1 in the morning, then left to return to Bratislava. But they did not sign the telegram nor approve its dispatch.

Tiso nevertheless knew when the cards were stacked too heavily against him. At 9 a.m. the following morning, March 14, he met the Sidor Cabinet and explained what had happened. At 11 he met the Slovak Assembly.[47] Sidor announced the resignation of his Cabinet. Drily and with irony Tiso explained the nature of the choice with which Hitler had faced them. He made no recommendations or proposals. This was left to Martin Sokol, Speaker of the Assembly, who put the vote on a declaration of independence to the Assembly. 'All in favour, rise to their feet.' All present, fifty-seven of the sixty-three members of the Assembly, rose to their feet. Sokol declared, 'I confirm that the Assembly of the Slovakian region, as the sole organ competent to express the political will of the Slovak nation, is decided on the proclamation of an independent Slovak state.' It was just after midday.

Monsignor Tiso was now entrusted with the formation of a new Cabinet. Ďurčanský became Minister of Foreign Affairs. Messages were at once sent off to all states announcing that Slovakia had proclaimed its independence.[48] That to Hitler remarked pointedly that Slovakia was sure that Hitler would always protect and guarantee the victorious principle of national independence.[49] Another message, passed through the German Consul in Bratislava, conveyed the Assembly's views that Slovakia could defend its own frontiers.[50]

This was rank mutiny. That same day elements of the German naval flotilla on the Danube appeared off Bratislava and trained their guns on the offices of the Slovak Government. The following day urgent instructions were sent to Vienna.[51] Ďurčanský and Tuka were to draft a new telegram to the Führer asking for his recognition of Slovakia. The telegram had to include the word 'protection' (*Schutz*), which the Slovaks wished to avoid at all costs. Tiso hit on a formula calling on Hitler to guarantee the protection of Slovakia's political independence and territorial integrity; to no avail. Hitler's reply, of March 16, bore no relationship to Tiso's message. The definition of 'protection' that Tiso had inserted was simply omitted.[52]

What was happening in the meantime to the Czechs and the

Ruthenes? Since its constitution in December 1938, the Czech Cabinet had been leaning over backwards to convince Hitler of its good will. It had great hopes of a German guarantee. But when Chvalkovský went to see Hitler and Ribbentrop on January 21 he found himself confronted with a long list of grievances.[53] Hitler was lofty, aloof, and spoke 'more in sorrow than in anger'. How extraordinary that Czech opinion still had not adapted itself to realities, and was still hoping for a miraculous turn in European politics. The followers of Dr Beneš were still grasping at straws, failing to realize the overwhelming strength of Germany, and the weakness and indifference to what happened in Czechoslovakia of the Western powers. Czechoslovakia was still full of Jews, its offices still full of Beneš followers. Why did it still maintain an army of 120,000 men? Why was the Czech press filled with hostile articles (he produced two examples)?

Ribbentrop aped Hitler's style.[54] But it was his role to produce more specific charges. Where Hitler had spoken with aloof contempt, Ribbentrop was vindictive. Sinister symptoms were becoming apparent. He demanded action to redress them.

Chvalkovský returned to Prague, however, with one inexplicable illusion.[55] If the Czech Government 'set its house in order' as Hitler had demanded, then Germany would guarantee the new Czech state. The Czech Cabinet fell over itself to comply. General Franco's Government in Spain was recognized at once *de jure*. The journal of the Czech Legion was suppressed. The trades unions were dissolved and the co-operative societies followed them. A series of senior officials, including General Krejci, the Chief of Staff, were dismissed. The Germans remaining on Czech territory were lauded and appeased, and the Nazi party legitimized. The defence budget was cut by one-third. A series of anti-Jewish measures were introduced. Part of the Czech gold reserves were surrendered to the Reichsbank. All in vain. Dr Chvalkovský hoped in return to extract from Germany approval for a Czech declaration of neutrality. On February 22 he approached the French and British Governments as well as the German with a proposal along these lines.[56] He repeated the approach on March 1, sending a special emissary to Berlin for the purpose.[57] Ribbentrop showed the minute on the conversation to Hitler who said he was 'not interested'. Czechoslovakia had to go. The only question was how and when.

To arrange this was supposed to be the task of Messrs Keppler, Bürckel and Seyss-Inquart, who were working on the Slovaks. As we have seen, their efforts nearly foundered on Slovak obstinacy. Hitler had to intervene in the crudest possible manner to induce Monsignor Tiso to get the Slovak Cabinet and Assembly to claim independence.

The German press campaign against the Czechs was not unleashed until March 12, a Sunday. The incidents they seized on had in most cases been provoked. In Brno German students were roused to create trouble and a German troop marched through the streets singing battle songs. They had a difficult task. A German representative even complained to the German Chargé in Prague of the 'perfectly correct, even accommodating, attitude of the Czechs'.[58] A *VdM* representative the following day, returning from a tour of Brno, Olomouc and Jihlova, reported 'very great difficulty in rousing feeling among Czechs. . . . more violent action required to create serious incidents.'[59] On March 13, two German students had their ears boxed in Prague. German Nazi anti-Jewish demonstrators were actually supported by anti-Jewish Czech organizations.[60] Out of this the German press and radio made tortures, beatings, massacres. A pregnant woman had been kicked and trampled on. Blood was flowing in torrents. Czech troops were bayonetting Germans; and this on the day they were peacefully celebrating War Heroes Day. Czech mobs were 'giving full vent' to their passions.[61]

German troops had begun to move towards the frontier on the evening of March 11, from garrisons in central Germany. They were presumably still operating on the assumption that a Slovak declaration of independence would be forthcoming on demand, on March 12, which being a Sunday would have the advantage of catching the world's statesmen away from their offices. It was not, however, until the morning of March 14 that a declaration of independence could be obtained from Bratislava, and even then it was not accompanied by the appeal for German help and protection Ribbentrop had so carefully drafted. On March 13 Ribbentrop ordered the German Legation in Prague to have no more contact with the Czech authorities.[62] Hencke, the Chargé d'affaires, had in fact already seen Dr Chvalkovský once that day and had arranged to go to the Hradcany Palace to see President Hácha that evening.[63] Instead Chvalkovský telephoned his message. President Hácha would like to come to Berlin to see Hitler. Hencke insisted on having this in writing. The request duly arrived, at 11.25 a.m. on March 14.[64]

Hácha was old and sick. He could not fly. Instead he left Prague by special train at 4 in the afternoon, with Chvalkovský, his secretary Dr Pavelka, and his daughter. He arrived at the Anhalt railway station in Berlin at 9 p.m., where he was received with full military honours by the pompous figure of Otto Meissner, senior civil servant in the Presidential Chancellery since the 1920s;[65] he had to scramble through heavy snow to inspect the guard of honour. Then Meissner conducted him to the Hotel Adlon. Chvalkovský called on Ribbentrop, who then called himself at the Adlon to present Hácha's daughter with a bouquet of flowers. This courtesy, paid to the head of a state they were about to blot out, hid yet another minor blunder. Hitler was furiously angry because Hácha's train was an hour late. As a result Hitler kept him waiting until 1.15 a.m. on Wednesday, March 15.

The course of the meeting followed the classic pattern of such meetings.[66] Hácha was made to sit on one of the deep leather-cushioned chairs at the great round table where Tiso had sat thirty hours previously. But Hácha was no Tiso. He had neither his strength, nor his youth, nor his support. He could do nothing but appeal to what might laughingly be called Hitler's better nature. He knew already that German troops had crossed into Czechoslovakia in force. He was an old, sick man. He had never wanted to become President. He had accepted in the very vain, the microscopically tenuous hope that he could prevent the worst happening to his beloved country, which he had served all his life, honestly and with little or no personal reward. He had lived with the fear of German intervention, as a matter of high probability, for five months. For the last four days it must have struck him as a virtual certainty. He had had five long hours on the train and another four at the Adlon to prepare what he had to say, to crawl, to eat crow, to sacrifice virtually the only possession still left to him, his personal integrity and dignity, in the hope of staying Hitler's hand. He would crawl, he would flatter, he would take whatever lies and insults Hitler chose to give him if in any way he could preserve a modicum of Czech independence. He did all of this before an audience consisting not only of Hitler and Ribbentrop, but also Goering, General Keitel, State Secretary von Weizsäcker, Meissner, Hitler's Press Chief Otto Dietrich, Schmidt the interpreter, and the secretary, Walter Hewel. His only support was Chvalkovský.

Hitler heard his pathetic speech out. Then he launched into one of his special tirades, egotistical, self-laudatory, full of wonder at his own beneficent restraint, reproachful, but definite. At 6 o'clock that morning the German army would march. There was one German division, he was almost ashamed to say, for every Czech battalion. No one would support the Czechs abroad. 'The Moor has done his duty, the Moor can go' would be their attitude. Hácha had four hours in which to arrange things so that the Czechs offered no resistance. If there was any resistance Czechoslovakia would be annihilated. Hitler then told the two Czechs, who had sat through his harangues in shocked silence, to withdraw. They left with all the other Germans, led by Goering, Ribbentrop and Keitel. He would be sorry to have to bomb Prague, that beautiful city, said Goering (conveniently forgetting its fifty thousand German inhabitants and Hitler's own claims that it had been a German city for a thousand years), but it would be a salutary warning to Britain and France. At this Hácha fainted, or had a minor heart attack, and had to be revived by Hitler's personal physician Dr Theodor Morell, who gave him an injection. Shortly after Hitler had left them, Hácha and Chvalkovský telephoned Prague to urge there should be no resistance. But it took an hour and a half longer before Goering and Ribbentrop, bullying the two Czechs round and round the table on which the text of the agreement had been lying since they entered the room, and thrusting pens into their hands, could finally overcome their resistance. Finally the two Czechs gave in. They were ushered back into Hitler's presence, in a state of collapse, and the agreement was signed.[67] Hácha 'confidently placed the fate of the Czech people and country' (so the document states) in the hands of the Führer. It was 4 in the morning. Chvalkovský said, as they left the Chancellery, 'Our people will curse us, but we have saved their existence. We have preserved them from a horrible massacre.' As the Czechs left, Hitler burst into the room where his Private Secretaries sat, wan and tired but ready lest they be needed for more declarations. He pulled them to their feet and kissed them soundly. 'Children,' he said, 'this is the greatest day of my life. I shall enter history as the greatest German of them all.'[68]

The Czechs were to face six long years of occupation. They still had an easier time than the unfortunate Ruthenians. Since November 1938 the Ruthenian Provincial Government had consisted virtually of two men: Father Vološin, the short-sighted, slightly truculent Uniate priest who was Prime Minister, and Julius Revay, a thirty-two-year-old ex-schoolmaster and Deputy in the Czech Parliament. On January 16, 1939, the Czech Government appointed a third member, General Lev Prchala, a Czech who had once commanded the garrison in the Carpatho-Ukraine. This tactless reminder of the days when the Carpatho-Ukraine had been the most neglected province in Czechoslovakia was made worse by the fact that Prchala's wife was a Russian. As a result, when Prchala arrived in Chust he was completely boycotted, and very soon left again for Prague.

In practice the Carpatho-Ukraine was run by the Czech garrison, who represented the only real check on the extreme Ukrainian nationalists, by the Sič, and by the small handful of people around Vološin, who included two Germans, Kleiss, the *SD* agent masquerading as the *Völkischer Beobachter* correspondent, and the German State Secretary, Oldofredi, a Sudeten German from Eger sent by the *VdM* to make the local German minority 'conscious of their destiny'. Authority was limited, the Sič leaders behaved like local feudal barons, recruits poured in from the Polish Ukrainian minority and money came in part from Germany, in part from the Ukrainian communities in Canada and the United States. In February elections were held, though their 'freedom' was farcical. The Ruthenian Government did its best to persuade the Czechs to allot them more funds at the same time as the Slovak Government was negotiating on the same issue in Prague. And when the Czechs ran out of confidence in the Slovak Government, they also acted in Ruthenia.

On March 6 the Czechs announced that Julius Revay and his brother Fedor, the President, had been dismissed.[69] Prchala's troops occupied the Sič barracks and confiscated what arms they could find. But the action was pointless and too late. Father Vološin refused to have the Sič suppressed. Julius Revay was popularly believed to have taken refuge in Berlin, where the Germans would soon restore him to power. But Hitler had decided to make an end of the Carpatho-Ukraine. Revay found Berlin cold and unresponsive and soon left for Vienna.[70] Kleiss was recalled and with him the SD's separate Ukrainian policy disappears from the scene.[71] On March 12, in the evening, Hitler summoned the Hungarian Minister in Berlin, Count Sztójay. He advised him that Germany was about to smash Czechoslovakia and would withdraw her protection from Ruthenia. He suggested the Hungarian Government should act quickly as others, the Poles for example, no doubt had their eyes on the country. He suggested Hungary should content herself with Ruthenia. The time for Slovakia would always come later. Sztójay was to take this message personally to Horthy.[72] The message was delivered the following day, March 13. Horthy was delighted and sent Hitler a fulsome telegram of gratitude.[73] Only four days earlier on March 9, Sztójay had again been told by Ribbentrop to be patient.[74] The Hungarian Chief of Staff had to be told in no uncertain terms that if he did not act immediately there was no point.[75] Hungarian troops in fact crossed the frontier in strength on the morning of March 14; the ultimatum announcing this was not given to the Czech Minister in Budapest until noon the same day.[76]

Things had already begun to happen in Chust on Monday, March 13. Vološin ordered the Czech gendarmerie to hand their arms over to the Sič. On March 14 General Prchala re-asserted his authority, and rounded up and disarmed the Sič. He then proposed to resist the Hungarians. But the news of the Slovakian declaration of independence determined Vološin to follow suit. He proclaimed Ruthenian independence to a small and unenthusiastic crowd outside the government building in Chust, appointed Revay his Foreign Minister, and appealed to Germany to take the new state under its protection. On the morning of March 15 the Hungarian invasion began in earnest. The Czech troops pulled out before the Hungarians came. Chust was left to the nationalist enthusiasm of the Sič, and to the advancing Hungarians. The Sič, illiterate peasant boys, brilliantly visible in their sky-blue uniforms against the drab greens and browns of the Carpathian foothills in March, fought bravely but in vain. Several hundred were killed; a large number escaped into Slovakia, finding eventual refuge in German labour camps. Julius Revay escaped to Vienna, Father Vološin to Romania and eventually to Yugoslavia. All appeals to Berlin were rejected, and the Ruthenians had to settle down to be Hungarians. The Carpatho-Ukraine was no more.[77]

Hitler's next move came even faster. At Versailles Germany had been forced to renounce sovereignty over the old German seaport of the Memel. Since 1924 its largely German population had enjoyed autonomy under a League of Nations statute, with a directorate whose President was appointed by a Lithuanian governor. In 1935 the Lithuanians had moved to stamp out the growth of Nazism in the Memel in a way which did more credit to their fear of Germany than their respect for justice. Thereafter Lithuania's main quarrels were with Poland. In March 1938 the German army had prepared plans for the immediate occupation of the Memel in the event of a Polish-Lithuanian war. These plans had been re-affirmed in October 1938.[78]

German hopes of a Lithuanian-Polish conflict were in fact in vain. In the aftermath of Munich the Lithuanian Government began to do its best to mend its fences with Germany. Martial law, which had reigned since 1926, was ended on October 29. Directed by the *Volksdeutsche Mittelstelle*, the Nazi organization in the Memel began to clamour for union with Germany. The Polish-Soviet agreement of November 26, and the overriding importance to Hitler of an agreement with Poland, caused the Führer on December 3 to order the Memel Germans to behave themselves for the time being.[79] Early in February Gauleiter Koch of East Prussia intervened very forcibly. The leader of the Memel Germans, Dr Neumann, was summoned to Königsberg, together with the head of the Gestapo office, and told, on the Führer's instructions, that they would be shot if they did not obey orders and avoid any conflict with the Lithuanian Government.[80] There followed a brief and bitter battle of wills and Koch was forced to withdraw. Neumann was instructed to make a statement to the Memel Assembly calling for a fundamental change.[81] On March 20 it was the turn of the Lithuanian Foreign Minister, Joseph Urbšys, to sit where Tiso and Hácha had sat and receive the same treatment.[82] Plenipotentiaries should be sent at once, said Ribbentrop, to reach an agreement on the Memel. Pleni-potentiaries duly arrived on March 22, after the Lithuanians, under threat of the air bombardment of their capital, had withdrawn a public communiqué revealing the pressure that had been brought to bear on them.[83] The German-Lithuanian Agreement transferring the Memel to Germany was signed at 1.30 a.m. on March 23.[84] Hitler entered the Memel by sea, on board the pocket battleship *Deutschland*. The sea was very rough, and it was a very sick Führer who landed at the quayside in bitterly cold weather to take possession of this, Germany's newest gain.[85]

The German moves into Memel and into Bohemia and the estab-lishment of Slovakia as a virtual German protectorate extended German power significantly along the northern and southern frontiers of Poland. It was greeted by Polish opinion with alarm and disgust. Attacks on the policy of maintaining good relations with Germany, on Colonel Beck and on Józef Lipski, the Ambassador in Berlin, broke out into the open.[86] Beck and Szembek were heckled in the Polish parlia-ment and the police made various arrests among Polish opposition journalists and others. Polish opinion had already been much incensed by incidents in Danzig between German and Polish students. After incidents at the Café Langfuhr, a favourite haunt of students of the Danzig Polytechnic, German students had, early in February, placed a notice at the café door: 'To dogs and Polish students entrance is forbidden. Poor dogs!' Anti-German demonstrations had followed in various Polish university towns, and in Warsaw on February 25 a group of Polish students had demonstrated outside the German Embassy and a thrown stone had broken an Embassy window pane.[87]

Colonel Beck had done his utmost to counteract these demon-strations. The Chef de Protocole apologized to Ambassador von Moltke, and Lipski did his best to assuage Ribbentrop, Hitler and Goering on February 28[88] and on March 1.[89] The Germans were, in part at least, impelled to this by reports of British-Polish contacts and of Beck's forthcoming visit to Britain. Goering was particularly cordial.

It was therefore to Goering that Lipski turned on March 17 when the Slovak-German treaty was announced. Goering did his best to calm Lipski down but in vain.[90] Lipski, usually so strong and courageous, had an attack of the blackest pessimism, played on and added to by two conversations with Robert Coulondre, his French colleague in Berlin,[91] who was convinced that no real obstacles could now be put in the way of Hitler's expansionism. The techniques employed against President Hácha of threatening massacre from the air of the cities of those who opposed him struck Coulondre as impossible for the minor states of

Eastern Europe and the Balkans to resist. He could see nothing that France and Britain could do, in the current state of their armaments, to stop this process. Lipski saw his life's work in maintaining German-Polish relations called into question. On March 19 he left for Warsaw to tender his resignation.[92]

His resignation was not accepted; the same day he was telephoned from Berlin. Ribbentrop was waiting to see him at once. The interview, two days later, did nothing to calm Lipski's anxieties.[93] Ribbentrop was reproachful at Polish anxieties, still more over the manifestations of Polish opinion. The Führer was 'increasingly amazed' at the Polish attitude. The German press could not be restrained much longer; in plain English, Germany would start a press war. The Führer would welcome an early visit to Berlin by Colonel Beck. Germany had played its part in creating Poland. If Germany had pursued a different policy with Russia, Poland would never have come into existence. He repeated the Danzig and Corridor proposals which Lipski and Beck had opposed so firmly since Lipski's visit to Berchtesgaden the previous October and dangled the bait of Polish participation in the management and exploitation of Slovakia and the Ukraine.

Still more depressed, if not momentarily unmanned, Lipski returned to Warsaw.[94] On March 23 Marshal Smigly-Rydz issued military orders for the protection of frontiers in the east and in the west. About ten thousand reservists and a number of specialists were recalled to the colours so that the frontier units were at full strength.[95] The following day Beck held a conference of the senior officials in the Polish Foreign Ministry.[96] He had already come to one decision. On March 22, he had sent instructions to the Polish Ambassador in London, Count Raczyński, to propose a confidential bilateral agreement with the British.[97] The proposal was made the same day as he explained his view of the situation to his senior officials.[98]

Colonel Beck had clearly been shaken. His rather simplistic view of Poland's position between Germany and the Soviet Union rested on the belief that the behaviour of each of his two neighbours was clearly rational and predictable. Now he admitted that he had been wrong about Germany. He believed that the German leaders had lost their sense of realities, simply because no one had stood up to them. The mighty had shown themselves humble, the weak had capitulated. But if they now encountered determined opposition, the German leaders would recover their sense of balance. Germany had been marching across Europe with a mere nine divisions. No one could overwhelm Poland with this kind of force. All the trumps were really in Poland's hands.

On Danzig and the Corridor the position was quite clear. There was a definite set of limits, a line beyond which Poland's direct interests were involved. Poland could not accept any attempt to impose a unilateral solution of Danzig's problems upon her. Nor could she accept any threats to her own territory. This was the Polish *non possumus*. Beyond this line Poland would fight. Poland was not going to join that category of East European states that allowed the rules of the game to be dictated to them. It was wiser to go forward to meet the enemy rather than to wait for him to attack. Within this line, a normal policy could be conducted. The question in Beck's mind was whether a direct collision could be avoided.

Ribbentrop had already drafted a set of instructions to his Ambassador in Warsaw,[99] which, had they been sent, would have made it clear that a head-on collision was inevitable. Moltke was to make it clear that Hitler wanted the Danzig issue settled as soon as possible. In return Poland was to be given her head in relation to the Ukraine and to be offered as well a partition of Slovakia with Germany and Hungary. Beck was to be invited to come as soon as possible to Berlin to discuss this. If the Poles rejected the offer, it would be withdrawn at once and Poland would be considered as an enemy. This went a little too far for Hitler. On March 25, he said he did not want to solve the Danzig question by force as this would drive Poland into the arms of Britain.[100]

But there was to be no escape. Beck's instructions to Lipski left no way out.[101] The German proposals were simply ignored. In their place, Beck offered a joint German-Polish guarantee of Danzig, and far-reaching concessions on transport across the Corridor. But before Lipski had even reached Berlin, reports of Polish mobilization, and the strengthening of the Polish garrison in the Corridor and at Gdynia, had reached Ribbentrop.[102] State Secretary Weizsäcker suggested a warning to the Poles not to let things develop so that Germany was confronted with a public demonstration of Polish strength likely both to face her with open humiliation and to stir Hitler into a decision to avenge this by destroying Poland.[103] Ribbentrop as usual mishandled things.

March 26 was the vital day. Lipski presented himself at 12.30.[104] Ribbentrop had only three basic styles of diplomatic conversation, all modelled on his master. There was the angry 'Germany will no longer endure this' style. There was the style of cold *de haut en bas*, hauteur and arrogance as befitted a champagne salesman with a 'von' to his name. And there was the frankly smarmy and ingratiating. On March 26 he varied between the first and the second. Lipski began by handing over a written memorandum, which followed Beck's instructions very closely. Ribbentrop read it, with dawning realization that his whole

Polish policy was in ruins. His coldness disappeared immediately, to be replaced with anger. On March 21 he had offered a wide measure of agreement. Now Poland was replying by military measures. It reminded him of the Czechs. Any Polish aggression against Danzig, he stormed, would be treated as aggression against Germany.

In saying this Ribbentrop was going a long way further than Hitler had authorized him to go. Moreover, he knew that General Keitel of the OKW did not believe the Poles were planning to attack Danzig, though there were officers in the Army General Staff who disagreed with Keitel. Indeed Ribbentrop told Hitler that he did not believe Poland had any plans to intervene by force in Danzig. He was also, clearly, trying to do what Weizsäcker suggested, to give the Poles a warning. He succeeded only in sounding like a bully, and his reference to the Czechs, in view of Beck's view (which was shared by all of Polish opinion) that it had to be made clear to the Germans that the Poles were not Czechs and were not to be treated or considered as Czechs, was singularly unfortunate. Lipski for once was provoked into some very plain speaking about Poland's commitment to her own independence.

Ribbentrop's own recommendations to Hitler make it clear that he had no idea what he had done with his threats over Danzig. They include the gradual escalation of German press attacks on Poland; a second interview with Lipski, at which he should be told that the Polish proposals were unacceptable; and, should the Polish military measures not be scaled down after a certain interval, a warning to Lipski that such measures could well escalate and 'end badly'. In accordance with this view the Nazi leadership in Danzig were told to do nothing to provoke the Poles. Ribbentrop said he thought the present crisis had already reached its climax.[105]

Polish opinion was, however, in a very excitable state. There were wild rumours that Beck had been kidnapped and carried off to Germany. There were anti-German riots in a number of provincial towns. At Linicno, the local Nazi party had its meeting broken up by Poles who sacked their headquarters and tore up a portrait of Hitler and a German flag.[106] Ribbentrop protested one set of incidents to Lipski on March 27.[107] But the Polish press was full of bellicose language; the gist of the German proposals was steadily leaking out, despite Beck's attempts to smother it. Under the circumstances Beck could not possibly have left Ribbentrop's remarks about Danzig unanswered. On the evening of March 28, having read and digested Lipski's report of his interviews with Ribbentrop, he summoned the unhappy von Moltke before him.[108] Ribbentrop's comment that Germany would regard a Polish coup against Danzig as an attack on Germany to be answered by war left him no option, Beck said, but to state in turn that if Germany attempted to alter the status of Danzig unilaterally, or if the Danzig Senate made a similar attempt, Poland would regard this as a *casus belli*, an occasion to warrant a Polish declaration of war against Germany. Ribbentrop's angry incompetence, and that national pride which kept Poland alive through 150 years of partition, had drawn the lines for the second great European war. And this, much more than the first, would engulf the whole world in its progress.

CHAPTER 10

CHAMBERLAIN CHOOSES CONTAINMENT

On the evening of March 9, 1939, the day the Czech Cabinet moved against the Slovaks and six days before Hitler entered Prague, Neville Chamberlain summoned the lobby correspondents, the members of the British press responsible for parliamentary reporting, to give them an off-the-record briefing. He spoke of an upturn in relations between France and Italy, of great things to be hoped for from a forthcoming visit to Berlin by a Cabinet Minister, Oliver Stanley, to discuss Anglo-German trade, and of the possibility that a disarmament conference might meet before the end of the year. In a word, he was euphoric.[1] Journalists and some Cabinet colleagues took him at his word. *The Times* and the *Daily Telegraph* carried optimistic, forward-looking leading articles the following day. Sir Bernard Partridge, the mild but patriotic political cartoonist of *Punch*, whose amply bosomed Britannias and broadchested John Bulls had epitomized the upbeat side of the British establishment view of life for years, drew a cartoon headed 'The Ides of March' which showed John Bull awakening on March 15, a ghostly nightmare labelled 'War Scare' fleeing out of the open window. 'Thank goodness that's over', his John Bull said, the wall calendar showing March 15 (presumably John Bull had changed the date before going to bed the night before). A footnote explained the point for the less 'in-touch' among *Punch*'s readership: 'Pessimists predicted another "major crisis" in the middle of this month.'

Worse hit than poor Sir Bernard, who must have drawn the cartoon on March 9 or 10 at the latest, was Sir Samuel Hoare, the Home Secretary. Due to make his annual appearance before his Chelsea constituency party on March 10, he enquired of Chamberlain what he should say.[2] 'Do what you can to discourage the view that war is inevitable,' replied the Prime Minister. Hoare took him at his word. 'Suppose,' he said on March 10, 'that political confidence could be

162

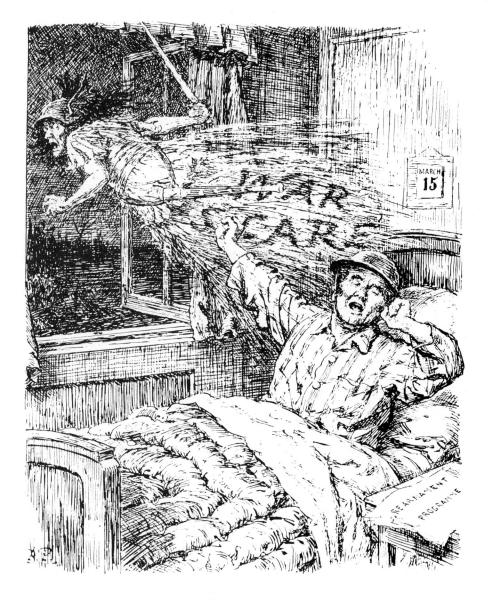

THE IDES OF MARCH

John Bull. "Thank goodness that's over!"

[Pessimists predicted "another major crisis" in the middle of this month.]

restored in Europe . . . suppose that the peoples of Europe were able to free themselves from the nightmare that haunts them, and from an expenditure on armaments that beggars them, could we not then devote the inventions and discoveries of our time to the creation of a golden age? . . . Five men in Europe, if they worked with a singleness of purpose and a unity of action, might in an incredibly short space of time transform the whole history of the world. . . . The world could look forward to a golden age of prosperity.' Sir Samuel was as carefully conditional as ever. But just as with his great speech to the League of Nations on 11 September 1935, the press and the public ignored his 'ifs and ans' to embrace his general air of optimism. Five days later the unhappy Sir Samuel was forced to realize that he had done it again.

There had been a fair amount of warning to be sure, especially from the Secret Services. But it had been ignored or overlooked in the general plethora of conflicting signals. Neville Chamberlain's optimism rested on a number of a priori convictions. In the first place, despite all the rumours and Foreign Office scares, Hitler had made no hostile move since Munich. Chamberlain believed this to be in part the result of a change in the balance of forces.[3] British rearmament was now in full swing and was rapidly catching up with German rates of aircraft construction. Germany was feeling the increasing economic strains of too rapid a rearmament effort. President Roosevelt's New Year speech to Congress and his carefully leaked briefing of the Senate Military Affairs Committee displayed a firmer will to resist aggression on the part of the United States Government. Economic consultations with German industry seemed to be going well. Mr Ashton-Gwatkin of the Foreign Office Economic Section had been to Berlin between February 19 and 26 and had been told by Marshal Goering that there would be no war.[4] Even Ribbentrop was friendly, and Ashton-Gwatkin concluded that definite German proposals for Anglo-German co-operation were on their way.[5]

Economic weakness, so Chamberlain believed, was driving Hitler into searching for a way to approach Britain 'without the danger of a snub'. 'We have at last got on top of the dictators,' he wrote in the middle of February.[6] On March 3, an Anglo-German coal agreement was signed in Berlin. Oliver Stanley was to visit Berlin in the middle of March when, no doubt, further progress could be made. 'It will take some time before the atmosphere is right,' but Hitler had 'definitely missed the bus'. Britain was stronger then, and on February 6, speaking in the Commons, Chamberlain had made it quite clear to both Germany and Italy that there could be no thought of driving a wedge between Britain and France.[7] Each was pledged to come to the aid of the other if she was attacked. Patience, toughness, rearmament and avoidance of confrontation would do the trick.

Sir Nevile Henderson also played his part in encouraging the Prime Minister's euphoria. In the middle of February he returned to Berlin fully recovered from the operation for cancer of the throat which had removed him from his post in November. His first step was to summon the Embassy staff and rebuke them for the tone of the reports made to London during his absence.[8] He did his best to correct their pessimism by telegram[9] ('my definite impression . . . is that Hitler does not contemplate any adventures at present and rumours to the contrary are completely without real foundation')[10] and by private letters to Chamberlain and Halifax.[11]

The only warning note in all this euphoria (apart from the speech of February 6) was struck with Chamberlain's full consent, by Leslie Hore-Belisha, the Minister for War, in his speech introducing the Army Estimates into Parliament on March 8.[12] After a long struggle fought in the full face of *The Times*, the Treasury and a great deal of other opposition, Hore-Belisha had converted the Cabinet to the view that if there was war in Europe Britain would have to send a considerable army to the Continent. No longer was there to be any talk of a war of 'limited liability'. The army's strength stood at six regular divisions, including two armoured, and thirteen territorial divisions, including one armoured. Seven anti-aircraft divisions had been raised to protect Britain against air attack. In the event of war, he said, Britain had an inescapable obligation to assist France.

His speech followed, as Chamberlain well knew, a thoroughly pessimistic 'European Appreciation' for the years 1939 and 1940, produced in February by the Chiefs of Staff.[13] Despite its title, the document surveyed Britain's prospects of success in a global war with Germany, Italy and Japan and pronounced them wanting. In the event of war Britain faced the immediate loss either of her control of the Mediterranean or of her possessions in the Far East. To retain the Fleet in the Mediterranean would be to renege on Britain's frequently respected pledges to defend Australia; to send a battle squadron adequate to deter the Japanese would mean losing control over south-east Europe and probably the Middle East. There ensued a long and bitter battle between Admiral Lord Chatfield, the Minister for the Co-ordination of Defence, for whom imperial defence was all-important, and the new First Sea Lord, backed by the ablest and most incisive of the navy's strategists, Admiral Drax, for whom the only course was to knock Italy out in the first six months of the war.[14] Chamberlain was well aware of these arguments. But his convictions stemmed from his belief that there was not going to be a war. Britain's growth in strength would deter Hitler. And without Hitler, neither 'Musso', as he always called him, nor the Japanese would act.

Chamberlain's first reactions to Hitler's entry into Prague were more concerned with the effects of the dissolution of Czechoslovakia at the apparent instance of the Slovaks than with the perfidy of Hitler. During the run-in to the occupation he prevaricated to Parliament.[15] This was the more unpardonable in that the Secret Intelligence Service (SIS) had given very precise warning of Hitler's intentions at least a fortnight earlier. On March 15 itself Chamberlain said in so many words that the action of the Slovak Diet in proclaiming the independence of Slovakia

Chamberlain bedauert sehr
'Chamberlain sincerely regrets' (March 1939: Germany occupies Czechoslovakia. Britain, France and Russia content themselves with protests)

made the British guarantee of Czechoslovakia meaningless.[16] He was, in fact, badly rattled, and for the moment, way out of touch with the movement of opinion in Britain. 'The feeling in the lobbies,' noted Harold Nicolson on March 17, 'is that Chamberlain will either have to go or completely reverse his policy.'[17] *The Times*, the *Daily Telegraph* and the mass-circulation *Daily Express* all roundly denounced Hitler's action.[18] From the Dominions, whose attitude always caused Chamberlain the deepest concern, evidence flooded in of a change of opinion.[19] Even the most isolationist after the Boers of all streams of opinion in the Commonwealth, the French Canadians, were said to be up in arms. For Hitler to conquer and occupy the Czech lands and people was naked imperialism, an abandonment of racial in-gathering for territorial aggrandizement.

In this situation, while Chamberlain, like some amputee needing time to recognize the full extent of his loss, was arguing in favour of a delaying action until the effects of Hitler's action were fully assessed, Lord Halifax moved with unhabitual certainty. Less concerned, in his aristocratic aloofness from the vulgar brawling of the House of Commons, to justify himself to his party he saw the movement of opinion and the implications of the occupation of Prague clearly. No doubt he was aided by the crashing failure of the attempt by Sir John Simon, the Chancellor of the Exchequer, to defend Chamberlain's stand in the Commons on March 15.[20] He was also in the centre of the storm at the Foreign Office. His permanent Under Secretary, Sir Alexander Cadogan, had shared much of his scepticism at the more alarmist reports which reached the Foreign Office from Sir Robert Vansittart's private intelligence service as well as from the Secret Service proper. Now he was totally converted.[21] Even Sir Nevile Henderson cabled in a fury that the 'cynicism and immorality of the German action defied description'.[22] Hitler, he wrote privately to Lord Halifax, 'has gone straight off the deep end again'.[23] The ministerial visit to Berlin should be postponed. He himself should probably be recalled. Lord Halifax himself spoke in terms of strong and biting scepticism to the German Ambassador in London, von Dirksen, who, not for the first or the last time, toned down and doctored his report of the interview.[24]

On the Friday of that week, March 17, the day before his seventieth birthday, Neville Chamberlain was due to speak in Birmingham, the family's bailiwick and stronghold since his father had taken hold of the Liberal Party organization there sixty years or more before. He had intended to speak about economic recovery and about the social services, subjects very near to his heart. Instead, on advice from Halifax, he altered the text of the speech drastically, sitting in his reserved compartment in the train travelling from London to Birmingham. The brief he worked to on the Great Western Express, whistling at the tunnels and rocking round the curves and bends of the permanent way, had been prepared in the Foreign Office and Halifax took good care for once that both the American and Soviet ambassadors were told of its contents in advance.[25]

Chamberlain defended himself and the policy he had followed at Munich and since in strong terms.[26] If it had not been for his visits to Germany in September 1938 hundreds of thousands of families would today have been in mourning for the flower of Europe's manhood. But he had not only gone to Germany to secure peace. He went to further appeasement. For that policy to succeed it was essential that no power should seek to obtain dominance over Europe. Hitler swore he had no wish to rule others than Germans. Now he had annexed the Czechs. What reliance could be placed on his assurances in the future? Was this a step towards an attempt to dominate the world by force? Britain would turn to her partners in the Commonwealth and to France. Britain was not disinterested in what went on in south-east Europe. She would review her policy. She would not take on any new commitments. There was no sacrifice he would not make for peace, but Britain would never surrender her liberty. No greater mistake could be made than to suppose that Britain had so lost its fibre that it would not take part to the utmost of its power in resisting any attempt to dominate the world by force.

The speech was a subtle and careful construction, a mixture of plain speaking on the feelings of alarm and loathing which the extremely ill concealed character of Hitler's machinations, intrigues and bullying had aroused in Britain, with a continuation of Chamberlain's old line, the refusal to plunge into new commitments in the effort to shore up peace. This last, no doubt, reflected the continuing influence of Sir John Simon and of the Treasury. It did, however, contain two new notes which can safely be ascribed to Lord Halifax's very different advice.

First, it spoke openly of war as a possible course of action into which Britain could be forced. Hints of this kind had been made before Munich, but in so oblique and conditional a manner as to lack much conviction even to their English listeners, to alarm rather than to warn. This speech for the first time spoke of war as an evil, but one preferable to surrender. By implication it accepted that German policy was really concerned to challenge and threaten Britain, even though each separate German action might be justified and defended in terms which related to it and it alone. That challenge was now openly named. Second, the speech marked a major reversal of British policy in Eastern and south-eastern Europe. The attempt to isolate Western Europe as the sole defensible frontier against Germany, which had been the centre of British policy since 1937, if not before, was abandoned. Within two weeks in fact Britain was to plunge headlong into a series, a web, of new commitments in Eastern and south-eastern Europe. Before six months were ended, Britain would be at war, ostensibly over a residual dispute resulting from the Treaty of Versailles, and involving a German minority. The process which was to bring Britain to this had begun even as the Prime Minister's train was pulling into Birmingham, even as the clouds of steam from its piston heads marked the end of its journey.

As Chamberlain spoke, his Foreign Secretary, Lord Halifax, had already acted to commit Britain irretrievably to the newer and tougher tactics foreshadowed in Chamberlain's speech, and to a return to the politics of Eastern Europe from which he and Chamberlain had so recently been trying to withdraw her. The occasion for this reversal was provided by a man who otherwise has little more than a walk-on part in the play of events leading up to the outbreak of the war, one among several hundreds of the corps of European diplomatists in whose curiously artificial and confined world each major event produced ripples and cross-ripples of action and reaction in patterns of the most geometrical complexity. His name was Virgil Tilea; he was Romanian Minister in London. And what he had to say to Halifax was both extremely alarming and in its most important aspects almost certainly not true.

Virgil Tilea at that date was forty-three years old. He had been Minister for his country in London for less than a year. Before his entry into the Romanian diplomatic service he had been Under Secretary of State in his country's Ministry of Finance where, it was alleged, he had 'encouraged and financed' the Romanian Fascist movement, the Iron Guard.[27] He was a football enthusiast, an Anglophile who had studied at the London School of Economics and founded the first Anglo-Romanian Cultural Society. He came from Transylvania, which Romania had won from Hungary at the peace settlement, the target of Hungarian revisionist ambitions. He was a dapper, excitable man, active in London society, still ambitious politically, still urging his country to lean towards Britain; indeed he was involved as an intermediary in the discussion which had followed King Carol's visit to London the previous November to establish, with the aid of the Romanian Jewish millionaire, Max Aušnit, a British-Romanian Corporation for the development of trade between the two countries.[28] He had not hesitated, in support of the project, to drag in the name of George VI who, he said, had 'insisted' on Romania intensifying her commercial relations with Britain.[29]

M. Tilea had already been exhibiting signs of alarm at the progress of the German action against Czechoslovakia. On March 14 he had visited the Foreign Office in London to advise the cancellation of Mr Stanley's visit to Berlin, and to make public the imminent dispatch of a British commercial mission to Bucharest.[30] On March 16, he asked Sir Orme Sargent of the Foreign Office what would be Britain's reactions if Germany reduced Hungary to 'vassalage' and 'proceeded to disintegrate Romania'.[31] He suggested a major loan to enable Romania to replace the arms she had on order with the great Czech armaments factory of Skoda, which the Germans had now taken over.

He was, in this move, acting on instructions from Bucharest to go to the Foreign Office and urge the British to do something to counteract the everspreading belief that Germany had now become the only arbiter of the security, peace and independence of the states of Europe[32] – magniloquent language, but nothing to authorize the action he was to take the next day. In one of the several different accounts he subsequently gave of his actions,[33] he was woken early on the following morning, March 17, by a telephone call from Paris; according to one version, his caller was a senior official of the Romanian court acting on instructions from King Carol of Romania with information about the current state of the economic negotiations between Romania and Germany. Another account attributes the call to the Romanian industrialist, Max Aušnit. From this Tilea deduced that Romania was next on the list of nations against whom Germany was to act.

That afternoon he called on Lord Halifax in a state of considerable excitement.[34] Before that towering figure, those sceptical eyebrows, those fingers pressed lightly together, he poured forth a story of imminent German action against Romania, of economic demands presented as a virtual ultimatum. What would Britain do? If Romania fought, would Britain support her? Would Britain draw a line beyond which Hitler must not go? Germany, he said, had demanded that Romania grant her oil concessions, suppress certain industries likely to be in competition with German industries and become, in particular, an agricultural satellite of Germany. He again asked for a loan to enable Romania to buy armaments from Britain.

Having alarmed Lord Halifax, he went on to do his best with the less flappable Cadogan, and to spread his story as widely as he could among the diplomatic corps in London. He had already spoken with the American Ambassador, Joseph Kennedy, before calling on Halifax.[35]

He took the trouble also to call on the Polish, French, Turkish and Soviet Ambassadors and the Greek Minister and give them the same story.[36] His Military Attaché alerted Leslie Hore-Belisha, the War Minister,[37] and somewhere along the line the same story was given to the press by M. Dimancescu, his Press Attaché, where it was headlined the next day alongside reports of Chamberlain's Birmingham speech. There was even a rumour that King Carol had spoken directly to George VI of Britain, by telephone. Tilea subsequently boasted to his Yugoslav colleague that he had used his instructions to the full.[38] He did not, however, admit the extent of his action in his own reports to Bucharest; his colleague in Paris, who passed the same story in rather more circumspect form to the French, said that 'his young colleague' had been dealing with matters which were 'some weeks old'. The Germans were now behaving more reasonably.[39]

The Foreign Office's reaction was immediate. Lord Halifax had already heard the same story from a fellow Cabinet minister, Walter Elliot. He in turn had had it via his junior minister, Robert Bernays, who had had it from Princess Marthe Bibescu, a woman-of-letters, an inveterate habitué of political and artistic salons in London and Paris. She in turn claimed to have heard the story directly from the Romanian Premier, Călinescu, by phone from Bucharest. She had in fact been urgently invited to London by M. Tilea to aid his intrigue. Robert Boothby, Churchill's maverick ally, later claimed to have master-minded the scheme. It is possible that a similar story had reached Vansittart by his private grapevine. A cipher clerk in the German Legation in Bucharest, a former member of the Austrian diplomatic service, was ordered to commit suicide in April for what he said about the Tilea episode in his cups in a Bucharest nightclub.[40] Within hours of Tilea's dramatic appearance, telegrams were on their way to Athens, Ankara, Bucharest, Belgrade, Paris, Warsaw and Moscow with the news he had brought with him.[41] The telegrams asked for reactions to Tilea's news. Moscow was asked to ascertain whether the Soviet Union would aid Romania to resist oppression if King Carol asked for aid. Romania's partners in the Balkan Entente and her Polish ally were asked how they would react if the Polish-Romanian alliance was agreed to be applicable to German aggression and if the Balkan Entente agreed to guarantee the countries' frontiers. At noon the next day Sir Reginald Hoare, Britain's Minister in Bucharest, phoned through an urgent telegram,[42] asking that all these instructions should be cancelled. As a second telegram[43] from him, also phoned through in the middle of that Saturday afternoon, made clear, Grigore Gafencu, the Romanian Foreign Minister, denied completely that any ultimatum had been received from Germany. The Germans, he said, had in fact showed themselves, remarkably, more conciliatory in the negotiations since the occupation of Prague than before. For the moment there was no threat to Romania's political or economic independence. M. Gafencu was, no doubt, more than a little embarrassed by the degree to which M. Tilea had improved on his original instructions. He was, however, shading the truth a little himself; as well he knew.

Romanian governing circles had been watching the growth of German influence and the increasing boldness of German foreign policy with very much divided feelings. They were tied to Czechoslovakia and Yugoslavia by their membership of the Little Entente. They were allied to France. They were tied to Yugoslavia, Turkey and Greece by the terms of the Balkan Entente. Both ententes involved regular Staff conversations between the participants. Romania herself was surrounded by enemies. The Soviet authorities pressed for the return of Bessarabia, seized in 1918. The Hungarians hoped and schemed for the return of Transylvania, lost by the Treaty of Trianon in 1919. The Bulgarians had lost the Dobrudja area on the Black Sea coast by the Treaty of Neuilly. But then Hungary and Bulgaria were among the vanquished of the First World War. At immense expense in lives and treasure, Romanian had backed the winners.

Like all the states of the Danubian area, Romania had suffered desperately from the Great Depression. With a single exception her staple exports were all raw materials and agricultural products, though she was trying to build up her iron industry. That exception was oil, from the great Romanian oilfields of Ploesti, exploited by a mixture of French, Anglo-Dutch and American capital, threatened by Italian, German and Russian ambitions for its control.

Romania's ruling circles were divided in their reactions to Munich. Elements of the Liberal party grouped around George Bratianu pressed consistently for a pro-German policy. There was a smaller pro-Italian group. The main current of thought, however, preferred a Western orientation, if the Western powers could be persuaded to act to ease Romania's parlous economic situation, to provide Romania with loans for trade and capital investment, and to show signs of standing up to German pressure in the Balkans. Evidence that British and French policy was inclined to take this kind of line was, however, singularly lacking.

In economic terms matters were rather different. The Romanians had deliberately accepted the terms of the payments agreement with Britain in early September 1938, with its effective devaluation of the lei by about half its formal relationship with sterling, in the hope of British investment in Romania and a substantial new loan. This King Carol and Militza Constantinescu of the Romanian National Bank had failed to secure, despite the support of Lord Lloyd, the super-imperialist, former High Commissioner in Egypt. But the British did in fact buy some 200,000 tons of Romanian wheat at the end of October 1938, with an option, which they took up, for a further 400,000 tons. The general information that King Carol got and the impression he formed on a visit to London in mid-November 1938 cannot but have convinced him for the moment that Britain was unable or unwilling to help to any considerable degree, and that her Government had largely left it to him to make what terms he could with Berlin.[44]

To do this was not an easy matter. The Germans were pressing hard for a similar devaluation of the lei in relation to the Reichsmark, and for increased deliveries of Romanian oil and cereals. King Carol did however manage to secure an invitation to visit Hitler in secret at Berchtesgaden at the end of November. His intermediary also succeeded in getting assurances that Germany was not encouraging Hungarian aspirations against Romania; the assurances were however secret. Carol wanted something more public, to dish the Hungarians openly and to strengthen himself with opinion in Romania.

His visit was not altogether a happy experience, although the German records indicate that the meeting was polite and friendly.[45] Carol mentioned Romania's armaments needs, and received a very sympathetic hearing. He was much less happy at German indifference to his two pet projects, an *Autobahn* from Berlin to Bucharest through Ruthenia, and the elevation of the German Legation to the rank of Embassy. Nor did he obtain any assurances that Germany would recognize Romania's existing frontiers and disappoint Hungarian hopes of German support for their claims on Transylvania, the disputed province taken by Romania in 1919, the gold and other minerals from which were adding substantially to Romanian foreign trade. The Germans preferred to keep both sides in this particular conflict suppliants for their support. They had, however, as we have seen, squashed Hungary's plans against the Carpatho-Ukraine just before Carol's visit to Berlin.

Carol seems to have been particularly disturbed by Ribbentrop's pointed enquiries as to the position of Codreanu, the leader of the Romanian Fascist movement, the Iron Guard. Directly after the King's return to Bucharest it was reported that Codreanu and thirteen other leaders of the Iron Guard had been 'shot while attempting to escape', a formula which, to say the least, carried very little credence in German eyes. Carol was violently attacked in the German press for murderous inclinations and for keeping a Jewish mistress (the famous Madame Magda Lupescu).[46] Orders and decorations conferred by King Carol on German leaders during his visit to Germany were ostentatiously returned.[47] Economic agreements were signed with Germany in December. The Germans found them signally unsatisfactory. German trade with Romania continued to suffer, while Anglo-Romanian trade boomed. Politically, too, German influence in Romania had plummeted – which may very well have been King Carol's intention. And the Germans were forced to abandon their demand for a devaluation of the lei and accept, instead of the oil and cereals they demanded, further deliveries of Romanian wheat (which they did not want). Walther Darré, Reichs Minister for Agriculture, complained furiously that, if he had been consulted, the agreements would never have been signed.[48]

In December King Carol changed his Foreign Minister. The new appointee, Grigore Gafencu, was from the King's own generation, one of the King's companions in childhood and adolescence.[49] From a Moldavian aristocratic family, he had a Scottish grandparent, an education divided between Switzerland, France and Britain, and a French wife. He had been in turn a journalist (editing *Timpul*, Bucharest's leading daily), a politician (National Peasant Party), and had already served a stint as Under Secretary in the Foreign Ministry. Carol chose him, in part because he was believed to be friendly with Colonel Beck, the Polish Foreign Minister, in part because he was bored with his predecessor, the cautious and colourless Petrescu-Comnéne, who was appointed Romania's representative to the Vatican.

In a word Gafencu was Carol's man, servant of a monarch who had the reputation of regarding his ministers as superior waiters. Gafencu was no coward. He had won Romania's highest distinction for bravery in action. As Foreign Minister, his actions were, however, to be marked by the volatility, the tendency to panic suddenly for which Romanian public opinion was notorious. He was to show himself an opportunist rather than a man of principle, more so than the new Prime Minister, Armand Călinescu, a tiny, one-armed, 'almost freakish-looking' man who was to provide the resolution his King and his colleague sometimes lacked.[50] Faced with real difficulties, Gafencu could, on occasion, lie; though whether he lied to himself or to others, is still unclear. Gafencu was to develop four lines of policy. First, he was to try to activate Romania's associates in the Balkan Entente and in the alliance with Poland. Second, he was to do his best to quieten down the conflicts with Hungary and Bulgaria. Third, he was to do his best to cultivate and encourage a revival of Western interest in the Balkans. Lastly, he would make noises as reassuring as possible towards Berlin and Rome.[51] The Romanian Ambassador in Paris did his best at the end of January to convince M. Daladier and M. Bonnet that Germany was about to 'enfeudalize' Romania unless the West supported Romania's efforts to maintain her political and economic independence.[52] Memoranda urging the granting of economic assistance to Romania had been given to Lord Halifax and to M. Bonnet the previous September when both were in Geneva.[53] A second private British mission, headed by Lord Sempill, visited Bucharest early in February, but the economic circumstances were no more favourable and Gafencu was forced back once more on Germany.

The Germans were in fact getting desperate. The Four Year Plan had been revamped in January 1939, as a result of Hitler's plans for war with Britain. Projected German needs for petroleum now stood at 9 million tons for 1939, rising to 13 million in 1940, 20 million in 1941 and 22 million by 1943.[54] Half of this was to have been covered by the production of synthetic petrol from German lignite coal. But the manpower, the production facilities and the extra coal production were grossly behind their target dates. Germany needed to import a minimum of 400,000 tons of oil a month. From September to December, Germany was only importing 61,000 tons a month. Britain was taking Romania away from the German orbit.

The German delegation arrived in Bucharest on February 21, determined to redress the balance. It was led by Helmut Wohltat, Goering's bureaucratic deputy in charge of the whole Four Year Plan.

The German demands were of a formidable character.[55] Romanian production was to be adapted to German requirements, and a joint German-Romanian petroleum industry was to be developed. Germany was to participate in the exploitation of Romania's forests, and her mineral resources were to be explored and exploited together. Romania was to 'respect German export interests' and to standardize her armaments entirely on German lines. Germany, in brief, would achieve economic predominance in Romania. Despite the fact that he was both host and Chairman, Gafencu won no support from the Balkan Entente which met in Bucharest in the third week in February;[56] and his visit to Warsaw on March 6 was also unsuccessful.[57] With Wohltat he procrastinated bravely, but German tempers were getting short. There was therefore some excuse for Tilea's misrepresentations, especially when the German delegation at Bucharest presented a revised version of its terms on March 10,[56] and Hungarian troops began massing near Romania's borders to move into Ruthenia.

The Romanian Government mobilized five infantry corps on March

16 in fear of an imminent German-Hungarian invasion. A sixth corps was mobilized on March 19. The Hungarians, in equal panic, mobilized in their turn. Appeals to Berlin for mediation went unanswered. It is a measure of how little credibility London enjoyed in Central Europe at this time that no similar appeal was made to the British. Nor was any British or French pressure exerted in Budapest to calm things down. Under these circumstances the Romanian Cabinet gave way. The German-Romanian Economic Agreement was, in fact, signed on March 23 in Bucharest.[59] The terms were, however, left very vague. The agreement was a framework, the development of which would depend on Romanian fears of further German action. King Carol justified Romania's acceptance of the agreement as a means of gaining time.[60] It was, in fact, to be another year before German imports of Romanian oil exceeded those by Britain, and Germany took final control of the Romanian economy. The British initiative was not as frivolous as Gafencu maintained, even though the reports which had inspired it were not strictly in accordance with the facts.

Lord Halifax's initiative was purely a first reaction, a request for information. As such it could also carry, as it was clearly meant to carry, the inference that Britain was planning some move of her own which implied or could imply that Britain would support whatever actions other powers were planning. This, in fact, reflected Chamberlain's refusal in Cabinet to consider, as yet, any definite British commitment. What he wanted was sufficient assurances from other countries to justify a British declaration which might deter Germany for the moment and produce a breathing space. What he and Halifax had not bargained for was the degree of distrust Britain's record over the previous eighteen months had created with all the powers to whom this request for information was addressed. Thus the Greek reply made action in defence of Romania conditional on the views of the Yugoslavs.[61] Prince Paul, the Anglophile Regent of Yugoslavia, replied by asking what Britain's intentions were.[62] Colonel Beck said he would have to consult with the Romanians first.[63] In fact, independent of each other, both Colonel Beck and King Carol decided to reject any proposal that required them to take sides between Germany and Britain, still less to accept support against Germany from the Soviet Union.[64] In Beck's view any such association with the Soviets would probably provoke the German attack it was supposed to deter.

Only the Turks said they would give any British proposals a sympathetic hearing,[65] and, even then, their first reaction was to ask what Britain's intentions were.[66] Most suspicious of all were the Soviets.

Litvinov asked outright whether Britain was planning to engage the Soviet Union while leaving her own hands free.[67] To underline the point, the Soviet news agency, Tass, issued a statement denying that any promises had been made to Romania,[68] even though a promise of Soviet aid had been made on March 1 and was to be reiterated on March 30.[69] Litvinov proposed the immediate summoning of a conference at Bucharest, to which Poland, Romania, Britain, France and the Soviet Union should send delegates to discuss common action.[70] The proposal was deliberately designed, so Maisky, the Soviet Ambassador in London explained,[71] to test British intentions.

Chamberlain in the meantime was hard at work drafting the follow-up to Halifax's enquiries. On one point he was quite clear. He did not want a conference; he disliked conferences, he distrusted the motives of those who called them, and he thought them a waste of time, devices which so often left matters worse than they had been before they were assembled. What he wanted was mutual undertakings in advance of any meeting. Second, he was determined to avoid an ideological line-up or the appearance of one, since this would inevitably, so he believed and so he was warned,[72] drive Mussolini into Hitler's arms. Find a device to restrain Hitler and German expansion, and peace might still be preserved. To present that device as a front against Fascism was to hand Goebbels a perfect propaganda slogan to rally European support behind Hitler.

Chamberlain was in fact inordinately pleased with the results of his labours. He thought his proposal pretty bold and startling.[73] If Hitler should persist in wanting a war, he would be forced to fight on two fronts. On this Chamberlain was admirably clear. 'We would attack Germany not in order to save a particular nation', he told the Cabinet,[74] 'but to pull down a bully'. Faced with this certainty, Hitler would be forced to pause, time would be gained and a way out or round whatever excuse he was planning to justify his next move would be found. His first draft was strengthened after Charles Corbin, Counsellor to the French Ambassador in London, had expressed horror at its vagueness.[75]

What Chamberlain proposed briefly was a declaration of intent, to be made by Britain, France, the Soviet Union and Poland. If any further threats to the independence of any state in Europe were made, these four bound themselves to consult together as to how to offer joint resistance to the threat. Detailed consultations on specific cases would follow. Behind this lay the idea, to be elaborated much more plainly in another ten days, that a line had to be drawn in Europe beyond which any more German transgression meant war. If this line was drawn, and was seen to be drawn clearly and openly, then Hitler would understand and return to his senses. What Chamberlain had hit on, though he failed to phrase it that way, was the idea of deterrence coupled with negotiation from strength. War might be stopped, if Germany could be convinced, not merely that her abuse of force would be instantly resisted, but that she would get consideration for any rational demand. Deterrence, not preventive, pre-emptive war, was his aim; not alliances but co-operative, co-ordinated, temporally coincidental 'declarations of intent'.

For the moment Romania was the most vulnerable sector. It was to Moscow, Paris and Warsaw that the proposal went out late on the evening of March 20,[76] for a joint formal declaration that if the political independence of any European state was threatened, then the four Governments would consult together as to what steps should be taken to offer joint resistance to such action. The final phrase including the vital three words 'offer joint resistance' was the fruit of M. Corbin's intervention.

The reactions of those approached were not overly enthusiastic. Litvinov had been deeply insulted by the use of the word 'premature' to describe his proposal for a six-power conference in Bucharest, and no amount of assurance from Sir William Seeds would mollify him.[77] He must have seen, with how sinking a feeling we can only guess, that once again the British Government was evading his advances. Nevertheless, he was still in the saddle, he still had Stalin's ear. After a day's cogitation he sent for Sir William late in the evening of March 22 and said that the Soviet Union would sign the proposed declaration as soon as France and Poland had accepted and promised their signatures.[78] He was perhaps forced into this by the leakage of the British proposal to the London press, at whose instance is still not clear.

M. Georges Bonnet, the French Foreign Minister, was already, though fortuitously, in London, accompanying M. Lebrun, the French President, on his formal state visit. On March 20 he met Halifax in the Foreign Office and discussed the situation.[79] M. Bonnet's immediate reaction, on March 18, had been to urge the Romanians to accept aid from the Soviets.[80] The reply, that Romanians, on the whole, preferred Hitler to Stalin, only made him turn to the Soviets.[81] Jakob Suritz, the Soviet Ambassador in Paris, replied that the Soviets would do nothing unless France took the lead. Stymied in his search for someone on whom to off-load French responsibilities, M. Bonnet, as always, was forced back on Britain. To Lord Halifax, M. Bonnet laid great stress (it was a habit of his) on the necessity of Polish participation. Russian help to Romania would only be effective if Poland collaborated. She would be mad not to. His view incidentally was shared by the Polish Ambassador in London, Count Raczyński.[82]

It was at this stage, however, that M. Bonnet threw his own little spanner in the works. On March 23 President Lebrun drove out in state to take luncheon with the British Royal Family at Windsor. While Their Majesties were entertaining M. Lebrun after luncheon with views of St George's Chapel and of Queen Mary's famous doll's house, M. Bonnet sought out Lord Halifax. He had, he said, received a series of telegrams from M. François-Poncet in Rome, most concerned for the effect it might have on Mussolini if Britain and France gave the impression they were about to launch on an ideological crusade alongside the Soviets against the dictatorships.[83] Nothing would be more likely to drive Mussolini into Hitler's camp. His view was strongly supported the following day by the Earl of Perth, who called his lordship's attention to the resolution passed by the Fascist Grand Council the previous day.[84]

At a further conversation, held the same day at a *soirée* staged at the India Office by Sir Robert Vansittart (who regaled his audience with a recital of his sub-Fleckerian verse in praise of France),[85] the idea of overcoming Polish resistance to aid Romania by guaranteeing British and French aid against Germany was first mooted.

The Poles, however, remained obdurate. In instructions drafted before the German entrance into the Memel, Colonel Beck told Count Raczyński that Poland was unwilling to make any gesture that would provoke a hostile reaction in Germany.[86] So far as Romania was concerned, there was no common Romanian-German frontier. Any assault on Romania would have to come through Hungary. The Polish Ambassador in Paris, Juliusz Lukasziewicz, had already provoked Alexis St Léger Léger, the cold genius that had presided over the Quai d'Orsay under successive Foreign Ministers from 1933, into the venomous accusation, 'Poland refuses to join France and England in protecting Romania.'[87] Léger had revenged himself by warning London that Beck, being totally untrustworthy, was about to do a deal with Hitler.[88] Now Raczyński had to break it to Halifax that Poland was quite unwilling to associate herself with the Soviet Union.[89] Instead he proposed a secret bilateral agreement, providing for British support in the case of German action against Danzig, to be secret even for a time from France. Such a suggestion was so far from Halifax's and Chamberlain's conception of an open deterrent, and so irrelevant to the current centre of British anxieties, the problem of Romania, as to produce the suspicion that Beck intended to use such an agreement, were he to have obtained it, as a private deterrent against Germany, leaking its existence himself to Germany whenever the occasion seemed to warrant it. Indeed, ignorance of the course of the German-Polish discussions and rumours of disagreements between Beck and Smigly-Rydz led to such suspicion, in both London and Paris, of Beck's willingness to compromise, that nailing Poland down became one of the main themes in British and French discussions.

There followed, so far as Moscow was concerned, a three-day hiatus. Maisky was told that Britain was waiting for a final reply from the Poles. In fact the Cabinet was arguing bitterly about the relative merits of Soviet and Polish support.[90] If it had been left to Halifax and his advisers in the Foreign Office, they would probably have come back to some revised form of declaration. Leslie Hore-Belisha, the War Minister, and Lord Chatfield, the former First Sea Lord, who in January had succeeded Sir Thomas Inskip as Minister for the Co-ordination of Defence, supported them. Sir Samuel Hoare made a strong fourth. But others, notably Sir John Simon, were much less favourably disposed.

Above all, Neville Chamberlain himself was doubtful and suspicious. He thought Russia an 'unreliable friend with very little capacity for active assistance but with an enormous irritative effect on others.'[91] Military[92] and Secret Service advice[93] was that the Soviets were incapable of any real action. In any case, as Chamberlain told a Labour Party delegation on March 23,[94] 'the key to the position is not Russia, which has no common frontier with Germany, but Poland, which has common frontiers with both Germany and Romania.' In a letter written on March 26 after the Cabinet had decided to support him[95], he confessed to 'the most profound distrust of Russia', of her 'ability to mount an effective offensive . . . even if she wanted to' and 'her motives, which seem to me to have little connection with our ideas of liberty.' He bitterly resented Maisky's lobbying activities with the Liberal and Labour opposition, considering these irregular and often a good deal less than totally truthful.

Moreover, he of all the Cabinet was most struck by the plea voiced by Bonnet and Perth, and supported by pressure from Finland,[96] Japan,[97] Portugal,[98] Canada and South Africa,[99] that Europe should not be divided into ideological blocs.[100] It had not yet struck him that he was allowing crypto- and philo-Fascists in Canada and South Africa to hinder and obstruct his resistance to the threat to Britain's vital interests and existence which Nazi Germany and Fascist Italy presented. He was always more tender to representations from the Commonwealth. A much more cogent argument was that a line-up with the Soviet Union might tip the balance in Tokyo in favour of an alliance with Germany and Italy, realizing the worst fears expressed by the Chiefs of Staff in their 'European Appreciation' the previous month.

Thus it was that, by March 27, the Foreign Policy Committee of the Cabinet had arrived at the conclusion that while 'we must keep Russia with us,' a coalition built around the Soviet Union was impossible.[101] The alternative was to build one around Poland. Hitler could only be deterred by the prospect of a war on two fronts. The Foreign Office evolved the idea of a joint Anglo-French undertaking to support Poland and Romania if the latter was prepared to resist any threats to its independence and if Poland would aid in such resistance. If the positions of these two states could be consolidated, then Turkey and Greece could be rallied to the common cause. The Soviets would be asked if they would guarantee their benevolent neutrality. The plan was approved in principle by Chamberlain on March 26 as by the Cabinet Foreign Policy Committee the following day.[102] It was clear that something had to be done. 'All the little states are weakening and showing funk,' wrote Cadogan in his diary.[103] Rumours of imminent German action came from all sides. On March 25, while at a state banquet at Buckingham Palace, Chamberlain was told of twenty German divisions massing on the French and Belgian frontiers.[104] 'This is like the Brussels Ball' (before Waterloo), his informant remarked. Under this pressure, the idea that the guarantee was to depend on a Polish commitment to Romania disappeared. The French thought the Russians deceitful, unreliable and unable to give any real help. It was imperative to secure Polish loyalty.

The telegrams for Warsaw and Bucharest were held up all of March 27,[105] because of conflicting anxieties and reports. At one moment the 'slippery' Colonel Beck seemed on the verge of a corrupt bargain with Germany.[106] The conclusion of the German-Romanian trade treaty on March 23, and the widespread impression that Britain and France were retreating, were threatening even the British position in Greece and Turkey. On the other hand, 'we did not know that Poland might not be invaded within a term which could be measured by hours and not by days,' Neville Chamberlain later recalled.[107] On March 20, Joseph Kennedy passed on information from his colleague, the superbly named Anthony J. Drexel Biddle IV, in Warsaw,[108] to the effect that Ribbentrop was now pressing for immediate action against Poland, on the assumption that Britain and France would not support her. His informant was an anonymous German journalist with connections to the United Press bureau in Berlin. Other warnings were coming in from the Military Attachés in Warsaw and Berlin and from Secret Service sources.

In the meantime, to demonstrate British resolve to those who felt that London's only weapons were paper, the Cabinet decided, on March 29, to double the size of the Territorial Army.[109]

The final report which was to spur the Cabinet into action came from a young British journalist, Mr Ian Colvin, then the Berlin correspondent of the *News Chronicle*. Mr Colvin was an occasional informant for Sir Robert Vansittart's private intelligence service. Sir Robert was not, however, the only one to have his own private secret service. At least as formidable a figure was Lord Lloyd, the former High Commissioner in Egypt and since 1935 head of the newly founded British Council. While the Council was entirely above board in its activities, his position as its head, coupled with his own formidable personality, enabled Lord Lloyd to travel where he wished, see whom he wished and virtually do as he pleased in the service of his country. In November 1938 he had played a considerable role behind the scenes in arranging King Carol of Romania's visit to London and in lobbying for British financial and commercial support for Romania.[110] In January 1939 he was in Rome observing Mussolini's efforts to damp down the popular enthusiasm for Chamberlain.[111] February had found him in Athens attempting to persuade the King of the Hellenes to rid Greece of its dictator, General Metaxas.[112] His papers reveal that he had access to the SIS reports and corresponded privately with its head.[113] Ian Colvin was one of his most regular correspondents. Already on January 27 he had reported to Lord Lloyd that German military preparations included the possibility of an attack on Poland in March.[114]

In this, as we have seen, he was premature and wrong. But this did nothing to destroy confidence in him. Throughout February he continued to maintain that Hitler was planning to attack Poland at the end of March.[115] In mid March, while on a tour through the Baltic states, he wrote warning of an imminent German drive into the Baltic states and maintaining that Colonel Beck, the Polish Foreign Minister, was completely in the Germans' pocket.[116] Poland would fall to Germany with Beck playing the Quisling in the autumn. In this, as he later realized,[117] his German sources were gulling him, a typical *Abwehr* trick. But on his return to Berlin two days later, he found that the Germans, who he feared had long been gunning for him, had picked him for expulsion from Berlin in retaliation for the expulsion of two German pressmen from Britain on charges of subversive activities and espionage. His case became known and his German informants, members of the bureaucratic opposition to Hitler, impressed him with the belief that the attack on Poland he had first reported in January was imminent.[118] His fears were added to by the British Military Attaché in

Berlin, Colonel Mason-MacFarlane, a courageous eccentric who once contemplated personally assassinating Hitler.[119] Mason-Mac, as he was generally known, confirmed Colvin's reports via official channels, timing one report to arrive the day after Colvin arrived in London to lobby against his expulsion.[120]

On the afternoon of March 29, Colvin called at the Foreign Office to see Sir Alexander Cadogan, the Permanent Under Secretary, to whom all Britain's clandestine agencies operating abroad were subordinate.[121] His information came as a godsend. The Cabinet was still divided over what to do, Chamberlain, with the support of Sir John Simon, still leaning towards the side of caution. Cadogan himself had only recently abandoned his scepticism towards Vansittart's constant reports of new German plans for aggression. He took Colvin at once to Halifax, then with Halifax to Chamberlain, who was even then donning evening dress to receive George VI and his Queen at a dinner at 10 Downing Street.[122] To each Colvin poured out his story, filled as it was with circumstantial evidence of the accumulation of rations for military purposes on the German-Polish borders. Hitler, he reported, was going to occupy a considerable section of Poland, leaving only a narrow strip, a German protectorate, to act as a buffer between German-occupied territory and the Soviet frontier.

Moreover, Hitler was not stopping there. Lithuania was next on his list. Its absorption would be followed by that of other states. That would make possible a Russo-German alliance and finally 'the British Empire, the ultimate goal', would fall helplessly into German hands. Ribbentrop was urging the Führer to strike now while Britain was still undecided whether to make an alliance with Poland and Romania.

This detailed description of Hitler's alleged plans makes possible the pinpointing of Colvin's sources of information, though not the individual responsible. For they could only have come from someone with access to the directive Hitler gave General von Brauchitsch, the Commander-in-Chief of the Army, on March 25, or someone privy to Hitler's most intimate circle. General Keitel, the head of the OKW, did not learn of this directive for one or two days, and his planning staff had only produced the initial draft instruction for *Case White*, the codename for the military orders for action against Poland, by April 1, when Keitel took them to Hitler on board the battle cruiser *Scharnhorst* in Wilhelmshaven harbour that afternoon. The timetable would thus suggest that the information came to Colvin from Brauchitsch's staff perhaps on March 26 or 27 at the latest, before the OKW had already got to work on the military orders, but at the moment when that work was about to begin. It is, in fact, alleged that at this time the Chief of the Army Staff, General Franz Halder,[123] warned the British Embassy that plans to attack Poland were under preparation.

Mr Colvin's information was thus a concoction of accurate information and grossly exaggerated inference, and the inference supplied to him, also in the guise of information, was clearly deliberately exaggerated to produce the maximum effect on the recipient, since it carried the idea that an attack on Poland was imminent. This was, in fact, untrue. No date was named in any German document until April 1, after the British had acted on Colvin's report; the date then named was September 1, five months off. Here, as in January, the intention of the individual or individuals who fed this misleading information to the British was clearly to provoke Britain into some major action to oppose, block, restrain or thwart the Führer. Whoever they were, they had the satisfaction of knowing within days that they had succeeded magnificently.

On its own and at another time Colvin's story might have been doubted. Chamberlain, for one, found much of what Colvin said 'so fantastic as to doubt its reliability'. But it seemed to confirm the American reports from Warsaw passed on by Joe Kennedy. Similar reports came from Colonel Mason-MacFarlane in Berlin. Against an imminent 'weekend swoop', something needed to be done very quickly. The following afternoon, March 30, Lord Halifax arranged for a question to be put down at the House of Commons for the following day, by Arthur Greenwood, the Labour leader, suggesting that a German attack on Poland was imminent and asking what action the British Government proposed to take. As the clerks and typists gathered around the tea urns in the corridors of the Foreign Office for their afternoon break, telegrams were dispatched to Paris and Warsaw, telegrams drafted by Chamberlain in his own hand, with Halifax and Cadogan adding amendments to the draft.[124] Chamberlain proposed to say that if any action was taken to threaten Polish independence, so that the Polish Government felt bound to resist with their armed forces, Britain and France would at once lend Poland all the support in their power.

The British Ambassador in Warsaw, Sir Howard Kennard, had already received instructions from London,[125] embodying the rather vague proposals Chamberlain had drafted on March 27. Himself a hard-nosed realist, tough in mind and body, he found them far from satisfactory. He had already suggested they be given as little publicity as possible.[126] As a reply to the Polish offer of an alliance, even a clandestine one, they must have struck him as likely to convey a deplorable picture of caution, pusillanimity, even dithering old-maidishness. He had nevertheless made it his business to see Colonel Beck that evening, March 30, having arranged with his somewhat excitable French colleague, M. Léon Noël, that he should convey a similar message to Marshal Smigly-Rydz.[127] He was in fact closeted with Colonel Beck, who was reacting in the worst possible manner to Chamberlain's proposals, questioning whether they might not drive Hungary into Germany's arms, when his First Secretary, Mr Robin Hankey, burst in on them with the telegram from London.[128] Colonel Beck changed his attitude at once. Here was something definite, concrete, open and forceful. 'Between two flicks of a cigarette', he accepted.[129] Sir Howard returned hastily to the Embassy to phone the news of Beck's reaction to London. His report[130] reveals the depths of his surprise. 'Any comments on my part would doubtless seem redundant,' he wrote, 'especially as your lordship doubtless possesses much information not available to me.' He even ventured to suggest that the declaration be watered down slightly, lest the Poles be nerved to some rash adventure against Danzig. But Lord Halifax would have none of this. The German technique of aggression, he wrote,[131] is 'so varied and insidious' that Poland, in self-defence, could well be driven to commit 'a technical act of provocation'.

On the afternoon of March 31, Chamberlain rose to a crowded House of Commons. He struck observers as ill and sick, aged and withdrawn.[132] But there was nothing of this in his delivery. Consultations, he said, were in progress with other Governments on the questions and disputes of the moment. While these were in progress, if any action clearly threatened Polish independence and if the Poles felt it vital to resist such action by force, Britain would come to their aid; as would France.[133] The House cheered.

It was in fact an extraordinary statement that Chamberlain made to the House. The restless yet motorized teenagers of California, whom Tom Wolfe has so startlingly celebrated, long ago developed a game called 'Chicken'. Each in their own jalopy, two will drive straight and fast at each other down an open highway so that a head-on collision seems unavoidable. Whoever flinches, grabs the wheel and first swerves aside is adjudged 'chicken': coward, gutless, lacking in manhood. The ultimate ploy in this game is to dismantle the steering wheel, and throw it out ostentatiously over the side. The opposing driver then has a clear choice, swerve or crash to self-destruction.

Mr Chamberlain's declaration bore many similarities to this ultimate manœuvre in the Californian game of Chicken. It left no option whatever for the British Government. If the Poles took up arms, then

Britain fought too. The decision, war or peace, had been voluntarily surrendered by Chamberlain and his Cabinet into the nervous hands of Colonel Beck and his junta comrades-in-arms. It was unprecedented. It was also unconstitutional. It is also clear that Chamberlain, for once, did not understand what he had done. On April 2 he told his sister Hilda[134] that the declaration only dealt with Poland's independence, not her territorial integrity. 'And it is we who will judge whether that independence is threatened or not,' he wrote (a contradiction of the terms of the guarantee which implicitly left the question of determination to the Polish Government).

The declaration was, of course, only intended to cover the period until the British had succeeded in constructing a unified Eastern Front. That moment never came. The declaration was intended to dismay and deter. The tragedy for Chamberlain's foreign policy was that Hitler did not, could not, believe in the firmness of Britain's determination to honour the guarantee until the moment his troops had been given the orders to march. Though all his allies and advisers (all but one) assured him that an attack on Poland meant, inevitably, unquestionably, without a shadow of a doubt, war with Britain, he preferred to listen to his own private oracle and to von Ribbentrop, who aped, aided, echoed and abetted it. Against stupidity even the gods fight in vain.

Not that there were not voices in Britain who, themselves appalled at what Chamberlain had done, sought to argue, to interpret, to mollify his statement out of existence. On March 31, the *Evening Standard*, on direct instructions from its owner Lord Beaverbrook, and, on April 1, *The Times*, aware of the terms of the debate which had riven the Cabinet the previous week, pointed out in the words Chamberlain himself had used in that debate, that the key word in the Prime Minister's statement was 'independence' not 'integrity'.[135] 'The new obligation does not bind Great Britain to defend every inch of the present frontiers of Poland.' *The Times* seemed to hint that there would be no objection in London to such minor adjustments as the return of Danzig to the Reich, the construction of an *Autobahn* with extra-territorial status through the Corridor, perhaps even the disappearance of the Corridor itself. The egregious Dr Theo Kordt of the German Embassy in London, whose opposition to Hitler's policy might have been expected to counsel restraint in such matters, had already picked up the question of integrity, in a telegram received in Berlin in the early hours of April 1.[136] The Soviets were equally suspicious. The Foreign Office was forced to intervene to secure a disclaimer. The communiqué which the Foreign Office News Department drafted for publication on April 3[137] adminis-

tered a magisterial rebuke to all who attempted 'to minimize' a statement of such 'outstanding importance, the meaning of which is clear
and logical. His Majesty's Government . . . do not seek in any way to
influence the Polish Government in the conduct of their relations with
the German Government.'

The Foreign Office had every reason for its magisterial rebuke; the
more so as it struck Maisky as 'weak and rather vague'.[138] When Count
Raczyński protested to the *Evening Standard*'s diplomatic correspondent
he was told that Lord Beaverbrook had written the paragraph himself,
claiming to base it on information from Chamberlain's immediate
entourage.[139] After *The Times* had echoed this report the next day, Beck
threatened to cancel his visit to London unless a *démenti* was
published.[140] It should, however, be noted that Beck was already
entrained for London in the afternoon of April 2,[141] before he could be
certain such a *démenti* would be published.

CHAPTER 11

HITLER TURNS AGAINST POLAND

On March 24 Hitler returned from his somewhat seasick triumph over Memel. Lipski, the Polish Ambassador, was due back from Warsaw on March 26, a Sunday. It was beginning to dawn on Hitler that the Poles would not fall in with his plan. The discovery placed him in considerable difficulty. For some time now he had been considering a *coup de main* against Danzig. Now any attempt to solve the Danzig issue by force (the 'little solution', as it came to be labelled) would undoubtedly drive Poland into Britain's arms. On the other hand, the Polish mobilization on March 23 seemed to demonstrate Polish hostility. If this proved correct, then the Polish state would have to be destroyed as a political factor and the German frontier advanced into central Poland. This was not an urgent matter; it could only be dealt with in the near future if especially favourable conditions arose. Nevertheless, the military should begin planning.

Hitler unburdened himself of these thoughts in a conversation with his tame soldier, General von Brauchitsch, the Commander-in-Chief Army, on March 25.[1] Characteristically, von Brauchitsch, whose divorce in 1938 to remarry an ardent devotee of Hitler the Führer himself had financed, did nothing. It was General Keitel (Lakeitel=Lackey to the anti-Nazis in the General Staff), Chief Staff Officer to Hitler in his role as Supreme Commander of the Armed Forces, the OKW, who acted. Between the OKW and the Army General Staff, the OKH, there was a long-standing conflict over whose responsibility it was to draft and issue general military planning orders. Keitel and the few other fanatic devotees of Hitler in the OKW had been incensed by army opposition to Hitler in the summer and autumn of 1938. In October Keitel had drafted an 'Address by the Führer to his officers' which called for faith in Hitler, and blind obedience and loyalty in their professional duties.[2] Goering had even attacked attachment to military tradition as incompatible with Nazism.[3] Officers were forbidden to talk of military policy. Policy was for the Führer to decide. On February 10,[4] Hitler had addressed a gathering of army commanders at the Kroll Opera House in Berlin on 'the tasks and duties of the officers in the National-Socialist State' and rebuked them for their pessimism.

Keitel now saw his chance of putting the OKH firmly in its place. By March 27 he had General Walter Warlimont, the new head of the OKW planning staff, at work. The task was disguised as a revision of the annual directive for the co-ordination of the armed forces in war, a task which had been left uncompleted since the previous autumn, though special orders had been issued covering the occupation of Bohemia and the Memel, and planning for a *coup de main* against Danzig was already considerably advanced. So far as war in the West was concerned, the only valid orders had been issued by the army in January 1939.[5] These were defensive in spirit, designed to defend Germany against a French attack. Three armies, the First, the Fifth and the Seventh, were to be engaged under the command of Army Group C; the rest of the German army was engaged in the East, guarding the frontiers with Poland and Lithuania.

Warlimont was a fast worker and an able one. More than this, despite his role in the OKW, set up by Hitler to curb army pretensions, he was an army man through and through and found the new defence structure Hitler had erected the previous year stupid, over-elaborate and full of unnecessary duplication. He speedily got hold of the Deputy Chief of Army Staff, General Heinrich von Stulpnagel, who warned General Halder, the Chief of Army Staff, of what was happening. Then he and Stulpnagel drafted the new directive loosely so as to give the army planners as free a hand in the detailed execution of the new directive as possible.[6]

By the end of March the first draft of the directive was ready. It fell into three parts, one dealing with the taking of precautions against sudden attack by land or air, one dealing with war against Poland, which was given the codename '*Fall Weiss*' (*Case White*), and one covering a *coup de main* against Danzig. Only the second part had in fact been completed when the initial draft was shown to Hitler. It was typed up in the large jumbo type which Hitler preferred as he could read it without glasses, and taken by the head of the OKW, Keitel himself, to the Reichs Chancellery. Much had happened in the intervening five days.

Since March 25, Hitler's never less than precarious balance had suffered a series of shocks at the hands of the Poles and the British. Lipski had rejected his last offer. Beck had presented von Moltke, the

German Ambassador in Warsaw, with a solemn warning about Danzig.[7] On March 25, Hitler had spoken of his plans to Josef Goebbels, his Propaganda Minister. He was going to step up the pressure on the Poles. Perhaps this might have an effect. But he would have 'to bite on the apple and guarantee Poland's frontiers'.[8] By March 27, all had changed. 'The Polacks are, and remain by nature, our enemies,' Goebbels confided to his diary.[9] News had begun coming in of the British moves to assist Romania, against whom Hitler at that moment had no designs whatever. British contacts with the Soviet Union at once raised the age-old spectre of 'encirclement'. Then on March 31 came the news of the British guarantee to Poland, clearly involving British support for the Polish position over Danzig. As the news reached Hitler he was sitting in front of the great marble table in his new Reichs Chancellery. With clenched fists he hammered on its marble top, enraged at this new evidence of England's betrayal of his belief in her complacency. 'I will brew them a devil's drink,' he shouted.[10]

The following day, April 1, found him at the great German naval base of Wilhelmshaven. Before him the vast bulk of the new 41,000-ton battleship, the *Tirpitz*, reared itself against the sky. Vice Admiral von Trotha welcomed him, the crowds shouted '*Sieg Heil*', the wife of his bitter enemy, Ambassador von Hassell, a daughter of the great Admiral von Tirpitz, creator of the imperial German fleet that had been scuttled so ignominiously at anchor in Scapa Flow that bright June morning twenty years before, pressed the button; the champagne (German, of course) foamed over the great hull, as she named the ship *Tirpitz*.

From the dock Hitler boarded the battle cruiser *Scharnhorst* which lay moored nearby. Here he proclaimed the promotion of Admiral Raeder, Commander-in-Chief of the German Navy, to Grand Admiral.[11] Here too he looked over the drafts Keitel had brought with him. Preparations for an attack on Poland he ordered should be ready, so that he could act any time after September 1.[12] The OKW was to prepare a timetable to which the preparations must conform. All material for this, together with the views of the three services, were to be ready by May 1.

At five in the evening he left the *Scharnhorst*, and drove to the *Rathaus*, the Town Hall, of Wilhelmshaven. After a reception at which he was made an honorary citizen of Wilhelmshaven, he appeared in front of the *Rathaus* – behind a bullet proof glass screen, it was noticed – perhaps the Gestapo's fantasies about the British Secret Service were already at work – and launched into a fiery tirade against Britain and Poland.[13] The place was well chosen, deliberately chosen. Here more than anywhere else in imperial Germany had lain the main drive against Britain. Here Admiral Tirpitz had assembled the great battleships and battle cruisers of the High Seas Fleet, with their heavy armour, massive guns and cruising range so limited as to confine their action to the North Sea and to the Royal Navy as their only available enemy. The German battleships had steamed out of Wilhelmshaven to Jutland, a battle which, so Hitler believed, with two more battleships and two cruisers and an opening earlier in the day, Germany could have won and forced Britain to her knees. But Britain had won and made of Wilhelmshaven, so Hitler implied, a place without any right to exist or any prospect for the future. She had won not by beating or defeating Germany but by the power of lies and by the poison of propaganda against which Germany, the innocent, was defenceless.

From this beginning he launched into a lengthy attack on British statesmen for constantly interfering, for insisting on being consulted on matters which had nothing to do with them, for practising brutality in Palestine while preaching legitimacy to Germany. 'Once,' he said, 'I concluded an agreement with Britain,' the naval agreement. 'It was based on the earnest desire, which we all have, never again to be drawn into a war with Britain. But this desire must obtain on both sides. If it no longer obtains in England, then the practical preconditions for this agreement are removed. Germany will also let these go. We are so sure of ourselves, because we are strong, and we are strong because we are united and because the world can see this.' With this Hitler left for a two-day cruise on the new cruise liner *Robert Ley*. He liked it so much that he extended the cruise for a third day, arriving at Hamburg on April 4, returning by special train to Berlin the same day.[14] The German press took up his slogans. That same day Goebbels advised the press to publish 'as many sharp attacks on Britain on present and historical grounds as circumstances allow'.[15] For once, Goebbels' propaganda had struck a note. British reports noted that the cry of encirclement was meeting with a large measure of success.[16]

While Hitler was enjoyed the only sea cruise of his life, watching the other guests playing deck games, being photographed with photogenic blonde Aryan maidens in bathing suits, sporting a blue yachting cap of his own design, General Keitel had returned to Berlin. On April 3, he issued the orders that Hitler had agreed on board the *Scharnhorst*; they carried a lengthy political introduction and a section headed 'Military Consequences' (i.e. of the political section) added on Hitler's instructions.[17] For the moment political disturbance was to be avoided until the moment came to strike Poland down. An internal crisis in France with a consequent withdrawal of Britain could very well intervene to make it possible to do this in the not-too-distant future. The armed forces should, however, continue to make preparations for war with the Western democracies as their major aim. *Case White* was only a precautionary complement not a necessary prerequisite to these preparations. When the time came Poland was to be isolated, struck at suddenly and heavily, and conquered quickly. Everything was to be made ready so that the assembly and concentration of the reserve forces could take place with the utmost secrecy.

These orders followed a familiar pattern. Hitler has gone down in history as the exponent of the *Blitzkrieg*. Rarely, however, did the actual offensives – carried out so ably by his army and air force according to the tactics and techniques they had worked out in the late 1920s on the manœuvre grounds in western Russia lent them by the Red Army, and practised and perfected in Spain – correspond to the ideas laid out in Hitler's own instructions. Militarily, tactical surprise was occasionally achieved – most of all in the attack on Norway in April 1940. But political, strategic surprise never. Hitler's own methods of political preparation telegraphed his punches only too obviously and clearly. Indeed the political effect he hoped again and again to achieve by surprise – the attack should take place 'as quick as lightning' (*blitzartig schnell*), he had ordered in the case of Czechoslovakia the previous year – was achieved by giving so much advance warning of his intentions as to warn off all but the most determined or foolhardy of opponents. In this his military-political concepts and his instinctive proclivities were at war with one another. When planning aggression, his model was always the footpad's ambush; he imagined himself lurking around dark corners, club or dagger ready to strike the unwary and distracted. Yet once the planning had begun to be put into action, he was unable to avoid warning his quarry, shouting threats and insults in a manner reminiscent of the formalized rituals of some primitive tribe, posturing and exhibiting himself for all to see in a fashion that suggests some deep-rooted internal compulsions totally at odds with the normal patterns of his political thought. In part it must have been the contemplation of violence that excited him. His military language was larded with the rhetoric of the street-brawl, save only when he hid behind the even more terrible euphemisms of the SS vocabulary. His language was incapable of pausing between the crude comic-strip violence of 'smash', 'crush', 'utterly destroy' and the refined circum-locutions such as 'solve the Polish question', 'exclude all threats from this direction for all time', and, most deadly of all, 'final solution of the Jewish question'. But he should have deceived no one. Whoever read these orders knew Hitler was determined on war.

For the moment, however, Hitler was on the defensive. On March 22 the local German press in the areas bordering on Poland had begun to print attacks on Polish 'atrocities' against members of the German minority in Poland, with a major spread in the *Nationale Zeitung*, alleging that British and French agencies were inspiring this Polish 'agitation'. The German national press began to follow this example, though still with a certain restraint, as the month of April advanced. The Ministry of the Interior circulated a memorandum on German-Polish negotiations on the linked questions of the Polish minority in Germany and the German minority in Poland, drawing the conclusion that the Poles were driven by a consciousness of their national inferiority to 'arrogate to themselves the right to torment and persecute' the German community in Poland.[18] Apart from this, however, everything was kept quiet. The Danzig Senate were told to lie low and do nothing.[19] The German Embassy in Poland were told to maintain complete reserve.[20]

In the meantime, Colonel Beck had completed his visit to Britain. The preparation of an Anglo-Polish treaty of alliance was announced on April 6, followed by the issue of British guarantees for Romania, Greece and Turkey, and the opening of serious Anglo-Soviet negotiations. There were reports of British diplomatic activity in the Baltic states.[21] The Swedish Government refused to make a declaration guaranteeing that German imports from Sweden would not suffer in the event of war.[22] Portugal resisted an indirect invitation to join the anti-Comintern pact.[23] And the Japanese still seemed unable to resolve their own internal difficulties. On April 10, the Dutch Government proclaimed a state of emergency and brought its frontier units up to strength,[24] following similar action by the Swiss Government on March 24, which the Swiss defended quite unashamedly against German protests.[25] The Swiss press was consistently hostile to Germany.[26] Hitler was reduced to desperate pressure on Yugoslavia, Romania and Turkey in the hope of preventing the front which British diplomacy appeared to be building against him.

It was under these circumstances that Hitler assembled the Reichstag, that curious collection of party henchmen masquerading as Nazi parliamentarians which he preserved mainly as an alternative sounding board to the mass rallies at Nuremberg and elsewhere and as a tame audience for his more dramatic announcements. The immediate occasion for this was a telegram received on April 15 from President Roosevelt asking for assurances that he, Hitler, was not planning to invade or attack the territory of some thirty-one states, including all those outside the Axis in Europe and adding Iraq, Arabia, Syria, Palestine, Egypt and Iran from the Middle East.[27] The receipt of the telegram had galvanized the German Foreign Ministry into frantic activity, as a result of which

Hitler had in his hand by April 28 assurances of somewhat dubious validity from seventeen countries that they did not feel threatened by Germany. It was noticed, however, that Switzerland, Romania and Latvia evaded the attempt to extort similar assurances from them and that no effort was made to extract such assurances from Britain, France, Ireland, Poland or the Soviet Union.

Before Hitler could convene the Reichstag, however, he had another jolt to survive. On April 23, Mr Chamberlain announced to the House of Commons that Britain intended to adopt conscription. Sir Nevile Henderson, the British Ambassador, returned from London especially to break the news to Berlin and to play down the importance of the decision as much as he could. It was not much of a birthday present, even at that, for Hitler, who had celebrated his fiftieth birthday on April 20 with peculiar pomp and circumstance, the famous Unter den Linden thoroughfare being decorated with golden eagles uncomfortably festooned with swastikas, and floodlit from the Brandenburger Tor to the Adolf Hitlerplatz. The occasion had been seized on for a demonstration both of the Führer's own popularity and of German military might. On April 19 Hitler drove along Unter den Linden standing in the back of an open car, his hand outstretched to receive the plaudits of the carefully assembled crowds, at the head of a motorized cavalcade filled with Nazi *Prominenten*. On April 20, he took the salute at a parade of some fifty thousand troops, infantry, cavalry, and armour, sitting on a large golden chair upholstered in red plush, flanked by Ribbentrop and his predecessor, Baron von Neurath, now ensconced as Reichs Protector of Bohemia. The two unfortunate Slovaks, Monsignor Tiso and M. Hácha, who had been brought to Berlin to receive their orders, sat with Ribbentrop and von Neurath, with the German military commanders, Goering, Grand Admiral Raeder, General von Brauchitsch and General Keitel, seated behind the Führer. Overflights by Luftwaffe squadrons drowned out the military bands and, if Hitler himself derived any peculiar thrill from the display, it was observed that the Berlin crowds, as walkers-on to this theatrical spectacle, played their parts with remarkably feeble enthusiasm.[28]

The lukewarmness of the German crowds had little effect on Hitler's general sense of well-being. He was about to see off Franklin D. Roosevelt. His economic advisers were still bursting with the euphoria the German-Romanian Agreement had inspired in them. Helmut Wohltat, Goering's deputy as Head of the Four Year Plan, had written an enthusiastic memorandum at the end of March envisaging the economic conquest of south-east Europe[29] (whose statesmen, led by Grigore Gafencu, the Romanian Foreign Minister, were now, one after the other, making pilgrimage to Berlin) by the same means. The Luftwaffe, who were in fact coming to the reluctant conclusion that their forces were totally inadequate for a bombing offensive against London, had convinced Hitler that the populations of London and Paris, struck with panic in September 1938 by fear of air attack, would make Britain's new encirclement policy a bluff.[30]

But most of all his surveyors had finished their examination of the booty captured with the occupation of Bohemia and Moravia. Enough arms had fallen into his hands to equip a further twenty divisions. Two thousand anti-tank guns, 800 tanks, 2,000 pieces of artillery, 57,000 machine guns, 750,000 rifles, and 1,200 aircraft were ready for use. The enormous armament manufacturing complexes, those of Skoda at Pilsen and Prague and those of the Czech Armaments Company at Brno, which had made Czechoslovakia the fourth largest exporter of arms in the world, lifted Germany's part in world arms production by 15 per cent, making her second only to the United States among the world's industrial powers. Eight hundred thousand ounces of gold and vast stores of non-ferrous metals eased the shortages from which the Four Year Plan was suffering – all save one, labour. For this Hitler needed not only the mineral resources of the Danube basin and the Balkans, which now seemed open to him, but cheap labour, especially in the agricultural sector. Czechoslovakia had been the major source of armaments for every Balkan state, from Yugoslavia to Turkey. To whom, other than Germany, could they turn, if Germany chose to turn off the tap?

Conscription was, by contrast, a very mixed blessing for the British. Since January 1939 the army had been ordered to prepare for a continental war. The Territorial Army had been doubled from thirteen to twenty-six divisions. Britain's aircraft production was rapidly overtaking Germany's. But her production of infantry and artillery weapons, let alone tanks, was grossly inadequate for her own needs. She had nothing to spare for Turkey, Romania, Poland or Yugoslavia; no arsenal for democracy there.

The Reichstag assembled at noon on April 28. It is unnecessary to rehearse yet again with what unctuous self-justification the Führer could defend his actions in the past, proclaim his desire for peace, enumerate the 'sacrifices', now rapidly diminishing in number, he had made in order to secure that peace in Europe, or outline the gratuitous insults, so-called, his long-suffering nation had to endure from interfering foreign statesmen. The main purport of his speech[31] could be summarized in three points: to throw back President Roosevelt's telegram in its author's face; to denounce the German-Polish Non-

Aggression Pact; and to denounce the Anglo-German Naval Agreement. The first task he performed with vulgar gusto, enumerating in detail all the assurances he had received from the states Roosevelt had listed, and breaking Roosevelt's telegram down into twenty-one points, which he answered in detail, point by individual point, piling sarcasm on thunder in a manner which no doubt delighted the President's hard-core Republican opponents (or so the German Chargé d'affaires in Washington reported in his attempt to gloss over the almost uniformly hostile reactions of the American press).[32]

The second and third parts of Hitler's task were performed with more seriousness. Lengthy memoranda were handed over by the German Embassies in Warsaw and London in interviews timed to coincide with the opening of Hitler's speech. That to Poland based the denunciation of the German-Polish Non-Aggression Pact on Poland's action in aligning herself with Britain against Germany, the Polish refusal of Germany's 'offer' to settle the Danzig/Polish Corridor complex of questions, and the Polish mobilization at the end of March.[33] That to Britain justified the denunciation of the Anglo-German Naval Agreement by reference to the British policy of encirclement.[34] There were, however, other reasons behind these two missives, at first sight so difficult to reconcile with Hitler's hope of secrecy in the development of his military plans towards Poland.

To take the Polish memorandum first. The real significance of this lies in the first of the reasons given for the denunciation of the German-Polish Non-Aggression Pact, the Polish alignment with Britain. Hitler still had not committed himself thoroughly to war with Poland that year. He still believed that the Polish Government could be coerced into joining his side and accepting his terms. He still had not unleashed the Danzig Senate even as a means of manufacturing the incidents necessary to the provision of an occasion for an attack on Poland. He was not able to do this for another month. The big stick might yet coerce the Poles into joining him.

Where the Anglo-German Naval Agreement was concerned there were other, far more urgent reasons for denouncing it. Most obnoxious of its provisions to the German Naval Staff were those that bound them to give notice to the British of every new warship laid down, with details of its displacement, gun calibre, and so on. The construction programme for 1939 contained two new battleships whose planned tonnage figures would bring the total tonnage of German battleships well above 35 per cent of that of the British battle fleet. A little time, six weeks perhaps, could be won by camouflaging them as 'floating docks'.[35] But as soon as serious construction began it would be obvious

"Fühlst du dich bedroht?"
'"Do you feel threatened?"' (April 1939: Hitler poses the question in Switzerland and the other small European states)

to the British that Germany had abandoned any attempt to stay within the limitations of the treaty. The German Naval Staff were curiously sensitive to accusations of bad faith from their British colleagues. They had therefore been urging the Führer, since at least the turn of the year, to denounce the agreement, despite the deliberate omission from its original text of any provision for denunciation. The Führer's speech therefore closely fulfilled their recommendations. It was a curious example of double-think, justified only by their own not altogether baseless suspicions that the British were deliberately restricting their own new construction as a means of limiting the German battle fleet to a manageable size.[36]

In the meantime planning went steadily forward, for a *coup de main* against Danzig, for an attack on Poland, for 'frontier protection in the west' and, because members of the General Staff were more than a little sceptical of Hitler's belief that he would isolate Poland and deal with her on her own, for economic warfare against Britain. Material for the timetable duly flowed in by the end of April 1939. And on May 16 the initial directive went out from the Commanders-in-Chief of the Army and Navy to the Senior Commanders in the field outlining the intention to attack Poland if Polish policy should cease to be based 'on the principle' of avoiding friction with Germany.[37] The usual euphemisms were employed, the usual circumlocutions trotted out. Great emphasis was placed on the political presupposition of such an attack – the diplomatic isolation of Poland. But none who saw the directive could have been in any doubt as to its purpose. Inevitably speculation followed. Could the Führer really isolate Poland? What would Britain, and France, and above all the Soviet Union do?

CHAPTER 12

ANGER IN ROME

The news from Prague struck Count Ciano and Mussolini with anger and dismay. Of the two men, Count Ciano was the more bitter. Here was a power, Italy's would-be ally, on whose side Italy had been prepared to go to war against France and Britain only six months previously; a power whose leader had assured everyone that he had no terrorist designs, that his aim was simply to reunite his people into the German Reich, that he 'did not want to annex a single Czech', incorporating six million non-Germans into the German state. What confidence could be placed in his other declarations and promises which directly concerned Italy? What was the point of the Axis if it functioned only in Germany's favour?

Hitler had, after all, given the Italians only the barest possible warning. Ribbentrop did not see Attolico, the Italian Ambassador in Berlin, until the day Hacha's train arrived in Berlin.[1] Hitler's defence of his action was only conveyed to the Italians the next day as his own motor cavalcade crossed into Bohemia proper, when he sent the inevitable Prince Philip of Hesse, King Victor Emmanuel's son-in-law, with a letter to Mussolini.[2] His justification of his action, even then, struck Count Ciano as good enough for Goebbels' propaganda but hardly proper between members of the Axis. As for Mussolini he was unhappy and depressed, unwilling even to announce Prince Philip's mission for fear of being laughed at by his people. 'Every time Hitler occupies a country, he sends a message,' he commented bitterly to his son-in-law. 'What need had he to put his hand on the Slavs? If he starts this kind of thing, what will he do next March?' After sleeping, or rather not sleeping on the matter the night of March 18, he arrived at the sullen conclusion that German hegemony in Europe was now established beyond any chance of dismantlement. Even if Italy was to join an anti-German coalition, this would only check German expansion, not undo it. Italy's interests therefore would be best served by allying herself with Germany.[3] A day's further reflection brought him no lessening of his gloom. Where would Hitler strike next? If there was anything in the theories of those who saw him as an Austrian intending to recover the lands of the Holy Roman Empire, he would very soon be pressing down on Trieste, whose economic hinterland in any case he now controlled entirely, and pushing his influence down the Danube towards Belgrade and the one-time Adriatic coastline of the Austrian crown. This would make war with Germany unavoidable.[4]

Throughout the next few days Mussolini continued to waver. At one time he was decided firmly against a German alliance. 'The very stones would cry out against it.'[5] Italian troops were concentrated on the borders of Venezia. The next day he was back on his pro-German line ('we cannot change our policy now, we are not prostitutes').[6] Talk of a 'democratic bloc' against the dictators in the British and French press hardened his views,[7] as did reports of British contacts with the Soviet Union. By March 21 he had finally made up his mind. In the face of the cynical comments of the old Fascist leader and one-time flamboyant air-ace, Italo Balbo, Mussolini addressed the Fascist Grand Council.[8] If he had been Hitler, he said, he would have done the same. The Axis was all the stronger for the German action against Bohemia. In international relations there was only one moral law, success. What did people want of Italy? To give up her friends? To make a half-turn? He blushed at the thought that people could think Italy still capable of this. The problem for Italy was the inner power relationship within the Axis which had shifted in Germany's favour. But Italy still held the decisive card in her hands. Without her aid, Germany could not be encircled. But she must increase her stature against Germany. 'When? Where? We will see.'

Count Ciano had some reason to be angry, as did Mussolini. Up to the time of Hitler's coup against Prague, the overt lead in the Axis had, since Munich, been left to Italy. The Italian conflict with France had dominated the headlines. Mussolini had come to assume that for the moment Germany, satiated by her gains the previous year, was supporting Italy against France, and that the alliance negotiations were likely to show advantage to Italy very soon. On March 10, after all, the Germans had at last accepted the idea he had been pressing since mid-February, that military Staff conversations between the German and Italian High Commands should be initiated.[9] The Italian Ambassador in Berlin reported that Hitler 'is fully committed to solidarity with Italy and is ready to march with us'.[10]

The Duce's thoughts were for the moment all concentrated on the dispute with France, and his claims in the Mediterranean. In January he had failed to induce Chamberlain and Halifax to make any move to

mediate in his claims on France, and early in February secret negotiations via Paul Baudouin, a director of the French bank that since
January 1935 had shared the direction of the railway between the capital
of Italian Ethiopia and the French Somaliland port of Djibouti, had also
failed.[11] He had therefore turned to a steady reinforcement of his troops
in Libya and around the frontiers of French Somaliland. He talked of
war, but he was convinced that the French, whom he affected to
despise, would give way in the end.

Ciano had more grandiose and far-reaching plans. Already in 1937,
worried by the steady growth of German influence and power in
Central Europe, he had become convinced that the only hope of
maintaining Italy on a footing of equality with Germany was to do all he
could to maintain Italian influence in Eastern Europe. His thoughts on a
'third Europe' echoed and paralleled those of Colonel Beck. And the
series of visits to the capital cities of Eastern Europe he had embarked on
in the winter of 1938/9 had culminated in a visit to Warsaw at the end of
February.[12] It had not been a success. Colonel Beck had been deliberately non-committal. Italy's abandonment of support for Germany in
November 1938 had not impressed him. There had been numerous
anti-German demonstrations which had embarrassed Count Ciano.
And he had been irritated in the extreme to find that the Poles regarded
Italy merely as a land of poets and painters, and that he was expected to
visit endless examples of Polish baroque architecture. Poland, said the
Duce, was 'an empty nut'.[13] Ciano was forced to agree; but the idea of
an Italian-Polish bloc persisted, at least where the states of the Danube
were concerned.

The centrepiece of his Danubian policy was Yugoslavia; and here
everything depended on the man who had been Prime Minister of that
divided country since 1935, Milan Stojadinovic. Before 1914 there had
been no Yugoslavia. Two small kingdoms, Serbia on the Danube and
Montenegro in the hills, had won their independence from the Turks in
the nineteenth century, worshipped according to the Orthodox rite,
wrote in the Russian Cyrillic script and hatched vast ambitions of
empire in the Balkans at the expense of the Hapsburg and Ottoman
empires. Bosnia-Herzegovina, with her largely Muslim population,
was occupied and treated as a colony by the Hapsburgs before its formal
annexation to their Empire in 1908. The kingdom of Croatia, whose
inhabitants were Catholics and used the Roman script, had been united
with the Hungarian crown in the seventeenth century, passed with
Hungary to Maria Theresa in the eighteenth and looked to the Hapsburgs to protect them against Magyar oppression. Other Croats in
Dalmatia, once ruled successively by the Venetians and by Napoleon's

youngest marshal, Marmont, and at least partly Italianized, looked to the Adriatic. The Slovenes of the north lived partly in the south of the German-speaking provinces of Styria and Carinthia, where they grew an excellent light wine and rioted for schools where the teaching would be in their own tongue, partly in the Slovene-speaking province of Carniola. They too were largely Catholics.

The kingdom that had been put together under King Alexander of Serbia in 1919 out of all these disparate elements had been dominated by the Serbs, and divided bitterly between Serbs and Croats. Political parties naturally followed these communal lines, and extremist nationalists had followed the Serb example set by Gavrilo Princip, the Bosnian student member of the Serbian Black Hand, who had assassinated Franz Ferdinand, heir to the Hapsburg throne, and precipitated the outbreak of the First World War. When King Alexander of Yugoslavia had allied his country to France and linked it with Czechoslovakia and Romania in the Little Entente and with Turkey and Greece in the Balkan Entente, they had turned to Italy, to Hungary and to Bulgaria. The moderate Croat leader, Stepan Radić, was shot down by a Montenegran in 1928. Macedonian terrorists raided into the south from Bulgaria. And in October 1934, Croat separatist terrorists of the *Ustaše*, operating from secret camps in Hungary, shot and killed King Alexander as he landed in Marseilles at the beginning of a state visit to France.

Alexander left a young son, Peter, who would not come of age until 1941. In the meantime the regency was exercised by Prince Paul, a man whose 'incontestable qualities of character, balance and taste . . . Oxonian dilettantism and charm which he exercised on his visitors were useless in the present circumstances and in a country where arguments of might are the only ones which count'. The verdict was that of a French diplomatist;[14] he might have added that Prince Paul's nerves tended to betray him under stress and that he was by nature inclined to yield to pressure rather than to withstand it. By sentiment he was Anglophile, anti-German, anti-Italian and pro-Greek (his wife was Greek). He wanted an end to Croat-Serb tension. In 1935 he had been seduced into the belief that a single national party forged out of Slovene, Bosnian and Serb groups was the answer. The Croats, led by the Peasant Party leader, Vladko Maček, remained in opposition. Milan Stojadinovic headed a new Yugoslav Radical Union.

In 1937, Stojadinovic had taken Yugoslavia into an agreement with Italy. One of his rewards had been the internment or deportation of the *Ustaše* leadership in Italy, but as his own internal position grew steadily less secure he began to toy with the idea of using Italian aid to establish himself as dictator. The elections of December 1938, which saw a 6 per cent drop in the votes collected by his coalition of Serbs, Slovenes and radicals, and a corresponding rise in the Croat, Serb and Montenegran coalitions led by Maček, weakened him still further. At his meetings with Count Ciano in Belje and Belgrade in January 1939 he had announced his intention of making the Yugoslav Radical Union into a Fascist-style party, and said that he intended to lean on Italy 'to find a balanced situation and security within the framework of the Axis.'[15] As only three days earlier all the Croat deputies in the Yugoslav parliament had called on the great powers to intervene in Yugoslavia to assure the Croats 'liberty of choice and destiny', and denounced all acts of the Belgrade Government, including its treaties with foreign powers,[16] Stojadinovic was acting under extreme pressure. Less than three weeks later, on February 4, after five members of his Cabinet had resigned, accusing him of having no solution to the Croat question, Prince Paul dismissed him in favour of a new premier, a man acceptable to the Croat leader, Maček, with whom Paul had been in private contact for much of the previous month.

The fall of Stojadinovic was alarming enough to Count Ciano. For a time he was seduced, first by a Croatian landowner, the Marquis de Bombelles,[17] who turned out to be a Yugoslav spy, and then by an Italianate Croat called Carnelutti, with a brother in the Italian consular service, a relative of Dino Alfieri, the Italian Minister of Propaganda, who sought a subsidy to finance a Croat uprising.[18] Both represented themselves as being sent by Maček; while Carnelutti was certainly in touch with the Croat leader, the hopes he inspired in Count Ciano's breast were quite baseless. What was real, and frightening to the Count, was the evidence which reached him of Croat approaches to the Germans and of German encouragement which included the formation of a Croatian legion in Munich and broadcasts in Serbo-Croat from the SS-controlled Vienna radio.[19] It was this news which provoked Mussolini to his talk of war with Germany. Yugoslavia was Mussolini's tenderest point; while for Ciano the fall of Stojadinovic and the uncertainty he felt about the new regime and Prince Paul's known Anglophilia was a defeat in itself. The German occupation of Bohemia, coming hot-foot upon this, meant in fact the complete destruction of his East European policy; but the German permissiveness, in allowing Hungary to occupy Ruthenia, merely underlined this still further. Italy's political influence in the Balkans had taken a bad beating.

In reaction, Ciano moved momentarily to try to repair relations with France. With Mussolini's agreement the contacts with Baudouin were re-activated.[20] The French Ambassador in Rome urged his Government to seize the opportunity. A scheme was hatched to bring in Pierre

Laval, the former French premier and Mussolini's collaborator before and during the Ethiopian war, but Daladier, backed by the hard-liners of the French Cabinet, turned the proposal down flat.[21] When the whole of Daladier's Czechoslovak policy lay in ruins at the feet of one dictator, it was not the moment from the point of view of French domestic politics to make concessions to another, even though clandestine contacts had narrowed the real area of disagreement down to the question of Tunis. First, the Italian press attacks on France would have to cease. Then Mussolini's speech, due to be delivered at the Fascist celebration of the anniversary of the March on Rome in 1922, would have to contain some open gesture of reconciliation.

This it might have done, had the Germans not moved swiftly to mend their fences. On March 18, Mussolini was pressing Prince Paul to hasten negotiations with Maček, and ordering troop concentrations on the Venetian borders with Austria and Yugoslavia.[22] On March 20 the German Ambassador appeared to give Ciano the most definite of assurances that Hitler had no aims in the Mediterranean or in Croatia.[23] The following day, he returned with a long and unctuous letter to Ciano, intended for Mussolini.[24] 'Interesting, providing we can believe in it,' said Mussolini. But it had its effect. 'We cannot change policies; after all, we are not prostitutes,' he added.[25] Reports in the French press the following day that Britain was preparing to build a 'front against the dictators', a 'democratic bloc', hardened his views,[26] as already noted.

The next day, however, saw him again bitter with Germany. His speech to the Fascist Grand Council had provoked the French press into depicting him again as Hitler's jackal. In this frame of mind he met Bernardo Attolico, the Italian Ambassador in Berlin. Balding and, but for his immense Roman nose, faintly elf-like in appearance, Attolico was, of all Mussolini's diplomatists, the most accomplished in the Byzantine intrigues by which his master's mind could be influenced. Sent to Berlin in 1935 to replace the violently anti-Nazi and Francophile Vittorio Cerruti and his disastrously indiscreet wife, Attolico disliked the Nazi leadership as much as, or more than, any of his colleagues in the Berlin diplomatic corps. He found the city obscenely violent, the atmosphere brutally vulgar and depressing. But it was not his instinct (he was too much a Roman) to ruin his chance to influence history, by making his repugnance so obvious as to destroy his acceptability to these bibulous barbarians among whom his lot was cast. He made the firmest friends with Ernst von Weizsäcker, Ribbentrop's State Secretary, and with the British Ambassador, Sir Nevile Henderson. These three on occasion collaborated in attempts to avoid, if this were humanly or rather bureaucratically possible, the issues of war and peace coming to the crunch. But his main exertions were directed at preventing his own country at all costs from being involved in the ruin and death his sensitive nostrils picked up so strongly from the atmosphere of the Third Reich. Now the moment seemed to him to have come for another little push to keep his master's own self-destructiveness from exposing itself.

On the evening of March 20 he left Berlin for Rome to report in person. Shortly before his departure, Ribbentrop had summoned him to a meeting with Hitler, at which the Führer had switched on his well-worn charm.[27] Hitler assured Attolico that Germany would support Italy if she was involved in war with France, but gave him to understand that it was the German view that such a conflict were best postponed for a few years. All this was intended to add to the effect of Ribbentrop's letter and to prevent Mussolini's reaction to the German occupation of Prague driving him either into a conflict or an accommodation with France. Two further steps, with the same end, were undertaken. On March 22, the German Military Attaché in Rome announced the initiation of the Staff conversations for which the Italians had been pressing so long.[28] And on March 25 Hitler sent Mussolini a letter so fulsome in tone that the German Foreign Ministry did all it could to preserve its secrecy.[29] Hitler flattered Mussolini's vanity in praising his role in preventing the 'Bolshevization' of Italy, spoke of the 'similarity in the development of our two ideologies and our two revolutions' in which 'one was tempted to believe in a single decision by Providence', referred to the 'hellish hatred' poured on them both by 'the rest of the world' and announced his unalterable decision: 'whatever may be the path you tread, Duce, you shall see in me and in the Germans your unchanging friends.'

The trouble was that in his own revolting way Hitler meant this. He had admired Mussolini and taken him as his model[30] ever since the days when as an obscure nationalist agitator he had conceived an immediate admiration for the 'great man south of the Alps' who had saved Italy from the 'Jewish-Bolshevist world hydra'. He was never to lose this admiration, even when Mussolini's press, after the 'night of the long knives' in 1934, were abusing Nazism as the party of pederasts and pimps. Even when Mussolini was ignominiously dismissed in 1943, in the days of Italy's defeat, Hitler sent his commandos under Otto Skorzeny to rescue the fallen Duce from his imprisonment, and bring him back to reign, if not to rule, over German-occupied North Italy, the puppet republic of Salo. He had cast Mussolini as his fellow hero, fellow Nietzschean superman; and nothing Mussolini could do, short of an outright declaration of war on Germany, could have disturbed him.

Under the circumstances there was not much Attolico could do with his master.[31] His strong emphasis on the need for clarification in the internal relations of the Axis was in itself a threat. The Axis, a metaphor indefinable to an extent which made ambiguity seem clarity, could not have survived such a definition; as well he knew. He did, however, feed Mussolini's own consciousness of this, warning him that Germany was 'on the skids . . . from the plane of overbearing power to that of annoyance, and might strike at our interests'. Suspicion, vacillation and doubt were the only weapons he could call on, and while in open court Mussolini was overwhelmed by Hitler's flattery, in practice his suspicions remained.

Count Ciano had already hit on a way to re-establish the prestige of the Fascist regime. To annex Albania was a project he had been urging since March 1938. Now, on March 23, Mussolini decided to move on the matter. Yet in re-asserting Italian power by such an action, demonstrating as both men thought their independence of Berlin, they were to confirm the belief of the democracies that they were acting in collaboration with Germany.

The kingdom of Albania seemed to present everything that in this imperfect world could be desired as the target for a continuing demonstration of Italian power. Small, mountainous, its people divided between warring tribes of Muslim, Orthodox and Catholics, it had, since 1921, been under a virtual Italian mandate, recognized by all the powers as such. The only other great power with interest in Albania, Britain, whose Anglo-Persian Oil Company was interested in the very high-quality Albanian oil, had accepted the preponderance of Italian influence in the 1920s. The British Mission in Albania resembled nothing so much as one of the minor British Balkan embassies depicted by Mr Lawrence Durrell.[32] The Albanian monarch, King Zog, with his Hungarian queen, had an inescapably operetta-ish Ruritanian air about him. A tribal leader, from the hereditary lords of the mountainous Mathi region, who had overthrown his principal rival with an army of White Russians armed by Yugoslavia and allegedly paid by the Anglo-Persian Oil Company, he had turned to Italy for support when it was proposed to change his presidency into a kingdom. But his slight frame and handsome appearance hid a mind as ruthless with those weaker than himself and as devious with those stronger as any the Balkans ever produced.

Count Ciano had been pressing for Italian occupation and annexation of Albania since the middle of 1937.[33] He had put up a proposal to the

Duce for a 'radical solution' after returning from attending King Zog's wedding in April 1938.[34] The Duce had then agreed to action in twelve months' time, returning from Florence on May 9, 1938 after seeing Hitler off to Germany.[35] Preparations had been made to subvert the dissident tribes,[36] and the Albanian Minister in Rome, King Zog's adjutant, General Zoff Sereggi, was won over to the Italian side.[37] For a time, as the occasion for a coup, even the assassination of King Zog seems to have been considered.[38] This had, however, been dropped as a result of the Duce's anxieties over Yugoslavia; in its place a scheme had been evolved for the partition of Albania between Yugoslavia and Italy, the details of which had been discussed between Count Ciano and Milan Stojadinovic during Count Ciano's visit to Belje in Yugoslavia in January 1939.[39] This plan was rendered useless by Stojadinovic's fall from power; Prince Paul rejected the Italian proposals with contumely. Italy was left to go it alone.

Mussolini, as was his wont, had blown hot and cold about the project from its inception. As always he liked the idea of bold, uncompromising, piratical, ruthless action. It suited him, pandered to his view of himself as the embodiment of Fascist activism. And yet there were dangers, risks that no one could foresee. His instincts warned him against such precipitate action. He was far from convinced that Italian public opinion would accept the occupation of Albania as an answer to the occupation of Prague. Bombastic, ridden with anxieties, indecisive as always, he was only really nerved to decision by the abundant evidence of German goodwill; and his final choice was less for the bold piracy Ciano planned than for the imposition of a new agreement upon a king who had already shown himself willingly pliant under Italian pressure.

King Zog was, however, not having any of this. Colonel Mario de Ferraris, the Italian intelligence agent who was sent on March 25 to negotiate with King Zog over the acceptance of a protectorate, found him agreeable but evasive.[40] His ministers said one thing, he another, a game he had been playing on Italian diplomatists since the 1920s. Pushed by Ciano and needled by the King of Italy, who told him that it was not worth taking these risks just to grab 'four rocks', and that the Germans in Munich were calling him 'Gauleiter of Italy', Mussolini decided to push ahead with an occupation by force.[41] Zog's queen was very near her time with their first child, and Ciano calculated that the King would do anything rather than risk their lives. He reckoned, however, without Zog's sense of honour, the honour of a man bred in a society where the vendetta was a normal part of life. Life as an Italian puppet was not for him. He would fight while he could and then withdraw across the frontier as he had in 1921 before he ever became king to evade his rival, Fan Noli. On April 4, he warned the British Minister in Tirane that he believed Italian invasion to be imminent.[42] The warning did not reach London. The following day, all Italian citizens in Albania were summoned by Italy to evacuate the country. Italian ships appeared off the Albanian coast. King Zog's son was born. Two days later, on Good Friday, the day of Judas Iscariot, the Italian invasion began. There was scattered shooting at the four ports where the landings took place but no serious resistance. Had there been, the Italians could well, in the view of at least one prominent Italian, have been driven into the sea, so chaotic and muddled were the Italian command arrangements for the landing. But the tribes had been too well subverted and many of Zog's own entourage turned against him. On April 8 he withdrew across the frontier[43] into Greece to the embarrassment and fury of the Greek Government, abandoning his subjects and making a nationalist resistance to Italy impossible. His wife and newborn child were all that he was prepared to save.[44] Thereafter he disappeared from the pages of history. He died in exile in Egypt.

Mussolini's action had, he thought, been more than adequately prepared. Although his Ambassador in London had had only two meetings with Lord Halifax in the two months which had followed the visit of Chamberlain and Halifax to Rome, and there had been no sign during all that period of any change in the rigidity of the French position or in London's unwillingness to play the mediator, the new turn in British foreign policy in the last weeks of March seemed to presage a new approach. On March 31 when Chamberlain was officially announcing the guarantee to Poland, he penned a special message, to go by the 'secret channel', Sir Joseph Ball to Dingli, to tell Mussolini that Britain was only awaiting a formal request from him for mediation to put pressure on the French to negotiate.[45]

Sir Joseph saw Dingli on April 4. Dingli did not take the message to the Italian Embassy until two days later. Crolla, the Counsellor in the Italian Embassy, commented sceptically before transmitting the message, that while he could understand that Britain and France desired Italian support against Germany, he could not see, in the light of Daladier's public statement that he would never negotiate with Italy, what the two democracies could offer to make it worth Italy's while.

The following day, Crolla asked to see the Prime Minister urgently, with a personal message from Mussolini.[46] Told that the Prime Minister was in Scotland for ten days, he was forced to content himself with handing the message to Halifax.[47] Ciano saw Lord Perth the same day.[48] Both were told of the numerous breaches of Italian trust allegedly perpetrated by King Zog. Both reacted so calmly as to give Ciano and Mussolini to believe that London was already reconciled to the Italian action against Albania.[49]

The Italian action against Albania was conceived, by Count Ciano at least, as a demonstration of Italian independence from Germany. To the statesmen of Europe, confronted as they were with all the familiar appearances of yet another Axis weekend coup, with their missions in Albania cut off from the international cable offices, the flood of justificatory propaganda and congratulatory military communiqués from Rome seemed to prove the Italian action the exact opposite. 'One step in a wider movement for the achievement of the expansionist aims of the Axis powers, who, it must be presumed, are acting in collusion,' was how it struck Lord Halifax.[50] The Turkish Premier, Inönü, put it more subtly to the German Minister in Ankara, Hans Kroll.[51] Either Hitler had incited Mussolini into action, in which case the Axis had to be treated as a hostile whole; or, as he told Kroll, 'if Mussolini did not inform your government, that is a further proof for us that Italy apparently needs to pay no attention to German opinion.'

The news of the Italian action struck four capitals with particular panic: Athens, Belgrade, Bucharest and Paris. In Athens the Greek Government, dominated by King George II and the military dictator, General John Metaxas, had been living for some time in a paranoiac world of its own imaginings. Son of an impecunious Ionian aristocrat, proud of the threadbare title of Count which he traced back to the seventeenth century, Metaxas was a long-term admirer of King Constantine (who had, as heir-apparent, already taken him under his wing before 1909) and a long-term enemy of democracy, whether Greek, French or British. Pro-German in World War I, Metaxas was deported to Corsica by the pro-Allied Greek Premier of the day in 1917. After the war he had returned, a convinced enemy of democracy still, a monarchist, looking for an opportunity, as he had put it before 1914, 'to drink a little parliamentary blood'.

His King, George II, restored to power in November 1935, was, however, completely Anglophile. Metaxas was able to foil a republican *coup d'état*, but was unable himself to win power by electoral means. Instead in August 1936 he persuaded the King to allow him to proclaim a dictatorship. This the British actually tolerated and supported, Anthony Eden defending Metaxas in April 1937 against charges of working with Germany. This did not prevent Metaxas, who remained in his own mind so convinced a monarchist as to consider himself totally dependent on George II, from being convinced that the British

Government wanted his overthrow. However, so long as Britain and Germany remained on friendly terms, General Metaxas was not too unhappy, but the growing division between the two great powers and the move of Italy towards Germany revived his convictions. In October 1938, while his King was visiting London, he had discussed an alliance with Britain with the British Ambassador in Athens, in the hope that the inevitable British refusal would free his hands in the Anglo-German conflict he now believed to be only a matter of time.[52] He failed to get George II to visit Germany and see Hitler, and in March 1939 he was again confiding to his journal his fears that Britain was seeking his fall.[53] He was not altogether wrong. Lord Lloyd had made a special trip to Athens in February to try to persuade King George to dismiss him, but in vain.[54]

The Greek Foreign Ministry had therefore regarded the initial efforts of the British to create a Balkan bloc against Axis expansion with a rather jaundiced eye.[55] The British approaches struck them a little like an invitation *à travailler pour le roi de Prusse*. But the Italian invasion of Albania, on a scale more suited to an invasion of France (some twenty Italian divisions were reported to be involved), aroused all their old fears of Italy. In 1925 Mussolini had shocked the whole world by bombarding the beautiful Greek island of Corfu, in the course of a minor difference with the Greek Government. On April 8, the Greek Military Attaché in Rome reported that the same source which had given him advance warning, to the day, of the Italian attack on Albania, had told him that Italy intended to attack Corfu between April 10 and 12.[56] The same information reached the Greek representative in Geneva from a source believed to be in touch with Italian General Staff circles, and from the Greek Minister in London who had it from a German source via Reuters news agency.[57] At midnight General Metaxas sent for the British Minister and told him that Italy would be resisted to the utmost.[58] The legatees of the traditions of Athens and Sparta had no love for the new imperialists of Rome. What would Britain do?

The Greek reaction was paralleled by that in Bucharest. The Romanians had had their hands full after the stir caused by M. Tilea's personal interpretation of his instructions, partly in sorting out what had actually been said in London, partly in attempting to resolve the continuing internal argument between the advocates of an agreement with Germany and those of King Carol's new appointments the previous winter, Grigore Gafencu, the Foreign Minister, Armand Călinescu, the Prime Minister, Alexandru Cretzianu, the State Secretary in the Foreign Ministry, who were attempting to keep all Romania's options open. Their biggest anxiety, however, was Hungary, whom they saw as as much Germany's forerunner and agent as Italy was in the Mediterranean. The Hungarian action against the Carpatho-Ukraine aroused their deepest anxieties. In December 1938 Romanian intelligence had come into possession of what was believed to be German military orders for an attack on Romania. The German troops which moved into Czechoslovakia were widely believed to have had in their possession maps and poster material printed in the Romanian language. Only the most careful diplomacy, with British mediation, had secured a degree of demobilization and the string of proposals for some kind of non-aggression pact between Romania and Hungary thereafter; Romanian anxieties were fed by Hungarian intransigence and refusal to abandon Hungarian claims on Romania. The Hungarians were, in fact, on the verge of an agreement with Romania on a mutual demobilization,[59] but their intimation of this was accompanied by the threat conveyed through Belgrade and Warsaw that if Romania failed to demobilize within six days, Hungary would march.[60]

The Romanians had other worries too. Reports of Colonel Beck's visit to London suggested they were about to be pressed into a general alliance against Germany and Italy. A Cabinet meeting hastily assembled on April 6 decided on further steps to avoid this, to secure a separation of Romania's links with south-east Europe from her link with Poland, and to win a unilateral guarantee from Britain and France.[61] M. Gafencu was to go to Ankara, to ensure agreement with Turkey on keeping the Balkan bloc neutral. M. Cretzianu, his deputy in the Foreign Ministry, was to go to Paris and London. The news from Albania broke the following morning. Britain and France seemed to do nothing. Carol immediately cancelled Romanian demobilization.[62] M. Gafencu left hot-foot for Ankara. The impression he left there was deplorable. M. Saracoğlu, with whom he spent three hours on April 8, thought his nerves had betrayed him,[63] and that he was in terror of 'damaging the teeth of the tiger who is seeking to devour him'. Saracoğlu did his best to restore Gafencu's courage, but it was not the best of preparations for his forthcoming visit to Warsaw and Berlin.

The nervous state of opinion in Bucharest and Athens was, if anything, surpassed in Paris. French military intelligence, always appallingly inclined to over-estimate hostile strength and intentions (they had credited Germany with fifty divisions on the French frontier in September 1938 as against the five inadequately equipped divisions which were all the Reichswehr could muster), had been repeating scare stories of imminent Axis attacks since the beginning of April. On April 3 and April 7, a sudden attack on France's western frontier by mechanized divisions moved from Prague was said to be imminent.[64]

An imminent Italian attack on Gibraltar was reported on April 7,[65] a surprise German air attack on London and Paris,[66] attacks on Yugoslavia,[67] Poland and Danzig,[68] and on Egypt,[69] all were mentioned. A different note was struck by rumours that Turkey was about to invade Syria.[70] A week later (April 15) there was to be a similar alarm over an alleged Spanish plan to attack Tangier and the Pyrenees.[71] Such alarms, as we have seen, were not unknown in London, but the involvement of French intelligence in them, when coupled with the persistent over-estimation of German strength, does cast considerable doubts on the balance and competence of French sources, if not on their loyalty.

This excitability was shared by M. Daladier himself. M. Daladier had been under strong pressure from the Italophile elements in his Cabinet and from M. François-Poncet to bury his distrust of Italy and open conversations with the Italians so as to free France's hands against Germany. On the eve of the Italian attack on Albania,[72] Chamberlain, as we have seen, had been about to add delicately to this pressure. The reports of imminent German movement, of troop movements towards Germany's frontiers on April 8, when taken with the Italian attack on Albania, were, however, too much for M. Daladier. On April 9, at a hastily summoned meeting of the Permanent Committee for National Defence,[73] it was decided, on his urging, to place the French Mediterranean fleet on an emergency footing and to put the frontier forces in a state of readiness by the call-up of reservists. On the hypothesis of an immediate war with both Axis powers, with Britain and the Soviet Union as allies and the Soviets holding the bulk of Germany's forces in the East, it was decided to launch an immediate all-out assault by land and air on Italy.

The new Romanian *démarche* appears to have unnerved M. Daladier entirely.[74] M. Cretzianu launched his appeal in Paris on April 11. The following day the French Cabinet met in conditions of renewed alarm.[75] While M. François-Poncet, recalled from Rome, preserved a saturnine silence, M. Daladier demanded an immediate French guarantee of Romania to be issued that very afternoon. A German attack on Romania in concert with Hungary was imminent. A German ultimatum would be presented in Bucharest within hours. Germany was determined to gain control of Romania's oil, which was the key to the entire situation. Daladier wanted to issue the declaration at noon that day; for the sake of preserving Anglo-French concord and unity, he was prepared, against his better judgment, to wait twenty-four hours, but no longer.[76]

The Romanian importunity, the French panic, struck Lord Halifax and his advisers as singularly unfortunate and ill-considered.[77] The basis of the British guarantee policy, as it had originally been conceived in the last week in March before Mr Ian Colvin and his unknown co-informants had succeeded in startling them into issuing a unilateral guarantee for Poland, was to use the offer of guarantees as a weapon to bring together Poland, Romania and the Balkan powers, especially Turkey, into an interlocking system, by which an attack on any one state would bring in all its neighbours as well as activating the British and French guarantees. They had already found it difficult to persuade Colonel Beck, safe in the possession of a public guarantee, to adjust his alliance with Romania so as to make it operative against Germany as well as the Soviet Union. It had already become clear that as long as Hungarian tension with Romania persisted, Colonel Beck would use this to avoid entering into any serious commitment to Romania.

As for the Romanians, their fears of being drawn into an 'encircle-ment' of Germany had been more than adequately explained at the beginning of April.[78] But it was still difficult to see their policy as anything but procrastination in the hope of evading a decision and preserving Romanian neutrality. To concede a second unilateral guarantee to M. Cretzianu's new importunity would be to abandon any hope of bringing Poland and Turkey to her support. Instead of an interlocking dam against further German expansion in Eastern Europe, its stones well cemented together by mutual alliances and guarantees, Britain would be left with a series of stones, each supported only by the strut of unilateral guarantees from the far side of the flood water. It was difficult to imagine any dam functioning adequately under such conditions.

Lord Halifax therefore did his best to restrain M. Daladier, but in vain. British attention, despite the Italian guarantees given so hurriedly to Greece in response to his peremptory demand, had turned to the need to stabilize the eastern Mediterranean. Whether Mussolini's action against Albania was concerted with Hitler or not, it was clear that he had to be regarded as a potential disturber of the peace. Central to British thoughts on the restraint of Italy, as to any hopes of bringing about a Balkan bloc to withstand Germany, was Turkey. In the event of war, the British planned to take Italy out first. Turkey's role was so 'pivotal' that every effort should be made, so the Cabinet were advised, to persuade Turkey into an alliance, even if this meant giving Greece a parallel guarantee.[79]

Previously Chamberlain had been worried about alienating Musso-lini. This worried him no more. When the Italians sought to use the 'secret channel' further to reassure Britain, Sir Joseph Ball told Mr

Dingli that his master was extremely angry and that the Italian gestures would not deceive a baby.[80] 'I have been at the nadir all week . . . profoundly distressed and unhappy,' Chamberlain wrote to his sister.[81] 'Musso has behaved to me like a sneak and a cad . . . he'has carried through his smash and grab raid with complete cynicism. . . . Any chance of a future rapprochement with Italy has been blocked by Musso just as Hitler has blocked any German rapprochement.'

The Foreign Policy Committee and the Cabinet determined therefore on a guarantee for Greece.[82] But the French could not be shaken. Confronted with the alternative of a French guarantee and a joint Anglo-French guarantee for Greece and Poland; with secret intelligence now suggesting that the German preparations against Poland were a piece of deliberate deception and that Germany's real target was Romania;[83] and faced with a personal appeal from M. Daladier, Halifax had no alternative but to yield.[84] On April 13, Mr Chamberlain, speaking in the House of Commons,[85] and M. Daladier in the French Assembly, announced British and French guarantees for Romania and Greece.[86] The guarantee policy, from being just a military nonsense, had now become a general *mélange* of nonsense. Such residual hopes as the British authorities entertained of putting them together into a single structure of sense had to rest on whatever powers of persuasion Lord Halifax could exercise on M. Gafencu, and on the staunchness and single-mindedness of the Turks. If one guarantee does not deter, because the power to be deterred is not convinced it will be implemented, it will become less credible rather than more if other guarantees equally questionable on their own are added to it. But then M. Daladier never really understood the notion of deterrence, and he counted unthinkingly on the Soviet Union. Lord Halifax's powers of persuasion; M. Daladier's automatic reliance on Soviet hostility to Germany; Turkish steadfastness under pressure; these three had to form the basis on which the policy of Balkan guarantees now rested. Only the third was to prove reliable. Josef Stalin had begun to calculate.

CHAPTER 13

STALIN BEGINS TO CALCULATE

The British guarantee for Poland, with its vaguest of mentions of the Soviet Union, was extraordinarily badly received in Moscow. The Soviets had been kept almost completely in the dark as to what was afoot. The precipitancy of the British action did not prevent her consultation with, among other states, France, Poland, the Dominions and Portugal.[1] The only contact with the Soviet Union, however, was a conversation between Ivan Maisky, the Soviet Ambassador in London, and Sir Alexander Cadogan on March 29, at which Cadogan explained that Britain had dropped the idea of a four-power declaration and was contemplating giving assurances of direct military assistance to Poland and Romania.[2] Then at lunchtime on March 31, shortly before Chamberlain and Halifax rose in the Commons and the Lords to read the text of the guarantee, Halifax gave Maisky the text, asking that he might say that the Soviet Government approved the statement.[3] There was far too little time for Maisky to cable Moscow for approval of any formula, and he was far too adept a survivor of the years of Stalin's purges to stick his neck out by giving such an assurance without direct instructions.

The best Halifax could get Maisky to accept was his agreement to Chamberlain saying that he believed that the principles behind the guarantee were 'understood and appreciated by' the Soviet Government. After all, such a statement could always be represented to his lords and masters in Moscow as having been made by Chamberlain on his own initiative. For the record Maisky spread the story all around London that he had not been consulted at all, complaining to all his contacts that Chamberlain was taking an extreme liberty in associating the Soviet Union with the guarantee.[4] He was subsequently forced to admit that, speaking to Cadogan on March 29, he had called the proposed guarantee a revolution in British policy.[5] But it also appears that he did not take it seriously and may very well not have reported on it to Moscow. He did, however, report, on the basis of a conversation with the French Ambassador in London, M. Corbin, that the subject of guarantees for Poland and Romania was on the table and that, in French eyes at least, the British seemed 'more willing than at any time in the past' to accept obligations in respect of Eastern Europe.[6] But both at the time and in their subsequent historiography, the Soviets have always insisted that they did not know the four-power declaration had been dropped until April 1.

It is hardly surprising, therefore, that the announcement of the guarantee struck the Soviets like a thunderclap. Litvinov could hardly conceal his rage. Addressing the unfortunate British Ambassador, he complained bitterly that all his efforts for Anglo-Soviet co-operation had been 'summarily dropped'. The Soviet Government had 'had enough, and would henceforth stand apart free of any commitments'. Seeds used his best Russian to attempt to calm the Soviet Commissar, usually so suave and witty; but in vain. Litvinov was fighting for his political life, possibly his actual life itself. He told Seeds he found the guarantee literally incredible. He could not believe Britain would ever fight for Danzig or the Polish Corridor.[7] And if Litvinov could not believe it, what of the cold mind of his master, so little experienced in dealing with foreign ways of thought, so crushingly sure in his reduction of all he could not understand to the level of suspicion, intrigue and universal enmity that he understood only too well? Nor were Maisky's reports any help; he chose rather to concentrate on the views of Chamberlain's critics, of Lloyd George and the Labour leadership, and gave the impression that the Foreign Office's indignant rebuke for the combined *Times*, Reuters and Beaverbrook press attempt to devalue the British guarantee to Poland was merely a 'weak and rather vague refutation' which carried no conviction.[8]

To enter into the minds of the Soviet leadership in this period is extraordinarily difficult. And yet if their speeches and writings, their memoirs and their historians reflect their view of the world, one cannot help distinguishing two kinds of thought at odds with one another. The one, cold, monumentally suspicious, viewed the entire world as, in varying degrees, evil and hostile. Like the paranoiac convinced that each man's hand is turned against him, that the most accidental, innocent and irrelevant of moves hides deep and sinister designs for his destruction, the representatives of this line of thought remained convinced that the Governments of the West waited only for the day of all-out war against the Soviet Union; their every manœuvre, be it towards the Soviet Union, be it between themselves, cloaked yet another long-term move towards the ultimate day when, to save its own existence and solve its otherwise self-destructive contradictions, the capitalist world would launch an all-out attack on the citadel of Socialism. Such men excelled in discovering selfish motives, if not thoroughly sinister ones, for every Western action. Their world was peopled with spies, saboteurs, *provocateurs* and plotters. They more than half-believed the Kafka-like inventions displayed in the scenarios written for the big show trials by the agents of the NKVD. Stalin himself, Molotov, Beria, and most of Stalin's immediate entourage, survivors of and destroyers in the purges, were more than touched by this miasma.

Against these were ranged those who saw divisions in the outside world between the agents of ultimate evil and pro-Soviet, socialistically-inclined forces. Their world was an extraordinary *mélange* of OK names to be appealed to, enlisted or manipulated, of mass appeals to be secured, of organizations to be incited, of points to be scored and speeches to be made, a world exciting, gratifying, filled with agitation, peopled with the same dark forces of evil as their more suspicious opposites recognized; but those forces could be denounced, identified, unmasked. This was the school of agitprop diplomacy; its members were, by nature, agitators, organizers, intriguers, men attempting to tie the bourgeoisie up in its own contradictory and hypocritical morality, counting the names of the near-great whom they had enlisted, exulting in the lists of resolutions they had secured for party or trades union congresses, finding in the activity which filled their days a refuge from the realization that their efforts were pointless froth, their agitation unrewarded, and their lists of well-known names lists of those who were prominent but powerless.

Ivan Maisky was an arch-example of this type. To do his job properly in Britain at this time he would have needed to cultivate not the long-discredited Lloyd George, the parliamentary leaders of the Labour and Liberal parties, or the 'premature' (a good Soviet word that) anti-Germans of Eden's and Churchill's rival entourages, whom he fed with half-truths about his diplomatic conversations. His task would rather have been to do his utmost to convince the Conservative Cabinet of Soviet military strength and determination, of what the Soviets could and would do to oppose Hitler. But this would have meant befriending and cultivating men whom he, the eternal café-revolutionary, regarded as beyond cultivation. He preferred to intrigue, to 'leak' to sympathetic journalists, to agitate and organize political pressure against them. And then he complained of the lack of confidence obtaining in Anglo-Soviet relations. Lost in admiration at his own skill in agitation, snobbishly proud of the half-great was-men he had been able to organize into his schemes, delighted with his powers in penetrating the anti-establishment (which is in Britain so much a part of the establishment as to cause real radicals to talk of a mutual conspiracy), he failed to see that he was juggling with a collection of political nulls and minuses and that his own folly was working on and multiplying that of the British authorities with whom he had to deal.

In some ways he is a sad, even a tragic figure still, this epitome of the British image of a Soviet diplomatist, with his 'sad Tartar' eyes, longing always for an Anglo-Soviet *rapprochement*, loving much in both the countries with which his destiny was tied, denounced in his dotage still by *Sovetskaya Kultura* for that most hideous of Soviet literary crimes, 'subjectivity', and, even in his latter years, tried and sentenced under Khrushchev for his links with Molotov, after the latter's defeat and downfall.[9] His sentence was, it is true, quashed on appeal to the Supreme Court. But it is a sad end to the life of even a successful survivor.

Such feelings, however, cannot survive long exposure to the eternal adolescent cleverness of his pronouncements on those among whom his life lay, his pettiness towards those he disliked, his meanness and lack of generosity, above all the tediousness of his perpetual intrigues and the consistency with which he misunderstood and misrepresented the subjects of his obscurations. Picture a Soviet leadership immured in the Kremlin, attempting to see straight through a haze of its own ideological suspicions and fed regular doses of Maisky's eternal vanities and posturings, and one can begin to understand quite how they were to walk so blindly into the disaster of June 22, 1941, deaf to all warnings, seeing even in the most overt German acts of war simply 'provocations' invented by Britain.

Nor was Litvinov any less guilty of doctrinaire stupidity. The published Soviet documents show him expending great efforts trying to check the British statement that Polish refusal to take part in a 'combination' with the Soviet Union against Germany had made the issue of a unilateral guarantee the only way of stopping Hitler.[10] British worries about the deep hostility towards co-operation with the Soviet Union manifest in the Dominions, he dismissed. And fed with every scrap of evidence Maisky could dredge from Lloyd George and the Liberal opposition to Chamberlain to show that the change in British policy was less than totally supported within the Cabinet, he seems to have concluded that what he took to be the basic aim of Chamberlain's policy, to embroil Germany and the Soviet Union in a war of mutual destruction, perhaps over Lithuania and the Balkan states (which Britain had not guaranteed), was still unchanged.

Instead, Litvinov fell back on what can only be described as the language and attitudes of the slighted teenage lover. 'It is intolerable', he wrote to Maisky on April 4,[11] 'for us to be in the situation of the man who is invited to a party and then asked not to come because the other guests do not wish to meet him. We would prefer to be crossed off the list of guests altogether.' Since, in his view, the British Government was only making gestures towards Russia in order to defend its policy against public opinion in Britain, he told Maisky to keep his distance from the Foreign Office. 'We do not need advice as to how to protect our own interests,' he wrote to Suritz in Paris.[12] The best judges of Litvinov's assertion should be the Soviet people, who in June 1941 had to face the onslaught of a Nazi empire in command of all Europe, untrammelled by any fears of a two-front war; with a war economy not only preserved against the weakening effects of Britain's blockade, but greatly strengthened by the years of Soviet deliveries of raw materials essential to that machine. He had, however, only one month more in office.

Soviet assessment of British motives was further derailed from a correct assessment by the visit during the last ten days of March 1939 of a British trade mission, headed by Robert Hudson, then Parliamentary Under Secretary at the Department of Overseas Trade. Normally, a mere parliamentary under secretary is the lowest, the most cribbed and confined of political figures, whose role is merely to deputize for his minister in answering the less controversial of parliamentary questions. Any step out of line brings immediate rebuke from minister and senior officials alike. But the Department of Overseas Trade, as Maisky wrote to Litvinov,[13] was unique, a hybrid sub-department nominally responsible to, yet in fact independent of, the Board of Trade and the Foreign Office. In practice this meant that Hudson was his own master.

Politically Hudson's views lay towards the right wing of the Conservative Party. He disliked and resented the disproportionate share of senior posts lavished on the Conservatives' partners in the so-called National Government – the National Liberals and the National Labour. Nor, with his landed gentry background, was he particularly drawn to the lawyers and provincial businessmen of Chamberlainite Conservatism. This ambitious and driving young Conservative hopeful had nearly come unstuck in December 1938 for his part in a conspiracy to overthrow the hated Minister of War, the Jewish National Liberal leader, Leslie Hore-Belisha, and Sir Thomas Inskip, the Minister for Co-ordination of Defence. Despite the strictest of instructions from the Foreign Office that he was to confine himself to the question of a new trade and payments agreement with the Soviet authorities, he was apparently determined to return with some kind of personal political coup, at least to the extent of linking an economic agreement with closer political relations. Such, at any rate, was the burden of his private conversations with Sefton Delmer, the foreign correspondent of the *Daily Express*, who accompanied him to Moscow, which were naturally blazoned all over the British press; and in his first conversation with M. Litvinov, the Soviet Commissar, he devoted himself entirely to political matters.[14]

His main conversations, however, were with Anastas Mikoyan, the Soviet Commissar for Foreign Trade, who was beginning to edge Litvinov out of some of the policy areas for which he had formerly been responsible. He found both Litvinov and Mikoyan at first even prepared to discuss a settlement of the long-outstanding issue of the Tsarist Government's debts in Britain, as a means of serving 'political advantage'.[15] Seeds noted that press 'sneers' at Britain's 'capitulatory policy' had ceased temporarily, though there was no mention in the Soviet press of Hudson's visit. But by March 27 the wind had changed; Hudson's hopes of seeing Stalin were disappointed, though he met Molotov as well as Litvinov and Mikoyan at the final reception. Whatever hopes Hudson still retained were ruined entirely by a too belated attempt by Halifax to eliminate from the final press communiqué, which the Soviets had already approved, any mention of political discussions having taken place.

Conscientious to a fault, Sir William Seeds did his best to fulfil these instructions; but he was too late to suppress the communiqué, and only succeeded in adding to Litvinov's suspicions at this attempt to censor a harmless and uncharacteristically graceful Soviet-inspired reference to the advantage of the personal contacts established by the meeting,[16] from the point of view of 'the consolidation of Anglo-Soviet relations' and 'international collaboration' to solve the problems of peace. Seeds himself telegraphed that the communiqué could only be found objectionable 'on the supposition that HMG desire publicly to abandon after about a week's trial their recent policy of consulting the Soviet government and to relapse into an aloofness which has poisoned relations since Munich'.[17] Cadogan did his best to explain the matter away to Maisky on March 29,[18] but this characteristic example of Halifax's flappability under fire contributed more than its fair share to Soviet suspicions. The Soviet press renewed its attacks on British 'capitulationism' the day after Hudson left Moscow. Litvinov's position, and the chances of genuine Anglo-Soviet co-operation, had been still further unnecessarily and gratuitously weakened. Soviet historians now interpret the Hudson mission as yet another gambit in Chamberlain's supposed policy of threatening 'Germany with a *rapprochement* with the Soviet Union'.

This was to credit the members of the British Cabinet with a combined capacity for Machiavellianism beyond any of their individual capabilities. The collectivist approach to history, today alas all too common even in countries where it lacks any ideological *raison d'être*, has always been baffled by the doctrine of the collective responsibility of members of the British Cabinet for its decisions. There were, in fact, at this moment, serious divisions within the Cabinet on the policy to be followed towards the Soviet Union. Lord Chatfield, formerly First Sea Lord and quondam Chairman of the Chiefs of Staff Committee, now Minister for the Co-ordination of Defence, Hore-Belisha certainly, and Hoare and Halifax to a certain extent, all urged that the Soviets should not be neglected and pushed to one side. But Chamberlain, backed by Sir John Simon, remained cautious and suspicious.

They had plenty of material with which to back their suspicions. British military opinion dismissed the Red Army as of little use, save in a defensive role.[19] Poland was considered the more useful military ally. Even Sir William Seeds on March 21 provided them with arguments, alluding to the 'considerable satisfaction' with which Stalin could be expected to stay aloof from 'an international conflict from which all the participants would be likely to emerge considerably weakened.'[20] The collective view of the Foreign Office was that Soviet policy was 'invariably opportunist'.[21] This was Chamberlain's own view, strengthened by the violent protests against Soviet participation in their protection which came from Warsaw, Bucharest and the capitals of the Baltic states, as well as from Rome, Lisbon and the Dominions. Not that Chamberlain was not capable of overriding these prejudices, but he did not find it an easy task; against the solid evidence of those whom he regarded as the experts – the diplomatists, Service Chiefs and the Secret Intelligence Service – and the thoroughly ungentlemanly methods of the Soviet Ambassador, the last things likely to inspire his slow mind and deep concern for personal integrity, all he could find to set on the opposite side of the balance were the 'hysterical passion of the opposition' and its 'pathetic belief that in Russia is the key to the situation'.[22]

The real responsibility therefore lay with the one Cabinet colleague to whom Chamberlain always listened, the Foreign Secretary. Infinitely non-involved, Lord Halifax was inclined at the moment to see a middle way. The Soviet Union must not be alienated or allowed to feel that she was being pushed to one side,[23] a sentiment Halifax found easier to enunciate than to practise, as we have seen. But she was to be kept in reserve, 'invited to lend a hand in certain circumstances in the most convenient form'.[24] Best of all would be Soviet benevolent neutrality, the supply of arms to Warsaw from the Soviet arsenals, but no military involvement, since this was totally rejected by the states with whose security Britain was now most immediately concerned, Poland and Romania.

As a long-term policy, given the difficulties the British Government faced in its attempt to produce a diplomatic deterrent to Nazi extremism, this had a certain amount to commend it, on three assumptions: that the Soviet leadership considered the maintenance of the status quo in Eastern Europe to be in its own best interests; that the states of Eastern Europe could be induced not only to accept but to facilitate some degree of Anglo-Soviet co-operation; and that the diplomatic deterrent would deter Hitler rather than provoke him into a pre-emptive strike. The first of these assumptions failed to allow for Molotov's myopia and Stalin's greed. The second was only valid so long as the states to be guaranteed remained more fearful of Germany than of the Soviet Union. This implied that the British guarantee should be made a diplomatic weapon to coerce the states guaranteed into accepting what they otherwise would reject. With the governments of both Poland and Romania, Britain abandoned this advantage in the panic of the moment. Once the guarantees were given, Poland and Romania had secured all they could hope for. If the diplomatic deterrent failed, the Soviet Union represented nothing they could recognize as salvation. By April 13, Halifax had reduced himself and his Government to the ludicrous position where the only way Britain's pledged word could be made good was by the threat of its recision.

This was immediately apparent when Colonel Beck visited London. Short-sighted and parochial as ever, Beck was obsessed with the possibility of conflict over Danzig and ignored anything else. On Danzig there was a real danger. Possibly the Germans might start something even while he was in London, he told his military and diplomatic advisers. Indeed until he could obtain something better than the British guarantee, which he professed to find rather vague and fragile,[25] the risk of an immediate conflict with Germany had somewhat increased. Nevertheless he remained confident that, given half a chance, he could manage and control things. What he wanted above all was a firm bilateral alliance with Britain. This would give Germany pause, strengthen his own position at home and keep the French in line. Beyond this he could not or would not look. He especially would not look at any closer connection with the Soviet Union, or at a transformation of the Polish alliance with Romania from one directed purely against the Soviet Union to a general alliance. He thought the Germans would find it provocative; and he did not think the Romanians had either the guts to stand up to the Germans or any army capable of anything but running away.

His determination was maintained throughout the three days of his visit to London. The visit passed smoothly, the formalities were all observed. With the lanky figure of Count Raczyński, the hawkish Polish Ambassador in London, at his side, the egregious Colonel Beck lunched with the King, gave a reception at the Polish Embassy, and attended lengthy meetings with Lord Halifax and Neville Chamberlain at the Foreign Office and in the Prime Minister's room at the House of Commons.[26] Halifax was abstract and circuitous, approaching his proposals with step-by-step, circumambient logic, leading Beck through all the stages of his own argument to the proposals which seemed to him to stem ineluctably from them; but in vain. Colonel Beck had logic as well disciplined as he had the members of the Polish democratic parties. Neither Halifax's patient stalking nor the more direct methods preferred by the Prime Minister produced any result. Lacking any hold over Beck, neither could induce him to take part in the kind of multilateral arrangement the British wanted, by which 'a number of states would band themselves round Great Britain, France and Poland as a nucleus', as the Prime Minister put it. No Polish participation in any arrangement to protect Romania, no Polish countenance to any contacts with the Soviet Union; these were Beck's negative achievements during his stay in London. As he returned to Poland he could congratulate himself that he had completely limited his liabilities; and that Germany, which, so he was advised, was not ready for a major European war, had been warned off any attack on Poland.[27]

As British policy was driven further and further away from the attempt to create a viable bloc of states in East Europe, pledged to help each other's defence and backed by British, French and Soviet guarantees, Litvinov's attempts to create a similar bloc under Soviet leadership were proving equally unsuccessful. For the time being, Britain had frozen him out over Poland and Romania. Tentative conversations with the Turks had likewise failed to produce any result as yet. And at the end of March he drew a similar blank with the small independent Baltic states of Estonia and Latvia. On March 28, Soviet declarations had been made to both the Latvian and Estonian Governments, warning them of the immense importance the Soviets attached to the maintenance of their independence. Any agreement with a third power which could diminish that independence would be regarded by the Soviet Union as a violation of their existing non-aggression pacts with the Soviet Union.[28] The detailed description of the type of agreement the Soviets had in mind showed very clearly that they feared German acquisition of bases and the like in Latvia and Estonia as a result of the kind of pressure to which the Czechs, Lithuanians and Romanians had already been subjected since March 13. The Estonian and Latvian replies, produced, after consultation between the two states, at the end of the first week in April, constituted a robust rebuttal of the Soviet position. Estonia intended to defend her independence herself, so ran the Estonian reply of April 7, and could not allow anyone else to judge how she fulfilled her international responsibilities.[29] In fact she was to move towards a non-aggression pact with Germany. A large-scale Soviet military demonstration on her borders on April 10 probably confirmed the Estonians in their reluctance to have anything to do with the Soviet approaches.

It is worth noticing here the beginnings of a Soviet obsession with the possibility of a German attack bypassing Poland and Romania, and directed at the Soviet north through the Baltic republics. This may, of course, have been simply the outcome of a Soviet military 'worst case' analysis. It is possible too that it had something to do with the rise in Stalin's councils of Andrei Zhdanov, party boss of Leningrad, who was to play a prominent part in the public oratory side of the forthcoming Anglo-Soviet negotiations. Stalin came to hate him, isolating him in the besieged Leningrad from 1942 to 1944 and purging him in 1947. It is most likely, however, that Stalin, remembering the British influence in the three Baltic capitals, whose successful resistance to the Red Army in 1917–19 had been buttressed by British ships and troops, found in their resistance, and in British reluctance to involve them in any eastern system of guarantees, proof of his continuing suspicions of British motives.

Baulked, here, Litvinov turned back to Britain. Since April 1 and his first bitter complaints about the British guarantee for Poland, Litvinov's representative, M. Maisky, had had two friendly but extremely critical meetings with Halifax in eleven days. One had been devoted to Beck's visit to London,[30] the other to the British reactions to Italy's attack on Albania.[31] Neither could have been said to have advanced the Soviet position one jot. Nor did they in any way diminish Halifax's distrust for Maisky or Maisky's general belief that British policy was all bluff and not serious. Halifax found Maisky 'cynical about the whole situation', or so he told Joseph Kennedy, the American Ambassador. Indeed he made an even more curious and suggestive comment that he was convinced that what he told Maisky was 'given over to the enemies'.[32]

Litvinov was left to search desperately for a way back into the

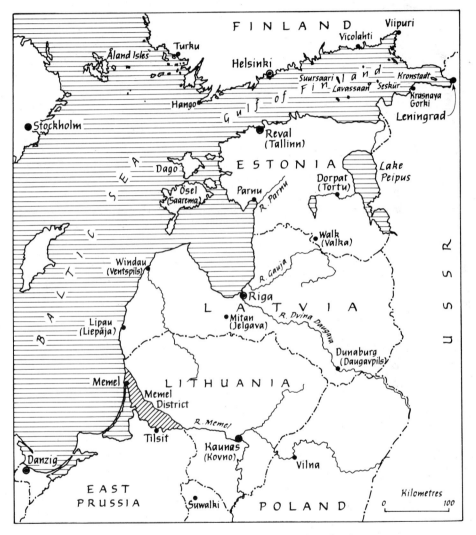

The Baltic coast line from Danzig to South Finland

British-controlled game. The British guarantee to Romania, which closed off what had hitherto seemed the really dangerous part of Germany's road to the east, offered him an opportunity. On April 11, Maisky believed Halifax to have asked him whether the Soviet Union would supply Romania with arms and materials in the event of war.[33] On April 14 therefore Maisky, on Litvinov's instructions, told Halifax that the Soviet Union was ready to give assistance to Romania.[34] How did the British Government think this would best be done?

A piece missing, Tovarish

The offer was reiterated by the Soviet Ambassador in Paris, Suritz, to M. Georges Bonnet.[35] It was undoubtedly genuine. At the very least it was designed to elicit from Halifax whether Britain definitely intended to come to Romania's aid militarily. It went, however, a long way further than Lord Halifax was as yet prepared to go. What he wanted was an open Soviet commitment, something which was essential to the diplomatic deterrent he was trying to create, and which, so far, since they could not secure it on their own terms, the Soviets had managed to avoid. All Halifax wanted was the commitment. He therefore thanked Maisky kindly for his offer and pressed ahead with his proposal, that the Soviet Union should make a unilateral declaration that, in the event of aggression against any of its European neighbours, the Soviet Union would make its assistance available. Maisky was so taken aback he forgot to press the request for information he had been instructed to make.[36] Litvinov, when he heard the proposal from the unfortunate Sir William Seeds, was friendly but obstinate: so friendly as to suggest that he hardly took the British proposal seriously, so obstinate as to suggest that he wanted at all costs to retain the diplomatic initiative.[37]

This seemed to be offered him by a French proposal, evolved in the nervous aftermath of the Italian invasion of Albania, when the French were expecting almost hourly an invasion of Romania by either the Germans or the Hungarians or both, who were, so Polish sources had informed them, about to conclude an alliance.[38] M. Bonnet therefore suggested to Suritz, the day after the guarantee to Romania had been announced, that the Soviet Union should sign an Annexe to the pact concluded between France and itself in May 1935, by which the Soviet Union would be bound to come to France's assistance if a war with Germany developed out of the guarantees for Poland and Romania.[39]

On April 17 in the late evening (his telegram recording the interview was dispatched at twenty-six minutes past four in the morning of April 18), the British Ambassador was called to the Kremlin and handed a written Soviet proposal for a triple alliance against aggression, either against themselves or against the states of Eastern Europe between the Black Sea and the Baltic, to be backed by a military convention.[40] That done, Litvinov recalled his ambassadors, Maisky from London and Merekalov from Berlin, and waited for a reaction from London; and waited, and waited.

Maisky could do nothing for him, sitting in Moscow. He neither had nor sought any contact with Sir William Seeds. And as Litvinov waited, British influence in the Balkans seemed to increase. M. Gafencu, the Romanian Foreign Minister, visited Warsaw, Berlin, London, Paris and Rome.[41] The powers of the Balkan Entente began pressing Bulgaria, the odd state out, to come in and join the neutral bloc.[42] The Yugoslav and Polish authorities were equally active in attempting to damp down Hungary's conflict with Romania.[43] Once again the Soviet Union was excluded. Her only friend in the Balkans, Turkey, seemed to be slipping irretrievably into the British sphere of influence. Everywhere Litvinov turned, Soviet Russia was excluded and his hopes of taking control baulked.

It was in these circumstances that Molotov, his rival and eventual successor, first became active. On April 15, he telegraphed directly to the Soviet Ambassador in Turkey, proposing a Soviet-Turkish meeting as soon as possible, in Tbilisi or Batum.[44] At the same time Litvinov enquired directly of the Turkish Ambassador in Moscow, Apaydin, about the Anglo-Turkish negotiations.[45] Why had not the Turks told him what was going on? On April 21, Apaydin reassured him.[46] The Turks, he said, had told the British that, in the event of a Balkan or Mediterranean war, they anticipated an attack on the Dardanelles, and asked what assistance they could count on from Britain and France. For that matter, Apaydin asked, what assistance could they count on from the Soviets? Litvinov could not answer. Instead he mentioned that the Soviet Deputy Foreign Minister, Vladimir Potemkin, would visit Ankara at the end of April. His real mission was to investigate the position in the Balkans. Advantage was taken of his visit for him to pass through Sofia on the way down to Istanbul, and to visit Bucharest and Warsaw on his return.

On his arrival at Istanbul, Potemkin was treated with high honours. He was well-known in Turkey. While his somewhat clerical unctuous-ness, his involved and somewhat archaic courtesies (he had been a professor of history in Tsarist Russia), had been penetrated by his Turkish acquaintances, he still inspired a considerable degree of con-fidence in the breasts of Kemal Atatürk's successors. On arriving in Istanbul he informed the French Ambassador, M. René Massigli,[47] that his object was to harmonize Turkish and Soviet policy and to synchron-ize the negotiations between Britain, France and Turkey on the one hand and the Soviet Union and Turkey on the other. He wanted very much to see the Balkan Entente strengthened and backed up by an Anglo-Franco-Soviet-Turkish agreement, a view which he repeated to his Turkish hosts. He was more than a little peeved to find that the British negotiations with Turkey had gone as far as they had. He was also worried by the very marked reserve the Turks showed towards Germany, as compared with their open hostility to Italy. The Turks, by his own account,[48] treated him openly, giving him a somewhat edited version of their talks with the Romanians and their exchanges with the British. Their version emphasized the Turkish reluctance to be in-volved in any guarantee system against Germany which was not backed by Soviet arms and Soviet aid. They proposed a direct Turkish-Soviet agreement to make the Anglo-Soviet and Anglo-Turkish agreements, whose conclusion they anticipated, into a triangular relationship. They asked for the terms of the Soviet proposal of April 17 to the British; and they asked, as Potemkin reported, for Soviet blessing for their negotia-tions with Britain. They asked too for Soviet aid in pressing Romania to cede the Dobrudja to Bulgaria so as to include Bulgaria in the Balkan Entente. They discussed a separate Black Sea security pact. And they wanted Soviet arms and 20,000 tons of Soviet sugar. Potemkin duly approved their stand in the Anglo-Turkish negotiations. His instructions, however, reached him on May 3; they may well have been the last dying gasp of Litvinov's ministry.

It will not have escaped notice that the other Soviet Ambassador recalled with Maisky was the Soviet Ambassador in Berlin, Alexsei Merekalov. Maisky has told us[49] that he felt it his duty at this conference to tell the truth, as he saw it, about British intentions. His disquisition would have leant heavily on the machinations of the Astor family and the Cliveden Set, the sinister influence of the American Ambassador, Joseph Kennedy (who, the total and resented outsider in American business circles, seems to have been cast in the Moscow screenplay as the representative wirepuller of American monopoly capitalism), and on the pre-eminence of class consciousness as the driving force in British suspicions of the Soviet Union. Nevertheless he recommended persistence with the alliance negotiations.

What would Merekalov have contributed to this discussion? The egregious Maisky, like the writer of some Victorian shilling shocker, always intent on his sad story of virtue confounded but persistent, and vice triumphant but doomed, does not tell us. But we can fill in his remarks from German sources. He would have been able to report at least two tentative yet surprising approaches from the German side early in April. One came from Karl Schnurre, head of the economic section of the German Foreign Ministry, a long-standing advocate of good German-Soviet relations, the man whose mission to Moscow Ribbentrop had cancelled in January rather than spoil his hopes of agreement with the Poles.[50] If the Soviets' German experts were observing with clear eyes, rather than through the dialectical spectacles worn by M. Maisky, they would have known that Schnurre and his friends in the German Embassy in Moscow had taken the hint dropped by Stalin in his speech of March 11. They would also have known that they had no importance and significance in the formulation of Nazi foreign policy. Schnurre's move seems to have been a straightforward initiative by one of the middle-ranking German diplomatic advocates of good German-Soviet economic solutions.

But what of the NKVD diplomats? Somehow, somewhere, contacts between some Germans and the Soviets were in progress by the end of March. Renzetti, the Italian Consul General in Munich, trapped an admission out of Erich Koch, Goering's associate and Gauleiter of East Prussia, at the end of March.[51] And on April 12 a member of the German Legation in Belgrade, in the course of a bitter complaint to his Turkish colleague over Turkey's bias towards the British policy of encircling Germany, blurted out that, in reaction, the Germans had decided to reach an agreement with the Soviets.[52] Negotiations, he said, between Berlin and Moscow had been in progress for two weeks. Early in April, Ribbentrop had clearly got wind of something, for he ordered Peter Kleist of his private office, the Büro Ribbentrop, to improve his contacts with the Soviet Embassy.[53] Kleist met Astakhov, Counsellor at the Soviet Embassy, and reported so enthusiastically that Ribbentrop in anger told him to break off the contact. The anxiety stayed with him, however. During the April 20 celebrations for Hitler's birthday, he warned Oshima and the Japanese Envoy to Italy, Shiratori, who was also present,[54] that unless the Japanese could solve their problems and conclude the alliance with Germany that both desired, Germany would be forced to sound out Russia on the prospects of a non-aggression pact. It was noticeable too that in his speech on April 28 Hitler omitted his usual ritual denunciations of Soviet Bolshevism. All attacks on the Soviet Union ceased in the German press too, the last one appearing in the SS journal, *Das Schwarze Korps*, on April 28.

Merekalov had also seen Ernst von Weizsäcker, Ribbentrop's deputy in the German Foreign Ministry, on April 17 before leaving for Moscow. The Soviet Military Attaché in Berlin, who accompanied his Ambassador to Moscow, where he took over the direction of Soviet military intelligence, is reported to have seen his opposite numbers at the OKW before leaving. We know what Weizsäcker made of this interview. His memorandum to Ribbentrop[55] was strongly slanted towards convincing his much-despised boss that the Soviet Union was ready to slide into a neutralist stance. What we do not know is what the Soviet participants in these conversations reported. We do not even know if, as Weizsäcker claimed then and subsequently, Merekalov was acting in accordance with instructions from his masters or if the initiative was taken by the Germans.

Having made his report, presumably to the day-long conference of which Maisky has told us, Merekalov disappeared. He never returned to Berlin. From April until September the matter of Soviet contacts with the Germans in Berlin was handled, at least in the formal interchanges, by Astakhov, his deputy, a man so unlike the normal run of Soviet diplomatists in the freedom of his speech and the scope for initiative allowed him (at least in German eyes) that he may well have been of the NKVD himself. On September 2, the appointment of A. A. Shkvartsev, a textile engineer, as Soviet Ambassador in Berlin was announced. Merekalov appears to have spent fifteen years in detention before being released into retirement. He died in 1983. Perhaps he saw better than Litvinov or Molotov where Soviet interests lay.

There is a further pointer to the fine hand of the NKVD. In 1935, as already stated, Mr John Herbert King, of the Foreign Office Communications Centre, had been recruited by the NKVD, but cast afloat when his controller, Theodore Maly, had been recalled to Moscow and disappeared. Shortly after the issue of the British guarantee to Poland had caught Litvinov so unawares, Mr King appears to have been reactivated. On April 19, the German Embassy in London reported from a 'most secret source' details of the Anglo-Polish exchanges and of the Soviet offer to Britain and France.[56] It was to receive similar reports, sometimes as little as five hours elapsing between the receipt of a telegram by the Foreign Office in London and the dispatch of a telegram from the German Embassy in London to Berlin summarizing its contents.[57] These reports did not, however, cover all the exchanges between London and Moscow, only those that coincided with interruptions in the German-Soviet exchanges or hesitancies on the German side. Nor were they always accurate, tending rather to play down any evidence of Soviet enthusiasm and to play up Britain's keenness in the negotiations for an alliance. The 'most secret source' of the German Embassy was, in short, a Soviet agent, working to the NKVD, resident in the Soviet Embassy in London, feeding directly to the Germans the results of Mr King's treason. And through this 'most secret source' the NKVD, acting to Soviet foreign policy directions, could play on German fears. Mr King gave them entrée into the British hand. He could also be used to force cards on the Germans. Meanwhile, in Tokyo, Richard Sorge kept Moscow informed on all that passed between Berlin and the Japanese. Given these three controls, whoever conducted the Soviet side of the negotiations with Britain and Germany was able to play on their partners like a poker player with marked cards.

As M. Potemkin made his round trip; as successively depressing reports came in from Soviet diplomatic missions of the degree of German penetration and German influence in Finland, Estonia and Latvia, all along the Soviet Union's most sensitive borders; as it became increasingly clear that British policy, whatever its original aims, was not likely to result in the establishment of a collective grouping of East and south-east European states united against Germany and dependent on Soviet arms and aid; as it became more and more apparent that Litvinov's offer of an alliance was completely unwelcome not only in London but also in Paris, Warsaw and Bucharest, and that even in Ankara the climate had changed, two further developments must have made their impact on the Soviet leadership. The first was the British adoption of conscription; the second Hitler's denunciation of the Anglo-German Naval Treaty and the non-aggression pact with

Poland. Seen from Moscow these signs would have pointed so plainly to an Anglo-Polish-German war that British hopes of averting this by a parade of strength must have seemed at best illusory, at worst a plot to embroil the Soviet Union in war with Germany. Britain, so it must have seemed, whether she realized it or not, was heading into serious danger. Under the circumstances, the British Government needed the aid of the Soviet Union far more than the Soviets did that of Britain. It remained the conviction of the Soviet leaders, their ears glued firmly to the wire between Berlin and Tokyo, that the Germans were determined on war with the West not with the Soviet Union. Hitler's public ranting was confirmed by Ribbentrop's secret diplomacy.

Just as a precaution, however, Soviet military intelligence was regrouping. In the winter and spring of 1939, Soviet agents were laying the ground in Belgium, France, Switzerland and Sweden for what was to become the famous Red Orchestra, the network of Soviet espionage which the Gestapo was to uncover in 1943. Soviet military intelligence had been freed of NKVD control in January 1939. The new preparations were the work of some of its most experienced field officers. In April 1939, the German end of the Red Orchestra, quiescent since 1937, was also re-activated. Neutrality, as well as war, needs its agents-in-place.

Therefore was it not time to abandon a style of diplomacy that had left the Soviet Union still in April 1939, as in September 1938, the great outsider? The course of British success and Soviet failure in March and April was shamingly wrong. The British were still acting as though they had something to offer, a ticket to the 'democratic' club perhaps. It was time for hard bargaining, for jolting Lord Halifax and his gentlemanly advisers out of their satisfaction with themselves, for rubbing their noses in reality, Soviet reality. A new man was needed, more senior, closer to Stalin, hard, obstinate, unclubbable, uncharmable, a man to keep everything in his own hands, a man capable of calculated obtuseness or deliberate rudeness if necessary. It would be of advantage too if he was less obviously *persona non grata* with the Nazis than Litvinov, a Jew. On May 3, Maxim Litvinov was dismissed. Vyacheslav Molotov, Stalin's right-hand man since 1917, Chairman of the Council of Ministers since 1930, the man who in January 1936 in a speech to the Central Executive Committee had said frankly that the 'Soviet government would have desired the establishment of better relations with Germany than at the present' and that 'the development of commercial and economic relations with other states, irrespective of the political forces that are temporarily ruling these countries, is in conformity with the policy of the Soviet Union', was now appointed

Commissar for Foreign Affairs in Litvinov's place. And Vladimir Dekanosov left the Foreign Department of the NKVD to become his deputy.

CHAPTER 14

DECISION IN MAY

On the morning of May 4, large headlines in the Soviet press announced Molotov's appointment. Litvinov's vacation of his post appeared briefly, in a four-line paragraph under 'News in Brief' on the back pages.[1] The Soviet Foreign Ministry had, in fact, issued a very short communiqué a few minutes after midnight on May 3/4, stressing that Litvinov had been relieved of his duties at his own request. It was clearly a very sudden decision. Litvinov had appeared with Stalin at the May Day parade in Moscow, and the press of May 3 had listed his name among the 'guests of honour' attending the celebrations. Sir William Seeds had seen him that same morning.[2] Other diplomatists had visited the Foreign Ministry later in the day. No one had been given a shadow of an inkling of the Minister's impending disappearance.

The news struck the Foreign Office and Lord Halifax in London as surprising, baffling even. Little was known of the new Foreign Minister. Sir William Seeds sent an alarmist, though admittedly speculative, telegram. For some reason, unlike the usual transmissions from Moscow, which took some three hours only to reach London, this was delayed more than fifteen hours overnight. Seeds felt the change might mean an abandonment of Litvinov's policy of collective security and a decision 'to enter instead on a policy of isolation more in accordance' with M. Stalin's speeches. Calling the following afternoon, May 5, at the Foreign Office, William Bullitt, the American Ambassador to Paris, who was in London for a brief visit, found Sir Robert Vansittart 'intensely apprehensive'. A Soviet turn towards isolationism, he told Bullitt, would ensure a collapse in resistance to Hitler in Eastern Europe and the Balkans.[3] Yet he was unable to imagine what alternative proposals Britain could make to the Soviet Union to avoid this.

The British Cabinet had in fact just decided on its reply to M. Litvinov's offer of an alliance, now some three weeks old. Reaching a decision on this reply had been a long and agonizing process, and one whose outcome few felt to be particularly happy. Yet what else could they do? Litvinov's proposal went a lot further than the majority of the Cabinet felt inclined to go at that moment. It was, said Lord Halifax, extremely embarrassing.[4] It clearly offended Polish sensibilities.[5] It was obviously more than unwelcome to the Baltic states and the Finns.[6] M. Gafencu spoke out most strongly against it during his visit to London.[7]

This negative view was shared in the Foreign Office. The British Embassy had reported that 'while Russia may be good for defence of her territory she would not, if she could, offer useful active service outside her territories. Her army is undermined by the purges; her air force, though formidable in numbers, is not up to date; her navy could probably not do much against the German navy in the Baltic. She might supply certain reserves of material but except in the air her potentiality in this respect is limited by the inefficiency of her transport system.' In short, it was felt the Soviet offer would 'alienate our friends and reinforce the propaganda of our enemies without bringing in exchange any material contribution to the strength' of the front Britain was trying to construct in Eastern Europe. In Paris, on the other hand, it was welcomed with some enthusiasm, provided that it was shorn of any reference to Poland.[8]

Behind this enthusiasm it is not difficult to see the automatic French drive to increase their own security. Such sensible and simple, if ignoble anxieties had no place in Lord Halifax's approach. His thinking was governed by a quartet of negatives: not to forgo Soviet assistance in case of war; not to jeopardize the still much desired common front by disregarding Poland's and Romania's susceptibilities; not to 'forfeit the sympathy of the world at large' by giving a handle to Germany's anti-Comintern propaganda; and not to provoke Hitler into doing something abruptly and drastically bellicose.[9] All these negatives seemed to be safeguarded by the original idea of a unilateral Soviet declaration to match those already made by Britain and France to Romania, Poland and Greece.

Thus ran Lord Halifax's arguments. They are distinguished by two very striking assumptions. The first of these, by contrast with the position taken by Britain twelve months earlier during the Czech crisis, is an entire absence of anxiety about the relative military positions of Britain and Germany. The policy of guarantees implied that Britain was lending to Poland and Romania a panoply of British strength such as would give Hitler complete pause. Soviet assistance was not, apparently, believed to be an absolute necessity, though of course every extra help was useful. The second assumption was that the Soviet Union would accept this new policy of benevolent imperial protection extended to states on her own borders as genuine, realizable and a welcome addition to her own defences. That the minds of the Kremlin, rendered hyper-suspicious by the processes of survival through the murderous politics of Stalin's Russia, might find it difficult to see things in the same light, hardly seems to have crossed Lord Halifax's mind. When Maisky or Seeds hinted at such things he was offended and thought them irritatingly unreasonable.

The Soviet leadership, on the other hand, had only their own obsession with secrecy and espionage to thank for the low opinion Europe held of their military capabilities. From 1937 onwards they had systematically closed to foreign access every opportunity of displaying how successful their so drastically enforced programme of industrial development and modernization had been. To cite one crucial example, Colonel Firebrace, the British Military Attaché, had visited in 1937, and been impressed by the standards of Soviet infantry and artillery units and officer-cadet training schools. In May 1939 he complained to Marshal Voroshilov, with whose command abilities he was not so impressed, that he had seen nothing for over a year.[10] The set military parades on the anniversary of the Revolution and on May Day did not impress him. His naval and RAF colleagues shared his views and experience. To be taken seriously in the calculations of power, military forces had to be seen, and be seen by experts. Throughout Europe only the ignorant and the believers took Soviet military power seriously. And if the politicians of Eastern Europe feared that an invitation to supply military assistance would present Stalin with an irresistible temptation to exchange those who invited him for a government more immediately under his control, the pattern of Soviet domestic politics between 1935 and 1938 provided more than adequate justification for their fears.

It was thus that, on May 6, after sending instructions to enquire cautiously whether the change from Litvinov to Molotov meant a change in policy,[11] Lord Halifax instructed Sir William Seeds to put the idea (and a draft text) of a unilateral declaration to the new Foreign Minister.[12]

Lord Halifax's formulation enjoyed a good deal less than enthusiastic support from the French. M. Bonnet, the Foreign Minister, was resigned to allowing Lord Halifax his head. At this time, as during the previous year over the Czech crisis, he was content to let Britain take the lead as the price for ensuring British support. Besides, he was never very effective in argument with Lord Halifax, whose physical endowments (he towered over Bonnet) only emphasized his intellectual aloofness, phrased as it always was in meticulous yet insufferably Anglo-Saxon French. But M. Bonnet was profoundly sceptical of the chances of success for the new British initiative.[13] Driven by the abiding French passion for over-insurance, he continued to prefer an outright tripartite alliance with the Soviet Union. Indeed in a moment of carefully planned indiscretion he had said as much to the Soviet Ambassador in Paris, Jakob Suritz, the day before Litvinov's fall.[14]

His anxieties can only have been reinforced by Litvinov's dismissal. That same day, M. François-Poncet propounded to the new British Ambassador in Rome his view that Stalin had sacked Litvinov in order to reach an accommodation with Hitler at the expense of Poland.[15] This was to be followed by a long report from M. Coulondre in Berlin of a conversation between the French Air Attaché, Paul Stehlin, and General Karl Bodenschatz, who had served under Goering in the famous Richthofen fighter squadron in 1918 and since 1933 had acted as his personal liaison officer with Hitler. Bodenschatz warned that Hitler was waiting his time carefully to strike at Poland, that Ribbentrop had received Merekalov before the latter left for Moscow and that the Soviet Military Attaché had also been received by senior German military figures before he too had been recalled. A fourth partition of Poland was in preparation. *'Etwas im Osten im Gange ist'* (something is brewing in the East), he said. Poland might count on Soviet aid to back her insolence towards Germany, but she was deceiving herself.[16]

M. Coulondre was to continue his warnings, though Bonnet, with that curious facility for shutting his eyes and ears to all that might disturb him in his views, remained content to let the British make the running. M. Coulondre reported his anxieties to his British colleague, Sir Nevile Henderson, who duly relayed them to London.[17] The Foreign Office, curiously enough, had also heard from General Bodenschatz.[18] Similar reports also came from Dr Karl Goerdeler, the former Lord Mayor of Leipzig, one of the central figures of the underground opposition to Hitler and an old friend and contact of Vansittart.[19] Hence, no doubt, Vansittart's alarm. The official Foreign Office view, however, attributed this 'very persistent' story to German and Italian efforts to disturb the Anglo-Soviet negotiations.[20]

The ubiquitous presence of General Bodenschatz tends to reinforce the view that Goering was urging Hitler to abandon Ribbentrop's vision of an alliance with Japan and to play for Russian aid to isolate Poland. Goering's subsequent conduct suggests very strongly that he encouraged the Soviet contacts as part of an internal struggle with Ribbentrop, and possibly as a means of persuading both the British and Poles to see reason. But the dismissal of Litvinov, and the Soviet approaches, both on the diplomatic level and on clandestine lines, showed a degree of Soviet seriousness which went much further than he could have expected. Moreover he was soon to be faced with a take-over both of his bilateral approaches to Italy and of his Soviet contacts by his hated rival, Ribbentrop.

The news of Litvinov's dismissal found Ribbentrop at Munich dancing attendance on Hitler. He was in fact immersed in preparations for his visit to Italy where, at the Italians' request, he was due to meet Count Ciano in Milan. Germany's Soviet experts were scattered far and wide. Schliep, the head of the Eastern European section in the Foreign Ministry in Berlin, was not greatly loved by Ribbentrop. Count Friedrich Werner von der Schulenburg, German Ambassador to the Soviet Union since 1934, was in Tehran, representing his country at the wedding of the Crown Prince to Princess Fawzia of Egypt. Tall, handsome in the perfect clubman style, of great personal charm, with few enemies, Count von der Schulenburg personally detested Hitler and von Ribbentrop and all they stood for. He was in fact to die for his part in the plot of July 1944 against Hitler's life, but at this time conviction that Germany would survive Nazism, provided that enough non-Nazis stayed at their posts, had led him to dissemble his feelings. He was in any case by nature an executant rather than an originator of policy.

His two best-informed deputies were Werner von Tippelskirch, Chargé d'affaires at the Moscow Embassy in his absence, and Gustav Hilger, a Moscow-born German who had served German economic and trade interests in Moscow since 1917. Tippelskirch could not be spared from Moscow. So it was Hilger who was immediately summoned to Germany to report to Hitler in the interim, before von der Schulenburg could make the long flight back from Tehran.

Hilger arrived in Munich, where Ribbentrop had returned after his visit to Milan, on May 9. He found Ribbentrop arrogant after the triumph of his Italian visit, but otherwise disgruntled. Until the Milan visit his position *vis-à-vis* the Führer had been getting steadily rockier. Of the three lines of policy into which he had followed and persuaded Hitler after Munich, the elimination of Czechoslovakia had been a thoroughly botched job with diplomatic consequences which were still operating to Germany's disadvantage. The approach to Poland had collapsed entirely and preparations for war were now going ahead. The negotiations for a tripartite pact with Japan had reached a complete impasse. At the beginning of April he had made a new and desperate approach to the Japanese after receiving on April 2, from his Japanese crony in Berlin, Ambassador Oshima, a further Japanese draft which still effectively deprived the treaty of any element of deterrence against

Britain and America.[21] This continuing frustration of his hopes had driven him to a plethora of suggestions, proposals and demands, with which he had bombarded the Italians, and the Japanese both in Berlin and in Tokyo, as well as his own advisers. In the meantime the Führer was getting impatient and Ribbentrop's old rival, Marshal Goering, was moving into action again.

The two new initiatives which Germany was to undertake in May 1939, the signature of the Pact of Steel with Italy and the first approaches to the Soviets, were in fact both to be traced back to the Goering-Koch group. Goering had been urging a bilateral alliance with Italy on the Führer since October. Less relentless an habitué of Hitler's ante-chamber than von Ribbentrop, he had lost out to the latter's more grandiose plans for a 'world alliance' with Japan. But the total ship-wreck of Ribbentrop's hopes of Poland with the British guarantee and the continuing deadlock in the negotiations with Japan had given him a second chance. It was from his group, Koch, Bodenschatz and others, and from the former nationalists of the High Command, remembering German collaboration with the Red Army in the days of the Weimar Republic, that talk of a *rapprochement* with the Soviet Union against Poland was now being heard.

On April 15, Goering had visited Rome and held official conversations with Mussolini and Count Ciano. The visit was cleverly arranged, being camouflaged at first as a visit to the Marshal's medical specialist who resided in the tiny independent republic of San Marino. The details were arranged by the Foreign Ministry's Chef de Protocole as a routine matter, and von Ribbentrop only got wind of what was brewing when his rival was already touring the Italian colony of Libya as Mussolini's guest. His furious telegram only reached Goering two days before the latter's arrival in Rome[22] and the Marshal was able therefore to act entirely freely.[23] Goering's main aim, it developed, was to reassure the Italian dictator over the very sensitive question of Italian interests in Yugoslavia and the Danube basin, and to sound out Mussolini on his view of a possible German approach to the Soviet Union. He also hinted very strongly at Hitler's increasing determination to solve the Polish question that year, though he agreed with Mussolini on the need for several years' peace before tackling the 'inevitable' conflict with the Western democracies. He did not refer in so many words to the desirability of a bilateral alliance between the two partners of the Axis, but the entire framework of his remarks was confined to a bilateral relationship and the information with which he returned to Germany must have been used to reinforce support for his challenge to what remained of Ribbentrop's 'grand design'. Most advantageous of all was the enthusiastic support Mussolini himself voiced for the idea of a *rapprochement* with the Soviet Union.

Goering had thus played his trumps against von Ribbentrop at a time when Hitler was turning most violently against the Poles. On April 28, he had denounced the Non-Aggression Pact with Poland. On May 5, Colonel Beck replied,[24] amidst a barrage of mutual attacks exchanged between the Polish and German press. His reply was calm but sharply worded. It must have struck Hitler, when taken with the increasingly intransigent state of Polish public opinion, as verging on the insolent. At the same time Ribbentrop received a further negative from Japan.[25] He was to keep vainly hoping; but it was becoming clearer and clearer that to survive with Hitler it was becoming essential to capture Goering's policy from him, to make the bilateral pact with Italy and the idea of a *rapprochement* with the Soviet Union his own.

Ribbentrop left for Italy on the afternoon of May 5. He met Count Ciano in Milan, deliberately chosen by Mussolini to counter reports of anti-German demonstrations among the Italians of that city. He brought with him two drafts of an alliance between the two countries. He did not, however, show either to Count Ciano. His job was to reassure the Italians; to get some control over them lest Germany be involved in a Franco-Italian war; to calm their fears over Poland; to sound them out as to the idea of an approach to the Soviets. For once, too, he decided to play it cool, to omit the bombast and pomp which had so alienated Italian sympathies on his previous visits. To the final dinner of his visit, held at the Villa d'Este on Lake Como, the nobility of Lombardy, the Sforzas, Crespis, Borommeos and Trivulzios, fell over themselves to obtain invitations. Camellias, rhododendrons, magnolias and azaleas adorned the gardens, and Paris fashions in the salons mingled with the grey diplomatic uniforms of the young men of Ribbentrop's entourage, clicking heels and kissing hands.[26] Ciano, impressed, noted that Ribbentrop was 'pleasantly calm'[27] and had a 'fair personal success, even in that useless and snobbish world of so-called society'.[28]

At the end of the first evening, spent over dinner in Milan, Count Ciano was called to the telephone by Mussolini, to urge that a public announcement be made of the imminent conclusion of an alliance between Italy and Germany. Once again Mussolini was playing for public effect, to demonstrate Italy's strength to the world, to rebuke the sneers of the French press and, so he hoped, to bring the French to the negotiating table. Ribbentrop had reassured Ciano on one vital point. Germany was not ready for war, so there was no danger this year of being dragged into battle behind the German chariot. Ribbentrop was a

The end of the Anglo-German war. Field-Marshal Montgomery receives the German surrender, 4 May 1945

Hitler in triumph. Entry into the Sudetenland, 8 October 1938

Anglo-French concord. From left to right: Cadogan, Strang, Lord Halifax, Neville Chamberlain, Georges Bonnet; Paris, 25 November 1938

Anglo-French concord. Daladier and Chamberlain; Paris, 25 November 1938

Anglo–Italian misunderstanding. Count Ciano, Lord Halifax, Chamberlain, Mussolini; 9 January 1939

The Pact of Steel. Ribbentrop, Admiral Raeder, Count Ciano, Hitler, Goering, General Pariani; Berlin, 22 May 1939

Four Under-Secretaries for Foreign Affairs: Sir Alexander Cadogan, UK (above left); Alexis St Léger Léger, France (below left); Ernst von Weizsäcker, Germany (above right); Sumner Welles, USA (below right)

Allied soldiers: General Lord Gort (above left), General Sir Edmund Ironside (above right), General Georges Gamelin (below)

Ambassadors in Berlin: André François-Poncet (above left), Robert Coulondre (above right), Bernardo Attolico (below left), Józef Lipski (below right)

Ambassadors in Ankara; Sir Hugh Knatchbull-Hugessen (left), René Massigli

Ambassadors of appeasement: Sir Eric Phipps (left), Sir Nevile Henderson

Admiral Raeder

General Keitel

Generals Halder (left) and von
Brauchitsch

Prague falls to the
Wehrmacht, 15 March 1939

The underground war in Germany: Colonel Hans Oster (above left), Reinhard Heydrich (above right), Admiral Canaris (below left), Dr Goerdeler (below right)

Marshal Smigly-Rydz (above left), President Mościcky (above right), Józef
Beck with Ciano (below left), Jozef Lukasiewicz, Poland's ambassador in Paris
(below right)

Herbert von Dirksen, German Ambassador in London (above left), Grigore Gafencu, Romanian Foreign Minister (above right), Virgil Tilea, Romania's minister in London (below left), Arthur Greiser and Albert Forster in Danzig (below right)

Before the war. The inner harbour of Danzig

Balkan kings under threat: Carol of Romania (left), Boris of Bulgaria

Victims: King Zog of Albania (above); The Slovaks: Ribbentrop with
Dr Tuka and Father Josef Tiso

Prince Paul of Yugoslavia

Saracoğlu of Turkey resists
Franz von Papen's 'oily charm'

Ismet İnönü, the indomitable
Turkish President

Pius XII

Dekanosov: from NKVD to
Foreign Ministry

General Zhukhov, victor over
the Japanese

Maxim Litvinov with V. Maisky,
Soviet Ambassador in London

Vladimir Potemkin

President Franklin D. Roosevelt

America's leaders: (above left) Senator Key Pittman of Nevada, Chairman of the Senate Foreign Relations Committee; (above right) Secretary of State Cordell Hull; (below left) William Bullitt, US Ambassador in Paris; (below right) Senator William Borah of Idaho

The Japanese: the Emperor relaxes (above left); Prince Saionji and Inukai (above right); Admiral Nomura (below left); Admiral Yonai (below right)

Hitler's birthday parade in Berlin, 20 April 1939

Hitler declares war on Poland in the Reichstag, 1 September 1939

Courting the Soviets: Mr and Mrs Neville Chamberlain enter the Soviet Embassy (above left); After the Nazi-Soviet Pact, Molotov, Stalin, Ambassador Count von der Schulenburg, Andor Henke (Ribbentrop's assistant), Ribbentrop (above right); Disappointed suitors: the Anglo-French military mission – (from the left) Admiral Drax, General Doumenc, Air-Marshal Stuart-Burnett, Major-General Heywood

General Eberhard, Commander of Danzig's clandestine forces

Carl Jacob Burckhardt,
League High Commissioner
in Danzig

1 September 1939: Germany attacks Poland. The Vistula bridge at Dirschau, destroyed by the Poles despite the Abwehr (above); The German battleship *Schleswig Holstein* bombards the Westerplatte (below)

Britain unafraid: Do-it-yourself Anderson backyard air-raid shelters being delivered to a London suburb (above); Outside 10 Downing Street, 2 September 1939

Sir Horace Wilson,
Chamberlain's equivocal
adviser

Sir Robert Vansittart, Chief
Diplomatic Adviser to the
Cabinet

Chamberlain's War Cabinet, 3 September 1939: back row, from left to right,
Sir John Anderson, Lord Hankey, Hore-Belisha, Churchill, Kingsley Wood,
Eden, Edward Bridges (Secretary to the Cabinet); front row, Lord Halifax,
Simon, Neville Chamberlain, Hoare, Lord Chatfield

little taken aback by Mussolini's urgency; but he too could use the telephone. Then and there he rang his master in Berchtesgaden. At midnight the unmistakably hoarse and vulgar tones of the Führer gave him the go-ahead. Ciano, far from enthusiastic about his master's instructions, helped draft a joint communiqué for the press and then retired to bed. Concerned only with the public effect of the alliance, he readily agreed to let the draft of the treaty be prepared in Berlin; he omitted to give Ribbentrop any statement of the points the Italians wished to see included.

The actual treaty was to be so blatant a confidence trick that it is extraordinary how Count Ciano, a man who prided himself on his astuteness and perceptiveness, could be so deceived. But the truth is that both Ciano and Mussolini were essentially lazy men. In this instance, Mussolini was beguiled by pride and over-confidence, lured by the prospect of alliance with the might and majesty of the German nation and Wehrmacht as Hitler had most carefully displayed it to him two years earlier on his visits to Berlin and to the military manœuvres in East Prussia. He was appallingly ignorant of the United States. And the only visit he ever paid to Britain was in 1922 when he saw only that part of London which lies between Victoria and Whitehall. Perhaps a visit to a British naval review, those massive cold grey silhouettes sliding inexorably through the empty sea, might have balanced matters; Mussolini was not a fool where naval matters were concerned. But all he had to set against the terrifying theatricality of German power were his encounters with Eden, Chamberlain and Halifax, and these men had come to Italy by train.

Ciano, on the other hand, was bored by the minutiae of diplomacy. World-rulers (and he liked to picture himself as such) do not chase commas or haggle over clauses. And he had thoughtlessly so broken the Italian Foreign Ministry organization as to lose any opportunity of keeping by his side the kind of ruthless and far-seeing legal advice Ribbentrop secured in Germany from Friedrich Gaus, the German Foreign Ministry's legal chief. There was no one therefore to point out to him that nowhere had he secured in writing any definition of when and how the alliance was to become operative, any secret clause obliging the partners not to provoke war for three years, or conditions relating to the vexed problems of the South Tyrol, Yugoslavia or even Poland. Yet in Hitler's mind, as he listened to Ribbentrop's telephoned explanations, weighing the effects of the announcement on London and Paris, exploring with all care the possibilities aroused by Litvinov's dismissal, the substitution of Soviet Russia for Japan as the trump card to force Britain to abandon its support for Poland, the use of Italian pressure to break up the Balkan bloc Britain was attempting to form around Turkey, and the unleashing against Poland of the Nazis in Danzig, of the whole Nazi propaganda machine under Goebbels' control, all stemmed inevitably from the alliance.

In the meantime Ribbentrop returned to Munich, where on May 9 he was joined by Gustav Hilger.[29] For most of that morning he subjected Hilger to a prolonged questioning as to the significance of Litvinov's dismissal and his estimates of Molotov's and Stalin's intentions. In the afternoon he reported to Berchtesgaden, bringing Hilger with him in anticipation of one of the Führer's interminable all-night conferences. Ribbentrop, however, had to cope with the Führer alone. Not until the following day, as Ribbentrop lay still asleep in a Salzburg hotel, was Hilger called to the Führer. Torn from his bed, unbreakfasted and in a foul temper, Ribbentrop rushed Hilger by car to the Obersalzberg. He was joined by General Keitel, Schnurre from Berlin and the only man in Hitler's entourage everyone liked, Walter Hewel.

For once Hitler listened as Hilger expounded the German Embassy's view. Stalin had dismissed Litvinov because he thought Litvinov was letting the British manœuvre Russia into being a British cat's-paw. Stalin was ready for an agreement with Germany if approached. Stalin was taking the ideology out of Soviet government and attempting to foster a new Soviet patriotism, resurrecting the old Tsarist military heroes, suppressing experiment in the arts, exalting parental authority and school discipline, building up Soviet industrial strength. Hitler heard him through and then dismissed him with a few formal words. Afterwards he told Ribbentrop that if Hilger was telling the truth and not being taken in by Soviet propaganda, something would have to be done about the Soviet Union as a matter of urgency. This is perhaps why he did not bother, apparently, to see von der Schulenburg who arrived the next day, leaving him to Ribbentrop to deal with.

Schulenburg spent a week in Berlin conferring with Ribbentrop. It is a measure of the impression Hilger had made on Hitler that the unfortunate Ambassador got a Hitlerized version of Hilger hot and strong from Ribbentrop's highly adaptable lips. Communism had ceased to exist in the Soviet Union. The Communist International was no longer a factor of any importance. There was consequently no ideological barrier remaining between Germany and the Soviet Union. He was therefore to return to Moscow, see Molotov and propose to him a resumption of the German-Soviet trade talks which had run into the sand in March. He was to play it very cautiously as there was the utmost danger of alarming the Japanese. Ribbentrop declared himself not to be worried in the least by the prospect of the Anglo-Soviet negotiations as he was convinced that neither Britain nor France would actually give military aid to any country in Eastern Europe. He still wanted an agreement with the Poles, but if it actually came to war Germany had no intention of occupying all of Poland. Schulenburg was to play the whole thing by ear and see what happened. But he was to be very, very, very cautious.

Ribbentrop personally still hoped that the Japanese would come through. On his return from Milan he had composed a lengthy explanatory telegram to his Ambassador, Colonel Ott, in Tokyo, and had had lengthy talks with General Oshima, the Japanese Ambassador in Berlin.[30] He explained why he and Ciano had decided to conclude a bilateral pact. This was not intended to exclude Japan, and he addressed an urgent appeal that the Japanese should initial the text of a three-power pact the day the Axis alliance was signed. At the same time it was clear that, whatever Ribbentrop's own feelings, Hitler was losing patience with the Japanese. To save his brainchild, Ribbentrop was even prepared to allow the Japanese to represent the pact as an answer to the 'acute menace' of the Soviet Union, should any enquiries come from Britain or the United States. This was the point at which the negotiations had stuck for so long. Ribbentrop had always refused to concede this, as he wanted the pact to deter Britain and distract America. It is a measure of his desperation that he was now giving that away. It was also plain stupid, though he was not to know this. Ott showed all important telegrams to Richard Sorge, the shrewd, womanizing drunk who was the Tokyo correspondent of the *Völkischer Beobachter*. Sorge, as we have seen, was head of one of Moscow's most successful spy-rings. Hitherto his messages had reassured Moscow that Hitler was set on war not with the Soviet Union but with the West. His report of Ribbentrop's new concession[31] must have given the Soviets more than a moment's doubt whether their estimate of Hitler's intentions was correct. The outbreak of serious fighting with Japan on the borders of Mongolia that same month must have intensified their anxieties.

Not that any of these doubts showed themselves to the West, or to poor Sir William Seeds. On May 8 he duly presented himself at the Soviet Foreign Ministry in a state of some curiosity as to the personality of the new Soviet Foreign Minister.[32] He was personally a great deal less than happy with the instructions he had been given, which he thought so likely to offend Soviet susceptibilities as to have little chance of acceptance. Nevertheless he did his best to set out the somewhat long-winded and periphrastic arguments with which Lord Halifax had armed him. He had one advantage over Molotov: he spoke Russian and could therefore use the time spent in interpreting his remarks to Molotov, and vice versa, in considering his next move. The stream of questions to which Molotov subjected him made this doubly useful. He did not know, however, that Molotov thought himself to be in possession of three pieces of information which destroyed any chance of Seeds' arguments being accepted as sincere by his interlocutor.

Two of these pieces were in fact false. M. Molotov had interpreted a remark made by Sir John Simon in the Commons on April 13 to the effect that Britain had no objection in principle to a military alliance with the Soviet Union as a literal statement of intent rather than a piece of legalistic evasiveness. (No doubt Maisky had overblown the remark to justify his own support for an Anglo-Soviet alliance.) And on May 8 Molotov had seen Grzybowski, the Polish Ambassador in Moscow, and had understood him to say that his Government had no objection to being publicly associated with the Soviet Union.[33] Now Seeds was denying Simon's statement and contradicting Grzybowski. (Grzybowski was himself to put the record straight on May 11, when he admitted to Molotov that he had misrepresented Polish opposition to a direct link with Russia.)[34]

It was the third item of information, however, that scuppered Seeds entirely. London had somehow failed to give him any warning of Bonnet's indiscretion to Suritz. France, said Molotov, had virtually accepted the Soviet proposals of an alliance. Britain had not. Had France approved the British position, or Britain that of France? Seeds did the best he could. But his later reference to this as either 'a gross and deliberate error of tactics' or 'the foolish amateurishness of a politician', shows the depths of his disgust, his feeling of betrayal.[35] To get off on the wrong foot so markedly in a first interview with a new Foreign Minister is the kind of nightmare that wakes diplomatists in a cold sweat in the small hours of the night. Under the circumstances Molotov's final comments that Soviet policy had not changed but was of course liable to change if other governments changed their policy, and that the Soviet reply would not be as dilatory as Britain's had been, were remarkably mild.

Molotov was in fact as good as his word. The very next day Maisky was round at the Foreign Office expressing Soviet doubts as to whether the British proposals might not result in the Soviet Union having to face Germany alone.[36] On May 11, *Izvestiya* carried a long article,[37] of which Molotov was, in fact, the author, revealing the British proposals and criticizing them for placing the Soviet Union in an unequal position. The Soviet Union was to be obliged to come to the aid of Britain and France. But Britain and France were assuming no such obligation to Russia (though they were to Poland and Romania!). Moreover, the British and French were reserving to themselves the right to commit Soviet military aid without any reference to the Soviet Union. As Suritz had commented in a telegram to Moscow on May 10, Britain was allotting to Russia the 'role of a blind companion in the coalition'.[38] Maisky pursued the same line with Halifax on May 11;[39] and he spread his arguments freely through his contacts with the British press and the parliamentary opposition. He also claimed to have discovered that the 'appeasers', the 'advocates of a Munich policy', were staging a strong comeback, a view he pressed upon his new boss.[40] He added a very significant time limit – it was vital that some Anglo-Soviet arrangement be reached within a month. The course of subsequent events suggests that such a time limit had in fact been set by Molotov and Stalin either in the conference in April in which he had taken part, or on Molotov's assumption of office.

Molotov gave Seeds the Soviet reply on May 14.[41] It amounted to a flat rejection of the British proposals. They did not contain the principle of reciprocity. They left the Soviet frontiers with Finland, Latvia and Estonia uncovered. The Soviet Union insisted on an effective alliance, with the obligation to wage war and declare peace together, the extension of guarantees to cover Estonia, Latvia and Finland, and a concrete military agreement. Seeds suggested that Molotov should go to Geneva for the meeting of the Council of the League of Nations where he and Halifax could talk personally. This Molotov politely refused. The meeting ended, like its predecessor, in laughter. Seeds could still make Molotov laugh. Even that facility was not to remain with him much longer.

The Soviet rejection of the British proposals was followed by ten days of bitter debate, both public and private, in Britain. Neville Chamberlain, supported only by Sir John Simon and W. S. Morrison in the Cabinet, fought in private a bitter rearguard action against the alliance. But he found himself deserted by all his former allies, and subjected to a mounting tide of public pressure orchestrated from behind the scenes, as MI5's telephone tapping revealed to Chamberlain's disgust and contempt, by the ubiquitous M. Maisky.[42] The rudimentary public opinion polls being carried out by Mass Observation and by the British Institution of Public Opinion at this time, showed an overwhelming weight of public opinion in favour of an alliance with the Soviets.[43] The Chiefs of Staff changed their position entirely and came out strongly for the alliance they had dismissed as being of little military value only a month earlier.[44] The French and Turkish Governments made the strongest representations.[45] Vansittart was already loudly in favour of overriding the Romanian, Polish and Baltic objections to a Soviet guarantee.[46] Cadogan was driven reluctantly to the same conclusions. In the Commons on May 19, Chamberlain was subjected to heavy and well-informed pressure, Maisky having briefed Churchill carefully before the debate began.[47] The Cabinet's Foreign Policy Committee could see no alternative to acceptance of a Soviet alliance other than a total breakdown of the negotiations. A heavy majority, led by Hoare and Inskip with the backing of Lord Chatfield and the Service Ministers, favoured the alliance.[48] Chamberlain was driven to irritable threats of resignation. But now, as before, it was Halifax who brought him to see reason.

Lord Halifax had been instrumental in persuading Sir Robert Vansittart to act as an unofficial intermediary with M. Maisky on May 16–17, to see if the Soviet Union would accept a pledge of an alliance once war had broken out and Staff conversations before that event.[49] But Molotov, well briefed by his intelligence sources in London and Tokyo, conscious that the British were just thrashing about in an effort to avoid the obvious, insisted on the alliance and nothing but the alliance.[50] And on May 20 Lord Halifax, *en route* for Geneva, was driven into a corner by Daladier and Bonnet with Alexis St Léger in support.[51] He had already in fact submitted proposals for a direct tripartite alliance to the Poles and the Romanians for their comments,[52] though he added that he thought it unlikely the British Cabinet would accept such a draft. The alternative was to make the operation of the alliance dependent entirely on the operation of the guarantees already given. This Daladier dismissed as unacceptable to the Soviets in their current mood, and strongly supported the direct alliance.

In Geneva Halifax proved quite unable to shake Maisky, to whom the job of representing the Soviet Union had fallen, on the main points. We are faced, he reported to London, with alternatives that are 'disagreeably plain': a breakdown of negotiations or agreement to a tripartite alliance.[53] Neither Colonel Beck nor M. Gafencu was prepared to impose a veto on the tripartite alliance.[54] M. Maisky, and M. Suritz in conversations with the French,[55] made much of the danger Russia faced from a sudden internal collapse in Poland or Romania under German pressure (King Carol's assassination and an Iron Guard takeover were mentioned), as a result of which Russia might find that the British and French guarantees had lapsed and Russia was left to face Germany alone. The history of the Anglo-French guarantee for Czechoslovakia given at Munich made this a justified – if unkind – observation. Halifax returned to London convinced that the alliance would have to be accepted.

Armed with a lengthy memorandum prepared in the Foreign Office during his absence,[56] Halifax, though confessing himself 'not enamoured' of the Soviet proposals,[57] bearded the Cabinet. Among the arguments he used were the fear of a Nazi-Soviet *rapprochement* (in addition to the more imaginative reports of direct German-Soviet contacts through the former Czech War Minister, General Syrovy, which were flooding in from all sides,[58] the Foreign Office was adequately informed by Helmut Wohltat of Goering's Four Year Plan and of the German proposal to send Dr Schnurre to Moscow);[59] the encouragement a breakdown of the negotiations would give to German aggressiveness in Eastern Europe; and the need, if there was to be a war, to ensure that it did not end with Germany and Britain in ruins, and a neutral Soviet Union with her army intact, poised to dominate Europe. There were indications, in the Foreign Office view, that this was the real aim of Soviet policy. Reluctantly Chamberlain agreed. That afternoon in Parliament he rashly announced that new British proposals under preparation made early agreement with the Soviet Union possible.[60]

In reality, however, Chamberlain had made one last desperate wriggle. Convinced that both Parliament and Cabinet were against a refusal of the Soviet proposals, but still distrustful of Soviet aims, doubtful of Soviet military strength and desperate to avoid a division of Europe into Fascist and anti-Fascist teams (a process which he felt could well drive Spain, Portugal, Italy, Japan, and possibly Finland and Yugoslavia into the German camp), he had adopted Sir Horace Wilson's suggestion of linking the treaty with the 'principles' of the covenant of the League. This would, in his view, 'catch all the mugwumps', yet give the treaty a 'temporary character', as Article XVI of the covenant, the article whose 'principles' of collective resistance to aggression were particularly objectionable, was bound to be 'amended or repealed some day or other', and substitute a declaration of intentions in fulfilment of League obligations for an outright, automatic military alliance.[61] That done, Chamberlain wrote, 'I recovered my equanimity.' It was a poisonously stupid and criminally asinine piece of ingenuity, which neither Halifax nor his advisers and certainly not the unfortunate Sir William Seeds seem to have spotted, so great was the mystique of the covenant of the League.

Nor curiously did the French. Bonnet and Daladier approved the draft on May 26.[62] On May 27 Sir William Seeds, together with his French colleague, presented the draft to M. Molotov in the Kremlin.[63] It proved to be a most painful occasion. Molotov, who received them sitting at a large desk on a raised dais, had already been sent the text from Paris (and, presumably, thanks to Mr King, from London). He proved to be in one of his most obtuse and offensive moods. The draft, he said, struck him as an attempt to keep discussions going *ad infinitum*. The reference to the League was an attempt to make effective co-operation dependent on the 'interminable delays of League of Nations procedure', where Bolivia, for example, could block any action while Russia was being bombed by the aggressor. Seeds, in despair after shouting at Molotov for most of the interview during intervals between repeated Molotovian references to Bolivia, all carefully and excellently translated by M. Potemkin, tried again two days later.[64] But after a conversation which lasted until nearly midnight he found it impossible to shift Molotov from his view that the British proposals showed they were not serious. 'It is my fate', he wrote, 'to deal with a man totally ignorant of foreign affairs and to whom the idea of negotiation – as distinct from imposing the will of his party leader – is utterly alien.'

Molotov's 'foolish cunning of the peasant type', of which Seeds wrote, was well displayed in those two interviews, though not in the sense that Seeds construed it. As we have seen, he had good reason not to greet the new British offer with cries of rapture even on its own merits. But most of what he objected to could well have been cleared up by a man who realized, as Maisky did, that 'Britain had come 75% of the way and was bound to come the whole way'.[65] But in the meantime two things had happened. The signature of the German-Italian Pact on May 22 had confirmed the Soviet view that Germany was, after all, determined on war in the West not the East. And confirming this, but even more importantly, the Germans had taken the Soviet bait, even when displayed with the rudeness from which Sir William Seeds was now suffering.

To take the German-Soviet side first: Count von der Schulenburg, as we have seen, had returned to Moscow on May 19. To encourage him he had two warnings from the Soviet feed to the German Embassy in London and three fairly broad hints dropped from the Soviet side in Berlin over the previous fortnight.

The mysterious source on which the London Embassy depended had passed to them two oddly timed pieces of information. The first was the text of the British proposals sent to Sir William Seeds on May 6, which, very oddly, were accompanied by a note of the possible Soviet objec-tions, from which could be seen 'how suspicious' the Russians were of the pact negotiations as a whole.[66] (Molotov's reactions were, in fact, only being registered as the German report was under way.) The second was a version of the Soviet reply of May 14, which, again, ahead of the debate this caused in London, summarized that debate and explained

Soviet anxieties over the Baltic republics.[67] Both reports effectually depicted Soviet hostility to the British approaches.

So much for the NKVD's role in London. From the Soviet diplomatic service, the Germans had had three broad hints and had passed on one of their own that we know of (leaving aside the whole story of a direct German offer to Stalin carried by the former Czech War Minister, General Syrový, and rejected by Stalin). On May 5, the Soviet Chargé d'affaires in the Embassy in Berlin, Georgi Astakhov, had called at the Foreign Ministry in Berlin and tried to pump Julius Schnurre, the head of the Foreign Ministry's section dealing with economic relations with the Soviet Union, on whether Litvinov's dismissal would have any effect on the German attitude to the Soviet Union.[68] Four days later, he had called again to introduce the new Berlin correspondent of Tass, the Soviet news agency, to the Foreign Ministry's press department. This time he played down the question of whether Molotov's appointment implied a change of policy and commented on the changed attitude of the German press to the Soviet Union.[69] Moscow, he said, was still suspicious, not knowing how to interpret this change – none of the usual denunciations of 'Soviet intrigue' or 'Bolshevist machinations' had appeared in the German press since April 28. Significantly, the instructions to the German press to desist from all attacks on the Soviet Union and on Bolshevism had been issued on May 5, the day after Litvinov's 'resignation' had been announced.[70] Finally, he had called again on May 17 to see Julius Schnurre.[71] This time he went a lot further. He hoped that a permanent state of affairs would develop from the current press truce. There were no conflicts in principle between Germany and the Soviet Union, and no reason for enmity. The Soviet Union felt threatened but it would undoubtedly be possible to eliminate this feeling. It must have been on this occasion or around it that von Weizsäcker used the Bulgarian Minister in Berlin, Draganov,[72] to tell Astakhov that Germany was ready for political and economic negotiations with the Soviets, and that the OKW was strongly in favour. Broader hints than this could hardly be expected.

Despite all this butter, von der Schulenburg approached his interview with Molotov with considerable trepidation.[73] Were Soviet hints to be taken seriously? Or were the Soviets, as Ribbentrop and Schulenburg half-suspected, simply trying to provoke German proposals to be used as a lever against the British? The effect of these suspicions was that Molotov very nearly overplayed his hand. He seemed to have arranged matters with Potemkin, Litvinov's suave deputy who had survived his master's removal, so that Potemkin would play the 'soft man' while Molotov played the tough. To

Schulenburg's cautious question, whether the Soviets were prepared to re-open negotiations on a trade agreement, Molotov replied bluntly that the Germans had only been toying with these matters in the past for political reasons. The Soviets therefore could only agree to a resumption of trade negotiations if the necessary 'political bases' for them were to be constructed. Schulenburg rose warmly to the bait, and asked what Molotov meant. Molotov said that both governments would obviously have to think this over. Beyond this he would not be budged. Schulenburg hastened to Potemkin, who was his usual suave self, begging him to find out what Molotov meant.

Schulenburg's telegram[74] reporting these conversations caused renewed debate in Berlin. Ribbentrop's immediate reaction was to tell Schulenburg to draw his horns in, sit tight and wait for the Soviets to speak more openly.[75] There followed a week of dithering in which, quite clearly, Ribbentrop's continued hopes of Japan played a major part. Since his meeting with Count Ciano in Milan, Ribbentrop had been in regular conference with General Oshima. In fact the news of the Milan meeting, and the decision to conclude a bilateral alliance between Germany and Italy, had greatly weakened the Japanese army in the internal debate in Tokyo. But their desperate fears of defeat led the proponents of the tripartite alliance in Tokyo to deny the effects the rising tide of anti-Axis feeling in the Japanese Cabinet was having on the chances of an agreement. They went on maintaining that it was only a matter of days before the Japanese army succeeded in overriding the resistance of the Naval High Command and the Foreign Ministry to the alliance.[76]

During the week before Schulenburg's return to Moscow, Ribbentrop reached two other decisions. The first, as we have seen, was to make one last appeal to the Japanese at least to initial the draft of a tripartite alliance on the same day as the German-Italian alliance was signed in public.[77] The other decision was to make the text of the treaty with Italy far more general and aggressive in tone. The new draft, prepared by Gaus,[78] heavily emphasized the 'close relationship of friendship and homogeneity existing between the two countries', the 'inner affinity between their ideologies and the comprehensive solidarity of their interests', and their common resolve 'to act side by side and with united forces for the realization of their eternal rights to life'. The provisions of the treaty envisaged 'the closest and continuous political and military relations in a common alliance to wage war'. No reference was made to 'unprovoked aggression' or offensive purposes at all, and all reference to the settlement of disputes between the two powers was dropped. So, too, was any reference, overt or secret, to the

Italian understanding that there would be no major adventures in Europe for three years. 'It contains some real dynamite,' noted Count Ciano in his diary.[79] But he did nothing about it; nor did Mussolini. The changes which Mussolini suggested in the text were of very minor importance and accepted by the Germans without question.[80]

On the evening of May 20, when Count von der Schulenburg's disappointing account of his interview with Molotov arrived, von Ribbentrop received another telegram from Tokyo. In it the German Ambassador reported fresh information from General Machijiri, the personal assistant to the Japanese Minister of War. That day the conference of five ministers, the inner ring of the Japanese Cabinet, had reached a decision. Germany's demands had been accepted in principle. General Machijiri read Ott the text of an official communication from the War Minister himself. The Japanese Foreign Minister would inform the German Government by Sunday, May 21 at the latest.[81]

No wonder Ribbentrop ordered von der Schulenburg to sit tight. His hopes of Japan, it seemed, had not been disappointed. His policy was still going to pay off. In the meantime there was plenty to do, while he waited on more formal news from Tokyo. On Sunday morning Count Ciano had arrived to sign the Pact of Steel.

There were conferences, consultations and ceremonies in the mosaic room of the new Reichs Chancellery.[82] Count Ciano was invested with the newly created Golden Cross of the Order of the German Eagle. And Ribbentrop, to his abiding joy, was publicly invested by Ciano with the much coveted Order of the Annunciata. His great rival, Marshal Goering, had tears of frustrated and jealous rage in his eyes at the ceremony,[83] which made Ribbentrop officially a 'cousin' of the Italian crown. Ribbentrop himself gave a dinner in the garden of his house in Dahlem in the evening of the Monday the treaty was signed. Count Ciano, surrounded by the flower of Germany's film stars, shivered in the cold despite the braziers scattered throughout the gardens. He would much rather have spent the evening in that curious temple of sexual perversion, the Salon Kitty.[84] Hitler appeared in a uniform of white with a gold belt, serene and less aggressive than before, or so Ciano found him. Well he might be. Not only was this re-establishment of the Axis on a deeper and more martial basis something dear to his sense of destiny, the linking irretrievably of his own personality with that of the one other man whom he felt destiny had selected to make a nation great and to conquer the 'Jewish-Capitalist-Bolshevik world hydra'. (Under the circumstances the total lack of enthusiasm of the population of Berlin, who had to be bribed and dragooned into playing their part in the ceremonies, was completely overlooked.) He had also reached a decision about Poland and was ready to impart it to his Generals.

The next morning, as Ciano's train steamed out of Berlin on its long journey across the Alps, Hitler attended the funeral of another von der Schulenburg, Count Friedrich von der Schulenburg, ex-Commander of the Imperial Cavalry Guards of Prussia, SS-Obergruppenführer and ardent Nazi since 1930. The Commanders-in-Chief of the three armed services, the Commanders of the Waffen-SS, Generals, Reichsleiters and Gauleiters galore attended the ceremonial. General von Brauchitsch spoke in von der Schulenburg's memory; Hitler laid a wreath. He was saving his voice for the afternoon.[85]

In the Reichs Chancellery that afternoon they all assembled, Goering, Grand Admiral Raeder, Generals von Brauchitsch, Keitel, Milch, Halder and Bodenschatz, Admiral Schniewind, Raeder's deputy, Colonels Jeschonnek, Warlimont and Schmundt of the General Staff, and three more junior officers. So secret was the affair that Schmundt, Hitler's military adjutant, made two copies of the minutes only, both in his own hand,[86] and that at some time after the event.

To be gathered and harangued in this way was not an unusual experience for Hitler's military advisers, but this was something special. For six weeks they had been working on the military plans against Poland, without being certain how far the plans were for real or how far Hitler had deviated from the long-term planning against Britain and France. Doubts they certainly had. General von Brauchitsch had just returned from a tour of Italian military establishments in Italy and Libya. He had returned totally unimpressed by what he had seen and determined to do what he could to block Ribbentrop's play. Milch, Halder, Bodenschatz and Warlimont were other sceptics. Moreover, the course on which Hitler was about to embark ran directly against their most deep-rooted convictions born of the years 1914–18: that, pitted against Britain, France and the United States, Germany was doomed to defeat, and that any policy which seemed openly to embrace that hazard was lunacy.

They sat therefore and listened. It was not one of Hitler's best speeches.[87] He rambled from specific to general and back again. But the gist was quite clear. Hitler had decided to attack Poland at the first available opportunity. He was convinced that Poland could be isolated diplomatically. If not, then the West must be tackled together with Poland. He lost himself in a long diatribe about war with Britain and Britain's weaknesses even at sea. He seemed to envisage a kind of Pearl Harbor against the British fleet, 'this only possible if we do not "slide" into war with England on account of Poland'. As for the West, he ordered the setting up of a small staff to plan operations against Britain. But the only date he named was 1943 or 1944. The Generals must have breathed again as they left the Reichs Chancellery, not realizing the role Colonel Schmundt's record was to play in the charges of conspiracy to commit aggressive war they were to face eight years later; not realizing either that Hitler was determined on war with Poland that summer, believed Britain could be discouraged, but, as his megalomania grew, was becoming increasingly less concerned and more careless than he had been in such matters in the past. This was no longer the Hitler who had displayed so faultless a sense of timing and anticipation of foreign reactions in proclaiming German rearmament or marching into the Rhineland. This was the Hitler who had so botched the march into Prague that he had raised the spectre of 'encirclement' against him and had re-established British interest in Eastern Europe. One other hint he gave. 'It is not ruled out that Russia might disinterest herself in the destruction of Poland. If Russia continues to agitate against us, relations with Japan may become closer.'

The alternatives Hitler posed were to worry Ribbentrop the rest of that week and into the next. The following day he was facing a second telegram from Ott with quite a different account of the Japanese Cabinet's decision.[88] He also learnt from General Oshima that the Japanese Foreign Ministry's version of that decision was so unaccept- able that both he and Shiratori in Rome had refused to pass it on.[89] Japan wished to reserve her position if war broke out in Europe. That same day came Chamberlain's announcement in the Commons that an Anglo-Soviet alliance was in sight. Armed with a personal letter from Count von der Schulenburg expounding his account of his interview with Molotov, Weizsäcker persuaded Ribbentrop there was still room for manœuvre.[90] A long telegram was drafted to send to Moscow, instructing the Count to try Molotov again.[91] Hilger was ordered back to Moscow to brief his Ambassador. But on the Friday Hitler vetoed this move. Instead Schulenburg was again ordered to hold his hand.[92]

On the morning of May 27, driven desperate by waiting, Ribbentrop telephoned from his home at Sonnenburg-bei-Salzburg, where he was spending the Whit Sunday weekend, to the Italian Ambassador in Berlin, Bernardo Attolico.[93] Racking his brains for a way of blocking the Anglo-Soviet treaty he had come to the belief that only fear of Germany and Japan was bringing Russia to ally herself with Britain. A German assurance to Moscow was not enough. He had appealed to Oshima to telegraph Tokyo to secure a Japanese assurance to Moscow. Oshima had flatly refused. Such a request would destroy any hope of a tripartite alliance with Japan. Attolico recommended pressure on

Tokyo of a more orthodox kind. And Weizsäcker had to spend Whit Sunday drafting a telegram to Tokyo in this sense.[94]

But on Whit Sunday Ribbentrop phoned again.[95] Could not the Italians intervene indirectly in Moscow? Attolico was driven to go down to Sonnenburg, where Weizsäcker and Gaus were also spending the holiday, engaged apparently on a line-by-line scrutiny of Schulenburg's report. Did Molotov intend his reference to a political basis to be followed up – or was he choking them off? Attolico observed mildly that he was of course unable to say one way or another, but if an Anglo-Soviet agreement was in the offing, an approach in Moscow seemed pointless. Ribbentrop then suggested that Weizsäcker should turn back to the source of all the hints which had led Schulenburg to Molotov's door, the Soviet Chargé in Berlin, Georgi Astakhov. Hitler's approval was secured, and on the Tuesday morning von Weizsäcker tackled M. Astakhov.[96] The interview was prolonged, friendly and informal. At its close von Weizsäcker concluded that Molotov had not intended to reject the German approach; it was decided to re-open trade negotiations slowly and tentatively. But Hitler had been reassured. The Soviet card was there to be played.

Confirmation came the very next day. Molotov had not been plagued by the same self-doubts. Conviction that a divided Japan would not attack Russia and that Germany was aiming west not east ruled out the kind of anxious debate that was raging between Berlin and Sonnenburg.[97] The Germans had bitten once, adequately enough to enable him to deal firmly with the unfortunate Sir William Seeds. As he rose the next day, May 31, to address the Supreme Soviet,[98] Molotov would have had Astakhov's report on his interview with Weizsäcker as confirmation. The Axis powers, he said, are clearly determined on aggression. The democracies are anxious to draw the USSR into collaboration against this. But their proposals left the Soviet Union in a less protected position than the democracies themselves would enjoy. 'Might it not turn out that their anxiety to restrict aggression in some areas will facilitate the removal of obstacles to the unleashing of aggression elsewhere?' The Soviet Union was strong. But it must be vigilant. In the meantime it was not impossible that trade negotiations with Germany might be resumed. As von der Schulenburg reported,[99] Molotov avoided sallies against Germany, he made no allegations that the Soviet Union was threatened, and he showed readiness to continue the trade talks. The long road to the Nazi-Soviet pact of August was now clearly open.

CHAPTER 15

MUDDLED SIGNALS FROM WASHINGTON

Throughout the summer of 1938, Hitler had faced a spirit of defeatism, near-mutiny and, though he never knew it, conspiracy among sections of the German military to arrest him and declare him insane, if he should actually involve Germany in war with Britain. The collapse of the conspiracy, together with Hitler's hopes of war, at the end of September 1938, had led the Führer to embark on a full-scale process of indoctrination of his military at all levels and ranks; it had led to a similar drive by his Propaganda Ministry to counter the widespread public demonstrations in favour of Britain and Chamberlain, as the proponents of peace in Europe, a drive which the stigmatization of British policy after March 15, 1939, as 'encirclement' certainly aided and reinforced. But behind these campaigns, which were to leave the military and bureaucratic opposition to Hitler divided and confused, there was a further factor, the role of the United States.

Axiomatic to the thinking of the conventional opposition to Hitler's policy among the old German aristocracy, the military, the senior bureaucracy and the thinking professional classes, as among the industrial and mercantile leadership, was the belief that in any war with Britain, Germany would, sooner or later, find herself opposed not only by the money and industrial strength, but ultimately by the military might of the United States. The German press under Goebbels' direction, in depicting Roosevelt from early on as a tool of international Jewry and the focus of all the dark forces of hostility to the Nazi revolution and the German rebirth, had fed those fears. Skilled, as all citizens of totalitarian states who cultivate their own sources of information must be, in decoding the public statements of their regime, the German élites stripped off the trappings and understood the undoubted truth: Nazi Germany had no friends in Roosevelt's Washington, and precious few elsewhere in the United States.

Why then did this understanding not exercise the same restraint in 1939 as it certainly had done a year earlier? For it is clear that it did not. In 1939, Adolf Hitler spent part of each of his great oratorical efforts to indoctrinate his military and political lieutenants with his own convictions, in doing his best to allay their anxieties over Britain, to emphasize the element of chance in the British and French victory in 1918, to underline the differences between the divisions, treacheries, and vulnerability to blockade, hunger and British propaganda, which had allegedly brought about the German collapse in October–November 1918, and the moral unity of the German *Volk* under Nazi leadership. He did not devote a single word in any of his great set pieces to the United States. He behaved as if Columbus had never sailed, Pershing never led American troops into their brief occupation of the German Rhineland in 1919, or American bankers bailed out the German economy after the runaway inflation of 1923. America as a power factor he totally ignored.

A generation of historians have combined to argue that this only demonstrates the innate provincialism he derived from his Central European origins; his inability to understand the deep underlying unity of purpose that a democracy by consensus can achieve; the stultifying effect of his racialism, which denied strength and determination, denied even the reality of nationhood to so mixed, so 'mongrelized' a state as the United States of America. All of this is, no doubt, in some sense true. But to explain why these factors did not operate in 1939 where, to an important extent, they did a year earlier, most of these arguments are irrelevant. Hitler did not enter on the eleven months between October 1, 1938, the aftermath of the Munich conference, and September 1, 1939, when his armies attacked Poland, with the same view of the United States as that with which he ended it. His conception of America changed radically.

He began by trying to come to terms with Poland and by looking for an alliance with Japan so worded that it would deter and distract both Britain and the United States. He ended by attacking Poland after abandoning Japan and concluding a non-aggression pact with the Soviet Union, an action which, he expected, would provide Britain with a pretext for abandoning Poland; its effect on America was nil, and not relevant to his change of direction. He no longer saw any need to divert America.

His conviction that the British Government would not show the courage to back up its protestations bore, of course, very heavily upon his decision to ignore the power of the United States in his calculations. The final measure of his conception of international politics, the stalking of and isolation of the individual nation, its fascination and immobilization by propaganda and subversion, then its annihilation in the sudden pounce of a short campaign, left little room for the long-drawn-out war of attrition, the slow mobilization and militarization of resources that was part of the British and American approach to war. And as far as Japan was concerned, when Roosevelt moved the US fleet from the Atlantic to the Pacific in April 1939, in response to British pleas, the invocation of the Japanese threat had done all that it could for Hitler in distracting American power.

In themselves these considerations are not enough to explain either his abandonment of the Japanese for the Soviet connection or the persistence of his other, even odder fixation, as we shall see, that Britain could be persuaded into her last-minute desertion of Poland by the offer of a German alliance, a German guarantee of the British empire. Against whom was this guarantee intended? Not against the Soviet Union, with whom Hitler had just concluded a non-aggression pact; that Hitler made plain to Sir Nevile Henderson, to whom he made the 'offer' on the afternoon of August 25, in Berlin.[1] No, the guarantee was intended to be against the United States; it stemmed from Hitler's longstanding conviction that successive United States governments and the industrial, mercantile, capitalist and Jewish interests that manipulated them were fundamentally hostile to the continuation of the British empire and to British imperialist-capitalism; and that in the final German assault on the United States which would follow the destruction of the 'Jewish-Capitalist-Bolshevik world hydra', Germany would need the British fleet and the British imperial position as Germany's ally.

The timing of the offer clearly indicated that it was envisaged as a manœuvre to unbalance the British Cabinet at the moment when Hitler was about to unleash his armed forces against Poland, but that is neither here nor there. Hitler more than half expected the Chamberlain Cabinet to fall anyway. He did, however, expect his offer to attract support from the forces which backed the Chamberlain Government. He hoped to offer Britain an alternative, that of becoming a junior partner in Roosevelt's crusade against Nazism. And he was, as he saw it, laying down a marker for a possible future.

In the short run, he no longer expected any significant American reaction. If he had feared any American move, it was not a military one that he expected. What he had feared, earlier in 1939, was some action that might tip the balance in London or Paris.

He no longer feared any such move. He felt he had taken the measure of the American President and his government; no real action or determination need be expected of them. The German Embassy in Washington might do its best repeatedly to emphasize that Roosevelt's aim was the 'annihilation of Nazi Germany and the nullification of the New Order in Europe'.[2] Roosevelt, it reported, was 'Hitler's most dangerous opponent'.[3] Roosevelt's 'pathological hatred' of Hitler and Mussolini had led him to hope for their assassination. Roosevelt's 'ruthless propaganda', in conjunction with 'Britain, Jewry and the Communists in brotherly association', had induced the 'credulous and mentally dull American people'[4] completely to succumb to the view that 'Germany was America's "Enemy No. 1"'.[5] None of these reports now worried him at all. He was convinced that there were counter-vailing forces in America which would restrain Roosevelt. This conviction is the measure of America's contribution to the failure of deterrence in 1939.

It was not as great a contribution as that of Stalin in concluding the Non-Aggression Pact of August 23, 1939, or that of all the amateur interventionists, all those who believed that Hitler needed the sight of a carrot to reward him for not resorting to force, as well as the threat of a stick if he did. But it is none the less significant. There were too many conflicting signals coming out of the United States in 1939. Nor was Roosevelt's style of leadership such that he could impose any harmony, let alone any unison, upon the cacophony of discordant notes they sounded.

The immediate American reaction to the annexation of Bohemia and Moravia was severe and condemnatory. Morgenthau had already taken legal powers in 1938 to impose extra, 'countervailing' duties on foreign goods whose import into America was subsidized by foreign governments. From October to March he had been battling with the State Department for the application of these duties against Germany. The German march into Prague destroyed State Department opposition overnight. The duties were applied within days. Morgenthau froze all Czechoslovak funds in America until the Treasury's lawyers advised him he would have to let them go. He tried hard to stop the export of American-made arms and ammunition to Germany, but in vain.[6] As a demonstration of 'methods short of war' the reality was not calculated to carry all that much conviction in Berlin. Nor was the steady rise in American investments in German industry, led by heavy industrial and technology firms such as General Motors, International Business Machines, Du Pont Chemicals and Standard Oil; a growth rate of 36 per cent in 1936–40, of $206 million, which stood second only, in US investments abroad, to the $275 million invested in Britain.

Roosevelt was soon to take other action. British anxieties over

Europe and the Mediterranean led Halifax, prompted by the Admiralty, to ask that the secret agreement reached in January 1938 between the US Navy and the British Admiralty should be re-opened.[7] The school of thought currently dominant in the Admiralty believed that Britain's main naval effort would have to be focused on the Mediterranean. In January 1939 when the matter had been discussed with the US Naval Attaché in London, Captain Wilson USN, the British were still contemplating sending a battle fleet to the Far East, albeit one reduced a little in size.[8] On March 19, following the Cabinet meeting the previous day, Sir Ronald Lindsay, the British Ambassador in Washington, was instructed to warn the Americans that if Britain was involved in war in Europe, it might not be possible to reinforce British naval forces in the Pacific. Commander T. C. Hampton of the Admiralty's Plans Division visited Washington in great secrecy in June; he had to commit Britain's Far Eastern War Plans to memory and travel without any official papers. His own report was pessimistic: 'the US Navy have no detailed plans at present for co-operation with the Royal Navy in the event of war.' But the Admiralty never expected anything so far-reaching; and the warmth of the greeting Hampton received from Admiral Leahy and Admiral Ghormley of the US Navy was encouraging.[9] Drafting of the US naval war plan, *Rainbow Two*, began a week later.

More important for British anxieties about the Far East was the strength of the US fleet in the Pacific. In February a substantial part of the US battle fleet was in the Caribbean on manœuvres. On April 11, overwhelmed by the need to concentrate British naval forces so as to contain Italy in the Mediterranean, Halifax appealed to Roosevelt to move the US Atlantic squadron to the Pacific without delay. His request was given more strength by the French, who seemed to have concluded from the early stages of the Anglo-French Staff talks that the British were still dominated by their Far Eastern anxieties. Bullitt was fed Deuxième Bureau reports that co-ordinated German attacks on Poland, Italian on the Mediterranean and a Japanese attack on Singapore were to be unleashed simultaneously.[10] Both Léger and Daladier, no doubt aware of how to play on American suspicions, alleged that pressure from the City of London had led the British to consider dividing their fleet and sending the major part of it to Singapore.[11] Daladier threatened to abandon any resistance to Hitler in the Balkans. Convinced that he was saving the entire peace front from collapse through Chamberlain's abdication of his responsibilities in the Mediterranean, Roosevelt had in fact ordered the transfer of the US fleet to the Pacific before Halifax's message was received.[12]

The origin of this quite unwarranted panic on the French side appears to have been a theoretical paper produced by the British participants in the Anglo-French Staff talks in London on March 31 in which the need to dispatch 'a British fleet' to the Far East in the event of Japan entering the war was emphasized.[13] The effect, it was admitted, would be that Italy would obtain control of the sea communications in the eastern Mediterranean. At the same meeting, the French had revealed that they had no intention of launching an offensive against Italy in the opening stages of a war. The weekly liaison meeting of the Deuxième Bureau on April 12 showed no mark of the interpretations given to Bullitt;[14] he, it would seem, had his gullibility and that of his President played upon, essentially for the purposes of a government which was determined to do nothing militarily positive itself.

As has already been shown, the move to the Pacific of the US fleet, the only part of the US forces capable of immediate action, removed one restraint on Hitler. Roosevelt, by his folly, and in part at the urging of the French and of the German opposition to Hitler, was about to remove another. Battleships were something Hitler, an avid reader of *Weyers Taschenbuch*, the German equivalent of Jane's *All the World's Fighting Ships*, thought he understood. But he understood even more the role and importance of the charismatic national leader. He prized Mussolini for his overblown *persona* in much the same way he had convinced himself that Chamberlain and Halifax could be despised, while Churchill, Eden and Duff Cooper should be consistently denigrated, at least to prevent their personalities being impressed on the German people, even if they could not be deflated in British eyes.

Among Americans, Roosevelt was the only politician whose speeches, actions and public appearances filled the world's headlines. Until the winter of 1938/9, he had been a figure too distant to be of great importance to Hitler. But his increasing oratorical prominence, coupled with America's undoubted wealth and industrial potential, made it necessary for Hitler to find a role for Roosevelt to play in the private pseudo-Wagnerian drama which constituted Hitler's vision of coming history. Was Roosevelt to be Hitler's evil antagonist, to epitomize the dark forces against which Hitler, to others a somewhat improbable crusader, saw himself taking armour and horse? Or was he to be simply another democratic halfling, half-dolt, half-dupe? By his message to Hitler and Mussolini of April 15, 1939, Roosevelt cast himself irretrievably as the latter.

The message illustrated only too clearly the disordered priorities, the lack of grasp of realities and perceptions outside the United States, the desire to play the great mediator, the preoccupation with American public opinion, and the concentration on easy rhetoric, rather than on politically hazardous and difficult action, to which all American presidents are prone. Even Roosevelt himself estimated its chances of success at only one in five. But Roosevelt felt that the message would 'put the dictators on the spot'. The dictators' replies would 'make it clear to people everywhere that they were intent on the conquest and domination of Europe'.[15] The most recent Gallup Poll in America had shown that 82 per cent of those questioned felt that America should support Britain and France in a European war with provisions and goods, and 66 per cent felt that Americans should furnish aircraft and war materials: evidence enough that American opinion already realized where Hitler and Mussolini were going.[16] If the President believed European opinion to be in any doubt, he was singularly ill-informed. Europe's worry was where the lightning would strike next, and how to divert it. On this the President's message offered little or no reassurance.

The idea for the message arose in the President's mind immediately after the Italian attack on Albania. Curiously enough, it had its origin in a memorandum written on March 16 for a British intermediary, a businessman named A. P. Young, by Karl Goerdeler, the former Burgomaster of Leipzig and Reichs Commissioner for Prices, proposing a conference to discuss 'legitimate' German claims. Hitler's rejection of the proposal would, Goerdeler felt, swing German opinion back against the Führer. Young got the memorandum to Hull, via Messersmith. It bore all the hallmarks of Goerdeler's particular brand of unrealism.[17] Bullitt warned that 'words, no matter how wise, have small effect on Hitler and Mussolini. They are still sensitive to acts.' He suggested asking Congress to increase the size of the army or navy or both. His message coincided with an appeal from the French for some visible progress in Congress on the neutrality issue.[18] Roosevelt expressed himself optimistically to the French Ambassador, the Marquis de St Quentin, but said it would take time. He was, he said, searching for a means of making the dictators 'declare their intentions and assume their responsibilities in public, especially in American opinion'.[19]

The message[20] called, in the interests of 'the cause of world peace', for a 'frank statement of policy' to be made to Roosevelt, which he as an 'intermediary' could pass on to the governments concerned. Were the dictators ready to give assurances that they would not attack or invade the territory of some thirty-one 'independent' European and Asian 'nations', for a period of ten years? Roosevelt undertook to enquire of the thirty-one states whether they would give similar assurances. Once that was done, Roosevelt pledged that America would take part in discussions, first, to reduce the crushing burden of armament, and, second, to look to the 'most practical manner' of opening the world up to a free trade market. At the same time, 'those governments other than the United States, who were directly interested, could undertake such political discussions as they wished or thought desirable'.

The list of thirty-one countries lumped Ireland with Great Britain, to the fury of Ireland's Premier Eamon de Valera,[21] and included Syria and Palestine, respectively French and British mandated territories. As Mussolini remarked to Goering on April 16, the President was 'not very well up on his geography'.[22] (He also commented that Roosevelt seemed to be 'suffering from an incipient mental disease'.) All in all, neither the somewhat pedestrian drafting of the message nor the failure to anticipate its effects can be said to reflect particularly well on the State Department's level of professional expertise. The main effect of the message was not to put the dictators on the spot. They, despite the reports which reached London, Paris and Washington of Hitler's rage and Mussolini's fury,[23] seem to have reacted with uncharacteristic equanimity. It was the Foreign Ministers of the twenty states which were neither British or French satellites, nor Poland and Russia, who were to find themselves on the spot, as Ribbentrop followed the President's message to each of the addressees with two enquiries: did the country concerned feel itself threatened by Germany? Had it authorized Roosevelt to make such an enquiry on its behalf?[24] Ribbentrop's initiative anticipated and largely nullified efforts undertaken by Hull and Halifax three days later to collect material in support of Roosevelt's action.

The weaker countries, Estonia, Latvia and Lithuania, for example, found themselves in an impossible situation. They had been pressing Germany for non-aggression pacts for some time. Roosevelt's message enabled them to extract non-aggression pacts from Hitler; but the effect of these agreements, which they had originally sought as a guarantee of neutrality, was to give many, the Soviets especially, the impression that they had joined the German camp.

Much the same dilemma was faced by the leaders of Romania, Greece, Yugoslavia and the Balkan states. All felt threatened: by Hungary or by Italy, if not by Germany. None of them, least of all M. Gafencu, due to arrive in Berlin on April 18, were likely to risk alienating Hitler in the face of so direct a question. Norway, Denmark, the Netherlands, Belgium and Luxemburg faced a similar dilemma. Colijn, the Dutch Foreign Minister, said as much to Gordon, the American Minister to The Hague. 'If we open our mouths, that will naturally draw Germany's anger.'[25]

The way was therefore clear for Hitler's reply. This was given in the

'Warmonger!'

same speech of April 28 in which he denounced the 1934 Non-Aggression Pact with Poland and the naval agreements with Britain. More than a third of the speech was devoted to making heavy fun of Roosevelt's initiative, which the German and Italian press had already made the centre of a campaign of vilification for the previous twelve days. Each repetition of the President's name sent his audience into heavily reported peals of scornful laughter. He had, he said, asked all the states mentioned whether they felt threatened and whether they had asked the President to secure guarantees for them. All had answered in the negative. Still, he would gladly guarantee each and every one of them – even the United States if they wished it.[26]

One can judge the damage his reply did to Roosevelt by the welcome given it by the isolationist Senators and the speed with which his court hurried to reassure him.[27] Senator Hiram Johnson's comments were typical: 'Hitler had the better of the argument. . . . Roosevelt put his chin out and got a resounding whack. I have reached the conclusion that there will be no war.'[28] The chief of the State Department's Division of European Affairs, the egregious liberal Jay Pierrepont Moffatt, complained bitterly that Hitler had treated the President's message as 'a trick', a comment that indicates, to say the least, a certain unfamiliarity, for someone in his position, with the Führer's style, methods and personality. All in all, the episode of the President's message left Hitler with a feeling of oneupmanship over a man he should have regarded as potentially his most dangerous enemy. It does not bode well for the peace of the world when the President of the United States allows himself to be manœuvred into appearing as an inept and ignorant fool.

The isolationist minority in Congress were soon to add to this image of ineptness one of impotence. Hitler's most valued source of information in the United States was to become the German Military Attaché, General von Boetticher. Von Boetticher had excellent contacts in US army circles. He was a personal friend of General Wedemeyer, a man widely regarded as one of the ablest of the coming generation of younger officers and one of the foremost of the names in the little black book General Marshall was keeping of those he proposed to promote in place of all the dead wood in the upper echelons of the US Army once he became Chief of Staff. Indeed in 1935 von Boetticher had arranged for Wedemeyer's two-year attachment to the German War College. Isolationism, America Firstism and a good dose of Anglophobia were common sentiments among the senior American military officers of the period. From his contacts Boetticher reported on the strength of isolationism in the US Army and among the middle-class Midwestern and Southern society among which so many of the principal US military stations had, ever since the Indian wars, been located.[29] He reported too that no American expeditionary force could be dispatched overseas for at least six months after America's entry into war.[30]

The US Navy was in the Pacific; the US Army was out of sympathy with the President, and unprepared. Now it was to emerge that Roosevelt could not control Congress. The American reaction to the German march into Czechoslovakia stirred Senator Pittman into fresh action. With help from the State Department a new bill, dubbed the Peace Act of 1939, was drafted, repealing the arms embargo section of the 1937 legislation and authorizing the sale of arms to any belligerent who could pay cash for them in America and transport them, not in American ships, to belligerent ports. There were still to be no loans for belligerents, no Americans were to travel on the ships of belligerents, and American merchant shipping was not to be armed. The President was to be given discretion to proclaim combat zones from which all American ships and travellers could be banned. Pittman launched the bill with a nationwide broadcast on March 19, emphasizing that it was his bill and not that of the administration. The bill divided the Senate bitterly. The isolationists opposed it. Other groups favoured going much further. The Chinese Government pointed out that there was no way they could carry goods to China through the Japanese navy. Pittman answered this with a separate Senate resolution authorizing the President to embargo imports from and exports to any country violating the 1922 Treaties on China.

Hearings on the new bill began on April 5. Pittman was unable to persuade his Senate committee to dispense with them or to impose a time limit. The House Committee on Foreign Affairs held parallel hearings. Public interest waned as week after week dragged on. Roosevelt held his peace. Opinion in the press and at the hearings remained divided. Labour itself divided, the American Federation of Labor favouring the arms embargo, the Congress of Industrial Organizations supporting repeal. The Churches were also divided, with the Catholics firmly in support of the 1937 Act. The peace movement divided bitterly between true pacifists and believers in international security. Even the college campuses split on the issue. Both parties were divided, both in Congress and in the country.[31] Pittman hit the bottle harder and more frequently. Hull was driven to cancel his own appearance before the Committee for fear of hostile questioning,[32] while London and Paris grew increasingly anxious.[33] On May 16, Pittman announced that 'the situation in Europe does not seem to induce any urgent action on neutrality legislation' and that further consideration of neutrality legislation would be postponed.[34]

In despair Hull and Roosevelt turned to the House of Representatives. The House Committee for Foreign Affairs was chaired by Representative Sol Bloom of New York, a flamboyant figure who had built up a fortune, first in music publishing and then in real estate.[35] Brash, bouncy and famous for antics which made him an easy target for ridicule, he affected Hull like chalk scraped across a blackboard. On May 19, however, at a conference at the White House, it was decided to give him his head.[36] The existing legislation, in the view of the State Department's legal advisers, would cripple British and French resistance to Germany, should war come. Repeal of the arms embargo, in Roosevelt's view, 'would actually prevent the outbreak of war in Europe', or, if it failed to do that, 'would make less likely a victory for the powers unfriendly to the United States'. Roosevelt hoped the House would act favourably before June 12, when King George VI and Queen Elizabeth were due to arrive from Canada as his guests.[37]

Bloom was no more adept a manager than Pittman. So far from having reached agreement by June 12, the House Committee adjourned for the space of the Royal visit. When the bill eventually reached the floor of the House, Luther Johnson, a Representative from Texas, introduced it and managed the business. The bill reached the point of a favourable vote when, at the last minute, an amendment was introduced enacting a limited embargo, covering the export of arms and ammunition. Defeated on a show of hands, it was passed by 159 to 157 when tellers were brought in. Roosevelt had his bill; but it virtually nullified all he had hoped for. The next day a renewed attempt to get the unamended bill agreed failed by four votes. Among the sixty-one Democrats who opposed their President, Irish, Italian and German names predominate. Only the South remained loyal.[38]

The outcome filled the Italian press with rejoicing.[39] The German press treated it in a low-key fashion.[40] The French, talking to Bullitt, were beside themselves with anxiety. Did the House of Representatives desire to precipitate war at this moment? Did it really desire the defeat of Great Britain, France and Poland?[41] The action of the House of Representatives, Daladier told Bullitt, had encouraged Hitler to believe that the democracies would get no arms or ammunition from the United States.[42] The coincidence of the House vote with the French panic over a possible coup against Danzig over the weekend of July 1 no doubt went some way to explain French alarm. The State Department was itself cognizant of and alarmed by the same reports.[43] Their coincidence with the worst moments of the crisis in the Far East over Tientsin strengthened its belief in the conspiratorial co-ordination of Axis and Japanese plans for aggression.

Roosevelt, ignoring the advice of his Vice President, Garner, and Harold Ickes, that the constitutional responsibility for foreign affairs freed him from the constraints imposed by the Neutrality Act, understood the importance of the signals that were coming out of Washington. Bribing Pittman by persuading the Senate to raise the subsidy for American-produced silver (of which Pittman's state, Nevada, was the major producer), Roosevelt pressed him to re-open the original Senate Foreign Relations Committee action he had abandoned in May. The twenty-three Senators on the Committee were split eleven against ten in favour with two undecided. Neither of the two waverers, both Democrats, Senators Walter George of Georgia, and Guy Gillette of Iowa, were dyed-in-the-wool isolationists; both had previously expressed their support for the total repeal of all neutrality legislation. But neither of them owed the President, who had refused to endorse their re-election in the mid-term elections the previous November, a favour. They yielded therefore to a suggestion from the leader of the opponents, Senator Champ Clark of Massachusetts, and voted to postpone consideration of the neutrality legislation until the next session of Congress, to begin in January 1940. Of the sixteen members of his own party on the Committee, and their two progressive and Farmer-Labor allies, Roosevelt could only command eleven votes.[44]

Roosevelt's first reaction was to draft a message calling his opponents contemptible and pitiable. Hull talked him out of this. Instead he appealed to the Senate majority to override its Committee. On July 18, he invited Hull, Vice President Garner and half a dozen leading Senators from both parties to meet him at the White House. Among them was the arch-isolationist, Senator William Borah of Idaho.

Borah had a record stretching back over two and a half decades of thwarting presidential foreign policy initiatives.[45] In 1919, he had been one of the 'irreconcilable' opponents of Senate ratification of the Versailles Treaty. It was his motion calling for a naval disarmament conference which coerced the 1921 Congress and Administration, perhaps the most nationalist and 'Big Navy' to be elected in this century, into taking the initiative which led to the Washington Naval Conference and Treaties of 1921–22. A progressive, even by some standards an imperialist in his youth,[46] he had developed, through long membership of the Senate Foreign Relations Committee, into a constant critic of successive administrations contaminating themselves, as he saw it, by involvement in the unjust and un-American system of compromise with power politics, by which Europe regulated or, more often, failed to regulate its affairs. He had attended, on July 7, the meeting of senatorial opponents of any revision of the neutrality legislation in the office of Senator Johnson which had stated their opposition to any repeal of the arms embargo and objected to 'any discretion being lodged in the hands of any Chief Executive to determine an aggressor or aggressors during any war abroad'.[47]

He was present at the meeting in the White House only by virtue of his position as senior Republican member of the Foreign Relations Committee. The others present were the Majority and Minority Senate leaders, Senators Alben Barkley of Kentucky and Charles McNary of Oregon, with, in the latter case, his deputy, Warren Austin of Vermont; the Vice President, John Nance Garner of Texas; and Key Pittman. All were there *ex officio*, rather than by virtue of their position on the neutrality legislation.

Borah had, in fact, been on record as early as January 1939 as saying that war might break out in 1939.[48] But he was irremediably opposed to trusting any President, least of all Franklin Roosevelt. Hull played into his hands by naming Gerald P. Nye as an extreme isolationist whose views were blocking repeal. Borah interrupted: 'there are others, Mr

President'. Roosevelt's famous charm could not move him. Borah insisted there would be no war that summer. White with anger, Hull invited the Senator to come to the State Department and examine the State Department cables. Disdainfully, Borah replied, 'So far as the reports in your Department are concerned, I wouldn't be bound by them. I have my own sources of information, and on several occasions, I've found them more reliable than the State Department.'[49] Close to tears of rage, Hull held his peace. Garner canvassed those present, then told Roosevelt bluntly, 'You haven't got the votes, and that's all there is to it.' Roosevelt took his defeat gracefully and made a joke. The meeting 'broke up in laughter'.[50]

The absence of positive support in Congress was, of course, the real issue, not Borah's sources, which, it turned out, consisted simply and solely of Claud Cockburn's *The Week*,[51] and reflected the beliefs and suspicions of West European Communists, fellow-travellers and all who shared their ineradicable distrust of the Chamberlain and Daladier Governments, if not those of Moscow as well. Roosevelt, and not only Roosevelt but the whole of Europe, were to pay for his failure to command the confidence of Congress in the degree to which he respected the balance of powers written into the American constitution. American domestic politics are always more real than those of the outside world to those who live in the Washington goldfish bowl under the glare of the so-called American Fourth Estate.

Lacking a clear lead, American opinion remained divided and confused. Roosevelt, apart from infrequent outbursts of public oratory, had done nothing practical to rally his allies, to win over the waverers or to remove the deep distrust which a majority of Congressmen, already aware that there was nothing to stop him running again for President in 1940, so great was his domination of his party, felt towards him. He was a man who preferred stealth to openness, who encouraged division even among his own supporters, and who looked for and complained of the lack of courage and leadership in Britain and France; in the field of American foreign policy he had yet to supply or demonstrate these qualities himself.

His style betrays a deep-seated if hidden insecurity which is, paradoxically, the last term his still-active supporters would admit. It is perhaps symbolized in his physical disabilities. A man who projected the appearance of enormous leonine strength, he could not stand for any length of time without being supported. The crippling disability left by the polio which struck him down in the 1920s seems reflected in the position of the presidency and the manner in which he chose to occupy it. No American president is as strong as he seems. His powers are checked, reviewed, scrutinized by Congress. Rarely if ever can he control the feudal barons who dominate the state sections of the two parties and who are normally deeply entrenched in the political and economic life of their own states. But Roosevelt could not, and would not, even control his own administration, tolerating division and feuding among his own appointees,[52] partly to keep his party happy, partly to protect his own position.

He could, however, see clearly, and he could act in stealth. And unbeknown to those who advised him that his powers could be used despite the neutrality legislation, he was following up the clandestine contacts with Britain established between navy and navy in January 1938. On June 30 he had summoned Sir Ronald Lindsay to the White House and unfolded to him a new plan, one which sprang from his and Admiral Leahy's reflections on the manœuvres of April 1939 in the Caribbean.[53] In the event of war, he told Lindsay, he proposed to establish an American naval patrol over the whole Western Atlantic up to 500 miles from the coasts of the Americas, with the aim of declaring the Western Atlantic a neutral zone and denying it in effect to Axis warships. In that way all ships with goods from the Americas bound for the Allies could collect at Halifax unchallenged and Britain need only provide convoy escorts to cover them once they passed outside the neutral zone. To this end he asked that air and naval bases should be leased to America in the British West Indies, on Trinidad and Tobago, on St Lucia and on Bermuda.

Lindsay, while 'aghast at the light-hearted manner in which the President was prepared to defy all ordinary concepts of neutrality at the outset of a war', recommended the idea to London very strongly. It struck the Foreign Office's own legal advisers as open to 'grave objections'. They thought allowing a neutral power to use the ports of one belligerent to deny 'certain waters to the other belligerent hardly within the realm of practical politics'. The Cabinet, like the rest of the Foreign Office, welcomed the idea. Malcolm MacDonald, the Colonial Secretary, told the Governors of Bermuda and of Trinidad and Tobago that, 'in view of the overriding political considerations, His Majesty's Government were anxious to give speedy acceptance.'

The legal advisers insisted, however, on exploring some of the implications. When Lindsay duly saw the President on July 8, to put some of their points to him, Roosevelt was at first 'stunned and angered'. Hull told him the British seemed to display 'a mis-apprehension of his intentions'[54] as well as a lack of appreciation of the constraints imposed on him by domestic considerations. Since this was only a week after Representative Bloom's defeat and a day after Borah's manifesto, Roosevelt's reaction is understandable. He was, however, to persist with the plan. By the middle of August, US naval missions, no more than one or two men in each case, were engaged discreetly in leasing land for seaplane bases from Pan-American Airways in Trinidad and in Bermuda and from private citizens in St Lucia.[55] Their action was in fact suspended for a little once war broke out, for fear of compromising Roosevelt's new and ultimately successful attempts to lift the arms embargo and partly as a result of the US Navy's discovery that it had neither the men nor the planes to make use of the bases. But the whole episode explains why London viewed Roosevelt's failure to dragoon Congress into a repeal of the arms embargo with more equanimity than did Paris.[56] Roosevelt failed to impress Hitler; but in his own way he strengthened the resolve of the British Cabinet.

CHAPTER 16

THE STRUGGLE FOR THE BALKANS: ROUND I — TURKEY

'The primary task', wrote Lord Halifax to Sir Eric Phipps on April 21, 1939, 'must be to erect the first essential barrier against aggression in Eastern Europe by making arrangements for the safety of those states most directly menaced. . . . In the scheme which we are in the process of organizing the key positions are occupied by Poland and Turkey.'[1] A glance at the map shows how vital the position of Turkey was in the British scheme. The archipelago of independent states which lay between the borders of the Axis states and the Soviet Union, is anchored firmly at its southern end by the great bulge of Asiatic Turkey. Turkey's European territories lie across the frontiers of Greece and Bulgaria, and block the entrance to the Black Sea at the Dardanelles. Both Romania and the Soviet Union depend on the friendship of Turkey for their sea links with the outside world. And it had long been the policy of the Soviet Union to establish a regime over the Straits that would confine access to the Black Sea to the shipping of the riparian states alone.

In 1939, Turkey was governed by the immediate followers of Kemal Atatürk, the generation of young officers which, despising the more flashy leaders of the Young Turk revolution who had led Turkey to defeat, occupation and the loss of her empire in 1918, had united Turkey in the troubled days of 1919–22. They had fought, defeated and outmanœuvred the French and Italians, they had suppressed the Armenians and the Azerbaijanis, they had broken and expelled the invading armies of Greece, and they had 'kept their cool' in the confrontation at Chanak with Britain. They were the soldier-statesmen of a revolution which had thereafter made Turkey over into a modern Western state in the teeth of the innately conservative Muhammadanism of its largely peasant population. Atatürk himself had winnowed these men through the first eighteen years of the new state, and they were, in their own way, as impressive a group as the Founding Fathers of the United States. Three lessons they had learnt in this long and testing period: the strength that a determined and decided man has over one who is not; the folly of an uncalculated, hotheaded challenge to a European great power; and the overriding importance of controlled and disciplined judgment. Two other principles governed their actions: an abiding contempt for those whom they had once ruled – Greeks, Armenians, Arabs, Bulgarians; and a deep respect for, and desire for the friendship of, both the Soviet Union, their sole ally in the war of independence, and Great Britain, the one power they had neither outfaced, outmanœuvred nor overborne. To retain the amity and support of the Soviet Union and to maintain and deepen friendly relations with Great Britain were the guiding principles of their foreign policy; but no power was capable of pushing them around.

Their country occupied a position of great natural defensive strength, and their military genius also lay in defence. In 1877, Turkish forces had prolonged the war with Tsarist Russia for nearly a year by their dogged defence of the fortress of Plevna. In 1915 they had held the heights of Gallipoli against the best troops of the British empire, and smashed Churchill's hopes of opening the seaway to Russia. The lines around Chatalja, which run from the Black Sea to the Sea of Marmora, had never fallen to military attack. Since the Treaty of Montreux in 1936 the Turks had been refortifying the Dardanelles. Even Hitler, at the height of his powers, did not attack Turkey. Alone among the armies of the Balkan states, the Turkish army had the unquestioning respect of the Military Staffs of the European great powers.

The Turkish forces had been in a state of semi-mobilization for some time. Since the Bulgarians had been granted increased armaments in an agreement with the powers of the Balkan Entente signed at Salonika in August 1938 as part of a move to defuse Bulgarian revisionism, the Turkish army had felt discretion to be the better part of valour. In December 1938 the Turkish high command had strengthened the garrisons of the frontier fortifications in Thrace by the creation of a new army corps. Anxieties about the vulnerability of the Anatolian coast-line to amphibious attack from the Italian bases in the Dodecanese, had caused a similar strengthening of those forces based on Izmir.[2] Turkey's leaders reacted to the Italian invasion of Albania by calling three classes back to the colours, approving a new credit of 215 million Turkish pounds and recalling various specialist troops to give them in all 250,000 men under arms;[3] of these, the bulk, 100,000 or so, were in Thrace, 50,000 or so were in western Anatolia and the remainder scattered through the country. German military reports put eight infantry and one cavalry division in Thrace with steady reinforcement through the spring and summer.[4] Whoever else was to be caught out, it was not to be the Turkish high command, which eyed the steady building up of Italian forces in Albania (some twenty Italian divisions were widely reported there) with the deepest suspicion.[5]

Since 1934, the Turks had been members, with Greece, Romania and Yugoslavia, of the Balkan Entente. The terms of the Entente bound its members to come to one another's aid, if one of the four signatories was attacked by their common enemy, Bulgaria. All had profited at Bulgaria's expense by the peace treaties in 1919, save only Turkey. Bulgaria had lost her Aegean coast-line to Greece, and half her Black Sea coast-line, the area known as the Dobrudja, to Romania. Bulgarian claims on Macedonia, divided between Yugoslavia and Greece, made her natural enemies with both countries. Only Turkey had no real quarrel with Bulgaria and it was to Ankara that the Bulgarians looked for a guarantee that the Balkan Entente would never function aggressively against her.

Kemal Atatürk, the great architect of modern Turkey, died on November 10, 1938. His successor as President of Turkey was Ismet Inönü, his friend from before 1914 and right-hand man ever thereafter. Inönü had even faced up to the great Lord Curzon at Lausanne in 1923 and won his grudging respect. In 1939 he was fifty-four years old, his hair already turning white, but still the same calm, imperturbable little man with the hesitant feeble voice which so much belied his inner determination, who had impressed the delegates of Europe and the United States at Lausanne. Honest, conscientious, straight as a die, brutal and brutally direct, he was going slightly deaf, a defect which he made into an asset in his interviews with foreign statesmen and diplomats. He had the reputation, especially with the French, of being pro-German and pro-Russian, of wishing to revive Turkish nationalist aspirations in Syria and the Caucasus, and of being the champion of the 'Asiatic tendency' in Turkey. This is the kind of a priori nonsense which for so long passed in Europe for expertise on the Middle East. Ismet Inönü was a Turk, no man's fool, no fool's servant and no follower of any predetermined ideological, nationalist or geopolitical theories.

His Foreign Minister, Sükrü Saracoğlu, was another of the same stamp. Successively Minister of Finance and of Justice under Atatürk, he had taken part in some of the hardest and toughest measures of the Atatürk regime. Like Inönü he was calm and forceful, with an inner self-confidence that made him disdainful of finesse. There was nothing feeble or hesitant about his way of speaking. Though his delivery was slow, it was strong, direct and simple. He had little finesse but much patience; he feared nobody. His deputy, Numan Rifaat Menemencioğlu, was closer to the traditional idea of a diplomatist. Deeply imbued with French culture, he was on equally good terms with British and German diplomatists. He was the ablest brain in the Turkish Foreign Ministry and, despite perpetual ill-health, its most tireless worker and most impressive negotiator – not to mention its heaviest drinker. Like Inönü, he had the reputation of being a Germanophile, especially in Berlin; but those who gave him this reputation mistook him, as they did his master.

The fourth figure in this gallery of Turkish diplomatists was Tevfik Rüştü Aras, Saracoğlu's predecessor as Foreign Minister and now Ambassador in Britain. A close personal friend of Atatürk since their days as young officers together – he was an army doctor – he was the comic in Atatürk's entourage. He spoke several languages besides his own, all of them with a volubility and a garrulity which made him the exact opposite of his successor. His convivial, affable manner endeared him to foreigners while at the same time preventing them from taking him seriously. He was apt to bemuse himself by his own flood of words, and to lose the thread of his argument in his admiration of his own eloquence. In certain moods he resembled a perambulating Algerian carpet-seller; but the resemblance was misleading. The appearance of the Orient in his manner concealed a mind as direct, as cold, as ruthless, in a word as Turkish, as was possessed by any of Atatürk's *epigoni*. He had been the architect of the *rapprochement* with Britain which was the main theme of Turkish foreign policy in the 1930s.

The first British approach to Turkey had been made in March 1939 at the time of M. Tilea's dramatic descent upon the Foreign Office. It had not been altogether successful. The new British Ambassador, Sir Hugh Knatchbull-Hugessen, was not a man to whom history has been altogether fair. To posterity his name, unpronounceable as it is to all but native-born English speakers – M. Saracoğlu could never get closer than 'Knatenbull' – is irretrievably overlaid by the stories of 'Cicero', his traitorous Turkish valet. But this is not the only instance of his tendency to attract misfortune. While serving as Ambassador in China in 1937 he had been shot up by a Japanese aeroplane and badly wounded while driving on the road between Nanking and Shanghai. So perverse is human nature that in British governmental circles there were not lacking advocates of an Anglo-Japanese settlement who felt that he was in some obscure way at fault for being so attacked. This feeling was not strong enough to prevent him succeeding to the Ankara Embassy, one of the 'plums', though not the largest, of a diplomatic career, when the popular and tough-minded Sir Percy Loraine was promoted to Rome. But his influence in 'the office', let alone with Halifax or Chamberlain, never amounted to very much. Vansittart and Cadogan dismissed him vulgarly as 'Snatch'. His finesse, his sense of humour, his ironical approach to the problems of his job, his underlying sensibility, went down excellently with the Turks as with his French colleague, René Massigli. They did not endear him to Lord Halifax, nor to Neville Chamberlain. They were not, for that matter, to endear him to Churchill or Eden either. What he was given to do, he did well, intelligently, and with success. But he was not often able to influence his masters in London.

The first British approaches to Turkey were not altogether very happy. To an initial enquiry as to the Turkish attitude in the event of a German attack on Romania, Saracoğlu replied that Turkey was well disposed to any British proposals but had no treaty obligations.[6] Rüştü Aras explained that it was a fixed principle of Turkish policy not to depart from existing commitments unless certain of British co-operation.[7] Meeting Bonnet during the latter's visit to London, Aras remarked that war would certainly come by September that year. A policy of neutrality based on strengthening the Balkan Entente and settling the feud with Bulgaria was called for. Of course, if the Soviets entered such a war they would win. He did not believe the Western theories that there would be a revolt against Stalin. As for the British proposal he did not understand it, sensed harm in it, and could not recommend it to his government.[8] On March 24 Saracoğlu remarked to Massigli that it was essential that France and Britain stop seeking advice from other countries and made their own minds up as to what to do.[9] He had already been put under pressure by the determinedly rotund German Chargé d'affaires in Ankara, Hans Kroll, who was to end a stormy diplomatic career in 1962 as one of the *ancients terribles* of the Federal German foreign service as Ambassador in Moscow.[10] The more diplomatic Numan had felt it wise to assure Kroll that Turkey would co-operate if it was a question of Germany making the Balkans her economic hinterland, while warning him that things would be much easier if Germany would not insist on the Balkans adopting 'a unilateral and manifestly partisan attitude in the coming struggle'.[11] On March 29, Saracoğlu went as far as to offer France a pact of assistance,[12] to cover France's frontiers in the Middle East and Turkey's in Eastern Europe against any aggression, a pact which could be extended provided that Britain would come in.

Lord Halifax, however, was still concentrating on Poland and Romania, and his contacts with the Turks remained intermittent. His first reactions to the Italian attack on Albania struck M. Saracoğlu as hesitant and lacking in firmness.[13] For a moment M. Saracoğlu was baffled and discouraged, and his first reactions to the news of the British guarantees to Romania and Greece and the British proposal that Turkey should extend her alliance with Greece to cover attack from Italy[14] were cold and on the sniffy side. Bluntly Saracoğlu remarked to Sir Hugh that his government were not prepared to put themselves irretrievably on the side of Britain without some definite British guarantee of Turkey's own security. No doubt he was thinking of the Italian naval and air bases in the islands of the Dodecanese, a barrier across the entry to the Aegean, and only minutes' flying time away from the cities of Turkey's Aegean coast-line.

The position, however, was immediately altered by the British decision to guarantee Romania without waiting to straighten out the Polish–Romanian relationship. On April 13 Sir Hugh was empowered to offer Turkey a guarantee against any attack by Italy in return for a Turkish alliance and assistance with the question of Romanian and Balkan security generally.[15] This the Turks accepted in three days flat. They were not prepared to come to the aid of Romania with their military forces, which they anticipated would be fully engaged in the defence of the Dardanelles. They insisted on Soviet collaboration. They emphasized the importance of attempting to settle Romania's difficulties with Bulgaria. But in the event of war in the Mediterranean, and on these terms, Turkey would fight on Britain's side.[16]

The Turks were well aware that if they could remove Romanian anxieties about their southern frontier with Bulgaria they would go some way both towards strengthening Romania's resistance to German pressure and towards increasing the chances of Balkan solidarity. As the one member of the Balkan Entente regarded in Sofia as reasonably friendly, Turkey hoped to use her influence with the Bulgarians to secure a settlement. And the initial Bulgarian reaction to the German occupation of Prague offered some support for their optimism.

Policy in Bulgaria was made by two men, the King and the man who combined the two posts of Prime Minister and Foreign Minister, Gheorgi Kiossievanov. As a descendant of the house of Coburg, King Boris was a distant relative of the British Royal Family, for whom he had an intense admiration. But the Coburg heritage of intrigue, so apparent in Queen Victoria's uncle, Léopold I of Belgium, had been sharpened and strengthened to the point of obsessiveness in the Bulgarian Royal Family. King Boris's father, having survived decades of Russian, Austrian and Ottoman pressure, had been forced to abdicate in 1919 after Bulgaria's defeat in the world war. Boris never forgot this, nor the terrible intrigues and bloodshed of the following decade, when Bulgarian politics were dominated by the terrorists of the International Macedonian Revolutionary Organization. He looked like a Latin, and worked and organized his life like a German; but his natural, open and outgoing courtesy hid a positively Byzantine mind. Reversing Occam, he always preferred the involved and intricate to the simple explanation. And he was obsessed by the fear of creating a national leader capable of overthrowing him. He was not naturally a strong man, either in physique or in character, and he knew it. And, while 80 per cent of the Bulgarian people were instinctively Russophile, Boris was influenced in all he did by fears both of Russia and of Communism. Neither, he felt instinctively, had any place in its cosmos for an independent Bulgarian monarchy.

His current Chief Minister, Gheorgi Kiossievanov, was a rather different personality. Fat and friendly, he wanted an independent Bulgaria as much as his King. But he was a lot more suspicious of Germany, and, so far as can be seen, a lot less obsessed by the loss of the Dobrudja than was Boris. He was, however, weighed down by Bulgaria's dependence on Germany for arms and markets. In mid-April he wrote to all Bulgarian missions abroad. 'Bulgaria', he wrote, 'conducts an independent foreign policy without obligations to anyone and will continue to do so, so far as is possible. . . . Her economic ties to Germany make it impossible for her to put herself on the side of the democracies and against the totalitarian states. The search for credits in the West remains fruitless.'[17] And he complained that the West was not interested in the Bulgarian market. Germany, by contrast, pressed credits on him: 45 million Reichsmarks in April, and a special mission in June.

Kiossievanov was unmoved. Bulgarians took the enslavement of their fellow Slavs in Prague very badly,[18] but with their conquest of Czechoslovakia the Germans now controlled 75 per cent of Bulgaria's foreign trade.[19] Kiossievanov distrusted such a state of affairs. It was he who, visiting Ankara in the days immediately after the German annexation of Prague, expressed to the Turks his great anxieties over German pressure on the Balkans and asked the Turks what they could do to resist it.[20] It was through him that the Turks hoped to secure a settlement of the Dobrudja issue.

The issue was put to M. Gafencu, the Romanian Foreign Minister, when he visited Ankara on April 8, at the time of the Italian attack on Albania.[21] Saracoğlu succeeded in persuading the Romanians to make friendly noises towards Sofia, inviting the Bulgarians to join in with the Balkan Entente in economic and cultural co-operation.[22] The

Bulgarians were invited to send a representative to the Economic Conference of the Balkan Entente due to meet in Bucharest in mid-May. But with the Italians invading Albania and a new panic in Bucharest that Hungarian attack was imminent, the idea of any Romanian territorial concessions to Bulgaria was simply ruled out of court by M. Gafencu.[23] The Greeks supported him in this.[24] Bulgarian revisionism included claims for the return of Dede Agach on the Aegean coast of Thrace and an outlet to the Mediterranean. The Turks hoped to get round this problem by persuading their Balkan allies to admit Bulgaria to full membership of the Balkan Entente, in the hope that frontier issues would then lose much of their force. But again it proved difficult to make any impression on the Romanians once they had secured the Anglo-French guarantee they wanted.

The truth would seem to be that the experience of being courted instead of isolated was beginning to go to King Boris's head, especially when coupled with German pressure exerted on him through the negotiations on German arms deliveries to the Bulgarian army.[25] Boris therefore instructed Kiossievanov to make it quite clear that Bulgaria was interested only in territorial concessions; and the Bulgarians appear to have found some support or at least understanding for their viewpoint from Yugoslavia.

In the meantime, however, the Turks, having secured the necessary display of firmness and reassurance from Britain, pushed ahead with the negotiations for an alliance. On April 23 Saracoğlu suggested three steps: a public declaration, secret negotiations on a treaty, and a public treaty.[26] Halifax explained that he thought the Germans were feeling around to create apprehension wherever they could, and that when they found a weak place they would exploit it. Hence the importance he attached to a rapid and public strengthening of the ties of solidarity between all the states that felt themselves threatened.[27] This was, very broadly, the Turkish view, but the Turks drew a considerable practical distinction between Germany and Italy, based on the limits of their own effective action. What they hoped for was a triangular structure of agreements, between Britain and the Soviet Union, between themselves and the Soviet Union and between themselves and Britain. To the first of these they attached immense importance but had little practical to offer. The second they envisaged as covering the Balkans and the Black Sea only. The third fell into two parts: against Italy, automatic collaboration in the event of war in the Mediterranean; against Germany, co-operation only if war spread to the Balkans.[28] This division was explained by reference to the Soviet Union. It was picked up by Lord Halifax and incorporated in the British draft of the declaration. The Turks approved this on May 6.[29] The Balkans were more complicated and less urgent and Lord Halifax had had enough of being stampeded.

In the meantime the Turks had three other great powers to deal with: Germany, the Soviet Union and France. The German Government were more than adequately informed as to the progress of the Anglo-Turkish negotiations owing to the primitive character of the Turkish diplomatic ciphers and the fact that the land cable between Ankara and London ran through German territory.[30] The Germans had also sub-orned a clerk in the Turkish Foreign Ministry archives.[31] The vital Turkish telegram containing the Turkish proposals of April 16 to Britain duly fell into German hands.[32] But its decipherment took the German authorities some time, and was never totally completed (possibly the Turks had adopted a new cipher), and it was not until April 25 that the German Foreign Ministry were in a position to warn their missions in Ankara and in Europe generally that the Anglo-Turkish conversations had gone a lot further 'than the Turks would care to tell us'.[33]

The news stung the German Foreign Ministry into rapid action. Since the retirement of the last German Ambassador to Turkey, Friedrich von Keller, in November 1938, they had been in no real hurry to fill this post. Intrigue had finally secured it for Franz von Papen, perhaps the most curious of all those German aristocrats who collaborated with and made themselves the cat's-paws of Adolf Hitler. Franz von Papen throughout his life had a reputation for intrigue and foxiness. Even as late as 1944, *Punch* could still depict him as the 'Octo-papen', stretching his tentacles throughout the Balkans from his Embassy in Ankara. But he could only enjoy the reputation of a fox in countries which rely on shotguns to keep foxes under control. In Britain, he would have fallen to the first outing of any reasonably competent local pack of hounds. (In German politics, however, he was to display an extraordinary gift for personal survival, forever bobbing up again just when everyone thought they had seen the last of him.) As an intriguer he was assiduous, crafty, devious and totally incompetent. As Military Attaché in Washington in the period of American neutrality during the First World War, he was so careless of his secret documents as to betray to British intelligence most of the activities of the German sabotage ring organized by Captain von Rintelen. What was not captured in the United States he thoughtfully preserved among his papers, which fell into British hands when his ship was boarded and his baggage searched after the Americans had expelled him. He took great care to confide all the remaining details to a personal diary which he took with him on his next assignment, a posting to the German troops fighting alongside the Turks in Palestine. There he took it with him on patrol, so that it might fall into British hands when he was surprised by British cavalry and fled, leaving his baggage behind him.

His greatest moment came in 1932. After a brief period as Chancellor (he had entered German politics on the right wing of the Catholic centre party), he had been a central figure both in the renewal of the industrialists' support of Hitler in November 1932, and in persuading the aged President, Field Marshal von Hindenburg, to appoint Hitler as Chancellor. His own appointment as Vice Chancellor was intended to give him constant control of Hitler's every action. His one achievement, in fact, was to negotiate a concordat with the Vatican and cast the mantle of the Vicar of Christ over one who bid fair to be His satanic opposite. In the summer of 1934 he believed Hitler's regime to be on the verge of collapse, and spoke publicly against it. In the 'night of the long knives' he escaped with his life through an accident in timing on the part of his would-be Nazi assassins. His secretary, Edgar Jung, who had urged him into action and drafted the vital speech, was shot at his desk by the SS. The disastrous outcome of the attempted Nazi coup in Austria a month later enabled him to persuade Hitler to send him as special envoy to Vienna where, as one Catholic soldier to another, he hoped to be able to win the confidence of Kurt von Schuschnigg, who had succeeded the murdered Engelbert von Dollfuss as Chancellor of Austria.

Four years in Vienna again nearly sealed his fate, and he was due to be purged in February 1938 with von Ribbentrop's promotion to be Hitler's Foreign Minister. But forewarning enabled him to escape dismissal by arranging the fateful visit of Schuschnigg to Berchtesgaden, which set in motion the German invasion and annexation of Austria on March 11, 1938, and again put him out of a job. Since that date he had apparently been proposed three times as German Ambassador in Ankara. Atatürk had turned his nomination down flat in April 1938, remembering him with distaste from the years of the First World War. İnönü had turned his name down again in November 1938 and in February 1939. And it was only when Saracoğlu rashly demanded of Kroll whether Germany ever intended to fill the Embassy, that Ribbentrop, who felt happier with von Papen well away from Hitler's ear, returned, this time successfully, to the charge. İnönü and Saracoğlu felt unable to refuse his nomination and accepted 'without enthusiasm', as Sir Hugh Knatchbull-Hugessen sardonically reported.[34]

The imminent signature of the Anglo-Turkish Agreement hurried von Papen to Ankara. He arrived on April 27, and called on Saracoğlu the same day. He found the conversation an upsetting experience. His attempt to persuade the Turkish Foreign Minister that, so long as Turkey was Germany's friend, she need not fear Italy, was met by the blunt remark that Turkey did not appreciate dependence on the friendship of others for her security. As for the Italians, the Turks were not afraid of them. 'They have their Italians and we have our Turks.' Papen suggested an Italian declaration of friendship, only to hear Saracoğlu retort that such a thing 'would displease Turkey enormously'. Did Germany intend to proceed further in the Balkans? '*Jamais de la vie,*' replied Papen. Then Germans can sleep quietly in their beds, replied Saracoğlu. Papen retired, visibly disconcerted.[35]

Two days later he tried again, when presenting his credentials to President Inönü. Inönü was gentler with him, but equally frank. But his gentleness gave von Papen the opening he needed. His report[36] showed that he believed, or at least wished the German Foreign Ministry to believe, that he was succeeding in choking off the issue of an Anglo-Turkish declaration. The Foreign Ministry, still following the Anglo-Turkish negotiations through the reports of the German cipher office, remained unconvinced.[37] Von Papen's second meeting with Inönü on May 2 destroyed his own optimism. He found Inönü obsessed by the threat from Italy, and wired Berlin urgently of the need to effect a reduction in the Italian troop concentrations in Albania.[38] On May 3, Count Ciano, to whom Papen's reports on his first meeting with Saracoğlu and Inönü had been forwarded from Berlin,[39] spoke, half-reassuringly, half-threateningly, to the Turkish Ambassador in Rome, Hussein Ragip Baydur.[40] As Papen was to discover over the next few days from both Inönü and Menemencioğlu,[41] this Italian gesture, being so obviously due to Papen's intervention, left the Turks unmoved; or so Saracoğlu told Massigli.[42] Papen's ever more despairing appeals drove Weizsäcker's deputy, Woermann, to order that they no longer be forwarded to Milan.[43] The matter of Turkey was barely touched upon by Ciano and Ribbentrop at Milan[44] on May 6. Papen was forced to confess his failure.[45]

The Turks had a great deal to set against von Papen's arrival on the scene. From May 1 to 5, Inönü, Saracoğlu and the Turkish Chief of Staff, Marshal Çakmak, had been entertaining the former French Chief of Staff, and Commander-in-Chief of France's armies in Syria, General Weygand.[46] This stroke of genius had been provoked by M. Massigli, the French Ambassador. The Turks made his visit into a major military occasion. Moreover, Inönü, who knew Weygand from the General's service on the French delegation to the Lausanne Conference in 1923, felt able to speak with unusual freedom. Germany, he said, had embarked on the path of universal domination. She had to be opposed.

Britain and France were about to construct an Eastern Front in the Balkans. Turkey had chosen her side. 'Your security is ours,' he remarked to Weygand.

He had, however, more to say. Russian aid, he pointed out, was essential. Indeed it was vital that Russian forces should be drawn into any fighting. The existence of fresh Soviet forces at the end of a war which had exhausted and drained those of the West was a danger to be avoided. The Turks would welcome the Red Air Force and Soviet ground forces in Thrace and Macedonia. Militarily, however, it was clear that he was, in true Turkish style, thinking defensively. French aid and technical advice was needed to fortify Turkey's Balkan frontiers. Gas-masks, anti-aircraft guns, anti-tank guns, heavy artillery, pilots and tank crews to be trained in France, these were Turkey's needs. But, above all, Turkey needed an Anglo-Soviet alliance. The obstacles were, he said, psychological rather than real. Britain and France would, he hoped, do all they could to overcome them. Menemencioğlu revealed that, by a secret agreement of 1929, Turkey was bound not to enter into an alliance with Britain without prior consultation and agreement with the Soviets. This agreement, he believed, M. Potemkin had given him, before leaving for Sofia. In the event, he was to be proved wrong. And in the end Turkey would sign the Anglo-French-Turkish alliance despite outright Soviet opposition. In early May, however, all this lay in the future. 'We consider Germany the adversary,' was the message from Ankara.

The Germans were to have more success in their pressure on Hungary and Yugoslavia. Admiral Horthy and Count Csáky had been led by the German occupation of Bohemia, the break in German-Polish relations and the German economic agreement with Romania to feel that the day of revenge was at hand, revenge on Romania for her acquisition of Transylvania at the Versailles Peace Conference and her continuing oppression of the Magyar minority. The Hungarian invasion and occupation of the Carpatho-Ukraine had been followed by the mutual mobilization of the Romanian and Hungarian armies. Fear of Hungary played a large part in the Romanian panic of early April which resulted in the British guarantee. This much was clear to everyone: to Colonel Beck in Lausanne, who had promised Halifax to do what he could to alleviate relations between Budapest and Bucharest; to Prince Paul and his Foreign Minister, Aleksandar Cincar-Marković, in Belgrade, glancing uneasily at their two over-mighty neighbours, Germany and Italy, and only too aware how their frontier with Hungary ran down towards Belgrade itself; to Hitler and Ribbentrop in Berlin, never quite sure what could be done with a state whose leaders alternated so rapidly between excessive caution and overweaning ambition; and to Mussolini and Ciano in Rome, anxious not to lose Budapest to German influence, but unwilling to drive Prince Paul and Gafencu into British or French arms. Contempt for the Magyars among the great powers and fear among the minor ones made an odd reward for individuals so determinedly proud, so exclusively ethnocentric as the Hungarian leadership. But watching their single-minded obsession throughout the summer of 1939, their discussions of possible bacteriological warfare against Romania,[47] and the constant menace of war their troops represented in a Europe filled with tinder of all kinds, it is difficult not to feel that the destruction by the war of the social system on which their power rested was richly deserved.

Count Csáky in fact had rather a rough time during April. Pressure to ease the tension in Hungarian-Romanian relations came from all sides: from Beck,[48] from the Yugoslavs,[49] from Britain.[50] On his visit to Rome on April 18–20, he was roundly lectured by Mussolini, who told him in so many words that Axis interests demanded benevolent neutrality from all the Balkan and Danubian states, and advised him to reach a settlement with Romania and Yugoslavia.[51] And at the end of the month he again found himself being severely lectured by Hitler and von Ribbentrop on the need for good relations with these same two countries.[52]

With Yugoslavia the Axis powers had a ready means of pressure. Before his dismissal, Milan Stojadinovic had committed the Yugoslav army and air force to large-scale purchases of anti-aircraft guns and aircraft on credit in Germany, over the opposition of those who preferred to buy from the smaller arms-producing nations such as Czechoslovakia, Sweden or Belgium. Goering and Ribbentrop deliberately stalled the negotiations so as to retain an effective means of control over Stojadinovic's successors.[53] Cincar-Marković attempted to negotiate some of Yugoslavia's needs with the Italians; on his visit to Venice for conversations with Ciano in the third week of April he succeeded not only in reassuring the Italians of Yugoslavia's general benevolence and unwillingness to join any British- or French-led front against the Axis powers but also in securing an arms credit of 500 million lire. Indeed he made an excellent impression on Ciano.[54] The Turks had already dismissed the Yugoslavs as beneath contempt for their failure to react in any way to the invasion of Albania. Cincar-Marković's reward, when he visited Berlin on April 25–27, was not only a go-ahead on the arms and credit transaction but also a German guarantee against any Hungarian claims on Yugoslavia's frontiers.[55]

The effects of these moves by Germany and Italy were to leave the

Turks very much isolated, when they went to sign the Anglo-Turkish Declaration on May 12. For Lord Halifax and his advisers, the declaration itself, even the alliance, was important mainly for the anchor it would provide for the security line they were attempting to call into existence in south-east Europe. The role of the Turks was to bolster and buttress Romania, and through Romania, Poland. Turkey was to persuade her partners in the Balkan Entente to damp down the conflict with Bulgaria, and to bring Bulgaria, so far as was possible, within the bloc. Yet once more Britain was to be left with an isolated guarantee but no link. The British system of guarantees in Eastern Europe was coming to resemble less a dam against aggression than the architecture of Stonehenge.

This may very well have been the impression carried back from his round trip through the Balkans by Vladimir Potemkin, Litvinov's deputy, in the last days of April and early May. Saracoğlu and Inönü laid the greatest of importance on the supplementation of any Anglo-Turkish agreement by similar agreements between Britain and the Soviets and themselves and the Soviets.[56] Whatever Potemkin's purpose in undertaking the visit, however great his surprise in learning how far advanced the negotiations were between Turkey and Britain, whatever the impressions he conveyed to his new lords and masters, neither of whom had any first-hand experience of Turkey, he made no effort then or later either to dissuade the Turks from signing the agreement with Britain or to accelerate the negotiations for an agreement between Turkey and the Soviet Union. He did apparently sound out Kiossievanov and King Boris on his return from Ankara, suggesting that Bulgaria should enter the Balkan Entente in return for the concession of southern Dobrudja,[57] but he was rebuffed both by the Bulgarians and a day later in Bucharest by an excessively nervous Gafencu.[58] On his return to Moscow he gave the general impression that the Soviet Union was prepared to leave the Anglo-Turkish negotiations alone until the fate of the Soviet Union's own negotiations with the West was settled.

The most difficult negotiations for the Turks were those that were to take place with France. The French were under the illusion that they could count on a fund of Turkish goodwill arising from their early recognition of Atatürk's republic. But if any such goodwill had ever existed, it had been dissipated by the long aftermath of the Conference of Lausanne when Atatürk's drive to free Turkey from the regime of special privileges and capitulations, imposed on the Ottomans by their need for European money, ran foul at every turn of French interests, French investments, French privileges and French protests.

Moreover, France had the mandate over Syria, with whom Turkey had more than 500 miles of frontiers. Just across these frontiers lay the cities of Alexandretta and Antioch with their surrounding mountains, with a population among whom Turks were the largest national group but among whom, like currants in a cake, were embedded very sizeable minorities of Armenians, Christian Arabs, members of the deviant Muslim sect of Alawites, and Sunni Arab Muslims. The area had never been part of Syria, enjoying a separate administrative status under the Ottoman empire as a Sanjaq, and this status had been confirmed by agreements between France and Turkey in 1921 and 1926; whereas France's relations with the rest of Syria were governed by the mandate awarded to her by the League of Nations, as far as the Sanjaq was concerned, the French had to contend with the Turks.

This had become immediately apparent in 1936 when the French were at last brought to terms by the Arab nationalists of Syria proper and signed a treaty granting a limited degree of self-government to a Syrian Arab state, ruled from Damascus. The prospect of the Sanjaq Turks passing under Arab rule, rule by their former subjects, roused strong tides of Turkish nationalism. What had been conceded to France in 1921 was not to be handed over to a group of wishy-washy Arab city dwellers. The Turkish Government was driven to protest both to Paris and to the League of Nations. More to the point, it concentrated sizeable forces on the Turkish border. There were disturbances, riots and deaths among the Turks of Antioch and Alexandretta, made worse by the French use of the largely Arab forces they had raised for internal security to maintain order. The sudden, explosive and atrociously violent Turkish temper manifested itself and the French, distracted by the danger from Spain, Italy and Germany, yielded. A Franco-Turkish treaty maintained the special status of the Sanjaq. It was to have its own government, its own assembly, and its own elections. But the treaty only exacerbated the local situation.

Elections were to be held by communities, each being guaranteed a minimum number of seats. Apart from that, representation was to be proportionate to the number of members registered as belonging to each community: Turkish, Muslim, Arab, Alawi, Armenian and Greek Orthodox Christian Arab. Such a solution, beloved of electoral statisticians and constitutional lawyers, was more redolent of French academic logic than of knowledge of Middle Eastern politics. Each community set about 'encouraging' its own faithful to register and discouraging others. Individuals were forced to declare their communal loyalties publicly. There was intimidation, more riots and deaths, and further reports of Turkish troop movements. In the summer of 1938, with the spectre of war looming over Czechoslovakia, the French gave way again. Martial law was proclaimed and Turkish troops were admitted to the Sanjaq to help maintain order. An assembly was elected, met, chose as its head one of Atatürk's personal friends, and proclaimed itself the Republic of the Hatay. But this was still a part of the French mandate and still within the monetary and tariff system of Syria, and Turkish national aspirations were a long way short of being satisfied.

The new Government in Turkey, moreover, the successors of Atatürk, were by no means as securely in control of those aspirations as the Ghazi himself had been. Within the National Party feuds were seething, ambitions stirring. Inönü himself had succeeded in driving his great rival, Celal Bayar, into private life in December 1938. But it was far from clear whether Reyfik Seydam, the new Premier, or Saracoğlu could withstand the pressure from or intrigues of other elements which remained in the party. The immobilism of the French position was a source of as much alarm and resentment to the Turks as it was to the new French Ambassador, René Massigli, himself.

On this issue, however, the French Government was as vulnerable as the Turkish. The aspirations of the Turks might be understandable; their methods of pursuing them struck the jurists of the Quai d'Orsay and the Ministère des Colonies as hardly distinguishable from those used by Hitler or Mussolini themselves. *Chantage*, blackmail, was a word with which the French cryptographers encoding and decoding the telegrams between Ankara and Paris must have become all too familiar. Moreover, the whole issue bore on one of France's most sacred cows, her *mission civilisatrice*, in the Middle East, which interested parties, organized in a pressure group quite as effective as the China lobby in the United States in the 1940s, were careful to trace back to the Crusades. 'Champagne, Alsace have been French for a much shorter period of time than Antioch,' wrote their most sedulous propagandist, Paul La Véou in June 1939.[59]

Les Syriens, as their critics in France called them, could do more than merely damage Franco-Turkish relations. They were strongly opposed to Britain, deeply suspicious of British cultivation of both Arab and Turkish nationalism, convinced beyond a peradventure that the single aim of British policy in the Levant was to exclude France from Damascus, Aleppo and Beirut as effectively as she had been excluded in the days of Garnett Wolseley and Kitchener, of Cromer and Curzon, from Cairo and Alexandria. That French banks continued to draw large profits from these two cities; that educated cultured Egyptians almost to a man sought refuge from the cold and discomfort of London in the warmth and permissiveness of Paris; that the Suez Canal Company still operated out of Paris with a board of directors only two of whom were nominees of the British Government, was neither here nor there. Gossiping over their *fines* along the Paris boulevards, 'ante-chambriering' in the Chambre des Députés or the Senate, dining over bankers' tables covered with green baize or mess-tables alight with silver candlesticks, the one burden of their argument was the sinister Machiavellian imperialist manoeuvres of the British. The extreme right-wing press in Paris might shout across its columns, '*Pourquoi mourir pour Danzig?*' 'Rather Hitler than Blum'. But for many it was rather Hitler than Chamberlain. They were not a factor Daladier or Bonnet could easily ignore.

René Massigli regarded this group and their allies, in the offices of Paris and in the High Commission in Beirut, with a massive intellectual contempt.[60] He set himself to circumvent them with an equally massive patience. After two months of correspondence with Paris and one further visit, he descended upon Beirut to beard the French High Commission. He found it consumed by fantasy, the victim of too great a reliance on the incredible misinformation fed to it by its local intelligence services.[61] An image of Turkish imperialism gripped its members, an expansionism which would not stop until all Syria had been re-incorporated in a revived Ottoman empire. Massigli was able to allay some of these fears. More successfully, he was able to nail down with Turkish assistance some of the local troublemakers operating across the Turkish borders with Syria. And in the aftermath of Prague he was finally able to secure from M. Bonnet, as always reluctant to grasp any problem which might have repercussions in domestic politics, instructions to open negotiations with Turkey.

In the first ten days of these negotiations M. Saracoğlu, as already noted, proposed a ten-year pact of assistance between Turkey, France and Britain. The proposal revealed by M. Bonnet to the Cabinet provoked a major counter-attack from *Les Syriens*. No mention was made of the pact; but *Le Temps* and *Le Figaro* carried violent articles and letters of protest. Deputations of influential deputies waited on Bonnet. A communiqué was issued by the deputies and senators of the Federal Republican Party.[62] It was a sign of Bonnet's political nervousness that, a few days later, he jumped at the chance of posing as the defender of France's empire. A rumour spread that a Turkish invasion of the Sanjaq was imminent.[63] Sixty thousand troops were said to be massed on the frontier. Without stopping to check the truth of the report in any way, Bonnet summoned the Turkish Ambassador. A cruiser was to be sent to Alexandretta and reinforcements dispatched, by a decision of the

Cabinet itself. It was a strange decision. The French Admiralty had little desire to detach one of its cruisers to the eastern Mediterranean. To reinforce Alexandretta in the face of such a concentration of Turkish troops was to reinforce the indefensible. The Cabinet rescinded its decision. The Turks meanwhile remained unmoved, but their distrust of such emotional instability was to show itself in the subsequent negotiations.

In the meantime the British had proposed and the Turks accepted the idea of a declaration followed by an alliance. Romania, Greece and Poland all stood guaranteed. The long attempt to bring in the Soviets began. Under Massigli's relentless pressure, behind which he was able to enlist the massive prestige of General Weygand himself, Bonnet began to move. The Turks would accept nothing short of complete cession of the Hatay to Turkey. *Les Syriens* in Paris set their face against even 'the least abandonment' as likely to have 'the most formidable repercussions, not only in the Middle East and in the whole basin of the Mediterranean, but throughout all Europe'.[64]

These were powerful arguments. On the other hand the Anglo-Turkish negotiations were moving to their conclusion. Neither Daladier nor Bonnet relished the kind of questioning they would face from the centre and left of the French Parliament if they seemed to lag behind Britain in standing up against Italy in the Mediterranean. They insisted that the Anglo-Turkish Declaration should be tripartite, should include France too. A way round seemed to have been found by a Turkish proposal that France should make a statement of her intention to conclude an agreement on the Hatay by a fixed date. Daladier announced the imminence of the declaration. By the evening of May 11, everything seemed settled. But at midnight, Numan Menemencioğlu called on Massigli.[65] The Turks did not trust such a statement. The consequences of subsequent disagreement would be too great. Massigli retired for the night, angry and hurt. To his English colleague's tactful enquiries he was for once a little less than polite. And on May 12, Reyfik Seydam in Ankara and Neville Chamberlain in London announced the terms of the Anglo-Turkish Declaration to their respective Parliaments, without an accompanying echo from Paris.[66]

CHAPTER 17

THE STRUGGLE FOR THE BALKANS: ROUND 2 — YUGOSLAVIA AND THE DRIFT TO THE WEST

'The Turks', so Sir Hugh Knatchbull-Hugessen, the British Ambassador to Ankara, confided to his diary,[1] 'are brave, honourable and straightforward to deal with, and it is a pleasure to treat with them.' The same could not be said of the leaders of the other Balkan states. Even before Reyfik Seydam and Neville Chamberlain had announced the terms of the Anglo-Turkish Declaration to their respective Parliaments on the afternoon of May 12, it was clear that the larger hopes pinned on Turkey by the British were not to be fulfilled. The Turkish Cabinet and people were tough, resolute and determined not to be pushed around by either Hitler or Mussolini. Their resolution was shared by the Greeks, but by few others in the Balkans. And as Lord Halifax had feared at the time, once the Romanian Government had infected the French with their own fears and stampeded London and Paris into giving them a guarantee, all hopes of including them to join a collective bloc with Poland and Turkey, let alone of persuading them into making concessions to Bulgaria, were ended. What neither Lord Halifax nor the Turks, apt as they were to regard their Balkan associates as lacking in resolution, had expected, was the degree to which they would bend to service German pressure on Turkey.

General Weygand was to have an early lesson in this. On leaving Turkey on May 5 he had taken the train to Bucharest. Over a ceremonial luncheon he had exhorted King Carol to follow the Turkish example in helping to create a strong Eastern Front with Poland and the Soviet Union. The Romanian Premier, Călinescu, had answered him directly. Turkey, he said, had a common frontier with the Soviet Union, but not with Germany. Should it come to war, Romania would welcome Soviet aid; but not if the price was the entry of Soviet troops into Romanian territory. As for any link with the Soviets in peacetime, that was out of the question. Apart from the danger of Romania's Fascists, the Iron Guard, exploiting public antipathy to Russia and memories of Russian conduct in World War I, any sign of Romania negotiating for Soviet assistance could lead to an immediate German or German-Hungarian invasion.

'I do not', said King Carol pathetically, 'wish to let my country be engaged in a war which would result, in a few weeks, in the destruction of its army and the occupation of its territory. . . . We do not', he added, 'wish to be the lightning conductor for the coming storm.' Romania could barely equip two-thirds of the thirty-two divisions of its army. She had no tanks, no heavy artillery, no anti-aircraft or anti-tank guns and only four hundred or so obsolescent aircraft, half of which were not working. Without massive arms deliveries, Romania was defenceless against German motorized forces, with or without Hungarian assistance.[2]

The Romanians, so the French Minister to Belgrade, M. Brugère, concluded, believed that they could stay out of war until they were ready and the time was right. In the meantime their policy was to convince Berlin and Rome of their devotion to neutrality. In common with their colleagues in Belgrade (Prince Paul, M. Cvetković, the Premier, and M. Cincar-Marković, the Foreign Minister, who followed M. Gafencu, the Romanian Foreign Minister, from Rome to Venice, Berlin and Warsaw and with whom they consulted frequently), the Romanians remembered the bitter cost of World War I, as well as the gains they had won from being on the winning side. They remembered too the outcome of the visits Herr Schuschnigg of Austria, and President Hácha of Czechoslovakia and Monsignor Tiso had paid to Berlin: merciless bullying, followed within days by the occupation and subjection of their countries. They dreaded the invitations to Berlin or Rome; but they had felt forced to accept them.

M. Gafencu had been the first. His visit to Berlin in April had been preceded by one to Warsaw and had been followed by calls in Brussels, London, Paris and Rome.[3] In Warsaw he professed to believe that Colonel Beck had agreed to the extension of the Polish-Romanian alliance to cover a German attack on Romania;[4] whether he deceived himself or lied to his French and British hosts is unclear. The Polish records show Beck's determination not to be drawn into any further moves which might unnecessarily enlarge the area of German antagonism.[5] They show too the low opinion held by the Polish military of Romanian resolution and of the Romanian armed forces.[6] German propaganda, moreover, had convinced the Romanians that Britain and France could do nothing to breach Germany's western fortifications, and that, in the event of war, Romania would find herself isolated. Given the state of her armaments, Romania would be committing suicide by allying herself with the Western democracies.[7]

M. Gafencu and his Yugoslav colleague, M. Aleksandar Cincar-Marković, had learned of the terms of the Anglo-Turkish Declaration four days before its publication on May 12. Both were alarmed by Article VI, with its hint of Anglo-Turkish action 'to ensure the estab-lishment of security in the Balkans'. The Turkish Ambassador in Belgrade even told M. Cincar-Marković that the Turks hoped the declaration would change his attitude to remaining neutral.[8] As Prince Paul and he were just about to pay a ceremonial visit to Rome following his success, on his visit to Venice a fortnight earlier, in smoothing away the effects of Italy's Albanian adventure, Marković found this sugges-tion badly timed and in poor taste; this may have something to do with the extraordinary idea he aired to Count Ciano amidst the pomp and panoply of the five-day state visit, that Yugoslavia, Romania and Bulgaria should get together against the Turks.[9]

M. Gafencu was equally annoyed. Only hours before leaving for Rome, M. Cincar-Marković had summoned the Romanian Ambassa-dor in Belgrade to his side and threatened Yugoslav withdrawal from the Balkan Entente in favour of the Axis if the Anglo-Turkish Declara-tion were, in fact, made.[10] Gafencu begged him to talk things over first; the two met on May 21 at Turnu-Severin, on the Danube, immediately below the Iron Gates, that fantastic gorge through which the penned-up Danube rushes to the sea. The meeting was preceded by a week of violent polemic in the Yugoslav press,[11] which had led Sir Ronald Campbell, the British Minister in Belgrade and one of the tougher, rougher members of the British Foreign Service, to dress M. Cincar-Marković down in no uncertain manner.[12] This was perhaps unwise. It stung the Yugoslav Foreign Minister into insisting that the Turks had acted contrary to the spirit and letter of the Balkan Entente and that M. Gafencu, as President of the Council of the Entente, should tell them this.[13]

M. Gafencu had come to believe that the ties of the Balkan Entente, however frail and irrelevant, were all he had to haul the Romanian ship of state into safe anchorage. To pacify the Yugoslavs, he promised to undertake this task. At the same time he sent M. Cretzianu off to Geneva to see Lord Halifax and try to explain all this away.[14]

Prince Paul was about to visit Berlin officially so there was, therefore, some reason for poor M. Markovic's alarm. There was much less for either M. Gafencu's attempt to convince the Yugoslavs that he had already succeeded in modifying the form of the Anglo-Turkish Dec-laration on the Balkans or his attempt to persuade the Turks not to go any further with the negotiations for an alliance with Britain.[15] Even Lord Halifax professed himself 'surprised and not a little discouraged'.[16] M. Saracoğlu's reaction was that Gafencu was in a fright;[17] and when M. Gafencu did arrive in Ankara on June 12, he made so many different statements to his various interlocutors that, despite his position and arguments, M. Saracoğlu wrote him off entirely, and with him all hopes of inducing a settlement with Bulgaria such as would enable the states of the Balkans to stand together against the Axis threat.[18]

Saracoğlu had in fact proposed to the Bulgarian Minister, Todor Christov, at the end of May that Bulgaria should enter the Balkan pact at once under a guarantee that Turkey, Greece and Yugoslavia would help her obtain a redress of her territorial claims on the Dobrudja. Only one proviso was made: that Bulgarian claims on Greece should be dropped. Christov duly returned to Sofia. But King Boris was too much for Saracoğlu. Kiossievanov simply told Christov that the idea was impossible.[19] Boris secured that Christov sought out Gafencu as publicly as possible to say that Bulgaria's claims included not only the Dobrudja but also Thrace and an outlet to the Aegean.[20] Saracoğlu affected to believe that Christov had been 'got at' by the Germans; Christov had served as Bulgarian Minister in Berlin and was a notorious and violent Germanophile. But Saracoğlu admitted that his action had made any further attempt to build up a Balkan front impossible. Gafencu, despite an urgent appeal from Lord Halifax,[21] remained adamantly opposed to any territorial concessions to the Bulgarians.

With this the original British idea of a 'peace front' in Eastern Europe had, to all intents and purposes, collapsed. All that remained were three isolated pillars: the British guarantees to Poland, Romania and Turkey. The view from London was not encouraging. The view from Berlin was, however, much worse. Behind what appeared to be the German victory in smashing British hopes of a solid Eastern Front against the Axis, the German position was deteriorating rapidly.

Cincar-Marković might seem to be toying for the moment with the idea of a line-up of genuine neutrals, Yugoslavia, Bulgaria and Hungary,[22] but Prince Paul (and the Yugoslav General Staff) had very different ideas. He courted the Bulgarians, and followed the Turkish example in urging his Romanian friends to make concessions to Sofia with one aim only: to get Bulgaria off his back so that he could concentrate on driving Italy out of Albania, and on preventing an Italian strike against Salonika. Early in May General Simovic, the Yugoslav Chief of Staff, made a preliminary approach to his opposite number, General Papagas, in Athens, for Staff talks. Planning continued through the next two months.[23]

292

But to carry out such plans Yugoslavia needed both arms and credits. Paul's tactics were aimed at winning credits and securing arms deliveries wherever he could, in Berlin, Paris or London. By playing on Goering's dislike of von Ribbentrop, Cincar-Marković had, on his visit to Berlin in April,[24] wheedled out of the Reichsmarschall the promise of German arms credits and of the delivery of over one hundred aircraft. At the end of May, indications of a forthcoming Italian attack on Salonika and of the German offer of credits caused M. Brugère, the French Minister in Belgrade, to hurry to Paris to secure military aid for Yugoslavia.[25] On June 29, Puric, the Yugoslav Minister in Paris, announced that the Bank Seligmann of Paris had granted the Yugoslav Government a loan of 600 million francs to be spent on arms and equipment for Yugoslav industry.[26]

Given the lack of security of the Yugoslav ciphers, the game Prince Paul was playing was a dangerous one. Yugoslavia's safety lay, however, in Hitler's single-minded concentration on Poland, which imposed on him a need to court rather than bully, to rein in his *Volksdeutsch*, the German minorities in Yugoslavia, whom the SS would have liked to use as a subversive force, to keep a firm hand on Hungary, and to avoid offending Mussolini, who believed that Yugoslavia lay in the Italian sphere of influence.

Prince Paul's visit to Berlin was thus not an occasion for pressure, but for pomp and persuasion.[27] Nothing was spared to impress upon the German people that Britain's 'encirclement' policy was failing. Nothing was spared to impress upon the world that Germany was marching from triumph to triumph. Not one but two major military parades were staged. There was a gala at the opera, a visit to Potsdam, a solemn reception at the Reichs Chancellery, and a grand dinner at which von Ribbentrop and Goebbels played the hosts. The Führer himself met Prince Paul at the station. He was lodged at Bellevue, the old imperial residence. He was shown the newest tanks and the latest aircraft. The final ceremonies surpassed those staged for Count Ciano and the signature of the Pact of Steel. At the end of the formal visit, the Prince and Princess, to von Ribbentrop's fury, spent three days as Goering's private guests at his country estate at Karinhall.

The Germans hoped for a treaty subjugating Yugoslavia's economy in the same manner as they hoped to subjugate that of Romania. They hoped to force Prince Paul into some overt commitment, withdrawal of his country from the League of Nations or accession to the anti-Comintern pact. They got nothing bar a small change in the exchange rate between the dinar and the Reichsmark.[28] Ribbentrop was left in a very bad humour. 'He is a log,' he remarked of the

Prince to one of his aides.[29] Hitler was left angry and hurt by Paul's behaviour.[30]

Hitler had good reason to be worried. While Cincar-Marković continued to go through the motions of courting Bulgaria·and talking of a Hungarian-Romanian-Bulgarian bloc, Paul sent General Pesic on a special mission to London and Paris to discuss Yugoslav war plans and to discover what he could of British and French plans for war in the Mediterranean. Pesic was to explain that while Yugoslavia would be constrained to declare her neutrality on the outbreak of war, this would end as soon as the Mediterranean and Adriatic came under Allied control. The Yugoslav army would be ready to intervene at the most opportune moment. The main thing was to prevent the Axis gaining control of Yugoslavia and her economic resources. Pesic spoke to General Gamelin in Paris.[31] In London he saw General Gort, the Chief of the Imperial General Staff, Lord Halifax and Lord Chatfield.[32] He found the two capitals somewhat divided on the question of Yugoslav neutrality and the immediacy of an Allied landing at Salonika.[33] Of the two he preferred to believe the French, whose obsession with fighting anywhere rather than on France's eastern frontiers had already earmarked General Weygand and the French army in Syria for a Balkan campaign; this would form the southern flank of a front stretching up to Poland and the Baltic.[34]

Pesic was followed by the Yugoslav Minister of Finance, Djuricic, to arrange for the spending of the Seligmann credit. Cvetković, the Yugoslav Premier, spoke angrily of the Germans' bad behaviour in holding up the delivery of arms, already paid for, from the Skoda factories in Bohemia.[35] On July 14, Djuricic and Daladier agreed on a massive delivery to Yugoslavia of howitzers, anti-aircraft guns, trucks, tanks, mobile workshops, tank transporters, anti-tank guns and machine guns.[36] Before leaving for Paris, Djuricic had stampeded the Germans into signing a protocol to the existing German-Yugoslav arms credit.[37] On July 17 the Yugoslav Minister in Berlin demanded that the delivery of the promised aircraft and anti-aircraft guns should be accelerated. If necessary, he argued, delivery could come from those stocks previously earmarked for Turkey. Yugoslavia could not be expected to preserve her neutrality without arms.[38]

In the meantime the wooing of Bulgaria continued. On July 9, Cincar-Marković met Kiossievanov of Bulgaria at Bled. The outcome was a communiqué announcing their determination to continue to pursue a policy of independence and neutrality which would be in the best interests of both countries and contribute to the pacification of the Balkans.[39] Italians and Germans remained unimpressed. But the

Italians seem no longer to have enjoyed their easy access to the Yugoslav ciphers; nor for that matter was the *Forschungsamt*, the German cipher agency, reading Yugoslav telegrams with any ease.[40] German intelligence learned little or nothing about Prince Paul's visit to London; or about Pesic and Djuricic, until German forces captured the French archives in 1940.[41] It would seem therefore that, at some time in May, either the Yugoslav ciphers were changed or Prince Paul began to play his cards exceptionally close to his chest. He certainly warned the Americans in June that the Germans were reading all diplomatic cables between Belgrade and the outside world, the American cables included.[42]

Prince Paul left Belgrade for London on July 15. While passing through France he stopped off at Châlons to meet General Pesic and hear his report. What he heard encouraged him in his hopes that he might succeed in persuading his British hosts into undertaking a pre-emptive war against Italy. He proposed to tell them that the bonds which had tied Yugoslavia and all the other Balkan powers in so immovable a stance were loosening. The Balkan powers were on the move towards a common front against the Axis. His visit was not improvised at the last moment, as the Yugoslav Embassy in London so successfully protested to all enquirers, nor did it have much to do with family affairs, although he and his wife were undoubtedly concerned to support their young son, Prince Nicholas, at school in Britain, who was about to undergo a minor operation.[43] Paul had been warmly encouraged by Gafencu, the Romanian Foreign Minister, when Gafencu visited Belgrade in May. The strength of his confidence can be seen in the transfer of the Yugoslav National Bank gold reserves to London while Paul was visiting Rome.[44]

The Germans were left suspicious and angry. The news, from Kiossievanov,[45] that Prince Paul was about to be made a member of the Order of the Garter struck Hitler, always sensitive to such gestures, as particularly ominous. He spoke bitterly to Count Csáky, the Hungarian Foreign Minister, and to Count Ciano, of Yugoslavia's bad faith.[46] Both members of the Axis redoubled their pressure on Belgrade, demanding again that Yugoslavia should definitely leave the League of Nations and make a public declaration of loyalty and benevolence towards the Axis. Cincar-Marković, who, conceivably, may not have been as privy to Paul's designs as some of his colleagues, fielded such representations gracefully, inviting his German interlocutors to have the fullest confidence in Yugoslavia's friendship and declarations of neutrality. Yugoslav policy, he told von Heeren, the German Minister in Belgrade, on August 9, 'had not arisen overnight nor sprung from a whim, but had developed, slowly it was true, but inevitably, from the facts of the situation.' Ribbentrop minuted von Heeren's report for Hitler.[47] Admiral Canaris, head of the *Abwehr*, the German intelligence service, professed himself convinced;[48] reluctantly, the Germans went ahead with the arms credits.

The 'facts of the situation' were, however, about to betray Paul. His plans, his hopes, his expectations depended on the successful conclusion of the Anglo-Soviet negotiations. The day he left for London, Colonel Vauhnik, the Yugoslav Military and Air Attaché in Berlin, reported that Germany and the Soviet Union had concluded a pact of friendship. Like all such reports, it was premature but prophetic. General Simovic consigned the report to the archives, calling it 'unrealistic' and 'improbable'.[49]

Despite the ceremony and hospitality with which he and his wife were treated, Paul cannot have been altogether satisfied by what he heard in London. Lord Halifax evaded his questions as to whether Britain could be sure of finishing Italy off quickly, should it come to war. Britain could, of course, deal with the Italian fleet. Strategic questions were, however, not within his area of responsibility. The truth was, as Halifax well knew, that refit and remodelling requirements had cut the British battle fleet from fifteen to eleven capital ships, and that the lengthy discussions in the spring of 1939 had shown that a pre-emptive strike against Italy was impossible without the conversion of French strategists from their obsession with defence. Halifax and Chamberlain were still hoping that Italian influence might convince Hitler that the rocks towards which he seemed determined to steer were very real, and persuade him to change course.[50] The two British men had been conspiring with Bonnet for over a month to drive Daladier and the hawks in the French Cabinet to yield a little to Mussolini's importunities.

As June gave way to July and the Anglo-Soviet negotiations continued, the degree to which the Balkan states were moving towards the West can be seen most clearly with Bulgaria. Most Balkan governments, and most Western diplomatists in Balkan capitals, assumed Bulgaria to be irrevocably tied to Germany. Kiossievanov, who combined the Bulgarian offices of Prime Minister and Foreign Secretary, on occasion made considerable play with this in conversation with Western diplomatists. It was a situation, however, that he did not intend to allow to cramp him or force him into making the same mistake as his predecessors had made during the First World War, taking Bulgaria into war on what turned out to be the losing side. He served a monarch for whom the recovery of the territories lost in 1919, the Dobrudja to Romania, Macedonia to Yugoslavia, and Aegean Thrace to Greece, was the main goal of his foreign policy; Kiossieva-nov, however, did not think Thrace was recoverable as long as the ties between Athens and Ankara remained. He was prepared to dispense with Bulgarian claims on Macedonia, to keep Yugoslavia sweet. The build-up of Turkish troops on the Turco-Bulgarian and Turco-Greek frontiers in Thrace he took as an ominous warning.[51]

From Britain and France, and from the Turks, there came continuous pressure on Bulgaria to join the other Balkan powers in the bloc they were trying to construct. None of this interested Kiossievanov. Should it come to war, and Romania be engaged on her Western Front, then Bulgarian support or benevolent neutrality was something Romania might find herself forced to buy with concessions on the Dobrudja issue. In the meantime he could rely on Romanian high-handedness to keep the treatment of the Bulgarian minority in Romania alive for Bulgarian opinion, and prevent any premature weakening of the Romanians' determination not to disgorge any of their gains from 1919 for fear of losing the lot.

In Berlin, however, Bulgaria seemed an even better bet than Yugo-slavia as the key to destroying Britain's drive to enlist the Balkans on the Western side. Since the loss of Turkey, that Bulgaria was more than ever 'our political and military fall-back position' was the view of the German Foreign Ministry, as stated in May.[52] The German counter-offensive against the effects of the Anglo-Turkish Declaration on the Balkans, which sent von Papen to Ankara, also picked up Count von Richthofen, hitherto acting as a deputy head of the political division of the German Foreign Ministry, and by his own account the last German to leave Bulgaria in 1918 when Bulgaria sued for an armistice; he became the new German Minister to Sofia.

Von Richthofen could play the German aristocratic diplomatist to King Boris's hereditary connections with the princedoms of imperial Germany. Boris hated and suspected the Soviet Union, and more than half-sympathized with the idea of a German-dominated *Mitteleuropa*. His Premier, his army, his diplomatists, his politicians and his people felt otherwise. Von Richthofen and his Italian colleague, Talamo, took turns in pressing on Boris and his Premier the advisability, the desirabil-ity, nay the necessity of Bulgaria joining the anti-Comintern pact.[53] Towards the end of June none other than Hans Frank, Reichs Minister for Justice and an occasional adventurer in the fields of German foreign policy, came to Sofia to convey to Kiossievanov the most pressing of invitations to visit Berlin.[54]

Such invitations were not to be turned down by the leaders of

Europe's minor powers. Kiossievanov duly visited Berlin from July 5 to 7, as Prince Paul had before him. He had a surprisingly easy ride. No pressure was put on him to declare his country's adhesion to the anti-Comintern pact.[55] This was not altogether surprising, as the Bulgarian Minister in Berlin since May 1939 had been acting as an occasional but vital intermediary between the German Foreign Ministry and Astakhov, the Soviet Chargé d'affaires in Berlin, who seems, at least until mid-August, to have enjoyed Stalin's and Molotov's confidence.[56] Ribbentrop indeed told Kiossievanov that there were no real conflicts of interest or unsurmountable obstacles in the way of a German-Soviet understanding, a view which echoed the remarks of his master.[57]

Kiossievanov had in fact a double play. While he again took up the Yugoslav approaches and joined Cincar-Marković at Bled to re-affirm their common interest in independence and neutrality – itself a rude shock to his German hosts – the news that Stoika Mošanov, President of the Bulgarian Parliament, was in London was far more unwelcome. Kiossievanov denounced Mošanov to the Germans as an over-ambitious and disloyal self-seeker. King Boris, he said, had asked Mošanov to abandon the trip which he had embarked upon while he, Kiossievanov, was still on his way back from Berlin. Bulgarian diplomats in London and Paris, he said, had been instructed to ignore him.[58] The Germans, in fact, intercepted the telegram which contained these instructions.[59] To Talamo, Kiossievanov spoke obscurely of a masonic conspiracy, pointing to the role of Britain's king in the formal structure of freemasonry in Britain.[60] The Italian Chargé in London noted, however, that the publicity in London for Mošanov's visit only followed the sudden return to London, by air possibly, of the Bulgarian Minister, Nikolas Momčilov; and that in addition to being received by George VI and by Lord Halifax, the Bulgarian parliamentarian also met Sir Frederick Leith-Ross, Chief Economic Adviser to the Cabinet.[61]

Mošanov returned to Sofia in an ostentatious state of disillusion. His visit, he said, had been entirely formal and he had found no real understanding of Bulgaria's situation or of her fears of Turkey.[62] Indeed, the Bulgarian Government spent the first weeks of August in a state of carefully publicized trepidation; carefully publicized, that is, to Germany.[63] British aircraft and aircrews were arriving in Salonika. A Romanian military mission was about to visit Thrace. Bulgaria expected an ultimatum demanding Bulgarian adhesion to the Balkan pact. The Romanians were reinforcing their frontiers in the Dobrudja. To ward off Soviet naval attack on Bulgaria's Black Sea coast, Bulgaria urgently needed two U-boats. This concoction of fantasies drove the Germans, though sceptical, to extreme measures. Arms deliveries were accelerated; the request for U-boats was politely evaded. General noises of goodwill were made. At the same time an Anglo-Bulgarian credit agreement was signed. Mošanov and Momčilov between them had done something to ease their country's economic dependence on Germany. Britain's credits were extended to cover Bulgarian trade with Egypt and Palestine, countries where Bulgaria's staple export, tobacco, was more welcome than in Britain.

Bulgaria's real salvation from Hitlerite economic pressure, as with much of the economic well-being of Turkey, Romania and Yugoslavia, depended on the tastes of the millions of British cigarette smokers. Before 1914, British smokers had largely confined themselves to Balkan tobacco, Virginian being regarded as too strong (Virginian cigarettes were known as 'gaspers'). War and blockade made Balkan tobacco unobtainable. By 1919 the tastes of the mass British public and the investments of the big tobacco companies were irretrievably switched to Virginian tobacco. In 1939 the tobacco companies, despite intervention at Cabinet level, could only be brought to consider purchasing Balkan tobacco (from which another German war was about to cut Britain off for a second time) with the utmost reluctance.[64] The issue had been opened with Greek tobacco in the winter of 1938. The tobacco companies' objections, however, applied with equal strength to Bulgarian tobacco (or Turkish, for that matter). The tobacco was too coarse and pungent even to be stored in the same warehouses as their Virginian imports. Blending would be very difficult. It would require a lengthy and preferably subsidized period of technical and market research; and so on, and so on.

The effect of this on the Bulgarian, Turkish or Greek tobacco-growers was just too bad. No cloth-capped British working man, no British 'flannelled fool', flaunting his pipe as a sign of masculinity, no housewife or housemaid having a quick 'drag' to enliven the dreary round, would give up their Woodbines, ounce of pipe-tobacco, or cork-tips to save Bulgaria from dependence on the German smoker and the Nazi market. Moreover, Britain had only just signed a trade agreement with the United States. The tobacco lobby in America was strong and well organized. It was unlikely that the American Government could be persuaded to overlook any preferential treatment given to Balkan tobacco-growers at the United States' expense. But in the end it was the British smoker who counted. Even in the worst days of the Battle of the Atlantic, sailors died, valuable shipping space had to be earmarked, precious dollars spent, to keep the morale of the smoking majority in Britain high. Bulgarian tobacco-growers had little chance against so rooted an addiction.[65]

Despite all this, however, Kiossievanov kept Bulgaria neutral, and German pressure was resisted. The drift towards the West and the Anglo-Franco-Soviet line-up that all expected to be established, can be seen equally in Romania. Gafencu might make himself ridiculous by his efforts to divert the Turks from overtly expressing their hostility towards the Axis powers as in Article VI of the Anglo-Turkish and Franco-Turkish Declarations. He might very well have preferred everything to be done in secret; he certainly misrepresented the outcome of his conversations in Ankara to both the Italian and German Ministers, even producing misleading 'agreed minutes' of his conversations for Italian and German inspection.[66]

But he was constrained by three factors. King Carol, and most of Romanian opinion with him, was set against any territorial concessions, either to Hungary or to Bulgaria; they were equally determined to resist as long as possible becoming either a German or a Soviet satellite; and they were determined to preserve the Balkan Entente and retain the link between Belgrade, with its external and internal vulnerability to both Italy and Germany, and Athens and Ankara, with their increasingly strong ties with Britain. Gafencu also had a credit of £5 million sterling, made available by an Anglo-Romanian economic agreement signed on May 11, firmly under his belt, together with a British promise to buy another 200,000 tons of cereals. Some of this Gafencu put into his speech of June 9 to the Romanian House of Deputies,[67] in which he responded to British and Turkish pressure by inviting Bulgaria to join the Balkan Entente and promised that she would encounter nothing but goodwill and sincerity. These assurances aroused little but anger and alarm in Sofia.[68] But they carried Gafencu with success, in his own eyes at least, through his round trip to Ankara and Athens, and enabled Cincar-Marković to provide Kiossievanov with a few more arguments to nerve himself for his visit to Berlin.[69]

Gafencu's contacts with Ankara had, however, a more secret agenda. For him, as for Călinescu, the Romanian Premier, the Romanians could use the Turkish-Soviet connection to link themselves with the Soviet Union and the Anglo-Franco-Soviet agreement, the inevitable conclusion of which all accepted. Romania would have nothing to do with direct negotiations with the Soviet Union, for fear of Germany's reactions. The Turkish proposal for a Black Sea security pact was firmly knocked on the head.[70] But if Turkey was linked with Britain and France by one alliance and with the Soviet Union by another, then Romania could declare her loyalties strongly enough to warn off

Hungarian and Bulgarian revisionists, with or without German encouragement. In the last week in July, Carol, meeting with Călinescu and Gafencu, decided that if the Turco-Soviet negotiations succeeded, they would seek Turkish mediation for the negotiation of a non-aggression pact with the Soviet Union.[71]

The Romanians were brought to their decision in part by the patient diplomacy of the Turks, in part by the continuous posturing of the Hungarians, and in part by their increasing conviction of German hostility. This last was the product of two factors. The first was the German diplomatic offensive against the progress of British and French diplomacy in the Balkans, an offensive concerted with the Italians at the beginning of June in an effort to defuse the effect of Article VI of the Anglo-Turkish Declaration and to prevent its incorporation into the parallel Franco-Turkish Declaration.[72] The second, following on the failure of the first, was directed against the Anglo-Franco-Turkish negotiations for an alliance which followed. The Germans found themselves, however, in a cleft stick. The end of June was marked by a series of agreements on the delivery of arms and the provision of credits to Yugoslavia, Romania and Bulgaria, so much so as to awaken alarm in Budapest. But the only leverage this gave the Germans was the ability to delay deliveries; taken with the attention lavished on Bulgaria, this only awoke more suspicions in Romanian breasts.[73]

These suspicions were reinforced by a series of reports on German intentions which reached Bucharest from sources in Germany. Early in July, during the Bulgarian visit to Berlin, information reached the French Embassy in the German capital to the effect that the alleged crisis over Danzig was a cover for German planning against Romania, and that 'Germany's principal objective remains the South-East.' In London there was talk of the overthrow of the Hungarian Government and its replacement by a more actively pro-German regime, which, in return for part of Slovakia, would place the Hungarian economy and army under German control. On August 1, Călinescu confided to the French that Romania had been receiving intelligence from Germany for the last year and a half pointing to an Axis drive into south-east Europe for the control of the Mediterranean.[74] The principal sources were an unnamed German industrialist close to the former German Defence Minister, General von Blomberg, and the Prince zu Wied.[75]

These reports were entirely untrue. So far from the German agitation against Poland being a cover for an attack on Romania, these reports were, either intentionally or inadvertently, a distraction from German planning against Poland. So impossible is it to find any evidence of German military planning for a drive into south-east Europe at this time, and so clear is it that the Germans were trying desperately to damp down all the various ambitions filling Hungarian heads, that it is difficult to see what could have given rise to these reports. Indeed one may take leave to wonder whether the Romanians were wise to trust any Prince zu Wied. There were, in fact, several princes of that name. The Romanian contact appears to have been the eldest brother of the reigning Prince, the ex-King of Albania, Prince Wilhelm Friedrich Heinrich, a man so hostile to Nazism that in 1938 he had withdrawn from Germany to live on his family estates in Romania. His younger brother, Prince Wilhelm Viktor zu Wied, was a German diplomat of markedly Nazi sympathies. He had joined the Nazi party in 1932, but the dominant group in the Foreign Ministry, intent on depoliticizing the Foreign Service, forced his retirement in March 1933. Six months later he was recalled and appointed German Minister to Stockholm. In 1935 he had denounced Gerhard Köpke, the head of Department II in the Foreign Ministry, to Hitler. Köpke, whose wife was Jewish though his sentiments were peculiarly nationalistic, was dismissed under the anti-semitic Nuremberg Laws that same year. The Prince remained Minister to Stockholm until 1943, when he retired at the age of seventy. There is a distinct smell of disinformation, possibly unwitting, about his brother's alleged services to Romanian intelligence.

The degree to which the Romanians had recovered their courage and the extent to which the Germans were prepared to go to avoid a head-on row were shown in July when Călinescu, the Romanian Premier, acted decisively to restrain the leader of the 800,000-strong German minority in Romania, Fritz Fabritius. In January, the German National Party in Romania had been admitted to membership of the Government coalition. By July this had gone completely to their heads. Fabritius had assumed the title of Führer. He had raised two paramilitary organizations, the National Workers' Front and the German Youth, put them into uniform and required their members to swear loyalty oaths to him. Early in July Călinescu was given the text of a speech Fabritius had made in Munich. In the course of this Fabritius had said that the frontiers of the Greater German Reich would have to be secured by a ring of armed peasant settlements along the Carpathians, the Urals and the Caucasus. Within this *Grossraum* (the term is virtually untranslatable) those alien peoples who lived there at present would be allowed to stay, but eventually those that could not be Germanized would be replaced by settlers of German racial stock repatriated from North and South America.

On July 13, Călinescu carpeted Fabritius. Enough was enough, he said. Fabritius was in breach of all agreements and he was imperilling the German community in Romania. The oaths, the illegal storm-troopers, the speeches could not be tolerated any longer. If his activities were generally known to the Romanian public, there would be such a backlash that Călinescu and King Carol would be forced to take legal action. The German Legation in Bucharest had been watching Fabritius' growing megalomania with increasing distaste and alarm. The German Minister was now able to secure Fabritius' temporary recall to Germany. He returned, sending a letter to Călinescu which attempted to bluster it out, but in his absence one of his staff had left on a train a briefcase full of compromising documents ordering paramilitary manœuvres. This too came into Călinescu's hands. The German Minister hustled Fabritius back to Germany where the SS agency which controlled him, the *Volksdeutsche Mittelstelle*, under pressure from the German Foreign Ministry, promptly sacked him. A major German intelligence agent, Edith von Coler, was expelled at the same time.[76]

At the end of July morale in Bucharest was high. A week later, M. Cretzianu, the Romanian Minister in Berlin, just back from a visit to his country, boasted to his French colleague that his country was united behind King Carol (then cruising on the Romanian Royal yacht on the Black Sea). Confidence in the Romanian army was high.[77]

Even as he spoke, however, a new panic was on its way. It was provoked, in part, by an ill-judged move on the part of the British Foreign Office, faced in mid-June with a Hungarian complaint that since Britain had guaranteed Romania, treatment of the Hungarian minority in Romania had greatly deteriorated. That complaint had in turn been generated by a Magyarophile member of the War Office, Colonel Bonfield. After attempting a direct approach to Bucharest and an indirect one via Turkey, the Hungarians had come back to London, presenting Orme Sargent, Cadogan's deputy in the Foreign Office, with a long catalogue of Hungarian complaints at the end of July.[78]

The reaction in Bucharest, when this memorandum was duly passed on there for comment, was loud and bitter. Even Mussolini and Hitler had refused to endorse Hungary's claims against Romania, Gafencu remarked to the French with some justice. To see himself faced with British endorsement of such claims, only ten days after Count Csáky had declared his loyalty to the Axis, was a bit much. The British had implied that, if Romania fought on the Allied side, she could not rely on keeping the same frontiers once the war ended. The British move raised the ghost of Lord Runciman.[79] When King Carol returned, he and Călinescu would have to submit their resignations. Le Rougetel, the British Chargé d'affaires, toned Gafencu's remarks down a bit (to his French colleagues, he described his Government's action as 'inappropriate', which for a junior British diplomatist of that era is strong language), but his Government duly backed off.[80] The coincidence of the British move with a fresh crop of reports of imminent German action (the German military was in the penultimate stages of preparation for the attack on Poland) was too much. The Romanians mobilized and King Carol took his yacht direct to Istanbul.[81]

In Istanbul, he spent three hours with Ismet Inönü and Saracoğlu. The Turks bolstered his morale by promising him the immediate mobilization of Turkish forces if Romania was attacked and pressing him to make an approach to the Soviet Union. Carol asked the Turks to make such an approach but said that Soviet recognition of the Romanian frontiers was essential.[82] For a fortnight, Romania's morale remained high and King Carol's determination remained strong. The Hungarians' nerve failed; and the Hungarian Foreign Ministry declared that Hungary's claims on Romania were without urgency or standing at the moment.[83] Real events were on the move. Count Ciano had seen Hitler and Ribbentrop at Berchtesgaden. Germany was clearly determined on war with Poland. Hitler and von Ribbentrop were obviously under the illusion that Britain would not fight, an illusion which no one save possibly Stalin and Molotov shared. Within a week the news of Ribbentrop's dramatic dash to Moscow was to break. The Hungarian conviction that everything would end in another great power conference at which, if they and the Bulgarians played their cards cleverly, all the wrongs done them in 1919 would be righted, disappeared overnight. Hitler wanted war, not talk. Nor would Britain and France back down. By the last week in August, the capitals of the Balkans were filled with politicians and monarchs running for cover. Only Ankara remained resolute.

The Turks had had to face a great deal of German and Italian pressure. The discovery that the Anglo-Turkish Declaration was to be followed by negotiations for a treaty had awoken in von Papen's ever-sanguine heart the thought that something might be done to abort these talks by reassuring Turkey on her fears of Italy.[84] He duly returned to Berlin on May 15 to lobby for his new ideas, but found Ribbentrop and Hitler in a bellicose and uncompromising mood. Hitler had already arranged for the cancellation of a Turkish order for six heavy howitzers from the Skoda works, which were both ready for delivery and paid for.[85] The bureaucrats in Berlin were being prodded by Ribbentrop into discussing ways and means of exercising economic pressure on Turkey. To their credit the officials of the German trade and financial agencies protested strongly against their instructions, but they were brusquely told that Hitler's decision was fixed; their job was simply to carry it out as best they could.[86] Papen returned to Ankara to a series of abrupt and stormy interviews with Saracoğlu and Inönü; his reports painted a picture of himself bullying and dominating the cowering tongue-tied Turks.[87] One may take leave to doubt whether they represented the strict truth. As Bernardo Attolico, the Italian Ambassador in Berlin, who cordially disliked von Papen, remarked to von Weizsäcker, speeches remained speeches and facts remained facts.[88] And the facts were that, despite von Papen's oily charm, despite Ribbentrop's stormy interviews with the Turkish Ambassador in Berlin, the stolid Mehmet Hamdi Arpag,[89] the Franco-Turkish Declaration made on June 24 had the identical text on the Balkans, Article VI, to which Gafencu and the Yugoslavs had made such extreme objections when it was originally included in the Anglo-Turkish Declaration.[90]

None of this was lost on the Turks; but it made very little difference to them. Hamdi Arpag replied firmly to Ribbentrop that the openly affirmed determination of Germany and Italy to acquire by conquest their 'vital living space' made it natural for Turkey, which had never staged a *coup de force* and had no aggressive designs, to range herself on the side of those powers which were defending peace.[91] And on July 9, in a speech to the Turkish National Assembly, Saracoğlu remarked ironically that considering how strongly the basic text of the Nazi regime (*Mein Kampf*) recommended an alliance with Britain, it was difficult to understand why Turkey's choice of the same policy of friendship with Britain should be so condemned in the German press.[92]

Having declared where they stood, the Turks now found themselves faced with a number of serious obstacles. Most serious in the short run were their discovery of how little Britain had to offer them by way of arms and financial aid, and the superior, paternalistic, if not outright colonialist attitudes they met in London. Where the French sent them General Weygand, an ex-Chief of Staff and the General Officer commanding in Syria, and followed him at the end of July with General Huntziger, a member of the Conseil Supérieur de la Guerre (the highest military-political committee in the French Government) and an army-commander designate in the event of war, the British sent a mere brigadier, Brigadier Lund of the General Staff. It is hardly surprising therefore that he never met Marshal Çakmak, the head of the Turkish army, who departed abruptly on a tour of inspection of the remote parts of the Turkish frontiers; or that Çakmak remarked sourly to the French that 'this is a hint we shall have to take into account when we appoint the head of our own military mission.'[93] As M. Massigli reported, Britain should have sent an admiral. 'The Turks respect the Royal Navy; they no longer believe in the British army.'[94]

The Turkish military mission to London was in fact headed by General Orbay, one of Marshal Çakmak's inner circle. He made little progress; until the unfortunate Brigadier Lund had reported on Turkey's war plans, the British professed themselves unable to judge whether Turkish statements of their needs were justifiable. Despite the respect normally expressed in British military circles for 'Johnny Turk's' fighting qualities, the military capabilities of their senior officers were dismissed, and the members of Orbay's mission came close to being treated as ignorant natives, suddenly offered a shopping spree at Harrod's and unable to judge for themselves what was genuinely necessary and what was not.

On the British side it must be said that Britain had nothing to spare. In January the army had suddenly found that it had to equip fifteen divisions for a continental war instead of five. In February this figure was raised to nineteen, and in May to thirty-two. Also in May, to make things worse, a new Ministry, that of Supply, had been set up to develop Britain's new rearmament programme for a mass continental army. The armaments firms simply had no surplus production whatever.[95] This was small consolation to the Turks, offered only twenty anti-aircraft guns and fifty Fairey Battle light bombers, whose obsolescence was to be demonstrated by the catastrophic losses the RAF squadrons flying Battles were to suffer in France a year later.[96]

This was not of much use to the Turks, who faced the loss of six heavy howitzers from the Skoda works and nineteen 190 mm guns from Krupps, together with 125 million Reichsmarks of other war material from Germany and German-controlled territories. But the British reply to the Turks' financial demands was even more embarrassing. At the end of June Lord Halifax was authorized to offer a defence credit of £10 million sterling with which *one-tenth* of the total Turkish demands could be met over the next eighteen months without damage to the British rearmament programme. There was an extra £5 million sterling left over from the 1938 credit agreement. But, even with the Mediterranean open to trade, Halifax did not see how Britain could help Turkey find alternative markets to those the Germans threatened to close.[97]

The first Turkish reaction was to propose the establishment of an equalization fund to keep the Turkish pound stable.[98] This was followed a fortnight later by the full unveiling of Turkey's military and financial needs: £35 million sterling credit for war materials, some to be available in free currency to be spent in Sweden, Belgium and the United States; a loan of £15 million sterling in gold; and a credit of £10 million sterling to enable Turkey to unfreeze her balances in Central

Europe. The Turks declared that these loans were not more than they had enjoyed from Germany and were entirely within Turkey's capacity to service. The bullion loan could be paid for in tobacco deliveries.[99] The effect, as Massigli and Knatchbull-Hugessen both pointed out, would be to tie Turkey firmly into the free currency bloc and to unglue Eastern Europe from Germany.[100] It seems to have been greeted in London as convincing evidence that the Turks were unable any more to distinguish funny money from the real thing.

On July 5, as the Turks were beginning to stoke up their indignation, the British Cabinet was in fact contemplating an extremely gloomy 'Note on the Financial Situation', produced by the Treasury.[101] The memorandum pointed out that Britain's gold stocks had been run down from £800 to £500 million in fifteen months, partly for economic reasons and partly through panic transfers to New York. Britain had already promised £10 million in credits to the Soviet Union and the same sum again to Turkey. Other credit promised included a further £6 million to Turkey, £4 million to Czechoslovakia, £5 million to China, and £30 million to India for army re-equipment. This, plus other sums promised to Poland, New Zealand, Romania, etc., brought the total to £60 million. Up to the present the disadvantage of the gold loss lay, in the Treasury's view, in the discouragement it gave to Britain's friends and the encouragement it gave to the Axis; but it could also soon affect Britain's 'staying power in war'. 'Our gold stock, together with such assets as we may be able to sell or mortgage in war-time to countries overseas, constitutes our sole war chest.'

Armaments increased the pressure on the gold resources in three ways. If made at home in Britain, about 25–30 per cent of the cost had to be paid in foreign exchange to cover the import of the necessary raw materials. Purchased abroad, they cost gold. Loans and credits to other countries, if the money was spent on arms produced in Britain, also cost 25–30 per cent in raw material import costs; if spent abroad, they added to the gold loss. The balance of trade was adverse anyway. Britain's capacity for waging a long war, barred as she was by US legislation from borrowing any money from America, was steadily bleeding away.

It was a sign of the increased determination of the majority of Cabinet members that collectively, following Lord Halifax's lead, they took a fairly robust view of the Treasury's presentation.[102] On only one point was the Treasury wrong. No one abroad would have believed such a presentation. Britain's friends were discouraged and her enemies cheered by the parsimonious face the Treasury turned towards her would-be allies.

Under these circumstances, however, the Turkish demands of July 13 were not such that the Treasury could be stirred into speedy action. General Pownall, the Director of Operations at the War Office, noted in his diary[103] that the Turks seemed 'past praying for'. Without a convention they would not reveal their dispositions for war. 'But until we know what their dispositions are,' he remarked, quite unconscious of how such arrogance would sound to the Turks, 'how can we judge what quality and quantity of help they may require?' Three days later, in conversation with General Huntziger and M. Massigli, speaking angrily and bitterly, his voice raised in uncharacteristic passion, the normally quiet and restrained Turkish President blew his top. It was two months, he said, since Turkey had declared for the West. Today she was much the weaker for it. Germany had cut her arms deliveries on which Turkey had counted, and Britain and France had delivered nothing.[104] A fortnight later nothing had changed, and Knatchbull-Hugessen reported a feeling of disillusionment among the Turks which was 'growing and harmful'.[105]

Early in July the Turkish Government was in the habit of escaping the arid heat of Ankara to take refuge in Istanbul where, as Knatchbull-Hugessen noted in his diary, it 'more or less disappears'. Most of the conversations with Saracoğlu and Menemencioğlu took place at the Yacht Club.[106] General Huntziger met Saracoğlu at the latter's villa at Moda. His sessions with Marshal Çakmak and the Turkish General Staff also took place in Istanbul. In the shadows of that extraordinary city, Huntziger's tact, seniority and diplomacy worked wonders. Colonel Ross, the British Military Attaché, who was courteously invited to participate, was given an object lesson in how to handle Turkish pride. General Huntziger could also move the French bureaucracy. For two months Massigli had been urging France to supply Turkey with the heavy guns Germany was withholding from her. Within a week General Huntziger had brought Paris to commit itself to their delivery.[107] At the same time M. Bonnet finally plucked up courage to approach both his colleague, Paul Reynaud, the French Minister for Finance, and the British to propose French participation in providing the financial aid Turkey demanded.[108] The British reply was immediate. Faced with a Turkish proposal which involved the devaluation of the Turkish pound from 5.93 to 9 to the pound sterling, and the establishment of a compensation agreement which would have forced Turkish goods on to the British market, the British proposed joint Anglo-French discussions on financial support for Turkey as the only alternative to losing her aid as an ally.[109] The French Treasury, whose purblindness made Britain seem a model of generosity, had hitherto insisted that France had paid Turkey quite enough by giving her Alexandretta: a view of which German and Italian propaganda to the Arab Middle East had made much use. Now it yielded, albeit with the peculiar gracelessness of the French *fonctionnaire* at his worst. By the end of August the two countries had at last agreed to co-operate in meeting some of Turkey's needs.[110]

What is so extraordinary, at first sight, in this catalogue is the lack of a sense of urgency in London and Paris. The French, especially the military with their plans for a joint Franco-Turkish military expedition to Salonika, were well aware of the importance of Turkey. Politically, Turkey's adhesion to the West was the rock on which all German and Italian efforts to intimidate the only too easily alarmed Balkans broke and failed. Strategically Turkey's ties with the West isolated the Italian colonies on the Dodecanese and confirmed the British navy's dominance of the eastern Mediterranean. Moreover, Turkish support was essential if Allied ships were to be able to use the Black Sea route to support Romania and supply the Soviet Union in time of war. Many thousands of brave men had died on the Gallipoli peninsula in the 1914–18 war to win what Turkish courage and determination would give without bloodshed by the alliance to be negotiated in July and August 1939. If war came, Turkey's role would be crucial.

It was on that 'if' that the sense of urgency was dissipated. For, it cannot be too often repeated, British and French policy in 1939 was aimed at the prevention of war and the deterrence of the would-be aggressor. That required the façade of an alliance; the serious underpinning might come later. Deterrence in 1939 and, please God, through into 1940 and beyond, was all that was aimed for. The trouble is that deterrence may well require the reality of military preparations for real war to be credible to those to be deterred and to those whom the deterrence is intended to protect. Otherwise there will always be the element of a Hollywood stage set, of two-dimensional façades about it.

The support of Turkey worked, as long as the rest of the Balkans believed that the Anglo-French-Turkish alliance negotiations and those between Britain and the Soviet Union were headed for success. The Turks themselves insisted on this, as they did on the triangle being completed by a Soviet-Turkish agreement. From M. Potemkin's visit to Ankara at the beginning of May 1939, Saracoğlu and the Turkish Foreign Ministry believed that they had Soviet approval of their agreement with Britain.[111] They were a little surprised by the issue on May 29 of a *démenti* by Tass, the official Soviet news agency, of a report that a Turco-Soviet agreement had already been signed.[112] But the general line of Turkish policy became to wait until the precise shape of the Anglo-French-Soviet Pact emerged before making a direct approach to Moscow. From the end of June, however, Saracoğlu heard nothing, either from Moscow or from the Soviet Ambassador in Ankara, Alexei Terentiev, of how the Moscow negotiations were going. Their lack of progress was sufficiently worrying for Saracoğlu to offer Turkish mediation in Moscow to accelerate the negotiations.[113] M. Bonnet found this an excellent idea, and the Turkish Embassy in Moscow was duly instructed. Molotov anticipated the enquiry by asking if the Turks were still disposed to conclude a bilateral treaty with the Soviets.[114]

On August 4, the Soviet Ambassador, Terentiev, invited Saracoğlu to come to Moscow to conclude a private and secret agreement with the Soviet Union.[115] Saracoğlu replied, accepting the invitation; he added, however, that Turkey was in no position to assume unlimited responsibilities towards the Soviets.[116] She was prepared to accept a pact, the scope of which could be discussed together. He suggested to Terentiev that the Soviets should send a preliminary draft to Ankara.[117] The Soviets replied,[118] expressing their willingness to do so but sending a list of questions to be answered first, a delaying tactic explicable by the definite signs of urgency, desperate urgency, in Berlin's approaches. Within seven days word of Ribbentrop's imminent visit to Moscow had hit Ankara as it had everywhere else.

The news of the Nazi-Soviet Pact caused the Turkish Foreign Minister, for the only time, to suffer a brief loss of nerve. On the morning of August 23 he was confronted with the news of Ribbentrop's dramatic descent on Moscow, and the realization that the Soviets had been deceiving him for some time; he also saw as a major threat the German quasi-ultimatum of August 21,[119] proposing a cancellation of all extant arms contracts and of the credit agreement of January, a prolongation of the 1938 agreements being made conditional on Turkish acceptance of this. 'Distinctly upset',[120] he told Knatchbull-Hugessen that he could no longer resist this pressure. For months he had been attempting to create a situation in which his country could withstand Germany; but he had not succeeded.[121]

His failure of courage was only momentary. Later the same day, Massigli found him as resolute as ever. Turkey, Saracoğlu said, had no intention of sitting down under German threats.[122] Two days later he told von Papen Germany had broken all its promises. Turkey would not submit to German domination. All Turkish economic and technical missions in Germany would be withdrawn.[123] İnönü reinforced this two days later. Turkey, he told von Papen, would act in accordance with her interests and commitments and would be found in any camp opposed to Germany.[124] Papen, 'thoroughly uneasy', was reported to have left the interview in a state of 'acute perspiration'. As well he should have. Hitler, listening to General Keitel, had already reversed his decision on the German arms contracts.[125] Germany might not need Turkish tobacco, but she needed Turkish chrome very badly.

Inönü, Saracoğlu, Menemencioğlu, Marshal Çakmak and their colleagues were not easy to bully or deceive. The onset of war made their loyalty and support the more valuable to Britain and France, but they would be of little value unless they could be relied on. After war broke out Saracoğlu did go to Moscow, where Molotov and Stalin kept him waiting for several days and then tried to bully him into abandoning the alliance with Britain and France; but in vain. Saracoğlu returned to Ankara in a fury. The alliance, so long a matter of the exchange of proposals and arguments over drafting, was signed within days. Turkish friendship towards the Soviet Union has still to recover. Atatürk's Turkey would accept aid and friendship between equals, but she would be nobody's satellite; least of all Stalin's.

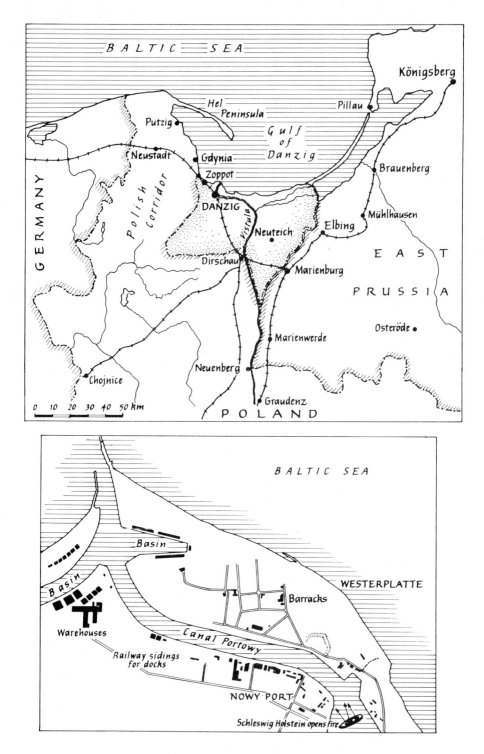

Danzig (i) The Free State and the Polish Corridors
(ii) The Polish defence of the Westerplatte

CHAPTER 18

HITLER STEPS UP THE PRESSURE: 'DIE FOR DANZIG?'

The city of Danzig stands at the mouth of the River Vistula, a German city (until 1945) dominating the mouth of a purely Polish river. (To the Poles Danzig was and is Gdansk. To the Germans the Vistula was the Weichsel.) It had once been an independent Hanseatic city, bound to Poland by a union with the Polish crown, the natural outlet for Polish grain, amber, furs and lumber, floated down the Vistula by barge and transhipped at Danzig's wharves near the Crane Gate. Architecturally, it was Dutch rather than German, set out around a core of public buildings and private houses, a city hall and the Marienkirche, built by imported architects from the sixteenth-century Dutch Renaissance. In the nineteenth century, after the partition of Poland between Prussia, Austria and Russia had cut it off from Warsaw and its Polish hinterland, it was the administrative capital of West Prussia. The local architects copied the older Dutch style. By 1918 it was just another typical north German coastal city. It boasted an imperial navy yard, a shipbuilding industry and a reasonable turnover as a port. Politically and emotionally it was German.

Its status as a free city was created by the Treaty of Versailles, as an unhappy compromise between President Wilson's Thirteenth Point, which promised a resurrected Polish state 'free and secure access to the sea', and his equally loudly proclaimed principle of national self-determination. It lay at the head of the 'Corridor' which linked Poland to the sea, separating East and West Prussia. Its waterways and harbour were run by a board composed equally of Poles and Danzigers. Its foreign affairs were formally controlled by Poland, which operated its railways, maintained a post office in the harbour area, and collected its customs revenues. Its constitution, however, was guaranteed by the League of Nations, as was its independence and its military protection, although this last was always a dead letter. There was a resident high commissioner to represent the League, a German consul general, a president and senate chosen by an elected popular assembly (*Volkstag*), and a Polish high commissioner whom Danzigers referred to as the 'Polish diplomatic representative'.

Among Danzig's 400,000 inhabitants, there was a 17,000-strong Polish-speaking population, largely composed of immigrant Poles, and a Polish-Jewish minority of a further 3,000 or so; but the vast majority of Danzigers were German in thought, sympathy and personal identification. The political parties were, in the main, extensions of German parties. Many of Danzig's officials came from Germany proper and returned there when their term of service was over. Danzig's legislation largely followed that of Germany, and there were open and covert German subsidies.

To both Germans and Poles the status of Danzig as a 'free city' was an unhappy and unwelcome compromise. In 1920, Danzig's dockers, then largely Communist in sympathy, had refused to unload arms for Poland's forces when the Soviet Red Army swept on to its defeat before Warsaw. From 1924 Poland had retaliated by building a rival port at a tiny fishing village, Gdynia, outside Danzig's limits, where the Polish Corridor touched the Baltic. Gdynia developed into a port of some 150,000 inhabitants, and, once the world slump had begun, a competitor for trade with Danzig. Indeed, by 1933 Gdynia was handling more freight than Danzig.

On January 30, 1933, Hitler was appointed Chancellor of Germany. By the end of June he had swept away all other political parties, trades unions and non-Nazi organizations. He had split the Protestant churches and signed a concordat with the Catholics. In Danzig, as in Germany proper, the Nazi party had grown in strength and violence as the slump bit deeper and unemployment rose. Poles and Jews were made equal scapegoats. In June 1933 the Nazis won an outright majority, 38 out of 72 seats, in the elections to the *Volkstag*. In March 1933 the Poles had reinforced their troops on the Westerplatte, the Polish arms depot on the edge of Danzig, in reply to local Nazi talk of an early return of Danzig to Germany, and this may well have tipped the vote over the 50 per cent mark. Hitler took immediate steps to damp down any inclination the Nazi majority in Danzig might have to try odds with the Poles. In return for a Polish agreement to send specified quantities of goods through Danzig and not to discriminate against the free city, Polish and Polish-Jewish minority rights in Danzig were to be respected. Neither side failed to cheat on the agreement; but so long as Hitler needed a quiescent Poland to free him to concentrate on recovering the right to rearm Germany, remilitarize the Rhineland, annex

Austria and destroy Czechoslovakia, the Nazis in Danzig were restrained.

It took until 1937 before the non-Nazi parties in Danzig could be wound up and the Nazi party had unquestioned control. The League of Nations Commissioner, Sean Lester from Ireland, resigned, as did the head of the Catholic Church in Danzig, another Irishman, Bishop O'Rourke. The Bishop was replaced by the administrator of the cathedral, a German who put his nationalist Polonophobia before the faith he shared with the Poles. Sean Lester was replaced by the Swiss historian Carl J. Burckhardt, a conservative, a believer in strong though not authoritarian government, a professional neutral from a country where neutrality is the dominant principle of foreign policy, and a man under instructions from the Secretary General of the League, as from the British and French Governments, not to be unduly concerned with Danzig's internal affairs so long as Danzig's relations with Poland could be kept in order. Burckhardt had come to know the State Secretary of the German Foreign Ministry, Ernst von Weizsäcker, when he was German Minister to Switzerland. Von Weizsäcker, seeing in Burckhardt a means of controlling Hitler, arranged for the Führer to get none but the most favourable reports on Burckhardt's respect for and sympathies with Germany, Hitler and National Socialism.[1] Burckhardt, who found the Nazi leadership in Danzig difficult at best when they were not brutal and repulsive, played along in the hope that Hitler would control them. Of the two leading Nazis, Burckhardt preferred the city's President, Arthur Greiser (who, he believed, preferred his current rank to the insignificance which would overtake him once Danzig became part of Germany), to Albert Forster, the Gauleiter.[2] But he could do little against Forster, who was a man after Hitler's own heart, and dominated the party in Danzig.

During the winter of 1938–9, Forster took a further step to increase the Germanization of Danzig on Hitler's instructions, introducing the full range of German anti-semitic legislation into Danzig.[3] For a moment a head-on clash with the League of Nations, the guarantor of Danzig's constitution, seemed likely. But von Ribbentrop's assiduous pursuit of an agreement with Poland required that the status quo in Danzig be maintained for the time being. Forster was reined in, and actually assured Burckhardt that his presence in Danzig was desirable.[4] London and Paris preferred to do nothing to upset Hitler until they were sure it was unavoidable. The British Consul General in Danzig, who felt that to accept the anti-semitic legislation was to abandon League control, was ignored.

Behind these manœuvres can be seen the struggle for power around

Hitler. By instinct Forster belonged to the radical revolutionary wing of the Nazi hierarchy. Son of a Bavarian prison official, he had joined the Nazi party in September 1923, just before the Bierkeller Putsch. Trained as a bank-teller, he lost his job and remained unemployed until 1928 when he found work with the nationalist Commercial Employees' Association. In 1930 he was elected, on the Nazi party ticket, to the Reichstag. That same October, on Goering's recommendation, he had been sent to Danzig to take over the local Nazi party.[5] By 1938, however, he was at loggerheads with Goering's ally, Erich Koch, Gauleiter of East Prussia. Koch was an advocate of the 'large solution', a German-Polish alliance which could compensate Poland for the loss of Danzig and the Corridor with an opening to the Black Sea through the Ukraine. Forster wanted the 'little solution', an immediate annexation of Danzig and the Memel. In November Forster briefly won the upper hand. On November 29, 1938, Hitler accompanied his orders to the Wehrmacht to prepare for a war in the West with special orders to plan for a *coup de force* against Danzig. This was to be carried out at 'a politically opportune moment' without war with Poland. The necessary planning was to allow for a simultaneous coup against Memel.[6]

In the meantime Forster and Greiser (who, like Forster, had spent the 1920s as a strong-arm man with the Nazi party in Munich and had direct links with the SS leadership)[7] began to build up a military position in Danzig. They justified this by the presence of Polish troops on the Westerplatte, and the military training given to the Polish public servants who worked in the railway station and the harbour post office. If a coup was to be prepared against Danzig, something had to be done to prevent the Polish military forces getting into the city first. Efforts to build up an SS presence in Danzig, however, were prohibited as long as von Ribbentrop still hoped for a Polish agreement. From the beginning of 1939 the tension in Danzig grew steadily. Student hotheads, always difficult to control, clashed repeatedly with their Polish opposite numbers in February, making Burckhardt's task more difficult. The disorders found their echo in Warsaw, where demonstrators broke the windows of the German Embassy during Count Ciano's visit to Warsaw.[8] It cost the Polish Foreign Minister and the Germans some effort to put the matter to rest. The incident did nothing to improve Hitler's increasing impatience with the Poles.

Forster took the annexation of Bohemia and Moravia on March 15 as a sign that his faction in Berlin had won the upper hand. On March 22, he announced that no elections would be held in Danzig that year.[9] There were strong indications that the elections, if held, would have resulted in a considerable defeat for the Nazi party. The Polish mobilization that same day, which put four thousand troops into Gdynia and moved troops up to the southern borders of the free city,[10] was a warning. Greiser travelled to Berlin[11] and invoked the support of his SS allies. Himmler himself is said to have intervened to attempt to secure Forster's dismissal, but the Gauleiter's close links with Hitler enabled him to survive.[12] And although the military plans for *Case White*, which Hitler approved on April 3, continued the notion of planning for a coup in Danzig, the British guarantee for Poland, and the unequivocal Polish declarations that any action against the Polish position in Danzig would be treated as an attack on Poland, effectively ruled the 'little solution' out of court; though the mechanisms of Nazi politics kept Forster's and von Ribbentrop's rivals, to whom Goebbels was now added, actively agitating for the coup, to the general alarm of those British, French and Poles to whom reports of their advocacy were conveyed.

Effectively, however, Danzig ceased to be an issue in itself, becoming instead both an instrument for Hitler to manipulate and an arsenal where at any time random sparks might provoke a premature explosion. To German and Polish propagandists it became simply a stage on and from which dramas of confrontation, provocation, even atrocities could be arranged, invented and propagated. German propagandists now drew for their attacks on Poland on a larger issue: the persecution of the German minorities throughout Poland. Genuine incidents were not lacking, but the German press was not usually prepared to wait for these to happen. Hyperbole and embroidery of the actual were not enough. Incidents of Polish 'terrorist' attacks on the innocent pure Germans, whom the victors of 1914–18 had so freely and inimically subjected to the rule of the Slav *Untermenschen* (sub-humans), were grossly exaggerated where they were not freely invented.[13] The Polish and German newspapers traded insults and allegations. The Polish Government, urged on by British and French representatives, did their best to exercise restraint. They lived under the difficulty, however, of facing a national opposition which found it only too tempting to manœuvre Beck and his allies into what could be represented as an ignominious if not a positively 'appeasing' stance.[14]

Poland was for Hitler still a cover for his newly found hatred of Britain. The attacks on Britain began with his speech of April 3 and the launching of the battleship *Tirpitz*.[15] Assaults on the British policy of encirclement were not without their effect on German opinion. Britain was to blame for Polish intransigence in turning down Hitler's 'generous offer'.[16] The British guarantee for Poland reinforced Hitler's view, enshrined in his military orders the previous November, that there could be no final crusade against Bolshevik Russia until Britain had been driven from the Continent.[17] Beck's visit to London convinced Hitler, as he told his generals on August 22, that Poland would fight on Britain's side and that, unless he 'took Poland out' first, he would be faced with a two-front war.[18] As the planning for *Case White*, the initial orders for which he had signed at the beginning of April, proceeded, so his resolution against Poland hardened. The orders were originally issued on April 11, as a 'temporary measure' until he could issue final orders for the 1939 'Instruction for the Unified Preparations for War by the Armed Forces for 1939'. *Case White* was the second annexe to these orders, the first covering preparations against sudden attack by land or air, and the third orders for 'taking possession of Danzig'. The draft of April 11 specifically stated that relations with Poland continued to be guided by the principle of avoiding disturbances. Should Poland take a threatening attitude, though, it would be necessary to isolate her and destroy her armed forces. This might happen if there was a domestic crisis in France such as to prevent her coming to Poland's aid, and a consequent withdrawal of Britain. The main goal in the build-up of the German armed forces, however, would continue to be determined by the enmity of the Western powers.

The German officer corps, with only a few exceptions, took its orders, at first, as merely pro-forma military planning. Having strong links with Prussian land-owners, the officers found the idea of war with Poland and the recovery of the lands lost to her an idea in itself to be commended.[19] The larger implications, that Britain and France could not be expected to behave as they had done in 1938 over Czechoslovakia, only dawned gradually upon them as Hitler's own views hardened. On May 10 Hitler ordered that the three Commanders-in-Chief were to report to him by August 1 at the latest on the measures taken in accordance with the directive.[20] By mid-June the detailed planning had gone sufficiently far and the documentation gone to the individual commands for the probable date of execution, August 25, to be fairly widely accepted.[21]

The orders for an occupation of Danzig to be effected by units of the peacetime armed forces acting from East Prussia without any mobilization of reservists continued to be worked on side by side with the work on *Case White*.[22] This appears to have been largely a means of distracting attention within the German officer corps and among Hitler's advisers from his determination to crush Poland. Hitler was well aware, from the events of 1938, that his entourage leaked like a sieve in all directions, partly due to the struggle for his favour which constituted the main issue of Nazi court politics, partly because of the inability of others, loud-mouths by nature, to avoid public posturing. Real secrecy consisted, in his view, either of limiting discussion of his real plans to the smallest and most intimate of circles, or of maintaining a kind of controlled indecision until his instincts told him the time for action had come. His growing hostility towards Poland and the violence with which he expressed himself to his intimates on the subject show, however, that a sudden stealthy coup against Danzig and Danzig alone had no place in his thinking. He wanted real war, real destruction to assuage the black apocalypse on which his deepest feelings fed. He does, nevertheless, seem to have successfully misled some of the more violently minded of his followers: Goebbels, Himmler, even von Ribbentrop, and certainly Forster, the Gauleiter of Danzig.

By instinct Hitler preferred to plan for war against Poland, as he had against Czechoslovakia, to take place as late in the summer campaigning season as possible. To get the German harvest in before calling up the reservists among the agricultural labour force; to allow long enough to overcome the enemy before bad weather or winter set in; to leave his potential opponents in the West the winter for reflection and the demoralization of morale his instincts told him were always at work in capitalist democracies, while he regrouped his forces for a new offensive; these seemed to him only sensible. The various dates of his planned offensives – September 30 for Czechoslovakia in 1938, August 26 for Poland in 1939, May 10 for France in 1940, and June 22 for the Soviet Union in 1941 – in each case reflect Hitler's conception of how soon victory could be achieved before winter set in, even though he proved grossly pessimistic in 1940 and totally mistaken in 1941. The problem, for one who preferred to direct the opening of war like a Hitchcock or a Cecil B. deMille, was to prevent the escalation of incidents and the enflaming of opinion (including his own, so overcome could he be by the propaganda of atrocities for which he himself had written the script) from getting out of hand, from 'peaking' before the chosen date.

At first all went reasonably well. The denunciation of the Non-Aggression Pact with Poland was preceded by orders to Germany's diplomatic representatives in Warsaw that no encouragement was to be given to any Polish gestures intended to re-open the conversations on Danzig and the Corridor.[23] The Führer had made his generous offer. It had been rejected and was not to be repeated. The Polish counter-proposal, made on March 26, for a joint Polish-German guarantee of Danzig and for a customs-free transit route, both road and rail, across the Corridor by which Germans could travel to and from East Prussia without hindrance, was rejected.[24] The Poles produced a counter-memorandum to that denouncing the German-Polish Pact.[25] Beck replied to Hitler's speech of April 28 with a speech to the Polish Parliament, the Sejm, on May 5.[26] The position of Danzig, he said, was the result of a 'positive interplay of German and Polish interests'. 'I have to ask myself', he added, 'what is the real object of this? Is it the freedom of the German population of Danzig, which is not threatened, or a matter of prestige – or is it a matter of barring Poland from the Baltic, from which Poland will not allow herself to be barred?'

What indeed? Polish intelligence was reporting massive movements of German motorized troops into Silesia, Moravia and Pomerania, all along the western flank of the Corridor.[27] Reserve divisions were being brought up. At the end of April a Polish light cavalry regiment with artillery support was stationed at Starograd across the Danzig frontier, 9 miles (15 km) from the city, with orders to oppose any coup which involved the intrusion of German troops into Danzig.[28] The bridge across the Vistula at Dirschau was mined. Beck's ringing declaration – 'For us Poles, the idea of peace at any price does not exist. There is only one thing which is without price . . . that is honour' – was roundly applauded, both in the Sejm and in the Polish press, where the notions that 'the eyes of the world are fixed on Poland' and that 'Poland will decide the fate of Eastern Europe' were a matter of national pride. Beck, hitting his fist on the rostrum to emphasize each gesture, gave a superb performance. Spontaneous demonstrations outside the Polish Ministry of Foreign Affairs followed that afternoon. Banks, offices and factories in Warsaw shut as the crowds gathered. Beck was called to the balcony, to the acclamation of the crowds.[29] He had voiced Polish pride and determination, the indomitable spirit which was to carry his fellow countrymen through defeat, occupation by the Soviets, the imposition of a Soviet-sponsored government, and the mass movement of population consequent on the redrawing of Poland's frontiers, to the 'Polish October' of 1956, to Solidarity even. The historian cannot but note this spirit. The historian cannot but note the terrible cost in life and freedom paid for it.

Beck's rhetoric was, however, to disturb his friends as well as his enemies. On May 4, writing in the Parisian daily, *L'oeuvre*, a journal which, though few knew it, was subsidized by the German Embassy, Marcel Déat, a former French Minister, published the first of a number of articles under the headline 'Die for Danzig?',[30] a question to which he gave a resounding negative. 'It is not a question of bending before the conquest-centred fantasies of M. Hitler . . . to shove Europe into war because of Danzig is a little strong . . . to fight beside our Polish comrades in the common defence of our territories, our goods, our liberties, that is a prospect one can view with courage, if it will contribute to the maintenance of peace. But to die for Danzig? No.' A second article[31] was to maintain that the Anglo-French guarantee gave to Poland the right to decide between war and peace.

M. Déat's articles were taken up resoundingly by the German press.[32] It took speeches by M. Albert Lebrun, President of France,[33] and Neville Chamberlain, speaking on May 11 to the massed ranks of Tory femininity, to restore the balance.[34] Britain, he said, would take orders from no one. But German actions had given rise to the suspicion that Germany wanted to devour state after state, with the intention, at the end, of dominating the world. On the subject of Danzig, he concluded: 'We have given Poland clear and secure assurances . . . if any attempt is made to change the situation by force in such a way that Poland's independence is threatened, there will inevitably follow a general conflagration in which Britain will be involved.'

It was no longer a matter of Danzig, even of the Corridor. Hitler too made this clear on May 23, speaking to his Generals.[35] 'It is not Danzig that is at stake. For us it is a matter of expanding our living space in the East. . . . The Pole is not a fresh enemy. Poland will always be on the side of our enemies. . . . The problem "Poland" cannot be disassociated from the show-down with the West. . . . There is no question of sparing Poland and we are left with the decision, to attack Poland at the first opportunity.' In his audience were Goering, Grand Admiral Raeder, Generals von Brauchitsch, Halder, Keitel, Milch, Bodenschatz, Rear Admiral Schniewind and six staff officers and adjutants. They were sworn to secrecy. None of Hitler's political associates, not even von Ribbentrop, was present. They were left to pursue their own courses, courses which were to result in a serious crisis at the end of June.

Among those not in on the secret appears to have been Gauleiter Forster. Under his direction the Danzig press had reprinted British press reports that Beck was to demand a Polish protectorate over Danzig, a Polish veto over the decisions of the Danzig Senate, Polish control over Danzig's heavy industry and a Polish military occupation of Danzig.[36] The Danzig Senate then declared that if Beck were to make such demands, German troops would immediately occupy Danzig.[37] Beck's failure to advance such demands was then hailed as a Polish retreat. At this point Forster fell ill with pleurisy. In his absence in hospital, his rival, the Senate President, Greiser, was able to calm things down a good deal. His comment on Forster's illness was, 'What a pity, he did not croak it'.[38] On his recovery, Forster was warned by Hitler to keep things quiet for a time.[39]

Forster's absence through illness was just as well. During May there were a number of incidents involving Polish authorities with the German minority in Poland. The worst incident occurred in Danzig where, after disturbances in the frontier hamlet of Kalthof involving an attack on the Polish customs inspectors' billets, the chauffeur of the Polish acting High Commissioner in Danzig, being threatened by three Danzig SA men, fired and killed one of them, a butcher by profession, Max Grubnau.[40] Both Greiser and Forster subsequently dismissed the issue in conversations with the League of Nations High Commissioner, Carl Burckhardt.[41] All the same, it was to arm them with an issue which, when revived two months later, was to provide the excuse on which the Germans were to force war upon Poland. The issue was that of the powers of the Polish customs inspectors. On June 3, Greiser delivered two notes to the Polish diplomatic representative in Danzig, Chodacki, breaking off relations with the Polish officials involved in the Kalthof incident (the Poles had refused to admit that the Danzig Senate was entitled to demand their recall), and complaining about the increasing numbers and bad behaviour of Polish customs officials operating in Danzig.[42] The Poles, as might be expected, rejected these notes. Since the Kalthof incident they had increased the number of their customs officials from 77 to 106.[43]

Burckhardt, though he does not seem to have realized this, had in fact been cast by the Germans since early May in the role of a muffler to prevent matters in Danzig getting out of hand before the appointed time. Since March he had been languishing in Geneva, where the League of Nations Committee, to which he was responsible, was agonizing in its own slow-moving way over what to do in the matter of Danzig.[44] The Senate was clearly getting out of hand. Hitler's contempt for the League was taken for granted. The Polish representative on the Council seemed to be determined to make any action impossible.[45] Well-founded reports were current of a Polish proposal to substitute what would be in effect either a partition of or a joint condominium over Danzig between Poland and Germany.[46] In May, however, Burckhardt came under increasing pressure to return to Danzig. Halifax and Bonnet thought this a good idea.[47] Burckhardt returned to Danzig via Warsaw, where on Whit Sunday he saw Beck in his private residence over dinner.[48] Burckhardt was amused to note that the autographed pictures of Hitler and Mussolini, which had stood so prominently on the piano on his previous visit, had disappeared. Beck's tone of voice, he also noted, appeared to have frosted a little and he addressed Burckhardt as though he was issuing instructions.

Beck asked Burckhardt to see Hitler in Berlin. Burckhardt thought

Beck was simply playing for time. Nevertheless, after stopping over in Danzig where Forster, still somewhat bruised by his recent calling-to-heel, complained that he was merely a puppet in Hitler's hands, Burckhardt was summoned to Berlin. There he met Ribbentrop, who received him in the new all-white diplomatic uniform into which the unhappy servants of the Reichs Foreign Service had now been forced. The exchanges between the two men were somewhat heated. Ribbentrop tried, but failed, to bully the usually imperturbable Swiss. For once nettled, if so uncharacteristic a sentiment can be attributed to a citizen of that country where detachment from the deplorably war-like affairs of the outside world is as Alpine as its landscape, Burckhardt tried to convince Ribbentrop that Britain and France would back Poland if she went to war over Danzig.[49] Ribbentrop was totally unconvinced. Any French government which involved France in war would fail, he said. Opinion in the provinces did not echo the notions of the Parisians. A recent enquiry by the Paris correspondent of the *Deutsche Allgemeine Zeitung*, Herr Krug von Nidda, had proved this. Baffled, Burckhardt returned to Danzig.

It was immediately apparent to Burckhardt that the extremists among Hitler's entourage were getting out of hand. During the second week in June the Danzig authorities staged a week of culture. Josef Goebbels, Minister of Propaganda, film tsar, was the guest of honour. In two violent and apparently extempore speeches,[50] he hailed the Danzigers' desire to be part of the Great German Reich. 'I am come', he said, 'to fortify you in your resolution. Germany is everywhere there are Germans. Only the jealousy, the defiance, the stupidity of the other nations oppose you. Then again, political frontiers can be displaced for a time. The frontiers which are drawn by language, race and blood are fixed eternally.'

The German and the Danzig press took up the cry. The Poles played the matter down, seeing in Goebbels' oratory an attempt to provoke them into some ill-judged action.[51] They were influenced in this by the undoubtedly accurate reports of a German military and paramilitary build-up in Danzig.[52] This took three forms: German soldiers, volunteers from Danzig serving in East Prussia, were instructed to return to Danzig to join the police, which was in the process of being militarized under the direction of a Reichswehr officer, General Eberhardt.[53] Members of the SS in East Prussia travelled to Danzig as tourists or business representatives to build up a Danzig armed SS; with them arrived the head of the East Prussian SS, Rodiess. The 3rd Sturm Battalion of the SS Death's Head group of Hitler's own bodyguard, stationed at the Adlershof in Berlin, were also moved, on Himmler's orders, to Danzig in June.[54] Himmler visited Danzig incognito. Martin Bormann from Hitler's own personal staff was said to be in Danzig to organize the coup or to report on it to his master.

Most of this is unverifiable. What does seem to have been going on behind the reinforcement of the military and paramilitary forces in Danzig and Forster's frequent visits to Berlin, was a back-stage contest for Hitler's ear; on the one side were Ribbentrop and Goebbels, with Forster egging them on by provocative speeches in Danzig, and on the other Goering, Koch and Himmler. Of these Goering and Himmler were well aware of Hitler's timetable. Koch, who did his best to convince Burckhardt that Hitler's real target lay in south-east Europe,[55] may have been a partner in this great game of misdirection and disinformation that Goering was playing; as we shall see, Goering also encouraged the procession of amateur intermediaries who now began to troop through Whitehall's offices and London's salons in a well-meaning but ill-timed attempt to avert war and qualify for the next Nobel Peace Prize.

For the moment it was necessary to spur the West into action, so that Hitler would curb his firebrands. General Bodenschatz, Goering's personal adjutant, who was himself listed among those present for Hitler's speech of May 23, was one of the chosen actors. On June 26 he spoke to Colonel Stehlin of the French Embassy in Berlin.[56] He showed himself so evasive on the question of Danzig as to arouse the French Ambassador to telegraph Paris. His move was followed by a leakage from one of Dr Lammers' staff in the Reichs Chancellery,[57] and by another from a Gestapo source,[58] also in Berlin. At the same time, two journalists separately passed to the Counsellor of the British Embassy what was roughly the same story.[59] On July 20, Hitler would visit Danzig, of which city he was a freeman. Goering would follow him. Danzig would fill up with 'tourists' and after Hitler and Goering had left, the free city would unilaterally declare its adhesion to the Reich. If Poland reacted, she would be the aggressor. The British and French guarantees would be in doubt, and if Poland thus exposed herself, Germany would smash her. Britain was, after all, heavily involved at the end of June in a crisis in the Far East over the Japanese blockade of the British concession in Tientsin. The French would not act on their own.

Two days later, on June 30, the final part of the deception was enacted. This time it was M. Daladier himself who was involved.[60] Hitler, he was told, had given Gauleiter Forster full powers to settle the Danzig issue over the weekend, July 1–2. Recent information from France had led Hitler to hope that the former Foreign Ministers of the mid-1930s, Pierre Laval and Pierre-Etienne Flandin, would prevent any reaction. M. Daladier linked this with some public boasting by Ribbentrop's personal representative in Paris, Otto Abetz, whose telephone the French were tapping.[61] Abetz had been boasting to all and sundry that there would be a coup in Danzig over the weekend and that the West could do nothing.

At precisely the same moment, M. Coulondre, the French Ambassador in Berlin, was having it explained to him by the State Secretary in the German Foreign Ministry, Ernst von Weizsäcker, that all these reports about Hitler's forthcoming visit to Danzig were fantasies.[62] M. Burckhardt in Danzig, commenting rather acidly on the stampede of the world's press to Danzig to cover the forthcoming coup, saw the head of the Danzig municipal police who spoke bitterly of Forster's gestures as 'puerile and senseless'.[63] The French, to Ribbentrop's fury and outrage and to the alarm of the staff of the German Embassy in Paris, made it clear that Abetz should leave France quietly.[64] In his wake, two French journalists, M. Aubin of *Le Temps*, and M. Moirier of *Le Figaro*, were arrested.[65] M. Bonnet received the German Ambassador, whose absence in Berlin during the build-up of the crisis, and whose equally sudden return, had done nothing to calm French nerves, on the Saturday, July 1. M. Bonnet handed over a note which stated unequivocally that any modifications in the status quo in Danzig which provoked the Poles into armed resistance would oblige France to come to Poland's assistance.[66]

The French had had a very bad fright. The Foreign Office and the Cabinet in Britain were left unsure what all the fuss had been about. The Poles, with their ability to read the German military ciphers – despite a momentary panic[67] – remained calm and damped down any excitement in their press;[68] indeed Colonel Beck recommended the same degree of unexcitability should be practised in London and Paris. If Ribbentrop, the degree of whose rage over the treatment of Otto Abetz was to lead him into bitter attacks on the German Ambassador in Paris, Count Welczeck, for not successfully forcing the French to take Abetz back,[69] had planned together with Goebbels and Forster to drive the Poles into a demonstration either of aggression or impotence, then they were blocked. The world breathed again. That Hitler had no hand in all this; that he was determined to smash Poland rather than re-incorporate Danzig; that he was holding to his military timetable is clear from all those who worked close to him.

Goering had, however, pushed his feud with Ribbentrop a little too far. For, as will be seen later, he had frightened Mussolini and sown distrust in Count Ciano's heart. He had, moreover, tested and strengthened the links between France, Britain and Poland. This may well have been part of his aim; to discredit Ribbentrop, who kept up his constant reassurances to Hitler that Britain and France were bluffing, was always one of his main aims.

The slow build-up of German forces in Danzig continued. In July, on Hitler's orders, the Danzig police was re-organized on a military basis, and armed and equipped so that it could be re-incorporated at short notice into the Reichswehr, as the *Landespolizei* in the demilitarized Rhineland had been when Hitler moved in his troops in March 1936.[70] Given the proximity of Polish military forces to Danzig, and Polish military plans, this was from Hitler's viewpoint an eminently sensible precaution. In addition to the motorized battalion stationed on the borders of the free city, the Poles were known to be fortifying seven points inside Danzig – the post office, the Polish Railways' office at the main railway station, the main railway directorate office building, the office of the Polish diplomatic representative, two school buildings and a block of flats – with a view to holding out until the Polish troops arrived.[71]

The first three weeks of July were quiet, save for continued reports of German military movements, a continuing row between Forster and Greiser, and the steady build-up of German forces. Forster continued to shuttle between Danzig and wherever Hitler was, using the private aeroplane Hitler had given him.[72] Ribbentrop took it upon himself to engage in a personal polemic with the French Foreign Minister, accusing Bonnet of going back on the undertaking he alleged Bonnet had given the previous December, to withdraw French interest from Eastern Europe, and refusing to discuss any part of Germany's relations with Poland over Danzig or anything else.[73] His decision to launch this somewhat pointless polemic, together with his rage over Abetz's removal from the scene, underlined how badly he felt his whole position with Hitler had been undermined. To add to the picture, Hitler had temporarily broken off the back-stage political conversations with the Soviets, for which Ribbentrop had made himself personally responsible; Ribbentrop was soon to learn that Goering's deputy, Helmut Wohltat, was negotiating with the British behind his back. Bonnet had no difficulty in refuting Ribbentrop's version of the Franco-German Agreement of December 6, 1938.[74] Waiting for August was preying on Ribbentrop's nerves.

Not so with Forster. At the end of the third week in July he launched himself on a complicated piece of deception and disinformation involving Burckhardt. He began by asking Burckhardt to arrange an informal meeting between himself and Marjan Chodacki, the Polish diplomatic representative, for which he said he was just off to seek Hitler's approval.[75] On his return on July 20, he told Burckhardt that after the publication of a newspaper article stating Danzig's case, the matter was to be laid to rest for a year or two.[76] M. Zarske, the editor of the *Danziger Vorposten*, Forster's lackey and public relations expert, fed the international press with stories of an imminent *détente*.[77] Burckhardt would have breathed again, had it not been for the sudden re-emergence of the SS on to the streets of Danzig,[78] the revival of the customs inspectors issue,[79] a series of German allegations that the Poles were smuggling troops through Danzig in sealed trains in breach of established agreements,[80] a panic over an alleged Polish plan to occupy the railways through Danzig[81] (it was traced to the establishment of a single armed guard on Polish territory), and a new frontier incident in which an armed member of the Danzig SA shot and killed a Polish frontier guard.[82] A group of Polish boy scouts who had strayed across the border were sentenced to a month in gaol.[83] In general, neither Burckhardt nor the Poles could see any sign of the will to *détente* of which Forster spoke. Burckhardt, however, believed Forster when the latter blurted out that a 'surprise could be expected in some other part of Europe' in August. The deception was furthered by various leaks, notably one to the British Embassy in Berlin, to the effect that Hitler was contemplating a new peace gesture, a proposal for a summit conference of the heads of government of the United States, Britain, France, Germany, Italy and, possibly, Japan.[84] The Nuremberg party meeting this year was to be named the Congress of Peace.

Of all these issues that of the customs inspectors was the one chosen to force the Poles' hand. Throughout June there had been a series of minor incidents. The Poles had actually arrested and imprisoned a member of the Danzig Customs Service. The Danzig authorities had arrested a Polish official.[85] On this issue Colonel Beck believed that Danzig was vulnerable to economic pressure. On July 19, therefore, he demanded an unequivocal statement as to whether the Danzig Senate was prepared to guarantee conditions in which the Polish customs inspectors could carry out their duties, and threatened measures against one of Danzig's largest businesses, the Amada-Unida margarine factory (the property of the Anglo-Dutch firm, Unilever), which produced almost entirely for the Polish market.[86] On July 29, the Danzig Senate replied.[87] Its reply was insolent: it withdrew recognition from all but actual members of the Polish Customs Inspectorate, disputed their number in relation to the volume of trade passing through Danzig and threatened economic counter-measures. M. Chodacki refused to relay the notes to his Government,[88] and accused the Danzig Senate of wishing to limit the activities of the Polish customs officials 'to pave the way for the widespread smuggling of arms and ammunition into Danzig'. All Polish customs officials, he said, in a second note of August 4,[89] would perform their duties in uniform and would be armed in the light of information from their opposite numbers in the Danzig Customs Service that the exercise of their functions would be resisted. Ribbentrop now had his issue. On August 9, on his instructions, the German Ambassador in Warsaw was told not to return to his post.[90] Von Weizsäcker read an official statement to the Polish Chargé d'affaires in Berlin, Prince Lubomirksi, labelling the Polish step as an action which, if repeated, would lead to an aggravation of German-Polish relations.[91] The following day, August 10, the Poles replied.[92] There was no legal justification for German intervention. The Poles would continue to react as they saw fit to any attempt by the Danzig Senate to impair Polish rights in the free city. Any German intervention to the detriment of these rights would be regarded as an act of aggression. The relevant documents were transmitted by teleprinter to Berchtesgaden where Hitler, Ribbentrop and Forster were already ensconced. According to Hitler's timetable the attack on Poland was scheduled for August 26.

First, however, he had to get Britain and France off his back. He was convinced that the will to war did not exist in London and Paris. This conviction stemmed in part from the difficulties which had beset the realization of the Anglo-Polish and Franco-Polish negotiations since Beck's visit to London in April. There was no treaty of alliance. Poland had failed to secure any substantial loan in London or Paris. In military terms the Polish position was as isolated and unstrengthened in August as it had been in April. All that could be set against this were a number of spoken warnings. These, Ribbentrop had convinced Hitler, were a bluff – or not to be taken seriously.

In view of Hitler's notorious unwillingness to listen to warnings and opinions which did not agree with his intuitions, and his determination, if need be, to drive Britain from Europe by destroying France, Britain's base for intervention on the Continent, it is possible that if the arguments which convinced him that Britain and France would abandon Poland had lost their validity, they would simply have been replaced by others. After Munich his hatred for Britain grew steadily. Ribbentrop, that relentless pursuer of Hitler's ear, whose hatred of the country which had rejected his embassy matched where it did not exceed Hitler's, did all he could to feed it. Wherever Hitler went, he followed, if he possibly could. He fed Hitler's hatred, his sense of rejection, his belief in the nobility of the offers he had made to Britain (and which had been rejected), and his belief in the existence in Britain of an American-Jewish-Freemasonry conspiracy (to which, by virtue of the British Royal Family's own masonic links, the British ruling class was so susceptible.)

Goering found Ribbentrop unendurable. Goebbels could only treat him as an ally when he, Goebbels, was out of favour with Hitler. At other times he was an unwelcome competitor for that deep and often maudlin fervour for Hitler which drove Goebbels throughout his life and led to his final self-immolation in the ruins of Hitler's bunker as the Soviet troops closed in. Rosenberg, the Nazi philosopher, despised Ribbentrop, as did most of the *Altkämpfer*, the Nazi street fighters of 1923 and the *Kampfzeit* of 1930–2, as a lily-handed Johnny-come-lately. Goaded by Heydrich's unquenchable ambition, Himmler targeted the Foreign Ministry (as he did the rest of the German state machinery and the armed forces) for infiltration and eventual take-over by the SS. Ribbentrop was hated, when he was not despised, by all but Hitler. Any chances of peace lay in someone breaking Ribbentrop's hold, or in Ribbentrop failing in such a fashion that he could not explain that failure away.

That being said, there is no doubt that the British, French and Polish Governments had by early April talked or conceptualized themselves into positions which were entirely contradictory. Central to each was the conviction that there were interests and positions for which in the end they would have to fight. Equally important was their belief that the clear demonstration to Germany of this fact, if accompanied by tactful handling, the avoidance of a head-on confrontation, and the assembly of a diplomatic, rather than a military line-up, would give Hitler pause.

The Polish position was the least realistic of the three, since it rested on the conviction that if things came to war, Poland was strong enough to hold out and Germany not strong enough to overwhelm her. This belief was the easier to maintain for lack of any serious military consideration over the previous twenty years to planning for war with Germany. Planning for such a war was made no easier by the division of responsibility for control of the Polish armed forces between the Ministry for Military Affairs and the Inspectorate General. Study of war with Germany had begun in 1936.[93] It had swiftly become clear that the Polish army, without a major programme of modernization, was no match for the Reichswehr. It was entirely unmechanized. Its artillery and machine guns were old and few in number. Its tanks were light and only fit for reconnaissance duties. The work of modernization had begun in 1936 but was still far from completed. Poland had defeated the onrush of the Red Army before Warsaw in 1920. The army was dominated by those who had fought in that war, none of whom had commanded any unit larger than a division. Poland's armies, her ammunition dumps, and her military infrastructure (so far as it existed) all faced east. Even in September 1939, six months after her acceptance of the Anglo-French guarantee, Poland had no overall plan of campaign against Germany. Moreover, the German military occupation of Slovakia had opened a new flank which hitherto there had been no need to consider. The only serious hope Poland had of successfully resisting Germany lay in obtaining Soviet aid. This the military junta ruled out of court. Apart from this, Poland would have to stock-pile all she needed for war before its outbreak. There was little chance of any Western aid reaching Poland once war had begun.

It was therefore essential not to provoke Germany unnecessarily. Efforts were made to persuade Hitler that the acceptance of the British guarantee was not intended as a hostile act towards Germany.[94] The Poles took particular care not to be trapped into helping Britain to create a unified Eastern Front by changing Poland's alliance with Romania, which was restricted to war against Russia, into a general agreement which would also operate against Germany. Beck and his colleagues were unable to believe that Hitler would risk a general war over Danzig, however he might huff and threaten.[95] They were agreed not to provoke him by concluding any agreement with the Soviet Union or becoming in any way involved in the British and French negotiations with the Soviets.[96]

In the meantime, however, Poland needed money from Britain and France with which to buy arms and stock-pile war supplies. She needed to know what Britain and France proposed to do should war come. And even at the cost of opening themselves to attack from the political opposition in either the Sejm or the press, anti-German feeling and individual action against the German minority in Poland needed to be damped down, a necessity of which the members of the Polish leadership were well aware even without the recurrent warnings passed on to them by the British and French Embassies in Warsaw.[97] It was to take some time before their conviction that Hitler was bluffing, even in Danzig, began to slip; by which time Polish pride and sense of national honour had carried them to the point where compromise, even had Hitler been prepared to accept it, was unthinkable if it involved any derogation of Poland's independence.

The British and French Governments were in an equally difficult position. The British Cabinet had been panicked into the guarantee of Poland by fears of an imminent German action. The guarantee had been only *ad interim*, a stop-gap measure to give Hitler pause while a more effective Eastern Front was created. It was generally agreed that to restrain Hitler at least the threat of a two-front war was required. The British Chiefs of Staff had no very strong hopes of Polish resistance being of any great duration.[98] The Anglo-French Staff talks of April 25 to May 4 in London agreed that Polish resistance would collapse in the early stages of fighting.[99]

It emerged that neither the British nor the French military was thinking of any major offensive action in the West. The French Permanent Committee of National Defence, meeting on April 9, had decided to give operations in the Mediterranean priority, should a war with both Axis powers break out.[100] With the minute striking force which was all the British army could provide until the results of the introduction of conscription and the arms necessary to supply the new territorial divisions were available, the only contribution to the defence of Poland Britain could envisage was in the air.[101] Here British military planning was itself diverted successively by the lure of a war with Italy who they believed could be easily and swiftly defeated, and the fears of a conflict in the Far East. It was not until mid-July that the British Chiefs of Staff returned to the idea of pressure on Italy as a means of helping Poland against Germany.[102] The outcome of their discussions of this possibility was depressingly negative. 'The fate of Poland will depend upon our ability to bring about the eventual defeat of Germany,' they stated.

It is hardly surprising therefore to find that the Anglo-Polish Staff talks held in Warsaw in late May amounted to little more than an exchange of information.[103] The Franco-Polish talks in Paris, however, constituted an outright deception.[104] The French agreed that if the major German military effort was unleashed against Poland 'France would undertake an offensive against Germany with the mass of her forces (beginning on the fifteenth day after mobilization).' This military agreement was not to come into effect until the political agreement, of which it was part, was signed.[105] General Gamelin, who signed the agreement, knew that there was no intention on France's side to assail the German fortifications in the West, not on the fifteenth day, not on the thirtieth, not within the first year of war. General Gamelin had three alternative answers if he was taxed on this point.[106] France would in fact remain on the defensive until Germany had been thoroughly weakened; or, she would undertake 'limited offensives on land in the West', whatever that meant; or, military decisions should be reserved to the moment of crisis and would not be taken in advance. This was how Gamelin's views struck Colonel Ismay, Secretary of the British Committee of Imperial Defence, the man who was to spend the war as Churchill's personal staff officer. None of these three alternatives covered General Gamelin's undertakings to the Poles. Poland was in fact overrun, her valiant forces obliterated, her cities devastated and Warsaw shelled into surrender, without any serious French action, let alone '*une action offensive avec le gros de ses forces*', being undertaken. The British undertaking to answer German air attacks on Polish civilian targets by all-out attacks on German civilian targets[107] (which was also not honoured) is only a minor betrayal by comparison.

Poland's Generals seem simply to have misunderstood. To them it was inconceivable that Britain and France had already written them off, with their thirty-seven divisions, eleven cavalry brigades and one brigade of light tanks.[108] They were confirmed in this misunderstanding by the dispatch to Poland of General Sir Edmund Ironside in July. General Sir Edmund Ironside had just returned from the Governor Generalship of Gibraltar to become Inspector General of British forces overseas. He, and many others, assumed he was being groomed to command the British Expeditionary Force. Nicknamed 'Tiny', he was 6 foot 4 inches in height, dashing, handsome, had a commanding presence, was a personal aide-de-camp to the King, and spoke excellent French.[109] Sir Alexander Cadogan thought him so stupid as to be impervious to anything.[110] General Pownall, the Director of Military Planning, commented on his appointment to Gibraltar: 'it is a mercy his soldiering days are over . . . more bluff and brawn than brain.'[111] A cavalry man himself, Ironside got on with the Polish soldiers like a house on fire. He had, after all, served with them in 1920. He left them unfortunately confirmed in all their illusions,[112] while, on return to London, he found it difficult to get any hearing from his military superiors. They recognized, as he did not, that the exiguous state of Britain's forces in 1939 gave them no way in which to press the French to move out of their enormously expensive defensive shell. Militarily the size of Britain's land forces in 1939 put her well below Poland, Romania, Greece or Turkey, and on a par with the Netherlands or Norway. By 1940 things would, it was hoped, be different. But in 1939, the British empire had no military aid to bring to Poland's rescue; nor, although the Poles understood this still less, did she have much to offer by way of financial aid.

It is perhaps here, even more than in the evasive manner in which the British and French dealt with the issue of military aid to Poland, that the ambivalence of the British Cabinet, the divisions within its ranks and the reluctance with which the onset of war was accepted can be seen most clearly. 'The worst times for me', Neville Chamberlain wrote to his sister Hilda,[113] 'and the only ones which really cause me worry are when I have to take a decision and don't clearly see how it is to come out.' Much of the Cabinet's discussions on aid to Poland demonstrates an unwillingness to take such decisions, or to reconcile the Foreign Office's demonstration of the clear need to do everything possible to sustain Poland's position (as well as to control her hotheads), and the Treasury's reluctance to do anything to weaken Britain's already shaky financial position, or to provoke a flight of capital from sterling or a run on the pound. Even before Colonel Beck's arrival in London in April, the Treasury, in the person of Sir Robert Waley, was expressing the hope that 'Colonel Beck would not be encouraged, as there was no money for Poland'.[114]

In May the Treasury invaded the Foreign Office's area of responsibility to argue that a loan to Poland would have the result that 'the feeling that we were encircling Germany by paying for Polish mobilization would be inevitable,'[115] adding for good measure, 'our losses of gold continue to be most disquieting and we have a transfer problem of our own which we are at our wits' end to resolve.' The Treasury was, however, not supported, for once, by the Board of Trade, so sticky on the subject of Balkan tobacco or buying off Bulgaria.[116] The Chiefs of Staff, aware that they could do nothing military for Poland, once fighting started, were also strongly in favour of offering money before the event.[117]

The Poles were in fact slower in asking for financial aid than the Foreign Office or the Embassy in Warsaw expected, demonstrating Beck's continuing belief that the limited acceptance of a British guarantee would bring Hitler back to the negotiating table.[118] It was not until the need arose to reply to the denunciation of the Non-Aggression Pact (as Beck did in his speech to the Sejm on May 5) that he yielded to Poland's financial authorities. The semi-mobilization of Poland's armed forces and economy, begun on March 22, was estimated by the British Embassy to be costing £2⅓ million sterling every month.[119] The Polish armed forces were short of everything and needed to stock-pile before war began. The Polish Minister of Finance, Eugeniusz Kwiatkowski, prophesied bankruptcy unless a British loan was forthcoming.[120] Without it Poland might have to yield to Germany. No more than the military could Poland's financial experts believe that Poland had not finally entered into her hour as the centrepiece of Britain's eastern strategy.

On May 12, the Polish Ambassador to London, Count Raczyński, asked for a forty-year loan to the extent of £60–65 million sterling, including £24 million in gold or convertible currency to buy outside

Britain.[121] As befits military men trapped in the unfamiliar world of finance and commerce (the principal Polish negotiating figure, Colonel Koc, head of the Bank Handlowy, was also a member of the Polish General Staff), the Poles anticipated a bargaining process. They would have been satisfied with £20 million, £10 million in disposable currencies.[122] They were, however, not dealing with a set of Oriental hucksters, anxious to achieve social advancement by aiding the aristocracy, but with the Treasury and the Bank of England, professional guardians of public funds and of Britain's world position, on whom the financial unrealism of the aristocrat (still less the aristocrat's imitators), on whom living beyond one's means was genetically imprinted, only made an impression of spendthrift frivolity. On April 20, the Committee of Imperial Defence (CID) had put Poland ninth in order of priority among the countries seeking aid from Britain, whose demands, given the enormous increase in Britain's own needs consequent on the imminent adoption of conscription, threatened to interfere with Britain's own rearmament programme.[123] Ahead of Poland lay Egypt, Iraq, Belgium, Portugal, Turkey, Greece, the Netherlands and Romania. Poland's needs were, however, put ahead of those of Yugoslavia and Afghanistan. If the Polish conception of financial bargaining lacked total contact with British patterns of financial behaviour, the CID's conception of strategic priorities seemed equally distant from reality.

The subsequent internal debates in Britain were bitter and protracted.[124] The Polish currency, the zloty, which was still tied to the value of gold, was, in the Treasury's view, unrealistically high. Poland was capable of raising at least £22 million by internal credits. Moreover, Poland's coal export quotas under the Anglo-Polish Coal Agreement required adjusting downwards. By the time the arguments were resolved it was June 28. The Treasury had succeeded in limiting the British offer to a mere £7.5 million in credits with the possibility of a small cash loan, on condition Poland took steps to deal with her currency position and agreed to a reasonable settlement of the Anglo-Polish Coal Agreement.[125] As always, the Treasury took the view of an old-fashioned banker extending an overdraft rather than of someone negotiating with an independent, sovereign state, let alone one as conscious of its pride as the Colonels' Poland.

Chamberlain's failure to exert any decisive leadership on this issue is very striking. Halifax pressed strongly for the abandonment of 'the commercial view': 'On the political side we were living in what was virtually a state of concealed war . . . the time had come when Poland . . . must be regarded from the military rather than the commercial point of view. . . . It might be claimed that the whole future of Europe might depend on Poland being sufficiently strengthened,' he claimed;[126] but, without Chamberlain's support, he could not carry the day. The Treasury offer was duly put to the Polish delegation on July 1.[127] It consisted of £8 million in export credit guarantees for orders for the land forces, together with 100 obsolescent Fairey Battle light bombers and 14 Hurricanes; £2 million for electrification; and £1.5 million for the purchase of key supplies. The issue of a cash loan (£5 million), to which it was hoped France would add 500 million francs, was made contingent on Polish devaluation and on concessions in the long-term trade talks. The Poles found meetings with the Treasury representatives, Sir Robert Waley (a member of one of the oldest Anglo-Jewish families) and Sir Frederick Leith-Ross, highly unpleasant.[128] Leith-Ross, in particular, treated them as potential de-faulting debtors, on discovering that they proposed to spend the £1.5 million not on industrial goods but on munitions. Waley, seething with rage, prophesied that Britain would have to allow Poland to spend all the money on military expenses; that it would be wasted; and that the Poles would very quickly be back, clamouring for more money to avert a financial collapse.[129]

Under these circumstances the Polish Government broke off the negotiations.[130] The Poles were not convinced by the arguments over devaluation. They thought Britain's attempt to limit Poland's exports of coal took back with one hand the very limited supplies of foreign exchange they were being offered by the other. And they resented most of all the control that the Treasury proposed to exercise over their drawings on the money loaned them. Their own delegation in London advised them to sign.[131] The British used the exigencies of the par-liamentary timetable (the loan could not be given without parliamen-tary legislation) to press them.[132] A part was played in the Poles' decision to reject the loan on the terms offered, by the illusion that the French were prepared to be more generous[133] and, once again, by the blustering assurances of General Ironside that he would explain the real situation to Mr Chamberlain on his return to Britain.[134] In the end, however, national pride and the deep sense of Polish independence ruled. The Polish Government had not rejected Hitler's invitation to become a German satellite to put itself under the dictates of Sir Frederick Leith-Ross. As for the latter, he seems to have held the Poles largely responsible for the inflammation of the Danzig issue – if not for the outbreak of war.[135]

Chamberlain remained silent. At the crucial period he was enraged: with the Cabinet and with the Tory opposition for pushing him steadily towards alliance with Russia; and with Robert Hudson for embroiling him publicly in an intrigue with Helmut Wohltat and Goering. The details of the negotiations with Poland were a matter for the appropriate officials, and Chamberlain usually trusted his officials unless they came from the Foreign Office. Like all neo-Wilsonian liberals (and in all but his marginal preference for nationalist authoritarians of the right, over internationalist authoritarians of the left, Chamberlain was a typical Wilsonian liberal), he would not accept that the senior officials of the Foreign Office were as much experts in the conduct of Britain's foreign relations and the methodology of protecting Britain's interests in general as the senior officials of the Board of Trade, the Chiefs of Staff or the Treasury were in matters economic, military or financial.

There remained the issue of the alliance with Poland. Discussions of an alliance to replace or consolidate the terms of the reciprocal guarantees agreed during Colonel Beck's visit to London were not pursued with great urgency by either side. In the third week in May Mr William Strang of the Foreign Office Central Department told the French[136] that the memoranda agreed on that occasion, which bound Britain to come to Poland's aid and Poland to Britain's in the event of German attack, and extended this even to German attack on the Netherlands, Belgium, Switzerland and Denmark, amounted to an alliance and certainly covered the case of a German attack on Danzig, even though Colonel Beck subsequently removed Switzerland from the list. Strang also called attention to the speech made by Chamberlain to an audience of Conservative women on May 11 at the Albert Hall. The memoranda were kept secret; their intention, however, was a constant theme in Halifax's and Chamberlain's speeches.

Draft memoranda on the proposed alliance were in fact exchanged early in June 1939.[137] The Poles were not inclined to hurry the matter until the Anglo-French negotiations with Russia were concluded.[138] Beck, on his side, made no attempt to press for a speedy end to the negotiations. He was, in fact, determined that they should be kept separate from the Anglo-Soviet negotiations for fear of Poland being drawn in. Not until August 2 did the Poles request the resumption of talks.[139] The collapse of the financial negotiations and the increased tempo of the Danzig crisis had much to do with their decision. The British, however, delayed for another fortnight, only changing their minds when the Soviet military, in the course of the Moscow Staff talks in August, demanded an undertaking on Polish co-operation in planning for war on the Eastern Front.[140] When Ribbentrop descended on Moscow on August 22, the Anglo-Polish alliance was still unsigned and the protocol to the Franco-Polish alliance, approved by the French Cabinet on May 11[141] and the signature of which had been adjourned by Bonnet on May 20,[142] remained equally unsettled.

In their place there were a series of British public assurances, most notably those given in a speech by Lord Halifax to the Royal Institute of International Affairs on June 28[143] and another given to Parliament on July 10 by Neville Chamberlain.[144] The German Ambassador in London explained the first away as the outcome of Jewish-French propaganda to sabotage the tendency to seek a 'constructive policy' towards Germany.[145] The second was regarded by the German Foreign Ministry as a 'harmful new factor', which had brought about 'a deterioration in rather than an improvement to the international situation'.[146] The speeches being thus mediated in transmission to Hitler and Ribbentrop, it was easy for the latter to play down their importance. The conclusion of a treaty might have been more difficult.

Hitler, however, was in no mood to listen to British blandishments. There were always people, Unity Mitford for example, to assure him that Britain, with only eight anti-aircraft batteries for London and equipment for two divisions only, could not fight a war.[147] His hostility towards Britain broke out regularly in his conversations with his intimates and with visiting statesmen alike. His growing hatred towards Poland, for which the Polish people were to pay terribly (more than six million Poles died under the German occupation), grew out of his hatred for Britain and those who had rejected him. For those who fawned on him he had nothing but contempt. While the British negotiations with the Soviets continued, these seem to have exercised some restraint. They were a useful argument in the hands of advocates of the 'little solution'. But this had little appeal to Hitler. He wanted his war; as he told his military adjutant, Major Gerhard Engel, in August[148] he was consumed with anxiety lest some 'blöder Gefühlsakrobat mit windelweichen Vorschlägen' (stupid acrobat of the emotions with wishy-washy proposals) would thwart him at the last moment.

If blame must be attached to diplomatists rather than statesmen, it must be to Sir Nevile Henderson, as to all the amateur intermediaries whom the prospect of war called into activity. Their reports and their conceptions failed to convey the raw hatred, the unswervable and determined hostility with which Hitler now regarded Britain. There were not lacking those who did their best to convey warnings. General Halder seems to have tried his best,[149] as did, apparently, General von Reichenau,[150] Fabrian von Schlabrendorff,[151] and Lieutenant Colonel von Schwerin of the General Staff.[152] All failed. At the end of July Chamberlain wrote to his sister:[153] 'All my information indicates that

Hitler now realizes he cannot get anything without a major war and has decided therefore to put Danzig into cold storage.' In one calendar month the German warship *Schleswig-Holstein* would open fire on the Polish garrison of the Westerplatte. The Soviet Union had destroyed British hopes of an Eastern Front. Hitler would have his war.

'If the British don't, maybe we will'

CHAPTER 19

THE JAPANESE ARMY OVERPLAYS
ITS HAND

The borders of Manchuria and Mongolia must be among the most desolate parts of the world. The border itself runs through a plain, covered in marsh and bogland, along the Khalkin-Gol (Halha to the Japanese), a slow-running river some 130–150 yards (120–140 m) wide, and 6 or more feet (2 m) deep. From it a tributary, the Khailastyn-Gol (Japanese: Holsten), runs eastwards into Manchurian territory. East of the river, three small hills, the Bolshegve Heights, rise some 150 feet (45 m) above the plain, the highest being the hill called Nomonhan. The border as always was in dispute, the Soviets claiming it lay some 10 miles (16 km) east of the Khalkin-Gol, the puppet Government of Manchukuo, dominated by the Japanese Kwantung Army, claiming it lay along the river itself.

Soviet influence had been firmly established in the nominally independent Mongolian People's Republic since 1936. In the winter of 1938/9, Stalin's man, Choibalsan, overthrew the nationalist and independently minded Premier, and put down mutinies among the people's armed forces, on the border with Manchuria near Nomonhan, moving troops loyal to him into the area. He certainly would have welcomed an external enemy, as would Stalin, conscious of the vulnerability of the Soviet position to Japanese adventurism. Soviet troops in Mongolia were steadily reinforced. At the beginning of March a mixed Soviet-Mongolian detachment was moved to Tamsag, the principal Mongolian town in the Nomonhan sector. On March 10, in his speech to the 18th Party Congress, Stalin boasted that any invasion of the USSR would be met by double strength. In 1936 Mongolia and the Soviet Union had signed a treaty of friendship and mutual defence. In practice any attack on Mongol territory would be regarded as an attack on the Soviet Union.

On the Japanese side, the Kwantung Army had been virtually a law unto itself, the agency in which the young extremist military faction

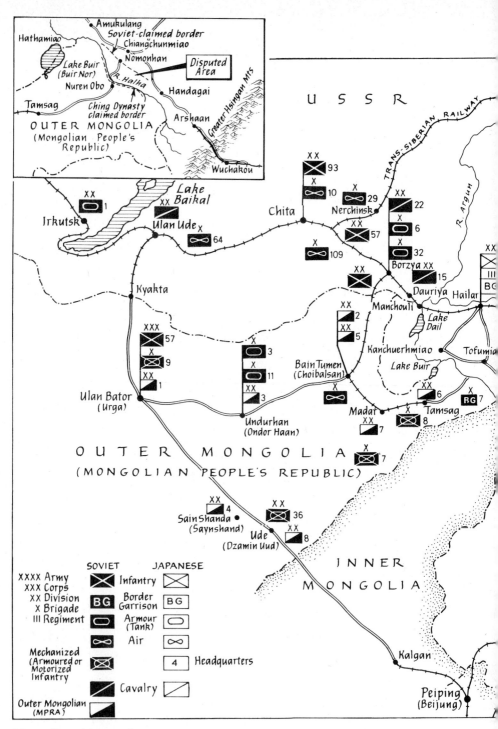

Mongolia and Nomonhan

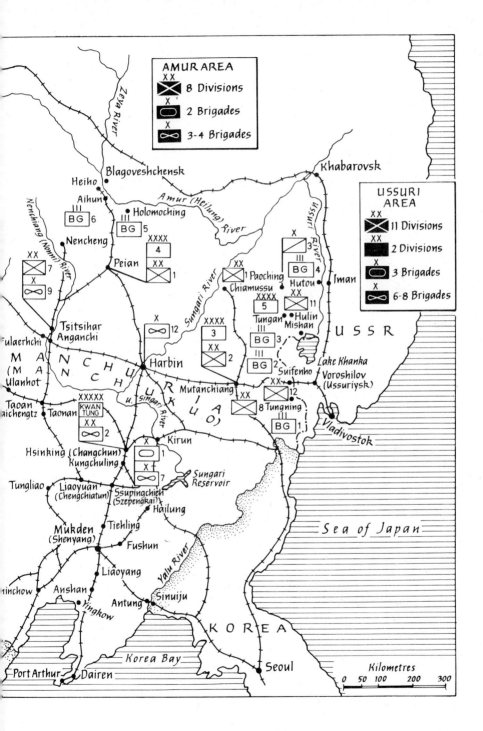

AMUR AREA

XX 8 Divisions

X 2 Brigades

X 3-4 Brigades

USSURI AREA

XX 11 Divisions

■ 2 Divisions

X 3 Brigades

X 6-8 Brigades

Zeya River

Nenchiang (Nonni) River

Blagoveshchensk

Khabarovsk

Heiho

Aihun

III
BG 6

Holomoching

III
BG 5

Amur (Heilung) River

Ussuri River

Nencheng

XXXX
4

XX
1

Peian

X
3

III
BG 4

Iman

XX
7

X
9

Sungari River

XX
1 Paoching

Chiamussu

Hutou

XXXX
5

XX
11

Tungan

Hulin

Mishan

U S S R

Tsitsihar

Anganchi

Fulaerhchi

M A N C H U

(M A

Ulanhot

X
12

XXXX
3

XX
2

III
BG 3

Lake Khanka

III
BG 2

Voroshilov
(Ussuriysk)

Harbin

R I

u. Sungari River

Mutanchiang

Suifenho

XX
12

Taoan
aichengtz Taonan

XXXX
KWAN
TUNG

XX
2

Kirun

K U O)

XX
8 Tungning

III
BG 1

Vladivostok

Hsinking (Changchun)

Kungchuling

X
1

X
7

Sungari
Reservoir

Sea of Japan

Tungliao

Liaoyuan
(Chengchiatun)

Ssupingchieh
(Szepengkai)

Hailung

Tiehling

Mukden
(Shenyang)

Fushun

Liaoyang

Yalu River

inchow Anshan

Yingkow

Antung Sinuiju

K O R E A

Port Arthur Dairen

Korea Bay

Seoul

Kilometres

0 50 100 200 300

had the most influence, for some eight years. Much of its original strength since the Japanese coup of 1931 had been diverted into the now separate North China Army, deeply embroiled in the war with Chiang Kai-shek's China. In April 1939, worried by the increasing frequency of frontier incidents between Mongolian border guards and the Manchurian frontier forces, the Kwantung Army commander, General Ueda, had laid down strict rules for dealing with frontier clashes. While prohibiting any invasion of Mongolian territory these rules devolved responsibility for dealing with border incidents upon the local divisional commanders.

Such incidents had been increasing since January; they had not, in the main, involved any Japanese units. On May 4, however, a party of some fifty Mongolian horsemen had crossed the Khalkin-Gol and ridden as far as the Bolshegve Heights. After an exchange of fire lasting some ten hours, Manchurian border guards had driven them back. There were further incidents on May 10 and 11. The area fell into that covered by the Kwantung Army's 23rd Division, a recently raised unit which had still to complete its training. Its commander, General Komatsubara, decided that his orders required him to act. He asked for, and was given, generous air support, and dispatched a task force consisting of the divisional reconnaissance regiment with two infantry companies and all available Manchurian forces. On May 15, Japanese air attack drove the Mongolian forces back across the river; the task force then retired, its duty done.

Two days later, on May 17, Soviet troops recrossed the river. This time they were in strength, a rapid deployment force with guns, tanks and anti-tank guns; Soviet engineers built several bridges across the river; Soviet air activity increased. Determined to teach them a lesson, at dawn on May 28, the Japanese attacked in force: Japanese infantry, Manchurian cavalry, and light motorized Japanese forces, supported by forty aircraft.

The Soviet forces had been built up too, though not to quite the same numerical strength, some 2,000 Japanese and Manchurians facing some 1,500 Soviet infantry and Mongolian cavalry. The Japanese had a light tank, the Soviets some ten tanks, fourteen field guns and howitzers. The original Japanese task force ran into a trap; the supporting Japanese forces, having lost their way and their bearings and lacking contact with their superiors, failed to come to its assistance, and the encircled task force was wiped out. The Soviets did not do much better. Various groups blundered into the other Japanese forces and took heavy casualties. Sporadic fighting took place over the next few days until on June 1 the Japanese exercised a 'lateral advance' (Japan army-speak for retreat), leaving the Soviets firmly established across the Khalkin-Gol. Neither side was very satisfied with the outcome. Soviet intelligence was extremely faulty and the movements of the individual units on both sides in the almost featureless terrain were far from well co-ordinated. Both sides rushed to build up their forces. On June 14–17, Soviet air forces attacked Japanese targets on the edge of the war zone. The Kwantung Army, fearing that its decision would be countermanded in Tokyo, launched its own air offensive deep into Mongolia, without clearing the matter with its superiors. The authorities in Tokyo were already deeply involved in a parallel crisis with Britain over the Tientsin concession. Furious, the Emperor called for the punishment of the Kwantung Army Commander.[1] The Kwantung reply, penned by the most hawkish of its junior staff officers, still further angered the Army Command in Tokyo. General Itagaki issued a restraining order and the air offensives into Mongolia were halted. The Kwantung Army was still, however, free to attack the Soviets, now firmly established across the Khalkin-Gol in what the Japanese still regarded as Manchurian territory.

It was at this juncture that the Soviet High Command, worried by the low effectiveness of its Far Eastern forces after the Stalinist purges had struck down Marshal Blyukher and the bulk of his commanding officers, turned to an obscure Corps Commander, General Georgy Konstantinovich Zhukhov. Once a non-commissioned officer of the 10th Novgorod Dragoons of the 10th Cavalry Division of the Imperial Russian Army, Zhukhov was a protégé of Stalin's favourite, Marshal Timoshenko, and shielded by him from the Stalinist purge; he was a veteran of the civil war, and one of the boldest experimenters with mobile armoured warfare in the Soviet manœuvres of the early 1930s. He was also a man who believed in thorough reconnaissance and massive preparations. He asked for massive reinforcements and got them: one tank brigade, three mechanized brigades, a motorized rifle division, heavy artillery and one hundred fighter aircraft. Thereafter the Japanese were consistently out-gunned and out-numbered in all arms and soon lost the command of the air.

The Soviets had another advantage. In June 1939 Richard Sorge, the head of the Soviet military intelligence ring in Tokyo, reported that the Japanese armed forces required fundamental re-organization which would take another one and a half to two years.[2] He added for good measure that there was 'no basis for fears this incident will lead to widespread war with the Soviet Union'.

The Japanese were also reinforcing. At the beginning of July General Komatsubara had under his command the entire tank strength of the

Kwantung Army, some 38 medium and 35 light tanks. To these, towards the end of July, there was to be added its small stock of heavy guns. The Japanese sense of *amour propre*, however, prevented him being superseded in command, as major reinforcement on the Soviet side would have necessitated. Japanese forces were supplemented by the addition of élite units from other parts of the Kwantung Army, but the conviction that the Soviets could easily be dealt with and that, despite all the Japanese intelligence to the contrary, this was still only a frontier skirmish, blinded the Kwantung Army to the realities.

Throughout July the Japanese were to launch a series of offensives against the Soviet forces on both sides of the Khalkin-Gol. The attempt to clear the left bank was a failure, depending as it did on a single bridge which, unlike the Soviet bridges, was not strong enough to take the Japanese armour. The armoured regiments had to be withdrawn after half their strength had been lost in three days' fighting at the beginning of July. The Japanese infantry, doggedly attacking at night, managed to drive the Soviet forces back to the river, but they were unable to cope with the accuracy and range of the Soviet artillery. The Japanese heavy guns proved equally ineffective. And the Japanese supply system never really coped with the problem of transport over Manchurian roads to a front some 90 miles (140 km) from the nearest railhead. Japanese infantry were brave and persistent under fire, but the deification of individual courage and the primitive nature of communications meant that command and control disappeared with the first charge (much as with the Cavalier cavalry in the English Civil War), leaving the commanding officers at all levels in complete ignorance of where their forces were in relation to one another. The older Soviet tanks, invulnerable to Japanese artillery fire, proved, with their petrol-fuelled engines, giving off inflammable vapours in the intense summer heat, vulnerable to Japanese-style 'Molotov cocktails', discarded apple-juice bottles half-filled with petrol and supplied with inflammable wicks. But more modern Soviet tanks, diesel-engined and immune to such weapons, were on their way to reinforce the front. By the end of July, the Japanese, with 4,500 casualties, were ordered to go over to the defensive.

In the meantime, however, the Japanese army in North China, bitterly angry with the indecisiveness displayed by the Government in Tokyo over the pact negotiations with Germany and totally ignoring what was happening in Manchuria, was doing its best to provoke war with Britain. The Japanese Cabinet had in fact since early April been deadlocked over the vital issues of whether the alliance with Germany should be confined in its operations to the Soviet Union and whether its operation should be automatic or left to the judgment of the individual signatories. The five Ministers – Ishiwata for Finance, General Seishiro Itagaki, the broad-shouldered firebrand who was Minister of War, a veteran of Japan's invasion of Siberia and closely involved in the Mukden conspiracy which had set off the aggression against Manchuria in 1931, the ageing, white-haired Hachiro Arita, Foreign Minister, the smooth, handsome, arrogant Admiral Mitsumasa Yonai, Navy Minister, and the imperturbable Baron Kuchiro Hiranuma, the Premier – met regularly throughout April and May in efforts to find a compromise between the army's insistence on a general alliance and the navy's determination not to be dragged into a Pacific war at the heels of an irresponsible European dictator.

Arita was convinced that a European war was inevitable, at the latest by the spring of 1940. Ishiwata and his Ministry were obsessed by the mounting cost of the war in China which they had convinced themselves, as had the army, was only kept going by the support given to Chiang Kai-shek by Britain, America and the Soviet Union. In China, moreover, two currencies were at war, the Chinese nationalist scrip, called *fapi*, and the notes issued by the Japanese-sponsored puppet Governments. Major efforts were being expended by the British on keeping the *fapi* going; it was still the principal currency employed in the very considerable volume of British trade and investment in China. Ishiwata found himself obliged to find funds not only to finance the substantial expenses of the campaign and occupation of China but also to back the Japanese puppet currency in China against *fapi*, behind which lay the financial support of Britain.

Behind these five men lay other forces rooted more deeply in the soil of Japan. The terrorist nationalist societies, comparatively quiescent since the failure of the army mutiny in February 1936, were active again. The young staff officers, the colonels and majors who despised the whole civilian side of Japanese life, were muttering against the sinister influences around the Emperor. Against them stood in the shadows the last of the five statesmen, the *Genro*, who had created modern Japan, the ageing Prince Kimmochi Saionji, with his amanuensis and right arm, Baron Harada. They were of the Japanese aristocracy, stable, courteous, reserved, dedicated to the maintenance of the essential institutions of Japan and to the position of the Emperor, and determined not to yield to the demands of people one of them stigmatized as 'cheap and unpresentable'. In the group around these two men were the Lord Privy Seal, Kurakei Yuasa, the Minister for the Royal Household, the tubby Tsuneo Matsudaira, and other former Ministers.

There were, however, among their number a certain number of appeasers. One was Baron Kiou, the Home Minister, who acted as an intermediary in efforts to convert Yuasa to the army's way of thinking. Fearing for the Emperor's position if the army and the right wing turned against him, Kiou exerted himself to persuade the *Genro* of the need to appease the army's feelings.[3] Baron Hiranuma, the Premier, was another. From the beginning of May he moved over to full support of the army advocacy of the alliance, despite knowing the repugnance of the Emperor himself to the army viewpoint and to alliance with Italy and Germany.[4] For this was the final crux. The Emperor, the Tenno or 'son of heaven', declared in the constitution to be 'sacred and inviolable', blood relation to Amaterasu Omikamir, the Sun Goddess, the Showa Emperor, whom few Japanese knew by his given name of Hirohito, was a scientifically minded liberal. He thought General Itagaki a fool.[5] When Prince Kanin, Chief of the Army General Staff, came to him at Itagaki's insistence to attempt to convert him to the idea of an alliance with Germany, he refused to listen and reprimanded him.[6]

Baron Hiranuma began to weaken towards the end of April. One factor in his change of heart may have been the unremitting pressure of the extreme nationalist Japanese-language press. Another may have been Oshima's and Shiratori's demands to be allowed to resign their Embassies (in Berlin and Rome respectively) rather than carry out the instructions sent to them on March 22.[7] Hiranuma decided to make a personal appeal to Hitler and Mussolini, and the Inner Cabinet met repeatedly to agree on the terms in which this was to be couched. The idea was certainly a dramatic one, and the assurances Baron Hiranuma wished to give, that Japan was finally and unshakeably resolved to come to Germany's and Italy's aid, even if they were attacked by a country other than the Soviet Union, went most of the way to meeting the demands of the army and of Hitler. But there were two initial qualifications to those assurances: for the time being Japan was in no position to fulfil her resolve; and in view of Japan's international situation she would be forced to be very careful in the explanations given to other powers when the alliance was signed. The whole appeal was to be bound up with solemn assurances of the sincerity and the considerations of a moral and spiritual nature which had led Hiranuma to make the gesture.

The text of the message was finally agreed on May 3, and given by Arita to Ambassadors Ott for Germany and Auriti for Italy the following day, with an ill grace so obvious as to provoke Ott to comment on it.[8] Arita had, however, some reason for congratulating himself. The two vital reservations followed his draft; and he had successfully squashed Baron Hiranuma's desire to include a further assurance that if Germany was involved in war *before* Japan was in a position to fulfil her resolve, Japan would adopt a position of non-belligerency. He had also thwarted General Itagaki's desire to see the message spell out in more detail what changes in Japan's circumstances would free her to fulfil her resolve.

The dramatic gesture, the invocation of Baron Hiranuma's secret word, did nothing, however, to ease the strains either between Tokyo and Berlin or inside the Baron's Cabinet. With astonishing discourtesy neither Hitler nor Mussolini answered or even acknowledged the Japanese message. General Oshima cabled instead the text of his own alternative compromise, which had been drafted in consultation with Friedrich Gaus, the German Foreign Ministry's legal expert. This was too much for Arita. He accused General Itagaki of giving Oshima prior warning of the message and declared that, in view of Hiranuma's support of the General, he, Arita, would have to resign. Admiral Yonai refused to discuss Oshima's draft until a formal reply was received to the Baron's message.[9]

The deliberations of the Inner Cabinet were to continue throughout May, the signs of Germany's and Italy's determination to sign an alliance without Japan rather weakening Hiranuma's resolve and the army's stand for a time. The bitterness of the younger officers, especially in China, grew steadily for this frustration. The apparent progress of the Anglo-Soviet negotiations alarmed them still further and seems to have given Arita second thoughts; but the navy remained adamant. For Yonai, firmly backed by his deputy, Admiral Yamamoto, one of Japan's great naval strategists, what was at stake was not the possibility of an Anglo-Soviet alliance but the certainty, if Japan joined the Axis, of an alliance between Britain and the United States. They were determined that it should be for them to say when, how and against whom their fleet was to fight.

It was in the midst of this division that Ribbentrop's last despairing appeal of May 15 arrived. At the Five Ministers' Conference on May 20, after long talks between General Itagaki and Admiral Yonai and their Staffs, agreement seemed to have been reached on a new formulation. The matter was greatly complicated by General Oshima's action in giving the Germans an assurance that the operation of the alliance would be automatic, a promise that he had never been authorized to give. Arita, furious, demanded that Oshima be instructed to retract this; being told by Hiranuma that there was no question of this, he seems to have decided to combat his Ambassador's chicanery with equal chicanery of his own. The Cabinet decided on May 20 to accept Ribbentrop's draft with some small changes in wording, but when Arita cabled this decision to Rome and Berlin he added that Japan's decision to honour any alliance she might sign with Germany would not be automatic on German involvement in war but would depend on the prevailing circumstances.[10]

This was going too far, and the army scented victory. Demands for Arita's resignation grew, and General Itagaki, in triumph, cabled Oshima to stop any further pressure as the atmosphere in Tokyo was now thoroughly in the army's favour.[11] Arita was saved by the Navy Minister, Admiral Yonai, and Yamamoto, his deputy, who found the army intrigues scandalous and disloyal to the Emperor. On May 27 a new conspiracy was uncovered by the secret police, directed at the assassination of Admirals Yonai and Yamamoto, together with Yuasa and Matsudaira, Ministers in the Royal entourage whom the extremists held particularly responsible for the pernicious liberalism of the Emperor's views. What alarmed the court most was evidence that the secret police would have joined the conspirators had there been any evidence of substantial army support for them.[12] May 27 was the anniversary of the great Japanese naval victory over Russia at Tsushima in 1905. The streets filled with nationalist demonstrations and processions in favour of the alliance.

Behind the shuttered windows of the Navy and War Ministries further conferences were in progress to evolve a new formula to replace that which Arita had successfully scotched and Oshima and Shiratori again rejected. The formula they agreed on was adopted by the Inner Cabinet on June 5 and cabled to Oshima and Shiratori the following day. If Germany was involved in war with the Soviet Union, Japan would honour her obligations at once. If Germany was involved in war with any other power, Japan would enter the war when the three allies agreed that this would be in the common interest of the alliance.[13] This was, so the army spokesman assured Ott, a great step forward.[14] The navy had abandoned its insistence that Japan's entry into a war should depend entirely on Japan's interests.

It is here that one is tempted to agree with the Emperor's verdict on General Itagaki. His assurances were nonsense. The navy had agreed to no such thing. As Admiral Yamamoto put it, in the event of war 'we have no obligation from beginning to end – in other words we would not take part in a war.'[15] But this time Itagaki had the bit between his teeth. On June 15 Oshima passed on to the Germans the lengthiest of assurances from General Itagaki as to the meaning and importance of these new instructions. The German drafts were to be accepted without restriction or reservation. It turned out, however, that the Japanese Cabinet still insisted on a formal but secret exchange of notes admitting Japan's military incapacity, something which Ribbentrop rejected at once on the sensible grounds that secrecy could not be maintained in such circumstances and that once the notes became known the effect of the treaty would be lost entirely.[16] Oshima cabled for new instructions. He never received an answer.

The Japanese army was now almost completely involved in the crisis which had developed over the British concession at Tientsin in northern China; in this large Chinese city under Japanese occupation, the British held a small enclave with a garrison of a single battalion of British infantry and a British municipal council. Adjoining it were still smaller French and Italian concessions with even weaker garrisons. Tientsin itself had a Japanese-sponsored puppet administration. Around it lay division after division of the Japanese army, with tanks, artillery and aircraft. From within the concession nationalist Chinese guerrillas carried out terrorist operations against the Japanese and their collaborators. In the vaults of the principal British bank in the concession lay £800,000 worth of silver, the property of the nationalist Central Bank of China, a sizeable part of Chinese currency reserves. Also within the concession Chinese nationalist bank-notes, *fapi*, circulated and percolated into Japanese-held Tientsin, depressing the value of the occupation *yuan* issued by the puppet Federal Reserve Bank in Peking.

The British and foreign-held concessions, from being a mere thorn in the Japanese flesh, were rapidly being promoted in the thinking of the occupying forces to the main cause of the continuing Chinese resistance. The presence of armed foreign, white, Caucasian troops, in the middle of the area over which the sun of Japan should exercise unchallenged sway, struck the young officers of the North China Army as verging on blasphemy, a defilement of all their ideals. Shanghai was bad enough. Throughout April and May there were constant thrusts at the international concession in Shanghai. A Japanese landing party was disembarked at Kulangsu, a small island with an international settlement opposite the Japanese-held port of Amoy. Houses were searched and arrests made after the assassination of the collaborationist head of the Amoy Chamber of Commerce. This attempt to take over an international enclave was blocked by the landing of British, French and American armed bluejackets. And Shanghai was on the whole too big a nut to crack, though there was some nervousness for a time that the local Japanese forces might try a *coup d'état* on their own.

Tientsin, was, however, a different matter. The only power

Some sort of victory urgently needed

seriously involved was Britain. There was no access to the concession by sea. And the British Government misunderstood and mishandled the Japanese case so as to make it easy for the local army authorities, backed by General Itagaki and the War Ministry, to provoke a crisis. The course of the crisis provides an outstanding example of failure of communication. Britain was only saved from war with Japan by the toughness and negotiating skill of Sir Robert Craigie, British Ambassador in Tokyo, who, with Sir Percy Loraine, is perhaps the ablest member of the British diplomatic service in this period to fail to win proper recognition for his stature and achievements from his fellow countrymen. Lesser men than they finished their careers as distinguished members of the House of Lords, directors of the Suez Canal Company, or holders of well-heeled sinecures, laden with high honours. Sir Robert Craigie's career ended when the outbreak of war with Japan terminated his tenure of the Tokyo Embassy. He was stigmatized, quite unfairly, as an appeaser, and his final report, with its critical notes on the handling of relations with Japan in 1940–1, was suppressed.

The British concession in Tientsin had been under Japanese pressure since the middle of 1935, when the Japanese had prevented the Chinese silver reserves in Tientsin from being sent to Shanghai. By October 1938, the Japanese were agitating against an alleged British plan to transport the silver to Shanghai on a British warship. At that time the French had proposed that the silver should be sealed into the vaults where it was lying and left untouched until the end of the Sino-Japanese hostilities. Japanese protests against the circulation of *fapi* inside the concessions and against the operations of Chinese guerillas had led to the removal from the concession area of all Japanese residents and forces and to the erection of Japanese-policed barriers at the exits to the concessions.

Things had seemed to get better in January 1939 when the former Japanese Military Attaché in London, Lieutenant General Masahuru Homma, was appointed commander of the local Japanese forces. He was no friend of the Axis powers and was hostile to the proposed alliance. He took down the barriers and proved courteous and friendly; but he was determined to stamp out terrorism, and his subordinates, especially Major General Tomoyuki Yamashita, his Chief of Staff, were hand-in-glove with the extremists and determined to use this issue to force Homma into a showdown. They replaced the barriers with an electrified fence totally surrounding the concessions, and began search-ing foreigners leaving the concessions for *fapi*. They demanded the 'dismissal' of 'undesirable elements' in the municipal police force, their replacement by Japanese, and the surrender of suspected terrorists. Craigie managed to secure an alleviation of this tension by pressure in Tokyo and by sending his Military Attaché, the thoroughly Japano-phile, Japanese-speaking Major General Piggott, to Tientsin to talk over matters with General Homma and with General Sugeyomo, the overall Japanese Commander in North China.

On April 9 the manager of the Japanese puppet Federal Reserve Bank in Tientsin was murdered by a Chinese terrorist in the Grand Theatre within the British concession. A Swiss businessman was killed, and a White Russian who tried to seize the assassin severely wounded. The gunman escaped.

General Piggott had already reported that the situation in Tientsin was more dangerous than any that had hitherto obtained. The Japanese could not understand why Britain allowed terrorist activities to con-tinue, and only interned guerrilla leaders when they were apprehended. Even Britain's friends were bewildered and resentful. The danger of a head-on clash existed. The British Consul General, Mr Jamieson, therefore took advantage of this assassination to offer his co-operation with the Japanese. They were invited to lend gendarmerie to the British municipal police and to co-operate in raids on any terrorist organiz-ations within the concession area that they could identify. Anyone arrested and shown to be connected with the crime would be handed over to them; others found in possession of bombs or arms would be detained.[17]

The Japanese police had already caught one man on a completely different charge, who, to save himself, had volunteered information about the assassins, a group of six men living in the British concession. At dead of night Japanese gendarmes, accompanied by British municipal police, swooped on the house where these men were living. Four men were arrested and handed over to the Japanese for questioning, under a personal assurance that they would not be tortured and that they would be returned to British custody within five days. On the evening of the fourth day the Japanese police stated that two of the men had confessed to complicity in the murder and that they would like to stage a reconstruction of the crime in the presence of British officials. Early the following morning, before the Chinese crowds were out, this duly took place in the presence of the Chief of Police, a British Major and a British Consul. The Consul questioned the two men, and formed the view that they were implicated in the murder. They were then taken away by the Japanese, and returned to British custody late that afternoon.

The two men must have known that unless something intervened to prevent it, they would shortly be handed back to the Japanese for trial and execution. On their return they alleged that they had been beaten and their stomachs filled with kerosene to make them confess. The British local police concluded that they had indeed been tortured by water, but that as only two out of the four had confessed, their confessions were probably genuine. The two officials who had seen the reconstruction of the crime had seen no signs of torture and had accepted the genuineness of the confessions. After seeing the reconstruction they had breakfasted with the Japanese officials at the race club and let them understand that the men would in fact be handed over. The other two men had simply admitted to membership of the gang and being accomplices before or after the crime. The confessions stated that the two men had been paid $100 each for their help in the murder (they had, it was alleged, covered the get-away by car of the assassin and his immediate assistant), and the Japanese produced $80 of the money in one case and the suspect's uncle, to whom it had been paid.[18]

On the return of the four men to British custody, Madame Chiang Kai-shek intervened almost at once with Sir Archibald Clark-Kerr, the British Ambassador in China, to attempt to prevent their return to Japanese custody.[19] The murdered man was one of three bank managers, all Japanese collaborators, to be murdered from bases in British concessions within the months of April and May, and the four men apprehended were officially said to be members of the Chinese 9th Route Army. Mme Chiang faced the possibility that if Britain acceded to the Japanese requests in the case of these four men, guerilla activities in occupied China would be made considerably more difficult.

It is at this point that the failure in communication and understanding began. Mr Jamieson, the Consul General, considered it obvious that whatever the strength of the evidence as to their involvement in the assassination, the men were admitted terrorists and should be handed over to the Japanese on the presentation of a warrant from the local court. The alternative seemed to be Japanese action against the concession as a whole, in favour of which the local Japanese authorities were now whipping up the local press,[20] the destruction of the very considerable British investments, and the imprisonment of the local British community with whose safety he was charged. The clarity of his own convictions led him to fail to appreciate the need to provide London with the full evidence on which these were based. He was not aided by a certain changeability of opinion among the local British police authorities as to the genuineness of the confessions. As a result it was not until mid-June that he provided London with full information on the reconstruction of the crime and not until June 25 that he revealed that the Japanese had been led to believe that the two men would be returned to them.[21]

In the absence of this information, Lord Halifax had an extremely ill-timed attack of moralism. In the absence of any prima facie evidence against the accused, he ruled that they could not be handed over to the Japanese. He was, however, prepared to authorize the handing-over to the Japanese of two other men who had been caught by the concession police with bombs in their possession.[22] Clearly these two *were* terrorists; and Lord Halifax had no objection to handing terrorists over. He ignored, however, Mr Jamieson's repeated recommendation that, whereas the four men might or might not have prima facie evidence against them for the assassination, they too were clearly and admittedly terrorists.

Even this decision had taken Lord Halifax nearly two months to reach. By June 5, the day he finally communicated it to the British Embassy in Tokyo, it was too late. General Homma's patience was at an end, and the extremists on his staff, led by General Yamashita, had seized their chance. On June 1, General Homma had felt obliged to ask for a definite decision on the two men to be reached by June 7.[23] His note requesting this was polite and carefully phrased, but the setting of a

353

time limit gave Yamashita a chance to approach the army authorities in Tokyo directly. They seized the opportunity, as a means of pushing their own Government into open conflict with Britain and mobilizing demonstrations against it to force the conclusion of the alliance with Germany. General Homma was ordered to prepare to blockade the concession. Orders were issued on June 10, and the blockade began on June 15.[24]

The Ministry of War in Tokyo envisaged occupation as the next step and did not anticipate any very marked British reaction.[25] On June 14 the blockade was duly begun. Everyone entering or leaving the concession was searched, the Japanese officers taking the greatest delight in inflicting indignities on male and female British citizens. Several were made to strip publicly at bayonet point. Food and fuel supplies were interrupted, shipping interfered with, business obstructed. The Japanese military authorities issued a statement declaring that the blockade would not be lifted until the British authorities agreed to eliminate the use of *fapi*, hand over the Chinese silver, suppress anti-Japanese wireless broadcasts and forbid the use of anti-Japanese textbooks in Chinese schools within the concession. All support for the Chinese nationalists was to end. The fate of the four men was unimportant, declared the Japanese military authorities, and a British concession on this point would not cause the blockade to be lifted. 'The arrow is already off the bow and therefore the question cannot be settled by the mere transfer of the four suspect assassins,' a Japanese military spokesman declared.[26] 'After Tientsin, it will be the turn of Shanghai,' said another.[27]

The failure of understanding between Lord Halifax and Mr Jamieson in Tientsin had thus led the British Government into a major confrontation with the Japanese at a time when military and naval advice to the Cabinet was emphasizing the total absence of any margin of extra strength in the face of the threat of war in Europe, and at a time when Lord Halifax was perfectly well aware that the accession of Japan to the Axis alliance hung on the precarious balance of opinion in Tokyo. So far as the general British public knew, there was no evidence against the four Chinese and the Japanese were trying to force the surrender of four innocents. Public opinion in Britain was incensed by the lurid reports carried in the press of the indignities inflicted by the Japanese soldiery on the British in Tientsin. The 'Yellow Peril' was evoked. White English women were being made publicly to strip. Children were being terrified. The feelings of anti-Asiatic racialism, always latent among the British people, leapt to the fore. The Oriental villain of a hundred films and a thousand cheap thrillers, sinister, alien, sadistic and lustful, was conjured up again and again in the popular press and on the newsreels. Lord Halifax's parliamentary statement of June 20 only confirmed this popular view.[28] The Chamberlain Cabinet seemed to face the two alternatives of an impossible and unnecessary war or a completely humiliating climb-down which would have deplorable effects on both her friends in America and her enemies in Europe, as both Sir Ronald Lindsay from Washington[29] and Sir Percy Loraine from Rome[30] pointed out with some force.

A considerable part was played in this confusion by the self-contained character of the Far Eastern section of the Foreign Office with its very definite pro-Chinese bias, personified especially by its adviser, Sir George Sansom. From Tokyo, Craigie argued consistently that what was at issue was the need not to play into the hands of the extremists, and to strengthen the moderate faction around the court. But to Sansom and his fellow Sinophiles there was no distinction between the moderates and the extremists. Both groups wanted the expansion of Japan at China's expense.[31] Everything had to be done therefore to strengthen China against them. This inability to distinguish between irrational extremists, who were on the whole not amenable to considerations of fear, prudence and practicability, and rational moderates who were; this insistence that friendliness must imply complete identity of views, otherwise the friendliness (as expressed by the moderates) was mere hypocrisy; this failure to consider things either in terms of Britain's overall commitments outside their own areas of expert knowledge, or to consider their own areas solely in the light of British interests, is characteristic of many self-styled experts in foreign affairs and often, as in this case, a cloak for a basically ideological approach to international politics.

This was to dawn on Lord Halifax with awful clarity five days after the blockade began, on his receipt of an extremely severe and critical telegram from Sir Robert Craigie.[32] Even if the general policy of backing Chiang Kai-shek as the means of restraining and absorbing Japanese energies in the Far East was strategically justifiable and morally correct, the truth was that it had failed in its purpose if it led to a direct Anglo-Japanese confrontation. Unless the British concessions with their sizeable British populations were to be abandoned entirely, so long as they were surrounded by Japanese forces their safety was pre-eminent. The only thing to do was to take advantage of the internal struggle in Tokyo, and play upon the unwillingness of the civilian members of the Japanese Cabinet to be pushed into action at the behest of the military they had so far contained on the alliance issue.

The news of the blockade did not find the British Cabinet or its advisers at their best.[33] Although the situation in Danzig was steadily deteriorating, and reports of Hitler's determination to settle the dispute by force were increasing, the Cabinet actually diverted the war-planners to grapple with the problems of an economic blockade of Japan. Lord Chatfield, the Minister for the Co-ordination of Defence, had spent the better part of his naval career, including six years as First Sea Lord, dedicated to the belief that the safety of the empire, especially that of Australia and New Zealand, depended on the abandonment of Britain's position in the Mediterranean if this was necessary to the dispatch of the main fleet to the Far East. Overruled, in the debates in March, in favour of a Mediterranean-first strategy, he now returned to the attack, aided by a change in the direction of the Admiralty, where his successor, Admiral Sir Roger Backhouse, had been forced by a terminal illness to resign.

The matter came to a head on June 26.[34] The Foreign Policy Committee of the Cabinet was confronted with the possibility of a world war in which neither America nor Russia would support Britain. With a Nazi coup threatened in Danzig over the coming weekend, it seemed highly probable that Hitler would take immediate advantage of any dispatch of the Fleet to the Far East. There were, in fact, only 11 of Britain's 15 capital ships available, as 4 were refitting. British naval doctrine had it that the 9 Japanese battleships could be held, given the 'Oriental' inefficiency of the Japanese, by 7 British ships. Nor was this the sole area where British racialism asserted itself. The Secretaries for the Colonies and India, Malcolm Macdonald and Lord Zetland, argued that failure to act against the insulting be-haviour of the Japanese troops in Tientsin would have a deplorable effect on British prestige in India and the colonies. But failure to come to the aid of Poland, Romania, Greece or Turkey would have destroyed British credibility in Europe. The Cabinet were reluctantly forced to admit that retaliation against Japan was out of the question.

Halifax toyed for a moment with the hope of French or American assistance. But the French, facing the possibility of British distraction in the Far East, were in what can only be described as a panic; their concession at Tientsin may have been equally under blockade through no fault of their own.[35] If America would support counter-measures against Japan, well and good; but they had no hope of restraining Hitler or Mussolini if the British fleet left the Mediterranean. The American Government could not be persuaded.[36] Both their Consul at Tientsin and the Chargé d'affaires in Tokyo (the Ambassador, Joseph Grew, who was equally unsympathetic, was on leave in Washington) thought the British had mishandled matters badly.[37] Lord Halifax, who had been inclined to make huffing noises, in the hope, no doubt, that the Japanese would recoil, washed his hands of the matter. Craigie was told to handle matters himself.[38] Faced with news reports that the Cabinet had abandoned the idea of counter-measures against the Japanese, he was forced to appeal to London to do nothing to confirm these reports.[39]

Sir Robert Craigie now faced, on his own, the formidable task of finding a way out of the impasse into which Lord Halifax and his advisers had trapped themselves. He was to be given a completely free hand so far as the actual negotiation went; though he was well aware that the constraints upon this freedom were strong and rigid. His first step, of necessity, had to be to persuade the Japanese to negotiate in Tokyo where he could himself handle the negotiations and at the same time play upon the Japanese moderates' dislike of their extremists. In this he succeeded on June 24 with the clandestine aid of the Japanese Premier, Baron Hiranuma.[40] Whatever his feelings about the alliance with Germany, Hiranuma was not the least disposed to let the army hotheads control an issue which could well lead to a war with Britain.

The next step, inevitably, was to settle the question of the agenda for discussion. Here Craigie found that the cost of moving the discussion to Tokyo was to expose himself and the Japanese Government not only to full-scale nationalist demonstrations,[41] in part organized by the Japanese political police, the *Kempei*, but also to a Japanese demand for agreement on general principles *before* the conversations on Tientsin opened.[42] This was more than Craigie felt able to resist. He devoted himself therefore to drawing the teeth of the Japanese proposals. In the course of these negotiations he found it necessary to advise the British Government to introduce legislation permitting the restriction of Japanese imports.[43] The final draft of the statement Craigie agreed with the Japanese omitted any of the phrases on which the Japanese had originally insisted, phrases which could have been used by Japanese propagandists in China to argue that Britain had betrayed the Chinese. It embodied only a statement of Britain's intentions not to allow anti-Japanese activities to be based on the British concessions or to be aided by British nationals or British authorities in China, intentions which had already been arrived at over the previous six months before the Tientsin crisis began.[44]

In the negotiations proper, which opened on July 24, Sir Robert found himself faced with a list of twelve demands, eight of which related to the activities of Chinese nationalists in Tientsin, while the remaining four dealt with the circulation of *fapi* and the removal of the Chinese silver reserves. The first eight demands, if conceded, would have virtually established a Japanese police protectorate over the British concession. Craigie devoted himself to the progressive scaling-down of these demands, sticking to the two clear principles that British sovereignty within the concession area should in no way be limited or overridden and that there should be no admission that the principles of British policy on these issues were being changed. And again his patient determination, his constant reminder to those with whom he was negotiating that they stood to lose as much as Britain or more by the breakdown of negotiations as a result of provocation by their military, worked the trick. The greatest compliments paid to his pertinacity were the continuous organization of demonstrations outside the Embassy, and the organization of a plot to assassinate him on his return from the Ministry of Foreign Affairs.[45] He was negotiating in the knowledge that there was no force available to back him up, whereas the Japanese Ministry of War had plans ready for the progressive occupation of all the British concessions, beginning with Tientsin. Yet he never lost heart and never lost control. He was backed in all this by the British population in Tientsin itself, who endured the Japanese insults and blockade with painfully British phlegm and stolidity, keeping themselves going by the traditional British activity of blaming everything on the incompetence and supine attitude of the Government of the day in London.

By mid-August Craigie had worn his collocutors down sufficiently for him to be able formally to separate the police issues from the issues raised by silver and *fapi*. The greatest compliment of all was that paid to him by the Japanese army leaders when on August 3 they renewed their pressure on the Japanese Cabinet for a conclusion of the alliance with Germany.[46] Their pressure revived the debate which had so convulsed the Five-Minister Conference in April and May. General Itagaki appealed to the Germans to hasten the conclusion of an alliance, and said that he was about to resign.[47] Early in August General Oshima and Ambassador Shiratori met hastily at the Villa d'Este on Lake Como to try to work out a fresh way of overcoming the opposition to the treaty.[48] There were renewed conversations between representatives of the Japanese Army and Navy Ministries.[49] Ambassador Shiratori emerged from his conference to give a series of press interviews, alleging that a tripartite alliance had been fully decided in principle.[50] Cabinet deliberations continued.[51] But nothing had changed in the old balance of forces; and time was running out. For the Nazi-Soviet contacts were about to destroy the whole basis of the army's agitation, to bring down the Cabinet and cause General Oshima, in despair, to talk of resignation.

Even before then, however, Craigie had won his victory. It was neither overwhelming, nor easily obtained. But by August 5, agreement had been reached in all the eight points concerned with the policing of the Tientsin concession. On the silver and *fapi* questions Sir Robert had stalled the negotiations successfully by insisting that France and the United States should also be consulted. The agreement on the police matters was announced on August 12, much to the anger of the Japanese military, who returned from the Tokyo conference to China in a state of high dudgeon, and on August 20 the conference was adjourned *sine die*. Sir Robert Craigie had won his victory. There was no Japanese occupation of the British concession, no humiliating withdrawal such as Lord Halifax and Sir George Sansom had envisaged, and no war in the Far East to force Japan into the arms of the Axis powers.

It was not a very noble victory. It left the British public and the American onlookers with a nasty taste in the mouth. Sir Robert earned no decorations or praise by it. He remained curiously unable to enlist the respect or the confidence of his professional contemporaries. Yet he had entered the negotiations with a hand devoid of realizable high cards, with his superiors in London in a spirit of black pessimism, and with his would-be allies in America and France convinced of his impending failure. The conflict was not of his choosing, resulting as it did from a combination of incompetence in Tientsin and doctrinairism in London. If he had failed, the Japanese military could have been relied on to move against the much more important British and international concessions in Shanghai. Indeed there were ominous troop moves on the borders of the Kowloon leased-territory of Hong Kong as the Tientsin conference adjourned. Craigie himself always believed the Japanese army had its military plans already laid for a war against Britain.

The bitterest pill inevitably was that the four Chinese had to be handed over to their deaths, and the restrictions on exit and entry to the concession in Tientsin continued, though on a milder and more correct basis, until a final agreement was reached on the silver issue in the spring of 1940. The residents in Tientsin suffered an extra hardship when torrential floods swept through the concession area and the city in general in late August. No gratitude was to be expected towards Sir Robert Craigie here. Yet the neutrality of Japan in the first year of the war must be traced largely to his skill and perseverance. The plot to assassinate him, the anger of the army extremists, and Goebbels' instructions to the German press to play the whole matter down, are the true measures of his success.

CHAPTER 20

MOLOTOV CALLS FOR BIDS

As Molotov stepped down from the dais at the Supreme Soviet on May 31, 1939, he must have been feeling more than the usual lift which accompanies the successful delivery of an oration to an audience which is drilled to applaud. He had been warned in adequate time that the British and French had accepted the original Soviet proposal for an alliance. He knew that their acceptance had been given reluctantly under the pressure of circumstances and, in Britain's case, of a steady movement of public opinion in favour of an alliance with the Soviet Union. He knew the French were consistently more enthusiastic than the British, and this gave him an additional lever to use against Chamberlain and his allies. How much he knew of the debate in Germany is unclear. He did know, however, that the Germans were taking up the bait he had dangled on May 20, and confirmed in his speech, of a new series of trade conversations. He was sufficiently confident that his rejection of the British proposals given him on May 27 would result in a new and improved offer, to secure from the Supreme Soviet, on June 3, a public endorsement of the alliance negotiations.

June was nevertheless to be a worrying month. The Germans were to prove much more hesitant in their approaches than he would have preferred, despite the detailed and distorted information on the context of the British-Soviet exchanges that the NKVD was supplying to the German Embassy in London, information which consistently over-stated the determination, not to say bellicosity towards Germany, that the British were displaying in the negotiations.[1] The British and French, on the other hand, proved dilatory, evasive on the points to which Molotov attached most importance, and, most of all, failed to behave in such a way as to convey that they regarded him and his country as equals. A hint was dropped that a visit by Lord Halifax must be welcomed; that hint was ignored.[2] Instead, William Strang, the head of the Central Department of the Foreign Office, came out to Moscow to brief Sir William Seeds, who had collapsed with influenza at the beginning of June.[3] No doubt the strain of negotiating with Molotov contributed to his illness.

William Strang was to become head of the Foreign Office in the late 1940s and to be ennobled. A slightly built man with, at least in his later years, a great capacity for warmth hidden behind a rather precise, marginally old-maidish manner, he had an excellent mind and very considerable powers of detachment. He was by no means standard Foreign Office material, being the son of a market gardener, a scholarship boy from a county grammar school, a graduate of University College, London, rather than 'Oxbridge', and a direct entrant into the Foreign Office by virtue of his service as an officer in World War I. He knew Russia well: he had been Chargé d'affaires in the early 1930s in Moscow. It was largely his strength of purpose and unflappability which had guided the British Government at the time Stalin's minions had accused a group of British engineers from Metro-Vickers Engineering of sabotage, making them scapegoats for the spectacular failure of one of Russia's earliest Five Year Plan constructions in the hydro-electric field. Britain had applied trade sanctions and forced the Soviets to disgorge their victims and pay them compensation.

Living in Moscow through the famines and repressions of the Five Year Plan and of collectivization, Strang had no liberal guilt complex for a Maisky or a Potemkin to play on; nor was he victim to the romantic Russophilia which Sir William Seeds had contracted in his student days at St Petersburg before the Revolution. He had observed and commented sardonically to his few close friends, how many eminent British visitors to the Soviet Union seemed to leave their sense of judgment and their normal suspicion of official utterances locked behind them in Britain, arriving in Leningrad or Moscow ready to believe anything they were told. Publicly, Russians tended to regard Strang as a political shrimp, whose dispatch to Moscow was insulting. Privately, those who remembered him cannot have been delighted to see someone as protected against their wiles, seductions and bullying as he was.

Strang's arrival in Moscow was not exactly what Molotov had hoped for. Molotov had, however, greater worries in the personality of his master, Stalin, and in the challenge to his position now being launched by Andrei Zhdanov, the head of the Leningrad party organization. These two problems manifested themselves in the same area, that of Finland and the three little Baltic republics, then independent (the

Soviets were to annexe them in the spring of 1940), of Lithuania, Latvia and Estonia.

The Soviet authorities had been worried about the growth of neutralism in the three Baltic countries and Finland since the turn of the year, if not before. They distrusted the Finnish Government with its strong Social Democratic element, as much as they did the unstable military-political regimes which governed the three Baltic republics. They were aware, for example, that in Estonia General Laidoner, the Commander-in-Chief of the army, advised by Colonel Maasing, the head of Estonian military intelligence, conducted his own foreign policy in spite, and sometimes behind the back, of the Estonian Foreign Minister. The Latvians suspected Laidoner and Maasing of having a special relationship with Germany.[4] The Soviets were aware, too, that Latvia had written off Britain and France, as well as the League of Nations, under the influence of Munich, and that its Sovietophile Minister of War, General Balodis, was at odds with the Latvian Foreign Minister, William Munters, who had fought on the German side in 1918.[5] The Lithuanians were even more worrying, even before the loss of Memel turned Lithuania into a German puppet.

The occupation of the Memel had been followed by the issue of a Soviet guarantee of the independence and neutrality of Latvia and Estonia.[6] This offer was unsolicited, embarrassing and unwelcome to its recipients. If anything, it pushed the three little republics further towards Germany. It was noticed that Hitler's birthday parade on April 20 in Berlin was attended by the Chiefs of Staff of the Estonian and Latvian armies, General Reek and General Hartmann, and by General Rastikis, the Lithuanian Commander-in-Chief and the 'strong man' in the Lithuanian Government.[7] Still worse from the Soviet view was the outcome of the speech Hitler made on April 28, which was to result in the conclusion, on June 7, of non-aggression pacts between Germany and the two Baltic states, Latvia and Estonia.

Under these circumstances the failure of the British to extend the system of guarantees she was scattering so liberally around Eastern and south-eastern Europe to the Baltic states led only too easily to the suspicion that Britain was trying to direct German aggression to the north-east and to a direct clash with the Soviet Union in this area. The suspicion was originally uttered by Litvinov, early in April, smarting from the rejection of his Baltic guarantees, his Black Sea pact proposals and his proposed five-power conference.[8] It seems to have infected Soviet thinking thereafter. With Maisky's assistance, Litvinov had then decided, quite wrongly, that the seizure by Poland of a Latvian port had been discussed between Beck and Halifax.[9] The Soviet alliance proposal of April 17 was intended to cover Finland, Estonia and Latvia as well as Poland and Romania. The British and French replies ignored this; and when taxed by Maisky at Geneva, Halifax pointed out that the Baltic states had shown a distinct reluctance to be guaranteed.[10] If the Soviets were aware – which, thanks to their agent in the Foreign Office Communications Department, may well have been the case – that Mr Le Gallienne, the British Minister in Tallinn, had been told by the Estonians that they would welcome a British but not a Soviet guarantee, they would have been the angrier.[11]

As things were, the speech of M. Erkkö, the Finnish Foreign Minister, to the Finnish Parliament on June 6, accusing Molotov of trying to drive a wedge between Finland and the other Nordic states, Norway, Denmark and Sweden, did not improve matters.[12] Finland, he said, explicitly rejected any idea of an automatic guarantee. 'Such a guarantee could not be accepted . . . [it would be] incompatible with the autonomy and sovereignty of Finland . . . the only attitude to take towards any state disposed by virtue of a guarantee undertaken on its own initiative to furnish its so-called assistance when it considers this to be requested by the state which it claims to protect, is to regard such a measure as aggression.'

Harsh words, not to be easily forgotten. The following day, the Estonian Minister in London spoke in the same vein to Lord Halifax.[13] On June 12 the Latvian Minister in Moscow told the Soviets roundly that his country did not recognize the right of any foreign state to acquire influence of a direct or indirect nature over its foreign, domestic and economic policy.[14] These were statements born either of courage or of despair. They could not but be linked in Molotov's mind with the conclusion of the Latvian and Estonian non-aggression pacts with Germany. A fortnight later it was announced that the Chief of Staff to the Reichswehr, General Halder, was to visit Latvia, Estonia and Finland. In Estonia, Halder inspected the two large islands at the month of the Gulf of Latvia, Saaremaa and Hiiumaa.[15] In Finland he inspected the frontier fortifications with the Soviet Union, on the development of which the Finns were spending 4.5 billion Finnish francs as a result of the talk of a Soviet guarantee for Finland.[16] A fortnight later, the *Admiral Hipper*, a German heavy cruiser, paid a formal visit to Reval (Tallinn), the Estonian capital and port which dominates the southern flanks of the sea-route to Leningrad.[17]

Among other German visitors to Reval in June were Admiral Canaris, the head of German military intelligence, and Peter Kleist, Ribbentrop's adviser on Baltic and Russian affairs.[18] Soviet military intelligence had one or more agents reporting on conversations held with Kleist in early March and on May 1, the first foreshadowing the occupation of Prague and the annexation of the Memel, bringing Lithuania under German control and giving the Germans a firm foothold in the Baltic, and the second outlining German plans for the military destruction of Poland and the alienation of the Baltic states from the Soviet Union; consequently the Soviets would be particularly alert to Dr Kleist's presence on their Baltic borders.[19] On a third occasion, Kleist also inadvertently repeated to his interlocutor Hitler's remarks to Ribbentrop in mid-June[20] about the need 'to stage a new Rapallo-phase in German–Russian relations', and 'for a certain period of time to pursue a policy of equilibrium and economic co-operation with Moscow'.

Stalin's anxieties about the vulnerability of Leningrad surfaced in February 1939. The new Military Commander of the Leningrad Military District, General Meretskov, was advised of Stalin's personal interest when he took up his command.[21] A tour of the district's defences revealed gross inadequacies, and Meretskov's report was followed by considerable transfers of men and equipment to his command. At the end of June, Stalin spoke with renewed anxiety to Meretskov about the whole situation.[22] Finland was showing herself increasingly hostile to the Soviet Union. The talks with Britain and France had still not produced any result. Germany was poised to pounce in any direction. Finland, said Stalin, 'may well become the springboard for anti-Soviet moves from either of the bourgeois-imperialist groupings – the German and the Anglo-French-American'. It was not to be excluded, he added, 'that they are plotting together for joint action against the USSR. . . . Finland might be urged against us as a skirmish for a major war.'

The concept of a Finnish attack on the Soviet Union might strike sceptics as the height of absurdity; Stalin's remarks do, however, demonstrate the degree to which his own particular ideologically grounded obsessions could dominate and distort his perceptions. They illustrate too the degree of uncertainty with which the Soviet leadership was beset at the end of June. Andrei Zhdanov was to voice these doubts with typical defensive aggressiveness of tone at the end of June, writing in *Pravda*.[23] As the representative, the feudal baron, the 'godfather', the party boss of Leningrad, he was particularly sensible to the strategic vulnerability of his city, the more so as he was associated directly with the oddest aspect of Stalin's personal megalomania, the desire to make of the Red Fleet a 'navy second to none'.[24] The Soviet naval budget was at the time being rapidly increased with a view to making it at least the equal of the German fleet in the Baltic.[25] Budgetary figures for 1939 showed an increase of 17.734 billion roubles over the naval budget for 1938. The first two Soviet battleships were being laid down in Leningrad and Odessa, with a third to follow. Leningrad was to become the most important centre of Soviet naval construction. Stalin had heralded this in his speech of March 11. Zhdanov had been appointed a member of the Naval Council to put his energy behind the drive. A new super-*Kirov*-type cruiser was being laid down. At the end of July, Navy Day was celebrated by fifty units of the Baltic Fleet in a three-day cruise down the Estonian coast, with Zhdanov on board the old Tsarist battleship *October Revolution*.[26] It was a brave, and rather un-Soviet, un-Russian display. It impressed but did not cheer the leaders of the Baltic states.

Central to the anxieties to which Stalin was subject was the position of Finland. The Finns were the Turks of northern Europe: resolute, determined and not easily scared. But they had a streak of Polishness in them and lacked the Turkish sense of realism. They had Germany and the Soviet Union to cope with where the Turks had only Italy. And, save at Petsamo in the extreme north, they had no access to the open sea. Their reaction to Munich and to the failure of the League and of the concept of collective security was to retreat into a position of armed neutrality, in which they hoped to be supported by the other members of the so-called Northern Entente, Sweden, Norway and Denmark. Whatever complexion of government ruled in Finland, suspicion of and hostility towards the Soviet Union and all forms of Great Russian nationalism were common to them all.

Finnish relations with the Soviet Union were further strained over the Åland Isles, a group of some thousand islands lying in the Gulf of Bothnia between Finland and Sweden. A bone of contention between Sweden, Finland and Russia (the inhabitants were Swedish-speaking, and the islands were Finnish but had, before the Russian Revolution, been under Russian sovereignty), the Åland Isles had been demilitarized by a ten-power convention of October 1921 under the auspices of the League of Nations. The Soviet Union was not a signatory.[27] In January, the Swedes and the Finns had proposed jointly to the signatories of the 1921 treaty that the islands, which controlled access by sea to their northern shores, should be fortified.[28] The Germans refused to allow the question to be referred to the League; they tried too to use the issue as a means of securing assurances from Sweden that in the event of war Germany could count on Swedish iron ore supplies.[29]

The Finnish Foreign Minister, Erkkö, eventually forced the Germans to agree to his proposals,[30] after he had intimated that their failure to answer his request would be regarded as inimical (or so he told the

French);[31] whereupon the Soviet delegate at Geneva, the ubiquitous M. Maisky, did his best to postpone any discussions of the matter by the League Council.[32] In the meantime Molotov, rejecting Finnish assurances with disdain, demanded the most detailed information about the 'objectives and character of the proposed fortifications'.[33] This the Finns refused to give; whereupon the Soviets, in effect, vetoed further discussions of the issue at Geneva, adding for good measure that they could not see what business, if any, it was of the Swedes.[34] In so doing, Molotov no doubt took a certain pleasure in disowning the asssurance given to the Swedes, on Litvinov's instructions, by Madame Kollontai, the veteran Soviet revolutionary, who represented Russia in Stockholm. Mme Kollontai was, no doubt, fortunate to escape unscathed from the great purges; but the price of Molotov's boorishness was a gratuitous row with the Swedes, and an inflammation of Stalin's suspicions that Finland was a possible spearhead for an Anglo-German crusade against the Soviet Union.

The Finns, once equally suspicious of Germans and Russians alike (the fortifications were intended to strengthen the armed neutrality the Finns were proposing to maintain in the event of a European war), now concluded that the Soviets were up to no good. Perhaps they wanted some of the smaller Finnish islands in the east of the Gulf of Finland. This, so Erkkö told the British Minister, the Finns might be prepared to concede – in return for compensation in the Arctic.[35] The Soviets, however, proved unwilling to bargain at all. They claimed equal rights with Sweden in the Åland Isles.[36] This the Finns, who were hoping that the Swedish air force would station aircraft on the islands to protect the Gulf of Bothnia, refused to recognize; instead they went ahead with fortifying the islands on their own,[37] which gave Halder's visit and other Finno-German military contacts an even more sinister tint in Soviet eyes.

M. Molotov might then have won a certain amount of ground by the determination he showed in May in the face of both the German and the Anglo-French approaches. He certainly used the secret information on the British and French deliberations which reached him from Mr King, the Soviet agent in the Foreign Office communications section, very effectively. Not only was he able to display (by comparison with normal Soviet bargaining practice) the most extreme speed in replying to the various Anglo-French proposals, providing answers and alternative proposals within twenty-four hours of receiving them; he was also enabled to follow the course of the German-Japanese negotiations, and to ascertain whether the Japanese Kwantung Army, in attacking the Soviet's satellite, Mongolia, was pursuing a policy in agreement with

Berlin and Tokyo, or acting on its own. This was a matter of some importance in view of the second Japanese offensive early in July, at a time when Berlin appeared to have given up on the approach to a political agreement. In addition Molotov could, as indeed he did at the end of June and again early in July, drop direct hints, via the secret informant to the German Embassy in London, that the Soviet Union was less than whole-hearted in its reception of the Anglo-French advances.[38]

It was this ability to leak British information to the Germans, a facility provided by the NKVD and created by the old Comintern intelligence, so drastically purged in 1936–7, that was to save him. Up to the middle of July Molotov had been displaying all the finesse of one attempting to play first-class lawn tennis with a heavy club. On June 29 Hitler decided that, in view of the difficulties the Soviets were making in the trade discussions in Moscow, they were to be told that Germany was no longer interested.[39] The German Ambassador in Moscow, Count von der Schulenburg, who had seen Molotov on June 28, did his best; but his various reports to Berlin[40] were unable to hide the fact that Molotov was still presenting a wooden, not to say unyieldingly suspicious front. Schulenburg was driven to send his second-in-command, Werner von Tippelskirch, to Berlin to find out exactly how his masters' minds were moving. Von Tippelskirch did not manage to see Ribbentrop; on July 12[41] he wrote to his Ambassador that the will to take a positive political stand was still lacking. He found it difficult to convince anyone that the idea that the Soviet Union, having started the negotiations with Britain and France, would let them fall 'without results and drift back into isolation' was at all possible, let alone something on which a sound policy could be based or risks taken. The German economic negotiators were depressed and defeatist.[42]

Much the same could be said of the British and French negotiators. Between the Soviet proposals of June 2 and July 1, they had made three separate proposals to the Soviets. Each had been rebuffed. To each a Soviet counter-draft had been presented. Being without any informal access to lower-level Soviet officials, who might let slip some item to enlighten them on Soviet thinking, the British had begun to disagree among themselves; and they found the need to refer everything back to London and Paris, and then to wait while London and Paris got their acts together, added to that sense of frustration. In London the Cabinet and the Foreign Office reacted with varying degrees of anger and depression to each rebuff. And after each rebuff, British opinion in Parliament and in the press, duly fed by the Soviet Embassy, became steadily more pressing. So did the French Cabinet and that part of

French opinion which supported a Russian alliance. (There was a vociferous right-wing press, partly subsidized by Berlin and Rome, to put an alternative view.)

Each party to the negotiations also had unseen agenda which, since the outbreak of war in September 1939, have almost totally disappeared from view; they did, however, have an element in common. Once the Anglo-Franco-Soviet agreement was struck, Germany would be restrained. That much was generally accepted. The one point shared by the different agenda in London and Moscow (Paris was so concerned as to what might happen if the agreement was not struck that it is almost impossible to discern any of the items on M. Bonnet's, let alone M. Daladier's, agenda) was concern as to how to exploit that agreement and what use might be made of it by their partners in the negotiations.

The constant theme in the reports from M. Maisky in London and M. Suritz in Paris, who were excluded from the negotiations by the fact of their taking place in Moscow, was that the hidden British agenda included a renewed attempt to come to an agreement with Germany. In the course of reaching this agreement, it was suggested, the British could well free themselves from their new partners and embrace the odious Hitler once more, urging him the while to pursue his long-term aims and attack the Soviet Union. This was varied from time to time, as plausible evidence presented itself, by the suggestion that the British would settle for an agreement with Germany, if it was offered, without waiting to consummate the relationship they were seeking with the Soviet Union. It was essential for the Soviets therefore to tie the British down as rigidly as possible, and to suspect, question, fight and, if necessary, denounce every ambiguity in the proposals which emanated from London. Maisky and Suritz managed to convince their masters in the Kremlin that the pressure of public opinion in London was such that in the face of Soviet firmness, the reluctance of the British Cabinet would yield and melt. The British Cabinet could not afford a break in the negotiations with the Soviet Union.

The Soviet leadership had, in turn, their own agenda. Central to Soviet thought appears to have been the conviction that, despite Stalin's suspicions, the main targets of Hitler's actions in 1939–40 were to be Britain and France. If Hitler was restrained, rather than overthrown, then there was the long-term danger that he would revert to the goals expressed in *Mein Kampf*. It was essential therefore to improve the defences of the Soviet Union and to remove as far from Leningrad, Moscow, Kiev, Kharkov and the Ukraine the bases in Europe from which Hitler would eventually launch his assault on the Soviet Union. Between Germany proper and the Soviet Union there lay a no man's land of small and unstable potential, if not actual, satellites of Germany. In so far as Britain could recapture the balance, as she seemed to be doing in Ankara at the time of M. Potemkin's visit in May, that was all to the good. Any benefit would disappear at once, however, if Maisky and Suritz were right, and an Anglo-German deal was being struck before the Soviets had their treaty with Britain under lock and key.

There was, however, a further danger to the Soviet position and this lay in the possibility that Hitler would not be deterred and that war might happen in 1939 after all. The British and French agendas included the possibility of war with Hitler in 1939. All available evidence suggests that the Soviet agenda did not. Yet the Soviet proposal for a tripartite alliance, military as well as political in nature, only made sense, only assumed political validity, if war really was the most probable outcome of the effort to restrain or deter Hitler. Indeed, if war were to break out in 1939 or 1940 the Soviet Union would inevitably have to bear the brunt of the fighting on land. Yet if war did not break out, it was quite conceivable that Britain rather than the Soviets would reap the maximum benefit.

Everything therefore turned, so far as Stalin's judgment (as opposed to his suspicions) was concerned, on the two questions of whether there would be war in 1939 and whether Britain and France would accept treaty terms which would make possible the advance of Soviet control and the Soviet defence system into Eastern Europe. From the beginning the Soviet treaty proposals contained three essential elements: there should be a tripartite military alliance with provision against the conclusion of a separate peace; this alliance should operate in the event of a German attack on any of the frontier states lying on the western frontiers of the Soviet Union, and on Belgium, the term 'operate' including military and Staff agreements; and the three signatories should be expected to act in the event of 'indirect aggression' of the kind Hitler had practised against Austria, Czechoslovakia or Lithuania (over the Memel). What the Soviet leadership seems at no point to have considered before it happened, was that Britain would go to war with Hitler whatever the Soviet Union did, or that the Soviet Union might soon need British and American aid to defeat a Hitler made very much stronger by his conquest of Europe.

At no point in Soviet thinking, either during the six months up to September 1939 or at any point from that date to this, can there be discerned any grasp of the one central idea by which British policy has been so severely judged: that the earlier Hitler was defeated and overthrown, the better for all concerned – for Europe as a whole, for

France, for Britain and, last but by no means the least, the Soviet Union, which was to suffer twenty million dead and the devastation of European Russia. If the appeasement of Germany, as practised by the British Government headed by Neville Chamberlain, was mistaken and wrong; if the failure to achieve an alliance against Hitler in 1939 was mistaken and wrong, then the Soviet conviction that Britain needed the alliance and the Soviets did not was also wrong. So too were the Soviet convictions that it was for Britain to court the Soviets, that the Soviets were free to choose whether the marriage contract being offered was reliable enough to make acceptance worth while, and that it was for the British to send Lord Halifax to Moscow in June or their Chiefs of Staff in August, rather than for the Soviets to send Molotov and Marshal Voroshilov to London. What mattered was the alliance. Without it, Hitler was to come close to defeating both Britain and the Soviet Union.

The historical verdict that British historians have accepted is the same as much of British opinion accepted in the summer of 1939. With war imminent, not to have done everything necessary to secure the Soviet alliance was, *from Britain's point of view*, an outstanding error of judgment. This should have no bearing on any judgment of Soviet behaviour in the pact negotiations. The events of 1941–2 were to prove, in retrospect, that the Soviets needed the alliance in 1939 just as much as Britain did. Molotov and Stalin, ably aided and abetted by Maisky and Suritz, were too suspicious, too sure that Britain needed them rather than the reverse, too greedy and, most of all, too unrealistic to see how greatly German strength outweighed what Britain and France could, in the short term, field against Hitler. Stalin's scientific Marxism was no more able to prophesy the fall of France, the German capture of the Balkans, or the occupation of seven-tenths of Russia west of the Urals, than were the British Chiefs of Staff.

British public opinion seems to have been more prescient than either the British or the Soviet Government. The majority of British opinion seems by June to have accepted that there would be war with Hitler before the summer of 1939 was over. British Government anxieties over the introduction of conscription proved baseless. The pacifist underpinning to the disarmament movement, the emotion-driven conciliators-at-all-costs who wrote to the newspapers, to their MPs, and to members of the Cabinet, as did the Germanophiles, the believers in semitic conspiracy, the sympathizers with Fascism, the anti-Bolsheviks, the imperial isolationists, indeed all the vociferous, convinced public figures who had persuaded so many foreign observers of Britain's softness, were still there and still as vociferous and active as ever. But they were revealed now as numerically insignificant, isolated minorities, who spoke only for themselves. No one wanted war. The hawks remained hooded. It was rather the day of the bulldog; or not quite yet. Chamberlain was still determined not to take Churchill into the Cabinet until war was declared. He was to hope for too long that the alternative strategy of deterrence would work. On July 23 he wrote to his sister Ida,[43] 'One thing I think is clear, namely, that Hitler has concluded we mean business and the time is not ripe for a major war. . . . That is what Winston and co[mpany] never realize. You don't need offensive forces sufficient to win a smashing victory. What you want are defensive forces sufficiently strong to make it impossible for the other side to win except at such a cost as not to make it worth while. That is what we are doing and though at present the German feeling is that it is not worth while *yet*, they will presently come to realize that it *never* will be worth while. Then we can talk. But the time to talk hasn't come yet because the Germans have not realized that they can't get what they want by force. . . .'

This was Chamberlain's policy and this underlay the reluctance with which he contemplated each step in the negotiations with the Soviets; he was not, however, master in his own Cabinet. At each stopping point he was overborne by the majority led, with habitual caution and tergiversation, by Lord Halifax, using not only the weight of parliamentary opinion, pressure from Paris and the arguments of the Chiefs of Staff, but also the logic of Chamberlain's own emphasis on deterrence. The Soviet alliance was the eventual underpinning to the whole 'Eastern Front' element in that policy. Its appearance was winning over the Balkans. Fears of a German agreement with the Soviets were the only restraint. Britain was playing for very high stakes. What Lord Halifax and the Foreign Office did not recognize was that they were playing with marked cards.

Not that there were not a number of warnings conveyed to the Foreign Office and to others in the Government about the contacts between the Germans and the Soviets.[44] A conservative estimate would put the number of known warnings at around a score; there may well have been more. The French received at least a dozen or so.[45] The Poles were so worried that they attached an extra intelligence officer to their Embassy in Russia to observe the comings and goings of German officers between Berlin and Moscow.[46] The Estonians and the Finns, always the best informed on Soviet actions of foreign intelligence sources, were convinced that, given the chance, the Soviets would pick Germany rather than Britain as their natural associate.[47] The rumours ran through Europe, worrying the Japanese and the Turks,[48] the

All you have to do is to sit down

Romanians and the Yugoslavs alike. Soviet diplomatists, genuinely not in the know, denounced and denied the rumours with indignation.[49]

The British Foreign Office, where rumours of Soviet-German contacts in January had, in February, provoked Sir Alexander Cadogan to the thought that the Soviets were capable of anything, seems to have been disarmed by the Soviet offers of an alliance. Thereafter all reports, even those from the Soviet defector, Walter Krivitzki, published in the United States before and after Litvinov's fall, were treated with incredulity and seen as either German or Soviet manœuvres.[50] Three elements seem to have combined to mislead the Foreign Office. The bulk of the rumours and reports which reached London did so in May, as an echo of the debate in Berlin which followed Litvinov's fall. They came from Goering's entourage or from the conservative German opposition, the degree of whose genuine antagonism to Hitler was never comprehended in London. And they were accompanied by other reports, which may have been deliberate disinformation from NKVD sources, to the effect that Stalin was so embittered by the discovery of German plans against the Ukraine and of a German plot to eliminate him that, while Stalin lived, a *rapprochement* with Germany was impossible. The reports tailed off markedly at the end of May. There were a few more in June, including two from the Kordt brothers, Erich and Theo, one set by the professionals of the Foreign Ministry to watch over Ribbentrop, the other Counsellor in the German Embassy in London,[51] and one from Admiral Canaris.[52] Theo Kordt did not, however, tell the British about the leakage to him of details of the Anglo-Soviet negotiations. During the last and most intense of Nazi-Soviet contacts from the end of July to August 22, there were no warnings that can be traced, save one, via the Americans, which came too late.

We return therefore to Sir William Seeds, magnificent in his height, his enthusiasm for things Russian, and his diplomatic uniform and cocked hat; William Strang, quiet, polite, self-effacing, but fluent with ideas; the shrewd French Ambassador, Emile Naggiar, but recently arrived in Moscow, loathing its atmosphere but cutting again and again through the complex formulations with which Lord Halifax tried to satisfy both the divided British Cabinet and the alternately suspicious and importunate M. Bonnet; and Molotov, aided as interpreter (he never dared act as more) by the deputy Foreign Minister, Vladimir Potemkin. Molotov habitually received his visitors sitting at a large desk on a raised dais in the right-hand corner of the room, with the windows on his left. His visitors sat on hard, straight-backed chairs in a semi-circle below him, Seeds on the left, then Strang, then M. Naggiar, then M. Potemkin, whose job it was to interpret from English and French into Russian and from Russian into French. On the left, far away, was a conference table; it was never used. Beyond that was a door; it always stood open. Molotov would fiddle from time to time with a switch on his desk-top at his left hand, presumably a tape recorder. The visitors had to balance any notes and papers they might have brought on their knees, and make notes as best they could.[53]

The matter of the dais grated much on British nerves. Chamberlain even mentioned it to a delegation from the British Labour Party as one of the factors which precluded any real discussion or negotiation.[54] There was no give and take in the discussions. Molotov seemed quite impervious to argument.[55]

Potemkin may have resented his demotion to a mere interpreter. If so, he took it out on his British interlocutors. On June 2 Molotov had replied to the British offer of May 27 with a draft treaty.[56] By the terms of this the Soviet Union undertook to come to the aid of the Western powers if they became involved in war as a result of aggression against Belgium, Greece, Turkey, Romania or Poland. In return the Western powers were to aid the Soviet Union if she was involved in war as a result of aggression against Latvia, Estonia or Finland. Making a separate peace was prohibited. There was to be a military agreement to come into operation at the same time as the political agreement. The Netherlands, Luxembourg and Switzerland were excluded from the Soviet guarantees. In avoiding the direct alliance proposed by Litvinov, the Soviets had made a kind of concession, but their draft was very vague as to what constituted a *casus belli*.

These proposals embarrassed the Western governments. They had already guaranteed Polish and Romanian independence. Neither country wished to have anything to do with the Soviets. M. Erkkö, the Finnish Foreign Minister, had told the British that any country which attempted to give the Finns armed assistance without being asked would be treated as an aggressor. Estonia and Latvia were just about to sign non-aggression pacts with Germany. Some members of their governments feared Soviet aid more than German protection. The proposals that Mr Strang brought to Moscow were designed to tone down the Soviet directness. The countries guaranteed were not to be enumerated and their number was to be confined to those which had consented to receiving a guarantee. If any other power came under such pressure that one of the three signatories felt their security to be threatened, then there would be consultation and assistance if the other two powers accepted the first signatory's diagnosis. They did not accept the 'no separate peace' clause; and they did not wish to hold up the political agreement by arguments over a parallel military agreement.

When this was presented to M. Molotov (who already knew the details from Mr King on June 15 and had indeed leaked them to the German Embassy on June 5 and 12),[57] he behaved like a prosecuting counsel cross-examining a recalcitrant witness.[58] The next day he made his formal reply.[59] The dull and colourless words of his Russian were made shocking and flamboyant by M. Potemkin. If the Western powers thought the Soviets likely to accept such proposals, they must take them for simpletons and imbeciles. The Soviet Union (even though her guarantees of the Baltic states had been rebuffed) must be treated on a basis of equality and reciprocity. Otherwise she would be humiliated.

Lord Halifax treated this outburst with all the sympathy of a dominant uncle dealing with a flighty, rather difficult young niece. A series of instructions, alternative wordings for different parts of the British draft, were telegraphed to Seeds,[60] and put by him to Molotov. Together Seeds and Naggiar, with Strang in attendance, saw Molotov on June 21[61] and 22.[62] Lord Halifax saw Maisky on June 23, to whom he remarked, with uncharacteristic brusqueness, that saying 'no' to everything was not his idea of negotiating and that it bore a striking resemblance to Nazi methods of dealing with international questions.[63] This M. Maisky, perhaps wisely, does not seem to have repeated to Moscow.

Lord Halifax could be forgiven for being a little huffy. M. Molotov was, as he pointed out to his colleagues on the Foreign Policy Committee on June 26,[64] insisting on raising the question not only of resisting aggression but of acting pre-emptively to prevent the states of the Soviet Union's boundaries from falling to Hitler by coups or other forms of pressure. Moreover, he was insisting that the Soviet Union should be the judge as to when such a danger threatened and pre-emptive action was required. The British Cabinet was inclined to take paltry refuge in a secret protocol naming the states concerned, on the somewhat implausible grounds that they could not object so strongly once its existence leaked out. Chamberlain noted[65] that 'even Halifax was beginning to get impatient' with the Russians but that his craven colleagues forced him to 'go very warily'. 'I should not feel so greatly weakened', he added, 'if we had to do without them.' But he was overruled.

A whole flood of telegrams, co-ordinated between London and Paris, was dispatched to Moscow between June 27 and 29.[66] By June 29 the German Embassy in London already had the details of Sir William Seeds' new instructions, and had drawn the conclusion their informants desired, that 'the Soviet government is conducting the pact negotiations without enthusiasm and would not be disappointed by its failure.' To force the point home, the Soviet Air Attaché in London, Brigade Commander Cherny, told his German colleague, Lieutenant General Wenninger, that the Soviet Government was not interested in concluding a pact with Britain and France.[67] To sweeten this information he also gave the Germans details of Britain's armaments in the air.

M. Molotov's commitment to the negotiations with Britain and France must have looked particularly shaky at the end of June. His master was fantasizing about a possible Anglo-German attack on the Soviet Union using Finland as the spearhead. General Halder was visiting Finland. The Soviet press was denouncing to the world the Japanese air attacks into the Mongolian People's Republic.[68] The Western press was proclaiming the imminence of a German attack on Danzig. On Molotov's instructions,[69] Suritz was alerting the French to the story that the Japanese were trying to scare Britain and France away from an agreement. Sorge was, it was true, reassuring Molotov that the log-jam in the Japanese negotiations with Germany was still unmoved, in that the Japanese were still unable to agree to the German demand for an open-ended alliance. On the other hand, they would sign an alliance which operated purely against the Soviet Union overnight – something which made any suggestion of an Anglo-German *rapprochement* the more suspicious and the more threatening. So far from standing up to the Japanese over the Tientsin crisis, the British showed every sign of a climb-down, something Moscow should have welcomed as a sign of realism, but chose instead to take as proof that the policy of appeasement still reigned in London.[70] The Germans were breaking off the commercial and economic negotiations and, with them, the chance of developing political discussions. And M. Zhdanov was proclaiming to the readers of *Pravda*[71] that the Western powers did not want an agreement on equal terms with the Soviets, and were introducing all kinds of unnecessary complications in order to string out the negotiations while they were pursuing quite other aims, a treaty in which the Soviet Union would 'play the part of a hired labourer bearing the brunt of the obligations on his shoulders'; 'by spreading the word about the alleged obstinacy of the Soviet Union' the Western powers were preparing 'public opinion in their countries for a deal with the aggressors', Zhdanov claimed.

The announcement on June 29 that the Red Army was to hold its annual manœuvres in the Leningrad Military District rather than on the borders of Poland as in 1938 is one measure of the genuineness of Stalin's anxieties over the Baltic gap. More significant perhaps is that when the new Anglo-French draft, with its concessions to Soviet views on the Baltic states, was presented to Molotov by Seeds and Naggiar on July 1, the Russian accepted the proposal that the countries guaranteed should be named in a secret protocol rather than in the text of the treaty. What shook him, however, and is a measure of how far his own narrow mind had dug him firmly into the mud of legalism, was the inclusion in the list of the Netherlands and Switzerland, neither of which had diplomatic relations with the Soviet Union. The obvious strategic considerations (both countries would clearly present strategic dangers to Britain and France if they should pass under German control) were irrelevant to him. In his view, Britain and France were only shielding three of the Soviet Union's neighbours and the Soviet Union was being asked to act if Germany attacked any one of seven countries with whom Britain and France were concerned (three of them were Russia's neighbours too). Nor did the new draft come clean on the issue of 'indirect aggression'.[72]

Nevertheless M. Molotov was still prepared to play the game. On July 3, he accepted most of the new draft.[73] He would even accept covering the Netherlands and Switzerland, on one condition: that Poland and Turkey conclude treaties of mutual assistance with the Soviet Union. 'Indirect aggression' he defined as 'an internal *coup d'état* or a reversal of policy in the interests of the aggressor'. With these two demands, M. Molotov seemed to play into the hands of all those in Paris and London whose suspicions of Soviet motives and doubts of Soviet reliability had been silenced by the anxieties of their colleagues as to Germany's intentions.

The reaction in London and Paris was immediate. The demand that the tripartite pact be held up until a Polish-Soviet treaty of mutual assistance had been concluded seemed likely to postpone this until the Greek calends. But it was the definition of 'indirect aggression' which awoke the most alarm. Sir Orme Sargent, Cadogan's deputy in the Foreign Office who was co-ordinating the British end of the negotiations, seemed very discouraged.[74] Lord Halifax was ready to drop the Netherlands and Switzerland, indeed to drop the whole list of 'guaranteed' states and to return to the original Soviet proposal of a simple alliance.[75] M. Bonnet agreed.[76] Lord Halifax, who had had to beat off an assault by the Finnish Minister in London, M. Gripenberg,[77] described M. Molotov's definition of indirect aggression as 'completely unacceptable' and impossible to defend 'either to the countries concerned or to public opinion here'.[78]

Public opinion was in fact giving him a good deal of trouble; the British press, nourished, it was discovered, by the Soviet Embassy and the Tass representative in London[79] with reports of the 'difficulties' the British and French Governments were putting in the way of accepting the Soviet position, continuously fed Soviet expectations that they had the 'appeasers' on the run.[80] Ivone Kirkpatrick of the Foreign Office told Richard Stokes of the Labour Party, 'if only your front bench would keep quiet for a little while, we could get an agreement.'[81]

If Molotov felt he had the British on the run he was mistaken. Indeed, British tempers were beginning to rise. For the time being, he felt he might have gone too far in his definition of indirect aggression, and withdrew the phrase about a 'reversal of policy in the interests of the aggressor' in favour of 'the use of the territory' of one of the named states 'for the purposes of aggression'.[82] This the French were prepared to accept; British questioning caused Molotov to withdraw the definition a day later in favour of a more complicated formulation.[83] He must have been cheered by the evidence which reached him from Mr King that Lord Halifax was thinking of yielding on the issue of a military convention,[84] while the French were willing to concede the point on indirect aggression.[85] He was soon to learn that on this last point the British were unshakeable; although divergencies appeared for a moment between London and Paris, and between M. Naggiar and his British colleague in Moscow, the French soon fell into line again.

Both sides were now thoroughly immersed in drafting and redrafting by telegram: between London and Paris; between London and Moscow; and between Molotov, Stalin and his legal advisers. Molotov himself gave every impression of being bored by the procedure, though the improving quality of the Soviet drafting suggested he was now calling on the legal resources he had inherited from his predecessor.[86] The British Cabinet was now half-resigned to keeping the negotiations going, simply to block any possibility of Moscow and Berlin getting together.[87] As for Molotov, he still seemed poised between his hopes that London and Paris would continue to be swept along by public opinion[88] and the possibility that, as Hitler's plans matured, he would come to realize that he needed Soviet neutrality. Molotov's own temper, however, was fraying. On July 17 he spoke of the British and French negotiators as 'crooked and cheats', and denounced their 'clumsy tricks'.[89] The same day General Pownall was confiding to his diary his belief that the Russians had no intention of signing any agreement.[90] 'As soon as our people give way on one point, the Russians produce a brand new obstacle which they say is essential or the deal's off. No doubt the F[oreign] O[ffice] will give way again.'

It was, no doubt, as a result of this impasse that various gestures were made towards the Germans. The German Embassy in London was given a version of Sir William Seeds' latest instructions,[91] which disguised any of the signs of weakness around the edges which were in fact affecting Lord Halifax's resolution. And M. Mikoyan was pushed into taking the initiative in Berlin to re-open the trade and credit negotiations, and to transfer the negotiations to the German capital. In addition, the Soviets offered to raise the value of their deliveries and to accept many of the German demands on the credit side.[92]

Molotov was thus taking advantage of a number of small breaches in Ribbentrop's determination to step back from the Russian conversations at the end of June. Early in July the Italian Ambassador in Moscow, Augusto Rosso, on instructions from Rome, had done his best to convince Potemkin that the Germans sincerely wanted an agreement.[93] On July 7, Ribbentrop murmured confidentially to Attolico that he was about to send new instructions which would be sufficient to catch Stalin's ear.[94] These led to an interview between Mikoyan and Hilger, the Commercial Attaché at the German Embassy in Moscow, on July 11, at which new German proposals were advanced as a sign of goodwill.[95]

The economic negotiators on the German side remained suspicious of the sincerity of the Soviet gesture.[96] But Hitler's timetable over Danzig was beginning to press on him. Astute Hitler-watchers in Berlin, in the German Embassy in Moscow and elsewhere were picking up the signs.

Among them was a young German diplomatist and military officer,

Hans von Herwarth, attached to the German Embassy in Moscow.[97] With a Jewish grandmother and a deep revulsion towards Nazism, von Herwarth had done his best in 1938 to alert the British to Hitler's plans through his friend and tennis partner from the British Embassy in Moscow, Fitzroy Maclean; like other such informants, he had seen his information neglected. Discouraged by this rejection and still more by Maclean's return to London, he had turned in early 1939 to another tennis partner, the young Charles (Chip) Bohlen of the US Embassy.[98] From January onwards von Herwarth kept the US Embassy in Moscow accurately and immediately informed of every move in the slow and disjointed German courtship of Moscow.[99] In the vain hope that Ciano would do something, he equally kept the Italian Embassy informed, securing only that Augusto Rosso, the Italian Ambassador, gave Schulenburg as the source of his information.[100] In the middle of July, he also spoke to Fitzroy Maclean's replacement in Moscow, Armine Dew.[101] Dew, who was killed in an air crash on his way to take part in the Yalta Conference in February 1945, presumably spoke to his Ambassador, but no report was made through official channels to London. Nor was Washington to break its silence towards the British until too late.

On July 23, Seeds and Naggiar met Molotov once again.[102] Molotov now swept aside the question of indirect aggression as of minor importance, something that could easily be settled in the time remaining. He insisted from the beginning of this conversation on the opening of military talks, the one concession Seeds and Naggiar had been instructed to yield only as a last resort. No doubt his prior knowledge of Sir William Seeds' instructions (which were passed to the German Embassy in London on July 21)[103] were of advantage to him. Now the British had to choose a Staff mission and, once the idea of conversations in Paris had been abandoned, find a means of dispatching it to Moscow.

The British decision coincided with the public discovery of Mr Robert Hudson's conversations with Dr Helmut Wohltat, Goering's deputy on the German Four Year Plan organization. These were unauthorized, 'premature' in Chamberlain's view,[104] and their details were greatly exaggerated in the public press. (They are covered in detail in the next chapter.) Their impact in Moscow can be imagined from the telegram Suritz sent on July 25 from Paris, linking Hudson's action with the British 'capitulation' over Tientsin.[105] The reaction can hardly be exaggerated. Everything Maisky and Suritz had gleaned from their contacts in the British and French opposition to Chamberlain, all the talk of Chamberlain's ineradicable and congenital wimpishness and lack of backbone, his preference for the appeasement of Germany rather than resistance to Hitler, all the rumours so sedulously spread by Claud Cockburn's private newsletter, *The Week*, a journal which seems to have served Roosevelt and the American Senate alike as a substitute for the intelligence service they had yet to create,[106] seemed to be confirmed. Vansittart was speechless with rage. Cadogan was on leave, so resolutely so that his diary is devoid of any comment on current affairs whatever. When M. Naggiar spoke of a 'recrudescence of lack of confidence' in Neville Chamberlain's intentions,[107] he was indulging in a French version of traditional British understatement.

It was therefore the more unfortunate that the whole question of the dispatch of a British Staff mission to Moscow was beset by an element of black comedy. Early in July the French had picked the head of their mission, General Joseph Doumenc, then commanding the first Military Region, and had announced the fact to the British delegates to the Anglo-French Army Staff talks on July 13.[108] At that stage, they were talking of a French mission designed to discuss Soviet military aid to Poland, Romania and Turkey. Neither General Gort, the Chief of the Imperial General Staff (CIGS) of the British Army, nor General Pownall, the 'thinking general' who, as Director of Operations in the War Office, accompanied Gort to Paris, seems to have paid any attention. William Strang, as early as July 20,[109] had warned that if a British military mission was sent to Moscow, it would have to be headed by an officer of at least equivalent rank to General Ironside, whose visit to Poland in July had been 'prominently reported' in the Soviet press. Ironside had, however, just been caught out in the unforgivable sin of fraternizing with the Secretary of State and giving him advice behind Gort's back.[110]

The British army representative was to be Major General T. G. G. Heywood, an ex-Military Attaché, although Sir John Dill, Alan Brooke and Sir Ronald Adam, the deputy CIGS, were all available. But the British generality had already realized that the dispatch of the British Expeditionary Force (BEF) to France was imminent (as early as the first week in July the War Office had been given mid-August as the date towards which the Reichswehr was preparing for action). No general worth his salt was voluntarily going to run the risk of being caught in Russia at the outbreak of war and miss the chance of commanding British armies in action. Indeed, no sooner had war broken out than Gort, Pownall and Adam all left for France, leaving the higher direction of the army lacking anyone with experience of planning for the war they were about to fight.

The command of the British Staff mission fell therefore to the navy. Here too the leading Admirals, all fighting men, had already selected their commands. The lot fell to Admiral Sir Reginald Plunket-Ernle-Erle-Drax. His name alone seemed to denote a naval equivalent of the cartoonist David Low's Colonel Blimp. He had, in fact, one of the sharpest minds in the Royal Navy. As a young officer he had been part of the modernizing Fronde that had engineered Lord Jellicoe's removal from the position of First Sea Lord in 1917, just in time to save Britain, by the introduction of the convoy system, from being starved into surrender by the German U-boat campaign. He was the first head of the Royal Naval Staff College. In early 1939 he had been the architect of the revision of British naval strategy to concentrate on the Mediterranean at the expense of Singapore and the Far East. He was the principal Naval Aide to King George VI.

His reward, as a result of the death of Admiral Sir Roger Backhouse, the First Sea Lord, from overwork (the Admiral did not believe in the need for a naval staff), was to be posted, together with Admiral Sir Bertram Ramsay, the other leading advocate of modern staff methods, to a land-based command. Between them they divided the command of Britain's southern coast. Ramsay was based at Dover. In 1940 it was his responsibility to organize the withdrawal by sea of the BEF from Dunkirk. His brilliant performance caught Churchill's eye and he ended the war, having organized the naval side of D-Day, as Admiral of the Fleet Sir Bertram Ramsay, justly laden with honours. Drax (as he signed himself) was not so fortunate. He was not blessed with luck, but he was not the obscure Blimpish Russophobe depicted by the enemies of the Prime Minister and by hostile historians ever since. The real problem, however, was how to convey to Moscow an Anglo-French Staff mission, laden with top-secret information on the war plans of the West, around, over or through the territory of their potential enemies. It was much too far to fly without landing on German-controlled territory. Any reader of spy fiction would know that a journey by train was much too open to skulduggery.

The Foreign Office Committee wanted to send the mission to Russia with a major fleet escort of cruisers and destroyers. This Halifax rejected as 'too provocative', a characteristic remark. There were perfectly sound military reasons for not sending British warships into the Baltic in August 1939 though the navy was prepared to waive them. It would not have made much sense to risk any of the navy's small number of convoy escort vessels being caught in the Baltic at the outbreak of war (and that included the newer, larger and faster passenger liners, whose hulls had been secretly strengthened and their speeds increased by Admiralty subsidy so that, armed with 6-inch guns, they could escort convoys and protect them against German merchant cruisers, similarly armed). What was left was the *City of Exeter* of the Ellerman line, roomy, comfortable, old and slow. It took her five days to get to Leningrad, and she arrived too late for the delegation to catch the midnight train to Moscow. It was not until the afternoon of August 11 that the Anglo-French delegation arrived in the Russian capital.[111]

By then it was very nearly too late. On July 26, Schnurre, the German economic negotiator, invited Georgi Astakhov, the Soviet Chargé d'affaires in Berlin, to dinner. The venue was a German Baltic restaurant, Ernest's. The ostensible guest was M. Babarin, the Soviet commercial negotiator, but it was Astakhov to whom Schnurre spoke, on Ribbentrop's instructions.[112] There existed, he told the startled Russian, no controversial problems of foreign policy between Germany and the Soviet Union 'anywhere along the line from the Baltic Sea to the Black Sea, or in the Far East. Both German and Soviet ideology had one thing in common: opposition to the capitalist democracies.' Schnurre added that German policy was aimed at Britain. He could imagine a far-reaching arrangement between Germany and the Soviets with due consideration for vital Soviet interests. All of this would be lost the moment the Soviet Union signed an agreement with Britain. The next day Schulenburg was sent a copy of Schnurre's record of the meeting, with instructions to press the same arguments upon Molotov. The Soviet Foreign Minister, however, proved difficult to pin down. Not until the evening of August 3, fully eight days later, could he find time to see Schulenburg. In the meantime, under Ribbentrop's urging, Schulenburg was battered with telegrams[113] and the Foreign Minister himself saw M. Astakhov.[114] Ribbentrop believed he had dropped a gentle hint as to a partition of Poland and an agreement on the Baltic states. He seems only to have awoken M. Astakhov's suspicions. On August 8,[115] he warned Moscow that the Germans had no intention of observing any obligations they might undertake 'seriously or for long'. They merely wished to reach a limited understanding and to 'neutralize us at this price' for the immediate future. For this stroke of wisdom M. Astakhov was subsequently recalled to Moscow and imprisoned, where he was to die in 1941.

M. Astakhov's prescience could not stand up to the whirlwind courtship which Ribbentrop now unleashed. The German timetable, the countdown to war, had begun. Soviet caution threatened to throw it totally out of kilter. Hitler still needed, desperately, a diplomatic trump to stop Britain and France from honouring their guarantee to Poland. It was true that Ribbentrop assured him that the British were bluffing. But even Chamberlain would need some kind of an excuse to go back on Britain's word. The pressure on Ribbentrop was increased by the emergence of yet another 'reliable source' on the progress of the Anglo-Soviet negotiations, this time in Moscow, where Schulenburg was informed that the British had conceded to the Soviets the right to move Soviet troops into the Baltic states in the event of their coming under attack.[116] It was, possibly, Molotov's own interpreter, Pavlov, named in a private memorandum in the German Embassy archives by Schulenburg on August 22 as 'our "friend" Pavlov'.[117] The following day Brigadier Firebrace, the British Military Attaché, was reported to have told the Russians that, after an early defeat of Poland, the Germans might offer Britain a separate peace in return for a free hand in the east.[118] On August 14, Ribbentrop instructed Schulenburg to broach the question of his coming to Moscow for discussions. Molotov was now in his element. All he had to do was to continue talking of a step-by-step amelioration of German-Soviet relations and the need for adequate preparation before Ribbentrop's visit. Even then someone felt that the 'reliable source' in London had not outlived his usefulness. On August 14 and 17, the German Embassy in London was told that the Anglo-Soviet talks were going well and that the Poles were ready to open Staff talks with the Russians.[119] Alas, this was far from true, but it added to Ribbentrop's urgency. His willingness to make concessions in advance increased daily. By August 20, Molotov had conceded a visit on August 26 or 27, and handed over the draft of a non-aggression pact to Schulenburg. It took a direct telegram from Hitler to Stalin to secure that Ribbentrop's visit be advanced to August 23. On August 21 Molotov finally yielded.[120] Ribbentrop's coup was secured.

CHAPTER 21

THE AMATEURS ATTEMPT TO
AVERT A WAR

Wars are made between governments, but they are fought between peoples. The war which was to break Europe into two, into the eastward- and westward-looking parts of today, was in the beginning fundamentally a war between the British and German peoples. Had British opinion shown itself as divided and irresolute in 1939 as in 1938, as inclined to see the issues as too complicated and remote to justify a recourse to arms, then Hitler would have had his way with Poland and the states of Europe would have joined in a mad *sauve-qui-peut* dash for Berlin and Berchtesgaden. Hitler was well aware of this. He preferred to believe that Britain would stand aside, that he could deal with Poland in isolation, that no armed resistance from Britain was to be expected. And in this view he was supported, despite everything, by von Ribbentrop. They were both to be disappointed.

In actuality opinion in Britain from Munich onwards was swinging so clearly and drastically against Germany that all over Europe anyone remotely sensitive could feel it. Parliament and Cabinet trailed uneasily in its wake, anxious or unwilling to believe how far and how fast it was moving, afraid, often, to do anything which might add to its momentum. The press, so often more in touch with 'informed' rather than mass opinion, failed adequately to reflect the swing, where it did not seek directly to oppose it, as did the mass circulation papers, the *Daily Mail* and the *Daily Express*. Even those leading figures who were moving with the current, feeling subconsciously in themselves the stirrings of emotions both strange and painful, deep atavisms rising to the surface, hatreds and bitternesses hitherto unknown in the civilized and Christian surroundings to their normal lives, hardly understood what was happening, until suggestions of compromise were made to them: rational, meaningful compromise which at other times they would have accepted without thought, but would now reject with contempt and hatred for those who advanced the idea.

385

The British generations which faced Germany in 1939 had grown to maturity during and after the First World War. Those of an age to fight had fought and survived where their friends, brothers and lovers had died. For twenty years they had honoured those deaths on Armistice Day with poppies, prayers and processions, culminating in the two-minute silence an hour before noon. Their cities, parks and village squares, their churches, schools and business offices, even the railway stations, each carried memorial rolls of the names of those who died in the 1914–18 war. It had, so they believed, been a war to end war. It had certainly been quite unlike the wars of their history books, as the disarmed tanks and spiked field guns which made up so many of the war memorials bore witness. They had lived to believe that there would be no more war, that disputes could be dealt with sensibly and peacefully round a table and that, failing this, the strength of world opinion and the threat of economic isolation would convince would-be aggressors that the game was no longer worth the candle.

But as the years of the 1930s succeeded each other in blood, assassination and turmoil, those beliefs became ever harder to sustain. The newsreels were constantly full of scenes of war, marching troops, machine guns in moving lorries, barbed wire, squat aircraft diving out of the sun on remote Asian towns. The wars of the 1930s had come steadily nearer, Manchuria, China and Paraguay giving way to Abyssinia and to Spain. The newspapers were filled with photographs of shattered cities, collapsing houses, weeping women and cowering children, refugees clutching a handful of possessions. The recruiting posters were alarming. The sensible preparations of government for war: the drawing up of evacuation schemes for the big cities; the issue of gas-masks; the digging of air raid shelters, their construction into the large blocks of flats the London boroughs were putting up as part of the slum clearance schemes – all these combined to convince the people that a new war was inevitable, that the hopes, prayers and poppies of twenty years had flourished in vain.

But it was not with a spirit of hopelessness that the people of Britain contemplated a major war with Germany for the second time in the life of anyone of age in 1939. They felt anger and a new hatred, building and feeding on those which had sustained them in the dark years of the First World War; and behind that hatred and that anger was a confidence so deep as to take little account of the realities of power, the calculus of weapons and strengths that looked, to the Chancelleries of Europe, so impossibly tilted against Britain. It was a Labour Party newspaper, the *Daily Herald*, that greeted the news of the Nazi-Soviet Pact, which Hitler had so confidently expected to give Britain pause, with the words

'At a critical juncture she [Russia] has left the line. But we shall not forget.'[1] But the conviction that Britain could fight and would win, no matter how long, how hard or how costly the struggle, was deep-rooted in the British people. And from the German march into Prague onwards nothing that happened in Europe seems to have shaken British people's conviction that war was inevitable that summer, and that it was inevitable because Hitler's Germany was incorrigibly and irrevocably determined on the conquest of Europe by force and had at all costs to be stopped.

It is hardly surprising, therefore, that there were to be a number of well-meaning attempts to avert the catastrophe. In the summer of 1939, before the last and ultimate crisis, these were to come basically from three quarters: the Vatican, the internal opposition to Hitler in Germany, and a concatenation of well-meaning amateurs working on Marshal Goering.

Of these, the Pope's intervention was the earliest and most cautious. Pius XII, Eugeneo Pacelli, had been Papal Nuncio in Germany in the 1920s, and Secretary of State since 1929. His election was only announced by the traditional puff of smoke on March 2, 1939, at 6 in the evening, after three votes had been taken in the conclave of cardinals. His first message to the faithful, read to the assembled princes of the Church in the Sistine Chapel, had been one of peace. It was a message which did more credit to the good intentions of the new Vicar of Christ than to his sense of political inevitability. For he was to see six years of war, years which were to leave his own image more than a little tarnished by the efforts he was to make to preserve his office from any overt and unneutral commitment to one side or the other. As Cardinal Pacelli, the new Pope had been above all a diplomatist. He had not hesitated to stand up to the Nazis during the years of direct conflict between the Nazi leadership and Catholicism in Germany. He had had more than a hand in penning the famous encyclical of 1937, *Mit brennender Sorge*, in which his predecessor had spoken out against the Nazi persecution of the Catholic Church. But it was the well-being and the interests, narrowly defined, of the Catholic Church that were to prove his greatest care. He would rather negotiate a truce, an armistice, a *modus vivendi* in any dispute than take it to the stake. He was no crusader and no would-be martyr, either, and though his election as Pope was hailed by the press of the West as a smack in the eye for the totalitarian powers, it was not so interpreted in Rome or Berlin.

In his private role the new Pope was an ascetic, almost a mystic, as suggested by his appearance, his air of total absorption in the magnificent ceremonial which surrounded his office. But in political matters he was cautious, hesitant, diplomatic and not engaged. During the First World War he had been sent by Benedict XV to Vienna and Berlin to investigate the possibilities of a negotiated peace. He had seen the disintegration of Germany in defeat and the brief days of the Soviet Republic of Bavaria in his three years as Nuncio in Munich from 1917 to 1920. In 1936 he had visited Roosevelt and seen the triumphs and failures of the New Deal at first hand. Perhaps, despite his air of non-alignment in the temporal struggle that was about to ravage Europe, it was these memories which restrained him from seeming openly to disapprove of the obscenities of Hitler's New Order in Europe. But whatever his motives, whatever his instincts, whatever his true inner judgment of the temporal world without the living confines of the Vatican enclave, he will always be remembered as the Pope who did *not* act, who did *not* denounce, who did *not* condemn, while millions were sacrificed not in the fortunes of war but as part of a deliberate campaign of extermination.

It was to be the same with the Pope's first intervention for peace. On April 21, a fortnight after the Italian desecration of Good Friday by the invasion of Albania, Pius XII sent for Father Tacchi-Venturi, the Papal intermediary between the Vatican and the Palazzo Venezia. It may be that he was stirred to this by President Roosevelt's action a week earlier, towards which Pius XII had exercised what was to become his all-habitual reserve. It may be that he was pricked by the constant stream of messages coming to him from the ordinary Catholics, particularly of the English-speaking countries, sentiments taken up by the British *Catholic Herald*, which was busying itself organizing a petition to demand a Papal initiative to call a peace conference.[2]

Whatever the final impulse, he instructed Father Tacchi-Venturi to sound out Mussolini first of all on the prospects of a successful outcome to a Papal call for a conference of peace. Father Tacchi-Venturi duly saw Mussolini, briefly on May 1, and for a longer period the following evening. He put to him the idea of calling a conference of five powers – Britain, France, Italy, Germany and Poland – charged with discussing ways of resolving the questions likely to lead to war. 'Germany', he said, 'can hardly deceive herself that she will be able to deal with Poland as she has dealt with the other powers without blood being shed. Poland will resist . . . and that will be the beginning of a European war.' He recommended the taking of diplomatic soundings of the other four powers. The Duce was his usual shrewd self, but was also lured by the idea of a new European stage for himself. 'Not even I could have dared suggest this to the Pope.'[3]

The following day instructions went from the Vatican to the Papal

Nuncios in Berlin, Paris and Warsaw and to Archbishop Godfrey, the Archbishop of Westminster, and Apostolic Delegate in London.[4] The same day Pius himself corrected the draft of a letter to Victor Emmanuel, suggesting that his 'beloved son' should act as host and convenor to this conference, which should have as its purpose the settlement of the questions outstanding between France and Italy on the one hand, and Germany and Poland on the other.[5] This letter was never to be sent.

The recipients of the appeal treated it to a man with courtesy and consideration. Lord Halifax was his usual distant and infinitely well-mannered self.[6] He did, however, make it clear that Britain would not contemplate another Munich.[7] Hitler received the Papal Nuncio, Monsignor Cesare Orsenigo, the sceptical Roman amidst the Teutonic barbarians, in Berchtesgaden, placing a special aeroplane at his disposal and offering him tea at the end of their conversation. But Hitler did not believe in the danger of war. The differences between France and Italy were capable of rational elucidation, such as to lead to a treaty but not to war. There was no danger with Poland, and his demands would not ripen in this quarter before 1942 or even 1945. No, the only real danger was Britain, who was inciting Poland against Germany as she had incited the Negroes of Abyssinia against Italy, 'the reds against Franco', Chiang Kai-shek against Japan and, by the machinations of the British Military Attaché in Berlin, General Mason-MacFarlane, and the British Chargé d'affaires in Prague, as she had fomented Czechoslovakia against Germany after Munich. Monsignor Orsenigo greeted this curious version of history in silence. But, Hitler continued, he was always loyal to his ally and friend, the Duce. He would have to consult him first.[8]

The Poles were cowed but bitter. The real source of difficulty in Europe, said Colonel Beck to Monsignor Filippo Cortesi,[9] Archbishop of Sirace and Nuncio in Poland, was the incomprehensible lack of courage displayed by Ciano and Mussolini, who, for fear of the Germans, were unwilling to show a real sense of the true interests of Italy by giving a stronger lead in Eastern Europe. If they were to follow such a policy, Poland would certainly be their ally. Poland, he continued, was working for peace by imposing restraint on the course of the Anglo-Soviet negotiations. A British guarantee for Poland was a measure *against* war; an alliance with Russia was a measure for war. He preferred a Papal offer of good offices rather than a conference where a probable lack of success might enhance the danger of war.

The real opposition curiously came from Paris. M. Bonnet was inclined to be on the distant side, exercising a diplomatic reserve worthy of Pius XII himself.[10] The really violent comments came from M. Alexis St Léger Léger. The whole affair, he told Sir Eric Phipps,[11] was a plot by Mussolini. He had been trying to inveigle the Western powers into a four-power conference like this for some time. Cardinal Maglione, the Pope's right-hand man, was acting as he had during the Abyssinian crisis, as an Italian rather than a servant of the Vatican. It would be far better for the Vatican to reserve itself for appeals 'on a general and usual plane for peace', and 'not get involved in political matters which it should leave to the Chancelleries'. On May 10, Cardinal Maglione announced[12] the abandonment for the time being of any Papal initiative, but he reserved the Vatican's right to return to the idea.

Where the Papacy was to show caution and hesitation, the various strands of the German opposition to Hitler were to find it impossible to cross the increasing barriers of national prejudice that were being raised at this period in their own hearts as well as those of their British contacts. At this period the two main centres of activity, those in the Army General Staff in touch with Oster in the *Abwehr* and with the group around Generals Beck and Witzleben, and the diplomatists centred on State Secretary von Weizsäcker, were operating entirely separately from one another and very largely at cross-purposes. The army officers had been desperately disheartened by the outcome of the Munich crisis. Not only had it seemed to prove Hitler's judgment right and their own wrong, but it had caused their seniors to withdraw in total panic at the lengths they had been prepared to go; the members of the army leadership now had their heads firmly down. In these circumstances any hope of reviving the conspiracy which had existed in the month of September 1938 seemed hopeless.[13] Oster resorted, as has been suggested earlier, to feeding the British with scare stories, designed to push them into ever more open opposition to Hitler. Whether the scare in mid-January was his work is possibly debatable. But the warning which caused the British fleet to man its anti-aircraft guns on April 3–4, while Lord Stanhope, the First Lord of the Admiralty, announced from the deck of the aircraft carrier *Ark Royal* that the navy was ready for anything, almost certainly came from the *Abwehr*.[14]

Oster's example was copied, though more openly, by the most dedicated officers of the General Staff. Among them was the forty-year-old Colonel Count von Schwerin, of the Atlantic Group of the War Ministry. In May he took up one of Colonel Mason-MacFarlane's more outspoken remarks about Britain's determination to fight against *Machtpolitik*; but his innocent enquiry as to whether 'Mason-Mac' was speaking officially, designed to strengthen his own arguments within the Staff that Britain's position was just as 'Mason-Mac' described it, offended Mason-MacFarlane's very delicate sense of propriety and only earned Schwerin a reprimand from his chief.[15] Undaunted, however, he followed in the footsteps of Ewald von Kleist, and came in the first week of July to London. British military intelligence refused to see him. 'If you want to know what I think of his coming over here, at a time when our country's relations with his are as bad as they are today,' an officer remarked to a British intermediary, 'I think it is a damned cheek.'[16] The navy was a good deal less stuffy, and Admiral Godfrey, the Director of Naval Intelligence, arranged for him to meet a Conservative whip, James Stuart, General Marshall-Cornwall, the former British Military Attaché in Berlin, and Mr Gladwyn Jebb, of the Foreign Office. But his proposals – for an ostentatious naval demonstration in the Baltic by units of the British fleet, for the appointment of Mr Churchill to the Cabinet, for the dispatch of RAF units to France, and the issuing of an invitation to General Milch, Goering's deputy, to see the extent of British civil preparations – fell on deaf ears.[17] Chamberlain was determined not to recall Winston until war had actually broken out, and all the other measures, which might at least have cracked the veneer of Hitler's conviction that Britain would not fight, struck Lord Halifax and his advisers as altogether too provocative. Count von Schwerin retired to Germany to play a brief part in von Weizsäcker's continuing intrigues in mid-August.

The misfortune of Count von Schwerin and his failure to get his message across to the British authorities were not entirely to be ascribed, however, to an upsurge of British nationalism in the breasts of his listeners. To those who might have been expected to have their ears attuned to the noises of opposition to Hitler in Germany there came a plethora of totally confusing reports among which it was only too easy to lose one's way. In the course of the summer men such as Vansittart, Godfrey and their juniors were visited by a succession of emissaries from different groups which were eventually to coalesce into the wartime conspiracy against Hitler, but at this time could only speak from an amorphous sense of alarm. Brave men all, they represented nothing sufficiently tangible or organized to make any impression on their listeners, save to fill the more sanguine of them with the belief that, should it come to war, Germany might well collapse from a breakdown in morale.

The two exceptions to this general confusion of faces were only to add to the confusion in the minds of their listeners. The one was Adam von Trott zu Solz, a young and dedicated idealist and a Rhodes scholar at Oxford, whose name appears on the war memorial of Balliol

College. His very striking looks and his intelligence had won him a circle of Oxford friends stretching from All Souls to Wadham, from A. L. Rowse, the historian of Elizabethan England, and Isaiah Berlin, the philosopher, to Lord David Cecil and Sir Maurice Bowra. Outside Oxford his friends included not only the formidable Lady Astor, but Sir Stafford Cripps and R. H. Tawney, the great economic historian.

Adam von Trott was to become for this summer an agent of Ernst von Weizsäcker's desperate fight to prevent war. In its course he was to do himself moral damage in the eyes of most of his English friends, from which he has never quite been redeemed, even by the most devoted of his friends and his own death at the hands of the SS after the failure of the 1944 attempt on Hitler's life. The fault for this lies not with his own confusion of mind. Neither his upbringing nor Oxford had given him any political sense, and he had spent much of 1938 in China and the Far East. It lies more with the confusion of purpose and motive of those who sent him, particularly that of Ernst von Weizsäcker, the State Secretary in the German Foreign Ministry.

Weizsäcker was a dedicated opponent of Hitler's foreign policy and the Nazi system of government. To doubt that, as some historians in Britain and France have done, is to be both ungenerous and crude in judgment. But his motives in opposing Hitler and von Ribbentrop and in accepting the calvary of working alongside that vain and stupid fool, though they sprang from a deep-rooted devotion to his country, led him and those who followed him very closely into a conflict of choice which they never succeeded in resolving. Put very crudely, the choice lay between attempting to sharpen the points of international conflict so that a general realization of the perils into which Hitler was leading Germany would cause the army leadership to remove him, and working to deter the oncoming conflict so that Germany should not be involved in a European war which could only end in disaster. Throughout Weizsäcker inclined towards the second of these choices. This was to lead him again and again into advocating a solution which, to British opponents of Hitler, seemed to differ hardly at all from surrender, from ignominious appeasement. It was to just such a scheme that Adam von Trott lent himself in May and June of 1939.

Behind this scheme there lay the aim of unseating von Ribbentrop as the first step. Adam von Trott was particularly suited to Weizsäcker's latest intrigue in that he had a line to Hitler through the most internationally experienced and least unpleasant of Hitler's personal entourage, Walter Hewel. Equally, his friendship with Lady Astor could bring him directly to Lord Halifax and Chamberlain. The scheme envisaged a restoration of Czechoslovak independence and the compensation of Germany by Poland, presumably by a change in the frontier of the Polish Corridor. No doubt a good deal of pressure on Poland would be required to secure this by way of the kind of international conference for which Pius XII had been taking soundings. But the removal of the British guarantee for Poland would, so it was felt, leave Poland no alternative but to adjust to the realities of her situation; while the magnificence of the gesture over Czechoslovakia would disarm suspicion of German expansionism in the West. Hitler himself would be deprived of the sense of conflict on which he thrived and, if he proved intransigent, this might then stir the army conspirators into action; and the German people, always, so von Weizsäcker believed, more easily incensed against Poland than against the Czechs, would not be able to accuse any government which might follow Hitler of abandoning the legitimate aims of the German nation, the restoration of the Bismarckian frontiers.

The scheme, without its anti-Hitlerian overtones, was discussed between Adam von Trott, Weizsäcker and Hewel. Adam von Trott duly came to Britain and spent the weekend of June 2–3 at the Astors' house, Cliveden, where he dined with Lord Halifax and Sir Thomas Inskip, going on to London on June 7 to talk to Chamberlain. He found a sympathetic hearing for his general position, though no commitment whatever. He also had to listen to some very plain speaking on the state of British opinion, 'passionately stirred', in Chamberlain's words, by the occupation of Prague and determined to fight rather than see another independent nation 'destroyed'. Trott returned to Germany to concoct a report which attempted to portray both his proposals and their reception in Britain as seen from the standpoint of a dedicated Nazi.[18] He succeeded only too effectively in his attempt at a pastiche of the Nazi literary style, but Ribbentrop prevented the report from reaching Hitler, and intervened also to prevent Trott's reception by Goering. A shortened version of his report did, however, reach Hitler via Walter Hewel. Trott returned to Britain for a second brief visit; quite why has never been made clear. Its only effect was to convince many of his friends that he had gone over to the Nazis. Everywhere he collided with the new mood in Britain. His friends were no longer thinking of the injustices of Versailles, wallowing in the guilt in which only the wealthy, the contented and the satisfied can indulge. Britain was threatened and the German nation was beginning to assume the lineaments depicted by British intellectual propaganda during the First World War. With the British in this mood the proposals which Adam von Trott had advanced simply appeared to be a means of adding Poland to Czechoslovakia as Germany's satellites. By a simple transference von Trott was obviously a Nazi agent.[19] Weizsäcker's own emissary, Erich Kordt, whose brother, Theo, was Counsellor in the German Embassy in London, received a similar treatment at Vansittart's hands in July[20] (though he did his best to gloss over this in his memoirs), as did Theo Kordt when he broached a variant of the plan to Gladwyn Jebb on August 18.[21] Whatever the justice of these proposals, they were simply not negotiable after the events of the preceding eighteen months and as long as Hitler was in power.

Nor were the British authorities likely in any way to be impressed by the total absence in the proposals of an alternative to Hitler's leadership. Today, with the benefit of hindsight, the structure of a permanent opposition to Nazism can be perceived underlying the variety of individual intimations to which the British authorities were to be subjected, an opposition which proved its bona fides by its belated attempt to overthrow Hitler; it must have been almost impossible, however, for even the well-intentioned in London, if there were any, to make anything of the little genuine information that was given them by their visitors.

No doubt this is why the other main enterprise undertaken from the German side seems to have been treated with a great deal more respect, though just as much caution, by the British Cabinet and Foreign Office. This was a group of three initiatives all leading back to Goering, though all undertaken at the instance of the intermediaries rather than by Goering himself. No doubt their actions were greatly welcomed by Goering, so long as they promised success. By the last week of May his position had been very much shaken. Ribbentrop had annexed both his previous initiatives in foreign policy: the bilateral pact with Italy and the approach to the Soviet Union. Relations with Poland were steadily worsening and his idiot rival was assuring Hitler night and day that Britain would not come to Poland's support. Goering never believed this. But by the beginning of June his star had sunk so low that diplomatic gossip depicted him and Ribbentrop as surrounding themselves with armed men to guard against the possibility of assassination at each other's hands. To prove Ribbentrop wrong, to bring about an agreement with England, must have seemed to Goering his one real chance of a comeback.

Whatever his motives, he did nothing to discourage the three amateur diplomatists who now rushed to put their services at his disposal. The first of these was the Swedish millionaire, Axel Wenner-Gren. He met Goering in the last week of May, when Goering took the initiative in talking of the need for peace between Britain and Germany.[22] He still believed in peace, he said, not like the Ribbentrop-

Goebbels–Himmler group who wanted war. To the Swedish suggestion that he might report these views in Britain, Goering agreed, with the proviso that Wenner-Gren should only approach Chamberlain, as there were those in the Foreign Office who were opposed to any Anglo-German settlement. Armed with a letter from the Crown Prince of Sweden, Wenner-Gren approached the Premier through the Conservative Chief Whip, the all-powerful Captain David Margesson. Chamberlain listened to the Swede sympathetically but his sense of outrage shows clearly through his own notes of the conversation.[23] Goering, he said, seemed to be inviting new British proposals on Poland and the colonies in return for German assurances. He found Hitler totally untrustworthy and if he was to suggest colonial concessions at that point he would be swept from office the next day. It was for Hitler to undo the mischief he had done and take more drastic steps to restore confidence in himself.

With this highly unpromising message, Wenner-Gren returned to Goering very full of his own importance. He not only sent Goering a seventeen-page outline of a peace programme suggesting the liquidation of concentration camps, a political amnesty, the release from imprisonment of Pastor Niemöller, the most famous of Hitler's religious internees, and Kurt von Schuschnigg, the Austrian Chancellor, an end to racial persecution and other similar proposals; he also revived the old idea of a restoration of Czechoslovakia. After this revelation of Swedish realism, Goering abandoned Mr Wenner-Gren and made no effort to introduce him to Hitler, though he was to keep stringing him along with the occasional message until well into August.[24]

At this point Goering already had approved a more promising series of contacts. The intermediary in this case, Helmut Wohltat, was the deputy head of his own Four Year Plan Organization, an accomplished negotiator (he had negotiated the German-Romanian trade treaty of March 23, 1939), and a man who was visiting Britain regularly in connection with both the International Committee on Refugees and the International Whaling Conference. He had excellent contacts in the German business world and could speak with Schacht's authority as well as Goering's (the old banker was developing his own support operation in Basle through Montagu Norman, Chancellor of the Bank of England, and desperately trying to get out of Germany on the pretext of wishing to be sent to China to advise on Chinese currency problems); and Wohltat was well known to Sir Horace Wilson, the head of the Civil Service, on whose advice Chamberlain leaned as much as or more than on anyone else.

The Wohltat mission has been subject to more misunderstanding than any other single question of the years before the war. Like Trott, Wohltat wrote a grotesquely pastiche-Nazi account of his negotiations which his friend and ally in them, the Ambassador Herbert von Dirksen, backed up.[25] They were under a double pressure to paint things the way they did, not only to influence Hitler but to protect themselves against Ribbentrop's fury when reports of Wohltat's activities got into the press and gave him the first intimation of what had been going on behind his back. These reports were published by the Russians in 1948 as a counterblast to American publication of the documents on the Nazi-Soviet negotiations between 1939 and 1941.[26] It is now clear that as historical evidence of the actual course of the negotiations they are as good as worthless.

Wohltat acted, as he subsequently admitted, on his own initiative.[27] He had excellent contacts in Britain. Before joining the German Civil Service in 1934 as the head of the new office for foreign exchange transactions, he had been active on the international market for oils and fats as a private businessman, and had maintained regular contacts in the City of London since the early 1920s. He had also been passing secret information and warnings of the Nazi-Soviet contacts to Sir Robert Vansittart, a fact which may explain why his file in the Foreign Office archives, one ostensibly dealing with the International Whaling Conference, remains closed to researchers until the year 2015.[28] At the beginning of June he announced to Goering his intention of conducting conversations in London on the possibilities of an Anglo-German understanding. Goering expressly forbade him to give these conversations an official character. He was at this moment unwilling to give Ribbentrop any new handle against him until he had something to take to Hitler, but he was prepared to let Wohltat go ahead and explore matters.

It is for debate how much Wohltat had been misled by a British amateur interloper into these great affairs. Henry Drummond-Wolff, former MP for Basingstoke, had been a frequent visitor to Germany in his capacity as a member of the Council of Empire Industries Association. In May he announced that he was to make a private visit to Berlin, letting the German Embassy know that he was undertaking this with the knowledge of Sir Horace Wilson,[29] a convenient phrase which can very well be used to cover anything from clandestine encouragement to simple information on the user's current travel plans. In Berlin he was entertained by both Wohltat and Dr Rüter, formerly concerned with economic matters on the staff of the German Embassy in London and now head of the Foreign Ministry section dealing with economic relations with Britain and the Commonwealth.[30] What he said to

Wohltat is unknown but to Rüter he gave a series of dark hints as to a possible British willingness to make Germany economic concessions in south-east Europe and a loan to cover her foreign exchange problems. The closeness of his contact with Sir Horace Wilson and the demi-official status he seemed to be claiming for his proposals may be judged by Rüter's comment that he did not seem 'quite *au courant*' with the circumstances of the discussions either between British and German industrial associations or the official trade discussions on an increase of German exports to Britain and the British colonies. Nor did he know about the Anglo-German discussions due to begin in London a few days later on the regulation of payments between German-occupied Czechoslovakia and Britain.

Wohltat was aware of this latter question, but he could well have shared Drummond-Wolff's ignorance of the other matters. He had after all had a very full programme of negotiations with Romania and was about to embark on another with Franco's Spain. He was also active on the Intergovernmental Committee on Refugees, a highly complicated and technical matter involving a regulation of international payments when Germany was totally unwilling to release any of her own foreign exchange earnings for the purpose. He was also involved in the International Whaling Conference. It is quite on the cards, therefore, that he never received any detailed briefing on the current state of Anglo-German trade negotiations and that his ignorance on their course over the previous nine months was as great as that of Mr Drummond-Wolff.

Wohltat arrived in London on June 6. He met Sir Horace Wilson privately the same day, at the London residence of the Duke of Westminster, a singularly curious meeting place. The Duke was not present. Those who were included Drummond-Wolff and Sir Joseph Ball, the head of the Conservative Party Research Department. Sir Joseph, who had formerly been associated with MI5 as we have seen, had been handling the 'secret channel' of contacts between No. 10 and the Italian Embassy for the last two years. He was also involved in the clandestine organization of British radio propaganda against Germany. Whenever one looks into the more shadowy aspects of Chamberlain's personal actions, Ball is there.

The conversation, of which no direct record seems to have survived, appears to have been a tough one, Sir Horace following very much the same line that the Prime Minister was following the same day with Wenner-Gren. He listened to Dr Wohltat's ideas and proposals politely and without commitment or rejection. His own side of the conversation was confined to making it as clear as possible that, however desirable and promising the proposals being advanced, the current tension in Anglo-German relations for which both Government and opinion held the German Government solely responsible, made them purely academic until and unless measures were taken by the German Government to reduce the tension and restore confidence in its good intentions.[31] This lesson was repeated to Dr Wohltat the following day by Frank Ashton-Gwatkin, head of the Foreign Office Economic Section, with a direct warning that if Germany attacked Poland, Britain would fight.[32] Lord Halifax had dealt with similar suggestions from the German Ambassador three weeks earlier with equal firmness; so much so that von Dirksen had not seen any point in reporting to Berlin on the conversation.[33]

Wohltat, however, seems to have been misled by the normal courtesies paid by his British listeners to his proposals. He returned to Berlin and gave Goering a written report on his activities and conversations. He then disappeared to Spain for a month's economic negotiations. On his return to Berlin in mid-July, Goering was not to be reached, so that Wohltat was forced to follow up on the June conversations in a still greater state of isolation and independence than he had enjoyed during them, without instructions and without any idea of Goering's own position in relation to Hitler or von Ribbentrop.

This was perhaps as well, as in the meantime a second Swede had become part of Goering's contacts with the British. This was Mr Birger Dahlerus, a Swedish industrialist who had long been a close friend of Goering and who had taken Goering's stepson on to his personal staff. Unlike Mr Wenner-Gren and Dr Wohltat, Mr Dahlerus began by approaching the British, meeting at the end of June in London a small group of internationally minded British businessmen.[34] Dahlerus saw it as his task to convince Goering and, through him, Hitler, that Britain would go to war if pushed too hard, although the British Government was genuinely prepared to negotiate a settlement if the pressure was removed. He started from the belief that there was increasing ignorance on each side of the real state of mind of the other – a failure of communication. It was his belief – it is a long-standing liberal heresy – that a face-to-face meeting between men of good faith would repair this failure and pave the way to a settlement once the mutual misunderstandings had been removed. It was unfortunate therefore that he proved in practice unable properly to comprehend the real position of either of the two sides between whom he was to attempt to mediate.

Dahlerus saw Goering on July 6 at Karinhall, Goering's superb residence outside Berlin. He found Goering worried and truculent. The worry seems to have stemmed from his conviction that Britain would fight if the Polish question was pushed into a war, a belief which the German diplomatic monitoring service, the *Forschungsamt*, which was directly under his control, was doing its best to strengthen and confirm. He made one very curious remark that Dahlerus recorded without showing any sign of appreciating its significance. Approaches by third parties, he said, 'which we can trace to England or believe have come from England, are a sign of weakness on the part of England. Mr Wenner-Gren came to see me with a message, so he said, or I understood it to be, from Mr Chamberlain.' If Goering's use of the word 'we' means anything, then he was clearly echoing Hitler's reaction to all this amateur mediation. That it was not his own view is shown by his willingness to explore Mr Dahlerus's proposals further, once he had given this warning.[35] The meeting between Dahlerus and his three British contacts was fixed, after a second meeting on July 8, for the beginning of August.

Before that date could be reached, however, the unfortunate Dr Wohltat's initiative blew up in his face. He had returned to London on July 17 in his capacity as leader of the German delegation to the annual International Whaling Conference. The following day he met Sir Horace Wilson in the late afternoon. According to the documentation that he and his ally, Ambassador von Dirksen, prepared for Goering and Hitler, Wilson had with him a memorandum which he had had prepared in the Foreign Office and which he made clear that Chamberlain had approved.[36] This memorandum has never been produced; Wohltat's report on his conversations with Sir Horace Wilson and with Robert Hudson brought the arguments he alleged had been used by the two men into one memorandum headed 'Programme for German-British Co-operation (Sir Horace W.)', which he wrote up after his return to Berlin.

One may take leave to doubt whether there ever was such a memorandum; if there was, it was certainly not produced in the Foreign Office, who were left completely in the dark about the whole business.[37] Sir Horace Wilson's own notes of the conversation make it clear that the only thing he gave Wohltat was a copy of *The Times* of June 30, containing the text of Lord Halifax's speech of June 29 at Chatham House. He was, he wrote, 'most anxious to maintain the position that had been adopted in the June conversation, namely that we were not unduly apprehensive about things and that the initiative must come from the German side'.[38] In view of Wohltat's admission that he had no idea what had happened to the memorandum he had given Goering on the June round of talks, Sir Horace may be forgiven for not taking the whole approach very seriously, the more so as Wohltat said that his framework for peace was contained in Hitler's April speech at the Reichstag. Sir Horace also recorded, in tones of some contempt, Wohltat's suggestion that some British personality of standing should visit Hitler to talk about the political, military and economic questions which might be of interest to the two countries.

Sir Horace Wilson's discretion, his restraint and his dry dismissal of Wohltat's initiative stand in considerable contrast to the action of Mr Robert Hudson, the political head of the Department of Overseas Trade, whom Wohltat saw on July 20. Hudson says he was asked to meet Wohltat by the German Embassy. Wohltat and Dirksen maintained that an invitation to call on Hudson was passed on to Wohltat by the highly embarrassed head of the Norwegian whaling delegation.[39] Hudson was, as has been seen, an ambitious man teetering on the edge of political failure. His intrigue against Hore-Belisha in January had failed. His visit to Berlin had been called off. His visit to Moscow had produced only a few thousand tons of Soviet dried herring. Small wonder, then, that Hudson rushed in where Wilson had refused to tread. His own note of his conversation is full of self-glorification. He spoke of the need to find markets for German heavy industries when rearmament came to an end. He speculated at great length and with a considerable degree of vagueness about co-operation between the heavy industries of Britain, Germany and the United States in the capital development of Russia, China and the various European colonial dependencies. He spoke of Anglo-American help for Germany's shortage of capital. He spoke of the joint administration of Africa as a means of satisfying German colonial claims. He warned Wohltat that all this was meaningless unless economic considerations played a part in the formulation of foreign policy in Germany. And when Wohltat said that they played very little part in the Führer's mind, he authorized Wohltat to report his remarks to Goering in the hope they could get through to him.

Hudson seems to have come out of this meeting in a state of high euphoria. His note of its course[40] was almost certainly written after Wohltat left him, which was fairly late in the evening. The following evening, still in extremely high spirits over his own cleverness, he let the cat out of the bag at a dinner attended by one or more unfriendly journalists. The following morning, July 22, Victor Gordon-Lennox in the *Daily Telegraph* and Vernon Bartlett in the *News Chronicle* went to town on the story. Britain had offered Germany a loan, the value of which was put in hundreds of millions of pounds sterling, in return for international control of German armaments, the monies to be used to place German industry on a sound peacetime commercial basis, after a conference had negotiated the return of Danzig to the Reich.[41] Hudson attempted to restore matters by giving an interview to the *Daily Express* in which he put the onus of the entire affair on Wohltat and posed as the 'strong man' who had put this Nazi intriguer in his place; and he accused the Germans of leaking lying reports to the press. But he was not to save himself. The *Sunday Times* published on July 23 an official denial that any such plan had been considered and on July 24 Chamberlain denied that any loan was under consideration, stating to a particularly ruffled House of Commons that Hudson had acted entirely on his own initiative and had been expressing his private opinions.[42] The Foreign Office files are singularly void of comment on the whole affair. Cadogan was on leave. Vansittart was almost incoherent with rage. Even Chamberlain was furiously angry over the whole episode. After a stormy interview at which Hudson denied ever mentioning a loan, Chamberlain wrote to his sister Ida[43] that Hudson was a 'clever fellow with a persuasive tongue', who had a 'very bad reputation as a disloyal colleague' and was always trying to advance his own interests at the expense of his friends; Chamberlain was not at all sure that Hudson had told him the whole truth. A week later, he was still fuming; 'Hudson's gaffe', he wrote to his sister, 'has clearly done a lot of harm and has clearly shown how completely he lacks the sense of responsibility which a Minister should have. I did not want to add to my troubles by sacking him, but . . .' He returned to his Pollyanna-ish mood, however, consoling himself that the episode showed that 'Hitler has concluded we mean business and the time is not ripe for a major war,' and again, 'Hitler has now realized that he cannot get anything else without a major war and has decided to put Danzig into cold storage.' 'In the meantime', he added ominously, 'there are other and discreeter channels by which contact can be maintained, for it is important that those in Germany who would like to see us come to an understanding should not be discouraged.'

The press reports unleashed a flood of angry speculation in the press of France and Poland, as well as in Germany and Italy. Reassured by Chamberlain's categorical denials, the French and Polish press accepted that this was another German manœuvre.[44] The Italian and German press affected to take the matter seriously and waxed monstrously sarcastic over Britain's Shylockian belief that everything could be bought if only a high enough price was offered.[45]

Soviet comments show that, from that day to this,[46] they took the episode as proof beyond peradventure of the duplicity of British policy, and as confirmation of their suspicions of British insincerity in the Anglo-Soviet negotiations for an alliance, even as justification for their

own, ultimately successful, negotiations with the Germans. Gladwyn
Jebb was not much wide of the mark when he wrote to Cadogan,[47] 'the
immediate effect of this piece of super-appeasement has been to arouse
all the suspicions of the Bolsheviks – I must say I doubt whether folly
could be pushed to a fuller extreme.'

More seriously, Hudson's indiscretion promised to spoil entirely any
chance of Wohltat's action fulfilling his and von Dirksen's expectations.
Von Dirksen was well aware of the general line Wohltat proposed to
take, and had indeed discussed this in some detail with him. He had had
very little chance, however, of seeing Wohltat after the meetings with
Wilson and Hudson, as Wohltat had left for Berlin on July 21. It was not
until late in August that he saw the full report Wohltat had made to
Goering and Hitler. Wohltat wrote the report on July 24. Ribbentrop
was on retirement at Fuschl in the Salzkammergut and does not seem to
have tumbled to what had been going on until the end of the month,
possibly because it was then that Goering had finally got through to
Hitler. There followed an angry series of telegrams between Berlin and
London, asking for detailed reports on the conversations;[48] but von
Dirksen had taken care to cover himself and Ribbentrop's wrath did not
fall on his head.

The report which Wohltat wrote[49] was a superb statement of the
ideas Wohltat himself had been advocating for much of that year: an
Anglo-German declaration that they would not use force against each
other; mutual declarations of non-interference; a fundamental revision
of the mandates provisions of the Treaty of Versailles; navy, army and
air force arms limitations agreements; common policy on raw materials
and markets; a colonial condominium in Africa; a declaration linking
the Reichsmark with the pound, with an international debt settlement
for Germany; and loans for the Reichsbank. Here was jam for everyone,
and a mish-mash of ideas that had been floating around centres of liberal
international gossip for a decade.

Wohltat got the idea of a declaration of no force from a book on the
Kellogg Pact, one which had attempted to fit the ideas of the Kellogg
Pact into the Nazi ethos of *Grossraumordnung* and *Lebensraum*, of there
being areas which were part of the spatial requirements of individual
powers and where other powers were alien interlopers (*raumfremde
Machte*).[50] Other ideas he drew from the international regime over the
Chinese customs. The idea of a condominium with access to raw
materials had been floated repeatedly through the years, and had been
the subject of an official enquiry organized for the League of Nations by
the Premier of Belgium, van Zeeland, in 1938.[51] Wohltat himself had
raised the idea of abandoning the most-favoured nation clause in an

article in a leading German economic journal, *Der deutsche Volkswirt*, the previous December. Yet all of this he fastened on Wilson.

Von Dirksen did his best to back him up. On August 3, he had a final conversation with Wilson, on which his report differs almost completely from that of Sir Horace, which insisted continuously on the need for a German initiative to reduce tension and define the situation.[52] What instructions has the Führer given to follow up Wohltat's report? . . . What will the Chancellor do to prevent the position from becoming worse? . . . Will he so arrange events during these weeks that they are non-provocative? . . . What will the German Chancellor do to show his determination to give the lead in creating a suitable atmosphere? . . . Hitler was in complete control of the situation; he had no critics to meet, no opposition forces to consider. . . . It was no use saying that he could not control the situation. . . . Only Hitler has it in his power to attack. Von Dirksen's report is the subtlest of variants on this, retaining all the Wohltatian proposals as though they came from Sir Horace, reproducing some of Sir Horace's warnings but representing them only as expressions of anxiety. All in vain: the report was never read. Hitler had already secured the assurances he was seeking from Russia.

Goering had already turned in his continuing exploration of approaches to Britain to the waiting Dahlerus. While Wohltat in all ignorance was devoting his weekend to the creation of diplomatic fiction in the service of peace and the salvation of his career, Dahlerus was meeting Goering in secrecy during the Marshal's visit to Hamburg for an immense evening celebration at the Hansehalle. Dahlerus had been in London conferring with his business friends. He had also been to Stockholm to see Wenner-Gren to ask if they might borrow the Swedish millionaire's yacht for the meeting. Wenner-Gren had done his best to warn Goering off this new intervention, writing to Goering that he had received direct warning from Neville Chamberlain that the planned meeting might result in the fall of his Government, a statement totally unsupported by any British evidence at present available, and trying to impress on Goering that his proposals offered the only chance of peace. Goering, in Dahlerus's version at least, said that Wenner-Gren's proposals were totally unacceptable, and mentioned too that he thought Wohltat's proposals absurd and not to be taken seriously. (Since Goering would not yet have received Wohltat's memorandum of July 24, either Wenner-Gren was referring to Wohltat's record of his June conversation or, probably, either he or Dahlerus himself was trying to impress on the British the need to use Dahlerus alone.) Goering certainly seems to have found Dahlerus's approach more promising than either of the two previous interventions, if Mr Dahlerus has given us an accurate record of the meeting, since he spoke of consulting with Hitler before his meeting with the British businessmen took place.[53]

On the Monday, Dahlerus returned to Britain and the following day, July 25, for the first time met Lord Halifax, using Sir Harold Wernher, the well-known race-horse owner and President of the Anglo-Swedish Society, to introduce him. Halifax encouraged the proposal, which was presented to him mainly as a means of impressing the genuineness of the change in British opinion on Goering, and through him on Hitler. Otherwise, apart from giving the shortest of shrifts to Dahlerus's attempt to blame the British press for the growth of British hostility to Germany, he made it clear that he did not want to know officially of the meeting at all.[54]

The meeting duly took place on August 7 at Soonke Nissen Koog, the estate of Dahlerus's wife on the island of Sylt. The British business-men, seven in number, led by a Mr Charles F. Spencer, brought with them a long memorandum, which Goering besprinkled with sarcastic marginalia. As they expounded their view of the development of opinion in Britain, Goering scribbled furious notes for his reply, doodling a brooding and ferocious face over the first page of them and breaking into furious polemic as soon as the British had finished.[55] The British record, equally besprinkled with marginalia, included a pathetic protest from Chamberlain – 'I am certain there is nothing in any of the speeches of mine which would justify this protest'; the record ended with proposals 'of the nature of an ultimatum', in Mr Spencer's words, for Britain and Poland to settle Danzig with Germany, for there to be direct Anglo-German conversations and a four-power conference to follow to settle all outstanding matters.[56]

Mr Chamberlain's verdict on this is not recorded. He was at the time on holiday in Scotland. He certainly did not think it worth confiding to his sisters or his journal. The Foreign Office view was that the meeting had done not much good but probably not much harm. Goering's proposals were unacceptable. There was nothing to do but keep to the present policy and wait. It was very nerve-racking, but there were signs that British policy was seriously bothering the Germans. If they saw there was no opportunity for a bloodless victory, then they might accept a peaceful settlement. This judgment contained three gross errors. It failed to recognize that Goering's communication of the facts of the meeting to Hitler would confirm him in his view that Britain would fail to come to Poland's aid. It assumed that the diplomatic scene was a constant, though the Nazi-Soviet Pact lay a bare ten days away.

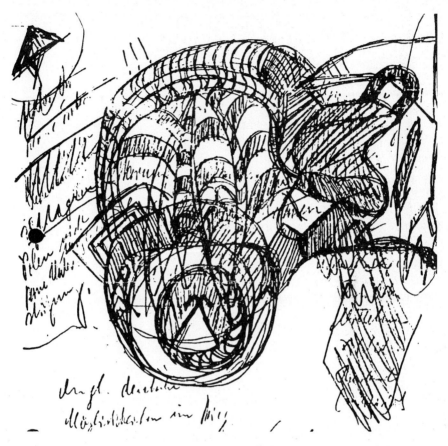

A graphologist, shown this sample of a doodle by Goering, wrote: 'He was feeling very much in control and rather unresponsive . . . the whole suggests him attempting to work his way . . . very triumphant.'

And it assumed that the prospect of victory with bloodshed repelled Hitler. It did not. He wallowed in it. Everything conspired to convince him that the British, who could not share his hunger for war, would recoil at the last moment.

One of the less happy of those who were to contribute to his conviction even at the end of July 1939 was Lord Kemsley, proprietor of the *Daily Sketch* and the *Sunday Times*, and brother of Lord Camrose, proprietor of the *Daily Telegraph*. Lord Kemsley had been an ardent supporter of the Prime Minister.[57] Like Chamberlain, he had been bitterly disillusioned by the German march into Bohemia and Moravia. Like others in Chamberlain's circle he saw value in 'keeping open a "direct wire"' to someone in Hitler's entourage, if not to the Führer himself. The most dubious aspect of his visit, and one which betrays the

'Just in case there's any mistake'

strained relations obtaining between the staff of the Foreign Office and Sir Horace Wilson and the staff of No. 10 Downing Street, is that apart from Lord Halifax himself and Sir Alexander Cadogan, the Foreign Office was kept in the dark about the mission. Henderson, who was in on the secret, corresponded directly and privately with Sir Horace Wilson and Lord Halifax. Not that Wilson was to show himself simple-minded; he was well aware that the invitation extended to Lord Kemsley might be a trick 'to throw dust in our eyes'; but he strongly suspected the Foreign Office Press Department, not altogether without reason, of leaking all it could to those organs of the press that were consistently opposed to the conciliation of Hitler.

At the end of July, Otto Dietrich, Hitler's Press Chief, engineered a meeting between Lord Kemsley and Hitler.[58] The idea was to counter the build-up of Anglo-German hatred in the two countries by an exchange of newspaper articles, British authors writing in the German press and Germans in the *Daily Telegraph*. Ribbentrop followed the meeting, which was exceptional, even by Hitler's standards, for the volume of windy but empty rhetoric indulged in, and Arthur Bryant actually prepared an article as the first British contribution. Lord Halifax did his best to control the issue, writing to Lord Londonderry, another Pan-Anglo-Germanist of the period, who owed his dismissal from the Cabinet in 1935 to the failure of the Air Ministry, which he headed, to take Hitler's claims to have an air force equal to the RAF seriously. Any British initiative, he wrote, would be seen by Hitler as a sign that Britain was weakening.[59]

This view did not seem to be understood by Sir Horace Wilson. As late as August 20, he can be found meeting Dr Fritz Hesse, the head of the official German news agency in London. Hesse returned from Germany with a copy of a letter Ribbentrop had written to Lord Rothermere. It was a great mistake, Hesse said, to go on stressing British determination to fulfil her obligations to Hitler. The only effect was to irritate and annoy Hitler who was fully alive to the situation. 'I took particular note of this assertion,' Sir Horace Wilson noted;[60] 'the point was, of course, very much in my mind.' Not quite the note that was likely to deter a man who had already set the attack on Poland for six days ahead. The net result of these well-meant efforts by Wohltat, Dahlerus, Rothermere, Sir Horace Wilson and, no doubt, still others unknown, was to confirm Hitler in his view of Britain: that its policy was not seriously intended and that the British guarantee to Poland was a piece of traditional British hypocrisy *nicht ernst zu nehmen*, not to be taken really seriously. In the meantime Hitler had turned towards Moscow, and Europe had only two weeks of peace remaining.

CHAPTER 22

ITALY BETRAYED

In September 1938 Mussolini's last-minute intervention had been the final element in the balance of considerations which had brought Hitler to the negotiating table and secured a Czech surrender without war. Mussolini's role in Hitler's fantasy world has already been noted. Hitler's speeches and thinking in 1939 show that Mussolini's Italy also continued to play a role in his strategic thinking. In November 1938, when Hitler had been planning a war with France, whose defeat was to be encompassed by a break through the Maginot line, Italy's role had been to protect Germany's back and to distract France in the Mediterranean. Italy hardly featured at all in the speech of May 23, 1939 which was devoted mainly to discussing the projects of war with Poland and of the vulnerability of Britain in war;[1] Italy was considered only as an ally, with Japan, against an alliance of Britain and France with Russia, and as a possible participant in a break through the Maginot line; nor did Italy figure in the directions for *Case White*. But, in the last fortnight of peace, in Hitler's speech of August 22 to the Commanders-in-Chief, Mussolini was named as a decisive factor, without whose existence Italy's loyalty could not be counted on. Equally, the rivalry between Italy, France and England in the Mediterranean counted for Hitler as a favourable political factor. In Hitler's dream of world conquest, Mussolini's Italy was cast as his partner.

Hitler's military advisers were by no means so enthusiastic. They had no very great or exalted opinion of the Italian military record. In a war against Britain, they regarded Italy as a military handicap which would make great inroads on Germany's economy without offering any real military advantages. Only the German navy, conscious of Italy's sizeable battle fleet and submarine strength, could see some limited advantage in co-operation with Italy in war. But then Hitler's military advisers regarded the prospects of war with Britain and France with no more enthusiasm in 1939 than in 1938. They relied on the Führer to keep the war with Poland limited and bilateral, as he had promised. This was particularly true for the Commander-in-Chief of the Navy, Admiral Raeder.[2] Mussolini's role as Hitler's indispensable ally rested in Hitler's mind and there alone.

That being said, could Mussolini have restrained Hitler from attacking Poland in 1939? Indeed, why did Mussolini not restrain Hitler in August 1939 as he had done in September 1938? There were some people, a dwindling band, in London who still hoped for such an eventuality. There were more in Paris, especially in the last few desperate days of peace, who hoped in vain for an Italian intervention to save France from being dragged into war at Britain's heels, as will be shown in a later chapter. That secret diplomatic conjuration which at various times encompassed Ernst von Weizsäcker, the State Secretary in the German Foreign Ministry, Bernardo Attolico, the Italian Ambassador in Berlin, Sir Nevile Henderson, his British colleague, Carl Burckhardt, the Swiss High Commissioner for the League of Nations in Danzig, and André François-Poncet, who had moved from Berlin in October 1938 to be French Ambassador in Rome, they too hoped that Mussolini might introduce a sense of realism into Hitler's fantasies. The new Pope, as we have seen, was prepared to provide Mussolini with spiritual encouragement. All was to be in vain. Where Roosevelt failed to convince Congress, and Stalin preferred the rewards of connivance to the perils of opposition, Mussolini, like some baritone in a Verdi opera, was to find himself *abbandonato e tradito*, abandoned and betrayed.

In that betrayal, that abandonment, he was to be the complaisant and naïve accomplice. He was gulled and cozened, and his son-in-law, Count Galeazzo Ciano, his Foreign Minister, with him. He was warned, it was true. But his sense of suspicion never got further than the motives of those who warned him, whose correspondence he was reading, whose telephone calls he was overhearing and whose safes his minions were burgling. Nor was he very good at calculating military realities, being apt to be carried away by his own rhetoric and to believe that once he had made a speech about anything, the issue was settled. Since in military matters his rhetoric was, as political rhetoric so often is, somewhat technologically out-moded, this made him doubly vulnerable. His famous phrase describing Italy's fighting strength,[3] *otto milioni di baionette*, eight million bayonets, was not only not true, but irrelevant in a war of tanks and dive-bombers, blockades and amphibious warfare. In fact in August 1939, his army did not have enough bayonets for the 1¼ million pre-1914 rifles which was all it had in store.

None of this, however, worried him as he celebrated the signature, on May 22, of the Pact of Steel. But as the summer wound its long hot way towards August, a certain sense of having been marginalized, of having been shunted to the verges of the main thoroughfare of international politics, began to overtake him. It was a slow process, this process of enlightenment. Like all politicians of the theatre, Mussolini played his part to an audience of one, his own imagination. It was just that, after the magic months of April and May, when his magnificent conquest of Albania had reconquered the headlines grabbed by Hitler with the march into Prague, the annexation of the Memel, and the challenge to the Poles over Danzig; when all the Balkan and East European statesmen who believed in insurance (save only the Greeks, whom he affected to despise, and the accursed Turks) had come to Rome or Venice to pay homage; when Ribbentrop came to Milan and Mussolini, to contradict the foreign press, which had pretended to find signs of anti-German sentiment in the streets of Milan, had ordered Ciano to propose a bilateral alliance, and Ciano had travelled to Berlin to sign that alliance; since then, June and July seemed rather empty of visitors and victories to feed his sense of destiny. He could make no progress with the Balkan states, except for the Hungarians whom he, with some reason, affected to despise. Led by the indomitable Turks, who made no bones about telling the Italian Ambassador, Ottavio de Peppo, what they thought of his master, Romania, Bulgaria, even Yugoslavia seemed to be turning more and more to London and Paris. As for the headlines, they were increasingly filled with talk of Danzig, with political gossip from Warsaw or Berlin, and above all with reports of the progress of the British and French negotiations with the Russians.

The announcement and conclusion of the Pact of Steel had been intended above all to strengthen him *vis-à-vis* the French. The more deeply the British became embroiled over Danzig, the more they would need his services, as would Germany, to secure a reasonable settlement. The more the British needed him, the more amenable they and the French would be to giving him what he wanted in the Mediterranean and on the Red Sea. What he wanted, it turned out, was already much less than that which had been demanded so 'spontaneously' by the Fascist Chamber of Deputies in November 1938. There was no talk now of recovering Corsica, Nice or the French Savoy. A free port in Djibouti, the capital of French Somalia and the railhead for the only rail connection between Addis Ababa and the open sea; the right to purchase that part of the Addis Ababa-Djibouti railway which lay within Ethiopia from its French owners; representation on the board of directors of the Suez Canal; and 'substantiation', whatever that meant, of the status of the large Italian minority in the French protectorate of Tunisia; this was the sum total of Italian claims. They had been discussed with Baudouin, the French unofficial intermediary, in February and early March 1939.[4] Details had been given to the British Ambassador, Lord Perth, in April.[5] M. Gafencu had carried a secret message from Paris to Rome, indicating French willingness to negotiate – or at least the readiness of M. Bonnet, the French Foreign Minister,[6] which was not quite the same thing. Mussolini's intelligence authorities told him of M. François-Poncet's efforts in the same direction. Mussolini liked Lord Perth, up to a point. He thought M. François-Poncet shifty, gutless, pompous and conceited. That was, however, a minor irritation beside the undoubted fact that nothing was happening. The British expressed goodwill, but there was no sign of their putting any real pressure on M. Daladier, the French Premier. And in the meantime their ridiculous guarantee of Poland was making Warsaw intransigent. To a man who could not believe either that there was any real justice in the Polish refusal to allow the German population of Danzig the right to rejoin their fellow Germans in the Third Reich, or that anyone would be mad enough to start a European war over Danzig,[7] it was all too much.

Like generations of egotistical actor-managers, Mussolini began by venting his rage on the bit players. His own Ambassadors in London and Paris, Dino Grandi and Raffaele Guariglia, were the villains of the piece. Grandi had been his Foreign Minister up to 1932, when Mussolini had taken over the Foreign Ministry himself and sent Grandi to London. He had been there too long; he had gone native.[8] Count Ciano disliked him. He should be got rid of. But he was also one of Mussolini's longest associates, a member of the Fascist Grand Council, one of the *Gerarchi*, the original Fascist leadership. Moreover, he was almost certainly in league with King Victor Emmanuel, and a closet monarchist. Goebbels and Ribbentrop, who disliked Grandi, a dislike he openly reciprocated, used their rumour factories in the French press to depict him as a leader of the secret Italian opposition to the Pact of Steel; or so Grandi believed.[9]

In February already, Mussolini, angry at the depths of response to Neville Chamberlain shown by the populace of Rome, recalled Grandi and told him he was to consider his mission at an end.[10] He was allowed to return to London in April, and finally recalled at the beginning of June. In September, he was made Minister for Justice. In 1943, together with Count Ciano, he was to take part in the formal deposition of Mussolini by the Grand Council. Ciano later fell into German hands and, despite being Mussolini's son-in-law, was tried and, on German insistence, executed for treachery by Mussolini's Fascist minions. Grandi survived to tell the tale.

Raffaele Guariglia, by contrast, was a professional diplomatist. He had joined the Italian diplomatic service in 1918, serving in Brussels, Madrid and Buenos Aires, and being appointed to Paris in October 1938. Mussolini was already threatening to recall him in early March. Ciano thought him a Francophile, and a democrat by inclination, though otherwise a mere functionary who would do what he was told.[11] Guariglia too, however, was regarded as too much of a monarchist, and entrusted with little or no work of any authority.[12]

Next to feel Mussolini's wrath was Lord Perth's successor at the British Embassy, Sir Percy Loraine. Loraine was among the tougher-minded members of the British foreign service. He had served in Persia in the early 1920s when Mohammad Reza was smashing his way to the throne of Persia, and in Greece, Egypt and Turkey. For most of his career, that is, he had served in those areas where the British imperialist interest required that face be maintained and British prestige be upheld. In December 1937 he was reported to the Italians as having remarked to a fellow diplomatist in Istanbul that 'when Britain was ready she would quickly destroy Italy and smash the Duce'.[13] Mussolini, to whose ears these and other similar comments had been relayed, characteristically had arranged for Loraine to be sent various anonymous and insulting letters and newspaper photographs of Italy's armed might.[14] Loraine, a horseman with his own stable of racehorses, membership of the Italian Jockey Club, and a natural eye for beautiful architecture, found Rome pleasant and congenial 'after the pathetic bleakness of Ankara'.[15] He was under instructions to uphold the Anglo-Italian Agreement of Easter 1938 and 'to burn no bridges which one day the Italians might wish to recross'.[16] Ciano's first impression of him was that he was 'naturally timid', a view which throws a certain light on Ciano's inability to distinguish between good manners and fawning. To judge from his diary, Ciano came to revise his early impressions of a man whom he described in 1940 as 'intelligent and frank'.[17]

Loraine was only to see Mussolini on two occasions during his stay in Rome, which was perhaps unfortunate. His first interview was delayed until May 27 (he arrived in Rome on May 2); by then Mussolini would have learnt from his intelligence of Loraine's belief that while Ciano was fully committed to Germany, Mussolini still had reservations. Had Loraine been able to see Mussolini before the Ciano-Ribbentrop en-counter, he might have been able to discover how Mussolini's mind was working.[18] Mussolini would also have been aware of Loraine's comment that however much the Duce might cry out for peace and justice, the peace was to be on Axis terms and without any guarantee that the 'highwayman will become a law-abiding citizen'.[19] The launching of a major radio offensive against Italy by the BBC Arabic service, using the Italian attack on the Muslim state of Albania to create prejudice against Italy throughout the Muslim world, also struck the Italians as a breach of the Anglo-Italian Agreement.[20]

Whatever the reason, Mussolini, with the Pact of Steel firmly signed and sealed, appears to have decided to teach Loraine a lesson. Ushered into the vast office in the Palazzo Venezia by the Italian Chef de Protocole, Loraine found Mussolini ensconced behind his vast desk with Ciano hovering at his elbow, and sensed immediately that 'something was in the air'. Mussolini chose to speak in Italian, knowing full well that Loraine did not understand it, and leaving Ciano to interpret into French. With stern 'impenetrable' visage, his face 'like that of an Oriental God sculptured in stone' (the description is Ciano's), the Duce launched a major attack on British policy, ending with the question as to whether the Anglo-Italian Agreement had any further value. Loraine somewhat punctured his oratorical fervour at this point by asking whether this was a question Mussolini *might* put to the British Government or whether he *was* definitely putting the question. Mussolini said he *was* putting this question. So Loraine carefully wrote it down. Count Ciano was so taken with his master's theatre that he misinterpreted Loraine's efforts to master his rage as a blush, an error compounded by the Chef de Protocole, who reported Loraine as having muttered under his breath and looked like a man who had received a slap in the face, all the way back to the Embassy.[21]

Loraine came from a long line of border reivers from the English side of the borders with Scotland, an area which still produces some of the most ferocious Rugby players in both countries. He had Royal Navy blood on both sides of the family. In 1901–2, as a volunteer in the Imperial Yeomanry, he had fought against Boer guerrillas in South Africa, spending days at a time in the saddle in pursuit of the Boer commandos and being wounded. Only chair-bound Italian prophets of braggadocio like Mussolini and Ciano could have mistaken Loraine for a wimp. He retained his balance and the sense of his instructions. Under François-Poncet's importunities, he was for a time to play his part in urging British pressure on France at least to explore the prospects of an agreement with the Italians, a view for which there were serious strategic arguments.

But any inclination Loraine might have had to ape his predecessor or Sir Nevile Henderson (and it is doubtful whether he ever suffered from that diplomatist's disease of desiring to be hail-fellow-well-met, if not actually liked by those to whom he is accredited) did not survive this encounter. Mussolini's unparalleled gift for miscasting, in the private grand drama which inhabited his head, all those he met, was never better demonstrated. Loraine's conclusion was that 'the visibility of overwhelming strength' was the only language Mussolini respected.[22] His peers in the British Foreign Office felt he stood up to Mussolini manfully.[23] His friend, Sir Walter Smart, wrote from Cairo that it was nice at last 'to see some backbone in our attitude to Rome'.[24]

It is by no means inconceivable that Ciano had already seen some of these comments when he met Loraine again on June 1 for what was a much less stormy encounter.[25] Mussolini, however, was still riding high. Hungary and Spain must join the Pact of Steel. Japan's entrance into the Axis must be facilitated. Bulgaria's position towards the Axis must be fixed. Yugoslavia's must be clarified. Negotiations with Maček must be continued. Perhaps once Croatia was set up as a separate state, Italy could content herself with a common Italo-Croatian Foreign Ministry and control over the army.[26] The air was full of unhatched chickens.

This bombast hid, however, a nagging worry, generated by the mean, cautious but realistically minded deutero-Mussolini who co-existed with the merchant of braggadocio behind Mussolini's famous profile. In Victorian fiction adventuresses were said always to bear in mind the precept: 'Get it in writing.' This Mussolini had neglected to do. Ciano and Ribbentrop had agreed that war with the democracies was inevitable. They had also agreed that it was neither in Germany's nor in Italy's interest for it to happen for a few years. With his usual incompetence, disguised as contempt for haggling over piddling details, Ciano had accepted and signed a German draft of the alliance which omitted any mention of German agreement on this point. Such matters were to be left to the German-Italian joint commission to settle. General Ugo Cavallero was to go to Berlin. With him was to go a long private letter from Mussolini to Hitler, setting out in detail Mussolini's reasons for delaying any war with the West ('a period of preparation') until the end of 1942.[27]

Mussolini anticipated a long and bitter war of attrition in which Germany and Italy could only hold their own by careful military and economic organization in time of peace. Italy would need to move her heavy industries out of reach of air attack, from the Po Valley to southern Italy. She would need to build up her foreign exchange reserves (which had dropped between 1927 and 1939 from 20,000 million lire to 3,200 million lire, 500 million short of what would be needed to cover Italian outgoings before the end of the year).[28] In addition, Italy needed to develop her system of economic autarchy,[29] to bring home to Italy the substantial Italian minority living in France, to hold the World Exhibition in 1942 in Rome, from which it was hoped to replenish Italy's foreign exchange reserves, and to reconstruct and recondition Italy's six battleships.

When General Cavallero arrived in Berlin he was kept waiting until the visit of Prince Paul of Yugoslavia was over. Thereafter he was given a polite but definite 'run-around'. He met Ribbentrop, Karl Ritter, the Foreign Ministry's economic expert, General Keitel, von Weizsäcker, General von Brauchitsch; various sub-commissions were established.[30] At the same time a series of Staff contacts, opening between the two Chiefs of Staff in March 1939 and continuing with separate army, air force and navy sections, were organized and duly took place.[31] By July, despite a fleeting personal visit by Ritter to Rome to discuss the composition of the economic commission, nothing had been agreed, nothing concluded. Above all, Mussolini's pre-conditions had remained without any answer whatever.[32] Instead Ribbentrop had generally suggested a meeting between the Führer and the Duce, possibly at the Brenner, some time in the summer.[33] He spoke also of his making a private visit to Florence in October. On June 11, Attolico conveyed the Duce's welcome for the idea and said that the Duce would leave it to Berlin to fix a date. Ten days later Ribbentrop suggested the first week in August.[34]

Attolico began to feel a certain degree of alarm, however, as the advocates of a coup against Danzig began to come to the fore. He was aware of the increasing impatience towards Japan that both Ribbentrop and Goering were beginning to manifest in June (indeed, he did his best to feed it).[35] He was also aware of the rivalry between Goering and Ribbentrop (both of whom from time to time spoke to him quite freely), and the complications this was introducing into the negotiations with Japan and the more hesitant approaches being made to the Soviets. Goebbels' philippics in Danzig worried him considerably, as did the evidence of Hitler's own fury with both Poland and Britain. The forthcoming meeting with Mussolini assumed even greater importance in his eyes as the only means of restoring the Führer's sense of realities.[36] The widespread stories that Count Welczeck, the German Ambassador in Paris, had, on Ribbentrop's instructions, told Bonnet in so many words that Germany was determined to solve the question of Danzig by force in the middle of August, and that if Britain intervened it would only be to the destruction of her empire, worried him further. Ribbentrop's remarks to Welczeck, as he wrote, plunged the diplomatic world in Berlin into a phase not so much of alarm, but of desperation.[37] (Abetz may have said something of the sort before the French expelled him, but, as we have seen, the stories about Welczeck were entirely untrue.)

By the beginning of July Attolico had stirred Ciano sufficiently to instruct him to discover from Ribbentrop 'with the greatest precision possible' what the Germans' intentions in relation to Danzig really were.[38] In the meantime the Italian Consul at Katowice on the Polish-German frontier was instructed to report any new military developments in his area.[39] Ciano, who had been virtually prostrated by the death of his father (to whose qualities he devoted all his diary between June 26 and July 3), tended to regard the whole 'weekend crisis' over Danzig as a false alarm, apparently on the grounds that the Germans had not said a word on the subject which could not be reconciled with the terms of the Pact of Steel.[40] Mussolini, however, scented a chance to mediate, and drafted a scheme for a plebiscite to be held in Danzig under international supervision.[41] Thoughts of intervention, however, reminded him of the monstrous and continuing refusal of the British to respond to his hints as to their mediating with (Mussolini-speak for 'twisting the arm of') the French to yield to his steadily diminishing demands. Instead, the British were protesting over the intensity of the Italian press campaign against them, and Bonnet, of all people, was laying down the law to Count Welczeck and to M. Guariglia on France's resolve to honour her obligations to Poland, if German action against Danzig should lead to a German-Polish war.[42] Similar assurances of British determination reached Mussolini from the Vatican[43] and were confirmed by an extremely strong warning conveyed by Sir Percy Loraine in Chamberlain's name on July 7.[44] Nor could his temper have been mollified by the story that reached him from a French Deputy in Bonnet's entourage, that Daladier had declared himself personally well disposed to resolve the Italian question but that the British had forbidden it.[45]

Sir Percy found Mussolini less dour on this occasion,[46] but he still seemed determined to play the part of the loyal ally and the true Fascist. 'It was as if yesterday morning I was talking about cricket and Mussolini was talking about chess,' Loraine wrote to Halifax.[47] Nevertheless, Loraine's warning, coming soon after the weekend scare over Danzig, seems to have played on Mussolini's fear of being marginalized. Whatever was going on, he wanted a major role. He might play the loyal ally, but he did not wish to play second fiddle. That same day Mussolini set out his views on Danzig for Ciano's benefit, remarking the necessity for ceasing to excite Poland into a warlike psychosis. If Britain supported the Polish thesis with force, Italy would fight on Germany's side. Clearly, however, neither he nor Ciano thought this a real issue.[48] Ciano immediately broke the promise he had exacted from Loraine that the issue should be kept secret, by talking to the German Ambassador, Hans von Mackensen,[49] and giving him a copy of Mussolini's notes. Ciano then departed on a ten-day visit to Spain.

In the meantime Attolico had two further interviews with Ribbentrop. In the first Ribbentrop expressed his belief that a coup in Danzig could be carried out without a war, and that Britain and France would do nothing. To continue the war of nerves he was about to announce the visit of a German cruiser, the *Königsberg*, to Danzig.[50] In the second,[51] on July 7, he said that the stories of a German coup in Danzig were pure invention, part of the war of nerves out of which Germany would emerge victorious, and treated Attolico (as in a dream) to a global tour in which the Maginot line (by contrast with the German western fortifications) was called a 'boy's joke'. Paris, if France chose war, would be pulverized by five thousand bombers; Britain's empire would be destroyed. Russia would do nothing – *niente*; America would do nothing for fear of Japan. Attolico had to remark drily that, according to the agreement between the Duce and the Führer, Italy and Germany were preparing for a war 'which was *not* to be immediate'.

Attolico found the meeting alarmingly and annoyingly unsatisfactory. He had secured a 'truly remarkable' vision of 'a certain German victory in everything and over everyone, today, in six months, in six years'. In everything one should have confidence in the wisdom and the genius of the Führer, which, Attolico added, he had, at least for the moment. For the moment, there was nothing to fear. As for the meeting between the Duce and the Führer, Ribbentrop suggested August 4 or 5.

Ciano was sufficiently reassured to reply from Spain that the end of September would be better.[52] Attolico, writing in Ciano's absence to Ciano's Chef de Cabinet, Filippo Anfuso, was not.[53] The Italians, as he pointed out, were being given the run-around. Ribbentrop had settled himself in Salzburg, close to Hitler's side. Goering had done the same. Von Weizsäcker had cancelled his holidays. It had proved impossible to hurry the meetings of any of the commissions set up by General Cavallero's mission. Arms were continuing to pour into Danzig. All German troop movements were to end on August 15. New army corps were being created. It was clear that some time between August 10 and 15 Hitler would decide for peace or war. It was essential that there should be a meeting between the dictators before that date.

Attolico reinforced this with detailed reports from the network of Italian Consuls in Germany of large-scale German troop movements.[54] He then left for Munich for four days, leaving Massimo Magistrati,

Ciano's son-in-law and the Counsellor in the Italian Embassy, as Chargé d'affaires in Berlin. In Munich, Attolico had met Hitler and given him the Duce's reply as to the date of their meeting. Hitler, though enormously pleased by Mussolini's reply to Sir Percy Loraine, was not particularly happy about the postponement of his meeting with Mussolini. Nor was Attolico with what he learnt from Walter Hewel.[55]

Hewel, who had shared Hitler's cell after the collapse of the Bierkeller putsch and Hitler's imprisonment in 1922–4, seems to have been unique among Hitler's entourage in that everyone liked him, and that he was straightforward and honest. He confirmed to Attolico that something was definitely being planned for Danzig and for July 28 when the *Königsberg* was due to arrive there, but that Hitler seemed to have had second thoughts (he was in fact withholding his decision).[56] In any case Hitler attached almost decisive importance to the attitude of the Soviet Union and had no idea whatever of trying a coup against Danzig and the Corridor until he was certain he could isolate Poland. Mussolini's influence would be crucial.

Ciano should have been worried. Attolico was now warning him that German promises of arms deliveries to Italy were more hopes than security;[57] Admiral Canaris,[58] the head of German military intelligence, warned him that Germany, though by no means ready for war by comparison with Britain, was being led into war by the Führer. Hitler, said Canaris, was driven by the faction which wanted war, and lied to about the effectiveness of the German armed forces by Goering and General Keitel; Hitler, Canaris warned, was determined to smash Poland, realized that the Danzig question could not be resolved without a war, and possibly through the SS, was planning incidents in Danzig to trigger off a conflict. From Warsaw[59] there came reports of the success of General Ironside's visit. Despite all this Ciano remained in a state of euphoria. Attolico was having another of his 'crises of fear'.[60] The Italian Consul in Prague was also reporting 'troop movements on a vast scale'.[61] But the Germans had said nothing. Attolico had 'lost his head'.[62] Ciano recalled his son-in-law, Magistrati, from Berlin. Together they assembled Mussolini's grandiloquent ideas of a six-power international but purely European conference together in a message for Hitler and a draft communiqué to follow their meeting. Ciano did not think such a conference would ever meet; but the invitation would sow confusion and dissension among the democracies.[63]

Attolico was certainly being encouraged by von Weizsäcker in his desperate attempts to warn Mussolini of what Hitler was planning; he was also clearly being fed information by the group of anti-Nazis around Admiral Canaris. The Italian Military Attaché in Berlin, General Mario Roatta, was on excellent terms with the German military. Attolico and von Weizsäcker were, nevertheless, not immune from mistakes and misjudgments. Their treatment of Mussolini's message to Hitler is a prime example. The message itself[64] assured Hitler that, if Germany felt obliged to mobilize, Italy would follow the German example and mobilize all her forces. Assuming, however, that Hitler had not decided on mobilization, Mussolini argued strongly against going to war at that moment. Opinion in the democracies, he wrote with truth, was prepared for war. There could be no strategic surprise. Italy was *not* ready for war. To undermine the determination of the democracies, Mussolini suggested a conference. It should be attended by the leaders of Germany, Italy, France, Britain, Poland and Spain, with perhaps one 'neutral' observer from Sweden, Switzerland or the Netherlands. The United States, the Soviet Union and Japan were to be excluded. At such a conference, the dictatorships, free from the need to worry about public opinion, would stand a good chance of success; whereas, if the conference failed, the fault would be with the democracies.

Attolico received this memorandum in Berlin. There was time for a brief discussion of tactics with von Weizsäcker,[65] who once again found his hopes of attaining the recovery by his country of the frontiers of 1914 (towards which, in common with many of his fellow members of the German foreign service, he had for so long directed his hopes and efforts) at odds with his fears of a general war in which his country could be defeated. He took the risk of alerting Ribbentrop to the Italian proposals in advance.[66] Still worse he muddled Mussolini's insistence on a conference with his own idea of bilateral German-Polish (and Franco-Italian) discussions, putting the stress on his own idea. Mussolini's memorandum was flown to Fuschl, Ribbentrop's lake-side country house near Salzburg, which Ribbentrop had expropriated from its Jewish owner after the annexation of Austria; it arrived ahead of the Italians, who motored to Munich where they met a member of the Foreign Ministry's protocol department who escorted them to Fuschl. There, amidst 'perfect German scenery', Ribbentrop met them, dressed informally and talking of trout fishing and bathing in the limpid water of the lake. Such conversation, remarked Magistrati, did nothing to calm or divert the distraught Italian Ambassador.[67]

Despite the idyllic surroundings, the conversation was not a happy one for the Italians.[68] Ribbentrop assured them that Hitler did not want or expect a war. At present Germany was engaged in a war of nerves, in which she could not afford to show any signs of yielding or weakness.

Among her opponents, on the other hand, signs of weakness were multiplying. The British had sold out completely to the Japanese over Tientsin. They were about to abandon their negotiations with Russia in confusion. Roosevelt had been defeated in his attempts to repeal the neutrality legislation by a campaign of opposition and propaganda; the Germans had contributed to his defeat by distributing hundreds of thousands of copies of Hitler's riposte to Roosevelt. As for the conference, Ribbentrop could not, of course, speak for the Führer, but he thought it would be impossible to sit at the same table as the Poles, who, he alleged, had replied to the Führer's 'generous offer' by saying (in the words of Ambassador Lipski, the Polish Ambassador in Berlin) that they would prefer war with Germany. As for the communiqué (which Mussolini had so proudly drafted), the Germans said it was 'obviously the work of Magistrati and had not been seen by Mussolini'. Attolico reported Ribbentrop's dismissal of it as 'banal'.

Ciano took the failure of his master's initiative with equanimity.[69] From Attolico's lengthy report he extracted only the assurances that there would be no war.[70] 'Attolico was frightened by his own shadow' and, he wrote shrewdly, probably working with someone in the German Foreign Ministry, 'has been trying to save his country from a non-existent danger'.

On August 2, Ciano bragged to the Portuguese Minister in Rome, José Lobo d'Avila Lima, of his confidence in the solidarity of the Axis. The international situation, he remarked, was loose and uncertain, but there was no immediate danger of conflict.[71] Ciano and Mussolini considered postponing the Duce's meeting with Hitler, something Hitler himself proposed on July 31.[72] The episode must have awoken Hitler's instincts of self-protection. Conferences, as Attolico underlined in his report, were something the Führer loathed. They made him weary and they made him unhappy. Besides, he had Mussolini's assurance of support in war. Above all he, like Ribbentrop, had convinced himself that Britain and France would stand aside. Mussolini's elaborate arguments were predicated on a danger he knew did not exist.

Mussolini's approach to Hitler had been made and rejected; yet he and Ciano still resisted any suspicion that their ally was not playing them fair. At the same time the forces in Britain and France who were hoping that Mussolini could be used to restrain Hitler in 1939, as he had in 1938, were overridden and defeated. Ironically it was Mussolini's own behaviour and the lessons drawn from it in London and Paris which were the most cogent arguments employed against those who were tempted to try to win him over by the offer of negotiations. In

France this faction was led by M. Bonnet, always in search of something which would avoid war and the forced dependence of France on Britain's leadership which war with Germany would inevitably imply. His main support came from M. François-Poncet in the French Embassy in Rome, and from the more conciliatory-minded members of the French Cabinet, from a cluster of former Ministers such as Laval and Flandin, and from the Anglophobe element in the Chamber who were so opposed to the cession of Alexandretta to Britain's ally, Turkey. Opposed to him, as Bonnet told the British Ambassador in Paris, Sir Eric Phipps,[73] were M. Daladier, the Prime Minister, Paul Reynaud, the Finance Minister, César Campinchi, the Minister for the Navy, Albert Sarraut, Minister of the Interior, and Georges Mandel, the Minister for the Colonies; formerly M. Clemenceau's hatchet man, the latter was Jewish and the most resolute opponent in the French Government of the appeasement of the dictators. These men were supported, to Bonnet's dismay, by Alexis Léger, the Secretary General of the French Foreign Ministry, and by the French Ambassador in London, Charles Corbin, whom M. François-Poncet accused of strengthening Daladier's hand by reporting British approval of his policy.[74]

The British cabal fell into two groups. There were certainly those in Chamberlain's entourage, with the 'secret channel' to the Italian Embassy in London, who still pinned their hopes on Mussolini's supposed influence with Hitler.[75] Grandi's recall to Rome, however, greatly diminished their scope; and hopes that Grandi in Rome would be able to exercise more influence than he had in London were largely dashed by Mussolini's initial reluctance to give him new employment once he had been recalled.[76] As a member of the *Gerarchi*, Grandi's influence and connections in Rome were clearly an asset to Anglophiles, but only when the *Gerarchi* were united, and only when Mussolini felt under pressure to consult them. And in the delicate manipulation of stick and carrot on which, in theory, Chamberlain's policy towards Germany (of deterrence plus eventual negotiation through strength) depended, Mussolini was only one of the channels by which Ribbentrop could be circumvented and direct contact with the Führer advanced.

There were, however, other arguments in favour of pressing M. Daladier to turn a less resolute face towards Rome. If war with Germany was inevitable, then her enemies were faced with two options: to treat Italy as an inevitable enemy or to attempt to secure her neutrality. Each carried with it further choices. If Italy was to be treated as a necessary enemy, then there was much to be said for making her the first target; there was even the possibility, given the strategic role she played in the Mediterranean, where she threatened Britain's Suez routes to the Far East and India and France's position in North Africa, of carrying out a pre-emptive strike against her. The same strategic arguments, however, also operated in favour of pressing the French to make some offer to buy Italy off, or at least to explore the chances of doing so, so the British defence planners argued as late as mid-July 1939 in a paper which explored both the options of a pre-emptive strike against Italy and of 'paying the genuinely high price which she will doubtless demand' to secure her strict neutrality.[77]

There were forces in the British defence establishment who, as we have seen, led by Admiral Drax, had been arguing since February for the abandonment of the Far East in favour of the Mediterranean and a 'knock-out blow' against Italy. Lord Chatfield, who, in the early 1920s, as deputy to the First Sea Lord of the day, had played a large part in drafting the 'Main Fleet to Singapore' strategy, and had himself been First Sea Lord during the Abyssinian crisis in 1935–6, was now Minister for the Co-ordination of Defence. His rearguard resistance to the new school of thought was suddenly revived when, at the end of June, the Tientsin crisis seemed to threaten war in the Far East. More urgent, however, was the discovery that the French refused to consider any early offensive against Italy in North Africa. Assuming Franco's Spain would be Italy's ally, they felt that the first target in any North African campaign must be the elimination of the Spanish garrisons in Morocco, which had been reinforced at the end of the Spanish Civil War.[78]

With this the advocates of a pre-emptive strike, weakened by the retirement and death of the First Sea Lord, Sir Roger Backhouse, found themselves in retreat. The new First Sea Lord, Admiral Sir Dudley Pound, came, it was true, directly from commanding the Mediterranean fleet. But he was no strategist; nor was he a particularly strong representative of the Admiralty's views.[79] The case, if case there still were, went therefore by default.

The rejection of the idea of a pre-emptive strike against Italy (which, in any case, only turned on war actually breaking out) had little effect on the development of the idea of pressing the French into taking up the Italian approaches. M. François-Poncet succeeded in panicking Loraine into talking of a 'veiled ultimatum' on May 23, before Loraine's first meeting with Mussolini, while he was still finding his feet and acting under the immediate impact of the signature of the Pact of Steel.[80] The main centre of the intrigue which Bonnet and his cabal were launching against Daladier was in Paris, and centred on Bonnet's relationship with Sir Eric Phipps.

The British Ambassador to Paris was related to Sir Robert Vansittart by marriage. He had, however, fallen out with his brother-in-law in 1934 when Vansittart had sent him to Berlin, which he detested, instead of Paris, which he loved. Phipps loathed the Nazis, on whom he exercised his malicious wit in a series of reports, including one on Goering's wedding ceremony that was so instantly quotable as to lead Cabinet Ministers to dine out for months on its ironies. Inevitably, the story got back to Berlin, where it did nothing to ease Phipps's difficulties.

In 1937 he finally obtained the Paris Embassy, where he attached himself most closely to the wealthier, more capitulationist elements in Paris society and politics, including M. Caillaux, Clemenceau's rival, Prime Minister before 1914, and M. Flandin. In a famous telegram at the height of the Munich crisis he described the capitulationists as 'all that is best in France'.[81] He was one of the dwindling band who could see only the hidden hand of Moscow behind the arguments that France and Britain should have honoured France's obligations to Czechoslovakia in 1938. He persisted in seeing Soviet influence in the views of the hard-liners in the French Cabinet.[82] His professional sense told him that the strains of war would imperil the never less than precarious balance of forces that made up the French Third Republic. His equally professional ignorance of France, outside those elements among whom his career lay, made him fear that what might replace the Third Republic would be a French revolutionary Soviet regime. In London, his main source of strength lay in the Prime Minister's entourage, especially with Sir Horace Wilson, whom he kept supplied with reports on his brother-in-law's intrigues with the French press;[83] in the pro-Chamberlain press, such as The Times, whose uncooperative correspondent in Paris he did his best to remove;[84] in Sir Maurice Hankey, the outgoing Secretary to the Cabinet;[85] and in the Chamberlainite faction in Parliament and among the Junior Ministers. It was these elements who put pressure on the Foreign Office to postpone his retirement, due in April 1939; he finally retired on the outbreak of war in 1939, at a time when Cadogan, the Permanent Under Secretary, felt his behaviour during the Munich crisis had made him dispensable.[86]

Phipps's friendship with M. François-Poncet was established during their joint service in Berlin. Their views on the importance of not driving Mussolini into Hitler's arms were aligned before François-Poncet left for Rome in November 1938.[87] Phipps had tried once to shift Daladier on his hostility towards Italy and had warned him against Léger's 'Italophobia' early in April. Primed by François-Poncet with details of how limited were the actual Italian claims on France,[88] he had tried again on April 28, hoping to take advantage of French gratitude at the British adoption of conscription. Daladier had, however, remained obdurate; his tone against Italy was violent; the Italians, he said, were 'gangsters' who were laying a trap to turn Arab opinion in North Africa and Syria against France.

The experience led Phipps and Bonnet to advise delaying any further pressure on Daladier until the negotiations with Russia were concluded and the French Parliament had adjourned for the summer. The Cabinet therefore took no action in response to Loraine's messages in May until July 11 when Bonnet finally gave the nod.[89] On July 13, after the Australian High Commissioner, Bruce, had added his two penny-worth of strategic anxiety over the Far East, Chamberlain's long and very much redrafted letter to Daladier was finally delivered by Phipps.

The timing could not have been worse. The Italians had wind of the British discussions on making the French 'see sense', almost certainly via the Horace Wilson-Ball connection ('sources very close to the Prime Minister').[90] The Italians had just protested bitterly over the French cession of Alexandretta to Turkey,[91] and the Italian press and radio were engaged in bitter philippics against France, in a vain effort to recover some of the ground lost in the propaganda war for Arab opinion to British and French exploitation of the Italian attack on Muslim Albania. Arab nationalist opinion regarded Alexandretta as an Arab city, and had taken a consistently hostile line to Turkish claims on the city and its surroundings ever since 1936, despite the Turks putting out their own radio propaganda in Arabic as a counter-measure. France had installed an Arab Government in Syria in 1936 in execution of the terms of the mandate from the League of Nations by which they had obtained dominion over Syria and the Lebanon at the Peace Settlement. But they had been in constant contention with those they had installed. Indeed, on July 8 after several weeks of crisis and the resignation of the Syrian President, the French High Commissioner in Syria had dis-solved the Syrian Parliament and appointed a council of five bureaucrats to act as the Syrian executive. Italian propaganda seized gleefully on the whole issue of the French mandate. Having defied the French 'Syrians', the Anglophobe right, over the cession of Alexandretta to Turkey, the last thing Daladier should have been asked to do was to discuss any further concessions to Italy in Tunisia. Perhaps Bonnet hoped to bring Daladier down. Phipps seems to have ignored these issues entirely.

Daladier, however, was at his best. He delayed his reply to Chamber-lain for ten days. His reply was firm,[92] not to say forceful. He enumerated the occasions on which the French had made gestures designed to cajole the Italians into discussions, but in vain. He outlined the evidence that Italy supported Hitler openly in his enthusiasm in

Central Europe. He called attention to Italian claims to control the Mediterranean and the four 'keys' to it: Suez, Gibraltar, the Turkish Straits, and Djibouti. He emphasized that Italy was more likely to be restrained if Mussolini could be convinced of the moral determination and solidarity of the democracies, that he had not got them on the run.

Daladier's letter followed on a series of messages from Loraine[93] advising that Mussolini should be left with the impression that his policy was not going well, and that British (and French) firmness in defending their interests could not be stronger. Loraine advised relying on 'the chances of the Germans making a mistake with him, so long as he and they are left à deux'. He advised Halifax to abstain from any offer of loans to Italy. 'We have got, or must be getting very near to the moment when the totalitarians must understand that for some things we *are* going to fight. Let us . . . keep Mussolini uncomfortable . . . for the time being . . . it is best for you to maintain your *silence menaçant* in London and me my *silence souriant* in Rome.' Chamberlain commented: 'A very sensible letter.' His own reply to Daladier on August 3 accepted Daladier's arguments.[94]

'The Germans may make a mistake with him.' Loraine could not know it, but they already had. The question was rather when the Italians would realize this, now that Ciano, preferring the naïve optimism of his son-in-law, Magistrati, had dropped the idea of a conference and dismissed Attolico as the panic-stricken tool of Hitler's enemies in the German Foreign Ministry. Characteristically, Ciano did nothing to move or choke off Attolico. His bombastic dismissal of his Ambassador in Berlin hid a continuing sense of unease. General Roatta's reports of troop movements, based on information from Canaris, to which Attolico drew Ciano's attention the following day;[95] Ambassador Arone's reports from Warsaw of the intensification of the Danzig conflict; Consul Spechel's reports from Danzig;[96] all began to convince Ciano something was wrong. Italy could be about to be dragged into war 'in the most unfavourable conditions for the Axis, and especially for Italy'. Ciano conceived the idea that he should see Ribbentrop. Mussolini approved.

On August 10, Ciano, accompanied by his German SS interpreter, Eugen Dollman, recalled from a glutton's holiday in Etruria, took train from Rome to Salzburg. He crossed the frontier in the early hours of August 11. Travelling with him were Leonardo Vitetti, the Director General of the Italian Foreign Ministry, his friend, the future ambassador Marcello del Drago, Hans von Mackensen, the German Ambassador to Rome, and a group of Italian journalists. In a state of some euphoria[97] – for were they not travelling to an historic meeting at which the fate of Europe would be decided? – and having picked up Attolico and Magistrati at Rosenheim, in Bavaria, they arrived in Salzburg around midday. Ciano brought with him a draft communiqué. It spoke of the 'perfect identity of views' obtaining between the German and Italian Governments. It spoke of their common determination to resist the policy of encirclement and to defend their vital interests against aggression. It confirmed the common desire of the two Governments for peace and for negotiations conducted by normal diplomatic channels through which to arrive at a satisfactory solution for the problems which so seriously disturbed the life of Europe.[98] And, Ciano was at once to discover, it did not in any way correspond with Ribbentrop's state of mind.

Von Ribbentrop, accompanied by Friedrich Gaus, the German Foreign Ministry's legal chief, met the Italian party at Salzburg's railway station. Both, to the surprise of the Italians, accustomed to the universality of uniforms in Nazi Germany, were informally dressed. After a brief reception at their hotel, the Oesterreichisches Hof, they were piled into a convoy of grey Mercedes saloons to be driven to Ribbentrop's country house, Schloss Fuschl, for a preliminary lunch and informal conversation.[99] Luncheon was a grisly occasion. As they sat down, Ciano asked his host, 'Is it only Danzig that you want?' 'No,' replied von Ribbentrop. 'We want much more than that. We want war.'[100] After such a conversation-stopper, lunch proceeded largely in silence, broken only by Ribbentrop's idea of small talk. After lunch the two Foreign Ministers disappeared into the salon for conversations *à deux*. Ironically, the two men conversed in English. The other members of their entourage spent the afternoon gloomily contemplating the Wolfgangsee, that most beautiful of the Salzkammergut's many lakes, on whose shores Schloss Fuschl stood.[101]

Ribbentrop, as if to emphasize the informality of the occasion, kept no records. Ciano's record is written in the heroic style he affected for what he regarded as great historical documents.[102] One may take leave to doubt its details, save that the two men, who detested and distrusted one another, preferred speechifying at one another to conversing. Ciano tried to convince Ribbentrop that any German attack on Poland would lead to a general European war. Ribbentrop maintained the opposite. If France and Britain intervened, the war would inevitably end in an Axis victory. Ciano did his best to argue the contrary; but it had no effect (*niente da fare*). Ribbentrop repeated that both his information and, above all, 'his knowledge of the English psychology' ('*sic*', wrote Ciano viciously) made him certain that any armed intervention on Britain's part could be excluded. Russia would not intervene, as he was in secret negotiations with her. Nor would any other power. In America German propaganda had brought about a profound change of opinion towards neutrality and isolationism. 'After two hours of continuous discussion,' wrote Ciano, 'I was left with the profound conviction that he intended to provoke a conflict and block any initiative which could peacefully resolve the crisis.'

The two men emerged at about 5.30 p.m., Ribbentrop repeating, as if mechanically, 'the localization of the conflict is certain,' 'the probability of victory is infinite.' His Italian guests, Vitetti, Attolico and Magistrati (Dollman, to his great relief, had been left in Salzburg), had a bare five minutes before a new convoy of Mercedes drove them across the valley to St Wolfgang, to the White Horse Inn, celebrated in the musical of that name, 'where good fortune stands by the door'. The lake was filled with gaily beflagged boats, the streets with Austrians celebrating. The dinner in the inn was another funereal occasion, enlivened only by the unhappy Burgomaster of St Wolfgang, who told stories of the Emperor Franz Josef and his mistress, Katerina Witt, who occupied an apartment in the town when the Hapsburg court summered at nearby Bad Ischl.[103]

Finally the Italians were allowed to return to their hotel. They met in the bathroom of Ciano's suite, where, to the sound of taps turned on full blast to blanket the Nazi microphones they assumed to be planted, Ciano's entourage heard what had happened. The conversation was animated and fruitless. The diplomatists urged the necessity of neutrality. Others urged the dangers of Fascism seeming to break with its fellow ideology. Ciano pledged that he would 'shipwreck' any attempt by Ribbentrop to produce a communiqué alleging German and Italian agreements; again, in vain.[104]

On the following two days, Ciano was to have successive meetings with Hitler himself at the 'Eagle's Nest', the mountain-top villa that Hitler had built at Berchtesgaden, in what was before 1938 and is again today a spur of the Bavarian Alps thrust so far into Austria that the road from Salzburg to Zell-am-See has to cross it. The uncertain weather of the previous day had given way to thick cloud. The famous view over the Austrian mountains was hidden. Once more the proceedings began with lunch. Hitler, who had presumably sat up late awaiting Ribbentrop's report, emerged from his bedroom about noon, looking wan and fidgety. Lunch, 'served at speed and eaten without appetite', consisted of ill-prepared vegetables and ill-dressed salads, at which Hitler picked listlessly. Ciano relieved his feelings by commenting on the excess of flour in the sauce and vinegar in the dressing, and poked fun at the flower arrangements.[105]

The subsequent conversation was a re-run of that between Ciano and Ribbentrop. Hitler spoke at length of the humiliations and disgrace heaped on Germany by the Poles, and gave Ciano the original of Ribbentrop's strategic *tour d'horizon*.[106] Ciano deployed all his arguments as to Italian weakness, war weariness, financial collapse and need for recuperation. He did not, as perhaps he should have, mention the number of occasions on which Hitler and his representatives had assured Italy of Germany's desire to postpone war for a few more years. He interrupted Hitler's peroration by asking for a glass of water. Hitler strode up and down, Ribbentrop stood wrapped in grandeur like a Homeric god of war, and Ciano was starting to scratch himself – always a sign of extreme agitation – when Hewel rushed in with telegrams from Tokyo and Moscow. That from Tokyo[107] reported a further deadlock on the alliance negotiations, which the Japanese War Minister was proposing to resolve by offering his resignation. The resulting Cabinet crisis would bring a set-back which would eventually be resolved in Germany's favour. That from Berlin reported a Soviet proposal for political discussions in Moscow. It was, almost certainly, a piece of theatre invented by Ribbentrop,[108] although it may have referred to a conversation in Berlin which took place that same afternoon between Astakhov, the Soviet Chargé d'affaires in Berlin, and Julius Schnurre, the chief German negotiator with the Soviets on economic issues.[109]

With that, the discussions were broken off. Ciano and his Italian companions were carried up in the bronze lift to the Eagle's Nest itself. The Wagnerian atmosphere was enhanced by a recording of the 'Ride of the Valkyries'. Outside the windows eagles circled. Neither Wagner nor mountains, neither eagles nor the hot tea which was all the teetotal dictator offered, held any warmth for Ciano and his companions. Shivering with cold and shock the Italians returned to Salzburg, to yet another fruitless discussion of what form, if any, the final communiqué should take. Ribbentrop's draft, with its evocation of the 'impassive unity of two nations', was clearly unsuitable.

Ciano had given up. The next morning he visited Berchtesgaden again. He did his best, but his heart was not in it. 'Inert' and 'apathetic' in manner, he listened to Hitler reject his attempt to postpone the German action. Once winter started, Hitler said, Poland could strangle Danzig economically, even occupy the city with impunity. Major military operations would be impossible. Danzig would be reduced to ruins. The Luftwaffe would be useless. Any concessions would be seen as weakness. If the West had decided to act, it would not wait while Italy rearmed. If it was still undetermined, swift action against Poland would deter it. If there were any new Polish provocation, he would take swift action. If Poland did not make her political attitude clear and unmistakable, she would have to be forced to do so. To Ciano's question, he replied that this would have to take place by the end of August.[110] (He did not reveal, as we shall see, that he planned to create the 'provocation' he required.)

Ciano did not attempt to cope with this. He replied only with the hope that Hitler would be proved right. 'Perhaps you see the problems more clearly than we do in Rome.'[111] With that he and his entourage left for Salzburg. Attolico and Magistrati returned to Berlin by air in Ribbentrop's own plane, to prepare new ammunition for the battle to come, the battle to convert Mussolini to neutrality. Ciano and his companions took plane back to Rome to report to Mussolini. The effort to restrain Hitler had failed.

So had the effort to restrain Ribbentrop from publishing the communiqué he desired. The morning of August 15, the *Völkischer Beobachter*, under the heading 'Danzig and the Axis', with a by-line from Salzburg, spoke of the 'absolute unanimity' of views on the current situation and the way of resolving it achieved at the meeting.[112] The DNB (Deutsche Nachrichten Büro), the official German news agency, had apparently issued a newsflash on August 13 only two hours after Ciano's plane left Salzburg airport,[113] a newsflash specifically designed for the foreign press. It spoke of the '100 per cent concordance of views', 'of the extraordinary amity and cordiality' of the meeting of the two Foreign Ministers. 'No more conversation would be necessary.' Not only had Ciano been defeated; he had been conned, gulled, lied to, betrayed, abandoned and cheated. Hitler's famous world view had no room in it for allies; only for enemies or for followers.

CHAPTER 23

HITLER WILLS HIS WAR

While Ciano was still winging his way back to Rome, furious, humiliated, feeling that he had encountered the raw edge of insanity, and determined to convince his master that the real Italy had no place in Hitler's cosmos and should no longer attempt to find one, the Führer was proceeding with his timetable. The political part of the timetable depended on three factors. He had to be careful to avoid any Polish move that might be interpreted as a will to concessions and thus reduce the Poles' plausibility as Germany's implacable enemy and persecutor. He had to ward off or evade any attempt, from whatever quarter, to pin him down to an international conference. And he had to bring the Soviets to show their hand publicly *before* his military timetable unwound its final inexorable way to war.

The first precaution taken was to break off effective diplomatic relations with Warsaw, Paris and London. The task was made the easier for him by the normal diplomatic timetable, by which ambassadors tended to take their annual holidays in August, when the governments to which they were accredited closed down their parliaments, and capital cities emptied their more powerful and prominent citizens to holiday in the coolth of the countryside, to cruise the Mediterranean or the Baltic, to shoot grouse or to take the waters in France, Switzerland or the spas of Central Europe. The British and French Ambassadors in Rome and Berlin had, wisely, taken their annual leaves in June or July. Herbert von Dirksen in London, Johannes Count von Welczeck in Paris, and Hans Adolf von Moltke in Warsaw had not. Each in turn, as he returned to Berlin to report, prior to taking his annual leave, was forbidden to return to his post until ordered.

Von Moltke was the first. On the evening of August 9, Dr Brücklmeier of von Ribbentrop's secretariat telephoned from Salzburg.[1] Von Moltke was to remain in Berlin. He was not even to telephone his staff in Warsaw. He was to have no contact with any Polish authority. The

430

Embassy in Warsaw was to maintain a 'purely receptive attitude', receiving any Polish communications that might come that way and reporting to Berlin. The same instructions were to be binding on the Foreign Ministry in Berlin. Von Moltke, son of the famous Field Marshal and a man of honour, protested repeatedly.[2] He was responsible for the safety of German citizens in Poland; he was responsible for the safety of his staff. He felt 'like a captain who had deserted his company at the critical moment'. He was ignored. The safety of the Reichs Germans in Poland was not the highest priority in Ribbentrop's mind. Indeed the larger the number of victims of Polish 'atrocities', the better. The Embassy in Warsaw was to report on 'significant events' which might be turned to propaganda advantage.[3] A telegram from Polish Silesia appealing for Hitler's protection against Polish persecution was to be used in conversations with foreign diplomatists, at a suitable moment,[4] so Ribbentrop's instructions ran.

As Moltke's deputy in Warsaw, Johann von Wühlisch, reported,[5] the Polish arrests in Upper Silesia were actually to be 'attributed to the organization of diversionary groups from various centres in Germany'. He knew of similar groups in Poznan, Pommerellen and central Poland. He requested that these activities should be suspended. The Foreign Ministry, recognizing the hand of Heydrich and the SS, and of Obergruppenführer Lorenz of the SS *Volkdeutsche Mittelstelle*, who had masterminded similar activities among the Sudeten Germans in Czechoslovakia, fumed, but did nothing. The German press, in the meantime, unleashed a new campaign of vilification against the Poles.[6] The French Ambassador in Berlin, Robert Coulondre, noted the invocation,[7] for the first time, of German honour, a type of argument, he noted ominously, invoked in September 1938 against the Czechs. 'The Hitlerian plan', he concluded, 'continues to develop according to a well-known procedure.'

In the meantime, the process of 'breaking the bridges' continued. On August 14, Herbert von Dirksen arrived in Berlin. He was immediately informed by von Weizsäcker that he was on no account to return to London without explicit instructions.[8] Von Dirksen was rash enough to spill his views to Attolico, the Italian Ambassador in Berlin; Attolico's report[9] was deciphered and given to von Ribbentrop. Dirksen was then banned from all political discussions,[10] and left for his estates in East Prussia,[11] and virtual retirement. His conviction that Britain would intervene if Germany attacked Poland, was not a view von Ribbentrop wanted bruited abroad in Berlin, especially from someone whose mother had, in the past, enjoyed Hitler's ear. Count von Welczeck arrived in Berlin at the same time. He too was forbidden to return to his post and placed in semi-retirement. His failure to secure Abetz's reinstatement made him doubly unacceptable to the German Foreign Minister.

Weizsäcker noted somewhat nervously in his diary on August 14[12] that, since the beginning of the month, opinion in Fuschl and on the Berghof as to whether Britain and France would stand by Poland seemed to have swung around completely. Other earlier diary entries ascribe the change to the rapid progress of the German approaches to Moscow and the Soviet refusal to clinch matters with the British.[13] Himmler, Ribbentrop and Forster, each in his own sphere of activity, were strengthening Hitler's will to war.[14] Ribbentrop particularly was guaranteeing British and French neutrality. This was all the odder, in that in the last days of July Ribbentrop had been confronted from two normally Germanophile sources, the newspaper owner Lord Rothermere[15] and the merchant banker (and MI6 confidant) Ernest Tennant,[16] with the most flat and direct assurances that Germany was on course for a head-on collision with Britain. Characteristically, he had reacted to both with bombastic boasting as to Germany's might and determination, and reiterations of the contempt with which Hitler regarded both the Poles and the British guarantee.

Hitler for his part had shown his hand to Count Csàky, the Hungarian Foreign Minister, on August 8 at the Berghof.[17] The Poles, he remarked with justice, were 'labouring under a dangerous delusion as to their strength and that of the German army'. 'Had they gone mad in Warsaw?' he asked. 'The tension with Poland had brought him [Hitler] the fanatical 100 per cent support of the German army as well as that of the last remaining opposition, namely certain Prussian aristocratic families.' 'The face of the Polish army already had the appearance of death.' As for the Soviet Government, they apparently wanted to bind themselves to no one; nor would the Soviets fight against Germany, as they were equally afraid of defeat as of victory for their army. Amidst his rabid talk of Polish 'bestial behaviour' towards the German minority in Poland, including the allegations of castration which betray the sexual side of his oratorical hysteria, the Führer's shrewdness was asserting itself again; but not towards Italy or Britain. Csáky was so shaken, he withdrew his Premier's letter stating Hungarian unwillingness to fight against Poland.

Hitler devoted himself now to four tasks: to laying a trap for the Poles by ostensibly showing signs of willingness to negotiate over Danzig; to laying various other false trails as to the timing of his next move, if move there was to be; to pressing the Soviets, since they were now his trump card by which British intervention – France hardly figures in his language in the next fortnight – was to be choked off; and to polishing the military preparations, which, for him, included the instillation into his military leadership of the will to war and the conviction of victory.

The Poles were living up to Hitler's estimates of them. Their diplomatists positively glowed with confidence. Polish nerves were strong, the Polish Ambassador to the United States, Count Jerzy Potocki, boasted to Sumner Welles on his return from Poland.[18] If it came to war, the Polish General Staff had determined to undertake an offensive into Germany with their highly mobile forces, especially the cavalry. (This was, as will be seen, quite untrue.) Beck was convinced things would not come to war. The German Generals had advised that, if Britain and France were involved, they could give Hitler no guarantee as to the outcome. If no war broke out this autumn, the internal situation in Germany would become so serious by mid-winter that Hitler would be overthrown by the spring. Similar views were to be heard from the young Lukasziewicz in Paris, from Count Raczyński in London, and from Beck himself, speaking to his Under Secretary Count Szembek, recalled from leave on August 14.[19] The Polish Ambassador in Rome, the independent-minded Boleslaw Wienawa-Dlugoszowski, had spoken in a more sombre, but equally determined manner to Ciano on the eve of the Italian Foreign Minister's visit to the Berghof.[20]

Polish sang-froid was improved by the tactics adopted by the Danzig leadership. After the delivery of the Polish note of August 10, which, in Moltke's absence in Berlin, Beck was forced to depute to an official of the Polish Foreign Ministry to be transmitted to the German Chargé d'affaires in Warsaw, the Poles found it impossible to open any direct conversations with the Germans, either in Berlin or in Warsaw, or indeed anywhere else. The one unofficial approach they did succeed in making, through the Secretary of the German-Polish Society in Berlin on August 12, was easily choked off;[21] which was just as well, from Ribbentrop's point of view, since the Poles who made the contact stated clearly that Danzig, the Corridor or any other questions could easily be made the subject of discussion.

The German press campaign alleging massive mistreatment of the German minority in Poland and the actual campaign waged against the Polish minority in Germany confused the Poles the more, as did perhaps the master-stroke, an invitation Hermann Goering sent to Józef Lipski, the Polish Ambassador in Berlin, to go shooting with him in the German state forests in October or November.[22] A similar invitation was sent to Sir Nevile Henderson, the British Ambassador. Goering's reputation as the voice of reason in Hitler's entourage made this the more baffling. Goering was clearly fully aware of Hitler's military timetable; but in the last month before the war he was so often to be found playing 'soft man' to Ribbentrop's and his master's 'hard men' that this invitation can only be seen as part of Hitler's deception strategy. The invitations also sent to all members of the diplomatic corps in Berlin to celebrate the twenty-fifth anniversary of Hindenburg's decisive victory in 1914 over the Russian armies at Tannenberg, and to the annual party conference in Nuremberg, should be seen in the same light.

This strategy of deception was given a major advance the day Ciano arrived in Salzburg; even as he and Ribbentrop were shouting at one another in Fuschl, even as he arrived in Salzburg, Hitler was entertaining Carl Burckhardt, the League of Nations Commissioner in Danzig, in his Eagle's Nest at Berchtesgaden. The evening of August 10, Burckhardt gave a dinner for Tadeusz Perkowski, the Polish Deputy High Commissioner in Danzig, whose chauffeur had fired the fatal shot at Kalthof in May. From that day on, Perkowski had been a marked man. The Danzig authorities had refused to have anything to do with him. Despite threats to his life (the German press had called him the 'murder diplomat'), he had continued to walk every day from his home in Danzig to his office. Early in August Beck had decided to cut his losses and recall Perkowski to Warsaw. Over Forster's protests, Burckhardt had insisted on giving him a farewell dinner. Even as they were rising from the dinner table, Burckhardt was called to the telephone. It was Forster. Hitler, he said, was sending his personal plane to Danzig at 9 a.m. the following morning to fly Forster and Burckhardt to Salzburg. At all costs the visit was to be kept secret.[23]

Burckhardt returned to his guest of honour. Frantic telephoning finally located Perkowski's boss, Chodacki, in a Gdynia night-club. By midnight Burckhardt had consulted or notified the French, British and Swedish representatives in Danzig, the local representatives of the three members of the League of Nations Committee on Danzig. Beck gave his approval; but not his confidence. The British representative brought Lord Halifax's approval to Burckhardt's home early the next morning. Punctually at 9 a.m. Hitler's personal plane, a two-engined Fokker-Wolff Condor 200, *Immelmann III*, took off from Danzig airport, closed since the previous evening, with Burckhardt and Forster aboard. It was the third such flight in as many days for Forster, who had only returned from Salzburg on August 9.[24] It was not the most entertaining of flights. Forster talked the entire trip, boasting of German invincibility, reminiscing about his exploits as a 'steward' fighting Communist hecklers at Nazi meetings and breaking up Communist meetings before

1923, and falling into a kind of patriotic ecstasy as the plane passed over Prague.[25]

If Burckhardt found Forster's behaviour on the journey bizarre, the behaviour of his host in the Eagle's Nest on the heights above his Berchtesgaden abode disturbed him considerably. Burckhardt's account of the conversation[26] is scored like a Wagnerian opera: 'crescendo', 'fortissimo', 'angry', 'furious', 'pause', 'hysterical laughter', 'calm', 'tapping the table'. 'Herr Hitler was so carried away by anger that he was unable to speak for several moments.'

The Führer began with a bitter attack on the Poles for the 'ultimatum' of August 10, and for the manner in which the Polish and French press had 'trumpeted' Polish courage and claimed that Hitler had lost his nerve (all of which had happened since Forster's invitation to Burckhardt). This was followed by the same kind of military-strategic rhodomontade of which Count Csàky had already been the victim, and which was to be unleashed the following day on Count Ciano.

There followed a dissertation on the reasonableness of the 'offer' Hitler had made to the Poles, which they had 'definitely ruled out'. Then came a brief episode of self-pity as he showed Burckhardt around his domain. 'How happy I am when I am here. I've had enough; now I need a rest.' Then followed the 'offer', the main reason for the invitation. If the Poles should leave Danzig calm, if the sufferings of the German minority should cease, then Hitler could wait. As for the British, Hitler only wanted to live in peace with them, to conclude a definite pact, 'to guarantee all the English possessions in the world and to co-operate'. Could not a German-speaking Englishman come to Berlin, perhaps General Ironside who had had such success in Poland?

The whole experience shook Burckhardt considerably. He thought Hitler 'older and whiter' than he had seen him two years previously. He seemed fearful, 'nervous, pathetic and almost shaken at times'. Burckhardt referred to his 'femininity'.

From Salzburg Burckhardt went on to Basle where, on August 13, he told the British and French members of the Committee of Three what had happened. His report was chewed to pieces in London and Paris without any new conclusions being drawn, save that it would be wise to impress on the Poles the need for restraint. This the Poles, watching the steady build-up of German troops already mobilized, and the steady movement towards the Polish frontier, were ready to accept.[27] Beck was, however, angered by Burckhardt's failure to see the Polish representative to the League; Burckhardt, he suspected, was acting as an Anglo-French agent.[28] Sensational reports in the French press, the work of an enterprising but over-imaginative French reporter in Danzig, that Burckhardt was charged with a secret message from Hitler to Chamberlain,[29] that he was to act as a new 'Runciman', did not help. Goebbels' propagandists having already started one canard, picked up by the British Communist newspaper, the *Daily Worker*, to the effect that the British had sent a commission to investigate the economic importance of Danzig to Poland, did their best to exploit the issue.[30] These reports were duly picked up by the Soviet Ambassador in Paris and reported to Moscow.[31]

Forster remained behind in Salzburg to obtain his orders for the next stage. Hitler's tactics in Danzig followed the standard pattern of hard play-soft play already used so tellingly against Czechoslovakia in 1938. On August 13, three Polish customs inspectors, who had turned the searchlight of their boat on a German vessel entering Danzig harbour without lights, were arrested on allegations of carrying pamphlets hostile to Herr Forster. On August 17 a Polish frontier guard was shot dead. In this latter case the Polish police acted firmly and promptly, arresting a number of members of the Nazi German minority organization, the Young German Party, one of whom shot a Polish policeman dead while resisting arrest.[32] In the meantime, Greiser, for the Danzig Senate, had, on Hitler's direct instructions (the German Foreign Ministry was kept in the dark), agreed to start discussions with the Poles in Danzig to settle the customs inspectors issue. The discussions actually opened on August 16 at Greiser's home.[33] Greiser promised that, if the Senate's desires were met, and the extra customs officials sent since May 'for military reasons', should be withdrawn, then those who remained would not be hindered in performing their duties. He asked for the frontier barriers to be lifted to demonstrate Polish goodwill.

Chodacki was firm, but as he had just been recalled to Warsaw for instructions, he made generally co-operative noises. He returned on August 18 for a second conversation.[34] He was empowered, he said, to withdraw the frontier guards, some of whom would be replaced by customs officials in civilian clothes. In return Greiser authorized the release of the Polish customs officers arrested on August 14. The same day Forster staged a major demonstration in Danzig. Units of the Danzig SS staged a great march through the streets of the city. The Gauleiter presented them with new colours. Technical discussions on the proposed measures were to follow on August 21. Reassured, the Polish Foreign Minister told Léon Noël, the French Ambassador in Warsaw, that matters were proceeding satisfactorily.

These signs of Polish conciliatoriness, by an odd accident, forced Forster to show his hand to the officials of the German Foreign

Ministry. Since June the German Consul in Danzig, Dr Janson, and Forster had been at such odds with each other that no information as to Forster's plan was reaching them at all. Even Ribbentrop was in the dark. Early in August Ribbentrop had sent Edmund Veesenmayer of the Foreign Ministry to Danzig as his personal representative.[35] Veesenmayer was not to be kept much more in the picture than was Janson. Excluded from Hitler's meetings with Forster,[36] he was reduced to referring the Foreign Ministry to Reinhard Heydrich, the SS deputy to Himmler, Chief of the Reichssicherheitshauptamt (RSHA), in charge of both the Gestapo and the regular police, and head of the burgeoning SS intelligence service.[37] On August 19, however, Forster was driven to ask, through Veesenmayer, whether he should proceed to raise his demands on the Poles to the immediate withdrawal of fifty customs officers, and if they yielded on this, to go on raising his demands so as to make agreement impossible.[38] This, it emerged on August 22[39] (after Forster had paid a further visit to Hitler), was part of a plan designed to provoke Polish action against Danzig; a breakdown in the negotiations, with the blame fixed on the Poles; the removal of all Polish customs officers; and the opening of the border with East Prussia. If the Poles did not react to that, then numerous Poles in Danzig would be arrested and 'numerous Polish arms dumps', the discovery of which was 'assured', would be 'closed'. Finally, if the Poles remained unmoved, the Polish garrison on the Westerplatte would be attacked.

If this elaborate charade was designed to fool the diplomatists in Berlin, it did not. Even the gullible, always optimistic Sir Nevile Henderson was glum and full of foreboding. The invitations to the Tannenberg celebration on August 27, and to the party celebrations in Nuremberg a week later, may have misled the diplomats in Berlin as to the date on which Hitler would make his move. But in common with most of the European capitals they were well aware that Hitler had ordered his military preparations to be complete by August 15. The belief that August 27–9 was the time of maximum danger merely led them to feel they had just a few days more in which to work a miracle. They had only two straws at which to clutch: a renewed intervention by Mussolini and the much-touted visit by the German-speaking Englishman, who would open Hitler's eyes to the certainty of British intervention.

The first required further activity on the part of the increasingly desperate Attolico. He had returned to Berlin from Salzburg on August 14 in a mixture of rage and depression. The rage was directed primarily at the British who, so he believed, following what Hitler had said at

Berchtesgaden, had encouraged the Poles into an intransigence over Danzig which they would not otherwise have adopted.

That evening he consulted von Weizsäcker.[40] Together they conceived the idea of a concerted British and Italian approach to Hitler. The following morning, Attolico had a somewhat strained meeting with Sir Nevile Henderson,[41] in which he told Sir Nevile that the biggest service he could do for peace was to convince the British Government that Hitler was not to be intimidated by the peace front and that something would have to be done quickly; the Führer was not going 'to sit with folded hands' while the various negotiations proceeded. Would Chamberlain be prepared to make a move in conjunction with Mussolini? Henderson, taken aback, could only reply that that would depend on what was proposed.

With that, Attolico left for Rome. Three days later he returned to tackle Ribbentrop at Fuschl. The meeting was, so Attolico reported to Rome, of no practical value,[42] despite the message he delivered from Mussolini, reiterating Italy's refusal to believe that a German-Polish war could be localized and her total lack of preparedness for a general war. The following day he returned to Salzburg to hear Hitler's reply to Mussolini's message.[43] Germany's decisions were already taken. Germany had not sought war. The war would remain localized; neither France nor Britain would dare attack the Axis powers. If the war became general, given the overwhelming predominance of the Axis, it would be soon over. In any case, with the Soviet frontiers open, the Axis could survive a long war. Attolico returned to Rome, disconsolate.

In Rome, he and Ciano prepared one last final appeal, a demand that Ciano and Ribbentrop should meet on the Brenner.[44] It was to be overtaken by the sudden acceleration of Ribbentrop's exchanges with Moscow. On August 21 Ciano insisted that he and Ribbentrop should meet.[45] At the other end of the phone, Ribbentrop stalled him. He was waiting, he said, for an important message from Moscow. That was at 5.40 in the evening. At 10.30 that same evening, he called Ciano back. He would rather see Ciano at Innsbruck than on the frontier. He had to leave on the afternoon of the next day to sign a political pact with the Soviet Union. Ciano gave up. With that, one of the two lines the diplomatic conspirators were pursuing fizzled out.

There remained the case of the German-speaking Englishman, so carefully planted on Burckhardt by Forster and echoed by Hitler that one suspects a trap; the more so, as Forster returned to the proposal at least once in the next ten days. A visit to Hitler by a senior British figure could not have been kept secret, least of all were the visitor the flamboyant General Ironside, with his towering height, his whiskers and his overblown personality. The ever-present suspicions of a new Munich in preparation, suspicions already blown into full flame by the unfortunately irrepressible Robert Hudson and fanned by the rumours surrounding M. Burckhardt's visit to Berchtesgaden, would have flamed into certainty. In Paris, Bonnet and his tail would have been able either to plead betrayal or to urge upon the Anglophile element in the Cabinet the necessity of following the British example. Daladier, wavering and irresolute, save towards Italy, would have deserted the few hawks at whose head he found himself at the moment. Morale in Warsaw, it could have been hoped, would have collapsed. And Hitler would have had a perfect occasion on which to stage the carefully manufactured incidents of Polish aggression Herr Heydrich and the SS were then preparing for him.

Something of this may already have been felt in Berlin, where Sir Nevile Henderson's daily importunities were doing nothing to enhance his already disintegrating reputation with his colleagues in the Foreign Office. It was under these circumstances that Weizsäcker felt obliged to risk a more direct warning, using once again the two Kordt brothers, Erich, on Ribbentrop's personal staff, and Theo, the Counsellor of the German Embassy in London. On August 16, Erich Kordt dispatched his young cousin, Susanne Simonis, to London with a message for his brother. She had acted in a similar role as courier in September 1938. On August 17, she arrived in London and briefed Theo Kordt.[46] That evening his remarks came to Strang's ears. 'The Italians', he was reported as saying, 'have not given a blank cheque over Danzig.'[47]

The next evening he sought out Vansittart and passed on his message. Hitler had chosen war. The date on which it would begin lay between August 25 and 28. Ciano had caused trouble at Salzburg. Italian anxieties were now allayed by Hitler's assurances that even if Britain and France joined in, all Hitler required of Italy was her friendly neutrality. In a state of nervous collapse, Vansittart telephoned Lord Halifax in Yorkshire, then rushed round to see his successor, Sir Alexander Cadogan, who fed him cold ham and calmed him down. Cadogan, who did not trust Theo Kordt (with reason, given Kordt's role in accepting information from a Foreign Office traitor as to the detailed exchanges between London and Moscow), wrote this off as possibly part of the 'war of nerves' which he believed the Germans to be waging. 'And I have seen the first casualty,' he noted sardonically in his diary.[48]

The date, however, fitted with the information which had been reaching MI6 from a source on the German railways. Other hints led

Halifax, who came hot-foot back from his family seat in Yorkshire, to feel something should be done.[49] He considered, and rejected, the 'Ironside approach', choosing instead the device of a personal letter to Hitler from Chamberlain, who was due to return to London from his fishing holiday in Scotland on Monday, August 21.[50] The following day the Cabinet met, with the news of Ribbentrop's forthcoming visit to Moscow before them, and approved a much-revised draft of Chamberlain's letter.[51]

Over the same three days an approach was made to Admiral Sinclair from someone unknown who claimed to be close to Goering, proposing that he should come to London in secret. Halifax waited three days only to learn on August 24 that Hitler had cancelled the visit.[52] Since MI6 records remain closed to historians, there is no way of knowing how or by whom this approach was made. Perhaps Hitler, having given up hope that the British would swallow his bait and send a general to Berlin, had decided to send the mountain to Muhammad. But it seems more likely that the whole story arose from the action of that extraordinary Australian airman, Sidney Cotton, who, with the approval of the deputy head of the Secret Service and with Chamberlain's knowledge, took time off from flying spy-photography flights for MI6 over Germany, to visit the German Foreign Ministry on August 23, to propose that Goering visit London. His move was dismissed out of hand by Under Secretary Ernst Woermann, head of the Political Department and, by coincidence, also the Foreign Ministry's liaison officer with the various German clandestine services.[53] Goering already had his own emissary to Britain in Birger Dahlerus,[54] who was busy pursuing his English contacts of August 8 and had made a further effort to stir something up on August 12, through Lord Runciman's son.[55] The effect of all this amateur diplomacy in London was to increase the scepticism with which the efforts of the intermediaries were regarded. That much was to the good. It seems also to have increased the scepticism with which their information and warnings were regarded; their dismissal as part of a 'war of nerves' was perhaps not so happy.

There was in fact no question either of a 'war of nerves' or of war arising out of a failure of communication or a runaway escalation, such as most then believed to have occurred in July–August 1914. Hitler fully intended war. The military planning ordered in April and confirmed on May 23 was specific, not contingent. The events of August 1939 were planned to happen, even if not planned to happen as they did. Hitler, as has been noticed before, most notably in the planning against the rump state of Czechoslovakia in February–March 1939, was not the most efficient of Machiavellis. May, June and July had been filled with the most detailed military planning. From early August onwards he left his military in no doubt as to what he planned.

Firm orders had been issued to General Keitel on August 12 before Count Ciano arrived. The army was to get ready. X-day, the day the German forces would attack Poland, was fixed for August 26.[56] That same day Admiral Canaris activated the clandestine group of the *Abwehr*, the army intelligence service, headed by General Lahousen, which was charged, among other things, with manufacturing a rising among the Ukrainian minority in Poland.[57] (This date itself had been fixed early in July.) Two days later Hitler began on the work of 'psyching up' his Generals, beginning with the army commander, General von Brauchitsch, and General Halder, the Army Chief of Staff.[58]

General Halder had spent the morning casting up the forces on either side of Germany's western frontier. Even on the assumption that no British troops reinforced those at France's disposal, he disliked what he saw. France had a superiority of ten divisions at her immediate disposal over the thirty-one divisions which was all Germany could spare in the west, and another forty-seven divisions at her disposal to use for an invasion of Germany through Belgium, Luxemburg and the Netherlands if she chose. After fifteen days, Halder expected some thirty Allied divisions to attack. Against them he could only muster some twenty-six under-equipped and under-gunned divisions. From Hitler he got a *tour d'horizon* designed to show the weaknesses of France and Britain, their lack of moral courage ('the grey heads of Munich will not take the risks upon themselves') and their military weakness. Hitler's main anxiety was that Britain would make the final decision more difficult by making some kind of offer. It would be months before British military strength could manifest itself. In any case Hitler was certain Britain and France, however they might huff and puff, would not intervene. The only thing he asked was that 'in eight to fourteen days' it should be clear to everyone that Poland was about to collapse. Brauchitsch and Halder listened in silence.

That would have been the moment for von Brauchitsch to act, if he had had it in him. He knew, as did Halder, that much of what Hitler said was, to say the least, improbable. Whatever Hitler said, neither of them believed Britain would just sit on her hands and do nothing. Halder took the trouble to check Hitler's remarks with von Weizsäcker.[59] He remained in touch with Colonel Oster,[60] the centre of the anti-Nazi group under Admiral Canaris in the *Abwehr*. Mostly, however, his days and his diary were filled with the details of military planning, as each operation against Poland's frontier defences required working out in detail.

For Hitler the time after August 14 was occupied in a welter of nostalgia. August 16 marked the twenty-fifth anniversary of his enlistment in the 16th Bavarian Infantry Regiment (Reserve), the 'List' regiment. It was also five years since Hitler had taken over the position of Commander-in-Chief of the Armed Forces when, on the death of the Reichs President and head of state Field Marshal von Hindenburg, he had abolished the Reichs Presidency and caused the officers of all the armed services to swear personal oaths of loyalty to himself. The festivities at the Obersalzberg began at midnight on the night of August 15 and lasted the whole day.[61] Himmler, Heydrich and Wolff of the SS, Goering, Ribbentrop, Bormann and Speer all appeared to offer personal congratulations. A delegation from the 19th Munich Infantry Regiment, the lineal successor to the 16th 'List', appeared in the afternoon to present the Führer with an illuminated address and for each man to be given a personally autographed photograph of their most famous veteran.

Mostly, however, Hitler waited and fretted. Consulted frequently on the details of the military planning, he was the more concerned that Stalin should be nailed down. Soviet working hours, the time difference between Berlin and Moscow, the need to transmit everything to Berlin to be enciphered and deciphered before it could be transmitted to Moscow or to Berchtesgaden, and the deliberation of Molotov in answering each increasingly importunate message from the Führer grated on his nerves. As for Molotov and his ultra-suspicious master, they suffered from the incompetence of the NKVD in the mid-1930s, when nothing had been done to replace the agents lost when Hitler cleaned out the German Communist party in 1933. For four years the NKVD resident in Berlin had sat on his chair, leaving active operations against Germany to be conducted from Prague. Some low- or medium-level agents they certainly had, but no Sorge, no King; nor is there any evidence in Soviet policy or behaviour of any ability to read the German diplomatic ciphers. Where Hitler's real intentions were concerned, what was happening at the Berghof or Fuschl, or how the planning for war in the German Army HQ on the Bendlerstrasse was going, Molotov and Stalin were without eyes or ears. Nazi psychology was unfamiliar ground. And every day a new, well-meaning English *prominenter* would blunder through Berlin in some new effort to prevent the lightning striking, to get men of goodwill around a table, or, so it was reasoned in Moscow, to buy Hitler off with promises of an open hand in the East.

Typical of the first was Charles Roden Buxton, a well-meaning Quaker with an excellent track record in 1919–20 in working among the German victims of the British blockade, a pacifist with connections with the British Labour Party.[62] More peculiar was the arrival as a visitor to Alfred Rosenberg of an anglicized Baltic German baron, Baron William de Ropp.

Baron 'Bill' de Ropp had been born a citizen of Tsarist Russia, where his father owned vast estates in what in 1919 was to become Lithuania. He had been educated in Germany, which he loathed, settled in England in 1910, married an English wife, took out nationalization papers, and served from 1915 to 1918 in the Wiltshire regiment and in the RAF as an interrogator of German prisoners of war. In the early 1920s he had settled in Berlin as the representative of an English business, and had been recruited to the British Intelligence by that unique system of recruitment in London clubland by which the SIS kept itself free of contamination by intellectuals and university men. His contacts, education and hostility towards the Lithuanians who had confiscated the family estates and towards the Bolsheviks, taken with his German education, won him an entrée first to the respectable German ultra-right and then to the Nazis. He had used this connection to meet his fellow Balt, the Nazi 'philosopher' Alfred Rosenberg, and through him Hitler. In turn he had introduced Group Captain Winterbotham, the head of the Air Force section of the British Secret Service, to leading Nazis. Winterbotham implies de Ropp was, in a way, a double agent.[63]

Just how seriously de Ropp's sales talk was intended remains locked in the archives of the British intelligence services. It is possible that the heads of the SIS, Admiral 'Quex' Sinclair and Sir Stewart Menzies, shared Winterbotham's critical attitude towards the guarantee of Poland and the approach to the Soviet Union. De Ropp may have been simply fishing for information; though his activities once war had broken out, when he was to re-appear in Germany with proposals for an Anglo-German settlement, suggest a more political purpose. De Ropp's line of patter, as Rosenberg reported it[64] – anti-Polish, anti-Soviet, with talk of a quick liquidation of the war once Poland had been quickly finished off, encouraging Germany to 'establish herself in the East' – was calculated to arouse every Soviet hackle. It may be that he, like his masters, saw this as an essential way in which to inveigle himself into Rosenberg's confidence; but Rosenberg, to whom no secrets were told, would have been useless as a contact, being not much more in Hitler's eyes than a token of Nazi intellectualism.

In the meantime Hitler waited. Saturday, August 19 was a particularly bad day.[65] The final signature of the economic agreement with the

Soviet Union hung fire all day. It was eventually signed at 2 a.m. on August 20. The Führer had to wait until late evening of that day before the Berlin teleprinter relayed Schulenburg's short telegram reporting that Molotov had handed him the draft of a non-aggression pact and agreed to Ribbentrop's coming to Moscow.[66] It was to cost him a further day and a half of waiting before Schulenburg could present Molotov with a personal appeal from Hitler to Stalin to receive Ribbentrop not later than August 23.[67] Schulenburg's report of Molotov's agreement did not arrive in Berlin until 7.55 p.m. on August 21.[68] The text of the communiqué prepared by Molotov did not reach the Berghof until after 10 p.m. that evening.[69] Tass and DNB had the text issued to the wire services before midnight.[70]

Already orders had gone out on August 19 to all the senior German military commanders to assemble in Munich by early morning, August 22, in front of the Nazi Brown House on the Königlichesplatz. They were to wear civilian clothes to avoid attracting attention. A convoy of cars picked them up, some forty or fifty Army and Army Group Commanders with their Chiefs of Staff, the Commanders of various naval divisions and air fleets, and Goering, fantastic in a white shirt under a green jacket with buttons of yellow leather, grey shorts, and a pair of massive laced boots, and sporting a scarlet sword belt with gold inlays and an ornamental dagger in a sheath of the same material. Ribbentrop joined them from Fuschl. Admiral Canaris mingled inconspicuously with the throng.[71]

By midday they were all seated in Hitler's long parlour at the Berghof on wooden chairs arranged in semi-circular rows with Goering, Brauchitsch and Admiral Raeder, Commander-in-Chief of the Navy, in the centre. The only other furniture was a grand piano with a bust of Wagner on it, and a long table under the great window with its marvellous view over the mountains. Hitler came into the room, in party uniform, leaned against the piano and began. There are various versions of what he said.[72] At least three of those present took notes, including Canaris. Others wrote down what they heard the same evening or the next day. One version, greatly rewritten to underline the bloodthirstiness of Hitler's expressions and to sabotage Goering's image of moderation, was passed to the British Embassy via the American journalist, Louis Lochner, and produced by the British prosecution, after 1945, at the main Nuremberg war crimes trial. Apart from this last the various versions differ only in small details of phrasing.

Hitler was determined to crush Poland. He did not think Britain and France would intervene. They might rattle a few sabres, impose economic sanctions, perhaps even try a blockade; but they would not act militarily – they lacked the necessary leadership. So far they had relied on the Soviet Union. 'But I have struck that card from their hands.' All the same, he realized that war with the democracies was inevitable. It could come in a few years. The war with Poland would be a useful exercise to prepare the German people for it. He had begun by trying to create an acceptable relationship with Poland so that he could turn against the West, but it soon became clear that the Poles could not be trusted; so it became necessary to deal with Poland first.

Germany had three great assets: its unity, which he personified; Mussolini, who alone could guarantee Italy's loyalty to the alliance; and Franco, who would guarantee Spain's benevolent neutrality. But at any time a criminal or a lunatic could eliminate any or all of these factors.

Britain, by contrast, had no outstanding personality, only politicians and parliamentarians. Her whole empire was at risk; she was threatened in the Mediterranean by Italy and in the Far East by Japan. In the Middle East Islam was turning against her. There was strife in Ireland. Concessions had had to be made in India. South Africa was becoming more independent. Nor were Britain's armaments in any real shape, even in the air. She would not even lend Poland a mere £8 million. France was in still worse shape, with a low birth-rate and obsolete artillery. 'Our enemies are small fry. I saw them at Munich.' Iron nerves, swift decisions, firm faith in the German soldier, and no pity for the weaklings were his final recommendations. Germany was invulnerable to blockade. A start had been made on the destruction of England's hegemony.

The audience heard him out in silence. They broke for a quick snack; then he resumed for another, shorter inspirational passage, some ten minutes or so. While the Führer remained, no one spoke a word. With set and anxious faces, they left to return to their units.[73] The Air Force Generals took it most lightly. The Admirals, suddenly faced with the possibility of a war with England, that Hitler had sworn lay at least four years in the future, were deep in gloom. Only Raeder took Hitler aside to ask for permission to withdraw the cadet training ship at present lying in the Gulf of Danzig, whose guns were outweighed and outranged by those of Gdynia. Hitler refused. 'If the old hulk sinks, no one will be the worse off.' Shocked, Raeder said that the loss of three hundred potential officers would be a serious blow for the navy. Hitler put him aside with the wave of a hand. (Nevertheless Raeder won his point a day or so later.) Brauchitsch said only, 'Gentlemen, back to your places as soon as possible.'

None of those present really believed Hitler's assurances that Britain and France would do nothing. On the other hand they were still reeling under the shock of the announcement of Ribbentrop's trip to Moscow. Colonel Schmundt, Hitler's military adjutant, tried to persuade Hitler that his speech had been a great success.[74] That does not seem to have been true. What was true was the unwillingness of most of his audience, save in the most intimate circle of their friends, to question either Hitler's role or his judgment. Five years of Nazism had already taught them to school their faces and to hold their tongues. Hitler, in fact, complained that he could get no reaction from them whatever. Their faces told him nothing. But they were not about to mutiny. The military conspirators of 1938 and 1944 were beaten. The military might doubt their Führer; but they would not refuse to fight his war.

CHAPTER 24

RIBBENTROP IN MOSCOW:
THE NAZI–SOVIET PACT SIGNED

At 10.35 on the evening of August 21, the Foreign Ministry in Berlin telexed the Berghof. Stalin had replied to Hitler's personal message. His message was formal rather than warm. But he agreed to the conclusion of a non-aggression pact. And he agreed to receive Ribbentrop in Moscow on August 23. Ensconced in Moscow since August 11, in the former imperial hotel which the Soviets used as a hospitality centre for visiting delegations of foreigners, comfortable, but surrounded by high fences and military guards, the French military mission had, however, noticed that workers had been labouring furiously both night and day since August 18, refurbishing the mansion next door.[1] It was the former Austrian Embassy; it had stood vacant since March 1938 when Hitler's troops had ended the independent life of the Austrian State. The Soviets were preparing it for Ribbentrop and his entourage. On August 17 Friedrich Werner von der Schulenburg, the German Ambassador, had urged Molotov to accept Ribbentrop's visit to Moscow as soon as possible, 'any day after August 18'. Molotov had stalled; the Soviet Government preferred to take things step by step.[2] But the Soviets knew he would come; they knew he would come very soon.

Ribbentrop took plane from Berlin on the evening of August 22. With him there travelled Friedrich Gaus, the Foreign Ministry's legal expert; Paul-Otto Schmidt, the leading Foreign Ministry interpreter, whom Hitler trusted not only as an interpreter but as a record-keeper; Walter Hewel; Paul Schmidt, head of the Foreign Ministry's press bureau; Peter Kleist, Ribbentrop's personal adviser on Polish and Soviet affairs; Ribbentrop's personal photographer; to Ribbentrop's annoyance and at Hitler's insistence, Heinrich Hoffmann, Hitler's court photographer and personal friend; the young 'Johnnie' Hans von Herwarth, who had been the American and Italian Embassies' inform-ant over the previous three months); and a slew of journalists.[3] The party, thirty in all, were too many to be accommodated on the

Fokker-Wolff Condor in which Ribbentrop intended to travel, so that a second one had to be chartered.

The party flew north over the Baltic, avoiding Polish air space, to land in Königsberg, where they were to refuel and spend the night. While most of the party filled the hotel bar, boozed, looked up old friends and slept, Ribbentrop was in a fury of activity. First he had to deal with an emergency. In his absence the British Ambassador, Sir Nevile Henderson, had telephoned the Berghof. He had a personal letter from the Prime Minister for the Führer. He would get to the Führer without Ribbentrop being there to monitor, divert or thwart him. Who knew what this letter might contain? Perhaps an offer that would make his visit to Moscow pointless. Perhaps it might say something to convince Hitler that Britain was determined on war, in contradiction of all Ribbentrop's assurances. Perhaps Goering was behind it. In a rage he telephoned von Weizsäcker, with whom Hitler had fixed Henderson's reception, rousing him from his bed to berate him.[4] Then he phoned the Führer to urge him to deal strongly with the British message. Next he turned to what he should say to Stalin, filling page after page with his scrawl, constantly telephoning Berlin and rousing members of his staff with requests for documents, briefings, information.[5] At last, well into the small hours, he slept, only to rise early as the adrenalin began to flow again.

The two Condors left Königsberg early, to arrive in Moscow at 1 p.m. The summer heat shimmered. The Soviet reception at the airport was low-key, though with odd details.[6] There was a band to play the Imperial German national anthem. There were swastika flags, some back to front, borrowed from a Moscow film studio where they had been props for an anti-Nazi film. The Deputy Foreign Minister, Vladimir Potemkin, and the Chief of Protocol, a large fleshy man, Nikolai Barkov, greeted the German visitors briefly and ushered them into a convoy of vehicles. Stalin had sent his personal limousine for Ribbentrop. But their real hosts were the staff of the German Embassy, from the Ambassador, Friedrich Werner Count von der Schulenburg, downwards. They were driven down the long, wide, empty streets to the former Austrian Embassy, to eat a cold collation and consume Georgian champagne. Then Ribbentrop, Schulenburg and Gustav Hilger, the Embassy's Economic Counsellor, who had been attached to the Embassy in one role or another since 1919, left for the Kremlin.

Neither of the two sets of participants was in any way certain of their welcome. One of Ribbentrop's most desperate worries was that Stalin was simply using him as a club to beat the British and French delegations into accepting his terms. Perhaps he would be greeted by the news that Stalin had just concluded an agreement with them. Even if that fear proved baseless, everyone knew that negotiating with the Soviets could be a long, painstaking, niggling business. He had made it clear from the beginning that he could only spend twenty-four hours in Moscow and that time was of the essence. He had arrived on a Wednesday. At 4 a.m. on the following Saturday, the attack on Poland was due to start. Even as he arrived, the Danzig Senate was proclaiming Gauleiter Forster its head of state. The *Schleswig-Holstein*, the old German battleship, was under way to anchor in the Danzig harbour alongside the Polish garrison on the Westerplatte on the Friday. Perhaps the Poles would react that day, and Stalin would simply sit on his hands. Perhaps. Perhaps.

On his side, too, Stalin's suspicions had yet to be quietened. The British and French military delegations had done nothing to allay his fears. Rather they seem to have confirmed his suspicions. Nothing had happened to allay his suspicions about an Anglo-German deal. One must presume that he knew the terms of the Prime Minister's letter to Hitler; but it is possible that he had only seen the first draft, since the letter had been drafted and redrafted several times to strengthen it, and the original had been the work of Sir Horace Wilson and Rab Butler, the latter the Parliamentary Under Secretary whom the Soviet Embassy's political informants had identified as the spokesman in Parliament for the appeasers in Chamberlain's administration.

Stalin was aware of all the unofficial visitors and intermediaries, from Wohltat to Kemsley (whose visit to Hitler, though reported in the British Communist *Daily Worker* on August 7, was only headlined in *Pravda* on August 19).[7] His diplomatists, following the French press, believed that Burckhardt's visit to Hitler had been part of another intrigue to arrange a new 'Munich'.[8] He was still obsessed by his fears of an attack on the Baltic side. Perhaps the whole visit was a piece of camouflage.

Sorge and the Soviet intelligence authorities had convinced his reason that no war was to be expected in the West. Western travellers on the Soviet railway system reported troop movements towards Siberia.[9] Apart from the concentration of forces for the annual manœuvres in the Leningrad area, and the long-standing army in the Ukraine, there seem to have been no major movements of troops (as there were, by contrast, in May 1941) towards Russia's western frontiers. But Stalin's suspicions, which rarely slept, would only have increased his fears of a trap and his concurrent sense of vulnerability. Hence the low-key nature of Ribbentrop's reception at the airfield.

The Anglo-French delegations had made their last separate appeals to the Soviets on August 22. Their arrival on August 11 had been greeted with the usual lavish banquet. Astute eyes noticed, however, that in addition to the members of the Soviet delegation who were to be their hosts, which included Marshal Voroshilov, Shaposhnikov, the ever-present, ever-deferential Chief of Staff, Smorodinov, his deputy, Flagman (Admiral) Kuznetzov, and Lokhtionov, Chief of Air Staff, there were present Marshal Budyenny, as the Commander of Moscow military district and the Generals Commanding White Russia and the Ukraine, whom even the British and French Military Attachés in Moscow had never met before.[10] The British and French delegations were also provided with an excellent concert, by three singers, soprano, tenor and bass, a pianist and a girl violinist. By Soviet standards the auguries had seemed good.

From then on it was all downhill. A considerable part of the problem arose from a conflict in military cultures, not only between the military delegations of Britain and France on the one hand and the Soviet military on the other, but between the military professionals in the Western delegations and their political chiefs in Britain and France. Indeed there were very considerable differences between the outlook and concepts of the British and French military delegations and their leaders. The British military had hardly begun to think about a war on the European mainland. Until January 1939 they had been specifically forbidden to do so. When this restraint was removed, they were left with an expeditionary force of exiguous strength, at least until the enormous expansion accepted by the Cabinet between January and April was mustered, trained and properly equipped. Their planners for war had so far digested the lessons of the First World War as to remain considerably uneasy at the prospects of side-show campaigns. But their military education had led them to concentrate their preparations for war on two concepts: the defence of Britain's vital overseas communications through the Mediterranean, Egypt and the Middle East; and a war of long duration, to be won by economic as much as by military pressure. The air force, with its dedication to the idea of strategic bombing, struck a discordant note in this thinking; but until the four-engined heavy bombers of the 1937 and 1938 programmes began to roll off the production lines in substantial numbers, it was confined to battlefield bombing in the extended, 50-miles-from-the-front-line concept of the battlefield already adopted in 1917.

Where land campaigning was concerned, the role of the British army was to support and strengthen that of France. Its ranks bustled with able and thrusting divisional and brigade commanders, the army and corps commanders of 1944–5. At the top, however, its leaders were slow, gallant, intellectually undistinguished, relatively unimaginative and riven by feuds. They deferred to the French: to General Gamelin, General Georges and the old men who had been the victors of 1918. But their thinking about war was inter-service and global. In France and in the Soviet Union the army was predominant. General Doumenc spoke for the whole of the French delegation as Marshal Voroshilov did for the Soviets. War to them was a matter for the masses, divisions, artillery and, possibly, tanks.

The French soldiers, however, differed from the Soviets in one vital respect. The sheer distances separating the separate sectors of the Soviet Union's potential battlefronts, whether against Germany, Britain in the Middle East, or Japan, seems to have made it quite impossible for the Soviet military to conceive of the Maginot mentality which the slaughter of 1914 and the experience of Verdun had instilled into French military thought. Fortifications in the Soviet view were for cities, not for armies in the field; still less for whole frontiers.

The Red Army had been forged in the Civil War of 1917–19 and the Red Army's sweep into Europe, which had ended so disastrously before Warsaw in the winter of 1920. Its manœuvres were carried out over vast distances. Its dominant school of thought, after the purges, followed Napoleon's practice in developing vast parks of artillery. But Soviet war was to be a war of movement, a war of numbers, it is true, a war of masses, in the name of the masses. But no Soviet general or military planner had ever had to face, as had their French equivalents, the relentless arithmetic of a falling national birth-rate.

Nor did Soviet military thought even begin to comprehend war in three elements. Stalin, Zhdanov, and Kalinin might brag of the Soviet Union's naval construction plans. But the sea existed in Soviet military thought only as an extension on the flanks of the land front or, in the hands of enemies, as an avenue by which those flanks might be turned by amphibious landings. Naval operations, supply routes at hazard across distances quite as great as those over which their enemies might fight on land, save as a theoretical exercise, lay entirely outside their cosmos. Nor had their airmen ever been encouraged to carry the war to the sites of their potential enemies' industrial strength. Like the Luftwaffe (or the British Fleet Air Arm) they were designed to serve as an extension of the army commander's eyes and as a reinforcement of his long-range artillery.

The plan of campaign against Germany towards which British and French Staff planners had been so obviously edging was therefore a defensive, hands-off war. From behind their defences, the two allies would build up their strength while sapping and destroying, by blockade and by bombardment from the air, that of their enemies. As to what would happen on Germany's eastern front, they had not even begun to address the subject. As has been seen, the separate British and French Staff discussions with the Poles had been exercises in deception on both sides. Polish military planning for war against Germany was, in any case, in a generous, well-intentioned, it-will-be-all-right-on-the-night, one-Pole-can-beat-any-three-Germans state of unpreparedness. Even were Soviet intentions as determinedly anti-German as they were presented as being, the impression that this combination of caution and defensiveness in the West and fecklessness in the East could have been expected to have made on the Soviet military, still less upon Stalin, would not have been encouraging. It is not surprising that Stalin's reaction then, and that of Soviet historians ever since, has been that the military Staff talks were not seriously intended by those who set them up.

Such an interpretation, however, can be supported only by a relentless refusal to examine the actual purpose in the minds of the British and French political leaders and in their relations with their own military. For Daladier and Bonnet it was quite simple. As Bonnet told General Doumenc, if he did not return with a Staff convention, war would be inevitable. A convention had to be secured, 'even at the cost of promises'. 'What promises?' asked the General, not unreasonably. 'Anything you judge necessary, but there must be a signed paper.' M. Daladier was less definite. 'They beat me about the head with this agreement, which won't do. Many say it is of extreme importance. Why are the Russians being so difficult? One must penetrate this attitude and clear it up. Make our position clear, get everything straight; then we will know what matters. *Au revoir* and good luck.' Doumenc retired.[11] Others advised him: be careful of your papers; expect microphones to overhear you everywhere. But the general tenor of his military instructions made his mission as much one of enquiry as of negotiation. He was, however, empowered to conclude and sign a military convention.

Admiral Drax, as he had to confess to his embarrassment at the first session with Voroshilov, did not have such powers. They were, however, soon sent to him – to the amusement of Voroshilov, who insisted on their being translated to him in full, when the interpreter stumbled over Drax's entitlement, Knight Commander of the Order of the Bath. 'Bath?' asked Voroshilov. 'That is what it says here,' replied the Russian interpreter in confusion. Much hearty Soviet laughter.[12]

Anything to prolong the farce. By then it was August 21 and the delegations were meeting for the last time.

Drax, like Doumenc, saw his political masters before he left. Chamberlain was uneasy and worried. The House of Commons had pushed him further than he wanted to go. Lord Halifax's view was that, even if the negotiations looked like failing, on the whole it would be preferable to keep them going as long as possible.[13] Almost a month earlier he had already expressed the same view. 'So long as the military conversations were taking place we should be preventing Soviet Russia from entering the German camp,' he told the Cabinet's Foreign Policy Committee on July 10.[14] Judging from the experience of negotiating with Molotov, the British expected the Staff talks to be lengthy and protracted. 'It is an infernal shame,' said Drax's friend, Admiral 'Quex' Sinclair, head of MI6, 'that they should send you out to Moscow to try to clear up the mess that has been made out there by the politicians.'[15]

Despite the misgivings which beset him, though him alone, during the ceremonial dinner on the evening of August 11, Drax seems to have been convinced that a Staff agreement was possible, at least on military grounds. It was the political grounds which defeated him. To be more accurate, what defeated him was the political conditions which the Soviets demanded, and the degree to which neither the British nor the French military delegation had thought through the political and strategic conditions necessary for the effective deployment of Soviet military forces.

Their political masters were still intent on the avoidance of war; the military convention, like the political agreement, was to deter Hitler rather than to defeat him. A few hoped that a frustrated and hemmed-in Hitler, faced with the economic breakdown of the Reich, might well give way to a different political constellation. The same forces which, so their 'moderate' German informants assured them, had driven Hitler into the arms of his extremists, would, if extremism seemed to lead only to disaster, turn him back to peace and internal reconstruction. Neither Chamberlain nor Halifax, neither Daladier nor Bonnet (the latter least of all), and only a minority in each of their respective Cabinets, had accepted the near-inevitability of war, let alone begun seriously to consider how the machinery of war (to the awakening of which an increasing amount of Cabinet time was now being devoted) should actually be used.

As to what the Soviet Union would or should do if, despite everything, Hitler was not deterred, the subject simply had not been broached anywhere in the British or French governmental systems, not in the Cabinets, nor among the diplomatists of the Foreign Office or the

Quai d'Orsay, nor among the military planners. Planners require data. For the last two years the denial of any reliable data whatever to the potentially hostile states of the outside world had been one of the major aims of Stalin's security forces. Here again Stalin's monumental, unsleeping suspicions were to work to his country's disadvantage.

The British and French delegations had spent a substantial part of their leisurely sea voyage planning the tactics they should employ in negotiating with the Soviets. Deprived of any real information as to Soviet military strength and capabilities (General Doumenc was witheringly critical of the deficiencies in French intelligence), they had decided to concentrate firstly on obtaining Soviet agreement to a set of principles, and then to signing a short convention which General Doumenc had drafted.

They were to be sorely disappointed. At the first session Voroshilov swept away the principles as so much high-faluting flap-doodle. When Drax and Doumenc invoked 'principles', Voroshilov replied 'plans of operations'. The most subtle and disingenuous of Soviet marshals, he played the simple soldier.[16] At one stroke he swept away the elaborate plans prepared on board the *City of Exeter*. At the third meeting, still on the first day of the discussions, Doumenc distributed the preamble and the first two articles of the draft convention. Voroshilov then cut the whole process short with a simple question. How did the British and French delegations envisage the participation of the Soviet Union in military operations in the case of an attack on France, Poland, Romania, together or separately, not forgetting Turkey?

The following day he repeated the same question, and added a further demand. Would Poland accept the entry of Soviet troops on to its territory in the north (the Vilno corridor), to enter into contact with the enemy? The third day, General Shaposhnikov outlined Soviet plans of action. If Britain and France were attacked, the Soviets would engage 70 per cent of the strength of the Anglo-French forces opposed to Germany. Poland would be expected to engage its full strength. France and Britain would be expected to obtain Polish consent to Soviet transit through Vilno to attack East Prussia, and if necessary through Galicia. If Romania were attacked, Poland must come to Romania's aid. The Soviet Union would only intervene, with its full strength, if Poland and Romania agreed to the passage of Soviet troops through Vilno, Galicia and Romania. If the aggressor used the territories of Finland, Latvia and Estonia to attack the Soviet Union directly, Britain and France would immediately enter the war and Poland, bound by its treaties with Britain and France, would be obliged to enter the war and allow Soviet transit through Galicia and Vilno.

In the first and second cases the Soviets required a major Anglo-French naval intervention in the Baltic to be based on the Åland Islands, on the Estonian archipelago, the islands of Osaf and Dagö and on the ports of Hangö in Finland, Parnu and Hasalu in Estonia, Ainazi and Libau (Liepāja) in Latvia. These bases should be used jointly by the British and French fleets and by the Red Fleet. In the Arctic and White Seas, British and French naval forces would co-operate with the Red Fleet against German cruiser warfare off Norway, and be based on Archangel.

The conversations continued on August 16 and 17, despite Marshal Voroshilov's efforts to adjourn them. On August 17 he succeeded. British and French pressure secured a new meeting on August 21; but as Voroshilov well knew, the main issue he posed rested now on the decision of the Poles. He had already shown his own hand informally, in remarking on August 14 to one of the French delegation, that he did not expect the Poles or the Romanians to agree.[17] Since the effort to burgle the French Embassy to get at the delegation's instructions on the night they arrived had failed, it is possible that the Soviets genuinely did not know whether the French had obtained some last-minute highly secret concessions from Beck or the Polish military. Stalin's purges of foreign Communists had hit the Polish Communists particularly severely. It is more than possible that, as with Mr King's original controller, whatever networks the NKVD, the Comintern, or Soviet military intelligence had built up in Warsaw in the 1920s and 1930s had been lost to contact in the vital years of 1937–8.

The Poles were, however, to prove obdurate. Despite the strongest pressure over August 16, from the British and French Ambassadors on M. Beck,[18] and of the French Military Attaché, General Musse, recalled from Paris and supported by Captain Beauffre from the French delegation to Moscow,[19] the Poles remained unmoved. General Stachiewicz, the Polish Chief of Staff, made it clear that he trusted the Soviets not at all and would not agree to their movement through Polish territory at any price. Under extreme pressure he agreed to receive a memorandum from the British and French delegations on military co-operation with the Soviet Union; essentially this concession, which accepted that the British and French should persuade the Soviets to produce a concerted plan, was meaningless. The French delegation in Moscow sent increasingly desperate messages. Bonnet's telegrams to Warsaw grew increasingly angry. In the end he instructed Doumenc to lie to the Soviets.[20] In London, the British felt unable to support this manœuvre.[21] By then it was, anyway, too late.

On August 19, the Soviets had announced the conclusion of the

German-Soviet economic agreement. That same day *Pravda* repub-
lished a story from the British Communist *Daily Worker* of August 7
alleging that Lord Kemsley's visit to Hitler had been to arrange a new
five-power conference on Danzig to meet without Soviet participation.
On August 21, as Captain Beauffre returned via Riga and Leningrad to
Moscow, *Pravda* and *Izvestiya* published a further canard from the *Daily
Worker*, one of the SS-planted pieces of disinformation, picked up from
the Stockholm *Aftonbladet*, about the alleged dispatch of a British
mission, headed by a Professor Reilly, sent to investigate the economic
importance of Danzig to Poland.[22] On the morning of August 22, the
Soviet press carried the Tass communiqué announcing von Ribbentrop's imminent visit 'in a few days'; the DNB communiqué gave the
date, August 23.

The news caught the British and French delegations at a low ebb.
That morning they had met Voroshilov and his colleagues as a delegation for the last time. Lacking anything from Warsaw to help them,
they had tried to postpone the meeting until August 23. Voroshilov had
refused. On August 21, after the comedy with Drax's titles was over, he
had demanded the suspension of the meeting for two to three days in the
absence of any Anglo-French reply to his cardinal problem. Drax and
Doumenc read a joint protest. They had been invited to Moscow to
conclude a military convention. Instead they had been presented with
difficult political issues. The Soviet reply, given after various interruptions and withdrawals, was easy to construct. How could the Soviet
Union, lacking a common frontier with Germany, make any serious
plans for action without knowing whether they would be allowed to
operate in Poland and Romania?

The following evening, as the British and French Ambassadors were,
by Soviet artifice, making their protests and enquiries separately
from one another and without time to compare notes, General
Doumenc endeavoured to carry out Bonnet's instructions, instructions
which had inexplicably been delayed seven hours in transit, arriving
only at 11 p.m. on August 21. For most of August 22, Doumenc had
tried in vain to contact Voroshilov. At length, at 7 p.m., one of
Voroshilov's staff officers collected him by car and took him to
Voroshilov's home.

Doumenc did his best. He had been authorized, he said, to sign a
military convention on the basis proposed by the Russians. Voroshilov
insisted on knowing whether his instructions committed the Poles. Did
the British agree? Doumenc said that Drax was awaiting instructions.
Had Doumenc possibly been instructed to proceed, without Polish or
Romanian consent being given? With a poker face, Doumenc replied

that he was not informed of the details of his Government's conversations with Poland and Romania. The conversation ended cordially, but not without a backward reference to the French failure to enlist Soviet military aid in September 1938, or a forward reference to Ribbentrop's forthcoming visit.

The conventions were maintained; Voroshilov gave Doumenc the Soviet record of the meeting, but it was in vain. Even if, as the French suspected, the delay in the arrival of Doumenc's instructions had been arranged to allow Soviet cryptographers the time to decipher the telegram,[23] this would have told the Soviets little that their 'man in the Foreign Office' had not told them, or that the Polish press had not been proclaiming all week. 'Are we to be obliged to beg for the right to fight the common enemy?' Voroshilov had asked. There was to be one final meeting on August 25 between Drax, Doumenc and Voroshilov, when they agreed, 'in view of the changed political situation', that they might as well go home. Voroshilov then repeated himself. 'Were we to have to conquer Poland in order to offer her our help, or were we to go on our knees and offer our help to Poland? The position was impossible.'[24]

Ribbentrop was, of course, under no such inhibitions as those restraining Admiral Drax and General Doumenc. His master was not about to save Poland, but to destroy her. He had no objection to Stalin participating in the task. On arriving at the former Austrian Embassy, Ribbentrop had insisted on the Soviets being informed that he had only twenty-four hours to spend in Moscow. Within the hour, he, Schulenburg and Hilger were on their way to the Kremlin.

Until he actually entered Molotov's office in the Kremlin, Ribbentrop had not realized that he was to meet Stalin himself. We have no photograph of this first meeting. For Stalin, it was a double first. Ribbentrop was the first minister of a foreign government he had encountered. This was Stalin's first venture into the personal diplomacy that was to be so much a feature of the years between 1942 and 1945. Schulenburg had been in Moscow four years but had never met Stalin before. Ambassadors wishing to go beyond the Soviet Foreign Minister tended to be fobbed off with President Kalinin. Expecting to meet Molotov only, Ribbentrop for once was in diplomatic gear, with black jacket and pin-stripe trousers. Stalin was in his habitual uniform: grey tunic, buttoned up to the neck, dark, baggy trousers, calf-length boots. His shortness of height, always concealed by photographers, passed unnoticed in the aura of menacing power he projected. At the moment his claws were sheathed.

After greetings, the four of them, Schulenburg, Molotov, Stalin and Ribbentrop, sat down together at a table. Pavlov, Stalin's young and trusted interpreter, sat behind his master. Hilger sat behind Ribbentrop to interpret what must have been the biggest and most successful sales pitch that quondam salesman of cheap champagne ever achieved. Ribbentrop laid it on with a trowel, speaking fulsomely, as to Hitler himself, of the historic nature of the meeting, of the friendship between Germany and the Soviet Union. In reply there was a brief and often-to-be-repeated comedy. Stalin asked Molotov to take the chair and reply for the Soviets. Molotov refused and from then on Stalin would lead the discussion, his replies to Ribbentrop, dry, factual and brief at first, becoming at once more heated and more demotic when they got down to details.[25]

First they discussed the Soviet text of the Non-Aggression Pact as Ribbentrop had amended it in Königsberg. The magnificent preamble, more suited to a meeting between Ribbentrop and Ciano, went at once. After six years of shovelling mountains of cow-dung over each other, said Stalin (his language was much coarser), they could not suddenly go public with this kind of profession of eternal friendship.[26] The rest of the text went easily. No aggression against each other; no support for any third party attacking one or other of the signatories; continuous contact and exchanges of information; no membership of a grouping of powers 'aimed directly or indirectly' at the other; disputes to be settled by the 'friendly exchange of views'; duration for ten years; the pact to come into force on signature[27] and not, as normal, when ratified.

That was, of course, for public consumption. The real meat was contained in the secret protocol.[28] Following on the clearest of statements made by Hitler and by Ribbentrop before his arrival, Stalin asked for a precisely defined division of spheres of influence. Poland was divided on the line of the Rivers Narev, Vistula and San. The future of what might be left of Poland was to be settled by joint agreement. Stalin expressed interest in the province of Bessarabia, with its large ethnic German minority, which Romania had annexed from a disintegrating Tsarist empire in 1918. Hitler wanted Lithuania and Latvia up to the Dvina River, including Riga. The rest of Latvia, Estonia and Finland went into Stalin's zone. Here Stalin's deep-rooted suspicion and fear of a Baltic invasion resurfaced. On the pretence that the Red Battle Fleet wanted Baltic harbours that would be ice-free all year round, he demanded all of Latvia, with the same ports the British had been expected to provide, Libau (Liepāja) and Windau (Ventspils). Ribbentrop had a free hand from Hitler, but not that free. This needed Hitler's agreement.[29]

At 6 p.m. Ribbentrop returned to the German Embassy, bubbling over with enthusiasm. Hyped up to the degree he was, nothing had struck him as fake or unusual in the atmosphere. He was full of admiration for the clarity and directness with which Stalin and Molotov had spoken.[30] A telegram, phoned in code to Berlin, obtained within three hours by the same means the Führer's permission to concede all Latvia.[31] An added instruction asked Ribbentrop to put on the record that the division of Eastern Europe into German and Soviet spheres of interest allowed no room for any other power to stake a claim.[32] With these concessions Ribbentrop returned to the Kremlin. This time he took with him a much larger section of the German delegation; though, out of sheer spite, he left Paul-Otto Schmidt, whom Hitler had sent specifically to keep a record, behind at the Embassy. The record was kept by one of the younger German diplomatists, Andor Hencke, attached to Ribbentrop's staff.[33] Ribbentrop began by announcing Hitler's agreement to the Soviet demand. As Stalin heard he need no longer fear a German invasion through the Baltic, a sudden tremor went through him. He did not at first grasp Ribbentrop's outstretched hand.[34] His suspicions could rest. Ribbentrop had, all unaware of the fact, passed (as the British had not) the acid test.

The draft pact was then taken off by the experts to be dressed up. Drinks were produced and the conversation reopened as the room filled with more Soviet participants: Beria, Kaganovitch, Mikoyan, who had signed the economic agreement four days previously, General Shaposhnikov. The conversation was still confined to Ribbentrop and Stalin, with Molotov in his usual role as Little Sir Echo to his master, the man who kept his, Molotov's, wife and children as hostages and from whose suspicions he had himself only narrowly escaped during the purges. Japan, Italy, Turkey, Britain, France – all were covered. Ribbentrop offered to help Japan and the Soviet Union bury the hatchet. Stalin interrogated Ribbentrop as to Mussolini's intentions, something on which Ribbentrop, with his certainty that Mussolini would fight on Hitler's side, was not perhaps the best authority. They shook their heads over Turkey where, said Ribbentrop, Britain had spent £5 million on anti-German propaganda; considerably more than that, said Stalin, on buying Turkish politicians.

Stalin and Molotov said the British military mission had never told them what they wanted, a trigger which exploded Ribbentrop into one of his ten-minute hate tirades against the country on which he was determined to avenge his diplomatic and social failure. Britain was weak, Britain wanted to let others do the fighting for her 'presumptuous claim to world domination'. Stalin echoed him. Britain's army was weak, her navy less important, and her air force short of pilots. Her domination rested on the stupidity of others who allowed themselves to be bluffed. Ribbentrop rose so rapidly to the bait that even Stalin felt obliged to warn him (or perhaps this was the German Foreign Ministry trying to get it on a record that Hitler might see – perhaps even read) that, despite her weakness, Britain would fight craftily and stubbornly.

The meeting ended with toasts and what passed for jokes in that ghastly atmosphere, shadowed, as it was, by those about to die at the hands of war or the political police about to be unleashed on Poland, the Baltic states, Finland and Bessarabia. The anti-Comintern pact had frightened the City of London and the British shopkeepers – this was Stalin's contribution. Stalin would join the anti-Comintern pact himself – Ribbentrop's version of the Berlin joke. Stalin raised his glass to Hitler. Molotov proposed the toast of Ribbentrop, then of Schulenburg. Molotov raised his glass to Stalin. Ribbentrop raised his glass to Stalin. The pact was brought in and signed by Ribbentrop and Molotov, as was the secret protocol. The photographers came in, Hoffmann with his message from Hitler (though his memoirs record the whole mission as spending four days in Moscow, the accuracy of his

Rendezvous

observation seems a little coloured by all the vodka), Ribbentrop's photographer, the Russian with an acetylene flare of the 'flash-bang-wallop – what a picture – what a photograph' type.

As they broke up, around 2 a.m. on August 24, Stalin addressed his last words to Ribbentrop. The Soviet Union, he said, took the new pact very seriously. He could guarantee his word of honour that the Soviet Union would not betray Germany. Ribbentrop's reply is not recorded; which is perhaps just as well.

CHAPTER 25

THE IMPACT OF THE NAZI–SOVIET PACT

Throughout the evening of August 23 Hitler waited for news from Moscow. Towards 8 p.m. he telephoned the Moscow Embassy. An hour ahead there, the staff were still waiting for Ribbentrop to return from his second visit to the Kremlin. Nothing was known. Hitler walked up and down the terrace of the Eagle's Nest, out of the sight of his staff, save for his adjutant, Nikolaus von Below. At that moment, Hitler said, he saw in the pact with Stalin a chance of keeping Britain out of his war with Poland. As he spoke, the northern sky turned a deep dark greenish colour, changing immediately through violet to a frighteningly deep red, as though reflecting a great fire in the distance north of the Unterberg. The red light filled the whole northern sky almost like the northern lights, something rarely seen that far south in Germany. Von Below remarked that this must foreshadow a most bloody war. Let it come then as soon as possible, Hitler replied.[1]

The waiting resumed. Latvia was duly conceded to Stalin. Then, a few hours later around 3 a.m., Ribbentrop reported. The pact was signed; he was coming back. Hitler wished him luck. As he put the phone down, Hitler whirled on his household. 'This will strike like a bomb,' he said. Champagne was ordered for all. Hitler, the ardent teetotaller, lifted a glass to his lips, then hammered both fists on the wall and shouted: 'Now Europe is mine. The others can have Asia.'[2]

That afternoon, Hitler flew back to Berlin to welcome Ribbentrop and to set his armies in motion. Ribbentrop slept late on August 24. His plane left Moscow at 1.20 p.m. with an escort of fighters. The Germans seem by now to have thoroughly deceived themselves with their own propaganda, and feared a Polish air attack. The second plane, un-escorted, flew a wide circle around the Baltic. As on the outward leg, they touched down at Königsberg where Erich Koch, the Gauleiter, who detested Ribbentrop and belonged to Goering's faction, nevertheless gave him a hero's welcome; then, on to Berlin, where Hitler welcomed him as a second Bismarck.[3]

Ribbentrop, convinced that Britain would withdraw and Poland sue for mercy, wallowed in the adulation. He spoke of Stalin with warmth; only when England was mentioned did his face cloud over. Jealous of Ribbentrop's success, Goering taxed him with not having worked hard enough for Anglo-German understanding. But Hitler would have none of it. Although he had returned from the Obersalzberg rather less sure that Britain was bluffing than before,[4] contact with Ribbentrop had restored his faith. Goebbels attended every meal, encouraging Hitler and Ribbentrop to talk more of the Moscow visit. Hoffmann played the hero of the hour, praising Stalin. Goebbels remarked cynically that Hoffmann had at last found a good drinking partner.[5]

There was, however, one cloud over Ribbentrop's hour of triumph. His great coup, his 'bombshell', like all real as opposed to metaphorical bombshells, obstinately refused to explode when it was supposed to. London, Warsaw, even Paris remained unmoved. In part that was his own fault. By insisting on releasing the news of his triumph on the night of August 21, two days before his arrival in Moscow and three days before the pact was actually concluded, he had weakened its impact.

The British Cabinet had met on the afternoon of August 22, its members returning to London from their summer holidays through streets placarded with the news. Taking their lead from the Prime Minister, they had simply shrugged the news away.[6] Instructions to British embassies abroad, and advice to the press at home was that the Soviet-German Non-Aggression Pact would not modify British attitudes or affect in any way Britain's obligations to Poland.[7] Instead, they had resolved to warn Hitler of Britain's determination to stick to its obligations to Poland. At Sir Nevile Henderson's suggestion,[8] the warning was to take the form of a personal letter from the Prime Minister to Hitler. The first draft was substantially strengthened by the hawks in the Cabinet. At 8.40 that evening Halifax warned Henderson that the letter was on its way and instructed him to ask to see Hitler as soon as possible.[9] Henderson's efforts to pin Hitler down and Hitler's efforts to evade this occupied most of the night of August 22.[10] By 9.30 a.m. on August 23, Henderson was on his way by air to the Berghof. At 1 p.m. he was already ensconced with Hitler. State Secretary von Weizsäcker accompanied him.

Since the text of Chamberlain's letter had been telegraphed *en clair*, Hitler was able to score a cheap point by telling Henderson as an opening gambit that he had already seen a translation of it. That said, he could only talk tough. The letter[11] was short and plain-spoken. Britain was preparing against the eventuality of war. The Führer should dismiss the idea that after the news of the German-Soviet Pact, intervention by Britain on Poland's side need no longer be reckoned with. If it was true that Britain's contribution to the outbreak of the First World War lay in not making her position clear, the Cabinet was resolved that 'on this occasion there should be no such tragic misunderstanding.' Nor should it be assumed that, once war started, it would come to an early end after 'a success on any one of the several fronts on which it will be engaged'. Britain was, however, sure that 'if a situation of confidence could be restored' and German-Polish discussions reopened, war could be avoided. One step would be a 'truce on press polemics and all incitement'. Any settlement that might be reached would have to be guaranteed by other powers. Britain would be prepared to act as one such guarantor.

Hitler was still convinced that this was bluff. Big talking cost nothing; he was prepared to reply in the same coin. If Britain took any further mobilization measures, Hitler would order general mobilization in Germany. As for Poland, he ranted and raved, revived the castration stories, talked of 100,000 German refugees from Poland, and attacked Britain for supporting the Czechs in 1938 and the Poles in 1939 against Germany. But for British support of Poland, Poland would have seen sense and the settlement would have been on the most generous terms. He abused the British press, attacked Britain for treating his every approach with contempt. As for the offer of direct Anglo-German discussions, he rejected it completely. He did not believe Britain was interested. After two hours of this, Henderson was dismissed to await the reply to Chamberlain which Hitler had drafted.

The second interview, at which his reply to Chamberlain[12] was handed over, was in much the same vein,[13] though Hitler had abandoned the ranting note. His voice was calm; but his language was even more categorical. He preferred war now, when he was in his fiftieth year, rather than in five or ten years' time. The only way war could be avoided was for Britain to change her policy entirely.

This Sir Nevile Henderson took as mere rhetoric. But Hitler meant it. As Henderson left him after their first meeting, Hitler turned his hysterical manner off like a tap, turned, laughing, to Weizsäcker and said, 'Chamberlain will not survive this conversation; his Cabinet will fall this evening.'[14] On the morning of August 25, he called in his press chief, Otto Dietrich. 'What news do you bring of Cabinet crises?' he asked. 'What Cabinet crises?' asked Dietrich, in bafflement. 'The ones in the British and French Cabinets of course. No democratic government can stand up to defeat and disgrace such as has been inflicted on Chamberlain and Daladier by our Moscow treaty,' Hitler replied.[15]

The British Cabinet were, however, still unmoved. They met briefly on August 24. Hitler's letter struck them as 'rough and full of reproaches'.[16] Reports of secret clauses in the Nazi-Soviet Agreement were already reaching them from Berlin over the previous night, even while Ribbentrop and Stalin were clinking glasses. On the morning of August 24 the British press were, with a few exceptions, either indifferent or angry, mainly the latter. The Conservative press, following the lead of the Foreign Office and Downing Street press officers, made it clear that the pact concluded in Moscow made no difference.[17] The Labour Party organ, the *Daily Herald*, was much more severe, calling Stalin's action in linking himself with Hitler 'one of the most indefensible and shocking reversals of policy in history', adding, 'If there is a war of aggression against Poland, heavy indeed will be the burden of Soviet guilt.'

The Soviet Embassy in London did its best to restrain those papers, notably the liberal *News Chronicle*, which relied upon it for leads, with stories that the pact contained a clause which allowed for its denunciation by one of the two signatories if the other attacked a third party.[18] But that did not survive the publication of the text of the pact on August 25. The press spoke, with one voice almost, of the unity with which Britain faced the prospect of war with Germany,[19] outdoing the somewhat less than whole-hearted manner in which the House of Commons greeted Neville Chamberlain's sober statement of British determination to fulfil her obligations to Poland,[20] despite the lead given by Arthur Greenwood, the acting leader of the Labour Party. Sir Samuel Hoare noted, 'the left suspicious and vindictive'.[21] But the Emergency Powers Bill went through all its stages the same day.

The British people were, in fact, retreating, as they were to in the summer of 1940, into one of those profoundly non-realistic states of conviction, incomprehensible to citizens and statesmen of other countries alike, with which by that very strength and single-mindedness the British can make nonsense of 'realism', as applied by such observers to their situation. Hitler might expect the fall of the Cabinet. The Under Secretary in the Canadian Department of External Affairs might write that 'not only Chamberlain and his Government, but Churchill and Eden and the Liberal leaders who have been egging the Government on, must share the responsibility for the greatest fiasco in British history.'[22] The British people's reaction was that, given what they saw as the deceit practised by the Soviet Government, or even, as outlined in the soberer press comments, the Soviets' very different view of where Russia's best interests lay, Britain was better off without Soviet assistance.

This supreme egocentricity was taken very badly in Moscow; Soviet journalists, as part of the 180-degree turn they were enjoined to make in order to justify the pact to their readers, no doubt over-emphasized British unreliability as the explanation for their leaders' new-found enthusiasm for Hitler, Ribbentrop and the Nazis. But there is also a genuine note of anger in reaction to the British press's dismissal of the Soviet Union as an unworthy ally. Maisky did his best to report the continuation of 'Munich-like' sentiments.[23] But he could hardly hide the extraordinary change which had come over British opinion in the eleven months since Munich. The Cabinet itself was already showing signs of the same change, to a degree which, in the last days of the peace, was to surprise even the Prime Minister.

The news of the imminent signature of the Nazi-Soviet Pact was received by the Poles with the equanimity of those who have nothing whatever to lose. For the last two weeks the Polish intelligence services had been reporting the steady concentration of German troops all along their East Prussian and Silesian frontiers. Incidents of German aircraft crossing into Polish air space were multiplying. Frontier guards were reacting to the tension by becoming increasingly trigger-happy. The pressure on the Poles to yield something, anything, to ease the task of the Anglo-French Staff missions in Moscow was intensifying. A German attack seemed imminent, a matter of days if not hours. Armed gangs of German irregulars were already active within Poland. There were German-inspired stirrings among the Ukrainian minority in the south. The German press maintained its ceaseless flow of atrocity stories, not all of which were invented, though none lost anything in the telling.[24] The impact of the Nazi-Soviet Agreement was somewhat numbed amidst all the welter of even more immediately threatening activity.

Beck's first reaction, therefore, was that, whatever the effect of this combined manœuvre by Moscow and Berlin on world opinion, it had in reality changed nothing. Poland had never taken the prospect of the Soviet Union entering a war very seriously. It is Ribbentrop's turn, Beck told M. Léon Noël,[25] the somewhat 'defeatist' Ambassador of France, to get the measure of Soviet good faith. It was clear that German-Soviet conversations had been in progress long before the Polish refusal to entertain Soviet troops on their soil. It was fortunate that Ribbentrop did not have the patience to wait a few days before going to Moscow. Poland was confirmed in its distrust of Moscow. General Stachiewicz said much the same, though more forcefully, to

General Musse.[26] Much the same message was conveyed to Sir Howard Kennard, the British Ambassador.[27]

The Poles, however, had not taken the full measure of the change in the Soviet position. They did not, so Sir Hugh was informed, anticipate any anti-Polish change in Soviet policy, though some minor military precautions were taken. This impression was increased by assurances given to M. Beck on August 24 by the Soviet Ambassador to Warsaw, M. Charanov, that the Nazi-Soviet Pact should be no obstacle to the Anglo-French negotiations in Moscow.[28] As Count Raczyński, the Polish Ambassador in London, told Lord Halifax, the Nazi-Soviet Pact struck the Poles as being more of a formal truce than anything else.[29] As long as Britain remained firm, and it was clear that Hitler would not get away with any easy success, Russia would be restrained from taking any advantage of Poland's problems; though no doubt Stalin would be happy to see Britain and Germany weaken one another.

It was in Paris, rather than in London, that Ribbentrop's coup struck hardest. As has been noted, opinion in Paris was much more desperate to bring about an agreement with the Soviet Union than in London. The French remained more hopeful that some last-minute concession could be wrung from the Poles with which to overcome Russian objections to being asked to come to their aid.

The French Council of Ministers met on the afternoon of August 22 at 5 p.m., just as their British colleagues were breaking up. Daladier and Bonnet, backed by Léger, the head of the French Foreign Ministry, were both persuaded that a last-minute effort could save the negotiations in Moscow.[30] As a result, the Council was not allowed to discuss anything else. Reynaud and Mandel, the hawks, suggested a general mobilization. That would make the Poles more intransigent towards Russia, was the reply. 'I do not ask for this,' said Bonnet; his remark was greeted with silence. Should an approach be made to Italy, perhaps by Anatole de Monzie, the Cabinet Minister, whom it was felt Mussolini would regard with the most sympathy? How would one reward Italy? She demands nothing, said de Monzie, a remark so palpably at odds with what the Italian press was saying, that that avenue too was closed.

M. Chautemps, the former Premier and future collaborator, wailed that this was the end of the peace front. Daladier's proposal for an intimidatory *démarche* in Warsaw to force the Poles to accept Soviet troops, was adopted. M. Beck, as we have seen, bent so far as to allow a non-committal formula to be used, while privately expressing his fury at the Russians' failure to approach Warsaw directly. Noël had encouraged this move. But Daladier's willingness to grasp it and Léger's support of it argue a certain parting of the anchor ropes to reality. As we have seen, Voroshilov needed only one question to block General Doumenc entirely.

The following day, at Bonnet's request, Daladier organized a meeting of the Standing Committee on National Defence. This committee, the nearest equivalent in France to Britain's Committee of Imperial Defence, was charged with keeping French foreign policy in line with the realities of France's military position. Its meetings were infrequent. The meeting on August 23 was presided over by M. Daladier who, wisely, had taken the portfolio of the Ministry of National Defence with responsibility for the army, as well as that of *Premier Ministre*. There were present Bonnet; César Campinchi, the Minister for the Navy, a hawk; Guy la Chambre, the Air Minister; the three Chiefs of Staff, General Gamelin for the Army, Admiral Darlan for the Navy, and General Vuillemin for the Air Force; General Jamet, Secretary General for the Ministry of National Defence; General Colson, Gamelin's deputy; General Tetu, deputy to Vuillemin; and General Aube, Anti-aircraft Defence. Neither Mandel, Minister for the Colonies, nor General Buhrer, the Chief of the General Staff for the Colonial Armies, was invited. General Decamp, Director of the Military Cabinet of Daladier's Ministry, kept the record.[31]

Daladier posed three questions. Could France assist in the disappearance of Poland and Romania by doing nothing? How could France oppose this? What should be done as a matter of urgency? Bonnet did his best to produce a satisfactorily gloomy picture. At the very least Poland would get no support from the Soviet Union. Romania would probably agree to supply Germany with all that she wanted. The Soviets would see that Turkey only entered the war if a Balkan power was attacked. Would it be better to remain faithful to France's engagements or to reconsider things and profit by the time gained to strengthen France's defences? It was decided that France had no choice but to fulfil her obligations to Poland, which had been entered into before negotiations with the Soviet Union were begun.

As for the state of France's forces, Guy la Chambre produced a favourable picture of French strength in the air. General Aube was gloomy about French civil defence. He feared for civilian morale and the effect of German air attacks on the civilian population. Gamelin and Darlan said the army and navy were ready. They could not do much to start with against Germany, but if Italy entered the war they could react vigorously against her. French mobilization would bring some support to Poland by distracting German forces. Daladier, summing up, said that with the fortifications on which France had spent so much and the fighter aircraft Guy la Chambre said were now in mass production, France, 'who would have to fight alone for several months', could appreciate her security.

On what was to be done, it was agreed to proceed to stage one of French mobilization, the recall of those reserves earmarked for *la couverture*, the full manning of the Maginot line. General mobilization would be the next step. The same day, Daladier passed to Gamelin the British proposals of August 17 for the establishment of a combined Anglo-French machinery for the conduct of war.[32] Whatever second thoughts Gamelin might have about the meeting of August 23 (and he was to develop a great many),[33] he was now committed to the hilt to war; it was to be a war in which the French army, despite the courage and desperation which so many of its forces were to show in combat, was to be out-manœuvred, out-generalled and defeated in detail within a year, its arteriosclerosis of thought and manœuvrability cruelly exposed and its pride humiliated.

Mobilization could only be ordered by the French Council of Ministers. On August 24, therefore, with Daladier's hopes of preventing a 'new partition of Poland' ebbing away, the Council of Ministers met at 10 a.m. Daladier declared that the Poles had accepted the passage of the Red Army and that an agreement with the Soviet Union was still possible.[34] He relied on a telegram of General Musse from Warsaw,[35] which two telegrams from Moscow had already stigmatized as overtaken by events.[36] General Doumenc had made his final appeal to Voroshilov, in vain.

News of the signature of the Nazi-Soviet Pact arrived while the Council was in session. The text soon followed. The clause present in most previous non-aggression pacts concluded by the Soviet Union, making its denunciation possible if either signatory attacked a third party, was conspicuous by its absence. By 3.45 that afternoon Bonnet was already instructing M. Naggiar, Ambassador in Moscow, to quiz Molotov on this departure from prior Soviet practice.[37]

The meeting was then interrupted by a further telegram from Warsaw declaring that the Poles had not accepted and never would accept the passage of Soviet troops. Daladier still remained hopeful. Robert Coulondre, the doughty French Ambassador in Berlin, had recommended not breaking with the Soviets. German mobilization was accelerating. The hawkish members of the Council were prepared to urge restraint on the Poles; but they were appalled by the ease with which the 'pacifists', joined by Daladier, seemed to envisage 'sacrificing Danzig' and the reserve which they showed towards Poland. Daladier saw himself faced with a possible Cabinet crisis. He summed up: all pressure would be brought to bear on Poland to see that she did not fire the first shot; but should Germany attack, France would be true to her obligations. It had been a 'close-run thing', as the Duke of Wellington is said to have remarked about the battle of Waterloo. But Hitler had again been disappointed. It should be noted, however, that Daladier did not summon another meeting of the Council of Ministers until August 31. The British Cabinet was to meet six times in the same period.

The Balkan states could not regard the news from Moscow and Berlin with the same equanimity. They were now confronted, at one and the same time, with all the signs of an imminent German attack upon Poland, and the collapse of the hopes or fears each of them had placed on the conclusion of an Anglo-French military alliance with the Soviet Union. If even M. Saracoğlu, the bravest of the brave, could for a moment lose his nerve, it was hardly to be expected that the Yugoslavs or the Romanians would keep theirs. Each had, however, gone further towards Paris and London than could easily be hidden from German eyes.

The Germans were not aware, for example, that Călinescu, the Romanian Premier, had promised the French that in the event of a German attack on Romania, the Romanian oil fields would be destroyed. Nor were they aware how far Călinescu had pushed King Carol towards the idea of joining the Anglo-Soviet line-up with Turkish assistance. They were, however, conscious of how far Romania had evaded the economic pressure they had hoped to apply through the March agreement, and of the degree to which British and French money and aid seemed to be pre-empting German hopes of colonializing the Romanian economy.

Until the news of Ribbentrop's visit to Moscow hit the Romanians on the morning of August 22, their main anxieties had centred on the possibility of a German-Hungarian attack on the one side and on the other an Anglo-French demand that Romania grant the Soviet Union the same transit rights London and Paris were pressing Warsaw to concede. The first fear stemmed in part from German disinformation, fed them to justify the movement of German troops into Slovakia and to mislead the Poles, and in part from the restless peregrinations of Count Csàky, the Hungarian Foreign Minister (who, like some small-time crook, sure that a major criminal operation was about to occur somewhere, kept rushing around trying to edge his way into the deal), to the Berghof on August 8 and to Rome ten days later,[38] peddling the idea of a tripartite German-Italian-Hungarian alliance. As for the second, Călinescu warned King Carol on August 21[39] to expect such a demand. He could not have expected Bonnet to advance it as late as the evening of August 23,[40] even as Ribbentrop and Ciano were celebrating their agreement, recognizing Romanian Bessarabia as part of the Soviet sphere of influence.

The news at once awoke in Călinescu the fear of a German-Soviet agreement to partition Poland and Romania.[41] The supporters of neutralism were reinforced in their views. Those Romanians who feared the Soviet threat more than that from Germany were now faced with the possibility of collusion between the two. No tears were lost over the fate of the Poles. In July, when Bucharest was panicking yet again over the machinations of its Hungarian neighbours, the Romanians had attempted to interest Warsaw in a military Staff agreement against an attack on their western frontiers. This the Poles had refused, well aware that Romanian fears of Hungarian attack were baseless.[42]

The conclusion and publication of the Nazi-Soviet Agreement had reinforced the Romanian reluctance to give Poland any assistance, now that a German attack seemed imminent.[43] Romania would not openly declare her neutrality; such a move might damage and isolate her Greek and Turkish associates in the Balkan Entente. She was still attached to the West, rather than to Hitler. But she would remain neutral, until the moment to enter the coming war on the side of the West seemed most suitable;[44] or so Gafencu represented King Carol as deciding.

What Gafencu did not say to M. Thierry, or to his British colleague, was that he was making very different noises to Berlin. On August 25, Gafencu claimed to the Germans that Romania had never compromised on her refusal to join the proposed Anglo-French-Soviet peace front. He had moreover pointed out that Germany and Romania had a common interest in freedom of navigation along the Danube from Germany to the Black Sea, which Romanian control of the Danube delta guaranteed.[45] Nor did he tell them of the way King Carol crawled to the German Air Attaché three days later, congratulating him on the great accession to German strength secured by the German-Soviet agreement, and boasting of his rejection of Anglo-French demands that he should allow the sabotage of the Romanian oil fields.[46]

On August 27 Gafencu told the German Minister in Bucharest, Fabricius, that Romania would be neutral.[47] Negotiations were already under way by which Romania agreed to lease to Germany 450,000 tons of oil, to the value of one and a half million Reichsmarks, in return for the German delivery of aircraft.[48] This was Romania's trump card. As the German Minister to Bucharest and his Air Attaché pointed out with some force when rumours of an SS conspiracy with the Hungarian army to march into the disputed areas of Romania reached them, any infringement of Romanian neutrality would result in the supply of Romanian oil coming to an end.[49] Arms deliveries to Romania in fact continued despite the military timetables for the attack on Poland.[50] As the Air Attaché remarked, the continuation without friction of petroleum supplies from Romania was much more important than the value of the armaments. Germany had no leverage here.[51] Without Romanian oil the Luftwaffe's campaign over Poland could well have been its last. All other oil supplies open to Germany had to come by sea and run the British blockade. Romanian oil could reach Germany by rail.

The Yugoslavs had no such trump card in their hands. The main source of their anxieties lay not in Berlin but in Rome. In his constant search for arms, M. Cvetković, the Yugoslav Premier, did his best to depict his country as a potential victim of German aggression and as one which Germany regarded as aligned with her enemies;[52] but the Yugoslavs' main fears lay in the constant movement of Italian troops into Albania. The visits to Albania of Marshal Badoglio, Chief of the Italian General Staff, in June and of Count Ciano in August alarmed and disturbed them:[53] with reason. One of the options Mussolini considered, in the wake of Count Ciano's visit to Salzburg, was a new adventure against Yugoslavia.[54] He gave directions to Marshal Badoglio;[55] an army command was set up under Marshal Graziani, and Count Ciano turned again to the sinister Marquis de Bombelles and to the infamous Anton Pavelič.[56] Raising an insurrection in Croatia was discussed, as was an offer of the crown of Croatia to a member of the Italian Royal Family.[57]

The Yugoslav Government was obsessed with the idea that Italy was preparing a coup against Salonika, their only outlet to seas not dominated by the Italian navy and the Strait of Otranto. General Simović, the Yugoslav Chief of Staff, unburdened himself of his anxieties to the German Air Attaché.[58] Prince Paul still pinned his hopes on an Allied occupation of Salonika in time to forestall any Italian plans in this direction. Still better would be a declaration of war on Italy and a pre-emptive strike. On August 26 he wrote to Lord Halifax,[59] warning Britain against allowing Italy to pretend to neutrality at the start of a German-Polish war. As soon as Poland had collapsed and German forces were released to protect Italy in the west, Italy would operate out of Albania with Bulgarian assistance. 'A rot throughout the Balkans' would follow, and the states of the Balkan Entente, perhaps even Turkey, would be driven to make what terms they could with Germany. The British Minister in Belgrade described Paul as being 'in the last stages of despair'.[60] Lord Halifax took this as typical of the

Prince in one of his manic-depressive moods and replied robustly that Britain was under no illusion as to how to treat Italy.

This apparent acceptance of Italian neutrality was not the response Prince Paul had been looking for. He turned therefore to M. Brugère, the French Minister in Belgrade, a man endlessly sympathetic and always inclined to take the Prince at his own valuation. Impressed by the Prince's lengthy, if not always accurate, catalogue of Italian deceits and misrepresentations, M. Brugère made the strongest of representations to Paris.[61] But the proposal 'to open a second front in the Balkans' now depended on an Inter-Allied War Council over whose deliberations Britain in fact had a veto.[62] No Allied troops were to intervene in south-eastern Europe until the British intrusion in January–March 1941 in support of Greece. By then Prince Paul had been driven so far into the German camp that the Yugoslav army and people, and Paul's young ward, King Peter, combined to overthrow him.

The Nazi-Soviet Pact had, in fact, ended Paul's hopes of an Anglo-French alliance to free Yugoslavia from Mussolini's constant threats. In freeing Hitler to attack Poland, it ensured a war in northern Europe rather than in the Mediterranean. The imminence of war in Europe had, however, one positive effect. It convinced the Croat leader, Vladko Maček, of the necessity of 'throwing a bridge across the abyss which separated Serb from Croat'.[63] On August 20, agreement (the *Sporazum*) was reached between Cvetković and Maček. Croatia, Dalmatia and seven other predominantly Croat regions were grouped into a single unit under a governor (*ban*) in Zagreb, with its own legislature and domestic budget. In return the Croat deputies took their seats in the Yugoslav Parliament and Maček, with three other members of his Croat Peasant Party, joined the Yugoslav Cabinet. Mussolini might go on financing the *Ustase* Croat extremists but Maček had the votes. The disruption of Yugoslavia, without a defeat in the field despite the hostility of the Serbian right, was no longer possible.

Worst hit among Germany's friends by the news of the Nazi-Soviet Pact were the Japanese, and among the Japanese it was General Hiroshi Oshima, the Japanese Ambassador in Berlin, who suffered most. His devotion to Hitler's Germany had been extreme. He had contributed articles to German and other journals, praising Hitler and National Socialism in what by any standard were extraordinarily fulsome tones.[64] His faith in his Nazi associates was deep-rooted in his own culture. To him Hitler and the Nazis were Japanese-style heroes bent on redeeming and re-awakening Germany, as he hoped Japan was also being awoken, cleansed and reborn. He had translated this enthusiasm into a whole-hearted drive for German-Japanese collaboration.

Oshima had been an associate of von Ribbentrop since 1935. In 1935 and 1936 they had conspired together, behind the backs of the German and Japanese Foreign Ministries, to bring about the anti-Comintern pact. Since the Japanese army had engineered his translation from Military Attaché to Ambassador in Berlin in October 1938, Oshima had been at constant odds with the Foreign Ministry in Tokyo over the German terms for the translation of the anti-Comintern pact into an alliance. With Toshio Shiratori, his colleague in Rome, he had, as we have seen, not only consistently refused to carry out instructions from Tokyo; he had also done his best to rally the other Japanese envoys in Europe in his support. The constant rumours of German-Soviet contacts which regularly swept the European capitals cannot but have disturbed him, but he had regularly denied their authenticity when questions came from Tokyo.[65]

The evening of August 21, Ribbentrop telephoned Oshima from the Berghof to break the news to him.[66] Oshima was hurt and angered. By Japanese standards of behaviour, he and his country had been betrayed and dishonoured. Germany, he told Ribbentrop, had violated the secret German-Japanese protocol to the anti-Comintern pact. His people and his Government would never accept it. At midnight he called on Weizsäcker to demand further explanations. His face was grey and set like a stone, Weizsäcker recalled.[67] He insisted on seeing Ribbentrop before he left for Moscow. If necessary, he would meet him at the Berlin airport. Ribbentrop did his best when they met,[68] but he was a bad liar under pressure. In one breath, he defended his action as the only way of avoiding encirclement by an Anglo-French-Soviet alliance; the necessity for a quick decision in Moscow left no time to consult his Japanese friends. The next he was advocating a German-Soviet-Japanese alignment against Britain, alleging that 'during the negotiations on the pact' the Soviets had repeatedly expressed their desire for a reconciliation with Japan, revealing that his visit was no last-minute improvisation. Oshima told him that he had already telegraphed his resignation to Tokyo.

Oshima left the Germans in no doubt of his dissatisfaction with Ribbentrop's explanations. He later told Prince Urach of the German Foreign Ministry's press department that he was both irate and disappointed at the manner in which he had been confronted with a *fait accompli*.[69]

The Japanese press received the first reports of the pact with rage, dismay, confusion and incomprehension.[70] The reports by their correspondents in Berlin did not help matters. Mr Adachi, the Berlin correspondent of the Japanese press agency Domei, had, like Oshima, hitherto been an ardent Germanophile. His reports revealed a sense of anger and betrayal. At the Propaganda Ministry press conference on August 22, he behaved so badly that complaints were made to Oshima. He had also ferreted out the information that the pact would contain secret clauses on the partition of Poland. The *Asahi* correspondent reported that Oshima had known nothing of the negotiations. The German Ambassador in Tokyo, General Ott, had been equally surprised by the news. He did his best; but he could not prevent a formal Japanese protest at the violation of the secret annexe to the anti-Comintern pact, nor the resignation of the Japanese Cabinet which followed the humiliating refusal of von Weizsäcker, on Ribbentrop's instructions, to accept delivery of that protest.[71]

At that moment it was not Britain but the Soviet Union that Tokyo felt to be most in need of restraint. Japanese nationalists and their supporters in the Japanese army were dismayed at the way Sir Robert Craigie, the British Ambassador in Tokyo, had manoeuvred them out of a war with Britain over Tientsin. Some of the extreme nationalists tried for a time to argue that the Nazi–Soviet Pact and the anti-Comintern pact could be reconciled. Where Ribbentrop and Stalin could joke, however, the Japanese 'double-patriots' were deadly serious. Their military supporters were far more worried that the Nazi–Soviet Pact would release the Soviet Union from fear as to its frontiers in Europe into a more active support for China in the Far East. As for the Kwantung Army, the news of the Nazi–Soviet Pact coincided with the launching of a major Soviet offensive against their forces at Nomonhan.[72]

In the first half of August the Japanese had successfully repelled three separate Soviet attacks, and severely mishandled the Mongolian 22nd Cavalry. Plans were going ahead for a new offensive. On August 20, however, the Soviet commander, General Zhukhov, beat them to the punch, achieving total operational surprise. Three Soviet rifle divisions, thirty-five infantry battalions and five hundred tanks including the T40 diesel-engined models, together with elements of the 262nd Air-borne Division, were launched against the tattered remnants of a division and a half of Japanese. The attack caught the Japanese surprised and disorganized. The Japanese did their best, gathering what forces they could to stage a counter-offensive on August 24 and 25. Their attacks across open ground against Soviet positions which overlooked them, with no proper artillery preparation and against Soviet armour, were a massacre. On August 27 Zhukhov renewed his offensive. The Japanese heavy artillery was overrun, the Japanese defending forces wiped out. Only a handful of men escaped at night. The remains of the

Japanese 23rd Division staged a final counter-attack the next day. They were surrounded, broken up, isolated and dealt with in detail. A smattering of survivors forced their way out of Soviet encirclement on the night of August 30/1. The Soviets halted on the frontier they recognized. The Japanese were left to count their losses.

The Japanese had committed the whole of their 23rd Division and ten thousand men of their 7th Division. Of the 15,000 men of the 23rd Division, nearly twelve thousand were dead, wounded, missing or ill. To these should be added 3,500 casualties from the 7th Division. The Japanese army was taught to lead from the front. Their casualties included an average of 80 per cent of the battalion, company and platoon commanders in the 23rd Division, 1,500 officer casualties in all. The 7th Division, committed piece-meal where reinforcements were needed, had not suffered so severely, but its casualties still represented a third of its strength. The Soviet casualties were probably about nineteen thousand, but they came from a much wider spread of units.

Even with this disaster and crippled by inadequate intelligence, the Kwantung Army refused to recognize the realities of the situation. The Nazi-Soviet Pact was, for them, a betrayal.[73] But this was soon overshadowed by the reversal of policy in Tokyo. For the Kwantung Army, honour was at stake. It was preparing to denude the rest of Manchuria of any protection, even to swallow its pride and ask for reinforcements it had previously turned down from the neighbouring North China Army. But Tokyo had had enough, the Emperor, who had seen his successive efforts to restrain his officers dismissed and ignored, particularly so. One direct imperial order, delivered in Hsinking on August 30 by General Nakajima, the Vice Chief of Army Staff, in person, was vigorously challenged. Indeed Nakajima himself was so infected by the atmosphere at the headquarters of the Kwantung Army that he was understood to have committed himself to a new offensive planned for September 10. On September 4, 1939, General Nakajima flew once more from Tokyo to Hsinking. This time he was not allowed to discuss the orders or to entertain argument whatever. General Ueda, in command of the Kwantung Army, was recalled with his Chief of Staff. The war was over.

In characteristically Japanese fashion, the Japanese Ambassador in Moscow, Shigenori Togo, had been in contact with the Soviets over a ceasefire at Nomonhan since July 20. The Soviets had, however, stalled him until August 22, when Zhukhov was reporting success in his offensive and Ribbentrop was taking plane to Moscow. It took until mid-September to agree to a ceasefire. Not until July 1940 did the

Japanese 'endure the unendurable' and accept the Soviet version of the frontier. The Kwantung Army had been broken.

So had the Hiranuma Cabinet. On August 28 it resigned. In part this was a formal expression of collective responsibility to the Emperor for a policy, that of seeking an agreement against Japan's British and Soviet enemies, which had so clearly been shipwrecked. In part it represented a revulsion within the Japanese army against its treacherous and dishonourable would-be allies. In part it reflected the justification of the suspicions the Japanese navy had always expressed of Germany's intentions and German loyalty. The 'Anglo-American group' around the court saw a chance of regaining some of the ground lost not only to the army in the pursuit of Germany as an ally, but also in external affairs generally as a result of the denunciation by the United States at the end of July of the Japanese-American Trade Agreement.

The days between August 24 and 28 had in fact been filled in Tokyo with the most bitter political infighting. There was too much at stake for the army leadership, whatever feelings its members might privately entertain towards Germany, for them to give up. They did their best to damp down the Japanese press and to circulate those arguments about the impact of the Nazi-Soviet Pact on Britain and France with which the German and Italian Embassies were feeding them.

The court, astute as ever, finally chose an army man, General Abe, as the new Premier. A hero of the war in China, he had also served as aide-de-camp to the Emperor. A major battle followed his acceptance of the mission to construct a new government.[74] The Emperor instructed Abe that the new Government should reject the pro-Axis policy of its predecessor and 'follow a conciliatory line with regard to Britain and America'. The navy, edgy about the degree of bitterness Admiral Yonai's stand had introduced into army-navy relations, produced a Minister less hostile towards their sister service.

But the real battle came over the appointment of a new Foreign Minister. The 'Anglo-American group', Prince Saionji and the court officials, lobbied hard for Ambassador Shigemitsu, Ambassador in London.[75] The army stuck out for Togo, the Ambassador in Moscow.[76] A new Foreign Minister was not appointed until nearly a month later. The choice fell on Admiral Nomura, once Naval Attaché in Washington and former head of the Peers' School where the scions of the Japanese nobility were educated. His appointment was a signal victory for the 'Anglo-Americans'. Unfortunately it was to awaken no echo in Washington.

Worst hit of all, however, among Germany's opponents were the dedicated anti-Fascists of the European Communist parties, those for whom the Popular Front years had meant a long, perilous, desperate but enthralling crusade against the Fascist enemies and their capitalist allies. For them the long agony of the Spanish Civil War had been a desperately disheartening process, only survivable by the belief that history in the end was on their side. To many of these the sight of Ribbentrop and Stalin drinking one another's health was both blasphemous and obscene.

The Comintern leadership in Moscow would say and do as it was told – when anyone got round to telling it what to say or do, which was not until mid-September. Communists in south-eastern Europe were so deeply at odds with their own Governments, so convinced that their loyalties lay only with Moscow, that the Nazi-Soviet Pact presented no problems to people like the young Milovan Djilas and his Yugoslav friends.[77] But for the Communists and their left-wing fellow-travelling allies in the democracies, things were much more difficult. For a time the leadership of the British and French Communist parties were able to justify Stalin's action as in the best interests of the Soviet State, the only existing embodiment of socialism; for themselves the struggle with Fascism and against war could continue.[78]

There were even those who hailed the Nazi-Soviet Pact as a 'blow struck for peace', in the words of the British *Daily Worker* and the French *L'Humanité*. Now they faced a double battle, against Chamberlain and Daladier, the allies of Fascism at home, and against Fascism in Germany and Italy. Moscow left them without directions until the middle of September, before cutting even this ground away from them. The war, came the message from Moscow, was entirely imperialistic. Communist parties should fight the imperialists at home in France and Britain and forget about Germany and Italy. 'Revolutionary defeatism' was the key phrase. The activist leadership in the small British Communist Party resisted this until the end of 1939. The French, much aided by the anti-Communist measures, including the suppression of *L'Humanité*, undertaken by the Daladier Government at the end of August, were more disciplined. This did not protect either party against catastrophic falls in their membership, violent demonstrations outside *L'Humanité*'s editorial buildings, and insults and accusations on the factory floor, where the parties' organizations had been strongest.

CHAPTER 26

WAR ORDERED — AND DEFERRED:
AUGUST 25 IN BERLIN

August 25 was a Friday. Two days earlier, on August 23, the hour of attack on Poland had been fixed for 4.30 a.m. on August 26. Hitler was always inclined to move over a weekend, if he could. In the old days, when he had declared Germany free of the shackles placed on the level of German armaments by the Treaty of Versailles, ordered his troops into the demilitarized Rhineland, or marched into Austria, he had always chosen a weekend for his actions. The world press had caught up with him, even to the point of crediting him with the intention of acting when no such plans were to hand. Over the weekend of May 20–21, 1938, with the aid of Czech military intelligence, there had been a 'crisis' in which, for once, Hitler had been wrongly accused. Press crowing over his failure to implement the plans he had never had enraged him into precipitating the crisis of September 1938, which ended at Munich. In 1939, the fact that a weekend was involved had much to do with the fears aroused over Danzig at the end of June. Given the importance attached by the army leadership to strategic surprise, it might have been thought Hitler would have chosen another day; but by now, action over a weekend seems to have become a tradition.

If the German army was to launch its assault across Poland's frontiers, its units needed to move up into their jumping-off points some time on August 25. To avoid giving the Poles any advance warning, especially so as to catch the Polish forces before they could mobilize, not only was Hitler prepared to dispense with the formal ritual of ultimatum and declaration of war, he was determined not to show his hand until the last moment. This determination had inspired the invitations to Lipski and Henderson to hunt with Goering in October, and to the diplomatic corps in general to attend the Tannenberg celebrations on August 27 and the *Parteitag* at Nuremberg at the beginning of September. Military men on both sides of the German-Polish border knew that every day brought closer the end of the campaigning season, when rain, mist and the treacherous Polish marshes would make any serious campaigning impossible. Their knowledge had been passed on to the diplomatists, to whom postponement of any confrontation became increasingly urgent, increasingly pressing.

Hitler had, however, given other hostages to time and to his military. Over and over again, he had assured them that Britain and France would not intervene, that his decision was for a localized war. Whether he spoke to his Generals and Chiefs of Staff as on August 14, 19 or 22, or to Count Csàky or Count Ciano, or to Keitel and his adjutant, Bernhard von Lossberg, at the end of July, his message was the same. 'I have met the umbrella men, Chamberlain and Daladier, at Munich and got to know them. They can never stop me solving the Polish question. The coffee-sippers in London and Paris will stay still this time too. . . . if it comes to war, then it will be limited to Poland. A world war will *never, never, never* come out of *Case White*'; with every repetition, he banged on the table. Then in a state of wild excitement, he left the room. That was how von Lossberg remembered him, at the end of July.[1]

The army leadership was not convinced. We have already seen General Halder, the Army Chief of Staff, anxiously counting the troops on either side of the Franco-German frontier prior to his meeting with Hitler at the Berghof on August 14. The need to deal with the Poles as quickly as possible was urged on the military planners by Hitler for political reasons. He wanted Poland crushed by the end of the campaigning season so as to be able to confront Britain, France and the world generally with a *fait accompli*. The overwhelming display of German military might which this feat would involve would give him added leverage throughout Europe. But his military planners had other, strictly military reasons for wanting to overwhelm Polish resistance as soon as possible. The Siegfried line was far from finished (something that seemingly escaped the French High Command). And the limited forces, of the second rank, which were all the Germans could spare for the defence of their western frontier, did not strike the German High Command as capable of holding out against the forces the Allies could bring against them for very long.

On the face of it the Polish position did not seem all that easy to defend. In the north some Polish forces had to be committed to defend Gdynia and the Polish Corridor to the sea. All along the northern frontier Poland faced German forces in East Prussia; while in the west the German occupation of Bohemia and Moravia and the extension of German forces into Slovakia confronted them with an enormous front from any part of which a major assault could be launched. But Poland is riven with rivers. In the north there were no easy routes out of East Prussia. The bridge over the Vistula could easily be blown. Poland's danger lay in the fact that her war-making capacity, her industries, her major centres of population lay west of Warsaw. Against German attack, Poland had no depth.

The German aim became therefore to destroy the Polish forces piece-meal before they could be completely assembled west of the Vistula–Narew Rivers. The German infantry had therefore to assemble as close to the frontier as possible, and the motorized infantry, light armoured and armoured divisions had to overrun the frontier defences and penetrate as deeply as possible without worrying about their flanks or rear, leaving the more slow-moving infantry with their horse-drawn guns to deal with the Polish forces they left behind. 'By swiftness of action and relentless attack, to gain the advantage over the enemy,' was the watchword.

The main German problems lay in the north where General von Bock's Army Group North was divided by the Corridor. The 4th Army, under General von Kluge, operating out of Pomerania, had to head for the Vistula, cutting the Corridor completely so as to be able to turn and drive south towards Warsaw. The aim was to control the road and rail communications through the Corridor and towards Warsaw. The 3rd Army (General von Küchler) had to use part of its forces to help capture the Vistula crossings. But its main weight was further east, due north of Warsaw, where its job was to destroy the Polish forces north of the Narew and drive east of Warsaw. It was to be the eastern end of the great encircling manœuvre planned by the German High Command on the model of a Zulu impi or Hannibal's armies against Rome at Cannae. This left no spare forces for Danzig. Danzig would have to defend itself with some aid from the German navy and the Luftwaffe. The fortifications at Gdynia could be mopped up later.

The three armies in Army Group South under General von Rundstedt, the 8th, 10th and 14th, were to close the other side of the circle. Over half Germany's motorized and armoured forces were assembled in the 10th Army, under General von Reichenau. On his northern flank, General von Blaskowitz's 8th Army was the weakest of the five German armies. Its job was to hold and follow, as befits the centre of a trap to be sprung by the two wings. In the south where General List commanded, the 14th Army's task was to contain the mountainous area on the Slovak-Polish border and protect the southern flank of the 10th Army's drive from any attempt to outflank it. The 14th Army had had to be reinforced as the true strength of the southern wing of the Polish forces became apparent. The Polish Cracow Army had seven infantry divisions; beyond it to the south lay two further divisions in reserve and the mountain brigades of the Carpathian Army. It became necessary for the 14th Army to take over part of the Slovak frontier and to absorb the Slovak army with its three divisions and obsolescent Czech arms.

All of this required preparation; and not all of it could be hidden. The Slovak side was fairly easy. In March the Germans had forced the infant Slovak state to accept a treaty of protection; this established a 'protected zone' which covered the Slovak-Polish frontier from the German-occupied Czech province of Moravia all the way to the Slovak-Hungarian frontier.[2] Within this the German military exercised military sovereignty, had jurisdiction over all German nationals, could requisition, use all means of transportation, supervise arms production and construct fortifications. The Slovaks had to live with the way in which Germany had sacrificed the unfortunate Carpatho-Ukrainians to Hungary, and the fear that for whatever reasons of high German policy, it might suit Hitler to sacrifice them in the same way. Until 1918 Slovakia had been a province of the Hungarian component of the Austro-Hungarian empire. The Slovaks were well aware that there were Hungarians for whom a return to the frontiers of 1914 was the major goal. They watched the peregrinations of Count Csáky, shuttling uneasily between Berlin and Rome, and saw not the figure of contempt that Hitler and Mussolini saw but a perpetual threat.[3]

Throughout the summer of 1939 a German military mission under General Franz Barckhausen had been in Bratislava, at the Slovak invitation, negotiating over the implementation of the March treaty.[4] It was only at the beginning of August that the military planners for *Case White* realized the need to take in Slovakia as a base for their plans against Poland. On August 17 the army planners met with the OKW and the Foreign Ministry to set the wheels in motion.[5] It was agreed that on Y-day, the day Poland was to be attacked, or a few hours earlier, the Slovaks were to be told that a Polish violation of Slovak territory was imminent and that German troops had been ordered into Slovakia to protect her. Slovakia was to be treated as a friendly state. There was to be no question of the civilian administration of Slovakia being interfered with; but it would be expected to do everything the military needed for operational purposes. A draft note to the Slovak Government was sent to the German Legation in Bratislava on August 21 to be held in readiness to be acted upon.[6]

These instructions were sent on August 23, at the same time as the orders were given fixing Y-day on August 26 at dawn. In return Germany offered to guarantee Slovakia's frontiers with Hungary and to help Slovakia recover the territories lost to Poland. Plagued by rumours that the alternative was to lose Slovakian independence to Hungary,[7] Monsignor Tiso, now the head of the Slovak state, accepted with relief. Monsignor Tiso was finding it increasingly necessary to exercise dictatorial powers to maintain national unity.[8] As the speech he made on August 15 showed, he saw his countrymen faced with a choice. They could base their nationhood on a realistic view of what was open to them, even if this involved a certain enforced amity towards Germany; or they could go the way of the Czechs. Tiso knew well that an 'independent' Slovakia had its uses to German propaganda to demonstrate that Germany was not, as such, anti-Slav. So the German demands were accepted;[9] and on August 25, Bratislava radio, as monitored in Budapest, did its little bit to envenom the airwaves, announcing that Slovakia would march side by side with Germany to recover the territories which Poland had annexed.[10]

Danzig was to be left to cope with the Polish forces in and around the city using the forces it had been secretly assembling over the past months. It was also supposed to supply the major justification for the German attack on Poland by provoking Polish military action against it.[11] Within the city, there had assembled a mixture of paramilitary units. Stationed in East Prussia were two regiments of *Landespolizei* under General Eberhard, made up of German soldiers of Danzig origin; each regiment consisted of three battalions, with light artillery and anti-tank companies after the model of the regular German army. Together they made up the Eberhard Brigade of about 6,500 men. There were also the customs officials and an SA *Standarte* which guarded the frontiers. There was also a largely raw SS Home Guard (*Heimwehr*), formed in May 1939, of enthusiastic volunteers from the Hitler Youth, high-school students and such like. They were only moved to Danzig in mid-August. They were, by contrast with the *Landespolizei*, excellently armed and equipped. They took part in a public parade in Danzig on August 18.[12]

Their role, they were told, was to hold Danzig against a Polish coup. They built fortifications and a pontoon bridge across the Vistula to East Prussia. The SS *Heimwehr* was given the job of seizing the main bridge over the Vistula at Dirschau (Tczew) before the Poles could destroy it and breach the main east-west road and rail link across the Corridor. The main reinforcement for the potentially beleaguered German forces in Danzig was to be provided by the German navy. In mid-June it had been announced that the German light cruiser *Königsberg* was to pay a courtesy visit to Danzig for the twenty-fifth commemoration of the dead of the cruiser *Magdeburg*, sunk by the Russians in 1914. By a curious coincidence the commemoration was to be held from

August 25 to 28. The Danzig and Polish authorities were formally notified.[13]

On August 15, very belatedly, these plans were changed.[14] The *Königsberg*'s guns were not thought powerful enough to cope with the Polish coastal batteries in Gdynia or on the Hel peninsula. Instead, the old *Schleswig-Holstein*, a battleship built in 1902 on the floating fortress lines of the day, was to be sent. The *Schleswig-Holstein* was usually used as a training ship. Its slow speed, four 11-inch guns and general obsoleteness ruled quite out of court its use as a battleship against anything built since 1906; but its combination of heavy guns and quick-firing secondary armament made it perfectly competent to deal with the garrison on the Westerplatte and on the Hel peninsula, or so it was thought. On August 23 it took on board a naval assault group from the Memel and sailed for Danzig.[15] Early on August 25 it entered Danzig harbour, mooring off the Westerplatte. The naval assault group remained out of sight, below decks. Its crew arranged the normal programme of complimentary visits,[16] invitations to come on board were extended to Burckhardt, the League of Nations Commissioner, to the foreign consuls, and even to M. Chodacki, the Polish diplomatic representative.

This last was, by his standards, exceptionally tactful. On August 23, Forster had sprung what was supposed to be the trap. That day, the Senate of Danzig, meeting at noon in solemn conclave, appointed Gauleiter Forster head of state of the free city of Danzig.[17] Greiser became Minister President, head of government. A Department of External Relations was set up. This represented the kind of major change in the Danzig constitution that, by the statute establishing the free city, could only be carried out with League of Nations agreement. Effectively it was a declaration of independence. The news was broken on the morning of August 24, to Mr Burckhardt by Greiser[18] and to the world by a DNB press release[19] from Berlin. At noon the same day the Polish delegation involved in the negotiations over the customs inspectors issue returned to Warsaw, after being confronted with the planned demand for the withdrawal of all frontier officials and a 50 per cent reduction in the customs inspectors.[20] Forster celebrated by arresting the head of the Polish railways administration in Danzig and several of his senior officials, and temporarily closing by force the Polish customs offices.[21]

According to the plans laid by Hitler and Forster, the Poles were now expected to react with some kind of move which could be hailed as provocation. Observers in Berlin noticed that the German press had temporarily dropped their emphasis on the alleged sufferings of the

German minority in Poland and returned on the morning of August 25 to the Danzig issue.[22] Marshal Smigly-Rydz and Colonel Beck were far too downy a pair of birds to be caught like that, even without the pleas for restraint showered on them by the hyper-nervous French Ambassador, Léon Noël.[23] They duly protested at the action of the Danzig Senate; but they did not think it really affected their interest.[24] No Polish 'provocation' over Danzig could be relied on in Berlin. Nor had the Poles done more than protest at the increasing number of frontier incidents in which the irregular forces organized among the German and other minorities in Poland were involved. Hitler was not worried, however. He proposed to stage his own acts of Polish provocation. For that he had turned to the SS, to Himmler and to the two men who gave Himmler his backbone and his teeth, Reinhard Heydrich and Heinrich Müller. Heydrich had been dismissed from the German navy with contumely, for making a habit of seducing the wives of his fellow officers. In 1942, as Reichs Protector of Bohemia (the title was a joke in singularly bad taste), he was assassinated by Czech agents parachuted in from Britain. Müller disappeared amidst the ruins of Berlin in April 1945 in the escape from Hitler's bunker after the Führer had killed himself. Himmler took his own life after falling into British hands in 1945. How and when Hitler briefed them we do not know.

The plotting, however, began on August 8,[25] when Heydrich briefed a small group of senior SS officials. Their job, should Poland not attack Germany, he said, was to simulate an attack. This was a direct order from the Führer. About 250 experienced SS men would be needed, of middle years, militarily trained and speaking Polish. The targets were three in number: the German radio station at Gleiwitz, a customs office at Hohnlinden and a small frontier post in Kreuzburg, all on the German-Polish frontier in Upper Silesia. The Gleiwitz radio station was to be held long enough to allow a Polish-speaking SS man to broadcast a provocative speech – in Polish. The SS men were to wear Polish military uniforms, which the *Abwehr* was to provide. And as a gruesome piece of authentic detail, a number of corpses had to be provided. The SS obligingly selected a number of prisoners from the concentration camps, to whom the grisly codename *Konserven* ('canned goods') was given. They too were to be dressed in Polish uniforms and their bodies strewn on the scene of action to add verisimilitude for the photographers. As Hitler said on August 22 to his Generals, 'I will provide a propagandistic *casus belli*. Its credibility does not matter. The victor will not be asked later if he has spoken the truth or not.' By August 25, the SS men, the uniforms, the *Konserven*, the transport and the weapons were all ready. The operation was given the codename *Tannenberg*; if this leaked, it would misdirect attention to East Prussia.

The SS planning was complicated by the *Abwehr*'s own organization of special forces to operate in advance of the German army, to prevent the destruction of strategically important bridges and railway tunnels and to harass, distract and mislead the Polish forces generally. The *Abwehr* had also raised and trained a substantial Ukrainian force from Ukrainians living in Germany, and put them in Polish uniforms with a view to launching them across the Polish-Slovak frontier to provoke an insurrection among the large Ukrainian minority in southern Poland.[26] This was cancelled on direct orders from Ribbentrop when he finally received his invitation to Moscow. There were enough already active, however, all in Polish uniforms, to necessitate special orders for the German uniformed forces as to how to recognize and treat these German agents.[27] One such group[28] was greatly to confuse matters on the night of August 25 by attacking and destroying the Polish customs office at Chwalentsitz across the Polish frontier from Hohnlinden.[29]

In the meantime, von Weizsäcker's desperate conspiracy to avoid war by bringing the Poles to some kind of negotiating offer was working its way through the system. After the stormy interview that Bernardo Attolico, the Italian Ambassador in Berlin, had had with Sir Nevile Henderson on August 15, Henderson was to bombard Lord Halifax with ever more desperately worded advice to press Warsaw to instruct the Polish Ambassador in Berlin to do something.[30] The German choice of the alleged mistreatment of the German minorities in Poland hit the Poles in what both London and Warsaw recognized to be the Poles' most vulnerable spot; so that while Henderson contrived to press the need for action, both Halifax and Lipski had, independently of each other, come to the same conclusion. On August 18 Lipski had already written to Warsaw on the issue.[31] That same day, Halifax instructed Sir Howard Kennard to ask Colonel Beck if some approach could not be made to the Germans on the matter.[32]

Attolico's last interview with Ribbentrop on August 19 added to the pressure. All that he could learn, so Henderson reported,[33] was that unless direct contact was re-established between Warsaw and Berlin by the end of that week (i.e. August 26) Hitler would proceed to direct action. This message reached London both from Henderson and from Sir Percy Loraine in Rome.[34] Halifax duly instructed Kennard again to urge Beck to make some move in Berlin, if only to test whether there was anything in these reports.[35]

Here Weizsäcker and Goering between them were operating a pair of already well-laid traps. The break in communications between Warsaw and Berlin was entirely of German making, as has already been seen. The only place in which that contact could effectively be re-opened, given the instructions issued to the German Embassy in Warsaw at the beginning of August, was in Berlin. And by the bogus invitation to go hunting in the German state forests in October, Goering had established himself with Lipski as still being Poland's best friend at Hitler's court.

Thus it was that Lipski was instructed as early as August 19 to see Goering.[36] On August 21, he returned to Warsaw to get detailed instructions out of Colonel Beck as to what he should say to Goering. He found Beck heavily under the influence of the Polish military, convinced that Poland could withstand German attack. All Beck would agree to was that Lipski should ask Goering who would benefit from a German-Polish war, and to make it clear that the Poles were determined not to yield.[37] The following day, shaken by the announcement of Ribbentrop's visit to Moscow and the imminence of a German-Soviet pact, Lipski returned to Berlin. He did not manage to see Goering until the afternoon of August 24; and despite further instructions from Beck to try to see von Weizsäcker, the State Secretary was in Berchtesgaden with Henderson seeing Hitler and could not be reached.[38]

Lipski found Goering dominated by one idea only, the need to persuade Poland to abandon the still-unconcluded alliance with Britain.[39] He could talk of nothing else. As Commander-in-Chief of the Luftwaffe, he knew perfectly well that Y-day had already been fixed for August 26. He had heard Hitler's address two days earlier. Hitler was in Berchtesgaden and Ribbentrop, his triumphant rival, on his way back from Moscow. In no way could he, nor would he have dared, take a positive initiative of the kind the whole conspiracy pre-supposed. He could have accepted a positive Polish offer to discuss the treatment of minorities, perhaps in a neutral capital. But the Nazi-Soviet Pact had made one thing clear in Warsaw: the Poles' choice lay, as it had always done, between resistance or total surrender. This last had no place in the mental cosmos of Marshal Pilsudski's young hawks. Even had he wanted to play the peacemaker, Goering had not the moral strength. He knew his master was determined on war.

This then was the position Hitler faced on the morning of August 25 when he asked Dietrich for the press clippings on the fall of the Chamberlain and Daladier Governments, and found that they had weathered the storm. It is not clear how far he knew that Goering had already understood the need for further misdirection to be given to confuse the British and French Governments. Goering had in fact sent General Bodenschatz to see Colonel Stehlin, his usual contact at the French Embassy in Berlin, on August 23.[40] Most of what Bodenschatz said was demonstrably true. On Danzig and Poland, however, he lied in his teeth. Germany was not intending to do anything over Poland or Danzig. 'We will not give the Poles the pleasure of playing the provocateur for them.' Germany did, however, anticipate an attack, perhaps towards Stettin, which was only 100 kilometres from the frontier. Colonel Beck was a reasonable man; but with Marshal Smigly-Rydz and his acolytes, nothing could be done. The whole action was designed to give verisimilitude to the reports the DNB was to carry on August 24 that Poland was mobilizing its forces, and to the rumours of an imminent Polish attack on Danzig.

Where Britain was concerned, any move by Goering towards Sir Nevile Henderson was likely to be intercepted by Ribbentrop. It was for just this reason that Goering's Swedish contact, Birger Dahlerus, was so useful. At 2 p.m. on the afternoon of August 24 Goering saw Dahlerus at his country house, Karinhall.[41] He then drove Dahlerus back to Berlin, to await the result of his meeting with Hitler and the impressions Ribbentrop had brought back from Moscow. That evening at 11.20 p.m. he telephoned Dahlerus at his hotel. He asked Dahlerus to explain in London the need for immediate negotiations and to stress Germany's 'absolute determination' to come to an agreement with Britain – this from a man who had just come from Hitler's celebrations with Ribbentrop and had heard his Führer at the Berghof only two days earlier.

Dahlerus arrived in London around 1.30 p.m. on August 25 and hurried to the Foreign Office. He brought with him four questions. Would Britain advise Poland to enter into direct negotiations with Germany and agree to a 'standstill' during the negotiations? Would the Poles accept an invitation from a neutral power to bring Germany and Poland together? Would Britain agree that no final settlement should be made with Germany until the Polish negotiations were concluded? Would Britain send a negotiator to Hitler with authority to say 'No' if German demands were too far-reaching? With our knowledge that the Gleiwitz incident was due to be staged within a day of Dahlerus's arrival in London, the intent of those questions is clear – to produce a situation in which German and British reasonableness could be reported as being brought to nothing by Polish criminality.

Hitler had, however, spoiled Goering's ploy by a much cruder one of his own. At 1 p.m. on August 25 he summoned Sir Nevile Henderson to the Reichs Chancellery.[42] Poland's provocations had become intolerable. Germany was determined to abolish these 'Macedonian' conditions on her frontiers. The problem of Danzig and the Corridor must be solved. If this was accepted he was ready to pledge himself personally to guarantee the existence of the British empire and to place German power at its disposal. If these ideas were rejected there would be war. He urged Henderson to fly back to London to convey his views. Henderson did his best to persuade the Cabinet to take them seriously.[43] Ribbentrop rubbed in the impossibility of the Poles by having his Under Secretary, Ernst Woermann, phone Henderson as soon as he got back to the Embassy to call his attention to yet another invented atrocity.[44]

At 2 p.m. the Italian Ambassador, Bernardo Attolico, was waiting to see Hitler.[45] Even as he waited his own Embassy telephoned. His instructions were cancelled.[46] Hitler called Attolico in, only to learn of this. Dismayed, he sent Ribbentrop off to try to telephone Ciano. He was told that neither Ciano nor Mussolini could be reached. They had gone off to the beach (a diplomatic untruth – they were still arguing). The hour for Hitler's decision was rapidly approaching. If he acted much later than 3 p.m., even the superb command machinery that Keitel and his planners had set up would not get the German troops into their jump-off positions in time to attack at 4 a.m. the following morning. At a minute before 3 p.m. Hitler emerged from his inner sanctum to see Keitel. The order to march was given. At 3.45 General Brauchitsch telephoned General Halder, head of Army Staff, from the Reichs Chancellery.[47] The order had reached 10th Army Command by 4 p.m.[48] The command to the individual units to move up to their jumping-off positions was issued at 4.30 p.m.; the order fixing Y-hour, 4.30 a.m. on August 26, followed an hour later. Orders went out at the same time to the German Consulate in Danzig. The navy received its orders at the same time. Its preparations were directed against Britain as much as against Poland.[49] On August 21, the 'pocket-battleship' *Graf Spee* had left the Kiel Canal to rendezvous in the South Atlantic south-west of the Canary Islands with its supply ship, *Altmark*. On August 24, a second pocket-battleship, the *Deutschland*, left to meet its supply ship, the *Westerwald*, east of Greenland. Between August 19 and 24, a dozen U-boats sailed to wait off the Shetlands and in the Channel. On August 23 the two German battle cruisers *Scharnhorst* and *Gneisenau* were ordered into the North Sea. German tankers at sea were diverted to Spanish harbours. The Naval High Command explained these as precautionary measures. They were – but against Britain and France, not Poland. The plans had been laid in June. The *Altmark* sailed on August 4 to take on US diesel oil in the Gulf of Mexico in time to meet the *Graf Spee* on the flank of Britain's main sea route through the Mediterranean or round the Cape to South-East Asia or Australasia.

All of this rested on the assumption that Britain and France could be misled and confused into not acting. Hitler had bidden the French Ambassador, Robert Coulondre, to see him at 5.30 p.m., but before Coulondre arrived, there came the first intimation that Hitler was mistaken. From his press office there came the news that the Anglo-Polish Treaty had been signed. His shoulders drooped; he collapsed into a chair and sat for a while. Then Coulondre was announced. The news had not really sunk in yet. Hitler launched into the same harangue he had unleashed on the unhappy Nevile Henderson.[50] Coulondre was not spared the ritual accusations of castration, mass murder at Bialice and Lódź, of Polish anti-aircraft guns firing on German civil airliners, even of a Polish ship firing at a plane carrying Wilhelm Stuckart, Secretary of State to the German Ministry of the Interior. Daladier was to be told all this. Hitler did not want war with France; but if it did come to war it would be war to the end. Much French and much German blood would be spilt. Hitler would be sorry if it came to that. 'Tell M. Daladier that from me.'

With that Hitler rose to take his leave of M. Coulondre. The French Ambassador was, however, a tougher man than Henderson. He gave as good as he got – even mentioning the alleged victim of Polish assassination who had actually died a month earlier in a domestic crime of passion. Hitler listened, shouted and repeated himself. Coulondre took his leave, the victor of that little encounter.

Barely had Coulondre left, when a new blow was struck at the edifice of assumptions on which Hitler was about to launch Germany into war with Poland. The news from London was in itself disastrous. So far from the British being baffled and bamboozled, bullied, frightened or bribed, they had signed the treaty with Poland, whose leisurely negotiation Hitler had always taken as proof they were not serious. His 'generous offer' to guarantee the British empire had been directly rejected. In actuality he had failed to allow for the effect of his treatment of Sir Nevile Henderson. So far from firing off an immediate telegram to London, Henderson had returned to his Embassy in a state of nervous collapse. For two hours he had dithered, composed arguments to convince London, discussed what to do with his staff. His telegrams to London were not dispatched until 5.30 p.m. Berlin time, long after the alliance had been signed in London. Their main effect was to convince Halifax that he could dispense with Mr Dahlerus; that evening, he informed the Swede courteously that since a direct channel of communication had been opened, his services were no longer needed.[51] Sir Nevile Henderson was coming to London with Hitler's message, of which he had sent an advance text. As Halifax had explained the previous evening to the 'nervous Nellies' among the Dominions High

Commissioners in London, Vincent Massey, the Canadian, Te Water, the South African, and Bruce, the Australian,[52] Hitler was not really open to reasoning. His whole outlook, philosophy, thought and language were centred on the overwhelming right of the 'virile, growing German race' to expansion, beside which the smaller nations and other races counted for nothing.

Hitler's new caller, the Italian Ambassador, brought what was for Hitler a stab to the heart. The previous news meant that Poland had acquired an ally, or rather allies. Now he was to learn that he could no longer count on Mussolini, whose steadfastness as an ally he had lauded only three days earlier to his Generals, as one of the three factors which made war in 1939 something Germany would win. Earlier that day he had witnessed a violent argument between Weizsäcker and Ribbentrop. Weizsäcker told Ribbentrop directly that after three months of war the Italians would be unable to continue ('to cook their soup any more') for lack of coal. Therefore they would stay out. Ribbentrop had replied angrily that he disagreed 100 per cent. 'Mussolini was too great a man.'[53] At 3.30 p.m. that afternoon Hitler had sent Mussolini a triumphant message,[54] justifying the conclusion of the Soviet agreement, pointing out that Romania and Turkey could now be regarded as completely neutralized, and that there had been the greatest possible gain in strength to the Axis. With Poland, however, the situation was becoming intolerable. The Poles could not control their own military. Germany was ready to act 'and in the case of intolerable events in Poland I will act immediately.' This message was handed within the hour by the German Ambassador in Rome, Hans von Mackensen, to whom it had been phoned directly, to Mussolini in the Palazzo Venezia, in Ciano's presence.[55] Mackensen had readied Ciano for the message at 2 p.m. Hitler's message followed a brief and desperate telegram from Attolico. Only a direct and personal appeal from the Duce to the Führer could save matters. Even if Britain were to demand that Poland should negotiate, there must be equivalent pressure on Hitler from Italy, 'but at once, at once, without losing a minute'.[56] The die was in Mussolini's hands.

Mussolini had spent the previous ten days swinging backwards and forwards between various positions, like a ham actor rehearsing different roles, practising different voices, for a command performance, but all along aware that the moment when he would have to go out on stage and play one role would clearly be upon him all too soon. Some of these roles were old and familiar ones: that of the loyal friend and reliable ally of Germany, the man who in September 1937 on the Maifeld, the vast parade ground outside Berlin, had declared, 'When I have a friend, I will go with him to the end,' the man who had pledged himself to the firm purposes of the Pact of Steel; that of the great mediator, the peacemaker, the man who had ended Franco-German enmity for a decade at Locarno in 1925, who had rescued peace from imminent war in September 1938 (Mussolini was apt to edit his memories more than somewhat). He did not want to have to admit publicly that his policy had been built on a bluff; that 'war' for him was a threat, a ploy, a piece of rhetoric that frightened him as much as he used it to frighten others, when Hitler seemed to lust after it; that his people hated and detested Germany.

He was also, as always, over-sensitive to what others were saying about him. One press agency, the Mediterranean Press Service of Anglo-American ownership, spread the most fantastic stories.[57] He had had a stand-up row with Marshal Badoglio, the chief of his military forces, which had come to blows and put Badoglio in hospital; he had fought a duel with Marshal Caviglia, who had committed suicide; Badoglio and the military were preparing a coup against him; King Victor Emmanuel had abdicated; there was a popular revolt. All were assiduously collected by his private secretariat. Guariglia protested to Bonnet, alleging that they originated with the entourage of the US Ambassador in Paris, William Bullitt.[58] A report on the Italian army's lack of preparations for war, carried in the sensationalist London tabloid, the *Sunday Dispatch*, of August 20, swung the Duce violently towards supporting Germany. 'We would be dishonoured for a century,' he told Ciano.[59]

For most of the weeks after Ciano returned from Salzburg, Mussolini had remained in almost total seclusion. He saw very few people; his relations of confidence with Count Ciano were badly shaken by the black hatred for Germany, Hitler and Ribbentrop with which Ciano returned from Salzburg. He shared with Ciano a sense of betrayal – sufficiently to appoint his own amanuensis, Barone Giacomo Paulucci di Carboli, to prepare a written and documented account of Hitler's betrayals.[60] On August 14, he charged Marshal de Bono with a military inspection of Italy's northern frontiers with Germany.[61] He instructed Starace, Secretary of the Fascist Party, on August 16, to rein in the pro-German propaganda action.[62] The instructions given to the Italian press and to the official Italian news service, the Agenzia Stefani, on August 18 emphasized the delicate nature of the negotiations necessary to bring about a German–Polish agreement which Italy, so it was said, regarded as the most probable outcome, and the need not to upset matters by exaggerated polemics.[63]

The message sent by Lord Halifax on August 19[64] and delivered by

Sir Percy Loraine on August 21, intended to encourage Mussolini, if he was so minded, towards pressing Hitler into direct negotiations with Poland, if necessary by proposing a conference (an idea it was believed in London Mussolini was entertaining), had for the moment the opposite effect. When it arrived, Ciano was in Albania. Loraine left it with Alfieri; he took it to Mussolini who chose to read into it a direct threat. His talk of entry into war alarmed Anfuso, Ciano's secretary, and led to Ciano's precipitous return from Albania. He found the Duce sufficiently calmed down to consider a new approach to Ribbentrop, which, as we have seen, was overtaken by Ribbentrop's flight to Moscow and the announcement of the Nazi-Soviet Pact which was released at midnight on August 21.

This announcement seems for a time to have brought all the Italian fire-eaters out of the woodwork.[65] All the firebrands and loudmouths, all the Anglo- and Francophobes, all who admired and hankered after the 'hardness' they found and admired in the image of Nazism and of the German army, emerged like termites from the woodwork. Badoglio was charged to examine the military possibilities of action against Greece and Yugoslavia or against Yugoslavia.[66] Marshal Graziani was put at the head of an *ad hoc* army command. Ciano, as we have seen, activated his Croat contacts.[67]

Sanity, however, set in more quickly in Rome than in Berlin, aided by the firmness and flexibility with which Loraine dealt with Count Ciano. The Italians could hardly fail to note that Britain was demonstrating a willingness to listen which was singularly absent in Berlin; nor that Lord Halifax was taking care to keep Rome informed in detail of the various British moves, by contrast with the deafening silence which was coming out of Berlin.[68] These diplomatic courtesies made the insouciance which Loraine displayed towards Ciano over the Nazi-Soviet Pact the more impressive:[69] no pregnant silences or solemn admissions that the pact had struck a severe blow at Berlin policy. 'The announcement', Loraine maliciously told a startled Ciano, 'had given me the first hearty laugh I had had for some weeks. . . . the Axis has scored a debating point but no more.' There followed a more formal warning which was accompanied by the news that, as a result of Mussolini's suggestion, the Polish Ambassador in Berlin was to see von Weizsäcker.[70] Mussolini remained inclined to take a rather high line,[71] but the contrast between the British and German attitudes could not fail in its effect when Ciano confronted Mussolini with his own dossier of all the German evasions, mendacities and deceits. Mussolini was never going to denounce the alliance, as Ciano wished him to do. Nor was he in any position to honour it, despite the degree to which General

Pariani, the Chief of the Army General Staff, tried to cover up the army's deficiencies.

Essentially the course Mussolini preferred was to write a letter to Hitler. If Germany attacked Poland, he wrote, and the attack remained 'localized', Italy would provide all the support requested of her. If Poland and the Allies attacked Germany the alliance would be honoured. If Germany attacked Poland and, as a result, Britain and France declared war on Germany, Italy would 'take no initiatives of a war-like character' by reason of Italy's lack of military preparation. If negotiations failed as a result of the intransigence of others, Italy would fight on Germany's side.[72]

This was, as was quickly realized, both illogical and untenable. Italy's inability to undertake or endure a war with Britain and France did not depend on the juridical niceties of who declared war on whom and when and why. By the morning of August 25 this statement had been reduced to three paragraphs. If the war was limited to Germany and Poland, Italy would give all the aid asked of her. If it was not, then Italy would take 'no initiative of a war-like character'. Italy's eventual action would depend on what war materials Germany could put at her disposal.[73]

A telegram in this sense was ready for dispatch to Attolico at midday on August 25. Attolico was primed to see Hitler. Then, after the instruction that a message from Hitler was on its way, Mussolini had a last-minute hesitation and Attolico had to be recalled from the Reichs Chancellery. Hitler's message duly arrived. Ciano and Mussolini could see nothing had changed. Attolico's panic-stricken appeal coincided with it. By contrast, Loraine sent in two polite notes indicating that Britain was still following Mussolini's advice and that military measures had been taken to avoid any untoward incidents on the borders between British-defended Egypt and the Italian colony of Libya.[74] Ciano was able to persuade Mussolini to strengthen and elaborate on the last part of the telegram already drafted. In the final version, Mussolini expressed perfect comprehension of the German position over Poland. There then followed the two paragraphs about action in the event of a limited war and an enlarged one. Italian intervention, the new draft continued, could be immediate if Germany could make immediate delivery of the armaments and war materials necessary to enable Italy to withstand the first Anglo-French offensive which would certainly be directed against Italy.

Attolico took Mussolini's message down as it was telephoned through to him. Then, accompanied by Magistrati, he hurried to the Reichs Chancellery. Its towering doors were guarded by SS guards in full battle gear. Its long corridors were filled with the multitude of persons that made up the Führer's court, all drawn by and infused with the excitement that surrounds historic decisions: ministers, elderly Nazi veterans of the street-fighting days of the 1920s, officials; even the Foreign Ministry staff were in the new grey 'campaign' uniforms. Telephones squealed, telegrams were delivered, dispatch riders scurried in and out. Amidst all this militarism, the two Italians, in their sober bourgeois civilian suits, caused a minor sensation. They were ushered into Hitler's inner sanctum where they found Ribbentrop, Goebbels and Goering's deputy, Bodenschatz. It was 6 p.m. Hitler knew the worst.[75]

The news came on him like a thunderbolt. He was 'completely beaten down', noted one observer. Hastily he summoned Ribbentrop.[76] Recall the troops, said Ribbentrop. He then telephoned Keitel. Could the order to attack and the staging of the provocative incidents be called off? Brauchitsch guaranteed they could be. Goering, Keitel and Brauchitsch were summoned. The recall orders went out at 7.30 that evening. Frantic telephoning, the dispatch of young officers all over the frontiers of Germany and Poland by car and motor cycle, managed the recall of virtually every unit, some almost as dawn was rising;[77] but not quite all units were contactable. The *Abwehr* and the SS ran into particular difficulties. One *Abwehr Kampfgruppe* crossed from Slovakia into Poland to try to prevent the strategic railway tunnel below the small village railway station of Mosty in the Polish Carpathians from being blown up. The railway line carried the main railway traffic from Poland through to the Balkans. The *Abwehr* duly captured Mosty railway station only to find that the German military engineer support team had failed to turn up and that the enraged Poles had blown the railway line by which they were supposed to arrive. Enlightened by a phone call from their Slovak base they successfully escaped back to Slovakia through the mountains, but the engineers who were supposed to follow them had taken forty Polish railway, customs and frontier guards prisoner and two Poles had been killed in various exchanges of fire. Nor was there to be any chance of their taking the Poles by surprise here again.

Where the *Abwehr* was concerned, the unit in question got itself involved by the sheer speed and efficiency of its thirty-odd ethnic German 'volunteers' under the young Lieutenant Hersner. In the SS case incompetence was the cause.[78] The units concerned were supposed to cross over into Polish territory opposite the German frontier post at Hohnlinden on the Silesian frontier, simulate a fire-fight with another SS unit drafted to replace the regular frontier guards, and then surrender. With luck it was reckoned the real Polish frontier guards would be alerted by the firing and add verisimilitude to the scenario.

Instead that part of the unit which was pretending to be Polish mistook the codeword for the alert warning for that comprising the action signal. They were, however, intercepted even after having crossed into Polish territory and brought back to Hohnlinden and their original quarters. The whole operation proved such a shambles that the group leader was immediately replaced. No harm was done, and the unfortunate *Konserven*, waiting in a drugged state in a number of SS cars nearby, were returned, alive, to store. Heydrich was enraged; the SS officer he had appointed in charge of the operation, who had consistently criticized the operation as shameful, ill considered and an unnecessary piece of deceit, was labelled an 'anti-counsellor' and left the SS to join the regular army, after a violent scene of mutual recrimination with Heydrich.

One other mess remained for the German diplomatists to conceal, apart from the aftermath of Mosty, Hohnlinden and some other minor frontier incidents.[79] The Gestapo and the *Abwehr*, for some time, had been keeping the various Polish Consulates in Germany under observation, suspecting them of acting as couriers for the Polish military intelligence. In the late afternoon of August 25, after the telephones of the Polish Embassy and the various Polish Consulates had been cut off, the local police took over the Polish Consulate in Marienwerder in East Prussia and arrested the Consul and his staff. They were later released and evacuated into Lithuania, escaping the fate of their colleagues, many of whom were to be arrested on August 31, to be executed or face death in German concentration camps.[80]

The soldiers returned to their jumping-off points with mixed sentiments. The German army, despite its reputation for efficiency, was no stranger to the kind of experience for which the US army a year or two later coined the acronym 'SNAFU' ('Situation normal, all fouled up' is the polite translation).[81] At the higher levels, however, opinion was divided. To many it only confirmed their professional prejudice against party politicians in general and the Führer in particular as the most extreme example of a pompous incompetent windbag. The would-be conspirators believed that Hitler could not survive so humiliating a withdrawal. Many others regarded it, however, as another piece of that magic legerdemain that Hitler had displayed so effectively in the past over the Rhineland, Austria and Czechoslovakia; these expected Poland to cave in, Britain to withdraw and the whole enterprise to be yet another 'battle of flowers'.[82] They were all to be proved wrong.

In the meantime, Hitler had to try to salvage something from the wreck of the hopes he had pinned on Italy and Mussolini. Privately, he realized that Italy had let him down. He even convinced himself that British foreknowledge of Mussolini's action had encouraged London finally to conclude the Anglo-Polish Alliance, making Italy doubly guilty of the actions which had caused him to call off the attack at the last moment.[83] He did, however, bring himself to draft one brief message to Mussolini, asking him for a list of what Italy needed in the way of war materials so that he could judge how far Germany could meet them.[84] It took Ribbentrop a little longer to remind himself of how far Italy had given the lie to the optimistic reassurances he had opposed to Weizsäcker's pessimism that same morning. His success in influencing Hitler into recalling the armies blinded him to the fact that if Hitler was going to have to make a new effort to separate and distract the Anglo-Franco-Polish front, it was Goering who could play the English card, and not he.[85]

One other man besides Hitler and Mussolini had spent Friday, August 25, in an agony of waiting. On August 27, Neville Chamberlain wrote to his sister Hilda:[86] 'Perhaps the worst trial came on Friday when at 12.45 I learnt that the Führer had sent for Henderson at 1.30. . . . Thereafter ensued a most trying period of waiting. By bad fortune my people could find me nothing to do and I sat with Anne [his wife] in the drawing room, unable to read, unable to talk, just sitting with folded hands and a growing pain in the stomach. It seemed only too likely that Henderson would be presented with an ultimatum and given but a few hours to get out. Yet as hour after hour went by and nothing was heard I began to cheer up a little.'

After Halifax had thanked him for his services, Dahlerus rejoined his British friends.[87] Peace, so he believed, had been saved. A celebratory dinner was called at the Carlton Hotel. After dinner it was decided that Dahlerus should phone Goering to get his reactions. Telephone communication with Germany was still difficult. Part of the German war plans had involved the interruption of all telephone lines between Germany and Britain, France and Poland. With aid from the British Foreign Office Dahlerus finally reached Goering at the Reichs Chancellery. Goering sounded in a state of extreme nervousness; his voice trembled so that he was hardly coherent. The situation was very grave; he feared that war might break out any minute. Dahlerus should do all he could to get Britain to realize the gravity of the situation. Dahlerus knew it was all to do over again.

CHAPTER 27

REGROUPING FOR WAR

After the shock of August 25, the surge of the German armies towards the Polish frontier and their last-minute recall, Europe had six more days without war. For Hitler and for those around him these were terrible days. The junior observers on his staff hoped in vain that sanity would re-assert itself. But as the days moved slowly from the Saturday the attack should have begun through the following week, they came to realize both the strength of those around Hitler who wanted war at all costs, and something of their Führer's own awesome qualities. For the diplomatists in Berlin, Sir Nevile Henderson for Britain, Robert Coulondre for France, Bernardo Attolico for Italy and Józef Lipski for Poland, these were days which began with a mixture of hope that the worst had been averted and that some way to avoid a repetition of the crisis could be found, and a belief that Hitler himself had shown that he would recoil before the certainty of war if only an exit could be found for him.

The first three of these men, with Ernst von Weizsäcker, who to some extent inspired and instigated their activities, realized how intimately the question whether Germany decided for or against war was bound up with the personality of Hitler. Each had, too, his own mental construction of Hitler, as each had his own view of what war would be and what would happen if war broke out. Common to all of them was the realization that Hitler was a man of great internal tensions, intensely vulnerable to any suspicion of being slighted, highly emotional, capable of being stampeded into decision, a daemonic character. Where Coulondre differed from Henderson was in his own willingness to stand up to Hitler and his attitude to war as a kind of challenge of honour, to avoid which could be purchased too dearly. For Sir Nevile Henderson, febrile, gripped by the cancer of the jaw which he had barely survived in the previous November and which was to kill him three years later, this attitude was just part of the higher lunacy which he was prepared to go to almost any lengths to avoid; so much so that Clifford Norton in Warsaw was driven to write in protest to William Strang[1] about Henderson's 'falsifying' British opinion and attempting to 'drag Britain's name in the mud again'. 'There is a worse hell for traitors and cowards than for those who go down because they kept their nerve.' These were not sentiments that Henderson would have shared, though he shared with all his colleagues a hatred for von Ribbentrop – and a dislike of being bullied.

It was on the manipulation of Hitler's moods, or rather on his docility as the supposed moderator between the factions in his entourage, that British and French policy was now to depend. It has to be said that, in London, very few had much hope of success. Lord Halifax's view of Hitler, as expressed to the Dominions High Commissioners, has already been cited. Nor should it be supposed that the British Cabinet, Lord Halifax or the serious men in the Foreign Office had any very high hopes of Birger Dahlerus's activities. Attempts to see in these last-minute negotiations a continuation of the policy of appease-ment – with all the pejorative undertones that a generation of British Churchillians, echoed by American, Soviet and other historians of both right and left have attached to the word – cannot long survive a full reading of the profusion of British sources now available. But even the most hawkish members of the British Cabinet or their critics were not prepared to deny the Cabinet the right to explore, even with the smallest of hopes of success, whether there were not some way, short of disowning Britain's obligations to Poland, by which a conflict might be avoided. There were a few criticisms of the manner in which those obligations had been entered into, though none of any great political weight or significance, mostly from the number of prominent impo-tents which are the inevitable concomitant of any democracy.

There were more divisions in Paris. A faction of M. Daladier's Cabinet, and some outside it, came very close to advocating the avoidance of war at almost any cost. They included, though one cannot say they were led by, Georges Bonnet.[2] Within the Cabinet they included de Monzie, Chautemps[3] and Marchandeau, even Guy la Chambre, the Air Minister, who on August 23 had unusually (and inaccurately) said that weakness in the air need no longer restrain France as it had in 1938. Bonnet was caught out by Daladier misrepresenting the Polish position on August 27.[4] Indeed Daladier went so far as to tell Juliusz Lukasziewicz, the Polish Ambassador in Paris, to deal with him and with Léger, rather than with Bonnet: in some of his many moods, Hitler was to see possibilities of dividing France from Britain. But M. Coulondre was not only not Sir Nevile Henderson. He too knew the importance of bypassing the French Foreign Minister. Bonnet was, however, effective in securing that his country was very largely to play a supporting role in the six days with which we are now concerned.

M. Lipski, as a professional diplomatist, was prepared to play his part in the diplomatic manœuvres; but he played them from a very different standpoint. As a Pole and a former member of the Polish minority in Germany, he made no mental distinction between Hitler and Germans generally. If they recognized Poland's rights and status, as with the 1934 Non-Aggression Pact concluded when he was already Polish Ambassador in Berlin, well and good. If they turned against Poland, this was only to be expected. He would not be a party to buying them off; and he would not be bullied by them or by anyone else.

In this he was characteristic of the generation which had power in Warsaw. It is doubtful if anything could have deterred Hitler from going to war with Poland once Poland had rejected what he found it very easy to convince himself was the 'generous offer' made in March. Polish diplomacy in those six days was conspicuous by its absence. No effort was made to steal Hitler's high ground from him, to play the diplomatic game in ways which would have wrested the initiative and the headlines away from him. Poland was prepared to be flexible, more so than Colonel Beck was given credit for. But he was the prisoner of the military junta, and they of their vulnerability to their own outraged public opinion. They felt under siege. They had nothing to give; and, the damnable legacy of Munich, they had no confidence in the firmness of their Western allies. Show firmness of purpose and Hitler would recoil, this was their belief. Play any other game and Poland would be lost. Besides, they, and for a vital few days the French, believed in the possibility of internal collapse and upheaval in Germany.

There was some reason for their belief. Hitler's condition for the first day and a half after the shock of August 26 was pitiable. There was talk of a serious breakdown. No one dared approach the Führer without definite orders.[5] Ribbentrop was in an explosive temper. His assurances to Hitler had turned out to be worthless. His prestige with Hitler was at stake. He had told Hitler Britain *would not* fight; and she clearly would. He had told Hitler that Mussolini *would* fight; and he clearly would not. Hitler was in a fury with the Italians. Ciano had warned the British of what had happened at Salzburg. General Roatta, the Italian Military Attaché, came under particular attack. He had learnt of the events of August 25 (from Admiral Canaris) and had, rashly, telephoned the news to General Pariani in Rome, not realizing that every phone call out of the Italian Embassy was monitored by Goering's so-called Research Office (*Forschungsamt*).[6] The King, the Italian army and the Italian diplomats were to blame. Ribbentrop had discovered Goering's ploy with Dahlerus, who was, he told Hitler, an employee of the British Secret Service.[7] Ribbentrop's predecessor as Foreign Minister, Baron von Neurath, now Viceroy over Bohemia and Moravia and always anxious to discredit von Ribbentrop, did his best to fan Hitler's anti-Italian feelings.[8] He could not shake Hitler's view of Mussolini; but he did nothing to restore Hitler's confidence.

The army leadership was loyal, but passively so. There were rumours of an SS putsch,[9] of an attempt to throw responsibility for the events of August 25 on the army's shoulders.[10] Hitler certainly surrounded himself with SS figures – Himmler, Heydrich, Wolff (one of the rising stars of the SS).[11] General Jodl and General Keitel, his two staunchest supporters among the Generals, and Friedrich Gaus of the Foreign Ministry did their best to restore his morale.[12] He uttered terrible threats as to how he would deal with the Wehrmacht leadership if they plotted against him, as the SS leadership no doubt was telling him they were doing.[13]

Over the Saturday and Sunday Hitler seems to have done very little, save to field the communications which flowed to him from Rome and Paris. The last message from Mussolini, with its open request for war materials as a condition of Italian support, required an answer, and that Hitler had duly sent; even though he suspected he was playing a card Mussolini had forced into his hand. The morning of August 26 Mussolini had duly convened his Chiefs of Staff. Ciano had made it clear to them that they must, for once, tell Mussolini the truth about Italy's stocks of war materials. The list was enormous. 'It's enough to kill a bull – if a bull could read it,' Ciano noted.[14] For a war of twelve months Italy needed 6 million tons of coal, 7 million tons of oil, 2 million tons of steel, 1 million tons of timber, and a list of fourteen other raw materials. To defend her war industry she needed the immediate dispatch of 150 batteries of 90 mm anti-aircraft guns. The list reached Berlin early in the afternoon of August 26.[15] Bernardo Attolico compounded its impact by insisting, when he was asked, that delivery should be immediate (*subito*).[16] It took much telephoning backwards and forwards between Rome and Berlin to straighten this out.[17] But as Hitler, after consulting his own military, was forced to explain,[18] Germany could only meet part of Italy's needs, and those only if Italy would provide Germany with manpower. The oil was impossible. He could only spare thirty anti-aircraft batteries. All he asked was that Mussolini should pin down as many French and British troops as possible by propaganda and by troop movements. This Mussolini promised to do, at least for the initial phase of the conflict. But he insisted too on the need for a political solution.[19] Hitler replied by stressing yet again the need for Italy not to show her hand[20] (he also begged Mussolini to send him Italian workers). We shall see later how Mussolini treated the former request.

The letter from Daladier was rather different. Ribbentrop despised and detested Daladier – Bonnet he could handle. Bonnet's twisted ambitions, his deathly fear of war as something which threatened his command of his office, and his whole personality were things Ribbentrop could understand. But Daladier was a front-line soldier, which gave him a means of appealing to Hitler which Ribbentrop could not match. Daladier's letter,[21] ostensibly in reply to the message Hitler had given to Coulondre the previous day, was an emotional evocation of French honour and France's desire not to allow the 'blood of two great peoples to be shed . . . like myself, you were a soldier in the last war – if the blood of France and that of Germany flows again, as it did twenty-five years ago, in a longer and even more murderous war, each of the two peoples will fight with confidence in its own victory, but the certain victors will be the forces of destruction and barbarism.'

Robert Coulondre delivered it at 7 p.m. on that Saturday.[22] Hitler read it, paid homage in a hard dry voice to Daladier's sentiments, and made to dismiss the French Ambassador. Once again Coulondre would not accept so easy a dismissal. He stirred Hitler, but did not shake him. He would have Danzig, Hitler said, and Poland would not cede it. Coulondre phoned Daladier to tell him the appeal had failed.[23] Hitler went in to dinner unwontedly silent and remained so for much of the meal, so Bodenschatz later told Colonel Stehlin.[24] Then he burst out. He should have told the French Ambassador that if the blood of women and children was shed, it would not be his fault. He would not be the first to order the bombardment of the civilian population. (Poles, of course, did not count.)

In the meantime Sir Nevile Henderson had taken the early plane to London. To understand the negotiations that were to follow it is essential to realize that these were entered into on the British side with very little expectation of success, but with the conviction that negotiation should be tried. No Cabinet member was prepared to accept the responsibility of not seeming to be willing to negotiate, to try any opening in the hope that somehow Hitler might be out-manœuvred. They were certainly not prepared to allow Hitler to say that a refusal to negotiate left him no option but war. Such optimism as was to emerge came only where there was ignorance of what had happened on August 25 or where, more commonly, the events of that day were shown as proof that Hitler could be deterred. The Cabinet seems not to have discovered for some days how narrowly war had been avoided and, by implication, the whole intended deceit behind Hitler's interview with Henderson.

There were three openings that seemed worth exploring. The first was that in response to a message from President Roosevelt addressed both to the President of Poland and to Hitler, sent on August 24, suggesting direct negotiation between Poland and Germany, President Mościcky had declared Poland's willingness to do so.[25] The second was that during the exchange between Hitler and Henderson on the afternoon of August 25, Henderson had suggested that as a solution to the persecution of the German minority in Poland of which Hitler was making so much, Poland and Germany should exchange populations as Turkey and Greece had in 1923. Since the whole aim of the interview for Hitler was to confuse the British and, if possible, get Henderson out of Berlin before the German attack on Poland, still then timed for 4.30 a.m. the following morning, Hitler had agreed to examine the question. The third idea, born in the Foreign Office, was that the minorities issue might be defused by the use of neutral observers who could perhaps report more accurately than Goebbels' press what was actually happening.

To understand the negotiations, it is essential also to understand that three separate plots were in progress. The first of them was a new attempt by Hitler to produce the favourable diplomatic line-up he usually demanded as a preliminary to each new military adventure. To isolate Poland, to drive a wedge, or wedges, between Britain, France and Poland was the aim. A second sub-plot involved Goering and an unwitting Dahlerus, and its main aim was to destroy Ribbentrop and show Hitler that Goering could bring about a British distraction where Ribbentrop had failed. The third sub-plot, already mentioned, involved Weizsäcker and Attolico, with unwitting support in Paris, in two ploys, the one to bring the Poles to negotiate, the other to draw a new offer of mediation out of Mussolini. Equivocal as always, Weizsäcker's encouragement of pressure on Poland was also playing Hitler's game. The evidence that he knew of the denouement Hitler was planning is, however, lacking.

In the meantime there was Henderson in London and Dahlerus, bursting with the conviction that he alone could circumvent Ribbentrop and get to Hitler directly. On August 26 Halifax gave Dahlerus what he described later as 'a platitudinous message' about Britain's desire for peace, and Dahlerus flew off to Berlin.[26] The message said in effect that Britain wanted to find a satisfactory solution; that it was vital to avoid any further inflammation of the atmosphere on both sides; that the British were urging the Poles to exercise control and they hoped Goering would do the same on the German side; and that the essential thing was to have a few days of inactivity.[27] With Dahlerus safely out of the way the Cabinet could get down to the business, on Saturday, of approving a reply to Hitler's message. It had already been exhaustively discussed at No. 10 Downing Street on the evening of August 25. Joseph Kennedy, the US Ambassador, had been called in to the discussion at one moment.[28] Halifax had worked on a draft overnight from 11.30 p.m. to 1 a.m.

On the morning of August 26, while they waited for Henderson to arrive from Berlin, R. A. Butler and Sir Horace Wilson took over the work of drafting. Halifax, Chamberlain and Sir Alex Cadogan sat in the garden of No. 10 'feeling pretty heavy-hearted'. Henderson's arrival added very little to what they knew. Halifax had to field enquiries from the French and Polish Ambassadors, and from the Romanian Minister, M. Tilea, with his rather different Hungarian obsessions. Mischief-making in the press over Henderson's return (the man smelt of Munich, unfortunately) informed their enquiries. Halifax had no problem re-assuring the Frenchman. Raczyński, the Pole, was not so easily assuaged. Tilea was his usual self. The Cabinet met finally at 6 p.m.[29] It was generally agreed that however little confidence one had in Hitler's promises – the offer to guarantee the British empire was variously regarded as either impudent or insolent – a reply would have to be sent and that the draft reply before the Cabinet was unacceptable. Above all the Cabinet was determined not to be rushed into anything, least of all over a weekend.

It met again on Sunday at 3 p.m., after two postponements. The second of these was due to the return of Dahlerus from Berlin. Dahlerus had arrived in Berlin at about 7 p.m. on the Saturday evening. He was taken to Karinhall, Goering's country abode, only to find that Goering had left by his private train *en route* for his secret Luftwaffe HQ near Berlin. Dahlerus and his escort eventually caught up with Goering at a small railway station named Friedrichsweide. After a heated discussion in which Goering told Dahlerus that Germany would be ready to attack Poland on August 30/1,[30] Dahlerus handed over the platitudinous message from Halifax which, said Dahlerus, made a deep impression on him. Now Goering had something to play against Ribbentrop. He did not realize that the news of Dahlerus's imminent arrival had been passed by Lufthansa to the Foreign Ministry and to Ribbentrop earlier that evening.[31] Goering and Dahlerus drove to Berlin. The Reichs Chancellery was in darkness. The Führer, a night owl who rarely went to bed before dawn, had dismissed his staff and gone disconsolately to bed.

Goering hurried in to wake him. Dahlerus returned to his hotel to wait. From there he telephoned his impressions to the British Embassy. When Dahlerus was summoned to the Chancellery some two hours later, the Reichs Chancellery was again ablaze with lights and full of people.

The conversation with Hitler which ensued[32] contained some somewhat bizarre elements. Dahlerus, an engineer who had managed a number of companies in Britain, talked of the British working classes, of which he claimed to have been a member, with all the insight and enthusiasm of a Swedish engineer graduate of substantial private means. Hitler boasted of the technical superiority of German weapons – then he suddenly was taken by a kind of hysterical seizure. If there is war, he shouted, 'I will build U-boats, build U-boats, build U-boats. . . . I will build aircraft, build aircraft, build aircraft, and I will destroy my enemies.' There was more in this vein. Eventually he calmed down and a six-point proposal emerged: a pact with Britain; Germany to get Danzig and the Corridor, Poland a free port in Danzig, a corridor to Gdynia and territory around it; a guarantee for Poland's frontiers; an agreement about Germany's colonies; guarantees for the German minority; and a German pledge to defend the British empire.

With this message Dahlerus sped back to his hotel, rang his business friend, Charles Spencer, in London and hot-footed it to Tempelhof airport. A German plane took him to London. He arrived at Croydon airport at noon, where Spencer and his colleagues from the Soonke Nissen Koog meeting were waiting to greet him, and was whisked away to London, the Foreign Office and Downing Street. Halifax noted that 'he did not really add much to what we know'; but taken with MI6 reports of dissension among the German military, Dahlerus's information added to the Cabinet's belief that things were by no means hopeless. Dahlerus insisted that Henderson stay one more day in London while he returned to Berlin. He and Sir Alexander Cadogan cobbled together a three-point message to Hitler: Britain was anxious to reach an understanding with Hitler; Britain would honour its guarantees to Poland; Britain recommended direct negotiations between Germany and Poland, any agreement to be guaranteed by the powers. With this Dahlerus returned to Berlin, leaving behind him a Foreign Secretary, a Cabinet and a Permanent Under Secretary, none of whom took him entirely seriously. The real work was going into the letter which Sir Nevile Henderson was to take back to Berlin the following day.

The main effect of the combination of Henderson's return from Berlin and Dahlerus's first shuttle was to drive all other proposals into limbo. The idea of an exchange of populations had been taken up assiduously by the French Ambassador to Warsaw on August 26. Beck and his Under Secretary, Count Szembek, had found it interesting enough to suggest that the French raise the issue in Berlin and had briefed their man in Berlin, Lipski, to expect it. The British Ambassador had suggested enlisting papal intervention. But neither Bonnet nor the Vatican seems to have followed it up,[33] perhaps because of the cold water poured on the idea by Charles Corbin, the French Ambassador in London. Nor did the idea of neutral observers fare any better. There remained direct negotiations between Germany and Poland. It was on this that Hitler's new plot was to turn.

This 2 a.m. *rencontre* with Dahlerus seems to have begun the work of restoring Hitler's confidence. Sunday had seen Hitler gradually recovering from the depths of the previous day. In part this was the result of the effort he put into drafting a reply to Daladier's letter. Matching Daladier's rhetoric with his own, reciting once again the catalogue of allegations of Polish persecutions, so often repeated that by now he had come implicitly to believe in them, had done much to restore his spirits.[34] Mussolini had promised him to fulfil his wishes 100 per cent (*cento per cento*).[35] Ribbentrop had done his puny best to keep matters on the boil, telling Coulondre matters were even more acute than before,[36] and telephoning Mackensen in Rome[37] to scotch any rumours that Attolico might have been spreading of an improvement in the situation. At 5.30 that evening Hitler was sufficiently recovered to address a collection of Reichstag deputies originally summoned to hear his justification of the attack on Poland and now fobbed off with a reception at the Reichs Chancellery.[38] To them he gave the impression that he was still hesitating between his minimum demand, Danzig and the Corridor, and his maximum, whatever the military situation would permit. To the party faithful, anti-Communist to a man, he defended the Soviet pact as an alliance with Satan to expel the devil. War is difficult, perhaps fruitless, he said. It would be brutal. So long as he lived Germany would never capitulate. His audience applauded on cue; but with no volume or enthusiasm. Nor were all present very impressed.

That same evening, August 27, Dahlerus returned to Berlin. He had spent the afternoon, while the Cabinet was meeting, in the Foreign Office, alternately being lectured by Sir Alexander Cadogan,[39] to whom Dahlerus was an unwelcome and unnecessary distraction, and hiding in an adjoining room while Cadogan denied knowing anything of him to a worried French Ambassador, half-convinced that the British were doing another deal with Germany behind their allies' backs. 'In his cultivated and sincere way' Cadogan told Dahlerus that Germany's 'gangster policy would have to cease'. Britain would have to 'present her demands and proposals in such a way as to preclude' the continued use of methods already introduced by Hitler. Until the armies were demobilized and the atmosphere had calmed down, no negotiations on outstanding questions between Britain and Germany would be possible. Chamberlain himself had put the crux of the British dilemma to Dahlerus, when he had asked 'how far one dared trust in the assurances of promises' given by Hitler 'in the light of the occurrences of the last twelve months'.

Dahlerus reached Berlin at midnight on August 27/8, and called on Goering at his private address. He felt ill at ease. The 'message' he had brought back was, thanks to Cadogan, redolent of British distrust of Hitler. Hitler's 'generous offer' had been variously stigmatized as 'ridiculous' and 'making no appeal to the British Government'. He does not seem to have been aware that the Cabinet, to whom his existence was disclosed that day, regarded him simply as an auxiliary arm, a punctuation, a means of testing the temperature of the water for their main negotiation, which was through Henderson. Nor was he to know that Goering's welcome for Lord Halifax's message, when taken with information from the Secret Intelligence Service,[40] whose own contact man with dissidents in the German army had travelled back with Dahlerus to Germany,[41] was seen as evidence of German weakening.[42]

The conversation with Goering, however, went well. Dahlerus was not allowed to see Hitler. Goering preferred to see Hitler alone to persuade him to issue a guarantee of Poland. From the Reichs Chancellery Goering rang Dahlerus at his hotel, at 1.30 a.m. He asked a question. Did the British idea of an understanding imply a treaty or an alliance? He said that Britain's guarantee of Poland was respected, as was the British desire to see direct negotiations between Germany and Poland. The idea of an international guarantee of Poland was also accepted. Highly gratified, Dahlerus hurried around to the British Embassy, got the Counsellor and, in Henderson's absence, Chargé d'affaires, Sir George Ogilvie-Forbes, who was not expecting him until 8 a.m.,[43] out of bed, and composed a message, the first of several he was to cause to be sent to London that day, reporting on the success he believed Goering to be having with Hitler.[44]

To understand the real nature of the success one has to turn to the German military planners. At 8 a.m. that same morning, General von Brauchitsch, the Commander-in-Chief of the German Army, met with General Halder, his Chief of Staff, to discuss the proposal that the army groups should attack Poland on August 31. At 3.22 that same afternoon

Brauchitsch telephoned Halder from the Reichs Chancellery. The attack on Poland was to start on September 1. The intention was to force Poland into an unfavourable position for negotiations and so achieve the maximum objective. Britain was said to be disposed to consider the comprehensive offer. Another report said that the decision as to whether Poland's vital interests were threatened lay with Britain (not Poland). 'Plan: we will demand Danzig, corridor through Corridor, and plebiscite. England will accept, Poland probably not. *Wedge between them!*' So Halder noted down Brauchitsch's message. 'Wait for Henderson.'

Dahlerus had brought Hitler the possibility of the opening he needed, an opening he proposed to exploit to isolate Poland for the killing-stroke. He had in fact described the technique he proposed to use two years earlier, speaking to senior party officials in 1937.[45] 'I will not', he said, 'use force to bring an opponent to battle. I do not use the word battle, although I wish battle; rather I say, canniness help me [*Klugheit hilft mir*] to manœuvre you into the corner so that you cannot thrust at me, and then you take the thrust in your own heart.'

The plot was made clearer to Halder the following day:[46] 'Basic principles: Raise a barrage of demographic and democratic demands. Plebiscite within six months, under international supervision. Those opting for Germany must remain German citizens; the same holds for the Poles. Poles will not want Germans in their territory.

30.8 Poles in Berlin
31.8 Blow up [i.e. break negotiations]
 1.9 Use of force.'

Its essence was the use of British pressure to secure a Polish negotiator in Berlin on August 30, the break of negotiations so as to put the blame on the Polish side and then, with the aid of the stage-managed incidents originally arranged for August 26, to justify the all-out attack on Poland to be launched at 4.30 a.m. on September 1.

Dahlerus's two visits had given Hitler the expectation both that Britain would secure a Polish negotiator in Berlin and, less certainly, that if the plot worked, Britain would be taken by surprise and fail to support the Poles. This was the chance Goering had perceived in the first message from Lord Halifax which, however platitudinous as it may have seemed to Halifax and his colleagues, enabled him to override Ribbentrop's deliberate refusal to keep the line to London open. The third point in the second message, on direct German-Polish talks, opened the prospect of British insistence that Poland would continue to be bound by President Mościcky's undertaking and enter into the German trap. Small wonder Goering would not let Dahlerus near Hitler or the Reichs Chancellery on his second visit. Hitler was under increasing pressure from his military advisers, who, hoping to panic him into a false move, insisted that the armies could not be long kept on the edge of the Polish frontiers.[47] Either they would have to attack or they would have to be withdrawn. It was that which imposed so tight a timetable on Hitler – that and Hitler's own calculation of the very limited campaigning time before the onset of the Polish autumn rains made a war of movement impossible.

There were, however, a number of things on the British side which Hitler either did not know, or to which he had shut his mind. The first was that in the effort to impress Dahlerus with the need for immediate British action, and possibly to mislead the Poles, Goering was giving away more military information than was strictly necessary. In the course of his stay in Berlin on August 28 and of his visits to Goering's headquarters, Dahlerus was told that the German army would be poised to attack Poland on the night of August 30/1. He was also shown a map of the planned German line of attack which covered the plan of attack of the whole of Army Group North and of the 14th Army in the south.[48] The major spearhead in the south, the attack by the 10th Army from Silesia, was not, however, mentioned. This news was passed on to Warsaw that evening by Lord Halifax.[49] Kennard saw Colonel Beck and gave him the news that same evening.[50]

Nor did Hitler realize that the astuter brains of the Foreign Office would spot much of the trap that he was laying, together with the probability that, once he had sprung it, Stalin would join him in exploiting it.[51] The Foreign Office was, however, wrong on one point. Having ruled out any question of not supporting Poland if she was attacked by German forces, they had not divined that Hitler's plot depended on his still believing it would be possible so to manœuvre things that Britain would not honour the Polish alliance.

Indeed, this was Hitler's blind spot. To be just, it was one shared by some Frenchmen,[52] by many Americans including, as has been seen, the Secretary of State, Cordell Hull, by many of Chamberlain's own opponents in Britain and by those sources of intelligence on British politics on which Stalin depended. So greatly had British opinion changed since Munich, not merely in the streets and in Parliament, but even within the Cabinet, that no British Government could have failed to support the obligation to Poland and stayed in office; the events of September 2 in the Commons and the Cabinet, as will be seen, were to prove that British opinion thoroughly understood that by the guarantee to Poland, the issue of Danzig and the Corridor, as 'faraway' and as unknown as the Sudetenland, had become a test case: the issue was not the justice or injustice of the status quo but the legitimacy or illegitimacy of the manner in which Hitler chose to alter it. This Hitler seemed incapable of grasping. What the Foreign Office advisers feared was that Hitler would content himself with two bites at the cherry, as he had with Czechoslovakia at Munich and in March 1939, the minimum solution of which he had spoken to the Reichstag deputies on August 27. In actuality, Dahlerus had unwittingly persuaded Hitler that he could go for the maximum solution. In doing so he had made inevitable the war that he was trying to prevent.

Henderson arrived in Berlin at 9.30 p.m. He put his visit to the Reichs Chancellery off for half an hour, ostensibly so that the German translation of the message he was bringing with him could be completed, actually, as he betrayed by his phone message to Coulondre, so that he could talk with his French colleague first.[53] According to Dahlerus,[54] the staff of the British Embassy in Berlin apparently believed that the only way the Germans could listen in to their telephone conversations was by a microphone in their building. Whether true or not, many of them, particularly Sir Nevile Henderson, were appallingly indiscreet in their use of the telephone. He told Coulondre that he was still deafened by the motors of the aeroplane. He was, however, as Coulondre noted with ironic satisfaction when he met him, still dapper and jaunty enough to have preserved that morning's carnation in his buttonhole.[55] It sheds an odd light on Henderson's relationship with Lord Halifax that he should have pretended later that he spent the half-hour before seeing Hitler over dinner and a bottle of champagne.[56]

The letter Sir Nevile Henderson brought with him[57] had gone through a great many drafts and two sessions of the Cabinet.[58] It largely dismissed the issues of Anglo-German relations as matters that could be taken up once there had been a settlement of those issues that lay between Germany and Poland. Whether or not that was satisfactory would turn, so the note remarked, 'on the nature of the settlement and the manner by which it is to be reached. On these points', it continued, Hitler's message was 'silent'. It proposed direct German-Polish discussions, the safeguarding of Poland's essential interests, an immediate cessation of the German press and propaganda campaign and the Polish counter-campaign launched in the last few days,[59] and an international guarantee for the settlement, if reached. 'Failure to reach' such a settlement, the note concluded, 'would ruin the hopes of a better understanding between Germany and Great Britain, would bring the two countries into conflict, and might well plunge the whole world into war. Such an outcome would be a calamity without parallel in history.'

The British note pleased the French.[60] Colonel Beck, for Poland, thought it excellent.[61] Attolico, the Italian Ambassador in Berlin, reporting on it to Rome, called it 'very friendly and convincing',[62] a phrase that the German Research Office picked out when it deciphered Attolico's telegram.[63] Hitler, playing soft man on August 28 so as to make the 'hard man role' he proposed to play the following day the more effective, allowed Henderson to lecture and hector him. He was surprisingly relaxed.[64] He pretended to find the document interesting, and for much of the following day Dahlerus was fed with tid-bits of information to keep up the illusion.[65] On the morning of August 29, therefore, a mood of relaxation spread out from the British Embassy, embracing Coulondre, Attolico and all who called on the Embassy for information. This mood spread to London, where the Home Secretary, Sir Samuel Hoare, found Horace Wilson 'very optimistic'.[66] In reality Hitler was preparing his thunderbolt: his military was making everything ready for war on September 1,[67] and more German troops were moving into Slovakia.[68]

After seeing Henderson, Hitler had gone to bed in a mood of great optimism, mainly as a result of Dahlerus's reportage. Goering said to him, 'we should stop playing *va banque*.' 'I have played *va banque* all my life,' replied Hitler.[69] When he rose, however, his mood was very different. His entourage found Hitler very difficult all that day,[70] August 29, 'unimaginably nervy, edgy and sharp', violently critical of the German army and the General Staff. 'Frederick the Great would turn in his grave if he could see the generals today.' Then he would fall into self-pity. He only wanted to liquidate the unjust conditions of Poland's relations with Germany. He did not want war with anyone else. If they were so stupid as to join in, that was their responsibility and they must be destroyed. All day his mood swung between outbursts of Anglophobia and a determination on war at all costs,[71] but he let it be known to his staff that the British note was conciliatory and that in relation to a major war Britain was 'soft'. This was the message conveyed by General von Brauchitsch to Halder.[72] State Secretary von Weizsäcker, watching this from the Foreign Ministry, bitterly noted Ribbentrop's contribution to all this. 'Whenever a constructive idea for a political solution arose, Ribbentrop knocked it on the head,' he confided to his private diary. There was a tendency towards a heroic death à la Wagner, a *Nibelungentod*.[73]

One such move had come from the Poles already. On August 27, Prince Lubomirski, the Counsellor at the Polish Embassy, together with the Polish Consul General in Berlin, had approached Peter Kleist, the expert on Poland and Russia in Ribbentrop's personal office, with a proposal for mediation.[74] Colonel Beck, they said, needed time to calm Polish national feeling. Given this he felt he could arrive at an acceptable settlement. There was an offer of good services from the monarchs of Belgium and the Netherlands. Mussolini's messages to Hitler constantly emphasized the opportunities for negotiation and urged acceptance of the opening offered by the British approach. On August 29, Colonel Beck held a meeting at his private house to discuss who would represent Poland in the negotiations in Berlin.[75] The memory of the visits paid to Berchtesgaden in February 1938 by Schuschnigg, the last Austrian Premier, and by President Hácha of Czechoslovakia to Berlin in March 1939, hung over him. He consulted the President and Marshal Smigly-Rydz by telephone. There should be no negotiations in Berlin; a town on the frontier or a railway carriage close to it were preferable. Various names were suggested. Eventually Józef Lipski, the Polish Ambassador in Berlin, was chosen as the Polish negotiator.

The Poles, however, took one further step. Throughout the days since Forster's declaration of Danzig's independence they had been steadily recalling men to their regiments. On August 29, in view of the warnings that were coming to them from Britain and from their own intelligence, it was decided to declare general mobilization. That afternoon, Count Szembek summoned the British and French Ambassadors. His hands shaking slightly, he read them an official note from his Government. In view of the increasing danger of German attack and the very precise information the British had given them, the Polish Government had irrevocably decided on general mobilization.[76] Sir Howard Kennard pointed out, very reasonably, that this was hardly the moment, when Hitler had accepted negotiation, to make public a move which was normally regarded as an immediate precedent to war. Léon Noël supported him. The process of general mobilization, it emerged, involved the private circulation of notices to all those to be recalled to the colours and the placarding of the public streets with notices. After talking with Beck, Szembek agreed to delay publication of the communiqué and the placarding of the streets. Beck said it would make no difference. This was not, of course, the position he took with Kennard, when he pressed that evening for the earliest possible news of Hitler's reply to the British note.[77]

The Poles had every reason to prepare for war. Conditions in Danzig were getting totally out of hand. The populations of the villages on the Danzig-Polish frontier were all evacuated by August 27. The Senate confiscated Polish-owned stocks of wheat, petrol and salt.[78] Two

hundred Polish shipworkers were sacked unpaid and their identification papers confiscated.[79] There were incidents on the frontiers every
day. Food was rationed, the newspapers full of sensational reports.[80]
The postal and rail services deteriorated noticeably. When the Poles sent
two officials to negotiate an agreement with their opposite numbers on
an improvement in the railway services, the Gestapo arrested them as
soon as they had left the conference chamber.[81] While Forster postured
and the Danzig storm-troopers could be seen everywhere, the general
population awoke to the realization that it was being treated as a small
chip in a game of poker.[82] And the *Schleswig-Holstein* continued to lie in
the harbour, the naval assault troops sweltering in the summer heat
below decks. Its commander confided to Burckhardt, the League of
Nations High Commissioner, 'I have a terrible duty, which I cannot
reconcile with my conscience.'[83] Burckhardt contented himself with
refusing Forster's invitation to celebrate the visit at the Danziger
Rathaus. In the meantime the frontier incidents, the acts of sabotage and
raids by 'freedom fighters', increased, in the effort to provoke a dossier
of incidents to be used by German propaganda.

At 7.15 p.m. Sir Nevile Henderson returned to the Reichs Chancellery to be given Hitler's reply.[84] It was already clear that, the cancer
from which he was to die upon him, he was not standing up well to the
tension. Von Hassell, the former German Ambassador to Rome, who
was to die for his part in the conspiracy against Hitler that so narrowly
failed to overthrow him in 1944, called at the Embassy at midday and
found him 'exhausted and under strain – though not entirely
pessimistic'.[85] Henderson had, however, persuaded himself that
Goering's influence on Hitler could be counted on to neutralize that of
Ribbentrop, whom he loathed and detested.

Dahlerus had seen Henderson in the late morning. Henderson
obviously resented Dahlerus's intrusion on the scene.[86] He also warned
Dahlerus against relying on Goering, who had lied frequently to him.
Dahlerus, like von Hassell, noted Henderson's nervous exhaustion and
the profound scepticism and worry with which he approached the
forthcoming meeting with Hitler.[87] He did, however, expect to pick up
some threads which a skilful diplomatist could embroider into a negotiation. He encountered Hitler in his 'hard man' role. As Weizsäcker
noted,[88] 'by evening every opinion again fully for war. Poland would
be defeated in two months, then we will make a great peace conference
with the West.' Henderson found Hitler in his most raucous mode. The
note which Hitler handed over was itself a kind of scream of rage, of
defiance, not of pain. The rage was directed against the Poles for their
blockade of Danzig, for the 'barbaric acts of maltreatment, which cry to

Heaven, against the German minority', which were 'unbearable' to a great power. Germany could no longer be a 'passive onlooker'. The German Government no longer shared 'as a matter of course' the British view that 'these grave differences can be resolved by way of direct negotiations'. But, though sceptical as to the prospects of a successful outcome, they were prepared to accept the British proposal and enter into direct negotiations, 'as a proof of the sincerity of Germany's intentions' – they never had any intention of attacking Poland's vital interests or questioning the existence of an independent Polish state. But Germany demanded Danzig, the Corridor and the safeguarding of German minorities in Poland. They would accept the dispatch of a Polish emissary to Berlin with full powers. He must arrive on Wednesday, August 30, that is, within twenty-four hours.

By his own account[89] Henderson lost his temper and shouted back at Hitler. This sounded, he said, unpleasantly like an ultimatum. Taken aback, Hitler and Ribbentrop denied this. The time limit is kept short, Hitler said, because of the danger of hostility breaking out at any minute as a result of some new provocation.[90] He accused the British of a total disregard for the Germans murdered in Poland. This provoked Henderson to more shouting. The interview ended with a welter of Hitlerian outpourings on the subject of his longing for friendship with Britain.

Henderson's return to the Embassy abruptly dispelled whatever remained of the mood of euphoria of that morning. Alerted by a despairing Ogilvie-Forbes, Dahlerus rushed to see Goering.[91] He was treated to a replay of the scene Hitler had acted out for Henderson; Goering added some variants of his own. He honestly believed the Poles were going to sabotage any chance of an agreement. The pact with the Soviet Union had been ratified (this was untrue) and Soviet forces were concentrating on the Polish frontier. Hitler was to propose a plebiscite for the Corridor under international supervision. And he added that Nevile Henderson's unbalanced behaviour in shouting at Hitler had incensed him and destroyed the good feeling towards Britain. Goering may well have felt that the Führer had overplayed his hand and driven Britain back into support of Poland. He ended by asking Dahlerus to fly once more to London. Dahlerus left at 5 a.m. on August 30, arriving in the Foreign Office at 10.30 a.m.

The state of mind, the deep depression and disturbance, in which Sir Nevile Henderson returned to his Embassy can be seen in the highly unprofessional sequence of disjointed and disorganized telegrams which began to arrive in London from 10.30 p.m. on August 29 onwards. Sir Alexander Cadogan digested them in the Foreign Office, then took them to No. 10 Downing Street to mull them over with Halifax and Chamberlain. They looked pretty bad at first; but the arrival after midnight of the full text of Hitler's note (which lacked the dreadful aura of elemental and unbalanced fury and terror conveyed by Hitler at the actual meeting) did not seem so bad.[92] Halifax, who had telegraphed Henderson's first summary of the meeting to Kennard in Warsaw with the comment that 'it did not close every door',[93] called it misleading when he saw the full text.[94] Further telegrams followed from London to Berlin at 2 a.m.[95] and to Rome a quarter of an hour later.[96] That to Rome envisaged proposing a military standstill; that to Berlin promised a reply by the afternoon and pointed out that to expect Britain to produce a Polish representative in Berlin within twelve hours was entirely unreasonable. Henderson, who could not bring himself to admit to 'shouting at the top of his voice at Hitler' until 2.30 a.m.,[97] had already read over Hitler's note to the Polish Ambassador, Józef Lipski, before midnight.[98] At 4 a.m. he rang Ribbentrop to give him Lord Halifax's message.[99] Both Lipski and Kennard from Warsaw said that the time limit was impossible.

Most of the telegrams and the first draft of a British note in reply to Hitler, though carrying Halifax's signature, were the work of Cadogan and the young Ivone Kirkpatrick, who as Permanent Under Secretary in 1956 was to live through much worse during the Suez crisis. Halifax went to bed. Chamberlain found time to tell the French Ambassador, Charles Corbin, what had happened.[100] It was, said Chamberlain, characteristic of Hitler that after all the threats and menaces, he still had not actually done anything decisive. Every day which went by was a day gained to safeguard peace. Only Hitler, he concluded, could imagine that to reconcile herself with Germany, Britain would embark on a general conference without regard for the country to which she had given a guarantee. The ease with which the Soviet pact had been concluded had impaired his judgment.

The gloom in London was not matched by the reactions in Rome and Paris. Whereas Coulondre learnt of Hitler's note directly from Henderson on his return from seeing Hitler, and realized at once that it was unacceptable and intended to be so ('more like a diktat imposed on a conquered country than an agreement to negotiate with a sovereign state', he commented),[101] M. Bonnet dismissed this and concentrated on Hitler's acceptance of direct conversations.[102] This could not be rejected. Sir Percy Loraine encountered much the same reaction from Ciano, when he saw him at midnight to convey Henderson's first summary of Hitler's note.[103] Ciano drew added satisfaction from his belief that Italian action had brought Hitler to accept direct negotiations with the Poles.[104] Attolico had seen Hitler immediately after Henderson, but Hitler's terms were much the same; however, he did not mention a time limit.[105] Attolico knew by 9.55 p.m. of Henderson's advice to Lipski, and of Coulondre's reluctant support for it. Coulondre noted an air of euphoria at the Italian Embassy on August 30.[106]

It was in this that the particular canniness (*Klugheit*) of Hitler's manœuvre lay. Once he had so ostentatiously yielded to international pressure to open direct conversations with Poland, having refused it for so long, it became virtually impossible for the British and others not to accept this and equally difficult for the Poles, no matter what they thought of Hitler's motives, to resist the pressure that London, Paris and Rome could be expected to exert upon them. Where the 'sting' went wrong, however, was in the impossible time schedule that Hitler set, and which his revised military timetable had imposed upon him.

Hitler was later to rail that the slowness with which Britain and Poland reacted to his 'generous proposal' (even the act of making a proposal rated as generosity in the vocabulary of Hitler's court) proved that they had no intention of taking it seriously. One could fly from Warsaw to Berlin in an hour and a half, he said to Henderson.[107] Given the necessary time for enciphering and deciphering of telegrams, and the late hour at which he received Henderson, his timetable hardly allowed time for his proposals even to reach Warsaw, let alone for any serious pressure to be exercised on the Polish Government by Britain and France, still less for the Poles to be convinced or bullied within a few hours into producing an emissary with plenipotentiary powers. Given that his hopes of isolating Poland depended on a degree of resentment being generated in Warsaw by the exercise of such pressure, and in London and Paris by the necessity of generating it, his insistence on a quite unrealistic timetable argues rather that he had already consciously accepted British and French intervention and was only going through the motions of trying to prevent it or was experiencing an unconscious compulsion to raise the odds against his success; it was this last which led Weizsäcker and von Hassell to talk of his Wagnerian impulses towards a Nibelung's death.

Goering does not seem to have shared this impulse. Both at his midnight *rencontre* with Dahlerus and in reply to Dahlerus's enquiries by telephone from London on August 30, he did his best to tone down the time limit and the necessity for a Polish plenipotentiary to appear. The time was important, but the Führer's proposals were merely a *Diskussionsvorlage*, a basis for discussion. But it was essential that someone should come from Warsaw to fetch the proposals; Lipski would not do.[108]

It was at this point that someone (who is unclear) drew a new red herring across the trail. During the day a German emissary, representing himself as being in touch with the military opposition to Hitler, came to the British Military Attaché with a story that Hitler had forced the German General Staff to alter their plan of attack on Poland.[109] General Halder had resigned and been replaced by General von Reichenau. Hitler had had a nervous breakdown and was under medical care. The General Staff wanted to stage a coup against Hitler, but needed to know that Ribbentrop's view that Britain would force Poland to yield Danzig and would back Germany's claims to a more satisfactory eastern frontier was untrue. A second military informant[110] gave rather a different picture, one of widespread dissatisfaction among the people, in the Nazi party and in the army, but warned that an army coup should not be expected.

The military and civilian opposition to Hitler at this time was in fact in a state of total disarray. Frau von Brauchitsch, the first, divorced wife of the Commander-in-Chief of the Army, warned von Hassell that her husband could not be relied upon; under the influence of her successor, a rabid admirer of Nazism and Hitler, he had become heavily involved with Nazism.[111] The second of the two informants has been tentatively identified[112] as Ewald von Kleist-Schmenzin. The first, it has been suggested, may have been Colonel Böhm-Tettelbach or Captain von Koerber, both retired officers who were involved at various stages in the military opposition to Hitler.[113] All of these are unlikely identifications. Von Kleist-Schmenzin was an East Prussian land-owner, a dedicated anti-Nazi and a devout Lutheran, who had, at risk to his life, travelled to London in the summer of 1938 to warn the British of Hitler's plans for war on Czechoslovakia. The two others had taken similar risks then and later. The first anonymous informant was a liar, possibly an *agent provocateur*, and was certainly fishing for information on Britain's war plans. In November 1939, a similar series of approaches from persons representing themselves as part of a military conspiracy against Hitler led to the two heads of the main British intelligence centre operating against Germany being lured to the German-Dutch frontier at Venlo and kidnapped across it. The perpetrators at that time were the secret intelligence wing of the SS, the *Sicherheitsdienst (SD)*. This episode has the same fishy odour about it. The SS, especially Heydrich, would have welcomed a chance of discrediting Ribbentrop and strengthening the hold on Hitler it had built up since August 26.

The mobilization notices were going up in the streets of Warsaw, Lódź, Cracow and the other Polish towns as Dahlerus was ushered into

No. 10 Downing Street. Kirkpatrick came over to see Halifax at his private house in Eaton Square at 9.20 a.m. with the result of his night's work. More discussion at the Foreign Office followed; then Halifax and Cadogan went on to Downing Street to meet Chamberlain. Dahlerus's report raised the issue of a plebiscite. While the Cabinet met to approve the draft British reply, Cadogan took Dahlerus over to the Foreign Office to phone Goering. The Cabinet made very little trouble over approving the reply which had kept Kirkpatrick up so late. There was none of the false optimism of the previous day. The general view was that Hitler was blustering, but 'the door was not shut.'[114] Hitler was trying to stage another Munich; but he was not going to be allowed to get away with it. Chamberlain himself spoke particularly strongly on this point. 'This definitely represented part of the old technique,' he said. 'It was essential that we should make it clear that we were not going to yield on this point.'

This last point carried a great deal of weight in the Cabinet's deliberations and elsewhere in Britain. That there was a good deal of dissatisfaction in Germany at this time struck a great many observers. The crisis of August 25 had been allowed to build up without any warning, so as not to alert the Poles and to preserve the element of strategic surprise. Severe rationing of food, petrol and other vital commodities had been introduced on August 27. German holiday-makers had had long and anxious journeys home. The filling stations had been low in petrol and long, disorderly queues at the pumps were the order of the day. Senior party members increased the discontent by their inbuilt propensity to jump to the head of all such queues. Nor, save in parts of East Prussia, Pomerania and Silesia, was the German public very easy to agitate against the Poles. Had war broken out on August 26, the disciplined German population might have accepted all this. But it had not; and many of them did not. British, French and other Consulates observed and reported, to the encouragement of the hawks at home and, in so far as Hitler heard of it, to the further detriment of his temper. In the meantime the German press was full of ideas of an Anglo-German entente; the Italian press was praising France; the Russo-German Pact was not ratified. A new Government in Japan, one hostile to the Axis, had been appointed. And above all, there was continuing news of dissension, anti-Nazi demonstrations and so on, in Germany. In Düsseldorf, a crowd was pulling down Nazi posters.[115] And the German military was getting restive.

The British note was meant to be firm and sharp. It was, however, to be preceded by a private message from Chamberlain to Hitler. This was delivered by Adrian Holman, the First Secretary of the British

Embassy, to the Reichs Chancellery at 5.30 p.m. that afternoon, August 30.[116] Its main import was to ask for German assurances that frontier incidents would be avoided and to say that pressure was being brought on Warsaw to do the same. That pressure was contained in Halifax's telegrams sent to Warsaw at 5.30 and 7.00 p.m. that day.[117] The first simply executed the promises contained in Chamberlain's note to Hitler. The second was to be executed at the same time as Henderson handed over the full British reply to Hitler. It was very carefully composed to contain no more pressure than the fact that it was being sent at all, though it emphasized the importance of not giving the Germans any opportunity of putting the blame for a conflict on Poland. It added, on Dahlerus's authority, that the British believed Hitler's note of the previous night not to be Hitler's last word. And it invited Beck's views and comments.

At much the same time Henderson was telephoned directly from the Foreign Office to warn him of the instructions that were on their way. The call, which Goering's *Forschungsamt* duly recorded, showed a desire to purge Sir Nevile Henderson of his belated feelings of guilt over his unprofessional behaviour in shouting at Hitler.[118] Henderson should not get so worked up about it, his caller said. The Prime Minister, who had looked into the matter, fully understood. He had after all been there himself. People were quite unperturbed in London. They thought they were on the right track now. The Germans really could not expect to succeed again by summoning people, handing them documents and having them sign on the dotted line. All that was over now. Berlin must come to realize this just as much as London. With that the caller lapsed into circumlocutions.

Whatever the attitude of the British Embassy staff in Berlin, the Foreign Office was well aware that anything said to the Embassy on the international line would be overheard by others than its legitimate audience. Indeed Halifax warned Henderson to use the telephone more discreetly less than twenty-four hours later.[119] Henderson's caller was, therefore, deliberately conveying two messages to the listening Germans. Henderson still had the complete confidence and support of the Foreign Office and the Prime Minister. They were, moreover, not going to settle for Hitler's latest technique of ultimata which were not ultimata, but still had a time limit. The most significant part of Henderson's instructions was sent in code: he was on no account to be drawn into discussing Anglo-German alliances, a point which, at the last minute, Robert Vansittart had insisted be spelt out.[120]

The actual text of the British reply was sent to Berlin at 7.40 p.m. *en clair*. This was the normal practice with documents to be handed over to foreign governments, so as to avoid providing hostile cryptographers with easy clues with which to break British codes and ciphers. It was thus safely in Hitler's hands well before Henderson arrived with the official text. Hitler had spent the evening sitting silently in a corner. His face was grey and set, his expression closed. While his staff chattered and speculated, he took no part in the discussion.[121] He left the business of checking with Henderson to von Ribbentrop. Dahlerus, ignorant of the British reply, had flown back to Berlin, sat around until well after 10 p.m. waiting for the British text to arrive at the Embassy, and then left to see Goering.

Ribbentrop met Henderson, not at the Reichs Chancellery but at the old Foreign Ministry building at 78 Wilhelmstrasse, in Bismarck's old office. He arrived from the Reichs Chancellery in a state of almost shivering excitement, his face pale, his lips set thin and tight, his eyes blazing.[122] According to a Foreign Ministry official who had seen him earlier that day, he was 'lusting for war'.[123] He may well have known that Hitler had decided that he could spare only one more day.[124] The attack on Poland could be postponed no later than September 2. If he could not achieve the diplomatic situation he wanted by then, the attack would be called off. He may also have been given the *Forschungsamt* report of an incautious phone conversation between Ogilvie-Forbes of the British Embassy and Attolico.[125] Ogilvie-Forbes said that they were all sitting there twiddling their thumbs, awaiting the reply from London. The longer they waited the better, as they would win time. Perhaps the British were deliberately delaying. If his Führer was not to be frustrated, it was up to Ribbentrop to cut short this diplomatic carousel.

The conversation which followed was largely conducted in German, a language over which Henderson had not as much command as he believed. The Foreign Ministry had spent the day drafting a sixteen-point programme for the German-Polish and Anglo-German conversations. A copy of this was sent to the Embassy in London in two parts, at 9.15 p.m. and 12.40 a.m., with instructions to take no action and to keep them secret.[126] Weizsäcker hailed their drafting as 'the first constructive idea for months', adding a question, 'but only for show?'[127]

The conversation opened with icy formality and soon degenerated.[128] Henderson began by repeating that it was unreasonable to expect the British Government to be able to produce a Polish plenipotentiary within twenty-four hours. Ribbentrop broke in at once. 'The set time is up,' he said. 'Where is the Pole that your Government was to produce?' Henderson continued to repeat Chamberlain's message. The

British had pressed Poland to avoid frontier incidents. Would the Germans do the same? 'The Poles are the provocateurs, not us,' Ribbentrop replied, his anger rising. 'You have come to the wrong address.' When Henderson then turned to ask the Germans to follow normal procedure and bring in the Polish Ambassador to Berlin as the channel by which the German proposals were to be given to the Poles, Ribbentrop's control went entirely and he began to shout. Henderson's control also began to slip. His hands shook and his face was flushed as he read out the British reply. The British proposal for a standstill in troop movements on both sides of the German-Polish frontier brought a fresh outburst of shouting. The British comment that there was evidence of German sabotage actions in Poland drove Ribbentrop quite out of control. 'That is a shameless Polish lie,' he shouted. 'I can tell you, Herr Henderson, the position is damned serious.'

Autre temps, autre mœurs. Henderson was shocked into anger by this mild swearword. He was surprised, he said stiffly, to hear such language from a Foreign Minister at so serious a moment. For a moment Ribbentrop hardly breathed. 'What did you say?' he said, leaping to his feet. Henderson rose simultaneously. The two men glared at each other. Paul-Otto Schmidt, the unhappy interpreter, waited, half-expecting Ribbentrop to throw Henderson out of the door. He drew a few doodles on his notepad, listened to the heavy breathing from both men. They both sat down again; Schmidt sighed with relief.

After a little more conversation, Ribbentrop drew the text of the German proposals from his pocket. He read them aloud, too fast for Henderson whose German was deserting him in the stress of the moment, and then refused to hand them over. Since no Polish nego-tiator had appeared, they were past history. The Führer had forbidden him to hand them over.

Both Schmidt and Henderson were shocked, part of the latter's inattention arising from his conviction that the list could be studied at his leisure, in peace and quiet, away from Ribbentrop's now intolerable presence. Schmidt gave Henderson a chance to note them down by asking if he would like them translated, but Henderson was too *bouleversé* to pick up his cue. Schmidt contented himself by decorating his note of Ribbentrop's refusal with a thick red line. Smiling and happy, Ribbentrop took himself off to report to his Führer. At one stroke he had blown Goering's mediation efforts away, destroyed Dahlerus and scored off that intolerable upper-class English representative[129] (whose heavily anglicized German Hitler used to delight to mimic[130]) who represented everything in Britain that had rejected him and made him inferior, non-U, *arriviste*, 'not quite-quite you know', a nearly-gentleman. It would make an excellent story, which he would, and did, delight in telling.

Ribbentrop's report sent Hitler into a sudden outburst, a storm against Britain.[131] The British signature of the treaty with Poland proved they wanted war. At the time he had questioned Henderson's assurance that the Poles were ready to negotiate. Now he knew this was a lie. The Poles were not ready to talk and never would be. It was pointless to negotiate any more. British policy was the same as in 1914. Every British note had one aim only, to divert the blame for war away from London. He stood in a circle with Goering and Ribbentrop. When Goering said he did not believe Britain would declare war, Hitler clapped him on the shoulder. 'My dear Goering,' he said, 'if the English sign a treaty one day, they are not going to break it in twenty-four hours.' Goering, who had been with Dahlerus when all this happened and had heard of it from a phone call from Ogilvie-Forbes to Dahlerus,[132] could do nothing with him. Hitler would not hear any more of the worthy Swede. Goering had, however, already shown Dahlerus the text and allowed him to dictate it over the phone to Ogilvie-Forbes. That was one phone call that did not end up on Hitler's desk. Later in the morning of August 31 at 8 a.m. he allowed Dahlerus to copy the German proposals and take them round to the British Embassy.

As with his encounter with Hitler the previous evening, Henderson arrived back at the Embassy in a state of shock, unable to do more than send off, at 2.45 a.m., two short telegrams.[133] A longer one[134] giving the gist of his interview with Ribbentrop did not follow until 5.15 a.m. and was delayed four hours in transit. As with many highly nervous, febrile types, shock and stress affected Henderson by driving him not into a state of stasis but into one of hyperactivity. Before sending the third, more detailed telegram he had got the Polish Ambassador out of bed at 2 a.m., called him to the British Embassy and urged him to call on Ribbentrop then and there to deliver him to the proposals he had refused to give to Henderson.[135] Lipski smelt a rat. If he went to Ribbentrop he would be asking Ribbentrop to serve an ultimatum on him. Henderson remembered very little of the document which, to his dying day, he maintained that Ribbentrop had deliberately gabbled through at break-neck speed so as to render it unintelligible. Only the provisions for a plebiscite stuck with him. He regarded those, so he told Lipski, as not unreasonable. Lipski refused to act without specific instructions. He promised to phone Warsaw. In actuality, since phone communications with Warsaw were increasingly difficult, Lipski, being without instructions from Beck, had already decided to send his Counsellor, Prince Lubomirski, to Warsaw by road and air.[136] Lubomirski took Lipski's note of his conversation with him. Lipski sent Warsaw a telegram at 9.30 a.m. that morning summarizing what Henderson had told him.[137]

Henderson also phoned Bernardo Attolico and gave him a long account of his meetings with Ribbentrop and Lipski, which Attolico put into a telegram to Rome at 2.25 a.m. That too took nearly four hours to get to Rome. With that the diplomatic Mafia, whose plotting had remained quiescent since August 25, sprang into action.

How and when von Weizsäcker heard of the débâcle of the Ribbentrop-Henderson conversation is not clear. It may have been from Albrecht von Kessel, of Weizsäcker's own Secretariat, who ran liaison between his office and that of von Ribbentrop. Whatever the source, he knew before 7.45 a.m. when he called Ulrich von Hassell to see him.[138] Hassell arrived at 8.20 a.m. By then Weizsäcker had also seen Attolico and sent him on a similar errand, with a similar story. There was, so the conspirators believed, only one very slender chance of averting war: to bring the Poles, by hook or by crook, to send someone to Berlin as soon as possible. Unaware that this would have completed Hitler's plot, they hurried and scurried, telephoned and implored, abjured and despaired. They had reason. At 6.30 that morning word was brought to General Halder from the Reichs Chancellery that the jump-off order had been given for the following day.[139] Although intervention by the West was not deemed inevitable, Hitler had decided to attack. To the fury of the *Reichsmarine* three of the Polish destroyers stationed at Gdynia had made a bolt for England.[140] The only gain was that it made possible the reinforcement of the German North Sea squadron. Four cruisers, three destroyers, two flotillas of torpedo boats and three U-boats were transferred from the Baltic.

The extra days had enabled the navy already to send U-26 with torpedoes and mines to watch the west coast of Britain. U-53 had sailed for the Atlantic; two U-boats were to watch the Channel, three the Dogger Bank; one lay off the British naval base at Rosyth watching the Firth of Forth; another lay off the Moray Firth.

Hassell began by calling on Henderson. He found him at breakfast. Henderson had finally got to bed at 4 a.m. By the time von Hassell arrived he had already phoned Lipski and failed to reach him. In Lipski's place there had appeared Lipski's First Secretary, Henryk Malhomme. Malhomme had found Henderson worn out and looking as if he had aged ten years.[141] He was also less than totally coherent, being mainly concerned to defend himself against Polish suspicions of his Germanophilia. He had also been visited by Attolico. Weizsäcker had primed both his emissaries with the dramatic but untrue story that, unless some Polish move was made within the next three hours, Hitler would declare war on Poland. The time limit for recalling the troops, who had already received their jumping-off orders, was 4 p.m., eight rather than three hours away. Nor was Hitler planning anything as formal as a declaration of war. Attolico's call had already primed Henderson to transmit the story to London.[142] After von Hassell's call he repeated it.[143] Just after calling on Henderson Attolico had cabled Rome.[144] If no new fact was produced, he said, there would be war in a few hours. A new fact would be either a direct telephone plea from Mussolini to Hitler, or the transformation of Lipski into an authorized negotiator.

From the British Embassy, Hassell enlisted the aid of Goering's sister, Olga Riegele, an old friend, to get him to see Goering. He arrived as Dahlerus, armed with his own transcription of the German 'offer', left for the British Embassy, where he found Henderson understandably tired and depressed. The situation, he said, was hopeless.[145] To get Dahlerus off his hands, however, he suggested that Ogilvie-Forbes should take him to call on the unfortunate Polish Ambassador and show him the German proposals. Dahlerus duly left to see Lipski.

In the meantime, Hassell was tackling Goering by phone.[146] Goering pretended not to have heard that the German proposal had been declared no longer valid by Ribbentrop. Since he had just dispatched Dahlerus to the British Embassy, he was forced to go through the motions of pretending to negotiate; as a participant in the discussions at the Reichs Chancellery after Ribbentrop's return and as the Commander-in-Chief of the Luftwaffe, he knew perfectly well how empty these negotiations were. If, however, they could produce a Polish negotiator, Hitler's original plot could still proceed. There was, after all, one extra day built into the timetable. To produce a negotiator would also be a personal triumph over Ribbentrop. He authorized Hassell to tell Henderson that at least the Poles must declare they would send a negotiator, even if there was not time for his arrival. Hassell returned to the British Embassy to Henderson, who at 11.24 phoned through a telegram in code to London.[147]

The pressure was now directed towards Lipski. Most of it was unnecessary after the visit of the French Ambassador, M. Robert Coulondre.[148] Henderson had alerted him by telephone immediately after seeing Attolico. Coulondre had called at the British Embassy, obtained more details from Henderson, including the sources of his information, and had hurried to see Lipski. By tactful handling he had got him to see that the Poles, having accepted the principle of direct negotiation, would be throwing the moral advantage away if they now appeared to be avoiding the direct contacts they had previously accepted. Lipski agreed to phone Warsaw again.[149] Coulondre returned to his Embassy to phone Henderson's story to Bonnet. Bonnet's pressure was now added to that bearing on Warsaw. Lipski found himself badgered also by Attolico, by the Hungarian Minister and by the Papal Nuncio.

The visit of Dahlerus was the last straw.[150] Full of himself and his mission, this (to Lipski) totally unknown Swede began to pour out some story about Goering's opposition to the Nazi extremists, and how necessary it was to satisfy Germany's demands for Danzig and the Corridor in order to avoid the total partition of Poland. Lipski should go immediately to Goering, sign whatever he wanted and 'then the whole problem would be settled and we would be able to shoot stags together.' With this Dahlerus began reading the famous sixteen articles. 'To stop this ghastly business' Lipski pretended not to be able to understand, and sent Dahlerus off to dictate his notes to Lipski's personal secretary.

Left alone with Ogilvie-Forbes, Lipski made his complete dissatisfaction with the whole business very clear. He was not prepared to discuss proposals infringing the territorial integrity of the Polish state with some unknown individual. Nor was he impressed with the British attitude; this kind of move would bring moral collapse and military breakdown in Poland. What was needed was a firm and united front. He was sure German morale was breaking. The German offer was cheap. Ogilvie-Forbes, as a dyed-in-the-wool professional diplomat, most probably shared Lipski's feelings. In sending Dahlerus to Lipski, Henderson was acting way beyond his instructions and aiding and abetting Dahlerus in his self-induced metamorphosis from courier into mediator. But Ogilvie-Forbes was also too good a professional to let any of this show to Lipski.

Lipski had, however, gained one thing from the sequence. He now had the famous German plan and could appreciate how dangerously innocent it could be made to appear. Reporting to Warsaw, he called it[151] 'a further symptom of pressure on us, which took especially drastic form today'. 'I react calmly, very firmly,' he added: the last telegram he sent to Warsaw.

Dahlerus returned to the British Embassy in a state of self-righteous fury. He was convinced the Poles were sabotaging his whole work. He rang London and spoke to Sir Horace Wilson.[152] Goering's terms were most liberal. The Führer had put them forward solely to show how anxious he was to receive a friendly settlement with Britain. He had been to see Lipski. Here Wilson heard a German voice repeating Dahlerus's words. He tried to warn Dahlerus, who was in full flood. When he said the Poles did not intend to give way and it was 'obvious' the Poles were obstructing everything, Wilson put down the receiver.

For Lord Halifax this was enough. A two-line telegram sent to Berlin within half an hour of Dahlerus's call said simply,[153] 'the Secretary of State . . . does not share the view . . . expressed as to obstructive attitude of Polish government.' Halifax had in fact convinced himself that Hitler's blustering inaction was the result of his being a defeated man. That day he lunched at the Carlton Club with the faithful Cadogan, joining the table of his Cabinet colleague, Euan Wallace.[154] Hitler had 'expected the Russian Treaty bluff to succeed, and finding that it has not done so, may be unwilling to risk a war,' was Wallace's view. We have 'the first view of a beaten fox', was Halifax's view. He had been a noted Master of Fox Hounds in his day.

Beck had instructed Lipski to ask for an interview with either Ribbentrop or Weizsäcker promising a formal reply that day.[155] The Polish Government was ready to enter into discussions with Germany, providing that they were on an equal footing and that Poland would not be faced with a *fait accompli*.[156] These instructions reached Lipski just as Dahlerus was giving his German listeners the notion that Goering's plot was working. It is hardly surprising therefore that when Dahlerus returned to see Goering that afternoon,[157] Goering staged a comedy, by which the text of Lipski's instructions, limiting the scope of his interview with Weizsäcker or Ribbentrop entirely to the message he was to deliver and instructing him on no account to enter into concrete negotiations, was turned against him. This proved, Goering stormed, how faithless the Poles were. With that Goering and Dahlerus went off for a late, but public lunch at the Hotel Esplanade.

In the meantime, Lipski was vainly trying to see either Ribbentrop or Weizsäcker. From 12.40 until 3 p.m. his calls to the Wilhelmstrasse were left unanswered. At 3 p.m. Weizsäcker phoned to ask whether he was acting as an ambassador or a plenipotentiary.[158] Lipski said he was acting in his capacity as an ambassador charged with communicating a message from his government. He did not get to see Ribbentrop until 6.30 p.m.[159] The meeting was icy; it lasted a bare ten minutes. Ribbentrop had won; Goering had been defeated. For the little that it was worth, the Poles had not fallen for Hitler's trap. Two hours later, Berlin radio broadcast the sixteen points, adding that Poland had rejected them. Thanks to Ribbentrop, they had never even seen them.

Next day Ribbentrop had to fend off the other part of Weizsäcker's conspiracy for peace, the Italian one. Attolico's letter calling for a 'new fact' reached Ciano just after 9 a.m.;[160] it was an 'ugly awakening'[161] for Ciano who had been up until 2.30 a.m. digesting the British reply which Henderson had given to Ribbentrop at midnight and which Loraine, faithful to his instructions, had delayed handing over to Ciano until Henderson's call at the Wilhelmstrasse was safely under way.[162] Ciano hurried to confer with Mussolini. The Duce's view was that unless he had something to offer Hitler, there was no point in his acting. The Duce remained convinced that Danzig was not only not worth a war; it was indubitably German. If he could offer Hitler Danzig, that might be something.

Ciano hurried to phone Halifax. From a raging Anglophobe, Ciano had now become so devoted a supporter of Anglo-Italian amity and co-operation that he had, only the previous day, rebuked Grandi for questioning Britain's motives.[163] Grandi was most amazed. Halifax, giving nothing away,[164] promised to consider the idea. As a quid pro quo he asked Ciano to press Berlin to establish direct contacts with the Poles. Ciano dutifully agreed. He also consulted Sir Percy Loraine, who promptly telephoned Halifax supporting Ciano's proposal.[165] He also suggested that he should put in train a well-pondered plan to detach Mussolini from the Axis.[166] Halifax knocked that on the head within the hour.[167] Ciano returned to Mussolini with a new idea. Mussolini should call a general conference for September 5, for the revision of the Treaty of Versailles. He put it to André François-Poncet, who phoned it to Bonnet;[168] Ciano then phoned Halifax directly.[169] What did Halifax think of the idea? No approach would be made to Germany without British and French approval. Once again, Loraine supported the idea.[170] Poland, Russia and Spain would also be invited.

Halifax, in truth, did not think much of the idea. Nor did the Prime Minister, whose first reaction was that it was impossible to agree to a conference under the threat of fully mobilized armies. A preliminary condition would have to be a measure of demobilization. Halifax's reaction was simpler. The crux was direct German-Polish negotiations. If they were initiated, then the conference would be unnecessary. If they were not, war would ensue and the proposal was no longer real. They called in Charles Corbin, the French Ambassador.[171] A phone call to Paris established three things. Bonnet had consulted Robert Coulondre in Berlin who, like Halifax, did not think the matter that urgent. Nor could he undertake anything without Daladier's consent and Daladier, sensing a threat to the cohesion of his government, wanted to hold a Cabinet meeting, something he had refrained from doing for the whole of the preceding week. Without waiting for the Cabinet meeting, however, Daladier took only an hour's consideration before telling the

British Ambassador in Paris that afternoon that he would rather resign than accept Mussolini's invitation to a second Munich.[172] In the meantime Halifax rang Rome to say that Britain did not feel able to urge Poland to give up Danzig in advance of negotiation. Danzig was the vital part of the dispute. He could not understand why Ribbentrop found it impossible to invite Lipski to the Wilhelmstrasse to give him the German proposals.[173]

At 8.20 that evening, the Italian telephone directorate informed Ciano that all telephone communication between Italy and Britain had been cut off by British action.[174] 'This is war,' said the Duce to Ciano.[175] 'But tomorrow we shall declare in the Grand Council that Italy will not march.' Ciano feared that tomorrow might open with a preemptive strike against Italian industry, the Italian fleet and the Franco-Italian frontiers. With Mussolini's approval, at 9.15 p.m., he called in Loraine and committed an 'indiscretion'.[176] If Germany went to war, he told him, Italy would stay neutral. Loraine had known this for over a week, but realizing what it cost Ciano to make such a declaration he pretended to be overjoyed. As for the telephone communications, he would take immediate action. The break turned out to be the result of inadequate briefing of the post and telecommunication censor department which the imminence of war had called into life in Britain.[177]

In the meantime there was Attolico in Berlin. Relations with Italy and with Attolico had been getting steadily colder since the traumatic experience of August 25. Ribbentrop had shown himself particularly difficult towards the man he had once treated so warmly. It was thus not hard for Attolico to press his advice on Józef Lipski. It was much trickier to persuade the Germans to see Lipski once he had accepted that advice. Ribbentrop was evasive.[178] Weizsäcker did what he could. Eventually Attolico got to see Ribbentrop at 5 p.m.[179] Ribbentrop, being told that Attolico was acting on the Duce's direct instructions, said that he would see Lipski 'as a unique favour to Italy'.[180] The only real concession to the Axis, or its memory, was that Hitler himself received Attolico at 7 p.m. to notify him of the Polish 'refusal' to accept the German proposals and the consequent failure of the British attempt at mediation.[181] He also gave Attolico a copy of the German proposals. Neither Coulondre nor Henderson rated higher than von Weizsäcker, and they had to wait, together with the Japanese Ambassador and the US and the Soviet Chargés d'affaires, until the DNB communiqué had already been broadcast on Berlin radio.[182] Attolico urged the Italian offer of mediation. Hitler made a virtue of refusing. He did not want to place the Duce in an awkward situation. So everything is now at an end? asked Attolico. Yes, said the Führer.

The Military line-up against Poland

German Troops

Army Group North
Reserve: 3 Inf Divs
1 Armoured Div
3rd Army: 7 Inf Divs in 2 Corps
5th Army: 6 Inf Divs in 3 Corps
3 Mot Divs
1 Pz Div

Army Group South
Reserve: 5 Inf Divs
8th Army: 4 Inf Divs in 2 Corps
SS div Adolf Hitler
10th Army: 6 Inf Divs
2 Mot Divs
2 Pz Divs
3 Lt Pz Divs in 5 Corps
14th Army: 6 Inf Divs
2 Pz Divs

1 Lt Pz Div
1 Mountain Div
SS Germania
Slovak Army: 3 Inf Divs
Luftflotte 1 & 2

Naval Command Group Baltic
Battleship *Schleswig-Holstein*
3 Destroyer Flotillas
8 U-boats
3 Gps Coastal Reconnaissance Aircraft
1 Lt Torpedo boat Flotilla
1 Minesweeper Flotilla

Polish troops
Army Pomorze: 5 Inf Divs
1 Cav Bde
Army Poznan: 4 Inf Divs
2 Cav Bdes

Army Lódź: 4 Inf Divs
2 Cav Bdes
Army Krakow: 7 Inf Divs
1 Cav Bde
1 Cav Bde (Armd)
1 Mountain Bde
Res. Wyszkow: 3 Inf Divs
Reserve South: 2 Inf Divs
Army Modlin: 2 Inf Divs
2 Cav Bdes
Army Prusy: 8 Inf Divs
1 Cav Bde
1 Cav Bde (Armd)
Army Karpaty: 2 Mountain Bdes
Op Gp Narew: 2 Inf Divs
2 Cav Bdes
Reserve Kutna: 2 Inf Divs

CHAPTER 28

POLAND ATTACKED:
THE WEST'S INGLORIOUS HOUR

At 4.45 on the morning of September 1, the sleeping city of Danzig was woken by the first explosions of the Second World War. The 11-inch guns of the *Schleswig-Holstein* had opened fire on the Polish garrison of the Westerplatte.[1] Stuka dive-bombers with their squat drooping wings swept over the city. Near Burckhardt's residence the Polish railway officials, holed up in their offices in the main railway station, were attacked by the Danzig forces of the *Landespolizei*.[2] Of all the other centres of Polish resistance, the post office on the Hevetiusplatz with its metre-thick stone walls held out the longest. Sandbags and bullet-proof steel shutters had turned it into a small fortress. A light field gun made a breach through the main entrance. But it was not until the fire brigade pumped petrol into the cellars of the building and set it on fire that the fifty-one strong garrison was smoked out. By German military law the defenders were not uniformed soldiers and so their defence was illegitimate. The survivors were shot as *francs-tireurs*, after a court martial, a month later.

The Westerplatte was a tougher nut to crack.[3] The *Schleswig-Holstein*'s guns with their flat trajectories could do little damage to the Polish concrete fortifications. The naval assault detachment which the *Schleswig-Holstein* had brought with it broke into the Polish lines, but was repulsed. A second attack at 9 a.m., in which the SS took part, was equally unsuccessful. The Poles, well dug into concrete bunkers with 88 mm guns, whose existence was unknown to German intelligence, resisted fiercely. The German assault troops lost 35 per cent of their strength in dead and wounded in the opening attacks. Low cloud prevented air attack until the late afternoon when sixty Stuka dive-bombers attacked without any noticeable success. There followed a violent row in the Reichs Chancellery as Himmler and Hess tried to take the operation out of the navy's hands and give it to the SS, whose record elsewhere was less than happy, owing to poor leadership. Eventually the army was entrusted with all further operations.[4] On the following day German destroyers were brought up to shell the Polish defences from the seaward side. Battered, bombed and bombarded, the Westerplatte was to hold out for another five days.

On the western side of the free city, Polish forces counter-attacked strongly in the effort to relieve the beleaguered garrison, driving the first attacks by the Danzig defence forces back across the frontier and bringing the most westerly township in the free state, Zoppot, under artillery fire; a brave but doomed effort, it ended when elements of the 19th Army Corps of the 4th Army, and of the 207th Infantry Division drove through the northernmost part of the Corridor to encircle Gdynia and the Polish fortifications on the Hel peninsula.

The garrison of Gdynia fought bravely, evacuating its forces to the Hel peninsula, whose fortifications were to hold out until October 2. The remaining ships of the Polish navy, the destroyer *Wicker* and the minelayer *Gryf*, beat off the first German naval attack, badly damaging two German destroyers, one of which sank on its way back to Danzig, before being sunk themselves by German dive-bombers. Of the five Polish submarines, two escaped to join the Free Polish Navy in Scottish waters, and three, damaged, sought refuge in internment in Sweden.

On land, the carefully planned attacks on the bridges across the Vistula at Dirschau and Graudenz went awry. The coup planned against Dirschau depended on smuggling a company of assault engineers on board a goods train timed to arrive at the bridge exactly at the moment the German attack on Poland was to begin. An armoured train following was to give covering fire. The arrival of the goods train, ostensibly in transit from East to West Prussia, was duly notified to the Poles in accordance with regular practice. It was announced for 4.30 a.m. on August 26, and then cancelled when the attack itself was cancelled. On August 31, however, Hitler had changed the hour of attack at the last minute from 4.30 to 4.45 a.m., on request from the Luftwaffe.

The goods train duly crossed the German-Polish frontier at Simonsdorf (Szymankowo). There was a Polish customs post and a small station, with about six Polish customs officials and twenty railway workers, in a predominantly German area where the local Nazis had been getting steadily more violent. On the night of August 31, they murdered a Polish railway official. The Poles spotted the subterfuge at once. The points were fixed to divert the armoured train following into a siding. A warning rocket was fired. The local Nazis took a terrible revenge. Every Pole they could find was hunted out and beaten to death. The bodies were shovelled into a mass grave with a wooden board planted on it. 'Here lies the Polish minority,' it read. Arriving at

Dirschau, the goods train came under fire. The bridge was blown. The bridge at Graudenz was supposed to be blown up by an *Abwehr* commando. It got off to a late start but penetrated the Polish lines successfully, only to be overrun by the advance wave of the German army. On trying to get through the retreating Polish lines, the *Abwehr* men were arrested by an officious German officer, and lost twelve hours arguing their way free. That afternoon the Poles blew up the Graudenz bridge.

It was to require the construction of emergency bridges by German army engineers before the 4th Army units, who were to cross the Corridor and swing on to the extreme wing of the 3rd Army, could complete their movement, and the main road and rail traffic across the Corridor took time to restore. Nor did the second enterprise against the Jablonka tunnel have any more success. Forewarned, the Poles blew it up in plenty of time.

The main body of the German armies had only encountered minor problems. The Germans had overwhelming numerical superiority where it mattered: in men, in weaponry, in training and in generalship, in all, in fact, but courage. The armour and the motorized troops swept across the Polish plains, the Luftwaffe swept Poland's skies and harried Polish troops wherever their officers rallied them. Behind them came Heydrich's police, Heydrich raving at the slow rate at which Polish 'criminals' were being sentenced and executed.[5]

The first casualty of the Second World War had, however, died before 4.45 when the guns began. His name was Franz Honiok.[6] He was a '*Konserve*'. He had been a salesman for agricultural machinery, who came from a small town near Gleiwitz. He was a sympathizer for Poland, had fought on the Polish side in 1921 in Silesia, and lived for a couple of years in Poland before returning to Germany. A German attempt to expel him had been foiled by his appeal to the League of Nations arbitration tribunal for issues of personal nationality in Geneva. He was arrested on August 30, 1939, in Hohnleben by order of the SS, who had picked him out of the Gestapo cells as a highly suitable example of the Polish irregulars whose attack on the Gleiwitz radio station they were about to simulate. He was forty-one years old. On the evening of August 31 he was taken away from the police cells at Gleiwitz in a black SS car. An SS doctor put him unconscious with an injection.

The attack was launched at 8 p.m. on August 31. The staff of the Gleiwitz radio station were driven into the cellar of the building at gunpoint. The SS radio expert then tried to make the microphone work. A comedy then ensued. The SS planners responsible for the choice of the Gleiwitz station as a suitable stage for their 'incident' had not realized that it was essentially only a relay station for Breslau radio. The only independent broadcasting carried out from Gleiwitz was emergency weather reporting. The weather microphone was found after a search. Eventually it was discovered how to make it work. 'Attention. This is Gleiwitz. The station is in Polish hands.' The director of the radio station, sitting in shirt sleeves over a late dinner in his home, heard the broadcast, called to his attention by his wife. He stormed over to the building, flung open the door to the studio, and saw a number of strangers, one of whom levelled a gun at him. He turned and fled, running home to ring the police and his superiors.

The broadcast in Polish was over. A few shots were fired in the air, there were a few shouts, and Honiok, still unconscious, was brought into the building and shot. His body was left by the side door to the station building. The intruders left, as the first police arrived from the local police station about half a mile (1 km) away. The whole episode had taken about thirteen minutes. In Berlin Heydrich was furious. By the time he had found Gleiwitz on his radio the action was long over. In any case, anyone who tuned in to Gleiwitz in Berlin would only pick up Breslau, which broadcast on the same frequency and carried a much stronger signal.

Two other corpses were in fact found at Gleiwitz. They were never identified; they seem to have come from the concentration camp at Sachsenhausen. The Gestapo took copious photographs. Some Poles living in the area were arrested and then released again. The attack on Gleiwitz made the German news bulletins. It was monitored by the French just before 10.30 p.m. on the evening of August 31, which was remarkably speedy news reporting by any standards.[7] But no one was very proud of the whole episode. No photographs were published, no articles written for the press. The whole matter was buried, until the Nuremberg trials in 1946 resurrected the matter.

Two other incidents were staged that night. In one, an attack on a deserted forest ranger's hut at Pitschen, no bodies were left or readied. In the other, the attack on the customs house at Hohnlinden (the usual occupants had been removed with their families, and the inhabitants of the small village warned to stay indoors), the SS who played the Poles demolished the empty building and its contents with sledge-hammers, after having fired live bullets in all directions. They were then arrested by another group of SS men, playing the part of the German frontier guards, and driven through Hohnlinden in open trucks. While the drama was being staged, six concentration camp inmates were brought, probably drugged, shot nearby and their corpses laid picturesquely around the landscape for the photographers to take pictures of this latest Polish 'atrocity'. When all was done the bodies were removed, their faces systematically beaten so as to make them unrecognizable. The perpetrators then drove smartly away. The Wehrmacht, who knew nothing of all this, was due to jump off against Poland within the hour. When the forces had safely passed through, the disfigured corpses were buried in the nearby forest.

From midday on August 31, the Reichs Chancellery had filled with Hitler's closest supporters.[8] Goebbels, Himmler, Bormann, Bühler, Dietrich, Lutze of the SA, Frick, Minister of the Interior, Bodenschatz, Hewel, Wolff, Goering, Ribbentrop, and Brauchitsch and Keitel with their adjutants; there was a continuous noise, a chaos of comings and goings. Hitler, always surrounded by brown uniforms, grew steadily more excitable. Everyone wanted to hear the latest news. All echoed Hitler's views. Goering and Ribbentrop, it was noted, hardly spoke to each other. They met only when Hitler was there. The military held their tongues and said little. Nothing of the real anxieties its members felt was allowed to show. The adjutants and aides, Walter Hewel, Bodenschatz, Captain von Puttkamer, Brandt the doctor, none of them party members, stood apart, discussing worriedly whether anything could be done. Their hopes were pinned on Goering. But Goering was in the plot, and he was much too taken with himself to do anything untoward, least of all anything which would damage his position as crown prince.

That evening Hitler signed Directive No. 1 for the Conduct of the War.[9] 'Now that every political possibility has been exhausted for ending by peaceful means the intolerable situation on Germany's eastern frontier,' it began, 'I have determined on a solution by force.' Most of it was concerned with possible counter-actions by France and Britain. 'In the west, it is important that the responsibility for the opening of hostilities should be made to rest squarely on Britain and France.' If Britain and France attack, then the west must be held in order to 'maintain the conditions for a victorious conclusion of the operations against Poland . . . warfare against merchant shipping – the better to be guarded against enemy raids – the Luftwaffe . . . to prevent the French and British air forces from attacking the German army and German living space. . . . Attacks on London are to be reserved for my decision.' This order had originally envisaged the evacuation of civilians from the German-French frontier. This was dropped, as Hitler did not expect France and Britain to march. He was soon to be shown wrong.

At 5.40 a.m. Berlin radio broadcast Hitler's proclamation to the Wehrmacht. This spoke of the bloodstained terror waged against the

Germans in Poland, of their being driven out of house and home, of innumerable Polish violations of Germany's frontiers. To end this insane behaviour nothing was left but to meet force with force. 'I expect every soldier, confident in the great tradition of eternal German soldierliness, to do his duty to his utmost.' At 8 a.m. long columns of SA and SS filed along Unter den Linden and the Wilhelmstrasse to line the route from the Reichs Chancellery to the Kroll Opera House, where the Reichstag met.

As Hitler drove along the route, the crowds were thin and the streets empty of traffic. Goering had packed the auditorium (over a hundred Reichstag deputies missed the meeting) with party members and others. Hitler wore a new uniform designed by the SS in field grey, with the SS flash instead of a swastika on the arm. He said he would not put it off until victory. It was not one of Hitler's better performances.[10] He seemed nervous and ill at ease. If he fell in the war, Goering was to be his successor and, after Goering, Rudolf Hess. There were distinct echoes of a death-wish when he spoke of the youth of Germany going with blazing hearts to make the sacrifice to the nation, the National Socialist state, expected and demanded of them. But mostly his speech repeated the themes of Polish insolence, the allegation that the Poles had begun firing on Germany; he boasted of the strength of the Wehrmacht. He did not want to make war on women and children. The Luftwaffe had been ordered to confine its attacks to military objectives. One lie followed another with hypnotic regularity. The applause was thin and struck some of those who heard it on the radio as forced. His eulogy of Molotov and the Soviet Pact was greeted with silence.[11]

In Danzig Gauleiter Forster, who had visited Berlin on August 27 and again on August 30 to settle the final arrangements with Hitler, had been active since the previous evening. His Gestapo heavies had burst into Burckhardt's house at 11 p.m. to put him under house arrest. His phone was cut off. He was told to expect a visit from Forster during the course of the night. Burckhardt replied that he was going to bed, he would see Forster in the morning. Forster duly arrived with a large following. Burckhardt, he said, represented the Treaty of Versailles. Hitler had torn up the Treaty of Versailles. In two hours the swastika would be hoisted above the High Commissioner's office. The Polish representatives were under arrest. He had two hours in which to leave Danzig. 'Personally,' added Forster, 'I have nothing against you,' which, says Burckhardt, added a touch of humour to the occasion. Burckhardt turned his back on him, packed, all the while harried by Gestapo visitors, got into his car with his secretary, and drove off through East Prussia to Kovno in Lithuania.[12] The German Foreign

Ministry, alerted from Danzig, smoothed his way, as they did that of the Dutch President of the Danzig Harbour Board.[13] The British Consul General asked for his passport and those of his staff, and left for Riga, through East Prussia, the same afternoon.[14] German troops arrived in Danzig in the course of the morning; they seemed to expect the tumultuous welcome given them in the Sudetenland the previous October, but the British Consul noted they were received with complete indifference.

Forster, as arranged, exchanged telegrams[15] with Hitler that same morning. Forster proclaimed a new basic law, setting aside the Danzig constitution, taking all authority to himself and declaring Danzig a constituent part of the German Reich. Hitler replied, recognizing his unilateral action and appointing Forster Chief of the Civil Administration for Danzig. In October, after the conquest of Poland, Hitler created a new *Reichsgau*, Danzig-West Prussia, comprising the northernmost segment of the Polish Corridor, including Gdynia, renamed Gdingen, and the northern part of the Polish province of Posen, including the city of Bydgoszcz (Bromberg).[16] Erich Koch, Gauleiter of East Prussia and Forster's old enemy, was forced to cede the five westernmost counties of East Prussia. Forster and his buddies settled down to run their new empire. Greiser was able to secure for himself the Gauleitership of the other new *Gau*, the Warthegau, which covered most of Posen, taking with him most of the anti-Forster faction. Forster was later to defy Himmler's racialist ideology and classify most of the Poles in his *Gau* as ethnic Germans, with the immortal words, 'if I looked like Himmler, I would not talk about race.'[17] This did not stop the new 'Germans' leaving their houses and farms to join the Polish partisan forces. Both Forster and Greiser were executed at war's end by the Poles on war crimes charges.

Danzig was only the excuse, not even the occasion, for the German attack on Poland and the war between Britain and Germany that was to follow. The British Cabinet, the Foreign Secretary, the Foreign Office, Parliament and the British people all knew that. In the last days of August, however, there were moments when the minute detail of the dispute and the day-to-day and hour-to-hour moves of the game so filled Lord Halifax's mind that he and those who followed his lead lost sight of the ends towards which the game itself was directed. Like Mussolini they found it difficult to believe that Hitler would go to war over Danzig, so minor an issue, still less over the rights and duties of Polish customs inspectors. They came therefore to see the game as one of pressure and counter-pressure, as a 'war of nerves' in which steadfastness and tenacity would prevail, provided care was taken not to be out-manœuvred. The Poles shared this view, opposing their own sense of *amour-propre* and honour to the situation. The notion that Hitler was intent not on winning the diplomatic game so much as on knocking the table over, drawing his gun and shooting it out, was one they understood intellectually but not in their hearts. Nor would British public opinion nor that of the neutrals have understood. Hitler's bitter complaint that the main aim of British diplomacy was to put the blame for starting the war on him was not altogether invalid. But then he wanted war.

It is to this refusal to accept that the many and detailed warnings of Hitler's military intentions represented his deep-rooted convictions rather than mere plans which diplomatic pressure might persuade him to change, that can be ascribed both the feeling that Hitler was on the run, which Halifax entertained on August 30–1, and the incredulity which greeted the first news of the German attack on Poland. Reuters flashed the DNB version of Hitler's appeal to the German army, very soon after it was broadcast on Berlin radio.[18] This was followed by a coded telephone call from Sir Howard Kennard in Warsaw at 8.30 a.m.[19] reporting the German air attacks on Cracow, Katowice and other Polish cities. Military movements across the frontiers seemed on the other hand to be small and isolated. Further incoherent telephone calls[20] from Warsaw followed at 12.15 and 2.00 p.m., by wireless at 4.00 p.m. and by telegraph at 7.59 p.m.[21] The last of these was not received until the following morning. Only at 2.00 p.m.[22] was Beck reported to be admitting that 'the various cases of armed German aggression which have occurred this morning on Polish soil cannot be taken any longer as isolated cases but constitute acts of war.' Since there was an air attack on Warsaw at the time, his waking up to reality is not surprising.

On August 31, Sir Horace Wilson had told Sir Samuel Hoare there was no likelihood of a sudden crash.[23] Sir Robert Vansittart, who rarely agreed with Sir Horace Wilson on anything, was equally sanguine. At luncheon, as we have seen, Halifax remarked that he had the first sight of a beaten fox. He told his Foreign Office Secretary, Oliver Harvey,[24] that he felt Hitler to be in difficulty; 'we must hold on to him' and not yield to blackmail. He wanted negotiations to start and then be very firm. The Poles had agreed to negotiate. The Italians had decided on neutrality; no sane person could imagine Hitler would choose as a pretext for war the non-appearance of a Polish negotiator within twenty-four hours of the first demand being made. Ribbentrop's extraordinary behaviour over the evening of August 30 made it even less likely.[25]

The Reuters news could not be doubted. Cadogan, who was woken by the Reuters office phoning through, rang Halifax and went over later to Eaton Square, returning to the Foreign Office to read the first of Kennard's fragmented and, without a map of the German-Polish frontier which gave the Polish place-names, almost unintelligible phone messages.[26] Dahlerus began trying to telephone at 6 a.m.; he broke off to visit Goering at 8 a.m., where he was given, and he swallowed, the German line on Gleiwitz and Dirschau (the Poles had opened fire on the Germans there, so it was alleged). At 9.50 he got through to Charles Spencer, his old English business friend.[27] He had, it will be remembered, spent a highly convivial lunch with Goering on the previous day; he had in fact persuaded Goering to meet Henderson together with Ogilvie-Forbes in the middle of the afternoon. Dahlerus's description of Henderson's behaviour suggests that, besides being dog-tired and near breaking point under the strain of seeing his mission in Germany ending in disaster, the Ambassador felt himself to be in a false position. Goering resurrected the notion of the unofficial distinguished British Germanophone personality who was to visit Hitler to discuss Anglo-German differences.

This may be the explanation for the suggestion, put forward by Attolico[28] on the evening of August 31 and telegraphed by Henderson[29] to London on that dreadful morning (he sent Ogilvie-Forbes to the Reichstag to hear Hitler's speech), that a visit by the Polish Marshal, Smigly-Rydz, to Goering might resolve German-Polish differences as between soldiers; alternatively, it may have been the last dying kick of the diplomatic conspiracy. In his immediately preceding telegram Henderson said[30] that he regarded the position as hopeless; his immediately subsequent telegram[31] commented that 'mutual distrust between German and Pole' was so complete that he did not think he could 'usefully acquiesce' in any further suggestions from Berlin. The suggestion about Marshal Smigly-Rydz has to be seen as an irrational proposal born of despair. Dahlerus, on the other hand, was still unconvinced. His first suggestion[32] combined General Ironside (the original 'distinguished German-speaking Englishman') and a Polish negotiator sitting in the British Embassy. At 12.20 he finally got through to Sir Alexander Cadogan to say that Hitler wanted Britain to mediate.[33] He should, he insisted, fly over at once with Ogilvie-Forbes. Cadogan brushed him off and when he rang again, told him in so many words that any suggestions of mediation while German forces were invading Poland was quite out of the question.[34] A world war could only be avoided by the immediate suspension of hostilities and the withdrawal of German troops from Polish territory.

At 10.30 a.m. Count Raczyński, the Polish Ambassador, called on Lord Halifax.[35] A phone call from Warsaw had informed him that German forces had crossed the frontier at four places. German planes had bombed Vilno, Grodno, Brest Litovsk, Lódź, Katowice and Cracow. At 9 a.m. an air attack on Warsaw had killed many civilians, including women and children. It was a plain case as provided for by the treaty. Halifax said that on the facts as reported he had no doubt that Britain would take the same view. Twenty minutes later Halifax summoned the German Chargé, the egregious Dr Theo Kordt, and asked him what light he could throw on all these reports of attacks on Poland.[36] Kordt, who had already delivered two notes that morning on the restrictions imposed on shipping and aircraft in the Gulf of Danzig, said he had no information. Three-quarters of an hour later Kordt telephoned[37] to say that, according to the news department of the German Foreign Ministry, the news of Warsaw and other Polish cities being bombed was untrue.

In the meantime the Cabinet met.[38] Chamberlain began with a plain statement. The events against which they had fought so long had come upon them. Their consciences were clear and their duty unmistakable. Halifax followed with a statement which inevitably reflected the fragmentary and confused nature of the reports of German actions then arriving. It was on this that the incredulity of the weaker and more reluctant members of the Cabinet, the 'do-nothing-until-we-are-sure brigade', fastened. Lord Chatfield said that the military wanted as short a period between an ultimatum being sent and its expiry as possible; if it was concluded that Britain was now bound to implement her guarantee, then an ultimatum should be sent 'without any more delay'.

The Cabinet still dithered. In the end they decided not to insert a time limit in the communication to be sent to Hitler, although in most other respects the note partook of the nature of an ultimatum; the need to consult the French, the question of how definite the information on the German attack on Poland was and, oddest of all, the notion that the insertion of a time limit would give a false sense of security which Hitler might exploit by attacking *before* the time limit expired, were all adduced. Such toughness as the weaker members of the Cabinet could summon was used in instructing Cadogan to choke off Mr Dahlerus. The Cabinet then declared full mobilization, instituted food control and radio censorship, and summoned Parliament for the afternoon. It was not an edifying performance. Some of the Cabinet thought that what they had drafted was an ultimatum.[39] Inskip, whose diary recorded grumpily,[40] 'this morning I was met by an unshaven fellow' who told him of Hitler's broadcast to his army, noted, 'At 11.30 a.m. we had a Cabinet meeting – nothing much to do except hear the news.'

The Cabinet in effect gave Chamberlain and Halifax *carte blanche* as to what to do next. Lord Halifax, as so often, was clear as to what should *not* be done. Even before the Cabinet met, he had phoned a message through to Rome,[41] thanking Mussolini for the offer of mediation made the previous day and regretting that German action 'has now rendered it impossible to proceed along those lines'. There had also been a message from the French Embassy[42] asking for agreement on the manner in which the respective British and French guarantees were to come into play. This message also argued strongly in favour of a time limit in order to prevent the Germans embarking on a delaying action by advancing counter-proposals which would discourage the Poles and distract public opinion in France and Great Britain. The deep divisions between the French Cabinet hawks and M. Bonnet, which were even then fully apparent in Paris, make it likely that M. Cambon, the Counsellor who transmitted the message and who shared the opinions of his Ambassador, the hawkish Charles Corbin, was either acting without instructions, or on instructions from Daladier or Léger rather than from Bonnet. Its divergence from the messages which were soon to come out of Paris only confused the issue still further. The French message to Mussolini, encouraging him to persist in his mediatory efforts, a copy of which was given to the Foreign Office at 10.15 that morning,[43] should have given a warning; but at that hour it was easy to see it as a left-over from the previous day, before Hitler's action had made mediation impossible.

Unlike the waverers in the Cabinet (about half the Cabinet at this moment), Lord Halifax understood perfectly that the news from Warsaw, so far as opinion in Parliament and the country was concerned, changed everything. He was far too much of a realist to clutch, as some of his colleagues seemed still to be doing, at the vain hope that this was some journalistic exaggeration, some error in translation or transmission, some minor power play or escalation by Hitler. It was what he had always feared and very largely expected. Hitler, as he had told the Dominions High Commissioners a week earlier, did not acknowledge the kind of consideration that restrained civilized states, accustomed to the restraints or rituals of international society. He had now embarked on war, and would have to be opposed in the same way. An ultimatum, and then a declaration of war, was the prescribed procedure; it was what public opinion in Britain, in the United States and in Eastern Europe expected. Any other course would destroy belief in Britain as a serious actor on the international stage.

This was not the view of hitherto influential sections of society in and around London, to whose anxieties other members of the Cabinet were especially sensitive, and unfortunately Halifax and the Prime Minister had to contend with this. The true pacifists were mostly outside the ranks of the Conservative Party and its National Liberal and National Labour allies. The pacifists for the sake of British economic and financial strength, for European or Christian cohesiveness, for Anglo-German amity, for social cohesion in Britain, and for imperial unity and overseas investment in the empire, were a rather different problem. Halifax was to deal in the months to come with a substantial post-bag from representatives of all these tendencies. Hitler's conclusion of the Nazi-Soviet Pact fortunately destroyed the anti-Bolshevik pro-Nazi position. With the rest Halifax was to deal with unfailing courtesy and unyielding determination.

So too did Neville Chamberlain, though with much greater distaste. The deplorable picture of irresolution which the Cabinet was now to project is belied by the steps he had already taken towards a reconciliation with his greatest critics within the Conservative opposition, Winston Churchill and Anthony Eden. Contacts with Winston had been in progress for more than a week. By September 1, Hoare, who was by no means as much in Chamberlain's confidence as he believed himself to be, was talking of Churchill as a Minister without Portfolio, Eden as Dominions Secretary, and Inskip's promotion to the Lord Chancellorship.[44] The real difficulty Chamberlain anticipated was reconciling his own inexperience of the problems of war leadership and the unease with which he contemplated the role, with Churchill's immense experience as a member of the various Cabinets which had taken Britain to victory in 1914–18, and the appetite for conflict that he so notoriously displayed.

In the meantime the British people were calmly preparing for war. Gas-masks had been issued in their millions after Munich. On August 31, the Cabinet, expecting war with Germany to open with wholesale devastation of Britain's cities by air attack, had voted to begin the evacuation of women and children from London, Birmingham, Manchester, Glasgow and the other big conurbations. The scheme required an enormous elaboration of reception areas, billeting officers with the law behind them, the organization of special train timetables, the registration of potential evacuees, and the identification of those who would provide homes and schooling for the thousands of children now separated from their parents. Throughout the previous months, all the arrangements had been quietly planned, households at both ends of the process surveyed and registered. The actual process of evacuation, with its natural accompaniment of heartbreak, anguish, homesickness, culture clashes and, in a fearful minority of cases, outright cruelty and exploitation, went, if not with military precision, with remarkable smoothness.

This is the more surprising in that, to the rage and despair of the military, general mobilization was called the day that the evacuation began.[45] The regular army had been quietly recalling reservists since the middle of August, with a view to bringing the first wave of the British Expeditionary Force, with the air arm which was to accompany it to France, into a state of readiness. The Royal Navy had been bringing its units up to strength, so as not to be taken off balance by the immediate operation of German cruiser or submarine warfare, and to intercept as much German sea-borne commerce is possible. The blockade of Germany was to begin as soon as war was declared. Warnings went out to the hundreds of British merchant ships at sea.

In every case the painstaking labour over the previous decade of all the multifarious sub-committees of the Committee of Imperial Defence, based on a series of detailed historical studies of the lessons of the 1914–18 war by leading academic and military historians in the Cabinet Office historical section, had been embodied in the War Book maintained by each department of government and spelling out what had to be done at each stage in the progress towards war. These War Books had been greatly revised in the light of the lessons learnt in September 1938. Hitler's attempt to force war and the British semi-mobilization had been an invaluable dress-rehearsal. Indeed a senior official at the Air Ministry remarked[46] that as a result of the experience of September 1938 things ran so smoothly that he had nothing to do but 'sit in his office and twiddle his thumbs'.

This was not the kind of atmosphere in which the distinction between a warning without a time limit and an ultimatum with one could be easily understood. Chamberlain's statement to Parliament at 6 p.m. on September 1 went therefore with very little difficulty. The London sky was already filling with barrage balloons, those great tattered airborne whales, whose pendant wires were supposed to deter or bring down diving bombers. Throughout London, barriers of sand-bags were appearing around the buildings of state. Arrangements to black out the buildings and turn off the street lighting at night were adopted. The House of Commons had lowered all lights which might be visible from the street. The House was filled. The Ambassadors thronged the Distinguished Strangers Gallery. Chamberlain's speech was clearly one he found great difficulty in delivering. He had prayed that it might never fall on him to ask his country to accept again the 'awful arbitrament of war', but the story that he told, of the negotiations of the previous few days, of the sixteen points denied to Henderson and never communicated to the Poles, and the text of the documents to be handed to the Germans that evening, made so deep an impression on his audience that no questions were asked. The spokesmen for the opposition, Arthur Greenwood for Labour and Archibald Sinclair for the Liberals, pledged the support of their parties. The Commons, so often rowdy and unsympathetic, recognized for a moment the moral agony, the misery which Chamberlain was undergoing and gave him its sympathy.[47]

Within a day this appearance of determination and national unity was to disappear. The fault lay, however, in Paris, with aid from Italy, rather than in any British failure of determination or the recurrence of a desire to buy peace by some last-minute measure of appeasement. Up to the morning of September 1, British policy had been to work for a German-Polish agreement, though not, as in 1938, by threats to abandon the Poles; indeed the last message that Halifax had sent Warsaw before catastrophe struck emphasized the British guarantee and the strength that that gave the Poles. The pressure was to be brought on Germany; and Halifax, and not only Halifax, had thought it was succeeding, not realizing either the depths of Hitler's determination or the degree to which Halifax's chosen instruments, Henderson and Dahlerus, were unsuited to the job they had to do because they basically shared Hitler's conviction that Polish interests were illegitimate beside Germany's will, and of the danger of an Anglo-German war. To do Sir Nevile justice, he did his best. But he was too associated in the minds of his German audience with the zeal with which he had pursued an Anglo-German understanding and with the manner in which he had dismissed the interests of lesser powers who had profited by the Versailles diktat, to carry conviction. His replacement had been under discussion for some time; but there were no very obvious candidates and the matter was postponed.

The trouble in Paris began with the meeting of the French Council of Ministers on August 31. The meeting of the Council had been called after a week or more in which its members had been left completely in the dark. The crisis of August 25/6 had passed without being remarked. Then suddenly, at 1.05 in the afternoon, M. François-Poncet had called from Rome with the Italian proposal for a conference.[48] At 1.30 p.m. M. Corbin had telephoned from London.[49] Halifax and Chamberlain accepted the Italian proposal on one condition: the demobilization of the opposing armies. Bonnet, delighted, consulted Daladier. The meeting of the Council of Ministers was summoned for 6 p.m. The leading Italophile in the Cabinet, de Monzie, had lunched with the Italian Ambassador, Guariglia, who was completely in the dark. De Monzie, alerted by Bonnet,[50] set out to fix some of the less extreme hawks in the French Cabinet, Henri Queuille, Charles Pomaret and Jean Zay. Zay was torn. So long as the conference was not a new Munich, so long as France acted in absolute agreement with Britain, then he would accept – the authentic voice of the Third Republic.

At the Council Bonnet pleaded strongly for the acceptance of the Italian proposal. It would gain several days.[51] The British proposal for demobilization should be rejected. Poland must be present at the conference, whose scope must be widened to cover all the problems threatening world peace. Daladier, whose hatred for his Foreign Minister was by now limitless, and who had in the meantime been briefed by Léger, 'bristled like a hedgehog. He turned his back on Bonnet from the first minute. His expression was one of contemptuous disgust.'[52] When he spoke he dismissed the Italian proposal as a new Munich. Léger had told him it was a trap. As for demobilization, General Gamelin had told him it would be mad and imprudent. A dictatorship could remobilize very quickly, a democracy could not. During the meeting, a note was brought in from the Ambassador in London. Halifax had called the Italian proposal a dangerous manœuvre. Daladier clinched the matter by reading a letter from Robert Coulondre. The letter had been written two days earlier, under the impact of Coulondre's discovery of Hitler's recall of the troops on August 25. He was convinced Hitler was bluffing. 'All that was necessary was to hold on, to hold on, to hold on.'[53] The letter convinced the waverers. It left Bonnet, who had not seen it and was taken by surprise, in a rage.[54]

Unlike the British Cabinet, the French Council of Ministers had no secretariat. No records were kept, no decision recorded. While Daladier and his supporters thought the Italian proposal had been squashed and the Minister of the Interior, Albert Sarraut, issued a press communiqué which seemed to imply this,[55] Bonnet and de Monzie were determined to continue to pursue the idea of a conference. Bonnet composed instructions for François-Poncet in this sense.[56] He also told the British Ambassador, Sir Eric Phipps, his confidant against Daladier's Italophobia, that the Italian proposal could not be declined out of hand.[57] A French draft reply, proposing a widening of the membership and scope of the conference, would be sent to London on September 1. It was this reply, arriving at 10.15 on September 1, which, as we have seen, Halifax ignored in view of Hitler's resort to war.

The news of the German attack, which reached Bonnet in two

telegrams from Léon Noël in Warsaw at 8.20 and 8.30 a.m.,[58] made no difference to him. At 9 a.m. that morning the Italian Ambassador, Raffaele Guariglia, was telephoned by his French cousin, the Comte de Ronceray.[59] Induced by de Monzie, the Count gave Guariglia the news that the French Council of Ministers had, the previous day, accepted the Italian proposal for a conference. Guariglia, who as usual had been kept completely in the dark by Count Ciano and knew nothing either of the proposal or its acceptance, wisely said nothing. Despite the unfortunate 'contretemps' which had intervened (so did the Count dismiss the German invasion of Poland), the French view was that the Italians should persist with their proposal. Following the phone call, his cousin came to the Italian Ambassador's house, followed by one of Bonnet's closest allies, the former Naval Minister and member of the Assembly, François Piétri.

At 10 a.m. Bonnet summoned Guariglia to the Quai d'Orsay, and told him that François-Poncet had been instructed to see Mussolini. Any question of waiting for London to approve the draft telegram had disappeared overnight. Guariglia noticed that, in addition to Piétri, Henri Béranger and Jean Mistler, the Chairmen of the Foreign Affairs Committees of both houses of the French Parliament, the Senate and the Chamber of Deputies, were waiting in Bonnet's anteroom. Guariglia then had a message sent by Guy la Chambre, the Air Minister, ostensibly from Daladier. France, it said, desired the restoration of Franco-Italian friendship with all the consequences that followed from it. Guariglia phoned the news through to Ciano at 11.25.

The Council of Ministers met that morning at 10.35 a.m.[60] It took two important decisions. It decreed that general mobilization should begin on September 2. And it decided to convoke Parliament for the afternoon of the same day to vote 75 milliard francs in supplementary military credits. Bonnet demanded once more that the Italian offer be accepted; he does not seem to have pressed the point. On emerging from the meeting, he sent François-Poncet his version of the decisions taken on August 31[61] (he had as usual lied to Guariglia: the telegram had not yet been sent when he saw him at 10 a.m.). François-Poncet saw Ciano at 12.35. He was pleased, but doubtful whether the Italian proposal now had any chance of success.[62] He had in fact just seen the British Ambassador, Sir Percy Loraine. Loraine did not seem to have taken in the force of Halifax's instructions.[63] He left Ciano[64] – and to judge by his own report, knew that he had left Ciano – still believing that Britain would not reject an Italian move.[65] Ciano's scepticism was based on his sense of 'the rabid determination of the Germans to fight'.[66]

Bonnet now had to bring the British and the Poles to accept the Italian proposal. He cannot have been sanguine that the Poles would accept. It is possible he hoped to use any refusal they might give to create prejudice against them. It is possible that Sir Eric Phipps, whose few telegrams of September 1 are models of brevity and reticence, may have misled him, if only by his silence, into thinking he had some prospects of success. In any case the gamble had to be taken. Bonnet was only of use to Daladier while he was maintaining a reasonable level of success in his diplomacy, and while Daladier felt that he needed Bonnet and the Parliamentary allies to maintain his Cabinet in office. Failure in the first would affect the value of the second. At 3.40 p.m. Bonnet phoned Corbin in London.[67] He told him that Ciano was of a mind to repeat his proposal for a conference and felt Poland should be present. Corbin should discover the exact terms in which Britain had replied to Italy. Bonnet then phoned Phipps and got a discouraging reply. Corbin returned his call at 4.10. Loraine had told Ciano that Britain would have favoured the Italian proposal had Hitler not gone to war. 'To do anything now would be to throw holy water over a man with a rope round his neck'; so Corbin reported the Foreign Office reply.[68]

To telephone Warsaw was more difficult. Bonnet finally reached Noël via Bucharest at 6.25 p.m.[69] Beck's reply,[70] made after consulting Marshal Smigly-Rydz, was understandably not only negative but irate. Warsaw had been attacked twice that day. The real question, he told Noël, was not whether a conference should be held but what common action should be taken by the Allies. None of this prevented Bonnet from continuing his pressure on Rome to attempt to convene a conference. 'If they encounter a refusal, then we will see.'[71]

Ciano was facing rather different problems. By September 1 Mussolini was convinced of the need for Italy to stay neutral. At 7.30 a.m. Attolico telephoned Rome. He feared that nothing more could be done. The German radio had broadcast Hitler's appeal to his armies to do their duty.[72] A quarter of an hour later he telephoned again. He could not get through to the German Foreign Ministry.[73] The Germans had annexed Danzig and barred all neutral shipping from the Gulf of Danzig while military operations were in progress. Mussolini reacted very quickly. By 8.30 a.m. he had instructed Attolico to secure from Hitler a note absolving Italy of any responsibilities under the alliance.[74] Using Hewel as his intermediary, Attolico managed to see Hitler without Ribbentrop being present, a condition Hitler had tried to insist on. Ribbentrop had apparently left instructions that no one was to see Hitler if he was not there. 'With no very great enthusiasm'[75] the Führer agreed to the Italian request. Hewel was told to tear up the telegram he was drafting and substitute one on the lines Mussolini requested. Attolico phoned the news at 9.15.[76] Ribbentrop then caused the SS guards to bar all entry to the Reichs Chancellery, with an SS officer to play 'the role of Cerberus' on his behalf. He also held up the offending telegram until after the Reichstag meeting.[77]

It was swiftly followed by a more self-justificatory telegram;[78] and then, as the telegraphic facilities were clearly unable to cope, the German Embassy in Rome was phoned simultaneously by Ribbentrop and Erich Kordt, and the text of both telegrams dictated by phone. The German Ambassador, Hans von Mackensen, called on Mussolini, to whom he was taken by Ciano at 1.10 p.m. According to his account[79] (which differs significantly in timing from that of the Italians), Mussolini fell over himself in gratitude, offering the support of the Italian press and saying that he hoped to be able to send considerable contingents of Italian workers, as Hitler had requested, from Venezia. Mackensen observed cautiously that Germany really needed coalminers. Mussolini replied that the average worker from Venezia was so versatile that, within a month or two, he would attain a miner's average output. Ciano told Mackensen[80] of the French support for a conference. Mackensen replied noncommittally that the word 'conference' rang unpleasantly in German ears. To which Ciano replied that Germany could not really complain at the results of Munich, the only conference Germany had attended.

At 3 o'clock the Fascist Grand Council met. On his way there, Grandi noted that the war-at-all-costs brigade, whose brave sailors were going to sink the Royal Navy and whose Blackshirts were going to be in Paris in three days, were strangely subdued. Their leader, Starace, the Fascist Party Secretary, was soon to be dismissed by the Duce. Mussolini himself was frowning, heavy, pale.[81] But the decision was firmly for 'non-belligerency', a word favoured by Mussolini as less wimpish than 'neutrality'. Ciano delivered himself of some of the resentment and hostility against Germany built up since his ill-fated meeting at Salzburg. Mussolini, however, said that Italy was firmly with Germany. The idea of a conference was at an end. The Poles had ignored it; they would without doubt be crushed. Ribbentrop was a liar; he had lied to the Führer. If anyone was betrayed, it was Italy. It was not a very connected or logical speech, but Mussolini had seen the whole rationality of his position totally challenged. The Poles, Hitler, Ribbentrop, the Allies, all had behaved out of character and, as he understood rational behaviour, quite irrationally. Still worse, they had forced him to discover, even if only briefly and fleetingly, how little the Italian people hankered after grandeur and war, and how vast the gap between Italy's strength as his rhetoric had persuaded him it was, and the reality. He was fighting for his self-esteem.

Ciano had another worry. Augusto Rosso, the Italian Ambassador in Moscow, had picked up something which the Soviets were doing their best to keep secret: the dispatch of the Soviet military mission to Berlin. The mission was actually intended to bring the Soviet Embassy in Berlin back to its proper strength. There had been no Soviet military attaché in Berlin for some time. The Soviet Ambassador, Merekalov, had not returned to Berlin in April. The Soviet Chargé d'affaires, Astakhov, who had conducted so much of the Berlin end of the negotiations which took Ribbentrop to Moscow, had been suddenly recalled to Moscow in the last few days before Ribbentrop's arrival. The Russians refused a German request that he be allowed to return to Berlin.[82] During his brief stay in Moscow, Ribbentrop had agreed with Molotov[83] that a new ambassador and a new military attaché should be sent to Berlin without delay, also that a special confidential representative should be sent by Molotov to be attached to Ribbentrop.[84] A new Soviet Chargé d'affaires, Ivanov, arrived on August 27 and was received by Hitler on August 29.[85]

The Soviets pleaded the lack of suitable personalities. On August 25 they named two new diplomatic personalities, Alexander Shkvartsev, as Counsellor, and as First Secretary, Kobulov, whom they described as an Armenian.[86] He was in fact Georgian, a younger brother to one of the three most senior NKVD appointments Beria had brought with him from Georgia when he took over the headship of the NKVD; Kobulov was a senior figure in the NKVD himself. The military mission was not appointed until August 29.[87] Its members' names were announced on August 31:[88] Corps Commander Purkayev, Brigadier General Belyakov and Colonel Major Nikolai Skornyakov (Assistant Attaché for Air Matters); they did not leave for Berlin until September 2. On September 2, Shkvartsev was nominated as Ambassador.[89] He was an engineer who, until his translation to the diplomatic service, had been running the textile industry in the Ukraine.[90] Molotov's former personal secretary and interpreter, Vladimir Pavlov, described by Schulenburg on August 22 in a handwritten memorandum written between midnight and 3 a.m. and kept in the secret files of the Moscow Embassy,[91] as '"our" friend Pavlov', accompanied Shkvartsev as Molotov's personal representative with Ribbentrop.[92]

Molotov had insisted, on the specious grounds that the mission's security might be endangered, on keeping the dispatch of the military mission secret until its safe arrival in Berlin.[93] This may have been part of the double game which was to lead the Soviet Ambassador in

Warsaw, on the first day of the German attack, to urge the Poles to ask for Soviet military supplies;[94] but it would seem more probable that it was a result of the total paralysis of all Soviet initiative other than that undertaken by Molotov in the face of so extraordinary and frightening a reversal of policy as the Nazi-Soviet Pact. Until Molotov's address to the Supreme Soviet on August 31,[95] which sought the sanction of Stalin's speech of March 11 as its justification, the rank and file of Soviet officialdom and of the party would simply not know what it was safe to do, say or think about the new course of Soviet policy.

Ciano feared this might be the precursor of a German-Soviet military alliance, as he remarked to Loraine on the morning of September 1. And coming out of the afternoon session of the Fascist Grand Council, he said angrily to Giuseppe Bottai, the Italian Minister for Education, and one of the *Gerarchi*, that if Germany brought Russia into Europe, Italy might find herself intervening on the opposite side.[96] Goering had, however, let the cat out of the bag to Henderson on August 31. Loraine, forewarned, kept an impassive face toward Ciano's anxieties.[97]

Bonnet had not, so far, extracted any real Italian support for his latest intrigue. Instead he could not escape going along with the instructions the British Cabinet was sending to Berlin. These were dispatched by Halifax to Henderson at 4.45 p.m. on September 1.[98] The instructions were to be carried out in conjunction with M. Coulondre. They were in the nature of a warning and not an ultimatum. If the German reply was not satisfactory, the next stage would be either an ultimatum with a time limit or an immediate declaration of war. Henderson was to make a very short statement. Its gist was that the German action appeared to the British and French Governments to call for the implementation of the Anglo-French undertakings to Poland. Unless Germany was prepared to give satisfactory assurances that she would suspend all aggressive action against Poland and withdraw her forces from Polish territory, Britain would without hesitation fulfil her obligations to Poland. This note was sent *en clair* and intercepted by the *Forschungsamt*.[99] It is hardly surprising, therefore, given Ribbentrop's moral cowardice and natural tendency to procrastinate, that it took Henderson four hours to get an interview with Ribbentrop, despite a formal application and two reminders.[100] He finally saw Ribbentrop at 9.30 p.m.[101] Ribbentrop said the message must be referred to Hitler. He also remarked that if Britain had been as active *vis-à-vis* Poland as she had been towards Germany, a settlement would have been reached at an early stage.

Corbin had phoned the text of Henderson's instructions through to Paris at 5.30 p.m.[102] Bonnet spared himself the need to argue. He simply instructed Coulondre to associate himself with Henderson's *démarche*,[103] which, as Coulondre remarked ironically, made his task that much easier.[104] Coulondre found that Ribbentrop would not subject himself to simultaneous pressure from both himself and Henderson. He did not get to see Ribbentrop until 10 p.m.[105] As with Henderson, Ribbentrop put the whole blame for the outbreak of hostilities on Poland, 'after having debited me with several lies', particularly by declaring that the Poles had invaded Germany at two points, said Coulondre. They parted on formal terms, Ribbentrop promising a formal reply. Bonnet continued with his pretence that a conference was in the offing. At midnight, Havas, the official French news agency, released an official communiqué, a masterpiece in suppression of the truth and suggestion of the false, by which, despite all discouragement, Bonnet could keep the prospect of Italian mediation open for another twenty-four hours. Its gist was as follows:[106] 'The French Government has today, as have several other Governments, received an Italian proposal looking to the resolution of Europe's difficulties. After due consideration the French Government has given a "positive response".'

Poland had then been under attack for sixteen hours.

CHAPTER 29

FENCING IN, FENCING OUT WAR: ROOSEVELT, PIUS XII, KING LÉOPOLD AND THE NEUTRALS

As the drumrolls of the German press and radio began their crescendo of hate and calumny against the Poles, the nations not directly involved in the Anglo-French guarantee system began to consider hard what to do. Feeling himself deceived or at least out-paced by Hitler, Mussolini, as we have seen, resorted to 'non-belligerency' and was entangled in M. Bonnet's desperate attempts to evade the operation of the French guarantee for Poland. Yugoslavia, Romania and Bulgaria tried to damp down their internecine conflict for fear of leaving some avenue open for Germany to lever them into its clutches. The Soviet leadership chose to collaborate with Hitler, in the hope of buying space and time against the day when Hitler remembered his ideological roots.

It is a measure of the degree to which Roosevelt thought of America as a part of or an eventual arbitrator in the European conflict that he was to match the efforts of the group of 'non-involved' European states and those of the other spiritual 'leader' of Europe, the Pope, to prevent the final breakdown of peace by appeals to the potential belligerents. It is a measure of the degree to which, like Stalin, he had already chosen his side that his open appeals were accompanied by a clandestine re-interpretation of the obligations of neutrality that was designed to work in favour of the democracies. In this, his views marched easily with those of the majority of the American people (though not of Congress). Like a spectator at a baseball game, he picked which side to root for; but, whatever his enemies might say then or later, he was far from intending to get down from the stands, don players' clothes and take a direct hand in the game. At best discreet hand signals from the dug-out was about as far as he was prepared to go.

The American press and radio had few such inhibitions. They were served by a generation of correspondents who had lived through the breakdown of democratic Europe, had seen democrats and dissidents buckle under the boots and blackjacks of Brown- and Blackshirts, be

551

hauled into vans and disappear into camps for 're-education'. They had reported on the civil war in Vienna and the riots in Paris in February 1934, on the murders of Dollfuss and King Alexander of Yugoslavia, on Ethiopia and on Spain. They had seen the aftermath of Hitler's march into Austria, and of the Gestapo's move into the Sudetenland in October 1938 and Bohemia and Moravia in March 1939. They had tangled with the police and the security authorities throughout Europe, and had no love for those who showed little or no love for them and their claims to uphold freedom of the press. They had believed all the rumours, picked up the misinformation and (like the ace American reporter in Evelyn Waugh's *Scoop*, who, sent to cover a revolution in a Balkan city, had provoked, by his reporting, a revolution in another state in whose capital he had alighted in error) their reportage had heavily enhanced and reinforced democratic perceptions of developments in Europe as a civil war between Fascism, authoritarianism, aristocratic élitist social organization and democracy, parliamentarianism, the common people.

For much of the 1930s they had found the British and French Governments difficult to place in this version of European history; they seemed to fail continually to pick up their cues. Aware up to a point of the repressive, managerial behaviour of the Conservative Government towards the British press and the degree to which some editors of the press, notably of *The Times*, co-operated with such management, it was easy for the American press and radio correspondents to believe, and to convince their readers, that there was a degree of conspiratorial collusion between the British establishment and European authoritarianism. For those who could make a hero out of Edvard Beneš, it was easy to make Chamberlain into a dupe, if not a collaborator, and the umbrella into a symbol of weak-kneed Mr Milquetoastianism, such that for the next two decades no American politician dared be seen carrying one. Reporters of the Cold War in 1930s Europe, they made of European politics – as they were, to Britain's benefit, to make of war in Europe – the kind of old-fashioned spectator sport in which there are true-blue heroes, low mean skunks, and corrupt gamblers tempting players to throw matches.

In the year 1939, this kind of reportage had had to face several shocks. The collapse of the Spanish Republican forces had ended one war in favour of the villains. The series of bold British initiatives between March and May had rather shaken the correspondents' view of the Chamberlain Cabinet's incurable tendency to buy peace at the expense of those Britain was supposed to protect, although there were enough would-be settlers of Anglo-German differences around still to confuse everybody. There was no British or French Cabinet member who lent himself to easy dramatization as a hero, least of all the mainspring of the changes in British policy, Lord Halifax. As for France, the reporters ran from Daladier to Bonnet, from Reynaud to Campinchi, and could find only ill-motivated confusion of motives or amiable, thick-headed, pompous French patriotism.

To crown it all came the Nazi-Soviet Pact, four months after the replacement of the always approachable and quotable Litvinov by Molotov, a man as invisible to the press as Stalin then was himself. This was coupled with an upsurging of the ordinary people of Britain and France. In the absence, at least until 1940, of heroic leaders, it was the common people, especially of London and Paris, displaying a degree of social patriotism and social discipline hitherto ignored or denigrated by the American press and radio, who became the heroes of their reportage and of the American public. Britain entered the war with an enormous reservoir of goodwill in America and – the pay-off to the seemingly endless lengths to which the pro-appeasement wing of the British Government had gone to avoid a direct challenge to Germany – a firm American conviction that Hitler's Germany was thoroughly in the wrong, even over Danzig and the German minority in Poland.

Roosevelt knew, however, that effective politics are not made by changes in the favour with which large but ill defined and ill organized numbers of the general American public regard a nation or an issue, but only limited by them. To be effective, policies have to be manœuvred through the thickets and prickly palm plantations of special interests, active and vociferous pressure groups, key states and their senators, key minorities and their spokesmen and spokeswomen. Many of these had no interest in the sport, where they did not want it abolished. One and all were determined to ban it from American stadia. It was essential, therefore, for the President to be seen to be above the mêlée. He moved very warily, where he moved openly.

Besides the President of the United States, there were two other forces involved in the efforts to prevent a European war: the Vatican and the so-called 'Oslo group' of states. The three appeals were to come within two days of each other: the Oslo group's through the mouth of King Léopold of the Belgians, by radio on August 23; the Pope's, also by radio, on August 24; and Roosevelt's in a series of messages to the King of Italy, to Hitler and to President Mościcky of Poland, all delivered on August 24. Given Hitler's progression from the address to his generals at the Berghof on August 22 to the celebrations of Ribbentrop's return from Moscow on the evening of August 24, his expectations that both the Chamberlain and Daladier Governments would fall, and the issue and rescission of the orders to attack Poland on August 25, it is clear that none of these appeals had the remotest chance of success. They were, however, made from different motives, had very different origins and those who made them derived very different lessons from them.

Roosevelt's appeal was made principally in response to Daladier's pressure on William Bullitt, the American Ambassador in Paris, under the numbing influence of the announcement at midnight on August 21/2 that Ribbentrop was about to visit Moscow to conclude a non-aggression pact with the Soviet Union. Daladier had already shown Bullitt information on German mobilization and troop movements pointing at German readiness to 'break loose' at the end of the week of August 21–6. On August 22 Bullitt twice telephoned Washington. On the first occasion he said that if there was anything Roosevelt could do 'to avert war, no time should be lost.' On the second he quoted Daladier as saying that an appeal by Roosevelt might act as a deterrent to Hitler. If the President were to summon everyone to Washington to a conference to settle all issues, Daladier would accept at once for France 'with deep gratitude'. The Nazi-Soviet Pact, Bullitt said, had destroyed the bones of French strategy, since it would take Britain two years before she developed a 'serious army'. France would either have to bear the brunt of the fighting for that period, and 'sacrifice French lives' in a war whose outcome was doubtful, to say the least, or renege on her commitment to Poland, take the shock to French morale, see Hitler overrun Poland and south-east Europe and become much stronger before he turned on France again. Welles duly passed all these telegrams to Roosevelt, who was then at sea on the USS *Tuscaloosa*.[1]

It is, of course, possible that Bullitt exaggerated the whingeing tone of Daladier's comments. He consistently represents the French Premier as a querulous Anglophobe, seeking American aid to replace French dependence on Britain, willing to express himself in a manner and a tone as singularly inconsistent with the pride of his fellow countrymen as with the position he occupied. But Daladier's own private military sources of information were all pessimistic, most notably Colonel Paul de Villelume, the French Staff officer charged with liaison between the Army General Staff and the French Foreign Ministry, a man who held both of those organizations in equal contempt for their failure to give their political overlords a true picture of French weakness and its likely consequences if France went to war.

Whatever his reasons, Roosevelt proceeded to a double manœuvre. An American president combines within his office two roles which in every other country (but Nazi Germany, oddly enough) are divided, that of head of state and head of government. He now donned the mantle of head of state, appealing in this capacity to the King of Italy, to President Mościcky of Poland and to Hitler himself. The appeal to the King of Italy was actually sent on August 23.[2] The King, however, was isolated in a remote mountain valley, an hour and three-quarters' drive from Turin. It took William Phillips, the US Ambassador to Rome, a day to get Mussolini's permission to see him. So it was on August 24, beneath lowering skies and a relentless drizzle, that he caught up with Victor Emmanuel on a trout-fishing holiday, living in a simple encampment of wood-frame houses. Phillips did not know[3] whether it was a sign of royal insouciance or powerlessness that at a moment of such severe crisis he should be so out of touch.

Roosevelt's message hinted at the kind of conference Daladier envisaged; but it amounted much more to a plea for Italian pressure on Germany to accept a pacific solution to 'the present crisis'. In this Roosevelt was, in part, following the clues Phillips had already given him as to the weaknesses in Mussolini's position *vis-à-vis* the Italian monarchy and the divisions within the *Gerarchi*. He also was well aware from British and other sources of the impact Ciano's visit to Salzburg had had on Italy's relationship with Germany.[4] He knew too of the British approaches to Mussolini and, from the British, had heard of the resistance shown by the King, the Italian military and some of the Fascist leadership to the *bellicistes* in Mussolini's entourage.[5] The approach to the Italian King was therefore seriously thought out, designed to outflank Mussolini and indeed Ciano, and push the Italian Government into further pressure on Hitler.

But what if it failed? Even before the announcement of Ribbentrop's visit to Moscow, the evidence coming in to Roosevelt from London, Paris and Warsaw, as well as from Berlin, pointed strongly to a degree of determination on Hitler's part from which no pressure, however strong, and no last-minute invitations to conferences were likely to divert him. The appeal to Hitler was, therefore, designed to make him show his hand, to put him on the spot. Shortly after sending the message to King Victor Emmanuel, Roosevelt would have seen Kennedy's report on Chamberlain's views.[6] Setting aside the despair and defeatism on the subject of avoiding war, the British inability to evade their Polish responsibilities was very strongly put; the message which Chamberlain sent to Hitler on August 23, which was also shown to Roosevelt,[7] confirmed the President in his views that, whatever Hull, his Secretary of State, might think, Britain was not preparing 'a new Munich'. A telegram from Bullitt[8] reporting Bonnet's conviction that 'there was no longer the slightest hope of preserving peace' would have reinforced these convictions.

The appeal to Hitler,[9] for a German-Polish agreement to refrain from hostilities for a set period while they solved their mutual problems by negotiation, arbitration or conciliation, was not therefore launched out of a naïve hope that Hitler's resolve might be weakened. It was designed to show outside opinion, especially in the United States, that Hitler was determined on war. The parallel message to President Mościcky of Poland[10] was to enhance this impression, since Mościcky replied on August 25 accepting direct negotiation,[11] enabling Roosevelt to renew his appeal to Hitler the following day.[12] The German Foreign Ministry and Hitler were well aware of this.[13] The only thing they could do was ride with the punch[14] until on August 31 Hitler finally felt free to reply that Polish intransigence had rendered the President's appeal no longer valid.[15] It was not Polish intransigence that brought Roosevelt's manœuvre to naught but Hitler's last-minute withdrawal of the orders to attack Poland on August 26 and their re-issue on August 31.

Nevertheless, the President's message lay on the record; and Mościcky's reply, as we have seen, encouraged Lord Halifax in his belief that direct German negotiations with the Poles might just provide a way out of a direct collision. What did not lie on the record was the instructions[16] given on August 21 by Hanes, Morgenthau's deputy in the US Treasury, to US customs officials and to the US coastguard that no irregularities were to be allowed in the clearance or departure of foreign vessels from American ports. Any attempt at a hurried or unscheduled departure was to be treated as suspicious and the offending ship thoroughly searched to see that there was no 'unmanifested merchandise aboard'. Roosevelt reinforced these instructions on August 25,[17] instructing that such ships should be searched for armaments that could be installed at sea. The effect was to hold German ships in American ports so as to improve the prospects of the Royal Navy – not exactly a neutral act. Roosevelt told Sir Ronald Lindsay that while it would take two to three days to search a German ship, British ships could rely on being away in half an hour. 'He spoke with a sort of impish glee,' reported Lindsay;[18] 'the whole business gave me the impression of resembling a schoolboy prank.' Once again, however, the delay in the attack on Poland from August 25 to August 31 and the two and a half days lost by M. Bonnet's delaying tactics between 4.45 a.m. on September 1, the hour of the German attack on Poland, and 11 a.m. on September 3, when the British ultimatum to Germany expired, meant that Roosevelt's manœuvre failed to catch any of the German merchant ships in American ports on August 22.

The Pope's intervention had rather different motives. Since the new Pope's accession, Osborne, the British Minister to the Vatican, had been establishing ever closer relations with the new Cardinal Secretary of State, Cardinal Maglione, and his two deputies, Monsignori Montini and Tardini. This policy was seen in London as one of the additional paths by which pressure could be brought to bear on Mussolini and the Italian Government. Halifax was to take as much care in keeping the Vatican informed of every exchange between London and Berlin as he was to show towards Roosevelt and Mussolini himself. On August 18 Osborne took Maglione detailed information about Burckhardt's visit to Hitler on August 11. Halifax had charged Osborne[19] to advise Maglione that, in his view, if the Vatican wished to be of service to the preservation of peace, there were two courses of action to follow. The first was a secret approach to the principal states to persuade them to open diplomatic exchanges and to act as an intermediary. The second, for later, 'should the crisis reach an acute stage', was a public approach urging a pacific solution. The approach should, however, concern itself with procedure not proposals, especially not of a return of Danzig to the Reich.

Osborne found Maglione over-worked, anxious, tired and depressed. He was, in fact, about to leave on holiday.[20] In part his anxiety arose from his inability to discover what had passed between Ciano and Hitler at Salzburg, or to derive any clear impression of which way Mussolini's indecision would be resolved;[21] the latter worry was shared, it will be remembered, by Count Ciano himself and the whole Fascist hierarchy. Maglione had been unable to get a clear answer out of the Italian Envoy to the Vatican. The anti-Polish tone of the Italian press worried him. There was much too much talk of war coming from the German and Polish press. The Poles told the Papal Nuncio in Warsaw[22] that they were at a loss what to suggest. The German military build-up on their frontiers was proceeding apace. Cardinal Maglione told Osborne that no papal initiative was being planned for the moment. In his absence papal business was to be conducted by Monsignor Tardini.

Tardini was a stocky little man, vehement of opinion, sardonic in expression, direct, often to the point of rudeness, of modest origins, the opposite of everything a Vatican functionary was supposed to be. He disliked Fascism, loathed the Nazis and had been heard to refer to Hitler as a 'mechanized Attila'.[23] This may well account, in some way, for the Vatican's decision to follow Halifax's advice but to reverse the order which Halifax had suggested. The public appeal – or rather, appeals – came first, rather than later. One was made on August 19, in an address to a group of pilgrims.[24] The second was to be made over Vatican radio on August 24.

It is possible to see this change in the Vatican's attitude as a response to the sudden acceleration of the German-Polish conflict whipped up by Hitler in preparation for the attack on Poland planned for 4.30 a.m. on August 26. The Vatican certainly found itself under considerable pressure from François Charles-Roux, the French Ambassador and doyen of the foreign diplomatic corps at the Vatican, a domineering, direct, persistent man who had a habit of browbeating the Vatican,[25] and who had lobbied shamelessly that year for Cardinal Pacelli's successful candidacy as the successor to Pius XI.[26] He wrote Tardini a strong letter on August 22;[27] one of his staff spoke strongly to Montini, the following day.[28] That same day he had a lengthy session with Father Ledochowski, General of the Jesuit order and a Pole whose Polishness was as passionate as his Catholicism.[29]

It is, however, a measure of Osborne's success that, following an appeal on August 22 from Lord Halifax for papal action,[30] and a private letter from Osborne to Monsignor Tardini the following day,[31] it was Osborne's suggestion of a radio address, to be published in *Osservatore Romano*, the Vatican's daily newspaper, that was adopted.[32] The Vatican, however, laboured under more difficulties than Lord Halifax allowed for, although the problems had in fact been explained to him in a letter written by Cardinal Maglione to Osborne in the middle of July.[33] The Vatican was faced with the possibility of a war between Germany and perhaps Italy against Britain, France and Poland. Poland was a profoundly Catholic country. The Vatican disliked Fascism and loathed and feared Nazism. Moreover, the Pope regarded Hitler, as did Chamberlain and Halifax, as impossible to trust. 'Religious persecution and the paganization of the young', he told the retiring Belgian Ambassador, M. de l'Escaille, had confronted him with a situation in which he literally did not know what to do.[34] The Vatican distrusted the secular authority of the French Third Republic, but maintained increasingly good relations with its Government. Seen as a war between one profoundly anti-Christian ideology and a profoundly Catholic country, a German-Polish conflict would have presented the Vatican with few problems. But Italy was infinitely more Catholic than Fascist and Germany had forty million Catholics, more than the whole population of France, a point the Pope was to make with some force to the French Ambassador, M. Charles-Roux, on August 28.[35] A war between two or more nation-states, each with large Catholic populations, was a war in which the Vatican could not, dared not take sides. As for the prospect of diplomatic negotiations, no more than Halifax could the

Vatican see any basis acceptable to both sides. 'Europe', said Cardinal Maglione to M. de l'Escaille, was 'like a sick man, who does not wish to die'.[36]

The Vatican's main aim was to keep Italy neutral. In that it saw eye to eye with Lord Halifax, with the Fascist Grand Council and with Mussolini most of the time. Vatican radio was not easily heard north and west of the Alps; Germans were forbidden to listen. It was audible throughout Italy. Nor was the Pope anxious gratuitously to provoke a new conflict with Hitler. In 1937 under his predecessor as Pope there had been a head-on collision. Pius XI had denounced Hitler's interference with the Catholic Church in Germany and the Gestapo's persecution of Catholic priests, nuns and laymen. He had rowed publicly with Mussolini over Italy's adoption of German anti-semitic legislation. Pius XII was conciliatory by nature. As Secretary of State to Pius XI he had borne much of the strain of battling with Hitler over the future of Catholicism in Germany. That conflict had ended in stalemate. The Vatican was not prepared to put the safety and loyalty of German Catholics at risk over any lesser issue.

The appeal broadcast by the Pope on August 24 is a moving document. It followed the least political of the four different drafts with which Tardini and Montini supplied him.[37] The evening of August 24, however, Hitler was celebrating Ribbentrop's return from Moscow and expecting the morning newspapers to report the fall of the Daladier and Chamberlain Governments. The next day he was to issue and rescind the order to attack Poland, after the news that the British alliance with Poland had been signed and that he could not expect Italian support. The papal appeal certainly did not make Mussolini's defection from the Axis any more difficult; but the manner in which Ciano and others brought him to this defection shows that the papal address played no direct part in it.

On August 27, Osborne spoke directly to the Pope, conveying Halifax's thanks and congratulations.[38] Pius XII placed some faint hopes for peace in the Anglo-German exchanges then in progress; otherwise he could see nothing further that he could do. He was in fact adding his pressure to that from London and Paris on the Poles to offer no pretext for a German attack.[39] In the meantime the Vatican was also doing its best to reinforce the division between Hitler and Mussolini. On August 28, Tardini observed in his characteristic manner that of the two dictators, Mussolini was 'the less mad of the two and this was the moment to influence him'.[40] The Pope, however, waited for another day, on the plain grounds that the Italian Government was already doing all it could to restrain Hitler.[41]

It needed the return of Cardinal Maglione from holiday to inveigle the Vatican into its least happy effort to bring about negotiations. He sent the Jesuit historian, Father Tacchi-Venturi, whom Mussolini had liked and trusted since 1922, to see Mussolini. The Duce suggested a scheme by which the Poles, in return for direct negotiations on Polish traffic in Danzig, on the Corridor and on the minorities (Poles in Germany, Germans in Poland), undertook not to oppose Danzig's return to Germany. The Pope should send this proposal via the Papal Nuncio in Warsaw directly to President Mościcky.[42]

Tardini fought the idea hard.[43] The Pope would be playing Hitler's game. Hitler would have a tasty morsel to satisfy his appetite and would start again in the spring. The Pope would be accused of arranging a new Munich and of being in Mussolini's pocket.

Maglione ignored this. Mussolini's proposal was telegraphed word for word to Warsaw.[44] Monsignor Cortesi, the Papal Nuncio, questioned the Vatican's wisdom.[15] He was told to go ahead and do as he was told.[46] The proposal was represented as one upon which Hitler was prepared to negotiate. The Polish Government was then confronting a very different set of demands from Berlin, the main element in which was the demand to produce a plenipotentiary in Berlin within twenty-four hours. Count Szembek saw Monsignor Cortesi on the afternoon of August 31.[47] Cortesi did his best, remarking that the Vatican was uniquely moved by its special attachment to Poland and its great fears for Poland in the presence of the danger of war. Szembek and Beck spotted Mussolini's hand at once. No action was taken. The German attack was just over twelve hours away.

The Pope made one final appeal that same day. His appeal to Germany, Poland, France and Italy to do all in their power to avoid an incident, and to abstain from any step that might aggravate the existing tension, was issued to Osborne, Charles-Roux, and Pignatti and von Bergen, the Italian and German Ministers, on the afternoon of August 31.[48] Von Bergen's telegram was received in the Wilhelmstrasse at 4.01 in the afternoon, a minute after the last point at which the orders for the attack could be rescinded, twelve hours and forty-five minutes before the guns of the *Schleswig-Holstein* opened fire on the Westerplatte. Though hard-pressed by Osborne and Charles-Roux to make some comments on the German action,[49] Cardinal Maglione refused. Instead he wanted absolution. Did Osborne feel the Vatican had done all it could in the interests of peace during the past weeks? Osborne, a Protestant, said that given the evident limitations on their action, he thought they had.

The third set of attempts to mediate between the prospective belligerents and to appeal for the preservation of peace came from a more secular, less ideologically motivated agency, the Oslo group of states. The Oslo group consisted of Norway, Denmark, Sweden, and Finland, Belgium, the Netherlands and Luxemburg. They had come together as an economic grouping in 1930 in a convention signed at Oslo in 1930 (Finland acceded to the group in 1932). In 1937 at The Hague they had signed a new convention on economic co-operation. They had acted together in similar fashion as the League of Nations security system had broken down in the face of Italy's assault on Ethiopia in 1935 and the German denunciation of the Locarno Treaty in March 1936. In July 1936 they had come together in a public refusal to consider the application of sanctions (Article XVI of the League of Nations Covenant) unless the other Articles of the Covenant looking to the prevention of war were reformed. In July 1938, faced with the imminent possibility of a European war breaking out over Czecho-slovakia, they had met at Copenhagen and issued a joint declaration that they no longer regarded the application of sanctions as compulsory. On September 24, 1938, six days before the Munich Conference ended the Czech crisis, the Foreign Ministers of the group met at Geneva during the meeting of the Assembly of the League of Nations. They agreed, as neutrals, to co-ordinate their trade policies in the event of war.

The initiative undertaken by the 'non-involved' Oslo group was, in fact, very largely the work of King Léopold III of the Belgians. It emerged from a conference, called at short notice, which met in Brussels on August 21–3, and took the form of a radio broadcast which he himself made in the other states' names over Brussels radio on the night of August 23. The conference emerged from his consultations with Queen Wilhelmina of the Netherlands, on the occasion of the state visit she paid to Belgium towards the end of May.[50] Both monarchies and their Governments had been alarmed by the war scare in January, even though the dire warnings then communicated to them had not been translated into reality. Reports of German designs against Belgium and the Netherlands, pressure from Paris on Brussels for Staff conversations, and German-spread reports of French plans against Belgium combined with the increasing signs of a German-Polish crisis over Danzig to worry them both; so that although much of the political side of the visit was taken up with discussions on a move towards a common market and the need for an international programme to overcome the general problems arising out of the breakdown of the world economy, Léopold and Wilhelmina also touched on the econ-omic problems the neutrals would face in the event of a new European war.

The development of their plans was delayed by constitutional difficulties in both countries. Both were constitutional and parliamentary
monarchies, governed by uneasy coalitions which, as in Britain, acted
in the name of the sovereign, but deprecated their sovereigns taking too
active a part in affairs of state. Léopold, like his forebears, had never
shaken off the traditions or outlook of German autocracy. A lonely man
since the tragic death of his popular queen, Astrid, he had become
increasingly isolated from his Cabinets[51] among a small group of
personal advisers. He took his constitutional position as Commander-
in-Chief of the Armed Forces very seriously. His sense of duty was to
betray him into surrendering himself into German custody in 1940,
when his Government and the Dutch Royal Family took refuge in exile.
He had little patience, faced with the possible enormity of a new war,
with constitutional niceties. Both he and Queen Wilhelmina, however,
faced a considerable degree of scepticism on the part of their Cabinets
over the urgency with which they sought to move from expressions of
pious but empty sentiment on the subject of the integration of the two
national economies to actual progress. This in turn delayed the development of closer co-operation in the defence of peace, despite the steady
worsening of the German-Polish crisis and the increasing evidence
of Hitler's military preparations. The Belgian military could see no
advantage in closer military co-operation between the two countries.[52]

Behind these differences there lay, however, the same dilemma as
beset President Roosevelt. Could active intervention, designed to
mobilize neutral opinion as a restraining force upon the potential
belligerents, be reconciled with neutrality? In 1936, after Hitler's
denunciation of the Locarno Treaty and remilitarization of the Rhineland, the Belgian Government, having already denounced twenty years
of Franco-Belgian Staff arrangements, had moved King Léopold in
September 1936 to declare from the throne a total refusal to become
involved in any future power bloc. During 1937, Britain, France and
Germany had all recognized this independence by separate declarations.
In May and June 1939, the Belgians had found themselves under
repeated pressure from the British Legation in Brussels to allow Staff
talks with Britain and France so that aid could be afforded them in the
event of a German violation of their neutrality.[53] Hubert Pierlot, a
devout Catholic, melancholy and reserved, 'serious to the point of
severity',[54] a man obsessed by detail, had added Foreign Affairs to the
premiership in April 1939. He would have agreed with Robert Walpole
not only in his horror of war, whatever the pretext, but also in his belief
that dogs asleep should never be disturbed. He had to bear the brunt of
the British pressure, while at the same time withstanding the alarm of

Parliament,[55] pressure from Germany,[56] and the efforts of the British and French to obtain from the Soviet Union, which he detested, Belgium's inclusion in the list of states to be guaranteed; Belgian opinion of all kinds took this as entirely contrary to their policy of neutrality. Henryk Colijn, the Dutch Premier, was if anything even more abstentionist in his views.

Towards the end of July, Léopold's impatience and mounting anxieties could be restrained no longer. On July 27 he unfolded his plan to his senior military adviser.[57] He wanted to bring together all the countries in Europe interested in the maintenance of peace. Although individually small, together they comprised over a hundred million Europeans. His chosen method was to address a letter to the heads of state of the Netherlands, Luxemburg, Norway, Sweden, Finland, Denmark, Portugal, Switzerland, and perhaps Romania, the Baltic and Balkan states, and Spain. (With the exception of Finland, Switzerland, Spain, Portugal and the three Baltic states, these were all monarchies.) Léopold drafted a letter to these monarchs that same day.

This idea had been privately discussed for a month or more between Baron Carton de Wiart of the Royal Secretariat and the senior officials of the Belgian Foreign Ministry. Tentative approaches to the Netherlands had found the Dutch Premier, Colijn, opposed. Nor was M. Pierlot an enthusiast for the idea. Léopold's action, however, was precipitated by the belief that Hitler would take advantage of either the Tannenberg celebrations or the Nuremberg *Parteitag*, scheduled for August 27 and September 2 respectively, to unleash an attack on Poland, and the necessity of launching an appeal before those dates, or so M. Pierlot explained it in retrospect to the Portuguese Minister in Brussels, Senhor Calheiros.[58] A meeting of foreign ministers at the September session of the League of Nations Assembly, favoured by Léopold's diplomatists, would be too late. Léopold sent Carton de Wiart directly to Queen Wilhelmina with a copy of his letter.[59] At the same time the Prince de Ligne toured the Scandinavian monarchies and M. Richard, a former Belgian Minister of Economics, took Léopold's letter to Lisbon to see Senhor A. Salazar de Oliveira, the Portuguese Premier and Foreign Minister. Baron Capelle, Léopold's personal secretary who inspired Léopold to this step, took the letter to King Carol of Romania.

It emerged very quickly that the Scandinavian Governments would have nothing to do with Spain, the Baltic and the Balkan countries, most especially Romania, tied to Poland by an alliance and to the Western powers by the British and French guarantees.[60] Wilhelmina, having rid herself of the obstructive Colijn, expressed her active support.[61] The new Dutch Foreign Minister and the Scandinavians also ruled out Portugal, Britain's oldest ally,[62] despite Richard's original approach; this in fact suited Salazar's preference for keeping Portugal out of the headlines,[63] especially in view of the uncertainty which still surrounded the Spanish position. Had Generalissimo Franco chosen to honour his engagements to Italy and Germany, Portugal's ties with Britain might well have provided a pretext for those ultra-nationalist Spaniards who wished to annex Portugal in the interests of a united Iberian peninsula. For his own part Salazar was profoundly pessimistic as to the prospects for peace, and said so in his reply to M. Richard.[64] 'The chances of success are minimal,' he stated.

The conference duly met in Brussels on August 23. Ribbentrop was on his way to Moscow, having spent the night in Königsberg. Sir Nevile Henderson was that morning in Berchtesgaden, the target of

Die Schweiz schirmt sich gegen fremde Einflüsse
'Switzerland protects itself against foreign influences'

Hitler's contrived hysteria over the sufferings of the German minority in Poland. Roosevelt and the Pope were considering their own initiatives. Hitler's generals, fresh, if that is the appropriate word, from their encounter with the Führer the previous day at Berchtesgaden, were making their last-minute preparations for an attack on Poland, to be launched at 4.30 a.m. on August 26, three days away. It was not the most encouraging of circumstances for an appeal for peace from the potential sheep to their potential butchers. Of the seven states that sent representatives to Brussels, five were, within a year, to find themselves under German occupation, and one had been forced into the Soviet sphere of influence.

The appeal was duly broadcast by Léopold himself in the name of the Kings of Denmark, Sweden and Norway, the Queen of the Netherlands, the Grand Duchess of Luxemburg and the President of Finland, over Brussels radio on the evening of August 23. The other powers had had the text since August 20. The Swiss had also been invited to send a representative.[65] Forewarned by their Legation in Stockholm, M. Etter, the President of the Swiss confederation, had already conferred with M. Motta, the Swiss Foreign Minister. With almost Ribbentropian delicacy they left the task of rejecting the Belgian invitation to the senior career head of the Swiss Ministry of Foreign Affairs, Hr Feldscher. He spoke quite frankly.[66] In view of the delicacy of the international situation, the Swiss would not take part in any collective action. In any case, the Swiss confederation did not have a simple head of state. The head of state, under the Swiss constitution, was the Federal Council in its collectivity. It could not meet in time (the invitation only arrived on August 22). It would, when it met, consider a separate Swiss appeal. Hr Feldscher had already denied that Switzerland had received an invitation to Brussels. In the Swiss view, no other state was as uniquely neutral as Switzerland. The Swiss record during World War II was to prove this, not always to the moral credit of the Swiss.

The conference did not run all that smoothly. Neither Pierlot nor his new Dutch colleague, E. N. van Kleffens, entirely approved of the initiative taken by their sovereigns. There was disagreement on the issue of whether the appeal to be made should be addressed to public opinion in general or to the Governments most closely involved in the incipient conflict.[67] The appeal was finally made general, 'to whomsoever it might concern'. It was not without its effect on German public opinion. It was carried by French radio and picked up by the French press.[68] M. Motta, though embarrassed, remained firm in rejecting an invitation to support it.[69] Lord Halifax, who never missed a trick, welcomed it.[70] King Carol of Romania, on the pretext of not wishing to weaken the position of his Polish allies, held his peace.[71] Roosevelt welcomed it.[72] Spanish opinion, revolting strongly against the German desertion of the cause of anti-Bolshevism, reacted favourably.[73] But, as with the appeals addressed by President Roosevelt to Hitler and Mościcky, and the radio address of August 24 made by Pius XII, the effect upon Hitler was as empty wind, a nullity.

The following week was to see Hitler's postponement of the attack on Poland from 4.30 a.m. on August 26 to 4.45 p.m. on September 1, while he and Goering sought a fresh way of manœuvring Poland into a trap and her Western guarantors into abandoning Poland. It also saw a movement of the Scandinavian states into a more neutral stance, apparent at the meeting of the Foreign Ministers of Norway, Sweden, Denmark and Finland at Oslo on August 31.

Léopold and Wilhelmina had one shot remaining. On August 28, as both countries mobilized their forces to guard their frontiers, the Dutch decided on a final appeal. Wilhelmina telephoned Léopold at 2 p.m. that afternoon to suggest a joint offer of their good offices to Britain, France, Poland, Germany and Italy. After a further exchange of messages, the two Foreign Ministers, Pierlot and van Kleffens, summoned the Ministers of the countries concerned and made their statement.[74] The Germans, who were preparing to dispatch economic missions to all the Oslo powers[75] – Ulrich von Hassell to the Scandinavian capitals, Karl Ritter to those of the future Benelux countries – were far more exercised over suggestions that they might be confronted with a single bloc with an agreed policy and again paid no attention; Hitler was already involved directly with Britain in the vain hope of bamboozling and browbeating Sir Nevile Henderson into providing his Government with a pretence for withdrawal. Mussolini had already decided effectively for non-belligerency. Lord Halifax once again expressed his warm appreciation, as did M. Moscicki (no relation of the Polish President), the Polish Minister in Brussels. Alas, it takes two to tango; and Hitler was, by now, resolutely determined on war.

It is here that the historical importance of these at first sight pointless and futile if well-meaning gestures by the neutral states lies. Their action, like much of that of Britain and France, was predicated on a model of how war might come, constructed from what they believed to have happened in 1914, reinforced by a sense of incredulity that anyone of an age to have lived through the events of 1914–18, let alone to have fought in them, could, wittingly, wish to go to war again. The outbreak of war in 1914 had come, so they believed, from an escalation of a petty conflict between Austria-Hungary and Serbia which could have been interrupted at several, if not at all stages in the process.

Should war come, despite their efforts, then their aim was, singly if necessary, collectively if possible, to fence themselves away from it by resolutely not thinking, saying or doing anything which one or other of the belligerents might think un-neutral and which might provide an excuse for them to intervene. The adage *inter arma silent leges* (amidst war the laws are silent) made it the more necessary for them not only to be neutral but to be seen clearly by the belligerents to be so. War had to be fenced out once it started; but before it started, everything must be done to avoid the psychological escalation which accompanied the actual move and counter-move, diplomatic and military, which led to war.

Such a process required that the potential belligerents should genuinely fear war, and that their difference should be resolvable by negotiations in good faith. In August/September 1939 that was not the case. Hitler wanted war with Poland; he was determined to destroy Poland. If this involved British and French hostilities against him, so be it. He did not believe it would; if Britain and France did go to war, he did not expect them to pursue war for very long or with very much determination. He had, in any case, resigned himself to war with Britain at some stage in his onrush to greatness. He paid no attention to the neutrals because he did not want a mediated settlement, least of all one from countries whose leadership he despised. He did not fall into war; nor was he pushed. He leapt into war, past the warnings of his more cautious advisers, past the efforts to appeal to his love of peace, past the clear statements from the British and French Governments, and despite the appeals from the Pope.

When war broke out, it was limited in scope to Britain, France and Poland on one side and Germany on the other. By October 2 the Baltic was as neutral a sea as the Mediterranean and the Black Sea. Germany was ringed with neutral states on her northern and southern frontiers. Scandinavia, the Benelux countries, Spain and Portugal, Italy and the Balkan countries, the Americas, even the Irish Free State declared themselves apart from the war. The seas were not so safe; though Roosevelt, as he promised, took steps to put the Western Atlantic out of bounds. On land and in the air, war was limited to the frontier between France and Germany, and to Germany's maritime frontier on the North Sea; but not for long.

CHAPTER 30

THUNDER IN LONDON

The morning of September 2 broke bright, sunny and early in London. Ministers and civil servants, diplomatists and soldiers who had found their way home through a blacked-out London, suddenly plunged into total darkness, awoke to a sky filled with barrage balloons. 'I don't think anyone expected to see so many,' Harry Crookshank, then a junior minister, wrote in his diary.[1] The day was calm, with that beautiful calm which, in London, is the earliest harbinger of autumn. Sir Alexander Cadogan walked with Lord and Lady Halifax through Buckingham Palace Gardens, through a sea of purple autumn crocuses. But there was no news from Berlin, where the failure to set a time limit to the British and French notes delivered the previous day had given Ribbentrop and Hitler what they most enjoyed, a chance to procrastinate.

The early morning was not so peaceful over Poland. The first day's fighting had not gone as easily or as well as the Germans had hoped. Indeed, there were reports in Berlin that the German army had suffered a significant setback[2] (there were also rumours of military discontent),[3] and 'Chips' Channon, the most determined advocate of peace *à l'outrance* in the Government (he was Parliamentary Private Secretary to R. A. Butler, the Foreign Office spokesman in the House of Commons) and an admirer of the Prime Minister to a hair's breadth this side of idolatry, wrote of a 'half-hearted war'.[4] These reports were given sufficient credit in London for the Dominions Minister, Sir Thomas Inskip, to tell the Dominions[5] that the fighting was 'of the lightest possible character' and that 'The Poles had not yet been forced to retreat.' Nor was the weather so welcome. Save for the mists of early morning, which had protected the defenders of the Westerplatte from the worst of the air attacks, the German air force had had fine weather and clear skies over most of Poland. The Polish air force had fought with the courage and *élan* for which the Poles were famous. Free Polish

Air Force squadrons flying Spitfires were to play an important part in the later stages of the Battle of Britain, twelve months later; but in September 1939 much of the Poles' strength was caught on the ground in the first hours of war. Their aircraft were obsolescent, significantly out-classed by those of the Luftwaffe.

The German bombers ranged freely over Poland, attacking towns, cities, railways, roads and bridges. Reports of deliberate attacks on civilian targets are difficult to assess through the fog of battle, in the air, on the ground and in the media. What is clear is that they were under no very great pressure to discriminate or to hold back where attacking military targets put civilians at risk. The reports of the British military mission even in the first day's fighting were full of the news of cities under attack from the air. Such stories came in to the capital much more easily than reports from the front, where Polish military communications were an early victim of the war of movement.[6]

The long hot summer had also prepared much of the terrain to the German advantage. River beds had dried out and water courses become dusty troughs, easily fordable by wheeled, let alone tracked, transport. The German Panzers had nothing to fear from marsh or inundations. From the morning of September 2, they began to cut deep into Poland, overrunning the Polish infantry and sweeping the cavalry, despite their courage, out of their way like chaff. September 2 was the first of a relentless series of disastrous days for the Polish army, under-gunned, under-supplied and led by senior commanders for whom this was as new a kind of war as it was for the greenest and youngest of the men they led.

The Polish Ambassadors in London and Paris were driven to desperation by the scattered reports of their country's agony which reached them and by the lack of any signs of positive action by the Governments to which they were accredited. In London, Count Raczyński remained outwardly calm and imperturbable, as befitted his lineage and upbringing. He was, he assured the opposition front-bench spokesman, Hugh Dalton, fully satisfied with what British Ministers had said to him. He had picked up the Foreign Office worries over the French; like everyone else in diplomatic circles he knew that the Havas communiqué of midnight on September 1/2 did not appear without ministerial sanction. His young colleague, Juliusz Lukasziewicz in Paris, was less old-school. At 9 a.m. he stormed into the Quai d'Orsay to see the French Foreign Minister.[7] As we have seen, he already distrusted Georges Bonnet. The French Premier, Edouard Daladier, had warned him to deal rather with the Secretary General of the Quai, Alexis Léger, or with Daladier himself. Bonnet told the fiery young Pole that no reply had been received from Ribbentrop. If a reply had not been received by the time the French Parliament was to meet, at 3 o'clock that afternoon, the Parliament would vote for a new ultimatum with a deadline. How long a deadline? asked Lukasziewicz. Forty-eight or twenty-four hours, replied Bonnet.

Lukasziewicz was appalled. This long a delay would, he said, be completely incompatible with the obligations Britain and France had assumed towards Poland. Hitler would exploit the delay to the utmost both in military and in propaganda terms. What motives could there possibly be for so long a delay? The delay, replied Bonnet, lying in his teeth, was the result of a British initiative, now a fortnight old.

Lukasziewicz in a fury returned to his Embassy. A phone call to Count Raczyński in London convinced him Bonnet was lying. There was, he surmised (the Havas notice seems to have evaded him), an Italian intrigue afoot. He went to see first William Bullitt, the US Ambassador, then Paul Reynaud, the Minister of Finance, one of the known hawks in the Council of Ministers. Reynaud told him the only motion to go to the French Parliament was a vote on war credits. This, it was to be argued, was an indispensable constitutional preliminary to empower a French government to declare war. Reynaud explained it as a way to protect French deputies against later accusations of voting for an 'aggressive' war.

Lukasziewicz then heard that the alleged inactivity on the Polish front covered a pause in hostilities, even a truce. He set his Embassy staff to counter these rumours. He then went to see Daladier with a note summarizing his conversation with Bonnet. Daladier was, he said, quite unaware of M. Lukasziewicz's meeting with M. Bonnet. What is the Quai d'Orsay waiting for? he asked. He told Lukasziewicz he would hurry things up. The Polish Ambassador returned to his office through a hurly-burly of French and foreign newsmen, all 'almost joyously' shouting questions about the truce in Poland. Lukasziewicz denied the reports with emphasis. They were pure German propaganda. They did not in any way correspond with the truth. The fighting, on land and in the air, was intensifying.

Lukasziewicz's suspicions were perfectly accurate. There was something going on between Paris and Rome, but, for once, the Italians were guiltless of any spirit of intrigue. Ciano had been led by Bonnet to believe that the proposal for a conference enjoyed British as well as French support. Bonnet, as has been seen, was acting on his interpretation of a decision, or rather an indecision, by the French Council of Ministers taken *before* the German attack on Poland had begun. At 9 a.m. Ciano had telephoned Bernardo Attolico in Berlin. There was, he told Attolico,[8] should the Führer agree, the chance of persuading France, Britain and Poland to accept a conference. The basis of such a conference was, first, an armistice, leaving the opposed forces where they were at the time of the armistice, and second, that the conference should meet in two to three days; a settlement of the Polish-German dispute, which, as things stood, would be in Germany's favour. Germany already had Danzig and pledges which would guarantee her the greater part of her claims. Attolico went round to the Wilhelmstrasse within the hour and handed the Italian proposals over to von Weizsäcker.[9] Ribbentrop, he was told, was ill, resting in bed, and could not get up[10] He still had not forgiven Attolico for reaching Hitler without him being there the previous day.

Weizsäcker's call soon got him out of bed. At 12.30, he received Attolico at the Wilhelmstrasse.[11] What, he asked, was the status of the British and French notes of the previous evening? They sounded like a collective ultimatum. In any case Germany would need time to reply. He could not hold out any prospect of a reply before Sunday evening at the earliest. Attolico insisted that the new proposal superseded everything else. Ribbentrop said the matter of the Anglo-French declarations would have to be settled. He proposed that Attolico should enquire of his British and French colleagues in Berlin. Were the notes 'ultimata' or not?

Attolico forgot his dignity and ran down the steps to the street.[12] Within twenty minutes, breathless, he was back.[13] He had asked Henderson and Coulondre if the notes were to be considered as ultimata. No, Sir Nevile Henderson had replied, they were in the nature of a warning.[14] Henderson also added that he could not see how anything could be done unless the German troops were at once withdrawn from Poland. Attolico reported this to Rome.[15] Wisely, for the moment he did not tell the German Foreign Minister. Henderson was, after all, only expressing his own opinion. Ribbentrop affected to consider the matter seriously. Could Attolico check once more with Rome? The Führer was examining the Duce's proposals. If Rome confirmed there was no question of an ultimatum in the Anglo-French declaration, his reply would be drafted in a day or two. Attolico said he needed a reply that evening. Procrastinatory to the last, Ribbentrop promised a reply by noon on the Sunday. Attolico phoned Rome.[16]

Ciano then turned to the British and French Ambassadors in Rome. He had already that morning warned his new-found ally, Sir Percy Loraine, of the initiative he was taking in Berlin.[17] At 2 o'clock that afternoon, he summoned both Loraine and his French colleague, André François-Poncet, to the Palazzo Chigi.[18] François-Poncet could not answer Ciano's question about the French note to Berlin – was it an ultimatum or not? Loraine, by contrast, was in a position to show Ciano a copy of the instructions on which Henderson had acted, sent to him as a matter of course. Not for the first time, the organization of business in the British diplomatic system had demonstrated its superiority. The Ambassadors waited while Ciano phoned Bonnet, who confirmed that the French note, too, was not an ultimatum.

To the rest of Ciano's proposal Bonnet, secretly delighted, gave his approval, subject, of course, to his reporting it to M. Daladier. His friends were in the meantime laying siege to the Italian Ambassador in Paris, Raffaele Guariglia.[19] That day, Guariglia had been visited by Hubert de Lagardelle, who had acted as an intermediary between Paris and Rome four years before at the opening of the Italo-Ethiopian crisis; by the Fascist Spanish Ambassador, who knew all about Bonnet's intrigue; and by François Piétri, Bonnet's ally in the Chamber. Piétri asked him to call on Sir Eric Phipps. The British had to be persuaded to drop any insistence on German evacuation of Poland as a pre-condition for a conference. Guariglia called on Phipps. He found him cold and sceptical. He would not intervene in London. Why, he remarked bitterly, did Ciano not approach Sir Percy Loraine, with whom he was on such friendly terms? (Apparently Phipps had been watching Loraine's sudden conquest of Count Ciano with a bitter and jaundiced eye since the failure of his and Bonnet's intrigue against Daladier in June and July.) Guariglia did not phone Rome.

Ciano, as we have seen, was not only consulting Sir Percy Loraine, he was conducting his office business with Loraine sitting alongside him. At 2.30 he managed to reach Lord Halifax,[20] to whom he explained the course of the negotiations in Berlin and his telephone conversation with M. Bonnet. To cut matters short, he asked Loraine to explain matters to Lord Halifax, who was apparently dictating what he said to Ciano to a shorthand typist at the same time. With Loraine's aid, Halifax gave as his personal opinion that the Cabinet would lay down as an indispensable condition to any conference that the German armies should first evacuate all Polish territory. Ciano said that the most Mussolini could hope to get out of Berlin was an armistice with a standstill, say on the next day, and a conference. The Germans would never hear of a withdrawal, which he himself thought unreasonable.

Halifax then had to act very quickly. Parliament was due to meet at 3 o'clock that afternoon. They would be expecting a statement. Was Britain at war or not? Was she going to war? There was no hard news, but rumours aplenty. The Havas message had not passed unnoticed. Even the story about Lukasziewicz's interview with Bonnet and letter to Daladier had reached London.[21] A British government, facing a parliament which is expecting an official statement which it is, for whatever reason, unable to give, may expect a very rough handling, in public from the opposition and in private from its own supporters. Not for the first time Sir John Simon had been put in to stonewall. Halifax and Oliver Harvey, the able young diplomatist who had served both Eden and Halifax as Private Secretary (and was to serve Eden again in this capacity from 1941 to 1945), rushed round to the Commons.[22] A brief announcement promising a statement at 6 p.m. was made. Simon, who was hourly increasing in hawkishness, agreed with Halifax that the Germans would have to get out of Poland before any conference could meet. His own view was that they faced a German-Italian plot to delay British entry into the war until all the German merchant ships were safely in port and the U-boats on station in the Atlantic and the North Sea, waiting to attack.

Halifax had not had an easy morning, waiting for news from Berlin. He had had a series of messages from Paris. France could not declare war without Parliament meeting. Its meeting was likely to be protracted. The French were very anxious that the British and French declarations of war should be simultaneous. There should be no question of Sir Nevile Henderson acting first.[23] Halifax had replied[24] inviting Sir Eric Phipps to infuse courage and determination into M. Bonnet, and speculating that the French might be delaying as a result of reports of disaffection and indecision in Germany. He had had an inconclusive meeting with the French Ambassador, Charles Corbin,[25] a man who did not share M. Bonnet's desire to run away before the first shot was fired. And he had sent Sir Eric Phipps the text of the statement that the British proposed to make to the Germans, looking to immediate consultation and action (an ultimatum to Berlin was implied) as soon as the French Parliament had voted.[26] Phipps had told him Bonnet's approval was on its way to M. Corbin,[27] and had done his best to assure him as to the French motives.[28] Phipps's last telegram, received at 1.30 p.m.,[29] had produced a very unwelcome surprise, with its disclosure (Bonnet's idea, as we have seen) of a forty-eight-hour time limit on any ultimatum. The French General Staff needed this to enable mobilization and the evacuation of France's vulnerable cities to take place unhindered.

At 4 p.m. M. Bonnet called Lord Halifax.[30] He recapitulated the Italian initiative in the terms Halifax had already heard from Count Ciano. Halifax replied that the Cabinet was about to consider the matter. He repeated the view that he could not see how a conference could meet while German troops remained on Polish soil. Bonnet affected to think German withdrawal desirable rather than essential. What was essential, in his view, was Polish representation at the conference. Bonnet then raised the question of a forty-eight-hour time limit on the ultimatum. Halifax said that that too would have to be considered.

M. Bonnet believed himself to be in a fairly strong position. The Italians had done what he asked of them. The Germans had not turned the matter down. He had successfully withstood a renewed assault in the early afternoon from the irate, the furious, the desperate M. Lukasiewicz to get the vital protocol to the Franco-Polish alliance, without which the Franco-Polish military agreements did not formally become valid, signed and sealed.[31] The text had been ready for signature in May when Bonnet had put it into cold storage and the Poles, in their pride and confidence, had failed to follow this up. The Chamber and Senate had met. Daladier had made what was, from Bonnet's point of view, a nearly masterly demonstration of French readiness to fight.[32] He had left the door open for both alternatives, a conference or a declaration of war, to equally massive applause. He had not called for a declaration of war. The only hostage he had given to fortune was that, like Lord Halifax, he apparently regarded a German withdrawal from Poland as an essential pre-condition to any new negotiation.

His audience had listened in a passion of patriotism. Why not? There was not only the tradition of the *Union Sacrée* by which, as in 1914, all political differences were sunk in the face of the national enemy. There was enough in the speech to feed both doves and hawks. Lord Halifax still had to face both Cabinet and Parliament. The Labour Party had already made it clear that it was not interested in entering a government of national unity under Neville Chamberlain's leadership.[33] Halifax was well aware of the strains that the alliance might face if war began without full French support. He was, however, attracted by the idea of a conference, if the Italians could prevail upon Germany to withdraw from Polish soil. As to the chances of that happening, he preferred not to speculate. He cannot have rated them very highly if at all. He needed, however, to close off the French options and to keep the Italians sweet.[34] He was also trying desperately to square a circle. 'I never remember spending such a miserable afternoon or evening,' he later recalled.[35]

The Cabinet met at 4.30 p.m. knowing very little more than that there had been no reply to the note presented in Berlin by Sir Nevile Henderson the previous evening, and that the statement which had been supposed to be made at 3 p.m. had been called off as a result of some Italian initiative. In the meantime, there was a good deal of disquiet. Why was Britain not already at war? The Cabinet now heard Halifax explain.[36] He began by reading the notes taken of his telephone conversations with Ciano[37] and Bonnet,[38] the latter somewhat edited to omit Bonnet's satisfaction at having insisted that Poland should be present at the conference. He had, he said, arrived at four conclusions, in conjunction with the Prime Minister. Henderson's note of the previous evening was not an ultimatum but a final warning. If the German Government wanted any more time, it should be allowed until noon on the next day, provided it accepted an armistice. The primary condition for any conference would be German withdrawal from Poland. Finally, while direct German-Polish negotiations were still thought to be the best course, other countries could be associated with this provided that the two countries agreed.

The Cabinet, very largely, was unwilling to accept any of this. It seemed to bear no relation to what public opinion was thinking. The Air Minister, Sir Kingsley Wood, the closest to a dove the Cabinet could boast of, opposed any further delays. Sir Samuel Hoare pointed out that so far as public opinion was concerned, the previous evening's note to Hitler had been regarded as an ultimatum. Public opinion, said Leslie Hore-Belisha, the War Minister, was strongly against yielding an inch. If the Germans were prepared to consider a standstill, it showed they were weakening. He thought Italy was acting in collusion with Germany. The Germans should be given until midnight to withdraw their troops, a demand which, as the Prime Minister pointed out, had already been made by Sir Nevile Henderson the previous evening; otherwise Britain should go to war. Even Lord Maugham, the Lord Chancellor, a man who was to defend the Munich Agreement until his dying day, called for a German withdrawal from Poland. Oliver Stanley, the President of the Board of Trade, said that the restoration of the status quo in Danzig must also be insisted upon. Chamberlain hastily put in that Halifax and he had intended that.

Nor were any of the Cabinet, despite the French plea, prepared to accept any presentation of the ultimatum later than midnight. The introduction at this point of a note from Count Raczyński, on Beck's instructions, to the effect that the German attack had greatly intensified, that the whole of the German air force was operating against Poland, and pleading for the engagement of German aircraft by Allied forces, strengthened the Cabinet's resistance. Ernest Brown, the Minister of Labour, Chatfield and Inskip all spoke in favour of an ultimatum at midnight. The Prime Minister summed up. There should be no negotiation without a German undertaking to withdraw her troops from Poland and Danzig. It was undesirable to allow Germany longer than until midnight to make up her mind. The precise terms of the ultimatum would have to be settled with the French. Chamberlain and Halifax were authorized to settle the terms in consultation with the French, also to draft a statement to be made in Parliament.

At 5 p.m. Sir Alexander Cadogan rang up M. Bonnet.[39] M. Bonnet had just been through a terrible scene with the Polish Ambassador.[40] M. Lukasziewicz had sat through M. Daladier's speech to the Chamber with increasing misgivings and mounting unhappiness.[41] Amidst the torrents of Gallic rhetoric he hoped for firm support for Poland, for an ultimatum with a time limit, for some indication as to how much longer his country would have to fight alone. His colleagues in the diplomatic box tried to cheer him up, but without success.[42] On returning to his Embassy at about 4.30 p.m. he had found the same message that Count Raczyński had carried to the British Cabinet meeting. Daladier was still at the Senate, the upper house of the French Parliament, where the vote of war credits passed by the Assembly was now being debated.

Lukasziewicz had therefore once again to beard Bonnet. He asked again about the timing of the ultimatum to be delivered to Germany. Bonnet again said forty-eight or twenty-four hours. It was a military matter. Personally he had nothing against a shorter period. He would, he said, speak to the meeting of the Council of Ministers which was due to assemble later that evening. Lukasziewicz's control snapped, and high words passed between the two men. More convinced than ever that there was some sub-plot of whose nature he was unaware, Lukasziewicz went to see the two Cabinet Ministers reputed to be the leading hawks, Paul Reynaud and Georges Mandel. He wrote a second letter to Daladier, protesting that a forty-eight-hour ultimatum hardly accorded with the terms of the alliance. Now M. Bonnet had to listen to the English.

Cadogan's opinion of Bonnet fell some way short of admiration. It is in a way surprising that Lord Halifax did not talk to his fellow Minister himself. Cadogan's message was very simple.[43] The British would accept nothing short of a German withdrawal from Poland. If Hitler did not withdraw by midnight, the British must fulfil their guarantee to Poland. If the troops were withdrawn and both Germany and Poland wanted the participation of other powers, then Britain would not object. Bonnet replied that the Council of Ministers was 'going to deliberate' whether a German withdrawal was a necessary pre-condition to tacit agreement to a conference. As for the time limit, the French held firmly to the view that the necessary limit was forty-eight hours. It was impossible to instruct the French Ambassador to deliver an ultimatum by midnight. Cadogan then asked if the Poles had made any representations about aid on the grounds that there was a big battle. Bonnet lied again. 'Not yet,' he said. He told Cadogan the French decision would probably be taken by 8 p.m.

At 6 p.m. Lord Halifax spoke to his Ambassador in Paris, Sir Eric Phipps.[44] A statement had to be made in Parliament that evening. It was proving impossible to get a French decision on either of the two points at issue: the withdrawal of German troops as a pre-condition for a conference, and the length of time to be mentioned in the ultimatum. Forty-eight hours was quite impossible. Could not M. Daladier be moved on this point? Phipps quoted Bonnet to the effect that the Poles had said they would be content with twenty-four hours, a statement not easily reconcilable with the terms of the appeal Colonel Beck had just delivered via Count Raczyński and M. Lukasziewicz. Lord Halifax had no option but to put off the announced time of the statement to be made to Parliament from 6 p.m. to 7.45 p.m. He returned to continue drafting the statement to Parliament.

At 6.38 p.m. Lord Halifax rang Count Ciano.[45] Britain, he said, could not favour any conference so long as German troops remained on Polish territory. Nor could Britain recognize that status which had been imposed on Danzig. Ciano said he did not think Hitler would accept. When the question of time came up, Ciano repeated that he did not think Hitler would accept the first condition. In fact he took it as the *coup de grâce* to the proposal to call a conference. At 7.22 p.m. Ciano phoned Loraine and François-Poncet.[46] Given Halifax's position and Daladier's speech to the French Assembly, which also mentioned a German withdrawal from Poland (Phipps and Halifax had missed the phrase), there was little possibility of the Italian initiative succeeding. At 8.20 p.m. accordingly, Ciano phoned Berlin, to speak to M. Attolico.[47] In view of the British 'fundamental condition', Italy did not propose to pursue the idea of a conference any more. At 8.30 he broke the final news to Loraine and François-Poncet.[48] Loraine's telegram to London did not arrive until 9.30 p.m.,[49] too late to save the Prime Minister from what was very nearly a major disaster, one which still ranks among the most dramatic scenes in the history of Britain's Parliament. It is M. Bonnet's unique achievement nearly to have overthrown an allied government on an issue that was stone cold and dead in the market at the moment when the crisis came.

The House of Commons had begun its session that afternoon at 2.45, expecting a statement. That had been postponed. The afternoon had been filled with minor defence legislation. A statement was promised for 6 p.m. The House filled; but the Speaker was forced to announce another adjournment until 7.45 p.m. The members adjourned to the bar, the tea-room, the corridors. Rumours spread easily in the absence of hard news. When they re-assembled the tension was apparent. Not a few had been drinking: 'Chips' Channon noted flushed faces and heavy breathing.[50] The diplomatic gallery was packed. Before the session began, Chamberlain had told the leaders of the two opposition parties, Arthur Greenwood for Labour and Sir Archibald Sinclair for the Liberals, what he was going to say and where the difficulty lay.[51] They dawdled a little in the Prime Minister's room, entering the chamber itself twelve minutes after the members had re-assembled. They sat down, and Chamberlain rose to speak.

The Prime Minister normally dominated the House of Commons, but on September 2 he was a mere shadow of his normal self. He was pale. His voice sounded as if he was sickening for a cold.[52] He had had a bad Cabinet meeting. For the last week Lord Halifax rather than he had provided the engine-room force for British policy. Halifax had called the interviews with foreign statesmen, Halifax had taken and shaped the British initiative, Halifax had held on to such control as Britain was exercising over events. Chamberlain had stood by, watching all his hopes of peace collapse. His letter to Hitler had been his last major action; and that had been the work of a committee, or rather of several committees. He must have known that he was not about to give Parliament what it expected. What is the more extraordinary is that he seemed to be going back on his Cabinet also. The statement he made had been most probably drafted by Sir Horace Wilson, that master of involved and complex sentence structure. What it said was much less significant than what it did not say. It did not say that an ultimatum had been sent. It did not say that the British Ambassador in Berlin had asked for his passports. It did not speak of Poland's heroism and of Britain's urgency in coming to Poland's aid. It did not speak of measures to intercept the German passenger liner, the *Bremen*, whose dramatic dash across the Atlantic for safety in German waters was the concern of the popular press.

Instead it opened with the German failure to reply to Henderson's warning message. It accounted for this by referring to the Italian proposal for an armistice and a conference. Britain, it said, could not take part in such a conference unless Germany withdrew from Poland and Danzig. Britain was in communication with France as to the limit in time to be allowed Germany to decide whether to effect that with-drawal. If Germany withdrew then Britain was prepared to accept that the position was the same as it was before the German forces crossed the Polish frontier. The way would be open for a German-Polish settlement and an international guarantee.

The statement betrayed very clearly Lord Halifax's capacity for intellectual detachment and his almost inhuman inability to rise to an occasion. The Italian proposal was never a starter, even without British insistence on a complete German withdrawal not only from Poland but also from Danzig. Both Halifax and Chamberlain had come to form views of Hitler, of his personality and his motivations, which ruled this out of court. They had heard the stories of military discontent, even of an incipient coup, but they had had similar stories in September 1938 and not credited them sufficiently to make them a basis for British policy. They wanted to turn the clock back: not far, only two or three days. That they could believe it remotely possible; that they felt no identification with Poland, invaded, bombed, devastated in the way their fears had so often pictured Britain devastated; that they could not identify with the feelings of their fellow-countrymen, their colleagues in Parliament, even their colleagues in the Cabinet; these facts provide an extraordinary illustration of the degree to which each man had been driven by the events and tensions since August 25 into his own private universe, Halifax of his Alpine logic, Chamberlain of his innermost personal fears.

The House of Commons was left aghast. The obvious inference, wrote one Junior Minister, was vacillation or dirty work.[53] 'I have never seen so sudden a reversion of feeling in my thirty years' experience of the House,' wrote Sir John Simon early next morning.[54] Arthur Greenwood rose to reply on behalf of the Labour Party. 'Speaking for the Labour Party,' he began. There was a storm from both sides of the House. 'Speak for England,' shouted Leo Amery, a former Cabinet Minister, on the hard right of the Tory Party (a call so instantly famous that Robert Boothby, one of Churchill's closest supporters, later claimed to have made it).[55] Chamberlain's head whipped around as if he had been stung. The Tory back-benchers were almost speechless with fury. So were many of Chamberlain's own Cabinet colleagues.[56] Greenwood made the speech of his life. He had not had time to prepare. 'I am greatly disturbed,' he said. 'An act of aggression took place thirty-eight hours ago. The moment that act of aggression took place one of the most important treaties of modern times automatically came into operation. . . . I wonder how long we are prepared to vacillate at a time when Britain, and all that Britain stands for, and human civilization are in peril.' He sat down amidst more shouting and disturbance. It was not the moment to make party capital, but such was the mood of the House that a motion of censure would have carried a majority easily. 'A puff would have brought the Government down.'[57]

One man might have spoken and provided that puff: Winston

Churchill. The previous day he had been called to No. 10 Downing Street by the Prime Minister.[58] Chamberlain said he saw no way of averting war with Germany. He proposed to form a small war cabinet of ministers without departments to run ('portfolios', in British parlance) to conduct the war. Would Winston serve as one? Churchill immediately accepted. He had waited all day, September 2, for a call to war; in vain. He knew war was coming. One thing he was determined on: Britain should enter the war against Germany so far as possible united. He, least of all people, with his past political record as both a Liberal and a Tory, a maverick who had stayed with Lloyd George and the coalition when the Tory Party had walked out in 1922, who had fought the Conservative leadership tooth and nail over the Government of India Act in 1931–2 and over the abdication crisis in 1936–7, could have divided the Conservative Party by bringing down its leader on the eve of war. It was not that Chamberlain had 'nobbled' him in advance, though there were those who were glad he had.[59] It was not the time, nor the occasion. Some of this he had to explain to his excited and disappointed allies later that evening.[60]

Chamberlain made a vain effort to repair some of the damage. Britain had to work *pari passu* with France. He did not for a moment believe the French were weakening. But his speech carried no conviction. Seen from the visitors' gallery, he seemed 'a dithering old dodderer with shaking voice and hands'.[61] James Maxton, a pacifist member of the extreme left of the Labour Party, a Glaswegian revolutionary in the 1920s and the last man ordinarily to support Chamberlain, called to him to continue his work for peace, but was shouted down.[62] The day was saved by the Tory Chief Whip, Captain David Margesson, who rose, solid and imperturbable, to move 'This House do now adjourn', as he did every night at the close of parliamentary business. The House duly adjourned. There was a swirl of disappointed and excited members into the lobbies, so darkened by the coming storm that 'a match struck flames like a beacon'.[63] One Cabinet Minister was cut dead by his oldest friends.[64]

As they left the Chamber, Greenwood spoke to Chamberlain.[65] 'You could not see your supporters,' he said. 'I could. I know their feeling is mine. I wish to tell you that unless you present an ultimatum to Germany before 11 o'clock tomorrow neither you nor I nor anyone else on earth will be able to hold the House of Commons.' Chamberlain knew that already. But he faced trouble closer to home than Sunday's reconvening of Parliament. A majority of his Cabinet, twelve out of twenty-two, were so incensed with what they saw as a complete reversal of the Cabinet decisions taken only two and a half hours previously that they had repaired at once to Sir John Simon's room in the House of Commons.[66] They were Sir Kingsley Wood, Oliver Stanley, Malcolm MacDonald, Captain Euan Wallace, Walter Elliot, John Colville, Earl de la Warr, Hore-Belisha, Sir John Anderson, and Morrison. A little later, Sir Reginald Dorman-Smith hurried in. Together, they constituted not only a majority of Chamberlain's Cabinet as a whole; only four Cabinet Ministers out of the sixteen who sat in the House of Commons were missing.

Lord Halifax had made the same statement in the House of Lords as Chamberlain in the Commons. It is not clear whether any of his Cabinet colleagues – Chatfield, Stanhope, Runciman, Zetland or Maugham – had stayed in the Lords to hear him. At least two of these, Chatfield and Stanhope, had spoken very strongly in favour of an ultimatum at midnight. The only members of the Cabinet who missed the meeting in Simon's room were Inskip, who for some reason was not in the Commons,[67] Brown and Burgin, who would both have supported the rebels if they had known of the meeting, and Hoare, who in disgust had gone home to bed.[68] He had lived through this sort of crisis in 1935 as Foreign Secretary when the House had reacted so strongly to the plan he had evolved with M. Laval, then the French Premier, to negotiate a settlement of the Italian invasion of Ethiopia. On that occasion the Cabinet members had thrown him to the wolves, to save their own collective skin. One can imagine he wanted no part of a similar auto-da-fé.

Halifax, however, was of sterner stuff. Having made the statement to the Lords, he had gone home.[69] He and his long-suffering wife were just going out to dinner when Chamberlain phoned. His statement had gone very badly in the Commons. There had been a very unpleasant scene. Halifax had never heard the Prime Minister 'so disturbed'. Halifax abandoned his wife and went straight round to Downing Street. The statement had infuriated the House, said Chamberlain, as he and Halifax sat down to dinner. Unless the position could be cleared, he did not believe the Government could maintain itself when it met Parliament on the morrow. Halifax pulled the unfortunate Sir Alex Cadogan away from his half-eaten dinner to come to Downing Street, where they were joined by Sir Horace Wilson for a time.[70]

Chamberlain would also have told Halifax that the rebel members of the Cabinet had already been to see him. He had spoken to them of the French insistence on a twenty-four-hour ultimatum and preference for one of forty-eight hours.[71] He had told them that the grave disadvantage of declaring war without France had in his view overridden the probable effect of further delay on the House of Commons and the country. As one man, the rebels had replied that unless the Commons could be told the next day that an ultimatum had been sent and that Britain was fulfilling its guarantee to Poland, the Government could not survive. In their name Simon had left a handwritten note with the Prime Minister.[72]

'The statement tonight', he wrote, 'they think will throw the Poles into dejection. German propaganda will see to that. We assume that Warsaw is getting a reassuring telephone message at once. Nothing will repair the injury but an announcement of our fixed decision as soon as possible.

'We all feel that 12 o'clock tomorrow is *too late*, and think that we ought to adhere to the Cabinet timetable of midnight. The only thing that could justify 12 noon tomorrow for the expiry of the ultimatum would be an announcement tonight that this had definitely been agreed with the French.

'Your colleagues here feel that if the French will *not* agree to expiry by 12 noon at the latest we are bound to act ourselves at once.'

Chamberlain had told his colleagues that he agreed with them. He had promised that he and Halifax would do their best to twist the arm of the French Government. The rebels had not, however, disbanded. They had gone back to Simon's room, pausing only to take an hour for dinner. Unwilling to face their fellow MPs in the restaurant at the Houses of Parliament, some had gone to the Savoy Grill on the Strand.[73] Even there they were not safe. Duff Cooper, who had resigned as First Lord of the Admiralty over Munich, was dining there with a group of like-minded MPs. Captain Euan Wallace refused to catch his eye. But when Duff Cooper left the restaurant he was handed a scribbled note. Wallace told him that the whole Cabinet had been taken by surprise.[74]

Halifax and Cadogan summoned the French and Polish Ambassadors,[75] and settled down to the telephone. According to the French records, they first called Sir Eric Phipps and sent him directly to see M. Daladier. M. Daladier had approved the statement which had caused so much disorder in the British Parliament at 7.10 p.m. that evening, just as the French Senate was ending. He had gone almost immediately into a meeting of the Council of Ministers. At this stage Bonnet found a new ally, General Gamelin, the Chief of the French army.

Gamelin was terrified that the French mobilization would become the target for an all-out German air attack.[76] He had convinced himself, as he told M. Frankowski, the Counsellor of the Polish Embassy, that two-thirds of the Luftwaffe were poised along the Rhine frontier,[77] waiting to descend upon French railroads, barracks and roads, while France was calling her reserves to the colours. He had convinced himself that the German fortifications in the west were completed and fully manned, and that there were substantial German forces in reserve capable of launching a counter-offensive. He had also convinced himself that no German attacks would come until France declared war – despite the clear evidence that no such legal restraint had operated to protect Poland. Despite the undertakings to Poland entered into in May, he had no intention, nor had the French military made any plans, for an immediate assault on Germany. Indeed, of the nineteen French Generals who made up the military membership of the Higher Council for War, only two, General Giraud and General Buhrer, spoke in favour of French entry into the war.

Gamelin was instead busy manufacturing convincing reasons for delay. The previous day he had written to Daladier regretting that he could not invade Belgium in order to find a way around the Siegfried line.[78] He was now to provide Bonnet with another excuse. He was prepared, he said, to risk an earlier declaration of war if the British were to dispatch their bomber forces at once to France,[79] a proviso that revealed not only his duplicity but also his inability to understand his own air force commanders. What was needed in France to ward off German air attack were fighters, not bombers. The British were, in fact, about to send an Air Striking Force to France, as Gamelin well knew. He also knew that the move, which involved providing the aircraft with bombs to carry and high-octane fuel to power their engines, let alone ground staff, mechanics and so on, was quite impossible to carry out in a day. As for actually bombing targets in Germany, Gamelin knew his own air force advisers had agreed with the British to hold back as long as possible owing to France's own vulnerability to attack from the air. Small wonder historians speak of the 'Gamelin mystery'.[80]

When the French Council of Ministers met, Bonnet and Daladier, nudged by Gamelin, whose ideal ultimatum would not have been delivered until noon the next day, Sunday, September 3, and not have expired until September 5,[81] were for once on the same side. There was a military interest in gaining twenty-four or forty-eight hours for mobilization, said Daladier. The Council agreed. Many of its members had been primed by Gamelin while waiting in the antechamber before the meeting began.[82]

Only Reynaud, Mandel and Campinchi, Minister for the Navy, disagreed when Bonnet proposed to use the time to explore the Italian offer[83] further. Reynaud, like Hore-Belisha in the British Cabinet three hours earlier, suspected Italy of trying to gain time for Germany. What if Germany, having got what she wants, proposes peace? he demanded. Would France not be worse off, declaring war on her then? There was a general view that in any case France would have to demand the evacuation of Poland. On this the Council voted to accept Bonnet's proposal. Only Mandel held out. As they were leaving, de Monzie, who knew that Count Ciano had already said that such a condition would be rejected by the Germans, protested to Bonnet that such a demand could not be sustained. Why not, he suggested, try for a symbolic retreat, a withdrawal of a few kilometres?[84]

That evening, Raffaele Guariglia was waiting in the salon of Mme Brunhes, one of the famous political salons of the Third Republic.[85] He was joined by de Monzie, then by his ally, Jean Mistler. Piétri soon followed. De Monzie told him that Ciano's proposal had been accepted by the French Council of Ministers. They were agreed that to demand the withdrawal of German troops was impossible. After telephoning Bonnet, de Monzie asked Guariglia in Bonnet's name to phone Ciano to propose a symbolic German withdrawal. Guariglia said that what was important was an armistice. Should France go to war, he hoped that French military action would be limited to a little bombardment, some military demonstrations; there must be no air attacks on Germany. An armistice would then be easy to arrange. Mistler agreed and went off to see General Gamelin. Guariglia returned to his Embassy to phone Count Ciano.[86]

'Symbolic withdrawal' may have salved Bonnet's feelings. It certainly provided the centre right, those dubious collaborationists of the future, with a reason for execrating Britain further. But by the time the French Council of Ministers was at an end, Attolico had already acted on Count Ciano's instructions and seen Ribbentrop.[87] The Duce, he said, given the British insistence on the immediate withdrawal of all German troops from Poland and Danzig, no longer considered the proposed mediation extant. Ribbentrop made no comment. He was in fact making his own final attempt, if only for the record, to derail the British. Ciano did not think Guariglia's proposal worth bothering with. Without informing Mussolini he threw the proposal in the waste-paper basket.[88] Bonnet had, after all, spoken with him on the phone at 9 p.m. and told him of the Council's decisions.[89] He had replied that Germany would not accept, and Bonnet had thanked him for his work for peace. Afterthoughts of this kind Ciano regarded as contemptible.

Ribbentrop's chosen messenger was Dr Fritz Hesse, the London correspondent of the official German news agency, the Deutsche

Nachrichten Büro. At 8 p.m. that evening, Ribbentrop telephoned him. He was to invite Sir Horace Wilson to come secretly at once to Berlin. Wilson had played a major role as Chamberlain's emissary to Berlin in September 1938. Wohltat and von Dirksen had both made much of his role in the initiative Wohltat had taken in July (but fathered on Wilson, when Ribbentrop got to hear of it). The anti-appeasers always depicted him as the arch-appeaser in the heart of the British Cabinet, the wire-puller *par excellence* of the doves, and the Prime Minister's closest adviser. Hesse phoned Downing Street and Wilson, in duty bound, took time off from the deliberations and phone calls to see him.[90] He took very little time over it. What was the purpose of his being invited to Berlin? he asked. To discuss the whole position, heart to heart, including Poland, replied Hesse. The position, replied Wilson, was as the Prime Minister had stated it to Parliament; and, he added, by no means flattered or gratified by the invitation, he would be glad if Dr Hesse would tell Ribbentrop that under no circumstances would Britain agree to any conversations with the German Government until German forces had been withdrawn and the status quo restored. Hesse retired, to phrase the rebuff as best he could in a telegram to Ribbentrop.[91]

In the meantime, Halifax, Cadogan and Chamberlain were wrestling with the telephone. When M. Corbin, the French Ambassador, arrived at Downing Street, he had already learnt from M. Bonnet of the rejection by the French Council of Ministers of the British proposal.[92] Phipps had in fact been rebuffed. But if M. Bonnet believed that this would block the British he was to be disappointed. M. Corbin's role in carrying out his instructions was severely hampered by his suspicions of M. Bonnet and his sympathy for Poland. Before his phone call from Paris he had caused his Counsellor, M. Cambon, on the pretext of enquiring whether Count Raczyński had informed the Prime Minister that a major German offensive had begun in Poland, to urge that the Prime Minister speak personally to M. Daladier. Cambon had in fact spoken with William Strang.[93] Strang had passed the message to Chamberlain's Personal Private Secretary, Leslie Rucker.

Corbin found the Prime Minister unusually distressed. He attacked M. Corbin strongly. The House of Commons was in a very hostile mood towards France. The gossip in the lobbies was that France wanted to withdraw. The mood had now turned on the Cabinet who, being the custodians of Britain's honour, were in danger of being compromised by France's hesitation. No one was interested in the Italian proposal. It was just a way of helping Germany. Nor could the French proposal for a long-fuse ultimatum be accepted. It was stopping the adoption of protective measures by British shipping and giving the Germans more time to position their U-boats in the Atlantic and the North Sea. Public opinion in France was directly responsible for this.

The French Ambassador was stung by these reproaches into violent protest. He spoke of French unity, of the determination with which France's youth was answering the call to arms. There could be no doubt as to France's intentions. But Chamberlain was not to be satisfied. He insisted on speaking with Daladier (as indeed M. Cambon had advised). At 9.30 p.m., he did speak with Daladier,[94] who was under the impression that the Italian initiative still held some hope. Count Ciano, he said, had observed there was hope of a German agreement if Britain and France stayed their hand until noon the next day. (It will be remembered that fifty minutes earlier M. Bonnet had been told by Count Ciano that he had abandoned any hope of persuading Germany to accept an armistice if its terms included a German withdrawal. Bonnet had, at the very least, delayed passing this on to his Prime Minister.) Moreover, Daladier added, playing Gamelin's card on top of Bonnet's, unless the British bombers were ready to act at once, it would be better for France to delay the German attacks on the French armies, if possible for some hours. Daladier then broke off the conversation. Chamberlain resumed his pressure on the unfortunate M. Corbin.

At this point the dissident Cabinet Ministers returned from their dinner to Sir John Simon's room at the House of Commons.[95] They agreed to charge Sir John Simon and Sir John Anderson to go over to Downing Street and put their collective view. It was essential to know before midnight that an ultimatum, to expire before noon the next day, would be sent to Germany. With that the dissidents sat down to wait. They would not leave that room, they resolved, until war was declared. They were, wrote one, on strike.[96] There was a feeling of great emotion. Their civilized control was gradually stripped by the strain of waiting. They grew hotter and sweatier. Only Malcolm MacDonald remained cool, calm and collected; he even told a few jokes. Hore-Belisha had wanted them all to go over with Simon, but had been talked out of it.

Simon went into No. 10 alone.[97] Anderson waited in the car they had used, so as to avoid being mobbed by the crowds, drawn to Downing Street, as always in a time of crisis. It was thought Simon would deliver his message and return, but his appearance gave Chamberlain an extra means of pressure on M. Corbin. Simon took M. Corbin aside to impress on him the depth of feeling in the Cabinet, and the impossibility of Parliament or public opinion accepting any more delay. The Prime Minister's position as leader of the nation into war was in danger of being challenged. Unless this could immediately be corrected, the blame would undoubtedly be put on the French unwillingness to give an immediate and direct answer. Corbin did his best, but even noon the next day was too late for Simon. Parliament met at noon. Much of this dialogue was couched in the form of questions put to Simon by Chamberlain, to which Corbin was simply the audience.

Before Simon arrived, the Prime Minister had had time for a quick meeting with the Chiefs of Staff and Lord Chatfield.[98] The military men had unanimously pressed for an ultimatum to be delivered at 2 a.m. to expire at 6.00 a.m. Like General Gamelin they feared a surprise, pre-emptive German attack. Unlike the French Generals, however, they feared that any statement that an ultimatum was on its way might provoke such an attack. They were equally concerned that there should be no appreciable lapse of time between the delivery of the British and French ultimata. The bulk of the regular army and the Advanced Air Striking Force were to cross to France as soon as possible. They could hardly start for France until France had declared war on Germany. More pressure was needed on the French.

At much the same time the Polish Ambassador arrived.[99] He brought news from the official Polish news agency of the bombing of central Warsaw. He asked if there would be any limit set to the time given to the Germans to answer the last British note. If the French contrived to make difficulties, would Britain act on her own, or only act with the French? He was restrained and courteous, but clearly desperate. Halifax told him straight: Britain would insist on a time limit, and on a short one. He still hoped to bring the French along with Britain. Raczynski expressed his suspicions: he thought the French dupes of the Italians. The moral effect of this delay on his countrymen was devastating.

At 10.30 p.m. Lord Halifax spoke directly with M. Bonnet.[100] The Government had to make an announcement, with a time limit, after which, if Germany had not given the required assurances, Britain would be at war. The Ambassadors would call on Ribbentrop at 8 a.m. and give him until midday to answer. If France felt she could not act on this timetable, Britain proposed to act on her own, provided the French Government would give an assurance it would follow suit within twenty-four hours. Bonnet tried to argue; but it was never easy to argue with Lord Halifax once he had made up his mind. Halifax finally said Britain would feel free to act on her own timetable. The French could act a few hours later, putting in whatever timetable they liked. The conversation lasted three-quarters of an hour.

M. Corbin realized that the British had in every way the edge on his own Government. They had had two long meetings of Parliament since the German attack on Poland. The French had delayed until September 2. The British Cabinet had met twice. It had been fully and accurately informed. The French Council of Ministers had not met until 7.30 p.m. that day. He strongly (and rightly) suspected it had not been so accurately informed. He prized the honour of his own country very highly. He was a devotee of the closest and warmest relations between Britain and France. He knew what a deplorable impression would be created if France appeared to be dragged into war on Britain's coat tails. But he realized that the Prime Minister was fighting for his political life. His defeat on this issue would be an even greater disaster for France. He left for his Embassy.

How great a disaster it would be was impressed upon him when he arrived at the Embassy.[101] The building itself was under siege by journalists. He was besieged with phone calls from France's closest friends. Winston Churchill was the most aroused. The telephone positively vibrated with his voice. If France failed again and ratted on the Poles as she had ratted on the Czechs, he, who had striven all his life for Anglo-French friendship, would be entirely indifferent to the fate of France.[102] Talk of technical difficulties he dismissed. 'I suppose you would call it a technical difficulty for a Pole if a German bomb fell on his head.' Corbin managed to calm him down and the conversation ended with Churchill promising fervently to do all he could to develop the military strength of Britain to a maximum.

At 11.20 p.m., Chamberlain called for an immediate Cabinet meeting at Downing Street.[103] As the Ministers made their way there, the dissidents from the House of Commons squashed into three cars, the others coming from their homes, the heavens opened above them. The Cabinet's decision to send an ultimatum to Germany was taken amidst peals of thunder, almost incessant lightning and the drumming of rain on the pavements outside. The meeting opened with a brief apology from the Prime Minister, explaining what had happened and stressing the difference between the French and British positions. He was icily cold in his delivery. Like Halifax he had felt his Ministers' revolt very keenly. Downing Street was flooded with the rain, as the Cabinet dispersed. The streets were pitch dark, except for the lightning. It was decided that Sir Nevile Henderson should present the ultimatum at 9 o'clock, to expire by 11, that Sunday. When Chamberlain put the question to his colleagues, did anyone disagree with the decision, no one spoke. 'Right, gentlemen,' he said. 'This means war.' 'There was a most enormous clap of thunder, and the whole Cabinet room was lit up by a blinding flash of lightning,' Sir Reginald Dorman-Smith later recalled.

As the members of the Cabinet slowly dispersed, some to their offices, others to their homes, M. Corbin returned to Downing Street. Neville Chamberlain broke the news of the Cabinet decision to him. While the Prime Minister was so engaged, Lord Halifax and Sir Alexander Cadogan were drafting the ultimatum to be delivered at 9 a.m. in Berlin. Sir William Malkin, the Foreign Office legal adviser, was already in waiting. Coming down the big central staircase in the Foreign Office, Hugh Dalton, once Under Secretary in the Foreign Office in the Labour Government of 1929–31, was passed by Malkin running up in a great hurry.[104] 'I have the declaration in the bag,' he shouted to Dalton. 'It is settled now.' Coming out of the side door of the Foreign Office on to Downing Street, Dalton met Halifax and Cadogan. To Dalton's query and warning, Halifax assured him that the French would follow. It would be 'all right tomorrow'. 'Chips' Channon, the last of the peace-lovers, was left to mourn,[105] 'In a few hours we will be at war and the PM will have lost his great battle for peace.'

CHAPTER 31

SEPTEMBER 3: THE BRITISH ULTIMATUM

Thanks to M. Bonnet and his small group of accomplices and allies, Daladier and his Council of Ministers had held too long to the illusion that the clock could be wound back. They had been accompanied in this belief for a brief period by Chamberlain and Halifax. It is easy to say that their willingness to grasp at this illusion does them no credit. But it is fairer to see in their reluctance to seize the hour, to order war, to proceed immediately to the kind of attack on Germany's western frontiers that the German military most feared and which, just conceivably, might have precipitated a military coup against the Führer, the evidence of a fear of war with which subsequent generations have become only too familiar. They remembered the 1914–18 war; anyone over forty remembered the years of European wealth and supremacy that had preceded July 1914. As always their memories were selectively edited. They remembered the easy, calm days, the settled horizons, youth, expectancy, ambition; they did not remember annual crises, social strife, strikes, violence in the streets, poverty, disease and overcrowding in the cities. A new war would, they feared to the point of conviction, destroy their country, destroy their cities, destroy their culture and destroy the society in which they enjoyed status, power, authority, influence, comfort and wealth.

Beyond the fire of war they saw the spectre of 'Bolshevism'. That none of those for whom the spectre was so compelling could have given a rational explanation of what they comprehended Bolshevism to be is not the issue. The depths of the fear are illustrated by the severity with which the French Communist party was treated, by the banning of *L'Humanité*, its newspaper, and most of all by the action taken against the political refugees from Fascism and Nazism, who had made Paris the centre of international resistance to Hitler and Mussolini in the name of anti-Fascism and who had been the most betrayed by the pact between Hitler and Stalin. From the viewpoint of the 'Bolshevikophobes,' they were the real threat. They were not French; their loyalty, such as it was, was given to ideals which the Bolshevikophobes feared as disruptive, anarchic, subversive. Many of them were Jewish; all were godless unbelievers. The French began the war against Nazism by interning the anti-Nazis, the refugees from Nazism in their midst.

These elements only represent one part of the France that was about to declare war on Hitler. They were, however, deeply enough entrenched in French political life, in the French Parliament and press, in the police and the military, among the 'Two Hundred Families' and the wealthier reaches of French society, particularly French society outside Paris, that their representatives in Parliament and in the governing coalition could exercise a significant braking effect on the upsurge of patriotism which the proceedings of the French Parliament on the afternoon of September 2 seemed, at least on the surface, to manifest. To enter the war against Germany was to enhance the processes which were tearing the Third Republic apart. To enter the war against Germany in Britain's train, to have to bow to the outrage of the House of Commons against a British Prime Minister who tried to accommodate the political needs of the French Government, was still worse. Defeat and occupation would accentuate these divisions. Liberation, the process of instant vengeance against those who collaborated, which the French called *l'épuration*, did nothing to heal them.

The differences which so occupied the telephone lines between London and Paris on the night of September 2/3 amounted simply to this: fear of war, fear of Bolshevism, memories of the hecatombs and hatreds of 1914–18, concern for a Europe which was ending, a social order which a second world war would almost certainly destroy, divided political society in both Britain and France. But it divided it in different proportions on each side of the Channel; and it divided it very much less deeply in Britain. British society retained a sense of national identity, a grasp of the priorities necessary for the maintenance of national unity, a common set of symbols of that unity – king, parliament, flag – and a consciousness of Englishness, Welshness, Scottishness reinforced by more local ties of identification; these were to give Britain a sense of social cohesion, a level of social discipline, a feeling of singleminded purpose which were to make possible a degree of mobilization of the national resources in manpower and money which, for all the technological backwardness, out-dated managerial and labour practices, prejudices and grievances that historians now maintain accompanied this mobilization in Britain, Germany was only to achieve after D-Day.

The difference between Britain and France lay not in the sense of vulnerability to war which filled the public imagination in each country. The British people anticipated that war would begin with massive bombardment from the air, the widespread use of poison gas, wholesale destruction of London by fire, a quarter of a million casualties in the first twenty-four hours. They were comforted by the machinery of air-raid precautions, the establishment of uniformed air-raid wardens, the wide distribution of gas-masks, and the development and construction everywhere of air-raid shelters – from the large deep-level shelters built by the London boroughs to the ubiquitous Anderson shelter, a family-sized bunker of steel and cement which millions assembled or had installed in their back gardens. The vast whales of the air, the barrage balloons, gave an image of airborne protection – illusory, as it was to prove, but none the less comforting. None of this, however, prevented the dreadful disharmony of the electrically driven air-raid sirens, ullulating up and down the scale, from striking fear in the hearts of all who heard them, especially the parents of small children.

The British believed themselves to be prepared. In most respects, save the organizational, this was far from true; but the machinery for a command economy and for a directorial state already existed. It had been worked out over the previous decade. It lay ready to be set in motion. The British, lulled by an informal system of press, radio and newsreel management which was much more extensive than was generally known at the time, still broadly trusted their political leaders and their machinery of government to a degree which would have been incredible in France. Despite a figure of unemployment which ran around the three million mark, over 15 per cent of the registered work-force, Britain had voted the Government a comfortable majority in the general election of 1935. There was every indication that, had Chamberlain held a general election in 1939, he would have maintained, perhaps even slightly raised, that majority. Six weeks earlier Daladier had had to beg Chamberlain not to announce that he intended to hold an election until after the French Parliament had broken up for the summer vacation.[1]

As the British Cabinet found its way home through the rain, the thunder and the lightning of London's darkened streets, Halifax and Chamberlain were left to reflect on the behaviour of their Cabinet and colleagues over the day that had just ended. On the face of it Halifax was the calmer. He returned to the Foreign Office with Sir Alexander Cadogan and Ivone Kirkpatrick. The telegrams, already drafted, were dispatched. Lord Halifax relaxed with his colleagues, calling for beer, which was brought to him by the junior official on night duty, sleepy and pyjamaed. When he came to record the events of the day, however, he was more severe. Of the 'general feeling' that 'the French were trying to run out of their engagement to Poland and were taking us with them,' he commented:[2] 'the whole thing, to my mind, showed democratic assemblies at their worst, and I could not acquit some members of the Cabinet of having fed the flames of suspicion.'

Chamberlain was even more bitter. 'The House of Commons was out of hand,' he wrote to his sister Hilda, on September 10,[3] 'torn with suspicions and ready (some of them, including, particularly, Amery, the most insulting of all) to believe the Government guilty of any cowardice and treachery. To crown it all,' he added, 'a certain number of my colleagues in the Govt. [sic] who always behave badly when there is any crisis about, took the opportunity to declare that they were being flouted or neglected,' and 'even tried to set up a sort of meeting. Even Lord Halifax found their behaviour unbearable and declared that I had the temper of an archangel.'

An ungenerous view, which Chamberlain's first biographer, Keith Feiling, omitted from the text of the letter when he first published it in 1946. It has the air of injured egoism which, apparent, as we shall see, in his public utterances on September 3, makes it difficult entirely to share his genuine agony and sense of personal failure, in his seventieth year, as the second Anglo-German war began. There is much of classic Greek tragedy in the course of his career, from his assumption of the prime ministership in 1937 to the final disaster which overtook him in May 1940. His attempt to save Europe and Britain from a new, even more destructive war than that of 1914–18 was not an ignoble aim, even if it contains an element of that quasi-divine arrogance, that hubris upon which the Greek gods were always so quick to take their vengeance. With it, however, there is always that element of almost petulant egoism, quick to take fault, quick to reward itself with a Pharisaical reflection upon the failings of others.

The events of the morning of September 3, however, revolve almost entirely around Chamberlain and Sir Nevile Henderson, the British Ambassador in Berlin. In their last meeting the Cabinet had been most exercised over the difficulty of reconciling the need to reassure the press – so that the British public did not face in their Sunday morning newspapers the same mixture of suspicion and innuendo, born of ignorance, that had swept the House of Commons – with the need to preserve total security vis-à-vis the Germans up to the moment when Henderson delivered the ultimatum, lest forewarned the Germans might stage the kind of massive pre-emptive air strike, the 'bolt from the blue', which had for so long been the nightmare of the British defence authorities. The armed forces had been put on alert before the first note had been delivered by Sir Nevile Henderson on Friday, September 1.[4] They had been alerted again shortly after midnight on September 1/2.[5] These messages had gone out on a secure code. On September 2, however, the Germans had intercepted the Admiralty's warning to all British merchant ships to seek a safe harbour.[6]

The worst breach of security occurred, however, in Berlin. Once again, the offenders were Sir Nevile Henderson and Sir George Ogilvie-Forbes. Henderson phoned Robert Coulondre at 8.28 p.m. on September 2,[7] to say that he had had a telegram warning him of another to follow,[8] exclaiming that he did not know what it was but he could guess. His call was duly intercepted by the *Forschungsamt*. The telegram instructing him to seek an appointment with Ribbentrop at 9 a.m. was sent *en clair*.[9] And at 7.43 a.m. Sir George Ogilvie-Forbes phoned[10] (the *Forschungsamt* could not, or would not, identify his listener) to say that 'Henderson would be going over at 9 a.m. and would request a reply by 11 a.m.; if that was not forthcoming, they would ask for their passports and all would be over.'

The British fears were, fortunately, baseless. The Luftwaffe had no plans to attack Britain at the outset of war. Indeed, as has been seen, it lacked the capacity to do so from bases in Germany. The Luftwaffe was, moreover, largely engaged in action on the Eastern Front where, more and more, civilian targets (including the home of the US Ambassador to Poland) were replacing military ones. It was soon to be Germany's turn to entertain what at this date would prove equally baseless fears of the RAF.

After the dramatic and torrential midnight thunderstorm, the skies over Britain had cleared to produce another characteristically beautiful September day, calm, peaceful, without a cloud in the sky, the air fresh and clean as if new-minted, the streets washed white and free of dirt by the overnight cloudburst. The Sunday newspapers were filled with the flavour of war, reports of the savage fighting in Poland intermingling with admonitions to carry gas-masks everywhere, advice on how to behave if there was an air-raid warning, and statements that while rationing of meat, bacon and ham, butter, margarine and cooking fat, and sugar was to be introduced, there was no shortage at the moment and 'no reason for hoarding'. The evacuation of children and their mothers, begun the previous Friday, was nearly completed. The London Zoo had evacuated its inmates. And everywhere volunteers were filling more sand-bags to reinforce the lower storeys of government and other public buildings against bomb blasts. As the sentries outside Buckingham Palace and the Horse Guards paraded in khaki battledress and tin helmets instead of scarlet and brass with bearskins, as orthodox Protestant and Catholic England left home to go to morning service, Britain waited for war. Foreign observers, diplomatists, press correspondents and the new corps of American radio correspondents who were to make the European war into a spectator sport for America's hundred-million-strong radio listeners, to a man spoke of the determination, the sense of unity and purpose, the single-mindedness they saw and sensed in the British people.

Paris was not so well prepared, nor so certain. Paris was resigned to war rather than, as London and Britain were, relieved that the period of doubt, hesitation and uncertainty was over. Paris, it was said, had a slightly dishevelled look that Sunday, like a woman surprised without the make-up with which she habitually confronted the world. But Paris also projected an appearance of purpose, and a reliance on strength: the strength of the Maginot line, the strength of the pound sterling and the Royal Navy, the strength of French industry and inventiveness as it began suddenly to emerge from the industrial strife of 1937–8. 'We will conquer because we are the stronger,' was the slogan that was to calm any disquiet that might beset French opinion. Paris was empty of tourists. Urged on by their Embassy and by the feeling that they had suddenly become *de trop* in a family quarrel, American visitors had poured out of Paris and across the Atlantic in the last week of August and the first days of September. No one who goes to an amphitheatre wishes to be caught on the sand when the gladiators enter or the lions and wolves are unleashed. The wealthier idlers of fashionable Paris had remained on or returned to the Riviera.

As the devout went to Mass, to pray in Notre Dame des Victoires, and in the church of the Sacred Heart where Masses were held for the departing conscripts, Paris was enveloped in rain, pouring from grey skies. The mood, despite the rhetoric with which the newspapers were filled, was sombre, resigned, serious; there were too many memories of the enthusiasms of July 1914 and the terrible rolls of the dead celebrated in every town and village by statues in lead and bronze of a solitary *poilu*.

In Berlin the public consistently refused to perform in the role written for it by Hitler and Goebbels. Ulrich von Hassell noted on August 29[11] a total absence of any audience reaction to the films intended to incite popular hatred against the Poles. Three days later, he commented that the public seemed to regard the war as a sort of Nazi party project.[12] Foreign observers noted the lack of any public will for war.[13] The Italian Ambassador found himself applauded when he left the Reichs Chancellery[14] by a crowd which manifested little or no enthusiasm for the comings and goings of Nazi dignitaries. Magistrati, the Counsellor, commented on the lack of any signs of collective emotion. Berlin struck him, especially at night, as a dead city: only a handful of pedestrians, streets almost empty of motor cars and transport, absolute silence even on the Kurfürstendamm, Berlin's equivalent of London's Regent Street or New York's Fifth Avenue.[15] Coulondre wandered incognito through Berlin on foot on September 2.[16] He saw no one laugh or joke. There were no signs of enthusiasm for the war, no patriotic fever, none of the high emotions of July 1914, any more than in Paris. Until the last the Germans trusted in the Führer's skill. He would have some new magic which would keep the war localized. But the Führer, for the moment, had run out of magic.

At 5 a.m. on Sunday, September 3, the text of the ultimatum to be delivered to the German Government was telephoned through to Sir Nevile Henderson, together with his instructions.[17] The ultimatum referred back to the British note of September 1. No reply to that note had been received by Britain, and German attacks on Poland had intensified. Unless satisfactory assurances were received by 11 a.m. British summer time, a state of war would exist between the two countries. Henderson was told to inform Halifax before 11 a.m., by any means at his disposal, if such assurances were received. If they were not, he was to ask for his passports and those of his Embassy staff.

It was to take Mr Holman of the Embassy staff some time before he could make it clear to the Wilhelmstrasse that the Ambassador insisted on being received at 9 a.m.[18] He could not, however, secure that Ribbentrop was there at the Wilhelmstrasse to receive him. Even before the German Foreign Minister went to bed around 4 a.m. on the morning of September 3, it was clear to him that his game of pro-crastination had come to an end. As we have seen, Ribbentrop was not only a moral coward. He disliked playing 'historic' scenes where he did not control the script. Not for the first or the last time, he passed the poisoned chalice to Paul-Otto Schmidt, the rotund, owl-like senior interpreter to the German Foreign Ministry.[19] Schmidt overslept that morning and only made it to the Wilhelmstrasse by taxi. Even then, as he was still paying off his cab he saw the dapper figure of Sir Nevile Henderson, elaborately uniformed in full ambassadorial fig, with cocked hat tucked under his arm, ascending the main steps of the Foreign Ministry ahead of him. He stepped in by a side entry and made it to Ribbentrop's office in time to receive His Majesty's Ambassador at 9 a.m. on the dot.

Sir Nevile was at his most formal.[20] He shook Schmidt's hand, refused a seat at the small table in the corner of the room, took his stance on the carpet in the middle of the room, and delivered himself of the ultimatum, reading it slowly and with emphasis. The document read, he then handed it over, unbent a moment to express his regrets that he should have had to hand it over to Schmidt, who had always 'been so ready to help', took his goodbye and left. Schmidt hurried over to the Reichs Chancellery, the ultimatum in his briefcase.

The outer room to Hitler's office was crowded with members of Hitler's Cabinet and other prominent party figures.[21] Schmidt had to force his way through their anxious queries. Hitler sat at his desk;

Zu spät?
'Too late?' (September 1939: Britain and France declare war on Germany, despite Hitler's hopes for peace. This cartoon was banned by the Swiss censor)

Ribbentrop stood to his right by the window. Both looked at him tensely. Schmidt then translated the British ultimatum slowly. Hitler sat as if turned to stone. He made no angry scenes; he sat still in his place. When Schmidt had finished, there was what seemed to him an age of silence. At last Hitler turned to Ribbentrop, who still stood staring out of the window. 'What happens next?' he asked with a gleam of anger in his eye. 'We must assume that the French will give us a similar ultimatum in the next few hours,' replied von Ribbentrop.

Schmidt left, to be mobbed by the crowd in the antechamber. Schmidt's announcement, that in two hours Britain and Germany would be in a state of war, brought total silence. One listener said, 'If we lose this war, may Heaven be merciful to us.' (Schmidt remembered the speaker as Goering; but, as will be seen, Goering was elsewhere.) Goebbels stood in a corner, withdrawn and introspective. Everywhere Schmidt saw drawn, pale faces.

Ribbentrop had, however, already arranged to have the last word. The British ultimatum expired at 11 a.m. Shortly afterwards he summoned Henderson to the Foreign Ministry and handed over a long, argumentative, not to say polemical, document restating the German case.[22] Its length demonstrates that it was no preparation of the moment but something the Foreign Ministry draughtsmen (the hand of Friedrich Gaus can be detected) had laboured over since the first indications that a British ultimatum was on its way. It was written for the record, to strengthen the convictions of the already convinced. The war was Britain's fault for allowing Poland to count on her open support for every Polish act of aggression. All Germany sought was the revision of the Versailles Treaty. Britain had rejected Mussolini's offer of mediation. Germany did not intend to endure on her eastern frontier the kind of anarchic guerrilla warfare which Britain was suffering from the Arab insurgents in Palestine. Britain had always refused the hand of friendship Germany had offered. Unlike Britain Germany did not 'intend to dominate the world', but she was determined to defend her liberty, her independence and her life. Henderson took this document in silence, remarking only that it would be for history to judge (a cliché which more than earned its wages on September 3). The two men did not shake hands.

The French ultimatum was presented at 12 noon by Robert Coulondre. Once again, Ribbentrop sent in a substitute, in this case the State Secretary, Ernst von Weizsäcker. Coulondre, as instructed, had insisted on being received at noon.[23] As Coulondre left the French Embassy,[24] a small crowd had gathered outside, drawn by the pall of smoke from its chimneys as the incinerator strove to consume the secret archives Coulondre and his staff had been burning since the early hours of the morning. The crowd watched in silence, without any demonstration of anger or hostility. Even then M. Coulondre was somewhat shaken when, as he was getting into the Embassy car, he saw a young adolescent come towards him; even more shaken, when the young man handed him a postcard and a fountain pen, and asked him for his autograph. Coulondre smiled and patted his face. There were still Germans for whom this was 'a phony war'.

When Coulondre saw von Weizsäcker,[25] he posed the same question as Henderson had put to Schmidt. Was there a satisfactory answer to the French note? Weizsäcker said he was unable to reply; nor was he in a position to receive any French communication. If M. Coulondre would wait but a few minutes, Ribbentrop, who, he said, was even then attending the ceremony of presentation to Hitler of the new Soviet Ambassador,[26] would be able to see him personally, at the Reichs Chancellery. The two men made nervous conversation for a few minutes, then Coulondre was escorted to the Reichs Chancellery. He found it in the same state of hurry and scurry that it had been in every day over the past week or more.[27] To Ribbentrop, Coulondre posed the same question.[28] Ribbentrop replied that the delay had been caused by the Duce's offer of mediation which, Ribbentrop said, in flat contradiction of the record, Germany had accepted and Britain rejected. Britain had since presented an ultimatum. Germany, for reasons set out in the German note which he then handed over to Coulondre, had rejected that too. Germany would regret it if France were to behave in the same way. She would regard it as an entirely unjustified war of aggression by France against Germany. Coulondre avoided any attempt to lure him into an argument. Was he to assume that Germany rejected the French proposals? Ribbentrop said that was the case. Coulondre then handed over the French note.

The French note cannot be called a masterpiece of anything but circumlocution.[29] It too harked back to the enquiries directed at the German Government on September 1. If the German reply to those enquiries was negative, then France would be obliged, as from 5 p.m. on September 3, to fulfil 'those obligations contracted towards Poland of which the German Government is aware'. A formal declaration of war, for whatever reasons, was evaded. The text of the note had been drawn up by Coulondre on the basis of Bonnet's instructions.[30] Its formulation was Bonnet's. It had been phoned through to the French Embassy at 10.50 that morning.[31] Even then it had delayed the operation of the ultimatum to 5 a.m. on September 4.[32] Coulondre had telephoned to ask what he should do if the Germans tried to stall him once again. Act as if the reply was negative, said Léger. Bonnet then took his phone and confirmed this. Then, and only then, did he authorize Coulondre to advance the timing of the state of war from the morning of September 4 to 5 p.m. on September 3. It was in this revised form, though still with the time of 10.20 a.m., that the French were later to publish Coulondre's instructions.

Ribbentrop read the note. Germany had no intention of attacking France; if it came to war, France would be the aggressor, he said tonelessly. History will be the judge, said Coulondre, and withdrew. He and Henderson were to repeat themselves to each other, when Coulondre returned to the French Embassy and they compared notes, for the edification of the *Forschungsamt*'s telephonic eavesdroppers.[33]

The news of the British ultimatum appears to have induced in Hitler a severe attack of logorrhoea. At 2.30 p.m. four separate proclamations[34] were read by the announcers on Berlin radio. The first was an appeal to the German people, some eight hundred words long. There followed shorter proclamations addressed to the armies in the east and west respectively. The last was addressed to the party. 'Our Jewish democratic global enemy has succeeded in placing the English people in a state of war with Germany,' it began. The appeal to the German people spoke of the 'Jewish plutocratic and democratic ruling élite that wishes only to see the peoples of the world as obedient slaves'. The address to the eastern armies announced that, as a veteran of the First World War and 'as your supreme commander', he was about to join them at the front.

More important than this unpleasant mixture of threats, maledictions, racialist execrations and exhortations, was Hitler's War Directive Number 2.[35] This ordered restraint in the west on land and in the air. At sea, war against merchant shipping was to be conducted according to prize regulations. Air attacks on British naval forces were only to be undertaken if the British had already attacked similar targets by air, and if prospects of success were particularly favourable. As for the Luftwaffe in the west, 'its fighting power must be conserved for the decision against the western powers after the defeat of Poland.' The German war objective remained for the time being the destruction of Poland.

How the German navy interpreted these orders was almost immediately illustrated. That afternoon, off the Hebrides, the British passenger liner SS *Athenia*, *en route* for the United States from Liverpool carrying eleven hundred passengers and three hundred crew, was torpedoed and sunk by a German U-boat. Despite the speedy arrival of the Norwegian tanker *Knute Nelson*, the Swedish yacht *Southern Cross* and two British destroyers, 128 passengers were drowned. There were three hundred Americans on board hurrying to return to the sanctuary of their country. Twenty-eight of them were among the dead.

In London the hour of 11 a.m. had come and gone without any communication from Berlin. The Service representatives, the war planners and the representatives of the other Ministries concerned had been waiting in the office of the Cabinet Secretary, Sir Edward Bridges, since 10.30 a.m., wanting to know whether war had been declared.[36] At 11 a.m. Bridges came in to say that a telegram from Berlin was being deciphered. Ten minutes later Bridges came in again to say that there had been no reply from the German Government. Chamberlain's instructions were that the war telegrams should be dispatched forth-with. Those waiting broke up immediately, and hurried back to their Ministries.

Neville Chamberlain had had a 'short but troubled night': he looked 'crumpled, despondent and old'.[37] 'Only the fact that one's mind works at three times its ordinary pace on such occasions' enabled him to get through all the tasks 'on that awful Sunday', he later wrote.[38] His broadcast has become one of the classics of media iconography, used repeatedly in films, television dramas and documentaries and on radio, to set at once the mood of that now long-distant day when Britain's peace ended and Britain embarked on the war which, even in victory, was to prove a significant step in the diminution of British power. That sad, resigned, melancholy voice, so different from the solid vibrant strength his successor Churchill was to project, rang out throughout Britain. He outlined the events of the previous days. That morning, he said, a further communication had been made to the German Govern-ment asking for an assurance that the German forces would suspend their attacks on Poland and retire to their own territories. No such assurance had been received. 'Consequently, this country is now at war with Germany.'

Both his broadcast and his subsequent speech to Parliament betray by a personal note that he had come so to identify himself with the preservation of peace that he assumed everyone among his listeners would accept, admire, understand and sympathize: 'You can imagine what a bitter blow it is to me that all my long struggle for peace has failed. Yet I cannot believe that there is anything more, or anything different that I could have done, and that would have been more successful . . . a situation in which no word given by Germany's ruler could be trusted and no people or country could feel themselves safe, had become intolerable. . . .' When he spoke in Parliament later that note was to be even stronger.[39] 'Everything that I have worked for, everything that I have hoped for, everything that I have believed in in my public life has crashed into ruins. There is only one thing left for me to do: that is to devote what strengths and powers I have to forward the victory of the cause for which we have to sacrifice so much. I cannot tell what part I may be allowed to play myself: I trust I may live to see the day when Hitlerism has been destroyed, and a liberated Europe has been re-established.' In this, as in everything else, he was to be disappointed. In May 1940, after a catastrophic debate in Parliament over the poor performance of the British forces in Norway, he resigned. Churchill replaced him. Before the year was out he was dead from cancer.

Even as Chamberlain sat before the microphone in Downing Street, the legal machinery for the declaration of war was moving into operation. On the steps of the Royal Exchange there gathered a group of incongruously dressed officials, two in cocked hats, short gold-fringed capes and long coats with brass buttons down to the floor, one in morning suit with a tall top hat with a gold band around it, and two City policemen wearing tin helmets and carrying gas-masks slung on khaki-web shoulder straps; a crowd of City maintenance workers watched a gowned official in a short barrister's wig read the official proclamation of war. All over the world British and Commonwealth ships, military, naval and air force stations were getting their war telegrams. And over in Carlton House Terrace, Robert Dunbar, head of the Foreign Office Treaty Department, was calling on Dr Theo Kordt, Chargé d'affaires in the German Embassy, to declare war and to arrange the departure for Germany of the German career diplomats, consuls, officials and employees of diplomatic status. They left, under police escort, for Berlin via Gravesend and Rotterdam on the evening of September 4. Lord Halifax took special care to provide a home for the Embassy's old black dog (a familiar sight, as he lay on the Embassy steps, to all passers-by).

But before Chamberlain could meet his Parliament, that element of black humour with which great, even tragic events are so often inextricably tangled, struck again. Radio listeners to Chamberlain's speech heard the announcer say, 'Now, an announcement about food', followed by a long silence, interrupted only by a shuffling noise, as of paper, and a low whisper. Then the National Anthem was played. In the middle came the scream of air-raid sirens. Police cleared the streets with whistles. Policemen cycled the streets with placards – 'There is an air warning.' Most of the British public trooped into the shelters, covering their uneasiness with jokes and laughter. Churchill, who wished to watch the fun, was persuaded to take shelter. He took the brandy bottle with him. For twenty minutes people took shelter. Then the all-clear went. Nothing had happened: no hyper-efficient German General Staff of the Air had had squadrons standing by with engines running and bombs primed to set off the moment Sir Nevile Henderson had presented the ultimatum, if not before. It was a false alarm. Some errant private plane (belated revellers returning from a weekend at Le Touquet in one version) had been spotted by the new radio-location towers.

There was one other bemused participant in the black humour of these last weeks still to make his bow. The mysterious recipient of Sir George Ogilvie-Forbes's indiscreet phone call at 7.40 a.m. had been Birger Dahlerus.[40] It has been seen how, throughout his well-intentioned intervention, he had been the unwitting tool of a power conflict between Goering and Ribbentrop, by which Goering sought to beguile the British into allowing Poland to go down alone, where Ribbentrop had already written them off. The news from the British Embassy stirred Dahlerus into one last effort.

He rushed to Goering's headquarters, arriving at 8.40 a.m.[41] He found Goering, so he said, in the dark as to the events of September 2 and surprised by the presentation in the form of an ultimatum of the British conditions. Goering's surprise was well feigned; the *Forschungsamt* regularly intercepted communications between Count Ciano and the Italian Embassy in Berlin. Ciano's communications with Attolico would already have alerted him to the offer and the abandonment of the Italian mediation, and of the reasons for it. He pretended indignation. Never in the history of the world had a victorious army been compelled to withdraw before negotiations had started. He broke off in mid-tirade to call first Ribbentrop and then Hitler. Dahlerus conceived the notion that so long as the Führer returned a soft answer to the British, something might still be solved. He rang the Foreign Office. The time was 10.15 a.m. He spoke to Frank Roberts, in the Central Department.[42] 'Without undue arrogance', he said, he thought he knew the Berlin end better than anyone else. He had done his damnedest to overcome the difficulties regarding the withdrawal of troops. These were, however, insurmountable. He was sure that with a little give-and-take on both sides a conference could be arranged, and there would be a good chance of world peace.

He returned to Goering. The Field Marshal, he said,[43] should offer to fly to London. His plane should take off before 11 a.m. (so as to forestall the expiry of the British ultimatum). Goering instructed his aide, General Bodenschatz, to arrange for a plane to be readied. Then he phoned the Reichs Chancellery to speak to Hitler. Before agreeing,

Hitler wanted to know whether Goering's mission would be acceptable to the British. Dahlerus phoned Ogilvie-Forbes at the Embassy. Ogilvie-Forbes, who appears throughout Dahlerus's narrative as playing stooge to his wise guy, like a feed to a music hall comedian, said that Britain would require assurances of complete sincerity. Dahlerus phoned London again.[44] It was then 10.50 a.m. The British ultimatum had ten minutes to run. He proposed that Goering should fly to London. Halifax was consulted. He had had enough. Britain was waiting for the German answer, Dahlerus was told. No one was prepared to wait for further discussion with Goering. Britain's attitude would depend on the German reply to the ultimatum. Cadogan summed it up more tersely. 'I said "rats",' he wrote in his diary.[45] Dahlerus and Goering waited,[46] Dahlerus unable to understand why Goering did not jump into a car and drive to beard his Führer. After twenty minutes, the news of Chamberlain's broadcast was brought to them. Britain was at war. Dahlerus's shuttle diplomacy was at an end. The comedy was over.

Parliament assembled at noon. Chamberlain made his apologia. All was unity again. The National Service (Armed Forces) Bill was passed through all its stages before lunch. At 3 p.m. the Direction of Plans Committee, now renamed the War Committee, met. At 5 o'clock the new War Cabinet met for the first time. Churchill attended it as the new head of the Admiralty. 'Winston is back,' ran the signal from the Admiralty to the Royal Navy at sea at 6 p.m. that evening. The battle lines for the second Anglo-German war had been drawn.

CHAPTER 32

AFTERTHOUGHTS

With the British declaration of war this story ends. It did not end for those who lived through it. One by one the smaller European nations fell victim as it spread. Some of their ruling groups tried in vain to accommodate themselves, only to find themselves bled of authority by their new overlords or repudiated by those in whose name they exercised authority. Prince Paul of Yugoslavia, King Boris of Bulgaria, Admiral Horthy in Hungary, Monsignor Tiso in Slovakia, all tried to walk the paths of accommodation in the hope of survival through the new order that the SS, Hitler's economists and the business leadership in Germany (who had already trodden a similar path) were to establish in the wake of the German army. Others were to be defeated, overrun, occupied. Some sought safety in exile, to return as junior members of the Grand Coalition, allies who had won their place by the courage of their forces in exile, the work of the underground movements in subversion and intelligence-gathering in the service of the British or American victors. The Dutch, Norwegian, Belgian and Greek Governments brought substantial overseas assets, ships and raw materials to the anti-Hitler coalition. Even the Polish merchant marine, some thirty-seven ships, was a useful adjunct to the Allies' maritime transport capacity.

Even with those who resisted Hitler after defeat, the period of occupation accelerated internal processes and exacerbated internal divisions. The Yugoslav army, or rather its dominating Serbian element, combined with the young King Peter to overthrow Prince Paul and repudiate his policy of accommodation. King Peter did not return from exile. His War Minister, General Mihailović, took to the mountains. He ended his life executed by his successful Communist rivals in the mountains, on charges of collaboration with the occupying powers. King Boris of Bulgaria died in mysterious circumstances before his country fell into the sphere of influence of the advancing Soviet armies.

Călinescu, the brave little Romanian Premier, was assassinated in October 1939 by members of the Iron Guard. King Carol was forced to resign in 1940 after the Soviet Union, Bulgaria and Hungary had each in turn forced Romania to give up Bessarabia, the Dobrudja and most of Transylvania. The train taking him and his Jewish mistress, Magda Lupescu, into exile was pursued across the Yugoslav border by Iron Guard gunmen, intent on avenging the murder of their leader, Codreanu, in 1938. Carol's successor, his young son Michael, saw Romania taken into Germany's attack on Russia in 1941. Three years later, he staged a successful *coup d'état* and surrendered his country to the advancing Soviet armies. In 1946 Romania recovered Transylvania, but not under the monarchy or the social system that had existed before it accepted the British guarantee. The Greek Royal Family returned to Greece to decades of civil war, sometimes open, more often suppressed; but it too has now become a thing of the past.

In Western Europe the governing systems were more stable. Norway and Denmark remained royalist social democracies. King Haakon of Norway continued as head of the Norwegian Government-in-exile. King Christian of Denmark, whose country was supposed to be a showpiece of German benevolence, remained obstinately unco-operative towards the German occupation authorities. King Léopold of Belgium, who surrendered his defeated army to Germany in 1940, was not so fortunate. At war's end charges of hidden collaboration and of sympathies with the conqueror drove him into abdication in favour of his son.

The Third Republic in France did not survive defeat in 1940. Its successor government and regime, pledged to rebirth in the name of French authoritarianism, became in practice ever more clearly an instrument of German policy, and ever more alienated from the rival embodiment of France's long traditions of patriotism and nationalism, General de Gaulle. De Gaulle triumphantly survived all attempts to provide alternative leadership and alternative versions of France, more welcome to one or other of the leading figures in the coalition created by Hitler. As General de Gaulle knew beyond a peradventure, where others could only see decline into social disorder, France was unique, given the right system of government, in its capacity to contain and unify within its consciousness of national unity, divisions and antagonisms which to others would seem impossible to survive.

Most unhappy in their fate were the people of Poland. Their terri-tory, as it existed in 1939, was divided between Germany and the Soviet Union. By the end of the war it was as though it had been picked up and moved bodily westwards. The western frontiers came to encompass not only all of East Prussia (save for Königsberg, annexed to the Soviet Union), but West Prussia too as far west as Stettin and German Silesia. Only the gravestones remained to show that here were once German cities. The Government of the Polish Colonels, having taken refuge in Romania on the defeat of Poland, was dissolved. A new Polish Government-in-exile was formed which strove to accommodate all the elements of inter-war Polish political life with the exception of the Polish Communist party, regarded as irretrievably compromised in its Polish-ness by its association with the power which had incorporated the eastern half of inter-war Poland into its own territories. Under German occupation a secret Polish state re-organized itself, with its own army to complement the Polish forces-in-exile. But Poland's inter-war independence could not be sustained. The Government-in-exile could not accommodate itself to the Soviet victors, and its Western supporters could not face another conflict with their Soviet allies. What remained, however, was indubitably Polish, even more so than in inter-war Poland since the German, Ukrainian, Jewish and Lithuanian minorities had gone, the Germans expelled, the Jews largely destroyed, the others absorbed into the Soviet Union.

The Baltic states, saving only Finland, fell into the Soviet sphere of influence. In 1940 the Soviet Union incorporated their territories into its own. Finland fought the Soviet Union twice, both times unsuccessfully, in 1939–40 on its own and in 1941–4 as an ally of Germany. The Soviet leadership found the Finns so integrated a society as to make the idea of absorption or Sovietization a non-starter. Finland survived, diminished in territory, deprived of access to the open sea in the north, but still recognizably the same Finland as before 1939.

The only neutrals to survive were those on the European periphery or in its dead centre. Spain and Portugal, Sweden and Turkey survived by different strategies and with different sympathies, Spain even sending a division of volunteers to fight against the Soviet Union. Franco's price for entering the war on Germany's side proved too high even for Hitler. After meeting Franco in 1940 he said, feelingly, that he would rather have all his teeth pulled out without anaesthesia than undergo such an experience again. Turkey remained obdurately unwilling to enter the war on the side of its British ally (the Anglo-Franco-Turkish Alliance was signed in the face of extreme Soviet pressure in September 1939), and as determinedly unsympathetic towards the German cause on the other. Swedish iron ore, Swedish conservatism and Sweden's sense of self-preservation kept that country neutral and at least not overtly unsympathetic towards the German state.

At the heart of Europe Switzerland remained the most resolutely neutral of all. Surrounded by Axis-controlled territory, it exacted a vigorous conformity with the laws of neutrality on the representatives of the belligerents on its soil – not with a high degree of success, as it was a centre of anti-German intelligence operations, carried out by both the Western powers and the Soviet Union. So long as its Alpine passes and tunnels remained open for north-south traffic, the Germans saw no advantage in attack. Its citizenry was ready to spring at once to its defence. The tunnels and passes were mined. It was more use to Germany as a neutral. Its long history of hostility towards the Soviet Union and its conservative bourgeois German and French culture made it less unsympathetic towards German policy, including German anti-semitic legislation, than its citizens are happy to remember. It seemed often to be neutralist as much as neutral in its sympathies. In the whole of Europe, few could be found who actively welcomed war save the extremists of right or left. On the right the restlessly violent, the political street-fighters of the Depression, now uniformed but not domesticated, welcomed war. Save in the Nazi and SS hierarchy, however, few were close to the levers of power or the trappings of success. And on the revolutionary left and the terrorist right of Eastern Europe, extreme nationalists such as the Croatian *Ustase*, or extreme revolutionary Communists such as Milovan Djilas, welcomed war as the harbinger of a just revolution. For these the fire of war was a cleansing flame; for the rest the blackened scorched corpses, stinking of petroleum jelly and melted flesh, hanging out of 'brewed-up' tanks or curled over where the napalm or the flame-throwers caught them, were the reality. There is nothing cleansing about the flames of war.

The world knows what happened to Hitler and Mussolini. Hitler killed himself. Mussolini was shot by Italian partisans as he tried to escape, together with his mistress, into Switzerland; their shrunken and drained bodies were left dangling over the pumps of an Italian petrol station. The unity of Germany as a single political territorial unit disappeared as the victorious Allies incorporated their various occupa-tion zones into their own socio-economic systems. Much of the subsequent 'Cold War' and the settlements of 1955, 1970 and 1975 which ended different phases of that quasi-conflict, turned on efforts by the different protagonists to win control of all rather than part of it.

This is what one school of historians likes to call dismissively the high politics of the Second World War and its aftermath. In this case the ebb and flow of high politics determined only too drastically the fate of the ordinary people. For the inhabitants of Europe the Second World War brought a return of the days of the wolf, as they had not existed since the Thirty Years War. The wolves were human. Often they wore uniform.

Often they acted under orders, in disciplined formations. Less often, but not that less often, they acted in the name of revenge. Sometimes the nationalism they revenged was that of an existing state. Sometimes it was in the name of a nationalism that existed in the minds of some *Abwehr* or SS planning staff, trading on the ambitions of that sad group of nationalisms that rarely if ever achieved nationhood: Sorbs, Ukrainians, Flemings, Bretons, Cossacks or the like. Some sought to destroy rival nations or groups in the name of anti-Bolshevism, racial purity, religious fidelity, social revolution, or the cause of the working classes. But the modus was the same, arbitrary authority backed by the gun. Criminality became law, murder masqueraded as military justice, revenge and the blood feud as legal punishment.

The only universal victims were Europe's wholly non-territorial nations, the gypsies and the Jews, made the targets of systematic, industrialized extermination. As the war ended, the German minorities in Eastern and Central Europe were hunted in retribution. Czech villagers posed above the bodies of those they had shot, heaped in piles, as the European aristocrats at pre-1914 shooting parties posed, their guns under their arms, above the battues of grouse, deer, pheasants or wild boar that had fallen to their guns. The silence of the farmstead, broken only by the noise of crows, the stilled and empty house, the church, roofless to the sky with fire-smoked walls, all betokening the return of the barbarian, became familiar sights throughout Europe from the massif of central France where the Maquis was active to the steadings of northern Norway, from the ordered fields and streets of the Netherlands to the partisan-ridden forests of central Russia or the slopes of the great Caucasian ranges. In Poland alone, besides the Jews, six million died.

This degree of human misery cannot be measured. Statistics only take away the humanity of the endlessly repeated tragedies. Novelists have tried to convey some of it: Curzio Malaparte, the former Italian Fascist, Arthur Koestler in *Arrival and Departure*, and more recently William Styron in *Sophie's Choice*. Few writers can live for more than the time it takes to write one book, contemplating or vicariously experiencing the terrible territories of the mind and the soul through which the subjects of their pens must wander. Artists have tried; but the realism of Jacques Callot's woodcuts of the Thirty Years War and the romanticism of Goya's *Los desastres de la guerra* could only be replaced by the fractured images of Picasso's *Guernica*. The real horrors can sometimes be found in the still photographs and the occasional piece of newsfilm that have survived. Many of the written records of the murders and the destruction were destroyed before the victors could seize them. The perpetrators of many of these acts went unidentified and unpunished. They were by no means all on the defeated side. Soon the relentless movement of time will have carried them away to join their victims; the books will be closed; new grass grows where they brought fire, death and torture, rape, robbery and refugeedom. Only the human capacity to descend to such depths and invent systems of thought and morality to justify them remains. *Homo hominis lupus est*: man is, and remains, the wolf of man.

What is so extraordinary in the events which led up to the outbreak of the Second World War is that Hitler's will for war was able to overcome the reluctance with which virtually everybody else approached it. Hitler willed, desired, lusted after war; though not war with France and Britain, at least not in 1939. No one else wanted it, though Mussolini came perilously close to talking himself into it. In every country the military advisers anticipated defeat, and the economic advisers expected ruin and bankruptcy. Most of their prophecies were realized. There were *bellicistes* in London and Paris. Few were to be found in either Government or Cabinet. The record of the British and French Cabinets, harried and hurried into guarantees that they could not or would not implement, into a system of deterrence they did not understand, and which left them in the last days of August desperately trying to avoid the realization that their policy had failed to deter, is neither a happy nor an edifying spectacle. But it is really open to doubt whether any alternative course would have made any difference.

Britain's success lay in the containment of the war for the first six months, in the avoidance of conflict with Japan and with Italy. In Italy's case Daladier's obstinacy held the line sufficiently long for Halifax, coached by Loraine, once he had got the measure of Mussolini, to avoid those marginal assaults on Mussolini's image of himself that might have tipped him, so narrow was the balance, towards entry into the war in 1939 rather than 1940. A man so marginally governed by the realities of his power as Mussolini could very well have been pushed the other way by too great a willingness to make concessions or too tough a demonstration of power. As for Japan, the balance there was so precarious that a lesser man than Craigie might have given away enough to encourage the belligerent, and a more antagonistic might well have provoked an invasion of the Tientsin concession. In both cases German insensibility and Ribbentrop's incompetence played into British hands.

The biggest British and French failure lay with the Soviet Union. Contrariwise the biggest Soviet failure lay with Britain and France. Soviet secrecy meant that nothing was available to counter the image of Soviet military weakness and military incompetence that made up the professional judgment of those whose job it was to advise Britain and France on Soviet strength. The approach to diplomacy of the Soviet Ambassadors abroad, especially of Maisky in London, made them blind to the changes in opinion and policy taking place in the British Cabinet. Soviet intelligence in the West was used as much, if not more, as a weapon of intrigue, than as a source of political information. Stalin's obsession with the *cauchemar* of a German invasion along the Baltic coast, which Zhdanov may have shared but certainly played upon, added an extra element of distortion to the Soviet viewpoint. Central, however, was the note of almost adolescent sensitivity which saw slights everywhere, in the dispatch of Mr Strang rather than Lord Halifax, and of Admiral Drax rather than the Chiefs of Staff to Moscow, a readiness to take offence which stemmed from the equally questionable assumption that since Hitler had no plans against the Soviet Union in 1939, Britain needed the Soviet Union more than the Soviet Union needed Britain and should behave as if she did. On any calculation the Soviet Union faced a much greater threat from Germany in 1941 than she did in 1939, when the German invasion of Russia had been planned and prepared for over the previous years, when Germany faced no armed resistance anywhere else on the European continent, and when Germany had absorbed and occupied south-eastern Europe.

That being said, the British and French began by feeling the Soviet Union could be marshalled to the service of a policy of deterrence already determined upon. They rejected Litvinov, who believed in collective action. They got instead Molotov, ignorant, short-sighted and dominated by his master's suspicions. They were not well served by their Ambassadors. M. Naggiar had an acuter mind than poor Sir William Seeds; but no more than Seeds could he imagine a Soviet government capable of believing a pact with Hitler, that destroyed the main British weapon of blockade against him, preferable to a pact designed to constrain and deter him. Nor had the British and French military done anything to come up with a convincing, let alone a coherent offensive strategy against a German enemy.

General Doumenc and Admiral Drax were sent to Moscow with grossly inadequate briefing and without a single card in their hands. The attitude taken by Marshal Voroshilov – what do you want us to do? We will only commit a percentage of the forces you commit – does not strike one as a serious approach to the problems of war against Nazi Germany either; though it is thoroughly consistent with Stalin's conviction that Britain needed Soviet aid so badly that she should expect to pay whatever price the Soviet Union demanded for Soviet support. It is, incidentally, odd that in one so quick to take offence, the essentially mercenary notion of the relationship with Anglo-French capitalism into which he was contemplating entering, never seems to have struck him.

Roosevelt and the United States ventured less than the Soviet Union, and the United States was to prove the only untrammelled victor in the Second World War. Under the stimulus first of British and French purchases and then of the massive demands of America's own war effort, the American economy, sluggish and barely ticking over at a quarter or less of its capacity in the decade before 1939, took off. Alone of the belligerents America enjoyed a massive rise in its standard of living and consumption in the years of war. In 1939, however, much of American opinion still believed that what happened in Europe, while it might be regrettable, was none of America's business. Roosevelt saw more clearly and truly even if, as with the British Cabinet, much of the evidence on which he acted was misleading or manufactured or both.

He, like Chamberlain, however, faced the same dilemma: whether to try to prevent war coming or to ensure that, when it did, its outcome was the most satisfactory for America's interests as he saw them. He did not share Chamberlain's views as to the desirability of preserving a European comity or harmony; but he did share his views as to the danger of a German victory. Roosevelt's opinion was that any further advance of Hitler's power in Europe endangered his America and his New Deal. Britain and France were the advance guards of America's interest. Their military power and their resolution to resist Hitler were inter-dependent. Both needed strengthening.

His difficulties lay elsewhere. His vision was not matched by his ability in practice to make either his administration or the general machinery of American politics work for him. His own Cabinet, even his most trusted associates such as Bullitt or Sumner Welles, did not share his convictions that an Anglo-German coalition against America was an entirely imaginary danger. The leaders of Congress were more concerned with the threat to American politics they discerned in the growth of Roosevelt's power and the ambitions of his entourage than with Hitler, Mussolini or Japan. American opinion in general supported Britain and thought Nazism un-American and a threat to American democracy. It believed that if a second world war broke out, America would be drawn in again. Such a prospect was regarded with fear and repulsion. It involved American soldiers fighting in 'foreign wars', American lives being lost in un-American conflicts. As a spectator sport war was OK. Like all-in wrestling, it involved 'goodies' to be cheered and 'baddies' to be hissed and booed. It most manifestly and certainly did not involve the spectators entering the ring.

Roosevelt had therefore to move in secrecy. It was, anyway, his habitual method of operating. He could not have kept together so ideologically divided, so geographically separated, so mutually incompatible a coalition as the Democratic Party in any other way. This ruled out the kind of overt and direct declaration Chamberlain was to make in 1939. Overtly, Roosevelt could only plead for peace. His aim was not the immediate deterrence of Hitler but the long-term education of American opinion. For him the reality of politics lay in Washington, Chicago, New York, in the valleys of the Ohio, the Mississippi and the Missouri, in the great plains of the Midwest, in the mountain states, in California, Texas and the Pacific states, not in Prague, Warsaw, Rome, Berlin, Paris or London, still less in Bratislava, the Memel or Danzig, Nice, Corsica, Savoy, Albania, Athens, Belgrade or Ankara. Moreover, here as with Britain, Hitler had his own informants, who told him what he wanted to hear. America was divided, ridden by Jews, interested only in making money, incurably isolationist, a view Senator Borah and the majority in the Senate Foreign Relations Committee and the House did their unwitting and ill-considered best to confirm.

In the end the war was Hitler's war. It was not, perhaps, the war he wanted. But it was the war he was prepared to risk, if he had to. Nothing could deter him. He preferred to trust his intuition and his creatures, Ribbentrop, Forster, Abetz, anyone who would tell him what at that moment he wanted or needed to hear. He was no longer prepared to wait on events. He needed to force them, to manipulate them, to manufacture incidents, to create pretexts for action. Thus he could enter the world of ghastly farce, where his minions picked a radio station that could not broadcast, or where his own change of a quarter of an hour in the timing of the attack could distort the timetable on which depended the coup against the bridge at Dirschau, on which he had personally spent so much time.

Placed alongside this obsessive determination, the chapter of misperceptions, misinformations and misunderstandings which propelled the British Government into the decision to commit a major military force to the Continent in January, to come to Romania's aid and to guarantee Poland in March, and to guarantee Romania, Greece and Turkey in April are historical events of much less consequence. It is of interest that much of this was the result of reports planted by Hitler's enemies in Germany, and much was the product of nerves strained by Hitler's unpredictability and the misunderstandings and misperceptions that two years of Sir Nevile Henderson's Embassy in Berlin had entrenched in British understanding of Hitler. It is ironic that one of Hitler's most perceptive enemies in Britain, Sir Robert Vansittart, should have fathered this disastrous appointment on his political masters.

Sir Nevile Henderson has had so bad a press that it is easy to forget how clearly he perceived the elements of imbalance in Hitler's personal make-up which made setbacks spurs into ever more violent action. But it was the acute form of *déformation professionnelle* from which he suffered (to which few diplomatists are immune), of thinking the maintenance of good relations with the host country the measure of success, which made him such a disaster. He misrepresented Britain to Hitler and Hitler to Britain; and not only to Britain, but to Britain's partners in the Commonwealth, who then fed back his views of German reasonableness as pressure on the British Cabinet to seek accommodation with Germany. It can hardly be a coincidence that a decisive turn in the Cabinet's perception of Hitler occurred during his absence in Britain from November 1938 to February 1939.

What too are we to think of the 'interlopers in diplomacy', as Sir Lewis Namier, once the doyen of British historians of the European diplomacy of the period, called Dahlerus?[1] There can be little doubt that their collective effect was to increase Hitler's belief in Britain's un-willingness to translate her guarantee of Poland into action, to confirm Stalin in his suspicions that another Anglo-German deal was in preparation, and to mislead Chamberlain into thinking there were ways of influencing German policy and viable alternatives to Hitler in waiting should he fail. Adam von Trott zu Solz, Helmut Wohltat, Erich and Theo Kordt, Sir Joseph Ball, Lord Kemsley, Robert Hudson, Corder Catchpool, even the eccentric Australian SIS pilot, Sidney Cotton, combined to create and confuse the efforts made by Chamberlain and Halifax to convince Britain's potential allies and enemies alike that Munich would not be repeated, that this time they and their country were resolved. That resolve was an essential element in their strategy to preserve peace.

As so often in the history of the practice of deterrence and of 'negotiation from strength', the prospect of war such concepts evoked scared some of those on whose support they should have been able to count, more than it did their potential enemies. Trott, Weizsäcker, the Kordts and Wohltat only confused their British interlocutors as to the real situation in Germany. Ball, Kemsley, Hudson, Catchpool and their kind, the peace at-any-price, peace-before-all brigade, blurred the clarity of British resolution. No one in the British Cabinet and few in the administration were peace-at-any-price men, as the extraordinary scenes on the evening of September 2 more than amply demonstrated.

The more determined, covert opposition to Hitler in Germany

produced a rather different effect. The policy of trying to frighten the British Government by feeding London with exaggerated reports of German military planning – against the Netherlands, or for a direct air attack on London or on the British fleet, as in January or April 1939 – ran the danger, when the reports were not confirmed, of discrediting both the channel by which the report was planted and those who were prepared to act upon it. At other times, as with the doctored report of Hitler's speech on the Obersalzberg on August 22, leaked to the British Embassy, it was unnecessary and to a certain extent buried amidst the welter of information on German troop movements which reached the British from other sources. It did not affect the willingness of Chamberlain and Halifax to listen to Dahlerus. Indeed there is some doubt as to whether they were even made aware of it.

The other, stronger warnings, carried for example by Lieutenant Colonel von Schwerin, failed because, even where they found a hearing, they urged political action within Britain (taking Churchill into the Cabinet, for example) which ran against Chamberlain's inclinations; like the proposals for fleet visits to the Baltic or a visit by RAF units to Poland, they struck Halifax as likely to confirm Hitler in his desperation rather than give him pause. The enormous problems of divided loyalty and unwillingness to cross the line between true patriotism and treacherous action that such Germans faced was complicated by the degree to which the conservative opposition had for so long pursued the ideal of restoring Germany to the frontiers of 1914; even men like Goerdeler, who had risked certain death repeatedly to convey valuable political intelligence to Britain, struck their British listeners as seeking the same dangerous goals as Hitler. More equivocal figures like von Weizsäcker, the Kordt brothers and others in their ambience, could very easily be seen as more subtle servants of Hitler's ends, which, where von Weizsäcker was concerned, was not always that far from the truth.

In the course of the twelve months, from Munich to the British declaration of war on Germany, the balance of power and influence within the British Cabinet shifted palpably. Chamberlain was the architect of Munich. The attempt to build on the Anglo-German declaration he had sprung on Hitler on the morning of September 30, 1938, the reassurance of the French and the cultivation of Mussolini were his policies, although he shared in their execution with Halifax. But with his return from Rome in January, the balance began to shift subtly towards Halifax. Chamberlain took no real part in handling the war-scare in mid-January. Its outcome, when taken with the evidence of Roosevelt's more active interest in Europe, lulled him into a feeling of satisfaction. He was prepared to play his part even in Halifax's attempt to mend Britain's fences in Europe. But the twin shocks of the German absorption of Czechoslovakia and the Italian attack on Albania destroyed the basis of his policy. If the dictators were not to be trusted, his approach was impossible.

The balance shifted to Halifax and, within the Cabinet, the majority turned in favour of guarantees, containment and an alliance with Russia. Chamberlain sensed and resented this shift, as his querulous comments ('even Halifax') to his sisters amply illustrate. In the end he found the House of Commons and the majority of his own Cabinet in near-mutiny against him. He entered the war reluctantly; to be fair his reluctance was from the heart not the head. He knew that Hitler had left him no alternative and that the hour had come to end the havering on the Friday Hitler's troops attacked Poland. He had known for two months or more that no agreement with Hitler could be relied upon. But it was the direction in which his heart pulled him that suckered him into Bonnet's last-minute efforts to lie his way out of war, and very nearly brought forward to September 2, 1939, the events of May 8, 1940, which were to end his premiership.

As the initiative moved into Halifax's hands, so the British hand came to be played by a man who was almost totally cerebral in his approach. Apart from a tendency to lose his calm under extreme pressure, as in the last days of March 1939 or in his immediate reactions to the Tientsin crisis and, *vis-à-vis* Turkey, to the Nazi-Soviet Pact, Halifax was resolute, balanced and endlessly patient. He was, however, constantly surprised by the visceral reactions of his colleagues in Parliament and in the Cabinet; and in his conversations with Bonnet, observers were often struck by their total failure to communicate on the same wavelength. Never could he have been a leader of the British people in war. But his tenure of the Foreign Office and his sceptical, enquiring mind, well served in most respects by the unflappable Cadogan, held Britain firmly to a course which ensured, save for such criminal pieces of freelancing as Robert Hudson so frequently indulged in, that British policy was clear and comprehensible. Where he failed it was because, although in his head he understood the burden of defeatism that Munich had stamped upon the image of British foreign policy abroad and among the opposition at home, to him this was just one of many phenomena. He could not grasp how deeply it had struck into the hearts of those whose perceptions of Britain would condition their responses to his moves.

Like Chamberlain he trusted his professional advisers too much and never set up his own private cabinet to check on them (Chamberlain's personal cabinet was less to inform him than to bypass those he did not trust). He was thus beguiled too long by the Sinophile majority in the Foreign Office's Far Eastern Department, and too dependent, even when he no longer had full confidence in them, on Nevile Henderson in Berlin or Eric Phipps in Paris. Nor can one feel that Seeds was up to the strain of negotiating with the Soviets. Halifax can be seen at his best and his worst in the last week of peace – withstanding Dominions pressure, handling Mussolini and Ciano with the minutest and most delicate of courtesy, urging Colonel Beck towards a reasonable settlement while refusing to apply any but entirely legitimate pressure; at the same time he was, despite Henderson's warnings, totally misconceiving Hitler's state of mind and ready to fall into Bonnet's web of deceit.

Little more needs to be said of France. The Third Republic was in its penultimate stage of decay, led by a politician who was nearly, but not quite, a strong man and a statesman, with a Cabinet whose majority tended towards the *inactiviste* rather than the *belliciste* wing. A Daladier who could tolerate or admire a Bonnet was a man divided in himself, offloading his indecisions upon Bonnet as Bonnet tried to offload France's responsibilities, and depending for his military advice on General Gamelin, a man whose equal aim was to divert responsibility for France's inability even to use the forces she had to back her foreign policy. Passing the buck, like 'Hunt-the-slipper', was central to the French system of government.

The Quai d'Orsay under Léger reflected the same divisions and distrust. The calibre of Coulondre, Corbin, Charles-Roux in the Vatican, Massigli and Naggiar was as good as or better than anything the British diplomatic service could provide, save perhaps for Loraine in Rome and Lindsay in Washington. They could not match Craigie in Tokyo. His skill as a negotiator was unique. Noël in Warsaw was weaker and more emotional than Sir Howard Kennard, his British colleague. The French diplomatists in south-eastern Europe were streets ahead of their British colleagues (with the possible exception of Campbell in Belgrade). The French diplomatic service batted all the way down the order. It had few duds and fewer time-servers, and its misfortunes, as with François-Poncet in Rome, lay in the personal likes and dislikes which governed both Ciano and his master.

And so the historian has to return to Germany. Here the most difficult area to explore is that of the factions within Hitler's court: Goering, Ribbentrop, backed by Goebbels, Ley and Darré, with the SS, manipulated by Heydrich, coming up fast on the outside. One has to allow too for mavericks such as Albert Forster, the Gauleiter of Danzig, who dealt with Hitler directly (the SS backed his rival and victim,

Arthur Greiser), and Hans Frank, whose occasional appearances on the stage are impossible to tie in with the little we know of Nazi factionalism. Contemporary observers tended to a simple equation, Goering on the side of moderation, Ribbentrop, Himmler, Goebbels, and so on among the extremists. But this picture is wrongly conceived. Goebbels played little or no part in any of the formulation of foreign policy. For much of the time he was in disgrace as a result of the sexual scandals which broke just after Munich (and which Goering's minions boasted their master had engineered). His brief appearance in Danzig may have been orchestrated by Hitler – Goebbels was always Hitler's creation. Himmler was merely the front man for Heydrich; and there was no love lost between Heydrich and Ribbentrop.

The rivalry between Goering and Ribbentrop was more personal than ideological. When Ribbentrop was working for a tripartite German-Japanese-Italian alliance, Goering made himself the advocate of a bilateral alliance with Italy. When Ribbentrop's effort to convert Poland into a German satellite began to break down, Goering began to cultivate the idea of a *rapprochement* with the Soviet Union. When Ribbentrop hijacked that policy, and visibly wrote Britain off, Goering began gently to encourage others to explore the settlement with Britain he knew his Führer still hankered after. When Ribbentrop stopped concerning himself with confusing the British, Goering allowed Dahlerus to invent himself in the role of mediator.

Goering's trouble was that Ribbentrop controlled the Foreign Ministry and the German missions abroad and he did not. He lacked the manpower to conduct anything but the occasional raid into foreign policy, which was after all Ribbentrop's allotted sphere. He was also lazy and, in a very real sense, satiated. As a young man he had been a courageous and daring fighter ace. Defeat, the destruction of his planes on the ground by fire in front of his eyes, had driven him into drug addiction until he hitched his star to Hitler's chariot. Hitler was his anchor and his meal-ticket. His fear of and contempt for Ribbentrop stemmed as much from jealousy and fear of displacement in Hitler's eyes as from any ideological grounds.

It is true that having all he needed and desired – power, wealth, luxury, and the opportunity for indulgence in his odder passions for dressing up in ever fancier uniforms, like some combination of the Emperor Nero and Marshal Murat – he had good reason to fear an Anglo-German war. He stood to lose too much if things went wrong – and like all who had lived through October and November 1918 on the Western Front (while Hitler lay in hospital on the Baltic coast, half-blinded and recovering from a gas attack), he remembered the British victories and the inexorable and relentless advance of Haig's armies. To go to war again with Britain struck him as too high a risk. He had had his fill of living dangerously. It is therefore not surprising to find him attempting to use Dahlerus to out-manœuvre and derail the British war machine. But the same basic cowardice, the same fear of losing all that being deputy head of state to Hitler meant to him, that led him to try to avoid a war with Britain, made it unthinkable that he would ever oppose Hitler. Against Ribbentrop, he lacked the energy, persistence and willingness to abase himself which made Ribbentrop so dangerous a rival. Ribbentrop was always with Hitler. When the crisis really broke Goering was on his command train, forty minutes by road from the Reichs Chancellery.

Always one returns to Hitler: Hitler exultant, Hitler vehement, Hitler indolent, Hitler playing the great commander, Hitler bullying the unfortunate President Hácha, raging at Dahlerus, ranting at Count Csáky, lecturing his Generals, hectoring his Army Commanders, threatening, cajoling, and appealing to German destiny. Above all, increasingly in a hurry, always raising the stakes, and losing, as he turned to manipulating events rather than waiting upon them, his uncanny gift for timing, setting himself ever tighter, more impossible timetables, steadily losing touch with reality, but never, as Paul Claudel once prophesied he would, going away.[2] Time's winged chariot urged him on. If there had to be war with Britain, then better in 1939 than ten years later, he said. He had no confidence in his health or his ability to age well. German destiny – world power or downfall – required the strongest, most ruthless, most decisive leadership. Age brought weakness, a loss of faculties, ill health. His doctor Morell lived off Hitler's fears of ageing, ill health and early death, devising ever more potent stimulants to feed his patient's obsession with his health, that same obsession which made him a vegetarian and seems to have kept his relationship with Eva Braun unconsummated.

In much the same way, he more than half-believed his propagandists, with their significant emphasis on castration as the worst of the atrocities they alleged the Poles to be committing against members of the German minority in Poland. The Polish Government had defied him. It had rejected his 'generous offer' (he became more convinced of his generosity every time he spoke of it) with contumely and arrogance. As a righteous punishment, Poland must be destroyed. The Poles, arrogant and proud, though they were of inferior race, would not have dared to defy him if Britain had not encouraged them and backed them. Britain too rejected his offer to guarantee her empire, as she was to reject the offers of peace he was to make in October 1939 and after the fall of France. The SS plans for the treatment of a defeated and occupied Britain were to be as draconian as those applied to a defeated Poland.

The Poles were mere sub-men, Slavs, aping civilization and the ways of the superior race. They were to be 'rotted out'. Bombs, fire, and his loyal Himmler and the SS would cleanse Polish soil and resettle its fertile plains and forests with German peasants. The Poles should have copied the Czechs, the members of whose Government he pensioned off and allowed to retire, or the Slovaks, who did as he wished. Slovakia survived. Slovak forces were to march, in the name of Christianity, alongside the Wehrmacht, against the godless Soviet Union. How could he not be regarded as generous, ever-merciful, slow to wrath, but when aroused as merciless as any divinely appointed judge in the earliest books of the Old Testament? Gods and heroes, agents of the force of history, do not, should not, cannot accept limitations or hindrances which lesser men, unwitting agents of evil, put in their way.

The rank and file of the German armed forces, the urban middle class, the aircraft workers and the German peasants entered the war for a whole variety of reasons, which had only a remote relationship to Hitler's dream of empire. Resignation, fear of identification as a subversive, a renewal of the feelings of isolation from the rest of the world, the habit of civil obedience, a blind confidence in Hitler's previous track record, a feeling of individual helplessness, the lack of

"He says he done it all to save 'is face"

any alternative voice, patriotism, loyalty to their fellow Germans as well as a dedicated acceptance of Nazi ideals, and, *vis-à-vis* Britain (as with British reactions towards Germany), a revival of the hatreds, antagonisms and resentments that had been building up before and during the 1914–18 war; all these motives were at work. Let Admiral Raeder, Commander-in-Chief of the German Navy, speak for these last[3]: 'Today', he noted on September 3, 'the war against England and France began – the war which according to the Führer's previous assertions, we had no reason to expect before 1944. The Führer believed up to the last moment that it could be avoided, even if this meant postponing a final settlement of the Polish question. (The Führer made a statement to this effect to the Commanders-in-Chief of the Armed Forces at the Obersalzberg on August 22.) At the turn of the year 1944–5, by which time according to the Führer's instructions the navy's Z-plan [for naval construction] would have been completed . . . in this way, especially with the co-operation of Japan and Italy, . . . the prospect of defeating the British fleet and of cutting off supplies, in other words of *settling the British question conclusively* would have been good. . . .'

Britain entered the war in 1939, barely equipped for survival and in no position to help her allies; but in certain crucial respects she had the edge. The combination of Spitfire and Hurricane eight-gun fighters, radar and ground-to-air communication, not in place in 1938 and barely in place in 1940, enabled her to survive the onslaught of the Luftwaffe by day. In the electronic war she held her own. Bomber Command and the four-engined heavy bombers of the 1938 programme devastated Germany's industrial cities and much else in the years 1941–3. Her atomic physicists, with the aid of the French team and the refugees from Hitler's persecution, started Britain towards the atomic bomb, while German scientists lost their way. Poland gave Britain its biggest edge, Polish knowledge of the Enigma cipher machine which, when developed with the mathematical genius of Alan Turing, among others, and the organizational genius that managed to keep Britain's possession of it secret from the Germans throughout the war and for two and a half decades thereafter, was of incalculable value to Britain. In the battle of the Atlantic its possession could well have been all that stood between Britain and the German victory at sea of which Raeder wrote so feelingly on September 3, 1939.

In all these important respects, the Polish gift of their work on Enigma, the transfer in 1940 to Britain of the French atomic scientists and their stock of heavy water, Vichy's co-operation in keeping British knowledge of Enigma secret from the Germans, the work of the refugee scientists, the placing at Britain's disposal of the Czech and Polish intelligence services (which were to bring Britain the first news of the German V1 and V2 guided missile programmes), Europe turned to Britain as the symbol of all in the European tradition that Hitler rejected. In turn Britain gave Europe, through the BBC, contact with the non-Nazi world and hope. In Germany, as in France, Italy, Yugoslavia, in Belgium, the Netherlands, Denmark and Norway, the BBC and the more covert radios run by the British political warfare executive gave Europe a point of resistance, of hope, of amusement even, and, with the 'V for victory' programme, a slogan and a logo. If Britain had faltered or compromised; if Hitler had not diverted himself against Russia, in part because he convinced himself that Russia had a hand in keeping Britain's hopes alive in 1940; if Roosevelt had not nailed his hopes of victory over Germany and Japan to Britain's survival under Churchill, Hitler might have succeeded for Europe's despair of any alternative.

By the end of 1941 the Anglo-German war had become the world war, Britain, the Commonwealth and the empire, the Soviet Union and the United States against a Europe forcibly united under Hitler; Britain, the Commonwealth and the empire with the United States and China against Japan. It was the dubious achievement of British diplomacy that in 1939 the war was limited to Britain and France, Germany and Poland, a limited war, constrained and fenced about. Its progressive widening, like its beginning, was Hitler's work. The propensity to resist him was there, as was the desire to avoid involvement. Britain's opposition to Hitler encouraged the propensity to resist him. Hitler brought those who tried to stay out of the war into the ever-widening conflict, some out of greed, most by force or the threat of force.

The Anglo-German conflict did not disappear, however. It was by virtue of the part Britain played that Britain became a founder of the United Nations with a permanent seat on the Security Council. Whatever status Britain has in the world today stems ineluctably from the course of action she followed in 1939, and from the revolt in the House of Commons and Cabinet on September 2, 1939. That revolt, which stemmed in turn from the degree to which British opinion accepted and supported the guarantees for Poland, understood that, whatever the rights and wrongs of Danzig and the Corridor, Poland had become a test case as to whether the 'law of the jungle' or the 'law of nations' was to rule Europe, and accepted that not only British credibility to others, but pride, self-respect, honour and very existence were bound up with the fulfilment of Britain's guarantee. Thus it was that the conclusion of the Nazi-Soviet Pact was dismissed, as the end of reliance on an untrustworthy ally, if not as a betrayal of what British opinion had thought was accepted as a common cause; and that in the end the fall of France itself was seen as a lightening of Britain's sword arm from the restraints of an unhappy and unenthusiastic ally, but in no way as a diminution of Britain's purpose.

In May 1945 Britain was the only power whose people could say that they had entered the war by choice, to fight for a principle, and not because their country was attacked. They entered to fight Hitler and those who supported him: that they made increasingly little distinction between Hitler and Nazism and Germany and its traditions is evidence of the degree to which in Europe the Second World War was both a war between nations and a pan-European civil war. But it is odd that the greatest reproach so often made against the Government which commanded a majority in the House of Commons and in the country is that it did not go to war against Hitler a year earlier. A Churchill, a Duff Cooper, an Eden, as a citizen of that country, has the right to lay such a charge; but not the citizens of countries whose Governments waited until their countries were attacked, still less citizens of countries whose Governments gave aid and encouragement to the power that was to attack them.

Few in Britain doubted, whatever injustices might be committed in the course of the war, that theirs was a just war and a just cause. For the British, old stereotypes die hard. The images formed *by* war and the images formed *in* war, to enable public morale to maintain itself *through* war, have a half-life of their own. It is not so long ago that a British press correspondent, appointed by his newspaper to cover events in Germany, was told, 'Remember, there is only one kind of news the British are interested in from Germany – old Nazis and new Nazis'; and, his instructor might have added, Nazi war criminals who survived and have reached positions of power and influence. The notion that Nazi rottenness lives on, that behind the door of every new German residence the SS uniform still can be found hanging, and that every closet door conceals a regularly polished pair of jackboots, still lingers on.

So do the fears of a war which stems from the will or miscalculation of a ruler or ruling group intent on global hegemony to the point of unreason or mental instability. Hitler willed, wanted, craved war and the destruction wrought by war. He did not want the war he got. Its origins lay through his own miscalculations and misperceptions, as much as through those of his eventual opponents, not least in their belief that he was bluffing, that he would recoil, that in Paul Claudel's words, '*Croque-mitaine se dégonflera*' (the bogeyman will go away). Be firm and it will not happen. If Hitler spoke on the Obersalzberg as Raeder recorded it on September 3, 1939, then he proved himself a liar. When it became clear that settling with Poland would, despite all his hopes, involve war with Britain, he did not postpone that settlement for more than a week.

Neither firmness nor appeasement, the piling up of more armaments nor the demonstration of more determination would stop him – or, if it did, it stopped him only from 7 p.m. on August 25 until 4 p.m. on August 31, 1939. The only people who could have stopped him permanently were those least conditioned to do so, his Generals, and their soldiers, if they had been ready to obey, by a *coup d'état*, or an assassin capable of penetrating into the Reichs Chancellery from which, in the last days of peace, Hitler never emerged. History knows this did not happen.

ABBREVIATIONS USED IN THE NOTES
AND BIBLIOGRAPHY*

AA	Auswärtiges Amt [German Foreign Ministry]
ADSS	Actes et Documents du Saint Siège
AHR	American Historical Review
AHHM	Allianz Hitler-Horthy-Mussolini
BBB	British Blue Book, Cmd. 6106
BDFA, SU	British Documents on Foreign Affairs, The Soviet Union, 1917–1939
BMh	Berliner Monatshefte
CDP	Ciano's Diplomatic Papers
DAFP	Documents on Australian Foreign Policy, 1937–1939
DAPE	Dez Anos de Politica Externa, 1936–1946
DBFP	Documents on British Foreign Policy, 1919–1939
DCER	Documents on Canadian External Relations, 1936–1939
DDB	Documents Diplomatiques Belges, 1920–1940
DDF	Documents Diplomatiques Français, 1932–1939
DDI	[I] Documenti Diplomatici Italiani, 1860–1943
DGFP	Documents on German Foreign Policy, 1918–1945
DIMK	Diplomaciai isatok magyarország külpolitikájához, 1936–1940
Dipl.Hist.	Diplomatic History
DKJG	Dokumente zum Konflikt mit Jugoslavien und Griechenland
DME	Documents and Materials Relating to the Eve of the Second World War
EHR	English Historical Review
EcHR	Economic History Review
Eristov	Documents Secrets du Ministère des Affaires Etrangères de l'Allemagne
ESR/Q	European Studies Review/Quarterly [title changed in 1987]
FRUS	Foreign Relations of the United States
FRUS, SU	Foreign Relations of the United States, The Soviet Union 1933–1939
FYB	French Yellow Book
GFG	die Geheimakten des französischen Generalstabes
GFM	German Foreign Ministry
GNA	German Naval Archives [Archiv der Marine], cited by serial and frame numbers and British Admiralty pg numbers
GrWB	Greek White Book
GWB	German White Book
H.C.Deb.	[Hansard's Parliamentary Debates], House of Commons 5th series
HJ	Historical Journal
HZ	Historische Zeitschrift
IHR	International History Review
IMT	International Military Tribunal. Trial of the Major War Criminals
IMT FE	International Military Tribunal. Trial of the Major War Criminals in the Far East.
Int.J.	International Journal
Int.Nat.Sec.	Intelligence and National Security
JAH	Journal of American History

JCEA	Journal of Central European Affairs
JCH	Journal of Contemporary History
JMH	Journal of Modern History
JRUSI	Journal of the Royal United Service Institute
JSS	Journal of Strategic Studies
Král	Vaclav Král, [Ed.], *Das Abkommen von München*
LES	Les Évènements Survenues en France
MAE	Ministère des Affaires Etrangères
MVHR	Mississippi Valley Historical Review
NCA	Nazi Conspiracy and Aggression
ND	Nuremberg Documents
Pol.Stud.	Politische Studien
PRO	Public Record Office [London]
PWA	Polish Western Affairs
PWB	Polish White Book
Rev.Hist.	Revue Historique
Rev.Pol.	Review of Politics
RHd'A	Revue Historique des Armées
RHDGM	Revue d'Histoire de la Deuxième Guerre Mondiale
RI	Relations Internationales
RIIA	Royal Institute of International Affairs, London
RRH	Revue Roumaine de l'Histoire
RSPI	Rivista di Studi Politici Internazionali
SPE	Soviet Peace Efforts on the Eve of the Second World War
USNIP	United States Naval Institute Proceedings
VjH Zg	Vierteljahreshaft für Zeitgeschichte
WWR	Wehrwissentschaftliches Rundschau

★ For elaboration of these references see the entry for Official Documents in the Bibliography.

Note on Citation

(i) All documents, diary entries, etc are cited with their date, author and recipient where this is not mentioned in the text. A series of documents is followed by the days, months and years; e.g. 12.1.39, 12/14.i/27.ii/1939.

(ii) Documents cited from published collections are cited by the number of the document, save for those cited from the *FRUS* volumes, where the citations are by page, no numbers being given to the documents in the original.

(iii) Citations of unpublished documents from the German Foreign Ministry, Army or Navy archives are from the microfilms retained in London or Washington when the originals were returned to the Federal German Republic; those retained in London are cited by serial and frame numbers, those from Washington by roll numbers.

(iv) Citations from diaries, whether manuscript or printed, are by the date of the entry.

(v) Citations from memoirs, monographs, collections of speeches, etc are by the name of the author, short title where relevant, and page.

(vi) Citations from articles in journals or collective works are by author, short title, journal or collective work, and year of publication. Full details of all works cited may be found in the Bibliography.

NOTES

Chapter 1 May 1945

This chapter is based on the following sources: (1) For the German surrender on the Lüneburg heath, contemporary reports in the British press and newsreels; (2) For the destruction of Europe's art treasures, (i) Reports of the British Committee on the Preservation and Restitution of Works of Art, Archives and Other Material in Enemy Hands; (ii) La Farge, *Lost Treasures of Europe*.

Chapter 3 *Hitler plans a new war*

Apart from the sources cited, this chapter is based on the following sources: (i) On Hitler's early career: Jetzinger, *Hitlers Jugend*; Jenks, *Vienna and the Young Hitler*; Bradley Smith, *Hitler, his Family and Youth*; Maser, *Frühgeschichte der NSDAP*; Hanfstaengel, *15 Jahre mit Hitler*; Jones, *Hitler in Vienna*; Wiedemann, *Der Mann der Feldherr werden wollte*; Franz-Willing, *Ursprung der Hitler-Bewegung*; Watt, 'Die bayerische Bemützungen um die Ausweisung Hitlers', *VjHZg*, 1958; (ii) On Hitler's views of Britain: Henke, *England in Hitlers politischen Kalkül, 1935–1939*; Hillgruber, 'England in Hitlers aussenpolitische konzeption', *HZ*, 218, 1974; (iii) On German propaganda after September 1938: Bramsted, *Goebbels and National-Socialist Propaganda*; Sywottek, *Mobilmachung für den totalen Krieg*; Sänger, *Politik der Taüschungen*; (iv) On German naval development and Britain: Dülffer, *Hitler, Weimar und die Marine*; Bensel, *Deutsche Flottenpolitik*; Gemzell, *Hitler, Raeder und Scandinavien*; Watt, 'Anglo-German Naval Negotiations', *JRUSI*, 1958.

1. Schacht testimony at Nuremberg, *IMT*, XII, p. 584; Görlitz, *Keitel*, p. 195; Meissner, *Staatssekretär*, p. 470; Hassell, *Diary*, 14.x.38.
2. Domarus, I, pp. 949–50.
3. *DGFP*, D, I, 19.
4. *ND*, 79-L; *DGFP*, D, VI, 433.
5. Dietrich, *12 Jahre mit Hitler*, pp. 154.
6. *ND*, 248-PS, *DGFP*, D, VII, 192; *ibid.*, App.I, Halder diary, 22.viii.39; *ND*, Raeder-27, *IMT*, vi, pp. 16–25.
7. *ND*, 789-PS, *DGFP*, D, VIII, 384.
8. Domarus, I, p. 745, 31.x.1937.
9. Henderson, *Failure of a Mission*, p. 111.
10. Luedecke, *I Knew Hitler*.
11. Hanfstaengel, *15 Jahre mit Hitler*.
12. Rumbold to his son, 18.ix.38, Gilbert, *Rumbold*, p. 437.
13. Jones, *A Life in Reuters*, pp. 396–97; Fitzrandolph, *Als Frühstucksattaché*, p. 19.
14. *DGFP*, D, I, 93, Ribbentrop memorandum, 2.i.1958.
15. Magistrati, *L'Italia a Berlino*, p. 255; Anfuso, *Du Palais de Venise*, p. 80; Donosti, *Mussolini e l'Europa*, p. 129.
16. *DBFP*, 3, II, 1228; Home, *The Way the Wind Blows*, p. 66; Strang, *At Home and Abroad*, pp. 147–48.
17. Pronay and Taylor, '"An improper use of broadcasting"', *JCH*, 18, 1983.

18. Domarus, I, pp. 952–53.
19. Domarus, I, pp. 945–56.
20. Treue, 'Rede Hitlers vor den deutschen Presse', *VjHZg*, 6, 1958; Domarus, I, pp. 973–77.
21. Sywottek, *Mobilmachung*, p. 166.
22. Dülffer, p. 57, fn. 92.
23. Dülffer, p. 468; Watt, 'Anglo-German Naval Negotiations', *JRUSI*, 1958.
24. Raeder, *Mein Leben*, II, p. 126.
25. *DGFP*, D, VII, Appendix II (K), (iv), 27.i.39; Salewski, *Seekriegsleitung*, I, pp. 252–53.
26. Dülffer, pp. 471–512.
27. Salewski, *Seekriegsleitung*, pp. 91–92; Dülffer, p. 543; *Führer Naval Conferences*; Raeder memorandum 3.ix.39.
28. *DGFP*, D, IV, 411.
29. Lipski papers, 124, 24.x.38; Lochner, *What About Germany?*, pp. 180–81.
30. *DDF*, 2, XIII, 139, Coulondre to Bonnet, 15.xii.38.
31. *ND*, 175-C.
32. *DGFP*, D, II, 221, ND, 388-PS.
33. Pfaff, 'Prag und der Fall Tukhachewski', *VjHZg*, 1987.

Chapter 4   Ribbentrop in difficulties

Where not otherwise stated, this chapter is based on the following sources and studies: (1) On Italy: Quartararo, *Roma tra Londra e Berlino*; Bolech Cecchi, *Non bruciare i ponti con Roma*; Wiskemann, *Rome-Berlin Axis*; Siebert, *Italiens Weg in den zweiten Weltkrieg*; Mack Smith, *Mussolini's Roman Empire*; Watt, 'The Rome-Berlin Axis: myth and reality', *Rev. Pol.*, 1960; de Felice, *Mussolini il Duce*, vol. II; von Rintelen, *Mussolini als Bundesgenosse*; Magistrati, *L'Italia a Berlino*; (2) On Japan: Boyd, *The Extraordinary Envoy*; Toscano, *Le Origini diplomatiche del Patto d'Acciaio*; Sommer, *Deutschland und Japan zwischen den Mächten*; Tokushiro Ohata, 'The Anti-Comintern Pact, 1935–1939', in Morley, *Deterrent Diplomacy*; Ferrati, 'La politica estera giapponese e i rapporti con l'Italia e la Germania (1935–1939), *Storia Contemporanea*, VII, 1976; (3) On Poland: Lipski papers; Woytak, *On the Borders of War and Peace*; (4) On Slovakia, Romania and Hungary: Hoensch, *Die Slowakei in Hitlers Ostpolitik*; idem., *Der ungarische Revisionismus und die Zerschlagung der Tschecho-slowakei*; C. A. Macartney, *October 15*; Stercho, *The Diplomacy of Double Morality*; (5) On France: Adamthwaite, *France and the Coming of the Second World War*; Duroselle, *La Décadence*.

1. Ciano, *Diario*, 23.x.38; *CDP*, pp. 239–40.
2. Ciano, *Diario*, 23.x.38.
3. Watt, 'An earlier model for the Pact of Steel', *International Affairs*, 1957; idem., 'Hitler's visit to Rome', *JCH*, 9, 1974.
4. Ciano, *Diario*, 23.x.38.
5. Watt, 'Gli accordi mediterranei anglo-italiani del 16 aprile 1938', *RSPI*, 1959; Bolech Cecchi, *L'accordo di due Imperi. L'accordo italo-inglese del 16 aprile 1938*, Milan 1977; Quartararo, *Roma*, Ch. 6.
6. *DBFP*, 3, III, 326.
7. *DBFP*, 3, III, 356.
8. *DBFP*, 3, III, 360.
9. Ciano, *Diario*, 28.x.38.
10. Ciano, *Diario*, 28.x.38.
11. Ciano, *Diario*, 28.x.38.
12. Ciano, *Diario*, 27.x.38.
13. Ciano, *Diario*, 27.x.38; *CDP*, pp. 242–46.
14. Ciano, *Diario*, 11/28.x.38.
15. Michaelis, *Mussolini and the Jews*, passim; Ciano, *Diario*, 6.xi.38.
16. Ciano, *Diario*, 7.x.38.
17. Ciano, *Diario*, 24/25.x./14.xi.38.
18. Ciano, *Diario*, 16.xi.38.
19. Ciano, *Diario*, 5.xi.38.
20. Ciano, *Diario*, 8/30.xi.38.
21. Ciano, *Diario*, 10.xi.38.
22. Ciano, Diario, 15.vii.38; *German Naval Archives*, M70/M002233, Lange to OKM, Gkdos S

667, 4.viii.38; *ibid.*, M70/M002219–20, Neubauer to Ob.d.M., IC 12029, Gkdos S, 18.viii.38.

23. *German Naval Archives*, PG 33744, reports of 3, 10, 19, 26.x./7.xi.39.
24. *DGFP*, D, IV, 403, 406.
25. *German Naval Archives*, 8230/E585423–25, Guse to OKM, Ia 17/38 Gkdos Chefssache, 26.iv.38.
26. Boyd, 'The role of Hiroshi Oshima in the preparation of the anti-Comintern pact', *J. Asian Studies*, 1971.
27. Boyd, 'The Berlin-Tokyo Axis and Japanese military initiative', *Modern Asian Studies*, 1981.
28. Boyd, *Extraordinary Envoy*, p. 84; Ohata, pp. 71–73.
29. Ohata, pp. 73–75; Ferrati, p. 810, citing Japanese records; Sommer, p. 152; *IMTFE*, p. 30, 308, Itagaki evidence.
30. Sommer, p. 194.
31. *DBFP*, 3, VIII, 200, Craigie to Halifax, 3.xi.38.
32. *CDP*, pp. 249–50, Ciano to Grandi, 14.xi.38.
33. Ciano, *Diario*, 29.xi.38.
34. Ciano, *Diario*, 30.xi.38; *DBFP*, 3, III, 464, Perth to Halifax, 1.xii.38; ibid., 468 & fn.1, Perth to Cadogan, 2.xii.38.
35. *HC Deb.*, 342, cols 2517–26; Bolech Cecchi, *Non brucciare* p. 43, fn. 132.
36. *DBFP*, 3, III, 475, Cadogan to Perth, 12.xii.38; *ibid.*, 478, Perth to Halifax, 16.xii.38; Ciano, *Diario*, 16.xii.38.
37. *DGFP*, D, IV, 421, Ciano to Ribbentrop, 2.i.39; *CDP*, pp. 258–59; Ciano, *Diario*, 1/2.i.39.
38. Woytak, *On the Border of War and Peace*, p. 22.
39. Woytak, pp. 52–54; Stercho, *Diplomacy of Double Morality*, pp. 256–57.
40. GFM collection of reports, October 1938, 2381/499128–140.
41. *DDF*, 2, XIII, 196, Noel to Bonnet, 21.xii.38.
42. *DGFP*, D, V, 72; *DDF*, 2, XII, 92, Noel to Bonnet, 12.x.38.
43. *DGFP*, D, V, 257, 1.xii.38; *DGFP*, D, IV, 146 and GFM 401/213686–91, Treaty of 7.xii.38; *DDF*, 2, XIII, 205, Coulondre to Bonnet, 22.xii.38.
44. *DDF*, 2, XIII, 116, Coulondre to Berlin, 13.xii.38.
45. *DDF*, 2, XIII, 44.
46. *DDF*, 2, XII, 136, François-Poncet to Bonnet, 15.x.38.
47. *DDF*, 2, XIII, 19, Corbin to Bonnet, 3.xii.38; Lloyd Papers, GLLD 17/58, Colvin to Lloyd, 22.xi.38.
48. Cienciala, *Poland and the Western Powers*, pp. 55–56.
49. Ciano, *Diario*, 6/7/8/9.iii.38.
50. *DGFP*, D, V, 67, Moltke to A.A., 8.x.38.
51. *DGFP*, D, V, 76, Moltke to A.A., 19.x.38.
52. *DGFP*, D, V, 72, 81, 82, 15/24/25.x.38; *DDF*, 2, XII, 92, Noel to Bonnet, 12.x.38; Stercho, *Diplomacy of Double Morality*, pp. 256–57.
53. *DGFP*, D, IV, 132, 133, 134; *Allianz Hitler-Horthy-Mussolini*, 46, Kanya to Sztójay, 21.xi.38.
54. *DGFP*, D, V, 100; Stercho, pp. 285–86, fn. 4; *Allianz Hitler-Horthy-Mussolini*, 40, Colonel Lengyel (Warsaw) to Hungarian C.G.S., 10.x.38.
55. Stercho, pp. 287–88, citing diaries of Miklos Kozma.
56. Stercho, p. 291.
57. Woytak, pp. 59–60; Szembek diary, 4/5.xi.38.
58. *Allianz Hitler-Horthy-Mussolini*, 42, Csáky to Kanya, 14.x.38.
59. Stercho, pp. 293–94.
60. Stercho, p. 295.
61. Stercho, pp. 295–96, citing Kozma diary.
62. *DGFP*, D, IV, 100.
63. Lipski papers, 124, memorandum of 24.x.38; *DGFP*, D, V, 81; *PWB*, 44.
64. Szembek diary, 29.x.38.
65. Szembek diary, 28.x.38.
66. *PWB*, 45; Lipski papers, p. 458, fn. 149.
67. Lipski papers, 127; *DGFP*, D, V, 101; *PWB*, 46.
68. Szembek diary, 22.xi.38.
69. *PWB*, 47, Beck memorandum.
70. *DGFP*, D, V, 104, Moltke to A.A., 22.xi.38.
71. *PWD*, 160, 161, 26.xi.38; *DGFP*, D, V, 105, 108; *SPE*, I, 54, 55.

72. Szembek diary, 7.xii.38.
73. Lipski papers, pp. 474–76, 130, 131; *DGFP*, D, V, 112, 113.
74. *DGFP*, D, V, 70.
75. *DGFP*, D, V, 99, von Twardowski minute, 12.xi.38.
76. *DGFP*, D, V, 110, 5.xii.38.
77. Burckhardt, pp. 203–04; *DBFP*, 3, III, Appendix VI, Burckhardt to Walters, 20.xii.38.
78. *DGFP*, D, V, 115, Moltke to Ribbentrop, 20.xii.38.
79. *DGFP*, D, V, 119, memorandum by Schmidt, 15.i.39; *PWB*, 48; Beck, *Final Report*, pp. 171–72; Schmidt, *Statist*, p. 426; Szembek diary, 8/10.i.39.
80. Beck, *Final Report*, p. 172.
81. *DGFP*, D, V, 120; *PWB*, 49.
82. Szembek diary, 8.i.39.
83. Král, 286, Czech Foreign Ministry memorandum, end January, 1939; *DBFP*, 3, IV, 82, Shepherd to Halifax, 6.ii.39.
84. *DBFP*, 3, IV, 47, Shepherd to Halifax, 28.i.39.
85. *DGFP*, D, V, 122, Hewel memorandum, 13.i.39.
86. Schmidt, *Statist*, pp. 425–26; Denne, p. 154.
87. *PWB*, 52, 53; Szembek diary, 26.i./1.ii.39.
88. *DGFP*, D, V, 126.
89. Meissner, *Staatssekretär*, pp. 485–86.
90. Domarus, II, pp. 1047–67.
91. Kleist, *Zwischen Hitler und Stalin*, pp. 19–23.
92. Duroselle, *La Décadence*, p. 382, fn. 57.
93. Phipps papers 1/21, Phipps to Halifax, 26.x.38; Duroselle, *La Décadence*, p. 369; Bedarida, 'La gouvernante anglaise', in *Édouard Daladier, Chef de Gouvernement*, p. 238.
94. *DGFP*, D, IV, 337, fn. 1, Mackensen to Weizsäcker, 12.x.38.
95. *DGFP*, D, IV, 338.
96. François-Poncet, *Souvenirs*, pp. 339–49; *DDF*, 2, XII, 197, François-Poncet to Bonnet, 20.x.38; *PYB*, 17, 18.
97. *DDF*, 2, XII, 199, Bonnet to François-Poncet, 21.x.38.
98. *DGFP*, D, IV, 347.
99. *DDF*, 2, XIII, 45, 58, 126; *DGFP*, D, IV, 370, 371; Schmidt, *Statist*, pp. 423–25; Coulondre, *De Staline à Hitler*, pp. 223–25; Scherer, 'Le Probleme des "Mains Libres" à l'Est', *R. d'H.DGM*, 1958.

Chapter 5   Chamberlain after Munich

Apart from the sources cited, this chapter relies on the following sources: (1) On Anglo-Italian relations: Quartararo, *Roma tra Londra e Berlino*; Bolech Cecchi, *Non bruciare i ponti con Roma*; Pratt, *East of Malta, West of Suez*; de Felice, *Mussolini il Duce*, vol. II; Mack Smith, *Mussolini*; Rotunda, 'The Rome Embassy of Sir Eric Drummond', London Ph.D. 1972; (2) On British rearmament policy: Peden, *British Rearmament and the Treasury*; Gibbs, *Grand Strategy*, vol. I; (3) On Britain's policy in South-East Europe: van Kessel, 'British reactions to German economic expansion in South-East Europe, 1938–39', London Ph.D. 1972; (4) On domestic British politics: Cowling, *The Impact of Hitler*; Fuchser, *Neville Chamberlain and Appeasement*; Watt, 'British Domestic Politics and the Onset of War', in *Les Relations Franco-Britanniques de 1935 à 1940*; (5) On Anglo-German Naval relations: Watt, 'Anglo-German Naval Negotiations', *JRUSI*, 1958; Dülffer, *Weimar, Hitler und die Marine*; Salewski, *Deutsche Seekriegsleitung*, vol. I; Roskill, *Naval Policy between the Wars*, vol. II.

1. Roosevelt papers, PSF I, Diplomatic Correspondence, Gn 3 1933–38, Box 7; *From the Morgenthau diaries*, pp. 458–67.
2. Watt, *Personalities and Policies*, Ch. V.
3. Cockburn, *I, Claud*; Patricia Cockburn, *The Years of the Week*; Watt, '*The Week* that was', *Encounter*, 1972.
4. *PRO*, PREM 1/266a, Stanley to Chamberlain.
5. Home, *The Way the Wind Blows*, p. 66.
6. *DBFP*, 3, III, 285, Halifax to Phipps, 1.xi.38.
7. Chamberlain papers, NC 18/1/1072, to Hilda Chamberlain, 15.x.38.

8. *DBFP*, 3, III, 329, Perth to Halifax, 3.x.38.
9. *DBFP*, 3, III, 331, 332, Perth to Halifax, 4.x.38.
10. *DBFP*, 3, III, 336, Halifax to Perth, 6.x.38.
11. Chamberlain papers, NC 18/1/1071, to Ida Chamberlain, 9.x.38.
12. *DBFP*, 3, III, 373, Perth to Halifax, 2.xi.38.
13. Chamberlain papers, NC 18/1/1075, 6.xi.38.
14. *DBFP*, 3, III, 378, 16.xi.38.
15. *DBFP*, 3, III, 164; *DGFP*, D, IV, 249.
16. Domarus, I, pp. 954–56.
17. *DBFP*, 3, III, 188, 198, 280, 290, 296.
18. *DBFP*, 3, III, Appendix I, (i)/(ii), Henderson to Halifax, 6/12.x.38.
19. Private information from former members of the staff of the British Embassy, Berlin.
20. *DGFP*, D, IV, 253, Weizsäcker to Dirksen, 17.x.38.
21. *DGFP*, D, IV, 251, Enclosure 2, memorandum by Fritz Hesse, 11.x.38; *ibid.*, 254, Weizsäcker to Dirksen, 17.x.38; Cadogan diary, 28/29/30.xi./1/2/5.xii.38.
22. *DGFP*, D, IV, 260; *Dirksen Papers*, 24.
23. *DGFP*, D, IV, 257.
24. *DBFP*, 3, III, 299, fn. 3; *ibid.*, 305, 306, 309, 313.
25. *DBFP*, 3, III, 302, 307, 308; *DGFP*, D, IV, 269, fn. 3.
26. *DGFP*, D, IV, 269, Dirksen to A.A., 17.xi.38.
27. Chamberlain papers, 18/1/1076, to Hilda Chamberlain, 13.xi.38.
28. *PRO*, FO 371/22344, R 8690/94/67, 31.x.38.
29. *PRO*, CAB 23/96, CAB 55(38) 8, 16.xi.38; *ibid.*, CAB 27/624, FP (34) 31st Mtg., 21.xi.38.
30. *PRO*, 371/22460, R 9438/223/37; van Kessel, pp. 188 ff.
31. *HC Deb*, 342, cols 445–502.
32. Van Kessel, pp. 210–14.
33. *PRO*, CAB 27/624, FP (35) 32nd Mtg.
34. Chamberlain papers, NC 18/1/1076.
35. *PRO*, CAB 23/96.
36. *DBFP*, 3, III, 422, 429, 431, 432, 433; *DGFP*, D, IV, 276, 278, 279.
37. Watt, 'Anglo-German Naval Negotiations', *JRUSI*, 1958.
38. *DGFP*, 3, III, 432, 15.xii.38.
39. *DBFP*, 3, III, 325; *DDF*, 2, XII, 418.
40. Murray, *Change in the European Balance of Power*, pp. 272–74.
41. *PRO*, FO 371/21593, C 15630/13/17, 12.xii.38; *ibid.*, C 15682/13/17, Phipps to Halifax, 19.xii.38; *DDF*, 2, XII, 120, 14.xii.38.
42. *DBFP*, 3, III, 509, 522 and fn. 1, 530, 536, 553; *PRO*, FO 371/22915, Colonel Fraser (Military Attaché, Paris) memorandum, 'The French strategic position after Munich', 22.xii.38.
43. Harvey diary, 4.xii.38.
44. *PRO*, PREM 1/327, Cadogan to Perth, 12.xii.38, Perth to Cadogan, 15.xii.38.
45. *PRO*, FO 371/23796, R 9/9/22, Perth to Halifax, 27.xii.38.
46. Quartararo, 'Appendice', *Storia Contemporanea*, 1976.
47. Quartararo, *Roma*, pp. 412–13.
48. Lloyd Papers, GLLD 19/2, Lloyd to Lady Lloyd, 17.i.39.
49. Ciano, *Diario*, 11.i.39.
50. *DBFP*, 3, III, 500, 502; *CDP*, pp. 259–66; Ciano, *Diario*, 11/12.i.39; Harvey diaries, 11/12/13/14.i.39; de Felice, *Il Duce*, II, pp. 574–76; Mack Smith, *Mussolini*, p. 268; Halifax, *Fulness of Days*, p. 201; Quartararo, *Roma*, pp. 416–22; Bolech Cecchi, *Non bruciare*, pp. 86–95.
51. Chamberlain Papers, NC 18/1/1082, to Hilda Chamberlain, 15.i.39.
52. Bottai, *Diario*, 4.ii.39; Mack Smith, *Mussolini's Roman Empire*, p. 139.

Chapter 6   Lord Halifax is alarmed

Where not otherwise stated, this chapter is based on the following sources: (1) On British intelligence on Germany: Aster, *1939*; Watt, 'British Intelligence and Germany', in May, *Knowing One's Enemies*; Dilks, 'Appeasement and Intelligence', in Dilks, *Retreat from Power*; Dilks, 'Flashes of Intelligence', in Andrew and Dilks, *The Missing Dimension*; Andrew, *Secret Service*; Strong, *Intelligence at the Top*; Wark, *The Ultimate Enemy*; (2) On Franco-Belgian relations: Martin S.

Alexander, 'Les réactions à la menace strategique allemande en Europe occidentale: La Grande Bretagne, la Belgique et le "cas Hollande", Décembre 1938 – Février 1939', *Cahiers d'Histoire de la Seconde Guerre Mondiale*, 1982; *Les relations militaires Franco-Belges de Mars 1936 au 10 Mai 1940*; (3) On British military policy: Gibbs, *Grand Strategy*, vol. 1: Howard, *The Continental Commitment*; Bond, *British Military Policy between two Wars*; Bialer, *The Shadow of the Bomber*; (4) On the Germany military/civil opposition to Hitler: Ritter, *Goerdeler*; Müller, *Das Heer und Hitler*; idem., *Armee und Drittes Reich*; Thun-Hohenstein, *Der Verschwörer*; (5) On French intelligence and on French military policy: Young, 'French military intelligence and Nazi Germany', in May, *Knowing One's Enemies*; Adamthwaite, 'French military intelligence and the coming of war', in Andrew and Noakes, *Intelligence and International Relations*.

1. Conwell-Evans, *None So Blind*, London 1947; Rose, *Vansittart*, p. 232.
2. Conwell-Evans, pp. 66–67, citing Christie papers.
3. Wark, *The Ultimate Enemy*, pp. 117–18.
4. Wark, *The Ultimate Enemy*, Appendix 6, pp. 245–46.
5. Watt, 'British Intelligence and Nazi Germany', in May, *Knowing One's Enemies*, pp. 253–54.
6. PRO, CAB 23/96, 21.xii.38.
7. Cadogan diary, 15.xii.38; Kirkpatrick, *The Inner Circle*, pp. 136–39; PRO, FO 371/22961, C 939/15/18; ibid., CAB 2/8, CID 342nd, 343rd Mtgs., 16/22.xii.38; Aster, pp. 44–45.
8. PRO, CAB 27/624, FPC 35th Mtg.; Inskip diary, 16/23.i.39; Harvey diary, 15/16/17.i.39.
9. PRO, CAB 27/627, FPC (36) 74, 19.i.39.
10. PRO, CAB 23/97, Cab 2 (39), 25.i.39.
11. DBFP, 3, IV, 5, Halifax to Mallet, 24.i.39; FRUS, 1939, I, pp. 2–6, Johnson to Hull, 24.i.39.
12. PRO, FO 371/22915, Strang to Ismay, 12.i.39.
13. PRO, CAB 58/44, COS 829, 830 (39), 24/25.i.39.
14. PRO, FO 371/21597, Phipps to Halifax, 23.xii.38; ibid., FO 371/22915, Fraser memorandum, 29.xii.38, cited Alexander, 'Réactions', p. 10, fn. 16.
15. Belgium Foreign Ministry Archives, Henry to Spaak, 22.xii.38, cited Alexander, 'Réactions', p. 10, fn. 17.
16. DDF, 2, XIII, 363, Bonnet to Campinchi, 13.i.39.
17. Minney, *Hore-Belisha*, citing diary, 1.i.39; PRO, FO 371/22915, Hore-Belisha to Halifax, 9.i.39, cited Alexander, 'Réactions', p. 11, fn. 21.
18. Inskip diary, 23.i.39; PRO FO 371/22963, C 1292/15/18 'An Estimation of German intentions'; ibid., Vansittart to Halifax, 18.i.39.
19. Vanwelkenhuysen, 'La Belgique et la menace d'invasion 1939–40', *Rev. Hist.*, CCLXIV; H. Graml, 'Der Fall Oster', *VjHZg*, 1966.
20. Andrew, *British Secret Service*, pp. 433–34; Macdonald, 'The Venlo Affair', *ESR*, 1978.
21. PRO, FO 371/21665, C 14809/62/18.
22. PRO, FO 371/21657, C 15084/42/18, Cadogan minute, 10.xii.38.
23. Cadogan diary, 11.xii.38.
24. PRO, CAB 23/96, C 59 (38) 5, C 60 (38) 3.
25. PRO, FO 371/22962, C 1096/15/18, Vansittart memorandum; ibid., C 1196/15/18, 26.i.39.
26. FRUS, 1939, I, pp. 18–20, Sumner Welles memorandum, 20.ii.39.
27. DBFP, 3, IV, 18, 26.i.39.
28. DBFP, 3, IV, 27, 27.i.39; ibid., 39, Enclosure, Washington to The Hague, 26.i.39; DDF, 2, XIII, 438, Enclosure.
29. DBFP, 3, IV, 30, 39, 27.i.39.
30. DBFP, 3, IV, 26, 28, 27.i.39; FRUS, 1939, I, pp. 6–7, Hull to Johnson, 27.i.39.
31. DBFP, 3, IV, 40, Halifax to Phipps and Clive, 28.i.39; ibid., 48, Halifax to Bland, 29.i.39.
32. DBFP, 3, IV, 44, Halifax to Phipps, 28.i.39.
33. DBFP, 3, IV, 49, 64, 72, 80, Clive to Halifax, 29/31.i./1/2.ii.39; Alexander, 'Réactions', p. 27; Van Overstraeten, *Albert I*, pp. 318–20.
34. DBFP, 3, IV, 80, Enclosure 2, Col. Paris to Sir Robert Clive, 2.ii.39; ibid., 70, fn. 2.
35. DDF, 2, XIII, 454, 460, 29/30.i.39; ibid., XIV, 5, 106; DBFP, 3, IV, 51, 53, 54, 29.i.39.

Chapter 7   Stalin makes a speech

Besides the sources quoted, this chapter is based on the following sources: Haslam, *The Soviet Union and the struggle for collective security in Europe, 1933–1939*; Aster, 'Ivan Maisky and Parliamentary Anti-Appeasement, 1938–39', in Taylor, *Lloyd George, Twelve Essays*; Niedhart, 'Der

Bündniswert der Sowjetunion im Urteil Grossbritanniens 1936–1939', *MgM*, 1971; Herndon, 'British Perceptions of Soviet Military Capability, 1935–1939', in Mommsen and Ketternacker, *The Fascist Challenge and the Policy of Appeasement*; Niedhart, *Grossbritannien und die Sowjetunion*; Conquest, 'The *Great Terror* revisited', *Survey*, 1971; Watt, 'The Initiation of the Negotiations leading to the Nazi-Soviet Pact', in Abramsky and Williams, *Essays in Honour of E. H. Carr*; idem, 'John Herbert King', *Intelligence and National Security*, 3 1988; idem, 'An Intelligence Failure. The Failure of the Foreign Office to anticipate the Nazi-Soviet Pact', *Intelligence and National Security*, 4 1989. On Soviet Intelligence organization, Höhne, *Krieg im Dunkeln*; *The Rote Kapelle: The CIA's History of Soviet Intelligence and Espionage Networks in Western Europe, 1936–1949*; Conquest, *Inside Stalin's Secret Police*; Poretzky, *Our Own People*; Prange, *Target Tokio*.

1. Degras, III, pp. 315–22.
2. Degras, III, pp. 363–71.
3. *DGFP*, D, VI, 441 and *IMT*, X, p. 267.
4. *DGFP*, D, VI, 1; German Foreign Ministry microfilms, 357/202529, 202530–34, Schulenburg to A.A., 11/13.iii.39.
5. *DBFP*, 3, IV, 452; *BDFA, SU*, XV, 40, Seeds to Halifax, 20.iii.39.
6. *FRUS, SU, 1933–1939*, pp. 344–45, Kirk to Hull, 14.iii.39.
7. *DGFP*, C, VI, 183, 195, 6/11.ii.39.
8. I. Pfaff, 'Prag und der Fall Tukhachewski', *VjH Zg*, 35/1, 1987.
9. *FRUS, SU, 1933–1939*, pp. 591–92, Kirk to Hull, 31.x.38; *DBFP*, 3, III, 217, Chilston to Halifax, 8.x.39; *DGFP*, D, IV, 476, 479, Tippelskirch to A.A., 3/10.x.38.
10. *SPE*, I, 15, 35, 37, 40.
11. Coulondre, *De Staline à Hitler*, p. 165.
12. Degras, III, pp. 308–11.
13. Thomas, *Spanish Civil War*, 3rd Edn, pp. 851–52; Cattell, *Soviet Diplomacy*, p. 128.
14. Thomas, *Spanish Civil War*, pp. 950–56; Koestler, *Scum of the Earth*, passim.
15. Prange, *Target Tokio*, passim.
16. *SPE*, I, 45, fn. citing *Pravda* 1.vii.67.
17. *The Rote Kapelle*, passim.
18. E. Poretzky, *Our Own People*, passim.
19. Watt, *Int. Nat. Sec.*, 1988.
20. *SPE*, I, 95.
21. *SPE*, I, 61, 77, 85, Litvinov to Suritz, 4/19/31.xii.38.
22. *SPE*, I, 5.
23. *SPE*, I, 90, Maisky to Litvinov, 10.i.39.
24. *SPE*, I, 114, 6.ii.39.
25. *SPE*, II, p. 290, fn. 44, Shtein to Litvinov; Toscano, 'L'Italia e gli accordi tedesco-sovietici', *RSPI*, 1951, pp. 556–57, 561, Rosso to Ciano, 13.i./12.iii.39.
26. Toscano, 'L'Italia', *RSPI*, 1951, pp. 561–63, Rosso to Ciano, 5.iv.39.
27. Aster, *1939*, pp. 152–53.
28. V. I. Popov, *SSSR i Angliya*, p. 375.
29. Watt, 'An Intelligence Failure', *Int. Nat. Sec.*, 1989.
30. *DBFP*, 3, IV, 76, 1.ii.39.
31. *DBFP*, 3, IV, 24, 46, 26/28.i.39.
32. *SPE*, I, 113, 3.ii.39; *DBFP*, 3, IV, 103.
33. *DBFP*, 3, IV, 121; *SPE*, I, 124, 19.ii.39.
34. *SPE*, I, 102, 27.i.39; *ibid.*, 130, 20.ii.39; *ibid.*, 131, 23.ii.39.
35. Aster, 'Maiski'.
36. *SPE*, I, 130.
37. *SPE*, I, 140, Maisky to Litvinov, 2.iii.39.
38. *DBFP*, 3, IV, 193.
39. *DBFP*, 3, IV, 194.
40. *DBFP*, 3, IV, 302, 314, 315, 321.
41. 'The Soviet Security System', *International Conciliation*, 1929.
42. Haslam, p. 198.
43. *DGFP*, D, V, 560. German Foreign Ministry microfilms, 257/202527, Kroll to A.A., 28.ii.39; *ibid.*, 257/202525, Heeren to A.A., 24.ii.39; *ibid.*, 257/202526, Fabricius to Berlin.
44. *DDF*, 2, XIV, 144, Thierry to Bonnet, 20.ii.39.

45. V. Moisuc, 'Orientations dans la politique exterieure de la Roumanie après Munich', *RRH*, 1966.
46. *Izvestija*, 9.iii.39.
47. *Survey of International Affairs, 1938*, III, p. 447; *DGFP*, D, V, 559.
48. *DGFP*, D, IV, 478, 26.x.38.
49. *DGFP*, D, IV, 483, 484.
50. *DGFP*, D, IV, 485.
51. *DGFP*, D, IV, 486, 487.
52. *DGFP*, D, IV, 490.
53. *DGFP*, D, IV, 495.
54. Domarus, II, pp. 1036–37; Wiedemann, *Der Mann der Feldherr werden wollte*, pp. 229–32.
55. Gannon, *British Press and Nazi Germany*, p. 40.
56. PRO, FO 371/23686, N588/243/38, Seeds to Halifax, 2.ii.39; *FRUS, 1939*, I, pp. 313–14, Kirk to Hull, 31.i.39; *DDF*, 2, XIV, 3, Payart to Bonnet, 1.ii.39.
57. *FRUS, SU, 1933–1939*, Kirk to Hull, 22.ii.39.

Chapter 8   Roosevelt backs Britain and France

Where not otherwise stated, this chapter is based on the following sources: Schewe, *Roosevelt and Foreign Affairs*, Vols. VII and VIII; Blum, *From the Morgenthau Diaries*, Vol. II; John McVickers Haight, *American Aid to France*; Orville Bullett (Ed.) *For the President: Secret and Personal*; Wayne S. Cole, *Roosevelt and the Isolationists*; Robert W. Divine, *The Illusion of Neutrality*; Betty Glad, *Key Pitmann*; Callum Macdonald, *The United States, Britain and Appeasement*; David Reynolds, *The Creation of the Anglo-American Alliance*; Robert Dallek, *Franklin D. Roosevelt and American Foreign Policy*; W. L. Langer and S. Everett Gleason, *The Challenge to Isolationism*; Michael Beschloss, *Kennedy and Roosevelt*; Alsop and Kintner, *American White Paper*.

1. Tugwell and Ickes, cited in Dallek, p. vii.
2. Watt, 'The Historiography of Yalta', *Dipl. Hist.* 13, 1989.
3. Bullitt, *For the President*, passim.
4. Biddle papers, passim.
5. Jones, *U.S. Diplomats in Europe*, pp. 113–28.
6. Watt, '*The Week* that was', *Encounter* 1972.
7. Acheson, *Present at the Creation*, p. 9.
8. Compton, *The Eagle and the Swastika*, p. 73; *DGFP.*, D, IV, 515.
9. Offner, 'Appeasement Revisited', *JAH*, 1974.
10. *Moffatt Journals*, June 1938, p. 190; Ickes, *Secret Diaries*, II, p. 377.
11. Pell to F.D.R., 21.x.1938; Bowers to F.D.R., 24.x.38. Roosevelt Papers (PSF Spain). Schewe, VII, 1366, 1368.
12. PRO, CAB 23/94, CP (38) 36.
13. *FRUS, 1938*, I, pp. 615–18.
14. Bullitt, *For the President*, pp. 297–300, Bullitt to F.D.R., 25.ix.38.
15. Lindbergh, *War Diaries*, entries of 1/2.x.38.
16. National Library of Scotland, Murray of Elibank Papers, Folio 8808, pp. 284, 294–95.
17. Elibank, 'Roosevelt'; Murray papers, Folio 8809, Murray to Halifax, 22.x.38; memorandum for the Prime Minister, 21.x.38.
18. Murray papers, Folio 8809, Murray to Kingsley Wood, 21.x.38; Murray memorandum, 23.x.38.
19. Postan, *British War Production*, pp. 56–57, 107 and Appendices 2 and 4.
20. Murray papers, Folio 8809, Murray to F.D.R., 15.xii.38; Schewe, *Roosevelt and Foreign Affairs*, vol. VIII, 1481; PRO, PREM 1/367, Chamberlain memorandum, 14.xii.38.
21. Haight, 'Les Negociations Françaises', pt 1, *Forces Aëriennes Françaises*, 1963.
22. Blum, *From the Morgenthau Diaries*, II, pp. 48–49.
23. Dallek, p. 175; Ickes, *Secret Diary*, II, entries of 9.x, 5.xi, 18.xii.38, 15.i.39.
24. Watt, 'Stalin's First Bid'; *USNIP*, 1964; Haight, *American Aid to France*, pp. 78–80; McFarland, 'Woodring v. Johnson', *Army*, 1976.
25. Haight, *American Aid to France*, p. 98; Blum, *Morgenthau*, II, pp. 66–71.
26. Haight, *American Aid to France*, pp. 94–95.
27. Schewe, VIII, 1503.

28. Roosevelt, *Public Papers*, 8, pp. 70–74.
29. Haight, *American Aid to France*, pp. 93–94.
30. Schewe, VIII, 1565; Haight, *American Aid to France*, pp. 98–99; Cole, *Roosevelt and the Isolationists*, pp. 305–06.
31. Cole, *Roosevelt and the Isolationists*, pp. 306–07.
32. Cole, *Roosevelt and the Isolationists*, p. 307; *Congressional Record, 76ia Congress*, 1st Session, 1939, 84, pp. 1010–14.
33. Schewe, VIII, 1574, 1598.
34. Divine, *Illusion of Neutrality*, pp. 236–39.
35. Glad, *Pittman*, pp. 280–82.
36. Divine, *Illusion*, pp. 235–36; Schewe, VIII, 1529.
37. Divine, *Illusion*, pp. 236–37; Hull, *Memoirs*, I, p. 613.
38. Bowers to F.D.R., 13.i.39, Schewe, VIII, 1530.
39. Halifax to F.D.R., 7.ii.39, Schewe, VIII, 1587b.
40. Ickes, *Secret Diary*, II, pp. 569–70.
41. Halifax to F.D.R., 30.i.39, Schewe, VIII, 1563a; the same to the same, 7.ii.39, Schewe, VIII, 1587a and b.
42. Bowers to F.D.R., 8/16.ii.39, Schewe, VIII, 1580, 1597a.
43. Biddle to F.D.R., 18.ii.39, Schewe, VIII, 1599 and 1599a.
44. Bullitt, *For the President*, pp. 308–11, Bullitt to Hull, 6.ii.39.
45. Ickes, *Secret Diary*, II, p. 571; F.D.R. to Merriman, 15.ii.39, Schewe, VIII, 1594.
46. *H.C. Deb.*, 353, cols. 80–81.
47. Feiling, *Chamberlain*, p. 344.
48. *FRUS, 1939*, I, pp. 14–17.
49. Messersmith papers, 3.ii.39, cited Macdonald, *The U.S., Britain and Appeasement*, p. 131.
50. *DBFP*, 3, VIII, 479, Mallett to Halifax, 7.ii.39; Early to F.D.R., (23.ii.39), Bullitt, *For the President*, pp. 311–12; Bullitt to Hull, 13.ii.39, Schewe, VIII, 1591; Bullitt to F.D.R., 16.ii.39, (PSF France), cited Macdonald, *The U.S., Britain and Appeasement*, p. 132; Sumner Welles memorandum, 20.ii.39, *FRUS, 1939*, I, pp. 18–20.
51. Watt, 'The Week that Was', *Encounter*, 1972.
52. Cecil Roberts, *And So to America*, cited Macdonald, *The U.S., Britain and Appeasement*, p. 137.
53. Moffatt Diaries, entry of 26.iii.39.
54. Macdonald, 'The U.S. and the Open Door', in Mommsen and Ketternacker (Eds.), *The Fascist Challenge*, p. 407, citing State Department files, Berle and Moffatt diaries, Joseph E. Davies papers.
55. Moffatt diaries, 10.v.39, cited Macdonald, 'U.S. view of British Appeasement'.

Chapter 9   Hitler enters Prague

Besides the sources cited, this chapter is based on the following sources: (1) For Slovakia, Hoensch, *Die Slovakei und Hitlers Ostpolitik*; Durica, *La Slovacchia e le sue relazioni politiche con la Germania*, vol. I. Both Hoensch and Durica draw heavily on the Slovak sources including the memoirs of Carol Sidor, Tiso's speeches and documents produced at the post-war trials of Tiso in Czechoslovakia and of the Wilhelmstrasse officials (Case XI) in Germany. Durica carries an Appendix of numbered documents. Lettrich, *Modern Slovakia*; Mikus, *La Slovaquie dans le drame de l'Europe*; Durčansky, 'Mit Tiso bei Hitler', *Pol. Stud.*, 1956; Delfiner, *Vienna broadcasts to Slovakia*. (2) For the Carpatho-Ukraine, Winch, *Republic for a Day*; Stercho, *Diplomacy of Double Morality*; Hoensch, *Ungarische Revisionismus*. (3) For the occupation of Bohemia-Moravia, Kennan, *From Prague after Munich*; Ronnefarth, *Die Sudetenkrise in der internationalen Politik*; Laffan, *Survey of International Affairs, 1938*, III; Ripka, *Munich before and after*; Woytak, *On the borders of War and Peace*; Macartney, *October 15*. On Hácha's visit to Berlin, the evidence of his daughter, Milada Radlova, née Hácha, to the Wilhelmstrasse Trial, Case XI, *Trials of the War Criminals*, XII, pp. 904–06; Schmidt, *Statist auf diplomatische Bühne*; Meissner, *Staatssekretär*.

1. Kennan, *From Prague*, personal notes, March 1939, pp. 80–87.
2. Domarus, II, pp. 1097–1103.
3. *DGFP*, D, IV, 81, 21.x.39.
4. *DGFP*, D, IV, 46.

5. *DGFP*, D, IV, 68, 69, 112.
6. Durica, 10, Frank memorandum, 2.xi.38.
7. *DGFP*, D, IV, 120; *DBFP*, 3, III, 214, 216, 251; Ronnefarth, pp. 205–07.
8. *DGFP*, D, IV, 152.
9. *DGFP*, D, V, 119, 120; *PWB*, 48, 49.
10. *DGFP*, D, V, 272, 273.
11. *DGFP*, D, IV, 109.
12. *DDF*, 2, XII, 109; Stercho, passim.
13. *DGFP*, D, IV, 146, 7.xii.38.
14. Winch, *Republic*, pp. 28–29.
15. *DGFP*, D, IV, 141.
16. *DDF*, 2, XIV, 80, 132.
17. Schellenberg, *Memoirs*, p. 58; Hoensch, p. 229.
18. Hoensch, p. 226; Durica, 18, von Druffel to A.A., 2.ii.39.
19. *DGFP*, D, IV, 168; Hoensch, pp. 226–28.
20. Durica, 19, von Druffel to A.A., 23.ii.39.
21. Delfiner, pp. 71–72, 102, 106–08.
22. Hoensch, pp. 232–33.
23. Hoensch, pp. 170–71, 231.
24. Hoensch, pp. 237–39.
25. Hoensch, pp. 240–42.
26. Hoensch, pp. 245–46, Durica, 24, and pp. 63 65.
27. Hoensch, pp. 248–49; Durica, p. 67.
28. Durica, pp. 69–73.
29. *DBFP*, 3, IV, 149.
30. Durica, p. 75; Hoensch, pp. 249–65.
31. *DBFP*, 3, IV, 210; Hoensch, p. 270.
32. Delfiner, pp. 114–16; *DBFP*, 3, IV, 208, 212.
33. Delfiner, p. 118; *DBFP*, IV, 209; *DGFP*, D, IV, 194; Hoensch, p. 264.
34. *DBFP*, 3, IV, 218, 219.
35. Durica, p. 76.
36. Durica, p. 76; Hoensch, p. 270.
37. *DBFP*, 3, IV, 203; Durica, 26, Druffel to A.A., 11.iii.39; Hoensch, pp. 270–72.
38. Durica, pp. 78–79; Hoensch, pp. 273–74, fn. 21, pp. 279–82.
39. *DGFP*, D, IV, 228.
40. *DGFP*, D, IV, 188.
41. *DGFP*, D, IV, 198, 199.
42. Durica, p. 80.
43. Durica, 43, Druffel to A.A., 13.iii.39; Hoensch, pp. 286–87.
44. *DBFP*, 3, IV, 231.
45. Durica, p. 81; Hoensch, pp. 287–88.
46. *DGFP*, D, IV, 202; Durica, 47, Tiso to Slovak assembly, 14.iii.39; Hoensch, pp. 290–97; Durčansky, *Pol.Stud.*, 1956.
47. Durica, 47, and pp. 84–85; Hoensch, pp. 298–303.
48. Durica, 50.
49. Durica, 51; Hoensch, p. 304, fn. 158.
50. Durica, 48; *DGFP*, D, IV, 212.
51. Durica, p. 92; Hoensch, p. 334.
52. *DGFP*, D, VI, 10; Hoensch, pp. 334–38.
53. *DGFP*, D, IV, 158.
54. *DGFP*, D, IV, 159; Ronnefarth, pp. 719–20.
55. *DBFP*, 3, IV, 126, Troutbeck to Strang, 20.ii.39; *DDF*, 2, XIV, 168, Lacroix to Bonnet, 21.ii.39; *ibid.*, 177, Lt. Colonel Albord to Daladier, 22.ii.39 with enclosures.
56. *DGFP*, D, IV, 171; *DBFP*, 3, IV, 138; *DDF*, 2, XIV, 184, Lacroix to Bonnet and fn. 3, 23.ii.39.
57. *DGFP*, D, IV, 177.
58. *DGFP*, D, IV, 189, Toussaint, Hencke to A.A., 12.iii.39.
59. *DGFP*, D, IV, 197; Hencke to A.A., 13.iii.39.
60. *DGFP*, D, IV, 203.
61. *DBFP*, 3, IV, 218, 219, 249, Henderson to Halifax, 13.iii.39.

62. *DGFP*, D, IV, 204 and fn. 1, Ribbentrop to Hencke, 13.iii.39.
63. *DGFP*, D, IV, 206, 207, 208.
64. *DGFP*, D, IV, 216.
65. Radlova, testimony; Meissner, *Staatssekretär*, p. 476.
66. *DGFP*, D, IV, 228; Meissner, pp. 476–77; Schmidt, *Statist*, pp. 429–32.
67. *DGFP*, D, IV, 229.
68. Zoller, *Hitler privat*, p. 84.
69. Ripka, *Munich, before and after*, p. 245.
70. Stercho, p. 371.
71. Winch, p. 272.
72. *DGFP*, D, IV, 197; *DIMK*, III, 413, Sztójay to Csáky.
73. *DGFP*, D, IV, 199.
74. *DIMK*, III, 400, Sztójay to Foreign Ministry.
75. *DGFP*, D, IV, 198, Erdmannsdorf to A.A., 13.iii.39.
76. *DIMK*, III, 423, *DGFP*, D, IV, 217.
77. Winch, pp. 280–86; *DGFP*, D, IV, 210, 215, 218, 235, 236, 237, 14/15.iii.39.
78. *ND* 136-C, IMT XXXIV, pp. 477–81, 18.iii/21.x.38; *ND*, 137-C, 24.xi.38.
79. *DGFP*, D, V, 390, 371, 372, 5.xii.38.
80. *DGFP*, D, V, 388, 390.
81. *DGFP*, D, V, 395, 396, 398.
82. *DGFP*, D, V, 399.
83. *DGFP*, D, V, 403.
84. *DGFP*, D, V, 405 and fn.
85. Domarus, II, pp. 1110–13.
86. Lipski papers, p. 501.
87. Lipski papers, p. 495.
88. *DGFP*, D, V, 131.
89. Lipski papers, 135, Lipski to Beck, 2.iii.39.
90. Lipski papers, 137, Lipski to Beck, 17.iii.39.
91. Lipski papers, p. 501.
92. Lipski papers, p. 501.
93. *PWB*, 61; *DGFP*, D, VI, 61.
94. Szembek diary, 22.iii.39.
95. Lipski papers, p. 501, fn. 9.
96. Lipski papers, 138.
97. *PWB*, 66; DBFP, 3, IV, 485.
98. *DBFP*, 3, IV, 518.
99. *DGFP*, D, VI, 73.
100. *DGFP*, D, VI, 99.
101. Lipski papers, 139.
102. *DGFP*, D, VI, 90.
103. *DGFP*, D, VI, 90, fn.
104. *DGFP*, D, VI, 101.
105. *DGFP*, D, VI, 101.
106. Biddle papers, 23, Biddle to Hull, 4.iv.39.
107. *DGFP*, D, VI, 108.
108. *DGFP*, D, VI, 118.

Chapter 10   Chamberlain chooses containment

Where not otherwise stated, this chapter is based on the following sources and studies: Aster, *1939*; Cienciala, *Poland and the Western Powers*; Newman, *March 1939*; Prazmowska, *Britain, Poland and the Eastern Front*; Gannon, *The British Press and Nazi Germany*; Marguerat, *Le IIIe Reich et le pétrole roumain*; Moisuc, 'Orientations dans la politique exterieure de la Roumanie', *RRH*, 1966; idem., 'Tratatul economie Romano-German din 25 Martie 1939', *Analele*, 1967; Lungu, *Romania and the European Great Powers*; idem, 'The European Crisis of March–April 1939', *IHR*, 1985; Colvin, *Vansittart in Office*; van Kessel, 'British Reactions to German Economic Expansion', London Ph.D., 1972; Rotunda, 'The Rome Embassy of Sir Eric Drummond, 16th Earl of Perth', London Ph.D., 1972; Petrescu-Comnéne, *Preludi del grande dramma*; Maisky, *Who Helped Hitler?*; Aster, 'Maiski', in Taylor, *Lloyd George: 12 Essays*.

1. Feiling, *Chamberlain*, pp. 396–97; Halifax, *Fulness of Days*, p. 232; Cadogan diary, 10.iii.39; *DBFP*, 3, IV, 39, Halifax to Lindsay, 27.ii.39; *DCER*, VI, 928, Dominions Secretary to Prime Minister, Canada, 7.iii.39.
2. Templewood, *Nine Troubled Years*, p. 328.
3. Chamberlain papers, NC 18/1/1083, 1084, 1085, 1086, to Ida Chamberlain, 28.i./12.ii.39, to Hilda Chamberlain, 5/19.ii.39.
4. *DBFP*, 3, IV, Appendix II (2).
5. *DBFP*, 3, IV, Appendix II (1).
6. Chamberlain papers, NC 18/1/1084, to Hilda Chamberlain, 5.ii.39; Chamberlain papers, NC 18/1/1086, to Hilda Chamberlain, 19.ii.39.
7. *H.C. Deb.*, 343, col. 623.
8. Private information; Mason-MacFarlane papers.
9. *DBFP*, 3, IV, 109, 118, 119, 127, 135, 162, 163.
10. *DBFP*, 3, IV, 118.
11. *DBFP*, 3, IV, Appendix I, (i)–(vii).
12. *H.C. Deb.*, 344, cols 2161–84.
13. Gibbs, *Grand Strategy*, vol. I, pp. 657–67; PRO, DP(P) 44, COS 848.
14. Pratt, *East of Malta*, pp. 169–75; Pritchard, *Far Eastern Influences*, pp. 138–43.
15. *H.C. Deb.*, 345, cols 435–40.
16. *H.C. Deb.*, 345, cols 435–40.
17. Nicolson diary, 16.iii.39.
18. Gannon, *British Press*, pp. 235–38, 239–40, 245–48, 252–54, 256–57, 259–61; DDF, 2, XV, 7, General Lelong to Daladier, 10.iii.39.
19. Ovendale, pp. 216–24; Feiling, *Chamberlain*, p. 400.
20. *H.C. Deb.*, 245, cols 545–59.
21. Cadogan diary, 26.iii.39.
22. *DBFP*, 3, IV, 285, 10.iii.39.
23. *DBFP*, 3, IV, Appendix I (viii).
24. *DBFP*, 3, IV, 279; *DGFP*, D, IV, 244.
25. *DBFP*, 3, IV, 344, Halifax to Lindsay, 17.iii.39.
26. Chamberlain, *Struggle for Peace*, pp. 413–20.
27. I. Spalatelu, 'Presa revolutionara si democrata din anii 1933–1937 despre sprijinut acordat organizatiilar fasciste de cercuri reactionare interna si externa', *Analele*, xiii/4, 1967, p. 116.
28. Van Kessel, 'British Reactions', pp. 206–08.
29. Tilea to Bucharest, 9.ii.39, Moisuc, 'Orientations', *RRH*, 1966, p. 332, fn. 18.
30. *DBFP*, 3, IV, 297.
31. *DBFP*, 3, IV, 298.
32. Gafencu to Tilea, 16.iii.39, Moisuc, 'Tratatul', *Analele*, 1967; Lungu, *IHR*, 1985, p. 392.
33. Aster, *1939*, pp. 61–63.
34. *DBFP*, 3, IV, 395.
35. *FRUS, 1939*, I, p. 72, Kennedy to Hull, 17.iii.39.
36. Lungu, *IHR*, 1985; *DDF*, 2, XV, 33, Corbin to Bonnet, 17.iii.39; *SPE*, I, 155, Maisky to Litvinov, 17.iii.39.
37. *PRO*, FO 371/23832, R 2195/113/37, Hore-Belisha minute, 17.iii. 39.
38. *Breach of Security*, p. 62, Cincar-Marković to Berlin, 21.iii.39.
39. *DDF*, 2, XV, 56, 18.iii.39.
40. Harvey diary, 18.iii.39; Bibescu, *Jurnal*, 16/19.iii.39; Aster, *1939*, pp. 63–64 and note; Newman, *March 1939*, pp. 115–16; PRO, FO 371/23847, R 5123/464/37; Boothby, *I fight to live*, p. 187; Channon diary, 18.iii.39; PRO, FO 371/22958, C 3709/3356/18, Jebb minutes, 18.iii.39.
41. *DBFP*, 3, IV, 389, 390.
42. *DBFP*, 3, V, 397.
43. *DBFP*, 3, V, 399.
44. Paul von Hohenzollern, *King Carol*, pp. 182–83; Comnéne, *Preludi*, pp. 378–96; PRO, FO 371/22460, R 9438/223/37, Halifax to Palairet, 17.xi.38; *ibid.*, FO 371/22446, R 9168/3/37, Minutes of conversation with King Carol, 17.xi.38; *ibid.*, FO 371/22446, Nichols minute, 24.xi.38; van Kessel, 'British Reactions', pp. 198–200; Aster, p. 67.
45. *DGFP*, D, V, 254, 24.xi.38; *DDF*, 2, XIII, 8, 13, 1/2.xii.38.
46. *DGFP*, D, V, 260, 261; *DDF*, 2, XIII, 34, 42.
47. *DGFP*, D, V, 264.

48. Marguerat, *Le IIIe Reich et le pétrole roumain*, p. 124, fn. 4.
49. *DDF*, 2, XVI, 474, Thierry to Bonnet, 19.vi.39.
50. Cretzianu, *Missed Opportunity*, p. 29.
51. Conference of 23.i.39, Moisuc, 'Orientations', *RRH*, 1966, pp. 329–30; Zaharia and Calafteanu, 'The International Situation and Romania's Foreign Policy', *RRH*, 1979.
52. Tatarescu to Bucharest, 23.i.39, Moisuc, 'Orientations', *RRH*, 1966, p. 329, fn. 6.
53. Van Kessel, 'British Reactions', pp. 139, 193.
54. Marguerat, *Le IIIe Reich et le pétrole roumain*, p. 96.
55. *DGFP*, D, V, 293, 294, 297, 298, 306.
56. *DGFP*, D, V, 299, 21.ii.39.
57. Lungu, *IHR*, 1985.
58. Romanian memorandum, 15.iii.39, cited Lungu, *IHR*, 1985.
59. *DGFP*, D, VI, 78.
60. Călinescu diary, 23.iii.39, 1.iv.39, cited Talpes, *'Politique militaire de la Roumanie'*, *RHDGM*, 1985, p. 45, fn. 17, Lungu, *IHR*, 1985, pp. 402–03.
61. *DBFP*, 3, IV, 425, 439, Waterlow to Halifax, 20.iii.39.
62. *DBFP*, 3, IV, 420, Campbell to Halifax, 19.iii.39.
63. *DBFP*, 3, IV, 400, Kennard to Halifax, 18.iii.39.
64. Călinescu diary, 20.iii.39.
65. *DBFP*, 3, IV, 423, Knatchbull-Hugessen to Halifax, 19.iii.39.
66. *DBFP*, 3, IV, 407, Knatchbull-Hugessen to Halifax, 18.iii.39.
67. *DBFP*, 3, IV, 403, Seeds to Halfax, 18.iii.39; *SPE*, I, 161, Litvinov to Maisky/Suritz, 18.iii.39.
68. *SPE*, I, 179, 22.iii.39.
69. Moisuc, 'Orientations', *RRH*, 1966, p. 335.
70. *DBFP*, 3, IV, 421, Seeds to Halifax, 19.iii.39; *SPE*, I, 162, Litvinov to Maisky/Suritz, 18.iii.39.
71. Aster, 'Maiski'.
72. *DBFP*, 3, IV, 376, Perth to Halifax, 21.iii.39; *PRO*, FO 371/22944, C 4311/421/62, Cadogan minute.
73. Chamberlain papers, NC 18/1/1090, to Hilda Chamberlain, 19.iii.39.
74. *PRO*, CAB 23/98, Cab 13(29), 20.iii.39.
75. Cadogan diary, 20.iii.39; *DDF*, 3, XV, 74, Corbin to Bonnet, 20.iii.39.
76. *DBFP*, 3, IV, 446; *DDF*, 2, XV, 105.
77. *DBFP*, 3, IV, 461, 462, Seeds to Halifax, 21.iii.39; *SPE*, I, 176, Litvinov memorandum.
78. *SPE*, I, 178, Litvinov to Maisky/Suritz, 22.iii.39; *DBFP*, 3, IV, 490.
79. *DBFP*, 3, IV, 458, Record of an Anglo-French conversation.
80. *DDF*, 2, XV, 56, Bonnet memorandum, 18.iii.39.
81. *DDF*, 2, XV, 57, Bonnet memorandum, 18.iii.39.
82. *DBFP*, 3, IV, 471, Halifax to Kennard, 21.iii.39.
83. *DBFP*, 3, IV, 507, Halifax to Campbell, 23.iii.39.
84. *DBFP*, 3, IV, 509, 24.iii.39.
85. Channon diary, 23.iii.39.
86. Potocki to Raczyński, Lubienski to Raczyński, 22.iii.39, cited in Cienciala, *Poland*, pp. 216–17.
87. *FRUS, 1939*, I, pp. 83–85, Bullitt to Hull, 21.iii.39.
88. *DBFP*, 3, IV, 405, Phipps to Halifax, 18.iii.39.
89. *DBFP*, 3, IV, 518.
90. *PRO*, CAB 23/98, Cab 14(39), 22.iii.39.
91. Chamberlain papers, 18/1/1093, Chamberlain to Ida Chamberlain, 9.iv.39.
92. *DBFP*, 3, IV, 183, 498.
93. *PRO*, FO 371/23061, C 8968/3356/18, Oliphant minute, 29.iii.39.
94. *PRO*, FO 371/22867, C 4317/15/18; Dalton, *The Fateful Years*, pp. 237–38.
95. Chamberlain papers, NC 18/1/1091, to Ida Chamberlain, 26.iii.39.
96. *PRO*, FO 371/23061, C 3849/3356/18, Snow to Halifax, 22.iii.39.
97. *PRO*, *ibid.*, C 3942/3356/18, Kirkpatrick minute, 23.iii.39.
98. *PRO*, FO 371/23062, C 4213/3356/18, Halifax to Selby, 25.iii.39.
99. *PRO*, FO 371/23062, C 4470/3356/18.
100. *PRO*, PREM 1/321, Cadogan/Strang memorandum, 26.iii.39.
101. *PRO*, CAB 27/624, FPC Mtg., 27.iii.39.

102. Cadogan diary, 26.iii.39.
103. Cadogan diary, 26.iii.39.
104. Chamberlain papers, NC 18/1/1091, to Ida Chamberlain, 26.iii.39.
105. *DBFP*, 3, IV, 538.
106. *DBFP*, 3, IV, 523, 534, 535, 540, 547, 550, 564.
107. Wheeler-Bennett, *King George VI*, p. 368.
108. *DBFP*, 3, IV, 571, 577.
109. *PRO*, CAB 23/98, Cab 15(39).
110. Lloyd papers, GLLD 19/7, Halifax to Lloyd, 19.x.38; *ibid.*, 19/8, Lloyd to Loraine, 20.x.38.
111. Lloyd papers, GLLD 19/9, Lloyd to Lady Lloyd.
112. Koliopoulos, p. 106; *PRO*, FO 371/23769, Sergent to Lloyd, 25.ii.39.
113. Lloyd papers, GLLD 19/8, Lloyd to Sinclair, 27.x.38.
114. Lloyd papers, GLLD 19/9.
115. Lloyd papers, GLLD 19/9, Colvin to Lloyd, 9/23.ii./7.iii.39.
116. Lloyd papers, GLLD 19/9, 23.iii.39.
117. Colvin, *Chief of Intelligence*, p. 78; Aster, *1939*, p. 192.
118. Colvin, *Vansittart in Office*, pp. 298–311; Cadogan diary, 29.iii.39.
119. Butler, *Mason-Mac*, pp. 75–76.
120. *DBFP*, 3, IV, Appendix V, Ogilvie-Forbes to Strang, 29.iii.39, Enclosure II, Mason-MacFarlane memorandum, 28.iii.39.
121. Cadogan diary, 29.iii.39.
122. Chamberlain Papers, NC 18/1/1092, to Hilda, 2.iv.39.
123. Krausnick, 'Vorgeschicht und Beginn des militärischen Widerstandes gegen Hitler' in *die Vollmacht des Gewissens*, p. 377; Mueller, 'die national-konservative Opposition gegen Hitler vor dem zweiten Weitkrieg' in *Militärgeschichte*; *Probleme, These, Wege*, p. 241; Schall-Riaucour, *Aufstand und Gehorsam*, p. 265.
124. *DBFP*, 3, IV, 656, 568, and fn. 2.
125. *DBFP*, 3, IV, 588, 561, 563.
126. *DBFP*, 3, IV, 557, 29.iii.39.
127. *DBFP*, 3, IV, 575.
128. *PWB*, 68.
129. Namier, *Diplomatic Prelude*, p. 101.
130. *DBFP*, 3, IV, 573.
131. *DBFP*, 3, IV, 584, 31.iii.39.
132. Nicolson diary, 31.iii.39.
133. *H.C. Deb.*, 345, col. 2415.
134. Chamberlain papers, NC 18/1/1092.
135. Aster, *1939*, p. 192, citing A. L. Kennedy diary; *SPE*, I, 206, Maisky to Litvinov, 2.iv.39; Newman, *March 1939*, p. 208; Gannon, *British Press*, citing Geoffrey Dawson diary, 3.iv.39.
136. *DGFP*, D, VI, 137, 21.iii.39.
137. *The Times*, 3.iv.39.
138. *SPE*, I, 206.
139. Raczyński, *In Allied London*, p. 14.
140. Raczyński, p. 14.
141. *DBFP*, 3, IV, 605, Kennard to Halifax, 2.iv.39.

Chapter 11   Hitler turns against Poland

Where not otherwise stated, this chapter is based on the following sources: Hencke, *England in Hitlers politischen Kalkül*; Sywottek, *Mobilmachung für den totalen Krieg*; Müller, *Armee und Dritte Reich*; Müller, *Das Heer und Hitler*; Domarus, *Hitlers Reden*, vol. II.

1. *DGFP*, D, VI, 99; *ND*, 100-R; *IMT*, XXXVIII, pp. 274–76.
2. Müller, *Armee und Dritte Reich*, doc. 45.
3. von Manstein, *Soldatenleben*, p. 74.
4. Domarus, II, p. 1075; Müller, *Das Heer und Hitler*, p. 388; *idem, Armee und Dritte Reich*, doc. 107.
5. Mueller-Hillebrand, *das Heer*, I, pp. 47–48; Absolon, IV, fn. 666; Meier et al, p. 92, fn 32.
6. Warlimont, *Im Hauptquartier*, pp. 34–35.

7. *DGFP*, D, VI, 118, 29.iii.39.
8. Goebbels diary, 26.iii.39.
9. Goebbels diary, 28.iii.39.
10. Gisevius, *Bis zum bitteren Ende*, Vol. II, p. 107; *To the Bitter End*, p. 363.
11. Domarus, II, pp. 1118–19.
12. Domarus, II, p. 1119.
13. Domarus, II, pp. 1119–27.
14. Domarus, II, p. 1127.
15. Hencke, *England*, p. 240, fn. 137, citing Bundesarchiv Koblenz, Bremmer, Z Sg 101/12, 3.iv.39.
16. Hencke, *England*, p. 240, fn. 139; Sywottek, *Mobilmachung*, pp. 199–201; Wette in *Das Deutsche Reich und der zweiten Weltkrieg*, I, pp. 135–36, esp. fn. 184; *PRO*, FO 408, FOCP 15906/47, C5157/53/18, Ogilvie-Forbes to Halifax, 12.iv.39.
17. *ND* 120-C; *DGFP*, C, VI, 149, 185 enclosure II.
18. *DGFP*, D, VI, 125, 29.iii.39.
19. *DGFP*, D, VI, 126, Schliep to Moltke, 29.iii.39.
20. *DGFP*, D, VI, 139, 5.iv.39.
21. *DGFP*, D, VI, 196, 14.iv.39.
22. *DGFP*, D, VI, 229, 18.iv.39.
23. *DGFP*, D, VI, 224, 241, 18/21.iv.39.
24. *DGFP*, D, VI, 263 and fn. 1.
25. *DGFP*, D, VI, 181, 11.iv.39.
26. *DGFP*, D, VI, 310, 2.v.39.
27. *DGFP*, D, VI, 200; *FRUS, 1939*, I, pp. 130–33; Hull, *Memoirs*, I, p. 620; see also Chapter XV below.
28. *DDF*, 2, XV, 460, de Vaux Saint-Cyr to Bonnet, 28.iv.39; Domarus, II, 1147.
29. *DGFP*, D, VI, 131 and enclosure.
30. Völker, *Dokumente zur Geschichte der Luftwaffe*, p. 149; Boog, *Die deutsche Luftwaffenführung*, p. 93; Gundelach, 'Gedanken', *WWR*, 1960, p. 46; Murray, *Strategy for Defeat*, p. 11.
31. Domarus, II, pp. 1148–63.
32. *DGFP*, D, VI, 283, 287, 301, 28/29.iv/1.v.39.
33. *DGFP*, D, VI, 276; *PWB*, 76.
34. *DGFP*, D, VI, 277; *DBFP*, 3, V, 307.
35. *ND*, C-126 C; *ND*, NOKW-229.

Chapter 12   Anger in Rome

Where not otherwise stated, this chapter is based on the following sources: (i) On Italy: de Felice, *Mussolini Il Duce*, Vol. II; Guerri, *Ciano*; Siebert, *Italiens Weg*; Toscano, *Le Origine diplomatiche del Patto d'Acciaio*; Quartararo, *Roma tra Londra e Berlino: Politica estera fascista del 1930 al 1940*; idem, 'Inghilterra e Italia dal Patto di Pasqua a Monaco: con un' appendice sul "canale segreto" italo-inglese', *Storia contemporanea*, 1976; Toscano, *Le Origini del Patto d'Acciaio*; Borejsza, 'L'Italia e la guerra tedesco-polacca del 1939', *Storia Contemporanea*, 1978. (ii) On Romania: Lungu, *Romania and the European Great Powers, 1933–1940*; Moisuc, 'Imperativul organizarii securitatu si pacii europene si politica externa a Romaniei in ultimele luni de pace (aprilie–august 1939)', in Moisuc (Ed.), *Probleme de politica externa a Romaniei 1919–1939*, 1971; Calafteanu, 'Eforturile diplomatice romanesti in vederea realizarii unitatii de actiune a statelor din sud-estul Europei in fata expansiunii fasciste (Martie 1938 – Iulie 1939)', in Moisuc, *Probleme de politica externa a Romaniei 1918–1940*, 1977. (iii) On Yugoslavia: Breccia, *Jugoslavia*; Hoptner, *Yugoslavia in Crisis*. (iv) On Greece: Koliopoulos, *Greece and the British Connection*. (v) On Turkey: Krecker, *Deutschland und die Turkei im zweiten Weltkrieg*; Kroll, *Lebenserrinerungen eines Botschafters*; Massigli, *La Turquie devant la guerre*.

1. *DGFP*, D, IV, 224.
2. Ciano, *Diario*, 15.iii.39.
3. Ciano, *Diario*, 16.iii.39.
4. Ciano, *Diario*, 17.iii.39.
5. Ciano, *Diario*, 19.iii.39.

HOW WAR CAME

6. Ciano, *Diario*, 20.iii.39.
7. Ciano, *Diario*, 21.iii.39.
8. Bottai, *Diario*, Ciano, *Diario*, 21.iii.39; Mussolini, *Opere Omnia*, XXIX, pp. 248–53.
9. *DGFP*, D, IV, 459.
10. Attolico to Ciano, 9.iii.39, Toscano, *Origine*, pp. 153–54, fn. 173; Ciano *Diario*, 10.iii.39.
11. Baudouin, 'Un Voyage à Rome: février 1939', *Revue des deux mondes*, 1.v.1962, pp. 69–85.
12. Ciano, *Diario*, 25/27/28.ii.39, 1.iii.39; *CDP*, pp. 273–75; Borejsza, 'L'Italia', pp. 610–13.
13. Ciano, *Diario*, 3.iii.39.
14. *DDF*, 2, XV, 382, Brugère to Bonnet, 13.iv.39.
15. Ciano, *Diario*, 19/23.i.39; Breccia, *Jugoslavia*, pp. 7–8, 12, 13; *CDP*, pp. 267–72; Hoptner, pp. 124–26.
16. Hoptner, pp. 128–29.
17. Hoptner, Breccia, passim.
18. Hoptner, Breccia, passim.
19. *CDP*, pp. 276–77; Ciano, *Diario*, 17/18.iii.39; *DBFP*, 3, IV, 375, 376, 377, Perth to Halifax, 16/21.iii.39; *FRUS, 1939*, I, pp. 47–48, Phillips to Hull, 17.iii.38; *ibid.*, pp. 82–83, Lane to Hull, 30.iii.39; *DGFP*, D, V, 300, 310; *DGFP*, D, VI, 55, fn. 1; Breccia, pp. 49–51, fns 72–74.
20. Ciano, *Diario*, 18/19.iii.39.
21. *DDF*, 2, XV, 91, 20.iii.39, Daladier to Baudouin.
22. Ciano, *Diario*, 17/19.iii.39; Ciano to Indelli, 19.iii.39; Breccia, *Jugoslavia*, pp. 54–55.
23. *DGFP*, D, VI, 45.
24. *DGFP*, D, VI, 55, 20.iii.34.
25. Ciano, *Diario*, 20.iii.39.
26. Ciano, *Diario*, 21.iii.39; *DBFP*, 3, IV, 376, 21.iii.39.
27. *DGFP*, D, VI, 52.
28. *DGFP*, D, VI, Appendix I (ii).
29. *DGFP*, D, VI, 100.
30. Watt, 'Rome-Berlin axis', *Rev.Pol.*, 1960.
31. Ciano, *Diario*, 22.iii.39.
32. Ryan, *Last of the Dragomans*, passim.
33. Guerra, *Ciano*, p. 363.
34. Ciano, *Diario*, 25/28.iv.38; Guerra, *Ciano*, pp. 365–66; *CDP*, pp. 203–05.
35. Ciano, *Diario*, 17/19.v.38.
36. Ciano, *Diario*, 8.ii.39; Mack-Smith, *Mussolini's Roman Empire*, p. 250.
37. Ciano, *Diario*, 1.iv.39.
38. Guerra, *Ciano*, p. 370.
39. Ciano, *Diario*, 15/16.i.39; *CDP*, pp. 370–73.
40. Ciano, *Diario*, 25.iii.39.
41. Ciano, *Diario*, 27.iii.39.
42. *DBFP*, D, V, 133, Ryan to Ingram, 11.iv.39; *DDF*, 2, XV, 250, Massigli to Bonnet, 4.iv.39.
43. *DBFP*, 3, V, 133, Ryan to Ingram, 11.iv.39; *ibid.*, 159, Ryan to Halifax, 19.iv.39; *GWB*, 39, Metaxas to Rome, 9.iv.39.
44. *DBFP*, 3, V, 91, Waterlow to Halifax, 8.iv.39.
45. Quartararo, 'Canale segreto', pp. 685–86; idem, *Roma*, p. 448.
46. Quartararo, *Roma*, p. 449.
47. *DBFP*, 3, V, 81; Quartararo, *Roma*, p. 782, fn. 101.
48. *DBFP*, 3, V, 82.
49. Ciano, *Diario*, 7.iv.39.
50. *DBFP*, 3, V, 138, Halifax to Knatchbull-Hugessen, 12.iv.39.
51. Kroll, p. 108.
52. Koliopoulos, pp. 89–91.
53. Metaxas diary, 4/5.iii.39 cited in Koliopoulos, p. 106.
54. *PRO* FO 371/23769, Sergent to Lloyd, 25.ii.39. Lloyd Papers, *GLLD* 19/9.
55. *DBFP*, 3, IV, 425, 439, 497.
56. *DBFP*, 3, V, 97, Waterlow to Halifax, 2.30 a.m., 9.iv.39.
57. *DBFP*, 3, V, 111, Halifax to Waterlow, 9.iv.39.
58. *DBFP*, 3, V, 97; Metaxas diary, 9.iv.39, Koliopoulos, p. 110, fn. 5.
59. *DGFP*, D, VI, 165, Erdmannsdorff to A.A., 6.iv.39.
60. Szembek diary, 13.iv.39; *DDF*, 2, XV, 376, Thierry to Bonnet, 13.iv.39.

61. Cǎlinescu diary, 8.iv.39, cited Lungu: Gafencu to Cretzianu, 7.iv.39, Moisuc, 'Imperativul' (1970) p. 378 and fn. 56.
62. *DGFP*, D, VI, Fabricius to A.A., 11.iv.39.
63. *DDF*, 2, XV, 334, Massigli to Bonnet, 10.iv.39; Moisuc, 'Imperativul', (1970) pp. 376–77; Calafteanu, 'Eforturile' (1977), p. 365.
64. *DBFP*, 3, V, 20, 21, 22, 23, Phipps to Halifax, 7.iv.39.
65. *DDF*, 2, XV, 260, 5.iv.39; *DBFP*, 3, V, 96, Phipps to Cadogan, 8.iv.39.
66. *DBFP*, 3, V, 24 and enclosure, 8.iv.39.
67. *DDF*, 2, XV, 341, 11.iv.39, Coulondre to Bonnet..
68. *DDF*, 2, XV, 301, 330, de Vaux Saint-Cyr to Bonnet, 8/10.iv.39; *ibid.*, 322, Noël to Bonnet, 10.iv.39.
69. *DBFP*, 3, V, 96.
70. *DDF*, 2, XV, 243, 302, 4/8.iv.39.
71. *DDF*, 2, XV, 390, 391, 404, 424.
72. *DBFP*, 3, V, 73, 76, 78, 79, 85.
73. *DDF*, 2, XV, 316; *DBFP*, 3, V, 106.
74. *DDF*, 2, XV, 354.
75. Zay, *Carnets Secrets*, 11.iv.39.
76. *DDF*, 2, XV, 354, Bonnet to Corbin, 12.iv.39.
77. *DBFP*, 3, V, 144, Halifax to Phipps, 12.iv.39; *ibid.*, 48, 49, 57, 66, 12/13.iv.39; *DDF*, 2, XV, 358, Corbin to Bonnet, 12.iv.39; *PRO*, CAB 27/624, FPC 41st Mtg., 10.iv.39; *CAB* 28/29, Cab 20(39), 13.iv.39.
78. *DBFP*, 3, IV, 601, 602, 603, R. Hoare to Halifax, 2.iv.39.
79. *PRO*, CAB 23/98, Cab 20(39), 13.iv.39.
80. Quartararo, *Roma*, pp. 452–53.
81. Chamberlain papers, NC 18/1/1094, Chamberlain to Hilda Chamberlain.
82. *PRO*, CAB 27/624, FPC 41st Mtg., 10.iv.39; *ibid.*, CAB 28/98, Cab 20(39), 13.iv.39.
83. Lloyd papers, GLLD 19/11, note (by Lord Lloyd) 13.iv.39.
84. *DBFP*, 3, V, 57, 58.
85. *H.C. Deb.*, 346, col. 13.
86. *DDF*, 2, XV, 370.

Chapter 13   *Stalin begins to calculate*

This chapter is based on the same sources as those listed at the head of the footnotes for Chapter VIII. Additional sources used are: Cienciala, *Poland and the Western Powers*; Breccia, *Jugoslavia*; Toscano, 'L'Italia e gli accordi tedesco-sovietici', *RSPI*, 1951; Newman, *March 1939*.

1. *DBFP*, 3, IV, 537, 538, 551, 558, 559, 561.
2. *DBFP*, 3, IV, 565.
3. *DBFP*, 3, IV, 589; *SPE*, I, 200.
4. Aster, 'Maiski', pp. 341–43, 344–45.
5. Aster, 'Maiski', p. 341.
6. *SPE*, I, 190.
7. *SPE*, I, 203; *DBFP*, B, IV, 597.
8. *SPE*, I, 202, 206, 207.
9. Nekrich, 'The Trial of Ivan Maiski', *Survey*, 1976.
10. *SPE*, I, 204, 205, 211.
11. *SPE*, I, 210.
12. *SPE*, I, 223, 11.iv.39.
13. *SPE*, I, 130, 20.ii.39.
14. *SPE*, I, 186; *DBFP*, 3, IV, 505.
15. *DBFP*, 3, IV, 519, 531, 593.
16. *DBFP*, 3, IV, 593 enclosure; *SPE*, I, 191.
17. *DBFP*, 3, IV, 545.
18. *DBFP*, 3, IV, 4, 4.iv.39.
19. *PRO* (CAB 53/11), COS, European Appreciation, 1939–40, 20.ii.39, DP (P) 44 (39).
20. *DBFP*, D, IV, 976.
21. *PRO*, FO 371/23061, Minutes on C 3928/3356/18.

22. Chamberlain papers, NC 18/1/1893, Chamberlain to Ida Chamberlain, 9.iv.39.
23. *DBFP*, 3, IV, 484, 22.iii.39.
24. *PRO CAB* 27/624, FPC 38th Mtg., 27.iii.39.
25. Polish archives, London, MFA B-6; note by Lubienski, 1.iv.39, cited in Cienciala, p. 229.
26. *DBFP*, B, IV, 16.
27. Cienciala, p. 238.
28. *SPE*, I. 192; *FRUS, 1939*, II, 934, Packer to Hall, 16.iv.39; Degras, III, 325–26; *DBFP*, III, 300, Enclosure, Le Gallienne to Orde, 21.iv.39, Enclosure 2, Soviet declaration, 28.iii.39.
29. *DBFP*, 3, V, 300, Enclosure 3, Estonian Embassy, Moscow, to Soviet Government, 7.iv.39.
30. *SPE*, I, 214; *DBFP*, 3, V, 19.
31. *SPE*, I, 226, 11.iv.39; *DBFP*, B, V, 42.
32. *FRUS, 1939*, I, pp. 125–26, 11.ii.39.
33. *SPE*, I, 226.
34. *SPE*, I, 230, 231; *DBFP*, 3, V, 166.
35. *DDF*, 2, XV, 349, 11.iv.39, Bonnet to Naggiar.
36. *SPE*, I, 224, Litvinov to Maisky, 11.iv.39.
37. *SPE*, I, 233; *DBFP*, 3, V, 182, 15.iv.39.
38. *DDF*, 2, XV, 405, Noël to Bonnet, 411, de Vaux Saint-Cyr to Bonnet, 15.iv.39.
39. *DDF*, 2, XV, 387, Bonnet to Naggiar, 14.iv.39; *SPE*, I, 232.
40. *DBFP*, 3, V, 201; *SPE*, I, 238, 239.
41. Gafencu, *Last Days of Europe*, passim.
42. *DGFP*, D, VI, 320, 3.v.39.
43. *DDF*, 2, XV, 376.
44. *SPE*, I, 234.
45. *SPE*, I, 246, 21.iv.39.
46. *SPE*, I, 246.
47. *DDF*, 2, XV, 527, Massigli to Bonnet, 30.iv.39; *SPE*, II, 264, Potemkin to Moscow, 29.iv.39.
48. *SPE*, II, 264, 265, 269, 271, 273, 29/30.iv./3.v.39.
49. Maisky, *Who Helped Hitler?* pp. 119–23; Bilainkin, *Maiski*, p. 246.
50. See p. 71 above.
51. Renzetti to Attolico, 7.v.39, Toscano, *L'Italia*, pp. 577–79, n. 24-bis.
52. Haydar Aktar to Ankara, 14.iv.39, Breccia, *Jugoslavia*, p. 100, n. 31.
53. Kleist, *Zwischen Hitler und Stalin*, pp. 26–30.
54. *IMT FE*, pp. 6079 ff., Oshima testimony, pp. 35642 ff., Shiratori testimony; *DGFP*, D, VI, 270, Ribbentrop to Ott, 26.iv.39; Attolico to Ciano, *Le Origine diplomatiche del Patto d'Acciaio*, p. 125.
55. *DGFP*, D, VI, 215, 217.
56. *DGFP*, D, VI, 233, 239, 19/21.iv.39.
57. Watt, 'John Herbert King', *Int.Nat.Sec.*, 1988.

Chapter 14   Decision in May

Save where otherwise stated, this chapter is based on the following sources: (1) On the Anglo-Soviet negotiations: Aster, *1939*; Watt, 'An Intelligence Failure', *Intelligence and National Security*, 1989; *idem*, 'John Herbert King', *Int.Nat.Sec.*, 1988; (2) On the German-Soviet negotiations: Weinberg, *Germany and the Soviet Union*; Hilger and Meyer, *The Incompatible Allies*; Toscano, 'L'Italia e gli accordi tedesco-sovietici dell'agosto 39', *RSPI*, 1951; (3) On the German-Italian-Japanese negotiations: Toscano, *Le Origine diplomatiche del Patto d'Acciaio*; Sommer, *Deutschland und Japan zwischen den Mächten*; Magistrati, *L'Italia a Berlino*.

1. *DBFP*, 3, V, 353; *DGFP*, D, VI, 325.
2. *DBFP*, 3, V, 359; Toscano, 'L'Italia', p. 571, 573–75, Rosso to Ciano, 5.v.39.
3. *FRUS*, 1939, I, pp. 248–51, Bullitt to Hull.
4. *PRO*, CAB 27/624, FPC 44th Mtg., 25.iv.39.
5. *DBFP*, 3, V, 222, Kennard to Halifax, 19.iv.39.
6. *DBFP*, 3, V, 195, Snow to Halifax, 17.iv.39; *BDFA, SU*, XV, 57.
7. *DBFP*, 3, V, 285, Record of conversation, 25.iv.39; *PRO*, CAB 23/99, Cab 22(39), 26.iv.39.
8. *DDF*, 2, XV, 482, 24.iv.39; *DBFP*, 3, V, 280, enclosure.

9. *DBFP*, 3, V, 305, Halifax to Phipps, 25.iv.39.
10. *BDFA, SU*, XV, 61, Col. Firebrace to Seeds, 12.v.39.
11. *DBFP*, 3, V, 389.
12. *DBFP*, 3, V, 389, 397.
13. *DBFP*, 3, V, 350, Phipps to Halifax, 3.v.39.
14. *DBFP*, 3, V, 351, Phipps to Halifax, 3.v.39.
15. *DBFP*, 3, V, 372; *DDF*, 2, XVI, 54.
16. *DDF*, 2, XVI, 100, Annex (memorandum by Capt. Stehlin), 6.v.39; Stehlin, *Témoignage*, pp. 147–52.
17. *DBFP*, 3, V, 413, 8.v.39.
18. *PRO*, FO 371/22972, Kirkpatrick minute, C 6794/15/18, 6.v.39.
19. *Ibid.*, Strang minute.
20. *PRO*, FO 371/22972, C 6785/15/18, Roberts minute [*DBFP*, 3, V, 413].
21. Toscano, *Origine*, pp. 253–54, Attolico to Ciano, 25.iv.39; RIIA, *Documents 1939–1946*, I, 156–58; Sommer, *Deutschland und Japan*, pp. 203–204 and fn. 43–44.
22. *DGFP*, D, VI, 178.
23. *DGFP*, D, VI, 205, 211, 15/16.v.39.
24. *PWB*, 78; *DGFP*, D, VI, 334 and enclosure.
25. *DGFP*, D, VI, 306, 326.
26. Magistrati, *L'Italia a Berlino*, pp. 339–42; Schmitt, *Statist*, p. 437. Dollmann, *Interpreter*, p. 155.
27. Ciano, *Diario*, 6.v.39.
28. Ciano, *Diario*, 7.v.39.
29. Hilger and Meyer, pp. 293–97; Teske, *Koestring*, pp. 133–36.
30. *DGFP*, D, VI, 382, 15.v.39.
31. *SPE*, I, 235, 236, 15/16.iv.39.
32. *DBFP*, 3, V, 421, 436; *SPE*, II, 278, 279.
33. *SPE*, II, 271, 8.v.39.
34. *SPE*, II, 289.
35. *DBFP*, 3, V, 533, Seeds to Oliphant, 16.v.39.
36. *DBFP*, 3, V, 433.
37. *DBFP*, 3, V, 481; *SPE*, II, 288.
38. *SPE*, II, 283.
39. *DBFP*, 3, V, 494.
40. *SPE*, II, 268, 281, 284, 2/9/10.v.39.
41. *DBFP*, 3, V, 520, 530; *SPE*, II, 291.
42. Chamberlain Papers, NC 18/1/1098, Chamberlain to Hilda, 14.v.39; *ibid.*, NC 18/1/1000, Chamberlain to Ida, 21.v.39; *ibid.*, NC 18/1/1101, Chamberlain to Hilda, 28.v.39.
43. Watt, 'British Domestic Politics and the Onset of War. Notes for a discussion', in *Les Relations Franco-Britanniques de 1935 à 1939*.
44. PRO, CAB 53/11, COS 295th, 296th Mtgs, 16.v.39.
45. *DBFP*, 3, V, 531, 535, 16/17.v.39.
46. *PRO* FO 371/20366, C 7169/3365/18.
47. Maisky, *Who helped Hitler?*, pp. 125–26.
48. PRO, CAB 23/59, Cab 27(39), 10.v.39; *ibid.*, Cab 28(39), 12.v.39; *ibid.*, Cab 30(39), 24.v.39; *PRO* CAB 27/625, FPC, 47th Mtg., 16.v.39; *ibid.*, FPC, 48th Mtg., 19.v.39.
49. *PRO* FO 371/20366, C 7169/3356/18, 16.v.39; *DBFP*, 3, V, 527, and fn. 2; *ibid.*, 589, fn. 1; Vansittart Papers, Vnst. 3/2.
50. *DBFP*, 3, V, 520, 15.v.39.
51. *DBFP*, 3, V, 569.
52. *DBFP*, 3, V, 556, 576, 19/20.v.39.
53. *DBFP*, 3, V, 582.
54. *DBFP*, 3, V, 620; *ibid.*, 567, 595.
55. *DBFP*, 3, V, 581, 582; *SPE*, I, 303, 294.
56. *DBFP*, 3, V, 589.
57. *PRO*, CAB 23/99, Cab 30(39), 24.v.39.
58. Watt, 'An Intelligence Failure', *Int.Nat.Sec.*, 1989.
59. Cadogan diary, 21.v.39.
60. *H.C. Deb.*, 347, col. 2267.
61. Chamberlain Papers, NC 18/1/1101, Chamberlain to Hilda Chamberlain, 28.v.39.

62. *DBFP*, 3, V, 643, Corbin to Halifax, 16.v.39; *DDF*, 2, XVI, 286.
63. *DBFP*, 3, V, 657; *DDF*, 2, XVI, 295; *SPE*, II, 311.
64. *DBFP*, 3, V, 665, 670.
65. Aster, 'Maiski', p. 550.
66. *DGFP*, D, VI, 362, 8.v.39.
67. *DGFP*, D, VI, 381, 15.v.39.
68. *DGFP*, D, VI, 332.
69. *DGFP*, D, VI, 351.
70. Hagemann, *Der Presselenkung im dritten Reich*, p. 160, n. 189.
71. *DGFP*, D, VI, 406.
72. Hoppe, p. 67.
73. *DGFP*, D, VI, 424, Schulenburg to Weizsäcker, 22.v.39.
74. *DGFP*, D, VI, 414, fn. 2.
75. *DGFP*, D, VI, 414, 21.v.39.
76. *DGFP*, D, VI, 410, 427, 444.
77. *DGFP*, D, VI, 383, 15.v.39.
78. *DGFP*, D, VI, 371.
79. Ciano, *Diario*, 18.v.39.
80. *DGFP*, D, VI, 386.
81. *DGFP*, D, VI, 410.
82. Domarus, II, pp. 1191–94; Magistrati, *L'Italia a Berlino*, pp. 346–48.
83. Ciano, *Diario*, 21.v.39.
84. Dollman, p. 159.
85. Domarus, II, 1195.
86. Washington microfilms, T-77, Roll 775 contains the second copy.
87. *DGFP*, D, VI, 433; IMT, XXXVII, pp. 546–56, 79-L.
88. *DGFP*, D, VI, 437, 23.v.39.
89. *DGFP*, D, VI. 447, Ribbentrop to O.H., 28.v.39; *DDI*, 8, XII, 14, Auriti to Ciano, 25.v.39.
90. *DGFP*, C, VI, 437.
91. *DGFP*, D, VI, 441; Sommer, *Deutschland und Japan*, p. 244 and fn. 33.
92. *DGFP*, D, VI, 442, 26.v.39.
93. *DDI*, 8, XII, 48, Attolico to Ciano, 27.v.39.
94. *DGFP*, D, VI, 447.
95. *DDI*, 8, XII, 53; Weizsäcker, *Errinerungen*, p. 331.
96. *DGFP*, D, VI, 447.
97. *DGFP*, D, VI, 441, 449, 450, 451, 452.
98. *SPE*, II, 314.
99. *DGFP*, D, VI, 463.

Chapter 15   Muddled signals from Washington

1. *DGFP*, D, VII, 265.
2. *DGFP*, D, VI, 107, 27.iii.39, Thomsen to A.A.
3. *DGFP*, D, VI, 222, 17.iv.39, Wiedemann to Weizsäcker.
4. *DGFP*, D, VI, 403, 17.v.39, Thomsen to A.A.
5. *DGFP*, D, VI, 107.
6. Blum, *Morgenthau*, pp. 82–83.
7. Pritchard, p. 183, citing US Naval Historical Division, and *PRO*, ADM 116/3922.
8. Pritchard, pp. 184–88; Lowe, p. 96–99; Roskill, *British Naval Policy*, II, pp. 496–97; *PRO*, Adm. 116/3922.
9. Halifax to Lindsay, *DBFP*, 3, V, 169.
10. Bullitt to F.D.R., 11.iv.39, SD 740.00/770, cited Macdonald, *The U.S., Britain and Appeasement*, p. 148; Bullitt to F.D.R., 10.iv.39, *FRUS, 1939*, I, p. 123.
11. Bullitt to F.D.R., 10.iv.39, SD 740.00/768; the same to the same, 11.iv.39, SD 740.00/770, both cited Macdonald, *The U.S., Britain and Appeasement*, pp. 148–49.
12. Leahy diary, 11.iv.39, cited Macdonald, *The U.S., Britain and Appeasement*, p. 156.
13. *DDF*, 2, XV, 214 and annexes, 5.iv.39.
14. *DDF*, 2, XV, 303.
15. Dallek, p. 186; Berle, *Negotiating the Rapids*, entries of 13/15/19.iv.39; Moltmann,

'Roosevelt's Friedensappel'; Langer and Gleason, *Struggle for Isolation*, pp. 75-90; Hull, *Memoirs*, I, 620-23.

16. *DDF*, 2, XV, 328, St Quentin to Bonnet, 10.iv.39.
17. Macdonald, *The U.S., Britain and Appeasement*, pp. 150-51, citing Hull papers and Messersmith papers; A. P. Young, *The X Documents*, pp. 185-86.
18. Bullitt to Hull, 10.iv.39, *For the President*, pp. 335-39; Bonnet to St Quentin, 10.iv.39, *DDF*, 2, XV, 317.
19. St Quentin to Bonnet, 11.iv.39, *DDF*, 2, XV, 338.
20. Schewe, IX, 1721; *FRUS, 1939*, I, pp. 130-33; *DGFP*, D, VI, 200.
21. *FRUS, 1939*, I, pp. 135-36, McVeagh (Dublin) to Hull, 17.iv.39.
22. *DGFP*, D, VI, 211, 16.iv.39.
23. Bullitt to Hull, 18.iv.39, *FRUS, 1939*, I, pp. 142-43; Noress (Kovno) to Hull, 19.iv.39, *ibid.*, p. 146; Dept. of State memorandum, 16.iv.39, Schewe, IX, 1722; Phillips to *F.D.R.*, Schewe IX, 1742.
24. *DGFP*, D, VI, 213, circular telegram, 17.iv.39.
25. Gordon to Hull, 21.iv.39, SD 740.00/1052, cited Moltmann, 'Roosevelt's Friedensappel', p. 105.
26. Moltmann, 'Roosevelt's Friedensappel', pp. 100-105.
27. Geist to Hull, 28.iv.39, *FRUS, 1939*, I, pp. 158-59; Lamont to Miss Le Hand, 28.iv.39, Schewe, IX, 1760; William E. Dodd to F.D.R., 28.iv.39, *ibid.*, 1762; *FRUS, 1939*, I, p. 162, 29.iv.39.
28. Cited Dallek, p. 187, from Hiram Johnson papers.
29. Watt, *Succeeding John Bull*, pp. 92-93; Compton, *The Eagle and the Swastika*, pp. 105-24; Wedemeyer, pp. 10-11.
30. Thomsen to A.A., 26.iv.39, *DGFP*, D, VI, 268; Boetticher to A.A., 25.viii.39, *DGFP*, D, VII, 260.
31. Divine, *Illusion of Neutrality*, pp. 246-60; Cole, *Roosevelt and the Isolationists*, pp. 312-15.
32. Divine, *Illusion of Neutrality*, p. 260; Hull, *Memoirs*, I, p. 642.
33. Bullitt to Hull, 10.v.39, *FRUS, 1939*, I, p. 185; Divine, *Illusion of Neutrality*, p. 260.
34. Divine, *Illusion of Neutrality*, p. 262.
35. Divine, *Illusion of Neutrality*, pp. 261-62.
36. Hull, *Memoirs*, vol. I, p. 643.
37. Langer and Gleason, pp. 138-39; Ickes, *Secret Diary*, II, p. 677; Hull, *Memoirs*, I, p. 643; Divine, *Illusion of Neutrality*, p. 263.
38. Divine, *Illusion of Neutrality*, pp. 267-74.
39. Phillips to Hull, 5.vii.39, *FRUS, 1939*, I, pp. 663-64; Attolico to Ciano, 26.vii.39, *DDI*, 8, XII, 687.
40. Kirk to Hull, 5.vii.39, *FRUS, 1939*, I, pp. 665-67.
41. Bullitt to Hull, 5.vii.39, SD 811.04418/454 cited in Divine, *Illusion of Neutrality*, p. 275.
42. Bullitt to Hull, 5.vii.39, *FRUS, 1939*, I, pp. 281-82.
43. Berle, *Negotiating the Rapids*, entries of 26/28/30.vi.39.
44. Divine, *Illusion of Neutrality*, pp. 276-78; Patterson, 'Eating Humble Pie', *Historian*, 1969.
45. McKenna, *Borah*; Maddox, *Borah*, passim.
46. Watt, *Succeeding John Bull*, p. 25 reviews the literature on this controversy.
47. Cole, *Roosevelt and the Isolationists*, p. 316.
48. Maddox, *Borah*, p. 239.
49. Hull, *Memoirs*, I, pp. 649-51; Divine, *Illusion of Neutrality*, pp. 280-81; Cole, *Roosevelt and the Isolationists*, pp. 317-18; Israel, *Nevada's Key Pitman*, p. 165.
50. Divine, *Illusion of Neutrality*, p. 251; Alsop and Kintner, *American White Paper*, pp. 58-59; Mazuzan, 'Warren R. Austin's Memorandum', *Vermont History*, 1974.
51. Maddox, *Borah*, p. 241; McKenna, *Borah*, p. 364; Cole, *Roosevelt and the Isolationists*, p. 318.
52. McFarland, 'Woodring v. Johnson', passim.
53. Lindsay to Halifax, 30.vi.39, PRO, FO 371/23901, W 10051/9058/49 cited Baptiste, 'The British Grant', *Caribbean Studies*, 1976, p. 7.
54. PRO, FO 371/23902, W 10369/9805/75, Lindsay to Halifax, 8.vii.39, cited Baptiste, pp. 20-22.
55. Baptiste, 'The British Grant', pp. 24-25; Watt, 'U.S. Strategic Anxieties', *JRUSI*, 1963.
56. Kennedy to Hull, 5.vii.39, *FRUS, 1939*, I, pp. 282-83.

Chapter 16   The struggle for the Balkans: Round 1 – Turkey

Where not otherwise stated, this chapter is based on the following sources: Massigli, *La Turquie devant la Guerre*; Knatchbull-Hugessen, *Diplomat in War and Peace*; Papen, *Memoirs*; Kroll, *Lebenserrinerungen*; Hoppe, *Bulgarien*; Deringil, 'Turkey's diplomatic position', *Boğazici Universitesi Dergisi*, 1980–81; Krecker, *Deutschland und die Türkei*; Zhivkova, *Anglo-Turkish relations*; Ataöv, 'The policy of the Great Powers towards Turkey', *Studia Balcanica*, 1973; *Survey of International Affairs*, vols for 1936–1938; Fleury, 'L'affaire du sandjak d'Alexandrette, 1921–1939', *RI*, 1979.

 1. *DBFP*, 3, V, 247.
 2. Weber, *Evasive Neutral*, p. 21, Loraine to Halifax, 16.xi.38; Campus, *Intelegere Balcanica*, p. 254, fn. 97 and p. 262; Popisteanu, *Romania si Antanta Balcanica*, p. 238.
 3. *DDF*, 2, XII, 690, 694, 788.
 4. *DDI*, I, XII, 108, 699, 734.
 5. Kroll, p. 108.
 6. *DBFP*, 3, IV, 423, 424, Knatchbull-Hugessen to Halifax, 19.iii.39.
 7. *DBFP*, 3, IV, 472, Halifax to Knatchbull-Hugessen, 21.iii.39.
 8. Ataöv, *Studia Balcanica*, 1973, pp. 326–27.
 9. *DDF*, 2, XV, 158.
10. *DGFP*, D, VI, 72; Kroll, pp. 108–09.
11. *DGFP*, D, VI, 32.
12. *DDF*, 2, XV, 198; Massigli, pp. 120–21.
13. *DBFP*, 3, V, 119, 120, 121, 124, Knatchbull-Hugessen to Halifax, 10.iv.39; Massigli, p. 132.
14. *DBFP*, 3, V, 128, 138, Halifax to Knatchbull-Hugessen, 11/12.iv.39; *ibid.*, 149, 151, 152, 153, Knatchbull-Hugessen to Halifax, 13.iv.39; Massigli, p. 139.
15. *DBFP*, 3, V, 155.
16. *DBFP*, 3, V, 199, enclosures 1 and 2, Saracoğlu to Knatchbull-Hugessen.
17. Hoppe, p. 62.
18. *DGFP*, D, VI, 673.
19. Hoppe, p. 56.
20. *DDF*, 2, XVI, 85.
21. *DBFP*, 3, V, 278, Record of Conversation with M. Gafencu.
22. *DBFP*, 3, V, 62, 63, 13.iv.39; *ibid.*, 173, 14.iv.39.
23. *DBFP*, 3, V, 278, 348; *DDF*, 2, XV, 505.
24. *DBFP*, 3, V, 299.
25. Hoppe, pp. 62–63.
26. *DBFP*, 3, V, 271.
27. *DBFP*, 3, V, 276, 24.iv.39.
28. *DBFP*, 3, V, 286, 287, 291, 26.iv.39.
29. *DBFP*, 3, V, 309, 311, 391, 29.iv/6.v.39.
30. Kroll, p. 110.
31. Kroll, p. 110.
32. *Breach of Security*, pp. 59–61.
33. *DGFP*, D, VI, 259.
34. Massigli, pp. 169–70; Papen, *Memoirs*, pp. 443, 450, 451; Knatchbull-Hugessen, *Diplomat*, p. 146; *DBFP*, 3, V, 302, fn. 1.
35. *DDF*, 2, XV, 511; *DBFP*, 3, V, 302.
36. *DGFP*, D, VI, 286; Massigli, p. 171.
37. *DGFP*, D, VI, 288.
38. *DGFP*, D, VI, 289, 303 fn. 6, 305.
39. *DGFP*, D, VI, 286.
40. *DGFP*, D, VI, 317; Ciano, *Diario*, 3.v.39; *DBFP*, 3, V, 387.
41. *DGFP*, D, VI, 317, 324, 333, 3/4/5.v.39.
42. Massigli, p. 172.
43. *DGFP*, D, VI, 333, fn. 2.
44. *DGFP*, D, VI, 341; *CDP*, pp. 283–86.
45. *DGFP*, D, VI, 336.
46. *DDF*, 2, XVI, 25, 37, 39, 110; Massigli, pp. 140–41.
47. *DIMK*, IV, 127, 134, General Werth to Csáky, Csáky to Werth, 8/11.v.39.

48. *DIMK*, IV, 76, 82, 13/15.iv.39.
49. *DIMK*, IV, 102, 112; Breccia, *Jugoslavia*, pp. 95–97, fn. 25, 27.
50. *DIMK*, IV, 79, 14.iv.39.
51. Ciano, *Diario*, 18/19/20.iv.39; *DIMK*, IV, 90.
52. *DIMK*, IV, 115, 116; *DGFP*, D, VI, 372, 376.
53. *DGFP*, D, VI, 142, Wiehl to Belgrade, 6.iv.39.
54. Ciano, *Diario*, 22.iv.39.
55. *DGFP*, D, VI, 262, 271, 25/26.iv.39.
56. *SPE*, II, 264, 265, 269, 271, 273; *DDF*, 2, XV, 527; Moisuc, 1971, p. 377 citing Stoica to Bucharest, 1.v.39; *DBFP*, 3, V, 322, 343, 357, 378, 379; Zhivkova, pp. 98–99.
57. *DGFP*, D, VI, 346; Hoppe, p. 64.
58. *DGFP*, D, VI, 349.
59. Paul de Véou, *Chrétiens en péril au Moussa Degh*, Paris 1939, pp. 170–71, cited in Massigli, pp. 128–29, fn. 1.
60. Massigli, pp. 53–54.
61. Massigli, pp. 107–08.
62. Massigli, p. 123.
63. *DDF*, 2, XV, 243, 302, 4/8.iv.39; Massigli, pp. 124–25.
64. Massigli, p. 150.
65. Massigli, pp. 159–61; *DBFP*, 3, V, 498.
66. *H.C. Deb.*, 347, Col. 953.

Chapter 17   *The struggle for the Balkans: Round 2 – Yugoslavia*

1. Knatchbull-Hugessen diary, entry of 9.v.39.
2. *DDF*, 2, XVI, 6.v.39, Thierry to Bonnet.
3. *DGFP*, D, VI, 227, 234, 18/19.iv.39; *DDF*, 2, XV, 453, 455, 464, 20/21.iv.39; *DDF*, 2, XV, 505, 22.iv.39. Gafencu.
4. *DDF*, 2, XV, 433; XVI, 4, fn. 2, 26, 46.
5. Szembek diary, 19.iv.39.
6. *DDF*, 2, XV, 422; XVI, 51.
7. *DDF*, 2, XV, 469, 21.iv.39.
8. Hoptner, p. 146, citing memorandum of 8.v.39; Breccia, p. 101.
9. Ciano, *Diario*, 10.v.39.
10. *DDF*, 2, XVI, 132, 133, 9/10.v.39; *DBFP*, 3, V, 440, 458, 10.v.39.
11. *DDF*, 2, XVI, 267, 277, 24/25.v.39; p. 522, fn. 2, 23.v.39.
12. *DBFP*, 3, V, 526, 553, 596, 16/19.v.39.
13. *DBFP*, 3, V, 618, 626, 25/26.v.39.
14. *DBFP*, 3, V, 602, 23.v.39.
15. *DBFP*, 3, V, 663, 29.v.39.
16. *DBFP*, 3, V, 647, 27.v.39.
17. *DBFP*, 3, V, 626, 633.
18. *DBFP*, 3, VI, 40, 13.vi.39.
19. *DDI*, 8, XII, 145, 7.vi.39.
20. *DBFP*, 3, VI, 28, 40, 12/13.vi.39.
21. *DBFP*, 3, VI, 13, fn. 1, 8.vi.39.
22. *DBFP*, D, VI, 544, 19.vi.39.
23. Breccia, p. 154, fn. 28, citing Simovic and Papagos memoirs.
24. *DGFP*, D, VI, 379, 27.iv.39; 683, 17.vii.39.
25. *DDF*, 2, XVI, 243, 24.v.39; 286, 25.v.39; 324, 31.v.39; 346, 3.vi.39.
26. *DDF*, 2, XVII, 47, 29.vi.39.
27. Balfour and Mackay, pp. 173–78.
28. *DDF*, 2, XVI, 327, 1.vi.39; 358, 369, 6/8.vi.39.
29. Breccia, p. 127, fn. 37.
30. Engel diary, 28.vi.39.
31. *Dokumenti o Jugoslavija*, 7, cited Breccia, p. 155, fn. 29; Wuescht, pp. 289–92, doc. 5.
32. *PRO*, FO 371/23876, Halifax, 21.v.39, cited Breccia, p. 155, fn. 30.
33. *Dokumenti o Jugoslavija*, 7, cited Breccia, p. 157; Wuescht, pp. 289–92.
34. *DDF*, 2, XVII, 144, 7.vii.39.

35. *DDF*, 2, XVII, 105, 6.vii.39.
36. *DDF*, 2, XVII, 213, 15.vii.39.
37. *DGFP*, D, VI, 573, 586, 615, 620, 27/29.vi.39, 5.vii.39; Yugoslav archives cited Breccia, p. 152, fn. 26.
38. *DGFP*, D, VI, 683, 17.vii.39.
39. Hoppe, pp. 65–66; Breccia, p. 151.
40. *Breach of Security*, pp. 68–69.
41. *DKJG*, passim, but especially 38, French military attaché, Belgrade, to Daladier, 18.iii.39; *ibid.*, 39, memorandum by W. Knoll, 9.vi.39; *ibid.*, 41, de Boisenges, Belgrade, to Bonnet, 9.vii.39.
42. *FRUS, 1939*, II, pp. 887–90, Bullitt to Hull, 27.v.39.
43. Breccia, pp. 167–68.
44. *DGFP*, D, VI, 691; *Aprilski Rat 1941*, 77, 80, cited Breccia, p. 160, fn. 38.
45. *DDI*, 8, XII, 628, Talamo to Ciano, 21.vii.39.
46. *DGFP*, D, VI, 784; *DGFP*, D, VII, 43; *DDI*, 8, XIII, 1–4; Ciano, *Diario*, entry of 12.viii.39.
47. *DGFP*, D, VII, 16, 10.viii.39.
48. *DDI*, 8, XII, 648, Italian Naval Intelligence, 22.vii.39.
49. Vauhnik, *Memoiren eines Militärattachés*, p. 187.
50. *DBFP*, 3, VI, 393, 421, 422, 21/24.vii.39; *FRUS, 1939*, I, pp. 287–88, Kennedy to Hull, 20.vii.39; Balfour and Mackay, *op. cit.*
51. *DDF*, 2, XVII, 412, 417, 3.vii.39; *DGFP*, D, VI, 656, 673, 689, 12/15/29.vii.39; *DBFP*, 3, VI, 393, 27.vii.39; *DDI*, 8, XII, 629, 757, 21/27.vii./3.viii.39.
52. Hoppe, p. 63, fn. 18, citing Bulow to Clodius, 2228/47504–05.
53. See, for example, *DDI*, 8, XII, 156; *DGFP*, D, VI, 500, 508.
54. Hoppe, p. 65, fn. 30.
55. Hoppe, pp. 67–68.
56. *DGFP*, D, VI, 529, Woermann memo, 15.vi.39.
57. *DGFP*, D, VI, 617, 618, 6/7.vii.39.
58. *DGFP*, D, VI, 689, 20.vii.39.
59. *Breach of Security*, p. 67.
60. *DDI*, 8, XII, 636, 21.vii.39, Talamo to Ciano.
61. *DDI*, 8, XII, 632, 21.vii.39.
62. *DDI*, 8, XII, 752, 3.vii.39, Talamo to Ciano.
63. *DDF*, 2, XVII, 412, 417, 3.viii.39; *DGFP*, D, VI, 673, 689, 14/20.vii.39; *DGFP*, D, VII, 1, 12, 60, 9/12/14.viii.39.
64. Churchill College, Lloyd papers, GLLD 19/11, Ingrams (FO) to Lloyd, 16.v.39, R 3982/2905/67.
65. van Kessel (Ph.D. 1972), pp. 351–58.
66. *DGFP*, D, VI, 567, 25.vi.39; *DDI*, 8, XII, 353, 24.vi.39.
67. Cited Moisuc, 1971, pp. 400–01; Calafteanu in Moisuc, 1977, p. 372.
68. *DGFP*, D, VI, 508.
69. Calafteanu, in Moisuc, 1977, pp. 373–75.
70. Gafencu to Ankara, cited Varga, 'Attitudinea', p. 64; *DBFP*, 3, VI, 41, 65, 148, 13/15/26.vi.39.
71. Călinescu Papers cited Moisuc, 1971, pp. 401–02.
72. *DDI*, 8, XII, 129, 137, 149; *DGFP*, D, VI, 476, 488.
73. *DGFP*, D, VI, 625, 627, 633, 651, 662, 7/13.vii.39.
74. *DDF*, 2, XVII, 124, 6.vii.39, Coulondre to Bonnet; *FRUS, 1939*, I. 19.vii.39, p. 286.
75. *DDF*, 2, XVII, 389, 1.viii.39; 484, 10.viii.39; *DDF*, 2, XVIII, 203, 18.viii.39; Moisuc, 1971, p. 406, fn. 114; Jacobsen memoirs, pp. 27, 468, 472; Moisuc, 'L'ecroulement des alliances', *RHDGM*, 1985, p. 20, fn. 62.
76. Bohm, pp. 98–102, citing German legation Bucarest archives; *DDF*, 2, XVII, 357, 28.vii.39; Moisuc, 1971, citing report by Romanian secret service: *DDF*, 2, XVII, 476, 8.viii.39.
77. *DDF*, 2, XVII, 476, 8.viii.39, de Saint-Hardouin to Bonnet.
78. *DIMK*, IV, 181, 187, 189, 190, 248, 250; *DBFP*, 3, VI, 58.
79. *DDF*, 2, XVII, 518, 11.vii.39.
80. *DBFP*, 3, VI, 570, 591, 603, 619; *DBFP*, 3, VII, 57.
81. *DDF*, 2, XVII, 483, 484, 486, 488, 10/11.viii.39; *DBFP*, 3, VI, 629, fn. 1.
82. *DDF*, 2, XVII, 540, 12.viii.39; *DDF*, 2, XVIII, 148, 19.viii.39; *DBFP*, 3, VI, 637.
83. *DIMK*, IV, 269, 273, 17.viii.39.

84. *DGFP*, D, VI, 374, 13.v.39.
85. von Papen, *Memoirs*, pp. 448–49; *DGFP*, D, VI, 321, 3.v.39.
86. *DGFP*, D, VI, 435, 454, 24/30.vi.39.
87. *DGFP*, D, VI, 475, 489, 512, 515.
88. *DDI*, 8, XII, 227, 14.vi.39.
89. *DGFP*, D, VI, 472, 5.vi.39; *DDF*, 2, XVI, 389, 6.vi.39.
90. *DDF*, 2, XVI, 517.
91. *DDF*, 2, XVI, 389, 10.vi.39, Coulondre to Bonnet.
92. Cited by Krecker, pp. 51–52.
93. *DDF*, 2, XVII, 147, fn. 3, Ankara to Paris, 23.vi.39.
94. *DDF*, 2, XVII, 147, fn. 3, Ankara to Paris, 5.vii.39.
95. Pownall diary, entry of 5.vi.39.
96. *DBFP*, 3, VI, 169, 29.vi.39.
97. *DBFP*, 3, VI, 169.
98. *DBFP*, 3, VI, 205, 1.vii.39.
99. *DBFP*, 3, VI, 320, 14.vi.39; *DDF*, 2, XVII, 195, 13.vii.39.
100. *DBFP*, 3, VI, 331, 14.vii.39; *DDF*, 2, XVII, 263, 21.vii.39.
101. *PRO*, CAB 24/287, C.P. 149 (39), 3.vii.39.
102. *PRO*, CAB 23/00, 5.vii.39.
103. Pownall diary, entry of 17.vii.39.
104. *DDF*, 2, XVII, 249, 20.vii.39; *DBFP*, 3, VI, 388.
105. *DBFP*, 3, VI, 526, 3.viii.39.
106. Knatchbull-Hugessen diary, entry of 14.vii.39.
107. *DDF*, 2, XVII.
108. *DDF*, 2, XVII, p. 488, fn. 1.
109. *DDF*, 2, XVII, 525 and Annex, 5.viii.39.
110. Massigli, *Mission à Ankara*, pp. 235–40.
111. *DDF*, 2, XVI, 389, 29.v.39.
112. *DDF*, 2, XVII, 66, 1.vii.39.
113. *DDF*, 2, XVII, 211, 15.vii.39.
114. *DDF*, 2, XVII, 215, 276, 16/22.vii.39.
115. *DBFP*, 3, VI, 579, 7.viii.39; *DDF*, 2, XVII, 472, 8.viii.39.
116. *DDF*, 2, XVII, 491, 9.viii.39.
117. *DBFP*, 3, VI, 620, 11.viii.39; *DDF*, 2, XVII, 506, 10.viii.39.
118. *DBFP*, 3, VII, 9, 15.viii.39.
119. *DGFP*, D, VII, 141 and fn. 6 thereto.
120. *DBFP*, 3, VII, 188, fn. 1.
121. *DBFP*, 3, VII, 161.
122. *DBFP*, 3, VII, 188.
123. *DBFP*, 3, VII, 260; *DGFP*, D, VII, 247.
124. *DBFP*, 3, VII, 370; *DGFP*, D, VII, 342, 393.
125. *DGFP*, D, VII, 219, 23.viii.39.

Chapter 18   Hitler steps up the pressure: 'die for Danzig?'

Where not otherwise stated, this chapter is based on the following sources: Levine, *Hitler's Free City*; Denne, *Das Danzig-problem*; Ruhnau, *Freie Stadt Danzigs*; Burckhardt, *Meine Danziger Mission*; Prazmowska, *Britain, Poland and the Eastern Front*; Mueller, *Das Heer und Hitler*; Woytak, *Border of War and Peace*; Skubiszewski, 'Did the War start for Danzig?', *PWA* 1969; Szembek, diaries; Roos, 'Militärpolitische Lage und Planung Polens', *WWR* 1957.

1. Levine, *Hitler's Free City*, p. 143.
2. Burckhardt, pp. 76–78.
3. *DGFP*, D, V, 671, 672, 673; *DBFP*, 3, V, 411.
4. *DBFP*, 3, VI, 36. Makins memorandum.
5. Burckhardt, p. 76; Levine, pp. 31–34.
6. *ND*, C-130, 8.xii.38.
7. Levine, pp. 26, 28, 29.
8. Ciano, *Diario*, 25.ii.39.
9. *DGFP*, D, VI, 74; Levine, pp. 147–48.

10. *DDF*, 2, XV, 93, 173; *DGFP*, D, VI, 85, 90; Woytak, pp. 79–82.
11. *DGFP*, D, VI, 124, 24.iii.39.
12. Denne, *Danzig-problem*, p. 182; *PYB*, 104, 25.iv.39.
13. Sywottek, *Mobilmachung*, pp. 213–19; M. Toscano, 'Di alcuni falsi e omissioni nel libro bianco tedesco sulle origini della seconda guerra mondiale', *Pagine di Storia Diplomatica Contemporanea*, vol. II, pp. 187–210.
14. *DBFP*, 3, IV, 515, 535.
15. Domarus, II, 119.
16. Hencke, p. 240–41, fns 139, 140.
17. Hencke, pp. 241–42.
18. *DGFP*, D, VII, 142.
19. Mueller, *Das Heer und Hitler*, p. 392.
20. *ND*, C-120, Anlage VI.
21. *ND*, 2337-PS, 14.vi.39; Grosscurth diary, 20.vi.39.
22. *ND*, C-120, Anlage III, 11.iv.39; *ND*, NOKW 2657, OKW to Command East, 28.iv.39.
23. *DGFP*, D, VI, 247, 22.iv.39.
24. *DGFP*, D, VI, 159, 5.iv.39.
25. *PWB*, 78; *DGFP*, D, VI, 334, enclosure; *DBFP*, 3, V, 402.
26. *PWB*, 79; *BBB*, (Cmd. 6106 (1939)), 15.
27. Woytak, p. 89, citing Szymański.
28. Woytak, p. 85.
29. *DDF*, 2, XVI, 67, 134, Noël to Bonnet, 5/10.v.39; Noel, *L'Aggression allemande*, pp. 358–61; *FYB*, 120, 121, 125.
30. *DDF*, 2, XVI, p. 53, fn. 3 (p. 118).
31. *DDF*, 2, XVI, 147, fn. 4 (p. 300).
32. *DDF*, 2, XVI, 53, 147, Coulondre to Bonnet, 4/11.v.39.
33. *DDF*, 2, XVI, p. 330, fn. 1.
34. *The Times*, 12.v.39.
35. *DGFP*, D, VI, 433; *ND*, 79-L.
36. Denne, p. 196.
37. *DBFP*, 3, V, 472.
38. *DBFP*, 3, VI, Appendix II (ii), Burckhardt memorandum.
39. *DBFP*, 3, VI, 36.
40. *DBFP*, 3, VI, 575, 577, 579, 585; *FYB*, 129; *DGFP*, D, VI, 417, 418; *DDI*, 8, XII, 37; Denne, pp. 210–11.
41. Burckhardt, p. 301.
42. *DBFP*, 3, V, 707, Shepherd to Halifax, 4.vi.39; *DGFP*, D, VI, 515.
43. *DBFP*, 3, V, 736, 7.vi.39.
44. Denne, p. 205.
45. Denne, p. 205.
46. *DBFP*, 3, VI, 164.
47. *DBFP*, 3, V, 628.
48. *DBFP*, 3, V, 656, Kennard to Halifax, 28.v.39; *DBFP*, 3, VI, 36 and Appendix II, (i) and (ii), Burckhardt memoranda.
49. *DBFP*, 3, V, 696, Shepherd to Halifax, 2.vi.39; *DBFP*, 3, VI, Appendix II (i) and (ii), Burckhardt, pp. 302–03.
50. *DBFP*, 3, VI, 93, 120, 19/21.vi.39.
51. *DDF*, 2, XVI, 508, Noël to Bonnet, 22.vi.39; *DDI*, 8, XII, 324, Arone to Ciano, 23.vi.39.
52. *DGFP*, D, VI, 547, 599, 670, 19.vi/1/14.vii.39; *DDF*, 2, XVII, 13; *DDI*, 8, XII, 384.
53. *DBFP*, 3, VI, 434, 502; *DDF*, 2, XVI, 394; Denne, p. 212.
54. Ruhnau, p. 169; *DDF*, 2, XVII, 27, p. 67, fn. 6.
55. *DBFP*, 3, VI, Appendix II (iii), Burckhardt to Makins, 5.vii.39.
56. *DDF*, 2, XVII, 23, 27.vi.39.
57. *DDF*, 2, XVII, 13, 27.vi.39; Stehlin, *Témoignage*, pp. 155–57.
58. *DDF*, 2, XVII, 27, fn. 6.
59. *DBFP*, 2, VI, 180.
60. *DBFP*, 3, VI, 186, Phipps to Halifax, 30.vi.39; *FRUS, 1939*, I, pp. 194–95, Bullitt to Hull, 28.vi.39.
61. *DDF*, 2, XVII, 56, p. 443, fn. 3; Bonnet, *Dans la Tourmente*, pp. 157–60.
62. *DDF*, 2, XVII, 55.

63. *DBFP*, 3, VI, Appendix II (iii), Burckhardt to Makins, 5.vii.39.
64. *DGFP*, D, VI, 640, fn. 2; *DBFP*, 3, VI, 180; Bonnet, *Dans la Tourmente*, pp. 157–60.
65. *DDF*, 2, XVII, 262, fn. 3; Deridan, *Chemin de la Defaite*, pp. 128–29.
66. *DDF*, 2, XVII, 67.
67. *DDF*, 2, XVII, 61.
68. *DDF*, 2, XVII, 80, Gauquié to Bonnet, 3.vii.39; *ibid.*, 91, Coulondre to Bonnet, 9.vii.39; *ibid.*, 109, Noël to Bonnet, 5.vii.39; *ibid.*, 113, 114, 115, 116, 6.vii.39.
69. *DGFP*, D, VI, 640, 658, 664, 9/12/13.vii.39; *ibid.*, 690, 755, 767, 20.vii/2/4.viii.39; *DGFP*, D, VII, 22, 49, 65, 11/14/15.viii.39.
70. Engel Papers, 4.vii.39.
71. Ruhnau, *Freie Stadt Danzigs*, p. 166.
72. *DBFP*, 3, VI, 353, 363; *DDF*, 2, XVII, 214, 245, 438.
73. *FYB*, 163; *DGFP*, D, VI, 669, enclosure; *DBFP*, 3, VI, 471, enclosure I, 14.vii.39.
74. *FYB*, 168; *DGFP*, D, VI, 722; *DBFP*, 3, VI, 471, enclosure II, 25.vii.39.
75. *DBFP*, 3, VI, 333, 17.vii.39; *DDF*, 2, XVII, 313.
76. *DBFP*, 3, VI, Appendix II (iv), Burckhardt to Makins, 27.vii.39; *ibid.*, 462, 26.vii.39.
77. *DBFP*, 3, VI, 461.
78. *DBFP*, 3, VI, 410, 22.vii.39.
79. See below, pp. 436–37.
80. *DBFP*, 3, VI, 407, 457, 484, 501, 516.
81. *DBFP*, 3, VI, 450.
82. *DBFP*, 3, VI, 364, 384, 417, 470.
83. *DBFP*, 3, VI, 477, fn. 1.
84. *DBFP*, 3, VI, 261, fn. 2, 14.vii.39.
85. *DGFP*, D, VI, 652, and fns 2 and 3, 11.vii.39.
86. *DGFP*, D, VI, 702.
87. *DGFP*, D, VI, 749, 31.vii.39; *DBFP*, 3, VI, 503, 523; *FYB*, 175, 178; *DDF*, 2, XVII, 375, 381.
88. *DGFP*, D, VI, 765, Chodacki to Greiser, 3.viii.39.
89. *DGFP*, D, VI, 774, enclosure, Chodacki to Greiser, 4.viii.39.
90. *DGFP*, D, VII, 2.
91. *DGFP*, D, VII, 5; *PWB*, 85.
92. *DGFP*, D, VII, 10; *PWB*, 86.
93. Woytak, p. 80, and fn. 32; Prazmowska, *Britain, Poland and the Eastern Front.* pp. 89–93; Roos, *WWR*, 1957.
94. *DGFP*, D, VI, 167, 169, 334.
95. Szembek diary, 27.v.39.
96. Szembek diary, 21.v/20.vi.39.
97. Szembek diary, 2.vii.39.
98. *PRO*, CAB 29/159, AFC 6, 4.iv.39; Prazmowska, pp. 80, 82.
99. *DDF*, 2, XV, 254, 274; *DDF*, 2, XVI, 79, 153, 193; *PRO*, CAB 29/159, AFC 7.
100. *DDF*, 2, XV, 316.
101. *PRO*, CAB 53/11, COS (39), 299th Mtg., 1.vi.39; CAB 2/8, CID (39), 369th Mtg.
102. *PRO*, CAB 2/9, CID (39), 369th Mtg., 24.vii.39.
103. Polish-British General Staff Meeting, Protocols, *Bellona*, 1957.
104. Polish-French General Staff Meeting, Protocols, *Bellona*, 1958; *DDF*, 2, XVI, 207, 214, 223.
105. *DDF*, 2, XVI, 245, Gamelin to Kazprzycki, 20.v.39.
106. Dutailly, pp. 67–68.
107. *Bellona*, 1957.
108. Szembek diary, 26.iv.39.
109. Mcleod and Kelly (Eds), *The Ironside Diaries*, introduction.
110. Cadogan diary, 17.v.1940.
111. Pownall diary, 13.vi.38.
112. *DBFP*, 3, VI, 341, 361, 374; *DDF*, 2, XVII, 241, General Musse to Daladier, 19.vii.39.
113. Chamberlain papers, NC 18/1/1101, Chamberlain to Hilda Chamberlain, 28.v.39.
114. *PRO*, FO 371/23129, C 5086/27/55, Prazmowska, p. 111.
115. *PRO*, FO 371/23144, C 6860/1110/55, Prazmowska, p. 112.
116. *PRO*, FO 371/23144, C 6996/1110/55, 5.v.39, Prazmowska, p. 112.
117. *PRO*, FO 371/23144, C 6996/1110/55, 5.v.39, Prazmowska, p. 112.
118. Prazmowska, p. 115.

119. *DBFP*, 3, V, 266, Kennard to Cadogan, 22.iv.39.
120. Szembek diary, 26.iv.39.
121. *DBFP*, 3, V, 508, Halifax to Kennard, 12.v.39.
122. Szembek diary, 20.vi.39.
123. *PRO*, CAB 2/8, CID (39), 368th Mtg., 20.iv.39, Prazmowska, pp. 116–17.
124. Prazmowska, pp. 108–10, 117–122, 127.
125. *DBFP*, 3, VI, 22, fn. 2.
126. *PRO*, CAB 23/100, CAB 33(39), 21.vi.39.
127. *DBFP*, 3, VI, 200, 222.
128. *DDF*, 2, XVII, 206, Corbin to Bonnet, 15, vii.39.
129. *PRO*, FO 371/23146, C 10029/1110/55, 12.vii.39; *PRO*, T 160, 16073/2, 13.vii.39., Prazmowska, p. 129.
130. *DBFP*, 3, VI, 436, 25.vii.39.
131. Prazmowska, pp. 130–31; Szembek diary, 21.vii.39; *DBFP*, 3, VI, 377, 21.vii.39.
132. *DBFP*, 3, VI, 362, 383, 406.
133. Prazmowska, p. 130.
134. Ironside diary, 18/19.vii.39; *DBFP*, 3, VI, 341; Szembek diary, 18.vii.39.
135. Leith-Ross, *Money Talks*, pp. 257–60.
136. *DDF*, 2, XVI, 254, 22.v.39.
137. *DDF*, 2, XVI, 383, 9.vi.39.
138. *DBFP*, 3, VI, 521.
139. *DBFP*, 3, VI, 521; Prazmowska, pp. 59–60.
140. Prazmowska, pp. 160–61.
141. *DDF*, 2, XVI, 202, 211, 222, 226, 255.
142. Lukasiewicz papers, pp. 219–20; *FRUS, 1939*, I, pp. 189–91, Bullitt to Hull, 22.v.39.
143. BBB, Cmd. 6106, 25.
144. *H.C.Deb.*, 349, Cols 1787–89.
145. *DGFP*, D, VI, 598, 606.
146. *DGFP*, D, VI, 671, Weizsäcker memorandum, 14.vii.39.
147. Engel diary, 28.vii.39.
148. Engel diary, 22.vii.39.
149. Mueller, *Das Heer und Hitler*, pp. 394–95.
150. *DBFP*, 3, VI, 4; *PRO*, FO 800/315, Rumbold to Halifax, H/XV/174.
151. von Schlabrendorff, *Secret War*, pp. 95–98.
152. See Chapter XXI below.
153. Chamberlain papers, NC 18/1/1110, Chamberlain to Ida Chamberlain, 30.vii.39.

Chapter 19   The Japanese army overplays its hand

Save where otherwise stated this chapter is based on the following sources: (i) Coox, *Nomonhan*, vol. 1; Hata, 'The Japanese-Soviet confrontation' in Morley (Ed.), *Deterrent Diplomacy*; Erickson, *The Soviet High Command*; Detweiler and Burdick (Eds), *War in Asia and the Pacific*, vol. XI; Hata in Morley (Ed.), *Deterrent Diplomacy*; Boyd, *Extraordinary Envoy*; Storry, *The Double Patriots*; Borg and Okamoto (Eds), *Pearl Harbour as History*; (iii) Pritchard, *Far Eastern Influences*; Clifford, *Retreat from China*; Jones, *Shanghai and Tientsin*; Roskill, *British Naval Policy*, vol. II; Usui, 'The Politics of War' in Morley (Ed.), *The China Quagmire*; (iv) Mario Toscano, *Le Origine Diplomatiche de Patto d'Acciaio*; Theo Sommer, *Deutschland und Japan zwischen den Mächten 1935–1940*.

1. Coox, *Nomonhan*, I, p. 279.
2. Prange, *Target Tokyo*, p. 265, citing Japanese sources.
3. Storry, pp. 251–55.
4. Hata in Morley (Ed.), *Deterrent Diplomacy*, pp. 85–87; Storry, citing Saionji-Harada memoirs, 5.v.39.
5. Saionji-Harada memoirs, 11.vii.39, cited Storry, p. 254.
6. Saionji-Harada memoirs, 16.v.39, cited Storry, pp. 249–50.
7. Storry, p. 246.
8. *DGFP*, D, VII, 326, Ott to A.A., 4.v.39; Hata in Morley, *Deterrent Diplomacy*, pp. 93–95.
9. Hata in Morley, *Deterrent Diplomacy*, pp. 96–98; Storry, pp. 248–50.
10. Hata in Morley, *Deterrent Diplomacy*, pp. 101–02.

11. Hata in Morley, *Deterrent Diplomacy*, p. 318, fn. 159; *DGFP*, D, VI, 447, Ribbentrop (citing Oshima), to Ott, 28.vi.39; *IMTFE*, p. 33, 700, Kawabe evidence; p. 34,010, Oshima evidence; *DDI*, 8, XII, 17, 32, 64, 25/26/31.v.39.
12. Storry, p. 253; Hata in Morley, *Deterrent Diplomacy*, pp. 106–07.
13. Hata in Morley, *Deterrent Diplomacy*, pp. 104–05; *DGFP*, D, VI, 487, 7.vi.39; *DDI*, 8, XII, 110, 111, 126, 5/6.vi.39.
14. *DGFP*, D, VI, 487.
15. Saionji-Harada memoirs, p. 2547.
16. *DGFP*, D, VI, 538, 553, Weizsäcker to Ott, 17.vi/21.vii.39; Hata in Morley, *Deterrent Diplomacy*, pp. 105–06.
17. *DBFP*, 3, IX, 2.
18. *DBFP*, 3, IX, 64, 180, 245, 249, Jamieson (Tientsin) to Halifax, 13.v.11/15/22.vi.39; *DBFP*, 3, IX, 381, 419, Craigie to Halifax, 25/30.vii.39.
19. *DBFP*, 3, IX, 30, 1.v.39, Clark Kerr to Halifax.
20. *DBFP*, 3, IX, 119, 138, 169.
21. *DBFP*, 3, IX, 205, 249, 15/22.vi.39.
22. *DBFP*, 3, IX, 139, Halifax to Clark Kerr, 148, Halifax to Jamieson, 149, Halifax to Craigie.
23. *DBFP*, 3, IX, 187.
24. *DBFP*, 3, IX, 196.
25. *DDI*, 8, XII, 191, Auriti to Ciano, 12.vi.39.
26. *DBFP*, 3, IX, 196, 242.
27. *DDI*, 8, XII, 273, Auriti to Ciano, 19.vi.39.
28. *H.C. Deb.*, 348, col. 2610.
29. *DBFP*, 3, IX, 264, 26.vi.39.
30. *DBFP*, 3, IX, 244, 21.vi.39.
31. Cadogan diary, 30.vii.30; *DBFP*, 3, IX, App. I, Sansom memorandum, 3.viii.39; Lee, *Britain and the Sino-Japanese War*, pp. 199–200.
32. *DBFP*, 3, IX, 227, 18.vi.39.
33. Pritchard, *Far Eastern Influences*, pp. 155–61; Lee, *Britain and the Sino-Japanese War*, pp. 188–91; Roskill, *British Naval Policy*, II, pp. 463–67.
34. CAP 27/625, FP 54(36)2, 26.vi.39; see also JPC 435 (39), 16.vi.39; COS 928, 301, 302 (39); CID 362 (39) 1, 26.vi.39.
35. *DDF*, 2, XVI, 451, Bonnet to St Quentin, 16.vi.39; *DDF*, 2, XVII, 146, Bonnet to St Quentin, 8.vii.39; *DBFP*, 3, IX, 22, Phipps to Halifax, 16.vi.39; *FRUS, 1939*, IV.
36. *FRUS, 1939*, IV, pp. 176–77, 199–200, Caldwell (Tientsin) to Hull, 12/26.vi.39, pp. 181–82, Doonan (Tokio), to Hull, 19.vi.39.
37. *DDF*, 2, XVII, 181, 208; *FRUS, 1939*, IV, pp. 220–21, Grew memo, 15.vii.39; *DBFP*, 3, IX, 235, 258, 272, 329, 330.
38. *DBFP*, 3, IX, 253, 23.vi.39.
39. *DBFP*, 3, IX, 247, 248.
40. *DBFP*, 3, IX, 240, 259, Craigie to Halifax, 20/29.vi.39.
41. Storry, pp. 252–55; Craigie, pp. 76–77; *DBFP*, 3, IX, 439 and fn 1; *DDI*, 8, XII, 755.
42. *DBFP*, 3, IX, 325.
43. *DBFP*, 3, IX, 276, 350, 385.
44. *DBFP*, 3, IX, 365.
45. Craigie, p. 77.
46. *DGFP*, D, VI, 762; *DGFP*, D, VII, 7; *DDI*, 8, XII, 763, 779; Hata in Morley, *Deterrent Diplomacy*, p. 105.
47. *DDI*, 8, XII, 778, 834; *DGFP*, D, VII, 25; *DBFP*, 3, IX, 509.
48. *IMT FE*, pp. 34, 140–41; *DDI*, 8, XII, 811; *FRUS, 1939*, III, p. 49, Phillips to Hull, 10.viii.39, Sommer, p. 267.
49. Sommer, pp. 268–69.
50. Ciano, *Diario*, 9.viii.39.
51. Hata in Morley, *Deterrent Diplomacy*, p. 109; *DDI*, 8, XII, 801, 802, 812, 821, 834, 835, 836, 837; *DDI*, 8, XIII, 26, 52, 70, 81; *FRUS, 1939*, III, p. 48, Doonan to Hull, 8.viii.39.

Chapter 20   Molotov calls for bids

1. Watt, 'John Herbert King', *Int. Nat. Sec.*, 1988.
2. *SPE*, II, 323, Molotov to Maisky, 10.vi.39.

3. Strang, *At Home and Abroad*, pp. 157–58, 169–72.
4. Myllieniemi, p. 37.
5. Myllieniemi, p. 39, citing Finnish Foreign Ministry archives, 24.xii., 5.x.38.
6. *SPE*, I, 192, 28.iii.39; Degras, III, pp. 325–36.
7. Myllieniemi, pp. 46–47.
8. *SPE*, I, 221, 226, 10/11.iv.36.
9. *SPE*, I, 239, 244, 17/19.iv.39.
10. *SPE*, II, 303, 21.vi.39.
11. *BDFA, SU*, XV, 57, 2.v.39.
12. *BDFA, SU*, XV, 71.
13. *BDFA, SU*, XV, 73, 7.vi.39.
14. *BDFA, SU*, XV, 83, 14.vi.39.
15. *SPE*, II, 337, 352, 21/28.vi.39.
16. *BDFA, SU*, XV, 96, 18.vii.39.
17. *BDFA, SU*, XV, 101, 3.viii.39; *SPE*, II, 369, 313, 13/14.vi.39.
18. *BDFA, SU*, XV, 91, 11.vii.39.
19. *SPE*, I, 149, 13.iii.39; *SPE*, II, 266, 2.v.39.
20. *SPE*, II, 333, 19.vi.39.
21. Meretzkov memoirs, p. 171, cited in Haslam, pp. 208–09.
22. Meretzkov memoirs, pp. 177–78, cited in Haslam, pp. 221–22.
23. *SPE*, II, 355, 29.vi.39.
24. Watt, 'Stalin's First Bid', *USNIP*, 1964.
25. *BDFA, SU*, XV, 65–67, 27.v.39.
26. *BDFA, SU*, XV, 100, 24.vii.39.
27. Barros, *The League of Nations and the Åland Islands Dispute.*
28. *DGFP*, D, V, 464.
29. *DGFP*, D, VI, 187, 212, 229, 232, 242.
30. *DGFP*, D, VI, 312, 2.v.39.
31. *DDF*, 2, XV, 52, 18.iii.39.
32. *DDF*, 2, XVI, 299.
33. *DGFP*, D, VI, 419, fn. 3, Blücher to A.A., 22.v.39; *SPE*, II, p. 73, Molotov speech, 31.v.39.
34. *DDF*, 2, XVI, 349, 4.vi.39.
35. *BDFA, SU*, XV, 87, 88, 17/19.vi.39.
36. *DGFP*, D, VI, 612, 4.vii.39.
37. *DGFP*, D, VI, 626, 7.vii.39.
38. *DGFP*, D, VI, 581, 657, 29.vi., 12.vii.39.
39. *DGFP*, D, VI, 570, 29.vi.39.
40. *DGFP*, D, VI, 579, 607, 29.vi./3.vii.39.
41. *DGFP*, D, VI, 661.
42. *DGFP*, D, VI, 576, 596.
43. Chamberlain papers, NC 18/1/1108, 23.vii.39.
44. Watt, 'An Intelligence Surprise', *Int.Nat.Sec.*, 1989.
45. *DDF*, 2, XVI, 48, 56, 100, 251, 329, 407, 510; *DDF*, 2, XVII, 15, 23, 56, 88, 279, 291.
46. Woytak, p. 88.
47. Myllieniemi, p. 48.
48. *DDF*, 2, XVII, 66.
49. *DDF*, 2, XVII, 151.
50. Watt, 'An Intelligence Surprise', *Int.Nat.Sec.* 1989.
51. *DBFP*, 3, VI, Appendix I (iii), 16.vi.39; Blasius, pp. 154, 161; *PRO*, FO 371/22973, C 8167/15/18, 5.vi.39; Thielenhaus, pp. 118–19.
52. Watt, 'An Intelligence Surprise', *Int.Nat.Sec.*, 1989.
53. Strang, *At Home and Abroad*, p. 175.
54. Chamberlain to Dalton, 23.vi.39, Pimlott, *Dalton*, p. 276.
55. *DBFP*, 3, VI, 122, Strang to Sargent, 21.vi.39.
56. *SPE*, II, 315; *DBFP*, 3, VI, 697; *DDF*, 2, xvi, 336, 335.
57. *DGFP*, D, VI, 473, 511.
58. *SPE*, II, 329, 331; *DBFP*, 3, VI, 60, 66, 103; *DDF*, 2, XVI, 422, 438.
59. *SPE*, II, 330; *DBFP*, 3, VI, 69, 73; *DDF*, 2, XVI, 457, 460.
60. *DBFP*, 3, VI, 94, 96, 97, 99, 112, 113.
61. *DBFP*, 3, VI, 119, 1122; *SPE*, II, 338.

62. *DBFP*, 3, VI, 123, 126, 127; *DDF*, 2, XVI, 507, 515; *SPE*, II, 339.
63. *DBFP*, 3, VI, 135.
64. *PRO*, CAB 27/625, FPC (/9), 54th Meeting.
65. Chamberlain Papers, NC 18/1/1105, to Hilda Chamberlain, 2.vii.39.
66. *DBFP*, 3, VI, 151, 157, 158, 159, 160, 171, 181, 182, 185, 199, 206.
67. *DGFP*, D, VI, 581.
68. *SPE*, II, 346, 349, 350, 354, *Tass* Communiqués, 26–30.vi.39.
69. *SPE*, II, 356, Molotov to Suritz, 30.vi.39.
70. *SPE*, II, 343, Maisky to Molotov, 24.vi.39.
71. *Pravda*, 29.vi.39, *SPE*, II, 355.
72. *DBFP*, 3, VI, 207; *DDF*, 2, XVII, 64; *SPE*, II, 357.
73. *DBFP*, 3, VI, 225, 226, 227, 247; *DDF*, 2, XVII, 85, 86; *SPE*, II, 360, 361.
74. *DDF*, 2, XVII, 89, Corbin to Bonnet, 4.vii.39.
75. *DDF*, 2, XVII, 99.
76. *DDF*, 2, XVII, 100, Bonnet to Corbin, 5.vii.39.
77. *DBFP*, 3, VI, 243, 5.vii.39.
78. *DBFP*, 3, VI, 251.
79. *DBFP*, 3, VI, 255.
80. *DDF*, 2, XVII, 75, 87, and fn. 2. See also *SPE*, II, 345, 347, 371, 372; *DBFP*, 3, VI, 339, 349.
81. Dalton diary, 10.vii.39.
82. *DBFP*, 3, VI, 279, 9.vii.39.
83. *DBFP*, 3, VI, 251, 10.vii.39.
84. *DBFP*, VI, 290, 11.vii.39.
85. *DDF*, 2, XVII, 162.
86. *DBFP*, 3, VI, 376, Strang to Sargent, 20.vii.39; *PRO*, CAB 27/265, FPC (36) 57th Meeting.
87. *BDFA*, *SU*, XV, 87, 88, 17/19.vi.39.
88. *SPE*, II, 365, 371, 372, 377.
89. *SPE*, II, 376, Molotov to Suritz, 17.vii.39.
90. Pownall diary, 17.vii.39.
91. *DGFP*, D, VI, 679; *DBFP*, 3, VI, 329.
92. *DGFP*, D, VI, 677, 685, 16/18.vii.39.
93. *DDI*, 8, XII, 451, 4.vii.39.
94. *DDI*, 8, XII, 503, Attolico to Ciano, 7.vii.39.
95. *DDI*, 8, XII, 537.
96. *DGFP*, D, VI, 685, 18.vii.39.
97. Hans Heinrich Herwarth von Bitternfeld, *Against two Evils*, pp. 144–61.
98. Charles Bohlen, *Witness to History*, pp. 67–87.
99. *FRUS, 1939*, I, pp. 312–350, passim.
100. Herwarth, p. 150.
101. Herwarth, pp. 152–53.
102. *DBFP*, 3, VI, 414, 415, 416; *DDF*, 2, XVII, 282.
103. *DGFP*, D, VI, 695.
104. Chamberlain papers, NC 18/1/1108, 23.vii.39.
105. *SPE*, II, 385.
106. Watt, '*The Week* that Was', *Encounter*, 1972.
107. *DDF*, 2, XVII, 309, 31.vii.39.
108. *DDF*, 2, XVII, 198.
109. *DBFP*, 3, VI, 376, Strang to Sargent.
110. Pownall diary, 31.vii.39.
111. Drax diary; Davidson diary; *PRO*, FO 371/23701; *PRO* CAB 54/2, DCOS (39) 45th mtg, 31.vii.39; FPC (39) 60th mtg, 1.viii.39; Aster, pp. 295–96.
112. *DGFP*, D, VI, 729.
113. *DGFP*, D, VI, 744, 757, 758, 759, 760, 761, 766.
114. *DGFP*, D, VI, 758.
115. Haslam, p. 226, citing Soviet sources.
116. *DGFP*, D, VII, 14, 10.viii.39.
117. *DGFP*, D, VII, 170, memorandum by Schulenburg, 22.viii.39.
118. *DGFP*, D, VII, 27, 11.viii.39.
119. *DGFP*, D, VII, 55, 99.
120. *DGFP*, D, VII, 70, 73, 75, 88, 89, 98, 105, 113, 125, 132, 133, 140, 142, 157, 158.

Chapter 21   *The amateurs attempt to avert a war*

Where not otherwise stated, this chapter is based on the following sources: (1) For the Vatican; F. Charles-Roux, *Huit Ans au Vatican, 1932–1940*; Owen Chadwick, *Britain and the Vatican during the Second World War*; Introduction to *ADSS*, vol. I; (2) For the German 'national-conservative' opposition to Hitler; K-J Müller, *Das Heer und Hitler, 1933–1940*; idem, *Armee und Drittes Reich, 1933–1939*; H. Krausnick, 'Vorgeschichte und Beginn des militärischen Widerstandes gegen Hitler', in *Vollmacht des Gewissens*; Paul Hoffmann, *History of the German Resistance*; Ueberschar, 'General Halder and the Resistance to Hitler in the German High Command, 1939–40', *EHQ*, 18/3, 1988; R. A. Blasius, *Für Grossdeutschland; gegen den grossen Krieg*; M. Thielenhaus, *Zwischen Anpassung und Widerstand*; Thun-Hohenstein, *der Verschwörer*; (3) On Adam von Trott zu Solz; David Astor, 'Why the revolt against Hitler was ignored', *Encounter*, 1969; Sykes, *Troubled loyalty*; H. O. Malone Jr., 'Adam von Trott, the Road to Conspiracy', Univ. Texas Ph.D.; idem, *Adam von Trott, Werdegang eines Verschwörers*; Shiela Grant Duff, *The Parting of the Ways*; (4) On Wohltat; Helmut Metzmacher, 'Deutsch-englische Ausgleichsbemühungen im Sommer 1939', *VjhZg*, 1966, and Wohltat's records therein cited; (5) On Dahlerus, B. Dahlerus, *The Last Attempt*; L. Namier, 'An Interloper in Diplomacy', *Diplomatic Prelude*; (6) On Lord Kemsley; Lenz und Ketternacker, 'Lord Kemsley's Gespräch', *VjhZg*, 1971; Dietrich, *12 Jahre mit Hitler*; Gannon, *The British Press and Nazi Germany*.

1. Cited Naylor, *Labour's International Policy*, p. 308.
2. *DSS*, I, pp. 11–13.
3. *ADSS*, I, 18, 2.v.39.
4. *ADSS*, I, 19.
5. *ADSS*, I, 20.
6. *DBFP*, 3, V, 385; *ADSS*, I, 23, 27.
7. Halifax to Godfrey, 4.v.39, FO 371/23790, and Osborne to Tardini, 7.v.39, FO 371/23790, cited Chadwick, *Britain and the Vatican*, pp. 62, 65; *DDF*, 2, XVI, 113, Charles-Roux to Bonnet, citing Mgr. Tardini, 9.v.39.
8. *DGFP*, D, VI, 331; *ADSS*, I, 29, 6.v.39.
9. *ADSS*, I, 34, 9.v.39.
10. *ADSS*, I, 23, 25; *DDF*, 2, XVI, 77; *FRUS, 1939*, I, pp. 179–81.
11. *DBFP*, 3, V, 418, 8.v.39; *FRUS, 1939*, I, pp. 182–84; Charles-Roux, *Huit Ans*, pp. 316–17.
12. *ADSS*, I, 36; *FRUS, 1939*, I, pp. 184–85; Charles-Roux, *Huit Ans*, p. 318.
13. Müller, *Das Heer und Hitler*, pp. 387–401; Thun-Hohenstein, *Der Verschwörer*, pp. 127–28.
14. Mclachlan, *Room 39*, pp. 245–46; Beesley, *Very Special Admiral*, p. 114. See also Lloyd papers, GLLD 19/19, unsigned memorandum 'Leakage of information that has occurred in London', n.d., probably by Ian Colvin.
15. *DBFP*, 3, V, App. I (x), Mason-MacFarlane to Henderson, 15.v.39.
16. Astor, 'Revolt against Hitler', *Encounter*, 1969.
17. *DBFP*, 3, VI, 269. Marshall-Cornwall memorandum; Gilbert, *Churchill, Companion*, V, pp. 1553–54, 1556; Godfrey memoirs, V, Pt 1, pp. 17–18; Aster, *1939*, pp. 235–38; Mclachlan, *Room 39*, pp. 17/324; Gladwyn, *Memoirs*, pp. 90–91; Beesley, *Very Special Admiral*, pp. 117–18; Marshall-Cornwall, *Wars and Rumours of Wars*, p. 125; Thun-Hohenstein, *der Verschwörer*, p. 128.
18. *DGFP*, D, VI, 497; Malone, 'Adam von Trott', pp. 563–64; Douglas-Home, *Half-Term Report*, p. 113; Sykes, *Troubled Loyalty*, pp. 233–35, 240–45.
19. Astor, 'Revolt against Hitler', *Encounter*, 1969; Malone, 'Adam von Trott', p. 565; idem, *Adam von Trott*, p. 218; Bowra, *Memoirs*, pp. 305–06; Rowse, *All Souls and Appeasement*, pp. 91–101; Sykes, *Troubled Loyalties*, pp. 233–68.
20. *DBFP*, 3, VI, Appendix I, (iii), (v), 16/23 (13).vi.39; Case XI, Protocol, Erich and Theo Kordt evidence, 4.vi./14.vii.1948, pp. 7443–48, 12131 ff; Blasius, pp. 150, 156–57; Aster, *1939*, p. 274; Colvin, *Vansittart*, p. 329; Rose, *Vansittart*, p. 236; Kordt, *Nicht aus den Akten*, pp. 313–19.
21. *DBFP*, 3, VII, Appendix I, (viii).
22. *DBFP*, 3, VI, Appendix III, (i), Annex, Wenner-Gren memorandum.
23. *DBFP*, 3, VI, Appendix III, (i), 5.vi.39.
24. *DBFP*, 3, VI, Appendix III, (ii), (iii), Wenner-Gren to Margesson, 10.vi.39; ibid., (iv), (vi), Wenner-Gren to Chamberlain, 3/19.vii.39; *DBFP*, 3, VII, 67 and Appendix I, (iii).
25. *DGFP*, D, VI, 716, 24.vii.39.

26. *Documents and materials relating to the Eve of the Second World War*, (Moscow 1948), Vol. II, *The Dirksen papers.*
27. Metzmacher, *VjhZg*, 1966, p. 374.
28. Aster, *1939*, pp. 183, 244, fn.
29. *DGFP*, D, VI, 368, Selzam (London) to Wiehl, 11.v.39.
30. *DGFP*, D, VI, 380, Rüter memorandum, 14.v.39.
31. *DBFP*, 3, VI, 354.
32. *DBFP*, 3, V, 741.
33. *DBFP*, 3, V, 539, 19.v.39.
34. *DBFP*, 3, VI, 192, Minute by Mr Roberts, 30.vi.39; *ibid.*, Appendix IV (i), memorandum by Charles Spencer, A. Holden, S. W. Rawson, 8.viii.39.
35. *DBFP*, 3, VI, Appendix IV (i); Dahlerus, *Last Attempt*, pp. 29–32.
36. *DGFP*, D, VI, 716.
37. Gladwyn, *Memoirs*, p. 93; Harvey diary, 24.vii.39.
38. *DBFP*, 3, VI, 354, 19.vii.39.
39. *DBFP*, 3, VI, 370, 20.vi.39; *DGFP*, D, VI, 716.
40. *DBFP*, 3.vi.370.
41. *DDF*, 2, XVII, 267, 268, 270, Corbin to Bonnet, 22.vii.39; *DGFP*, D, VI, 698, 22.vii.39.
42. *H.C.Deb.*, 350, cols. 1025–28; *DDF*, 2, XVII, 284, 285, Corbin to Bonnet, 24.vii.39.
43. Chamberlain papers, NC 18/1/1108, Chamberlain to Ida Chamberlain, 23.vii.39.
44. *DBFP*, 3, VI, 423, 439, Campbell to Halifax, 24/25.vii.39; *ibid.*, 442, Norton to Halifax, 25.vii.39; *DDF*, 2, XVII, 403, General Morse to Paris, 1.viii.39.
45. *DBFP*, 3, VI, 424, 440, Henderson to Halifax, 24/25.vii.39; *DDF*, 2, XVII, 302, 330, 331, 380, de St Hardouin to Bonnet, 25/27.vii./1.viii, 39; *DBFP*, 3, VI, 425, Loraine to Halifax, 24.vii.39.
46. *SPE*, II, 385, Suritz to Molotov, 25.vii.39; *DDF*, 2, XIII, 349, 367, 28/31.vii.39, Naggiar to Bonnet.
47. Gladwyn, *Memoirs*, p. 93.
48. *DGFP*, D, VI, 743, Ribbentrop to Dirksen, 31.vii.39.
49. *DGFP*, D. VI, 716.
50. Metzmacher, *VjhZg*, 1966, p. 389, fn. 126.
51. Crozier, *Appeasement and Germany's last bid*, pp. 241–63.
52. *DBFP*, 3, VI, 583; Dirksen, *Moskau, Tokyo, London*, pp. 251–52.
53. *DBFP*, 3, VI, Appendix IV, (ii), 24.vii.39; Dahlerus, *Last Attempt*, pp. 35–36.
54. *DBFP*, 3, VI, 443, Halifax Minute, 25.vii.39.
55. *DGFP*, D, VI, 783 and footnotes; Dahlerus, *Last Attempt*, pp. 43–48.
56. *DBFP*, 3, VI, Appendix IV, (iii).
57. Gannon, *British Press*, pp. 218–23.
58. Lenz and Ketternacker, 'Lord Kemsley's Gesprach', *VjhZg*, 1971; Dietrich, *Zwölf Jahre mit Hitler*, pp. 59–60.
59. PRO, FO 800/316, Halifax to Londonderry, 2.viii.39.
60. PRO, PREM I/331, Wilson memorandum, 20.viii.39.

Chapter 22   *Italy betrayed*

1. *DGFP*, D, VI, 433.
2. Raeder, *Mein Leben*, II, pp. 126–27.
3. Graziani, *Ho difeso la patria*, p. 178, cited Mack Smith, *Mussolini's Roman Empire*, p. 173.
4. Baudouin, 'Un voyage à Rome'.
5. Ciano, *Diario*, 4.iv.39; *PRO*, FO 371/28793, R 2392/7/22, Perth to Halifax, 6.iv.39.
6. Toscano, 'Colloqui con Gafencu' in *Pagine di Storia Contemporanea*, II; Gafencu, *Last Days*, pp. 123–32; Ciano, *Diario*, 30.iv.39.
7. Grandi, *Il mio paese*, p. 463.
8. Grandi, *Il mio paese*, pp. 400–61.
9. Grandi, *Il mio paese*, p. 463.
10. Grandi, *Il mio paese*, pp. 463–64; Ciano, *Diario*, 21/22.ii.39.
11. Ciano, *Ciario*, 3.iii.39.
12. Ciano, *Diario*, 9.xi.38.
13. Ciano, *Diario*, 1.xii.37.

14. Ciano, *Diario*, 16.xii.38.
15. Waterfield, *Professional Diplomat*, p. 22.
16. *DBFP*, 3, VI, 396, Loraine to Halifax, 21.vii.39.
17. Ciano, *Diario*, 31.i.40.
18. *DBFP*, 3, V, 424. 9.v.39.
19. Loraine to Halifax, 16.v.39, cited Waterfield, *Professional Diplomat*, p. 230.
20. Quartararo, p. 465, citing Italian archives.
21. Ciano, *Diario*, 27/28.v.39; *DGFP*, D, 456, Mackensen to Berlin, 31.v.39; *DBFP*, 3, 651, 652, 653, Loraine to Halifax, 28.v.39; *DDF*, 2, XVI, 312, François-Poncet to Bonnet, 30.v.39.
22. *DBFP*, 3.vi.353.
23. Harvey, *Diary*, 29.v.39; PRO, FO 371/23784, R 4399/1/22, minutes, 31.v., 1.vi.39.
24. Waterfield, *Professional Diplomat*, p. 253.
25. Ciano, *Diario*, 1.vi.39; *DBFP*, 3, V, 699.
26. Ciano, *Diario*, 31.v.39.
27. *DDI*, XII, 59; *DGFP*, D, VI, 459, Enclosure, IMT, XXI, 2818-PS.
28. Ciano, *Diario*, 2.vi.39; McGregor Knox, pp. 30–31.
29. A. Raspin, 'Wirtschaftliche und politische Aspekte der italienischen Rüstung', in Forstmeier and Volkmann, *Wirtschaft und Rüstung am Vorabend der zweiten Weltkrieges*.
30. *DDI*, 8, XII, 102, 134, 182, 186; Magistrati, pp. 355–60.
31. *DGFP*, D, VI, Appendix I, passim; Toscano, 'Le conversazioni militari italo-tedesche'. *Riv.Storica Italiani*, 1954.
32. *DDI*, 8, XII, 437, Attolico to Ciano, 3.vii.39.
33. *DDI*, 8, XII, 130, Attolico to Ciano, 6.vi.39; Toscano, *Origini*, p. 193.
34. *DGFP*, D, VI, 546, fn. 1.
35. *DDI*, 8, XII, 231, Attolico to Ciano, 14.vi.39.
36. *DDI*, 8, XII, 323, Attolico to Ciano, 23.vi.39.
37. *DDI*, 8, XII, 367, Attolico to Ciano, 26.vi.39.
38. *DDI*, 8, XII, 432.
39. *DDI*, 8, XII, 439, 3.vii.39.
40. Ciano, *Diario*, entries of 3/4.vii.39.
41. *DDI*, 8, XII, 443; Ciano, *Diario*, 3.vii.39.
42. *DDI*, 8, XII, 372, Crolla to Ciano, 27.vi.39; *DDI*, 8, XII, 464, Guariglia to Ciano, 4.vii.39.
43. *DDI*, 8, XII, 442, 3.vii.39.
44. Ciano, *Diario*, 7.vii.39; *DDI*, 8, XII, 463.
45. *DDI*, 8, XII, 464, Guariglia to Ciano, 4.vii.39.
46. *DBFP*, 3, VI, 261.
47. Loraine papers, Loraine to Halifax, 8.vii.39, Waterfield, *Professional Diplomat*, p. 235.
48. *DDI*, 8, XII, 505.
49. *DGFP*, D, VI, 629.
50. *DDI*, 8, XII, 466.
51. *DDI*, 8, XII, 495, 503, 504.
52. *DDI*, 8, XII, 518, Ciano to Attolico, 9.vii.39.
53. *DDI*, 8, XII, 535, 11.vii.39.
54. *DDI*, 8, XII, 550, 12.vii.39; *DDI*, 8, XII, 563, 13.vii.39.
55. *DDI*, 8, XII, 598, 17.vii.39.
56. *DGFP*, D, VI, 705, 23.vii.39.
57. *DDI*, 8, XII, 637.
58. *DDI*, 8, XII, 648, 22.vii.39.
59. *DDI*, 8, XII, 616, Arone to Ciano, 20.vii.39.
60. Ciano, *Diario*, 19.vii.39.
61. Ciano, *Diario*, 20.vii.39; *DDI*, 8, XII, 659, Caruso to Ciano, 24.vii.39.
62. Ciano, *Diario*, 23.vii.39.
63. Ciano, *Diario*, 21/22.vii.39; Magistrati, pp. 376–83.
64. *DDI*, 8, XII, 662; *DGFP*, D, VI, 718, Enclosure; Magistrati, pp. 380–82.
65. Blasius, pp. 106–07.
66. *DGFP*, D, VI, 711, Weizsäcker memorandum.
67. Magistrati, p. 384.
68. *DDI*, 8, XII, 674, 678, 689; *DGFP*, D, VI, 718; Magistrati, pp. 384–87.
69. Ciano, *Diario*, 27.vii.39.

70. Ciano, *Diario*, 28.vii.39.
71. *DAPE*, II, 800.
72. Ciano, *Diario*, 31.vii.39; *DGFP*, D, VI, 737.
73. Phipps papers I/22, 28.iv.39.
74. *DBFP*, 3, V, 85, 6.iv.39.
75. Quartararo, 'Appendice'.
76. Grandi, *Il mio paese*, passim.
77. PRO, FO 371/229351, DP (P) 65 Revise, July 1939.
78. PRO, CAB 2/8, CID, 360th Meeting, 20.vii.39; FO 371/22935, DP (P) 65 Revise; CAB 52/11, COS, 309th Meeting, 19.vii.39.
79. Roskill, *British Naval Strategy*, II, pp. 463–67.
80. *DBFP*, 3, V, 593, 603.
81. *DBFP*, 3, II, Phipps to Halifax, 24.ix.38; Harvey diary, 19/21/24/27.ix.38, 17.xi.38; Cadogan diary, 24.ix.38; Phipps papers, PHPP 1/21, Phipps to Halifax, 26.x.38.
82. Phipps papers, PHPP 1/23, Phipps to Halifax and Chamberlain, 22.vi.39.
83. Phipps papers, PHPP 3/1, Phipps to Horace Wilson, 13.vi.39.
84. Harvey diary, 10.i.39.
85. Roskill, *Hankey*, III, p. 294, 303–04, 389–91.
86. Harvey diary, 20.v.39; Roskill, Hankey, III, p. 393.
87. Phipps papers, PHPP 1/21, Phipps to Halifax, 31.x., 5.xi.38.
88. Phipps papers, PHPP 1/22, Phipps to Halifax, 22/27/28.iv.39; *DBFP*, 3, V, 251, 255, 289, 328.
89. *DBFP*, 3, VI, 48, 132, 162, 272, 273; PRO, FO 371/23795, R 4812/7/22, Sargent minute, 28.vi.39; PHPP 1/23, PRO, FO 371/23795, Phipps to Halifax, 11.vi.39; PRO, CAB 23/100, Cabinet Conclusions 83 (39) 4, 21.vi.39; Watt, 'Britain, France and the Italian Problem, 1937–1939' in *Les relations Franco-Britanniques de 1935 à 1939*.
90. *DDI*, 8, XII, 408, Crolla to Ciano, 30.vi.39.
91. *DDI*, 8, XII, 450, 545; *DBFP*, 3, VI, 313, 316; *DDF*, 2, XVII, 28, 166, 188, 210.
92. *DBFP*, 3, VI, 428.
93. *DBFP*, 3, VI, 398, Loraine to Halifax, 21.vii.39; *DBFP*, 3, VI, 509, 1.viii.39.
94. *DBFP*, 3, VI, 536.
95. *DDI*, 8, XII, 750, 767, 3/4.vii.39; Magistrati, p. 392.
96. *DDI*, 8, XII, 795, 796, 7.vii.39.
97. Marcello del Drago, unpublished memoirs, cited Guerri, *Ciano*, pp. 417–18.
98. *DDI*, 8, XII, 810.
99. Magistrati, pp. 395–97; Guerri, p. 418 citing del Drago.
100. Edda Ciano, *La mia testimonianza*, p. 149.
101. Magistrati, pp. 396–97; Schmidt, *Statist*, p. 438.
102. *DDI*, 8, XII, 1; *CDP*, pp. 297–99.
103. Magistrati, p. 397; Schmidt, *Statist*, pp. 438–39.
104. Magistrati, pp. 397–98.
105. Dollmann, p. 165.
106. *DGFP*, D, VII, 43; *DDI*, 8, XIII, 4; Dollmann, pp. 166–67; Schmidt, p. 439; Magistrati, pp. 399–400.
107. *DGFP*, D, VII, 25.
108. Siebert, pp. 242–43.
109. *DGFP*, D, VII, 50.
110. *DGFP*, D, VII, 47; *DDI*, 8, XIII, 21; Magistrati, pp. 402–03; Dollmann, p. 168.
111. Schmidt, p. 440; Dollmann, p. 168.
112. *DDI*, 8, XIII, 42; *DDF*, 2, XVIII, 35.
113. *DDI*, 8, XIII, 28, 29, 36, 47.

Chapter 23   Hitler wills his war

Where not otherwise stated, this chapter is based on the following sources: Burckhardt, *Meine Danziger Mission*; Magistrati, *L'Italia a Berlino*; diaries of von Weizsäcker, von Below, General Halder, Captain Engel; General Liebmann papers, 8; Lahousen diary, *Kriegstagebuch OKW, Abwehr II*; Halifax, 'A record of events'; Winterbotham, *Secret and Personal*; idem, *The Nazi Connection*; the diaries of Sir Alexander Cadogan, Captain Euan Wallace, Oliver Harvey, General

Pownall; Baumgart, 'Zur Ansprache Hitlers vor den Führern der Wehrmacht am 22 August 1939', *VjhZg*, 1968; General-Admiral Boehm, 'Zur Ansprache Hitlers vor den Führern der Wehrmacht am 22 August 1939', *VjhZg*, 1971.

1. *DGFP*, D, VII, 2.
2. *DGFP*, D, VII, 22, 82, 11/16.viii.39.
3. *DGFP*, D, VII, 46, 13.viii.39, Weizsäcker to Warsaw.
4. *DGFP*, D, VII, 91, 17.viii.39.
5. *DGFP*, D, VII, 106, 18.viii.39.
6. *DDF*, 2, XVIII, 2, 13.viii.39; *DDI*, 8, XIII, 58, 16.viii.39; *FRUS, 1939*, I, pp. 208–09, 10.viii.39.
7. *DDF*, 2, XVIII, 15, 14.viii.39; ibid., 48, 59, 97, 111, 15/18.viii.39.
8. *DGFP*, D, VII, 58, pp. 256–57.
9. *DDI*, 8, XIII, 44, 15.viii.39.
10. *DGFP*, D, VII, 115, 18.viii.39.
11. Dirksen, *Moskau, Tokio, London*, pp. 256–57.
12. Weizsäcker diary, 14.viii.39.
13. Weizsäcker diary, 6.viii.39.
14. Weizsäcker diary, 13.viii.39.
15. Rothermere-Ribbentrop correspondence 28.vi./20.vii./2/5.viii.39, in Simon MSS 85.
16. James Douglas-Hamilton, 'Ribbentrop and War', *JCH*, 1970; Tennant, *True Account*, pp. 217–26.
17. *DGFP*, D, VI, 784.
18. Sumner Welles memorandum, 9.viii.39, Schewe, X, 1976.
19. Szembek diary, 14.viii.39.
20. Borejsza, 'L'Italia e la guerra tedesca-polacca', *Storia Contemporanea*, 1976, pp. 629–30.
21. *DGFP*, D, VII, 44.
22. Lipski papers, 148, 11.viii.39; *DBFP*, 3, VII, 35, 16.viii.39.
23. Burckhardt, *Meine Danziger Mission*, pp. 336–39.
24. *DGFP*, D, VII, 4.
25. Burckhardt, p. 339.
26. *DBFP*, 3, VI, 659, pt. 2.
27. *FRUS, 1939*, I, pp. 211–12, Biddle to Hull, 11.viii.39; *ibid.*, p. 215, Biddle to Hull, 15.viii.39.
28. Szembek diary, 11.viii.39.
29. Burckhardt, pp. 337–38, 347–38.
30. *DBFP*, 3, VI, 16, 15.viii.39, Campbell to Cadogan.
31. *SPE*, II, 421, 16.viii.39.
32. *DBFP*, 3, VII, 11, 23, 39, 48.
33. *DGFP*, D, VII, 72.
34. *DGFP*, D, VII, 117.
35. *DGFP*, D, VII, 119, fn. 1.
36. *DGFP*, D, VII, 138.
37. *DGFP*, D, VII, 155, 21.viii.39.
38. *DGFP*, D, VII, 119.
39. *DGFP*, D, VII, 176.
40. Siebert, *Italiens Weg*, p. 252; Thielenhaus, p. 146.
41. *DBFP*, 3, VII, 5.
42. *DDI*, 8, XIII, 100, 101, 102; Magistrati, *L'Italia*, pp. 416–18.
43. *DDI*, 8, XIII, 108; Magistrati, pp. 418–19.
44. Magistrati, pp. 421–22.
45. Ciano, *Diario*, 21/22.viii.39.
46. Thielenhaus, pp. 137, 141; Blasius, pp. 121–22.
47. *PRO*, FO 371/22976, C 11375/15/18, Strang memorandum, 17.viii.39.
48. Cadogan diary, 18.viii.39.
49. *PRO*, FO 800/816, Halifax to Chamberlain, 19.viii.39.
50. Halifax, 'Record', 22.viii.39.
51. Euan Wallace diary, 22.viii.39. CAB 23/100, CAB 41(39).
52. Halifax, 'Record', 24.viii.39.
53. *DGFP*, D, VII, 221, 23.viii.39; Winterbotham, *Secret and Personal*, pp. 135–36; *idem, The Nazi Connection*, pp. 199–200; Barker, Aviator Extraordinary, pp. 130–36.

54. See Chapter XXI above; *DBFP*, 3, VII, Appendix I, (ii), (iii), (vii).
55. *DBFP*, 3, VII, Appendix I, (i).
56. Von Below diary, 12.viii.39; von Lossberg, *im Wehrmachtsführungstab*, pp. 31–32.
57. Lahousen diary, 16.viii.39.
58. Halder diary, 14.viii.39.
59. Halder diary, 14/15.viii.39.
60. Halder diary, 16.viii.39.
61. Domarus, II, 1230.
62. *DGFP*, D, VII, 87.
63. Winterbotham, *Secret and Personal*, pp. 23–24; *idem*, *The Nazi Connection*, pp. 20–24; Baron William de Ropp, 'I spied on Hitler', *Daily Mail* (London), 28–31.x., 1.xi.57.
64. *DGFP*, D, VII, 74, 151, 16/21.viii.39.
65. Read and Fisher, pp. 210–12.
66. *DGFP*, D, VII, 135.
67. *DGFP*, D, VII, 142.
68. *DGFP*, D, VII, 158.
69. *DGFP*, D, VII, 160.
70. *DBFP*, 3, VII, 128, 153.
71. Liebmann papers, 8, pp. 428–30; Boehm, 'Zur Ansprache', *VjhZg*, 1971.
72. Liebmann papers, 8, pp. 428–32; Boehm, 'Zur Ansprache'; Halder diary, 22.viii.39; *DGFP*, D, VII, 192, 193.
73. Liebmann papers, 8, pp. 430–32.
74. Engel diary, 22/24.viii.39.

Chapter 24   Ribbentrop in Moscow: the Nazi-Soviet Pact signed

Where not otherwise stated, this chapter is based on the following materials: (1) For Ribbentrop's visit to Moscow: Hoffmann, *I Was Hitler's Friend*; Hilger and Meyer, *The Incompatible Allies*; Kleist, *Zwischen Hitler und Stalin*; Schmidt, *Statist auf diplomatische Bühne*. (2) For the Anglo-French-Soviet staff talks: (i) The records of the staff meetings printed in *DBFP*, 3, VI, App. V and VII, App. II; in *DDF*, 2, XVIII, Add. I–IV; and in *SPE*, II; (ii) the diaries of Admiral Drax, General Davidson and Admiral Robertshaw; (iii) the final report of Corvette Capitaine Willaume, French naval delegate, *DDF*, 2, XVIII, Add. V; (iv) extracts from General Doumenc's memoir of his mission, *DDF*, 2, XVIII, Add. VI; (v) Beaufre, *Le Drâme de 1940*; (vi) Read and Fisher, *The Deadly Embrace*.

1. Doumenc memoir, *DDF*, 2, XVIII, p. 611.
2. *DGFP*, D. VII, 75, 105.
3. Read and Fisher, pp. 246–48; Hoffmann, pp. 246–48; Kleist, *Zwischen Hitler und Stalin*, pp. 54–55.
4. von Weizsäcker, *Errinerungen*, p. 252.
5. Schmidt, *Statist*, p. 441.
6. Kleist, *Zwischen Hitler und Stalin*, p. 55.
7. G.E.R. Gedye Papers, Box 21, p. 145; *DBFP*, 3, VII, 104, Seeds to Halifax, 21.viii.39.
8. *SPE*, II, 4–21, Suritz to Moscow, 16.vii.39.
9. *FRUS*, *The Soviet Union, 1933–1939*, pp. 775–79, Steinhart to Hull, 10.viii.39.
10. Davidson diary, 11.viii.39.
11. Doumenc memoir, *DDF*, 2, XVIII, p. 608.
12. Davidson diary, 12.viii.39.
13. Drax diary, 12.viii.39.
14. *PRO*, CAB 27/625, F.P.C., 57th mtg, 10.vii.39.
15. Drax diary and narrative, p. 5.
16. Willaume report, *DDF*, 2, XVIII, p. 596.
17. Willaume report, *DDF*, 2, XVIII, p. 598.
18. *DBFP*, 3, VII, 30, 38, 39, 52, 60, 70, 88, 90, 119; *DDF*, 2, XVIII, 51, 68, 92, 115, 120, 144, 153.
19. *DBFP*, 3, VII, 60, 87, 94; *DDF*, 2, XVIII, 69, 110, 114, 147, 150, 169; Beaufre, 1940, pp. 153–62; Noël, *L'Aggression Allemande*, pp. 422–24.
20. *DDF*, 2, XVIII, 182, fn. 5, Gamelin to Moscow, 21.viii.39; ibid, 167, 182.

21. *DBFP*, 3, VII, 115, Strang minute, 21.viii.39, ibid, 130 and fn.
22. *DBFP*, 3, VII, 104, Seeds to Halifax, 21.viii.39.
23. *DDF*, 2, XVIII, 182, fn. 5.
24. *DBFP*, 3, VII, App. II, 11.
25. Hilger and Meyer, *Incompatible Allies*, pp. 301–02.
26. IMT, Hess-16, Gaus Affidavit.
27. *DGFP*, D, VII, 228.
28. *DGFP*, D, VII, 229.
29. Hilger and Meyer, *Incompatible Allies*, p. 302; Schmidt, *Statist*, p. 444.
30. Schmidt, p. 444.
31. *DGFP*, D, VII, 205, 210.
32. *DGFP*, D, VII, 206.
33. *DGFP*, D, VII, 213.
34. Kleist, *Zwischen Hitler und Stalin*, p. 37.

Chapter 25   The impact of the Nazi-Soviet Pact

Where not otherwise stated, this chapter is based on the following sources: (1) For the reactions in Berlin: the diaries of von Below, and von Weizsäcker, and Kleist, *Zwischen Hitler und Stalin*; (2) For reactions in London, the diaries of Captain Euan Wallace, Sir Thomas Inskip, Sir Samuel Hoare and W. Crookshank; Halifax, *A record of events before the war*, 1939, PRO, FO 800/517; the diaries of Sir Alexander Cadogan, Harold Nicolson, MP, Hugh Dalton, Leo Amery, Oliver Harvey, General Sir Henry Pownall; (3) For reactions in Yugoslavia, Breccia, *Jugoslavia*; (4) For reactions in Romania, Lungu, *Romania and the European Great Powers*; (5) For reactions in Paris, *Les Carnets Secrets de Jean Zay*; (6) For reactions in Japan, Boyd, *The Extraordinary Envoy*; Chihiro Hosoya, 'The Tripartite Pact, 1939–40', in Morley (Ed.), *Deterrent Diplomacy*; (7) On the Japanese-Soviet fighting at Nomonhan, Coox, *Nomonhan*, vol. II, Hata, 'The Japanese-Soviet Confrontation', in Morley (Ed.), *Deterrent Diplomacy*, Erickson, *The Soviet High Command*; Detweiler and Burdick (Eds), *War in Asia and the Pacific*, vol. xi; (8) For reactions in the Communist Party of Great Britain, PRO, WP (43) 159 of 13.iii.43: in the *Parti Communiste Française*, Rossi, *Les Communistes français pendant la drôle de guerre*, J. C. Simmonds, 'The French Communist Party and the Beginnings of Resistance'. *ESR*, 1981. More generally, Leonhard, *Der Schock des Hitler-Stalin Paktes*.

1. Von Below diary, 23.viii.39.
2. Teske, *Koestring*, p. 142.
3. Von Below diary, 24.viii.39.
4. Von Weizsäcker diary, 24.viii.39; Jodl diary, 24.viii.39, *IMT*, 1788-PS.
5. Von Below, 24.viii.39.
6. Cadogan diary, 22.viii.39; Euan Wallace diary, 22.viii.39; Crookshank diary, 22.viii.39: Halifax, 'A record of events', FO 800/317 (22.viii.39); *PRO*, CAB 23/100, Cab 41 (59).
7. *DBFP*, 3, VII, 137.
8. *DBFP*, 3, VII, 56, 68, 73, 95, 119.
9. *DBFP*, 3, VII, 142, 145, 146.
10. *DBFP*, 3, VII, 200, Henderson to Halifax, 23.viii.39.
11. *DBFP*, 3, VII, 415; *DGFP*, D, VII, 200.
12. *DBFP*, 3, VII, 211.
13. *DBFP*, 3, VII, 248.
14. Weizsäcker, *Errinerungen*, p. 252.
15. Kleist, *Zwischen Hitler und Stalin*, p. 66.
16. Inskip diary, 25.viii.39; *PRO*, CAB 23/100, Cab 42 (39).
17. Gannon, *British Press*, pp. 279–84; *DDF*, 2, XVIII, 338, Cambon (London) to Bonnet, 24.viii.39; Naylor, *Labour's International Policy*, p. 308.
18. *DDF*, 2, XVIII, 224, Cambon (London) to Bonnet, 22.viii.39.
19. *DDF*, 2, XVIII, 404, 405, 25.viii.39. Naylor, *Labour's International Policy*, p. 306.
20. Euan Wallace diary, 24.viii.39; Nicolson diary, 24.viii.39.
21. Hoare diary, 24.viii.39; Naylor, *Labour's International Policy*, p. 307.
22. *DCER*, III, 992, Skelton memorandum, 22.viii.39.
23. *SPE*, II, 441, 444, 23/26.viii.39.
24. Sywottek, *Mobilmachung*, pp. 219–33; *DDF*, 2, XVIII, 96, 128, 141, 162, 192, 232, 370, 417;

DBFP, 3, VII, 251; *DDI*, 8, XIII, 126, 204; see also *DGFP*, VII, App. IV; M. Toscano, 'Di alcuni falsi e omissioni nel libro bianco tedesco sulle origini della seconda guerra mondiale', *Pagine di storia diplomatica contemporanea*, II, pp. 187–209.

25. *DDF*, 2, XVIII, 215, Noel to Bonnet, 22.viii.39; Lukasiewicz, *Diplomat in Paris*, pp. 254–55, Beck to Lukasiewicz, 22.viii.39; *DBFP*, 3, VII, 124, Kennard to Halifax, 22.viii.39; *DDI*, 8, XIII, Arone to Ciano, 22.viii.39.
26. *DDF*, 2, XVIII, 396, Musse to Daladier, 24.viii.39.
27. *DBFP*, 3, VII, 123, 124.
28. *DBFP*, 3, VII, 264; *DDF*, 2, XVIII, 374; Lipski, *Diplomat in Berlin*, 154, Beck to Grzybowski, 26.viii.39.
29. *DBFP*, 3, VII, 206.
30. *Carnets Secrets de Jean Zay*, 22.viii.39; Duroselle, *La Décadence*, p. 474.
31. *DDF*, 2, XVIII, 324; Gamelin, *Servir*, I, pp. 23–43; Bonnet, *Dans la Tourmente*, pp. 166–70; Reynaud, *Au Coeur de la Mêlée*, pp. 328–32.
32. *DDF*, 2, XVIII, 328; Daladier to Gamelin, 23.viii.39.
33. Gamelin, *Servir*, I, pp. 23–43.
34. *Carnets Secrets de Jean Zay*, 24.viii.39; Duroselle, *La Décadence*, p. 475.
35. *DDF*, 2, XVIII, 284, rec. Paris 6 p.m., 23.viii.39.
36. *DDF*, 2, XVIII, 306, 307, rec. Paris 1 a.m., 24.viii.39.
37. *DDF*, 2, XVIII, 343, 350.
38. Ciano, *Diario*, 18.viii.39.
39. Călinescu diary (cited in Lungu, *Romania and the European Great Powers*), 21.viii.39.
40. *DDF*, 2, XVIII, 303, Annex, Bonnet to Thierry, 23.viii.39, 11.35 p.m.
41. Călinescu diary (cited in Lungu, *Romania and the European Great Powers*), 24/25.viii.39.
42. *DDF*, 2, XVIII, Spitzenmüller (Bucharest) to Bonnet, 12.viii.39.
43. *DDF*, 2, XVIII, 400, Thierry to Bonnet, 24/25.viii.39.
44. *DDF*, 2, XVIII, 431, 25.viii.39.
45. Gafencu to Berlin, 25.viii.39 (cited from Romanian State Archives, AMEA f.71/Romania vol. 77, Lungu, *Romania and the European Great Powers*).
46. *DGFP*, D, VII, 386, 28.viii.39.
47. *DGFP*, D, VII, 361; *DDI*, 8, XIII, 388.
48. *DGFP*, D, VI, 78, 632, 638, 639; *DGFP*, D, VII, 97, 121, 127, 162, 230, 243, 345, 373.
49. *DGFP*, D, VII, 517, 547, 1.ix.39.
50. *DGFP*, D, VII, 497.
51. *DGFP*, D, VII, 454, 30.viii.39.
52. *DDF*, 2, XVIII, 216, Brugère to Bonnet, 22.viii.39.
53. Breccia, *Jugoslavia*, pp. 169–70.
54. Ciano, *Diario*, 13/15.viii.39.
55. *DDI*, 8, XIII, 162.
56. Ciano, *Diario*, 22.viii.39.
57. Breccia, pp. 177–81.
58. *DGFP*, D, VII, 112, 18.viii.39.
59. *DBFP*, 3, VII, 554 and fn. 1.
60. *DBFP*, 3, VII, 556, Campbell to Halifax, 30.viii.39.
61. Brugère, *Veni, Vidi, Vichy*, pp. 12, 161–63.
62. Woodward, *British Foreign Policy*, I, pp. 22–23; Balfour and McKay, *Prince Paul*, pp. 190–91.
63. Breccia, *Jugoslavia*, pp. 182–83; Balfour and McKay, *Prince Paul*, pp. 186–87.
64. Boyd, *Extraordinary Envoy*, pp. 119–23.
65. IMT FE, Exh. 2232; Boyd, *Extraordinary Envoy*, pp. 119–23.
66. *DGFP*, D, VII, 22.viii.39; Oshima to Arita, 22.viii.39, cited Hosoya in Morley (Ed.), *Deterrent Diplomacy*, p. 191.
67. von Weizsäcker, *Errinerungen*, p. 429.
68. Oshima to Arita, 23.viii.39, cited Hosoya in Morley (Ed.), *Deterrent Diplomacy*, p. 192; *DGFP*, D, VII, 183.
69. *DGFP*, D, VII, 223.
70. *DGFP*, D, VII, 209.
71. *DGFP*, D, VII, 262, 329, 24/26.viii.39.
72. Coox, *Nomonhan*, vol. II, passim; Hata in Morley (Ed.), *Deterrent Diplomacy*, pp. 169–70; Erickson, *Soviet High Command*, pp. 532–37.
73. *DDI*, 8, XIII, 253, 550, Guadagnini (Hsin King) to Ciano, 25.viii./1.ix.39.

74. *DDI*, 8, XIII, 435, 30.viii.39; Hosoya in Morley (Ed.), *Deterrent Diplomacy*, pp. 193–94.
75. Kido diary, 28.viii.39, cited Hosoya in Morley (Ed.), *Deterrent Diplomacy*, p. 194.
76. *DDI*, 8, XIII, 435; Hosoya in Morley (Ed.), *Deterrent Diplomacy*, pp. 194–95.
77. Djilas, *Memoirs of a Revolutionary*, pp. 329–30.
78. *PRO WP* (43) 159, 13.iii.43; Rossi, *Les Communistes français*, pp. 18–37; Simmonds, 'The French Communist Party', *ESR* 1981.

Chapter 26   War ordered – and deferred: August 25 in Berlin

Where not otherwise stated, this chapter is based on the following sources: (1) For the German military planning, Klaus Meier *et al.* (Eds), *Das Deutsche Reich und der Zweite Weltkrieg*, vol. II, die *Errichtung der Hegemonie auf dem europäischen Kontinent*, esp. pp. 79–103; *Kriegstagebuch der Marineleitung*; Spiess and Liechtenstein, *das Unternehmen Tannenberg*; *Kriegstagebuch Halder*; Lahousen diary, *Kriegstagebuch OKW Abwehr II*; Schmidt, *Statist auf diplomatische Bühne*; the diaries of von Weizsäcker, Engel and von Below; Jurgen Runzheimer, 'Der Ueberfall auf den Sender Gleiwitz' *VjHZg*, 1962; Charles Whiting, 'The Man who invaded Poland', *World War II Investigator*, 1988. (2) On the Italian side: *DDI*, 8, XIII, Appendice I, 'Cronologia dei principali avvenimenti precedenti lo scoppio della Guerra'; de Felice, *Mussolini il Duce*, vol. II, *Lo Stato totalitario, 1936–1940*; Dino Grandi, 'Il mio diario', in D. Grandi (ed. R. de Felice), *Il mio Paese*; Ciano, *Diario*. (3) On the Polish side, Józef Lipski, *Diplomat in Berlin*. (4) On the activities of Hr. Dahlerus, c.f. his original narrative in the Halifax Papers, with comments by Frank Roberts and Llewellyn Woodward, April 1943. This is less subject to *ex post facto* editing than Birger Dahlerus, *The Last Attempt*, which was published after Hr. Dahlerus had testified at the Nuremberg War Crimes Trial.

1. von Lossberg, *Im Wehrmachtsführungsstab*, pp. 31–32.
2. *DGFP*, D, VI, 40, 18.iii.39.
3. Mikus, *La republique Slovaque*, pp. 168–70.
4. Durica, *La Slovacchia*, pp. 97–108.
5. *DGFP*, D, VII, 100.
6. *DGFP*, D, VII, 165.
7. *DDI*, 8, XIII, 139, Lo Faro (Bratislava) to Ciano, 21.viii.39.
8. *DGFP*, D, VII, 237.
9. *DDI*, 8, XIII, 50, Lo Faro to Ciano, 15.viii.39.
10. *DDI*, 8, XIII, 277, Vinci (Budapest), to Ciano, 25.viii.39.
11. *DGFP*, D, VII, 176, Veesenmayer to A.A., 22.viii.39.
12. Ruhnau, *Freie Stadt Danzigs*, pp. 169–70.
13. *DGFP*, D, VI, 555, 580, 21/29.viii.39.
14. *KTB der Marine*, 15.viii.39; *ND*, C-126A, 21.viii.39.
15. *KTB der Marine*, 23.viii.39.
16. *DBFP*, 3, VII, 275, Shepherd to Halifax, 25.viii.39; *DDI*, 8, XIII, Spechel to Ciano, 26.viii.39.
17. *DGFP*, D, VII, 197, 224.
18. *DGFP*, D, VII, 231, Greiser memorandum.
19. *DDF*, 2, XVIII, 354.
20. *DGFP*, D, VII, 232, 254.
21. *DGFP*, D, VII, 259, Enclosure II, Chodacki to Greiser, 24.viii.39.
22. *DDF*, 2, XVIII, 407, 441.
23. *DDF*, 2, XVIII, 416.
24. *DBFP*, 3, VII, 245, 265, 273.
25. Spiess and Liechtenstein, *Unternehmen Tannenberg*; *KTB OKW Abwehr II*; *IMT*, 2751-PS, Naujocks Affidavit; Runzheimer, 'Der Ueberfall', passim.
26. *ND*-NOKW-423, 4.viii.39; *KTB OKW Abwehr II*, 15/18/20/23/28.viii.39.
27. *ND*-NOKW-083, 23.viii.39.
28. Spiess and Liechtenstein, *Unternehmen Tannenberg*, p. 28.
29. See chapter XXXI below.
30. *DBFP*, 3, VII, 112, 127, 158, 21/22.viii.39.
31. Lipski, *Diplomat*, 151, Lipski to Beck, 18.viii.39.
32. *DBFP*, 3, VII, 58.

33. *DBFP*, 3, VII, 127, 22.viii.39.
34. *DBFP*, 3, VII, 166, 23.viii.39.
35. *DBFP*, 3, VII, 140, 170, 22/23.viii.39.
36. Lipski, *Diplomat*, 152.
37. Lipski, *Diplomat*, pp. 565-66, 587-88.
38. *DBFP*, 3, VII, 221, 228, 263, Kennard to Halifax, 24/25.viii.39.
39. Lipski, *Diplomat*, pp. 590-91; *DBFP*, 3, VII, 263.
40. *DDF*, 2, XVIII, 333.
41. Dahlerus narrative, April 1943; *DBFP*, 3, VII, 285, minute by Hr. Dahlerus.
42. *DBFP*, 3, VII, 283, 301; *DGFP*, D, VII, 265.
43. *DBFP*, 3, VII, 284, 286.
44. *DBFP*, 3, VII, 287; *DGFP*, D, VII, 267.
45. Weizsäcker diary, 25.viii.39; Schmidt, *Statist*, p. 450.
46. *DDI*, 8, XIII, 232; Appendice I, 25.viii.39.
47. Halder diary, 25.viii.39.
48. *ND-NOKW* 2660, *KTB XV AOK, 14 Army*, 25.viii.39.
49. *KTB der Marine*, 4-25/viii.39.
50. *DDF*, 2, XVIII, 425.
51. Dahlerus narrative.
52. Inskip diary, 25.viii.39.
53. Weizsäcker diary, 25.viii.39.
54. *DGFP*, D, VII, 266; *DDI*, 8, XIII, 245.
55. *DGFP*, D, VII, 280, 25.viii.39; Ciano, *Diario*, 25.viii.39.
56. *DDI*, 8, XIII, 236.
57. de Felice, *Mussolini*, II, pp. 653-54.
58. *DDI*, 8, XIII, 320, Guariglia to Ciano, 26.viii.39.
59. Grandi diary, 21.viii.39.
60. de Felice, p. 655.
61. de Bono diary, cited in de Felice, p. 655.
62. Grandi diary, 17.viii.39.
63. Agence Stefani papers, cited in de Felice, p. 657.
64. *DBFP*, 3, VII, 79; *DDI*, 8, XIII, 117.
65. Grandi diary, 23.viii.39.
66. *DDI*, 8, XIII, 162.
67. Ciano, *Diario*, 22.viii.39.
68. de Felice, *Mussolini*, II, pp. 661-62.
69. *DBFP*, 3, VII, 214, Loraine to Halifax, 2.30 a.m., on 24.viii.39.
70. *DBFP*, 3, VII, 243.
71. Ciano, *Diario*, 24.viii.39.
72. de Felice, p. 661.
73. *DDI*, 8, XIII, 232.
74. *DDI*, 8, XIII, 231, 235.
75. *DDI*, 8, XIII, 250; *DGFP*, D, VII, 271; Magistrati, *L'Italia*, p. 431.
76. von Below, Engels, Weizsäcker, Halder diaries, 25.viii.39.
77. *ND-NOKW-2660*, *KTB XV AK*, *ND-NOKW-2882*, *KTB I AK*, 25.viii.39; *KTB OKW Abwehr* II, 25.viii.39.
78. Spiess and Liechtenstein, *Unternehmen Tannenberg*, pp. 113-123.
79. *DGFP*, D, VII, 330, Enclosures 1 and 2, Polish Embassy Berlin Notes-Verbales, 25.viii.39.
80. Lipski, *Diplomat*, pp. 592-93 and footnote 25; *DGFP*, D, VII, 336.
81. *ND-NOKW-2660*, *KTB XV AK*, 26.viii.39.
82. von Lossberg, pp. 34-35, Raeder, *Mein Leben*, II, p. 167.
83. Görlitz, *Keitel*, p. 212.
84. *DGFP*, D, VII, 277.
85. von Below diary, 25.viii.39.
86. Chamberlain papers, NC 18/1/1115.
87. Dahlerus narrative, 25.viii.39.

Chapter 27   Regrouping for war

Where not otherwise stated, this chapter is based on the following sources: (1) On the diaries of von Below, Grosscurth, Halder, Weizsäcker. (2) On the cabinet diaries of Walter Crookshank, Sir Samuel Hoare (Lord Templewood), Sir Thomas Inskip and Captain Euan Wallace, and on Lord Halifax, 'A Record of Events before the War 1939', PRO, FO 800/317. (3) On Birger Dahlerus 1943 Narrative, included in Halifax Papers, A4.410.3. 10, Reel 1, Churchill College, Cambridge, Halifax to Cadogan 29.iv.1943. (4) On the papers and diaries of Sir Alexander Cadogan, Churchill College, Cambridge. (5) On D. Irving (Ed.), *Breach of Security, the German Secret Intelligence File on Events leading to the Second World War* with an Introduction by D. C. Watt (London, 1968). (6) On the memoirs of Robert Coulondre, *de Staline à Hitler*, Leon Noël, *L'Aggression Allemande contre la Pologne*, Paul-Otto Schmidt, *Statist auf diplomatische Bühne* and Massimo Magistrati, *L'Italia a Berlino*. (7) On the collected papers of Józef Lipski, *Diplomat in Berlin*, J. Lukasiewicz, *Diplomat in Paris* and on the diaries of Count Jan Szembek.

1. William Strang papers, Norton to Strang, private letter, 30.viii.39.
2. René Girault in Rémond, *Daladier*, pp. 212–14.
3. *DBFP*, 3, VII, 346, Phipps to Halifax, 26.viii.39.
4. Lukasiewicz, *Diplomat in Paris*, p. 263.
5. von Below diary, 26.viii.39.
6. Halder diary, Grosscurth diary, 26.viii.39.
7. Kleist, *Zwischen Moskau und Berlin*, p. 72.
8. Halder diary, 26.viii.39.
9. Grosscurth diary, 26.viii.39.
10. Halder diary, 26.viii.39.
11. Halder diary, 28.viii.39.
12. Grosscurth diary, 27.viii.39.
13. Halder diary, Grosscurth diary, 28.viii.39.
14. Ciano, *Diario*, 26.viii.39.
15. *DDI*, 8, XIII, 293; *DGFP*, D, VII, 301.
16. Ciano, *Diario*, 26.viii.39; Magistrati, *L'Italia*.
17. *DGFP*, D, VII, 308, 311.
18. *DGFP*, D, VII, 307, Hitler to Mussolini, 3 p.m., 26.viii.39; *DDI*, 8, XIII, 298.
19. *DGFP*, D, VII, 317; *DDI*, 8, XIII, 304.
20. *DGFP*, D, VII, 341, 27.viii.39; *DDI*, 8, XIII, 329.
21. *FYB*, 253; *DGFP*, D, VII, 324.
22. Coulondre, *de Staline à Hitler*, pp. 290–91.
23. Grosscurth diary, 27.viii.39; *FYB*, 261.
24. Stehlin, *Témoignage*, p. 173.
25. *FRUS, 1939*, I, pp. 361–62, 24.viii.39, p. 368, 25.viii.39; *PWB*, 90.
26. Halifax, 'Record of Events', 26/27.viii.39; Dahlerus 1943 Narrative.
27. *DBFP*, 3, VII, 349, Annex I.
28. Halifax, 'Record'; *FRUS, 1939*, I, pp. 369–70, Kennedy to Hull.
29. Crookshank, Wallace, Hoare, Inskip diaries, 26.viii.39; Halifax, 'Record'; Cadogan diary, 26.viii.39; CAB 23/100, Cab 43(39).
30. Dahlerus 1943 Narrative, Woodward commentary, citing Ogilvie-Forbes to Halifax, 26.viii.39.
31. *DGFP*, D, VII, 319.
32. Dahlerus 1943 Narrative; *DBFP*, 3, VII, 349, Annex I, Dahlerus memo, 27.viii.39.
33. Szembek diary, 26.viii.39; Noël, *L'Aggression Allemande*, pp. 436–37; *FYB*, 246, 252, 258; *DBFP*, 3, VII, 212; *ADSS*, I, 135, 136.
34. *DGFP*, D, VII, 54; *FYB*, 266.
35. *DGFP*, D, VII, 349, Mackensen to A.A., 21.viii.39.
36. Coulondre, *de Staline à Hitler*, p. 291.
37. *DGFP*, D, VII, 357.
38. Domarus, II, pp. 1276–77; Halder diary, 27.viii.39; *DDI*, 8, XIII, 346.
39. Cadogan diary, 27.viii.39; Dahlerus 1943 narrative.
40. Halifax, 'Record'; Cadogan diary, 27.viii.39.
41. Cadogan diary, 27.viii.39.
42. *DBFP*, 3, VII, 397, Kirkpatrick minute, 27.viii.39.

43. *DBFP*, 3, VII, 403, fn. 1.
44. *DBFP*, 3, VII, 402, 408, 418, 27.viii.39.
45. Domarus, II, p. 1234, fn. 650.
46. Halder diary, 29.viii.39.
47. Greiner, *Oberste Wehrmachtsführung*, p. 56.
48. *DBFP*, 3, VII, 418, Ogilvie-Forbes to Halifax, 3.40 p.m. 28.viii.39; *DBFP*, 3, VII, 437, Ogilvie-Forbes to Halifax, 10.00 p.m., 28.viii.39.
49. *DBFP*, 3, VII, Halifax to Kennard, 6.50 p.m., 28.viii.39.
50. *DBFP*, 3, VII, 456, Kennard to Halifax, 3.44 p.m., 29.viii.39.
51. *DBFP*, 3, VII, 455, fn. 8, minutes by Kirkpatrick, Orme Sargent and Halifax.
52. *FRUS, 1939*, I, pp. 380–81, Bullitt to Hull, 29.viii.39.
53. *Breach of Security*, p. 99.
54. Dahlerus, *Last Attempt*, p. 80.
55. Coulondre, *de Staline à Hitler*, p. 295.
56. *DBFP*, 3, VII, 501.
57. *DBFP*, 3, VII, 426; *DGFP*, D, VII, 384, Enclosure.
58. Hore-Belisha Papers 5/67; Halifax, 'Record'; Wallace, Inskip, Hoare, Cadogan diaries, 27.viii.39.
59. *FYB*, 276, 281; *PWB*, 94; *DBFP*, 3, VII, 410; *FRUS, 1939*, I, pp. 274–75, Biddle to Hull, 26.viii.39.
60. *FRUS, 1939*, I, pp. 380–81, Bullitt to Hull, 29.viii.39.
61. Szembek diary, 29.viii.39.
62. *DDI*, 8, XIII, 399.
63. *Breach of Security*, p. 99.
64. Coulondre, *de Staline à Hitler*, p. 296; *DDI*, 8, XIII, 399, 400, 402.
65. *DBFP*, 3, VII, 458, 459, 467, 470, 477, 478; Dahlerus 1943 Narrative.
66. Hoare diary, 29.viii.39.
67. *ND-NOKW-2660*, *KTB XV AOK*, 29.viii.39; Halder diary, 29.viii.39.
68. *DGFP*, D, VII, 362, 401; *DDI*, 8, XIII, 412.
69. Weizsäcker diary, 29.viii.39.
70. Engel diary, 29.viii.39.
71. Weizsäcker diary, 28.viii.39.
72. Halder diary, 29.viii.39.
73. Weizsäcker diary, 28.viii.39.
74. Kleist, *Zwischen Stalin und Hitler*, pp. 75–76.
75. Lipski, *Diplomat in Berlin*, p. 601, citing note by Beck's secretary, Pawel Starzenski.
76. Szembek diary, 29.viii.39; Noel, *L'Aggression Allemande*, p. 463, *DBFP*, 3, VII, 473, 475, 482, 489.
77. *DBFP*, 3, VII, 492, Kennard to Halifax, 10.15 p.m., 29.viii.39.
78. *FYB*, 269, de la Tournelle (Danzig) to Bonnet, 27.viii.39.
79. *FYB*, 289, 29.viii.39.
80. *DDI*, 8, XIII, 359, Spechel (Danzig) to Ciano, 28.viii.39.
81. *DDI*, 8, XIII, 393, Spechel to Ciano, 29.viii.39; *DDI*, 8, XIII, 428, 429, Spechel to Ciano, 30.viii.39.
82. *FYB*, 305, 30.viii.39. See also *PWB*, 106, Zawadowski (Danzig) to Beck, 28.viii.39.
83. Burckhardt, *Meine Danziger Mission*, pp. 351–52.
84. *DBFP*, 3, VII, 490, 498, 502, 508, 565; *DGFP*, D, VII, 421.
85. Von Hassell diary, 29.viii.39.
86. Dahlerus 1943 Narrative.
87. Dahlerus, *Last Attempt*, pp. 84–85.
88. Weizsäcker diary, 29.viii.39.
89. *DBFP*, 3, VII, 508, 565.
90. Schmidt, *Statist*, p. 455.
91. *DBFP*, 3, VII, 514, Foreign Office minute; Dahlerus 1943 narrative.
92. Cadogan diary, 29.viii.39.
93. *DBFP*, 3, VII, 58, 495.
94. *DBFP*, 3, VII, 505, Halifax to Kennard.
95. *DBFP*, 3, VII, 509.
96. *DBFP*, 3, VII, 506.
97. *DBFP*, 3, VII, 508.

98. *DBFP*, 3, VII, 520.
99. *DBFP*, 3, VII, 512.
100. *FYB*, 293, Corbin to Bonnet, 11.55 p.m., 29.viii.39.
101. Coulondre, *de Staline à Hitler*, pp. 296–97; *FYB*, 300.
102. *FYB*, 294, Bonnet to Noël, 1 a.m., 30.viii.39.
103. *DBFP*, 3, VII, 507.
104. Ciano, *Diario*, 29.viii.39.
105. *DDI*, 8, XIII, 418, 419, 422.
106. Coulondre, *de Staline à Hitler*, p. 298.
107. *DBFP*, 3, VII, 520, 1 p.m., 30.viii.39.
108. *DBFP*, 3, VII, 519, 12.30 p.m., 30.viii.39.
109. *DBFP*, 3, VII, 546, Henderson to Halifax, 9.00 p.m., 30.viii.39.
110. *DBFP*, 3, VII, 551, Henderson to Halifax, 9.37 p.m., 30.viii.39.
111. von Hassell diary, 29.viii.39.
112. Bodo von Scheurig, *Ewald von Kleist-Schmenzin*, passim; *DBFP*, 3, II, App. IV, pp. 638–39; *DBFP*, 3, III, 386, 29.xi.39.
113. Strauch, *Henderson*, p. 298, fn. 52.
114. Wallace diary, Hoare diary, 30.viii.39.
115. Inskip diary, quoting Halifax.
116. *DGFP*, D, VII, 450; *DBFP*, 3, VII, 525.
117. *DBFP*, 3, VII, 532, 539.
118. *Breach of Security*, pp. 102–103.
119. *DBFP*, 3, VII, 592.
120. Cadogan diary, 30.viii.39; *DBFP*, 3, VII, 455, fn. 8; *DBFP*, 3, VII, 545.
121. Von Below diary, 30/31.viii.39.
122. Schmidt, *Statist*, pp. 458–57.
123. Von Hassell diary, 30.viii.39, quoting Ulrich von Kessel.
124. Halder diary, 30.viii.39.
125. *Breach of Security*, p. 104.
126. *DGFP*, D, VII, 458.
127. Weizsäcker diary, 30.viii.39.
128. Schmidt, *Statist*, pp. 457–60.
129. Weizsäcker diary, 31.viii.39.
130. Irving, *War Path*, pp. 255–56, citing Himmler diary.
131. Von Below diary, 30/31.viii.39.
132. Dahlerus 1943 Narrative.
133. *DBFP*, 3, VII, 570, 571.
134. *DBFP*, 3, VII, 574.
135. Lipski, *Diplomat in Berlin*, pp. 606–07; *DBFP*, 3, VII, 575, Henderson to Halifax, 5.15 a.m., 31.viii.39.
136. Lipski, *Diplomat in Berlin*, pp. 605–06.
137. Lipski, *Diplomat in Berlin*, 159, p. 571.
138. Von Hassell diary, 31.viii.39.
139. Halder diary, 31.viii.39.
140. *KTB der Marine*, 30.viii.39.
141. Lipski, *Diplomat in Berlin*, pp. 569–70, excerpts from Malhomme's undated notes.
142. *DBFP*, 3, VII, 577, 9.15 a.m., 31.viii.39.
143. *DBFP*, 3, VII, 579, 10.30 a.m., 31.viii.39.
144. *DDI*, 8, XIII, 487, 9.04 a.m., 31.viii.39.
145. Dahlerus 1943 Narrative.
146. Von Hassell diary, 31.viii.39.
147. *DBFP*, 3, VII, 581.
148. Coulondre, *de Staline à Hitler*, pp. 300–01.
149. Lipski, *Diplomat in Berlin*, 166, p. 575.
150. Lipski, *Diplomat in Berlin*, pp. 608–09; Dahlerus 1943 Narrative; Dahlerus, *Last Attempt*, pp. 104–05; *DBFP*, 3, VII, 597.
151. Lipski, *Diplomat in Berlin*, 163, p. 579, Lipski to Beck, 2.45 p.m., 31.viii.39.
152. *DBFP*, 3, VII, 589.
153. *DBFP*, 3, VII, 541, 1.15 p.m., 31.viii.39.
154. Wallace diary, 31.viii.39.

155. Lipski, *Diplomat in Berlin*, 161, p. 578; *PWB*, 110.
156. Lipski, *Diplomat in Berlin*, p. 609.
157. Dahlerus, *Last Attempt*, pp. 105–08.
158. Lipski, *Diplomat in Berlin*, p. 610; *PWB*, 111; *DGFP*, D, VII, 475.
159. Lipski, *Diplomat in Berlin*, p. 610; *PWB*, 112; *DGFP*, D, VII, 476; Schmidt, *Statist*, p. 460.
160. *DDI*, 8, XIII, 484.
161. Ciano, *Diario*, 31.viii.39.
162. *DBFP*, 3, VII, 567.
163. Grandi diary, 30.viii.39.
164. *DBFP*, 3, VII, 580.
165. *DBFP*, 3, VII, 584, 12.05 p.m.
166. *DBFP*, 3, VII, 585, 12.07 p.m.
167. *DBFP*, 3, VII, 594, 1.15 p.m.
168. *FYB*, 306.
169. *DBFP*, 3, VII, 590.
170. *DBFP*, 3, VII, 595, 1.30 p.m., 31.viii.39.
171. *DBFP*, 3, VII, 590.
172. *DBFP*, 3, VII, 604.
173. *DBFP*, 3, VII, 604.
174. *DDI*, 8, XIII, Appendix I, p. 408.
175. Ciano, *Diario*, 31.viii.39.
176. *DBFP*, 3, VII, 621, 11 p.m.
177. *DBFP*, 3, VII, 647, Halifax to Loraine, 1.ix.39.
178. *DDI*, 8, XIII, 491, Attolico to Ciano, 12.30 p.m., 31.viii.39; Magistrati, *L'Italia*, p. 443.
179. *DGFP*, D, VII, 474.
180. Magistrati, *L'Italia*, p. 444.
181. *DGFP*, D, VII, 478; *DDI*, 8, XIII, 507.
182. *DGFP*, D, VII, 482; *DBFP*, 3, VII, 619; *FYB*, 317.

Chapter 28   Poland attacked: the West's inglorious hour

Save where otherwise mentioned, this chapter is based on the following sources: (1) On the attack on Poland, Klaus Meier *et al.* (Eds), *Das Deutsche Reich und der zweite Weltkrieg*, vol. II, *die Errichtung der Hegemonie auf dem europäischen Kontinent*; Spiess and Liechtenstein, *den Unternehmen Tannenberg*; Ruhnau, *Die Freie Stadt Danzigs*; Levine, *Hitler's Free City*; Stjernfelt and Böhme, *Westerplatte 1939*; Schindler, *Mosty und Dirschau*; Pospieszalski, 'L'attaque manquée contre le pont sur la Vistule près de Tczew', *PWA*, 1987; Bachmann, 'der Kampf um Hela', *WWR*, 1970; Roos, 'der Feldzug in Polen', *WWR*, 1959; Burckhardt, *Meine Danziger Mission*; (2) On events in London, the diaries of Cadogan, Harvey, Inskip, Hoare, Nicolson, Pownall; Halifax, 'A record of events'; (3) On events in Paris, *Carnets Secrets de Jean Zay*; de Monzie, *Ci-Devant*; Guariglia, *Ricordi*; Duroselle, *La Décadence*; (4) On events in Rome, Ciano, *Diario*; Bottai, *Diario*; de Felice, *Mussolini*; (5) On events in Berlin, Henderson, *Failure of a Mission*; Coulondre, *de Stalin à Hitler*; Irving (Ed.), *Breach of Security*.

1. Burckhardt, *Meine Danziger Mission*, p. 352.
2. Ruhnau, *Die Freie Stadt Danzigs*, pp. 172–73.
3. *KTB der Marine*, 1/7.ix.39.
4. Grosscurth, private diary, 2.ix.39; 'Erfahrungsbericht Korps Kommando XIII (September 1939), Grosscurth, 18, pp. 367–70, on SS Leibstandarte Adolf Hitler; Halder diary, 2.ix.39.
5. Grosscurth, private diary, 8.ix.39.
6. Spiess and Liechtenstein, *Unternehmen Tannenberg*, pp. 74–84, 132–35.
7. *FYB*, 340, Bonnet circular to all French diplomatic missions, 7 p.m., 1.ix.39.
8. Von Below diary, 31.viii.39.
9. *ND* 126-C; *DGFP*, D, VII, 493.
10. Domarus, II.
11. *FYB*, 341, Coulondre to Bonnet.
12. Burckhardt, *Meine Danziger Mission*, pp. 352–53; *DBFP*, 3, VII, 714, Burckhardt to Halifax, 2.ix.39.
13. *DGFP*, D, VII, 458, 9.35 a.m., 1.ix.39.

14. *DBFP*, 3, VII, 657, 767.
15. Domarus, II, p. 1308.
16. Levine, *Hitler's Free City*, pp. 154–59.
17. Levine, *Hitler's Free City*, p. 159.
18. *DBFP*, 3, VII, 637, 7.28 a.m., 1.ix.39.
19. *DBFP*, 3, VII, 638.
20. *DBFP*, 3, VII, 650, 655, 662.
21. *DBFP*, 3, VII, 676.
22. *DBFP*, 3, VII, 652.
23. Hoare diary, 31.viii.39.
24. Harvey diary, 31.viii.39.
25. Pownall diary, 31.viii.39.
26. Halifax, 'Record', 1.ix.39.
27. Dahlerus 1943 Narrative; *DBFP*, 3, VII, 613, 31.viii.39, 643, 10.30 a.m., 1.ix.39.
28. *DDI*, 8, XIII, 510, 9.40 p.m., 31.viii.39.
29. *DBFP*, 3, VII, 645, Henderson to Halifax, by phone, 10.50 a.m., 1.ix.39.
30. *DBFP*, 3, VII, 644, 10.45 a.m.
31. *DBFP*, 3, VII, 653, 3.45 p.m.
32. *DBFP*, 3, VII, 639, note by Mr Spencer, 9.50 a.m., given to Foreign Office, 10.30 a.m.
33. *DBFP*, 3, VII, 651, Cadogan minute.
34. *DBFP*, 3, VII, 652, Cadogan minute.
35. *DBFP*, 3, VII, 689.
36. *DBFP*, 3, VII, 690; *DGFP*, D, VII, 501.
37. *DBFP*, 3, VII, 690; *DGFP*, D, VII, 502.
38. *PRO*, CAB 23/100, Cab. 47 (39).
39. Euan Wallace diary, 1.ix.39.
40. Inskip diary, 1.ix.39.
41. *DBFP*, 3, VII, 646, 11.20 a.m.
42. *DBFP*, 3, VII, 648.
43. *FYB*, 327; *DBFP*, 3, VII, 649.
44. Hoare diary, 1.ix.39.
45. Pownall diary, 1.ix.39.
46. Inskip diary, 25.viii.39.
47. Nicolson diary, 1.ix.39.
48. French MAE archives, cited Duroselle, *La Décadence*, p. 480.
49. French MAE archives, cited Duroselle, *La Décadence*, p. 480.
50. de Monzie, *Ci Devant*, pp. 145–46.
51. *Carnets Secrets de Jean Zay*, 31.viii.39.
52. de Monzie, *Ci Devant*, p. 146.
53. Coulondre, *de Staline à Hitler*, p. 298.
54. de Monzie, *Ci Devant*, p. 147.
55. Duroselle, *La Décadence*, p. 481; *DBFP*, 3, VII, 686.
56. de Monzie, *Ci Devant*, pp. 148–49.
57. *DBFP*, 3, VII, 634, Phipps to Halifax, 2 a.m., 1.ix.39.
58. *FYB*, 322, 323.
59. *DDI*, 8, XIII, 608, Guariglia to Ciano, 2.ix.39.
60. *Carnets Secrets de Jean Zay*, 1.ix.39; Reynard, *Au Coeur*.
61. *FYB*, 327.
62. *FYB*, 332; *DDI*, 8, XIII, 537 and Appendix 1, p. 410.
63. *DBFP*, 3, VII, 646, 11.30 a.m.
64. *DDI*, 8, XIII, Appendix 1, p. 410.
65. *DBFP*, 3, VII, 654.
66. Ciano, *Diario*, 1.ix.39.
67. Duroselle, *La Décadence*, p. 485.
68. Duroselle, *La Décadence*, p. 485; Villelume, *Journal*, 1.ix.39.
69. *FYB*, 338.
70. *FYB*, 343; *DBFP*, 3, VII, 693; Noel, *L'Aggression Allemande*, pp. 474–75.
71. Duroselle, *La Décadence*, p. 485.
72. *DDI*, 8, XIII, 525.
73. *DDI*, 8, XIII, Appendix 1, p. 409.

74. *DDI*, 8, XIII, Appendix 1, p. 409.
75. *DDI*, 8, XIII, 563.
76. *DDI*, 8, XIII, 529.
77. *DGFP*, D, VII, 500.
78. *DGFP*, D, VII, 504.
79. *DGFP*, D, VII, 505, Mackensen Memorandum, and 507.
80. *DGFP*, D, VII, 508.
81. Grandi diary, 1.ix.39; Bottai, *Diario*, 1.ix.39; Ciano, *Diario*, 1.ix.39; de Felice, *Mussolini*, pp. 670–74.
82. *DGFP*, D, VII, 425, Schulenburg to A.A., 29.viii.39.
83. *DGFP*, D, 285, Weizsäcker to Schulenburg, 26.viii.39.
84. *DGFP*, D, 387, 28.viii.39.
85. *DGFP*, D, VII, 431.
86. *DGFP*, D, VII, 381, fn. 2, Schulenburg to A.A., 25.viii.39.
87. *DGFP*, D, VII, 425, Schulenburg to A.A.
88. *DGFP*, D, VII, 471 and fn. 2, 480.
89. *DGFP*, D, VII, 540.
90. *PRO*, FO 371/23042, C 14029/170/18, Seeds to Halifax, 11.ix.39.
91. *DGFP*, D, VII, 170.
92. *DGFP*, D, VII, 540.
93. *DGFP*, D, VII, 514, 534.
94. *DBFP*, 3, VII, 694, Kennard to Halifax, 2.30 a.m., 2.ix.39.
95. *DBFP*, 3, VII, Appendix III.
96. Bottai, *Diario*, 1.ix.39.
97. *DBFP*, 3, VII, 678.
98. *DBFP*, 3, VII, 664, 669.
99. *Breach of Security*, p. 118.
100. *DBFP*, 3, VII, 680, Makins minute.
101. *DBFP*, 3, VII, 682, 684; *DGFP*, D, VII, 513.
102. *FYB*, 335.
103. *FYB*, 337, 5.55 p.m.
104. Coulondre, *de Staline à Hitler*, p. 308.
105. *FYB*, 344, Coulondre to Bonnet, 11 p.m., 1.ix.39; *DGFP*, D, VII, 515; Coulondre, *de Staline à Hitler*, p. 308.
106. *FYB*, 347.

Chapter 29 Fencing in, fencing out war

Where not otherwise stated, this chapter is based on the following sources: (1) For the Vatican, *Actes et Documents du Saint-Siège*, vol. I; Owen Chadwick, *Britain and the Vatican during the Second World War*; F. Charles-Roux, *Huit Ans au Vatican, 1932–1940*; (2) For the American press corps, Roger W. Buckley, 'The American Press Corps' view of Nazi Germany. Memoirs of selected correspondents', London M.A. thesis, 1965; (3) For the Oslo states, Nils Ørvik, *Sikkerhetspolitiken, 1920–1939*, Oslo, 2 vols, 1960–61; *idem*, 'Nordic Security, Great Britain and the League of Nations', in Bourne and Watt, *Studies in International History*; *idem*, *The Decline of Neutrality*; Ger van Roon, *Kleine Landen in Crisistijd; van Oslostaaten tot Benelux, 1930–1940*.

1. Schewe, X, 1992, 1993, 2000, 2001, 2002.
2. Schewe, X, 2007; *FRUS, 1939*, I, pp. 351–52, Welles to Phillips, 23.viii.39.
3. Schewe, X, 2024, Phillips to F.D.R., 25.viii.39.
4. *FRUS, 1939*, I, p. 214, Kirk to Hull; pp. 215–17, Bullitt to Hull, 15.viii.39; pp. 218–19, Kirk to Hull, 15.viii.39; pp. 221–22, Phillips to Hull, 17.viii.39.
5. *FRUS, 1939*, I, pp. 230–32, Johnson to Hull, 21.viii.39.
6. *FRUS, 1939*, I, 355–56, 23.viii.39.
7. *FRUS, 1939*, I, p. 355.
8. *FRUS, 1939*, I, pp. 356–58, 23.viii.39.
9. Schewe, X, 2009; *FRUS, 1939*, I, pp. 360–61.
10. Schewe, X, 2010; *FRUS, 1939*, I, pp. 361–62; *PWB*, 89.
11. Schewe, X, 2023; *PWB*, 90; *FRUS, 1939*, I, p. 368.

12. *FRUS, 1939*, I, pp. 368–69.
13. *DGFP*, D, VII, 306, Thomsen (Washington) to A.A.
14. *DGFP*, D, VII, 328.
15. *DGFP*, D, VII, 486, Ribbentrop to Washington.
16. Schewe, X, 2008.
17. Schewe, X, 2019, Roosevelt to Hanes.
18. *DBFP*, 3, VII, 318, 26.viii.39.
19. *DBFP*, 3, VII, 23, 16.viii.39.
20. *DBFP*, 3, VII, 65, 18.viii.39.
21. *DDF*, 2, XVIII, 100, 146, 17/19.viii.39, Charles-Roux to Bonnet.
22. *ADSS*, I, 102, Cortesi to Maglione.
23. Chadwick, *Britain and the Vatican*, pp. 54–55.
24. *ADSS*, I, 105.
25. Chadwick, pp. 15–16.
26. Chadwick, pp. 42–43.
27. *DDF*, 2, XVIII, 264.
28. *DDF*, 2, XVIII, 316.
29. *DDF*, 2, XVIII, 318.
30. *ADSS*, I, 110; *DBFP*, 3, VII, 126.
31. *ADSS*, I, 111, Osborne to Tardini.
32. *ADSS*, I, 111, footnote 1.
33. *DBFP*, 3, VI, 336, Enclosure; Chadwick, pp. 72–73.
34. *DDB*, V, 90, 14.viii.39.
35. *ADSS*, I, 144, note by Mgr. Tardini.
36. *DDB*, V, 90.
37. *ADSS*, I, 113; *DBFP*, 3, VII, 281, 311.
38. *DBFP*, 3, VII, 281, 385.
39. *DBFP*, 3, VII, 372; *DDI*, 8, XIII, 371, 26.viii.39.
40. *DBFP*, 3, VII, 454.
41. *ADSS*, I, 126.
42. *ADSS*, I, 148.
43. *ADSS*, I, 152.
44. *ADSS*, I, 153; *DBFP*, 3, VII, 526.
45. *ADSS*, I, 165, 31.viii.39.
46. *ADSS*, I, 166, 167.
47. Szembek diary, 31.viii.39.
48. *ADSS*, I, 160, 161; *DBFP*, 3, VII, 602; *FYB*, 310; *DDI*, 8, XIII, 494; *DGFP*, D, VII, 473.
49. *DBFP*, 2, VII, 687, 1.ix.39; *ADSS*, I, 171, Maglione notes.
50. van Roon, *Kleine Landen*, pp. 305–06, 311.
51. Spaak, *The Continuing Battle*, p. 19.
52. *DDB*, V, 57, 24.iii.39, General Dénis to M. Janson.
53. *DDB*, V, 65, 66, 70, 74; *DBFP*, 3, VII, 196 and footnote 1.
54. Spaak, pp. 16–17.
55. *DDB*, V, 72, 23.vi.39; *DDF*, 2, XVI, 239, 384.
56. *DDB*, V, 54, 61, 63, 64, 69, 73, 80, 82; *DGFP*, D, VI, 517, 575, 697, 701.
57. Van Overstraeten journal, 27.vii.39.
58. *DAPE*, II, 819, Calheiros (Brussels) to Salazar, 21.viii.39.
59. van Roon, pp. 306–07; *DDB*, V, 87.
60. *DDB*, V, 91, Annex 4, Ligne memorandum, 15.viii.39.
61. *DDB*, V, 92, 14.viii.39, Queen Wilhelmina to King Leopold.
62. van Roon, pp. 311–12.
63. *DAPE*, II, 820, Salazar to Calheiros, 22.viii.39.
64. *DDB*, V, 96, Richard to Pierlot, 18.viii.39.
65. *DDB*, V, 100, Pierlot to d'Ursel (Berne), 21.viii.39.
66. *DDB*, V, 102, d'Ursel to Pierlot, 22.viii.39.
67. van Roon, p. 312.
68. *DDB*, V, 107, La Tellier (Paris) to Pierlot, 24.viii.39.
69. *DDB*, V, 108, d'Ursel to Pierlot, 24.viii.39.
70. *DDB*, V, 109, British Note, 29.viii.39.
71. *DDB*, V, 110, du Parc (Bucharest) to Pierlot.

72. *DDB*, V, 111.
73. *DDB*, V, 113, de Romrée (Madrid) to Pierlot.
74. *DDB*, V, 135, 136, 137 and footnote 1; *FYB*, 284; *PWB*, 100; *DGFP*, D, VII, 390; *DDI*, 8, XIII, 397; *DBFP*, 3, VII, 451.
75. *DGFP*, D, VII, 402, 28.viii.39, Wiehl memorandum.

Chapter 30   Thunder in London

In addition to the sources listed in the footnotes, this chapter is based on the following sources: (1) For the British Cabinet, the diaries of Leslie Hore-Belisha, Sir Thomas Inskip, Sir Samuel Hoare, Sir John Simon and Captain Euan Wallace; on Lord Halifax, 'A record of events', FO 800/317; on Sir Reginald Dorman-Smith's *Recollections*, first printed in the *Sunday Times*, 6 October 1964, and reprinted in Gilbert, *Churchill, Companion*, V, *1936–1939*, pp. 1607–09. (i) For the proceedings in parliament on September 2, in addition to the preceding sources, the diaries of Leonard Amery, Sir Henry 'Chips' Channon, Blanche 'Baffy' Dugdale and Harold Nicolson; on the Dalton diaries and papers; and on Gilbert, *Churchill, Companion*, V, pp. 1109–1110. (ii) On the diaries of Sir Alexander Cadogan, Sir Oliver Harvey and General Sir Henry Pownall: (2) On the French side on J. B. Duroselle, *La Décadence*, pp. 486–93 and the sources therein quoted; *Les Carnets Secrets de Jean Zay*; Anatole de Monzie, *Ci-Devant*; Charles Corbin to Georges Bonnet, 7 September 1941 [1939] translated into German from *Le Gringoire*, 5 September 1941; 'Die letzte Friedensstunden in London: Corbins Schlussbericht' in *Berliner Monatshefte* (*BMh*), 19 November 1941, pp. 727–35; (3) On the Polish side on Juluisz Lukasiewicz, *Diplomat in Paris, 1936–1939*, and on Count Raczyński, *In Allied London*; (4) On the Italian side on Raffaele Guariglia, *Ricordi*; and on Guariglia to Ciano, 4 September 1939, *DDI*, 9, I, 23; Ciano, *Diario*, entries of 2/8 September 1939.

1. Crookshank diary, 2.ix.39.
2. *DBFP*, 3, VII, 719, Henderson to Halifax, 5.15 p.m., 2.ix.39.
3. *DBFP*, 3, VII, 725, Henderson to Halifax, 5.35 p.m., 2.ix.39.
4. Channon diary, 2.ix.39.
5. *DAFR*, III, 186, Bruce to Menzies, 2.ix.39; *DCER*, VI, 1048, Massey to Ottawa, 2.ix.39.
6. *DBFP*, 3, VII, 695, 720, 748, 754, 2.ix.39.
7. Lukasiewicz, *Diplomat*, pp. 274–76; *FRUS, 1939*, I, pp. 411–12, Bullitt to Hull, 2 p.m., 2.ix.39.
8. *DDI*, 8, XIII, 571 and Appendix 1, p. 412.
9. *DGFP*, D, VII, 535, 10 a.m., 2.ix.39.
10. *DDI*, 8, XIII, 572, 10.40 a.m., 2.ix.39.
11. *DGFP*, D, VII, 579, 12.30 p.m., 2.ix.39.
12. Schmidt, *Statist*, p. 462.
13. *DGFP*, D, VII, 541, 12.50 p.m., 2.ix.39.
14. *DBFP*, 3, VII, 707, Henderson to Halifax, 1.27 p.m., 2.ix.39.
15. *DDI*, 8, XIII, 574, Attolico to Ciano, 1.30 p.m., 2.ix.39.
16. *DDI*, 8, XIII, 581, 2.15 p.m., 2.ix.39.
17. *DBFP*, 3, VII, 717, time not recorded, 2.ix.39.
18. *DBFP*, 3, VII, 709, Loraine minute, 2.ix.39.
19. Guariglia, *Ricordi*, pp. 413–14; *DDI*, 9, I, 13, 4.ix.39.
20. *DBFP*, 3, VII, 710, minute by Harvey.
21. Nicolson diary, 2.ix.39.
22. Harvey diary, 2.ix.39.
23. *DBFP*, 3, VII, 696, with footnotes 2 and 3 thereto, 9.35 a.m., 2.ix.39.
24. *DBFP*, 3, VII, 699, 11.55 a.m., 2.ix.39.
25. *DBFP*, 3, VII, 713.
26. *DBFP*, 3, VII, 700, 12.30 p.m., 2.ix.39.
27. *DBFP*, 3, VII, 702.
28. *DBFP*, 3, VII, 706, 1.15 p.m., 2.ix.39.
29. *DBFP*, 3, VII, 708.
30. *DBFP*, 3, VII, 716; Bonnet, *Dans la Tourmente*, p. 187.
31. Lukasiewicz, *Diplomat*, pp. 278–79.
32. *FYB*, 356.
33. Dalton diary and papers, 3/2, 2.ix.39.

34. Hoare diary, 2.ix.39.
35. Halifax, 'Record', 2.ix.39.
36. CA 23/100, Cab 48 (39); Hoare, Hore-Belisha, Inskip, Simon, Euan Wallace diaries; Halifax, 'Record'.
37. *DBFP*, 3, VII, 710.
38. *DBFP*, 3, VII, 716.
39. *DBFP*, 3, VII, 718.
40. Lukasiewicz, *Diplomat*, pp. 282–83; Bonnet, *Dans la Tourmente*, p. 188; *FRUS, 1939*, I, 413, Bullitt to Hull, 8 p.m., 2.ix.39.
41. Lukesiewicz, *Diplomat*, pp. 279–802.
42. *DBFP*, 3, VII, 721, Phipps to Halifax, 5.30 p.m., 2.ix.39.
43. *DBFP*, 3, VII, 718.
44. *DBFP*, 3, VII, 727.
45. *DBFP*, 3, VII, 728; *DDI*, 8, XIII, Appendix 1, p. 413.
46. *DDI*, 8, XIII, Appendix 1, p. 413; *FYB*, 363; *DBFP*, 3, VII, 731.
47. *DDI*, 8, XIII, 589.
48. *DDI*, 8, XIII, Appendix 1, p. 413.
49. *DGFP*, D, VII, 739.
50. Channon diary.
51. Harvey diary.
52. Nicolson diary.
53 Crookshank diary; Amery diary.
54. Simon diary.
55. Nicolson, *A diary with letters*, p. 412, footnote 27.
56. Pownall diary, 2.ix.39.
57. Crookshank diary.
58. Gilbert, *Churchill*, V, p. 1109.
59. Hoare diary.
60. Gilbert, *Churchill*, V, pp. 1109–10.
61. Dugdale diary.
62. Channon diary.
63. Nicolson diary.
64. Dorman-Smith narrative.
65. Boothby to Churchill, 3.ix.39, Gilbert, *Churchill*, vol. V, p. 1612.
66. Simon, Hore-Belisha, Wallace diaries; Dorman-Smith narrative.
67. Inskip diary.
68. Hoare diary.
69. Halifax, 'Record'.
70. Cadogan diary.
71. Simon and Wallace diaries.
72. Neville Chamberlain papers, NC 7/K/32/321, Sir John Simon to Neville Chamberlain, 8.45 p.m., 2.ix.39.
73. Wallace diary.
74. Duff Cooper diary cited Gilbert, *Churchill*, V, pp. 1109–10.
75. Corbin to Bonnet, 7.ix.39, *BMh*, 1941; Simon diary; *DBFP*, 3, VII, 751 (10 p.m.), 2.ix.39. *DBFP*, 3, VII, 730, Phipps to Halifax.
76. Duroselle, *La Décadence*, p. 482.
77. Lukasiewicz, *Diplomat*, p. 284.
78. Gamelin to Daladier, 1.ix.39, *Die Geheimakten der französischen Generalstabs*, 3; Duroselle, *La Décadence*, p. 542, fn. 83.
79. Bonnet, *Dans la Tourmente*, p. 189; Corbin to Bonnet, 7.ix.39, *BMh*, 441; *DBFP*, 3, VII, 740.
80. P. le Goyet, *Le Mystère Gamelin*, Paris, 1977.
81. Daladier to Bonnet, 2.ix.39, cited Duroselle, *La Décadence*, pp. 490, 542, fn. 88.
82. *Carnets Secrets de Jean Zay*, 2.ix.39.
83. *Carnets Secrets de Jean Zay*, 2.ix.39.
84. de Monzie, *Ci-Devant*, p. 146.
85. Guariglia, *Ricordi*, note dated 2.ix.39, pp. 413–14.
86. *DDI*, 8, XIII, 616, 1.10 a.m., 3.ix.39.
87. *DDI*, 8, XIII, 589; *ibid.*, Appendix 1, p. 413, 8.20 p.m.; *DGFP*, D, VII, 554, 8.50 p.m.
88. Ciano, *Diario*, 3.ix.39.

89. *DDI*, 8, XIII, Appendix 1, p. 413.
90. *DBFP*, 3, IX, Appendix IV, note by H. J. W[ilson], 2.ix.39.
91. *DGFP*, D, VII, 558, 2 a.m., 3.ix.39.
92. Corbin to Bonnet, 7.ix.39, *BMh*, 1941.
93. *DBFP*, 3, VII, 747.
94. *DBFP*, 3, VII, 740, Cadogan minute, 9.50 p.m., 2.ix.39.
95. Simon, Hore-Belisha, Wallace diaries, 2.ix.39; Dorman-Smith narrative.
96. Dorman-Smith narrative.
97. Simon diary.
98. CAB 23/100, Cab 49 (100).
99. *DBFP*, 3, VII, 751, Halifax to Kennard, 2.ix.39.
100. *DBFP*, 3, VII, 791; Corbin to Bonnet, 7.ix.39, *BMh*, 1941.
101. Corbin to Bonnet, 7.ix.39, *BMh*, 1941.
102. Bracken to Dalton, 3.ix.39, Dalton diary and papers, 3/2; Corbin to Bonnet, 7.ix.39, *BMh*, 1941.
103. Cab 23/100, Cab 49 (39); Simon, Hoare, Hore-Belisha, Inskip, Wallace diaries; Halifax, 'Record'; Dorman-Smith narrative.
104. Dalton diaries and papers, 3/2, 12.55 a.m., 3.ix.39.
105. Channon diary, 1.15 a.m., 3.ix.39.

Chapter 31   September 3: the British ultimatum

Where not otherwise stated, this chapter is based on: Bell, *The Last Day of the Old World*; Kee, *The World We Left Behind*; Dahlerus 1943 narrative, and *The Last Attempt*; Halifax, 'A Record of Events'; Domarus, *Hitler, Reden und Proklamationen*, vol. II.

1. *DBFP*, 3, VI, 46, and fn. 1, Phipps to Chamberlain 13.vi.39, Chamberlain to Phipps, 14.vi.39; *DBFP*, 3, VI, 449, Campbell to Halifax, 25.vii.39 and 452, Halifax to Campbell, 26.vii.39.
2. Halifax, 'Record'.
3. Chamberlain papers, Chamberlain to Hilda Chamberlain, 10.ix.39.
4. Kennedy, *Business of War*, p. 15; *DCER*, VI, 1037, 1.ix.39; *DAFR*, III, 181, 2.30 p.m., 1.ix.39.
5. Kennedy, *Business of War*, p. 16.
6. Halder diary, 2.ix.39.
7. *Breach of Security*, p. 119.
8. *DBFP*, 3, VII, 752.
9. *DBFP*, 3, VII, 752.
10. *Breach of Security*, p. 119.
11. von Hassell diary, 29.viii.39.
12. von Hassell diary, 1.ix.39.
13. *DDI*, 8, XIII, 607, Attolico to Ciano; 2.ix.39.
14. *DDI*, 9, I, 20, Attolico to Ciano, 4.ix.39.
15. *DDI*, 9, I, 22, Magistrati to Ciano, 4.ix.39.
16. Coulondre, *de Staline à Hitler*, p. 310.
17. *DBFP*, 3, VII, 756, 757.
18. *Breach of Security*, p. 119.
19. Schmidt, *Statist*, pp. 462–64.
20. Schmidt, *Statist*, p. 463; *DBFP*, 3, VI, 760; Henderson, *Failure of a Mission*, pp. 284–85.
21. Schmidt, *Statist*, pp. 463–64.
22. *DGFP*, D, VII, 561; *DBFP*, VII, 766; Henderson, *Failure of a Mission*, pp. 284–85.
23. Coulondre, *de Staline à Hitler*, p. 312.
24. Coulondre, *de Staline à Hitler*, p. 313.
25. *DGFP*, D, VII, 562; Coulondre, p. 313.
26. Domarus, II, p. 13338.
27. Coulondre, *de Staline à Hitler*, pp. 313–14.
28. *DGFP*, D, VII, 563; Coulondre, *de Staline à Hitler*, p. 314.
29. *DGFP*, D, VII, 563, Enclosure.
30. *FYB*, 365.

31. Coulondre, *de Staline à Hitler*, p. 312.
32. Coulondre, *de Staline à Hitler*, p. 313.
33. *Breach of Security*, p. 120.
34. Domarus, II, pp. 1339–1342.
35. *DGFP*, D, VII, 576.
36. Kennedy, *Business of War*, p. 16.
37. Alvar Liddell, interview, *Daily Express*, 4.ix.67, cited Aster, *1939*, p. 389.
38. Feiling, *Chamberlain*, p. 415.
39. *H.C. Deb.*, 351, 3.ix.39, cols 291–92.
40. Dahlerus, 1943 narrative; *idem, Last Attempt*, p. 126.
41. Dahlerus, 1943 narrative; *idem, Last Attempt*, pp. 126–27.
42. *DBFP*, 3, VII, 762, footnote 1, Roberts minute, 3.ix.39.
43. Dahlerus, 1943 narrative; *idem, Last Attempt*, p. 129.
44. *DBFP*, 3, VII, 762, minute by Sir A. Cadogan, 3.ix.39; Dahlerus, *Last Attempt*, pp. 129–30.
45. Cadogan diary, 3.ix.39.
46. *Last Attempt*, pp. 130–131.

Chapter 32   Afterthoughts

1. *Diplomatic Prelude*, Part II, Chapter II, pp. 417–33.
2. Paul Claudel, 'Croquemitaine se dégonflera', *Le Figaro*, 19.vii.39, cited in de Monzie, 19.viii.39.
3. 'Führer Naval Conferences,' Raeder memorandum, 3.ix.39, *Brassey's Naval Annual*, 1948, pp. 37–38.

BIBLIOGRAPHY

Note: Selections from the papers and archives of the major and minor powers' participants in the events covered by this book have been widely published. The archives themselves vary in accessibility. Lacking expertise in the Slav languages, or the opportunity to visit Slav archives, I have relied on other authors who have cited original sources from the Finnish, Bulgarian, Yugoslav, Romanian and Polish archives. This bibliography lists the primary source materials, and to a lesser extent the secondary sources I have consulted. It is not intended to be comprehensive.

This bibliography is organized in the following sections:
- I. *Unpublished Sources*
    - 1. Official Papers (by countries)
    - 2. Unofficial Sources: Private Papers and Diaries (by countries)
- II. *Published Sources* (by countries)
    - 1. Official Documents
    - 2. Official and Demi-Official Histories
    - 3. Speeches
    - 4. Unofficial sources by country
        - (i) Diaries and Papers
        - (ii) Memoirs
        - (iii) Biographies
- III. *Secondary Sources*
    - 1. Books
    - 2. Collective Works
    - 3. Articles
    - 4. Doctoral Theses
    - 5. M.A. Theses

I. *Unpublished Sources*

1. *Official Papers* (Notes on availability and openness of archives to research)

Belgium
The Belgian records are now open to historical research, but still invite substantial exploitation.

Baltic States (Estonia, Latvia, Lithuania)
The archives of these three states passed into Soviet control with the union of the states into the Soviet Union in 1940. They are no more accessible than are the Soviet records.

Bulgaria
There has been no publication so far of documents from the Bulgarian archives for this period. Ludmila Zhivkova and Hans-Joachim Hoppe (see Section III.1. below) have had access to these and cite reports from Bulgarian diplomatic representatives. The Bulgarian diplomatic cipher was broken by the German *Forschungsamt* and Bulgarian reports are cited in their long report of September 1939 printed in David Irving (Ed.), *Breach of Security* (see bibliography).

Finland
The Finnish archives have been used by a number of Finnish and other historians including Seppo Myllyniemi, *die baltische Krise, 1938–1941* (Section III.1. below).

France
The records of the Quai d'Orsay were extensively destroyed in 1940. They have been reconstructed and used by a number of French historians since the early 1980s. The military records have been used by French and British historians.

Germany
The German records were damaged during the events of 1939–45, by their dispersal to avoid bombing and by the division of Germany. The bulk of the Foreign Ministry and other records fell into the hands of the Western allies and were extensively filmed by the tripartite Allied editors of Series C and D of *Documents on German Foreign Policy, 1918–45* (see Section II.1. below). Microfilms and photostats are available in London and in Washington. The originals were returned to the Federal German archives in 1960, together with the archives of the German Admiralty and a vast range of military and party records. Selected documents were used as evidence at the Trial of the Major War Criminals and at the eleven trials of war criminals conducted by the US occupation authorities (see Section II.1. below). Copies of these are available in London at the Imperial War Museum. Those archives which fell into Soviet hands were lodged with the archives of the Democratic Republic of Germany at Potsdam.

Great Britain
Save for the records with intelligence implications, the British official records are open to all at the Public Record Office. The CAB series (Cabinet and all its committees), FO (Foreign Office), and PREM (Prime Ministers) series are of particular relevance.

Hungary
Hungarian official records have been greatly exploited by Hungarian historians and extensively, if selectively, published, in English, French and German as well as in Hungarian.

Italy
The Italian records for the periods uncovered by the seventh and eighth series of *I Documenti Diplomatici Italiani* have been extensively used by historians such as Renzo de Felice, the late Mario Toscano, Alfredo Breccia, D. Bolech Cecchi and Rosario Quartararo (see Section III.1. below).

Japan
The Japanese records were plundered for the use of the International Military Tribunal for the Far East. They were also used extensively in the collective semi-official history, *Teiheiyō sensō e no michi: kaisen gaikō shi*, 7 vols, Tokyo 1962–63 (see Section II.2. below).

Netherlands
The archives of the Netherlands have not been widely used so far in studies of the origins of the Second World War. Effective and relevant use has, however, been made of them by, among others, Ger van Roon, *Kleine Landen in Crisistijd. Van Oslostaaten tot Benelux 1930–1940*, (see Section III. 1. below). The official publication, *Documente betreffende de buitenslandse politik van Nederland* has not reached the years 1938–39 at the time of writing.

Norway
The Norwegian archives have been used by Nils Ørvik and Ger van Roon (see Section III. 1. below).

Poland
Polish records were extensively destroyed by the events of 1939–1945, and divided following the split between the London Polish government in exile and the post-war government of Poland. This division has been much mitigated by cooperation between centres of Polish emigré research and by archivists and historians resident in post-war Poland; it has been used extensively by post-war Polish and Polish-speaking historians, including Henryk Batowski and Anna Prazmowska (Section III. 1. and III. 2. below).

Sweden
The Swedish archives have been used by a number of historians whose work is relevant to this study, including Ger van Roon, W. M. Carlgren and E. Carlquist.

Yugoslavia
Virtually the whole of the Yugoslav records were destroyed in the German air attack on Belgrade in 1941. The records of the Yugoslav Embassy in London survived undamaged and were returned to Yugoslavia after the war. They have been used by Yugoslav historians and drawn on by Alfredo Breccia, *Jugoslavia 1939–1941* (Section III. 1. below). Some Yugoslav records survived in the United States and were used by J. B. Hoptner, *Jugoslavia in crisis 1934–1941* (Section III. 1. below).

2. *Unofficial Sources.* Private Papers, documents etc.

Bulgaria
Stoycho Moshanov: an unpublished autobiography has been used by Ludmila Zhivkova and by Hans-Joachim Hoppe (see Section III. 1. below).

France

Papiers Bonnet	Ministre des Affaires Etrangères
Papiers Daladier	Centre Nationale des Recherches Scientifiques
Papiers Hoppenot	Ministre des Affaires Etrangères
Papiers Massigli	Ministre des Affaires Etrangères

Germany
Most of the private collections of German and Nazi officials fell into Allied hands at the end of the war and, if they are in western Europe, are now to be found in the Bundesarchiv in Koblenz. The Institut für Zeitgeschichte in Munich has the largest collection, including the papers of General Liebmann and General Geyr von Schweppenburg.

Great Britain

Sir Alexander Cadogan, papers and diaries	Churchill College, Cambridge
Neville Chamberlain, papers	Birmingham University Library
Admiral of the Fleet, Lord Chatsfield	National Maritime Museum
Group Captain Christie, papers	Churchill College, Cambridge
Harry Crookshank, papers	Bodleian Library, Oxford
Hugh Dalton, diaries and papers	British Library of Political and Economic Science
General J. C. Davidson, diaries and papers	Liddell Hart Archives, King's College, London
Admiral Sir Reginald Drax, diary and narrative	Churchill College, Cambridge
Alfred Duff Cooper, Lord Norwich, diary and papers	Churchill College, Cambridge

Walter Elliot, papers	National Library of Scotland
G. E. R. Gedye, papers	Imperial War Museum
Admiral Sir James Godfrey, papers	Churchill College, Cambridge
Lord Halifax, papers	Churchill College and PRO FO800
Lord Hankey, papers	Churchill College, Cambridge
Sir Nevile Henderson, papers	PRO, FO800
Sir Samuel Hoare, Lord Templewood, papers and diary (1939)	Cambridge University Library
Leslie Hore-Belisha, papers and diaries	Churchill College, Cambridge
Sir Thomas Inskip, Lord Caldecote, diary	Churchill College, Cambridge
Sir Hugh Knatchbull-Hugessen, diary	Churchill College, Cambridge
Lord Lloyd, papers	Churchill College, Cambridge
Sir Percy Loraine, papers	PRO
Sir Victor Mallet, papers	Churchill College, Cambridge
General Mason-MacFarlane, papers	Imperial War Museum
Lord Murray of Elibank, papers	National Library of Scotland
Sir George Ogilvie-Forbes, papers	Aberdeen University Library
Sir Eric Phipps, papers	Churchill College, Cambridge
Lieutenant-General Sir Henry Pownall, diary	Liddell Hart Archives, King's College, London
Sir George Rendel, papers	National Library of Wales
Admiral Sir Ballin Robertshaw, diary	Imperial War Museum
Viscount Runciman, papers	University of Newcastle
Sir Orme Sargent, papers	PRO FO800
Sir John Simon, Viscount Simon, diary and papers	Bodleian Library, Oxford
Sir William Strang, Lord Strang, papers	Churchill College, Cambridge
Sir Robert Vansittart, Lord Vansittart, papers	Churchill College, Cambridge
Captain Euan Wallace, diaries	Bodleian Library, Oxford
Lord Zetland, papers	India Office Library

Greece
Simopoulos Papers, St Anthony's College, Oxford. These have been used by John Koliopoulos (see Section III.1. below).

Japan
Baron Kido diary, *IMT FE* Exhibit 3440, *Transcript*, pp. 16235 ff.

Poland
There is a considerable volume of Polish private papers extant in London and New York. They have been used by Woytak, *On the Border of War and Peace* (see Section III.1. below).

Romania
Călinescu Diary. This has been used by the Israeli historian Dov Lungu, now resident in Canada and by various Romanian historians (see Sections III.1. and III.2. below).

Others
The Halifax papers at Churchill College, Cambridge, contain a long narrative, written originally for the Swedish Foreign Minister in 1943 by the Swede, Birger Dahlerus, annotated by Mr Frank Roberts of the Central Department of the British Foreign Office, and by Llewellyn Woodward, the Foreign Office's official historian, in April 1943. This is to be preferred to his memoirs, *The Last Attempt* (see Section II.4(ii) below), which were published after Hr. Dahlerus had testified at the Nuremberg War Crimes Trial.

II. *Printed Sources*

1. *Official Documents*

Australia
Documents on Australian Foreign Policy, 1937–1939, vols. II & III [DAFP]

Belgium
Documents Diplomatiques Belges, *1920–1940*, vol. V, *La Politique de la Securité Extérieure*. Brussels 1966 [*DDB*, V]

Canada
Documents on Canadian External Relations, vol. VI, *1936–39*, Ottawa 1972 [*DCER*]

Czechoslovakia
Vacláv Král (Ed.), *Das Abkommen von München, Tschechoslowakische diplomatische Dokumente, 1937–1939*, Prague 1988 [Král]

France
Le Livre Jaune Français: documents diplomatiques, 1938–1939. [English Translation] *The French Yellow Book, Diplomatic documents, 1938–39*, Paris 1939. [*FYB*]
    Les Évènements Survenues en France de 1933 à 1945. Témoignages et documents receuillis par la Commission d'Enquête parlementaire, Paris 1947 [*LES*]
    Documents Diplomatiques français, 1932–1939, IIe Serie, *1936–1939*, vols XI–XVIII, Paris (in progress) [*DDF*, 2]
    'Die letzten Friedensstunden in London. Corbin's Schlussbericht.' [Corbin to Bonnet] '7.ix.41[39]'. *Berliner Monatshafte*, 19, 1941, pp. 727–35 [BMh]

Germany
Auswärtiges Amt, *Zweites Weissbuch der deutschen Regierung*, Berlin 1939 [GWB]
    Auswärtiges Amt, 1939/41, *die Geheimakten der franzözischen Generalstabs, Weissbuch, Nr. 6*, Berlin 1940 [GFG]
    Auswärtiges Amt, 1939/41, *Dokumente zum Konflikte mit Jugoslavien und Griechenland, 1941, Weissbuch Nr. 7*, Berlin 1941 [DKJG]
    Documents Secrets du Ministère des Affaires Etrangères de l'Allemagne, Trans. Michel and Madeleine Eristov, 3 vols, Paris 1946 [Eristov]
    Nazi Conspiracy and Aggression, 11 vols. [NCA] International Military Tribunal, *Trials of the Major War Criminals*, 42 vols, Nuremberg 1948 [IMT]
    Trials of the War Criminals before the Nuremberg Military Tribunals under Control Commission Law No. 10, XV vols, Case XI, The United States v. von Weizsäcker and others, vols XII–XIV; Case XII, The United States v. von Leeb and others, vols X–XI, Nürnberg 1947–48.
    Documents and Materials Relating to the Eve of the Second World War (English, French, German and Russian editions), 2 vols, Moscow 1948 [DME]
    Documents on German Foreign Policy, Series D, *1936–1941*, vols IV–VII (English, French and German editions), London 1954–57 [DGFP, D]
    David Irving (Ed.), *Breach of Security. The Secret German Intelligence File on Britain, 1938–39*, Introduction by D. C. Watt, London 1968 [*Breach of Security*]
    D. Eichholtz and W. Schumann (Eds), *Anatomie des Krieges. Neue Dokumente über den Rolle des Monopolkapitalismus bei der Vorbereitung und Durchführung des zweiten Weltkrieges*, Berlin 1969.
    Heinz Boberach (Ed.), *Meldungen aus dem Reich. Die geheime Lageberichte des Sicherheitsdienstes der SS 1938–1945*, Heersching 1984, vol. II, *1938–39*.
    'Fuehrer Conferences on Naval Affairs, 1939–1945', *Brassey's Naval Annual*, 1948.
    Karl Heinz Völcker (Ed.), *Dokumente und Dokumentfotos zur Geschichte der deutschen Luftwaffe. Aus den Geheimakten des Reichswehrministeriums und des Reichsluftministeriums, 1933–1939*, Stuttgart 1968.

Great Britain
Documents on British Foreign Policy, *1919–1939*, 3rd series, *1938–1939*, 9 vols, London 1949–57 [DBFP, 3]
    D. Bourne and D. Cameron Watt (Eds), *British Documents on Foreign Affairs: Reports and Papers from the Foreign Office Confidential Print*, Part II, *From the First to the Second World War*, various series, Washington DC (in progress) [BDFA]
    British Committee on the Preservation and Restitution of works of art, archives and other material in enemy hands: *Works of Art in Italy. Losses and Survivals in the War*, Part I, *South of Bologna*: Part I, *North of Bologna*, London 1945.
    idem: *Works of Art in Germany (British zone of occupation). Losses and Survivals in the War*, London 1946.

idem: Works of Art in Austria (British zone of occupation). Losses and Survivals in the War, London 1946.

idem: Works of Art in Greece, the Greek islands and the Dodecanese, London 1946.

Lieutenant-Colonel Sir Leonard Woolley, *A record of the work done by the military Authorities for the protection of the Treasures of Art and History in War Areas*, London 1947.

Cmd 6106 (1939): *Documents concerning German-Polish relations and the outbreak of hostilities between Great Britain and Germany in September 1939.* [BBB]

Greece
The Greek White Book, London 1942 [GrWB]

Hungary
Diplomaciai iratok magyarország Külpolitikjáhaz, 1936–1940, vols 2–3, 4, Budapest [DIMK]

Allianz Hitler-Horthy-Mussolini. Dokumente zur ungarischen Aussenpolitik, 1933–1944, Budapest 1966 [AHHM]

Magda Ádám (Ed.), 'Documents relatifs à la politique étrangère de la Hongrie dans la période de la crise tschechoslovaque (1938–1939)', *Acta Historica*, 10, 1963–64.

Italy
Count Galeazzo Ciano, *L'Europa verso la Catastrofe*, Rome 1947. [in Eng., Malcolm Muggeridge (Ed.), *Ciano's Diplomatic Papers*, trans. S. Hood, London 1948] [CDP]

I Documenti Diplomatici Italiani, ottava serie, 1935–1939, Rome, 1952–53, vols XII, XIII [DDI 8, XII/XIII]

Japan
International Military Tribunal for the Far East, Proceedings, Introduction by D. Cameron Watt, (Ed.) J. and S. Z. Pritchard, (New York, 1988) [IMTFE]

Poland
The Polish White Book: Official Documents concerning Polish-German and Polish-Soviet Relations, 1933–1939, London 1940 [PWB]

Polnische Dokumente zur Vorgeschichte des Krieges, vol. II (Printed, but not published, German Foreign Ministry Microfilms, Serial H1832), Berlin 1940.

'Protocols of the Polish-French General Staff Conferences in Paris, May 1939', *Bellona*, 1958.

'Protocols of the Polish-British General Staff Conferences in Warsaw, May 1939', *Bellona*, 1957.

Portugal
Dez Años de Politica externa, 1936–1939; A nação Portuguese e a Seconda Guerra Mondiale, vols I, II, Lisbon 1961 [DAPE]

Switzerland
Edgar Bonjour (Ed.), *Geschichte der schweizerische Neutralität*, Basel 1975, vols VII–IX, *Dokumente*

USA
Foreign Relations of the United States, 1938, 4 vols. [*FRUS, 1938*, I/IV]
Foreign Relations of the United States, 1939, 4 vols. [*FRUS, 1939*, I/IV]
Foreign Relations of the United States, the Soviet Union, 1938–1939, [*FRUS, SU*]

USSR
V. Filin *et al.* (Eds), *Soviet Peace Moves on the Eve of World War II*, 2 vols, (Moscow 1973) also in German and Russian versions [SPE, I/II]

Jane Degras (Ed.), *Soviet Documents on Foreign Policy, 1917–1941*, vol. III, London 1953.

Vatican
Actes et documents du Saint Siège relatifs à la seconde guerre mondiale, vol. I, Vatican City 1965. [ADSS].

Yugoslavia
Aprilski Rat 1941, vol. I, *Mart 1938 – December 1940*, Belgrade 1969. [cited by Breccia, section III(i) below].

D. Cvetković, *Dokumenti O Jugoslavija*, 10 vols., Paris, 1951–57. [cited by Breccia, Wuescht, section III(i) below].

BIBLIOGRAPHY

General
RIIA, *Documents on International Affairs, 1939–1946*, I, London 1958.

2. *Official and Demi-Official Histories*

Australia
Paul Hasluck, *The Government and the People 1929–41*, Canberra 1952.

Canada
J. M. Eayrs, *In Defence of Canada*, vol. I. *Appeasement and Rearmament*, Toronto 1965.

France
Lieutenant-Colonel Henri Dutailly, *Les Problèmes de L'Armée de Terre Française, 1935–1939*, Paris 1980.

Germany
The Military History Research Office of the Federal German Republic has published a multi-volume history of the Second World War. Relevant voiumes (vols I and II) are:
   Wilhelm Deist *et al.* (Eds) *Ursachen und Voraussetzungen der deutschen Kriegspolitik*, Stuttgart 1979.
   Klaus Meier *et al.* (eds) *Die Errichtung der Hegemonie auf dem europäischen Kontinent*, Stuttgart 1979.
   See also Rudolf Absolon, *Die Wehrmacht im dritten Reich*, 3 vols, Boppard/Rhein 1963/1971/1975.

Great Britain
Relevant volumes from the Cabinet Office Historical Section are:
1. *History of the Second World War: Civil Series*
   H. Duncan Hall, *North American Supply*, London 1952.
   W. K. Hancock and M. M. Gowing, *British War Economy*, London 1949.
   W. N. Medlicott, *The Economic Blockade*, vol. I, London 1952.
   M. M. Postan, *British War Production*, London 1952.
2. Sir Llewellyn Woodward, *British Foreign Policy in the Second World War*, vol. I, London 1970.
3. *History of the Second World War: Military Series*
   J. R. M. Butler, *Grand Strategy*, vol. II, London 1957.
   Basil Collier, *The Defence of the United Kingdom*, London 1957.
   Norman Gibbs, *Grand Strategy*, vol. I, London 1976.
   Stephen Roskill, *The War at Sea*, vol. I, London 1954.
   Major-General S. Woodburn Kirby, *The War in the Far East*, vol. I, London 1957.
   Major-General I. S. O. Playfair, *The War in the Mediterranean*, vol. I, London 1954.
   Sir Charles Webster and Noble Frankland, *The Strategic Bombing Offensive*, vols I and IV, London 1961.
4. F. H. Hinsley *et al.*, *British Intelligence in the Second World War*, vol. I, Cambridge 1979.

Italy
Ufficio Storico dello stato maggiore dell'esercito, *L'Esercito Italiano tra la Prima e la Seconda Guerra Mondiale, 1918–1940*, Rome 1954.

Japan
Teiheiyō sensō e no michi: kaisen gaikō shi, 7 vols, Tokyo 1962–1963 (*The Road to the Pacific War: A Diplomatic History of the Origins of the War*). Selections relevant to this study have been published in English translation in: James William Morley (Ed.) *Deterrent Diplomacy. Japan, Germany and the USSR, 1935–1940*, New York 1976, and *The China Quagmire. Japan's Expansion on the Asian Continent, 1933–1941*, New York 1983.

The Netherlands
L. de Jong, *Het Koninkrijk der Nederlanden in de Tweede Wereld Oorlog*, deel I, *Voorspiel*, s'Gravenhage 1969.

Poland
Komisja Historyczna Polskiego Sztabu Głównego w Londynia, *Polskie Siły Zborojne*, Tom I, *Kampania Wrześniowa 1939*, London 1951.
  Witold Berganski, Piotr Starecki, Janusz Wojtarik (Eds) *Histoire Militaire de la Pologne: Problèmes Choisis*, Warsaw, Ministry of National Defence, 1970.

USA
Stetson Conn and Byron Fairchild, *The Western Hemisphere: The Framework of Hemispheric Defence*, Washington 1960.
  William L. Langer and S. Everett Gleason, *The Challenge to Isolation 1937–1940*, New York 1952.
  Mark S. Watson, *Chief of Staff: Pre-War Plans and Preparations*, Washington 1950.

3. *Speeches*

Edouard Daladier, *Défense du Pays*, Paris 1939; [English translation], *In Defence of France*, London n.d. (1939).
Max Domarus (Ed.) *Hitler; Reden und Proklamationen 1932–1945*, II Bände, Würzburg 1963.
Neville A. Chamberlain, *The Struggle for Peace*, London 1939.
Bradley Smith and Agnes Peterson (Eds) *Himmlers Geheimreden 1933 bis 1945 und andere Anspräche*, Frankfurt 1974.
E. and D. Susmel (Eds) *Opera Omnia di Benito Mussolini*, 36 vols, Florence 1951–1963.
Donald B. Schewe (Ed.) *Franklin D. Roosevelt and Foreign Affairs, January 1937   August 1939*, XI vols, New York/London 1979.

4. *Unofficial sources*

(i) *Diaries and Papers*

Belgium
General van Overstraeten, *Albert I – Leopold II: Vingt Ans de Politique Militaire Belge, 1920–1940*, Brussels 1950.

France
Hervé Alphand, *L'Étonnement d'Être. Journal, 1939–1973*, Paris 1977.
Albert Fabre-Luce, *Journal de France, 1933–1940*, Paris 1969.
Jules Jeanneney, *Journal Politique*, Paris 1972.
A. de Monzie, *Çi-Devant*, Paris 1949.
Philippe Herriot (Ed.), *Les Carnets Secrets de Jean Zay, de Munich à la Guerre*, Paris 1942.

Germany
von Below diary: Nikolaus von Below, *Als Hitlers Adjutant, 1937–45*, Mainz 1980.
Herbert von Dirksen papers: *Documents and Materials Relating to the Eve of World War II*, vol. II, *The Dirksen Papers*, Moscow 1948.
Gerhard Engel diary and papers: Hildegarde von Kotze (Ed.) *Als Heeresadjutant bei Hitler, 1938–1940*, Stuttgart 1970.
Grosscurth diary: Helmut Krausnick and Harold C. Deutsch (Eds) *Tagebuch eines Abwehroffiziers, 1939–1940*, Stuttgart 1970.
Halder diary: Hans Adolf Jacobsen (Ed.) *Franz Halder. Kriegstagebuch*, Stuttgart 1962. (For English translation, see *DGFP*, D, VII, Appendix I.)
Ulrich von Hassell, *Von andern Deutschland*, Zurich 1946. (English translation, *The Von Hassell Diaries*, London 1947.)
Jodl diary: Historical Division, Headquarters, US Forces Europe: *Foreign Military Studies: Interpretation and Commentary on Jodl*. See also *ND*, 1780-PS.
Keitel papers: Walter Görlitz (Ed.) *Generalfeldmarschall Keitel. Verbrecher oder Offizier?* Göttingen 1961.
Köstring diary and papers: Herman Teske (Ed.), *General Ernst Köstring: der militärische Mittler zwischen dem deutschen Reich und der Sowjetunion, 1921–1941*, Frankfurt/M 1966.
von Leeb papers: Georg Meyer (Ed.) *Generalfeldmarshall Ritter von Leeb. Tagebuchaufzeichnungen und Lagebetrachtungen aus zwei Weltkriegen*, Stuttgart 1976.

Rosenberg diary: Hans-Gunther Seraphim (Ed.) *Das politische Tagebuch Alfred Rosenbergs aus dem Jahren 1933/34 und 1939–40*, Göttingen 1963.
Wagner papers: Eduard Wagner, *Der Generalquartermeister: Briefe und Tagebuchaufzeichnungen des Generalquartiermeisters des Heeres, General des Artillerie, Eduard Wagner*, Munich 1963.
von Weizsäcker diaries and papers: Leonidas Hill (Ed.) *Die Weizsäcker-papiere, 1938–1950*, Frankfurt/M 1974.

Great Britain
Amery Diaries: John Barnes and David Nicholson (Eds) *The Empire at Bay: The Leo Amery Diaries, 1939–1945*, London 1988.
Cadogan diaries: David Dilks (Ed.) *The Diaries of Sir Alexander Cadogan, O.M., 1938–1945*, London 1971.
Channon diaries: Robert Rhodes-James (Ed.) *'Chips'. The Diaries of Sir Henry Channon*, London 1967.
Churchill papers: Martin Gilbert (Ed.) *Churchill, Companion*, vol. V, *1936–1939*, London 1982.
Dalton diaries: B. Pimlott (Ed.) *The Political Diary of Hugh Dalton 1918–1940, 1945–60*, London 1986.
Blanche Dugdale diaries: N. A. Rose (Ed.) *'Baffy'. The Diaries of Blanche Dugdale, 1936–1947*, London 1973.
Harvey diaries: John Harvey (Ed.) *The Diplomatic Diaries of Oliver Harvey, 1937–1940*, London 1970.
Hore-Belisha diaries and papers: R. J. Minney (Ed.) *The Private Papers of Hore-Belisha*, London 1960.
Ironside diaries: Colonel Roderick Macleod and Dennis Kelly (Eds) *The Ironside Diaries, 1937–1940*, London 1962.
Nicolson diaries: Nigel Nicolson (Ed.) *Harold Nicolson. Diaries and Letters 1930–1939*, London 1966.
Pownall diaries: Brian Bond (Ed.) *Chief of Staff. The Diaries of Lieutenant-General Sir Henry Pownall*, vol. I, *1933–1940*, London 1972.

Greece
Metaxas Diary: P. Vranes (Ed.) *Ioannis Metaxas. To prosopiko tou imerologia*, vol. IV, *1933–1941*, Athens 1964. [Cited by Koliopoulos.]

Italy
G. Bottai, *Diario, 1936–1944* (Ed. Giordano Bruno Guerra), Milan 1982.
Galeazzo Ciano, *Diario, 1937–1943* (Ed. Renzo de Felice), Milan 1980.
Grandi Diaries: Dino Grandi, *Il mio Paese* (Ed. Renzo de Felice), Bologna 1985.
Leonardi Simone [Michele Lanza], *Berlino, Ambasciata d'Italia 1939–1943*, Rome 1946.
Leonardi Vitetti, 'Diario', *Nuova Antologia*, 519, 1973.

Japan
The Saionji-Harada Memoirs: Complete Translation into English, Washington DC 1978.

Poland
Szembek diaries: Jan Zaranski (Ed.) *Diariusz i Taki Jana Szembek*, 4 vols, London 1962.
Raczyński diaries: Edouard Raczyński, *In Allied London. The Wartime Diaries of the Polish Ambassador*, London 1962.

Romania
Marthe Bibescu, *Jurnal Politic, 1939–1941* (Ed. Cristian Popisteanu and Nicola Minei), Bucharest 1979.

USA
Berle papers: Beatrice Bishop Berle and Travis Beal Jacobs (Eds.) *Adolf A. Berle, Navigating the Rapids, 1918–1971*, New York 1973.
Biddle papers: Philip V. Canistraro, Edward A. Wynot Jr and Theodore P. Konaleff (Eds.) *Poland and the Coming of the Second World War. The Diplomatic Papers of Anthony J. Drexel Biddle IV, United States Ambassador to Poland, 1937–1939*, Columbus, Ohio 1976.

687

Bullitt papers: Orville Bullitt (Ed.) *For the President, Personal and Secret: Correspondence between Franklin D. Roosevelt and William C. Bullitt*, Boston, Mass. 1972.
Kennan papers: *From Prague after Munich. Diplomatic Papers, 1935–1940*, Princeton, NJ 1968.
Lindbergh diaries: Charles A. Lindbergh, *The War-Time Journals of Charles A. Lindbergh*, New York 1970.
MacVeagh papers: John Olatrides (Ed.) *Ambassador MacVeagh reports: Greece 1937–1947*, Princeton, NJ 1980.
Moffatt papers: Nancy Harrison Hooper (Ed.) *The Moffatt Papers: Selections from the Diplomatic Journals of Jay Pierrepont Moffatt, 1919–1943*, Cambridge, Mass. 1956.
Morgenthau papers: John Morton Blum (Ed.) *From the Morgenthau Diaries*, vol. III, Boston, Mass. 1967.
Roosevelt papers: Donald B. Schewe (Ed.) *Franklin D. Roosevelt and Foreign Affairs, January 1937 – August 1939*, XI vols, New York, London 1979.
Wilson Papers: Hugh R. Wilson Jr (Ed.) *A Career Diplomat. The Third Chapter. The Third Reich. The Papers of Hugh Wilson*, New York 1960.

(ii) *Memoirs*

Belgium
Jacques, Comte d'Avignon, *Berlin 1936–1940: Souvenirs d'une Mission*, Brussels 1951.
Paul Henri Spaak, *Combats Inachevés*, Paris 1970, translated, *The Continuing Battle: Memoirs of a European, 1931–1966*, London 1971.
Pierre van Zuylen, *Les Mains Libres: Politique Exterieure de la Belgique, 1914–1940*, Paris 1950.

Czechoslovakia
Herbert Ripka, *Before and After Munich*, London 1939.
Felix Durčansky, 'Mit Tiso bei Hitler', *Politische Studien*, VII, 1956.

France
Général J. Armengaud, *Batailles politiques et militaire sur l'Europe: Témoignages (1932–1940)* Paris 1948
Armand Bérard, *Un Ambassadeur se souvient*, vol. 1: *Au Temps du Danger Allemand*, Paris 1976.
André Beauffre, *La Drame de 1940*, Paris 1965; translated by D. Flower, *1940, The Fall of France*, London 1967.
Gustave Bertrand, *Enigme ou la plus grande Enigme de la Guerre, 1939–1945*, Paris 1975.
Georges Bonnet, *Défense de la Paix*, 2 vols, Geneva 1951.
idem, Dans la Tourmente, 1935–48, Paris 1971.
Robert Coulondre, *De Staline à Hitler*, Paris 1950.
Jean Deridan, *Le Chemin de la Défaite (1935–1940)*, Paris 1950.
Jean Fabry, *J'ai Connu: 1935–1945*, Paris 1960.
André François-Poncet, *Souvenirs d'une Ambassade à Berlin*, Paris 1947, translated, *The Fateful Years*, London 1949.
idem, Au Palais Farnèse. Souvenirs d'une Ambassade à Rome, Paris 1961.
G. Gamelin, *Servir*, 3 vols, Paris 1946–47.
M. Gauché, *Le Deuxième Bureau au Travail (1935–1940)*, Paris 1954.
R. Genebrier, *Septembre 1939. La France Entre en Guerre*, Paris 1982.
René Massigli, *La Turquie devant la Guerre. Mission à Ankara 1939–40*, Paris 1962.
Léon Noël, *L'Aggression Allemande contre la Pologne*, Paris 1946.
Paul Reynaud, *La France a Sauvé l'Europe*, Paris 1947.
idem, Au Coeur de la Mêlée, 1930–1945, Paris 1947; translated by J. D. Lambert, *In the Thick of the Fight, 1930–1945*, London 1955.
idem, Envers et Contre Tous, Mémoires, Paris 1960.
Paul Stehlin, *Témoignage pour l'Histoire*, Paris 1964.
Guy de la Tournelle, 'A Dantzig de Decembre 1939 à Septembre 1939', *Revue d'Histoire Diplomatique*, 92, 1978.

Germany
Otto Abetz, *Das offene Problem: ein Rückblick auf zwei Jahrzehnte deutsche Frankreichpolitik*, Cologne 1951.
Wipert von Blücher, *Gesandter zwischen Diktatur und Demokratie: Erlinerungen aus dem Jahren, 1935–1944*, Wiesbaden 1951.

Otto Dietrich, *12 Jahre mit Hitler*, Munich 1955, translated by R. and C. Winston, London 1957.
Herbert von Dirksen, *Moskau, Tokyo, London: Errinerungen und Betrachtungen zu zwanzig Jahre Aussenpolitik, 1919–1939*, Stuttgart 1949.
Eugene Dollmann, *The Interpreter*, London 1967.
Moritz von Faber zu Faur, *Macht und Ohnmacht: Errinerungen eines alten Offiziers*, Stuttgart 1953.
Sigismond 'Sizzo' Fitzrandolph, *Der Frühstucksattaché aus London*, Stuttgart 1954.
Hans Frank, *Im Angesicht des Galgens*, Munich 1955.
Hans-Bernd Gisevius, *Bis zum bitteren Ende*, 2 vols., Zurich 1946.
Ernst Hanfstaengel, *15 Jahre mit Hitler*, Munich 1980.
Werner von Hentig, *Meine Leben: Eine Dienstreise*, Göttingen 1962.
Hans Heinrich (Johnny) Herwarth von Bittenfeld, *Against Two Evils*, London 1981.
Fritz Hesse, *Das Spiel um Deutschland*, Munich 1953.
idem, *Das Vorspiel zum Krieg. England berichte und Erlebrisse eines Tatzeuges 1935–45*, Leone am Steinbergersee 1979.
Gustav Hilger, *Wir und die Kreml: deutsch-sowjetische Beziehungen, 1918–1941*, Frankfurt 1956. German version of Gustav Hilger and Alfred Meyer, *The Incompatible Allies*, New York and London 1953.
Heinrich Hoffmann, *Hitler was my Friend*, London 1955.
Peter Kleist, *Zwischen Hitler und Stalin, 1939–1945, Aufzeichnungen*, Bonn 1950.
Erich Kordt, *Nicht aus den Akten: die Wilhelmstrasse in Frieden und Krieg*, Stuttgart 1950.
Hans Kroll, *Lebenserrinerungen eines Botschafters*, Cologne 1967.
Wolfgang Leonhard, *Der Schock des Hitler-Stalin Paktes: Errinerungen aus der Sowjetunion, Westeuropa und USA*, Freiburg/Breisgau 1986.
Bernhard von Lossberg, *Im Wehrmachtsführungsstab*, Hamburg 1949.
Kurt Luedecke, *I Knew Hitler*, London 1938.
Erich von Manstein, *Aus einem Soldatenleben 1887–1939*, Bonn 1958.
Otto Meissner, *Staatssekretär unter Ebert, Hindenburg, Hitler*, Hamburg 1950.
Franz von Papen, *Die Wahrheit einer Gasse*, Munich 1952.
Wolfgang Gans Edler Herr zu Putlitz, *Unterwegs nach Deutschland. Errinerungen eines ehemaligen Diplomaten*, Berlin 1957.
Admiral Raeder, *Mein Leben*, 2 vols, Tübingen 1956–57.
Joachim von Ribbentrop, *The Ribbentrop Memoirs*, London 1954.
Hans Edmund Reisser, *Von Versailles zur UNO: Aus den Errinerungen eines Diplomaten*, Bonn 1962.
Enno von Rintelen, *Mussolini als Bundesgenosse: Errinerungen des deutschen Militärattachés in Rom, 1936–1943*, Tübingen 1951.
Hjalmar Schacht, *76 Jahre meines Lebens*, Bad Wörtshofen 1958.
Fabian von Schlabrendorff, *The Secret War Against Hitler*, London 1966.
Lutz Schwerin von Krosigk, *Es geschah in Deutschland*, Tübingen 1951.
idem, *Memoiren*, Stuttgart 1977.
Albert Speer, *Errinerungen*, Frankfurt/M 1969.
Georg Vogel, *Diplomat unter Hitler und Adenauer*, Dusseldorf 1969.
Walther Warlimont, *Im Hauptquartier der deutschen Wehrmacht, 1939–1945*, Bonn 1964.
Ernst von Weizsäcker, *Errinerungen*, Dortmund 1964.
F. Wiedemann, *Der Mann, der Feldherr werden wollte*, Velbert 1964.
A. Zoller, *Hitler Privat*, Dusseldorf 1949.

Great Britain
Leo Amery, *Memoirs*, vol. III, *The Unforgiving Years, 1929–1940*, London 1955.
Sir John Balfour, *Not too Correct an Aureole*, Salisbury 1983.
Robert Boothby, *I Fight to Live*, London 1967.
Maurice Bowra, *Memoirs, 1898–1939*, London 1966.
R. A. B. Butler, *The Art of the Possible*, London 1971.
Admiral of the Fleet Lord Chatfield, *It Might Happen Again*, vol. II, *The Navy and Defence*, London 1947.
Winston S. Churchill, *The Second World War*, vol. I, *The Gathering Storm*, London 1948.
Claud Cockburn, *In Time of Trouble*, London 1956.
idem, *I Claud*, London 1961.
Patricia Cockburn, *The Years of 'The Week'*, London 1968.
Alfred Duff Cooper, *Old Man Forget*, London 1954.
Aviator Extraordinary: The Sidney Cotton Story, as told to Ralph Barker, London 1969.

Sir Robert Craigie, *Behind the Japanese Mask*, London 1946.
Geoffrey Cox, *Countdown to War: A Personal Memoir of Europe, 1938–1940*, London 1988.
Hugh Dalton, *The Fateful Years: Memoirs, 1931–1945*, London 1957.
William Douglas-Home, *Half-Term Report*, London 1954.
Sefton Delmer, *Trail Sinister*, London 1962.
Shiela Grant Duff, *Fünf Jahre bis zum Krieg, 1934–1939*, Munich 1978.
idem., *The Parting of the Ways. A Personal Account of the 1930s*, London 1982.
Anthony Eden, *Facing the Dictators, 1928–1938*, London 1962.
Lord Halifax, *Fulness of Days*, London 1957.
Sir Nevile Henderson, *Failure of a Mission*, London 1940.
Lord Home of the Hirsel, *The Way the Wind blows: an Autobiography*, London 1976.
Baron Ismay, *Memoirs*, London 1960.
Gladwyn Jebb, *The Memoirs of Lord Gladwyn*, London 1962.
Sir Ivone Kirkpatrick, *The Inner Circle*, London 1959.
Sir Hugh Knatchbull-Hugessen, *Diplomat in War and Peace*, London 1949.
Arthur Koestler, *The Scum of the Earth*, London 1941.
Sir Roderick Jones, *A Life at Reuters*, London 1957.
Sir Frederick Leith-Ross, *Money Talks: Fifty Years of International Finance*, London 1968.
Sir Basil Liddell Hart, *Memoirs*, vol. II, London 1958.
Harold Macmillan, *Memoirs*, vol. I, *Winds of Change, 1914–1939*, London 1966.
Sir James Marshall-Cornwall, *Wars and Rumours of Wars. A Memoir*, London 1984.
Viscount Maugham, *At the End of the Day*, London 1956.
Sir Cecil Parrott, *The Tight-Rope*, London 1975.
Sir Maurice Peterson, *Both Sides of the Curtain*, London 1950.
Major-General Stuart Piggott, *Broken Thread*, London 1950.
Sir George Rendel, *The Sword and the Olive*, London 1957.
Baron William de Ropp, *I Spied on Hitler*, Daily Mail 28–31.x/1.xi.1957.
A. L. Rowse, *All Souls and Appeasement*, London 1948.
Sir Andrew Ryan, *The Last of the Dragomans*, London 1951.
Viscount Simon, *Retrospect*, London 1952.
Sir John Slessor, *The Central Blue*, London 1956.
Lord Strang, *At Home and Abroad*, London 1956.
Sir Kenneth Strong, *Intelligence at the Top; Recollections of an Intelligence Officer*, London 1968.
Viscount Templewood, *Nine Troubled Years*, London 1954.
Ernest W. P. Tennant, *True Account*, London 1957.
Sir Geoffrey Thompson, *Frontline Diplomat*, London 1959.
Major-General Carton de Wiart, *Happy Odyssey*, London 1955.
F. W. Winterbotham, *Secret and Personal*, London 1969.
idem, *The Nazi Connection*, London 1978.
Lord Winterton, *Orders of the Day*, London 1953.
Elizabeth Wiskermann, *The Europe I Saw*, London 1968.
Marquess of Zetland, *Essayez*, London 1956.

Italy
Dino Alfieri, *Due Dittatori di Fronte*, Milan 1948.
F. Anfuso, *Dal Palazzo Venezia al Lago di Garda, 1936–1945*, Bologna 1957.
idem, *Roma, Berlino, Salo, 1936–1945*, Milan 1950.
S. Bastianini, *Uomini, Cose, Fatti*, Milan 1959.
G. Bottai, *Vent'anni e un Giorno*, Milan 1949.
Edda Ciano, *La mia Testamonianza*, Milan 1975; translated G. Finletter, *My Truth*, London 1977.
Mario Donosti, *Mussolini e l'Europa. La politica estera fascista*, Rome 1945.
Dino Grandi (a cura di R. de Felice), *Il mio Paese: Ricordi Autobiografici*, Bologna 1985.
R. Guariglia, *Ricordi, 1922–1946*, Naples 1949.
Felice Guarneri, *Battaglie economiche tra le due guerre*, Milan 1953.
Mario Lucotti, *Palazzo Chigi: Anni Roventi. Ricordi di Vita Diplomatica Italiana dal 1933 al 1948*, Milan 1958.
Massimo Magistrati, *L'Italia a Berlino (1937–1939)*, Verona 1956.

Poland
Joseph Beck, *Dernier Rapport. Politique Polonaise 1926–1939*, Paris 1951.
Anton Szymański, 'Als polnische Militärattaché in Berlin', *Politische Studien*, 13, 1962.

Romania
Alexandru Cretzianu, *The Lost Opportunity*, London 1957.
Grigore Gafencu, *The Last Days of Europe*, London 1947.
N. Petrescu-Comnéne, *Preludi del grande dramma*, Rome 1947.
idem, I Responsabili, Milan 1949.

USA
Dean Acheson, *Present at the Creation*, London 1969.
Alben Barkley, *That Reminds Me*, New York 1954.
Charles E. Bohlen, *Witness to History, 1929–1949*, New York 1973.
Joseph Grew, *Ten Years in Japan, 1931–1941*, London 1944.
idem, Turbulent Era. A Diplomatic Record of Forty Years, London 1953.
Cordell Hull, *Memoirs*, 2 vols, New York 1948.
George Kennan, *Memoirs, 1929–1960*, London 1968.
Louis Lochner, *What About Germany?* London 1942.
William Phillips, *Ventures in Diplomacy*, London 1955.
Sumner Welles, *A Time for Decision*, London 1944.

USSR
Severyn Bialer (Ed.) *Stalin and his Generals: Soviet Military Memoirs of World War II*, New York
    1969.
N. Khrushchev, *Khrushchev Remembers*, vol. I, London 1971.
V. Maisky, *Who Helped Hitler?* London 1954.
The Memoirs of Marshal Zhukhov, London 1971.

Yugoslavia
Milovan Djilas, *Memoirs of a Revolutionary*, New York 1971.
Constantin Fotitch, *The War We Lost*, New York 1948.
Prince Paul of Yugoslavia, *A King's Heritage*, London 1955.
Vladimir Vauhnik, *Memoiren eines Militärattachés*, Buenos Aires 1967.

Others
Carl Burckhardt, *Meine Danziger Mission, 1937–1939*, Munich 1969.
Birger Dahlerus, *The Last Attempt*, London 1948.
G. A. Gripenberg, *Finland and the Great Powers. Memoirs of a Diplomat* (trans. Albin T. Anderson),
    Lincoln, Nebraska 1965.
Gunnar Hägglof, *Diplomat. Memoirs of a Swedish Envoy*, London 1972.
Vincent Massey, *What's Past is Prologue*, London 1963.
Elizabeth Poretzky, *Our own people: a Memoir of Ignace Reiss and his friends*, London 1969.

(iii) *Biographies*

Australia
D. Day, *Menzies and Churchill at War*, London 1985.

Belgium
D. du Chapois, *Paul van Zeeland*, Brussels 1971.
J. Stengers, *Leopold III et le Gouvernement*, Paris 1980.

Canada
Bruce Hutchinson, *The Incredible Canadian*, Toronto 1958.
J. W. Pickersgill, *The Mackenzie King Record*, vol. I, Toronto 1960.

France
Philip Bankwitz, *Maxime Weygand and Civil-Military Relations in Modern France*, Cambridge,
    Mass. 1966.
Evelyn Demey, *Paul Reynaud, Mon Père*, Paris 1980.
Pierre Le Goyet, *Le Mystère Gamelin*, Paris 1979.
John M. Sherwood, *Georges Mandel and the Third Republic*, Stanford, Ca. 1970.
G. Wormser, *Georges Mandel, l'Homme Politique*, Paris 1980.

Armand Teyssier, 'Le General Guillemin, Chef d'Etat-Major General de l'Armée de l'Air, 1938–1939: un haut responsable militaire face au danger allemand' *RHd'A*, 167, 1987.

Germany
Alan Bullock, *Hitler, A Study in Tyranny*, London 1952.
Gunther Deschner, *Heydrich. The Pursuit of Total Power*, London 1981.
Joachim Fest, *Hitler: eine Biographie*, Frankfurt/M 1974.
Helmut Heiber, *Joseph Goebbels*, London 1973.
Hans Hoehne, *Canaris, Patriot im Zwielicht*, Munich 1976.
W. Jenkins, *Vienna and the Young Hitler*, New York 1976.
Franz Jetzinger, *Hitlers Jugend – Phantasien, Lügen – und die Wahrheit*, Vienna 1956.
Louise Jodl, *Jenseits des Endes: Leben und Sterben des Generaloberst Alfred Jodl*, Vienna 1976.
F. Sidney Jones, *Hitler in Vienna, 1907–1913*, London 1983.
Seppo Kuusisto, *Alfred Rosenberg in der nationalsocialistisches Aussenpolitik, 1933–1939*, Helsinki 1984.
Ursula Laeck-Nickel, *Albrecht Haushofer und der National-Sozialismus*, Stuttgart 1974.
Joachim von Lang, *Bormann. The Man who Manipulated Hitler*, London 1979.
Henry Ozette Malone Jr., *Adam von Trott zu Solz. Werdegang eines Verschwörers, 1909–1938*, n.p., 1986.
W. Maser, *Hitler, Legende, Mythos, Wirklichkeit*, Munich 1971.
W. Michalka, *Ribbentrop und die deutsche Weltpolitik, 1938–1944*, Munich 1980.
R. Overy, *Goering, the Iron Man*, London 1984.
Gunther Peis, *The Man who Started the War*, London 1966.
Gerhard Ritter, *Carl Goerdeler und die deutsche Widerstandsbewegung*, Stuttgart 1956.
Heide-Marie, Gräfin Schall-Riaucour, *Aufstand und Gehorsam. Offizierstum und Generalstab im Umbruch; Leben und Wirken von General-Oberst Franz Halder*, Wiesbaden 1972.
Bodo von Scheurig, *Ewald von Kleist-Schmenzin*, Oldenburg 1958.
Bradley F. Smith, *Adolf Hitler, his Family, Childhood and Youth*, Stanford, Ca. 1967.
Christopher Sykes, *Troubled Loyalty. A Biography of Adam von Trott zu Solz*, London 1968.
Romadio Galeazzo, Graf von Thun-Hohenstein, *Der Verschwörer: General Oster und die Militär-opposition*, Berlin 1982.
John Toland, *Adolf Hitler*, London 1977.

Great Britain
J. S. Colville, *Man of Valour: The Life of Field Marshal The Lord Gort*, London 1981.
Colin Forbes Adam, *The Life of Lord Lloyd*, London 1948.
Mosa Anderson, *Noel-Buxton: A Life*, London 1952.
Patrick Beesley, *Very Special Admiral*, London 1986.
Earl of Birkenhead, *Halifax. The Life of Lord Halifax*, London 1966.
Ewan Butler, *Mason-Mac: The Life of Lieutenant-General Sir Noel Mason-MacFarlane*, London 1972.
J. R. M. Butler, *Lord Lothian, 1882–1940*, London 1966.
John Charmley, *Duff Cooper, The Authorised Biography*, London 1986.
idem, *Lord Lloyd and the Decline of the British Empire*, London 1987.
John Cross, *Sir Samuel Hoare: A Political Biography*, London 1977.
Ian Colvin, *Vansittart in Office*, London 1965.
Keith Feiling, *Neville Chamberlain*, London 1946.
Martin Gilbert, *Winston S. Churchill*, vol. V, *1922–1939, The Prophet of Truth*, London 1977.
idem, *Sir Horace Rumbold*, London 1973.
Anthony Howard, *Rab. The life of R. A. Butler*, London 1987.
H. Montgomery Hyde, *Neville Chamberlain*, London 1976.
Robert Rhodes James, *Churchill: A Study in Failure, 1900–1939*, London 1972.
Ben Pimlott, *Hugh Dalton*, London 1985.
Norman Rose, *Vansittart, Study of a Diplomat*, London 1978.
Stephen Roskill, *Hankey. Man of Secrets*, vol. III, *1931–1963*, London 1974.
Rudi Strauch, *Sir Nevile Henderson. Britische Botschafter in Berlin 1937 bis 1939*, Bonn 1959.
Gordon Waterfield, *Professional Diplomat*, London 1973.
Sir John Wheeler-Bennett, *King George VI. His Life and Reign*, London 1958.

Italy
Renzo de Felice, *Mussolini il Duce*, vol. II, *Lo Stato Totalitario, 1936–1940*, Turin 1981.

Giordano B. Guerra, *Galeazzo Ciano, Una Vita, 1903–1944*, Milan 1979.
D. Mack Smith, *Mussolini*, London 1983.

Japan
Carl Boyd, *The Extraordinary Envoy: General Hiroshi Oshima and Diplomacy in the Third Reich, 1934–1939*, Washington DC 1980.
Robert Butow, *Tojo and the Coming of the War*, Stanford, Ca. 1961.
L. A. Conners, *The Emperor's Adviser: Saionji Kimochi and pre-war Japanese Politics*, London 1987.

USA
Ralph F. de Bedlo, *Ambassador Joseph Kennedy 1938–1940. An Anatomy of Appeasement*, New York 1985.
Michael R. Beschloss, *Kennedy and Roosevelt: The Uneasy Alliance*, New York, 1986.
James M. Burns, *Roosevelt. The Lion and the Fox*, New York 1956.
Wayne S. Cole, *Senator Gerald P. Nye and American Foreign Relations*, Minneapolis 1962.
idem, *Charles A. Lindbergh and the Battle against American Intervention in World War II*, New York 1974.
Robert Dallek, *Franklin D. Roosevelt and American Foreign policy, 1932–1945*, New York 1979.
Henry C. Farrell, *Claude A. Swanson of Virginia. A Political Biography*, Lexington, Kentucky 1985.
Betty Glad, *Key Pittman. The Tragedy of a Senate Insider*, New York 1956.
Waldo Heinrichs, *American Ambassador. Joseph C. Grew and the Development of the United States Diplomatic Tradition*, Boston 1966.
Fred Israel, *Nevada's Key Pittman*, Lincoln, Nebraska 1966.
Neil M. Johnson, *George Sylvester Viereck. German-American Propagandist*, Urbana, Ill. 1972.
David E. Koskoff, *Joseph P. Kennedy. A Life and Times*, Eaglewood Cliffs, NJ 1974.
Richard Lowitt, *George W. Norris. The Triumph of a Progressive, 1933–1944*, Urbana, Ill. 1978.
Keith D. McFarland, *Henry D. Woodring*, Lawrence, Kansas 1975.
Marion C. McKenna, *Borah*, Ann Arbor 1961.
Robert Maddox, *William E. Borah and American Foreign Policy*, Baton Rouge 1969.
Forest W. Pogue, *George C. Marshall*, London 1964–65, 2 vols.
Julius W. Pratt, *Cordell Hull*, Vol. 2, New York 1964.

USSR
Isaac Deutscher, *Stalin. A Biography*, London 1949.

Others
Neill Balfour and Sally McKay, *Paul of Jugoslavia. Britain's Maligned Friend*, London 1940.
James Barros, *Betrayal from Within. Joseph Avenol, Secretary-General of the League of Nations, 1933–1940*, New Haven 1969.
Prince Paul of Hohenzollern-Roumania, *King Carol II: A Life of my Grandfather*, London 1988.

III. Secondary Sources

1 *Books*
Carl-Dietrich Abel, *Presselenkung im NS-Staat. Eine Studie zur Geschichte der Publizistik in den national-sozialistischen Zeit*, Berlin 1968.
A. P. Adamthwaite, *France and the Coming of the Second World War, 1936–1939*, London 1977.
idem, *The Lost Peace. International Relations in Europe 1919–1939*, London 1980.
Rolf Ahmann, *Nichtangriffspakte: Entwicklung und operative Nutzung in Europa 1922–1939*, Baden-Baden 1988.
Dietrich Aigner, *Das Ringen um England: Das deutsch-britische Verhältnis: die öffentliche Meinung 1933–1939: Tragödie zweier Völker*, Munich 1969.
Sven Allard, *Stalin und Hitler. Die sowjetrussische Aussenpolitik 1930–1941*, Munich 1974.
Joseph Alsop and Robert Kintner, *American White Paper*, New York 1940.
Christopher Andrew, *Secret Service. The Making of the British Intelligence Community*, London 1985.
John A. Armstrong, *Ukrainian Nationalism, 1929–1945*, New York 1963.
Nino d'Aroma, *Hitler: Rapporto a Mussolini*, Rome 1974.
Sidney Aster, *1939. The Making of the Second World War*, London 1973.
T. Ataöv, *Turkish Foreign Policy (1939–1945)*, Ankara 1965.

Adrian Ball, *The Last Day of the Old World*, London 1963.

Corelli Barnett, *The Collapse of British Power*, London 1972.

Heinrich Bartell, *Frankreich und die Sowjetunion, 1938–1940*, Wiesbaden 1986.

Charles A. Beard, *American Foreign Policy in the Making 1932–1940*, Hampden, Conn. 1946.

Max Beloff, *The Foreign Policy of Soviet Russia, vol. 2, 1936–1941*, London 1949.

P. M. H. Bell, *The Origins of the Second World War in Europe*, London 1986.

R. Bensel, *Die deutsche Flottenpolitik von 1933 bis 1939. Eine Studie über die Rolle der Flottenbaus im Hitlers Aussenpolitik* (Beiheft 3 zur *Marine Rundschau*), Frankfurt/ M 1958.

D. Bergamini, *Japan's Imperial Conspiracy*, London and New York 1971.

Walther Bernhardt, *Die deutsche Aufrüstung 1934–1939: Militärische und politische Konzeptionen und ihre Einschätzung durch die Allierten*, Frankfurt/ M 1969.

Uri Bialer, *The Shadow of the Bomber*, London 1976.

Rainer Blasius, *Für Grossdeutschland-gegen den grossen Krieg: Staatzekretär Ernst Freiherr von Weizsäcker in den Krisen um die Tchechoslowakei und Polen 1938/1939*, Cologne 1981.

Henry Blumenthal, *Illusion and Reality in Franco-American Diplomacy, 1914–1945*, Baton Rouge, La. 1986.

Johann Böhm, *Das Nazionalsozialistische Deutschland und die deutsche Volksgruppe in Rumanien, 1936–1944*, Frankfurt/ M 1985.

Willi A. Boelcke, *Die Macht des Radios: Weltpolitik und Auslandrundfunk, 1924–1976*, Frankfurt 1977.

D. Bolech Cecchi, *Non bruciare i Ponti con Roma: le Relazioni fra l'Italia, la Gran Bretagna e la Francia dall'Accordo di Monaco allo Scoppio della Seconda Guerra Mondiale*, Milan 1986.

R. Bollmus, *Der Amt Rosenberg und seine Gegner. Studien zum Machtkampf im nationalsozialistischen Herrschaftssystem*, Stuttgart 1970.

Brian Bond, *British Military Policy between Two World Wars*, Oxford 1980.

Horst Boog, *Die deutsche Luftwaffenführung, 1935–1945: Führungsprobleme, Spitzengliederung, Generalstabssausbildung*, Stuttgart 1982.

Dorothy Borg, *The United States and the Far Eastern Crisis of 1933–1938*, Cambridge, Mass. 1964.

Ernest K. Bramsted, *Goebbels and National-Socialist Propaganda 1925–1945*, East Lansing, Michigan 1965.

Max Braubach *Hitlers Weg zur Verständigung mit Russland im Jahre 1939*, Bonn 1960.

Alfredo Breccia, *Jugoslavia 1939–1941: Diplomazia della Neutralità*, Rome 1978.

J. W. Bruegel, *Tschechen und Deutsche, 1918–1939*, Munich 1967.

idem, *Stalin und Hitler: Pakt gegen Europa*, Vienna 1973.

Bohdan B. Budorowycz, *Polish-Soviet Relations, 1932–1939*, New York 1963.

Alan Bullock, *Hitler and the Origins of the Second World War*, Oxford 1967.

Trevor Burridge, *British Labour and Hitler's War*, London 1976.

Eliza Campus, *Intelegere Balcanica*, Bucarest 1972.

idem, *Mica Intelegere*, Bucarest 1968.

W. Carr, *Arms, Autarchy and Aggression: A Study in German Foreign Policy, 1933–1939*, London 1972.

B. A. Carroll, *Design for Total War. Arms and Economics in the Third Reich*, The Hague 1968.

David T. Cattell, *Communism and the Spanish Civil War*, Berkeley, 1955.

idem, *Soviet diplomacy and the Spanish Civil War*, Berkeley 1957.

Owen Chadwick, *Britain and the Vatican during the Second World War*, Cambridge 1986.

Anne M. Cienciala, *Poland and the Western Powers, 1938–1939. A Study in the Interdependence of Eastern and Western Europe*, London 1968.

Anthony Clayton, *The British Empire as a Super-Power*, London 1986.

Nicholas Clifford, *Retreat from China: British Policy in the Far East 1937–1941*, Seattle 1967.

Wayne S. Cole, *Roosevelt and the Isolationists, 1933–1945*, Lincoln, Nebraska 1983.

Ian Colvin, *The Chamberlain Cabinet*, London and New York 1971.

J. V. Compton, *The Eagle and the Swastika: Hitler, the United States and the Origins of World War II*, Boston 1967.

Matthew Cooper, *The German Army 1933–1945. Its Political and Military Failure*, London 1978.

Alvin D. Coox, *Nomonhan, Japan against Russia, 1939*, Stanford, Ca. 1985.

Maurice Cowling, *The Impact of Hitler: British Politics and British Policy, 1933–1940*, Cambridge 1935.

J. B. Crowley, *Japan's Quest for Autonomy. National Security and Foreign Policy, 1930–1938*, Princeton, NJ 1966.

Andrew J. Crozier, *Appeasement and Germany's Last Bid for Colonies*, London 1988.

Robert Dallek, *Franklin Roosevelt and American Foreign Policy 1932–1945*, Oxford 1979.

Roman Debicki, *Foreign Policy of Poland 1919–1939*, New York 1962.

Henry Delfiner, *Vienna Broadcasts to Slovakia: 1938–1939. A Case-Study in Subversion*, New York 1974.

L. Denne, *Das Danzig-problem in der deutschen Aussenpolitik, 1934–1939*, Bonn n.d. 1959.

Peter J. Dennis, *Decision by Default. Peacetime conscription and British Defence 1919–1939*, London and Durkem, NC 1972.

Selim Deringil, *Turkish foreign policy during the Second World War: an 'active' neutrality*, Cambridge 1989.

Harold C. Deutsch, *The Conspiracy against Hitler in the Twilight War*, Minneapolis 1970.

P. M. Dieudonnat, *Je Suis Partout, 1930–1944: les Maurassiens devant la Tentation Fasciste*, Paris 1973.

R. A. Divine, *The Reluctant Belligerent. American Entry into World War II*, New York 1969.

idem, Causes and Consequences of World War II, Chicago 1969.

idem, Roosevelt and World War II, Baltimore 1969.

idem, The Illusion of Neutrality, Chicago 1962.

J. C. Doherty, *Das Ende der Appeasement. Die britische Aussenpolitik, die Achsenmächte und Europa nach dem Muenchener Abkommen*, Berlin 1973.

K. Drechsler, *Deutschland, China, Japan 1933–1939*, Berlin 1964.

N. A. Dreisziger, *Hungary's Way into World War II*, Austin Park, Florida, 1968.

Donald Drummond, *The Passing of American Neutrality, 1933–1941*, Ann Arbor 1955.

J. Dülffer, *Weimar, Hitler und die Marine. Reichspolitik und Flottenbau 1920 bis 1939*, Dusseldorf 1973.

Milan Stanislao Durica, *La Slovacchia e le sue relazioni politiche con la Germania 1938/1945*, Padua 1964.

J. B. Duroselle, *La Décadence, 1932–1939*, Paris 1979.

W. Erfurth, *Die Geschichte des deutschen Generalstabes von 1918–1945*, 2nd Edn, Göttingen 1960.

John Erickson, *The Road to Stalingrad*, London and New York 1975.

idem, The Soviet High Command: A Military-Political History 1918–1941, London 1962.

Ph. W. Fabry, *Der Hitler-Stalin Pakt 1939–1941. Ein Beitrag zum Methode Sowjetischer Aussenpolitik*, Darmstadt 1962.

Ladislas Farrago, *The Game of Foxes*, London 1973.

Valdo Ferretti, *Il Giappone e la Politica Estera Italiana, 1935–1941*, Milan 1983.

Herbert Feis, *The Road to Pearl Harbor: The Coming of the War between the United States and Japan*, Princeton 1950.

Louis Fischer, *Russia's Road from Peace to War. Soviet Foreign Relations 1917–1941*, New York 1969.

Nicholas Fleming, *August 1939. The Last Days of Peace*, London 1979.

Antoine Fleury, *La Pénétration Allemande au Moyen Orient 1919–1939: le cas de la Turquie, de l'Iran et de l'Afghanistan*, Leiden 1977.

Robert Frankenstein, *Le Prix du Rearmament Français, 1935–1939*, Paris 1982.

Georg Franz-Willing, *Ursprung der Hitler-Bewegung, 1919–1922*, Oldendorf 1974.

Patrick Fridenson and Jean Lewin, *La France et la Grande Bretagne face au Problèmes Aériens (1935–Mai 1940)*, Vincennes 1976.

S. Friedlander, *Hitler et les Etats-Unis 1939–1941*, Geneva 1963.

Alton Frye, *Nazi Germany and the American Hemisphere, 1933–1941*, New Haven, Conn. 1967.

Larry William Fuchser, *Neville Chamberlain and Appeasement. A Study in the Politics of Appeasement*, London and New York 1982.

Franklin Reid Gannon, *The British Press and Nazi Germany, 1936–1939*, Oxford 1971.

Lloyd C. Gardner, *Economic Aspects of New Deal Diplomacy*, Madison, Wis. 1964.

C. A. Gemzell, *Raeder, Hitler und Skandinavien. Der Kampf für einen maritimen Operationsplan*, Lund 1965.

idem, Organisation, Conflict and Innovation: a Study of German Naval Strategic Planning, 1888–1940, Lund 1973.

Martin Gilbert, *The Roots of Appeasement*, London 1967.

Martin Gilbert and Richard Gott, *The Appeasers*, London 1963.

Johannes Glasneck, *Turkei und Afghanistan: Brennpunkte der Orientpolitik im zweiten Weltkrieg*, Berlin 1968.

Helmut Greiner, *Die Oberste Wehrmachtsführung, 1939–1943*, Wiesbaden 1951.

William L. Grenzebach, Jr, *Germany's informal empire in East-Central Europe: German economic policy towards Yugoslavia and Rumania, 1933–1939*, Wiesbaden 1988.

Lothar Gruchmann, *Nationalsozialistische Grossraumordnung: die Konstruktion eines 'deutsche Monroe-doktrin'*, Stuttgart 1962.

695

Jeffrey Gunsburg, *Divided and Conquered. The French High Command and the Defeat of the West, 1940*, Westport, Conn./London 1979.

Jürgen Hagemann, *Presselenkung im Dritten Reich*, Bonn 1970.
Nicholas Halasz, *Roosevelt through Foreign Eyes*, Princeton, NJ 1961.
John McVicar Haight Jr, *American Aid to France 1938–1940*, New York 1970.
Jonathan Haslam, *The Soviet Union and the Struggle for Collective Security in Europe, 1933–1939*, London 1984.
Oswald Hauser, *England und das dritte Reich. Eine dokumentierte Geschichte der englisch-deutschen Beziehungen von 1933 bis 1939*, Stuttgart 1972.
Jonathan Helmreich, *Belgium and Europe. A Study in Small Power Diplomacy*, The Hague 1976.
J. Henke, *England im Hitlers politischen Kalkül, 1935–1939*, Boppard am Rhein 1973.
John Hiden, *Germany and Europe 1919–1939*, London 1977.
Trumbull Higgins, *Hitler and Russia. The Third Reich in a Two-Front War, 1937–1943*, New York 1966.
Klaus Hildebrand, *Vom Reich zum Weltreich. Hitler, NSDAP und Koloniale Frage, 1919–1939*, Munich 1969.
idem, Deutsche Aussenpolitik, 1933–1945. Kalkül oder Dogma? Stuttgart 1971.
Andreas Hillgruber, *Deutschlands Rolle in der Vorgeschichte der beiden Weltkriegen*, Göttingen 1967.
idem, Hitler, König Carol und Antonescu. Die deutsch-rumänischen Beziehungen 1938–1944, Wiesbaden 1954.
idem, Hitlers Strategie, Politik und Kriegsführung 1940–1941, Frankfurt 1965.
Lukasz Hirszowicz, *The Third Reich and the Arab East*, Toronto 1966.
Heinz Höhne, *Der Orden unter dem Totenkopf. Die Geschichte der SS*, 1957.
J. K. Hoensch, *Der ungarische Revisionismus und die Zerschlagung der Tschechoslowakei*, Tübingen 1967.
idem, Die Slowakei und Hitlers Ostpolitik, Cologne 1965.
idem, Geschichte der tschechoslowakischen Republik, 1918–1965, Stuttgart 1966.
Walther Hofer, *Die Entfesselung der zweiten Weltkrieges. Eine Studie über die internationalen Beziehungen im Sommer 1939*, Frankfurt/M, 3rd Edn, 1964. Trans. S. Gerdman, *War Premeditated*, London 1955.
Peter Hoffmann, *Widerstand, Staatsstreich, Attentat; Das Kampf der Opposition gegen Hitler*, Munich 1979; English: *The History of the German Resistance*, trans. Richard Barry, London 1979.
Robert Holland, *Britain and the Commonwealth Alliance*, London 1981.
Edward L. Homze, *Arming the Luftwaffe: the Reichs Air Ministry and the German Aircraft Industry, 1919–1939*, Lincoln, Nebraska, 1976.
Hans-Joachim Hoppe, *Bulgarien – Hitlers eigenwilliger Verbundeter. Eine Fallstudie zur national-sozialistischen Sudosteuropapolitik*, Stuttgart 1979.
J. B. Hoptner, *Yugoslavia in Crisis 1934–1941*, New York 1962.
Michael Howard, *The Continental Commitment. The Dilemma of British Defence Policy on the Eve of the Two World Wars*, London 1972.
L. Montgomery Hyde, *British Air Policy between the Wars 1918–1939*, London 1976.

F. W. Iklé, *German-Japanese Relations 1936–1940*, New York 1956.
David Irving, *Die Tragödie der deutschen Luftwaffe. Aus den Akten und Errinerungen vom Feldmarschall Milch*, Frankfurt/M 1970.
idem, The War Path: Hitler's Germany, 1933–1939, London and New York 1978.
Viktor L. Israelyan and Leonid V. Kutakov, *Diplomacy of Aggression: Berlin-Rome-Tokyo Axis – its Rise and Fall*, Moscow 1970.

Hans Adolf Jacobsen, *Nationalsozialistische Aussenpolitik, 1933–1938*, Frankfurt/M 1968.
Max Jacobson, Robert Levine, William Schwabe, *Contingency Plans for War in Western Europe, 1920–1940*, Santa Monica, Cal., Rand, 1985.
Eberhard Jäckel, *Hitlers Weltanschaung: Entwurf einer Herrschaft*, Tübingen 1969.
idem, Frankreich in Hitlers Europa, Stuttgart 1966.
F. A. Johnson, *Defence by Committee: The British Committee of Imperial Defence*, London 1960.
Manfred Jonas, *Isolationism in America 1935–1941*, Ithaca, New York 1966.
F. C. Jones, *Japan's New Order in Asia. Its Rise and Fall 1937–1945*, London 1954.
Detlef Junker, *Der unteilbare Weltmarkt: das ökonomische Interesse in dem Aussenpolitik der USA, 1933–1941*, Stuttgart 1975.

David Kahn, *The Code Breakers*, New York 1973.

David Kaiser, *Economic diplomacy and the origins of the Second World War: Germany, Britain, France and Eastern Europe*, Princeton, N.J. 1980.

Robert Kee, *The World We Left Behind*, London 1987.

John F. Kennedy, *Why England Slept*, New York 1940.

David O. Kieft, *Belgium's Return to Neutrality*, Oxford 1972.

Jon Kimche, *The Unfought Battle*, London 1968.

Christopher Kimmich, *The Free City*, New Haven, Conn. 1968.

Charles P. Kindelberger, *The World in Depression 1929–1939*, London 1973.

Martin Kitchen, *Europe between the Wars. A Political History*, London 1988.

Peter Klefisch, *Das Dritte Reich und Belgien 1933–1939*, Frankfurt/Main 1988.

Burton Klein, *Germany's Economic Preparations for War*, Cambridge, Mass. 1959.

H. Macgregor Knox, *Mussolini unleashed. Politics and Strategy in Fascist Italy's last War*, Cambridge 1982.

John S. Koliopoulos, *Greece and the British Connection 1935–1941*, Oxford 1977.

Anthony Komjathy and Rebecca Stockwell, *German Minorities and the Third Reich: Ethnic Germans of East Central Europe between the Wars*, New York 1979.

Joseph Korbel, *Poland between East and West. Soviet and German Foreign Policy towards Poland 1919–1939*, Princeton NJ 1963.

Richard N. Kottman, *Reciprocity and the North Atlantic Triangle*, Ithaca, New York, 1968.

Dimitrios G. Kousoulas, *The Price of Freedom. Greece in World Affairs 1934–1953*, Syracuse 1953.

L. Krecker, *Deutschland und die Turkei im zweiten Weltkrieg*, Frankfurt 1968.

Axel Kuhn, *Hitlers aussenpolitisches Programm: Entstehung und Entwicklung 1919–1939*, Stuttgart 1970.

Henry La Farge, *Lost Treasures of Europe*, London 1946.

William L. Langer and S. Everett Gleason, *The Challenge to Isolation 1937–1940*, New York 1952.

Conrad F. Latour, *Sudtirol und die Achse Berlin-Rom 1938–1945*, Stuttgart 1962.

Bradford A. Lee, *Britain and the Sino-Japanese War, 1937–1939: A Study in the Dilemmas of British Decline*, Stanford, Cal. 1973.

Joachim Leuschner, *Volk und Raum: Zum Stil der nationalsozialistischen Aussenpolitik*, Göttingen 1958.

Josef Lettrich, *A History of Modern Slovakia*, London 1956.

William E. Leuchtenberg, *Franklin D. Roosevelt and the New Deal 1932–1939*, New York 1963.

James B. Leutze, *Bargaining for Supremacy: Anglo-American Naval Relations, 1937–1941*, Chapel Hill 1977.

Herbert S. Levine, *Hitler's Free City: A History of the Nazi Party in Danzig, 1935–1939*, Chicago 1973.

Lincoln Li, *The Japanese Army in North China, 1937–1941*, Tokyo 1975.

W. Roger Louis, *British Strategy in the Far East 1919–1939*, Oxford 1971.

Peter Lowe, *Great Britain and the Origins of the Pacific War: A Study of British Policy in East Asia 1937–1941*, Oxford 1977.

John A. Lukacs, *The Last European War, September 1939–December 1941*, New York 1976.

Dov Lungu, *Romania and the European Great Powers, 1933–1940*, Durham, NC 1989.

C. A. Macartney, *October Fifteenth: A History of Modern Hungary*, Edinburgh 1961.

Mary McCarthy, *The Stones of Florence*, London 1959.

Callum A. Macdonald, *The United States, Britain and Appeasement*, London 1981.

Donald M. McKale, *The Swastika outside Germany*, n.p. 1977.

Denis Mack Smith, *Mussolini's Roman Empire*, London 1976.

Donald McLachlan, *Room 39: A Study in Naval Intelligence*, London 1968.

James B. MacSherry, *Stalin, Hitler and Europe 1933–1939*, New York 1968.

Nicholas Mansergh, *Survey of British Commonwealth Affairs. Problems of External Policy 1931–1939*, London 1952.

Philippe Marguerat, *La IIIme Reich et la pétrole roumain, 1938–1940*, Leiden 1977.

Werner Maser, *Frühgeschichte der NSDAP*, Frankfurt 1965.

Timothy W. Mason, *Arbeiterklasse und Volksgemeinschaft: Dokumente und Materialen zur deutschen Arbeiterpolitik 1936–1939*, Opladen 1975.

idem, Sozialpolitik im Dritten Reich, Opladen 1977.

Vojtech Mastny, *The Czechs under Nazi Rule. The Failure of National Resistance, 1939–1942*, New York 1971.

Massimo Mazetti, *La Politica militare italiana tra le due guerre mondiali*, Salerno 1979.

W. N. Medlicott, *The Coming of War in 1939*, London 1963.

idem, British Foreign Policy since Versailles, 1919–1963, 2nd rev. edn, London 1968.

Meir Michaelis, *Mussolini and the Jews. German-Italian relations and the Jewish Question in Italy, 1922–1945*, Oxford 1978.

Keith Middlemas, *Diplomacy of Illusion. The British Government and Germany, 1937–1939*, London 1972.

Joseph A. Mikus, *La Slovaquie dans le drame de l'Europe. (Histoire politique de 1918 à 1950)*, Paris 1955.

'Miles', (pseud.), *Deutschlands Kriegsbereitschaft und Kriegsaussichten im Spiegel der deutschen Fachliteratur*, Zurich 1939.

Jacques Minart, *La Drame du Désarmement Française (Ses Aspects Politiques et Techniques): la Revanche Allemande 1918–1939*, Paris 1959.

V. L. Moisuc, *Diplomatia Romania si Problema Operarii Suveran Statii si Independentei Nationale in Perioada Martie 1938– Mai 1940*, Bucarest 1971.

Leonard Mosley, *On Borrowed Time*, New York 1964.

Klaus-Jurgen Müller, *Das Heer und Hitler: Armee und nationalsozialistisches Regime, 1933–1940*, Stuttgart 1969.

idem, Armee und Drittes Reich, 1933–1939, Paderborn 1987.

B. Mueller-Hillebrand, *Das Heer 1933–1945*, vol. I, *Das Heer bis zum Kriegsbeginn*, Darmstadt 1954.

Williamson Murray, *Strategy for Defeat. The Luftwaffe, 1933–1945*, Maxwell, Alabama 1983.

idem, The Change in the European Balance of Power, 1938–1939, The Path to Ruin, Princeton NJ 1984.

Seppo Myllyniemi, *Baltian Kriisi 1938–1941*, Helsinki 1977. German trans. *Die baltische Krise 1938–1941*, Stuttgart 1977.

Ladislas Mysyrowitz, *Autopsie d'une Défaite: Origines de l'Effondrement Militaire Française de 1940*, Lausanne 1973.

Sir Lewis Namier, *Diplomatic Prelude 1938–1939*, London 1948.

idem, Europe in Decay 1936–1940, London 1950.

idem, In the Nazi Era, London 1952.

John F. Naylor, *Labour's International Policy: The Labour Party in the 1930s*, London 1969.

Jacques Néré, *The Foreign Policy of France from 1914 to 1945*, London 1973.

Simon Newman, *March 1939. The Making of the British Guarantee to Poland*, Oxford 1976.

Gottfried Niedhart, *Grossbritannien und die Sowjetunion 1934–1939: Studien zur britischen Politik der Friedenssicherung zwischen den beiden Weltkriegen*, Munich 1972.

A. Niri, *Istoricul Unui Tratat Inrobitor. Tratatul Economie Romano-German din Martie 1939*, Bucarest 1965.

F. S. Northedge, *The Troubled Giant. Britain among the Great Powers 1916–1939*, London 1966.

Arnold Offner, *American Appeasement, United States Foreign Policy and Germany 1933–1938*, Cambridge, Mass. 1969.

idem, The Origins of the Second World War. American Foreign Policy and World Politics 1917–1941, New York 1975.

Robert J. O'Neill, *The German Army and the Nazi Party, 1933–1939*, London 1966.

Nils Orvik, *Sikkerhetspolitiken, 1920–1939*, Oslo, 2 vols, 1960–61.

Ritchie Ovendale, *'Appeasement' and the English-Speaking World: The United States, the Dominions and the Policy of 'Appeasement', 1937–1939*, Cardiff 1975.

Claude Paillat, *Doissiers Secrets de la France Contemporaine*, vol. IV, *Le Désastre de 1940*, Pt. I, *La Répétition Générale*, Paris 1983; Pt. II, *La Guerre Immobile, Avril 1939–10 Mai 1940*, Paris 1984.

Robert Paxton, *Parades and Politics at Vichy*, Princeton NJ 1966.

George Peden, *British Rearmament and the Treasury, 1932–1939*, Edinburgh 1979.

Steven Pelz, *Race to Pearl Harbor: The Failure of the Second London Naval Conference and the Onset of World War II*, Cambridge, Mass. 1974.

Dieter Petzina, *Autarkiepolitik im Dritten Reich: der nationalsozialistische Vierjahresplan*, Stuttgart 1968.

idem, Die deutsche Wirtschaft in der Zwischenkriegszeit, Wiesbaden 1967.

Ernst-Albrecht Plieg, *Das Memelland 1920–1939*, Wurzburg 1962.

A. Mellini Ponce de Leon, *L'Italia Entra in Guerra. Gli Eventi Diplomatici dal 1 Gennaio 1939 al 10 Giugno 1940*, Bologna 1963.

C. Popisteanu, *Romania si Antanta Balcanica*, Bucarest 1968.

Barry R. Posen, *The Sources of Military Doctrine. France, Britain and Germany between the World Wars*, Ithaca/London 1984.

Barry Powers, *Strategy without Slide-Rule. British Air Strategy 1914–1939*, London 1976.

Gordon W. Prange, *Target Tokyo. The Story of the Sorge Spy Ring*, New York 1984.

Lawrence R. Pratt, *East of Malta, West of Suez: Britain's Mediterranean Crisis 1936–1939*, Cambridge 1975.

Anita Prazmowska, *Britain, Poland and the Eastern Front, 1939*, Cambridge 1987.

Ernst L. Presseisen, *Germany and Japan: A Study in Totalitarian Diplomacy, 1933–1941*, The Hague 1958.

R. J. Pritchard, *Far Eastern Influences upon British Strategy towards the Great Powers, 1937–1939*, New York 1987.

Rosario Quartararo, *Roma tra Londra e Berlino: Politica Estera Fascista dal 1930 al 1940*, Rome 1980.

Anthony Read and David Fisher, *The Deadly Embrace: Hitler, Stalin and the Nazi-Soviet Pact 1939–1941*, London 1988.

David Reynolds, *The Creation of the Anglo-American Alliance 1931–1941. A Study in Competitive Cooperation*, London 1981.

Anthony Rhodes, *The Vatican in the Age of Dictators, 1922–1945*, London 1973.

Norman Rich, *Hitler's War Aims*, 2 vols, New York 1973–74.

H. W. Richardson, *Economic Recovery in Britain, 1932–1939*, London 1967.

E. M. Robertson, *Hitler's Pre-War Policy and Military Plans, 1933–1939*, London 1963.

William R. Rock, *Appeasement on Trial: British Foreign Policy and its Critics, 1938–1939*, Hamden, Conn. 1966.

Helmuth K. G. Ronnefarth, *Die Sudetenkrise in der internationalen Politik*, 2 vols, Wiesbaden 1961.

Ger van Roon, *Kleine Landen in Crisistijd: van Oslostaaten tot Benelux, 1930–1940*, Amsterdam 1985.

Hans Roos, *A History of Modern Poland*, New York 1966.

idem, *Polen und Europa: Studien zur polnischen Aussenpolitik 1931–1939*, Tübingen 1957.

Stephen W. Roskill, *Naval Policy between the Wars*, Vol. II, *1930–1939*, London 1976.

Graham Ross, *The Great Powers and the Decline of the European States System, 1914–1945*, London 1983.

A. Rossi, (pseud. Angelo Tasca), *Les Communistes français pendant la drôle de guerre*, Paris 1951.

The Rote Kapelle: The C.I.A.'s History of Soviet Intelligence and Espionage Networks in Western Europe, 1936–1949, Washington DC, 1979.

Benjamin A. Rowland, *Balance of Power or Hegemony: The Inter-War Monetary System*, New York 1976.

Rüdiger Ruhnau, *Die Freie Stadt Danzig, 1919–1939*, Berg am See 1979.

Leona Sabiliunas, *Lithuania in Crisis: Nationalism to Communism 1939–1940*, Bloomington, Ind. 1972.

Fritz Sänger, *Politik der Taüschungen, Missbrauch der Presse in dritten Reich. Weisungen, Informationen, Notizen 1933–1939*, Vienna 1975.

Thomas L. Sakmyster, *Hungary, the Great Powers and the Danubian Crisis, 1936–1939*, Athens, Georgia 1979.

Michael Salewski, *Die deutsche Seekriegsleitung, 1935–1945*, Frankfurt/M 1970–73.

A. Savu, *Dictatura Regale*, Bucarest 1970.

Herbert Schindler, *Mosty und Dirschau, 1939: zwei Handstreiche der Wehrmacht vor Beginn des Polendfeldzuges*, Freiburg 1971.

Wilhelm von Schramm, *. . . sprich von Frieden, wann du den Krieg willst: Die psychologischen Offensiven Hitlers gegen die Französen, 1933–1939*, Mainz 1973.

Ehrengard Schramm von Thadden, *Griechenland und die Grossmächte im zweiten Weltkrieg*, Wiesbaden 1955.

Gerhard Schreiber, *Revisionismus und Weltmachtstreben: Marineführung und deutsch-italienische Beziehungen, 1919–1944*, Stuttgart 1978.

Hans Jurgen Schroeder, *Deutschland und die Vereinigte Staaten 1933–1939: Wirtschaft und Politik in der Entwicklung des deutsch-amerikanischen Gegensatzes*, Wiesbaden 1970.

Paul Seabury, *The Wilhelmstrasse: A Study of German Diplomats under the Nazi Regime*, Berkeley 1954.

Hugh Seton-Watson, *Eastern Europe between the Wars 1918–1941*, Cambridge 1945.

Robert Paul Shay Jr, *British Rearmament in the 1930s: Politics and Profits*, Princeton NJ 1977.

F. Siebert, *Italiens Weg in dem zweiten Weltkrieg*, Frankfurt 1962.

V. I. Sipols, *Die Vorgeschichte des deutschen-soujetischen Nicht-Angriffs-vertrags*, trans. from the Russian, Cologne 1981.

Th. Sommer, *Deutschland und Japan zwischen den Mächten 1935–1945. Vom Antikominternpakt zum Dreimächtepakt. Eine Studie zur diplomatischen Vorgeschichtes der zweiten Weltkriegs*, Tübingen 1962.

Walther Sommer, *Die Weltmacht USA im Urteil der französischen Publizistik*, Tübingen 1967.

Martin K. Sorge, *The Other Price of Hitler's War. German Military and Civilian Losses resulting from World War II*, New York 1986.

Alfred Spiess and Heiner Lichtenstein, *Das Unternehmen Tannenberg*, Wiesbaden 1979.

Hans-Jakob Stehle, *Die Ostpolitik des Vatikans, 1917–1955*, Munich 1975.

Marlis Steinert, *Hitlers Krieg und die Deutschen; Stimmung und Haltung der deutschen Bevölkerung im zweiten Weltkrieg*, Dusseldorf 1970.

J. Stengers, *Leopold III et le Gouvernement: les deux politiques belges de 1940*, Paris 1980.

Peter Stercho, *Diplomacy of Double Morality*, New York 1971.

Bertil Stjernfelt and Klaus-Richard Böhme, *Westerplatte 1939*, Freiburg/Breisgau 1979.

Richard Storry, *The Double Patriots*, London 1957.

Joseph Swire, *Bulgarian Conspiracy*, London 1939.

Jutta Sywottek, *Mobilmachung fur den totalen Krieg. Die propagandistische Vorbereitung der deutschen Bevölkerung auf den zweiten Weltkrieg*, Opladen 1976.

A. J. P. Taylor, *The Origins of the Second World War*, London 1961.

Marian Thielenhaus, *Zwischen Anpassung und Widerstand: Deutsche Diplomaten, 1932–1941*, Paderborn 1984.

Jochen Thies, *Architekt der Weltherrenschaft: Die "Endziele" Hitlers*, Düsseldorf 1976.

Hugh Thomas, *The Spanish Civil War*, 3nd Edn, London 1966.

Neville Thompson, *The Anti-Appeasers. Conservative Opposition to Appeasement in the 1930s*, Oxford 1971.

Christopher Thorne, *The Approach of War, 1938–1939*, London 1967.

History of "The Times", 4, The 150th Anniversary and Beyond 1912–1948, Part II, 1952.

Mario Toscano, *Storia dei Trattati e Relazioni Internazionali*, 2 vols, Turin 1963.

idem, *Le Origini del Patto D'Acciaio*, Florence 1956 (2nd Edition), English trans., Baltimore 1967.

idem, *Pagine di Storia Diplomatica Contemporanea*, vol. II, Milan 1963. English trans., *Designs in Diplomacy*, Baltimore 1970.

idem, *L'Italia e gli Accordi Tedesco-Sovietici dell'Agosto 1939*, Florence 1955.

P. E. Tournaux, *Défense des Frontières*, Paris 1960.

David Tutaev, *The Consul of Florence*, London 1966.

Adam B. Ulam, *Expansion and Co-existence. The History of Soviet Foreign Policy 1917–1967*, New York 1968.

Roman Umiastowski, *Russia and the Polish Republic 1918–1945*, London 1945.

Karl Heinz Völker, *Die deutsche Luftwaffe 1933–1939: Aufbau, Führung, Rüstung*, Stuttgart 1967.

Von Tag zu Tag. Chronik der Weltereignisse von 25 August bis 31 Oktober 1939, n.p.n.d. 1940.

Nicholas von Vormann, *Der Feldzug 1939 im Polen*, Weissenburg 1958.

Wesley K. Wark, *The Ultimate Enemy: British Intelligence and Nazi Germany, 1933–1939*, Ithaca, NJ 1985.

D. C[ameron] Watt, *Personalities and Policies. Studies in the Formulation of British Foreign Policy in the 20th Century*, London and South Bond, Indiana, 1965.

idem, *Too Serious a Business. European Armed Forces and the Approach of the Second World War*, London and Los Angeles 1975.

idem, *Succeeding John Bull. America in Britain's Place 1900–1975*, Cambridge 1984.

idem (Ed.), *Hitler's Mein Kampf*, London 1969.

Franz G. Weber, *The Evasive Neutral: Germany, Britain and the Quest for a Turkish Alliance in the Second World War*, Columbia, Mo. 1979.

Reinhard Weber, *Die Entstehungsgeschichte der Hitler-Stalin Paktes 1939*, Munich 1980.

Gerhard Weinberg, *Germany and the Soviet Union, 1939–1941*, Leiden 1954.

idem, *The Foreign policy of Hitler's Germany, 1937–1939*, Chicago 1980.

Bernd Jurgen Wendt, *Economic Appeasement. Handel und Finanz in der britischen Deutschland-Politik, 1933–1939*, Dusseldorf 1971.

idem, *Grossdeutschland: Aussenpolitik und Kriegsvorbereitung des Hitlerregimes*, Munich 1987.

W. J. West, *Truth Betrayed*, London 1987.

John Wheeler-Bennett, *Munich, Prologue to Tragedy*, London 1948.

idem, *The Nemesis of Power: The German Army in Politics 1918–1945*, London 1953.

Elizabeth Wiskemann, *The Rome-Berlin Axis: A History of the Relations between Hitler and Mussolini*, London 1949.
idem, *Undeclared War*, London 1939; 2nd Edition, London 1967.
Richard A. Woytak, *On the Border of War and Peace. Polish Intelligence and Diplomacy in 1937–1939, and the Origins of the Ultra Secret*, Boulder, Col. 1979.
Johann Wuescht, *Jugoslawien und das Dritte Reich*, Stuttgart 1969.
Marcus Wüttrich von Trüb, *Die Verhandlungen der Westmächte mit der Sowjetunion im Sommer 1939. Ein Beitrag zur west-östlichen Kontroversie um die Entfesselung des zweiten Weltkrieges*, Munich 1967.

A. P. Young, *The X documents. The Secret History of Foreign Office Contacts with the German Resistance, 1937–1939*, London 1974.
Robert W. Young, *In Command of France. French Foreign Policy and Military Planning*, Cambridge, Mass. 1978.

Ludmila Zhivkova, *Anglo-Turkish Relations, 1933–1939*, London 1976.

2. *Collected and Collective Works*
Christopher Andrew and David Dilks (Eds), *The Missing Dimension*, London 1984.
Christopher Andrew and Jeremy Noakes (Eds), *Intelligence and International Relations 1900–1945*, Exeter 1987.
Wolfgang Benz and Hermann Graml (Eds), *Sommer 1939. Die Grossmächte und der europäische Krieg*, Stuttgart 1979.
Dorothy Borg and Shumpei Okamoto (Eds), *Pearl Harbor as History: Japanese-American Relations 1931–1941*, New York 1973.
Richard D. Burns and Edward H. Bennett (Eds), *Diplomats in Crisis: United States-Chinese-Japanese Relations, 1919–1941*, Santa Barbara, California 1974.
Gordon Craig and Felix Gilbert (Eds), *The Diplomats*, Princeton NJ 1963.
Roy Douglas (Ed.), *1939: A Retrospect 40 Years On*, London 1983.
Europäische Publikationen, *Vollmacht des Gewissens*, Frankfurt 1960.
Renzo de Felice, (Ed.), *L'Italia fra Tedeschi e Alleati*, Bologna 1973.
Erhard Forndran (Ed.), *Innen- und Aussenpolitik unter nationalsozialistische Bedrohung. Determinanten internationaler Beziehungen in historischen Fallstudien*, Wiesbaden 1977.
Friedrich Forstmeier and Hans Erich Volkmann (Eds), *Wirtschaft und Rüstung am Vorabend des zweiten Weltkrieges*, Düsseldorf 1975.
Manfred Funke (Ed.), *Hitler, Deutschland und die Mächte: Materialen zur Aussenpolitik des Dritten Reiches*, Düsseldorf 1976.
Hans W. Gatzke (Ed.), *European Diplomacy between Two Wars 1919–1939*, Chicago 1972.
Thaddeus V. Gromada (Ed.), *Essays on Polish Foreign Policy 1918–1939*, New York 1970.
Klaus Hildebrand, Karl Ferdinand Werner and Klaus Manfrass (Eds), *Deutschland und Frankreich, 1936–1939*, Munich 1981.
Gerhard Hirschfeld and Lothar Ketternacker (Eds), *"Der Führerstaat". Mythos und Realität. Studien zur Struktur und Politik des dritten Reiches*, Stuttgart 1981.
Kenneth Paul Jones (Ed.), *U.S. Diplomats in Europe, 1919–1941*, Santa Barbara, Cal. 1981.
Franz Knipping and Klaus-Jurgen Müller (Eds), *Machtbewusstsein in Deutschland am Vorabend des zweiten Weltkrieges*, Paderborn 1984.
H. W. Koch (Ed.), *Aspects of the Third Reich*, London 1985.
R. G. D. Laffan (Ed.), *Survey of International Affairs 1938*, vol. III, London/Oxford 1956.
Les Relations Franco-Allemandes, 1933–1939, Paris 1976.
Les Relations Franco-Britanniques de 1935 à 1939. Communications présentées aux colloques Franco-Britanniques, 1971–1972, Paris 1975 (CNRS 1975).
Les Relations Militaires Franco-Belges de Mars 1936 au 10 Mai 1940: Travaux d'un Colloque d'Historiens Belges et Françaises, Paris 1968 (CNRS 1968).
Ernest R. May, (Ed.), *Knowing One's Enemies: Intelligence Assessment before the Two World Wars*, Princeton, NJ 1984.
Wolfgang Michalka (Ed.), *Nationalsozialistische Aussenpolitik*, Darmstadt 1978.
Militärgeschichtliche Forschungsamt, *Aufstand des Gewissens. Militärisches Wilderstand gegen Hitler und das NS Regime 1933–1945*, Bonn 1984.
Viorica Moisuc (Ed.) *Probleme de politica externa a Romaniei 1919–1939: Culegere de Studii*, vol. I, Bucarest 1971.
idem (Ed.), *Probleme de politica externa a Romaniei, 1919–1940: Culegere de Studii*, vol. II, Bucarest 1977.

Wolfgang J. Mommsen and Lothar Ketternacker (Eds), *The Fascist Challenge and the Policy of Appeasement*, London 1983.

James W. Morley (Ed.), *Deterrent Diplomacy: Japan, Germany and the USSR 1935–1940*, New York 1976.

idem, The China Quagmire. Japan's Expansion on the Asian Continent, 1933–1941, New York 1983.

Gottfried Niedhart (Ed.), *Kriegsbeginn 1939: Entfesselung oder Ausbruch des zweites Weltkrieges*, Darmstadt 1976.

René Rémond and Janine Bourdin (Eds), *Edouard Daladier, Chef de Gouvernement*, Paris 1977.

Adrian Preston (Ed.) *General Staffs and Diplomacy before the Second World War*, Toronto and London 1978.

Henry A. Turner (Ed.) *Nazism and the Third Reich*, New York 1972.

Esmonde M. Robertson (Ed.) *The Origins of the Second World War*, London 1971.

Jurgen Schmädeke and Peter Steinach (Eds) *Der Widerstand gegen den Nationalsozialismus. Die deutsche Gesellschaft und der Widerstand gegen Hitler*, Munich 1985.

Arnold Toynbee and Frank Ashton-Gwatkin (Eds) *Survey of International Affairs, 1938–1939, The World in March 1939*, London 1952.

Arnold Toynbee and V. S. Toynbee (Eds) *Survey of International Affairs, 1938–1939. The Eve of the War*, London 1958.

3. *Articles*

Ch. R. Ageron, 'L'Opinion publique français pendant les crises internationales de septembre 1938 à juillet 1939', *Cahiers de l'Institute d'Histoire de la Presse et de l'Opinion*, vol. 1.

idem, 'La venalité de la presse française dans la première moitié du XX siècle. L'Action des Etats étrangers', *Cahiers de L'Institute d'Histoire de la Presse et de l'Opinion*, vol. 1.

Martin Alexander, 'Les réactions à la menace strategique en Europe occidentale. La Grande Bretagne, la Belgique et le 'cas' Hollande, Decembre 1938 – Février 1939', *Cahiers d'Histoire de la Deuxième Guerre Mondiale* (Brussels), 7, 1982.

Alex Alexandroff and Richard Rosecrance, 'Deterrence in 1939', *World Politics*, 29, 1977.

Marek Andrejewski, 'La propagande révisioniste allemande par rapport au problème de la ville libre Gdansk durant la periode d'entre les deux guerres', *PWA*, 25, 1984.

P. Angel, 'Les responsabilités hitlériennes dans le déclenchement de la Deuxième Guerre Mondiale', *RHDGM*, 15, 1965.

S. Aster, 'Ivan Maiski and parliamentary anti-appeasement, 1938–39', in A. J. P. Taylor (Ed.), *Lloyd George: Twelve Essays*, London 1970.

Turkkaya Ataöv, 'The policy of the Great Powers towards Turkey on the eve of the Second World War', *Studia Balcanica* (Sofia), 7, 1973.

A. Babin, 'The victory at Khalkin-Gol', *Int. Aff. (Moscow)*, 1979/9.

Hans R. Bachmann, 'Der Kampf um Hela, 1 September – 1 Oktober 1939', *WWR*, XX, 1970.

Vaughn Baker, 'Nevile Henderson in Berlin: A re-evaluation', *Red River Valley Historical Journal*, III, 1974.

F. A. Baptiste, 'The British grant of air and naval facilities to the United States in Trinidad, St Lucia and Bermuda in 1939', *Caribbean Studies*, 16, 1976.

Henryk Batowski, 'August 31 in Berlin', *PWA*, 10, 1969.

idem, 'Polish diplomacy and the outbreak of the Second World War', *PWA*, 21, 1980.

idem, 'The Polish-British and Polish-French alliances and treaties of 1939', *PWA*, 14, 1973.

idem, 'La désagregation de l'Entente Balcanique', *Studia Balcanica* (Sofia), 4, 1971.

Wilfred Baumgart, 'Zur Aussprache Hitlers vor den Führern der Wehrmacht am 22 August 1939', *VjHZg*, 16, 1968.

Hedva Ben-Israel, 'Cross-purposes: British reactions to the German anti-Nazi opposition', *JCH*, 20, 1985.

L. Berov, 'The withdrawing of Western capital from Bulgaria on the eve of the Second World War', *Studia Balcanica* (Sofia), IV, 1971.

G. Biedlungmaier, 'Die strategische und operativen Ueberlegungen der Marine, 1932–1942', *WWR*, 13, 1963.

W. Blayer, Roswitha Czollek, 'Die Vereitelung der Aggressionspläne der faschistischen deutschen Imperialismus gegenüber den baltischen Staaten durch die Sowjetunion im Sommer/Herbst 1939', *Militärgeschichte*, 19, 1980.

Charles Bloch, 'Les relations anglo-allemandes de L'Accord de Munich à la dénonciation du traité naval de 1935', *RHDGM*, 5/18/19, 1955.

General Admiral Hermann Boehm (with reply by Wilfred Baumgart), 'Zur Aussprache Hitlers vor den Führern des Wehrmacht am 22 August 1939', *VjHZg*, 19, 1971.

Jerzy W. Borejsza, 'L'Italia e la Guerra tedesco-polacca del 1939', *Storia Contemporanea*, IX, 1978.

Carl Boyd, 'The Berlin-Tokyo Axis and Japanese military initiative', *Modern Asian Studies*, 15, 1981.

idem, 'The role of Hiroshi Oshima in the preparation of the Anti-Comintern Pact', *J. Asian Studies*, 11, 1971.

Alfredo Breccia, 'La potenza dell'Asse e la neutralità della Jugoslavia alla vigilia della seconda guerra mondiale', *RSPI*, 41, 1974.

idem, 'Le fonti per lo studio della storia delle relazioni internazionali dei paesi jugoslavi nel periodo 1890–1945', *Storia e Politica*, 1970, 1971.

Martin Broszat, 'Deutschland-Ungarn-Romanien. Entwichlung eine Grundfaktoren national-sozialistisches Hegemonial und Bündnispolitik, 1938–1941', *H.Z.*, 1968.

idem, 'Die eiserne Garde und der dritte Reich', *Pol. Stud.*, 1958.

P. Buffetot, 'La perception du réarmement allemand par les organisations de renseignement français de 1936 à 1939', *RHd'A*, 3, 1979.

idem, 'The French High Command and the Franco-Soviet alliance, 1933–1939', *JSS*, 5, 1982.

Alan Bullock, 'Hitler and the origins of World War II', *Proceedings of the British Academy*, 53, 1967.

John C. Cairns, 'A nation of shopkeepers in search of a possible France, 1919–1940', *AHR*, 79, 1974.

L. Calafteanu, 'La Roumanie et le problème de la creation du bloc balcanique au début de la deuxième guerre mondiale, *RRH*, XIV, 1975.

idem, 'les relations économiques germano-roumaines de 1933 à 1944,' *RHDGM*, 35/1, 60, 1985.

Lucio Ceva, 'Appunti per una storia della Stato Maggiore generale fino alla vigilia della "non-belligerenza" (giugno 1925 – luglio 1939)', *Storia Contemporanea*, X, 1979.

idem, 'Altre notizie sulle conversazione italo-tedesche alla vigilia della seconda guerra mondiale, aprile-giugno 1939', *Risorgimento*, 30, 1978.

John W. Chapman, 'A Dance on Eggs: Intelligence and the Anti-Comintern', *JCH*, 22, 1987.

Michael J. Cohen, 'British strategy and the Palestine Question, 1936–1939', *JCH*, VII, 1972.

Wayne S. Cole, 'Senator Key Pittman and American neutrality policies, 1933–1940', *MHVR*, 46, 1960.

Enzo Collotti, 'Il ruolo della Bulgaria nel conflitto tra Italia e Germania per il nuovo ordine in Europa', *Studia Balcanica* (Sofia), VII, 1973.

Robert Conquest, 'The *Great Terror* revisited', *Survey*, 17, 1971.

Nicolai Constantinescu, 'Les contradictions économiques franco-allemandes et anglo-allemandes en Roumanie à la veille de la seconde guerre mondiale', *Studia Balcanica* (Sofia), VII, 1973.

John S. Conway, 'The Vatican, Great Britain and relations with Germany, 1938–1940', *H.J.*, 16, 1978.

F. Culinovic, 'La politique de l'Italie et les divergences german-italiennes dans les Balkans', *Studia Balcanica*, (Sofia) VII, 1974.

Lynn H. Curtwright, 'Great Britain, the Balkans and Turkey in the autumn of 1939', *IHR* 10, 1988.

Charles F. Delzell, 'Pius XII, Italy and the outbreak of war', *JCH*, 11, 1967.

Selim Deringil, 'Turkey's diplomatic position at the outbreak of the Second World War', *Boğazici Üniversitesi Dergisi*, 8–9, 1980–81.

James Douglas-Hamilton, 'Ribbentrop and War', *JCH*, 5, 1970.

Walter M. Drzewienecki, 'The Polish army on the eve of World War II, *Polish Review*, XXVI, 1981.

J. Dülffer, 'Weisungen an die Wehrmacht als Ausdruck ihrer Gleichschaltung 1938/1939', *WWR*, 18, 1968.

J. P. Duroselle, 'Les ambassadeurs français', *RI*, 7, 1976.

Lord Elibank, 'Franklin Roosevelt: friend of Britain', *Contemporary Review*, CLXXXVII, 1955.

Valentin Falin, 'Why in 1939? Reflections on the beginning of World War II', Article in four parts, *New Times*, Nos 38–41, 1987.

Valdo Ferretti, 'La politica estera giapponese e i rapporti con l'Italia e la Germania (1935–1939)', *Storia Contemporanea*, VII, 1976.

idem, 'Fra Inghilterra e Germania: un aspetto delle origini della seconda guerra mondiale secondo la recente storiografia giapponese', *Storia Contemporanea*, XIII, 1982.

Antoine Fleury, 'Le nouveau cours des relations franco-turques et l'affaire du Sandjak d'Alexandrette, 1921–1939', *R.I.*, 19, 1979.

T. Georgescu, 'La cinquième colonne en Roumanie', *RHDGM*, 70, 1968.

Aaron Goldman, 'Two Views of Germany: Nevile Henderson and Vansittart and the Foreign Office, 1937–1939', *BJIS*, 6, 1980.

Fred Greene, 'The military view of American national policy, 1904–1940', *AHR*, 65, 1960–61.

Karl Gundelach, 'Gedanken über die Führung eines Luftkrieges gegen England bei der Luftflotte 2 in dem Jahren 1938/1939: ein Beitrag zur Vorgeschichte der Luftschlacht gegen England', *WWR*, 10/1, 1960.

Thomas E. Hachey, 'Profiles in Politics: The British Embassy view of prominent Americans in 1939', *Wisconsin Magazine of History*, 54, 1970.

John McVicar Haight, 'Les négociations françaises pour la fourniture d'avions américains, 1ère partie – avant Munich', *Forces Aériennes Françaises*, 198, Dec. 1963.

idem, 'Les négociations relatives aux achats d'avions américains par la France pendant la période qui précéda immédiatement la Guerre', *RHDGM*, 58, 1965.

Gerald K. Haines, 'Under the Eagle's Wing. The Franklin Roosevelt administration forges an American Hemisphere', *Dipl. Hist.*, 1, 1977.

Jonathan Haslam, 'Soviet aid to China and Japan's place in Moscow's foreign policy 1937–1939', in Ian Nish (Ed.), *Some Aspects of Soviet-Japanese Relations in the 1930s*, London, *ICERD/LSE International Studies 1982/11*.

Milan Hauner, 'Did Hitler want world dominion?', *JCH*, 13, 1978.

Joszef Henke, 'Hitler und England: Mitte August 1939', *VjHZg*, 21, 1973.

Ludolf Herbst, 'Die Krise des nationalsozialistisches Regimes am Vorabend des zweiten Weltkrieges und die forcierte Aufrustung', *VjHZg*, 18, 1978.

John Herman, 'Soviet peace efforts on the eve of World War II. A review of the documents', *JCH*, 15, 1980.

John D. Heyl, 'The construction of the Westwall 1938. An exemplar for National-Socialist policy-making', *Central European History*, 14, 1981.

Leonidas Hill, 'Three crises, 1938–39', *JCH*, III, 1968.

Andreas Hillgruber, 'England's place in Hitler's plans for world dominion', *JCH*, 9, 1974.

idem, 'England in Hitlers aussenpolitsche Konzeption', *HZ*, 218, 1974.

idem, 'Der Faktor Amerika in Hitlers Strategie, 1938–1941', *Aus Politik und Geschichte*, Beilage zu Das Parlament, B.19, May 1966.

idem, 'Der Hitler-Stalin Pakt und die Entfesselung des zweiten Weltkrieges. Situationsanalyse und Machtkalkül der beiden Pakt-Partner', *HZ*, 230, 1978.

Norman Hillmer, 'The Anglo-Dominions Alliance, 1919–1939', *15e Congrès International des Sciences Historiques, Rapports* (Bucharest 1980).

Peter Hoffmann, 'Peace and the *coup d'etat*: the foreign contacts of the German Resistance', *Central European History*, 19, 1986.

J. M. d'Hoop, 'La politique militaire de la France dans les Balkans de l'Accord de Munich au début de la deuxième guerre mondiale', *Studia Balcanica*, (Sofia), 7, 1973.

G. Juhasz, 'La politique extérieure de la Hongrie de 1939 à 1943', *RHDGM*, 62, 1966.

Peter Kent, 'A Tale of Two Popes. Pius XI, Pius XII and the Rome-Berlin Axis', *JCH*, 23, 1988.

G. O. Kent, 'Pope Pius XII: Some aspects of German-Vatican relations, 1937–1939', *AHR*, 70, 1964.

V. Khvostov and A. Grylev, 'On the eve of the Great Patriotic War: the Soviet Union prepares to resist the Fascist aggression,' *Int. Aff.* (Moscow), October 1968.

Dimitri Kitsikis, 'La Grèce entre l'Angleterre et l'Allemagne 1936–1941', *Rev. Hist.*, 1967.

Klemens von Klemperer, 'Adam von Trott zu Solz and British Foreign Policy', *Central European History*, 14, 1981.

I. Koblyakov, 'The USSR battles against the War danger in 1937–1939', *Int. Aff.* (Moscow), 1979/10.

H. W. Koch, 'Hitler and the origins of the Second World War. Some thoughts on the status of some of the documents', *HJ*, 11, 1968.

Oya Koyman, Attila Sonmez, 'The social and economic background to Turkey's non-involvement in World War II', *Studia Balcanica*, (Sofia), VII, 1973.

Anthony Komjathy, 'The First Vienna Award (November 1938)', *Austrian History Yearbook*, 15/16, 1979–80.

Armand Krebs, 'Le bluff de Moscou en 1939 avant la Pacte Germano-Sovietique', *Ecrits de Paris*, 397, 1979.

Alfred Kupferman, 'Diplomatie parallèle et guerre psychologique: le role de la Dienstelle Ribbentrop dans les tentatives d'action sur l'opinion française, 1934–1939', *RI.*, 3, 1974.

Donald S. Lammers, 'Fascism, Communism and the Foreign Office, 1937–39', *JCH*, VI, 1971.

idem, 'From Whitehall after Munich: the Foreign Office and the future course of British policy', *HJ*, 16, 1973.

Wilhelm Lenz and Lothar Ketternacker, 'Lord Kemsley's Gespräch mit Hitler, Ende Juli 1939', *VjHZg*, 19, 1971.

Herbert S. Levine, 'The Mediator: Carl J. Burckhardt's efforts to avert a Second World War', *JMH*, 45, 1973.

Mark M. Lowenthal, 'Roosevelt and the coming of the war: the search for United States policy', *JCH*, 16, 1981.

C. Leonard Lunden, 'The Nazification of German Baltic minorities. A contribution to the story of diplomacy in 1939', *JCEA*, 7, 1947.

Callum A. MacDonald, 'Britain, France and the April Crisis of 1939', *ESR*, 2, 1972.

idem, 'Economic appeasement and the German "moderates", 1937–1939. An introductory essay', *Past and Present*, 56, 1972.

idem, 'The Venlo Affair', *ESR*, 8, 1978.

Keith D. McFarland, 'Woodring v. Johnson: F.D.R. and the Great War Department Feud', *Army*, 26, 1976.

Robert Manne, 'The British decision for alliance with Russia, May 1939', *JCH*, 8, 1974.

idem, 'Some British light on the Nazi-Soviet Pact', *ESR*, 11, 1981.

Philip Marguerat, 'L'Allemagne et la Roumanie à l'automne 1938: économie et diplomatie', *RI*, 1974.

Frederick A. Marks III, 'Six between Roosevelt and Hitler. America's role in the appeasement of Nazi Germany', *HJ*, 28, 1985.

F. Marzari, 'Projects for an Italian-led Balkan bloc of neutrals, September–December 1939', *HJ*, 13, 1970.

idem, 'Western-Soviet rivalry in Turkey', article in 2 parts, *Middle East Studies*, VII/1/2, 1971.

T. W. Mason, 'Some origins of the Second World War', *Past and Present*, 1964.

Carl T. Mazuzan, 'The Failure of Neutrality Legislation in mid-Summer 1939. Warren T. Austin's memorandum of the White House Conference of July 18', *Vermont History*, 42, 1974.

Hans Meier-Welcker, 'Zur deutsch-italienischen Militärpolitik und Beurteilung der italiensichen Wehrmacht vor dem zweiten Weltkrieg', *MGM*, 1/1, 1970.

Kneho Meneghalli-Dinčić, 'la politique étrangère de la Yugoslavie (1936–1941)', *RHDGM*, 58, 1965.

Herbert Metzmacher, 'Deutsch-Englische Ausgleichsbemühungen im Sommer 1939', *Vj HZg*, 14, 1966.

Fortunato Minnitti, 'Il problema degli armamenti nella preparazione militare italiana dal 1935 al 1943', *Storia Contemporanea*, IX, 1978.

V. Moisuc, 'Orientations dans la politique extérieure de la Roumanie après la Pacte de Munich', *RRH*, 5, 1966.

idem, 'Tratatul economie romano-German din 25 Martie 1939 si semnificati sa', *Analele*, 1967.

idem, 'L'ecroulement des alliances de la Roumanie à la veille de la deuxième guerre mondiale', *RHDGM*, 35/160, 1985.

idem, 'The offensive of Hitlerite Germany for seizing Romania's economy', *Rev. Roum. d'Etudes Int.*, 5/4, 1971.

Viorica Moisuc and Gheorge Zaharia, 'Politica Germanistica Nazistica de hegemonie in sud-estul europei si independente economica a Romanei in anii, 1938–1939', *Analele de Istoria*, 21, 1975.

Gunther Moltmann, 'Franklin D. Roosevelt's Friedensappel von 14 April 1939', *Jahrbuch für Amerikastudien*, 1964.

idem, 'Weltherrschaftsideen Hitlers', in *Festschrift für E. Zechlin*, Hamburg 1961.

Alexander Nekrich, 'The arrest and trial of I. M. Maiski', *Survey*, 22, 1976.

Gottfried Niedhart, 'Die britisch-französische Garantie-erklärung für Polen am 31 Marz 1939: aussenpolitische Kurswechsel der Westmächte', *Francia*, II, 1974.

idem, 'Europa in der britischen Weltpolitik vor dem zweiten Weltkrieg', *Francia*, V, 1977.

idem, 'Appeasement: die britische Antwort auf die krise der Weltreiches und das internationale Systems vor dem zweiten Weltkrieg', *HZ*, 226, 1978.

Arnold Ofner, 'Appeasement revisited: the United States, Great Britain and Germany, 1933–1940', *JAH*, 64, 1977.
Nils Ørvik, 'Nordic security, Great Britain and the League of Nations', in K. Bourne and D. C. Watt (Eds), *Studies in International History*, London 1967.
R. J. Overy, 'Hitler and Air Strategy', *JCH*, 15, 1980.
idem, 'From Ural bomber to Amerika-bomber; the Luftwaffe and strategic bombing', *JSS*, I, 1978.
idem, 'Hitler's War and the German economy: a reinterpretation', *EcHR*, 35, 1982.
idem, 'The German prewar aircraft production plans. November 1936 – April 1939', *EHR*, 90, 1975.

R. A. C. Parker, 'The economics of rearmament and foreign policy: the United Kingdom before 1939', *JCH*, 10, 1975.
idem, 'The pound sterling, the American Treasury and British preparations for war, 1938–1939', *EHR*, 98, 1983.
James T. Patterson, 'Eating humble pie. A note on Roosevelt, Congress and Neutrality Revision in 1939', *Historian*, 31, 1969.
George Peden, 'The burden of imperial defence and the continental commitment reconsidered', *HJ*, 27, 1984.
idem, 'A matter of timing. The economic background to British foreign policy, 1937–1939', *History*, 59, 1984.
I. Pfaff, 'Prag und der Fall Tukhachewski', *VjHZg*, 35, 1987.
Cristian Popisteanu, 'Diplomatic actions carried out by Rumania in the spring and summer of 1939', *Studia Balcanica*, (Sofia), VII, 1973.
K. M. Pospieszalski, 'Nazi attacks on German property: the Reichsführer's plan of summer 1939', *PWA*, 24, 1983.
idem, 'L'attaque manquée contre le pont sur la Vistule près de Tczew', *PWA*, 28, 1987.
A. J. Prazmowska, 'War over Danzig? The dilemma of Anglo-Polish relations in the months preceding the outbreak of the Second World War', *HJ*, 26, 1983.
idem, 'Poland's foreign policy September 1938 – September 1939', *HJ*, 29, 1986.
Nicholas Pronay and Philip M. Taylor, '"An improper use of Broadcasting". The British Government and clandestine radio propaganda operations against Germany during the Munich crisis and after', *JCH*, 18, 1983.

R. Quartararo, 'Appendice a Inghilterra e Italia. Dal Patto di Pasqua a Monaco', *Storia Contemporanea*, VII/4, 1976.

Hans Radondt, 'Die IG-Farbenindustrie in Sudosteuropa, 1938–1945', *Jahrbuch für Wirtschaftsgeschichte*, I, 1967.
Elizabeth du Reau, 'Enjeux strategiques et redeploiement diplomatique français: november 1938, september 1939', *R.I.*, 35, 1983.
idem, 'L'information du décideur et l'élaboration de la décision diplomatique française dans les dernières années de la IIIe République', *R.I.*, 32, 1980.
idem, 'Edouard Daladier et l'image de la puissance française en 1938', *RHdA*, 1983.
Benjamin D. Rhodes, 'The British Royal visit of 1939 and the "Psychological Approach" to the United States', *Dipl. Hist.*, 2, 1978.
idem, 'Sir Ronald Lindsay and the British view from Washington, 1930–1939' in Clifford L. Egar and Alexander W. Knott (Eds), *Essays in Twentieth Century American Diplomatic History dedicated to Professor Daniel H. Smith*, Washington DC, 1982.
Hans Roos, 'Die militärpolitische Lage und Planung Polens gegenüber Deutschland von 1939', *WWR*, 7, 1957.
idem, 'Der Feldzug in Polen vom September 1939', *WWR*, 9, 1959.
Jürgen Runzheimer, 'Der Ueberfall auf den Sender Gleiwitz im Jahre 1939', *Vj HZg*, 10, 1962.

Patrick Salmon, 'British plans for economic warfare against Germany 1937–1939. The problem of Swedish iron ore', *JCH*, 16, 1981.
Andre Scherer, 'Le problème des mains libres a l'Est', *RHDGM*, 8/14, 1958.
Hans Schiefer, 'Deutschland und die Tschechoslowakei vom September 1938 bis März 1939', *Zeitschrift für Ostforschung*, 4, 1955.
H. J. Schroeder, 'Sudosteuropa als informal Empire Deutschlands 1933–1939. Das Beispiel Jugoslawiens', *Jahrbuch für Geschichte Osteuropas*, 1975.

idem, 'Economic Appeasement. Zur britischen und amerikanischen Deutschland-politik vor dem zweiten Weltkrieg', *VjHZg*, 30.

K. Schröder, 'Die Gedenken des Oberbefehlshabers der Kriegsmarine zum Kampf gegen England in Atlantik und im Mittelmeer 1939–1940', *Marine Rundschau*, 67, 1970.

Amnon Sella, 'Khalkin-Gol: the forgotten war', *JCH*, 22, 1987.

Stanislaw Sierpowski, 'Italy and the Nazi aggression on Poland in 1939', *PWA*, 19, 1978.

J. C. Simmonds, 'The French Communist Party and the beginnings of resistance: September 1939 – June 1941', *ESR*, 11, 1981.

K. Skubiszewski, 'Did the War start for Danzig?' *PWA*, 10, 1969.

Paul Stafford, 'The visit of Chamberlain and Halifax to Rome: a reappreciation', *EHR*, 1983.

Michael Stenton, 'British propaganda and *Raison de'Etat*, 1935–1940', *ESR*, 10, 1980.

L. Szigmond, 'La politique extèrieure de la Hongrie de 1933 à 1939', *RHDGM*, 62, 1966.

Commandant Joan Talpes, 'La politique militaire de la Roumanie (1938–1940)', *RHDGM*, 35/160, 1985.

Philip M. Taylor, 'If war should come. Repairing the Fifth Arm for Total War, 1935–1939', *JCH*, 16, 1981.

Mario Toscano, 'Le conversazioni militari italo-tedesche alla vigilia della seconda guerra mondiale', *Riv. Storica Italiana*, XIV, 1954.

Gerd R. Ueberschar, 'General Halder and the resistance to Hitler in the German High Command, 1938–40', *E. H. Q.*, 18/3, 1988.

idem, 'General Halder im militärischen Widerstand, 1938–40', *Wehrforschung*, 2, 1973.

Teddy Uldrichs, 'The impact of the Great Purges on the People's Commisariat for Foreign Affairs', *Slavic Review*, 36, 1977.

V. A. Varga, 'Attitudinie guvernului romin burghezo-mosieresc fată de tratarile anglo-franco-sovietice din anii 1939', *Studii revista de istorie*, XIII, 1960, 4.

Jan Vanwelkenhuysen, 'La Belgique et la menace d'invasion, 1939–1940', *Rev. Hist.* CCLXIV/536, 1980.

Georg Vigrabs, 'Die Stellungnehme der Westmächte und Deutschlands zu den baltischen Staaten im Frühling und Sommer 1939', *VjHZg*, 7, 1959.

D. C[ameron] Watt, 'Sir Lewis Namier and contemporary European history', *Cambridge Review*, 1954.

idem, 'Anglo-German naval negotiations on the eve of World War II', *JRUSI*, CIII/610–11, 1958.

idem, 'Die bayerische Bemühungen um die Ausweisung Hitlers, 1924', *VjHZg*, 4, 1958.

idem, 'German Strategic Planning and Spain, 1938–1939', *Army Quarterly*, LXXX/2, 1960.

idem, 'The Rome-Berlin Axis, 1936-1940. Myth and reality', *Rev. Pol.*, XXII/4, 1960.

idem, 'American strategic interests and anxieties in the West Indies, 1917–1940', *JRUSI*, CVIII/3, 1963.

idem, 'Stalin's first bid for sea power, 1935–41', *Proceedings of the US Naval Institute*, XC/6, 1964.

idem, 'South African attempts to mediate between Britain and Germany', in K. Bourne and D. C. Watt (Eds) *Studies in International History*, London 1967.

idem, 'Diplomatic History, 1930–1939', in C. L. Mowat (Ed.), *New Cambridge Modern History*, vol. XII, 2nd Edn, *The Shifting Balance of World Forces, 1895–1945*, Cambridge, 1969.

idem, '*The Week* that Was', *Encounter*, May 1972.

idem, 'Chamberlain and Roosevelt. Two appeasers', *Int. J.*, XXVIII/2, 1973.

idem, 'The initiation of negotiations leading to the Nazi-Soviet Pact. An historical problem', in Chimen Abramsky and Perry J. Williams (Eds) *Essays in Honour of E. H. Carr*, London 1974.

idem, 'Britain, France and the Italian Problem, 1937–1939' and 'British domestic politics and the onset of war. Notes for a discussion', in *Les Relations Franco-Britanniques de 1935 a 1939*, Paris 1975.

idem, 'The breakdown of the European Security System 1930–1939', in *Papers Presented to the XIV International Congress of Historical Sciences, San Francisco, 22–29 August 1975*, San Francisco 1975.

idem, 'European military leadership and the breakdown of Europe, 1919–1939', in Adrian Preston (Ed.) *General Staffs and Diplomacy before the Second World War*, London 1978.

idem, 'Błędne informacje, błędne koncepcje, brak zaufania z dziejów brytyjskiej polityki zagranicznej w latach 1938–1939', *Kwartalnik Historyczny*, LXXX/4, 1978.

idem, 'Restraints on war in the air: before 1945', in Michael Howard (Ed.) *Restraints on War. Studies in the Limitation of Armed Conflict*, Oxford 1979.

idem, 'Britain and Russia in 1939', *Britain-USSR*, 57–58, 1980–81.

idem, 'The European Civil War', in Wolfgang J. Mommsen and Lothar Ketternacker, *The Fascist Challenge and the Policy of Appeasement*, London 1983.

idem, 'Misinformation, misconception, mistrust: episodes in British policy and the approach of war, 1938–1939', in Michael Bentley and John Stevenson (Eds) *High and Low Politics in Modern Britain*, Oxford 1983.

idem, 'Les perceptions britanniques de la puissance militaire avant 1939', in René Girault et Robert Frank, *La Puissance en Europe 1938–1940*, Paris 1984.

idem, 'British intelligence and the coming of the Second World War in Europe', in Ernest R. May (Ed.), *Knowing One's Enemy. Intelligence Assessment before two World Wars*, Princeton, NJ 1985.

idem, 'The case of John Herbert King. A Soviet agent in the Foreign Office', *Intelligence and National Security*, 3/4, 1988.

idem, 'The Foreign Office failure to anticipate the Nazi-Soviet Pact', *Intelligence and National Security*, 4/3, 1989.

idem, 'The historiography of Yalta', *Dipl. Hist.*, 13/1, 1989.

Gerhard L. Weinberg, 'German colonial plans and policies, 1938–1942', in *Festschrift für H. Rothfels*, Göttingen 1963.

idem, 'A proposed compromise over Danzig in 1939', *JCEA*, 14, 1955.

idem, 'Hitler's image of the United States', *A.H.R.*, 69, 1963–64.

Charles Whiting, 'The man who invaded Poland – a week too early', *World War II Investigator*, I, 1988.

T. F. D. Williams 'Negotiations leading to the Anglo-Polish Alliance', *Irish Historical Studies*, 10, 1956.

Marian Wojciechowski, 'The Free City of Gdansk and Poland', *PWA*, 20, 1979.

Robert Young, 'Spokesmen for economic warfare', *ESR*, VI, 1976.

idem, 'The strategic dream: French air doctrine in the inter-war period, 1919–1939', *JCH*, 9, 1974.

idem, 'French military intelligence and the Franco-Italian alliance, 1933–1939', *HJ*, 28, 1985.

G. Zaharia, 'Sur la politique extérieure de la Roumanie avant la deuxième guerre mondiale', *RHDGM*, 70, 1968.

G. Zaharia and Ion Calafteanu, 'The international situation and Rumanian foreign policy between 1938 and 1940', *RRH*, 18, 1979.

M. Zgorniak, 'Les preparatifs de l'attaque contre la Pologne', *RHDGM*, 77, 1970.

Ludmila Zhivkova, 'British economic policy in the Balkans on the eve of World War II', *Studia Balcanica* (Sofia), 4, 1973.

4. *Doctoral Theses*

A. P. Adamthwaite, 'French Foreign Policy, April 1938 – September 1939, with special reference to the policy of Jean Bonnet', Leeds 1966.

S. Aster, 'British policy towards the USSR and the Onset of the Second World War, March 1938 – August 1939', London 1969.

J. S. Conway, 'German Foreign policy, 1937–1939', Cambridge 1955.

Selim Deringil. 'Turkish Foreign Policy during the Second World War. Turkish Reactions to European Crises', East Anglia 1978.

E. Gilman, 'Economic Aspects of Anglo-American Relations in the Era of Franklin Delano Roosevelt and Neville Chamberlain', London 1976.

H. Gotlieb, 'England and the Nature of the Nazi Regime: a Critical Assessment of British Opinion, 1938–1939', Oxford 1953.

T. K. McCulloch, 'Anglo-American Economic Diplomacy and the European Crises, 1938–1939', Oxford 1980.

Henry Ozelle Malone, 'Adam von Trott zu Solz: The Road to Conspiracy against Hitler, 1909–1938', University of Texas at Austin 1980.

F. Marzari, 'The Balkans, the Great Powers and the European War, 1939–40', London 1966.

R. J. Pritchard, 'Far Eastern Influences on British Strategy towards the Great Powers, 1937–1939', London 1980.

D. J. Rotunda, 'The Rome Embassy of Sir Eric Drummond, 16th Earl of Perth, 1933–1939', London 1972.

G. J. van Kessel, 'British Reactions to German Economic Expansion in South-East Europe, 1936–1939', London 1972.

5. *M. A. Theses* (*London*)

Elizabeth Breg. 'The Wohltat-Hudson negotiations of July 1939', 1975.

Gerrard Casey, 'The International repercussions of *Reichskristallennacht*', 1987.

A. T. Crozier, 'British foreign policy, 1936–39, and the published Portuguese documents', 1967.

David Gee, 'Neville Chamberlain's perception of Hitler's intentions, October 1938 – March 1939', 1987.

Ronald Hanhoff, 'Slow boat to Russia: the failure of Anglo-Soviet rapprochement, March–August 1939', 1984.

John Herman, 'Soviet peace efforts on the eve of World War II – a review of the Soviet literature', 1978.

Beatrice Heuser, 'Turkey and the Great Powers, from the occupation of Prague to the Anglo-Turkish declaration', 1982.

Neville Hughes, 'Britain's search for security between 15 March and the Anglo-Polish agreement of 31.iii.39', 1971.

Kenneth Ludlow, 'The visit of Neville Chamberlain and Lord Halifax to Rome, January 1939', 1972.

Alison Lunzer, 'The Attitude of the Foreign Office towards the Soviet Union between Munich and Prague', 1980.

Sheena MacDougal, 'The Flying Ambassador: A Study of the Impression made on the British Press by Joachim von Ribbentrop as Ambassador to Britain, 1936–1938', 1979.

Michael G. Paul, 'The Foreign policy of the Communist Party of Great Britain, 1935–1941', 1984.

R. J. Pritchard, 'German attitudes towards the Carpatho-Ukraine from Munich to Prague', 1968.

Gerald Prothero, 'Sir Nevile Henderson: the shaping of a mission', 1984.

S. E. Robinson, 'The Role of Sir Nevile Henderson: July–August 1939', 1974.

Philip Somerville, 'Foreign Office attitudes to Poland, October 1938–April 1939', 1970.

J. R. Stabler, 'British attitudes to Italy, 7 April–3 September 1939', 1979.

James M. Weinberger, 'The attitude of the British Embassy, Washington, and the Foreign Office towards Senator William T. Borah, 1931–1939', 1979.

CREDITS

PHOTOGRAPHS

Bilderdienst Suddeutscher Verlag: p.xix, above; The Franklin D. Roosevelt Library, New York: p.xvi; Count Herworth von Bitterfeld: p.xx, above right; BBC Hulton Picture Library: p.i, below; p.iii, above; p.iv, above left; p.v, above left & right; p.vii, above left & below; p.x, above left, below right; p.xi, below left; p.xiv, below right; p.xviii, above left & right; p.xix, below; p.xx, below; p.xxiv, above left & right; The Trustees of the Imperial War Museum, London: p. i, above; p. viii, above left & right, below left; p.ix, above right; p.xviii, below left & right; p.xxiii, above & below; The Polish Institute & Gen. Sikorski Museum; p.x, above right; Popperfoto: p.ii, above & below; p.iii, below; p.iv, above right, below left & right; p.v, below; p.vi, all four pictures; p.vii, above right; p.viii, below right; p.ix, above left, below left & right; p.x, below left; p.xi, above left & right; p.xii, below; p.xiii, above & below; p.xiv, above left & right, below left; p.xv, all four pictures; p.xvii, all four pictures; p.xx, above left; p.xxiv, below; Scherz Verlag: p.xxi below; Wissenschlaft-lichen Archiv der Freien und Hansestadt Danzig: p.xi, below right; p.xii, above; p.xxi, above; p.xxii, above & below.

ARCHIVE MATERIAL

The author and publishers are most grateful to the following for permission to quote from private papers and other archive material:
The Bodleian Library (Bod. Lib.)/Mrs Elizabeth Crookshank (papers of Harry Crookshank); Bod. Lib./Lord Simon (papers of Sir John Simon); Bod. Lib./Mrs Laura Morland (papers of Euan Wallace); The University of Birmingham (papers of Neville Chamberlain); The Syndics of Cambridge University Library (the Templewood papers); The Master, Fellows and Scholars of Churchill College in the University of Cambridge (CCC)/Sir Colville Barclay (papers of Lord Vansittart); CCC/Lord Caldecote (the Calde-cote papers); CCC/Lady Lloyd/Dr John Charmley (the Lloyd papers); CCC/ Lt. Commander H. W. Drax (papers of Admiral Drax); CCC/Farrer & Co. (papers of Sir Alexander Cadogan); CCC/Mrs Margaret Godfrey (papers of

Admiral John Henry Godfrey); CCC/Lord Halifax (papers of Lord Halifax); CCC (papers of Lord Hankey); CCC (papers of Leslie Hore-Belisha); CCC (papers of Sir Hugh Knatchbull-Hugessen); CCC/Philip Mallet (papers of Sir Victor Mallet); CCC (papers of Sir Eric Phipps); CCC/D.A. Shailer (papers of Group Captain Christie); CCC/Lord Strang (papers of Lord Strang); The Trustees of the Imperial War Museum (IWM) (papers of G.E.R. Gedye); Lieutenant-General Sir Noel Mason-MacFarlane); IWM/Mrs Margaret Robertshaw (Vice-Admiral Sir Ballin Robertshaw); The Trustees of the National Library of Scotland (the Murray of Elibank papers).

MAPS

The maps were drawn by Neil Hyslop. We are grateful to Alvin D. Coox for permission to re-draw the map on pp. 340–1 from his book *Nomonhan, Japan against Russia, 1939*, Stanford, Ca. 1985.

CARTOONS

We thank the following for permission to reproduce cartoons: Low/*The Evening Standard*/The Centre for the Study of Cartoons and Caricature, University of Kent at Canterbury (CSCC): p.99; p.226; p.263; p.351; p.373; p.338; p.406; p.460; Sir Bernard Partridge/*Punch*: p.163; Pont/*Punch*: p. 620; Vicky/*Courier*/CSCC: p.131; Vicky/*Time and Tide*/CSCC: p.39; Zollikofer AG: p.95; p.166; p.197; p.564; p.597.

INDEX

The index was compiled by Meg Davies (Society of Indexers).

INDEX